Windows 10
Inside Out

Ed Bott
Carl Siechert
Craig Stinson

PUBLISHED BY
Microsoft Press
A division of Microsoft Corporation
One Microsoft Way
Redmond, Washington 98052-6399

Library of Congress Control Number: 2014955516
ISBN: 978-07356-9796-6

Printed and bound in the United States of America.

Second Printing

Microsoft Press books are available through booksellers and distributors worldwide. If you need support related to this book, email Microsoft Press Support at mspinput@microsoft.com. Please tell us what you think of this book at http://aka.ms/tellpress.

This book is provided "as-is" and expresses the authors' views and opinions. The views, opinions, and information expressed in this book, including URL and other Internet website references, may change without notice.

Some examples depicted herein are provided for illustration only and are fictitious. No real association or connection is intended or should be inferred.

Microsoft and the trademarks listed at http://www.microsoft.com on the "Trademarks" webpage are trademarks of the Microsoft group of companies. All other marks are property of their respective owners.

Acquisitions and Developmental Editor: Rosemary Caperton
Editorial Production: Curtis Philips, Publishing.com
Technical Reviewer: Randall Galloway; Technical Review services provided by
Content Master, a member of CM Group, Ltd.
Copyeditor: John Pierce
Proofreader: Andrea Fox
Indexer: William Meyers
Cover: Twist Creative • Seattle

To our families, for their patience and understanding

Contents at a glance

Appendixes

Table of contents

What do you think of this book? We want to hear from you!

Microsoft is interested in hearing your feedback so we can improve our books and learning resources
for you. To participate in a brief survey, please visit:

http://aka.ms/tellpress

What do you think of this book? We want to hear from you!

Microsoft is interested in hearing your feedback so we can improve our books and learning resources for you. To participate in a brief survey, please visit:

http://aka.ms/tellpress

Introduction

We're back!

The three authors responsible for this edition began working together in 2001. Like many of you, we took a break a few years ago, watching from the sidelines as Microsoft released Windows 8 and Windows 8.1. We've returned for Windows 10 because, quite frankly, we're excited by the possibilities of "Windows as a Service." Unlike with previous versions, which remained largely static until the next big release, you can expect Windows 10 to evolve rapidly.

Much of what we found in Windows 10 is familiar, especially as we dug deep into its core features. The fundamentals of NTFS security and the registry, for example, have remained reassuringly consistent throughout many generations of Windows. But there is also plenty that's new in Windows 10, some of it obvious (the new Start menu) and some not so obvious (Windows Hello).

The challenge of writing a book like this one is that Microsoft plans to keep changing Windows 10, releasing new features every few months instead of every few years. Over time, that means step-by-step procedures for getting tasks accomplished will change (making those routines simpler, we hope). That's why, in this edition, we've tried to focus on the *why* and not just the *how*.

Who this book is for

This book offers a well-rounded look at the features most people use in Windows. It serves as an excellent starting point for anyone who wants a better understanding of how the central features in Windows 10 work. If you're a Windows expert-in-training, or if your day job involves IT responsibilities, or if you're the designated computer specialist managing computers and networks in a home or small business, you'll discover many sections we wrote just for you. And if you consider yourself a Windows enthusiast—well, we hope you'll find enough fun and interesting tidbits to keep you interested because, after all, we're unabashed enthusiasts ourselves.

Assumptions about you

This book was written for people who have some experience with Windows and are comfortable with and even curious about the technical details of what makes Windows work. It touches only briefly on some of the basic topics that you'll find covered in more detail elsewhere (for those, we recommend other Microsoft Press titles, such as *Windows 10 Step by Step* or *Windows 10 Plain & Simple*).

Whether your experience comes from using Windows 8.1 or Windows 7, we expect that you are comfortable finding your way around the desktop, launching programs, using copy and paste operations, and finding information in a web browser. We don't assume that you're a hardware tinkerer, a hacker, a hardcore gamer, or a developer.

How this book is organized

Part 1, "Getting started with Windows 10," offers an overview of what's new in this version, with details on installing and configuring Windows 10, personalizing the Windows experience, connecting to the Internet and local networks, and keeping your user accounts and devices secure.

Part 2, "Working and playing with Windows 10," covers the essentials of using and managing apps and desktop programs, with details on built-in productivity tools (including Mail) and the entertainment apps that help you enjoy your collection of digital photos and music. This section covers the two browsers in Windows 10, the all-new Microsoft Edge and the more familiar Internet Explorer. Finally, it explains how to organize your folders and files and how to find those files when you need them.

Part 3, "System maintenance and troubleshooting," starts with a detailed guide to the different types of hardware you can use with Windows 10, with storage devices getting their own chapter. Additional chapters cover routine maintenance tasks and explore tools and techniques for measuring and improving your computer's performance. The section closes with advice on how to back up your important files, how to recover quickly from problems, and how to troubleshoot issues when they arise.

Part 4, "Windows 10 for experts and IT pros," goes into detail about advanced system-management tools and explains how to set up an advanced network so that you can safely share files, printers, Internet connections, and other resources. Other topics include Windows PowerShell scripting and the powerful Hyper-V virtualization technology built in to the Pro, Enterprise, and Education editions of Windows 10.

Finally, we provide three appendixes of reference information, including a concise look at the differences between Windows 10 editions, an overview of help and support resources, and some details about how the OneDrive cloud storage service works with Windows 10.

Acknowledgments

For this edition of the book, like many before it, we're fortunate to have an expert production team led by Curtis Philips of Publishing.com. Along with technical editor Randall Galloway, copyeditor John Pierce, and proofreader Andrea Fox, our favorite team asked the right questions and made excellent suggestions to cover our lapses. And, as usual, they made it all happen quickly and efficiently, despite all the curveballs that we would throw them.

Although the publishing world has changed tremendously over the past two decades, one constant remains: the folks at Microsoft Press are a delight to work with. Product manager Rosemary Caperton and director of publishing Anne Hamilton carry on this tradition magnificently.

Our sincere thanks go to all these folks.

Errata, updates, & book support

We've made every effort to ensure the accuracy of this book. You can access updates to this book—in the form of a list of submitted errata and their related corrections—at

http://aka.ms/Win10InsideOut/errata

If you discover an error that is not already listed, please submit it to us at the same page.

If you need additional support, email Microsoft Press Book Support at

mspinput@microsoft.com

Please note that product support for Microsoft software and hardware is not offered through the previous addresses. For help with Microsoft software or hardware, go to

http://support.microsoft.com

Free ebooks from Microsoft Press

From technical overviews to in-depth information on special topics, the free ebooks from Microsoft Press cover a wide range of topics. These ebooks are available in PDF, EPUB, and Mobi for Kindle formats, ready for you to download at

http://aka.ms/mspressfree

Check back often to see what is new!

We want to hear from you

At Microsoft Press, your satisfaction is our top priority, and your feedback our most valuable asset. Please tell us what you think of this book at

http://aka.ms/tellpress

We know you're busy, so we've kept it short with just a few questions. Your answers go directly to the editors at Microsoft Press. (No personal information will be requested.) Thanks in advance for your input!

Stay in touch

Let's keep the conversation going! We're on Twitter: *http://twitter.com/MicrosoftPress*

What's new in Windows 10

Windows 10 is not just another incremental upgrade to the world's most popular PC operating system.

The first clue is the version number. No, you didn't miss Windows 9—Microsoft jumped straight from 8.1 to 10 to underscore the magnitude of change in this release. And make no mistake about it, Windows 10 is dramatically different from the version you're probably using today.

How you react to Windows 10 will be determined in no small part by how you feel about its predecessor.

With the launch of Windows 8 in October 2012, Microsoft removed the familiar touchstones of the Windows user experience—the Start button and Start menu—and replaced them with a radically redesigned Start screen created for use with touch-enabled devices. It also introduced a new class of touch-friendly apps, delivered through a new Windows Store.

The innovations in Windows 8 ushered in a new class of computing devices that a time traveler from 1995 would barely recognize as members of the PC family. But that new design also inspired some passionate and often blunt feedback from Windows users who weren't pleased with the radical changes to an operating system they had spent years mastering.

NOTE

The core code that makes up Windows 10 runs on a broad assortment of hardware, ranging from mobile phones and pocket-size tablets to oversize, touch-enabled smart displays mounted on the walls of corporate conference rooms. In this book, we focus primarily on devices designed to perform the functions associated with traditional PCs. For a discussion of what makes Windows 10 different on small devices, see "Windows 10 on phones and small tablets" in Chapter 13, "Hardware."

Microsoft has reacted to that feedback by reworking the user experience in Windows 10, bringing back the Start menu from Windows 7, combining it with live tiles and other features that were introduced in Windows 8, and tossing in some impressive all-new capabilities. The result should feel significantly more natural for anyone upgrading from Windows 7.

If you skipped Windows 8 and stuck with Windows 7, as we suspect many of our readers did, you have some catching up to do. If you're coming to Windows 10 after spending quality time with Windows 8 and Windows 8.1, you have a different kind of adjusting to do.

In this chapter, we offer a high-level overview of what's new in Windows 10. We start, naturally enough, with the hardware that unlocks many of the signature features in Windows 10.

Next-generation hardware

Every year, Microsoft's hardware partners sell hundreds of millions of PCs running the latest version of Windows. The majority of those PCs still follow traditional form factors: towers designed to fit under a desk, all-in-one PCs that pack the electronics behind a desktop display, and clamshell-shaped laptops with full keyboards and trackpads.

But an increasing percentage—roughly one in every four Windows devices, according to recent research—have diverged from those familiar designs.

The defining characteristic of these next-generation Windows 10 devices is a touchscreen. On touchscreen-equipped laptops, you can choose to perform a task by tapping the screen or by using the keyboard and trackpad. In the case of a tablet running Windows 10, the touchscreen offers the only way to navigate between and within apps.

Then there's the most intriguing category of all: so-called hybrid devices, with a keyboard that can be detached or folded out of the way. The models in Lenovo's perfectly named Yoga series, for example, include touchscreens that can rotate 360 degrees, turning a laptop into a tablet with the keyboard behind the display.

On Microsoft's popular Surface line, shown in Figure 1-1, the Type Cover clicks into place magnetically, allowing the keyboard to flip open for typing and then flip closed to cover the screen. With the Type Cover attached and the adjustable kickstand extended, the Surface Pro looks and acts like a laptop. When you remove the Type Cover and close the kickstand, the Surface Pro becomes a tablet that you can control with a finger or a pen.

On a touchscreen, you swipe and tap to interact with objects on the screen and use an on-screen keyboard to enter and edit text. For devices with detachable keyboards, Windows 10 includes features designed to ease the transition between the traditional PC way of working and the new Tablet Mode.

Figure 1-1 The Surface Pro 3 is the quintessential hybrid device. With the Type Cover attached (left) it works like a laptop. Remove the Type Cover, and it's a tablet.

We offer details on how to master the new user experience, on traditional PCs and touch-screen-equipped devices, in Chapter 3, "Using Windows 10." Our coverage of customization options is in Chapter 4, "Personalizing Windows 10."

The new generation of hardware isn't just defined by peripherals. Modern devices designed for Windows 10 incorporate new features that enhance the security of the startup process. If you've mastered the ins and out of BIOS setup on a legacy PC, you'll need to learn how to configure its replacement, the Unified Extensible Firmware Interface (UEFI). That hardware design in turn enables an additional security feature called Secure Boot, which protects your Windows 10 PC from an insidious form of malware called rootkits. We discuss these features in much greater detail in Chapter 7, "Securing Windows 10 devices."

The Windows 10 user experience

Ironically, if you skipped Windows 8 you missed several major iterations of the Windows user experience that some users found difficult to use on conventional PCs with a keyboard and mouse. By contrast, the Windows 10 user experience feels very much like a smooth evolution of Windows 7.

On a conventional PC, equipped with a keyboard and a mouse or trackpad, Windows 10 starts at the Windows desktop. If you're making the move from Windows 7, this environment, shown in Figure 1-2, should be familiar.

CHAPTER 1

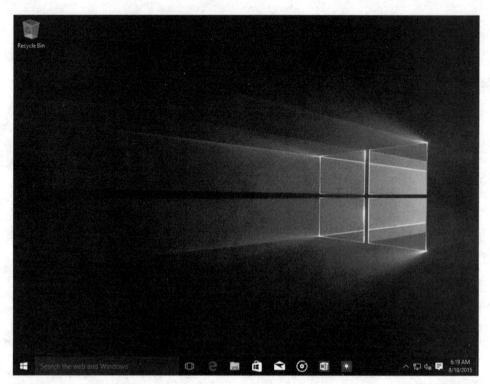

Figure 1-2 After you sign in to Windows 10, you're greeted with the familiar desktop and taskbar.

In the lower left corner is a stylized Windows logo. Clicking that button opens a menu like the one shown in Figure 1-3.

That configuration addresses one of the biggest complaints about Windows 8, which organized programs on a Start screen that occupied the entire display. The new Start menu can be resized to occupy nearly the entire display. If you prefer the Windows 8–style full-screen option, it's available by switching to Tablet Mode, which works even on traditional PCs.

Windows 10 introduces a new visual design, with flat icons and a monochromatic color scheme, as typified by the Settings app shown in Figure 1-4.

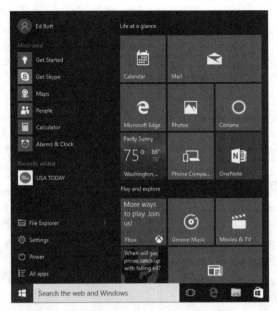

Figure 1-3 The Windows 10 Start menu combines the two-column layout from Windows 7 with live tiles from Windows 8.

Figure 1-4 The visual design and arrangement of the new Settings app are characteristic of the overall design of Windows 10.

The pieces of Windows 8 that didn't survive

The Windows 8 user interface was radically different from any previous version of Windows. Maybe too radical, based on the clear feedback Microsoft received from customers.

That feedback inspired a thorough rethinking of the Windows user experience, which in turn led to the design you see in Windows 10. In the process, these signature Windows 8 elements were retired:

- **Charms menu.** This vertical row of five buttons, with the Windows logo key at the center, appeared on the right side of Windows 8 PCs in response to a swipe from the right edge or the mouse moving to the upper right corner of the display. Its five functions have been broken up and moved to the new Start menu and to Action Center, which now appears where the Charms once did with a swipe from the right or a click of the Notifications button.

- **Hot corners.** For PCs without a touchscreen, a key navigation principle in Windows 8 involved moving the mouse to a corner and pausing until something happened. Moving the mouse pointer to the upper left corner and then sliding down, for example, exposed a column of thumbnails for switching between running apps. In Windows 10, moving the mouse to a corner does nothing special, and app switching has been moved to the Task View button and its keyboard shortcuts.

- **Start screen.** The Start screen, filled with colorful live tiles, was the first thing a new Windows 8 user saw. Over time, with Windows 8.1 and a subsequent update, the Start screen was modified to make it less jarring. In Windows 10, the desktop is the default first step. If you miss the Start screen, you can restore the experience by expanding the Start menu to full screen or switching to Tablet Mode.

Our experience suggests that the learning curve for Windows 10 is not that steep. But it's ironic that one of the biggest challenges in making the transition from Windows 8 is unlearning these now-missing elements.

Windows 10 isn't just an evolution of features you already knew, however; you'll also find plenty of new capabilities to explore.

Cortana, for example, is the Windows 10 "personal assistant," first seen in Windows Phone 8.1, who takes over the search box if you give her permission and then delivers news headlines, reminders, and answers based on your schedule and your interests. Which interests exactly? That's under your control, using the Notebook shown in Figure 1-5 to tailor your preferences.

We explain how to use and customize this feature in "Cortana and search" in Chapter 3.

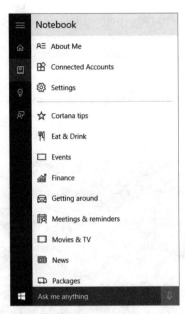

Figure 1-5 With Cortana enabled, clicking in the search box displays personalized reminders and alerts based on settings you specify in the Cortana Notebook.

Another major addition, all new in Windows 10, is the pane that appears on the right side when you swipe in from the right on a touchscreen or click the Notifications button, just to the left of the clock. (In a bit of naming confusion, this new feature is called Action Center, although it's unrelated to the identically named feature from earlier Windows versions.) The top of the pane contains notifications from apps (new messages, weather alerts, alarms, reminders), while the bottom contains handy buttons for performing common tasks, as shown in Figure 1-6.

Figure 1-6 These buttons, which appear beneath notifications in Action Center, allow quick access to system settings.

The new universal apps for Windows 10 are delivered through the Windows Store, just as their predecessors in Windows 8 were, but that's where the resemblance ends. In Windows 10, these so-called modern apps can work in resizable windows alongside conventional Windows desktop applications.

On a tablet, for example, the editing capabilities in the new Photos app work best in full screen. On a large desktop display (or two), the full-screen view is overkill and the app is perfectly usable in a window, as shown in Figure 1-7.

Figure 1-7 The editing controls in the new Photos app are designed so that they work well in a resizable window on desktop PCs with a large display, a keyboard, and a mouse.

For a more thorough look at how modern apps work, see Chapter 8, "Using and managing modern apps and desktop programs."

Fundamental changes in core features

If you're among the substantial population that has stuck with Windows 7 for the past few years, you've missed some interesting and deep-seated changes to some of the core features in Windows. We go into detail about three of those features in this book.

- **File Explorer.** It's no longer called Windows Explorer; beginning with Windows 8, the name officially changed to File Explorer. The addition of a Microsoft Office–style ribbon, shown in Figure 1-8, makes a number of formerly obscure operations more discoverable and dramatically improves search capabilities by adding a Search Tools tab when you click in the search box. Windows 10 adds a Quick Access region in the navigation pane. We cover File Explorer in exhaustive detail in Chapter 12, "Organizing and searching for files."

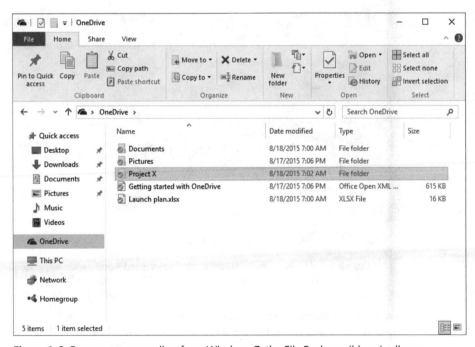

Figure 1-8 For anyone upgrading from Windows 7, the File Explorer ribbon is all new.

- **Backup and recovery.** If you've ever had to reinstall an older version of Windows, you know how tedious and time-consuming the process can be. Windows 8 introduced "push-button reset" options that automate the process of a clean install, with the option to keep your data or wipe it clean. Windows 10 refines those options impressively, as we explain in Chapter 16, "Backup, restore, and recovery." It also adds the ability to undo a Windows 10 upgrade and restore your previous Windows version, as shown in Figure 1-9.

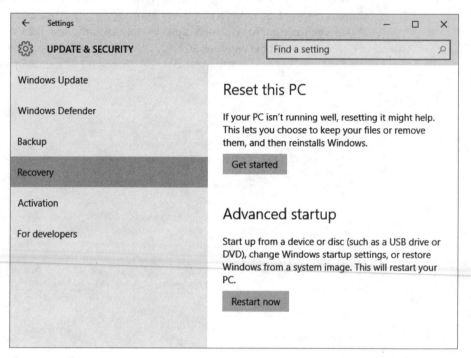

Figure 1-9 The Recovery options in Windows 8 are significantly enhanced in Windows 10, using less disk space and requiring fewer post-restore updates.

- **Task Manager.** This is another familiar Windows 7 utility that received a major make-over in Windows 8. The same improvements are visible in Windows 10: more information about running processes, a new tab for managing processes, and detailed performance information, as shown in Figure 1-10. For an in-depth look at the new Task Manager, see Chapter 15, "System maintenance and performance."

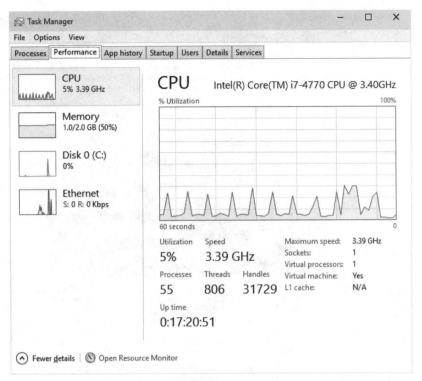

Figure 1-10 The Task Manager Performance tab in Windows 10 offers more information, more clearly organized, than its Windows 7 predecessor.

Windows 10, the web, and cloud services

Internet Explorer has been a part of every version of Windows released in the past 20 years. In Windows 10, for the first time, Internet Explorer isn't the default web browser. Instead, that honor goes to a new browser, Microsoft Edge.

Edge is touch friendly, with a minimal list of controls. Among its unique features is a Reading View button that reformats and rearranges the text of a cluttered webpage to make a less distracting reading experience. You can see this feature in action in Figure 1-11.

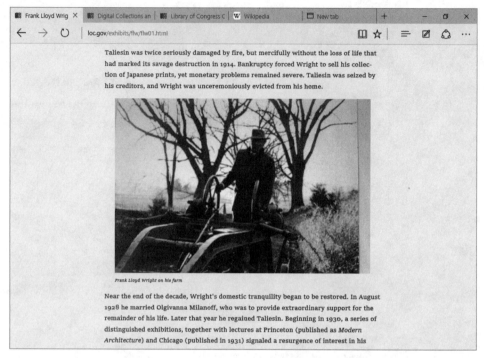

Figure 1-11 The Microsoft Edge web browser has simple controls and a Reading View option that reformats text and removes clutter from webpages.

Edge uses a new rendering engine designed with interoperability as a much higher priority than backward compatibility. Internet Explorer is still available for situations where its unique features are essential. We explain the differences between Internet Explorer and Edge, as well as how to configure each one to match your preferences, in Chapter 11, "Browsing the Internet."

Of course, a web browser isn't the only way to connect to shared resources online. When you sign in using a Microsoft account, Windows 10 automatically connects to shared files in the OneDrive service. You can also connect to business-class services using Office 365 and Azure Active Directory.

Working and playing with Windows 10

If you're looking for familiar names in the list of apps included with Windows 10, you'll find plenty—Windows Media Player, Notepad, and Paint, for example.

But much more interesting are the new universal apps that are designed to work on any device running Windows 10. Because these apps are updated automatically via the Windows Store, they can incorporate new features and fix bugs without requiring a separate installation. These apps also allow you to sync settings and data between Windows 10 devices without having to reconfigure accounts or import data.

Windows 10 includes several productivity apps as part of a default installation. Chief among them are the new Mail and Calendar apps, which work with a variety of Internet services, including Microsoft's Outlook.com and Office 365 services as well as Google's Gmail and Apple's iCloud. Figure 1-12 shows a week of appointments in the Calendar app.

Figure 1-12 The Calendar app, shown here, is included with a default installation of Windows 10. You can switch to the companion Mail app with a click of the icon in the lower left corner.

There are other productivity apps available in the Windows Store, including touch-friendly versions of Word, Excel, and PowerPoint that are included as part of a standard installation in some editions of Windows 10.

For more on work-oriented apps and utilities in Windows 10, see Chapter 9, "Productivity and communication tools."

Windows 10 is also a solid platform for entertainment apps, including digital music and video services that also work on Xbox consoles and Windows 10 phones. The Music app developed exclusively for Windows 10, shown in Figure 1-13, also allows you to access your own personal collection, stored in OneDrive.

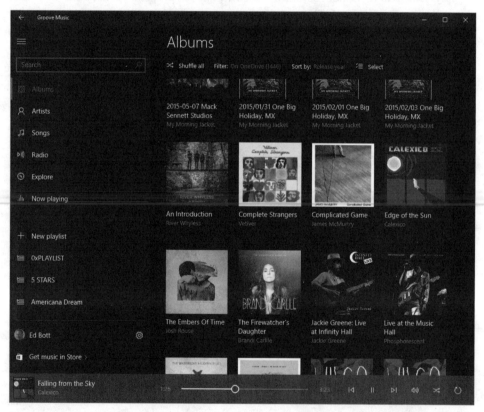

Figure 1-13 The Windows 10 Music app lets you connect via the cloud to a music collection stored in OneDrive's Music folder.

Another hidden gem among the new entertainment features in Windows 10 is built-in support for Miracast adapters, which plug in to an HDMI input on a high-definition TV. Using Miracast, you can tune in to an online video clip and project it to the big screen, with full support for surround sound.

You'll find more details about apps made for fun and games in Chapter 10, "Music, photos, movies, and games."

More updates, more often

Historically, the cadence of Windows has gone something like this: Roughly every three years, a new version of Windows comes out. When you buy a new PC, it includes the latest Windows version; for existing PCs, you can upgrade your current Windows version to the new one (or choose not to upgrade). You then live with that version of Windows until the next one is released and the cycle begins anew.

That's all history now.

Beginning with Windows 10, Microsoft has declared its intention to treat Windows as a service. In the first year after the release of Windows 10, upgrades are free to anyone running Windows 7 Service Pack 1 or Windows 8.1 (except for Windows Enterprise editions, which are available only through Volume License purchases and play by a different set of rules).

Whether you buy a new device with Windows 10 or upgrade an existing one, it is eligible for feature updates, which will be delivered through Windows Update. That's a major change for Windows users, who normally receive only security and reliability updates through these Microsoft-managed channels. Instead of waiting two or three years to be included in a new Windows version or a service pack, new features will be delivered automatically, when they're ready.

The new update process also allows Windows users to choose how soon they want to receive those updates.

Previously, Microsoft developed and tested new Windows features privately, occasionally offering the public an advance look in the form of preview versions before releasing them publicly.

Beginning with Windows 10, those preview releases are built into the development cycle. As new features make their way into Windows, they are delivered to different "flights," starting with internal testers in Microsoft's engineering group, then working out to customers who have opted in to receive preview releases. Each new flight reaches a larger number of people, with fixes for bugs discovered in previous flights incorporated into later ones. Figure 1-14 shows, conceptually, how the flight process works.

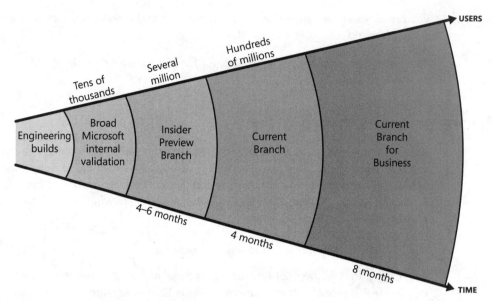

Figure 1-14 For Windows 10, Microsoft is delivering new features in "flights" that eventually reach consumers in the Current Branch.

The official release, installed by PC manufacturers and available to the general public, is officially called the Current Branch. It represents program code that has been thoroughly tested as part of the preview cycle and corresponds to what have traditionally been General Availability releases of new Windows versions or service packs.

This process also allows Microsoft to continue the Windows 10 Preview program, which it started in October 2014. Members of this program, called Windows Insiders, have full access to early test releases of Windows 10 along with frequent updates. In exchange, Microsoft's developers receive unprecedented levels of feedback that shape the development effort in real time. That feedback comes from automated data collection (known as telemetry) and a Feedback app, shown in Figure 1-15, which is installed with every preview release.

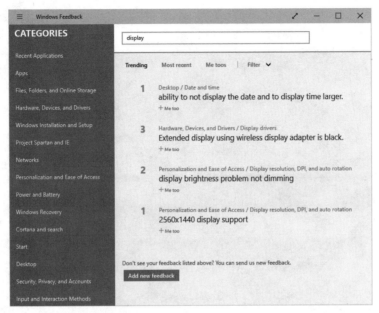

Figure 1-15 This Windows Feedback app allows anyone using a preview version of Windows 10 to report bugs and offer suggestions directly to Microsoft.

Windows 10 for IT pros and experts

The intended scope of this book covers consumers and small businesses using Windows 10. We would need hundreds of additional pages to cover the concerns of IT pros and network administrators responsible for integrating Windows 10 devices into Windows domains using Active Directory.

But if you fall into the IT pro classification, we haven't completely forgotten about you. In particular, we suggest you look at Part 4, where we've assembled information of special interest to power users and administrators.

In those chapters, you'll find information on arcane but incredibly useful topics like editing the Windows registry, troubleshooting performance-related issues, and automating routine tasks.

For those who really want to polish their expert skills, we especially recommend Chapter 21, "Working with Command Prompt and Windows PowerShell," and Chapter 22, "Running virtual machines with Hyper-V," which goes into depth with the powerful, built-in virtualization platform included with Pro and Enterprise editions of Windows 10.

Installing, configuring, and deploying Windows 10

Microsoft's ambitious goal for Windows 10 is to have it running on 1 billion devices within two or three years after its launch.

A few hundred million of those devices will be new PCs, laptops, tablets, and phones that come with Windows 10. But a potentially much larger number will be PCs currently running Windows 7 or Windows 8.1, thanks to Microsoft's unprecedented offer of a free upgrade for those devices. (That offer ends on July 29, 2016, one year after the official launch of Windows 10.)

Among some PC traditionalists, it is a badge of honor to wipe a newly purchased PC clean and then set up Windows from scratch. Even if you're not so fastidious, a clean install is sometimes unavoidable: it's the only option for PCs you build yourself and for virtual machines, and it's sometimes the fastest way to get back up and running after a disk failure.

The same Windows 10 setup program is used for both upgrades and clean installs. For upgrades, the installer is streamlined, offering a minimum of options. Booting from Windows 10 installation media offers a much more complete set of options: choosing a specific physical disk for use in dual-boot (or multiboot) scenarios, creating and formatting partitions, and setting up unattended installations, for example.

In this chapter, we cover both options. We don't include step-by-step instructions to document every possible upgrade or clean installation scenario. Given the nearly infinite number of combinations of PC hardware, comprehensive instructions would be impossible, and besides, we're confident that our readers can make their way through a setup wizard without handholding.

Instead, this chapter concentrates on the big picture, breaking each type of Windows setup into its major steps and explaining what happens (and what can go wrong) in each one. We finish with a checklist to run through after completing an upgrade or clean install.

But first, some suggestions on how to make the setup process as smooth as possible.

Before you start

If you're lucky, your Windows 10 upgrade will be uneventful and the results will be flawless. You can increase the odds of this ideal outcome by taking some common-sense precautions first.

At the top of this list is checking the hardware on which you plan to install Windows 10 to confirm that it meets the minimum requirements (note that this list is unchanged from the system requirements for Windows 7):

- Processor: 1 gigahertz (GHz) or faster

- RAM: 1 gigabyte (GB) (32-bit) or 2 GB (64-bit)

- Free disk space (system drive): 16 GB

- Graphics card: Microsoft DirectX 9 graphics device with WDDM driver

NOTE

The free disk space requirement varies, and Microsoft is continuing to work on improving upgrade scenarios for low disk space. On devices with very small amounts of built-in storage, you might be able to upgrade with as little as 10 free gigabytes. As you approach that threshold, however, you might find that setup fails in unpredictable ways. If you're stuck, check the Microsoft Community forums (*http://answers.microsoft.com*) to see whether there's a workaround for your situation.

Those are fairly modest requirements, and virtually every PC sold in the past six years with Windows 7 or a later version preinstalled should qualify.

For online upgrades to Windows 10, you also need a Microsoft account and Internet access. In fact, regular Internet access is a prerequisite for most of the tasks we describe in this book.

Inside OUT

RIP, Windows Media Center

One of the signature features of Windows for many years has been Windows Media Center. This feature, which debuted as a special edition of Windows XP in 2002, enabled a so-called 10-foot interface for using Windows PCs as an entertainment hub in a living room. Media Center grew steadily from its original design, adding support for high-definition TV and digital cable tuners, to become the centerpiece of the Windows 7 Home Premium, Professional, and Ultimate editions.

After Windows 7 launched, the Windows Media Center team was disbanded and development of the feature ceased. In Windows 8 and 8.1, the Media Center functionality was available as an extra-cost add-on, but it was a simple port of the Windows 7 version, with no new features.

With Windows 10, Windows Media Center is officially retired. When you run Windows 10 Setup to upgrade a PC that has the Windows Media Center feature enabled, it will be uninstalled, and the feature will be completely unavailable after the upgrade is complete. There's no registry magic or secret to enable the feature on Windows 10, either. If Media Center is a make-or-break feature for you, avoid the Windows 10 upgrade on that PC.

Check for potential compatibility problems

In broad terms, any device that is already running Windows 8.1 should be compatible with Windows 10, as should any apps or device drivers installed on that device. There are, however, exceptions to this rule—some of them minor, others more serious. Your likelihood of encountering (usually minor) compatibility issues goes up when upgrading Windows 7 (with Service Pack 1).

The Windows 10 setup program includes a compatibility checker that alerts you to any potential compatibility issues before performing the actual installation. We describe its workings in the section, "Upgrading to Windows 10."

Before you run the setup program, though, it's worth taking inventory of your critical apps and devices and checking with the developer or manufacturer to confirm that those products will be supported under Windows 10. Pay special attention to any app or device that's more than a decade old.

Inside OUT

Use dynamic updates

When you upgrade an existing Windows version using Windows Update, the setup program automatically checks for and downloads dynamic updates. When you start the upgrade process from installation media, you're asked whether you want to get the latest updates. If you have an active Internet connection, be sure to take advantage of this option.

Dynamic updates can include any or all of the following: critical updates to the setup program itself; improved or new versions of boot-critical drivers for storage, display, and network hardware detected on your system; and compatibility updates (also known as shims) for programs you're currently running. Rolling these updates in at the beginning of the process increases the likelihood that your Windows 10 upgrade will be successful. After completing installation, you'll still need to connect to Windows Update to check for critical updates for Windows and the most recent drivers for detected hardware.

Back up your data and settings

Having an up-to-date backup of important files is, of course, good advice for any time. But it's especially important when you're upgrading an operating system.

The simplest way to back up files is to sync them to the cloud. OneDrive sync capabilities are built in to Windows 8.1; a sync utility for Windows 7 is available for download from *http://onedrive.com/download*. Move or copy your files into the OneDrive folder and wait for them to be fully synchronized before proceeding.

With large file collections or slow Internet connections, a sufficiently large USB flash drive or an external hard drive makes a perfectly good target for a local backup. If you're upgrading from Windows 7, you can use its built-in backup program; individual files and folders from those backups can be restored in Windows 10 by using the helpfully labeled Backup And Restore (Windows 7) option. For a complete look at your options, see Chapter 16, "Backup, restore, and recovery."

If you're upgrading from Windows 8.1 and you've signed in with a Microsoft account, your personalized settings are already being synced to OneDrive. From Windows 7, there's no easy way to back up those settings. Although you can find third-party utilities that promise to accomplish this task, it's probably faster (and less risky) to re-create that handful of settings than it is to mess with transfer utilities.

Choose the right package

Those who are able to upgrade online can skip this section. The Windows 10 installer delivered through Windows Update chooses the correct successor to your current edition, downloads it for you in the background, and then walks you through setup.

But for every other Windows 10 installation scenario, you have some decisions to make. To do a clean install or to upgrade using Windows media, you typically download an ISO file, which you can then mount directly or use to create installation media. (Physical copies of Windows 10 are also available in packages in which the installer is on a bootable USB flash drive or a DVD.)

> **NOTE**
> The ISO name is ancient, by modern computing standards, dating back to the mid-1980s. And, strictly speaking, it's also meaningless. The name is shorthand for the file system originally used with CD-ROM media, which was designated ISO 9660 by the standards-setting body that published it. These days, an ISO image file is just as likely to use the UDF file system (ISO/IEC 13346), which is commonly found on larger-capacity optical media such as DVDs and Blu-ray Discs.

Choosing the correct installer involves finding the specific combination of three factors that match your needs:

- **Windows 10 edition.** For installing or upgrading a desktop PC, laptop, or hybrid device, there are two and only two choices: Windows 10 Home or Windows 10 Pro. (Large organizations with volume license contracts can install Windows 10 Enterprise as an upgrade.) We describe the differences between the editions in Appendix A, "Windows 10 editions at a glance."

- **Language.** Windows 10 is available in a large number of languages—111 languages, covering 190 countries and regions, at the time of its initial release. Choose the base language that is appropriate for your installation. You can add language interface packs to translate text that's displayed in commonly used wizards, dialog boxes, menus, and other items in the user interface; however, you can't change the parent language except by reinstalling Windows using an edition built for that language.

- **Architecture.** Windows 10 is available in 32-bit and 64-bit distributions. Most modern CPUs will support either version, and your preference should be for the 64-bit version. In general, 32-bit versions of Windows are appropriate for systems with 2 GB (or less) of RAM, with no option to add memory. Choose a 64-bit version if your system includes 4 GB or more of memory or if you rely on one or more programs that are available only in 64-bit editions. (And note that all of your 32-bit programs, including new and old versions of Microsoft Office, will work fine on a 64-bit copy of Windows, so you needn't fear in that regard.)

If your goal is to purchase a physical or electronic copy of Windows for installation on a new PC or in a virtual machine, the intricacies of Windows licensing require several additional decisions beyond those we just described.

You can choose from the following license types:

- **Full.** A full license is sold directly to consumers as an electronic distribution or a packaged product. With a full license, Windows can be installed on a computer that was not sold with Windows originally, or it can be used as an upgrade. A full license can be transferred to a different computer as long as the underlying copy of Windows is no longer being used on the original location.

- **OEM.** An OEM (original equipment manufacturer) license is one that's included with a new computer. This license is locked to the computer on which it's installed and cannot be transferred to a new computer. OEM System Builder packages are intended for use by small PC makers but are often used by consumers and hobbyists in place of a full license. The system builder is required to provide support for OEM Windows along with the device on which it is installed.

- **Upgrade.** An upgrade license is a discounted copy of Windows that can be installed only on a system that already has an OEM or full license.

- **Volume.** Volume licenses are sold in bulk to corporate, government, nonprofit, and educational customers and are typically deployed by using enterprise management tools. A volume license is available as an upgrade only.

Any PC that was purchased with Windows 7, Windows 8, or Windows 8.1 preinstalled (look for the sticker on the PC itself or on the power supply) is qualified for a free Windows 10 upgrade (the free upgrade offer is good until July 29, 2016). This is true whether the PC came from a large OEM or from a system builder.

You need a full license to install Windows in a virtual machine, on a Mac or other computer that does not come with Windows preinstalled, or in a dual-boot or multiboot setup. That condition can be satisfied with a full (retail or OEM) license of Windows 10 or a full license for an earlier Windows version that supports a Windows 10 upgrade.

> NOTE
>
> It's important to understand that the legal and contractual restrictions imposed by license agreements are completely independent of technical restrictions on installation. If you upgrade a system to Windows 10 from Windows 7 and then the system's hard disk fails, you can perform a clean install of Windows 10 and still be properly licensed. Conversely, it is technically possible to install and activate an upgrade version on a computer that doesn't have an underlying license, but doing so violates the license agreement.

Choose your upgrade method

Microsoft strongly encourages online upgrades for anyone running Windows 7 (with Service Pack 1) or Windows 8.1. But you also have the option to perform a custom installation. A custom installation of Windows 10 allows you to start from scratch, with or without your personal data files; you need to reinstall your programs and re-create or transfer settings from another system. An upgrade retains installed programs and settings, but at the risk of creating some compatibility issues.

You'll need to boot from the Windows 10 media and choose a custom installation if either of the following conditions is true:

- **You need to adjust the layout of the system disk.** The Windows 10 installation program includes disk-management tools that you can use to create, delete, format, and extend (but not shrink) partitions on hard disks installed in your computer. Knowing how these tools work can save you a significant amount of time when setting up Windows.

- **You want to install Windows 10 alongside another operating system.** If you want to set up a multiboot system, you'll need to understand how different startup files work so that you can manage your startup options effectively. We discuss this option later in this chapter, in the section "Configuring a multiboot system."

If the system on which you plan to install Windows 10 is already running Windows 7, Windows 8.1, or Windows 10, you can start the setup program from within Windows.

Running setup from within Windows allows you to upgrade from Windows 7 or Windows 8.1, transferring settings and desktop programs to the new installation—provided that the Windows 10 edition is equivalent to or higher than the currently installed Windows edition. If you attempt an unsupported upgrade path, you have the option to transfer personal files only. Table 2-1 shows the supported upgrade paths.

Table 2-1 Supported upgrade paths by edition

Current version	Supported upgrade
Windows 7 Starter, Home Basic, Home Premium	Windows 10 Home
Windows 7 Professional, Ultimate	Windows 10 Pro
Windows 8.1	Windows 10 Home
Windows 8.1 Pro, Windows 8.1 Pro for Students	Windows 10 Pro
Windows Phone 8.1	Windows 10 Mobile

Starting Setup from within Windows does not offer the option to perform a custom install. However, performing an upgrade and choosing Nothing from the list of what you want to keep has the same effect as performing a clean install. After Windows 10 is installed, the Reset option is the preferred way to accomplish the task of repairing a Windows installation that isn't working properly.

Note that the installation media must match the architecture of the installed Windows version. You cannot run the 64-bit setup program on a PC running a 32-bit version of Windows, or vice versa. In addition, you cannot make any changes to the layout of a disk when running Setup from within Windows; you must use existing partitions, and Setup will not recognize or use unallocated space on an attached hard drive.

If you boot from the Windows 10 installation media, you can delete existing partitions, create new partitions, extend an existing disk partition to unallocated space, or designate a block of unallocated space as the setup location. (We describe these actions later in this chapter.) After booting from the Windows installation media, you cannot upgrade an existing Windows installation. Your only option is a custom install.

Using either setup option, you can install Windows 10 on the same volume as an existing Windows version. (You'll find step-by-step instructions in "Performing a clean install" later in this chapter.)

In the next section, we explain what happens behind the scenes when you perform a Windows 10 upgrade or a clean install.

How Windows 10 Setup works

The Windows 10 setup program does its magic using two folders.

- **C:\\$Windows.~BT** is a hidden folder that contains the files used during both the online and offline phases of setup. These files are downloaded directly if you upgrade using Windows Update. When you launch Setup from installation media, such as an ISO file or a bootable DVD or USB flash drive, the initial phase of setup creates this folder and copies the setup files to it for temporary use, eliminating the possibility of a setup failure caused by prematurely removing or unmounting the installation media.

- **C:\Windows.old** is created only when you perform an upgrade or do a clean install on a volume that already contains a Windows installation. This folder does double duty. During upgrades, it's used as a transfer location to hold files and settings that are moving from the old installation to the new one. After setup is complete, this folder holds system files from the previous Windows installation as well as any user files that were not migrated during setup.

NOTE

These temporary installation files are deleted automatically after four weeks. Your previous Windows installation is saved indefinitely in Windows.old, allowing you to roll back to the previous version if necessary. On systems with limited storage, you can use the Disk Cleanup utility to remove these files manually. We describe this process in more detail in "Managing disk space" in Chapter 15, "System maintenance and performance."

Upgrading to Windows 10

The streamlined wizard that walks you through a Windows 10 upgrade should be familiar if you've used Windows 8 or 8.1. If most of your experience is with Windows 7, we predict you'll be pleasantly surprised by the improvements in speed (especially on systems with a large number of files) and the reduction in complexity of the entire setup process.

In Windows 10, the upgrade process is optimized for software distribution over the Internet. In those scenarios, the installer file is downloaded using Windows Update and the well-tested Background Intelligent Transfer Service.

No major upgrade is ever risk free, of course, but the Windows 10 installer is designed to be robust enough to roll back gracefully in case of a failure.

When you kick off a Windows 10 upgrade, the setup program performs a series of tasks. First, it runs a compatibility check, which determines whether your PC, peripheral devices, and installed Windows apps will work with Windows 10. (See "Checking compatibility" later in this section for details about warnings that might appear.)

Using Windows Update

Assuming you have a reasonably fast Internet connection, the simplest and fastest way to upgrade to Windows 10 is by using Windows Update. To start that process, click the Get Windows 10 icon in the notification area at the right side of the taskbar, or use the Get Windows 10 link in Windows Update, and then follow the instructions.

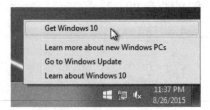

CHAPTER 2

Inside OUT

What if the Get Windows 10 icon isn't visible?

The Get Windows 10 app is a tiny helper app that is automatically installed (via Windows Update) on all PCs running up-to-date versions of Windows 8.1 or Windows 7. If you don't see the icon, here are some possible reasons:

- The KB3035583 update, which delivers the Get Windows 10 app, is not installed. Solution: Check Windows Update and, if necessary, confirm that the update hasn't been hidden. See *https://support.microsoft.com/kb/3035583*.

- Windows is out of date. Solution: For Windows 7, you must have Service Pack 1 installed. Windows 8 PCs must be updated via the Windows Store to Windows 8.1, and Windows 8.1 PCs must have the Windows 8.1 Update (KB2919355) installed. More details are at *http://windows.microsoft.com/en-us/windows-8/install-latest-update-windows-8-1*.

- Your PC is running an Enterprise edition of Windows or is joined to a domain. Solution: Talk with your network administrator about how your organization plans to deploy Windows 10.

That program checks your system configuration for compatibility issues. Assuming your system passes the compatibility test, the app then determines which Windows 10 edition (Home or Pro, 32-bit or 64-bit) is appropriate for the existing installation and configures Windows Update to receive upgrades.

After a restart, Windows Update runs automatically. You should see a dialog box like the one shown in Figure 2-1.

Click Get Started to begin.

Windows Update downloads the necessary installer files in the background, including one large Windows Image file in compressed ESD format, to the C:\Windows\SoftwareDistribution\Download folder. When the download is complete, Windows Update moves Install.esd to the hidden folder C:\$Windows.~BT (along with the other setup files). You can monitor the download progress from Windows Update.

Figure 2-1 Assuming your Internet connection is fast enough, Windows Update is the easiest way to upgrade to Windows 10.

At the end, you see the prompt shown in Figure 2-2. After you restart, the offline portion of the setup process begins.

Figure 2-2 Click Restart Now to switch Setup into offline mode, where the actual installation and migration of settings takes place.

Inside OUT

Upgrade directly from an ISO file

The ISO disc image format was originally devised to make it possible to share DVDs as files, without having to put shiny discs in the mail and wait a few days or weeks. Over time, they've evolved into a virtual alternative that doesn't require discs at all. Beginning with Windows 8, File Explorer supports the capability to mount ISO files directly. (For Windows 7, you need a utility program like the free Virtual CloneDrive from SlySoft, *http://slysoft.com*.)

Obviously, this option won't work for a clean install on a freshly formatted drive, but it's ideal for upgrades. Double-click a saved ISO file in File Explorer to map its contents to a virtual disk, which appears as a DVD drive in the Devices And Drives area of File Explorer, as in Figure 2-3.

Figure 2-3 In this File Explorer window, drive D is a physical drive, but drive E is a virtual drive created by double-clicking and mounting an ISO disc image file.

Double-click to open the mounted disk, and then run Setup to kick off an upgrade. When you no longer need the virtual drive, right-click its File Explorer icon and click Eject.

Using Windows installation media

When you start an online upgrade from within Windows 8.1, the upgrade keeps all your data files and migrates settings, Windows apps, and desktop programs. Upgrades from Windows 7 preserve data files and desktop programs but do not migrate personalized settings such as your desktop background.

If you have Windows 10 installation media, you can also start the upgrade process from within Windows. Open the DVD or USB flash drive in File Explorer and double-click Setup. The resulting wizard walks you through several steps that aren't part of the streamlined online upgrade. The most important of these is the option to transfer files, apps, and settings, a topic we cover shortly.

Checking compatibility

A comprehensive compatibility checker is built into the Windows 10 setup program (it replaces the Upgrade Advisor from Windows 7), and runs as one of the first steps when you kick off an upgrade. A more limited version runs on a clean install, checking for issues such as a BIOS that needs updating or a disk controller or network adapter that has no supported driver.

In most cases, this appraisal turns up nothing, and setup continues without interruption. If this routine finds any issues, however, it notifies you with a warning dialog box. When the compatibility checker turns up any "hard blocks," setup ends immediately, with a message like the one shown in Figure 2-4.

Setup will refuse to continue if your device doesn't have enough RAM or free disk space. Other causes of hard blocks include a CPU or a BIOS that is not supported, as well as the presence of a hard-disk controller or networking device that lacks a driver.

For less severe issues, Setup might warn you that specific apps or devices may not work correctly or will have reduced functionality in Windows 10. You may be given the option to fix the issue and try the upgrade again. In these cases, the compatibility checker offers instructions to deal with specific issues:

- You might need to install updates to your current version of Windows before continuing. If you are upgrading from Windows Update, this task is handled automatically.

- You might need to suspend disk encryption before upgrading.

- Some apps must be uninstalled before the upgrade can continue (in some cases, they can be reinstalled after the upgrade is complete).

- Some apps must be updated to a newer version before the upgrade can be completed.

- After the upgrade, you might need to reinstall language packs.

CHAPTER 2

Figure 2-4 A hard block, such as too little memory or an unsupported CPU or network device, will prevent you from installing Windows 10 on a PC.

If the upgrade process ends prematurely for any of these reasons, Setup generally cleans up after itself, although you might have to manually remove some leftovers.

Transferring files, apps, and settings

When you install Windows 10 on a disk volume that already contains a copy of Windows, you must choose what you want to do with user files, settings, and apps. As we noted earlier, online upgrades using Windows Update make this choice for you.

To choose an alternative option, run Setup from installation media or an ISO file. Figure 2-5 shows your options when upgrading from Windows 8.1 to Windows 10.

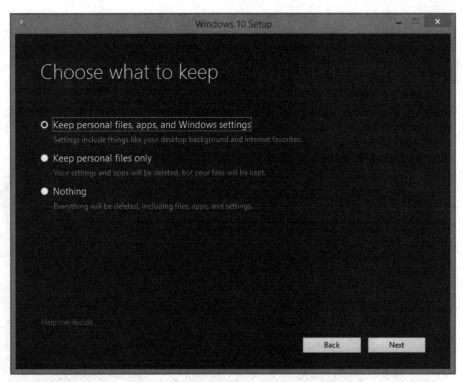

Figure 2-5 When you start a Windows 10 upgrade from installation media, you see the full range of options shown here.

Here's what happens with each option:

- **Keep Personal Files, Apps, And Windows Settings.** All Windows desktop programs and user accounts are migrated. After the upgrade is complete, you need to sign in with your Microsoft account to reinstall apps from the Windows Store and sync saved settings.

  ### NOTE
  This option is unavailable if you are installing a Windows edition that is not a supported upgrade path from the current edition.

- **Keep Personal Files Only.** This option is the equivalent of a repair installation. Each user's personal files are available in a user profile that otherwise contains only default apps and settings.

CHAPTER 2

- **Nothing.** Choose this option if you want to perform a clean install, with your exist-ing installation moved to Windows.old. Note that the descriptive text, "Everything will be deleted," is misleading. Your personal files, as well as those belonging to other user accounts in the current installation, are not deleted. Instead, they are moved to the Windows.old folder, where you can recover them by using File Explorer.

After the initial prep work, Setup restarts in offline mode, displaying a progress screen like the one shown in Figure 2-6.

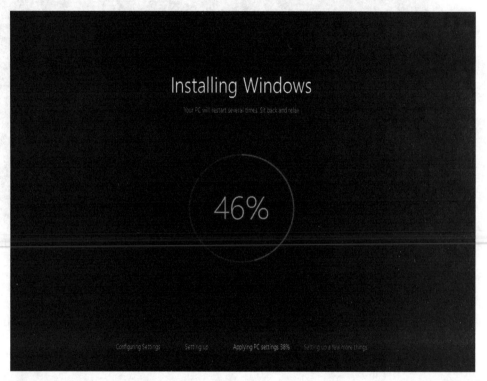

Figure 2-6 The progress circle in the center of this status screen makes one full revolution for each of the phases listed along the bottom of the screen.

In this mode, you can't interact with the PC at all. Your PC is effectively offline as the following actions occur.

Windows Setup first moves the following folders from the existing Windows installation on the root of the system drive into Windows.old:

- Windows

- Program files

- Program files (x86)

- Users

- Program data

During this offline phase, Setup extracts registry values and program data from the Windows.old folder, based on the type of upgrade, and then adds this data to the corresponding locations in the new Windows 10 installation.

Next, Setup lays down a new set of system folders for Windows 10 using the folder structure and files from the compressed Windows image. After that task is complete, Setup moves program files, registry values, and other settings it gathered earlier.

Moving folders minimizes the number of file operations that have to take place, making upgrade times consistent even when individual user accounts contain large numbers of files. (By contrast, the Windows 7 setup program moved files individually, which could lead to some painfully long upgrades.)

To further speed things up, Windows 10 Setup uses hard link operations to move files and folders from the transport location to the new Windows 10 hierarchy. Not having to physically move the file improves performance and also allows for easy rollback if something goes wrong during setup.

Folders associated with individual user accounts are moved when they meet the following criteria:

- Every file in the folder and all of its subfolders is preserved, with no rules defined to exclude some files or subfolders.

- The entire folder is placed within the fresh Windows 10 installation unchanged.

- The target Windows 10 destination doesn't already exist and thus there's no need to merge an existing folder in the target destination with one from the source operating system.

This activity is accompanied by several restarts and can take as long as a few hours, depending on your hardware. At the conclusion of this process, you're confronted with a sign-in screen like the one shown in Figure 2-7.

CHAPTER 2

Figure 2-7 In the final stage of setup, signing in with a Microsoft account restores synced settings and apps from OneDrive.

By signing in with a Microsoft account, you can continue setting up Windows 10 by using synced settings. The most current version of each installed app is downloaded and installed from the Windows Store, a process that may continue for several minutes after you sign in.

If you're upgrading from Windows 7 or from a Windows 8.1 PC that was configured to use a local user account, you'll need to sign in using the credentials for that account. After that, you'll have the option to link your account to a Microsoft account or to continue using a local account.

For more on your options when setting up a user account, see Chapter 6, "Managing user accounts, passwords, and credentials."

Performing a clean install

For some veteran Windows users, a clean install is the only option worth considering. Histori-cally, that option means starting up from a bootable USB flash drive containing the Windows 10 installation files and removing all traces of the currently installed Windows version before proceeding with setup.

This is still a perfectly valid installation method, one we'll describe in more detail shortly. But it's no longer the only option, nor is it always the best. For a system that's already running any modern version of Windows, you'll find it much easier to start Setup from within Windows, choose an upgrade install, and choose the option to keep Nothing. After you use Disk Cleanup Manager to remove the old Windows installation, the result is identical to an old-fashioned clean install.

> ## NOTE
> **For a thorough discussion of how the Push Button Reset option works, see Chapter 16.**

That neat option isn't possible if you are starting with a brand-new hard disk or you want to install a 64-bit Windows 10 edition on a device that's currently running 32-bit Windows, or you want to clean up a messy OEM's partition layout on the system disk, or . . . you get the idea.

For those scenarios, you need to boot into the Windows 10 setup program from a USB flash drive (or a DVD drive, if your PC is equipped with one of those increasingly rare peripherals). You might need to read the manual for your device to learn the magic combination of key-strokes and firmware settings that make it possible to start up using a bootable Windows 10 disc or drive.

After the setup process begins, you can follow the instructions as outlined in this section.

Making bootable media

You can't simply copy installation files to a flash drive and use it to perform a clean install. First, you have to make the disk bootable. When creating a bootable drive, you need to con-sider two factors:

- **Partitioning scheme: MBR or GPT?** You can use either scheme with a UEFI system; older BIOS-based systems might only be able to recognize MBR partitions.

- **Disk format: NTFS or FAT32?** If you plan to install Windows on a UEFI-based system (such as Microsoft's Surface Pro line), the boot files *must* reside on a FAT32 partition. If the drive is formatted using another file system, the PC will not recognize the device as bootable.

CHAPTER 2

One of the simplest ways to create a bootable install drive from an ISO file is to use the built-in Recovery Media Creator utility. In previous Windows versions, this tool was able to create a bootable drive that included the recovery partition provided by the OEM. If you performed a clean install or removed that recovery partition for space purposes, the recovery drive could be used only for simple repair operations.

In Windows 10, if the Recovery Media Creator can't find an OEM-supplied recovery image, it reconstructs one from currently installed system files. You can use that image to replace the underlying Windows 10 version, and you can use it to perform a clean install. Figure 2-8 shows this utility in operation.

Figure 2-8 Choose the option to add system files if you want to create a recovery drive that you can use to reset the current system.

If you have downloaded an ISO file containing the Windows installation files, you can burn that file to a DVD (assuming the target system has an optical drive from which it can start). Or you can create a blank recovery drive using Windows 8.1 or Windows 10, skipping the option to copy system files to the drive; then mount the ISO file and use File Explorer to copy all of its files and folders to the USB recovery drive.

NOTE

For maximum flexibility in creating installable media, we recommend the free, open source utility Rufus, available at *http://rufus.akeo.ie/*. **It allows precise control over partitioning, formatting, and copying installation files to a USB flash drive.**

When you boot from that media, you pass through a few introductory screens—choosing a language, accepting a license agreement—and eventually reach the Windows Setup dialog box shown in Figure 2-9. Although you're prompted to choose an installation type—Upgrade or Custom—that's actually a trick question.

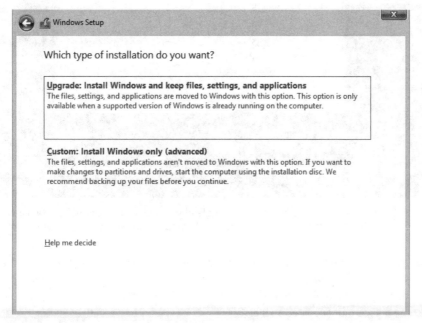

Figure 2-9 When you boot from a USB flash drive or DVD to perform a clean install of Windows, the only option that works from this screen is Custom.

Choosing the Upgrade option raises an error message; you can upgrade Windows only if you start Setup from within Windows.

The Custom option allows you to continue, and you're presented with a list of available disks and volumes. Figure 2-10 shows what you'll see on a system with a single, newly installed hard drive.

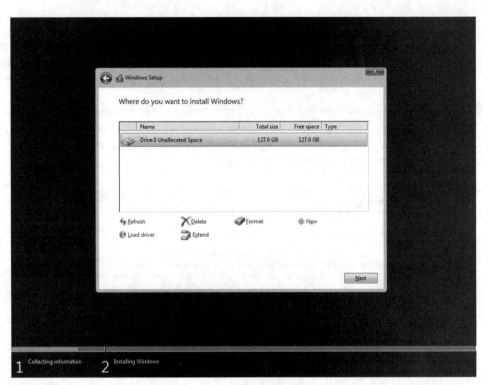

Figure 2-10 In this simple scenario, with a single physical disk that does not contain any partitions, you can click Next to create a partition and install Windows using the entire physical drive.

You can use the tools beneath the list of available drives to manage partitions on the selected drive. These tools allow you to delete an existing partition (for a truly fresh start on a drive that already contains files), create a new partition, format a partition, or extend a partition to include adjacent unallocated space.

For more on managing disks using the full array of Windows tools, see Chapter 14, "Managing disks and drives."

When you click Next, the setup process switches into a lengthy unattended phase in which it lays down the clean Windows 10 image. When that's complete, you get to choose default settings for all new accounts. The default settings are explained in detail in the Use Express Settings screen, shown in Figure 2-11. Click the small Customize Settings link in the lower left corner to open additional pages where you can adjust any of these settings.

If you do a clean install using bootable media for Windows 10 Pro, you're faced with one additional choice immediately after this phase of setup. The dialog box shown in Figure 2-12 asks you who owns your PC. (For an installation of Windows 10 Enterprise, the dialog box asks whether you want to join Azure AD or join a domain.)

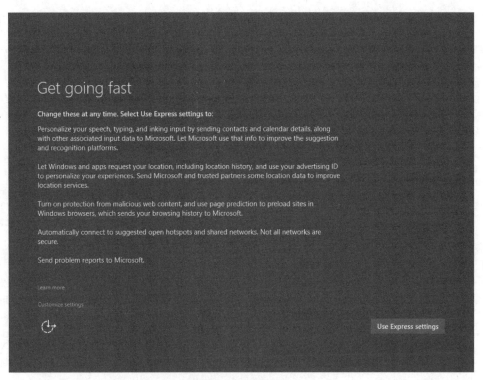

Figure 2-11 When you do a clean install, these default options allow you to configure a user account quickly, without fussing over individual options.

Figure 2-12 This option is available only when you do a clean install of Windows 10 Pro.

Choosing the first option (My Organization) and clicking Next leads you through a slightly confusing series of dialog boxes that allows you to set up a device for access to online services (from Microsoft and others). The credentials are managed in Azure Active Directory and can be linked to services such as an Office 365 account at a workplace or university.

If you own the device, or if it is a company PC that will be joined to a local Windows domain, choose the I Do option.

➤ **For more on setting up user accounts, during or after setup, see Chapter 6.**

Setup and your hard disk

In the previous section, we described the steps for a clean installation on the simplest of all PC configurations: a single hard disk containing unallocated space ready to be automatically partitioned for use as the system drive. Out in the real world, especially among Windows enthusiasts, we know that disk configurations can be much more complex.

On most desktop PCs and on some notebooks, you can connect multiple physical disk drives. You can choose to install Windows 10 to a volume on any IDE or SATA drive (including eSATA drives, which attach to the system via an external cable but appear to Windows as an ordinary internal drive). You cannot, however, install Windows to an external drive connected via USB or IEEE 1394 (FireWire), or to any form of removable media. (The sole exception is the Windows To Go feature, which requires specially built USB drives and an installed copy of Windows 10 Enterprise edition.)

With a new hard disk or an existing one, you might have any of several good reasons to tinker with disk partitions. You might prefer to segregate your operating system files from your data files by placing them on separate volumes, for example, or you might be planning to set up a dual-boot or multiboot system. In any event, it's always easier to make partitioning decisions before setup than it is to resize and rearrange volumes after they're in use.

➤ **For a full inventory of all disk-management tools and techniques available in Windows 10, see Chapter 14.**

Inside OUT

How Windows 10 divides a disk

If you install Windows 10 on a UEFI-based system with a single unformatted disk, Setup creates a default disk layout. Three of its partitions are visible in the Disk Management console, as shown here.

The small (300 MB) recovery partition at the start of the disk contains the Windows Recovery Environment, which allows the system to boot for repair and recovery operations. (For more information, see "Making repairs with the Windows Recovery Environment" in Chapter 17, "Troubleshooting.")

The EFI system partition is even smaller, at 100 MB. It contains the files required for the system to start up, including the Windows Hardware Abstraction Layer and the boot loader (NTLDR).

The largest partition is the primary partition, formatted using NTFS, which contains Windows system files, the paging file, and all user profiles.

A fourth partition, required for every GPT disk, is hidden and not visible in Disk Management. This partition, labeled MSR (Reserved), resides between the EFI system partition and the primary partition and is used for postinstallation tasks, such as converting a basic disk to a dynamic disk. It is visible when you use DiskPart or the partitioning tools available with a custom installation.

PC makers have the option to add custom OEM partitions to this layout, with those volumes containing files that are part of a custom installation. In addition, some PCs contain a second recovery partition, at the end of the drive, that contains files required to restore the original system configuration.

To make adjustments to existing disk partitions, boot from Windows 10 installation media (DVD or bootable USB flash drive) and run through Windows Setup until you reach the Where Do You Want To Install Windows page of the Windows Setup dialog box, shown earlier in Figure 2-10. The collection of tools below the list of disks and partitions is shown in Figure 2-13.

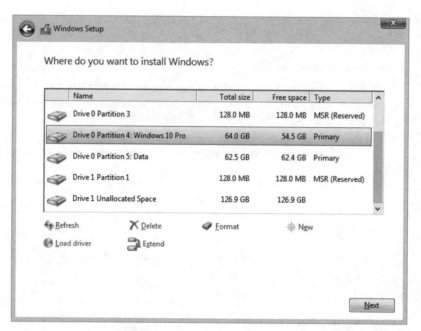

Figure 2-13 Use the disk-management tools in this phase of the Windows 10 setup process to manage disk partitions for more efficient data storage and multiboot configurations.

The system shown in Figure 2-13 includes two physical disks. The first, Drive 0, has been divided roughly in half, with a Windows installation on Partition 4, leaving a block of unallocated space. The second physical disk, Drive 1, has been partitioned but still has most of its space unallocated.

You can accomplish any of the following tasks here:

- **Select an existing partition or unallocated space on which to install Windows 10.** Setup is simple if you already created and formatted an empty partition in preparation for setting up Windows, or if you plan to install Windows 10 on an existing partition that currently contains data or programs but no operating system, or if you want to use unallocated space on an existing disk without disturbing the existing partition scheme. Select the partition or unallocated space, and click Next.

- **Delete an existing partition.** Select a partition, and then click Delete. This option is useful if you want to perform a clean installation on a drive that currently contains an earlier version of Windows. Because this operation deletes data irretrievably, you must respond to an "Are you sure?" confirmation request. After deleting the partition, you can select the unallocated space as the destination for your Windows 10 installation or create a new partition. Be sure to back up any data files before choosing this option.

- **Create a new partition from unallocated space.** Select a block of unallocated space on a new drive or on an existing drive after deleting partitions, and click New to set up a partition in that space.

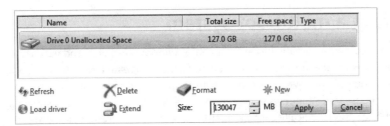

By default, Windows Setup offers to use all unallocated space on the current disk. You can specify a smaller partition size if you want to subdivide the disk into multiple drives. If you have a 1,500-GB drive, for example, you might choose to create a relatively small partition on which to install Windows and use the remaining space to create a second volume with its own drive letter on which to store data files such as music, pictures, documents, and videos or TV shows.

- **Extend an existing partition by using unallocated space.** If you're not happy with your existing partition scheme, you can use the Extend option to add unallocated space to any partition, provided that space is immediately to the right of the existing partition in Disk Management, with no intervening partitions. If you originally divided a 120-GB notebook hard disk into two equal volumes, you might decide to rejoin the two partitions to give your system drive more breathing room. After backing up your data files to an external drive or to cloud storage, delete the data partition, select the partition you want to make larger, and click Extend. Choose the total size of the extended partition in the Size box (the default is to use all available unallocated space), and click Apply. You can now continue with your installation, restoring your data files after setup is complete.

CAUTION

In both the Disk Management console and the disk-management tools available via Windows Setup, it can be confusing to tell which partition is which. Confusion, in this case, can have drastic consequences if you inadvertently wipe out a drive full of data instead of writing over an unwanted installation of Windows. One good way to reduce the risk of this sort of accident is to label drives well. In Figure 2-13, for instance, you can see at a glance that the first partition on Drive 0 contains a current installation of Windows 10 Pro, the second partition is formatted for data storage, and Drive 1 is empty.

Alert observers will no doubt notice that one option is missing from that list. Unfortunately, Setup does not allow you to shrink an existing disk partition to create unallocated space on which to install a fresh copy of Windows 10. The option to shrink a volume is available from the Disk Management console after Windows 10 is installed, but if you want to accomplish this task before or during setup, you'll need to use third-party disk-management tools.

Configuring a multiboot system

If your computer already has any version of Windows installed and you have a second disk partition available (or enough unallocated space to create a second partition), you can install a clean copy of Windows 10 without disturbing your existing Windows installation. At boot time, you choose your Windows version from a startup menu, like the one shown in Figure 2-14. Although this is typically called a dual-boot system, it's more accurate to call it a multiboot configuration, because you can install multiple copies of Windows or other PC-compatible operating systems.

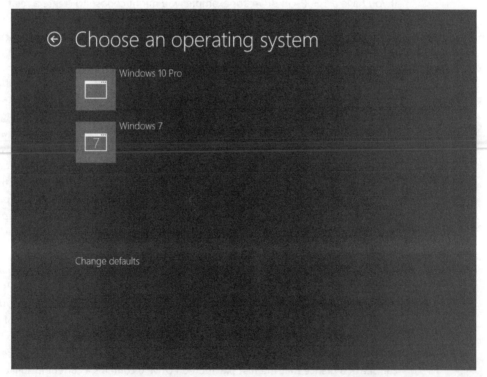

Figure 2-14 This system is configured to allow a choice of operating systems at startup.

Having the capability to choose your operating system at startup is handy if you have a program or device that simply won't work under Windows 10. When you need to use the legacy program or device, you can boot into your earlier Windows version without too much fuss.

This capability is also useful for software developers and IT professionals who need to be able to test how programs work under different operating systems using physical (not virtual) hardware.

For experienced Windows users, installing a second copy of Windows 10 in its own partition can also be helpful as a way to experiment with a potentially problematic program or device driver without compromising a working system. After you finish setting up the second, clean version of Windows 10, you'll see an additional entry on the startup menu that corresponds to your new installation. (The newly installed version is the default menu choice; it runs automatically if 30 seconds pass and you haven't made a choice.) Experiment with the program or driver and see how well it works. If, after testing thoroughly, you're satisfied that the program is safe to use, you can add it to the Windows 10 installation you use every day.

Inside OUT

Use virtual machines instead of hassling with multiboot menus

You can create truly elaborate multiboot configurations using more than a decade's worth of Windows versions. But unless you're running a hardware testing lab, there's no good reason to do that. The much simpler, smoother alternative is to use virtual hardware that faithfully re-creates the operating environment. During the course of researching and writing this book, we installed Windows 10 in virtual machines to capture details of several crucial tasks and processes that can't easily be documented on physical hardware, and we saved many hours compared to how long those tasks would have taken had we set up and restored physical hardware.

We strongly recommend Microsoft's Hyper-V virtualization software, which is a standard feature in the Pro editions of Windows 8.1 and Windows 10 and on recent Windows Server releases. (For more information about Client Hyper-V in Windows 10, see Chapter 22, "Running virtual machines with Hyper-V.")

To run Windows 10 on a Mac, try Parallels, available at *http://parallels.com*. For other operating systems, check out VMware (*http://vmware.com*), which offers excellent virtualization software for use on desktop Windows machines and servers, and the free VirtualBox package from Oracle (*http://virtualbox.org*).

Using any of these solutions, you can install even the most ancient Windows version. Backing up a machine's configuration and restoring it is as simple as copying a file. Legally, you'll need a license for every operating system you install in a virtual machine. If you have a license to use Windows for evaluation purposes, the option to run Windows in a virtual machine can be a lifesaver.

To add Windows 10 to a system on which an existing version of Windows is already installed, first make sure that you have an available partition (or unformatted disk space) separate from the partition that contains the system files for your current Windows version.

The target partition can be a separate partition on the same physical disk, or it can be on a different hard disk. If your system contains a single disk with a single partition used as drive C, you cannot create a multiboot system unless you add a new disk or use software tools to shrink the existing partition and create a new partition from the free space. (The Disk Management console, Diskmgmt.msc, includes this capability; to shrink partitions on a system running an older Windows version, you'll need third-party software. For details, see "Shrinking a volume" in Chapter 14.) The new partition does not need to be empty; if it contains system files for another Windows installation, they will be moved to Windows.old. Run Setup, choose the Custom (Advanced) option, and select the disk and partition you want to use for the new installation.

The setup program automatically handles details of adding the newly installed operating system to the Boot Configuration Data store.

And how do you edit and configure the Boot Configuration Data store? Surprisingly, the only official tool is a command-line utility called Bcdedit. Bcdedit isn't an interactive program; instead, you perform tasks by appending switches and parameters to the Bcdedit command line. To display the complete syntax for this tool, open an elevated Command Prompt window (using the Run As Administrator option) and type the command **bcdedit /?**.

For everyday use, most Bcdedit options are esoteric, unnecessary—and risky. In fact, the only option that we remember using more than once in the past four years is the command to change the text for each entry in the boot menu. By default, the setup program adds the generic entry "Windows 10" for each installation. If you set up a dual-boot system using two copies of Windows 10 (one for everyday use, one for testing), you'll be unable to tell which is which because the menu text will be the same for each. To make the menu more informative, follow these steps:

1. Start your computer, and choose either entry from the boot menu. After startup is complete, make a note of which installation is running.

2. Right-click Start, or press Windows key+X, and choose Command Prompt (Admin) from the Quick Link menu. Click Yes in the User Account Control box to open an elevated Command Prompt window.

3. Type the following command: **bcdedit /set description "*Menu description goes here*"** (substitute your own description for the placeholder text, and be sure to include the quotation marks). Press Enter.

4. Restart your computer, and note that the menu description you just entered now appears on the menu. Select the other menu option.

5. Repeat steps 2 and 3, again adding a menu description to replace the generic text and distinguish this installation from the other one.

A few startup options are available when you click or tap Change Defaults at the bottom of the boot menu, as shown here.

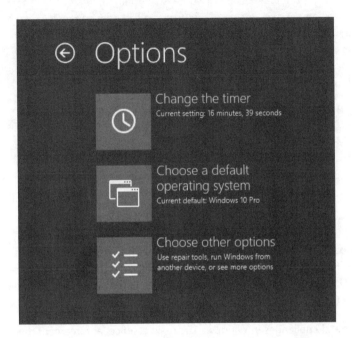

You can choose which installation is the default operating system (this is where descriptive menu choices come in handy) and change the timer that determines how long you want to display the list of operating systems. The default is 30 seconds; you can choose 5 seconds (allowing the default operating system to start virtually automatically) or 5 minutes, if you want to ensure that you have a choice even if you're distracted while the system is restarting. These options write data directly to the Boot Configuration Data store.

For slightly more control over the boot menu timer, use the System Configuration utility, Msconfig.exe. The Boot tab allows you to change the default operating system and set the Timeout interval in any amount between 3 and 999 seconds.

CHAPTER 2

Inside OUT

Installing Windows 10 and Linux in a multiboot configuration

It's possible to install Windows 10 and Linux in a multiboot configuration that works much like the Windows multiboot setup described on the preceding pages. You can set it up to use the Windows 10 boot menu, or you can use a Linux boot loader (most commonly, GRUB) if you prefer. The procedure is a bit more complex than the procedure for installing another version of Windows, and it varies somewhat depending on which Linux distribution you use and which Linux tools (such as partition editors, boot loaders, and the like) you prefer. It's generally easier to set up such a system if the Windows partition is set up first, but it can be done either way: Windows and then Linux, or Linux and then Windows.

An Internet search for "dual boot Linux Windows" turns up plenty of detailed instructions, and if you add the name of your Linux distribution to the search input, you're likely to find the specific steps needed to make it work with Windows 8.1 or Windows 10.

Activating Windows

For more than a dozen years, desktop versions of Windows have included a set of antipiracy and antitampering features. In the past, Microsoft has used different names for these capabilities: Windows Activation Technologies and Windows Genuine Advantage, for example. In Windows 10, these features are collectively referred to as the Software Protection Platform.

The various checks and challenges in Windows 10 are, in essence, enforcement mechanisms for the Windows 10 license agreement, which is displayed during the process of installing or deploying the operating system (you must provide your consent to complete setup). We're not lawyers, so we won't attempt to interpret this license agreement. We do recommend that you read the license agreement, which is fairly straightforward. In this section, we explain how the activation and validation mechanisms in Windows 10 affect your use of the operating system.

Product activation happens shortly after you set up a new PC with Windows 10. Typically, this involves a brief communication between your PC and Microsoft's licensing servers. If everything checks out, your copy of Windows is activated silently, and you never have to deal with product keys or activation prompts.

In the past, activating Windows required entering a 25-character alphanumeric product key. On OEM PCs, this product key is stored in the computer's firmware so it can be automatically retrieved and activated. For retail installations and upgrades, though, entering that product key was mandatory. That's no longer true.

With Windows 10, Microsoft has made a fundamental change to the way it performs product activation on upgrades. The biggest change of all is that the Windows 10 activation status for a device is stored online. After you successfully activate Windows 10 for the first time, that device will activate automatically in the future, with no product key required.

When you upgrade from Windows 7 or Windows 8.1, the Windows 10 setup program checks your current activation status and reports the result to the activation servers. If your current installation of Windows is "genuine" (that is, properly activated), the Windows activation server generates a Windows 10 license certificate (Microsoft calls it a "digital entitlement") for the version to which you just upgraded (Home or Pro). That proof of digital activation is stored in conjunction with your unique installation ID on Microsoft's activation servers.

That unique installation ID is essentially a fingerprint of your PC, based on a cryptographic hash derived from your hardware. That hash is reportedly not reversible and not tied to any other Microsoft services. So although it defines your device, it doesn't identify you. But it does make it possible to store activation status for that device online.

Once that online activation status is recorded, you can wipe your drive clean, boot from Windows 10 installation media, install a clean copy skipping right past the prompts for a product key, and at the end of the process you'll have a properly activated copy of Windows 10.

If you're building your own PC or installing Windows 10 in a virtual machine that doesn't currently have an activated copy of Windows 7 or Windows 8.1, you'll still need a product key for use with a retail Windows 10 package or an OEM System Builder license.

After you successfully activate your copy of Windows 10, you're still subject to periodic antipiracy checks from Microsoft. This process, called *validation*, verifies that your copy of Windows has not been tampered with to bypass activation. It also allows Microsoft to undo the activation process for a computer when it determines after the fact that the product key was stolen or used in violation of a volume licensing agreement.

Validation takes two forms: an internal tool that regularly checks licensing and activation files to determine that they haven't been tampered with, and an online tool that restricts access to some downloads and updates.

If your system fails validation, your computer continues to work, but you'll see some differences: the desktop background changes to black (and if you change it to something else, Windows changes it back to black after one hour), an "activate now" reminder that also tells you your copy of Windows is "Not Genuine" appears on the desktop, and an Activate Now dialog box appears periodically. In addition, your access to Windows Update is somewhat restricted; you won't be able to download optional updates, new drivers, or certain other programs from the Microsoft Download Center until your system passes the validation check.

NOTE

A device that has failed Windows validation can still be used. All Windows functions work normally, all your data files are accessible, and all your programs work as expected. The nagging reminders are intended to strongly encourage you to resolve the underlying issue. Some forms of malware can result in damage to system files that has the same effect as tampering with activation files. Another common cause of activation problems is a lazy or dishonest repair technician who installs a stolen or "cracked" copy of Windows instead of using your original licensed copy. Links in the Windows Activation messages lead to online support tools, where you might be able to identify and repair the issue that's affecting your system. Microsoft offers free support for activation issues via online forums and by telephone.

The activation mechanism is designed to enforce license restrictions by preventing the most common form of software piracy: casual copying. Typically, a Windows 10 license entitles you to install the operating system software on a single computer. If a system builder uses the same product key on a second (or third or fourth) device, you might be unable to activate the software automatically.

As we write this chapter, Microsoft has just begun rolling out the new product activation system in Windows 10. It is possible that some of the details we describe here will change over time.

Entering a product key

When you upgrade a PC that contains a properly activated copy of Windows 7 or Windows 8.1, the freshly upgraded copy is automatically activated as well, with no manual intervention required on your part. At any time, you can check the activation status of your device from the Activation page in Settings, Update & Security, as shown in Figure 2-15.

In some installation scenarios, you might be prompted to enter a 25-character alphanumeric product key that uniquely identifies your licensed copy of Windows. If you experience activation hassles caused by an incorrect product key, you can use the Change Product Key button to set things right, using the dialog box shown in Figure 2-16.

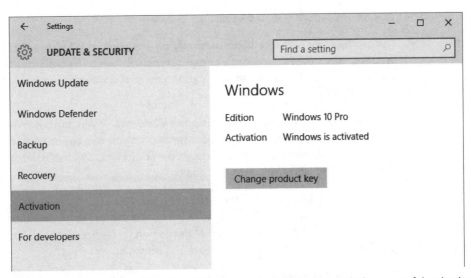

Figure 2-15 Most Windows 10 PCs will be automatically activated, with the successful activation status shown in this dialog box.

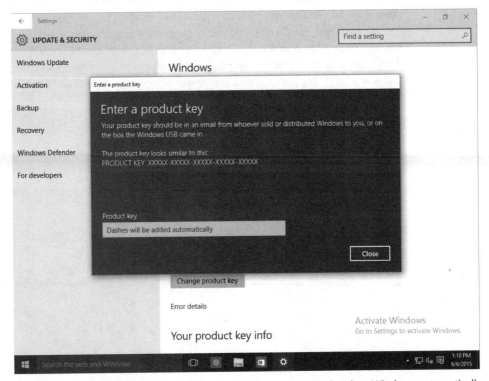

Figure 2-16 When you enter the 25-character alphanumeric product key, Windows automatically checks it and prompts you to complete activation.

Here are some key facts you should know about this procedure:

- **The product key is entered automatically on any copy of Windows that is pre-installed on a new PC by a large computer maker.** This configuration is called System Locked Preinstallation (SLP) and allows you to reinstall Windows from recovery media without entering a product key.

- **Your product key matches your edition of Windows.** If you purchase a boxed copy of Windows 10 from a retail outlet, the installation media (typically a DVD) contains a configuration file that automatically installs the edition you purchased: Home or Pro. The product key works only with that edition.

- **Most Windows 10 upgrades don't require a product key.** If you upgrade a properly activated copy of Windows 7 or Windows 8.1 during the free upgrade offer, you don't need to enter a product key. A record of the edition you're licensed to use, Home or Pro, is stored with your hardware ID on Microsoft's activation servers.

- **The architecture does not need to match your product key.** You can use the same key to replace a 32-bit Windows 10 edition with a 64-bit edition, or vice versa.

- **You are not required to enter a product key when performing a clean install of Windows 10.** You're prompted to enter a valid product key to install Windows 10 on a system that does not currently contain a properly activated ("genuine") Windows installation corresponding to the one you're trying to install. If you leave the Product Key box blank and click Next when attempting a clean install of an upgrade edition of Windows, Setup will not continue. You must click the tiny Skip link, just to the left of the Next button.

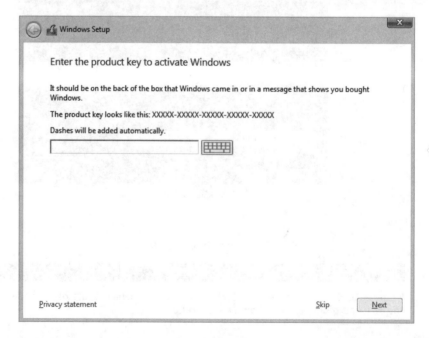

Activating a retail copy of Windows

When you install Windows 10 on a new PC, it will attempt to contact Microsoft's licensing servers and activate automatically within three days. If the activation process fails, you can activate Windows by connecting to a Microsoft activation server over the Internet or by making a toll-free call to an interactive telephone activation system.

Under most circumstances, activation over the Internet takes no more than a few seconds. If you need to use the telephone, the process takes longer because you have to enter a 50-digit identification key (either by using the phone's dial pad or by speaking to a customer service representative) and then input the 42-digit confirmation ID supplied in response.

The activation process is completely anonymous and does not require that you divulge any personal information. If you choose to register your copy of Windows 10, this is a completely separate (and optional) task.

You're allowed to reinstall Windows 10 an unlimited number of times on the same hardware. During the activation process, Windows transmits a hashed file that serves as a "fingerprint" of key components in your system. When you attempt to activate the same edition of Windows 10 you activated previously, the activation server calculates a fingerprint on the fly, using your current hardware setup, and compares the value against the one stored in its database. If you're reinstalling Windows 10 on hardware that is essentially the same, the fingerprints will match and activation will be automatic.

Just as with earlier Windows versions, the activation process is designed to prevent attempts to tamper with the activation files or to "clone" an activated copy of Windows and install it on another computer. What happens if you upgrade the hardware in your computer? When you activate your copy of Windows 10, a copy of the hardware fingerprint is stored on your hard disk and checked each time you start your computer. If you make substantial changes to your system hardware, you might be required to reactivate your copy of Windows.

Because the activation mechanism assumes (mistakenly) that you've tried to install your copy of Windows on a second computer, Internet activation might not work. In this case, you're required to manually enter a new activation code, which can be obtained from the telephone-based activation support center. You can upgrade almost all components in a system without requiring a new license. You can also replace a defective motherboard and retain the right to reactivate your copy of Windows. (If you upgrade your PC with a new motherboard, that is considered a new PC and might require a new license.)

Activation requirements for OEM installations

If you purchase a new computer with Windows 10 already installed on it, the licensing procedures are different, as are the rules for activation. In the arcane parlance of Windows, system makers are known as original equipment manufacturers, or OEMs. To make matters more confusing, not all OEMs are created equal; instead, they're divided into two classes:

- Large system builders (Microsoft refers to these firms as named or multinational OEMs or, informally, as royalty OEMs) are allowed to install and preactivate Windows using System Locked Preinstallation (SLP), mentioned earlier. The preinstalled copy of Windows (including the recovery disc) contains configuration files that look for specific information in the system BIOS or firmware. As long as this information matches, no activation is required. A new computer from one of these large companies may contain a sticker that certifies your installation, but unlike in earlier versions of Windows, that sticker contains no product key. The OEM uses a single master key to activate large numbers of computers. If you need to reinstall Windows, you must do so by using the recovery media from the same computer (or one with the same motherboard/BIOS combination).

- Smaller firms that build PCs can also preinstall Windows. These OEM copies are called System Builder copies, and they do require activation. The rules of the System Builder program require the PC manufacturer to use specific tools to preinstall Windows so that you accept a license agreement and activate the software when you first turn on the PC. In addition, the manufacturer is required to supply the purchaser with the Windows 10 media (typically a DVD) and affix a product key sticker to the PC's case. If you need to reinstall Windows on this computer, you must enter the product key and go through activation again.

The license agreement for a retail copy of Windows 10 allows you to transfer it to another computer provided that you completely remove it from the computer on which it was previously installed. An OEM copy, by contrast, is tied to the computer on which it was originally installed. You can reinstall an OEM copy of Windows an unlimited number of times on the same computer. However, you are prohibited by the license agreement from transferring that copy of Windows to another computer.

Product activation and corporate licensing

Businesses that purchase licenses through a Microsoft Volume Licensing (VL) program receive VL media and product keys that require activation under a different set of rules from those that apply to retail or OEM copies. Under the terms of a volume license agreement, each computer with a copy of Windows 10 must have a valid license and must be activated.

Enterprise editions of Windows 10 can be installed using Multiple Activation Keys, which allow activations on a specific number of devices within an organization, or they can use Key Management servers to activate computers within their organization. If you encounter activation issues with Windows 10 Pro or Enterprise in a VL deployment, contact the person in your organization who manages your VL agreement—the "Benefits Administrator" as this person is called.

Managing Windows activation from the command prompt

Windows 10 includes a command-line tool that you can use to examine the licensing status of a PC, change its product key, and perform other activation-related tasks. Although this feature is primarily intended for automating license administration activities, you can also run the Windows Software Licensing Management Tool interactively. Open a Command Prompt window with administrative privileges and then run the command `Slmgr.vbs`. Run without parameters, this command shows its full syntax in a series of dialog boxes.

One common use of this tool is to display the current licensing status for a device, using the syntax `slmgr.vbs /dli`. Figure 2-17, for example, shows the status of a device that has failed validation and is in Notification mode.

For a much more detailed display of information, use the same command with a switch that produces verbose output: `slmgr.vbs /dlv`.

Figure 2-17 This output from the Windows Software Licensing Management Tool shows a system that is in Notification mode. The Notification Reason code, in the last line, can be useful for troubleshooting.

Tweaking and tuning your Windows 10 installation

When Windows Setup completes, you're signed in and ready to begin using Windows 10. For upgrades and clean installs alike, we suggest following this simple checklist to confirm that basic functionality is enabled properly.

- **Look for missing device drivers.** Open Device Management and look for any devices that have a yellow exclamation mark over the icon or any devices that are listed under the Other category. This is also a good time to install any custom drivers supplied by the device maker and not available through Windows Update. For more on working with device drivers, see "How device drivers and hardware work together" in Chapter 13, "Hardware."

- **Adjust display settings.** You'll want to confirm that the display is set for its native resolution and that any additional tasks such as color calibration have been completed.

- **Check your network connection.** If you skipped network setup during a clean install, you can complete the task now. Open the Network folder in File Explorer to switch from a public network to a private network and allow local file sharing.

- **Verify security settings.** If you use third-party security software, install it now and get the latest updates.

- **Check Windows Update.** You'll get the latest updates automatically within the next 24 hours. Doing the update manually lets you avoid a scheduled overnight restart.

- **Change default programs.** Use this opportunity to set your preferred browser, email client, music playback software, and so on.

- **Adjust power and sleep settings.** The default settings are usually good enough, but they're rarely a perfect match for your preferences. Now is a good time to adjust when your device sleeps and whether it requires a password when it wakes.

Using Windows 10

Regardless of your upgrade path—from Windows 7 or from Windows 8.1—your day-to-day experience changes significantly with Windows 10.

The things you expect Windows to do on your behalf—launching programs, arranging windows on the screen, switching between tasks, finding files, setting notifications, interacting with cloud services, communicating with other people—are basically the same. But the steps you take to accomplish those tasks are different.

The change is more striking if you're moving from a conventional PC or laptop to a touchscreen device. Even if you still have access to a keyboard and mouse or trackpad, the addition of touch fundamentally changes how you interact with Windows and with apps. With a phone or small tablet added to the mix, you have still more options to explore.

In this chapter, we look at the things you tap, click, drag, and drop to make Windows do your bidding. Some, like the taskbar and notification icons, are similar enough to their predecessors that you might miss subtle but significant changes.

Our coverage also includes a section on the unique ways to interact with a tablet running Windows 10. And, of course, we introduce Cortana, the first Windows feature that can literally speak for itself.

A disclaimer, right up front: in this chapter, we are writing about a user experience that is evolving from month to month and that will continue to do so even after the initial release of Windows 10 on July 29, 2015. The screen shots and step-by-step instructions you see here are based on that initial release. It's not only possible, but practically certain, that some of the features we describe here will change in the months after we send this book to the printer as Microsoft delivers on its promise of "Windows as a service."

If you see subtle differences between what's on these pages and what's on your screen, that's the likely reason. We hope our descriptions make it possible to incorporate those changes into your learning.

An overview of the Windows 10 user experience

Before we dive into detailed descriptions of individual features, please join us for a brief tour of Windows 10. Our goal is to introduce the different parts of Windows, new and old, so that we can be sure you're on the same page . . . or at least looking at the same arrangement of pixels.

Figure 3-1 shows the basic building blocks of Windows 10 and offers a hint of its signature visual style.

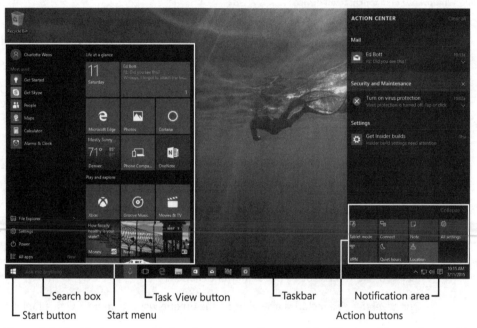

Figure 3-1 The Start menu and Action Center are at the core of the Windows 10 experience, with the familiar desktop front and center for conventional PCs.

When you first start up a conventional PC running Windows 10, you see the familiar Windows 7–style desktop and taskbar. Clicking the Start button—the Windows logo in the lower left corner—opens the Start menu, which is conceptually similar to its predecessor but differs dramatically in the details.

How the cloud changes your experience

One noteworthy difference between the initial Windows 10 experience and the traditional Windows experience that reached its zenith with Windows 7 is the amount of personalization you see when you sign in on a new PC or device. If you use a Microsoft account you've already used on a different device, the customized settings saved with your account appear automatically on the new device, making it feel familiar right away.

On a clean install or a refresh, you can create a local account, which gives you the standard default layout and themes, as defined by Microsoft. If you sign in to a corporate network, your personalized settings roam according to policies defined by your network administrator. (If your organization allows you to, you can attach a Microsoft account to your domain account, and both your personal and work settings roam together as you switch between devices.)

When you allow your Microsoft account to sync settings between devices, you don't have to go through a tedious process of tweaking the default settings to match those preferences; instead, your visual themes, browser settings, and saved Wi-Fi passwords appear exactly as you expect. If your Microsoft account is connected to OneDrive, your online files, photos, and music collection will be available too. We discuss these features in more detail in Chapter 5, "Networking essentials."

CHAPTER 3

A click on the right side of the taskbar opens Action Center, which is also shown in Figure 3-1. This pane, which uses the full height of your display, contains notifications from apps and services as well as action buttons that allow quick access to settings.

As with previous versions, Windows 10 offers multiple ways to switch between tasks. The Task View button, a new addition to the Windows 10 taskbar, produces the view shown in Figure 3-2, which also illustrates another new feature: virtual desktops. We discuss both features in more detail later in this chapter.

Figure 3-2 Task View allows you to switch quickly between available windows; the new virtual desktop feature allows you to group windows.

➤ For more details on how to set up notifications and configure Action Center, see Chapter 4, "Personalizing Windows 10."

Navigating Windows 10

Touchscreens might represent the future of computing, but the present is still ruled by more-or-less conventional desktop and laptop PCs, each equipped with a keyboard and a mouse or touchpad.

For that type of device, the desktop is where you'll likely spend most of your time, and it's what we concentrate on in this section. Tablet Mode has its own set of rules and gets its own section, immediately after this one.

Using and customizing the Start menu

The Windows 10 Start menu, like its Windows 7 counterpart, is divided into two vertical segments. On the left side is a comparatively thin column, with the current user's name and picture at the top. Below that identifying iconography is a list of installed programs, with dedicated shortcuts for File Explorer, Settings, and Power below that.

Inside OUT

Change your Start menu picture

The picture that appears at the top of the left side of the Start menu is the one associated with your user account (the one that also appears on the Welcome screen). If you're not happy with that picture, click it, and then click Change Account Settings. That takes you to the Settings page for your account, where you can choose a different picture or snap one with a webcam.

At the very bottom of the list, you can click or tap All Apps to change the contents of the Start menu's left side so that it looks like Figure 3-3.

Figure 3-3 Clicking All Apps changes the left column in the Start menu to an alphabetical list of available programs.

The scrolling All Apps list is arranged in alphabetical order, in a fashion that's similar to its Windows 7 predecessor. One noteworthy difference: program groups, such as the Windows

Accessories folder, slide downward to open instead of flying out to the right in cascading menus.

On a lightly used system, you can probably find what you're looking for by scrolling through the list of shortcuts on the All Apps menu. Swipe directly on a touchscreen, use two-finger scrolling gestures on a touchpad, or use the scroll wheel with a mouse.

For larger lists of programs, using the search box is the fastest way to find a specific program. For an alternative to scrolling, try this time-saving shortcut: Click or tap any of the letter headings in the list to see the entire alphabet, as shown in Figure 3-4. Then click or tap a letter to jump to the section of the list beginning with that letter.

Figure 3-4 Clicking or tapping any heading in the alphabetical list takes you to this index, where tapping a letter takes you to the programs whose names begin with that letter.

You can change the size and shape of the Start menu by dragging it up (to a maximum height that is 100 pixels below the top of the display), to the right, or both ways. Resizing the Start menu doesn't change the width of the left column, and making the menu wider can be done only in increments corresponding to the width of two Wide tiles. (More on that shortly.)

Customizing the contents of the Start menu

If you're accustomed to the extensive array of customization options for items on the Start menu in earlier Windows versions, you'll need to make some adjustments.

You can remove programs from the Most Used section, but you can't pin program shortcuts to the left side of the Start menu.

You can add or remove shortcuts from the group of options just above the All Apps shortcut and the Power button. Besides the default File Explorer and Settings menu items, locations available for this section include your personal folder, the default folders from your user profile (Documents, Downloads, Music, Pictures, and Videos), and the Network folder. You can also add a HomeGroup shortcut. To see the entire list, open Settings, open Personalization, click or tap Start, and then click or tap Choose Which Folders Appear On Start.

Inside OUT

Which programs are included in the Most Used list?

The list of most used programs—the items that appear below the pinned programs on the left side of the Start menu—is controlled by Windows. In previous Windows versions, this list included only shortcuts to executable files you open, such as .exe files and .msc files. Windows 10 continues this behavior.

Several types of items are excluded by default, so you won't see things like setup programs, installer and uninstaller packages, Control Panel modules, and MMC consoles. You can find a list of what's excluded in the AddRemoveApps value of the registry key HKLM\Software\Microsoft\Windows\CurrentVersion\Explorer\FileAssociation. We do not recommend trying to edit these values manually.

Pin any Windows app to the Start menu, the taskbar, or both, either by right-clicking the program's entry in the All Apps list or by dragging it from that list and dropping it on the right side of the Start menu.

Inside OUT

Master the powerful "other" Start menu

Here's some good news for anyone who misses the system shortcuts from earlier itera-tions of the Start menu. Most of those tools are available as part of a hidden menu that appears when you right-click the Start button or press Windows key+X, as shown here:

Programs and Features
Power Options
Event Viewer
System
Device Manager
Network Connections
Disk Management
Computer Management
Command Prompt
Command Prompt (Admin)

Task Manager
Control Panel
File Explorer
Search
Run

Shut down or sign out >
Desktop

Most of the major system management and troubleshooting tools are on that list, including Disk Management, Event Viewer, and the Computer Management console.

Windows traditionalists will appreciate the fact that the Shut Down Or Sign Out menu item is here, along with links to Control Panel and Task Manager. Our personal favorite is the Command Prompt (Admin) shortcut, which eliminates one minor hassle when it's time to get work done the old-fashioned way, by typing commands directly. If you're a PowerShell aficionado, an option on the Navigation tab of the Taskbar And Start Menu Properties dialog box lets you replace the two Command Prompt options with Power-Shell equivalents.

Adding and arranging tiles

Anything that appears on the All Apps menu can be dragged to the right side of the Start menu and placed as a tile. Tiles, which were found on a separate Start screen in Windows 8.1, behave much the same way in Windows 10, but they are constrained to the Start menu.

Clicking a tile has the same effect as clicking a Start menu program shortcut or a pinned task-bar button. What makes tiles different is the variety of sizes and their ability to display information or notifications from the app, making a tile *live*.

To pin a program as a tile to the right side of the Start menu, drag it into position. As an alternative, right-click its entry in All Apps or the Most Used list on the left side of the Start menu, and then click or tap Pin To Start. The item will take up residence as a medium size tile in the first available empty space on the right side of the menu, from where you can move and resize it as needed.

To remove a program from the right side of the Start menu, right-click it and then click Unpin From Start.

You can adjust the size of any tile by right-clicking the tile to see the menu shown in Figure 3-5.

Figure 3-5 These options are available for most programs acquired from the Windows Store. Not all apps support this full list of sizes.

Note that not all tiles support the full range of sizes shown in this figure. Windows desktop programs, for example, offer only the Small and Medium options.

On a touchscreen, you can accomplish the same tile customization tasks with a long press on the tile. That produces the two options shown in white circles on the right side of the tile in Figure 3-6. Tapping the top option unpins the tile, while tapping the ellipsis in the bottom right reveals a menu with Resize and Live Tile items.

Figure 3-6 On a touchscreen, a long press on any tile produces these controls, which lead to options identical to those on the right-click menu.

CHAPTER 3

NOTE

Options for a specific app might allow additional customization of the live tile. The Photos app, for example, allows you to choose a specific image for its tile.

Right-clicking the tile for a Windows desktop program produces a menu with an extra set of options: Run As Administrator, for example.

Tiles can be arranged into groups, with or without custom group names. Drag tiles, one at a time, into the position you prefer. If the position you choose is sufficiently far from the edge of an existing group, your tile ends up in a new group of its own. You can move it back to an existing group or add other tiles to the new group.

A slim bar sits above every group of tiles. By default, this bar is blank. Click (as we have in Figure 3-7) to display a text box where you can type a group name of your choosing. (We created a group named Microsoft Office here.) Click the horizontal line to the right of the name box to drag the entire group to a new location.

Figure 3-7 Click above any group of tiles to give that group a descriptive label.

Using and customizing the taskbar

The taskbar is that strip of real estate along one screen edge (bottom by default) that contains, from left to right, the Start button, the search box, program buttons, notification icons, and a clock. The taskbar made its first appearance in Windows 95. In the years since, it has slowly evolved without changing its basic shape

The Windows 10 taskbar continues to serve the same basic functions as its progenitors—launching programs, switching between programs, and providing notifications—with only subtle changes in functionality.

Every running program with a user interface has a corresponding taskbar button. When you close that program, the button vanishes as well, unless it's been pinned to the taskbar. A faint line appears underneath the icon for a running program, and the program with the current focus has a subtle but noticeable transparent shadow to identify it.

The Windows 10 taskbar offers a limited selection of customization options, most of which are available through the Taskbar And Start Menu Properties dialog box (see Figure 3-8). Open it by right-clicking an unoccupied area of the taskbar (if the taskbar is full, right-click the Task View button) and then clicking Properties.

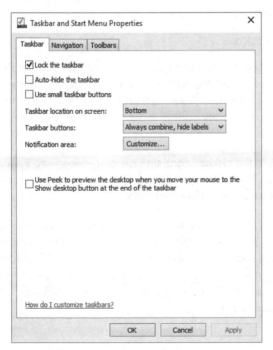

Figure 3-8 For most people, the default options here will be acceptable, especially Lock The Taskbar, which prevents you from accidentally dragging the taskbar to the side of the monitor.

Two items on the Taskbar tab of the Taskbar And Start Menu Properties dialog box control the size and appearance of taskbar buttons:

- **Use Small Taskbar Buttons.** Select this option if you want to reduce the height of taskbar buttons, making them similar in size to buttons in earlier Windows versions. In our experience, buttons of this size are too small for practical use. If you have the eyesight of a hawk, you might beg to differ.

- **Taskbar Buttons.** The default setting for Taskbar Buttons is Always Combine, Hide Labels. This setting instructs Windows to always group multiple windows from a single application (such as Microsoft Word documents) into a single taskbar button. The Hide Labels setting for this option is left over from an old Windows version; Windows 10 does not display labels (window titles) for taskbar buttons.

    With either of the other settings (Combine When Taskbar Is Full or Never Combine), Windows gives each window its own separate taskbar button. It groups windows only when the taskbar becomes too crowded or continues to shrink the size of taskbar buttons as you open more windows. We recommend the default setting here.

    ➤ **If you have more than one display attached to a Windows 10 PC, some extra customization options are available for the taskbar. See "Configuring the taskbar with multiple displays" in Chapter 4 for details.**

Pinning programs to the taskbar

Pinning a taskbar button makes it easy to find and run favorite programs without the need to open the Start menu or use the search box to find the program's shortcut. To pin a program to the taskbar, simply drag its icon or a shortcut (from the Start menu, from the desktop, or from any other folder) to the taskbar. Alternatively, right-click a program icon wherever you find it and then click Pin To Taskbar.

To remove a pinned program from the taskbar, right-click the pinned icon and then click Unpin This Program From Taskbar. This command also appears on other shortcuts to the program, including those on the desktop and on the Start menu.

You can use task buttons to launch a program that's not currently running or to switch from one running program to another. You can also click a task button to minimize an open window or to restore a minimized window. If those features sound too obvious, here's a trick you might not know: you can open a new instance of a program that's already running—a new Microsoft Word document, for example, or a fresh File Explorer window—by right-clicking the taskbar button and then clicking the program name.

Using Jump Lists for quick access to documents and folders

A Jump List is the official name of the menu that appears when you right-click a taskbar button. Each taskbar Jump List includes commands to open the program, to pin the program to the taskbar (or unpin it), and to close all open windows represented by the button.

In addition, for programs that have been developed to take advantage of this feature, Jump Lists can include shortcuts to common tasks that can be performed with that program, such as Open New Tab on a browser window. For Microsoft Office programs, Adobe Acrobat, and other, similarly document-centric programs, Jump Lists also typically include links to recently opened files.

Figure 3-9 shows the default Jump List for File Explorer.

Figure 3-9 Right-click an icon, such as File Explorer, to see a Jump List showing recently opened files and folders with the option to pin items for quick access.

Individual files and folders can't be pinned directly to the taskbar, but you can add them to Jump Lists by using the following techniques.

- To pin a document to the taskbar, drag its icon or a shortcut to any empty space on the taskbar. If the taskbar already has a button for the program associated with the document, Windows adds the document to the Pinned section of the program's Jump List. If the document's program is not on the taskbar, Windows pins the program to the taskbar and adds the document to the program's Jump List.

- To pin a folder to the taskbar, drag its icon or a shortcut to the taskbar. Windows adds the folder to the Pinned section of the Jump List for File Explorer.

- To open a pinned document or folder, right-click the taskbar button and then click the name of the document or folder.

- To remove a pinned document or folder from the Jump List, right-click the taskbar button and point to the name of the document or folder to be removed. Click the pushpin icon that appears.

Changing the order of taskbar buttons

To change the order of buttons on the taskbar, simply drag them into position. Pinned program icons retain their order between sessions, allowing you to quickly find your most-used programs in their familiar (to you) location.

Inside OUT

Use shortcut keys for taskbar buttons

The first 10 taskbar buttons are accessible by keyboard as well as by mouse. Press Windows key+1 for the first, Windows key+2 for the second, and so on (using 0 for the tenth). Using one of these shortcuts is equivalent to clicking the corresponding taskbar button: if the button's program isn't running, it starts; if it has a single open window, you switch to that window; if it has multiple open windows, Windows displays previews of all windows and a "peek" view of the first window.

Note that when you change the order of a taskbar button, you also change the Windows key+number combination that starts that particular program.

Another useful shortcut key is Windows key+T, which brings focus to the first item on the taskbar. At that point, you can repeatedly press Windows key+T, Shift+Windows key+T, or the arrow keys to select other taskbar buttons. When a taskbar button is selected, you can press Spacebar to "click" the button, press the Menu key to display its Jump List, or press Shift+F10 to display its shortcut menu.

Changing the taskbar's size and appearance

The default height of the taskbar is enough to display one button. (If you switch to small buttons, the taskbar automatically shrinks its height to fit.) You can enlarge it—and given the typical size and resolution of computer displays these days, enlarging it is often a great idea. Before you can change the taskbar's dimensions, you need to unlock it. Right-click an unoccupied area of the taskbar; if a check mark appears next to the Lock The Taskbar command, click the command to clear the check mark. Then position the mouse along the border of the taskbar farthest from the edge of the screen. When the mouse pointer becomes a two-headed arrow, drag toward the center of the screen to expand the taskbar. Drag the same border in the opposite direction to restore the original size.

Getting the taskbar out of your way

By default, the taskbar remains visible at all times. If that's inconvenient for any reason, you can tell it to get out of the way. In the Taskbar And Start Menu Properties dialog box, shown earlier in Figure 3-8, select Auto-Hide The Taskbar. With this option selected, the taskbar retreats into the edge of the desktop whenever any window has the focus. To display the task-bar, move the mouse pointer to the edge of the desktop where the taskbar is "hidden."

> ### NOTE
> **Regardless of how you set the auto-hide option in the Taskbar And Start Menu Proper-ties dialog box, you can make the taskbar visible at any time by tapping the Windows key or pressing Ctrl+Esc.**

Moving the taskbar

The taskbar docks by default at the bottom of the screen, but you can move it to any other edge, including any edge of a secondary screen. To move the taskbar, select a Taskbar Location On Screen option in the Taskbar And Start Menu Properties dialog box.

As an alternative, you can manipulate the taskbar directly: unlock it (right-click an unoccupied spot and then click Lock The Taskbar—unless no check mark appears beside that command, which means that the taskbar is already unlocked). Then drag any unoccupied part of the task-bar in the direction you want to go. (Don't drag the edge of the taskbar closest to the center of the screen; doing that changes the taskbar's size, not its position.)

Adding toolbars to the taskbar

A seldom-used feature of the taskbar is its ability to host other toolbars. Optional toolbars date back to much older versions of Windows, offering shortcuts to folders, documents, and applications. Third parties can also write add-ons that operate entirely within the confines of the taskbar. Built-in toolbars you can choose to install include the following:

- **Address.** The Address toolbar provides a place where you can type an Internet address or the name and path of a program, document, or folder. When you press Enter or click the Go button, Windows takes you to the Internet address, starts the program, opens the document, or displays the folder in a File Explorer window. The Address toolbar is functionally equivalent to the Start menu's Run command or the address bar in File Explorer or the Microsoft Edge browser.

CHAPTER 3

- **Links.** The Links toolbar provides shortcuts to Internet sites; it is equivalent to the Links toolbar in Internet Explorer.

- **Desktop.** The Desktop toolbar provides copies of all the icons currently displayed on your desktop. In addition, it includes links to your Libraries, Homegroup, This PC, Network, Control Panel, and other user profile folders. When you click the toolbar's double arrow, a cascading menu of all the folders and files on your system appears.

To install a new toolbar or remove one you're currently using, right-click any unoccupied part of the taskbar or any existing toolbar. Click Toolbars on the menu that appears, and then choose from the ensuing submenu. A check mark beside a toolbar's name means that it is already displayed on the taskbar. Clicking a selected toolbar name removes that toolbar.

NOTE

You can also display any of the predefined toolbars (listed earlier) or remove any currently displayed toolbar by using the Toolbars tab of the Taskbar And Start Menu Properties dialog box.

In addition, any folder on your system can become a toolbar. To create a new toolbar, right-click an existing toolbar or a spot on the taskbar, click Toolbars, and then click New Toolbar. In the next dialog box, navigate to a folder and click Select Folder.

The folder's name becomes the name of the new toolbar, and each item within the folder becomes a tool.

Controlling how notifications appear

Windows apps are continually notifying you that things have happened: you've received a new message, someone has mentioned you on Twitter or Facebook, or a news app has a breaking news headline to share. Windows gets in the act occasionally as well.

This type of notification appears in Action Center, where each such alert can be dismissed individually or you can clear the entire list with a single click or tap.

Confusingly, these new Action Center notifications, found only in Windows 10, share a name with a classic Windows feature: the notification area, also sometimes called the system tray or the status area, which appears at the right side of the taskbar, just to the left of the clock.

In previous versions of Windows, the taskbar often became crowded with tiny icons. Some of them supply notifications in the form of pop-up messages, but many don't "notify" you of anything and simply offer shortcuts to the parent program.

To deal with notification-area congestion, Windows 10 keeps a few essential icons visible at all times but hides those you aren't actually using. As a result, the notification area doesn't consume an increasingly large chunk of the taskbar; new icons are corralled in a box that appears only when you click the arrow at the left end of the notification area to display the hidden items.

To make an icon visible on the taskbar, drag it from the pop-up box containing hidden icons onto the taskbar. To hide an icon, drag it into the corral.

You can also see a list of notification area icons and specify exactly which ones will appear on the taskbar. To see how many taskbar icons you have and manually switch each one on or off, use your search skills to locate the Select Which Icons Appear On The Taskbar option. (If you want to open this Settings page manually, you'll find it in Settings under the System heading, on the Notifications & Actions tab.) That opens the Settings page shown in Figure 3-10.

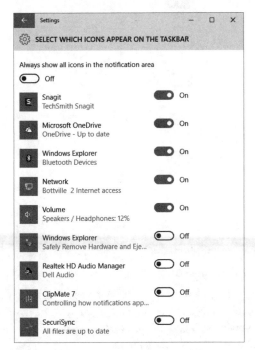

Figure 3-10 This well-hidden Settings page allows you to see a full list of tray icons and decide which ones should appear on the taskbar.

For each notification area icon, you can choose whether to show it on the taskbar at all times or to keep it hidden.

CHAPTER 3

The system icons (Clock, Volume, Network, and so on) can be remanded to the box of hidden icons as well. But if you'd rather banish one or more of them altogether, search for the Turn System Icons On Or Off option, which produces this Settings page. Note that the Power icon is available only on portable PCs.

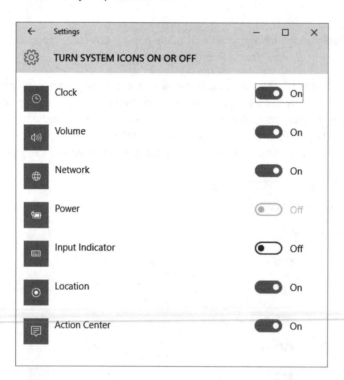

Inside OUT

Use a keyboard shortcut for notification area tasks

If you're one of those users whose fingers never leave the keyboard, you can press Windows key+B to move the focus to the Show Hidden Icons arrow in the notification area. Press Spacebar or Enter to open the box of hidden tray icons. Use the arrow keys to select an icon, and Shift+F10 to display the icon's menu.

Switching tasks

As in previous Windows versions, you can switch to a different program by clicking its taskbar button. And if you're not sure which icon your document is hidden under, hover the mouse pointer over a taskbar button to display a thumbnail image of the window above the button. If a taskbar button combines more than one window (representing multiple Microsoft Excel spreadsheets, for example), hovering the mouse pointer over the taskbar button displays a preview of each window.

If the live thumbnail isn't enough to help you select the correct window, hover the mouse pointer over one of the preview images. Windows brings that window to the fore, temporarily masking out the contents of all other open windows.

The alternative to this manual hunt-and-click technique is a new feature in Windows 10 called Task View, which displays large, live thumbnails of running programs on the screen so that you can switch with confidence.

To begin, click the Task View button or use the Windows key+Tab shortcut. On a touchscreen-equipped device, you can swipe in from the left edge. Figure 3-11 shows the results on a system with seven running programs on a PC operating in Tablet Mode.

└─Task View button

Figure 3-11 After you switch into Tablet Mode, opening Task View shows running programs using their windowed dimensions, but tapping any thumbnail opens it using the full screen.

Those thumbnails remain open until you do something, usually by clicking or tapping a thumbnail to switch to that window, or by pressing Esc to return to the current window.

If there are too many open windows to fit as thumbnails on the display, use the up and down arrows at the bottom of the screen to scroll through the full list.

The old-fashioned Alt+Tab task switcher, familiar to every Windows user of a certain age, is still available as well. The concept is similar, but the thumbnails are smaller and appear only as long as you continue to hold down the Alt key. Hold down Alt and tap the Tab key to cycle (left to right, top to bottom) through all open windows, with a display that looks like the one in Figure 3-12. When you've highlighted the window you want to bring to the fore, release the Alt and Tab keys.

Figure 3-12 Longtime Windows experts who have the Alt+Tab task-switching shortcut firmly ingrained will be relieved to know it still works in Windows 10.

When using Task View, you also have the option of closing a window by clicking the red X in the upper right corner of the preview or, if your mouse scroll wheel supports clicking, by middle-clicking anywhere in the preview image. Other basic window tasks are available on the shortcut menu that appears when you right-click the preview image.

Switching between virtual desktops

Virtual desktops have been reserved exclusively for power users in previous Windows versions, with the feature requiring the use of third-party utilities.

The idea is straightforward: instead of just a single desktop, you create a second, third, fourth, and so on. On each desktop, you arrange individual programs or combinations of apps you want to use for a specific task. Then, when it's time to tackle one of those tasks, you switch to the virtual desktop and get right to work.

Virtual desktops show up along the bottom of the Task View window. Figure 3-13, for example, shows a Windows 10 system with three virtual desktops configured.

Figure 3-13 In Task View, choose any desktop from the list above the taskbar to see its contents and close programs or drag them to a different desktop.

To create a desktop, click New Desktop in the lower right corner of the Task View window.

And no, there's no option to save virtual desktop configurations so that you can resume with your carefully constructed desktop layout after a restart. You have to start from scratch. We predict (perhaps from wishful thinking) that this feature will make it into a Windows 10 update in the near future.

CHAPTER 3

Using Windows 10 on a touchscreen device

Tablet Mode was specifically designed for sustained use with a touchscreen-equipped device such as a tablet or hybrid PC. We've already discussed the Windows user experience with a conventional PC. Tablet Mode introduces a series of significant changes, automatically if it detects that you're using a touchscreen device without a keyboard attached, or manually if you want to treat a touchscreen-equipped laptop as if it were a tablet. (In fact, you can enable Tablet Mode on a desktop PC without a touchscreen or even a touchpad; the resulting experience might be helpful for someone who occasionally wants that immersive, full-screen environment.)

Turning on Tablet Mode makes the following changes in the Windows 10 user experience:

- Reconfigures the taskbar, bumping up button sizes, adding a back button, replacing the search box with a search button, and hiding all taskbar buttons. The following comparison shows the normal taskbar on top and the same area in Tablet Mode below it.

- All apps run in full screen. It's possible to snap two apps side by side, but they have a thick sizing bar between them, similar to the one introduced in Windows 8.

- The Start menu opens in full screen, with the left column hidden by default and accessible only by tapping a so-called hamburger menu (a stack of three lines that resembles a beef patty between two buns) in the upper left corner of the display.

- Swiping from the left and right enables Task View and Action Center, respectively.

Windows 10 makes some assumptions about your preferences based on your hardware. On conventional PCs with a keyboard and mouse, Tablet Mode is off. On dedicated tablets, this mode is on by default. You can adjust these preferences by using the Settings page shown in Figure 3-14. On a hybrid device with a relatively small touchscreen, you might prefer to have Tablet Mode on full time, for example.

The other essential feature of a touchscreen-equipped device, especially one without a keyboard, is the presence of the extremely versatile Windows 10 Touch Keyboard. It allows text entry into dialog boxes, web forms, your browser's address bar, documents, the search box—anywhere you would normally need a physical keyboard to provide input.

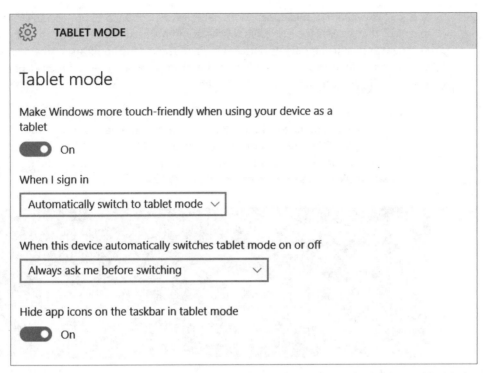

Figure 3-14 These settings are appropriate for a hybrid device that you switch into Tablet Mode occasionally.

Figure 3-15 shows the standard Touch Keyboard layout.

Figure 3-15 This is the standard Touch Keyboard; use the controls in the upper right to move, dock, or close the keyboard.

The Touch Keyboard should appear automatically when you tap to position the insertion point in a place that accepts text entry. On touchscreen-equipped devices, you can make the Touch Keyboard appear by tapping its button, which appears in the notification area on the right of the taskbar. (If this button is hidden, right-click or do a long press on the taskbar and then select the Show Touch Keyboard Button option.)

The limited screen space available for the Touch Keyboard means you have to switch layouts to enter symbols and numbers. Tap the &123 key in the lower left corner to switch between the standard QWERTY layout and the first of two symbol layouts, as shown in Figure 3-16. Note that the layout includes a dedicated number pad, which is extremely handy for working with spreadsheets and performing other data-entry tasks.

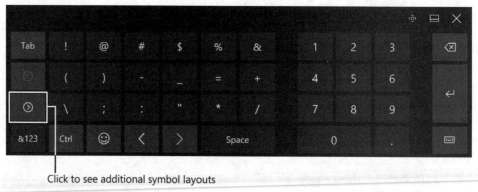

Click to see additional symbol layouts

Figure 3-16 Tap the &123 key in the lower left corner to switch between the standard QWERTY keys and this alternate view of symbols and numbers.

In some respects, the Touch Keyboard is more versatile than its physical counterparts. Entering typographic symbols like the interrobang or emoji—the whimsical characters available on all mobile platforms and on Windows 10—doesn't require the use of ANSI codes. Instead, you can enter characters directly. To show the first of more than 30 emoji keyboard layouts, each containing 30 symbols, click the "happy face" button on the bottom row.

With the emoji keyboard layout visible, the bottom row displays keys that you can use to switch between different categories, several of which have multiple layouts, accessible via the left and right arrows below the Tab key. Figure 3-17 shows a useful layout from the Objects & Symbols category.

Figure 3-17 Windows 10 supports hundreds of emoji characters. Pick a category from the bottom row and use the arrow keys to scroll through different character sets, 30 at a time.

NOTE

For a full list of officially supported Windows-compatible emoji characters, see *http://emojipedia.org/microsoft-emoji-list/*.

In addition to the conventional QWERTY layout, the Touch Keyboard comes in some variations, which are accessible by tapping the Switch key in the lower right corner, as shown in Figure 3-18.

Figure 3-18 Tap the Switch key in the lower right corner of any keyboard layout to change to a different arrangement or adjust language preferences.

The Handwriting panel, shown in Figure 3-19, is most useful with devices that support pen input, such as Microsoft's line of x86-based Surface and Surface Pro devices. (The ARM-based

CHAPTER 3

Surface RT and Surface 2 devices do not support Windows 10.) Text you enter in the input box is automatically translated into characters for entry at the current insertion point.

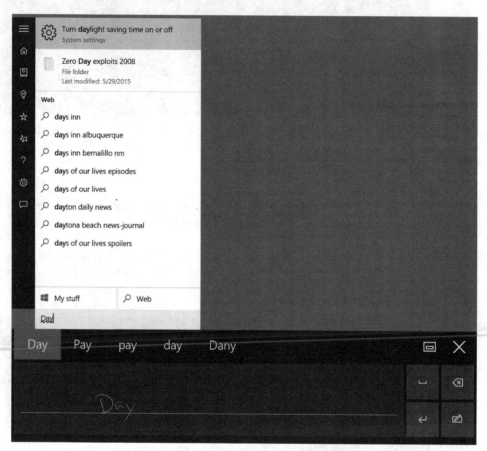

Figure 3-19 The handwriting input box does a frankly remarkable job at translating even sloppy penmanship into readable results.

Handwriting recognition is excellent, even for casual entry. As Figure 3-19 shows, you also have autocorrect options if the recognition engine guesses wrong.

Inside OUT

Using ink and handwriting

When you use a pen to scribble a handwritten note or sketch a figure within a pen-aware application, you create a type of data called ink. Although it superficially resembles a simple bitmap, ink-based data contains a wealth of information in addition to the simple shape. Windows records the direction, pressure, speed, and location of the tablet pen as it moves and stores the resulting marks as a compressed graphic. If you enlarge a piece of data that was stored as ink, Windows uses this stored data to ensure that it keeps its proper shape.

By recognizing the combinations of strokes that represent handwritten letters, the operating system can convert even bad handwriting into text, and with surprising accuracy. You don't have to convert ink into text to get the benefits of handwriting recognition, either. The handwriting recognizer automatically converts handwriting to text in the background, storing the resulting text along with the ink and adding the recognized words and phrases to the search index.

Applications that fully support ink as a data type are relatively rare, but you can perform some remarkable feats with those that do exist. Using Microsoft Word, for instance, you can insert handwritten comments and annotations into a document. Another member of the Office family, OneNote, goes even further, indexing your handwritten notes and allowing you to search through an entire notebook for a word or phrase.

Although you need a pen and a touchscreen that supports digitizing capabilities to add ink to a document using Windows 10, the resulting ink-based data is visible on any Windows-based system, with or without a touchscreen.

CHAPTER 3

The Split Keyboard layout, shown in Figure 3-20 on a Surface 3 in portrait orientation and in Tablet Mode, is extremely odd looking until you imagine trying to tap text with one finger as you hold a tablet in your other hand. With the split layout, you can grip a tablet in portrait or landscape mode and use your thumbs for typing. It takes some practice, but anyone who ever used an old-school BlackBerry phone can confirm that with practice you can achieve startling typing speed.

CHAPTER 3

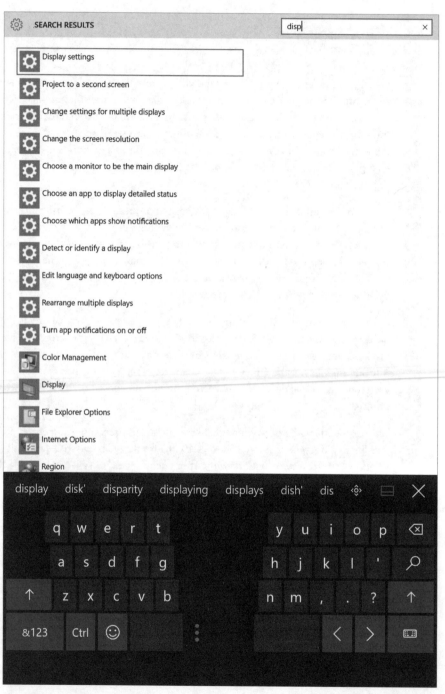

Figure 3-20 This split keyboard layout works best on a smaller tablet, where you can comfortably type with two thumbs.

By default, the Touch Keyboard appears at the bottom of the screen, pushing the contents of the page above it for unobstructed text entry. An X in the upper right corner lets you close any keyboard layout, a second button allows you to lock the keyboard into position, and the four-headed button lets you move a floating keyboard to a more comfortable position on a larger display.

Managing and arranging windows

Windows 10 includes a host of keyboard shortcuts and mouse gestures that greatly simplify the everyday tasks of resizing, moving, minimizing, arranging, and otherwise managing windows. The most useful trick is a collection of "snap" techniques. These have been around for several Windows versions, but Windows 10 adds some extremely useful new tricks to the old familiar methods.

The simplest window-snapping scenario is a PC with a single display, where you want to arrange two windows side by side. You might want to compare two Word documents, move files between the Documents folder and an archive, or do financial research in a web browser and plug the numbers into an Excel spreadsheet.

Drag a window title bar to the left or right edge of the screen, and it snaps to fill that half of the display. As soon as you let go of the title bar, the window snaps into its position and Windows helpfully offers thumbnails for all other open windows to help you choose what to run alongside your first snapped window.

In Figure 3-21, for example, we've just snapped a File Explorer window to the right side of the screen and now have a choice of four other running windows to snap opposite it. (If you don't feel like snapping a second window, just press Esc or click anywhere except on one of those thumbnails. They vanish immediately.)

Here are a few ways you can snap windows in Windows 10 by using a mouse or by dragging directly on a touchscreen:

- Drag the title bar to the top of the screen to maximize the window, or drag the title bar away from the top edge to restore it to its previous window size.

- Drag a window title bar to any corner of the screen, and it snaps to fill that quadrant of the display. This capability is new in Windows 10 and is most useful on large, high-resolution desktop displays.

- Drag the top window border (not the title bar) to the top edge of the screen, or drag the bottom border to the bottom edge of the screen. With either action, when you reach the edge, the window snaps to full height without changing its width. When you drag the border away from the window edge, the opposite border snaps to its previous position.

CHAPTER 3

Figure 3-21 When you snap a window to one edge of the display, Windows shows other open windows in thumbnails alongside the snapped window for easy side-by-side arrangement.

Note that the window resizes when the mouse pointer hits the edge of the screen. To use this feature with minimal mouse movement, start your drag action by pointing at the title bar near the edge you're going to snap to.

As soon as you begin dragging a snapped window away from the edge of the screen, it returns to its previous size and position.

Inside OUT

Snap side-by-side windows at different widths

Although Windows automatically arranges side-by-side windows at equal widths, you don't have to settle for symmetry. On a large desktop monitor, for example, you might want to arrange a news feed or Twitter stream along the right side of your display, using a third or less of the total display width and leaving room for Word or Excel to have a much larger share of the screen real estate.

The secret is to snap the first window and immediately drag its inside edge to adjust the window to your preferred width. Now grab the title bar of the window you want to see alongside it, and snap it to the opposite edge of the display. The newly snapped window expands to fill the space remaining after you adjusted the width of the first window.

The rules work the same with multimonitor setups. With two side-by-side monitors, for example, you can drag the mouse to the inside edge of a display and snap a window there, allowing for four equal-size windows lined up from left to right. Dragging the title bar also allows you to move a maximized window from one screen to another on a multimonitor system.

Inside OUT

Shake to minimize distractions

An ancient Windows feature called Aero Shake, first introduced with Windows Vista, survives into Windows 10. Grab the window's title bar with the mouse or a finger and quickly move it back and forth a few times. Suddenly, all windows retreat to the taskbar except the one whose title bar you just shook. This move takes a bit of practice, but it's worth mastering. It requires only three smooth "shakes"—a left, right, left motion is best—not maniacal shaking.

Windows 10 includes keyboard shortcuts that correspond with the preceding mouse gestures. These (and a few extras) are shown in Table 3-1.

Table 3-1 Keyboard shortcuts and gestures for resizing and moving windows

Task	Keyboard shortcut	Gesture
Maximize window	Windows key+ Up Arrow	Drag title bar to top of screen
Resize window to full screen height without changing its width	Shift+Windows key+ Up Arrow	Drag top or bottom border to edge of screen
Restore a maximized or full-height window	Windows key+ Down Arrow	Drag title bar or border away from screen edge
Minimize a restored window	Windows key+ Down Arrow	Click the Minimize button
Snap to the left half of the screen	Windows key+ Left Arrow*	Drag title bar to left edge
Snap to the right half of the screen	Windows key+ Right Arrow*	Drag title bar to right edge
Move to the next virtual desktop	Ctrl+Windows key+ Left/Right Arrow	Three-finger swipe on precision touchpad; none for mouse
Move to the next monitor	Shift+Windows key+ Left/Right Arrow	Drag title bar

CHAPTER 3

Task	Keyboard shortcut	Gesture
Minimize all windows except the active window (press again to restore windows previously minimized with this shortcut)	Windows key+ Home	"Shake" the title bar
Minimize all windows	Windows key+M	
Restore windows after minimizing	Shift+Windows key+M	

* Pressing this key repeatedly cycles through the left, right, and restored positions. If you have more than one monitor, it cycles these positions on each monitor in turn.

The Windows 10 taskbar also exposes some traditional window-management menus. The secret? Hold the Shift key as you right-click a taskbar button. For a button that represents a single window, the menu includes commands to Restore, Move, Size, Minimize, Maximize, and Close the window. For a grouped taskbar button, Shift+right-click displays commands to arrange, restore, minimize, or close all windows in the group.

If you find it disconcerting to have windows snap to a certain size and position when you drag their title bars, you can disable Snap. These options are well hidden on the Multitasking page in System Settings; it's easier to find them by typing **Snap** in the search box.

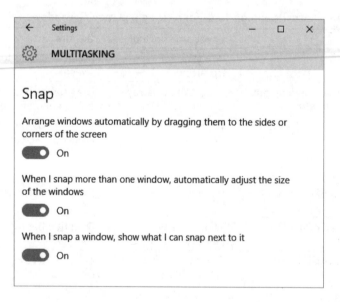

Cortana and search

We start this section with a disclaimer: Search, as a Windows 10 feature and as an online service, is evolving at breathtaking speed. The results that show up in the search box are delivered by online services that are constantly improving, as are the Windows features you use to make those requests. Our goal in this section is not to show you how to accomplish specific search tasks but to help you discover what search is capable of accomplishing for you.

Search is built into Windows 10 as an integral feature that gets prime real estate, just to the right of the Start button.

By default, on desktop and laptop PCs, this space is occupied by a search box. In Tablet Mode (or if you change the default setting), a search button appears, which expands into a box when you tap or click it.

By default, Windows Search is businesslike and efficient, with no personality. You type something in the search box and see results like those shown in Figure 3-22. Windows Search is very good at finding settings and apps, as you can see.

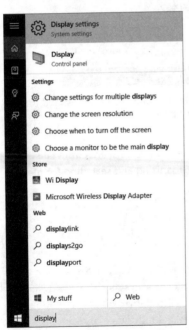

Figure 3-22 Type a word or phrase in the search box, and you get a list of settings and apps that match the search term, with options at the bottom to search personal files or the web.

If you're more interested in finding a photo or a PowerPoint presentation, enter your search term and then click or tap My Stuff to change the search scope. That immediately expands the size of the search results window, as shown in Figure 3-23, and displays results that match your search terms.

Figure 3-23 Changing the search scope to My Stuff expands the results list and turns up photos, documents, and more, with sort and filter options up top.

➤ For more detailed instructions on how to use Windows Search from File Explorer, see "Using Windows Search" in Chapter 12, "Organizing and searching for files."

Inside OUT

Don't want search? Hide it.

As with most things Windows, you can remove the search button or box completely if you're really convinced you won't use it. You can also specify that you want a button or a box, regardless of whether you're on a PC or tablet. All of these options are in the Taskbar And Start Menu Properties dialog box, on the Toolbars tab.

Cortana, the intelligent search assistant built into Windows 10, adds an adult's voice and a (programmed) sense of humor to the core search experience. It also adds the ability to perform additional tasks, such as adding items to a to-do list, and to deliver regular updates that match your interests, as defined in a notebook full of settings.

In many ways, Cortana today is like a two-year-old prodigy. Despite the pleasant female voice and the mostly natural intonations, "she" is really a web service, which is constantly learning and adding capabilities.

For a partial list of things Cortana can do for you, just ask. Click the microphone button in the search box and say, "What can you do?" That should produce a list like the one in Figure 3-24.

Figure 3-24 If you're not sure what Cortana can do, just ask, "What can you do?"

Because Cortana requires that you grant access to personal information, you need to go through a brief but important setup first. Pay special attention when the setup wizard asks for permission to use your microphone to accept spoken input. (Note: You're perfectly free to say no, but that changes the experience significantly.)

The icon bar along Cortana's left edge is cryptic at first. For a more thorough explanation of what each icon means, click the hamburger menu in the top left corner, next to Cortana's name, to see the list with descriptive labels attached, as in Figure 3-25.

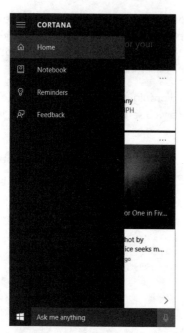

Figure 3-25 Click or tap the hamburger menu in the top left of the Cortana window to display labels identifying what each of the options along the left side does.

The tasks Cortana can complete on your behalf include adding appointments and reminders, creating notes, setting alarms, retrieving a weather forecast, and checking your calendar for upcoming events. Figure 3-26, for example, shows the response when you ask Cortana to set a reminder.

Cortana is most valuable on mobile devices, of course, where the ability to ask a question (literally) and get a useful answer is paramount. But she is a handy assistant in an office as well.

In addition to taking over search duties for files, folders, settings, music, and so on, Cortana can return results based on information you've allowed her to search. Just clicking in the search box allows Cortana to display a scrolling list of useful information: news headlines, stock prices from your watch list, results from your favorite team's latest game, weather forecasts, and reminders on when you need to leave to arrive on time for an appointment.

You establish those interests in an initial, brief interview, but you can expand or change those interests later by visiting the Cortana notebook. To start, click the Notebook icon, just below Home on Cortana's left side. That opens a dialog box like the one shown in Figure 3-27.

Figure 3-26 If you ask Cortana to set a reminder or create an appointment, she responds with this crisply efficient form.

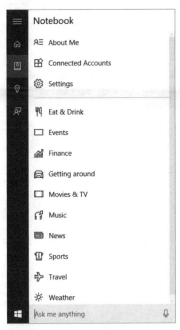

Figure 3-27 Use Cortana's notebook to customize your interests and help make the "Here's what's happening now" summaries more useful.

You have every right to be concerned about privacy when using a service that knows so much about your daily routine. You can read the Cortana privacy policy by following a link at the bottom of the Cortana Settings pane, shown in Figure 3-28.

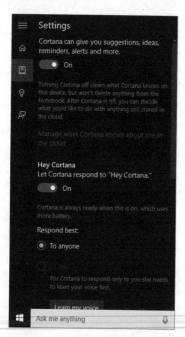

Figure 3-28 The Cortana Settings pane allows you to read the privacy policy, disable the service and clear local information, or go online and delete all saved information.

The top option on this window turns Cortana off and deletes any locally saved information. To delete personal information saved on Microsoft's servers, click or tap Manage What Cortana Knows About Me In The Cloud and follow the instructions.

Personalizing Windows 10

Every new version of Windows brings some changes to its visual appearance, and Windows 10 is no exception. Another constant is the ability to tweak and refine that appearance to better suit your tastes.

It's your operating system; make it reflect your preferences, your needs, your style. Make it work for you. Windows 10 provides myriad tools for doing just that—tools that we survey in this chapter.

Settings vs. Control Panel

Personalizing Windows to your liking is generally done by applying settings. So it makes sense that many personalization settings are made in a modern app called Settings, which is shown in Figure 4-1. The Settings app made its first appearance in Windows 8, beginning the transition of personalization and other settings from Control Panel, the desktop app that has served this function since the beginning of Windows back in 1985. That transition is not complete, however. In Windows 10 you'll find that some settings are made only in Settings, some can be made only in Control Panel, and some have equivalent functions in both places.

You'll find a shortcut to Settings in the lower left corner of the Start menu. Alternatively, you can launch it with a keyboard shortcut: Windows key+I. To open Control Panel, right-click or long-tap the Start button (or press Windows key+X), and then click or tap Control Panel. Of course, using the search box, you can find and launch either one, as well as find and launch the page or app for individual settings.

In this chapter we guide you to the most effective way to make a specific setting, be it via Settings or Control Panel. But there's no need to memorize a particular pathway. Use the search box in Settings; the results include matches from Settings *and* Control Panel. (The corresponding search box in Control Panel searches only within Control Panel.)

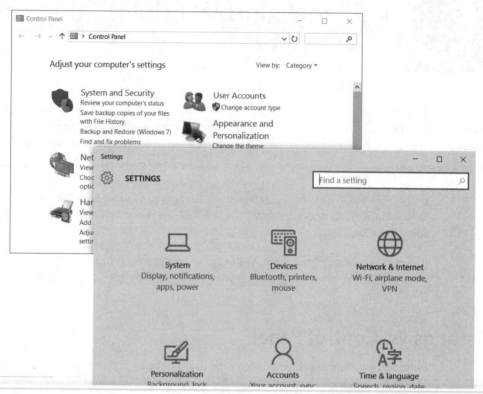

Figure 4-1 The modern Settings app will eventually supplant the old school Control Panel.

Customizing the visual appearance

The most obvious way to personalize your Windows experience is to customize its visual appearance—the desktop background, the window colors, and so on. These settings are made in the aptly named Personalization, a Settings tool that appears when you right-click the desktop and choose Personalize. See Figure 4-2.

NOTE

Confusingly, Control Panel also has a Personalization option—and you can't use it to set backgrounds and colors. Instead, it's the place for working with themes, a topic we take up in "Syncing your settings between computers" later in this chapter.

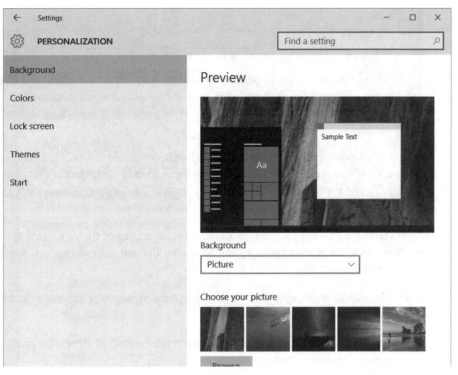

Figure 4-2 Personalization, your home base for setting backgrounds and colors, shows the effect of your settings in a Preview area.

Selecting the desktop background

You can perk up any desktop with a background image. Your background can be supplied by a graphics file in any of several common formats (including .bmp, .gif, .jpg, .png, and .tif). And you're not stuck with a static image, either. You can set up a slide show of images.

To select a background, in Settings choose Personalization, and then click Background. The Background box (see Figure 4-2) offers three types of backgrounds:

- **Picture** displays a photo or other image. Choose one of the pictures provided with Windows or click Browse to choose one of your own pictures.

- **Solid Color** covers the background with a color you select from a palette of two dozen shades.

- **Slideshow** is like the Picture option, but with a twist: At an interval you select (ranging from 1 minute to 1 day), Windows changes to a new picture from your selected picture albums. By default, Windows uses your local Pictures library and your Pictures folder on OneDrive as sources for the slide show. Click Browse to replace these choices.

Inside OUT

Restore the photographs furnished with Windows

When you click Browse to select a new picture, your selection replaces one of the five existing picture choices. But what if you decide you'd rather go back to one of those terrific photos provided with Windows? Getting any one of them back is simple, but not obvious.

Click Browse and navigate to %Windir%\Web\Wallpaper. (On most systems, %Windir% is C:\Windows.) You'll find a handful of nice pictures in subfolders of that folder—including the ones you've displaced.

After you choose an image or set up a slide show, select one of the six Choose A Fit options to let Windows know how you want to handle images that are not exactly the same size as your screen resolution.

- **Fill** reduces or enlarges the image so that it fits the shortest dimension and crops the other edges.

- **Fit** reduces or enlarges the image so that it fits the longest dimension and adds black bars on the other edges.

- **Stretch** reduces or enlarges the image so that it fits both dimensions, distorting the image as necessary.

- **Tile** repeats the image at its original size to fill the screen.

- **Center** displays the image at its original size in the center of the screen.

- **Span** works like Fill to display a single image across multiple monitors.

Here are some other ways to change the desktop background:

- Right-click an image file in File Explorer and choose Set As Desktop Background.

- Right-click an image in Internet Explorer and choose Set As Background.

- Open any image file in Paint, open the File menu, and choose Set As Desktop Background. A submenu lets you choose the Fill, Tile, or Center picture position.

- Use the Photos app to open an image file, click or tap the ellipsis at the right side of the menu bar, and then click or tap Set As Background.

Selecting colors

With a beautiful desktop background in place, your next personalization step might be to select a complementary color for the window borders, Start menu, and taskbar. To do that, right-click the desktop, choose Personalize, and then click Colors to see a screen like the one shown in Figure 4-3.

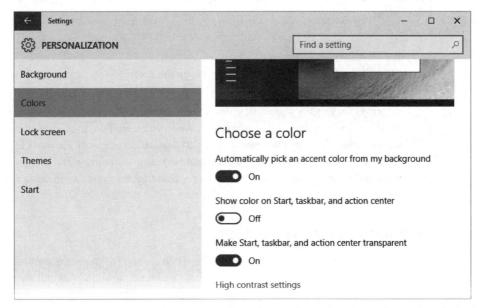

Figure 4-3 Compared with earlier versions of Windows, color options in Windows 10 are limited.

Unlike the dizzying array of options for setting colors for every individual screen element in earlier versions of Windows, Windows 10 offers only the following choices:

- **Automatically Pick An Accent Color From My Background.** The accent color, in varying intensities, is used to highlight selections (such as the word *Colors* in the left pane shown in Figure 4-3), as a background color for taskbar and Start menu icons, and for some text elements in modern apps. When this option is on, Windows selects a color that complements your current background, be it a solid color or a picture. (And if you use a slide show as your background, the accent color changes each time the background picture changes.) Turning this option off displays a selection of colors from which you can choose.

- **Show Color On Start, Taskbar, And Action Center.** Turning this option on applies the accent color as a background to the Start menu, the taskbar, and Action Center. When it's off, those areas have a dark background.

CHAPTER 4

- **Make Start, Taskbar, And Action Center Transparent.** Not "transparent" as in clear glass; more like darkly tinted glass, which allows you to see "through" each of these elements to the underlying desktop. To some, transparency is a cool effect, whereas others find it distracting.

One more option appears on the Colors tab: High Contrast Settings. That option is intended to help users with visual impairments. For more information, see "Overcoming challenges" later in this chapter.

TROUBLESHOOTING

The automatic color option doesn't change the color

Suppose you turn off the first option and select a color, and then later decide you'd rather go back to the automatic color. So you turn on the option to automatically select an accent color and . . . nothing happens. When you turn it on, the automatic option doesn't take effect until the *next time* the background changes. If you want to use the automatic color associated with the current background, return to the background page and select the same background again; that triggers Windows to "automatically" select an accent color.

Customizing mouse pointers

Sometimes it's the little things that make a difference . . . and make your computer uniquely yours. If you think an hourglass depicts the passage of time more unambiguously than a rolling doughnut, you can easily bring back the Windows XP–era shape. You can customize the entire array of pointer shapes your system uses by choosing Mouse in Control Panel, which opens a dialog box like the one shown in Figure 4-4. (If you find yourself on the Mouse & Touchpad page in Settings, scroll down to the bottom. Under Related Settings, click Additional Mouse Options to open the Mouse Properties dialog box.)

On the Pointers tab of the Mouse Properties dialog box, you can select a pointer type in the Customize box and then click Browse to select an alternative pointer shape. (The Browse button takes you to %Windir%\Cursors and displays files with the extensions .cur and .ani. The latter are animated cursors.)

Windows wraps up a gamut of pointer shapes as a mouse-pointer scheme. The system comes with an assortment of predefined schemes, making it easy for you to switch from one set of pointers to another as needs or whims suggest. Figure 4-4 shows the list.

Figure 4-4 Some of the predefined mouse-pointer schemes are better suited than the default scheme for working in challenging lighting conditions.

The pointers included with Windows won't win any cutting-edge design awards; some of them date back to an era when an hourglass actually *was* used for keeping time. However, there are situations where a switch is worthwhile. If you sometimes use your portable computer in lighting conditions that make it hard for you to find the pointer, consider switching to one of the large or extra large schemes. If nothing else, those will give your eyeballs a larger target to pursue.

If you're inclined to roll your own mouse scheme (by using the Browse button to assign cursor files to pointer types), be sure to use the Save As command and give your work a name. That way you'll be able to switch away from it and back to it again at will.

Configuring desktop icons

A fresh, cleanly installed Windows 10 desktop (as opposed to one generated by an upgrade installation) includes a single lonely icon—Recycle Bin. If you want to display other system icons, in the search box (any search box: on the taskbar, in Settings, or in Control Panel) type **desktop**, and then click Show Or Hide Common Icons On The Desktop. The Desktop Icon Settings dialog box, shown next, provides check boxes for five system folders—Computer, User's Files (the root folder of your own profile), Network, Recycle Bin, and Control Panel.

CHAPTER 4

If you're really into customization, you can change any of the five icons that appear in the large box in the center. Note that the Control Panel icon does not appear in this center box even if you select its check box; Windows doesn't provide a way to change it.

To change an icon, select it in the center box and click Change Icon. You'll find an interesting assortment of alternative icons in the file %Windir%\System32\Imageres.dll. (Be sure to use the horizontal scroll bar to see them all.) If none of these suit you, try browsing to %Windir%\System32\Shell32.dll.

After you've populated your desktop with icons, you might want to control their arrangement. If you right-click the desktop, you'll find two commands at the top of the shortcut menu that can help in this endeavor. To make your icons rearrange themselves when you delete one of their brethren, click View and then click Auto Arrange Icons. To ensure that each icon keeps a respectable distance from each of its neighbors (and that the whole gang stays together at the left side of your screen), click View, Align Icons To Grid. And if your icons occasionally get in the way (for example, if you want to take an unimpeded look at the current desktop background image), click View, and then click Show Desktop Icons. (Return to this command when you want the icons back.)

CHAPTER 4

To change the sort order of desktop icons, right-click the desktop and click Sort By. You can sort on any of four attributes: Name, Size, Item Type, or Date Modified. Sorting a second time on any attribute changes the sort order from ascending to descending (or vice versa).

Controlling the appearance of other icons

Windows displays icons around the perimeter of the desktop too: in the notification area (the right or bottom end of the taskbar), in Action Center, and on the Start menu.

The notification area ordinarily shows the date and time, icons that indicate network and battery status, a shortcut for setting speaker volume, and the like. In addition, many programs add icons that serve as shortcuts to various program functions as well as status indicators. And some programs display pop-up messages via the notification area.

Fortunately, you can manage the clutter and the distractions to include only the information you want. You'll find the tools to do so in Settings, System, Notifications & Actions. On that page, click Select Which Icons Appear On The Taskbar and Turn System Icons On Or Off to specify which icons appear. Scroll down a bit to the Show Notifications From These Apps section to specify which ones are allowed to display pop-up messages or play sounds. For more information, see "Controlling how notifications appear" in Chapter 3, Using Windows 10."

Action Center, which appears when you swipe from the right side of the screen or click the Action Center icon in the notification area, includes a collection of action buttons at the bottom of the pane, as shown here.

Other action buttons appear if you click Expand—but the top four buttons are designated as *quick actions*, because all it takes is a swipe and a tap to execute one of these actions. To select your four quick actions, make your choices at the top of the Notifications & Actions page in Settings, System.

The available action buttons depend on the capabilities of your computer, but they may include items such as Wi-Fi, Bluetooth, and Airplane Mode (which let you turn wireless communications on or off with a tap or click); Brightness, Battery Saver, Rotation Lock, and Tablet Mode (which control features normally used only on mobile PCs); and All Settings and Notes (shortcuts to Settings and OneNote, respectively). Quiet Hours turns off notifications temporarily.

CHAPTER 4

Inside OUT

Add or remove icons from the Start menu

By default, in the lower left corner of the Start menu you'll find icons for File Explorer, Settings, Power, and All Apps. If you like, you can add shortcuts to many other commonly used folders. In Settings, choose Personalization, Start, and then tap or click Choose Which Folders Appear On Start. For information about making other changes to the Start menu, see "Using and customizing the Start menu" in Chapter 3.

Configuring the taskbar with multiple displays

If your computer has more than one monitor attached, you have additional options for configuring the taskbar: you can show it on just the main display or on all displays, and you can vary its appearance on each display. To review these options, right-click the taskbar and choose Properties. You'll find them under Multiple Displays at the bottom of the Taskbar tab in the Taskbar And Start Menu Properties dialog box, shown next.

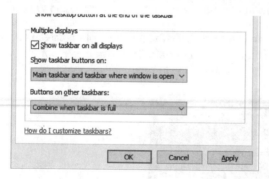

Selecting the first option shows a taskbar on each monitor; if you clear it, the taskbar appears only on the main display. (You specify the "main display" in Settings, System, Display. For details, see "Displays" in Chapter 13, "Hardware.")

The Show Taskbar Buttons On setting determines where the taskbar button for a particular app appears—on all taskbars or only the one where that app's window resides.

The last setting specifies how taskbar buttons are combined on displays other than the main display.

> ➤ For information about other taskbar settings, see "Using and customizing the taskbar" in Chapter 3.

Customizing the lock screen

The lock screen—the screen that's displayed while your computer is turned on but nobody is signed in—can be changed to your liking too. In Settings, click Personalization, Lock Screen to see your options, as shown in Figure 4-5.

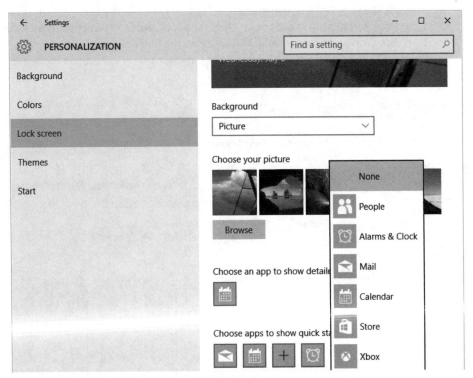

Figure 4-5 Tapping a status icon lets you select which apps you want to appear on the lock screen.

Here you can select a background, using options similar to those available for a desktop background. You can also select one or more apps to display their current status—such as the number of new email messages, upcoming appointments, alarms, and so on—on the lock screen. Tap one of the app icons to see a list of apps that support this feature. You can have only one app display detailed status and only seven apps show quick status. To add another you must first stop showing one of the existing apps.

Additional options for determining what appears on the lock screen can be found in Settings, System, Notifications & Actions. Under Notifications, two options control the ability of app notifications, alarms, reminders, and incoming calls to appear on the lock screen.

Working with fonts

The days when your choice of fonts ended just beyond Arial and Times New Roman are long gone; if you include all the language variants and style variants (bold, italic, and so on), Windows 10 comes with hundreds of fonts.

The headquarters for font management is Fonts in Control Panel, which is shown in Figure 4-6. From this list of fonts, you can select a font (or a font family, which appears as a stack) and then click Preview to open a window that shows the font's characters in sizes ranging from 12 point to 72 point. (A point is a printer's measurement that is still used in modern digital typography. There are 72 points to an inch.)

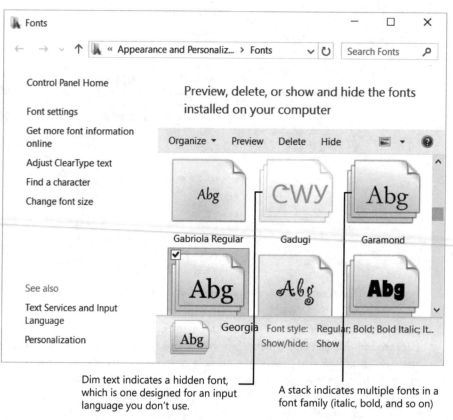

Dim text indicates a hidden font, which is one designed for an input language you don't use.

A stack indicates multiple fonts in a font family (italic, bold, and so on)

Figure 4-6 Hidden fonts don't appear in application font lists, but they do show up in Fonts.

The primary font format used by Windows is TrueType. Windows also supports OpenType and PostScript Type 1 fonts. To install a new font, you can drag its file from a folder or compressed .zip archive to Fonts in Control Panel. But it's not necessary to open Fonts; the simplest way to install a font is to right-click its file in File Explorer and choose Install. Because font file names are often somewhat cryptic, you might want to double-click the file, which opens the font preview window, to see what you're getting. If it's a font you want, click the Install button.

NOTE
PostScript Type 1 fonts normally consist of two or three files. The one you use to install the font—regardless of which method you use—is the .pfm file, whose file type is shown in File Explorer as Type 1 Font File.

Making text easier to read

If you like to work at high screen resolutions but find yourself straining to read the text, you can try the following:

- Look for scaling ("zoom") commands in the text-centric programs you use. Many programs, including most modern word processors, include these scaling features. Scaling text up to a readable size is a good solution for particular programs, but it doesn't change the size of icon text, system menus (such as the Start menu), or system dialog boxes.

- To enlarge part of the screen, use the Magnifier tool. (For more information, see "Overcoming challenges" later in this chapter.)

- Use the scaling options in Display settings. Adjusting the scaling to a higher level enables you to have readable text at higher screen resolutions.

To adjust display scaling, in Settings tap System, Display. Adjust the slider below Change The Size Of Text, Apps, And Other Items, as shown in Figure 4-7. The slider for adjusting display sizes has only three or four (depending on your display hardware) predefined settings; it's not continuously adjustable as a slider control might imply.

Your changes take effect only after you click Apply, which is below the Brightness Level slider (not visible in the figure), and sign out. After you sign in again, test some text-centric applications to see whether you like the result. If you don't, return to the Display settings and try another setting.

➤ **For information about screen resolution and other display configuration tasks, see "Displays" in Chapter 13.**

CHAPTER 4

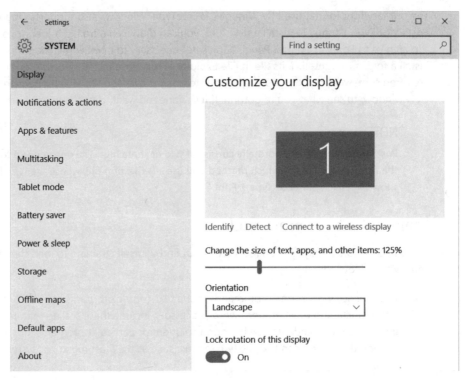

Figure 4-7 Unlike most other options in Settings, to effect your changes on the display size slider, you must scroll down and click Apply.

Using font smoothing to make text easier on the eyes

ClearType is a font-smoothing technology that reduces jagged edges of characters, thus easing eye strain.

To check or change your font-smoothing settings, type **cleartype** in the search box, and then click Adjust ClearType Text. Doing so opens the ClearType Text Tuner, which, in its first screen, has a check box that turns ClearType on when it is selected. The ensuing screens that appear each time you click Next offer optometrist-style choices ("Which is better, number 1 or number 2?") to help you reach ClearType perfection. If you have more than one monitor attached, the ClearType Text Tuner goes through this exercise for each one.

Windows includes seven fonts that are optimized for ClearType. The names of six of these—Constantia, Cambria, Corbel, Calibri, Candara, and Consolas—begin with the letter c—just to help cement the connection with ClearType. If you're particularly prone to eye fatigue, you might want to consider favoring these fonts in documents you create. (Constantia and Cambria are serif fonts, considered particularly suitable for longer documents and reports. The other four are sans serif fonts, good for headlines and advertising.) The seventh ClearType-optimized font, Segoe UI, is the typeface used for text elements throughout the Windows user interface. (Windows also includes a ClearType-optimized font called Meiryo that's designed to improve the readability of horizontally arrayed Asian languages.)

➤ For information about how ClearType works, visit Microsoft's ClearType site at *w7io.com/0404*.

Calibrating your display's colors

To get the most accurate rendition of images and colors on your screen, you should calibrate it. You've probably noticed, but perhaps not fiddled with, the buttons on your monitor that control various display settings. A tool included with Windows, Display Color Calibration, helps you to calibrate your screen by using your monitor's display controls as well as various Windows settings. With Display Color Calibration, you set gamma, brightness, contrast, color balance, and other settings, all of which are explained in the on-screen descriptions.

To run Display Color Calibration, in the search box, type **calibrate** and then click Calibrate Display Color. If you'd rather click or tap your way to it, open Settings, click System, Display, Advanced Display Settings, Color Calibration. Display Color Calibration opens a full-screen application that leads you through the steps of adjusting your display by making settings and adjusting monitor controls until the images displayed at each step look their best.

NOTE
If you work with color and you need more precise control over the way colors appear on your screen and on your printer, you should explore Color Management, a tool that lets you work with stored color profiles. In the search box, type **color management** to find this tool.

Making other small visual tweaks

Windows is alive with little animations, such as when you open or close a window. Along with other effects, these can help to direct your focus to the current window or activity. But some folks find them annoying, and an argument can be made that they do take a small bite out of your computer's performance. So if you don't like them, turn them off!

In the search box of Settings or Control Panel, type **performance** and then choose Adjust The Appearance And Performance Of Windows. Alternatively, you can tap your way through this lengthy path: Settings, System, About, System Info, Advanced System Settings, Settings (under Performance). A dialog box like the one shown next opens, allowing you to control animations and other effects on a granular level.

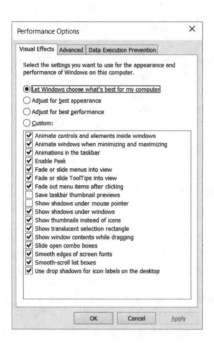

Working the way you like

It's important to look good, and that's what the previous sections of this chapter cover. But even more important is personalizing your computer to work in a way that's comfortable for you, and that's what we address here: specifying your mouse and keyboard preferences, selecting sounds for alerts, and even choosing a screen saver.

> ➤ Customizers often like to change a few other functionality-related features. For information about moving system folders and libraries, see "Relocating personal data folders" in Chapter 12, "Organizing and searching for files." For information about power-management settings, see "Power management and battery life" in Chapter 15, "System maintenance and performance."

Taming your mouse or other pointing device

To teach your mouse new tricks, in Settings visit Devices, Mouse & Touchpad. Settings here under Mouse let you swap the functions of your left and right mouse buttons (great for left-handed folks) and control how much to scroll each time you roll the mouse wheel. You'll find other mouse settings by scrolling to the bottom of the Mouse & Touchpad page and clicking Additional Mouse Options. Doing so opens the Mouse Properties dialog box, shown earlier in Figure 4-4.

Mouse Properties has settings that define a double-click (that is, how quickly you must twice press the mouse button for it to be detected as a double-click instead of two clicks), add visual highlights to the mouse as you move it, and more.

Depending on the mouse you have, you might find additional options in Mouse Properties or in a separate app. For example, if you have a Microsoft mouse, you might see the Mouse And Keyboard Center tab (as shown in Figure 4-4). That tab contains a link that launches an app where you can adjust many more settings, such as assigning useful functions to each mouse button.

If your computer has a precision touchpad, the Mouse & Touchpad page in Settings, Devices has a lot to explore, as shown in Figure 4-8.

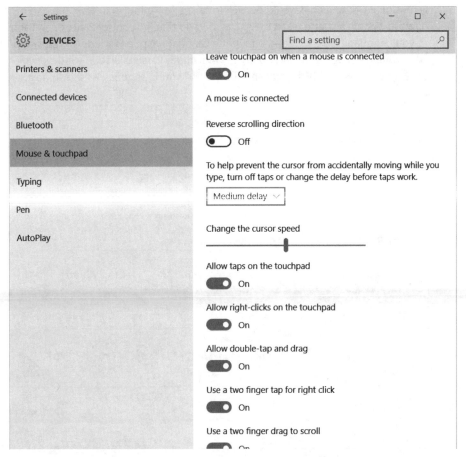

Figure 4-8 Touchpad users are richly rewarded by visiting Mouse & Touchpad and scrolling down to the settings under Touchpad.

Options here let you turn off the touchpad when you have a mouse attached or disable it altogether. Those who've been annoyed when the pointer suddenly hops to a new location while they type (usually because a thumb lightly grazed the touchpad) will appreciate—nay, shout hosannas about—the setting that delays cursor moves. Other settings determine what various gestures (tapping, double-tapping, tapping with two or three fingers, dragging with two or three fingers, and so on) will do.

If you use a pen with your computer, visit the Pen page in Settings, Devices. The modest number of settings here control the appearance of the pen cursor and offer another place for lefties to assert their rights.

Handwriting recognition in Windows is amazing; it has often correctly interpreted our own writing, which we could barely read ourselves. Nonetheless, pen users whose handwriting verges on indecipherable would do well to take a few minutes to train the handwriting recognition system to better read their scrawl. To do that, in Control Panel open Language. Next to your language, click Options, and in the Language Options window click or tap Personalize Handwriting Recognition. This opens a Handwriting Personalization window, which leads to a series of windows in which you can submit handwriting samples, as shown next.

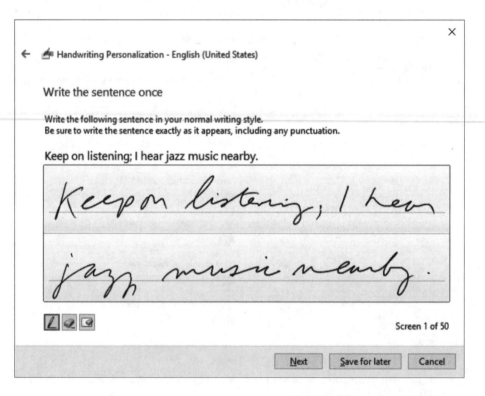

Managing keyboard settings

Keyboard users—yes, there are still a few—will find settings under Keyboard in Control Panel that control how quickly a key repeats when it's held down. And as with a mouse, you might find additional settings in a manufacturer-provided tab or app.

But wait; there's more! In Settings, open Devices, Typing to see options like those shown in Figure 4-9. The options under Spelling and the Add A Period option under Typing work only with modern apps. The other options under Typing work only with the Touch Keyboard. Adding to the confusion, some (but not all) options under Touch Keyboard also work with a physical keyboard. If you often use modern apps or the Touch Keyboard, you'll want to experiment with these settings.

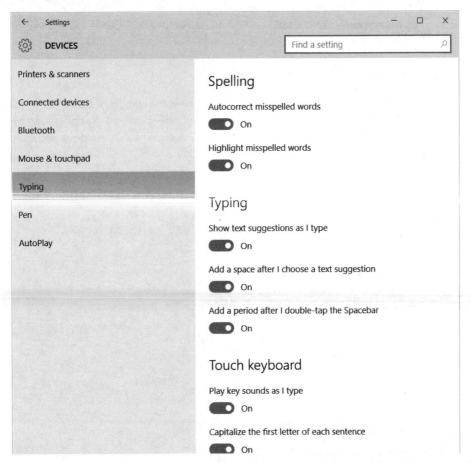

Figure 4-9 For the most part, the options on the Typing page work only with modern apps and with the Touch Keyboard.

Inside OUT

Reconfigure the Caps Lock key to avoid shouting

If you occasionally find yourself accidentally stuck in Caps Lock mode, so that your emails are shouting or your text documents look like a demand letter from a creditor, consider the following tweak.

You can disable the Caps Lock key so that it does nothing whatsoever: Open Registry Editor and navigate to HKLM\System\CurrentControlSet\Control\Keyboard Layout. Add a Binary value called Scancode Map. Set the data for this key to

00000000 00000000 02000000 00003A00 00000000

Close Registry Editor, restart, and you'll never be stuck in Caps Lock again.

Selecting sounds for events

To specify the sounds that Windows plays as it goes through its paces, in the search box type **sounds**, and then click Change System Sounds. In the Sound dialog box (shown here), you can select a predefined collection of beeps, gurgles, and chirps that Windows and various apps play in response to various system and application events.

You can select a sound scheme from the list (a new installation of Windows comes with only a single scheme, called Windows Default), or you can customize the sound schemes. To see which sounds are currently mapped to events, scroll through the Program Events list. If an event has a sound associated with it, its name is preceded by a speaker icon, and you can click Test to hear it. To switch to a different sound, scroll through the Sounds list or click Browse. The list displays .wav files in %Windir%\Media, but any .wav file is eligible. To silence an event, select None, the item at the top of the Sounds list.

If you rearrange the mapping of sounds to events, consider saving the new arrangement as a sound scheme. (Click Save As and supply a name.) That way, you can experiment further and still return to the saved configuration.

Inside OUT

Mute your computer

If you like event sounds in general but occasionally need complete silence from your computer, choose No Sounds in the Sound Scheme list when you want the machine to shut up. (Be sure to clear the Play Windows Startup Sound check box as well.) When sound is welcome again, you can return to the Windows Default scheme—or to any other scheme you have set up. Switching to the No Sounds scheme won't render your system mute (you'll still be able to play music when you want to hear it), but it will turn off the announcement of incoming mail and other events.

If you want to control sound levels on a more granular level—perhaps muting some applications altogether and adjusting volume levels on others—right-click the volume icon in the notification area and choose Open Volume Mixer. Volume Mixer provides a volume slider (and a mute button) for each output device and each running program that emits sounds.

CHAPTER 4

Choosing a screen saver

Screen savers don't save screens. (In long-gone days when screens were invariably CRTs and many offices displayed the same application at all hours of the working day, having an image move about during idle times probably did extend the service life of some displays.) And they certainly don't save energy. But they're fun to watch. To see the current offerings, in the search box type **screen saver**, and then click Change Screen Saver.

In the Screen Saver Settings dialog box (shown next), select an option under Screen Saver. Some screen savers have additional configuration options; click Settings to review your choices.

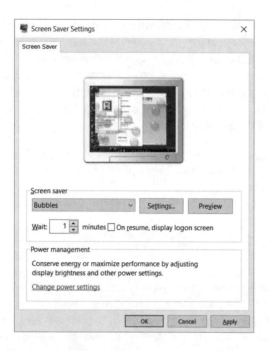

Tuning Windows to know about you

A personalized experience requires Windows to know some things about you. Not just how to read your handwriting, or your dining preferences, but some basic information: where are you?

Your location affects several settings, such as the current time (more specifically, the time zone), your language and keyboard, and the way dates, times, and numbers are displayed. To set your location, in Settings open Time & Language to display the Date & Time page, as shown in Figure 4-10.

First, be sure to select the proper time zone for your current location. If you're connected to the Internet, the time should be set automatically; Windows periodically synchronizes your computer's clock to an Internet-based time server. (Without an Internet connection, turn off automatic time setting and click Change to set the time manually.)

Then you'll want to review the samples under Formats; many apps use the formats you set here as their default format for displaying dates and times. Initially, these are set based on the country/region you specify during Windows setup, but you can easily change any or all of them by clicking Change Date And Time Formats.

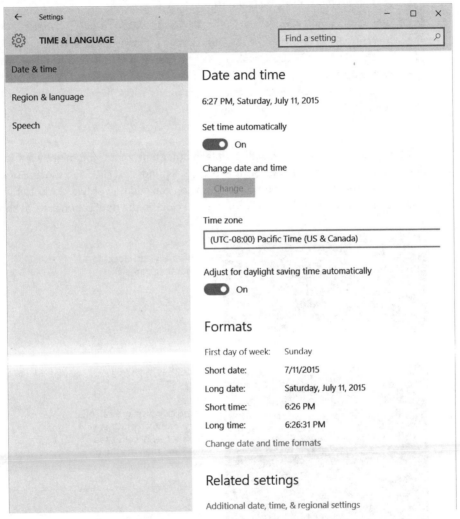

Figure 4-10 A quick way to display this page is to tap or click the clock in the notification area and then tap or click Date And Time Settings.

Inside OUT

Set formats for currency and numbers

Some apps also look to Windows for a default format for displaying monetary amounts (the currency symbol and number format) and numbers (items such as the thousands separator and the decimal symbol)—but you won't find those settings here. Instead, on the Date & Time page in Settings, tap or click Additional Date, Time, & Regional Settings. In the Control Panel window that opens, click Change Date, Time, Or Number Formats, and then click Additional Settings.

If you frequently communicate with people in other time zones, you might want to scroll down to the bottom of the Date & Time page in Settings and click Add Clocks For Different Time Zones. This opens a dialog box in which you can add one or two clocks to the top of the calendar that appears when you click or tap the clock in the notification area, as shown next.

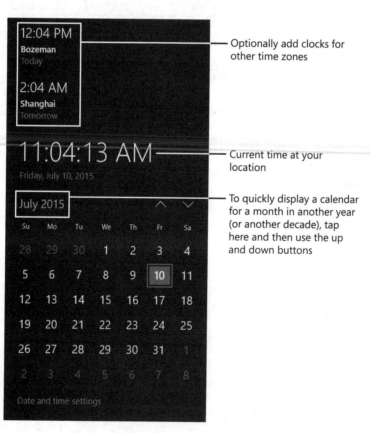

Optionally add clocks for other time zones

Current time at your location

To quickly display a calendar for a month in another year (or another decade), tap here and then use the up and down buttons

Syncing your settings between computers

Windows 10 offers two types of synchronization among computers:

- A *theme* is an über configuration that combines and names the various personalization settings that you can make. Themes can incorporate the desktop background, window color, sound scheme, screen saver, desktop icons, and mouse pointers.

- A more comprehensive collection of synchronization settings encompasses not only themes but various other personalization options:

  - **Web Browser Settings.** Settings you make using the Settings command in Microsoft Edge and the Internet Options command in Internet Explorer

  - **Passwords.** Passwords you've saved in your web browser

  - **Language Preferences.** Settings you make in Settings, Time & Language

  - **Ease Of Access.** Settings you make in Settings, Ease Of Access (for details, see the next section, "Overcoming challenges")

  - **Other Windows Settings.** Various other settings, ranging from window positions to Start menu arrangements to calendar settings—and many more

Note that these are all settings that pertain to your own Microsoft account or domain account (either a work domain or an Azure Active Directory domain). Settings that apply to all users at your computer, such as screen resolution, are not included in the current theme or other synchronized settings. Also, settings associated with a local user account don't get synchronized with other computers.

Working with themes

To select a theme, go to Settings, Personalization, Themes, and then click Theme Settings. A dialog box appears showing predefined themes included with Windows as well as themes you've saved. Simply click one to select it; the theme is applied right away, so if you don't like what you see and hear, you can select another before you close the window.

If you've got all the visual and aural aspects of your profile set up just the way you want them, and you want to be able to experiment further but still return to the current settings, it's time to revisit Theme Settings. At the top of the themes list, in the My Themes category, you'll see Unsaved Theme if you made changes to whatever theme was previously in effect. To make those changes reusable, click Save Theme and supply a name.

If you make additional changes, you'll once again generate an Unsaved Theme entry. There's no limit to the number of themes you can create. Windows saves each group of settings as a .theme file in your %LocalAppData%\Microsoft\Windows\Themes folder. (A .theme file is a standard text file that describes all the theme settings. For complete details about theme

CHAPTER 4

files, see "Theme File Format" at *w7io.com/0402*.) You can delete unwanted items from the My Themes list; simply right-click the item you no longer want and choose Delete Theme. Note that you can't delete the theme that's currently in use.

Inside OUT

Share themes with friends or from a local user account

Syncing themes among your devices is effortless when you sign in with a Microsoft account. But even if you use a local account, you still might want to use a theme on your other computers or share it with other users. Because a .theme file is just a text file, it doesn't contain the graphic images of your desktop, the sound files you use for various events, or other necessary files that make up the entire theme experience. For the purpose of sharing themes, Windows uses a .themepack file, which includes the .theme file as well as all other nonstandard theme elements. A .themepack file uses the standard compressed folder (.zip archive) format to envelop its component files. To create a .themepack file of an item in My Themes, right-click it and choose Save Theme For Sharing. Unless you specify otherwise, Windows saves the .themepack file in the default save location of your Documents library.

To use a theme that was saved in .theme or .themepack format, simply double-click it. (Of course, a .theme file won't offer the full experience if the theme's components aren't available on your computer in folders to which you have access. To create a .themepack file—which includes all the necessary files—see the preceding tip.)

Because themes are so easily portable, you can find many compelling Windows themes online. Start your quest by clicking Get More Themes Online (under My Themes in Personalization), where Microsoft offers a nice selection.

Synchronizing other settings

To manage synchronization of various other components, in Settings click Accounts, Sync Your Settings. Figure 4-11 shows the window that appears.

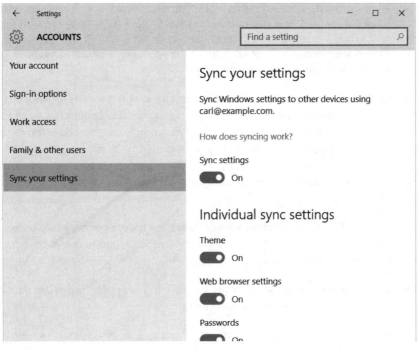

Figure 4-11 You can enable or disable all sync settings with a single setting, or you can control settings individually.

Overcoming challenges

Microsoft has a longstanding commitment to making computing accessible and easier to use for persons with vision, hearing, or mobility impairments. Windows 10 groups these options into the Ease Of Access section of Settings. (Alternatively, you can press Windows key+U to open Ease Of Access Center, the Control Panel equivalent.)

Ease Of Access in Settings provides a prominent link to each of the following settings, which can be used alone or in combination:

- **Narrator.** This tool converts on-screen text to speech and sends it to your computer's speakers. This option allows people who are blind or have severe vision impairments to use Windows.

- **Magnifier.** This tool enlarges part of the screen, making it easier for persons with vision impairments to see objects and read text. (You can also launch Magnifier with a keyboard shortcut: Press Windows key+plus sign to launch it and zoom in. Press again to zoom in more, or press Windows key+minus sign to zoom out.)

CHAPTER 4

- **High Contrast.** This tool uses a high-contrast color scheme (by default, white text on a black background) that makes it easier for visually impaired users to read the screen.

- **Closed Captions.** This tool lets you set the appearance of closed captioning in videos for apps that support closed captioning.

- **Keyboard.** This collection of tools includes an alternate means for Windows users with impaired mobility to enter text using a pointing device. Options that appear when you click Options in On-Screen Keyboard let you control how it works—you can choose whether to select a letter by clicking, for example, or by allowing the pointer to pause over a key for a specific amount of time. Other tools on the Keyboard page allow uses with impaired mobility to more easily deal with key combinations and repeated keystrokes.

- **Mouse.** This page includes tools that make the mouse pointer easier to see for visually impaired users. Another tool enables the numeric keypad to move the mouse pointer instead of by using a mouse.

- **Other Options.** This page includes a smattering of appearance-related options to assist those with visual or hearing impairments.

The easiest way to configure your computer for adaptive needs in one fell swoop is to open Ease Of Access Center in Control Panel and then click Get Recommendations To Make Your Computer Easier To Use, a link near the center of the page. The link launches a wizard, shown here, that walks you through the process of configuring accessibility options.

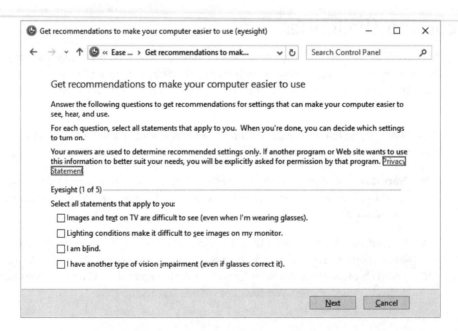

If you want accessibility options to be available at all times, even before signing in to the computer, click the Change Sign-In Settings link in the left pane of Ease Of Access Center in Control Panel. This option (shown next) applies any changes you make to the sign-in desktop. If you choose not to enable this option, you can still turn accessibility features on or off at the sign-in screen; click the small Ease Of Access icon in the lower right corner of the sign-in screen to display a list of available settings, and then press the Spacebar to enable each one.

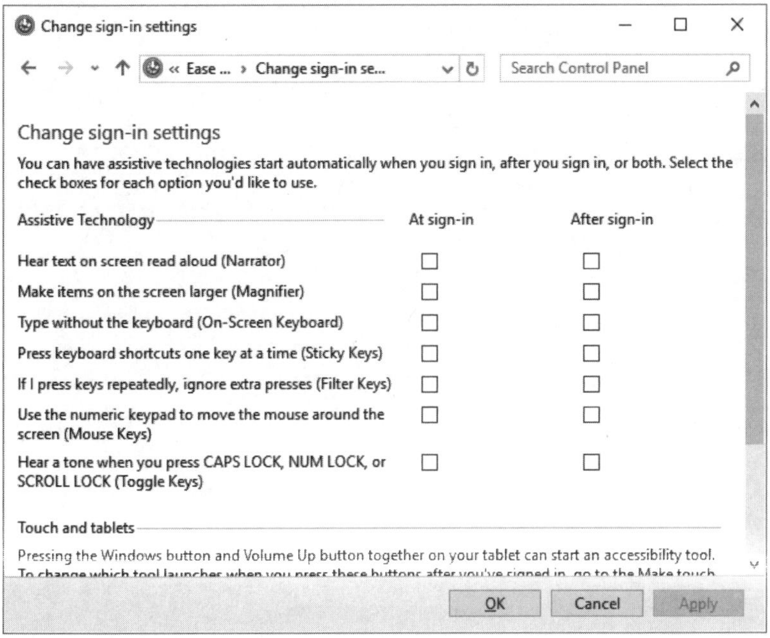

CHAPTER 4

Networking essentials

Modern computing is defined by our ability to communicate and share with one another by using devices of all shapes and sizes. These days, most of that activity happens over the world's largest global network, the Internet, using a variety of widely accepted hardware and software standards. The Internet is also the driving force behind cloud-based services, which are transforming the way we work and play.

The same network standards that allow connections to the Internet can also be used to create a local area network (LAN), which makes it possible to share files, printers, and other resources in a home or an office.

In the not-so-distant past, setting up a network connection was a painful process, one that often required professional help. Today, network hardware is ubiquitous, and setting up a network connection in Windows 10 requires little or no technical knowledge. That doesn't mean the process is entirely pain free; troubleshooting network problems can be maddeningly frustrating, and understanding the basics of networking is tremendously helpful in isolating and fixing problems.

In this chapter, we cover the essentials of connecting a Windows 10 device to wired and wireless networks in a home or small office. We also explain how to share resources securely and how to check the status of your network connection to confirm that it's working properly.

At the time we wrote this chapter, we wanted to include a discussion of OneDrive. Unfortunately, Microsoft's release schedule for the new OneDrive synchronization client didn't quite mesh up with the initial release of Windows 10. You'll find a summary of OneDrive and other cloud services in Appendix C, "OneDrive and other cloud services."

> ➤ In larger businesses, networks typically have a Windows server at their heart. We cover the ins and outs of managing and using these larger, more complex networks in Chapter 20, "Advanced networking."

CHAPTER 5

Getting started with Windows 10 networking

Before you can connect to the Internet or to a local area network, your Windows 10 device needs a network adapter, properly installed with working drivers.

Since the release of Windows 7, Microsoft's hardware certification requirements have mandated that every desktop PC, laptop, all-in-one, and portable device include a certified Ethernet or Wi-Fi adapter.

You'll typically find wired Ethernet adapters in desktop PCs and all-in-ones, where a permanent wired network connection is appropriate. These adapters can be integrated into the motherboard or installed in an expansion slot and accept RJ45 plugs at either end of shielded network cables.

Most modern wired adapters support either the Fast Ethernet standard (also known as 100Base-T), which transfers data at 100 megabits per second, or the more modern Gigabit Ethernet standard, which allows data transfers at 1 gigabit (1,000 megabits) per second. In an office or a home that is wired for Ethernet, you can plug your network adapter into a wall jack that connects to a router, hub, or switch at a central location called a patch panel. In a home or an office without structured wiring, you need to plug directly into a network device.

Inside OUT

Connect to a wired network using a USB port

If you crave the consistent connection speed and reliability of a wired network but have a portable PC or mobile device that lacks a built-in Ethernet connection, consider investing in a USB network adapter. A USB 2.0 port will support Fast Ethernet speeds, whereas a modern device with a USB 3.0 or USB Type-C port should be capable of Gigabit Ethernet speeds. Some network docking stations and USB hubs include an Ethernet adapter; this option allows you to use a single USB connection for instant access to a wired network and other expansion devices while you're at your desk, using Wi-Fi when you're on the go.

In recent years, wireless networking technology has enjoyed an explosion in popularity. Wireless access points are a standard feature in most home routers and cable modems, and Wi-Fi connections are practically ubiquitous. You can connect to Wi-Fi, often for free, in hotels, trains, buses, ferries, and airplanes in addition to the more traditional hotspot locations such as cafés and libraries.

All laptops and mobile devices designed for Windows 10 include a Wi-Fi adapter, which consists of a transceiver and an antenna capable of communicating with a wireless access point.

CHAPTER 5

Wireless adapters are also increasingly common in desktop and all-in-one computer designs, allowing them to be used in homes and offices where it is impractical or physically impossible to run network cables.

Ethernet and Wi-Fi are the dominant networking technologies in homes and offices. Alternatives include phone-line networks, which plug into telephone jacks in older homes, and power-line technology, which communicates using adapters that plug into the same AC jacks you use for power. The availability of inexpensive wireless network gear has relegated phone-line and power-line technologies to niche status; they are most attractive in older homes and offices, where adding network cable is impractical and wireless networks are unreliable because of distance, building materials, or interference. (A hybrid approach, useful in some environments, allows you to plug a Wi-Fi extender into an existing power line to increase signal strength in a remote location.)

You don't need to rely exclusively on one type of network. If your cable modem includes a router and a wireless access point, you can plug network cables into it and use its wireless signal for mobile devices or for computers located in areas where a network jack isn't available.

When you upgrade to Windows 10, the setup program preserves your existing network connection. If you perform a clean setup of Windows 10, your wired Internet connection should be detected automatically; you're prompted to enter the access key for a wireless connection during the setup process.

NOTE

In this chapter, we assume you have an always-on broadband connection in your home or office or that you are connecting to the Internet through a public or private Wi-Fi connection with Internet access. Although Windows 10 supports dial-up connections, we do not cover this option.

Checking your network's status

As we noted earlier, most network connections in Windows 10 should configure themselves automatically during setup. Three tools included with Windows 10 allow you to inspect the status of the current connection and either make changes or troubleshoot problems.

Using the network icon and flyout

The most easily accessible network tool is the status icon that appears by default in the notification area at the right side of the taskbar. Its icon indicates the current network type (wired or wireless) and the status of the network. Click that icon to display the network flyout, which displays options relevant to your type of network connection.

Figure 5-1 shows the network flyout for a Surface Pro 3 with a USB Ethernet adapter con-nected to a wired network and a Wi-Fi connection to the Bottville access point. Both networks appear to be operating properly. (As we explain later, a status of Limited would indicate prob-lems with the network's ability to connect to the Internet.)

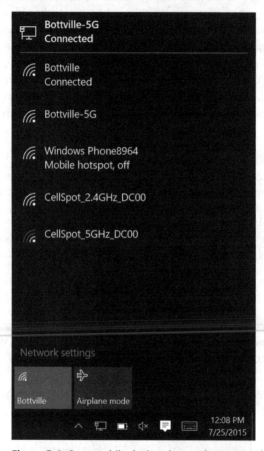

Figure 5-1 On a mobile device, the two buttons at the bottom of this network flyout allow you to enable or disable Wi-Fi (left) or turn on Airplane Mode (right) to shut down all radios temporarily.

Every available network is shown on this list, including wired connections and wireless access points that are broadcasting their names. In Figure 5-1, the PC is connected to both a wired network and a wireless access point. Because the wired connection is faster, it gets priority, sit-ting at the top of the list with a line separating it from the wireless networks.

The icon for each access point indicates its signal strength. In Figure 5-1, for example, the router named CellSpot is transmitting and receiving on two different frequencies, with each one getting its own name. The 2.4 GHz connection appears to be considerably stronger than the 5 GHz connection.

Two buttons at the bottom of the network flyout are available on laptops and mobile devices. The button on the left shows the name of the currently connected wireless network. Click or tap to temporarily disable Wi-Fi connections; tap again to reconnect to a wireless network. (We cover the details of wireless connections more fully later in this chapter.)

A red X or yellow triangle over the network icon means your Wi-Fi adapter is enabled but not working properly. In Figure 5-2, for example, the yellow triangle with an exclamation point is Windows 10's way of warning that something's wrong with that connection. The network flyout shows that the wireless adapter is connected to an access point but isn't able to reach the Internet.

└─ This yellow warning icon indicates a wireless problem

Figure 5-2 The familiar warning icon over the wireless icon means there's a problem with the connection. The flyout provides more details: The connection is limited, with no Internet access via Wi-Fi.

> ➤ For help with troubleshooting network problems (wired and wireless), see Chapter 20.

The Network Settings link at the bottom of the network flyout leads to the Network & Internet page in Settings, with details for the current network shown by default. On a desktop or all-in-one PC with only a wired connection, that page looks something like the one shown in Figure 5-3.

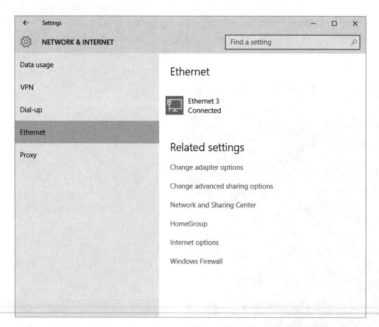

Figure 5-3 The Ethernet heading and the icon shown here confirm that the current connection is wired. All of the options under Related Settings lead to the classic desktop Control Panel.

Inside OUT

Mobile hotspots and other metered connections

Some devices with data connections on a cellular network allow you to turn the device into a mobile Wi-Fi hotspot, sometimes referred to as a "Mi-Fi" device. This capability is invaluable when you need to get some work done on a portable PC and an affordable, reliable Wi-Fi connection isn't available. The list of available network connections in Figure 5-1, for example, includes a phone running Windows 10 Mobile, which is capable of acting as a hotspot once the option is turned on. Most modern smartphones, including iPhones and Android devices, are capable of acting as a hotspot as well, although the cellular data provider must allow this capability.

A mobile hotspot looks like a Wi-Fi network, so you can connect your Windows 10 laptop by using its Wi-Fi adapter. A modern mobile network can be significantly faster than a public Wi-Fi connection. It also has the advantage of being more secure because you're connecting through your trusted mobile device to the carrier's (presumably secure) network rather than to a public Wi-Fi network that could be compromised.

The downside of using a mobile hotspot where you pay by the megabyte or gigabyte is potentially higher costs (especially if you're roaming outside your home network) or the risk that you'll hit your data limit and have your connection throttled or stopped completely. To avoid that possibility, Windows 10 identifies mobile hotspots as metered connections and automatically limits certain types of background activity. By default, the list of restricted activities includes downloads from Windows Update and always-on connections to an Exchange Server in Microsoft Outlook. The Data Usage option in Settings, Network & Internet allows you to see how much data a specific network connection has used in the past 30 days.

If Windows 10 doesn't realize that a specific network is on a pay-as-you-go connection, open the Wi-Fi page under the Network & Internet heading in Settings, and click or tap Advanced Options. Slide the Set As Metered Connection switch to the On position, as shown here:

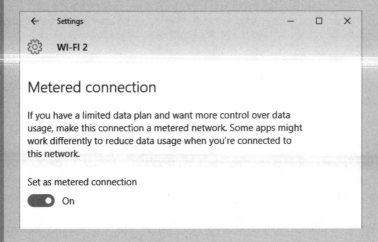

Clicking the icon for a connected wired network (the one labeled Ethernet 3 in Figure 5-3, for example) displays details about that connection: its IP addresses, Domain Name System (DNS) settings, and network adapter (including manufacturer name and current driver version). Figure 5-4 shows these properties for the virtual network adapter in a Hyper-V virtual machine we used for testing as we worked on this book.

CHAPTER 5

Figure 5-4 These details for a wired network connection are essential for troubleshooting networking problems. Click Copy to save the settings to the Clipboard to paste into a help desk ticket or an email message.

You can get to the equivalent information for a wireless connection by selecting the Wi-Fi option on the Network & Internet Settings page and then clicking or tapping Advanced Options.

On the Network & Internet Settings page (shown earlier in Figure 5-3), each item in the list under the Related Settings heading leads to an option in the classic desktop Control Panel. It's possible that some of these functions will have migrated to the modern Settings app by the time you read this.

> ➤ We cover Change Adapter Options and Change Advanced Sharing Options more fully in Chapter 20.

Network And Sharing Center

If you've managed a network in Windows 7, you're probably already familiar with the Network And Sharing Center, which was the hub of almost all networking activities. You can get to the Windows 10 version of the Network And Sharing Center in any of the following ways:

- In the notification area, click the Network icon and then click Open Network And Sharing Center.

- In the search box, begin typing **network** until the Network And Sharing Center item appears at the top of the menu; click it.

- In Settings, click or tap Network & Internet and then click or tap Network And Sharing Center under the Related Settings heading.

- In Control Panel, click Network And Internet, and then click Network And Sharing Center.

- In File Explorer, select the Network folder, open the Network tab on the ribbon, and then click the Network And Sharing Center button.

As you can see in Figure 5-5, this iteration of the Network And Sharing Center is a bit tidier than its predecessors but still firmly entrenched in the desktop Control Panel, offering access to most of the same information and functions.

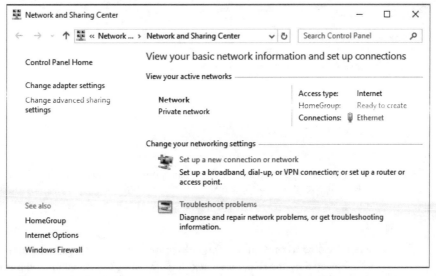

Figure 5-5 The Network And Sharing Center provides a snapshot of the active network and includes links to nearly every relevant related task or setting.

The block of options along the left side is essentially the same as the choices under the Related Settings heading in the newer Network & Internet page in Settings. The most useful information in the Network And Sharing Center appears in the center, under the heading View

Your Active Networks. In Figure 5-5, you can see that this network is using a wired connection and is configured to be private, allowing other PCs and devices on the same network to view shared resources. (We explain how and why to choose between public and private networks later in this chapter in "Setting network locations.")

Clicking the name of the active connection—in this example, Ethernet—leads to a status dialog box, where a Details button leads to additional information. The list of network details is a bit longer than its counterpart in the Settings app, as Figure 5-6 illustrates.

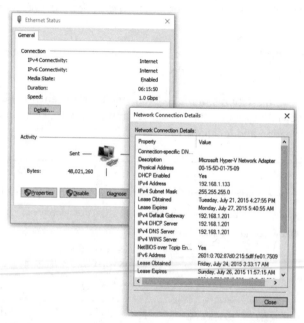

Figure 5-6 Click the Details button in the status dialog box for a connection (left) to open an information-dense listing of IP addresses and other details (right).

NOTE

Many tasks related to configuring networks require elevation to administrator privileges, as indicated by the shield icon next to commands and on command buttons.

Although there's no obvious way to copy information from the Network Connections Details box (to share with a support engineer, for example, or to paste into a post on a community support forum), it is possible to do so. Use your mouse to select a single row, or hold down Ctrl or Shift and click to select multiple rows, then press Ctrl+C to copy the selection to the Clipboard.

Monitoring network performance in Task Manager

Sometimes it's useful to know not just whether a network connection is working but how well it's handling its primary job of transmitting and receiving packets of data. For a real-time graph of network throughput, open Task Manager, click the Performance tab, and then select a connection name from the list on the left. Figure 5-7 shows a file upload in progress on a wired Ethernet connection.

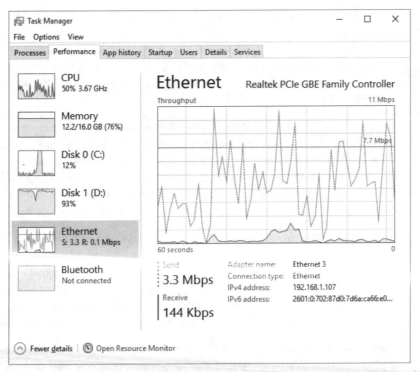

Figure 5-7 The real-time performance graph in Task Manager lets you see not just whether your network connection is working but also how well.

The scale of the real-time performance graph adjusts dynamically to allow you to see relative differences easily. In Figure 5-7, for example, the Gigabit Ethernet adapter is theoretically capable of sending and receiving data at roughly 1,000 megabits per second. Using that scale, the spikes in this upload, averaging an otherwise impressive 3.3 megabits per second, would be a tiny flat squiggle nearly indistinguishable from the bottom border. With a scale of 11 megabits per second, both the send and receive graphs are capable of telling the story of whether the connection is working as expected.

➤ For more information on basic techniques for identifying problems on Windows networks, see "Troubleshooting networking problems" in Chapter 17, "Troubleshooting." For more advanced troubleshooting help, see Chapter 20.

Inside OUT

IPv6 and Windows 10

The longer you've worked with Windows, the more likely you are to be familiar with the granddaddy of Windows networking, Internet Protocol version 4, also known as IPv4. A default network connection in Windows 10, wired or wireless, uses IPv4 but also enables the newer IP version 6. IPv6 is on by default and has been the preferred protocol in all desktop and server versions of Windows for nearly a decade, since the release of Windows Vista.

Without getting into the minutiae of network addressing, suffice it to say that IPv4, with its addresses based on four groups of numbers from 0 to 255, has a big problem. When the Internet was young, that address space, consisting of 4.3 billion unique combinations of dotted addresses, like 192.168.1.108 or 10.0.0.242, seemed huge. Unfortunately, nobody anticipated just how big the Internet would become, and the authorities who assign IP addresses on the Internet have literally run out of IPv4 addresses.

The solution is IPv6, which uses 128-bit addresses and therefore has a maximum address space of 3.4×10^{38} addresses, which we are confident is enough to last for the next few generations of Internet users. IPv6 is slowly but surely taking over large swaths of the Internet. The giant American Internet and cable provider Comcast has fully enabled its network for IPv6, with most of its competition not far behind. Major mobile carriers are also providing the majority of traffic on native IPv6 connections.

Major content providers are enabled for IPv6 as well. You can read about Microsoft's IPv6 efforts at *bit.ly/ms-ipv6*. Almost all of Google's services now work over IPv4 and IPv6, as does Yahoo. Facebook's giant data centers now run IPv6 exclusively, and Netflix has supported IPv6 for years.

Windows veterans might be tempted to shy away from IPv6, preferring the more familiar IPv4. In our experience, that's a mistake. IPv6 is here to stay. Learn about it and embrace it.

Setting network locations

A desktop PC connected to a wired home or small office network remains in a single location, by definition. In contrast, mobile devices running Windows 10 can connect to different types of networks—a corporate domain, a wireless hotspot at a coffee shop, or a private home network. Each type of network has its own security requirements. Windows uses network locations to categorize each network and then applies appropriate security settings. When you connect to a new network, Windows applies one of three security settings:

- **Public.** This is the default setting for any new, untrusted network connection. Network discovery is turned off for public networks, making it impossible for other people on the same access point to connect to your computer. This option is appropriate for networks in public places, such as wireless hotspots in coffee shops, hotels, airports, and libraries. It's also the correct choice if your desktop or laptop PC is directly connected to a cable modem or other broadband connection without the protection of a router and hardware firewall.

- **Private.** This option is appropriate when you're connecting to a trusted network, such as your own network at home—if and only if that network is protected by a router or residential gateway (a consumer device that combines a cable modem, router, and wireless access point in a single box) or comparable Internet defense. When you make this choice, Windows enables network discovery and allows you to enable the HomeGroup feature for sharing with other users on the network.

- **Domain.** This option is applied automatically when you sign in to Windows using a computer that is joined to a Windows domain, such as your company network. In this scenario, network discovery is enabled, allowing you to see other computers and servers on the network by using accounts and permissions controlled by a network administrator.

> ➤ If you have a mobile computer that connects to multiple networks, keep in mind that the Windows Firewall keeps separate network security profiles for private (home or work), public, and domain-based networks, For more information about Windows Firewall, see "Blocking intruders with Windows Firewall" in Chapter 7, "Securing Windows 10 devices."

The location of the current network is shown in the Network And Sharing Center, below the name of the network.

To change a public network to a private one, or vice-versa, open Settings, click or tap Network & Internet, and then select the Wi-Fi or Ethernet heading in the list on the left. Click or tap the icon for a wired connection or, for a wireless connection, click or tap Advanced Options. That opens the properties dialog box for the active connection, with the Find Devices And Content option, shown in Figure 5-8, at the top. When this setting is Off, the network is public. Slide the switch to On to make the network private.

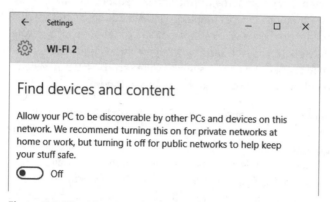

Figure 5-8 Flip this switch to the On position to notify Windows that this is a private network and it's safe to connect to other network devices. In the Off position, the network location is set to Public and outside access is blocked.

Inside OUT

Workgroups versus domains

Computers on a network can be part of a workgroup or a domain.

In a workgroup, the security database (including, most significantly, the list of user accounts and the privileges granted to each one) for each computer resides on that computer. When you sign in to a computer in a workgroup, Windows checks its local security database to see whether you've provided a user name and password that matches one in the database. Similarly, when network users attempt to connect to your computer, Windows again consults the local security database. All computers in a workgroup must be on the same subnet. A workgroup is sometimes called a peer-to-peer network.

By contrast, a domain consists of computers that share a security infrastructure, Active Directory, which in turn is managed on one or more domain controllers running Windows Server. Microsoft's cloud-based alternative, Azure Active Directory, provides the same infrastructure without requiring IT departments to manage local servers. Active Directory and Azure Active Directory can be combined to create effective hybrid environments. When you sign in using a domain account, Windows authenticates your credentials against the security database defined by your network administrator.

In this chapter (and throughout this book), we focus primarily on workgroup networks.

Connecting to a wireless network

In this section, we assume that you have already configured a wireless access point (often included as a feature in cable modems and DSL adapters supplied by your broadband provider) and confirmed that it is working correctly.

Whenever your computer's wireless network adapter is installed and turned on, Windows scans for available wireless access points. If it finds at least one (and you're not already connected to a wireless network), it alerts you via the wireless network icon, which looks a bit like an antenna. If you see a bright dot at the end of an otherwise gray antenna, that means connections are available.

Unless you're out in the country, far from civilization, you're likely to see lots of access points available for connection, most of them owned by your neighbors or nearby visitors. Assuming those networks are adequately secured with a password you don't know and can't guess, you'd have no luck connecting to them anyway.

Clicking or tapping the entry for a secured access point reveals a box in which you are expected to enter a passphrase, as in Figure 5-9. If what you enter matches what's stored in the access point's configuration, you're in. Getting in is easy on a network you control, where you set the password. For a secured access point controlled by someone else—a doctor's waiting room, a coffee shop, a friend's office—you'll need to ask the network owner for the passphrase or key.

Figure 5-9 Connecting to a secure network for the first time requires that you correctly enter a passphrase or security key.

Before you reach that security prompt, you're asked whether you want to connect automatically to that network in the future. If this is a place you expect to visit again (or in the case of a coffee shop, again and again and again . . .), say yes to save the credentials. Note that saved Wi-Fi passwords are synced between devices when you sign in with a Microsoft account, so you might find that a brand-new device, one you've never used before, automatically connects to your home or office Wi-Fi without having to ask you.

To disconnect from a Wi-Fi access point, click or tap its entry in the network flyout and then tap Disconnect. Doing so automatically turns off the option to connect automatically to that network in the future.

Windows 10 saves credentials for every Wi-Fi access point you connect to, giving you the option to connect with a tap when you revisit. If that thought makes you uncomfortable, you can see and manage the full list of networks by opening Network Settings and clicking Manage Wi-Fi Settings on the Wi-Fi page. That list can be startling, especially if you're a frequent traveler. Tap any name in the list, and you'll see either one or two buttons, as in Figure 5-10.

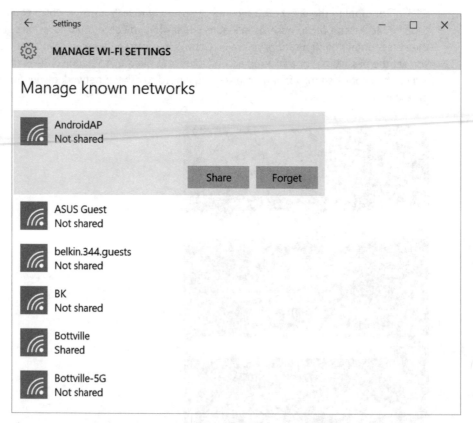

Figure 5-10 Wireless networks you connect to are saved in this list. Tap Forget to delete the saved passphrase and remove the network from the list.

CHAPTER 5

Tapping the Forget button deletes any saved security information and removes the network name from the list. The Share button is available only if you've turned on the option to share network settings with your contacts, a feature that's part of Wi-Fi Sense, which we describe later in this chapter.

Inside OUT

Decoding Wi-Fi standards

The most popular wireless networks use one of several variants of the IEEE (Institute of Electrical and Electronics Engineers) 802.11 standard, also known as Wi-Fi. On modern Wi-Fi networks, you are likely to encounter one of the following three standards (going from oldest to newest):

- **802.11g.** This standard was current up until 2009, just before the release of Windows 7. It's still in wide use on older PCs and wireless access points. It can transfer data at a maximum rate of 54 megabits per second using radio frequencies in the 2.4 GHz range. (Some manufacturers of wireless networking equipment have pushed the standard with proprietary variations that approximately double the speed.) 802.11g-based networks have largely supplanted those based on an earlier standard, 802.11b, which offers a maximum speed of 11 megabits per second.

- **802.11n.** Using this standard, adopted in 2009, you can expect to see dramatic improvements in speed (600 megabits per second) as well as significantly greater range. Unlike the earlier standards, the 802.11n standard allows use of the 5 GHz frequency range as well as 2.4 GHz. However, not all 802.11n hardware supports both bands.

- **802.11ac.** This standard, finalized in 2014, builds on the 802.11n specification and allows multiple links at both ends of the wireless connection, advertising throughput rates of 500 megabits per second per link, with a theoretical maximum speed of up to 2,600 megabits per second.

Although the newer Wi-Fi standards are backward compatible with hardware that uses the older, slower standards, be aware that all traffic on your network runs at the speed of the slowest wireless standard in use; if you've just bought an 802.11ac router, you will see the faster speed only if you replace your old network adapters.

For the maximum throughput, use 5 GHz 802.11ac devices throughout your network. The 5 GHz band is subject to less radio interference than 2.4 GHz and is capable of a higher maximum theoretical data rate. If you must maintain compatibility with older 2.4 GHz devices, the ideal solution is to use a dual-band wireless access point.

CHAPTER 5

Connecting to a hidden network

Every wireless network has a name, formally known as a *service set identifier* but typically referred to as an SSID. Some wireless networks are set up so that they don't broadcast their SSID. Connecting to such a hidden network is a bit more challenging because its name doesn't appear in the list of available networks on the network flyout or in Network & Internet Settings. Making such a connection is possible, however, as long as you know the network name and its security settings.

> **NOTE**
>
> Configuring a router so that it doesn't advertise its name has been incorrectly promoted by some as a security measure. Although it does make the network less accessible to casual snoops, lack of a broadcast SSID is no deterrent to a knowledgeable attacker. Furthermore, attackers can learn the SSID even when they're not near your wireless access point because it's periodically broadcast from your computer, wherever it happens to be. We provide these steps to help you connect to a hidden network managed by someone else; we don't recommend that you configure your home or office network in this fashion.

If one or more nearby networks aren't broadcasting their SSID, you'll see Hidden Network in the list of available networks. Click or tap that entry, and then you'll need to enter the correct SSID before you're allowed to the real security test, your passphrase or security key.

NETGEAR64

Walker's Wi-Fi Network

xfinitywifi

Hidden Network

Enter the name (SSID) for the network

Next   Cancel

Advanced options

Manage Wi-Fi settings

After you jump through that one extra hoop, the process is no different from connecting to a network that broadcasts its name.

To set up your computer so that it connects to a particular nonbroadcasting wireless network whenever you're in range, follow these steps:

1. Open Network And Sharing Center, and click Set Up A New Connection Or Network.

2. In the Set Up A Connection Or Network Wizard, select Manually Connect To A Wireless Network and click Next.

3. Specify the network name (SSID), the type of security used by the network, the encryption type if the network uses WPA or WPA2 security, and the security key or passphrase, as shown in Figure 5-11. Select Connect Even If The Network Is Not Broadcasting. (What is the privacy risk mentioned in the dialog box? When this option is turned on, your computer sends out probe requests to locate the wireless network; an attacker can detect these probe requests and use them to determine the network's SSID. Your computer continues to send these requests even when you're away from your network's access point.) Click Next.

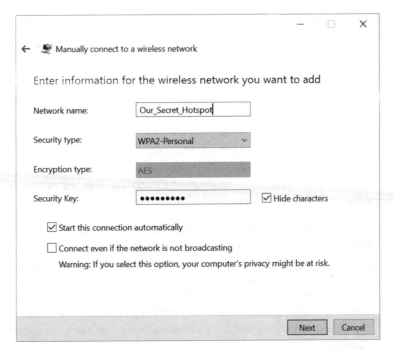

Figure 5-11 Use this well-hidden dialog box to configure a hidden network so that it's always available to connect to automatically.

4. Click Next, and then click Close.

Wireless security

On a conventional wired network, especially in a private home or office, physical security is reasonably easy to secure: if someone plugs a computer into a network jack or a switch, you can trace the physical wire back to the intruder's computer. On wireless networks, however, anyone who comes into range of your wireless access point can tap into your network and intercept signals from it.

If you run a small business, you might want to allow Internet access to your customers by using an open Internet connection. Some Internet service providers create secure guest accounts on their customers' cable modems that allow other customers of that service to connect using their network credentials.

Other than those scenarios, however, you probably want to secure your network so that the only people who can connect to it are those you specifically authorize. Doing that means configuring security settings on your wireless access point or router. When you connect to a network, known or unknown, the level of security is determined by the encryption standard chosen by the network owner and supported by network hardware on both sides of the connection.

Depending on the age of your hardware, you should have a choice of one or more of the following options, listed in order of preference:

- **Wi-Fi Protected Access 2 (WPA2).** Based on the 802.11i standard, WPA2 provides the strongest protection for consumer-grade wireless networks. It uses 802.1x-based authentication and Advanced Encryption Standard (AES) encryption; combined, these technologies ensure that only authorized users can access the network and that any intercepted data cannot be deciphered. WPA2 comes in two flavors: WPA2-Personal and WPA2-Enterprise. WPA2-Personal uses a passphrase to create its encryption keys and is currently the best available security for wireless networks in homes and small offices. WPA2-Enterprise requires a server to verify network users. All wireless products sold since early 2006 must support WPA2 to bear the Wi-Fi CERTIFIED label.

- **Wi-Fi Protected Access (WPA).** WPA is an earlier version of the encryption scheme that has since been replaced by WPA2. It was specifically designed to overcome weaknesses of WEP. On a small network that uses WPA, clients and access points use a shared network password (called a preshared key, or PSK) that consists of a 256-bit number or a passphrase that is from 8 to 63 bytes long. (A longer passphrase produces a stronger key.) With a sufficiently strong key based on a truly random sequence, the likelihood of a successful outside attack is slim. Most modern network hardware supports WPA only for backward compatibility.

- **Wired Equivalent Privacy (WEP).** WEP is a first-generation scheme that dates back before the turn of the century. It suffers from serious security flaws that make it inappropriate for use on any network that contains sensitive data. Most modern Wi-Fi equipment supports WEP for backward compatibility with older hardware, but we strongly advise against using it unless no other options are available.

You might see other encryption options, but those are typically designed for use on enterprise networks and are beyond the scope of this book.

Inside OUT

Beef up security at the access point

If your data is sensitive and your network is in an apartment building or an office complex where you can reasonably expect other people to wander into range with wireless adapters, you should take extra security precautions in addition to enabling WPA. Consider any or all of the following measures to protect your wireless access point from intruders:

- Change the network name (SSID) of your access point to one that doesn't match the hardware defaults and doesn't give away any information about you or your business.

- Disable remote administration of the access point; if you need to change settings, you can do so directly, using a wired connection.

- Whether you decide to allow remote administration of the access point or not, set a strong password so that a visitor can't tamper with your network settings.

- Check the firmware and drivers for wireless hardware (access points and adapters) at regular intervals and install the most recent versions, which might incorporate security fixes.

- Consider using a virtual private network (VPN) for wireless connections. A VPN sends all wireless traffic over an encrypted connection, making it impossible for others to snoop on your wireless traffic. Corporate network administrators can help set up a VPN using your company's security infrastructure. For unmanaged Windows 10 devices, VPN software and services are available.

When setting up a wireless access point for a home or small office, choose a strong passphrase. A passphrase for WPA or WPA2 can be up to 63 characters long and can contain letters (case-sensitive), numbers, and spaces (no spaces at the beginning or end, however). Many devices generate a random alphanumeric key, but you might prefer to use a memorable phrase instead of random characters. If you do, choose a phrase that's not easily guessed, make it long, and consider incorporating letter substitution or misspellings to thwart attackers. Because it can be saved and synced between devices, you shouldn't need to enter it often.

CHAPTER 5

You must use the same encryption option on all wireless devices on your network—access points, routers, network adapters, print servers, cameras, and so on—so choose the best option that is supported by all your devices. If you have an older device that supports only WEP (and it can't be upgraded with a firmware update), consider retiring or replacing that device.

TROUBLESHOOTING

You can't connect to other computers

If you're connecting to a network in your home or office (as opposed to a public hotspot, such as at an Internet café), be sure that the network is defined as a private network (either home or work). By default, Windows errs on the side of security, setting the location of all new networks as Public, and thus not open to connections from other devices on the same network. That's safe, but it also means you won't be able to see other local computers you trust. To see whether this is the problem, open the Network And Sharing Center. If Public Network appears beneath the name of your network, there's an easy fix.

Open File Explorer and click or tap Network in the list on the left. That should display a yellow banner at the top of the list noting that network discovery and file sharing are turned off. Click that banner, and then click Turn On Network Discovery And File Sharing in the resulting menu, as shown in Figure 5-12.

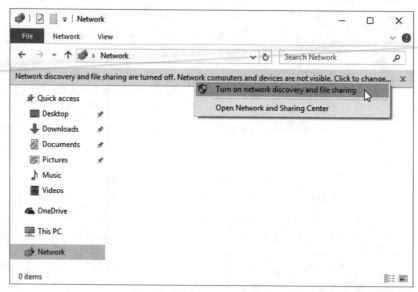

Figure 5-12 If your network location is set to Public, you'll see this banner in the Network folder; click it to make the network private and see other devices on the local network.

That click toggles the network location from Public to Private and should allow you to see the rest of the network (and vice versa). Do this only if you are certain that the other devices connected to this network can be trusted.

Sharing wireless connections with Wi-Fi Sense

Windows 10 includes a pair of new features under the collective heading of Wi-Fi Sense. What they share in common is a desire to make it easier to connect to and share trusted, secure Wi-Fi connections without you and your friends having to ask for passwords.

To manage Wi-Fi Sense, click the taskbar icon for your Wi-Fi network, click Network Settings, and then, on the Wi-Fi page, click Manage Wi-Fi Settings. Figure 5-13 shows the Wi-Fi Sense Settings page.

Figure 5-13 Wi-Fi Sense is designed to make it possible to automatically connect to an unfamiliar network that has been suggested by Microsoft or shared by a friend.

The top setting, Connect To Suggested Open Hotspots, allows you to connect automatically to hotspots that are in a database managed by Microsoft. The second group of settings, Connect To Networks Shared By My Contacts, allows you to share a network with friends and family members who are in your Outlook.com, Skype, or Facebook contact lists and are also using Windows 10. Your friends never see the password; instead, they're authenticated securely by Wi-Fi Sense, using encrypted credentials.

Although the option to share networks is on by default, none of your saved Wi-Fi networks are actually shared until you choose to do so. To control sharing for a network, find its entry in the Known Networks list (shown earlier in Figure 5-10) and then use the Share (or Stop Sharing) button for that network name to enable (or disable) sharing.

Sharing files, digital media, and printers in a homegroup

The HomeGroup feature, originally introduced as part of Windows 7 and maintained through Windows 10, allows Windows devices to share resources on a home network. The list of share-able things includes USB-connected printers as well as files from the default libraries: Docu-ments, Music, Pictures, and Videos. You can print a boarding pass, concert tickets delivered via email, or a Word document from your PC, with the documents emerging from a printer attached to a different PC on the same network. The HomeGroup feature also allows you to search across all computers in a homegroup to find pictures from a recent event. Files on other devices are almost as easily accessible as if they were on your own computer.

(Oh, and if you're confused by the capitalization of the term, you're not alone. Microsoft hasn't budged from the conventions it adopted when this feature appeared in Windows 7. The cor-rect spelling is HomeGroup when the term refers to the feature and the associated Control Panel option where you configure it. The collection of Windows computers joined together this way is called a homegroup, with no capitalization. In File Explorer, in dialog boxes and menus, and in this book, the term might be capitalized to indicate that it is part of the name of an option. We apologize profusely for the confusion.)

> ### NOTE
> The HomeGroup feature works only with computers running Windows 7 or later. To share files with computers running other operating systems (including earlier versions of Windows), or to enable users of those computers to access files on your Windows 10 computer, you must use network sharing methods compatible with those older ver-sions. For details, see "Sharing resources with other users" in Chapter 20.

The HomeGroup feature is specifically designed for environments where the connected computers are in a physically secure location (a private home or an office) with users who are fully trusted. Traditional network sharing requires matching account credentials on every device and will not work with devices for which the user has a blank password. HomeGroup is designed to work well regardless of whether computers and user accounts have passwords. Sharing is accomplished through the use of a special password-protected user account. If you're interested in the technical workings, see the "How HomeGroup works" sidebar.

How HomeGroup works

The simplicity of setting up and using HomeGroup belies its complexity. The basic sharing mechanism uses standard sharing protocols that have been part of Windows for many years. Here's the short version: HomeGroup grants share permissions and applies an access control entry (ACE) to each shared object, allowing access to a group called HomeUsers. A hidden, password-protected account (which is required for accessing shared objects over a network connection) named HomeGroupUser$ is a member of HomeUsers and acts as your proxy in accessing shared network resources. (In fact, even if your user account is password protected, HomeGroup still uses the HomeGroupUser$ account instead of your account to connect to a remote computer.) You can work around this setting by selecting the Use User Accounts And Passwords To Connect To Other Computers option in Advanced Sharing Settings. For more information about this setting, see "Configuring your network for sharing" in Chapter 20.

CAUTION

Do not change the password for the HomeGroupUser$ account; doing so is a recipe for disaster. (Note that the account password is *not* the same as the homegroup password.)

But there's much more going on with HomeGroup. Creating or joining a workgroup creates the HomeGroupUser$ account and the HomeUsers group and adds all local accounts to the group. HomeGroup setup also configures Windows Firewall. (Specifically, it enables certain rules in the Core Networking, Network Discovery, and HomeGroup groups. And for computers that are not joined to a domain, it enables rules in the File And Printer Sharing, Windows Media Player, and Windows Media Player Network Sharing Service groups.) In addition, it configures the HomeGroup Provider and HomeGroup Listener services. (HomeGroup also relies on Function Discovery and several other networking services.)

The requirements to implement and use HomeGroup are few:

- At least one computer running Windows 7 Home Premium or above or any edition of Windows 8, Windows 8.1, or Windows 10 to create the homegroup

- All computers in the homegroup running Windows 7 or later

- The network location for all computers must be set to Private. Although domain-joined PCs were able to access homegroup resources in earlier versions, that capability is not available in Windows 10.

For users, setting up HomeGroup is a straightforward process. On one computer—it doesn't matter which one because HomeGroup is a true peer-to-peer networking system without a designated server/controller—you create a homegroup. Then, on other computers, you join the homegroup.

Creating a homegroup

The current HomeGroup status is visible with the details of any active network in Network And Sharing Center. If no homegroup exists, click Ready To Create to begin the setup process. You can also set up the HomeGroup feature at a later time; type **homegroup** in the taskbar or Control Panel search box, and then click HomeGroup in the list of search results.

If no homegroup currently exists on your network, the HomeGroup page in Control Panel informs you of that fact, as in Figure 5-14. Click Create A Homegroup to open a wizard that walks you through the process.

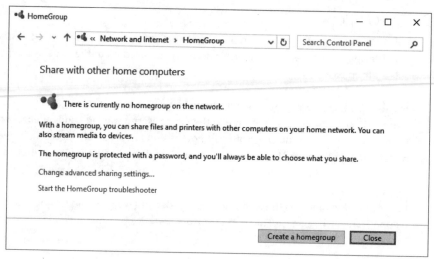

Figure 5-14 You'll see this Control Panel page only once. After your homegroup is created, this page offers options for you to change, join, or leave the homegroup.

Inside Out

Go ahead, change the homegroup password

The homegroup password isn't intended to be highly secure. The only machines that can connect to your homegroup are those that are connected to your wired or wireless network, so even a simple password is sufficient to keep out uninvited guests. To change the randomly generated alphanumeric password to one that's easier to remember, visit the HomeGroup Control Panel from any computer that's already joined the homegroup. Using an administrator's credentials, click the Change The Password option (shown here) and follow the prompts.

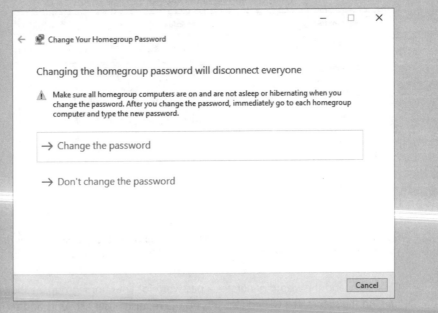

In the dialog box that follows, you can enter any password you like (we suggest a memorable passphrase), or click the refresh button until you're satisfied with one of the automatically generated options. As the instructions in this process make clear, you'll need to visit every other computer in the homegroup and manually replace the old password with the new one you just created.

The first step allows you to select which default libraries should be shared with other home-group members and which should remain out of bounds. As the example in Figure 5-15 shows, the Documents folder is excluded from sharing by default, whereas pictures, videos, music, and printers and other shareable devices are included. You can change any of these settings now or later.

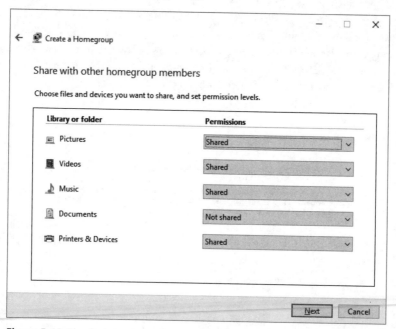

Figure 5-15 The first step in setting up a homegroup is to specify which of your default libraries you want to share as well as whether to share printers.

Click Next, and the wizard generates a password for your homegroup, as shown in Figure 5-16. (Behind the scenes, the wizard also sets up the requisite user accounts and security groups, services, firewall rules, and shares.) Click Finish, and you're done.

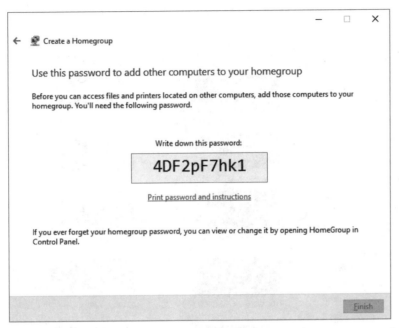

Figure 5-16 You'll use this same (shared) password to join other computers to the homegroup.

Joining a homegroup

After a homegroup has been created, other computers on the network can join it by using a similarly brief process. Open HomeGroup in Control Panel and click Join Now to reach a wizard that informs you that a homegroup already exists and gives you the opportunity to join it.

Click Next, and the wizard asks you to choose the resources you want to share with other devices that are part of the same homegroup. Click Next again to enter the homegroup password. Enter the password and click Next, and you're ready to view resources from other computers in the homegroup. To do that, open File Explorer. In the left pane, expand Homegroup to see a subfolder for each user account on each computer in the homegroup, as shown in Figure 5-17.

By default, every homegroup user has View (read-only) access to the shared personal libraries and folders on other computers in the homegroup.

Fortunately, you're not limited to sharing only the content of the Documents, Music, Pictures, or Videos libraries. If you would like to share other folders or files with users of other computers in your homegroup, you can add the folder (or folders) to an existing library or create a new custom library. (For instructions on working with libraries, see "Working with libraries" in Chapter 12, "Organizing and searching for files.")

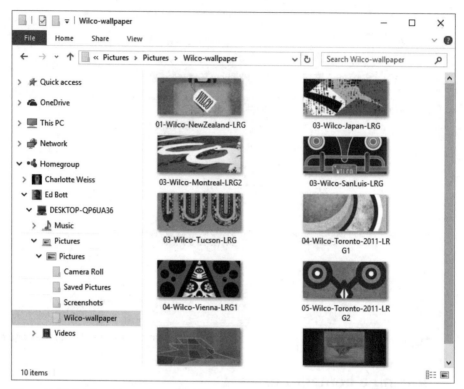

Figure 5-17 Joining a homegroup enables access to libraries on other computers.

To share a folder that's not in a library, locate that folder in File Explorer, right-click and click Share With, and then choose Homegroup (View) or Homegroup (View And Edit), as shown in Figure 5-18. (The same commands are also available on the Share tab of the File Explorer ribbon.)

CAUTION

Don't share the root folder of a drive (for example, D:\). Although sharing the root folder has long been common practice, we recommend against doing so. Because of the way permissions are inherited, changing permissions on the root folder can cause a variety of access problems. A better solution is to create a subfolder within that root folder to hold the files and subfolders you want to share, and then share the subfolder.

Which command you select, of course, determines whether a homegroup user on another computer can create, modify, and delete folders and files within the shared folder. Both options share the selected item with your entire homegroup.

CHAPTER 5

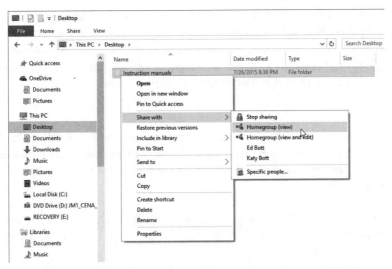

Figure 5-18 In a homegroup, you can choose to share individual folders using this well-hidden option.

To share with only certain individuals, choose Share With, Specific People. Doing so opens the File Sharing dialog box shown in Figure 5-19.

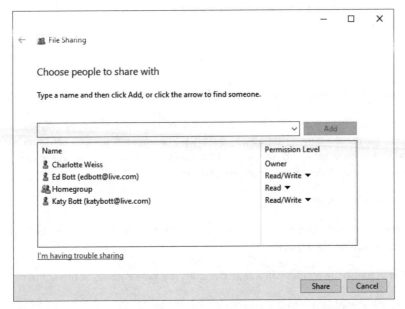

Figure 5-19 Clicking the arrow in the top box displays a list of local user accounts as well as homegroup users who have signed in using a Microsoft account.

CHAPTER 5

Using this feature with homegroups allows you to set per-user permissions that override homegroup permissions. So if you allow homegroup users View access, you can allow specific individuals Read/Write access. The time-honored Windows technique to implement this level of sharing is to set up user accounts with matching names and passwords on different PCs. That can lead to management hassles and messy sign-in screens.

NOTE

The File Sharing dialog box describes its two permission levels as Read and Read/ Write. In File Explorer's Share With menu, the Homegroup options are View and View And Edit. They are, for all practical purposes, the same set of permissions described differently.

You also use the Share With command on the ribbon or the shortcut menu to prevent sharing of a particular folder or file within a shared library or folder. Select the items, click Share With, and then click Stop Sharing.

Similarly, you can override the default sharing settings for private folder profiles within a library—normally these are shared with View access—by selecting a folder or file within the shared library or folder and clicking Share With.

NOTE

A computer joins a homegroup and, therefore, all users on that computer have access to the homegroup's shared resources. However, sharing options are maintained on a per-user basis; on a computer with more than one user account, each user decides which of his or her libraries to share.

Browsing shared folders and files

If your network location is set as Private, you've probably noticed the Homegroup node in File Explorer's navigation pane. After adding a device to a homegroup, you can work with folders and files from other computers in the Homegroup node just as you use folders and files in your own libraries. Tasks you can perform include:

- Preview and open files

- Play music or view pictures or video (in a folder filled with music files, look for the Play All button on the toolbar)

- Search through all files within a folder, a library, a user node, or the entire homegroup

- Add a shared folder to one of your local libraries

- Add, modify, and delete files (only in libraries or folders shared with Read/Write access)

The Homegroup node also responds politely to right-clicks, displaying a convenient menu that lets you change settings for the homegroup, view the homegroup password, or start a trouble-shooter to figure out why sharing isn't working properly.

Sharing a printer

Printer sharing isn't as big a deal today as it was when the HomeGroup feature debuted many years ago.

Today, we carry boarding passes and concert tickets on our smartphones. And for the rare pages we do need to commit to paper, it's often easiest to save a file to the cloud and then retrieve that file using the PC that has a printer attached.

Still, there's nothing quite like the convenience of sitting on the couch with a Windows 10 tablet and printing out a document to a printer in your home office.

If a homegroup member computer has a printer connected to one of its USB ports, and if the computer's user has chosen to share its printers (by selecting the Printers And Devices check box in HomeGroup), all homegroup users have access to that printer.

If the printer has been certified by the Windows Logo Program, it shows up automatically in Control Panel's Devices And Printers folder for all homegroup users. HomeGroup obtains the driver files from the host computer whenever possible or downloads them from the Internet if necessary (for example, if the host computer runs 32-bit Windows and your computer has 64-bit Windows installed), and then installs the driver without requiring any user intervention. (Note that it might take a few minutes after joining or connecting to a homegroup for HomeGroup to discover the shared printer and install the driver.)

If the shared printer is connected to a desktop computer (but not a laptop) that is in sleep mode, sending a print request to the printer uses Wake On LAN to awaken the computer so that it can perform the print job. After completing the print job, the computer returns to sleep.

Leaving a homegroup

If you decide that HomeGroup isn't for you (or, perhaps, you want to join a different homegroup), you can leave a homegroup. Open HomeGroup in Control Panel and click Leave The Homegroup. Because HomeGroup is a true peer-to-peer network, when any computer leaves the homegroup, the homegroup remains intact and all other members are unaffected (except they'll no longer be able to see your computer's resources, of course).

Note, however, that the Homegroup icon remains in File Explorer even after you leave the homegroup. Selecting the icon displays a message that includes an option to join a homegroup (if one is detected) or create one.

CHAPTER 5

Managing user accounts, passwords, and credentials

The user account, which uniquely identifies each person who uses the computer, is an essential component in security and in providing a personalized user experience in Windows. Windows allows you to restrict access to your computer so that only people you authorize can use the computer or view its files. User accounts in Windows provide the means by which you can

- Require each user to identify himself or herself when signing in.

- Control access to files and other resources that you own.

- Audit system events, such as sign-ins and the use of files and other resources.

- Sync files and settings between different computers that you use.

If your computer is in a secure location where only people you trust have physical access to it, you might not have such concerns. But you should still create a user account for each person who uses the computer because associated with each account is a user profile that stores all manner of information unique to that user: favorite websites, desktop background, document folders, and so on. With fast user switching, a feature described in this chapter, you can switch between user accounts with only a few clicks.

Working with user accounts

When you install Windows 10 on a new computer, the setup program creates a profile for one user account, which is an administrator account. (An *administrator account* is one that has full control over the computer. For details, see "User accounts and security groups" later in this chapter.) Depending on what type of account you select during setup, that initial account can be either a Microsoft account or a local user account. (For information about these account types, see the next section, "Microsoft account vs. local account.") If you upgrade to Windows 10 from Windows 7 or Windows 8 and you had local accounts set up in your previous operating system, Windows migrates those accounts to your Windows 10 installation.

Local user accounts that you migrate from Windows 7 or 8 maintain their group memberships and passwords.

Through Accounts in Settings, Windows provides a simple post-setup method for creating new accounts and making routine changes to existing accounts. When you launch Accounts in Settings, you'll see a window similar to the one shown in Figure 6-1.

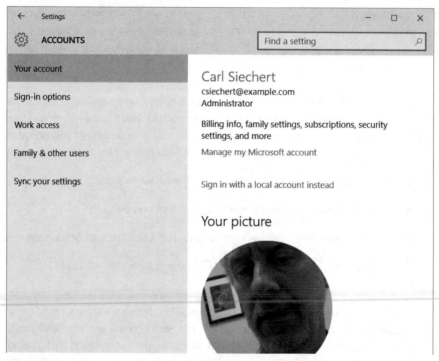

Figure 6-1 Accounts in Settings lets you manage your own account and, if you have an administrator account, manage other accounts.

You'll find different options and settings in Accounts depending on the type of account you use (Microsoft account or local account), whether your account is a member of the Administrators group, and—if your computer is joined to a domain—group policies in effect. In a domain environment, all management of user accounts beyond basic tasks such as selecting a picture is normally handled at the domain level.

And, because the transition from the old-school Control Panel to the modern Settings app is not complete, you'll find that some account-related settings can be made only with User Accounts in Control Panel, which is shown in Figure 6-2.

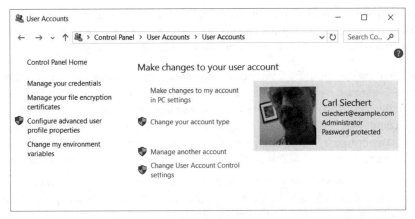

Figure 6-2 The link near the center of the page—Make Changes To My Account In PC Settings—opens Accounts in Settings. Most of the other links here lead to settings that aren't available in Settings, Accounts.

Microsoft account vs. local account

A *Microsoft account* is an online account system that can enhance security of your computer and its data, foster easy synchronization between computers, and enable many online services (such as OneDrive, Cortana, and Skype) as well as access to the Windows Store. Under various names (most recently, Windows Live ID), Microsoft accounts have been around for years. If you've registered for Microsoft services such as Hotmail, Xbox Live, or Zune, you already have a Microsoft account. If you have an email address that ends with msn.com, hotmail.com, live.com, or outlook.com, you have a Microsoft account. However, you do not need a Microsoft address to create a Microsoft account; you can set up a Microsoft account using an existing email address from any domain and any email provider.

A *local account* is one that stores its sign-in credentials and other account data on your PC. This type of account has been the standard in Windows for decades. A local account works only on a single computer.

> **NOTE**
> A third type of account, a work account using Azure Active Directory or Windows Server Active Directory, stores account information on a network server. It offers many of the advantages of a Microsoft account, subject to restrictions imposed by the network administrator. These accounts are more common in large businesses and schools. In this book we do not cover their use in depth.

CHAPTER 6

Beginning with Windows 8 and continuing in Windows 10, Microsoft recommends the use of a Microsoft account rather than a local user account. It's not a requirement, however; local accounts are still fully supported. So why use a Microsoft account?

- You can synchronize PC settings between multiple computers. If you use more than one PC—say, a desktop PC at work, a different desktop at home, a laptop for travel, and a tablet around the house—the ability to sync allows your settings to apply to all your computers. Settings include things like your desktop colors and background, your stored passwords, browser favorites and history, your account picture, your accessibility configuration, and so on. The synchronization happens automatically and nearly instantly.

  To view or modify your synchronization settings, open Settings and click or tap Accounts, Sync Your Settings. You can disable synchronization altogether (turn Sync Settings off) or you can turn individual settings on or off.

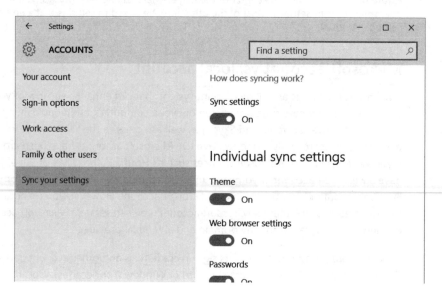

- You can use OneDrive cloud storage and gain access to your data from any computer. (For more information about OneDrive, see Appendix C, "OneDrive and other cloud services.")

- You can download modern apps using the Store app. Without a Microsoft account, you can browse in the Store, but you cannot download apps, music, or videos.

- Some features in preinstalled modern apps require the use of a Microsoft account.

- Cortana, the personal assistant that's part of Windows 10, is available only when you sign in with a Microsoft account.

- With built-in two-factor authentication, a Microsoft account provides security for your PC and its data.

CHAPTER 6

NOTE

It is possible to use OneDrive, make Store purchases, and use some other apps that depend on a Microsoft account even if you sign in with a local account. However, you must sign in to each app individually, and some features might be unavailable or, at a minimum, less convenient to use.

Are there any reasons *not* to use a Microsoft account?

- If you sign in using your Microsoft account password (rather than using a PIN or Windows Hello, as described later in this chapter in "Managing the sign-in process"), your password might be stolen. This could happen if someone is watching over your shoulder as you sign in, for example. Armed with your Microsoft account ID and password, a thief has access to much of your online life. (The moral here, of course, is not to eschew Microsoft accounts; rather, use a sign-in method that uses two-factor authentication and doesn't expose your password.)

- If your home network includes computers running Windows 7 or earlier (that is, versions that do not support the use of Microsoft accounts), connecting to shared resources can be more complicated. For information about working around this problem, see "Sharing resources with other users" in Chapter 20, "Advanced networking."

- Some folks have privacy and data security concerns about storing personal information on the servers of a large corporation, whether it be Microsoft, Google, Apple, Amazon, or others. Microsoft has implemented a single privacy statement that covers most of its consumer products and services. For information about the privacy policy and to make choices about how Microsoft uses your data, visit *account.microsoft.com/privacy*. For more information, see the sidebar "Configuring privacy options."

You can switch between using a Microsoft account and a local account by going to Settings, Accounts. On the Your Account page (shown earlier in Figure 6-1), click Sign In With A Local Account Instead. Windows then leads you through a few simple steps to create a local account, which you'll then use for signing in. If you're already using a local account, the link reads Sign In With A Microsoft Account Instead. A few screens later, you're connected to an existing Microsoft account or a new one you create.

Configuring privacy options

These days, you don't need to be a conspiracy theorist to be concerned about privacy. Some companies abuse your trust by taking your information—often without your knowledge or consent—and sharing it with others who hope to profit from that information. Because Windows 10 is tightly integrated with cloud services (meaning some of your information gets stored on Microsoft-owned servers), and because Microsoft acknowledges using some of your information to provide better service (for example, Windows collects information from your calendar so that Cortana can make better suggestions), some people have privacy concerns about Windows.

But Microsoft is forthcoming about the types of information it collects and, more importantly, what it does with that information. Here, for example, is part of the privacy statement regarding advertising:

> The ads we select may be based on your current location, search query, or the content you are viewing. Other ads are targeted based on your likely interests or other information that we learn about you over time using demographic data, search queries, interests and favorites, usage data, and location data—which we refer to as "interest-based advertising" in this statement. Microsoft does not use what you say in email, chat, video calls or voice mail, or your documents, photos or other personal files to target ads to you.

More important still, Windows includes a raft of options for controlling your privacy. You'll find them in Settings, Privacy, shown next. Here you can specify which apps are allowed to use each of your computer's many devices, whether to disclose your location, whether to let Cortana better know your voice and word pronunciations, and so on. You should examine each of these options carefully and decide for yourself where the proper balance is between your personal privacy and convenience.

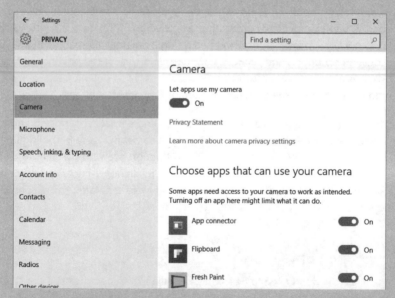

On each page in Settings, Privacy, you'll find a link to the Microsoft privacy statement and links to additional information as well as the controls for making settings. The privacy statement is detailed yet clearly written, and it is an important aid for deciding which options to enable.

Changing account settings

With options in Settings and Control Panel, you can make changes to your own account or another user's account.

To change your own account, open Settings, Accounts to open the Your Account page, shown earlier in Figure 6-1. If you start at User Accounts in Control Panel, click Make Changes To My Account In PC Settings to reach the same destination.

INSIDE OUT

Access the Your Account page quickly

You can jump straight to the Your Account page in Accounts without going through Control Panel or Settings. Simply open the Start menu, click or tap the account picture in the upper left corner of the Start menu, and choose Change Account Settings.

On the Your Account page, you can change your account picture, either by browsing for a picture file or by using your computer's built-in camera to take a picture. If you sign in with a Microsoft account, the Manage My Microsoft Account link opens your default web browser and loads your account page at *account.microsoft.com*. On that page, you can change your password or the name associated with your Microsoft account. Click other tabs along the top of the page to review your subscriptions and Store purchases, change your payment options, get information about all PCs and other devices associated with your Microsoft account, set privacy options, and more.

If you have added one or more users to your computer, you (as a computer administrator) can make changes to the account of each of those users. (For information about adding users, see "Adding a user to your computer" later in this chapter.)

To change a user's account type, in Settings, click Accounts, Family & Other Users. Then click the name of the account you want to change and click Change Account Type. (Your choices are Standard User or Administrator. For details, see "User accounts and security groups" later in this chapter.)

If the person signs in with a Microsoft account, there are no other changes you can make. (You can't make changes to someone else's Microsoft account at *account.microsoft.com*.) For users who sign in with a local user account, you can make a few additional changes, but you must start from User Accounts in Control Panel (shown earlier in Figure 6-2). Click Manage Another Account, and then click the name of the account you want to change. You can make the following changes:

- **Account Name.** The name you're changing here is the full name, which is the one that appears on the sign-in screen, on the Start menu, and in User Accounts.

- **Password.** You can create a password and store a hint that provides a reminder for a forgotten password. If the account is already password protected, User Accounts allows you to change the password or remove the password. For more information about passwords, see "Setting a password" later in this chapter.

- **Account Type.** Your choices here are the same as in Settings, Accounts: Administrator (which adds the account to the Administrators group) or Standard User (which adds the account to the Users group).

If you use a local user account, you can make the following additional changes to your own account (that is, the one with which you're currently signed in) by clicking links in the left pane:

- **Manage Your Credentials.** This link opens Credential Manager, which lets you manage stored credentials that you use to access network resources and websites. For more information, see "Managing and securing your credentials" later in this chapter.

- **Create A Password Reset Disk.** This link launches the Forgotten Password Wizard, from which you can create a password reset tool on removable media.

- **Manage Your File Encryption Certificates.** This link opens a wizard that you can use to create and manage certificates that enable the use of Encrypting File System (EFS). EFS, which is available only in Pro and Enterprise editions of Windows 10, is a method of encrypting folders and files so that they can be used only by someone who has the appropriate credentials. For more information, see "Encrypting information" in Chapter 7, "Securing Windows 10 devices."

- **Configure Advanced User Profile Properties.** This link is used to switch your profile between a local profile (one that is stored on the local computer) and a roaming profile (one that is stored on a network server in a domain environment). With a local profile, you end up with a different profile on each computer you use, whereas a roaming profile is the same regardless of which computer you use to sign in to the network. Roaming profiles require a domain network based on Windows Server. To work with user profiles other than your own, in Control Panel open System and click Advanced System Settings; on the Advanced tab, click Settings under User Profiles.

- **Change My Environment Variables.** Of interest primarily to programmers, this link opens a dialog box in which you can create and edit environment variables that are available only to your user account; in addition, you can view system environment variables, which are available to all accounts.

Deleting an account

You can delete any account except one that is currently signed in. To delete an account, in Settings, Accounts, click Family & Other Users, and click the name of the account you want to delete. Then click Remove. Windows then warns about the consequences of deleting an account, as shown in Figure 6-3.

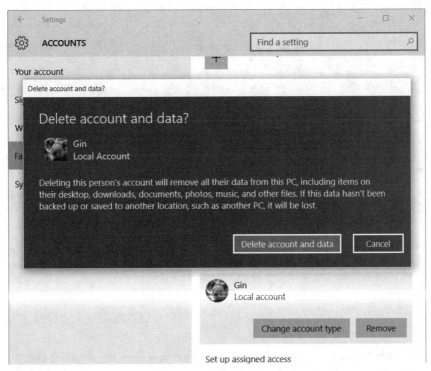

Figure 6-3 Before you click Delete Account And Data, be sure you have saved any data you don't want to lose.

NOTE
User Accounts won't let you delete the last local account on the computer, even if you're signed in using the account named Administrator. This limitation helps to enforce the sound security practice of using an account other than Administrator for your everyday computing.

After you delete an account, of course, that user can no longer sign in. Deleting an account also has another effect you should be aware of: you cannot restore access to resources that are currently shared with the user simply by re-creating the account. This includes files shared with the user and the user's encrypted files, personal certificates, and stored passwords for websites and network resources. That's because those permissions are linked to the user's original security identifier (SID)—not the user name. Even if you create a new account with the same name, password, and so on, it will have a new SID, which will not gain access to anything that was restricted to the original user account. (For more information about security identifiers, see "Introducing access control in Windows" later in this chapter.)

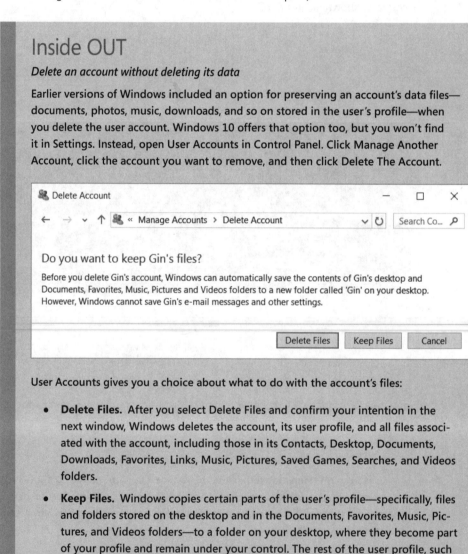

Inside OUT

Delete an account without deleting its data

Earlier versions of Windows included an option for preserving an account's data files—documents, photos, music, downloads, and so on stored in the user's profile—when you delete the user account. Windows 10 offers that option too, but you won't find it in Settings. Instead, open User Accounts in Control Panel. Click Manage Another Account, click the account you want to remove, and then click Delete The Account.

User Accounts gives you a choice about what to do with the account's files:

- **Delete Files.** After you select Delete Files and confirm your intention in the next window, Windows deletes the account, its user profile, and all files associated with the account, including those in its Contacts, Desktop, Documents, Downloads, Favorites, Links, Music, Pictures, Saved Games, Searches, and Videos folders.

- **Keep Files.** Windows copies certain parts of the user's profile—specifically, files and folders stored on the desktop and in the Documents, Favorites, Music, Pictures, and Videos folders—to a folder on your desktop, where they become part of your profile and remain under your control. The rest of the user profile, such as email messages and other data stored in the AppData folder; files stored in the Contacts, Downloads, Saved Games, and Searches folders; and settings stored in the registry are deleted after you confirm your intention in the next window that appears.

Managing the sign-in process

Users of Windows (as well as most other operating systems) are familiar with the time-honored sign-in method: at the sign-in screen, select your name (if it's not already selected) and then enter a password. This continues to be a valid technique in Windows 10.

NOTE

When you first turn on your computer or return to it after signing out, the *lock screen* is displayed. The lock screen normally shows a snazzy picture, the current time and date, and alerts from selected apps. (You can select your own lock screen picture and specify what information you want displayed on the lock screen. For details, see "Customizing the lock screen" in Chapter 4, "Personalizing Windows 10.") To get from the lock screen to the sign-in screen, click anywhere, press any key, or (if you have a touch screen) swipe up.

Inside OUT

Press Ctrl+Alt+Delete without a keyboard

Some network administrators enable a policy that requires you to press Ctrl+Alt+Delete to switch from the lock screen to the sign-in screen. That's tough to do on a tablet with no keyboard—until you know the trick: press the Windows button (usually on the bezel along the right or bottom edge of the screen) and the power button.

Windows 10 has other sign-in options that add security as well as convenience:

- You can enter a numeric PIN.

- You can trace a pattern of gestures on a picture.

- With appropriate hardware, you can use Windows Hello—a biometric sign-in method that scans your fingerprint, your face, or your iris.

These three methods each provide a form of *two-factor authentication*, a means of identifying yourself with multiple components. In the case of Windows sign-ins, the components include two of the following: something you know (such as a PIN or the gesture pattern), something you have (the device itself), and something that's inseparable from you (your fingerprint, face, or iris).

The device you sign in on acts as an authentication component because your information (the PIN or your biometric data) is stored, in encrypted form, on the device—not on a remote server. So, for example, if someone learns your PIN, they can use it only on that device; they

CHAPTER 6

can't use it to sign in to your account on any other device. Or if someone steals your computer, they can't sign in unless they know your PIN.

By comparison, passwords are not as secure. Even if you're vigilant about using a strong password, not writing it down, and ensuring that it's not stolen from you, your user name and password combination could be part of one of those huge data breaches that make the news on almost a weekly basis. Through no fault of your own, your data is in the hands of criminals, who can then use that data to sign in to your account using any computer. Using a PIN with Windows 10, a thief would need to know your PIN and steal your device. And it's even less likely that a thief could nab your device and spoof your biometric data.

In the following sections, we explain how to set up each of these sign-in methods: password, PIN, picture password, and biometric. You configure each of these options on the Sign-In Options page in Settings, Accounts, as shown in Figure 6-4.

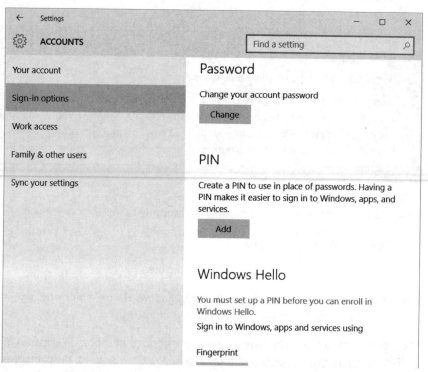

Figure 6-4 Options shown on the Sign-In Options page depend on your computer's hardware. For example, Windows Hello appears only if you have a compatible fingerprint reader or camera.

If you set up more than one option for signing in, you can choose a method other than the default by clicking Sign-In Options on the sign-in screen. This ability might come in handy, for example, if the fingerprint reader fails to recognize your grubby mitt. Icons for each of the options you've set up then appear as shown next; click or tap one to switch methods.

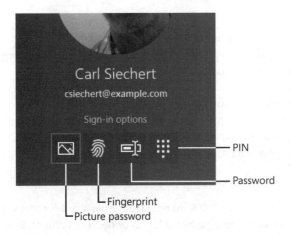

Setting a password

When you create a Microsoft account, you're required to create a password. Similarly, if you add a local user account to your computer, Windows 10 requires you to specify a password. Earlier versions of Windows did not have this requirement, however, so if you upgrade from an earlier version, you might have local accounts that are not password protected.

Now would be a good time to remedy that. After all, associating a password with your user account is your first line of defense against those who would like to snoop around in your files. Because the sign-in screen shows every user account, if you don't set passwords, anyone who has physical access to your computer can sign in simply by clicking a name on the sign-in screen. If the chosen name belongs to an administrator account, the person who clicks it has full, unfettered access to every file and setting on the computer. Requiring a password for each account (particularly administrator accounts) goes a long way toward securing your computer.

NOTE
If you sign in with a local account, you must add a password before you can use a PIN, picture password, or Windows Hello.

To set or change your own password, open Settings, Accounts. On the Sign-In Options page (Figure 6-4), click or tap Change under Password. You'll first need to enter your old password to confirm your identity. Windows then asks you to enter your new password twice. For a local account, you must specify a password hint. The password hint appears after you click your name on the sign-in screen and type your password incorrectly. Be sure

CHAPTER 6

your hint is only a subtle reminder, because any user can click your name and then view the hint. (Windows will not allow you to create a password hint that contains your password.)

NOTE

If you sign in with a local account, you can use a quicker alternative: Press Ctrl+Alt+Delete and click Change A Password. This method has one shortcoming, however: it does not let you enter a password hint.

You can also set or change the password for the local account of another user on your computer. To do so, open User Accounts in Control Panel, click Manage Another Account, and click the name of the user whose password you want to change. Then click Change The Password or (if the account doesn't currently have a password) Create A Password.

CAUTION

If another user has files encrypted with EFS, do not create a password for that user; instead, show the user how to create a password for his or her own account. Similarly, do not remove or change another user's password unless the user has forgotten the password and has absolutely no other way to access the account. (For more information, see the sidebar "Recovering from a lost password.") If you create, change, or remove another user's password, that user loses all personal certificates and stored passwords for websites and network resources. Without the personal certificates, the user loses access to all of his or her encrypted files and all email messages encrypted with the user's private key. Windows deletes the certificates and passwords to prevent the administrator who makes a password change from gaining access to them—but this security comes at a cost!

Recovering from a lost password

It's bound to happen: someday when you try to sign in to your computer and are faced with the password prompt, you will draw a blank.

For a Microsoft account, go to *account.live.com/password/reset*. (Presumably, you'll need to do this from another computer or a mobile device.) A series of questions there allows you to prove your identity and reset your password.

For a local account, Windows offers two tools that help you to deal with this dilemma:

- **Password hint.** Your hint (if you created one) appears below the password entry box after you make an incorrect entry and press Enter. You can create a hint when you set a password.

- **Password reset disk.** A password reset disk allows you (or anyone with your password reset disk) to change your password—without needing to know your old password. As standard practice, each user should create a password reset disk and keep it in a secure location. Then, if a user forgets the password, he or she can reset it using the password reset disk.

Both solutions require a little forethought on your part. You must create the hint when you set your password, and you must create the password reset disk before you actually need it.

To create a password reset disk, you need to know your current password and have removable media available. (You can use a floppy disk, USB flash drive, external hard drive, or memory card.) Follow these steps:

1. Sign in using the account for which you want to create a password reset disk.

2. Insert the removable media you plan to use as a password reset disk.

3. In Control Panel, open User Accounts.

4. In the left pane, click Create A Password Reset Disk to launch the Forgotten Password Wizard.

5. Follow the wizard's instructions.

You can have only one password reset disk for each user account. If you make a new one, the old one is no longer usable.

To use the password reset disk when password amnesia sets in:

1. On the sign-in screen, make an entry in the password box. If you guess right, you're in! If you're wrong, Windows informs you that the password is incorrect.

2. Click OK. The sign-in screen reappears, but with additional text below the password box.

3. If the first bit of additional text, your password hint, jogs your memory, enter your password. If not, click Reset Password to open the Password Reset Wizard.

   The Password Reset Wizard asks for the location of the password reset disk, reads the encrypted key, and then asks you to set a new password, which it then uses to sign you in. Your password reset disk remains usable for the next attack of forgetfulness; you don't need to make a new one.

If you can't remember the password, the hint doesn't refresh your memory, and you don't have a password reset disk, you're out of luck. An administrator can sign in and change or remove your password for you, but you'll lose access to your encrypted files and email messages and your stored credentials.

CHAPTER 6

Using a PIN

To set up a PIN for signing in to your computer, go to the Sign-In Options page (Figure 6-4) and click Add under PIN. After entering your password to confirm your identity, you enter numbers in a dialog box like the one shown here. The minimum length is four digits (0–9 only; no letters or special characters allowed), but your PIN can be as long as you want.

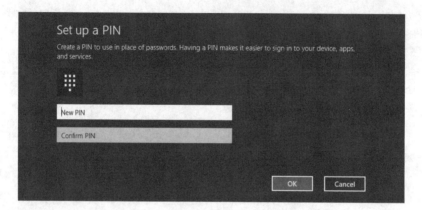

To sign in using a PIN, you can type the numbers on your keyboard. If your computer doesn't have a keyboard, a numeric pad appears on the screen so you can tap your PIN. (If the numeric pad does not appear, tap in the PIN-entry box.)

Using a picture password

A picture password allows you to sign in on a touchscreen using a combination of gestures (specifically, circles, straight lines, and taps) that you make on a picture displayed on the sign-in screen. The easiest way to get the hang of it is to go ahead and create one.

To get started, go to the Sign-In Options page in Settings, Accounts. Under Picture Password, click Add. Verify your identity by entering your password to display the introductory screen shown in Figure 6-5.

After reviewing the description, click Choose Picture. You then get to select one of your own pictures to appear on the sign-in screen. When you're satisfied with your selection, click Use This Picture.

On the next screen that appears, you specify the gestures you'll use to sign in. Your "password" must consist of three gestures. Upon successful entry of your gestures, click Finish.

To sign in with a picture password, on the sign-in screen you must perform the same three gestures: same order, same location, and same direction. You don't need to be *that* precise; Windows allows minor variations in location.

Figure 6-5 The first screen that appears when you set up a picture password explains how it works.

Using Windows Hello for biometric sign-ins

With the proper hardware, you can sign in simply by swiping your fingerprint or, even easier, showing your face in front of your computer's camera. When Windows Hello recognizes a fingerprint, face, or iris, it greets you by briefly displaying your name and a smiley face on the sign-in screen (as shown in Figure 6-6) before going to your desktop.

To use Windows Hello for biometric sign-ins, you need one of the following:

- A fingerprint reader that supports the Window Biometric Framework

- An illuminated 3-D infrared camera such as the Intel RealSense camera that is installed on some computers delivered in 2015 or later; a standard webcam will not work because it could easily be spoofed

CHAPTER 6

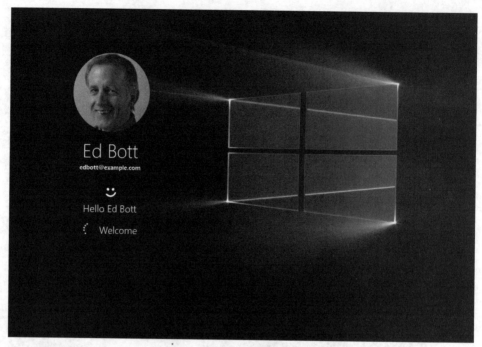

Figure 6-6 Windows Hello greets you, of course, by saying "Hello."

NOTE

You must add a PIN as described earlier in this chapter before you can use Windows Hello.

To set up Windows Hello, go to the Sign-In Options page in Settings, Accounts. Under Windows Hello, click Set Up for the biometric device you want to use. Windows asks you to enter your PIN to verify your identity. After that, you need to enter your biometric data. To be sure it's getting a good read, Windows asks you to scan several times, as shown in Figure 6-7.

If you are setting up fingerprint scanning, you can enroll additional fingers (so that you don't have to be particular about using the same finger all the time) by clicking Add Another after you complete registration for a fingerprint. (To add another fingerprint later, return to Settings, Accounts, Sign-In Options and click Add Another.) You can also associate an additional fingerprint with a different user account on the same device. Sign in to the alternate account and set up the second fingerprint there. When you restart, you can choose your account by choosing the fingerprint associated with that account.

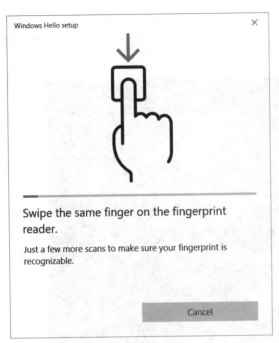

Swipe the same finger on the fingerprint reader.

Just a few more scans to make sure your fingerprint is recognizable.

Cancel

Figure 6-7 Setup for Windows Hello guides you through the brief process of scanning and storing your biometric data.

Signing out, switching accounts, or locking your computer

When you're finished using your computer, you want to be sure that you don't leave it in a condition in which others can use your credentials to access your files. To do that, you need to sign out, switch accounts, or lock your computer:

- **Sign Out.** With this option, all your programs close and the lock screen appears.

- **Switch Account.** With this option, your programs continue to run. The sign-in screen appears, ready for the sign-in credentials of the person you select. Your account is still signed in, but only you can return to your own session, which you can do when the user you switch to chooses to sign out, switch accounts, or lock the computer.

- **Lock.** With this option, your programs continue to run, but the lock screen appears so that no one can see your desktop or use the computer. Only you can unlock the computer to return to your session; however, other users can sign in to their own sessions without disturbing yours.

To sign out, switch accounts, or lock your computer, open the Start menu and click or tap your name at the top of the menu to display a menu like the one shown in Figure 6-8.

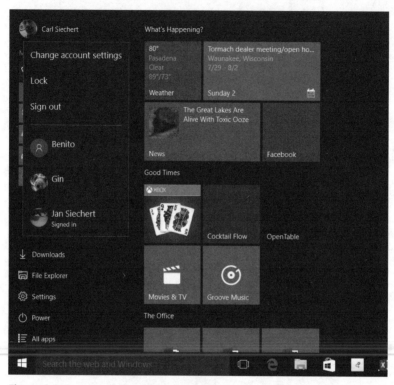

Figure 6-8 On a computer that's joined to a domain, Switch Account appears instead of individual account names. You can then enter an account name on the sign-in screen.

INSIDE OUT

Use keyboard shortcuts

To lock your computer, you can press Windows key+L. (You might also find it more convenient to use this shortcut for switching accounts; the only difference is that it takes you to the lock screen instead of to the sign-in screen.)

For any of these actions—sign out, switch accounts, or lock—you can start by pressing Ctrl+Alt+Delete, which displays a menu that includes all three options.

Sharing your PC with other users

Whether you're setting up a computer for your family to use at home or to be used in a business, it's prudent to set it up securely. Doing so helps to protect each user's data from inadvertent deletions and changes as well as malicious damage and theft. When you set up your computer, consider these suggestions:

- **Control who can sign in.** Create accounts only for users who need to use your computer's resources, either by signing in locally or over a network. Delete or disable other accounts (except the built-in accounts created by Windows).

- **Change all user accounts except one to standard accounts.** You'll need one administrative account for installing programs, creating and managing accounts, and so on. All other accounts can run with standard privileges.

- **Be sure that all accounts are password protected.** This is especially important for administrator accounts and for other accounts whose profiles contain important or sensitive documents. You might not want to set a password on your toddler's local account, but all other accounts should be protected from the possibility that the tyke (or your cat) will accidentally tap the wrong name on the sign-in screen.

- **Restrict sign-in times.** You might want to limit the computing hours for some users. The easiest way for home users to do this is with Microsoft Family; for details, see "Controlling your children's computer access" later in this chapter.

- **Restrict access to certain files.** You'll want to be sure that some files are available to all users, whereas other files are available only to the person who created them. The Public folder and a user's personal folders provide a general framework for this protection. You can further refine your file-protection scheme by selectively applying permissions to varying combinations of files, folders, and users.

Adding a user to your computer

To allow another user to sign in on your computer, you must add them through Settings, Accounts. Go to the Family & Other Users page, shown in Figure 6-9, which has separate controls for adding members of your family and adding "other users." The difference is that family members are subject to restrictions that an adult member of the family can specify (for details, see "Controlling your children's computer access" later in this chapter), whereas other users have full use of the computer (subject, of course, to limitations imposed by their account type).

> NOTE
> The Family & Other Users page is available only when you sign in with an administrator account.

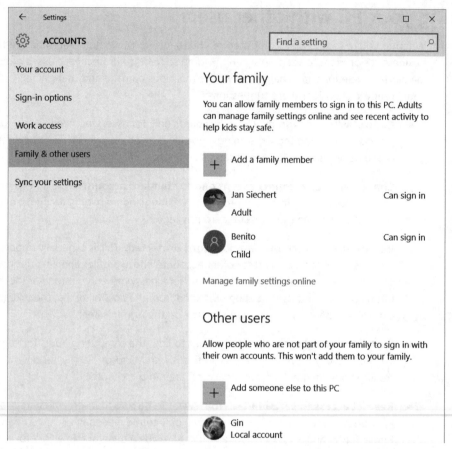

Figure 6-9 Under Other Users, you can add a local account or a Microsoft account. Family members must have a Microsoft account.

To add a user who's not a family member, under Other Users click Add Someone Else To This PC. Windows then asks for the email address of the new user. If the email address is already associated with a Microsoft account, all you need to do is click Next and the new user is ready to go. (The first time the new user signs in, the computer must be connected to the Internet.) If the email address you provide is not associated with a Microsoft account, Windows provides a link to sign up for a new Microsoft account. (Clearly, Windows tries to steer you toward using a Microsoft account at every opportunity.)

What if you want to add a local account? At the first screen—when Windows asks for an email address—instead click the link near the bottom: The Person I Want To Add Doesn't Have An Email Address. In the next dialog box that appears, shown next, Windows offers to set up a new Microsoft account.

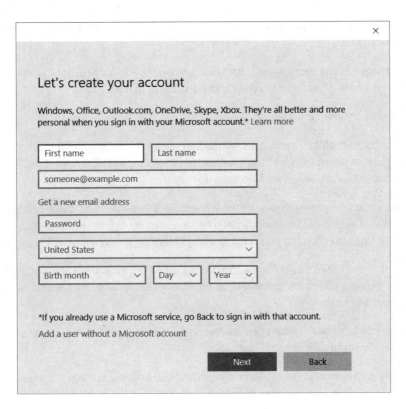

But you don't want a Microsoft account! Look to the bottom of the window, and click Add A User Without A Microsoft Account. Windows then asks you to specify a user name and password for the new user. (If your computer has only local accounts set up, you go directly to this final dialog box, skipping the two that guide you toward a Microsoft account.) Click Next, and your work is done.

Controlling your children's computer access

Previous versions of Windows had a feature called Parental Controls (Windows Vista and Windows 7) or Family Safety (Windows 8), which allowed parents to restrict and monitor their children's computer use. Windows 10 offers similar capabilities, but the implementation is completely different. Those earlier versions stored their settings on your PC, but in Windows 10 family settings are now stored and managed as part of your Microsoft account.

This architectural change has some obvious benefits:

- You don't need to make settings for each child on each computer. After you add a family member on one PC, you manage the settings for each child in the cloud, and those settings apply to all the family PCs where they sign in.

CHAPTER 6

- You can manage your children's computer use from any computer that's connected to the Internet.

Family settings has one requirement that some will perceive as a disadvantage: each family member must have a Microsoft account and sign in with that account.

What can you do with family settings?

- Monitor each child's computer use. You can see what they search for on the web and which sites they visit, which apps and games they use, and how much time they are signed in to each Windows 10 computer they use.

- Block inappropriate websites. When you enable this feature, Microsoft-curated lists of sites that are blocked or explicitly allowed are used by default, but you can supplement these lists with sites that you want to always block or always allow.

- Control each child's use of apps and games. Based on age ratings, you can limit the apps and games a child can download and purchase. You can also block specific apps and games from running.

- Restrict when your children can use the computer, and for how long. Figure 6-10 shows how you specify the hours of use.

At the time of the initial Windows 10 release in mid-2015, family settings features were still in development. By the time you read this, family settings might include changes to the preceding features as well as some additional features. Visit *account.microsoft.com/family* to see the newest adaptation.

To get started with family settings, open Settings, Accounts and click Family & Other Users. (See Figure 6-9.)

NOTE

To see the Your Family section of the Family & Other Users page, you must sign in with a Microsoft account, and your account type must be administrator.

Then click Add A Family Member. Windows asks whether you want to add an account for an adult or a child; the difference is that an adult can manage family settings, whereas a child is controlled by family settings.

You then enter the family member's email address, and if a Microsoft account is not associated with that address, Windows gathers the needed information to set one up. Unlike when you add an "other user," there is no option to use a local account.

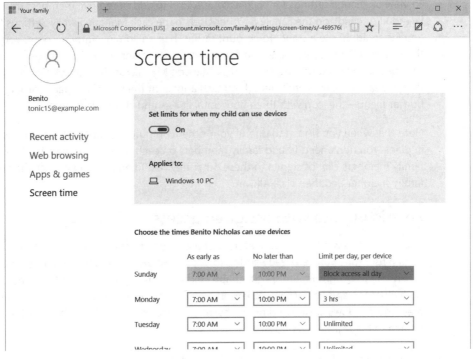

Figure 6-10 With Screen Time settings, for each day of the week you specify an allowable range of times for a child's computer use, plus an overall limit on the amount of computer time.

After you select a Microsoft account for the new family member, Microsoft Family sends an email invitation to that person. The new family member can sign in to your computer right away, but family settings take effect only after he or she opens the email message and clicks the Accept Invitation button. (Until that happens, the word *Pending* appears next to the family member's name on the Family & Other Users page.)

TROUBLESHOOTING

The email invitation never arrives

Despite repeated attempts on your part to use the Family & Other Users page, sometimes the invitation isn't sent. To get around this, click Manage Family Settings Online (alternatively, browse to *account.microsoft.com/family*). On the webpage that appears, click the Add button for a child or an adult.

CHAPTER 6

To view or change settings for child accounts, and to add or remove members from your family (adult or child), on the Family & Other Users page click Manage Family Settings Online. If you (as an adult) use a standard account rather than an administrator account, you won't see the Family & Other Users page. You can, however, still manage family settings. On the Your Account page in Settings, Accounts, click Manage My Microsoft Account. On the webpage that appears, click the Family tab. (If no tabs appear at the top of the page, click the hamburger menu—the icon with three horizontal lines—and choose Family.)

Note that when you sign in to one of your other computers, your family's accounts are already in place; you don't need to add family members on each device. However, by default the other family members cannot sign in to these other devices. To enable access, click the name of the family member and then click Allow.

Restricting use with assigned access

Assigned access is a rather odd feature that allows you to configure your computer so that a certain user (one you've already added to your computer) can run only a single modern app. When that user signs in, the specified app starts automatically and runs full-screen. The user can't close the app or start any others. In fact, the only way out is to press Ctrl+Alt+Delete (or press the Windows button and power button simultaneously), which signs out the user and returns to the sign-in screen.

The use cases for this feature are limited, but here are a few examples:

- A kiosk app for public use

- A point-of-sale app for your business

- A game for a very young child

If you can think of a use for this feature, click Set Up Assigned Access, at the bottom of the Family & Other Users page.

Introducing access control in Windows

The Windows approach to security is discretionary: each securable system resource—each file or printer, for example—has an owner who has discretion over who can and cannot access the resource. Usually, a resource is owned by the user who creates it. If you create a file, for example, you are the file's owner under ordinary circumstances. (Computer administrators, however, can take ownership of resources they didn't create.)

NOTE

To exercise full discretionary control over individual files, you must store those files on an NTFS volume. For the sake of compatibility, Windows 10 supports the FAT and FAT32 file systems used by early Windows versions and many USB flash drives, as well as the exFAT file system used on some removable drives. However, none of the FAT-based file systems support file permissions. To enjoy the full benefits of Windows security, you must use NTFS. For more information about file systems, see "Choosing a file system" in Chapter 14, "Managing disks and drives."

What are security identifiers?

Windows security relies on the use of a security identifier (SID) to identify a user. When you create a user account on your computer (local account or Microsoft account), Windows assigns a unique SID to that account. The SID remains uniquely associated with that user account until the account is deleted, whereupon the SID is never used again—for that user or any other user. Even if you re-create an account with identical information, a new SID is created.

A SID is a variable-length value that contains a revision level, a 48-bit identifier authority value, and a number of 32-bit subauthority values. The SID takes the form S-1-x-y1-y2- . . . . S-1 identifies it as a revision 1 SID; x is the value for the identifier authority; and y1, y2, and so on are values for subauthorities.

You'll sometimes see a SID in a security dialog box (for example, on the Security tab of a file's properties dialog box) before Windows has had time to look up the user account name. You'll also spot SIDs in the hidden and protected $RECYCLE.BIN folder (each SID you see in this folder represents the Recycle Bin for a particular user) and in the registry (the HKEY_USERS hive contains a key, identified by SID, for each user account on the computer), among other places. The easiest way to determine your own SID is with the Whoami command-line utility. For details, see the following tip.

Not all SIDs are unique (although the SID assigned to your user account is always unique). A number of commonly used SIDs are constant among all Windows installations. For example, S-1-5-18 is the SID for the built-in Local System account, a hidden member of the Administrators group that is used by the operating system and by services that sign in using the Local System account. You can find a complete list of such SIDs, called well-known SIDs, in Microsoft Knowledge Base article 243330 (*w7io.com/1601*).

To determine which users have access to a resource, Windows assigns a security identifier (SID) to each user account. Your SID (a gigantic number guaranteed to be unique) follows you around wherever you go in Windows. When you sign in, the operating system first validates your user name and password. Then it creates a security access token. You can think of this as the electronic equivalent of an ID badge. It includes your user name and SID, plus information about any security groups to which your account belongs. (Security groups are described later in this chapter.) Any program you start gets a copy of your security access token.

Inside OUT

Learn about your own account with Whoami

Windows includes a command-line utility called Whoami (Who Am I?). You can use Whoami to find out the name of the account that's currently signed in, its SID, the names of the security groups of which it's a member, and its privileges. To use Whoami, open a Command Prompt window. (You don't need elevated privileges.)

Then, to learn the name of the signed-in user, type **whoami**. (This is particularly useful if you're signed in as a standard user but running an elevated Command Prompt window—when it might not be obvious which account is currently "you.") If you're curious about your SID, type **whoami /user**. For a complete list of Whoami parameters, type **whoami /?**.

With User Account Control (UAC) turned on, administrators who sign in get two security access tokens—one that has the privileges of a standard user and one that has the full privileges of an administrator.

Whenever you attempt to walk through a controlled "door" in Windows (for example, when you connect to a shared printer), or any time a program attempts to do so on your behalf, the operating system examines your security access token and decides whether to let you pass. If access is permitted, you notice nothing. If access is denied, you get to hear a beep and read a refusal message.

In determining whom to let pass and whom to block, Windows consults the resource's access control list (ACL). This is simply a list of SIDs and the access privileges associated with each one. Every resource subject to access control has an ACL. This manner of allowing and blocking access to resources such as files and printers is essentially unchanged since Windows NT.

What are ACLs?

Each folder and each file on an NTFS-formatted volume has an ACL (also known as DACL, for discretionary access control list, and commonly called NTFS permissions). An ACL comprises an access control entry (ACE) for each user who is allowed access to the folder or file. With NTFS permissions, you can control access to any file or folder, allowing different types of access for different users or groups of users.

To view and edit NTFS permissions for a file or folder, right-click its icon and choose Properties. The Security tab lists all the groups and users with permissions set for the selected object, as shown here. Different permissions can be set for each user, as you can see by selecting each one.

To make changes to the settings for any user or group in the list, or to add or remove a user or group in the list, click Edit. (Use caution. Setting NTFS permissions without understanding the full consequences can lead to unexpected and unwelcome results, including a complete loss of access to files and folders. Before you delve into the inner workings of NTFS permissions on the Security tab, be sure to try the safer and less complicated homegroup sharing or the Share With command. For details, see "Sharing files, digital media, and printers in a homegroup" in Chapter 5 and "Sharing files and folders from any folder" in Chapter 20.)

The access granted by each permission type is as follows:

- **Full Control.** Users with Full Control can list contents of a folder, read and open files, create new files, delete files and subfolders, change permissions on files and subfolders, and take ownership of files.

- **Modify.** Allows the user to read, change, create, and delete files but not to change permissions or take ownership of files.

- **Read & Execute.** Allows the user to view files and execute programs.

- **List Folder Contents.** Provides the same permissions as Read & Execute but can be applied only to folders.

- **Read.** Allows the user to list the contents of a folder, read file attributes, read permissions, and synchronize files.

- **Write.** Allows the user to create files, write data, read attributes and permissions, and synchronize files.

- **Special Permissions.** The assigned permissions don't match any of the preceding permission descriptions. To see precisely which permissions are granted, click Advanced.

UAC, which was introduced in Windows Vista, adds another layer of restrictions based on user accounts. With UAC turned on, applications are normally launched using an administrator's standard user token. (Standard users, of course, have only a standard user token.) If an application requires administrator privileges, UAC asks for your consent (if you're signed in as an administrator) or the credentials of an administrator (if you're signed in as a standard user) before letting the application run. With UAC turned off, Windows works in the same (rather dangerous) manner as pre–Windows Vista versions: administrator accounts can do just about anything (sometimes getting those users in trouble), and standard accounts don't have the privileges needed to run many older programs.

➤ For more information about UAC, see "Preventing unsafe actions with User Account Control" in Chapter 7.

CHAPTER 6

Permissions and rights

Windows distinguishes two types of access privileges: permissions and rights. A permission is the ability to access a particular object in some defined manner—for example, to write to an NTFS file or to modify a printer queue. A right is the ability to perform a particular system-wide action, such as signing in or resetting the clock.

The owner of a resource (or an administrator) assigns permissions to the resource via its properties dialog box. For example, if you are the printer owner or have administrative privileges, you can restrict someone from using a particular printer by visiting the properties dialog box for that printer. Administrators set rights via the Local Security Policy console. For example, an administrator could grant someone the right to install a device driver. (The Local Security Policy console is available only in the Pro and Enterprise editions of Windows 10. In the Home edition, rights for various security groups are predefined and unchangeable.)

NOTE
In this book, as in many of the Windows messages and dialog boxes, *privileges* serves as an informal term encompassing both permissions and rights.

User accounts and security groups

The backbone of Windows security is the ability to uniquely identify each user. While setting up a computer—or at any later time—an administrator creates a user account for each user. The user account is identified by a user name and is normally secured by a password, which the user provides when signing in to the system. Windows then controls, monitors, and restricts access to system resources on the basis of the permissions and rights associated with each user account by the resource owners and the system administrator.

Account type is a simplified way of describing membership in a security group, a collection of user accounts. Windows classifies each user account as one of two account types:

- **Administrator.** Members of the Administrators group are classified as administrator accounts. By default, the Administrators group includes the first account you create when you set up the computer and an account named Administrator that is disabled and hidden by default. Unlike other account types, administrators have full control over the system. Among the tasks that only administrators can perform are the following:

  - Create, change, and delete user accounts and groups
  - Install and uninstall desktop programs

CHAPTER 6

- Configure automatic updating with Windows Update
- Install an ActiveX control
- Install or remove hardware device drivers
- Share folders
- Set permissions
- Access all files, including those in another user's folder
- Take ownership of files
- Copy or move files into the %ProgramFiles% or %SystemRoot% folders
- Restore backed-up system files
- Grant rights to other user accounts and to themselves
- Configure Windows Firewall

- **Standard user.** Members of the Users group are classified as standard user accounts. A partial list of tasks available to standard user accounts includes
  - Change the password and picture for their own user account
  - Use desktop programs that have been installed on the computer
  - Install system and driver updates using Windows Update
  - Install and run modern apps from the Windows Store
  - Install approved ActiveX controls
  - Configure a secure Wi-Fi connection
  - Refresh a network adapter and the system's IP address
  - View permissions
  - Create, change, and delete files in their document folders and in shared document folders
  - Restore their own backed-up files
  - View the system clock and calendar, and change the time zone
  - Set personalization options, such as themes, desktop background, and so on
  - Select a display dots-per-inch (DPI) setting to adjust text size
  - Configure power options
  - Sign in in Safe Mode
  - View Windows Firewall settings

Assigning an appropriate account type to the people who use your computer is straightforward. At least one user must be an administrator; naturally, that should be the person who administers the computer. All other regular users should each have a standard user account.

What happened to the Administrator account?

Every computer running Windows has a special account named Administrator. In versions of Windows before Windows 7, Administrator was the primary account for managing the computer. Like other administrator accounts, the Administrator account has full rights over the entire computer. But in Windows 10, the Administrator account is disabled by default.

In Windows 10, there's seldom a need to use the Administrator account instead of another administrator account. With default settings in Windows, the Administrator account does have one unique capability: it's not subject to UAC, even when UAC is turned on for all other users. All other administrator accounts (which are sometimes called Protected Administrator accounts) run with standard-user privileges unless the user consents to elevation. The Administrator account runs with full administrative privileges at all times and never needs your consent for elevation. (For this reason, of course, it's rather risky. Any application that runs as Administrator has full control of the computer—which means applications written by malicious or incompetent programmers can do significant damage to your system.)

Inside OUT

And the Guest account?

Historically, the built-in Guest account has provided a way to offer limited access to occasional users. Not so in Windows 10. Although this account still exists, it is disabled by default, and the supported tools for enabling it (the Local Users And Groups console, for example) do not work as expected. In our experience, trying to trick Windows 10 into enabling this capability is almost certain to end in frustration. In the cloud-centric world of Windows 10, the Guest account no longer works as it used to and enabling it can cause a variety of problems. A better solution (if your guests don't have their own device that can connect to your wireless network) is to set up a standard account for guest use.

Security groups allow a system administrator to create classes of users who share common privileges. For example, if everyone in the accounting department needs access to the Payables folder, the administrator can create a group called Accounting and grant the entire group access to that folder. If the administrator then adds all user accounts belonging to employees in the accounting department to the Accounting group, these users will automatically have access to the Payables folder. A user account can belong to one group, more than one group, or no group at all.

In large networks based on Active Directory domains, groups can be a valuable administrative tool. They simplify the job of ensuring that all members with common access needs have an identical set of privileges. We don't recommend creating or using groups other than the built-in Administrators and Users groups on standalone and workgroup-based computers, however.

Permissions and rights for group members are cumulative. That means that if a user account belongs to more than one group, the user enjoys all of the privileges accorded to all groups of which the user account is a member.

Managing and securing your credentials

When you sign in to a password-protected website using Microsoft Edge, the browser asks if you want it to save your user name and password. You might've wondered where Edge stores those credentials. You'll find the answer in Credential Manager, a Control Panel app that is shown in Figure 6-11.

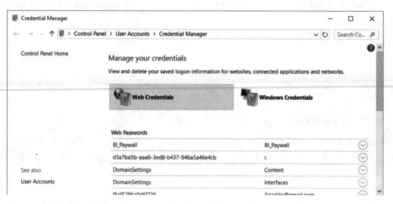

Figure 6-11 To see the details for a credential, click it to expand the entry.

To use Credential Manager, in the search box begin typing **credential** until Credential Manager appears; click it to open the app. Here you can see which credentials have been saved, view the details of each one (including the password for web credentials), and remove credentials you no longer need. Click Windows Credentials to display a list of network-related credentials. On this page, you can also add, back up, and restore credentials.

CHAPTER 7

Securing Windows 10 devices

We don't mean to be scaremongers, but they *are* out to get you. Computer attacks continue to increase in number and severity each year. And while the big data breaches—the loss of millions of credit card numbers from a major retailer or the loss of millions of personnel records from the U.S. government—command the most media attention, don't think that the bad guys wouldn't like to get into your computer too. Whether it's to steal your valuable personal data, appropriate your computing resources and bandwidth, or use your PC as a pathway into a bigger target with whom you do business, there are plenty of actors with bad intent.

According to the 2015 Internet Security Threat Report, published by Symantec, 60 percent of all targeted attacks struck small and medium-sized organizations. Like individuals, these organizations often don't have the resources to invest in security—making them juicy targets.

In this chapter, we examine the types of threats you're likely to face at home and at work. More importantly, we describe some of the more significant security improvements made in Windows 10—many of which are in layers you can't see, such as hardware-based protection that operates before Windows loads. Then we explain how to use the more visible security features, including Windows Firewall, User Account Control, BitLocker, and Windows Defender.

Understanding security threats

A decade ago, the threat landscape for Windows users was dominated by viruses and worms. Ah, for the good old days! The modern threat landscape is much more complex and, unfortunately, more insidious. Today, an attacker is likely to be part of an organized crime ring, not an attention-seeking vandal, and attacks are typically designed to go unnoticed for as long as possible.

A rogue program, installed without your knowledge and running without your awareness, can perform malicious tasks and transfer data without your consent. This category of software is often referred to as *malware*.

The goal of the bad guys is to get you to run their software. They might, for example, convince you to install a *Trojan*—a program that appears legitimate but actually performs malicious actions when it's installed. This category of malware doesn't spread on its own but instead uses social engineering (often using popular social networking sites such as Facebook and Twitter) to convince its victims to cooperate in the installation process. As part of its payload, a Trojan can include a downloader that installs additional malicious and unwanted programs. Some Trojans install a "backdoor" that allows an outside attacker to remotely control the infected computer.

What's in it for the bad guys? Money, mostly, gathered in a variety of ways, depending on how the attackers got through your defenses.

A *password stealer* runs in the background, gathers user names and passwords, and forwards them to an outside attacker. The stolen credentials can then be used to make purchases, clean out bank accounts, or commit identity theft.

Bad guys prey on fear with rogue security software (also known as *scareware*), which mimics the actions and appearance of legitimate antivirus software. If you install one of these programs, it inevitably reports the presence of a (nonexistent) virus and offers to remove it—for a fee, of course.

In 2015, the fastest rising star in the malware hall of shame is *ransomware*, a form of digital blackmail in which a program encrypts all your data files and offers to unlock them only upon payment of a ransom.

Phishing attacks, which use social engineering to convince visitors to give away their sign-in credentials, are a separate but potentially devastating avenue to identity theft that can strike in any browser using any operating system.

You can review lists of current malware threats, along with links to details about each one, at the Microsoft Malware Protection Center, *w7io.com/1518*. For a more comprehensive view of the changing threat landscape, the Microsoft Malware Protection Center issues a twice-yearly report, using data from hundreds of millions of Windows users and other sources. You'll find the latest Microsoft Security Intelligence Report at *w7io.com/1501*.

CHAPTER 7

Securing your computer: A defense-in-depth strategy

A multidimensional threat landscape requires a multilayered approach to protecting your PC and your network. The big picture goal is to secure your device, secure your data, secure your identity, and block malware. On a home or small business network, those layers of security include the following:

Use a hardware router to protect your broadband connection. This is an essential part of physical security, even if your network consists of a single PC. We provide an overview of the technology in "Getting started with Windows 10 networking" in Chapter 5, "Networking essentials."

Enable a software firewall and keep it turned on. You can use Windows Firewall, which is included with Windows 10, or a firewall that you obtain elsewhere. To learn more, see "Blocking intruders with Windows Firewall" later in this chapter.

Use biometric sign-in. Biometric sign-in using a fingerprint reader or facial recognition with Windows Hello offers much more than convenience. Because biometric sign-in is linked to a specific device, it provides effective two-factor authentication. If you don't have the necessary hardware, use a PIN or picture password for sign-in—both of which can be more secure than a traditional password. For more information, see "Managing the sign-in process" in Chapter 6, "Managing user accounts, passwords, and credentials."

Set up standard user accounts and keep User Account Control enabled. Standard accounts help to prevent (or at least minimize) the damage that an untrained user can do by installing untrusted programs. User Account Control (UAC) helps in this regard by restricting access to administrative tasks and virtualizing registry and file-system changes. For details, see "Introducing access control in Windows" in Chapter 6 and "Preventing unsafe actions with User Account Control" later in this chapter.

Keep Windows and vulnerable programs up to date. Windows Update handles this chore for Windows, Office, and other Microsoft programs. You're on your own for third-party programs. We provide an overview of security updates in "Staying on top of security updates" later in this chapter.

Use an antimalware program and keep it up to date. Windows Defender, which is included with Windows 10, provides antimalware protection, but many third-party solutions are also available. For details, see "Using Windows Defender to block malware" later in this chapter.

Protect yourself from threats in email messages. At a minimum, your email solution should block or quarantine executable files and other potentially dangerous attachments. In addition, effective antispam features can block scripts and prevent phishing attempts.

Use parental controls to keep kids safe. If you have children who use your computer, family safety features in Windows can help you keep them away from security threats. It also includes options you can use to restrict their computer activities in other ways. For details, see "Controlling your children's computer access" in Chapter 6.

Security And Maintenance, a Control Panel app, monitors many of these areas to be sure you're protected, and it displays an alert if something needs attention. For details, see "Monitoring your computer's security" later in this chapter.

The most important protective layer—and the one that is most easily overlooked—is user education and self-control. Everyone who uses a computer must have the discipline to read and evaluate security warnings when they're presented and to allow the installation only of software that is known to be safe. (Although a user with a standard account can't install or run a program that wipes out the entire computer, he can still inflict enough damage on his own user profile to cause considerable inconvenience.) Countless successful malware attacks worldwide have proven that many users do not have adequate awareness of safe computing methods.

What's new in Windows 10

Because the bad guys are always upping their game, a hallmark of each new version of Windows is a number of new and improved security features. Windows 10 is no exception. Here we enumerate changes available in Windows 10 Home and Windows 10 Pro; several additional features are included with Windows 10 Enterprise on a managed network.

Securing devices

Security features in Windows 10 begin with support for modern hardware designs. Although Windows 10 continues to support legacy hardware, some security features require two elements built in to most newer computers:

- **Unified Extensible Firmware Interface (UEFI).** UEFI is a firmware interface that replaces the BIOS, which has been a part of every PC since the beginning of personal computing. Among other improvements, UEFI enables Secure Boot and Device Encryption, features that are described in the following pages. PCs designed for Windows 8 and later must use UEFI.

- **Trusted Platform Module (TPM).** A TPM is a hardware chip that facilitates encryption and prevents altering or exporting encryption keys and certificates. With a TPM, BitLocker Drive Encryption (described later in this chapter) is more convenient to use as well as more secure. Other security features in Windows 10, such as Measured Boot and Device Guard, require the presence of a TPM.

With UEFI and TPM in place, Windows 10 is able to secure the boot process. (Many recent malware attacks take control of the system early in the boot process, before Windows is fully running and before antimalware programs spring into action. This type of malware is called a *rootkit*.) The Windows 10 boot process steps through the following features:

- **Secure Boot.** Secure Boot, a basic feature of UEFI, prevents the use of any alternative operating system (OS) loader. Only an OS loader that is digitally signed using a certificate stored by UEFI is allowed to run. (A conventional BIOS allows interruption of the boot process to use any OS loader, including one that's been corrupted.)

- **Early Launch Antimalware (ELAM).** Antimalware software—including compatible third-party programs as well as Windows Defender—that has been certified and signed by Microsoft loads its drivers before any other third-party drivers or programs. This allows the antimalware software to detect and block attempts to load malicious code.

- **Measured Boot.** Measurements of the UEFI firmware and each Windows component are taken as they load. The measurements are then digitally signed and stored in the TPM, where they can't be changed. During subsequent boots, measurements are compared against the stored measurements.

Securing data

The increased mobility of PCs also increases the risk of theft. Losing a computer is bad enough, but handing over all the data you've stored on the computer is by far the greater loss. Windows 10 includes new features to ensure the thief can't get your data.

- **Device encryption.** On devices that support InstantGo, data on the operating system volume is encrypted by default. (Formerly called Connected Standby, InstantGo is a Microsoft hardware specification that enables advanced power-management capabilities. Among other requirements, InstantGo devices must boot from a solid state drive.) The encryption initially uses a clear key, but when a local administrator first signs in with a Microsoft account, the volume is automatically encrypted. A recovery key is stored at *onedrive.com/recoverykey*; you'll need it if you reinstall the operating system or move the drive to a new PC.

- **BitLocker Drive Encryption.** BitLocker Drive Encryption offers similar (but stronger) whole-volume encryption, and on corporate networks it allows centralized management. In Windows 10, BitLocker encrypts drives more quickly than in previous Windows versions; additional speed comes from the new ability to encrypt only the part of a volume in use. For more information, see "Encrypting with BitLocker and BitLocker To Go" later in this chapter.

Securing identities

It seems like every week we hear about another data breach where millions of user names and passwords have been stolen. There's a thriving market for this type of information because it enables the thieves to sign in anywhere using your credentials. Furthermore, because many people use the same password for different accounts, criminals can often use the stolen information to hack into a theft victim's other accounts. Windows 10 marks the beginning of the end of passwords.

- **Windows Hello.** With Windows 10, enterprise-grade two-factor authentication is built in. After enrolling a device with an authentication service, the device itself becomes one factor; the second factor is a PIN or a biometric, such as a fingerprint, facial recognition, or an iris scan.

- **Microsoft Passport.** After Windows Hello signs you in, Microsoft Passport enables sign-in to networks and web services. Your biometric data remains securely stored in your computer's TPM; it's not sent over the network.

With this combination of authentication methods, an attacker who has a trove of user names and passwords is stymied. To unlock Microsoft Passport (and, by extension, gain the ability to sign in to your web services), he needs the enrolled device. And a thief who steals your computer needs your PIN or biometric data. Active Directory, Azure Active Directory, and Microsoft Accounts support this new form of credentials; other services are sure to follow.

For more information about Windows Hello, see "Managing the sign-in process" in Chapter 6.

Blocking malware

Since the days of Windows 7, several features that block malicious software have been beefed up:

- **Address Space Layout Randomization (ASLR).** ASLR is a feature that randomizes the location of program code and other data in memory, making it difficult to execute attacks that write directly to system memory because the malware can't find the memory location it needs. In Windows 10, memory locations are scrambled even more. And because the randomization is unique to each device, a successful attack on one device won't work on another.

- **Data Execution Prevention (DEP).** DEP is a hardware feature that marks blocks of memory so that they can store data but not execute program instructions. Windows 10 can't be installed on a system that doesn't support DEP.

- **Windows Defender.** In Windows 7, Windows Defender is a lightweight antispy-ware program. But starting with Windows 8 and continuing in Windows 10, Windows Defender includes the well-regarded antimalware capabilities of Windows Security Essentials, a free add-on for Windows 7. Windows Defender supports ELAM, described earlier in this chapter, which means that it can defend against rootkits that attempt to co-opt the boot process. For more information, see "Using Windows Defender to block malware" later in this chapter.

- **SmartScreen.** The goal of SmartScreen, introduced in Windows 7, is similar to that of Windows Defender: stop malicious code from running, which is much better than try-ing to clean up the damage after the fact. But SmartScreen takes a completely different approach: instead of looking for signatures of known bad programs, it checks a hash of each executable downloaded from an online source against Microsoft's application-reputation database. Files that have established a positive reputation are deemed safe and are allowed to run, whereas files with a negative reputation are blocked.

  In Windows 7, SmartScreen is a feature of Internet Explorer and checks files as they are downloaded. Beginning with Windows 8, SmartScreen is an integral part of Windows (and continues to be a feature of Internet Explorer and, in Windows 10, Microsoft Edge). Therefore, it blocks execution of unknown programs not just as you download them in a browser but any time you attempt to run a program from an online source—including those downloaded with a non-Microsoft browser.

Monitoring your computer's security

In Windows 10, security-related options have been gathered in Security And Maintenance in Control Panel, shown in Figure 7-1. (Veteran users of Windows 7 and Windows 8 will recognize this as the new name for what was called Action Center in those earlier operating systems. In Windows 10, *Action Center* refers to the list of notifications and buttons that can appear on the right side of the screen.) You can open Security And Maintenance from Control Panel or Settings: In the search box of either app, type **security** and then click Security And Mainte-nance. (No keyboard? Open Control Panel, tap System And Security, and then tap Security And Maintenance.)

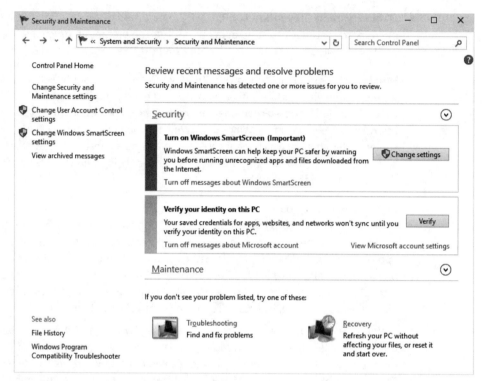

Figure 7-1 Security And Maintenance collects security, maintenance, and troubleshooting information and settings in a single window.

The Security section in Security And Maintenance provides at-a-glance information about your security settings. Items that need your attention have a red or yellow bar, as shown in Figure 7-1. A red bar identifies important items that need immediate attention, such as detection of a virus or spyware or that no firewall is enabled. A yellow bar denotes informational messages about suboptimal, but less critical, settings or status. Next to the bar appear explanatory text and buttons that let you correct the problem (or configure Security And Maintenance so that it won't bother you).

If all is well, the Security category is collapsed and you see nothing in that category when you open Security And Maintenance. Click the arrow to expand the category, and you'll see all the security-related items that Security And Maintenance monitors, as shown in Figure 7-2.

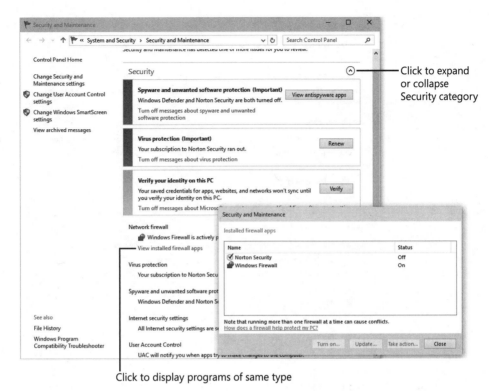

Click to display programs of same type

Figure 7-2 When multiple firewall programs are installed, you can click a link to show a list like this one. Use the Turn On button to enable a program that is currently disabled.

Security And Maintenance is designed to work with third-party firewall, antivirus, and anti-spyware programs, as well as with the programs built in to Windows (Windows Firewall and Windows Defender). Systems with more than one program installed in any of these categories include a link to show a list of such programs. For example, Figure 7-2 shows a system on which Norton Security is installed. The dialog box that appears when you click the link to view installed programs allows you to turn on any installed program that is currently turned off.

If you don't want to be bothered with alerts from Security And Maintenance about one or more security features, click Change Security And Maintenance Settings. After clearing items you don't want monitored in the dialog box shown in Figure 7-3, you won't receive any further alerts, and thereafter Security And Maintenance passively indicates the status as Currently Not Monitored.

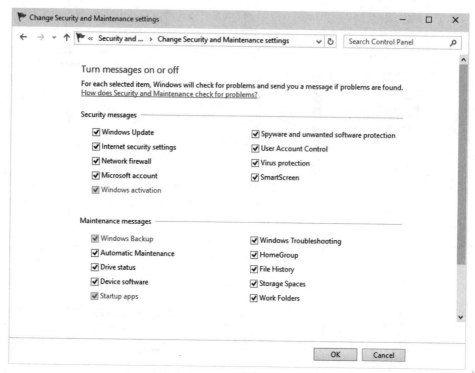

Figure 7-3 You can selectively disable and enable Security And Maintenance monitoring here, or you can manage monitored items individually by clicking links in the main Security And Maintenance window.

Staying on top of security updates

As we noted earlier in this chapter, Microsoft continues to beef up security in Windows. But as new threats emerge, the task is never done, so perhaps the most important step in keeping your system secure is to be sure that you stay current with updates to Windows and other programs. Microsoft issues frequent updates that provide replacements for installed device drivers as well as fixes to code that has been found to be faulty. Some updates provide new features or enhanced performance, while others patch security holes.

To install updates automatically, Windows uses Windows Update. In Windows 10, you'll find Windows Update in Settings under Update & Security. For more information about Windows Update, see "Keeping Windows up to date" in Chapter 15, "System maintenance and performance."

You might be interested in knowing more about current security threats, including those that are addressed by Windows Update: What, exactly, is the threat? How serious is it? What workarounds are available? Microsoft Security Response Center publishes detailed information, in the form of a *security bulletin*, about the threat and the response. To find this information, you can take either of two routes:

- In Windows Update, click Advanced Options, and then click View Your Update History. Click the link below an item for a brief description, and in the box that pops up click the Support Info link for details. Also notice that each item in the list includes a KB (knowledge base) number. You can get detailed information about the update and the problem it addresses by going to *https://support.microsoft.com/kb/nnnnnnn/*, replacing *nnnnnnn* with the seven-digit number following "KB."

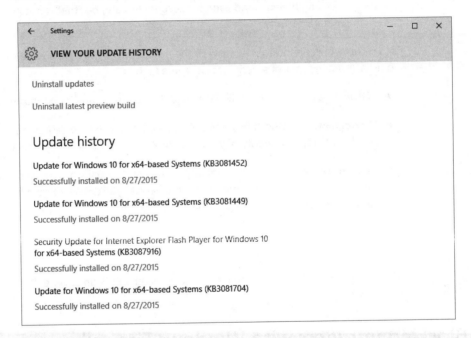

- Visit the Security Advisories and Bulletins page (*w7io.com/0702*). Here you'll find links to chronologically ordered information (most recent first) in the following formats:

  - **Security bulletin summaries.** A single document is published each month containing a complete list of security bulletins published during that month. For each bulletin in the list, you'll find a title and an executive summary, a severity rating (see the following page for more information about these ratings), a list of affected software, and a link to the bulletin.

    You can go directly to a security bulletin summary using this URL: https://technet.microsoft.com/library/security/ms*yy-mmm*/, replacing *yy* with the last two digits of the year (for example, use 15 for 2015) and *mmm* with the standard three-letter abbreviation for the month (for example, use "nov" for November).

- **Security bulletins.** Each bulletin contains detailed information about the issue, including a complete list—with version numbers—of software affected by the threat and, for each affected version, an assessment of the severity. Each security bulletin is assigned a name in the following format: MS*yy-nnn*, where *yy* is the last two digits of the year and *nnn* is a consecutive number that starts with 001 each year. For example, the twenty-seventh security bulletin of 2015 is called MS15-027.

  You can go directly to a security bulletin by appending the bulletin number to this URL: *https://technet.microsoft.com/library/security/*.

- **Security advisories.** Advisories describe security issues that might not require a security bulletin (and with it, a security update) but that can still affect your computer's security.

Each security bulletin includes a rating of the threat's severity. These are the four ratings that are used, listed in order of severity (most severe first):

- **Critical.** A critical vulnerability can lead to code execution with no user interaction.

- **Important.** An important vulnerability is one that can be exploited to compromise the confidentiality or integrity of your data or to cause a denial of service attack.

- **Moderate.** A moderate vulnerability is one that is usually mitigated by default settings and authentication requirements. In other words, you'd have to go a bit out of your way for one of these to damage your system or your data.

- **Low.** A vulnerability identified as low usually requires extensive interaction or an unusual configuration to cause damage.

For more information about these ratings, see "Security Bulletin Severity Rating System" at *w7io.com/0703*.

Blocking intruders with Windows Firewall

Typically, the first line of defense in securing your computer is to protect it from attacks by outsiders. Once your computer is connected to the Internet, it becomes just another node on a huge global network. A firewall provides a barrier between your computer and the network to which it's connected by preventing the entry of unwanted traffic while allowing transparent passage to authorized connections.

Using a firewall is simple, essential, and often overlooked. You'll want to be sure that all network connections are protected by a firewall. You might be comforted by the knowledge that your portable computer is protected by a corporate firewall when you're at work and that you use a firewalled broadband connection at home. But what about the public hotspots you use when you travel?

And it makes sense to run a firewall on your computer even when you're behind a residential router or corporate firewall. Other people on your network might not be as vigilant as you are about defending against viruses, so if someone brings in a portable computer infected with a worm and connects it to the network, you're toast—unless your network connection has its own firewall protection.

Windows includes a two-way, stateful-inspection, packet-filtering firewall called, cleverly enough, Windows Firewall. Windows Firewall is enabled by default for all connections, and it begins protecting your computer as it boots. The following actions take place by default:

- The firewall blocks all inbound traffic, with the exception of traffic sent in response to a request sent by your computer and unsolicited traffic that has been explicitly allowed by creating a rule.

- All outgoing traffic is allowed unless it matches a configured rule.

You notice nothing if a packet is dropped, but you can (at your option) create a log of all such events.

Using Windows Firewall with different network types

Windows Firewall maintains a separate profile (that is, a complete collection of settings, including rules for various programs, services, and ports) for each of three network types:

- **Domain.** Used when your computer is joined to an Active Directory domain. In this environment, firewall settings are typically (but not necessarily) controlled by a network administrator.

- **Private.** Used when your computer is connected to a home or work network in a workgroup configuration.

- **Guest or public.** Used when your computer is connected to a network in a public location, such as an airport or a library. It's common—indeed, recommended—to have fewer allowed programs and more restrictions when you use a public network.

If you're simultaneously connected to more than one network (for example, if you have a Wi-Fi connection to your home network while you're connected to your work domain through a virtual private network, or VPN, connection), Windows uses the appropriate profile for each connection with a feature called multiple active firewall profiles (MAFP).

You make settings in Windows Firewall independently for each network profile. The settings in a profile apply to all networks of the particular type to which you connect. (For example, if you allow a program through the firewall while connected to a public network, that program rule is then enabled whenever you connect to any other public network. It is not enabled when you're connected to a domain or private network unless you allow the program in those profiles.)

CHAPTER 7

➤ **For more information about network types, see "Setting network locations" in Chapter 5.**

Managing Windows Firewall

Windows Firewall is a Control Panel application that provides a simple interface for monitoring firewall status and performing routine tasks, such as allowing a program through the firewall or blocking all incoming connections. To open Windows Firewall, type **firewall** in the search box or in Control Panel. Click Windows Firewall to display a window similar to the one shown in Figure 7-4.

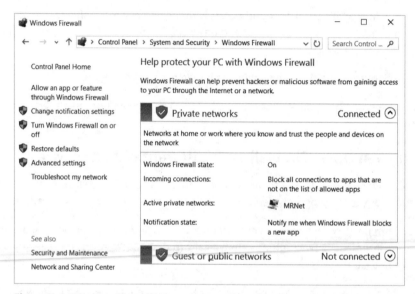

Figure 7-4 Windows Firewall shows status and settings for each currently connected network. The Domain Networks profile appears only on computers that have been joined to a domain.

Enabling or disabling Windows Firewall

The main Windows Firewall application, shown in Figure 7-4, is little more than a status window and launch pad for making various firewall settings. The first setting of interest is to enable or disable Windows Firewall. To do that, click Turn Windows Firewall On Or Off to open the screen shown next. From here you can enable (turn on) or disable (turn off) Windows Firewall for each network type. In general, the only reason to turn off Windows Firewall is if you have installed a third-party firewall that you plan to use instead of Windows Firewall. Most of those, however, perform this task as part of their installation.

As you'll discover throughout Windows Firewall, domain network settings are available only on computers that are joined to a domain. You can make settings for all network types—even those to which you're not currently connected. Settings for the domain profile, however, are often locked down by the network administrator using Group Policy.

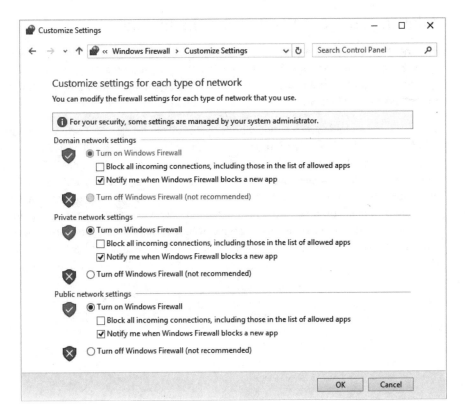

The Block All Incoming Connections check box in Customize Settings provides additional safety. When it's selected, Windows Firewall rejects all unsolicited incoming traffic—even traffic from allowed programs or that would ordinarily be permitted by a rule. (For information about firewall rules, see the next section, "Allowing connections through the firewall.") Invoke this mode when extra security against outside attack is needed. For example, you might block all connections when you're using a public wireless hotspot or when you know that your computer is actively under attack by others.

NOTE

Selecting Block All Incoming Connections does not disconnect your computer from the Internet. Even in this mode, you can still use your browser to connect to the Internet. Similarly, other outbound connections—whether they're legitimate services or some sort of spyware—continue unabated. If you really want to sever your ties to the outside world, open Network And Sharing Center and disable each network connection. (Alternatively, use brute force: physically disconnect wired network connections and turn off wireless adapters or access points.)

Allowing connections through the firewall

In some situations, you want to allow other computers to initiate a connection to your computer. For example, you might use Remote Desktop, play multiplayer games, or chat via an instant messaging program; these types of programs typically require inbound connections so that others can contact you.

The simplest way to enable a connection is to click Allow An App Or Feature Through Windows Firewall, a link in the left pane of the main Windows Firewall window. The list of programs and features that initially appears in Allowed Apps, shown in Figure 7-5, depends on which programs and services are installed on your computer; you can add others, as described in the following sections. In addition, program rules are created (but not enabled) when a program tries to set up an incoming connection. To allow connections for a program or service that's already been defined, simply select its check box for each network type on which you want to allow the program. (You'll need to click Change Settings before you can make changes.)

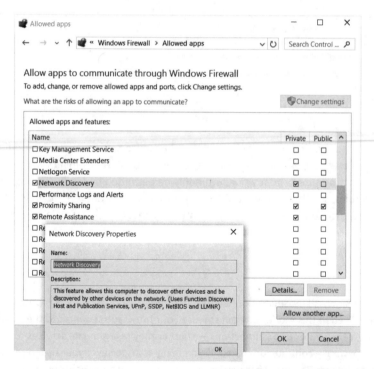

Figure 7-5 Selecting an item and clicking Details displays a description of the program or service.

In each of these cases, you enable a rule in Windows Firewall that pokes a small hole in the firewall and allows a certain type of traffic to pass through it. Each rule of this type increases your security risk to some degree, so you should clear the check box for all programs you don't need. If you're confident you won't ever need a particular program, you can select it and then click Remove. (Many of the list items included with Windows don't allow deletion, but as long as their check boxes are not selected, these apps present no danger.)

The first time you run a program that tries to set up an incoming connection, Windows Firewall asks for your permission by displaying a dialog box. You can add the program to the allowed programs list by clicking Allow Access.

When such a dialog box appears, read it carefully:

- Is the program one that you knowingly installed and ran?

- Is it reasonable for the program to require acceptance of incoming connections?

- Are you currently using a network type where it's okay for this program to accept incoming connections?

If the answer to any of these questions is no—or if you're unsure—click Cancel. If you later find that a needed program isn't working properly, you can open the allowed apps list in Windows Firewall and enable the rule.

Alternatively, you can set up the program from the Allowed Apps window shown in Figure 7-5 without waiting for a Windows Security Alert dialog box to appear. Follow these steps:

1. Click Allow Another App. The Add An App dialog box appears.

2. In Add An App, select the program for which you want to allow incoming connections. Or click Browse and navigate to the program's executable file if it isn't shown in the Apps list.

3. Click Network Types.

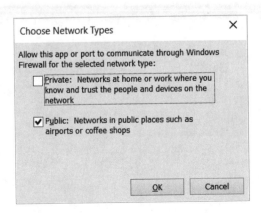

4. Select the network types on which you want to allow the program, click OK, and then click Add. (You can also select network types in Allowed Apps after you add the program.)

Restoring default settings

If you've played around a bit with Windows Firewall and perhaps allowed connections that you should not have, you can get back to a known secure state by clicking Restore Defaults in Windows Firewall. Be aware that doing so removes all rules that you've added for all programs. Although this gives you a secure setup, you might find that some of your network-connected programs no longer work properly. As that occurs, you can add again each legitimate program that needs to be allowed, as described on the previous pages.

Advanced tools for managing Windows Firewall

If you have any experience at all configuring firewalls, you'll quickly realize that the Windows Firewall application in Control Panel covers only the most basic tasks. Don't take that as an indication that Windows Firewall is underpowered. To the contrary, you can configure all manner of firewall rules, allowing or blocking traffic based on program, port, protocol, IP address, and so on. In addition, you can enable, disable, and monitor rules; configure logging; and much more. With advanced tools, you can also configure Windows Firewall on remote workstations. Because the interface to these advanced features is rather daunting, Windows Firewall provides the simplified interface described earlier. It's adequate not only for less experienced users, but also for performing the routine firewall tasks needed by information technology (IT) professionals and others.

Nonetheless, our tour of security essentials would not be complete without a visit to Windows Firewall With Advanced Security, a snap-in and predefined console for Microsoft Management Console (MMC) that offers granular control over rules, exceptions, and profiles. To open it, in Windows Firewall click Advanced Settings. Windows Firewall With Advanced Security appears, as shown in Figure 7-6.

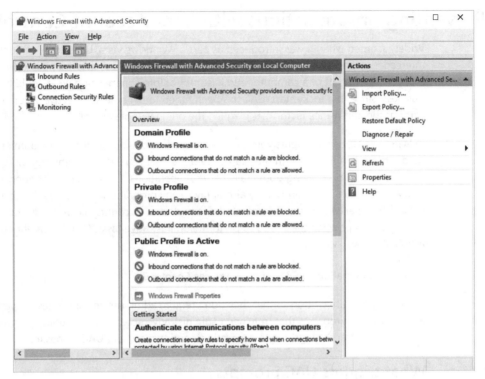

Figure 7-6 In the left pane, click Inbound Rules or Outbound Rules to view, configure, create, and delete firewall rules. The Domain Profile appears even on a computer that is not part of a Windows domain.

The initial view presents information similar to that shown in Windows Firewall. Go just a few steps farther into the cave, however, and you could be lost in no time. The "Windows Firewall with Advanced Security Getting Started Guide" can brighten your path; view it at *w7io.com/1502*. For additional details, see "Using Windows Firewall with Advanced Security" at *w7io.com/0701*.

Inside OUT

Open Windows Firewall With Advanced Security directly

You don't need to open Windows Firewall to get to Windows Firewall With Advanced Security. In the search box, type wf.msc and press Ctrl+Shift+Enter to run it as an administrator.

Preventing unsafe actions with User Account Control

Widely scorned when it was introduced as part of Windows Vista, User Account Control (UAC) intercedes whenever a user or program attempts to perform a system administrative task and asks for the consent of a computer administrator before commencing what could be risky business. Since that rocky start, UAC has been tuned to become an effective security aid— without the annoyance factor that plagued the original implementation.

In Windows 10, user accounts you set up after the first one are standard (nonadministrator) accounts by default; although they can carry out all the usual daily computing tasks, they're prevented from performing potentially harmful operations. These restrictions apply not just to the user; more importantly, they also apply to any programs launched by the user. Even administrator accounts run as "protected administrator" accounts allowed only standard-user privileges except when they need to perform administrative tasks. (This is sometimes called Admin Approval Mode.)

> ➤ **For information about user accounts, see Chapter 6.**

Most programs are written so that they don't require administrator privileges for performing everyday tasks. Programs that truly need administrative access (such as utility programs that change computer settings) request elevation—and that's where UAC comes in.

What triggers UAC prompts

The types of actions that require elevation to administrator status (and therefore display a UAC elevation prompt) include those that make changes to system-wide settings or to files in %SystemRoot% or %ProgramFiles%. (On a default Windows installation, these environment variables represent C:\Windows and C:\Program Files, respectively.) Among the actions that require elevation are the following:

- Installing and uninstalling desktop applications

- Installing device drivers that are not included in Windows or provided through Windows Update

- Installing ActiveX controls

- Changing settings for Windows Firewall

- Changing UAC settings

- Configuring Windows Update

- Adding or removing user accounts

- Changing a user's account type

- Running Task Scheduler

- Restoring backed-up system files

- Viewing or changing another user's folders and files

Within Windows, you can identify in advance many actions that require elevation. A shield icon next to a button or link indicates that a UAC prompt will appear if you're using a standard account.

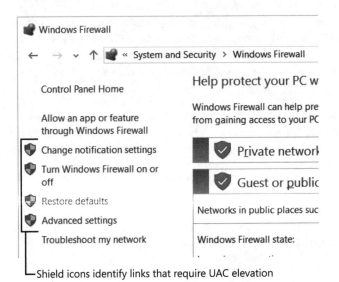

Shield icons identify links that require UAC elevation

If you sign in with an administrator account (and if you leave the default UAC settings unchanged), you'll see fewer consent prompts than if you use a standard account. That's because the default setting prompts only when a program tries to install software or make other changes to the computer, but not when you make changes to Windows settings—even those that would trigger a prompt for a standard user with default UAC settings. Windows uses autoelevation to elevate without prompting certain programs that are part of Windows. Programs that are elevated automatically are from a predefined list, they must be digitally signed by the Windows publisher, and they must be stored in certain secure folders.

Limitations of User Account Control

User Account Control isn't a security silver bullet. It's one layer of a defense-in-depth strategy.

Some Windows users assume that UAC consent dialog boxes represent a security boundary. They don't. They simply represent a place for an administrator to make a trust decision. If a bad guy uses social engineering to convince you that you need his program, you've already made a trust decision. You'll click at least a half-dozen times to download, save, and launch the bad guy's program. A UAC consent request is perfectly normal in this sequence, so why wouldn't you click one more time?

If this scenario bothers you, the obvious solution is to adjust UAC to its highest level. Among other changes, this setting disables the autoelevation behavior. (For details on how to do this, see "Modifying UAC settings" later in this chapter.) If a program tries to use this subterfuge to sneak system changes past you, you'll see an unexpected consent dialog box from the system. But as soon as you provide those elevated credentials, the code can do anything it wants.

A better alternative is to sign in using a standard account, which provides a real security boundary. A standard user who does not have the administrator password can make changes only in her own user profile, protecting the system from unintended tampering.

Even running as a standard user doesn't provide complete protection. Malware can be installed in your user profile without triggering any system alarms. It can log your keystrokes, steal your passwords, and send out email using your identity. Even if you reset UAC to its highest level, you could fall victim to malware that lies in wait for you to elevate your privileges and then does its own dirty work alongside you.

As we said, enabling UAC is only one part of a multilayered security strategy. It works best when supplemented by a healthy skepticism and up-to-date antimalware software.

Dealing with UAC prompts

At sign-in, Windows creates a token that is used to identify the privilege levels of your account. Standard users get a standard token, but administrators actually get two: a standard token and an administrator token. The standard token is used to open Explorer.exe (the Windows shell), from which all subsequent programs are launched. Child processes inherit the token of the process that launches them, so by default all applications run as a standard user—even when you're signed in with an administrator account. Certain programs request elevation to administrator privileges; that's when the UAC prompt is displayed. If you provide administrator credentials, Windows then uses the administrator token to open the program. Note that any processes that the successfully elevated program opens also run as an administrator.

As an elevation-requesting application attempts to open, UAC evaluates the application and the request and then displays an appropriate prompt. As an administrator, the most common prompt you're likely to see is the consent prompt, which is shown in Figure 7-7. Read it, check the name of the program, click Yes if you're confident that it's safe to proceed, and carry on.

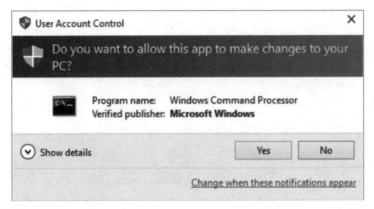

Figure 7-7 Clicking Show Details displays a link to the program's certificate.

If you use a standard account, when a program requires elevation you'll see the credentials prompt, which is shown in Figure 7-8. If the user is able to provide the credentials (that is, user name and password, smart card, or fingerprint, depending on how sign-in authentication is configured on the computer) of an administrator, the application opens using the administrator's access token.

By default, the UAC dialog box sits atop the secure desktop, a darkened representation of your desktop that runs in a separate process that no other application can interfere with. (If the secure desktop wasn't secure, a malicious program could put another dialog box in front of the UAC dialog box, perhaps with a message encouraging you to let the program proceed. Or a malicious program could grab your keystrokes, thereby learning your administrator sign-in password.) When the secure desktop is displayed, you can't switch tasks or click the windows on the desktop. (In fact, they're not really windows. When UAC invokes the secure desktop, it snaps a picture of the desktop, darkens it, and then displays that image behind the dialog box.)

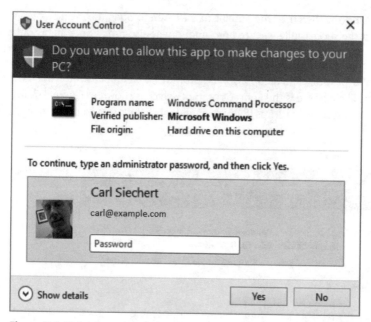

Figure 7-8 To perform an administrative task, a standard user must enter the password for an administrator account.

TROUBLESHOOTING

There's a delay before the secure desktop appears

On some systems, you have to wait a few seconds before the screen darkens and the UAC prompt appears on the secure desktop. There's no easy way to solve the slow-down, but you can easily work around it. In User Account Control Settings (described in the next section, "Modifying UAC settings"), you can take the protection level down a notch. The setting below the default provides the same level of UAC protection (albeit with a slight risk that malware could hijack the desktop), except that it does not dim the desktop.

NOTE

If an application other than the foreground application requests elevation, instead of interrupting your work (the foreground task) with a prompt, UAC signals its request with a flashing taskbar button. Click the taskbar button to see the prompt.

It becomes natural to click through dialog boxes without reading them or giving them a second thought. But it's important to recognize that security risks to your computer are real and that actions that trigger a UAC prompt are potentially dangerous. Clearly, if you know what you're doing and you click a button to, say, change Windows Update settings, you can blow past that security dialog box with no more than a quick glance to be sure it was raised by the expected application. But if a UAC prompt appears when you're not expecting it—stop, read it carefully, and think before you click.

Modifying UAC settings

To review your User Account Control options and make changes to the way it works, in the search box or in Control Panel, type **uac** and then click Change User Account Control Settings. A window similar to the one shown in Figure 7-9 appears.

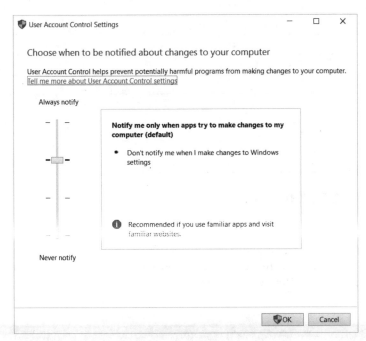

Figure 7-9 The topmost setting might overwhelm you with UAC prompts; the bottom setting turns off UAC.

Your choices in this window vary slightly depending on whether you use an administrator account or a standard account. For standard accounts, the top setting is the default; for administrator accounts, the second setting from the top is the default. Table 7-1 summarizes the available options.

To make changes, move the slider to the position you want. Be sure to take note of the advisory message in the bottom of the box as you move the slider. Click OK when you're done—and then respond to the UAC prompt that appears! Note that when you're signed in with a standard account, you can't select one of the bottom two options, even if you have the password for an administrator account. To select one of those options, you must sign in as an administrator and then make the change.

Table 7-1 User Account Control settings

Slider position	Prompts when a program tries to install software or make changes to the computer	Prompts when you make changes to Windows settings	Displays prompts on a secure desktop
Standard user account			
Top (default)	✔	✔	✔
Second	✔	✔	
Third	✔		
Bottom (off)			
Administrator account			
Top	✔	✔	✔
Second (default)	✔		✔
Third	✔		
Bottom (off)			

TROUBLESHOOTING

User Account Control settings don't stick

If you find that nothing happens when you make a change to User Account Control settings, be sure that you're the only one signed in to your computer. Simultaneous sign-ins that use Fast User Switching can cause this problem.

Inside OUT

Use Local Security Policy to customize UAC behavior

Users of the Pro and Enterprise editions of Windows 10 can use the Local Security Policy console to modify the behavior of UAC. Start Local Security Policy (Secpol.msc), and open Security Settings\Local Policies\Security Options. In the details pane, scroll down to the policies whose names begin with "User Account Control." For each policy, double-click it and then click the Explain tab for information before you decide on a setting. With these policies, you can make several refinements in the way UAC works—including some that are not possible in the User Account Control Settings window. (Administrators on Windows-based enterprise networks can also configure these options using Group Policy management tools.) For details about each of these policies, see "UAC Group Policy Settings" at *w7io.com/1523*.

Regardless of your UAC setting, the shield icons still appear throughout Control Panel, but you won't see UAC prompts if you've lowered the UAC protection level. Clicking a button or link identified with a shield immediately begins the action. Administrators run with full administrator privileges; standard users, of course, still have only standard privileges.

CAUTION

Don't forget that UAC is more than annoying prompts. Only when UAC is enabled does an administrator run with a standard token. Only when UAC is enabled does Internet Explorer run in a low-privilege Protected Mode. Only when UAC is enabled does it warn you when a rogue application attempts to perform a task with system-wide impact. And, of course, disabling UAC also disables file and registry virtualization, which can cause compatibility problems with applications that use fixes provided by the UAC feature. For these reasons, we urge you not to select the bottom option in User Account Control Settings, which turns off UAC completely.

Encrypting information

Windows provides the following encryption tools for preventing the loss of confidential data:

- Encrypting File System (EFS) encodes your files so that even if someone is able to obtain the files, he or she won't be able to read them. The files are readable only when you sign in to the computer using your user account.

- BitLocker Drive Encryption provides another layer of protection by encrypting entire hard-disk volumes. By linking this encryption to a key stored in a Trusted Platform Module (TPM) or USB flash drive, BitLocker reduces the risk of data being lost when a computer is stolen or when a hard disk is stolen and placed in another computer. A thief's standard approach in these situations is to boot into an alternate operating system and then try to retrieve data from the stolen computer or drive. With BitLocker, that type of offline attack is effectively neutered.

- BitLocker To Go extends BitLocker encryption to removable media, such as USB flash drives.

NOTE

Encrypting File System and BitLocker Drive Encryption are not available in Windows 10 Home. Encrypting a removable drive with BitLocker To Go requires Windows 10 Pro or Windows 10 Enterprise; the resulting encrypted drive can be opened and used on a device running Windows 10 Home.

Using the Encrypting File System

The Encrypting File System (EFS) provides a secure way to store your sensitive data. Windows creates a randomly generated file encryption key (FEK) and then transparently encrypts the data, using this FEK, as the data is being written to disk. Windows then encrypts the FEK using your public key. (Windows creates a personal encryption certificate with a public/private key pair for you the first time you use EFS.) The FEK, and therefore the data it encrypts, can be decrypted only with your certificate and its associated private key, which are available only when you sign in with your user account. (Designated data recovery agents can also decrypt your data.) Other users who attempt to use your encrypted files receive an "access denied" message. Even administrators and others who have permission to take ownership of files are unable to open your encrypted files.

You can encrypt individual files, folders, or entire drives. (You cannot encrypt the boot volume—the one with the Windows operating system files—using EFS, however. For that, you must use BitLocker.) We recommend that you encrypt folders or drives instead of individual files. When you encrypt a folder or drive, the files it contains are encrypted, and new files that you create in that folder or drive are encrypted automatically.

To encrypt a folder, follow these steps:

1.   In File Explorer, right-click the folder, choose Properties, click the General tab, and then click Advanced, which displays the dialog box shown next. (If the properties dialog box doesn't have an Advanced button, the folder is not on an NTFS-formatted volume and you can't use EFS.)

2. Select Encrypt Contents To Secure Data. (Note that you can't encrypt compressed files. If the files are already compressed, Windows clears the compressed attribute.)

3. Click OK twice. If the folder contains any files or subfolders, Windows then displays a confirmation message.

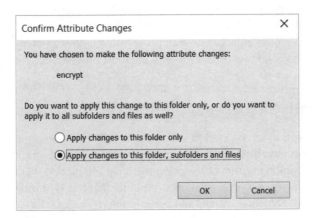

NOTE

If you select Apply Changes To This Folder Only, Windows doesn't encrypt any of the files currently in the folder. Any new files that you create in the folder, however, including files that you copy or move to the folder, will be encrypted.

After a file or folder has been encrypted, File Explorer displays its name in green. This minor cosmetic detail is the only change you are likely to notice. Windows decrypts your files on the fly as you use them and reencrypts them when you save.

CAUTION

Before you encrypt anything important, you should back up your file recovery certificate and your personal encryption certificate (with their associated private keys), as well as the data recovery agent certificate, to a USB flash drive or to your OneDrive. Store the flash drive in a secure location. To do this, open User Accounts in Control Panel, and then click Manage Your File Encryption Certificates. If you ever lose the certificate stored on your hard drive (because of a disk failure, for example), you can restore the backup copy and regain access to your files. If you lose all copies of your certificate (and no data recovery agent certificates exist), you won't be able to use your encrypted files. No backdoor exists (none that we know of, at any rate), nor is there any practical way to hack these files. (If there were, it wouldn't be very good encryption.)

To encrypt one or more files, follow the same procedure as for folders. You'll see a different confirmation message to remind you that the file's folder is not encrypted and to give you an opportunity to encrypt it. You generally don't want to encrypt individual files because the information you intend to protect can too easily become decrypted without your knowledge. For example, with some applications, when you open a document for editing, the application creates a copy of the original document. When you save the document after editing, the application saves the copy—which is not encrypted—and deletes the original encrypted document. Static files that you use for reference only—but never for editing—can safely be encrypted without encrypting the parent folder. Even in that situation, however, you'll probably find it simpler to encrypt the whole folder.

Encrypting with BitLocker and BitLocker To Go

BitLocker Drive Encryption can be used to encrypt entire NTFS volumes, which provides excellent protection against data theft. BitLocker can secure a drive against attacks that involve circumventing the operating system or removing the drive and placing it in another computer. BitLocker provides the greatest protection on a computer that has TPM version 1.2 or later; on these systems, the TPM stores the key and ensures that a computer has not been tampered with while offline. If your computer does not have TPM, you can still use BitLocker on your operating system volume, but you must insert a USB startup key or enter a password each time you start the computer or resume from hibernation. Non-TPM systems do not get the system integrity check at startup.

BitLocker To Go, a feature introduced in Windows 7, allows you to encrypt the entire contents of a USB flash drive or other removable device. If it's lost or stolen, the thief will be unable to access the data without the password.

To apply BitLocker Drive Encryption or BitLocker To Go, right-click the drive in File Explorer and then click Turn On BitLocker. BitLocker asks how you want to unlock the encrypted drive—with a password, a smart card, or both. After you have made your selections and confirmed your intentions, the software gives you the opportunity to save and print your recovery key, as shown in Figure 7-10.

Your recovery key is a system-generated, 48-character, numeric backup password. If you lose the password you assign to the encrypted disk, you can recover your data with the recovery key. BitLocker offers to save that key in a plain text file; you should accept the offer and store the file in a secure location.

CHAPTER 7

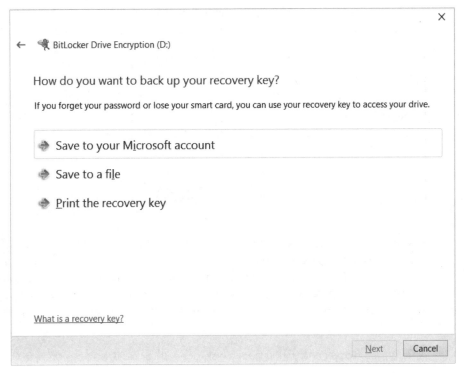

Figure 7-10 The option of saving the recovery key to your Microsoft account—that is, to your OneDrive—is new with Windows 10.

Inside OUT

Store your recovery keys on OneDrive

Clicking **Save To Your Microsoft Account** saves the recovery key on your OneDrive, making it accessible anywhere you have an Internet connection. But the trick is finding that key on OneDrive: Go to *onedrive.com/recoverykey*.

With all preliminaries out of the way, BitLocker begins encrypting your media. This process takes a few minutes, even if the disk is freshly formatted. However, if you are in a hurry, you can opt to encrypt only the used space on the drive. This choice can save you a considerable amount of time if your disk contains only a small number of files.

To read a BitLocker-encrypted removable disk, you need to unlock it by using whatever method you have stipulated. If you're prompted for a password that you have lost or forgotten, click More Options and then click Enter Recovery Key. In case you have several recovery-key text files, BitLocker To Go gives you the key's identification code:

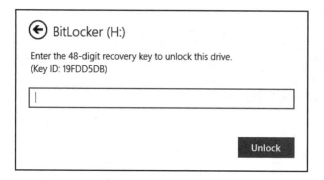

Find the entry on OneDrive (*onedrive.com/recoverykey*) or the text file whose name matches the identification code, copy the recovery key from this text file to the BitLocker dialog box, and you'll be granted temporary access to the files, which is good until you remove the disk or restart the computer. At this point, you might want to change the password; open BitLocker Drive Encryption in the System And Security section of Control Panel and click Change Password.

To remove BitLocker encryption from a disk, open BitLocker Drive Encryption in Control Panel and click Turn Off BitLocker. The software will decrypt the disk; allow some time for this process.

> ➤ For more information about BitLocker, see *bit.ly/bitlocker-overview*.

Using Windows Defender to block malware

The best way to fight unwanted and malicious software is to keep it from being installed on any PC that is part of your network. Over the years, malicious hackers have found a variety of ways to install malware: floppy disks, document files, email attachments, instant messaging attachments, AutoPlay on USB flash drives, scripts, browser add-ons . . . and the list goes on. Many of these transmission methods rely on social-engineering techniques designed to lure inattentive or gullible users into opening an infected attachment, visiting an infected website, and so on. Not satisfied with being able to pick off the inattentive and gullible, authors of hostile software are always on the lookout for techniques they can use to spread infections automatically.

Any program that tries to sneak onto your PC without your full knowledge and consent should be blocked. An important layer in a basic PC protection strategy, therefore, is to use up-to-date antimalware software. Into the breach steps Windows Defender, the antimalware program included in Windows 10.

Windows Defender runs as a system service and uses a scanning engine to compare files against a database of virus and spyware definitions. It also uses heuristic analysis of the behavior of programs to flag suspicious activity from a file that isn't included in the list of known threats. It scans each file that you access in any way, including downloads from the Internet and email attachments you receive. (This feature is called *real-time protection*—not to be confused with scheduled *scans*, which periodically inspect all files stored on your computer to root out malware.)

Using Windows Defender

In general, you don't need to "use" Windows Defender at all. As a system service, it works quietly in the background. The only time you'll know it's there is if it finds an infected file; one or more notifications will pop up to alert you to the fact.

Nonetheless, you might want to poke around a bit. To open Windows Defender, type **defender** in the search box, and click the program's shortcut. If a shortcut to Windows Defender doesn't appear or if you don't have a keyboard, open Settings, tap Update & Security, tap Windows Defender, scroll all the way to the bottom, and tap Use Windows Defender.

The Home tab, shown in Figure 7-11, shows the current status and the results of the most recent scan. This tab also tells you whether real-time protection is enabled.

Figure 7-11 The Home tab provides status and a launch pad for manual scans.

To temporarily disable real-time protection (if it is interfering with the installation of a legitimate program, for example), click Settings to open a window in which you can turn off real-time protection. Doing so causes the PC Status banner at the top of the program window to glow red and change from Protected to At Risk; a large Turn On button dominates the Home tab. Windows Defender is so anxious to restore real-time protection, in fact, that it automatically turns it back on when you restart your computer or after some time elapses.

Windows Defender uses Windows Update to retrieve definition files and periodic updates to the detection engine. The Update tab in Windows Defender shows when the definitions were last updated and also features an Update button in case you want to get the latest definitions immediately instead of waiting for Windows Update.

Manually scanning for malware

The combination of real-time protection and periodic scheduled scanning is normally sufficient for identifying and resolving problems with malware and spyware. However, if you suspect that you've been infected, you can initiate a scan on demand. To immediately scan for problems, on the Home tab (see Figure 7-11) under Scan Options, select the type of scan you want to perform and click Scan Now.

The Quick option kicks off a scan that checks only the places on your computer that malware and spyware are most likely to infect, and it is the recommended setting for frequent regular scans. Choose Full if you suspect infection (or you just want reassurance that your system is clean) and want to inspect all running programs and the complete contents of all local volumes. Click Custom if you want to restrict the scan to any combination of drives, folders, and files.

Inside OUT

Run a scan from a script or a scheduled task

Windows Defender includes a command-line utility that you can use to automate scans with a script or a scheduled task. You'll find MpCmdRun.exe in %ProgramFiles%\Windows Defender. For details about using the utility, open an elevated Command Prompt window and run the program with no parameters.

A full scan can be burdensome, especially if you have hundreds of thousands of files scattered around local disks. To minimize the time and system resources, you can specify that Windows Defender skip over locations and file types that you know are safe and haven't been tampered with. To do that, begin by clicking Settings. On the Windows Defender tab in Settings, click Add An Exclusion (under Exclusions) to display a window like the one shown in Figure 7-12.

Figure 7-12 Files, folders, file types, and processes that are excluded are ignored during scans. Click the plus icon to add items to the exclusion list.

There you'll find four options that affect scanning:

- **Exclude A File.** Specify files that you know to be safe.

- **Exclude A Folder.** Specify folders that you know to be safe. This is an appropriate option if you have a folder full of previously downloaded system utilities that routinely trigger alerts. Do not use this option with folders where you normally download new files.

- **Exclude A File Extension.** Similarly, you can exclude from scans all files with the file name extensions (such as common scripts) that you specify.

- **Exclude A .Exe, .Com Or .Scr Process.** If you find that a program is routinely detected as a potential threat despite your telling Windows Defender to allow it, consider adding the program to this list. Be sure to specify the process name (Myprogram.exe) and not the program name. This strategy is less risky than excluding the containing folder;

if you grant blanket approval for files in the containing folder, and later some real spyware ends up in the folder, you risk allowing malware to sneak onto your system with no warning.

To delete an exclusion (so it will no longer be excluded from scans), return to Add An Exclusion, click or tap the name of the exclusion you want to delete, and click Remove.

Dealing with detected threats

If Windows Defender detects the presence of malware or spyware as part of its real-time protection, it displays a warning above the notification area and, in most cases, resolves the problem without you lifting a finger.

To learn more about its findings, in Windows Defender click the History tab. Select Quarantined Items, and then click View Details. As Figure 7-13 shows, Windows Defender shows the name, alert level, and detection date of the quarantined item or items.

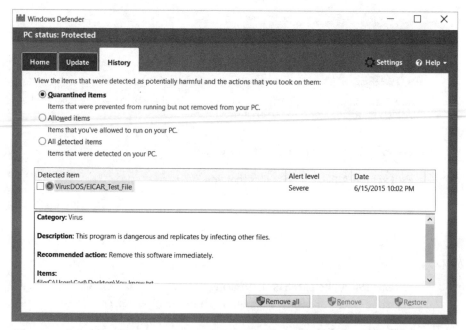

Figure 7-13 The box below the list shows details about the selected item; a link at the bottom of that box (not shown) leads to online information about the particular infection.

Detected items are moved to a restricted folder (%ProgramData%\Microsoft\Windows Defender\Quarantine) whose permissions include a Deny access control entry that locks out the built-in Users and Everyone groups. Executable files in this folder cannot be run, nor can the folder's contents be accessed from File Explorer. Items moved here can be managed only from the Windows Defender console (preferred) or an elevated Command Prompt window.

Stopping unknown or malicious programs with SmartScreen

SmartScreen, which began as a feature in Internet Explorer in Windows 7, is used to identify programs that other users have run safely. It does so by comparing a hash of a downloaded program with Microsoft's application-reputation database. This occurs when you download a program using Microsoft Edge or Internet Explorer, and when you attempt to run a program that you have downloaded from the Internet—regardless of what browser you use.

Programs with a positive reputation run without any ado. Programs that are known to be bad or that have not yet developed a reputation are blocked. A message similar to the one shown in Figure 7-14 appears.

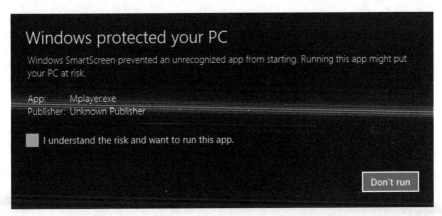

Figure 7-14 When you attempt to run a downloaded program that doesn't match one in Microsoft's database, a message like this appears.

If you're certain that a program is safe, you can override the block by selecting the check box, which adds a Run Anyway button you can then click. With default settings in place, you'll then need the approval of someone with an administrator account before the program runs. Don't say you weren't warned.

You can adjust the level of SmartScreen protection by going to Security And Maintenance (see Figure 7-1 earlier in this chapter) and clicking Change Windows SmartScreen Settings. Besides the default setting, you can remove the requirement for administrator approval or you can disable SmartScreen altogether.

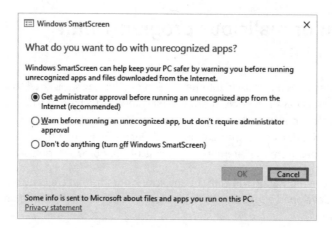

PART 2

Working and playing with Windows 10

Using and managing modern apps and desktop programs

As the title of this chapter suggests, the programs you can run on Windows 10 fall into two broad categories. One category consists of so-called desktop applications. These are the programs that you may have and could have run under Windows 7 and earlier versions. Windows 10 continues to support such programs. (You may also see these programs described as Win32 applications.) These traditional applications are designed, for the most part, for use with a keyboard and a mouse, and many of them first came into being during the era when desktop machines dominated the computing landscape.

The other category consists of programs delivered through the Windows Store. These programs, optimized for touch and mobile use (although equally usable on desktop systems with traditional input devices) are variously called *modern apps, trusted Windows Store apps,* or *UWP apps*. Windows favors the term *Trusted Windows Store apps*. If you enter the name of one of these programs in the search box on your taskbar, you will see something like the following:

Photos
Trusted Windows Store app

In this book, for the sake of simplicity, we use the designation *modern app*, but Windows opts for the wordier handle for good reason. These apps, available only through the Windows Store, have passed a stringent vetting process and can be trusted to be free of malware. They are also "sandboxed," which means they run in secure isolation, free from potentially hazardous interactions with other running processes.

The current name for the development platform is *Universal Windows Platform*, or *UWP*. The keyword here is *universal*. The platform offers a core application programming interface (API) that allows developers to create a single app package that can be installed on devices with a wide range of sizes and modalities, with adaptive controls that tailor the app to the size and feature set of the target machine. In short, a program you download from the Windows Store to your tablet is likely to work as well on your traditional desktop machine, your all-in-one, your Xbox console, your phone, and your notebook PC.

What's in a modern app

Here are some important characteristics of modern apps:

- **Tiles.** Each app gets a tile, which can be displayed on the Start menu or not, as you choose. To add an app to the Start menu, press the Windows key, click or tap All Apps, right-click the name of the app, and choose Pin To Start Menu. (Similar steps allow you to pin an app to the taskbar or to unpin an app from either location.)

- **Live tiles.** Tiles can be programmed to update dynamically when they're displayed on the Start menu—that is, they can become *live tiles*. Live tiles can, for example, display news headlines, cycle through a set of photos, show calendar information, and so on. If you find a tile to be livelier than you would like, you can render it inanimate by right-clicking it and then clicking Turn Live Tile Off.

- **Notifications and alerts.** Apps can trigger notifications and alerts. To take one example, your calendar app can display appointment information on your lock screen and issue reminders at the appropriate times.

- **Cortana.** Apps can be integrated with Cortana, allowing you to do such things as issue a voice command to send an email.

- **Security and safety.** Modern apps are prevented from accessing system resources. They also don't store their own configuration information in publicly accessible places, such as .ini files.

- **The ability to run without administrative consent.** Because modern apps are certified to be free of potential hazards, you don't need an administrative token to install or run them. You won't find Run As Administrator on the shortcut menus of modern apps; there is no need for it.

- **Power conservation.** By default, an app is suspended within a few seconds if you move away from it. This behavior is particularly valuable on battery-driven systems such as phones and tablets. Apps can be written to run in the background (allowing you, for example, to play music while you work), but this is an exceptional case.

- **Automatic updates.** Modern apps are updated automatically. The Windows Store manages this process for you when an app's publisher makes changes to a program.

- **Per-user installation.** When you install an app, that app is installed only for your user account. Other account holders who want to use the app have to install it as well. Depending on licensing provisions and the number of devices on which you have installed the app in question, other accounts on a system where an app has already been bought and installed might find, on visiting the Windows Store, that the app is identified as "owned." In that case, these users can install the app without going through a payment process. The same is true for other systems that you sign in to with the Microsoft account under which you bought the app.

- **Display adaptability.** If you have a modern app running on systems with disparate form factors, such as a phone and a notebook, you can easily see how the app adjusts its user interface to accommodate the different screen sizes. With many apps, you can see the same adaptability simply by adjusting window size. For example, if you display a month view in Calendar on a large display and then narrow the window from either side, you will note the following adjustment:

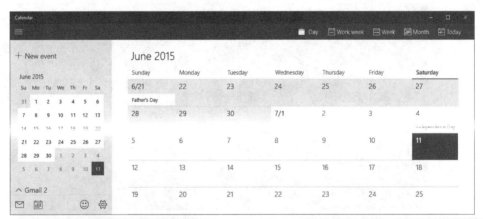

CHAPTER 8

Initially, as you reduce the window's width, Calendar compresses its display but maintains the layout. Eventually, to maintain readability, the program switches to a vertical layout comparable to what you would see on a phone.

Browsing the Windows Store

The Windows Store, much improved and expanded since its debut with Windows 8, is your emporium for games, music, movies, and TV shows, as well as modern Windows apps. The menu across the top of the Windows Store page allows you to switch between these various kinds of offerings. Below the display ad, you'll find some items that the Windows Store thinks you might be interested in, based on what you've downloaded earlier. Farther down is a sort of categorized bestseller list—top free games, games that have received stellar ratings from other users, "new and rising" items, and so on. Figure 8-1 shows how part of the Windows Store appeared on one of our systems around the time of the official launch of Windows 10.

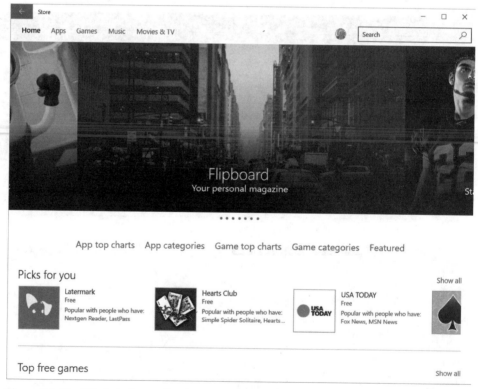

Figure 8-1 The Windows Store offers items it thinks you might want to download given the items you've chosen previously.

If you know more or less what you're looking for, you can use the handy search box to find it. You can search by name or publisher, and the search results will include entertainment offerings (albums and songs, for example), as well as apps.

> ➤ **For information about using the Windows Store to purchase music, movies, and TV shows, see Chapter 10, "Music, photos, movies, and games."**

If you just want to browse, you can start by clicking App Categories. An alphabetized list of categories appears. When you find something of interest, click it to see details. Figure 8-2 shows a sample of the kind of details you might find. Be sure to scroll down to the rating details and reviews.

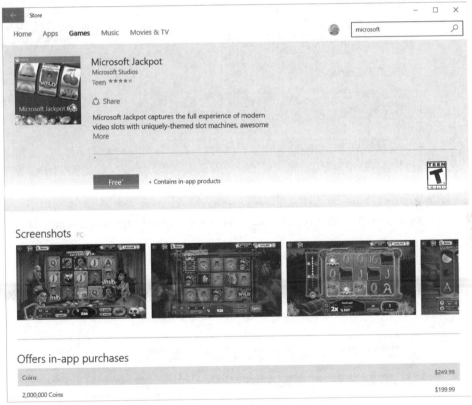

Figure 8-2 The details page for an app shows screen shots, reviews and ratings, and suggestions of what else you might like.

As Figure 8-2 shows, the price for some apps is adorned with an asterisk and the notation that the app comes with "in-app products." This is a delicate way of alerting you that the app, once installed, will be giving you the opportunity to buy extra goodies. Some apps are quite low-key about this; other have been known to be nearly useless without at least some of the extra items. A quick check of the reviews might help you spot an app whose effective price is not what it seems. As Figure 8-3 shows, the details screen should also enumerate the extra offerings:

Offers in-app purchases

Coins	$249.99
2,000,000 Coins	$199.99
900,000 Coins	$99.99
150,000 Coins	$24.99
48,000 Coins	$9.99
20,000 Coins	$4.99
750 Coins	Free

Figure 8-3 The details page for Microsoft Jackpot lists its in-app purchase offerings.

Finding additional information

Scrolling to the bottom of an app's details page reveals some additional useful details:

Features

- Stay up to date with the latest IT Innovations
- Cloud powered modern App provides latest IT Showcase contents leveraging latest Windows features
- Quickly find desired contents using key word search and semantic zoom
- Get Live Notifications, Pin your favorite contents on-to Favorites section for quick access
- Share contents over email, twitter or facebook or save it to OneDrive for any time access
- Read out contents, use app bar to quickly change themes, hide banner and perform more content functions!
- View & access IT Showcase content statistics by media type or by products through Trends Tile
- View localizaed contents specific to regions - click regions under settings to view available regions

Additional information

Published by Microsoft Corporation

Microsoft Corporation

Category
Business

Approximate size 6.9 MB

Age rating For ages 7 and up

Supported processors x86, x64, ARM

Installation Install this app on up to ten Windows 10 devices.

This app has permissions to use
- microphone
- internetClient

Supported languages
English (United States)

Learn more
Microsoft IT Showcase support
Microsoft IT Showcase website

Additional terms
Microsoft IT Showcase privacy policy
Store terms of use

Report this app
Report this app to Microsoft

Items of particular interest here might include the approximate size of the app, the system resources the app is permitted to use (in the example here, the microphone and Internet client), and the number of devices on which the app can be installed.

Buying an app

To begin the process of installing a new app simply click its price. If the app is free (many are), the download and installation process begins at once. If money is required, the payment process is managed through your Microsoft account. (If your Windows 10 user account signs in locally, as opposed to through a Microsoft account, you will be prompted at this point for Microsoft account credentials, and you will be guided to create such an account if you don't already have one.)

While the app is being downloaded and installed, you can follow its progress:

In the progress window, you can also pause or cancel a download. You might want to pause if you have several lengthy downloads going at once and want to prioritize them.

Uninstalling an app

The easiest way to uninstall a modern app is to right-click it on the Start menu or in the All Apps list and then click Uninstall. Because an app is installed per user, uninstalling is as well; if you want to be rid of a program everywhere it has been installed, you need to repeat the procedure to uninstall it.

You can also uninstall both modern and desktop apps by opening Settings, clicking System, and then clicking Apps & Features. The list of installed programs that appears provides useful information about when each app was installed and how much space on disk it is consuming (Figure 8-4). The list includes both modern and desktop apps and can be sorted by size, name, or installation date. Note that the size given for an app includes the data used as well as the application size itself. If you have large music and photo collections, for example, you will see much larger numbers in this column.

To uninstall an app from the Apps & Features list, simply click its name and then click the Uninstall button that appears.

Figure 8-4 The Apps & Features section of Settings provides a way to uninstall both modern and desktop apps.

TROUBLESHOOTING

Modern apps won't uninstall

If the normal uninstall routine for a modern app doesn't seem to work, you can remove the troublesome item by using Windows PowerShell. (See Chapter 21, "Working with Command Prompt and Windows PowerShell," for information about PowerShell.) Use the Get-AppxPackage cmdlet to obtain a list of packages installed on your system. Find the one you want to remove and note its *PackageFullName* property. Then supply this property as a parameter to the Remove-AppxPackage cmdlet. Note that you must be working in a PowerShell session with administrative privileges.

Managing line-of-business apps

Enterprises can develop line-of-business (LOB) apps for use within their organizations. Such apps can be deployed either through a private Business Store—managed and deployed by the Windows Store—or through a process called *sideloading*.

In addition to creating and deploying apps, administrators can also use Group Policy to control the use of all apps, including those that are supplied by Windows itself. For example, an organization might choose to remove the Sports app or prohibit it from running.

The process of distributing a Windows 10 app through a private Business Store requires that an enterprise have Azure Active Directory accounts for each user in the organization. (These accounts are used instead of Microsoft accounts.) Installation files are managed and deployed by the Windows Store, which also tracks license usage. Updates are delivered via normal update channels—Windows Update or Windows Server Update Services (WSUS).

LOB apps distributed within an organization without using the Windows Store don't need to be signed by Microsoft and don't require Azure Active Directory accounts. They do need to be signed with a certificate that is trusted by one of the trusted root authorities on the system.

Apps included with Windows 10

If you click through the Apps & Features list in Settings (see Figure 8-4), you will find that for some items, the Uninstall button is not available. These are apps that are supplied with a default installation of Windows 10, and Windows intends for you to keep them. (You will find a few other apps in the All Apps section of your Start menu that can't be uninstalled.) In the initial release of the operating system, the list of built-in programs included the following, among others:

- Alarms & Clock

- Calculator

- Camera

- Contact Support

- Cortana

- Groove Music

- Mail and Calendar

- Maps

- Movies & TV

- OneNote

- People

- Photos

- Settings

- Store

- Voice Recorder

- Weather

- Xbox

Several of these are relatively lightweight programs with no complexity worth discussing. You can read about some of the others in later chapters of this book. For the productivity and communication programs (including Mail and Calendar, OneNote, and People), see Chapter 9, "Productivity and communication tools." For the more right-brained items (Groove Music, Movies & TV, Photos, and Xbox), see Chapter 10.

Inside OUT

Don't overlook the humble Calculator

It's been around in one incarnation or another since the late 1980s, and it's no match for Excel, but the lowly Calculator app has a few tricks worth knowing about. It includes a programmer mode (specialized for bitwise operations on binary, octal, and hexadecimal values) along with the more common standard and scientific modes. And it can serve as a handy converter for measurements of volume, length, angles, time, and so on. (No, it doesn't do currencies.) Click the hamburger menu (three horizontal lines) in the upper left corner to see its repertoire.

Installing, running, and managing desktop applications

Windows 10 supports virtually all desktop applications that are compatible with Windows 7. If you have upgraded from Windows 7 (or from a Windows 8.1 system that itself was upgraded from Windows 7), all your desktop applications from the earlier environment should be happy and ready to go. Desktop programs can be installed anew in the usual ways, from installation media or by download from the Internet.

Desktop programs appear in the Start menu's All Apps list (or on the Start menu itself if you put them there) alongside modern apps. The only difference you're likely to see there is the absence of a live tile and the shortcut menu that appears if you right-click:

The Run As Administrator and Open File Location commands do not appear on this menu for modern apps. Running modern apps with administrative privileges is never required because such apps don't have the ability to mess with system files. Open File Location is absent from modern app shortcut menus because, as mentioned earlier, modern apps are defined by *package* data structures (in %LocalAppData%\Packages), and Windows assumes you have no need to inspect these structures.

The file locations for desktop apps (usually in a subfolder of %ProgramData%) are useful if you like to create shortcuts to your programs. For example, if you were accustomed to having shortcuts on your desktop to the programs you most frequently use, there's no reason not to populate your Windows 10 desktop the same way. Use the Start menu's shortcut menu to go to a program's file location. Then right-click the item in that folder and click Create Shortcut. The shortcut will appear in the same folder. Copy it, navigate to the desktop, and paste it there.

Running desktop applications as an administrator or another user

As in Windows 7, some desktop applications must be run with an administrative token. If you want to edit the registry, for example, you need to run Registry Editor (regedit.exe) as an administrator. You can run a program as an administrator by right-clicking any shortcut for the program (on the Start menu or elsewhere), choosing Run As Administrator, and satisfying the User Account Control (UAC) prompt with either consent or credentials. Here are two additional ways to do it:

- Start a Command Prompt session as Administrator: press Windows key+X and then choose Command Prompt (Admin). Then, in the Command Prompt window, type the name of the executable file for whichever program you want to run as an administrator. To run Registry Editor, for example, type **regedit**. Because you've already passed UAC inspection for the Command Prompt session, and because whatever you run from Command Prompt is a child process of Command Prompt, you don't have to deal with

CHAPTER 8

any further UAC prompts. This method is excellent for situations where you need to run a sequence of programs as an administrator. Keep one administrative-level Command Prompt window open, and run your programs from the command line.

- Type the name of the program you want to run in the taskbar search box, and then press Ctrl+Shift+Enter.

To run a program under a different user account, you can use the Runas command. You can do this from Command Prompt. The syntax is

```
Runas /user:username programname
```

After you issue the command, you'll be prompted to enter the password for the specified user account. Note that the Runas command does not work with File Explorer or with Microsoft Management Console (MMC) snap-ins.

Inside OUT

Use Steps Recorder to troubleshoot misbehaving software

When you need to report details about a software problem to a tech support person, the Steps Recorder tool can prove valuable. Run this program by typing **steps** in the taskbar search box and then clicking the Steps Recorder item that appears. Click Start Record, retrace your steps through the problematic program, and then click Stop Record. Steps Recorder takes a screen shot and time stamp at each crucial juncture (each mouse click or command), and then appends a verbal description of each step. You can add your own comments along the way. After you stop and save your recording, you can share it with tech support. (Steps Recorder is also an excellent tool for creating documentation to be used by others in your organization.)

Dealing with compatibility issues

As mentioned, programs that run without problems on Windows 7 will run equally well on Windows 10. Certain older desktop applications might create problems, however. Windows will attempt to flag potential compatibility problems when you first run such a program. The Program Compatibility Assistant that appears will offer you the alternatives of checking online for solutions (such as downloading a more recent version) or going ahead and running the program.

If you install a program and subsequently run into compatibility issues, a program compatibility troubleshooter may appear. Alternatively, you can run the troubleshooter yourself from Control Panel. You can find it by typing **compatibility** in the Control Panel search box. Under the heading Programs And Features, you will find the link Run Programs Made For Previous

Versions Of Windows. Click this link to launch the troubleshooter, and then click past the opening screen.

The troubleshooter begins by scanning for problems that it can detect automatically. If it finds none, it will present a list of applications installed on your system and let you select the one that's giving you difficulty. Select the offending program and follow the prompts to try to resolve your problem.

Managing programs and processes with Task Manager

Task Manager is a tool that serves two essential purposes. You can use it to track aspects of your system's performance and to see what programs and processes are running and terminate items when the normal shutdown methods aren't working.

➤ **For information about using Task Manager to monitor system performance, see Chapter 15, "System maintenance and performance."**

The easiest way to run Task Manager is by means of its keyboard shortcut, Ctrl+Shift+Esc. Figure 8-5 shows the Processes tab of Task Manager. If you don't see a tabular layout similar to that shown in Figure 8-5, click More Details at the bottom of the window.

Figure 8-5 Task Manager is useful for terminating recalcitrant applications and processes, as well as for monitoring system performance.

By default, the items listed on the Processes tab are grouped by type—apps at the top, followed by background processes, Windows processes, and so on. Grouping is optional; clear
Group By Type on the View menu if you want a single list.

Note that some of the items in the Apps list have outline controls. You can expand these to see
what files or documents are open. In Figure 8-5, for example, the Microsoft Word entry has
been expanded to reveal the name of the document that's currently open. The lists are initially
sorted in ascending alphabetical order. Click a heading to reverse the sort. You can also click
one of the performance headings to see which processes are using resources on your system.
Clicking CPU, for example, will give you a constantly updating readout of how your apps and
background processes are taxing the CPU.

Terminating a program with Task Manager

The Processes tab also includes a Status column. Most of the time, the entries in this column
will be blank, indicating that everything is humming along. If an app hangs for any reason,
you will see the words *Not Responding* in this column. In that case, you can attempt to shut
down the miscreant by right-clicking its name and clicking End Task. Don't be too quick on the
trigger, however; Not Responding doesn't necessarily mean permanently out to lunch. If the
program is using every bit of resources to handle a different task, it might simply be too busy
to communicate with Task Manager. Before you decide to end the program, give it a chance to
finish whatever it's doing. How long should you wait? That depends on the task. If the operation involves a large data set (performing a global search and replace in a large Microsoft
Access database, for instance), it's appropriate to wait several minutes, especially if you can
hear the hard disk chattering or see the disk activity light flickering. But if the task in question
normally completes in a few seconds, you needn't wait that long.

Inside OUT

Be smart about shutdowns

When you shut down an app by clicking End Task, Task Manager zaps the item immediately and irrevocably, closing any open files without giving you a chance to save them.
(This is equivalent to choosing End Process on the Processes tab of the Windows 7
Task Manager.) Whenever possible, you should try to close the program by the normal
methods before resorting to End Task.

Finding detailed information about a program

To see detailed information about the process that's running an app, right-click the app and choose Go To Details. This takes you to a related item on the Details tab. Right-clicking Microsoft Word, for example, takes you to Winword.exe, the name of Word's executable file. (See Figure 8-6.)

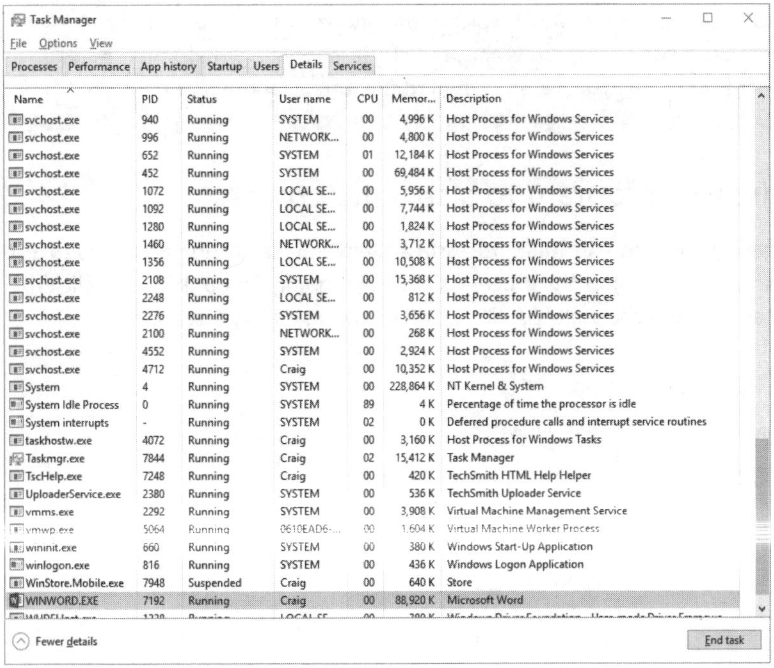

Figure 8-6 Right-clicking an item on the Processes tab takes you straight to the related item on the Details tab.

For each process, Task Manager includes the following information by default: image name (the name of the process), process ID (PID), status (running or suspended, for example), user name (the name of the person or account that initiated the process), CPU (the percentage of the CPU's capacity that the process is currently using), memory (the amount of memory the process requires to perform its regular functions, also known as the private working set), and description (a text field identifying the process). To display additional information for each process, right-click one of the headings and choose Select Columns.

CHAPTER 8

Inside OUT

Go online to read about programs and processes

Task Manager makes it easy to learn more about items on the Processes or Details tab. Simply right-click an item and choose Search Online. Task Manager opens a browser window and funnels the name of the app and the name of its process to your default search engine. There you'll typically find numerous links to official and unofficial information. If you're suspicious about the legitimacy of anything that shows up in Task Manager, by all means use this tool to find out what others are saying.

Assigning a program to a specific processor

If you have a multi-core or multiprocessor system, you can assign a process to a specific processor—but only after the process is already running. To do this, right-click the process on the Details tab and choose Set Affinity. The following dialog box appears:

To assign a process to a particular CPU, clear the check boxes for the other entries in this dialog box.

Reviewing history

The App History tab, like the Processes tab, provides information about how programs are using system resources. But App History, shown in Figure 8-7, knows only about modern apps; you won't find your desktop applications listed here. App History accumulates its information over some range of time, giving you an approximate idea of how you have been using your computer. If you never clear and restart the history, it will record everything going back to your installation of Windows 10. You can start fresh by clicking Delete Usage History.

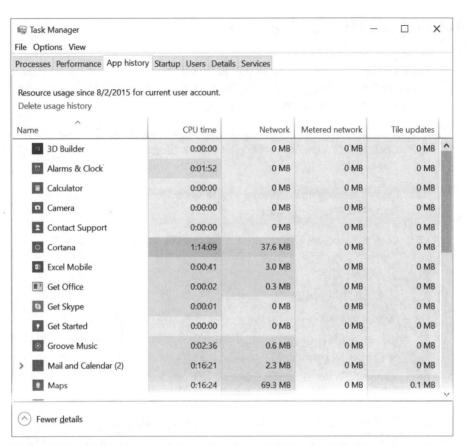

Figure 8-7 The App History tab tells you how much CPU time and other resources each modern app has used over a period of time.

As on other Task Manager tabs, you can sort information on the App History tab by clicking column headings. Clicking CPU Time, for example, brings the heavy hitters to the top of the list. Note, however, that Task Manager already calls your attention to the biggest consumers by means of color mapping, with the darkest colors assigned to the largest numbers.

History is interesting, but you might also find the App History tab useful as a program launcher. Right-click any item in any column, and you'll find a Switch To command. If the program is running, this command brings it front and center. If it's not running, Task Manager launches it.

Managing startup programs

Setting up a desktop application to run automatically when you start Windows is easy. If the program's installer doesn't offer to do this for you (many do) and you want the program to run every time you begin a Windows session, create a shortcut for the program in the Startup folder of your Start menu. Here's one way to do it:

1. On your Start menu, right-click the program you want to run at startup and choose Open File Location. You will find a shortcut for the program in the File Explorer window that appears.

2. Open a second File Explorer window and navigate to %AppData%\Microsoft\Windows\ Start Menu\Programs\Startup.

3. Copy the program's shortcut from the first File Explorer window to the second.

Inside OUT

Run a modern app at startup

You will find it challenging to launch a modern app from your Startup folder. You can find the app's executable by starting the program, running Task Manager, right-clicking the program on the Processes tab, clicking Go To Details, right-clicking the process name on the Details tab, and then clicking Open File Location. From there you can create a shortcut and copy it to your Startup folder. At the beginning of your next Windows session, you may find a warning from Windows SmartScreen:

Windows protected your PC

Windows SmartScreen prevented an unrecognized app from starting. Running this app might put your PC at risk.

App: Microsoft.Photos.exe
Publisher: Unknown Publisher

☐ I understand the risk and want to run this app.

Don't run

Windows SmartScreen is a security feature that helps protect you from potential malware. (See Chapter 7, "Securing Windows 10 devices.") Although the app in this example is clearly not a threat, SmartScreen may become wary on seeing it run from an unaccustomed location.

You can bypass SmartScreen by selecting the check box and clicking Run Anyway. But the next obstacle is more problematic:

The problem is that modern apps, unlike desktop programs, must be run within the context of elaborate data structures called *packages*. (You can see a list of the packages installed on your system and drill down to their component folders by visiting %LocalAppData%\Packages in File Explorer.) A workaround is to create your Startup folder shortcut not to the app but to a data file associated with the app. If .jpg files are associated with the modern Photos app, for example, create a startup shortcut to one of your .jpg files. At startup, Windows will execute the shortcut, which will launch the app.

Suspending or removing startup items

The problem that many users have with startup programs is not with creating them (that's easy, and in many cases it happens more or less automatically) but getting rid of them. Having too many startup programs not only makes your system take longer to start, it also has the potential to waste memory. If you don't require a program at startup, it's a good idea to get it out of your startup path.

If you've created the startup item in the first place by the method just described, you can remove it by revisiting the Startup folder and exercising the Delete key. Often, the situation is not so simple, however, because—as you'll see next—there are many other ways by which a program can be made to run at startup.

You can see a list of startup processes on the Startup tab of Task Manager. As Figure 8-8 shows, the Startup tab identifies each item by its estimated impact on the time required to start your Windows environment. In the figure, we've sorted on the Startup Impact column, bringing the high-impact items to the top.

You can't remove a startup item from this list, but you can disable it so that the item will not run automatically at your next startup. To do this, right-click the item and then click Disable.

Figure 8-8 The Startup tab in Task Manager shows you which startup programs are enabled and how much impact each is estimated to have on your startup time.

If you're not sure whether an item on the Startup tab is justifying its existence there, try disabling it and restarting. Alternatively, or additionally, you can right-click the item and use the handy Search Online command to learn more about it.

Other ways a program can be made to run at startup

As mentioned, a shortcut in the Startup folder is only one of many ways in which a program can be made to run at startup. Programs that set themselves up to run automatically and administrators who configure systems for others to use have a great many other methods at their disposal, including the following:

- **Run key (machine).** Programs listed in the registry's HKLM\Software\Microsoft\ Windows\CurrentVersion\Run key are available at startup to all users.

- **Run key (user).** Programs listed in the HKCU\Software\Microsoft\Windows\Current-Version\Run key run when the current user signs in. A similar subkey, HKCU\Software\ Microsoft\Windows NT\CurrentVersion\Windows\Run, can also be used.

- **Load value.** Programs listed in the Load value of the registry key HKCU\Software\ Microsoft\Windows NT\CurrentVersion\Windows run when any user signs in.

- **Scheduled tasks.** The Windows Task Scheduler (see Chapter 19, "Automating tasks and activities") can specify tasks that run at startup. In addition, an administrator can set up tasks for your computer to run at startup that are not available for you to change or delete.

- **Win.ini.** Programs written for 16-bit Windows versions can add commands to the Load= and Run= lines in the [Windows] section of this startup file, which is located in %SystemRoot%. The Win.ini file is a legacy of the Windows 3.1 era.

- **RunOnce and RunOnceEx keys.** This group of registry keys identifies programs that run only once, at startup. These keys can be assigned to a specific user account or to the machine:

  - HKLM\Software\Microsoft\Windows\CurrentVersion\RunOnce

  - HKLM\Software\Microsoft\Windows\CurrentVersion\RunOnceEx

  - HKCU\Software\Microsoft\Windows\CurrentVersion\RunOnce

  - HKCU\Software\Microsoft\Windows\CurrentVersion\RunOnceEx

- **RunServices and RunServicesOnce keys.** As their names suggest, these rarely used keys can control automatic startup of services. They can be assigned to a specific user account or to a computer.

- **Winlogon key.** The Winlogon key controls actions that occur when you sign in to a computer running Windows. Most of these actions are under the control of the operating system, but you can also add custom actions here. The HKLM\Software\Microsoft\Windows NT\CurrentVersion\Winlogon\Userinit and HKLM\Software\Microsoft\Windows NT\CurrentVersion\Winlogon\Shell subkeys can automatically launch programs.

- **Group Policy.** The Group Policy console includes two policies (one in Computer Configuration\Administrative Templates\System\Logon, and one in the comparable User Configuration folder) called Run These Programs At User Logon that specify a list of programs to be run whenever any user signs in.

- **Policies\Explorer\Run keys.** Using policy settings to specify startup programs, as described in the previous paragraph, creates corresponding values in either of two registry keys: HKLM\Software\Microsoft\Windows\CurrentVersion\Policies\Explorer\Run or HKCU\Software\Microsoft\Windows\CurrentVersion\Policies\Explorer\Run.

- **Logon scripts.** Logon scripts, which run automatically at startup, can open other programs. Logon scripts are specified in Group Policy in Computer Configuration\Windows Settings\Scripts (Startup/Shutdown) and User Configuration\Windows Settings\Scripts (Logon/Logoff).

The Startup tab in Task Manager is a fine way to disable startup behavior established by registry keys. Note, however, that Task Manager may not list every startup item; in particular, the list does not include items established by Group Policy or Task Scheduler. For a somewhat more complete list, run System Information (type **system information** in the taskbar search box; the utility should appear at or near the top of the search results). Unlike Task Manager, System Information includes items in the All Users startup folder (%ProgramData%\Microsoft\ Windows\Start Menu\Programs\Startup) as well as those in the startup folder for your own account. It also tells you *which* registry keys are responsible for a program's startup status, instead of simply indicating "Registry." Unfortunately, System Information, like Task Manager, also omits Group Policy and Scheduled Tasks items.

For the most comprehensive listing of items that run at startup, as well as a handy tool to prevent certain programs from starting, we recommend Autoruns, a free utility from Windows Sysinternals. Autoruns, which you can download from *w7io.com/2001*, shows all the registry keys and startup locations listed earlier, and it also shows Explorer shell extensions, services, browser helper objects, and more. Autoruns is particularly useful for finding processes that don't belong (such as a Trojan horse or other malware) or that you suspect of causing problems. You can then disable these items without removing them while you test your theory, or you can delete their autorun command altogether.

Select an item, and its details appear at the bottom of the screen, as shown here. Disable an item by clearing the check box next to its name; you can later reenable it by selecting the check box. To clear an item from the autorun list, select it and click Entry, Delete. (Note that deleting removes only the entry in the registry or other location that causes the item to run; it does not delete the program.)

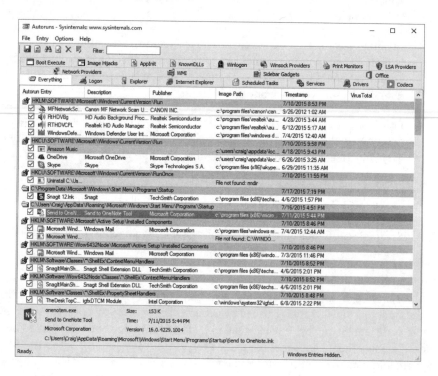

Although the tabs at the top of the Autoruns window filter the list of autorun items into various categories, the number of items can still be daunting. One nice feature of Autoruns is its ability to filter out components that are part of Windows or are digitally signed by Microsoft, as these are presumably safe to run. Commands on the Options menu control the appearance of these items.

You can also use the Compare feature in Autoruns to compare before and after snapshots of the data the program finds. Run Autoruns before you install a new program, save the data, run Autoruns again after you install the program, and compare the results to see what changes to autorun behavior were made by the program's installation.

Setting default programs and file-type associations

Most of the programs you use in Windows are associated with particular file types and protocols. These associations are what enable you, for example, to open an MP3 file in File Explorer and have your favorite audio program play the file, or click an Internet hyperlink in a document or an email message and have your choice of browser take you to the appropriate website. Some of these associations were probably established by the operating system when you performed a clean install or an upgrade from an earlier version of Windows. (The Windows setup program gives you choices in this matter during the installation process, allowing you, for example, to accept the associations that Windows proposes or keep the ones you had established before upgrading.) Regardless of how the associations between programs and file types and protocols are currently set, Windows allows you to see and modify the settings.

Some parts of the user interface used for managing file-type associations and default programs have been migrated to the Windows 10 Settings app, while other parts remain in the old-style Control Panel. Microsoft has indicated that, over time, all of these configuration settings will be available in the Settings app. But as of the July 2015 rollout of Windows 10, this work was still incomplete. You may find yourself using both Settings and Control Panel to get everything set up the way you want it.

For a quick and easy way to set the default app for certain kinds of documents, open Settings, System, and click Default Apps. Figure 8-9 shows an example of what you're likely to see.

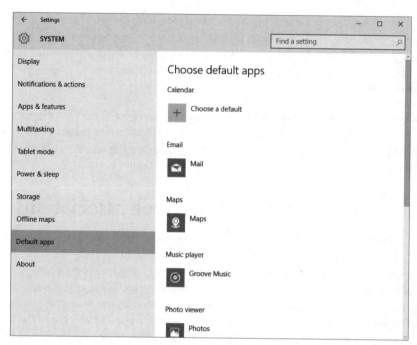

Figure 8-9 The Default Apps page in Settings provides a quick way to change the program associated with certain types of documents.

In the figure, you can see that, for example, the modern Mail app is the default handler for email documents or *mailto* links. To change that, click the Mail icon:

Here, two programs capable of handling email are installed on the system: the modern Mail app and the desktop version of Microsoft Outlook. Mail is currently assigned to this file type. You could change to Outlook or visit the Store to look for something else.

But just because a program is identified in Settings as the default for a file type does not mean that that program is assigned to open *every* file type that it can open. For example, Figure 8-9 shows Groove Music as the default music player. If you scroll to the bottom of the Default Apps list in Settings and click Set Default Apps By Type, however, you arrive in the Set Default Programs section of Control Panel, where you'll discover that Groove Music is the designated player for only 13 of 15 possible file types:

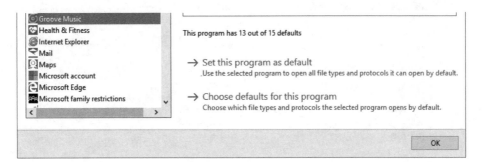

To see which file types Groove Music is assigned to handle and which ones it is not, click Choose Defaults For This Program. A quick glance at the file-type list that appears shows that Windows Media Player is the default for .wav and .wma files, while the rest of the file types are assigned to Groove Music, as shown next.

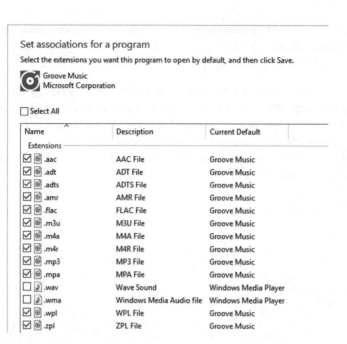

Clicking Select All (or selecting the individual check boxes for .wav and .wma) puts everything in the Groove Music camp.

What if, for some reason, you want to assign a file type in this list—say .mp3—to an altogether different program, perhaps an app that you intend to download from the Windows Store? To do this, return to the Default Apps page in Settings and click Choose Default Apps By File Type. As Figure 8-10 shows, Windows responds with a long alphabetized list of all the file types known to your system.

Figure 8-10 By clicking Choose Default Apps By File Type in Settings, you can control the associations for every file type recognized by your system.

Scrolling through the list to the .mp3 entry and clicking the name of the program currently associated with this type allows you to choose a different installed program or visit the Store:

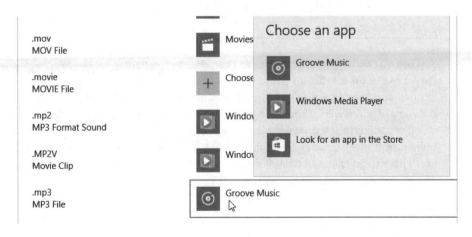

Using a nondefault program ad hoc

If you just want to open a file now and then in an application that's not the default for that file type, there's no need to go through all the business of changing the default application. Simply right-click the file in File Explorer and choose Open With. Windows displays a menu offering the various applications that can open the selected file type. If you don't find the one you want, click Choose Another App. This time a menu similar to the following appears:

You can do two things in this menu. You can change the default for the selected file type (select one of the listed apps and then click Always Use This App), or you can go for something altogether different by clicking More Apps. Doing this brings up a list of programs, many if not most of which will be completely unsuitable for the selected file type. Select one of these if you're curious to see what will happen. But don't click Always Use This App unless you are quite sure. If the program isn't what you want, it will simply make a nuisance of itself, and you'll have to go to the trouble of making something else the default.

Turning Windows features on or off

If you want to disable or enable certain default Windows features, open Settings and type **turn windows features on or off** in the search box. The dialog box shown in Figure 8-11 appears.

Figure 8-11 The Windows Features dialog box provides a simple way to disable or enable selected programs.

Here you can enable Hyper-V Management Tools (if they're not already enabled), disable Internet Explorer 11 if you have no further need of it, and so on. Note that some of the items in the list have subentries. Those marked by a filled check box have some components enabled and some not.

Setting AutoPlay options

AutoPlay is the feature that enables Windows to take appropriate action when you insert a removable device such as a CD, DVD, or memory card into a drive. The operating system detects the kind of disc or media you have inserted and takes the action that you have requested for that type of media. If you have not already made a decision about what the operating system should do, a window similar to this one appears:

If you don't want Windows to take any action, you can simply click the Close button. Otherwise, clicking or tapping brings you to the screen shown next.

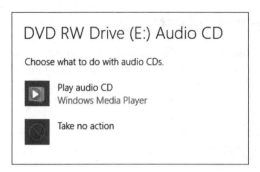

Notice that your choices here are limited to the current default program for the media type (Windows Media Player in this example) and Take No Action. If you don't want to commit to either of these, press Esc.

In any case, if you set a default action for a particular media type and subsequently change your mind and want a different default, you can open Settings and search for **AutoPlay**. Shown in Figure 8-12, AutoPlay in Settings lets you configure some types of media but not (as of July 2015) others. You might need to search for AutoPlay in Control Panel to see the rest.

Figure 8-12 The AutoPlay page in Settings lets you configure AutoPlay behavior for some types of media. You might need to visit Control Panel to configure other types.

In the Control Panel counterpart for this corner of Settings, you will see a dialog box comparable to the one shown in Figure 8-13.

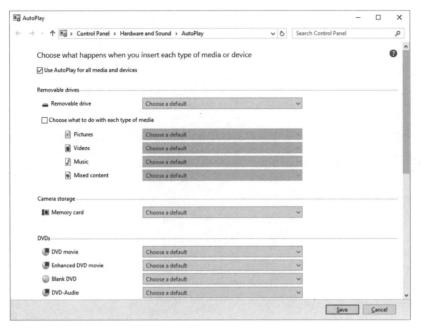

Figure 8-13 For each media type, Windows lets you choose from a list of appropriate possibilities.

Inside OUT

You don't want a default action?

To have no default action for a given media type, choose Ask Me Every Time. To suppress the AutoPlay dialog box completely, choose Take No Action.

Productivity and communication tools

In this chapter and Chapter 10, "Music, photos, movies, and games," we discuss specific programs that are included with a default installation of Windows 10 or available as free downloads from the Windows Store. We break these programs into two large categories, covering those that serve productive purposes in this chapter and those that entertain in the next. (Although we are well aware that the distinction is fuzzy—one person's amusement may certainly be another's business, and some of us find occasional entertainment in the exploration of mundane workaday programs.)

➤ **For information about Microsoft Edge and Internet Explorer, see Chapter 11, "Browsing the Internet."**

The list of tools that come with Windows grows longer with each iteration, largely because every new version, in addition to introducing new items, must continue to support the work habits developed by users of its predecessors. If you have routinely covered your Windows 7 desktop with color-coded sticky notes, for example, you will be pleased to know that the Sticky Notes desktop application is alive and well in Windows 10. (But you might want to explore the Store to see whether a comparable but more richly featured program is available.)

In addition to the obligatory legacy applications, Windows 10 offers a whole set of modern productivity and communication apps, all designed for touch and stylus as well as more traditional input methods. In addition, not installed by default but available without charge from the Store are mobile versions of three Microsoft Office applications—Word, Excel, and PowerPoint. A fourth member of the Office suite, OneNote, is installed by default; you don't have to go to the Store to get it.

We begin our survey with a look at the modern communication and productivity apps.

CHAPTER 9

Mail, Calendar, and People

Although they have separate entries on the Start menu, Mail, Calendar, and People are three faces of a common application. You can switch between Mail and Calendar by tapping or clicking icons in the lower left corner of the window. And the People app, populated by the accounts you set up in Mail or Calendar, provides a directory of potential addressees when you create Mail messages or invite associates to a meeting. Type the beginning of a contact's name or email address on the To line of a message, and if that name or address is among your contacts in People, the To line will be completed for you.

Setting up and using Mail

The first time you open the Mail app, you'll be asked to set up accounts:

At the top of the list is the Microsoft account you use to sign in to Windows or to Microsoft services such as Outlook.com. Below, you can add more email accounts as needed. Mail supports Exchange, Outlook.com, Gmail, iCloud, POP, and IMAP accounts. The setup process is straightforward, prompting you for your email address and password. You might see additional requests for information and permissions. For a Gmail account, for example, you are presented with the following:

Adding and configuring accounts

To add email accounts subsequently, click the Gear icon in or near the lower left corner of your screen:

The gear is your gateway to settings options for Mail (as for many other modern Windows apps). Click Accounts, then Add Account. To delete or reconfigure an existing account, select it in Settings. Note that you cannot delete (but you can reconfigure) the address associated with your Microsoft account.

Options for reconfiguring an account in Mail are shown in Figure 9-1. The default settings, shown in the figure, reflect the program's intended use as a mail client for users on the go. To save battery and disk space, Mail bases its sync frequency on your usage patterns. If you use Mail now and then only on this computer, the program dials back the sync frequency and reports its decision next to the Currently Syncing heading. In the figure, Mail is fetching your mail only once a day, but if you use the app with any significant frequency, it will fetch messages at shorter time intervals. In any case, you can override the program's decision making and configure a predetermined sync interval by opening the drop-down list at the top of the dialog box.

Figure 9-1 By default, the frequency with which Mail syncs messages from your mail server is based on your usage patterns. You can opt to sync more frequently.

Reading and responding to mail

Mail devotes the majority of its screen space to a list of message headers on the left and a reading area on the right. To read a message, tap or click it in the headers pane. To delete a message click or tap the trash can icon near the upper right corner of the header entry:

The icons to the left and right of the trash can let you archive a message or flag it as important. All three of these functions are also available via a shortcut menu if you right-click a message heading.

Creating a new message

To create a new message, click the New Mail icon. Note that the new message window provides an elaborate set of editing tools, derived from Microsoft Word. For example, a wealth of styling options is available via the Format tab on the ribbon. Use the arrows on the ribbon to see the full set of options at your disposal.

To attach a file to your message, click the Insert tab. You can use that part of the ribbon to insert tables, pictures, and hyperlinks as well. Mail also provides a proofreader; click Options and then click Spelling to check the spelling of your messages.

Using folders

The pane to the left of the message headers provides access to the Drafts and Sent Items system folders. Other folders that you may have created on your mail server appear in an additional pane that appears if you click More, below the system folders. You can move a message from the headers pane to one of your own subfolders by right-clicking the header and then clicking Move.

Setting Quick Actions and other options

On a touchscreen or tablet, you can make quick work of mail-handling tasks by means of Mail's Quick Actions feature (Figure 9-2). Click or tap the gear icon and choose Settings, Options to configure Quick Actions.

CHAPTER 9

Figure 9-2 The Quick Actions section of the Options pane lets you configure the way Mail responds to swipes with your finger or a stylus and provides easy ways to manage incoming messages.

You can assign one action to a right swipe and another for swiping left. By default, as shown in the figure, putting your finger or stylus on a message and whisking it off to the right flags the message as important (or clears the flag if it has already been set). Dragging in the other direction deletes the message. Alternatives for either direction include marking the message as read or unread and moving a message to a folder.

As Figure 9-2 shows, other parts of the Options pane let you configure a signature that is appended to outgoing messages, turn on automatic replies, and specify how and whether you want to be notified of incoming mail. If you turn on automatic replies, the pane expands so that you can enter your preferred message—for example, "I'm out of the office until the end of the month." You can specify one message for senders within your organization and another for those outside, and you can limit the automatic response sent to people on the outside to those who are on your contacts list.

Once you have flagged a set of messages, you might want to change the message list to show only those you have flagged. To do this, click the arrow to the right of Inbox and then choose Flagged. You can apply a similar filter if you want to see only those messages not marked as read.

One more command worth mentioning is Zoom. If your mobile device is just too small for comfortable reading, click the three dots at the upper right corner of the window, and then choose Zoom from the menu that descends. Magnification options range from 50 percent to 400 percent.

Setting up and using Calendar

In both Mail and Calendar, two icons at the lower left corner let you switch from one app to the other. If you're already running Mail, a quick tap takes you straight to Calendar. Alternatively, you'll find Calendar on your Start menu or the All Apps list.

Accounts set up in Mail are used in Calendar and vice versa. You can add or modify accounts in Calendar as you would in Mail; click the gear icon, and then click Accounts in the Settings pane. If you're using multiple accounts, your Calendar events will be distinguished by color, and if the display gets noisy, you can use the check boxes in the left pane, below the thumbnail calendar, to suppress particular components of your composite calendar, as shown next.

If you don't see this pane at the left of your screen, click or tap the so-called hamburger icon in the upper left corner. Doing this removes or redisplays the left pane (you'll find it useful particularly on a small display).

Adding an event

To add an event to your calendar, either click or tap New Event, or click the calendar itself. If you click New Event, you get the full Details window for the event, shown in Figure 9-3. If you click a day or an hour on the calendar, you get a smaller version of this window, and you can move to the full view by clicking More Details. In either case, if you have Calendar configured to use more than one account, you'll want to specify which account the new event should belong to.

Use the Reminder list to specify your preferences regarding alerts. Calendar defaults to a 15-minute heads-up, but you have lots of alternatives, including None. Note that Calendar's live tile (if you have the app on your Start menu) will also alert you to upcoming events. Cortana can offer reminders as well, of course, depending on how you have configured her.

Figure 9-3 shows the details of a recurring event. To create such an item, simply click Repeat and specify your parameters. Calendar offers daily, weekly, monthly, and yearly options.

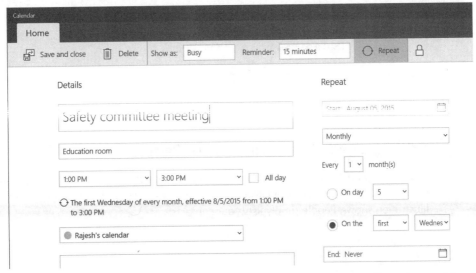

Figure 9-3 Clicking Repeat opens a new set of options, where you can specify yearly, monthly, weekly, or daily parameters for a recurring event.

Inviting others to a meeting

To create a meeting event and invite others to join, add the email addresses of your invitees to the People section of your Details view. Then click Send. Each of the invitees will get a message allowing him or her to send back a yes-no-maybe response:

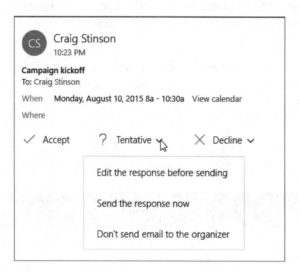

Recipients can expand the lists next to the Tentative and Decline buttons to add a message of explanation.

Adding or editing contacts with People

People is a simple app that acts as a repository for contacts derived from the accounts you set up in Mail or Calendar. (You can also add or delete accounts in People itself.) As the following illustration shows, People simply lists your contacts:

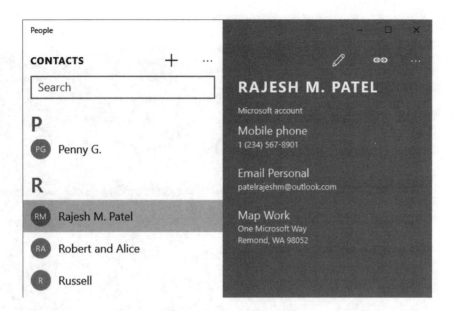

You can edit a contact's information by selecting the contact in the left pane and clicking the Edit icon (shaped like a pencil) on the right. If you have more than one entry for a contact, you can use the Link icon (to the right of the Edit icon) to consolidate them.

Downloading and using Skype

Skype, Microsoft's Internet video telephony and conferencing tool, is not part of a default installation of Windows 10, but you can download the free version by running Get Skype from the Start menu. (If you don't find Get Skype, go to *www.skype.com*.) Microsoft also offers a more richly featured product called Skype for Business (formerly known as Lync), either as a standalone item or as part of the business versions of Office 365. For information about features and pricing of Skype for Business, see *www.skype.com/business*.

After you download the app, Skype will prompt you to create an account or sign in to an existing one. Figure 9-4 shows how your screen might look after you have created your account but before you have added any contacts.

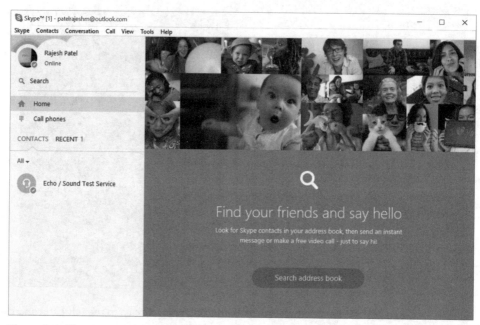

Figure 9-4 After you create a Skype account and sign in, your first actions might be to use the Echo/Sound Test Service link to verify that your camera and microphone are functioning and the Search link to add contacts.

Before you start making calls, you might want to check your video, microphone, and speaker settings. You can do this by clicking Echo/Sound Test Service in the Contacts pane. Alternatively, open the Tools menu, choose Options, and then click either Audio Settings or Video Settings.

To add contacts, click Search (below your name in the upper left corner of the window). Type your contact's Skype account name if you know it or an email address. You can also simply type the contact's name, but this approach might produce a long list of Skype users with identical first and last names. When you find the person you want to add, select the name and click Add To Contacts. Your contact will then receive a request message:

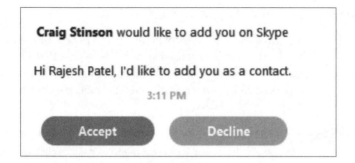

Note that if you receive an unwanted contact solicitation and choose to decline, the Decline button provides additional options to simply block the request or report it as spam.

With your equipment checked out and your contacts list populated, you might then want to flesh out your own profile—the information that your contacts will see about you. The profile screen appears when you click your own name in the upper left corner of the window, and here you can add phone information and many other details. (Click Show Full Profile to see the complete list of fields you can change.) If you shot your profile with the rear-facing camera by mistake or simply want to transmit a different image (there's no requirement that it be you!), click Change Picture.

Placing or answering an audio or video call

To initiate an Internet-to-Internet call, click your contact's name, and then choose one of the options that appear on the right side of the screen:

Click the icon on the right (the one with the plus sign) to add more people to the call. The phone icon in the center makes the call audio only. Choose the camera icon on the left to send video as well. You can also switch in and out of video during the call if the need arises— for example, if the quality of your Internet connection is not strong enough to support video transmission.

Similar buttons appear if someone places a call to you. Before you answer, you'll also get an audio signal to alert you to the call.

Calling people who don't have Skype or aren't online

Skype also lets you place Voice-over-Internet-Protocol (VoIP) calls to people who don't have Skype accounts or are not online. The calls are charged at per-minute rates that vary by country or region. Before placing a call, you can buy credit by opening the Skype menu and choosing Buy Skype Credit. For users in the United States, credit is available in increments of $10 and $25.

When you're ready to call, click Call Phones. On the dialer that appears, open the Choose Country/Region drop-down list, select the country or region you're calling, click the numbers to dial, and then click the phone icon.

Sending text or video messages, pictures, or files

To send a text message, select a contact name, and then type in the text box that appears at the bottom of the window. (You can also send text while you're in an audio or video call.) To send a video message to someone, click the paper-clip icon to the left of the text box, and then click Send Video Message. Your camera will come to life, your shining visage will appear on the screen, and you can click the red Record button when you're ready to start. Click the Send button when you're satisfied and ready to transmit.

To send a photo or a file, click the paper-clip icon and choose Send Photo or Send File.

Using the mobile and desktop versions of OneNote

Windows 10 comes with a modern OneNote app preinstalled. You don't have to grab it from the Store; it should already be there on your system. (If for any reason it's not, you *can* get it from the Store, free of charge.) This is a lightweight mobile version of Microsoft's excellent note-taking application, optimized by the size and spacing of the ribbon's tabs and commands to be used with fingers or a stylus. (It also works fine on systems without touchscreens, of course.)

Also free, but a download away (from *www.onenote.com/download*), is the full-featured desktop version of OneNote, a component of Microsoft Office. (As we write, the downloadable product is OneNote 2013, but OneNote 2016 is standing only a few feet offstage.) If you have a tablet or other touchscreen system, you can use your fingers or stylus with this version of OneNote as well, although the targets on the user interface will be a little smaller.

Because the mobile OneNote is a modern app, it is updated automatically by the Windows Store. The desktop Office applications, including OneNote, may also be updated periodically via Windows Update, but it's possible that Microsoft will be putting more development effort into the modern app.

In any case, there's no compelling reason to choose one or the other. You can use both, and your notebooks will be synced automatically and accessible from either version (as well as from your phone if you have OneNote installed there). OneNote Mobile may be ideal when you're on the go or when you're concerned with reading your notes (and those that others have shared with you) and making simple annotations. For more extensive editing and note taking, and for such things as inserting recorded audio or video notes, you'll probably want the much larger feature set provided by the desktop program.

If you're new to OneNote, the most essential things to know are these:

- Like the other Office mobile apps (Excel, Word, and PowerPoint), OneNote saves everything you enter immediately and instantly. If your notebook is stored on OneDrive, you have access to it from anywhere.

- Notes are stored in *notebooks*, which are subdivided into *sections*. Each section consists of one or more *pages*. OneNote gives you a notebook to start with, and that notebook contains a single section (called New Section 1) consisting of a single page (called Untitled Page). Sections are identified by tabs arrayed across the top, and pages are listed vertically, on the left (in the mobile version) or the right (in the desktop version). Click the plus signs to add sections or pages.

- OneNote is a free-form editor. You can type or jot anywhere on the page. With drawing tools, you can annotate your annotations.

With the desktop version of OneNote, you can create shared notebooks for collaborative projects. Click File to see a list of your notebooks. To share an existing notebook, click Invite People To This Notebook, below a notebook's name. (The notebook must be stored on OneDrive for this link to be available.) To create a new shared notebook, click File, then New. Choose a location, supply a name, and then click Create Notebook. In a moment, the following prompt will appear:

CHAPTER 9

Click Invite People, and then supply email addresses.

Shared notebooks, like all others, are usable in both versions of OneNote, but in the mobile version you're limited to sharing the current page. To do that, click the Share icon at the upper right corner of the window.

Using the mobile versions of Word, Excel, and PowerPoint

Microsoft also provides touch-optimized versions of three major Office programs—Word, Excel, and PowerPoint. Comparable to the mobile edition of OneNote described in the previous section, these mobile Office apps are modern apps that are ideal for quick reads and edits on tablets. Their large and well-spaced user-interface controls make them easy to manage with fingers and styli.

NOTE
The mobile Office apps are free (you can find them in the Windows Store), but their full functionality requires an Office 365 subscription. Without a subscription, you can open and read Office documents, but you cannot edit or save documents. In any case, you should consider these mobile items as on-the-go complements to their desktop suitemates. For extensive document generation and editing, you'll want the larger feature set that comes with Office 365.

Features common to the mobile Office apps

Here are some important features shared by all three mobile Office apps:

- **Autosave.** Changes are saved instantly and automatically. The name under which the current document is being saved appears in the center of the screen, above the ribbon:

You can change the name by clicking it and typing a new one, but you might find it easier to tap the File menu and then tap Save. As Figure 9-5 shows, the Save command serves the function that is assigned to the Save As command in other programs.

Figure 9-5 The Save command shows you where and under what name your file is being automatically saved. You can rename or copy the file here.

If you are making tentative edits, or if you are concerned that an errant press of your finger or hand might change the file's content awkwardly, consider working with a copy instead of the original. You can make a copy by visiting the Save command.

- **Sharing.** Clicking the Share icon in the upper right corner of the ribbon lets you extend read or read/write privileges to other people. As Figure 9-6 shows, you can attach a message to your invitation. Below the message appear the names of everyone who already has access to the document.

- **Help.** Near the Share icon on all three apps is a lightbulb icon. This provides access to the "Tell me what you want to do" feature (which will also be part of the Office 2016 desktop applications). When you indicate what you want to accomplish here, the program will—if it can—carry out the action you request instead of directing you to an explanation of how to do it. To save you stylus-strokes, a list of commonly requested actions appears, under the heading Try. (See Figure 9-7.) If what you want isn't there, you can type the task. If all else fails—for example, if the program can't understand or carry out your order—you'll be redirected to an Internet help source.

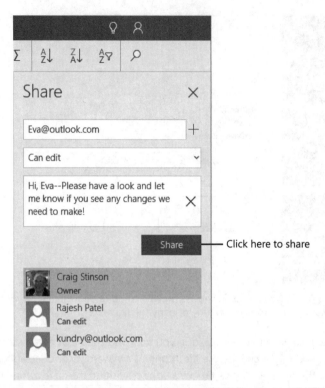

Figure 9-6 Clicking the Share icon lets you send a personalized invitation to a friend or coworker and shows you who is already on the team.

Figure 9-7 "Tell me what you want to do" can provide a quicker alternative to traditional Help commands. If it can, the mobile Office app will carry out your instructions directly, without telling you what to do.

Exploring the mobile Office apps

If you are familiar with the desktop counterparts of the three mobile Office apps, you might want to start exploring the mobile apps by looking at the comparison topics available via the "Tell me what you want to do" feature. These appear below the list of suggested entries. Figure 9-7, for example, shows the topic Compare Word Versions at the bottom of Word Mobile's "Tell me" list. These commands lead you to useful comparisons. Beyond comparing, the best way to learn about these apps is, quite literally, by poking around. Here are a few highlights.

Using Reading view in Word Mobile

Word Mobile has a Reading view that makes perusing a document on a small screen more comfortable. To get there, tap Read on the View tab or click the Read icon, between the "Tell me" icon and the Share icon, near the upper right edge of the screen. As Figure 9-8 shows, the Read tab offers a number of useful options for sizing, coloring, and spacing text. Reading view opens in full-screen mode; to see the Read tab, click the three dots at the upper right side of the window. To get out of Reading view, click Edit on the Read tab.

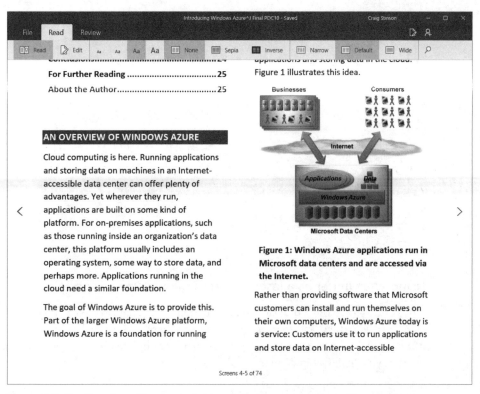

Figure 9-8 Reading view offers a set of sizing, coloring, and spacing options to ease your eyes on a small screen.

CHAPTER 9

Simplifying formula entry in Excel Mobile

Options on the Home tab provide quick access to many of Excel Mobile's commonly used commands. You can create sums here, for example, sort rows in a table, insert rows and columns, and so on. For more complex formula entry, however, click the Formula icon (*fx*) at the left edge, below the ribbon. Using the categorized function list that descends, you can enter the formula you need with a minimum of typing:

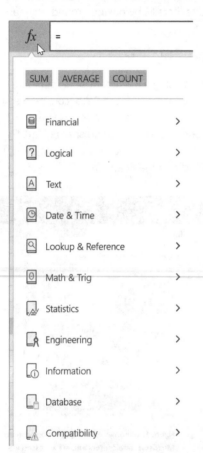

Using your finger as a laser pointer in PowerPoint Mobile

There's no need to use a mouse to highlight important points in a PowerPoint presentation. Start your slide show, and then use your finger to point to the places you want to underscore. After a pause, your finger press will produce a red dot on the presentation, which you can move as you would a highlighter.

Using Maps

Mapping applications have long been one of the indispensable tools of modern life. Microsoft's modern Maps app should serve you well, whether you want to explore a new city, plot a road trip, find a restaurant, print a set of turn-by-turn directions to take with you on the road, or just enjoy aerial views of the world or your neighborhood. (If you search for a restaurant known to Maps, you'll be rewarded with reviews, hours, and website information in addition to a map.)

On first run, Maps asks for permission to track your location information. If you consent, Maps will plant a marker at your current location. When you start Maps, it always opens to whatever map or view you were using last, but pressing Ctrl+Home displays your current location, assuming the program knows what that is.

To find a location, click the Search tool on the left or press Ctrl+F. You can type an address or the name of a place known to Maps—an institution or a restaurant, for example. As in Figure 9-9, Maps shows the location on the map and a couple of street-side pictures below the search string, on the left. A Nearby icon below the pictures provides categorized entries for potential items of interest near the selected location.

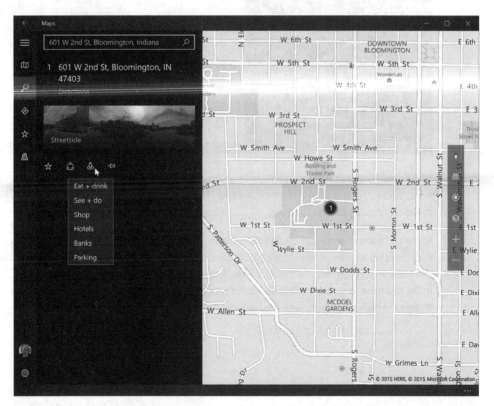

Figure 9-9 In addition to displaying your search item on the map, Maps shows pictures and can lead you to nearby attractions.

To get directions, click the Directions icon, directly below the Search icon, and then type your starting and ending points (one of them may already be in place if you just searched for it). Maps responds with a set of turn-by-turn instructions:

Above the turn instructions, you'll find a summary of the route—the distance, traffic conditions, and expected time of travel. Use the printer icon directly below this summary to print the directions as well as the map.

Maps defaults to showing driving directions. To see public transportation information instead, click the bus icon near the upper right corner of the directions pane. For a walking route, click the humanoid icon next to the bus icon. Maps calculates its walking time at a rate of about 2.3 miles per hour. If you usually walk or ride public transit, you can change the default by clicking the gear-shaped Settings icon and opening the Preferred Directions list.

With a set of directions in place, you can click the Go button, at the right side of the summary information, and you can expand the turn information to show maps and route at each point along the way:

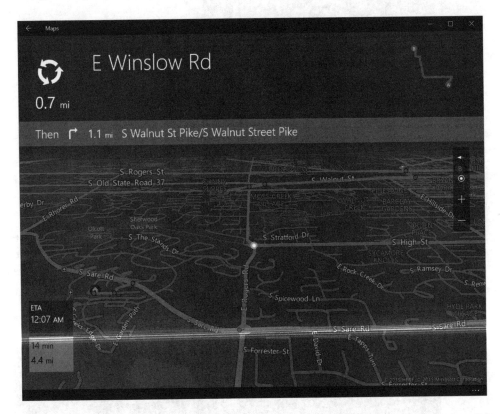

On a GPS-enabled device, such as a phone with Windows 10, Maps will give you spoken directions. If your device does not have GPS capability, silent images such as this will appear. (Please don't attempt to read these images and instructions while you drive; your passenger will be happy to act as navigator.)

On the right side of a map's display, Maps offers a panel of additional options, allowing you to change the compass heading, switch between plane and elevation views, display your current location, switch between aerial and street views, and zoom in and out. Clicking Map Views, the fourth of these icons, yields the flyout options shown next.

CHAPTER 9

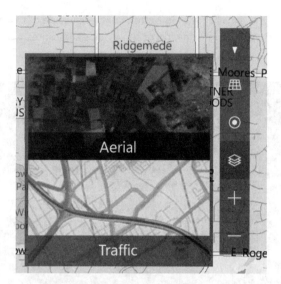

Maps also includes a 3D Cities feature (the last icon in the panel on the left side of the screen), which lets you display aerial images of a large selection of cities in various parts of the world. When you need a break from your labors, you can travel vicariously to Aix-en-Provence or drop in for an overhead look at the Dresden Frauenkirche:

Using Alarms & Clock

As the name implies, Alarms & Clock will give you a nudge at a prescribed time. You can configure an alarm to sound once only or to repeat on particular days. For example, if you use an
alarm to rouse you from sleep, you can have one alarm for workdays and another for week-
ends. As this image shows, you can also attach a text message to an alarm—to let you know
why you're being roused.

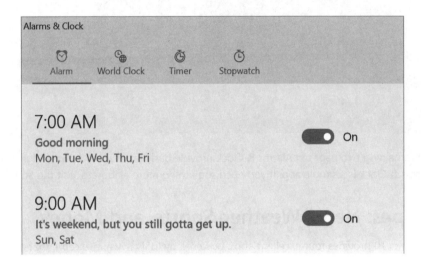

Alarms will also wake your computer from sleep—provided your hardware supports InstantGo.
For more information about this feature, previously known as Connected Standby, see
bit.ly/InstantGo.

To set a new alarm, click the plus sign on the Alarm page. Be sure to click the Save icon on
the New Alarm page when you have things set up as you want them. To remove an item from
your collection of alarms, right-click it and click Delete.

On the World Clock page, you can check out the time in any part of the world and compare it
with your local time. Click the plus sign to add a city. The display uses shading to show where
the sun is up and where it's not, as shown next.

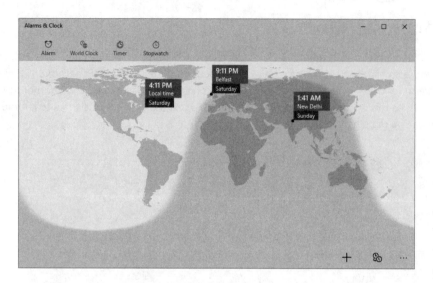

The remaining two pages in Alarms & Clock provide basic timer and stopwatch functionality. Alarms & Clock is a simple app. If you need something more elaborate, visit the Store.

The info apps: News, Weather, Sports, and Money

Windows 10 provides four excellent apps, powered by MSN (*www.msn.com*), that can keep you up to date about things going on around you (or lead you down the path to total self-distraction, depending on your inclinations). You can peruse the current headlines, drill down by category, search for anything you don't immediately find—and either read immediately or save items to your reading list to look at later. (The Reading List app is discussed in the next section.) All the info apps implement live tiles; pin them to your Start menu to get quick headlines.

News

The News app presents large tiles for recent headline stories, smaller tiles for stories of subordinate interest (be sure to scroll to see the whole list), and a menu across the top that lets you filter by category:

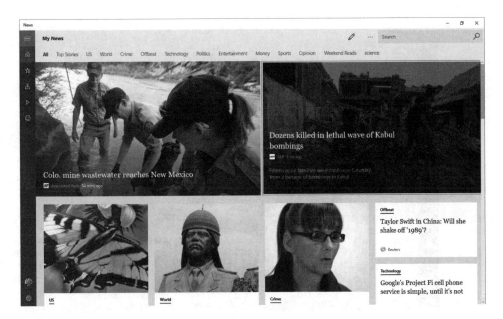

The horizontal menu across the top covers many categories but doesn't include local news. For that, click the fourth icon in the vertical toolbar on the left:

If you're looking for a story about a particular topic that doesn't happen to bubble up to the top of one of the category pages, try the Search field. As Figure 9-10 shows, News will present what MSN has about your search topic, along with other items judged to be related.

The horizontal menu of news categories might not include some you'd like to see and others you never want to bother with. To customize, click the Interests icon:

The My Interests page shows all your current categories. To remove a category, click the green check mark. To add others, select one of the items in the menu on the left, and then click the plus sign for a category you want to add.

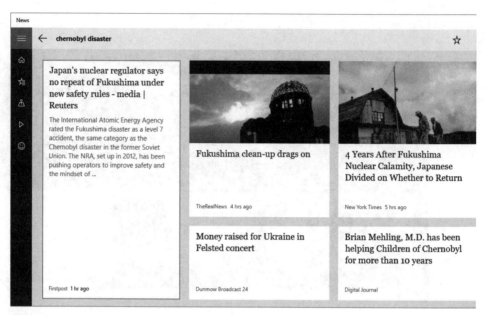

Figure 9-10 Here a search for "Chernobyl disaster" summons a few Chernobyl items plus several others that MSN judges to be related.

Weather

The Weather app offers a wealth of forecasted and historical information about virtually any city in the world, including your own:

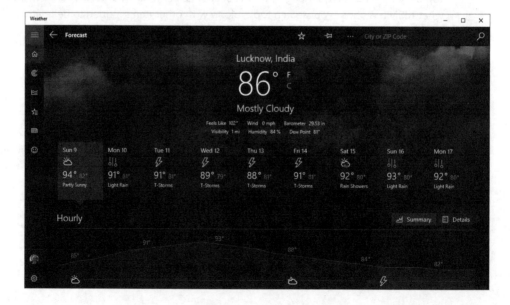

Scroll down the Forecast page to see details about the day—sunrise, sunset, wind speed, humidity, and more. Below that you'll find record highs, lows, and rainfall. You might also find such tidbits as the number of times thunderstorms have occurred on this day over the past 30 years. More interesting details await you on the Maps and Historical Weather pages. Click the icons in the panel on the left to display these.

If there are cities you regularly track, visit the Places page, shown next:

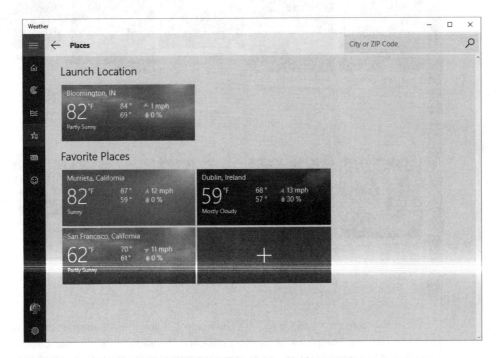

Click the plus sign to add a city. Right-click a city to remove it.

Finally, visit the News page for current weather stories.

Sports

With the Sports app, you can follow news stories about your favorite teams or sports:

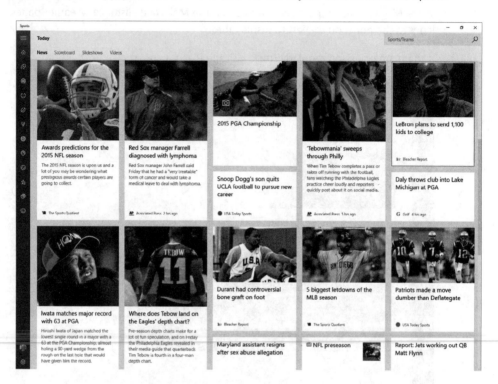

The list of available sports and leagues is truly global. If you like American football, you can follow the NFL, but Europeans who have a different definition of football can choose from no fewer than 42 separate leagues on the continent. You can also track Australian Rules football, cricket, and rugby. Or you can see a scoreboard of all the games currently going on:

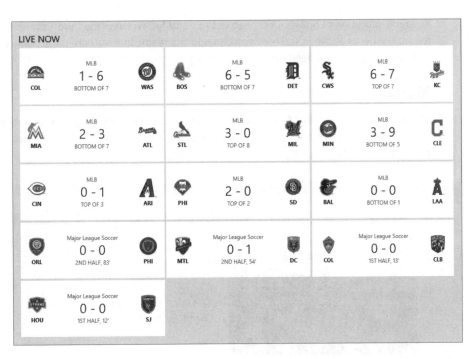

By drilling down on one of the current games, you can view detailed information in something close to real time:

In your exploration of Sports, don't neglect to visit My Favorites (the third icon from the bottom in the panel at the left). There you can add the teams that you are particularly interested in following. Sports will feed updates from these teams to its live tile.

Money

As Sports does for games, Money lets you track market action in an approximation of real time. Below the news stories on the Home page, a dashboard shows the current action in several major markets:

Click a market to see more detail:

The Money app covers stocks, bonds, commodities, and currencies. Click the World Markets icon (sixth from the top in the panel at the left) to see a map of the world with summaries of many regional markets. Click the Currency Converter icon (fourth in the panel) to check current conversion rates. The Watchlist icon (third from the top) lets you add stock symbols of particular interest. On your Watchlist page, Money supplies news stories as well as price data.

Sharing and saving news stories

When you find a story that you want to keep or send to someone else, open the story and then click the Share icon:

A menu will appear showing sharing options:

Choosing Mail opens your default mail client. If you choose OneNote, you'll see OneNote's proposed destination notebook and section. Use the drop-down list to change the destination.

If you choose Reading List App, a confirmation appears providing the name and source of your story. Open the Categorize list to specify which Reading List category will serve as your destination. (See the following section for information about Reading List app categories.)

Preserving items of interest with Windows Reading List

The first thing to know about the Windows Reading List app is that it is completely separate from the reading list *feature* that's part of the Microsoft Edge web browser. (Introduced in Windows 8, the app predates the browser.) Moreover, the reading list the app maintains is also separate from the one you might create in Edge. Windows Reading List is not installed by default; you can install it for free from the Store.

> ➤ **For information about using the reading list feature in Microsoft Edge, see "Using Reading List, an alternative to Favorites" in Chapter 11.**

The Reading List app is ideal for those who browse news stories with the expectation of reading them thoroughly later. Nearly any story that you open in one of the info apps (described in the previous section) can be saved to the Reading List app. Most webpages that you open in Edge (but not in browsers that are desktop applications) can be saved either to the Reading List app or to the reading list in Edge. Stories that you save to the Reading List app are available on any computer on which you sign in using the Microsoft account under which the item was saved. For example, you can browse at home and then read your selections on your tablet or laptop as you ride the train to work.

The Reading List app organizes saved items in categories. The app gives you six categories to start with—Finance, Food, Health, News, Sports, and Travel. You can create and delete categories at will. Anything not stored in a category goes into an additional bin called Uncategorized:

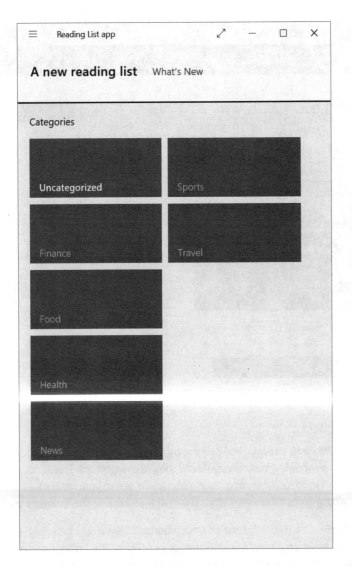

To save a story or webpage to the Reading List app, click the Share icon near the upper right corner of the window, and then select Reading List from the list of sharing options. You'll have an opportunity to choose a category in the confirmation dialog box that the Reading List app presents, as shown next.

CHAPTER 9

CHAPTER 9

When you open the Reading List app, you see the most recent items you have added (in descending chronological order) regardless of how they're categorized. This time-ordered display gives you another method of finding your material. To get to your categories, right-click anywhere in the window other than on a story tile, and then choose the category you want.

To open a story, simply click its tile. To put an uncategorized item into a category, right-click its tile. A menu that shows your current categories pops up from the bottom of the screen, and you can make a selection. An item at the bottom of this category list lets you create a new category.

You can keep stories in the Reading List app for as long as you like, but as a space-saving measure, the app removes the image from a story's tile after three months.

To delete an item, right-click it and then click Delete. Deleted items are kept in an archived state for, by default, 30 days. If you want another look at something you've deleted, right-click in the app (not on a tile) and click Recently Deleted. You can change the archival time to either

10 days or 60 days. To do this, click the hamburger menu, choose Settings, and then choose Options.

Voice Recorder

The Sound Recorder application that was included with Windows versions dating back to the Middle Ages (well, perhaps not *quite* that long) has been replaced by a shiny new modern app called Voice Recorder. The Voice Recorder app, which creates files in the .m4a format, is great for recording speeches, lectures, and interviews. There is no maximum time for a recording, and you can mark the recording at interesting junctures while your speaker speaks. During subsequent playback, a simple click on the marked timeline will bring you back to a place you found noteworthy.

To start recording, click the microphone icon in the left pane. While recording is in progress, Voice Recorder presents a flag icon that you can use to mark points of interest. The three time indications at the bottom of the following illustration indicate marks that have already been made.

When you have finished recording, Voice Recorder's left pane adds the new recording to the list of those you've already made, as shown next.

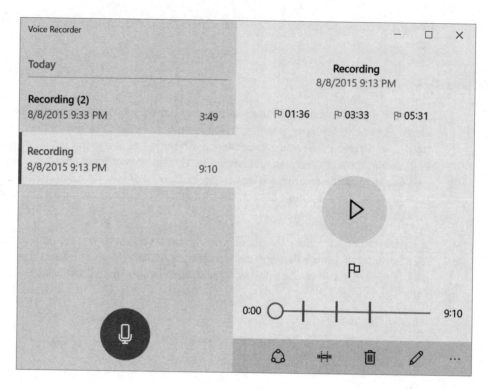

To change a recording's name to something descriptive, click the pencil icon on the toolbar in the right pane.

Voice Recorder includes a Trim command, by means of which you can shorten a recording. When you click the second icon on the toolbar, black handles appear at the beginning and end of the timeline:

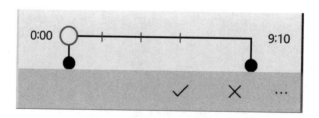

Drag the handles forward or backward and click the check mark to trim your recording.

CHAPTER 10

Music, photos, movies, and games

Not that long ago, your PC was the indispensable hub of digital media. Music and movies were delivered on shiny discs, and you needed a desktop or laptop PC to rip CDs, watch DVDs, transfer photos from your digital camera, and share your photos on social media.

Today, the explosion of mobile devices and cloud-based entertainment services means the PC is no longer a hub, and shiny discs are now an endangered species. The PC is still uniquely qualified for tasks that involve editing and managing a media collection and syncing it with cloud services, but for playing those files you're more likely to use a smaller mobile device.

The three core media apps included with Windows 10—Groove Music, Photos, and Movies & TV—are tightly connected to the cloud. Like other apps built on the Universal Windows Platform, they're touch-friendly but also work well in a window on a conventional PC.

If you're worried that the digital media landscape in Windows 10 will be completely alien, we can reassure you that a few of your familiar touchstones remain: Windows Media Player is still available for playing music and movies on a desktop or portable PC. Likewise, the venerable Windows Photo Viewer and, yes, Microsoft Paint are still around, virtually unchanged from their Windows 7 incarnations.

In the living room, it's still possible to connect a PC to a home entertainment system directly, although the experience is less enjoyable than it used to be now that Windows Media Center is no longer available with any edition of Windows 10 (in fact, Media Center is removed from your system when you upgrade from a prior edition). More modern alternatives include streaming content from a Windows tablet or PC to a large display (like your big-screen TV) by using built-in support for the Miracast standard. And if your living room or rec room includes an Xbox One game console, it's easy to connect to a Windows 10 PC.

But before we talk about apps, let's review the basics of how Windows 10 organizes media files.

Managing your digital media libraries

In the Windows world, digital media files are managed just like other files. As with earlier versions, Windows 10 creates default libraries for Music, Pictures, and Videos, and it uses metadata in files stored within folders in those libraries to organize their contents.

➤ For a detailed discussion of how to view and manage metadata in files, see "Managing file properties and metadata" in Chapter 12, "Organizing and searching for files."

In Details view, files in these locations are arranged in columns that reflect their content. The default Music folder, for example, displays song titles, contributing artists, and the name of the album containing those songs. After selecting multiple MP3 files, you can use the properties dialog box to change the album or artist title for the entire group, as shown in Figure 10-1. (This editing is supported in all widely used digital media formats, including Windows Media Audio and several lossless formats we discuss later in this chapter.)

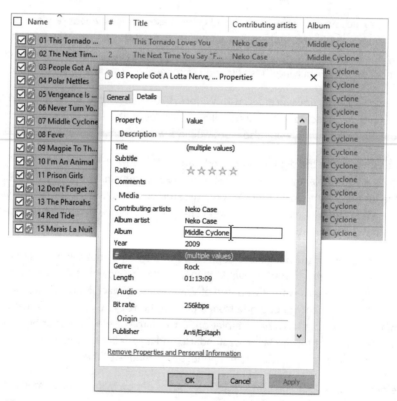

Figure 10-1 Use the properties dialog box to edit metadata for music files, such as changing the album title for a selection of tracks.

When you use File Explorer to open folders that contain music, photos, or videos, Windows adds a custom tab to the ribbon, with tasks appropriate for that type of data. Figure 10-2, for example, shows the Music Tools tab, with options to play files from the current folder, add them to a playlist, or "cast" them to a device such as a Miracast-enabled TV or an Xbox One (a topic we discuss in more detail later in this chapter).

Figure 10-2 For folders containing music files, the File Explorer ribbon adds a custom Music Tools tab with commands for direct playback to the default player app.

Likewise, folders containing digital image files contain a custom Picture Tools tab like the one shown in Figure 10-3, which offers an extremely limited set of customization options as well as the ability to bore your friends and family with a slide show cast to your Xbox One or other compatible device.

Despite the new look, all the new digital media apps use the tried-and-true library capabilities in Windows 10 to determine which files to display when you open the respective app. You can customize the selection of folders included in each library by clicking the gear icon to open Settings in any of the three apps. Figure 10-4, for example, shows the dialog box that appears when you click or tap Choose Where We Look For Music in the Groove Music app.

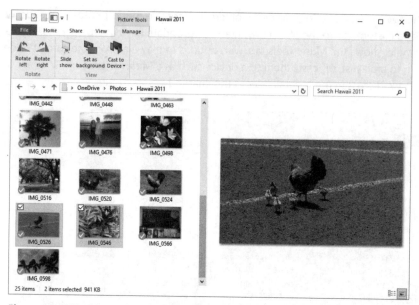

Figure 10-3 The Picture Tools tab appears automatically on folders containing images, offering simple rotation tools and slide-show capabilities.

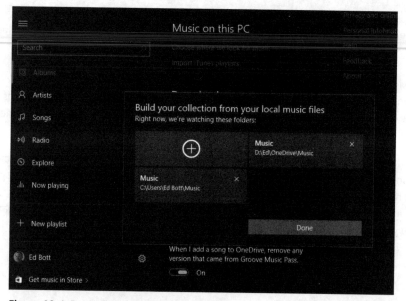

Figure 10-4 Every digital media app in Windows 10 includes a setting to adjust which folders are included in the corresponding library.

Note that any changes you make to the selection of folders in any of the three core digital media apps are automatically reflected in the corresponding Windows 10 library and vice versa.

And, of course, as befits a cloud-centric operating system, all those apps are also integrated with OneDrive. The Photos app, for example, includes the contents of your OneDrive Camera Roll folder, which contains photos you upload from mobile devices (iPhones and Android devices are supported, as are Windows phones). You can upload pictures to OneDrive manually or configure your phone so that new photos are automatically uploaded to OneDrive for safekeeping and sharing.

Similarly, you can store your music collection in OneDrive and stream or download its contents to any Windows 10 device using the Groove Music app.

Music

No, you're not seeing double. Windows 10 includes two programs whose primary purpose is to play digital music files.

- Groove Music is a Universal Windows app and the default app for playing music files in Windows 10. It's the direct successor to the Xbox Music app from Windows 8.1, and it traces its ancestry (at least indirectly) to the late, lamented Zune Music app. Using Groove Music, you can stream or download your music collection from OneDrive, play music files in a variety of formats, and stream customized playlists from the Groove Music service based on a single track, an album, or an artist. With a Groove Music Pass, you can listen to any album in the service's vast collection and download those album tracks for offline listening on up to four devices.

- Windows Media Player in Windows 10 is virtually identical to the version shipped with Windows 7. (The single, very large exception is support for files saved using formats based on lossless compression.) The most distinctive feature of Windows Media Player compared with Groove Music is its ability to play CDs and rip their contents to digital formats. It can also sync content with some older models of portable music players.

Both programs create indexed libraries from the contents of folders in your Music library. The indexes are stored separately.

CHAPTER 10

Groove Music

Every installation of Windows 10 sets Groove Music as the default music player. Figure 10-5 offers an overview of the program's interface.

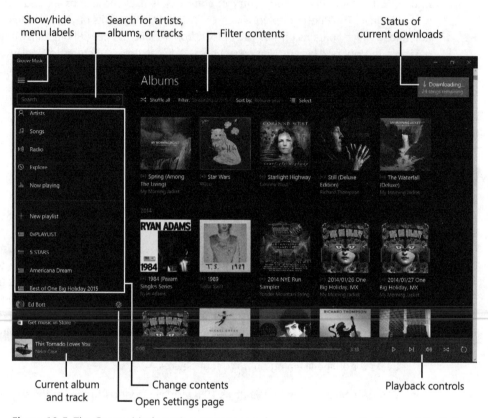

Show/hide menu labels · **Search for artists, albums, or tracks** · **Filter contents** · **Status of current downloads**

Current album and track · **Change contents** · **Open Settings page** · **Playback controls**

Figure 10-5 The Groove Music app's contents pane shows your entire collection by default. You can switch to a view by artist or show all songs by using links on the left.

The design of the Groove Music app isn't difficult to figure out. A menu pane on the left allows you to change the way your collection is displayed (Albums, Artists, or Songs). You can start a customized streaming playlist by clicking Radio, browse new albums available for purchase (or for playback with a Groove Music Pass) by using the Explore button, or display the current playlist by clicking Now Playing. Your custom playlists appear at the bottom of the left pane.

Figure 10-6 shows the options when you click to display the contents of an individual album. (The four options to the right of the album cover are visible because we clicked More.)

Figure 10-6 The options at the bottom apply only to the current selection. Use the Add To option to send tracks or an entire album to a custom playlist.

As we noted earlier, Groove Music integrates neatly with OneDrive. Any compatible files you save to the Music folder in OneDrive are available for playback when you sign in on any Windows 10 device. The resulting collection can be displayed along with locally stored files or maintained separately. Use the Filter menu, as shown in Figure 10-7, to specify your preferences.

Search terms you enter in the box at the top of the menu show results from your collection by default, as shown in Figure 10-8. You can change the scope to Full Catalog to show additional results, which are available for purchase or, with a Groove Music Pass, for streaming and download.

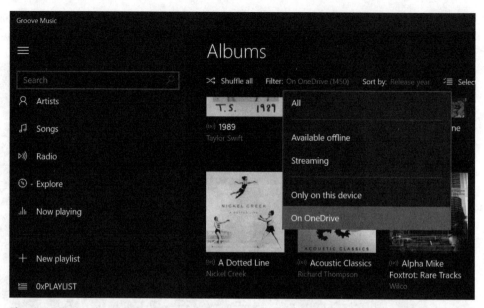

Figure 10-7 Use the Filter menu to show only a subset: albums saved in the OneDrive Music folder, for example, or those available offline.

Figure 10-8 Searches display results that match artists, albums, and songs from your collection by default. Use the Full Catalog option to see additional results from the Store.

TROUBLESHOOTING

You can't hear any sound from your speakers

Modern PCs often have multiple playback channels, in both digital and analog formats. Audio playback hardware can be found in a variety of locations: on your motherboard; as an optional feature on an add-in video card, with multichannel sound typically delivered over an HDMI cable; on an add-in sound card; or through headphones connected physically or wirelessly using a Bluetooth connection. It's not unusual to find multiple audio playback options in a single PC, especially one that has been upgraded extensively.

If your hardware and drivers appear to be installed correctly but you're unable to hear any sound, right-click the speaker icon in the notification area at the right side of the taskbar and choose Playback Devices. This opens the Sound dialog box from Control Panel, with the Playback tab selected. Look for a green check mark next to the device currently designated as the default playback device. In the following example, the built-in speakers are disabled, and headphones connected via Bluetooth are used for communications programs and for playback. To change the default playback device, click the Speakers/Headphones option (the exact wording varies depending on how the driver developer chose to implement it) and then click Set Default.

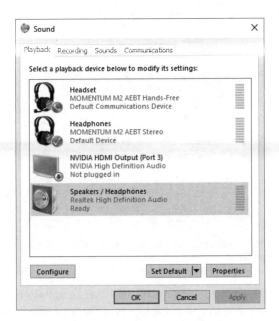

➤ For details on how to configure hardware and install drivers to unlock the functionality of those devices, see Chapter 13, "Hardware."

Using Windows Media Player to rip CDs

If you prefer the familiar Windows Media Player interface to the more modern Groove Music app, relief is a search away. We don't recommend Windows Media Player for new Windows 10 users, but if you're already comfortable with its quirks and you don't want to access your music collection from the cloud, it's a thoroughly appropriate choice.

We don't include exhaustive instructions for Windows Media Player in this edition (if you're interested in that, pick up a copy of *Windows 7 Inside Out*). The one task Windows Media Player can perform that Groove Music can't is to convert ("rip") tracks from an audio CD and save them in digital formats on your local hard drive.

Figure 10-9 shows a CD (selected in the left pane in Windows Media Player) with its tracks being ripped to the local hard drive.

Figure 10-9 The best reason to use Windows Media Player is to rip an audio CD to digital format, a task that Groove Music can't perform.

When you're connected to the Internet, Windows Media Player consults its online data sources to determine the name of your disc, as well as the names of the artist(s) and tracks and the genre of music the disc contains. This information is used to automatically tag and name tracks. You can use Windows Media Player or File Explorer to change those tags if necessary.

Windows Media Player copies each CD track to a separate file and stores it, by default, in the Music folder of the currently signed-in user (%UserProfile%\Music). Using the album metadata, Windows Media Player creates a folder for each artist and a subfolder for each album by that artist.

The digital files you create by ripping a CD are completely free of technical restrictions on your ability to play them back or make identical copies: you can listen to the saved tracks on your PC or on a mobile device, burn a collection of tracks to a custom CD, or copy those tracks to another PC or to OneDrive. Before you use Windows Media Player to rip a CD, however, it's wise to check the program's settings.

For practical purposes, files copied from audio CDs to your hard disk must be compressed; if you rip tracks to your hard disk using the uncompressed WAV format, a typical 60-minute CD will consume more than half a gigabyte of disk space. Compressing the files means you can store more music on your hard disk, and it makes the process of backing up and streaming music files easier and more efficient.

When it comes to compression, your first choice is simple: lossy or lossless? Most popular algorithms used to compress audio (and video) files are lossy, which means that they achieve compression by eliminating data. In the case of audio files, the data that's tossed out during the compression process consists mostly of frequencies that are outside the normal range of human hearing. However, the more you compress a file, the more likely you are to degrade its audio quality to the point where you'll notice it.

Windows 10 allows you to rip tracks using three different lossless compressed formats: Windows Media Audio Lossless, Apple Lossless Audio Codec (ALAC), or Free Lossless Audio Codec (FLAC). We recommend FLAC, which is widely supported and stores music files efficiently without sacrificing any information. In theory, at least, a track ripped in a lossless format should be indistinguishable from the original.

CHAPTER 10

NOTE

Although you can play files saved in FLAC format from a local disk, you cannot stream this format from OneDrive.

Deciding on the type and amount of compression involves a tradeoff between disk space and audio quality. The level of compression is determined by the bit rate you select for your copied files. Higher bit rates preserve more of the original sound quality of your audio tracks but result in larger files on your hard disk or portable player. Lower bit rates allow you to pack more music into limited space at a cost in fidelity.

For compatibility with the maximum number of devices, the widely used MP3 format is best.

To set your preferences after inserting a CD, click the Rip Settings button on the Player toolbar. (You can also reach this dialog box by clicking Organize and then Options, and then clicking the Rip Music tab.) Click Format, and then choose one of the six available formats, as shown in Figure 10-10. If you choose a format that allows lossy compression, use the slider at the bottom of the dialog box to choose a quality level.

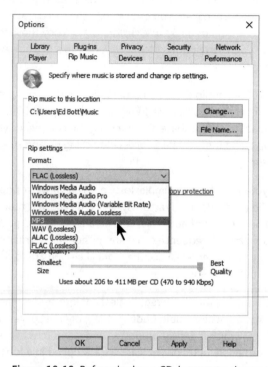

Figure 10-10 Before ripping a CD, be sure to choose a format and quality level here.

As long as you have that dialog box open, use the options at the top to change the location where your ripped files are saved and to define the default naming convention for individual tracks.

Managing photos and digital images

Windows 10 includes three built-in apps suitable for viewing, managing, and editing photos in digital image formats. In this section, we concentrate on the Photos app, with a nod to two older desktop programs—Windows Photo Viewer and Paint—which exist primarily for compatibility's sake.

As with its music and movie counterparts, the Photos app displays the contents of all files it finds in your Pictures library. It also includes the option to show photos and videos from One-Drive, even if those files are not synchronized with your PC or tablet.

Figure 10-11 shows the relatively simple user interface of the Photos app, with the entire collection available for browsing and editing.

Figure 10-11 By default, the Photos app organizes your collection of digital pictures by date, with the newest photos displayed first.

Several options in the Photos app's Settings page are worth checking before you invest a lot of time and energy learning its inner workings. Figure 10-12 shows these options, with the two most important at the top of the list.

CHAPTER 10

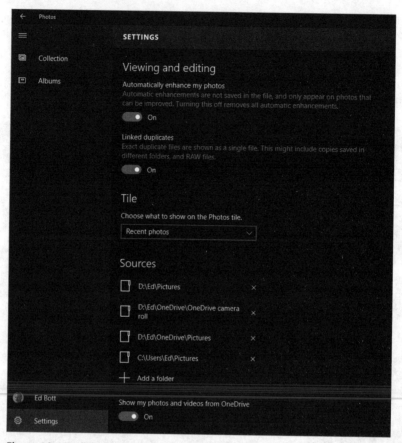

Figure 10-12 Click Settings (the gear icon in the lower left corner) to display these options.

Digital photography purists will probably want to disable both of the options at the top of this list, or at least be aware that they're enabled.

The first option automatically "enhances" photos as they're displayed. The underlying file isn't altered, but the image you (and your audience) see in the app might be changed to make it look better—at least in the eyes of the Photos app's algorithms.

The Linked Duplicates setting is intended to eliminate the frustration of seeing multiple copies of the same image. This can occur if your camera captures images in RAW format but also saves a lower-resolution copy for easier downloading on space-sensitive mobile devices. You can see the full selection of image files by using File Explorer.

Finally, at the bottom of the list is a switch that allows you to include photos and videos from OneDrive. This option includes every photo and every video in every folder. If you prefer to see only files in selected folders that are synced to your local PC or device, turn this option off and add the local synced OneDrive folders to your Pictures library.

Clicking an individual photo opens it for viewing, sharing, and editing, with an array of tools appearing in a bar above the image, as shown in Figure 10-13. Note that we've clicked the ellipsis at the end of the menu bar to show a drop-down menu of additional options.

Figure 10-13 By default, the Enhance option is selected in the menu bar. In addition to options for sharing and editing this photo, you can click the ellipsis to the right of the menu bar for more options.

Choose the File Info option to see selected details about the image, as shown here, with a clickable link to open the folder containing the image in File Explorer.

Using the Photos app to crop and edit pictures

The greatest strength of the Photos app is its collection of lightweight editing tools. After opening an image, click or tap the pen icon to see the full set of editing tools, as shown in Figure 10-14.

For quickly turning a casual shot into something worth keeping and sharing, the tools in the Basic Fixes category are extremely useful. Here's what each one does:

- **Enhance.** Use this option to allow the app's algorithms to analyze the image and make basic changes. You're likely to see the image straightened and the color balance or contrast corrected, for example.

- **Rotate.** This control lets you shift the angle of the picture 90 degrees at a time, to fix images that are sideways or upside down.

- **Crop.** Cut out extraneous material, using either a free-form selection or a standard aspect ratio. (See more details following this list.)

- **Straighten.** This option lets you move the horizon of the image in either direction, one degree at a time, for those occasions when you were holding the camera at a slight angle when the picture was snapped.

- **Red Eye.** Removes the red-eye effect caused by using a flash when snapping photos of people. (Note that this has no effect on pictures of dogs and cats and other nonhuman species.)

- **Retouch.** Click this tool to change the mouse pointer to a tool that blurs anything you click with it. Use it to remove distractions and clutter from an image.

Figure 10-14 Select one of the five options on the left to see editing tools in that category on the right.

The Crop tool is probably the one you'll use most often. Figure 10-15 shows it in action.

Figure 10-15 When cropping, use the tool on the menu bar to display this list of preset aspect ratios.

Drag any corner to make the crop area larger or smaller. After setting the correct size, click the photo and drag the portion you want to keep into the crop area. Click the check mark to save your changes.

The photo editing options available on the right side of the image change based on what you select on the left side. The following options are available in addition to the Basic Fixes tools we listed previously:

- **Filters.** Select from six predefined tones that highlight different shades (blue, gold, and so on); the final choice is black and white.

- **Light.** Change the brightness and contrast or emphasize or deemphasize highlights and shadows. The figure following this list shows an example of this feature in use.

- **Color.** Change the temperature, tint, or saturation of the image—for example, to compensate for a blue tint from indoor lighting. The final option in this group allows you to "color boost" a specific area by dragging a pin icon onto the spot to get the boost.

- **Effects.** The two options here allow you to create a vignette, with the center section you select in focus and the surrounding area slightly out of focus (you can see this effect applied to the image in Figure 10-16), or use the Selective Focus option to highlight a key portion of the image while blurring the rest.

Figure 10-16 shows the editing tools available for the Light category.

Figure 10-16 Selecting Light on the left exposes a set of editing tools on the right. Using these tools effectively takes a little practice.

Using these editing controls takes a little practice. When you click Brightness, for example, a circle appears to its left with a large white dot next to it, as shown on the right here. Drag that circle clockwise or counterclockwise to make the image brighter or dimmer (with the number in the center of the circle increasing or decreasing according to your changes). The other controls work in a similar fashion.

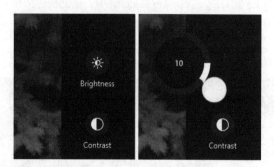

After making changes to a photo, you can save it (replacing the original) or save a copy. The respective controls are available above the photo itself.

Organizing photos into albums

Previously, we've discussed tools for managing an entire collection. The second option in the menu bar on the left side of the Photos app allows a more focused view of photos.

The Albums feature also illustrates a theme we've discussed repeatedly in this book. Our coverage is based on the Photos app as it existed at the time of the initial Windows 10 release, on July 29, 2015. In that release, the Albums feature feels decidedly unfinished, and we're confident that the app you're using as you read this section will be more polished (and will continue to improve over time).

One of the biggest disconnects in the release we discuss here is between the Albums feature at *OneDrive.com* and the feature of the same name in this app. In OneDrive, you create albums manually and can add photos from any folder. In the Photos app, albums are created automatically, based on dates and events. You can refine the selection by removing photos, but you can't combine two albums into one.

Switching to Albums view in the Photos app produces a scrolling list of all automatically created albums, as shown in Figure 10-17.

Figure 10-17 In the initial release of the Photos app, there's no way to create an album manually. These albums were automatically generated by the app.

The algorithm that creates albums adds a label to each one, based on the date the photos were taken, and then picks a cover photo and a selection of photos to include in the album. You can customize the name, change the cover photo, and select a different batch of photos. To start, open the album and then click or tap the pen-shaped Edit button. That opens an editing window like the one shown in Figure 10-18.

As with all such changes, be sure to click or tap the check mark (at the top of the page) to save your changes.

CHAPTER 10

Figure 10-18 In this editing view, you can change the title of an album, replace the cover photo, and add or remove photos from the album itself.

Windows Photo Viewer and Paint

For compatibility purposes, Windows 10 includes the Windows Photo Viewer desktop app. Figure 10-19 shows this app, which is capable of displaying a single photo at a time and has no editing options aside from the capability to rotate a photo 90 degrees. Its user interface clearly dates back to a bygone era.

Figure 10-19 The Windows Photo Viewer app, still included with Windows 10, sports a user interface from the Windows Vista era.

We can't really think of a good reason why someone would use this legacy app in place of the more modern Photos app. Its only distinguishing feature is the capability to burn a slide show to CD or DVD, a task you can also accomplish with any number of third-party apps.

And then there's Microsoft Paint (Mspaint.exe), which has been a part of Windows since version 1.0. Despite its age, Paint still has a few useful tricks up its sleeve. Its most useful feature is the capability to save an image in an alternative format—if you've saved an image in the space-hogging Windows Bitmap format, for example, you can quickly convert it to a much more efficient, compressed format, such as PNG or JPEG, by using the Save As option on the File menu, as shown in Figure 10-20.

CHAPTER 10

The Paint app also allows you to resize an image, a capability that is useful if your original image was captured at a very high resolution (with a correspondingly large file size) and you plan to post it on a webpage or share it via email, where the large file size might be unwelcome.

Figure 10-20 Use Paint's File menu to convert an image to a different format.

To shrink an image using Paint, click Resize on the Home tab. That opens the dialog box shown in Figure 10-21, which allows you to specify a percentage or an actual height or width, measured in pixels. The decrease in file size can be substantial.

Figure 10-21 Use Paint to change the size of an image file; this option is useful when you plan to post an image online and file size is a concern.

Watching movies, recorded TV shows, and video clips

The Movies & TV app is similar in design to Groove Music and Photos. Of the three, it is probably the simplest to use, doing its handful of required tasks very well.

Inside OUT

What about DVDs?

In a significant break from the past, Windows 10 doesn't include the capability to play DVDs (or MPEG-2 files ripped from DVDs). That decision is a reflection of two market realities: Most new PCs don't include optical disc drives at all, and the cost of royalties for DVD playback software is significant. Microsoft offers a DVD Player app that is free for anyone who upgrades a Windows 7, Windows 8, or Windows 8.1 PC that included Windows Media Center; this app should be installed automatically and be available in the All Apps list on any device that was upgraded from a previous version of Windows that contained Windows Media Center.. If you don't qualify for that app, we recommend the free VLC software, which contains the necessary codecs and is available in a desktop version (from *videolan.org*) and also in a modern version from the Windows Store.

The left-side menu bar in the Movies & TV app allows you to see content you've purchased from the Windows Store (previous purchases from the Xbox store are also included and can be played back). Figure 10-22 shows a typical TV library.

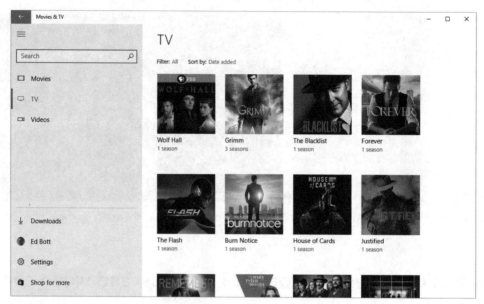

Figure 10-22 Movies and TV programs you've purchased through an Xbox or from the Windows Store are available for playback here.

The Videos page allows you to see your collection of personal video files captured in compatible formats, such as those in MP4 formats recorded on a modern smartphone. The player window, shown in Figure 10-23, includes the typical controls for playback, with a slider bar that allows you to move to a specific point in the file.

Figure 10-23 Click the double-headed diagonal arrow to zoom a video to full screen, hiding elements such as the title bar and playback controls.

Miracast

You have a high-definition video on your Windows 10 laptop or tablet. You have a large high-definition TV connected to a surround-sound system in your living room. If you have a long enough HDMI cable, you can connect your laptop's video output to a spare HDMI input on the big-screen TV. That option works, but it's an awkward solution at best. So how do you bring that video to the big screen without tripping over a 15-foot cord?

One answer, if you have the right hardware, is to stream your laptop display (with 5.1 surround sound) to the larger, louder living-room system. For this task, you can choose from a variety of wireless standards, each one backed by a large hardware or software company. Windows 10 natively supports a standard called Miracast, which is designed for wirelessly mirroring a mobile display and streaming high-quality sound between mobile devices and large displays, with (in theory) perfect fidelity.

In homes, Miracast is mostly an entertainment option, good for projecting YouTube videos and the occasional webcast to a larger screen. This setup is also effective for a conference room or a classroom, where the Miracast adapter can be permanently attached to a large-screen display and available for connection from any Windows 10 device.

CHAPTER 10

To project your laptop or tablet display using Miracast, you need a compatible receiver, such as a TV or Blu-ray player that also supports the standard, or an external adapter that connects to your TV's HDMI port. Although the Miracast standard is relatively new, the technology behind it is well tested, and there are an increasing number of compatible devices on the market. The most versatile option is a thumb drive–sized adapter like the Microsoft Wireless Display adapter shown in Figure 10-24, which plugs into an HDMI input on a TV or monitor and draws power via a USB adapter.

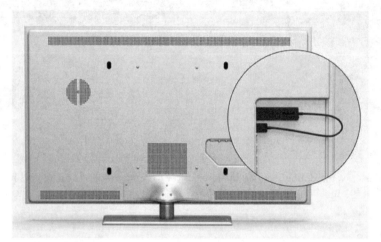

Figure 10-24 The Microsoft Wireless Display adapter plugs into an HDMI port and draws power via a USB connection, turning a TV into a Miracast receiver.

A Miracast receiver uses Wi-Fi Direct to turn itself into a special-purpose wireless hotspot. Connecting a Miracast-compatible device to that invisible hotspot allows the device to mirror or extend its display to the larger screen.

After preparing the Miracast receiver to accept incoming connections (usually a simple matter of turning it on and selecting the matching input on the TV), open Windows 10's Action Center and click or tap the Connect button. That opens up a panel that lists available devices, where you can click or tap the entry for your Miracast receiver, with the goal of making a connection like the one shown in Figure 10-25.

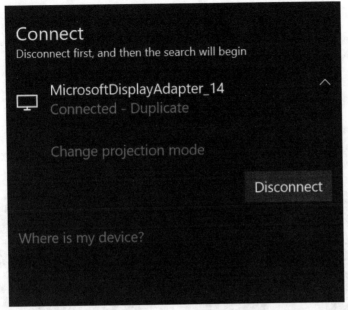

Figure 10-25 Tapping the Connect button at the bottom of the Windows 10 Action Center allows you to connect to a Miracast device and mirror your laptop or tablet display to a larger device such as a TV.

The first time you encounter a Miracast adapter, you're prompted to add it, installing a device driver in the process. (You can see previously paired and available devices in the Connect pane.) On subsequent visits, that device should be available as a target you can tap or click in the Connect pane. After successfully connecting to the Miracast receiver, you can duplicate the display on your laptop or tablet to the larger screen, allowing you to wirelessly project a PowerPoint presentation to a conference room TV, watch a livestream in your living room, or cue up a music playlist for a party.

All three built-in Windows 10 media apps include a Cast option that allows you to send the current video and audio output to a previously configured device.

After you make a Miracast connection, you can change the projection mode just as you would with a second display connected directly to your PC. Options available in the Connect pane allow you to extend the display, so that you can watch a webcast or a video conference call on the large screen while you work on your laptop; use the second screen only; or use the PC screen only, severing the Miracast connection.

CHAPTER 10

Xbox and other forms of online entertainment

Microsoft's Xbox One game console connects with Windows 10 devices in several ways. (In fact, as we write this section, Microsoft has announced plans to run a customized edition of Windows 10 on the Xbox One, an upgrade that should happen in November 2015.)

If you own an Xbox One console, we recommend that you check out two Windows 10 apps.

Xbox One SmartGlass, shown in Figure 10-26, turns a Windows 10 touchscreen device into a very capable remote control for your console. You can tap, slide, and type to control games, navigate the Xbox home screen, and pause or play back media files.

Figure 10-26 The Xbox One SmartGlass app for Windows 10 allows you to use a touchscreen device to control your Xbox One console remotely.

The Xbox app for Windows 10 allows more direct connections to an Xbox One, including the capability to stream games directly from the console to a Windows 10 device for immediate play even if someone else is using the TV that the Xbox One is connected to.

As Figure 10-27 shows, you can see your entire activity feed, connect with friends, and record games by using this versatile app.

Figure 10-27 The Xbox app includes most of the capabilities that diehard Xbox gamers want to see.

Browsing the Internet

It's a well-known phenomenon in software development: as applications get simpler and easier to use, they get more complex under the covers. Microsoft says that in developing its new web browser, Microsoft Edge, some 220,000 lines of code were deleted from the old browser, Internet Explorer 11. But more than 300,000 lines of code were added. The deletions removed baggage from the past—no longer needed or wanted in a modern browser. The additions brought new and useful features, such as the reading list and web notes, and integration with Cortana, plus support for new web-development standards and better interoperability with other modern browsers.

For the Windows 10 user, the one apparent complexity introduced by Edge is the presence of two Microsoft browsers. Edge is the default, but Internet Explorer remains as an alternative. (You'll find it in the All Apps section of your Start menu, within the subfolder Windows Accessories.) Quite unlike the situation in Windows 8.1, however, which had both a modern and a desktop variant of Internet Explorer, the two browsers in Windows 10 are totally distinct. Edge is a modern browser built to modern standards; Internet Explorer is an aging browser encumbered in many ways over the years by the need to maintain compatibility with old-style web-design practices. In the years ahead, Microsoft will continue to provide technical support and security updates for Internet Explorer 11, but development will be focused entirely on Edge.

Large organizations and other users who rely on older web technologies such as ActiveX for their intranets or line-of-business web applications might have reason to make Internet Explorer the default browser. Most others will prefer Edge for its uncluttered design, touch-friendliness, new features, speed, and, above all, its enhanced security. Like all other modern apps adhering to the Universal Windows Platform, Edge *always* runs in a protected environment. This is not to say you can't damage your system by downloading malicious goods or falling for phishing scams. (SmartScreen Filter will warn you about sites that might be dangerous, but it can't restrain you from choosing unwisely.) But Edge does eliminate many of the

CHAPTER 11

security hazards—particularly rogue ActiveX controls and browser helper objects—that have plagued Internet Explorer over the years.

➤ **For information about SmartScreen Filter, see "Using SmartScreen Filter to avoid phishing scams and dicey downloads" later in this chapter.**

For most users the choice is straightforward: use and enjoy Edge, but keep Internet Explorer on hand for the occasional website that requires it. (A simple command in Edge lets you open the current page in Internet Explorer.)

In this chapter, we survey Edge—with frequent comparisons with the still-present, still-useful Internet Explorer 11.

NOTE

Edge, like Windows 10 itself, is a work in progress and will receive frequent updates. Certain features that are not in place as we write (shortly after the official launch of Windows 10 in July 2015) may in fact be part of the version of Edge that you are using. For example, the ability to sync favorites between computers using the same Microsoft account was only a promise at launch; by the time you read this book, it may be an actuality. An extension model, based on JavaScript and HTML technologies, is also promised for later in 2015. At initial release, the only extensions supported by Edge were Adobe Flash Player and PDF rendering, both built in to the browser.

Why the new browser?

From a high altitude, the history of Internet Explorer, from its inception in 1995 to the present, can be seen as a competition between antagonistic ambitions—to adapt to new web-development standards (and to new competing browsers, such as Mozilla Firefox and Google Chrome) while maintaining compatibility with the past. Each new version of the browser made improvements to its predecessors. But because so many sites had been developed on the assumption that they would be viewed through older versions of browsers, the newer browsers had to include the means to emulate the older. So, for example, the Compatibility View option introduced in Internet Explorer 8 allowed users to correct some display problems that arose with sites that had been written for Internet Explorer 7. Moreover, older releases remained in use as newer releases arrived, presenting developers with the headache-inducing need to support numerous variant browser versions. (As of spring 2014, Internet Explorer 8 was reported to still have 20 percent of the browser market, despite the release of three later versions; developers could not comfortably ignore that large a user population.)

With Edge, Microsoft has set out to create a clean-slate, modern browser, free of compatibility freight and free of the most egregious security hazards. The focus is on support for current and forthcoming web standards and interoperability, so that sites developed for other modern browsers will run with minimal or no modifications on Edge.

After 20 years of service, the Trident rendering engine of Internet Explorer, Mshtml.dll, has been rewritten for the new Edge rendering engine, Edgehtml.dll. (The *rendering engine* is what translates HTML and other web code into an intelligible, navigable website.) Among the technologies not included in the new rendering engine are the following:

- ActiveX

- Browser helper objects

- Document modes

- Vector Markup Language (VML)

- VBScript

➤ **For more detailed information about the changes in EdgeHTML, see the Microsoft Edge Dev Blog, at** *http://blogs.windows.com/msedgedev*, **as well as the blog post "Microsoft Edge: Building a safer browser," at** *bit.ly/ms-edge-intro*. **For more about technologies that are either in development or under consideration for Edge, see** *http://dev.modern.ie*.

Browser basics

The following sections outline some of the essentials of browsing in either Edge or Internet Explorer. We discuss, among other things, how to make your choice of default browser and default search engine.

Setting or changing your default browser

Edge is Microsoft's recommended default browser. To make a different browser your default, open Settings and search for **default apps**. Under Choose Default Apps, click Web Browser. The menu that appears will list Edge, Internet Explorer, and any other browsers you happen to have installed on your system. (You'll also see the option to visit the Store.)

➤ **For information about fine-tuning your default settings—for example, assigning particular browsers to particular web protocols—see "Setting default programs and file-type associations" in Chapter 8, "Using and managing modern apps and desktop programs."**

Within Edge, you can open the current page in Internet Explorer by clicking the ellipsis icon at the far right of the toolbar (see Figure 11-1) and then clicking Open With Internet Explorer. If you are working in an environment in which Enterprise Mode has been enabled, sites configured to open in Enterprise Mode will automatically be displayed in Internet Explorer.

CHAPTER 11

User interface basics in Edge

Edge continues the trend toward visual simplicity (the minimization of "chrome") that has been characteristic of recent iterations of Internet Explorer. But whereas the menu bar in Internet Explorer is optional (you can make it appear or disappear by pressing the Alt key), Edge has no menu bar. What you see is what there is—with the exception of two possible customizations:

- You can add the Home button to your toolbar by clicking More Actions (the ellipsis icon), choosing Settings, scrolling to the bottom of the Settings pane, clicking View Advanced Settings, and then turning on the switch below Show The Home Button. There you can also type the address of the home page you want to use. On narrow screens, the Home button might push other controls too close together for finger navigation, but otherwise it's a handy item to have on board.

- You can display the Favorites bar by clicking More Actions, then Settings, then Show The Favorites Bar.

Figure 11-1 shows the landmarks in Edge (with the Home button displayed) and Internet Explorer 11. Note that controls in Edge are spaced to ease use on touchscreens.

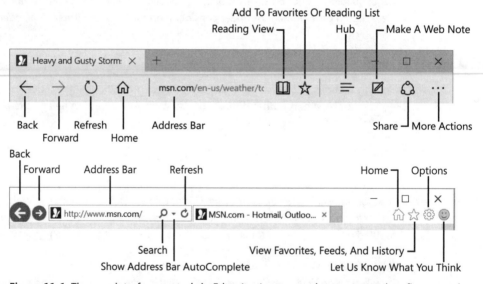

Figure 11-1 The user-interface controls in Edge (top) are spaced to accommodate fingers and a stylus. Internet Explorer (bottom) offers similar controls in a more traditional layout.

Using the Start page in Edge

Unless you have configured it to do otherwise, a new instance of Edge opens on the Start page. (You can also reach the Start page by entering **about:start** in the address bar.) As Figure 11-2 shows, the Start page asks for your next destination and presents a large field in which you can respond. You can enter either a Uniform Resource Locator (URL) or a search string here.

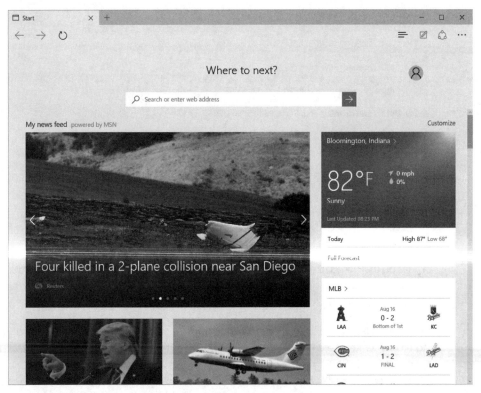

Figure 11-2 In the large input field atop Edge's Start page, you can type either a web address or a search string.

If Edge can parse your input as a web address, it takes you there directly. Otherwise, it passes your keystrokes to your default search provider.

CHAPTER 11

If the Start page is not present, simply type in the address bar, which functions the same way as the Start page's input field. In either place, Edge does its best to simplify your typing task. While you type, the browser offers a list of potential sites and search suggestions:

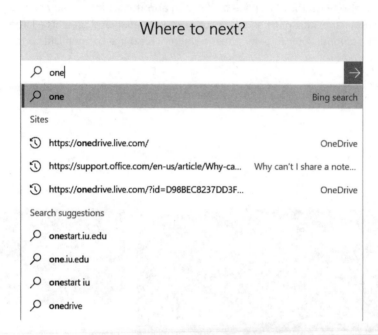

The icon that looks like a clock in retrograde motion marks sites derived from your browsing history. The search suggestions that appear below this group are based on information gathered by Cortana about your interests and location.

As Figure 11-2 shows, the rest of the Edge Start page, below the input field, is not given over to empty white space (the browser is not *that* Spartan); instead, it's filled with news-feed tiles, perhaps also including some tips about how to use Edge effectively. Here again, the browser does its best to track your interests, based on choices you have made in the info apps, your location, your selections in the Cortana Notebook, and so on. You can customize the news feed by clicking Customize in the upper right corner.

Cortana may pop up in your browser immediately if you type something about which she is particularly knowledgeable. Enter a flight number or the name of a currency, for example, and you will get status or rate information:

Cortana already knows a great many useful facts, and as time goes on you can expect the breadth of her expertise to expand.

Using tabs

Like all modern browsers, Internet Explorer and Edge allow you to keep multiple pages open on separate tabs in the same application window and switch between them quickly. This feature is a tremendous timesaver for anyone doing research or trying to juggle multiple tasks.

Tab grouping in Internet Explorer

The tab grouping feature in Internet Explorer allows you to identify groups of related tabs visually. When you open a new tab by clicking a link in the current tab, Internet Explorer displays the original tab and the newcomer in the same color, showing you at a glance that the two tabs hold related content. Any additional tabs you generate from pages also acquire the same color. Right-clicking a tab within a tab group reveals commands to close all tabs in the current group, close all tabs not in the current group, and remove the current tab from the group.

Creating and manipulating tabs

In either browser, you can open a new tab in any of several ways:

- To open a new blank tab, press Ctrl+T, or click the New Tab button, just to the right of the current tabs.

- To open a link in a new tab without shifting focus from the current tab, right-click the link and choose Open In New Tab, or hold down Ctrl while you click the link.

- To open a link in a new tab and shift focus to the newly opened tab, hold down Ctrl+Shift and click.

- To duplicate a tab, press Ctrl+K, or right-click the tab and choose Duplicate Tab.

To close any open tab, click the X at the right side of its tab or press Ctrl+W.

To reposition a tab within an array of tabs, drag the tab you want to move laterally. To peel a tab off from the current browser window and make it appear in a new window, drag the tab upward or downward.

If more tabs are open than will fit in the browser window, a scrolling arrow appears to the left of the first tab or the right of the last (or both). Click the arrow to scroll in the indicated direction. You can also use keyboard shortcuts to cycle between tabs: press Ctrl+Tab to move from left to right or Ctrl+Shift+Tab to go from right to left.

When you have a lot of tabs open, particularly if you are working with more than one browser window, you might prefer to navigate by hovering your mouse pointer over the Edge or Internet Explorer icon on the taskbar. In Internet Explorer, Windows displays either thumbnails or names for all open tabs, and you can point to the one you want. If you point to a tab in a browser window, a ScreenTip shows the page title and web address. In Edge, each separate browser window gets its own thumbnail, but seeing individual tabs requires switching to that window.

Setting tabbed browsing options

If you regularly open large numbers of tabs, you will probably want to tweak the way your browser handles tabs. To see the options available in Edge, click More Actions, then Settings. Toward the bottom of the pane you'll find Open New Tabs With. Click the field below to unfurl this set of choices:

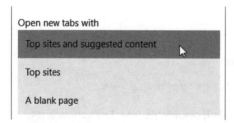

If you choose the first option or second option, new tabs will open with one or two rows (depending on screen width) of "top sites" suggestions:

After you've used Edge for a while, the Top Sites section of the new tab page should reflect your actual browsing history and become a useful navigational tool. Initially, however, you might find the selection a bit arbitrary. You can eliminate any sites that you don't want to see by pointing to the thumbnail and clicking the X.

A comparable but slightly different set of options is available in Internet Explorer. To find them, click Tools, then Internet Options. On the General tab of the Internet Options dialog box, click Tabs. In the Tabbed Browsing Settings dialog box, open the drop-down list below When A New Tab Is Opened, Open.

Reopening closed tabs

Did you accidentally close a tab before you were quite finished with it? No problem. In either browser, right-click any tab that's currently open and choose Reopen Closed Tab. Your most recently closed page will reappear in its previous location. You can repeat this procedure for other tabs you may have closed. If you like keyboard shortcuts, Ctrl+Shift+Tab reopens closed tabs without you having to move the mouse.

Internet Explorer, but not Edge, includes a command that lets you reopen a particular closed tab without having to reopen others that were closed later. Right-click a tab and choose Recently Closed Tabs. A menu will appear from which you can choose the page you want to revisit.

Restoring your last session

The new tab page in Internet Explorer includes a Reopen Last Session link that reloads every page that was open the last time you closed Internet Explorer. This can spare you some anguish if you accidentally close the browser when you meant to close only the current tab.

It can really rescue you if you sit down at your machine and find that your system has been restarted in your absence.

Be aware that if you have two or more Internet Explorer sessions open, each in a separate window, Reopen Last Session revives only the tabs that were open in the session that was closed last.

Edge automatically opens all tabs that were previously open if you restart Windows without closing Edge first. A separate setting will open each new session with the tabs that were open in the previous session even if you close Edge first. To avail yourself of this option, click More Actions, then Settings. Under Open With, choose Previous Pages.

Customizing your home and startup pages

Edge distinguishes between a home page and startup pages. Startup pages, of which you may have one or more, appear at the beginning of each new session. The home page, of which you may have but one, arrives only when you click the Home button—which is not displayed by default but can easily be added to your toolbar.

To configure startup pages, click More Actions, then Settings. As Figure 11-3 shows, your options are to open with the default Start page (about:start), the new tab page, the pages you had open when you last closed the browser, or one or more pages of your own choosing.

If you select A Specific Page Or Pages, Edge will propose MSN and Bing. If you want something else, click Custom. Then use the plus sign and address box to express your preferences. (If you're already looking at a page you want at startup, click in the address bar, press Ctrl+C to copy the page's URL, and then click in the Settings pane address box and press Ctrl+V to paste.)

Figure 11-3 You can use the Open With section of the Settings pane to tell Edge how you want to begin a session.

To use a home page, open the Settings pane, click View Advanced Settings, and then turn on the switch below Show The Home Button. Once the button has been enabled, a box will appear in which you can name a home page:

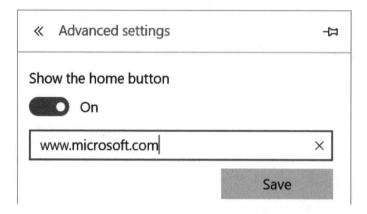

You can think of the Home button as a favorite-favorite shortcut. Link it to a page that you use frequently but not invariably. Assign as startup pages those that you must see every time you go to work in Edge.

Internet Explorer makes no comparable distinction between home and startup pages. But you can set multiple home pages by clicking Tools, then Internet Options. Fill out the Home Page section of the General tab with one or more URLs, each on a separate line:

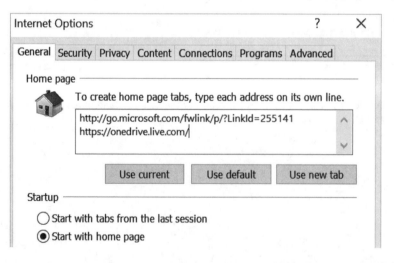

Note that the Startup section of this dialog box lets you dispense with home pages altogether and stipulate that each new session should begin with the tabs that were open in the last one.

Changing your default search provider

On a clean installation, Microsoft Bing, unsurprisingly, is the default search provider for both of Microsoft's browsers. With a few simple steps, you can change the default in either browser. The one gotcha is that to change the search provider in Edge, you must first have visited the search provider's website. You don't have to do anything there; you just have to have been there at least once for the provider to show up on the list of available search engines.

With that excursion completed, start in Edge by clicking More Actions, Settings, View Advanced Settings. Toward the bottom of the Advanced Settings pane, you'll see the name of your current default search provider:

Search in the address bar with

Bing (www.bing.com)   ∨

To make a change, open this drop-down list and choose Add New. On the screen that follows, you will find a list of search candidates (sites that you have visited that support the OpenSearch standard):

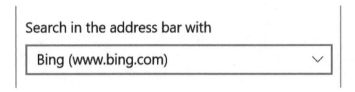

Select one and then click either Add As Default or Add (or Remove, if you want it off the list). If you click Add, Edge will not make it the default but will make it available in the Advanced Settings pane. If you want to use a certain search provider only some of the time, you can go to Advanced Settings and select it, without changing the default that will apply to searches in subsequent sessions.

To change providers in Internet Explorer, start by clicking Tools, Manage Add-Ons. The Search Providers section of the Manage Add-Ons dialog box, shown in Figure 11-4, displays a list of your current providers.

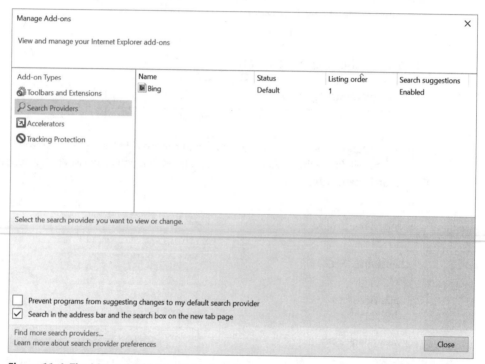

Figure 11-4 The Manage Add-Ons dialog box lists your current providers and offers a link whereby you can add more.

Near the lower left corner of the dialog box, if your eyes are good, you will find the link Find More Search Providers. Clicking this link takes you to the Internet Explorer Gallery, where you can make a selection. Click a provider, then click Add To Internet Explorer. In the confirmation dialog box that arrives next, you will have the opportunity to make your new provider the default:

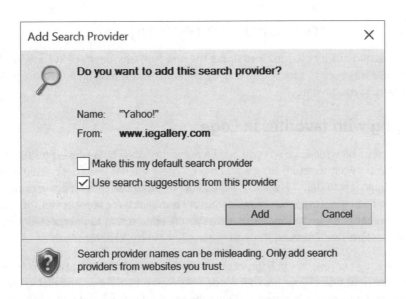

If you choose not to make the added provider the new default, you can still easily use the new search engine as an occasional alternative to the current default. When you search in the address bar, below the list of suggested sites, you'll find small icons for all your listed search providers (Figure 11-5). Click here to perform an ad hoc search with a nondefault provider.

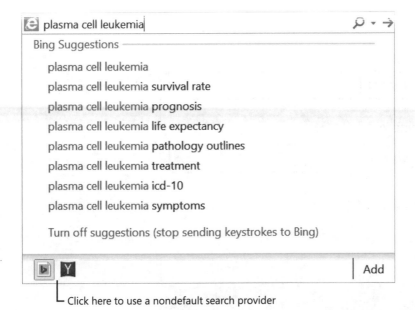

Click here to use a nondefault search provider

Figure 11-5 When you search in the address bar, Internet Explorer offers icons to let you select a nondefault search provider.

Using favorites, history, and the reading list

The favorites and history lists, grouped under the new Hub user interface in Edge, will help you find your way back to sites you've already visited. The new reading list feature in Edge is a handy alternative to favorites.

Browsing with favorites in Edge

Like every other browser, Edge lets you build a repository of favorite sites—sites that you know or suspect you'll want to return to now and then. Once a site has been designated a favorite, you can reopen it with only a few clicks, instead of having to search for it again or pull it up from your browsing history. (Your browsing history is available for reuse as well, of course, but it's often better to use history for sites that you need to return to unexpectedly. For more about this feature, see "Browsing through history" later in this chapter.)

To add a site to your favorites in Edge, click Add To Favorites Or Reading List. That's the star icon near the right side of your browser window. As Figure 11-6 shows, the dialog box that appears gives you a choice between adding a site to your favorites and adding to your reading list. Click Favorites if that's not already underscored.

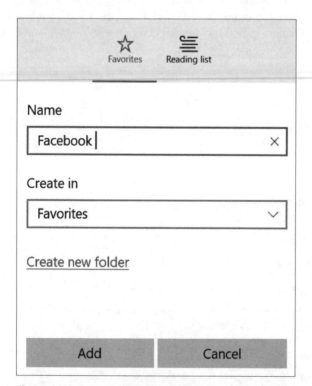

Figure 11-6 As part of its effort to keep the user interface controls well spaced for touch friendliness, Edge combines Add To Favorites and Add To Reading List in a single dialog box, accessed via the star icon on the toolbar.

Edge proposes the title of the current website as the name for your favorite and a folder destination for the new shortcut. Initially you may have only two folders, called Favorites and Favorites Bar. You can use the Create New Folder link to expand this repertory. (The Favorites Bar folder is special because the favorites you store there can be displayed as a toolbar at the top of your screen. To display the Favorites Bar, click More Actions, then Settings, and then click the switch labeled Show The Favorites Bar.)

NOTE

The quickest way to add the current page to your favorites is by pressing Ctrl+D.

Inside OUT

Always rename favorites

Get in the habit of assigning a descriptive name when you save a favorite. Make sure the name you choose contains the words your future self is likely to use as search terms. Steer clear of extra-long file names. Web designers often create outrageously long page titles, packing descriptions and keywords together with the goal of ranking higher on search engines. Shorter, more meaningful names are easier to spot when you're scrolling through a folder full of favorites. And speaking of folders, by all means use them to categorize your favorites. The more favorites you accumulate, the gladder you'll be that you did.

Navigating to a favorite site in Edge

To use your favorites, once you have created them, click the Hub icon. That's the one that looks like this:

You can also get to the Hub by pressing Ctrl+I.

As Figure 11-7 shows, the Hub is a multipurpose affair. The four icons at the top take you, from left to right, to Favorites, Reading List, History, and Downloads. We'll look at the other three Hub sections at later points in this chapter.

Figure 11-7 Favorites are accessed via the Hub, which also provides entrée to your reading list, history, and downloads.

Click a favorite to launch it in the current tab. To launch it in a new tab, right-click it and then click Open In New Tab. The menu that appears when you right-click also gives you the means to rename or remove a shortcut.

> **NOTE**
> If you have enough room on your screen and you expect to be working with several shortcuts, pin the Hub. The pane will remain open until you click the X, which replaces the pin icon in the upper right corner.

Importing favorites from other browsers

To import favorites that you have created in another browser, open the Hub, click the Favorites tab, and then click Import Favorites. (You have to be in the Favorites folder, not a subfolder, when you do this.) Edge will offer a selection consisting of whatever other browsers it finds on your system:

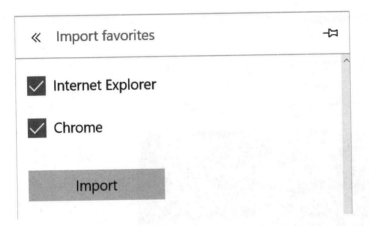

Select the check boxes for the browsers from which you want to import favorites.

> **TROUBLESHOOTING**
>
> *You can't find your Edge favorites*
>
> Internet Explorer saves its favorites in a subfolder of your user profile, %UserProfile%\ Favorites; Edge does not, at least in its current incarnation. (That feature is scheduled to be added in a future upgrade, perhaps even by the time you read this.) Like the executable files for modern apps, favorites that you create in Edge, a modern app, are tucked away in a folder deeply nested under %LocalAppData%\Packages. To be exact, the location is %LocalAppData%\Packages\Microsoft.MicrosoftEdge_8wekyb3d8bbwe\ AC\MicrosoftEdge\User\Default\Favorites. If you find that address difficult to remember, don't despair; you can't do anything useful with the File Explorer entries there anyway. For example, if you try to add a favorite by creating a file alongside the others, Edge will simply ignore it. And no, you can't sync your favorites with other devices by syncing that obscure folder.

Using the reading list, an alternative to favorites, in Edge

Favorites are a great way to preserve and categorize website addresses to which you expect to be returning periodically. When you just need to save something for later perusal, the reading list in Edge might be a better alternative. Any webpage can be saved to the reading list. It doesn't have to be text-oriented, although the reading list feature is perfect for long articles that you don't have time to read at the moment.

To save the current page to the reading list, click the Add To Favorites Or Reading List icon. A simple dialog box appears:

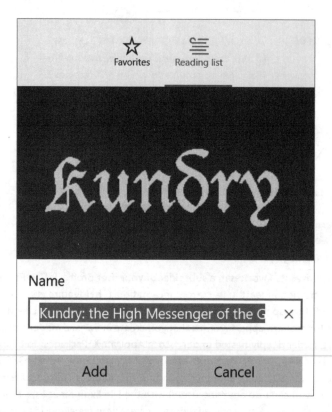

Edge proposes the name of the page as the name of your reading list item, but you can (and often should) replace that with something easier to recognize. Above the name field, Edge displays an image taken from the page you're saving, assuming that it finds one near the beginning of the page.

When you're ready to read your saved item, click the Hub, then the Reading List tab. Your pages are ordered chronologically with the most recent on top (see Figure 11-8). Click and read.

Figure 11-8 Edge sorts your reading list in descending chronological order.

When you've finished with an item, right-click it and choose Remove.

> ➤ The reading list maintained by Edge is separate from the one created by Windows Reading List. For information about the latter, see "Preserving items of interest with Windows Reading List" in Chapter 9, "Productivity and communication tools."

Browsing with favorites in Internet Explorer

To add a site to your favorites in Internet Explorer, do any of the following:

● Press Ctrl+D.

● Click Favorites, or press Alt+C or Ctrl+I to open the Favorites Center, and then click Add To Favorites.

● Pin the Favorites Center, and then drag the icon to the left of the webpage address in the address bar to the Favorites list. If you want the item to go inside an existing subfolder that isn't open, point to the folder icon and wait. After a pause, the folder opens, and you can drop the shortcut in its proper place within the subfolder.

● Right-click anywhere within the current page, and then click Add To Favorites. This action adds the current page to the Favorites folder. If you point to a link on the page and choose this menu option, the newly created shortcut picks up the title and address of the link.

All of these methods, except the drag-and-drop procedure, produce the Add A Favorite dialog box, shown in Figure 11-9.

Figure 11-9 Internet Explorer proposes to use the page title as the name for the favorite. Replace the default page title with a shorter, simpler name to make the favorite easier to find.

The Create In drop-down box allows you to save the new favorite within the top level of the Favorites folder or choose a subfolder. You can also create a new subfolder. Each favorite is saved as an Internet shortcut (a file with the extension .url) in the Favorites folder in your user profile.

You can edit these shortcuts the same way you edit any other kind of shortcut. Right-click the shortcut or folder in the Favorites Center to rename, copy, or delete the shortcut. You can also use File Explorer to rename your favorites and organize them into folders. A quick way to get to your Favorites folder in File Explorer is to type **favorites** in the search box.

To save all open tabs in the current window as a folder of new favorites, open the Favorites Center, click the down arrow next to Add To Favorites, and choose Add Current Tabs To Favorites. After you specify a folder name and location, Internet Explorer saves all open tabs in that folder. If the folder name you enter already exists, the current tabs are added to that folder.

Syncing favorites in Internet Explorer

Synchronizing your Internet Explorer favorites is simple and automatic if your systems are set up to sync settings via a Microsoft account. In Settings, search for **sync**. Choose Sync Your Settings, and then make sure that Web Browser Settings is turned on:

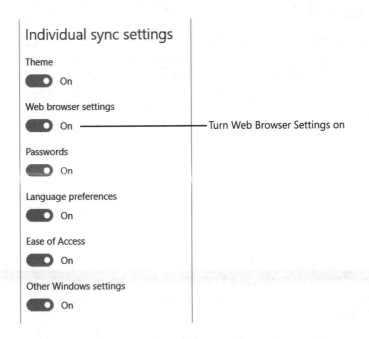

If Web Browser Settings is on, then any Internet Explorer favorite you create on one system will appear on all other systems you sign in to with the same Microsoft account.

Working with pinned sites in Internet Explorer

The idea behind pinned sites in Internet Explorer is straightforward: you can open a website in a tab and then drag an icon from the address bar (or drag the tab itself) onto the taskbar, where it's pinned just like a program. If the site has a custom icon (also known as a *favicon*), the shortcut for the pinned site uses it instead of the generic Internet Explorer icon.

CHAPTER 11

Here, for example, we've created pinned sites for four news sources and lined them up side by side on the right side of the taskbar:

When you open a pinned site, its appearance is subtly different from a normal website. It maintains its privileged position on the taskbar, complete with personalized icon, which makes it easy for you to quickly get back to a site you use regularly. The personalized icon appears in the upper left corner of the browser window as well, and the Back and Forward buttons take on the same color as the icon.

Browsing through history

Edge and Internet Explorer each maintain their own history of the sites you visit. If you need to return to a site and you neglected to make it a favorite (or save it to your reading list in Edge), you should be able to find it by looking through the history listings. It's not an ideal way to retrace your steps because the history is exhaustive and duplicative. You're likely to find an individual entry for each visit you made to a particular site, for example. More problematic, the sites are listed by their official titles, not by the friendly names you would probably have assigned to favorites. So to get back to a site via history, you might need to comb through a lot of distractions. It helps greatly, of course, if you know when you last opened the site you want to revisit. Both browsers gather their entries into time-interval bins such as Today or Last Week. Edge also adds a time stamp to sites that you opened during the last several days; if you know you discovered a site yesterday evening, this time stamping can help narrow your search.

History in Edge

To inspect your history in Edge, click Hub, and then click History (it's the third icon from the left). Alternatively, press Ctrl+H. As Figure 11-10 shows, Edge presents sites in descending chronological order, beginning with a category called Last Hour if it happens that the current day has barely begun.

Use the outline controls at the left to expand date categories. Don't click the X at the right side of a date heading unless you'd like to expunge that segment of your history. As you move your mouse pointer down through the sites, X icons appear to the right of each in turn. You might want to use those icons to get rid of sites that happen to be in the historical record but that you know you'll never need to reopen; doing so might make it easier to find the sites you do want.

Should it happen that history records that you went to Contoso.com every day in the last three weeks, you might want to avail yourself of another expunging option. Right-click one of the entries for this site and choose Delete All Visits To Contoso.com. (You probably don't need this history to find your way back.)

If you want to erase the entire history, click Clear All History at the top of the list. (You can also clear your browsing history via the Settings pane, as we'll see later in this chapter.)

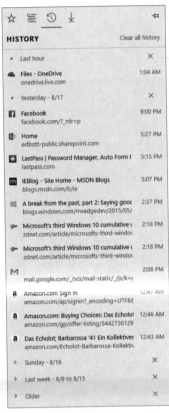

Figure 11-10 Edge organizes your browsing history in descending chronological order.

History in Internet Explorer

Internet Explorer hides your browsing history on the third tab in the Favorites Center. You can get there by clicking Favorites and then clicking the History tab or by pressing Ctrl+H. At the top of the history pane, you'll find a handy drop-down list that lets you arrange entries by date, site, most visited, or the order visited today (see Figure 11-11). Most important, perhaps, the list includes a Search History option. The search tool won't find content buried on a page, but it will find words that appear in page titles. For example, suppose you visited the website of an airport shuttle service and looked at the home page, a page called Rates, and another called Reservations. You don't remember the name of the company or which day you were pondering a limo ride, but you do remember that you went to the Reservations page. Search your history for "reservations," and you'll find what you need.

Figure 11-11 You can sort Internet Explorer's History list in a variety of memory-jogging ways. For best results, try the Search History option.

Managing downloads

Downloading documents and programs is straightforward. Both browsers provide progress reports such as the following while the download is under way:

If you change your mind midstream, you can click Cancel. If you need to pause while you do something else, there's a button for that as well. When the download is complete, another message asks you what you want to do with it:

For an executable, you'll have the option to run the new download. For a document, an Open button will appear in place of Run.

Clicking View Downloads in Edge takes you to a list of your downloads.

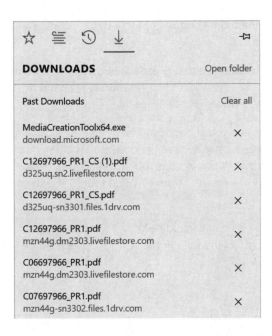

You can also get to this list in Edge by clicking the Hub icon and selecting the fourth icon from the left. Clicking entries in this list lets you open any downloaded document or run any downloaded executable—just as you could do in your Downloads folder (by default, This PC\ Downloads) in File Explorer; you can go to that folder directly by clicking Open Folder. If the Downloads list in Edge becomes cluttered, you can use the X controls to eliminate particular items, or clear the whole list at once with the Clear All link. Note that these actions delete nothing from your store of downloads; they simply tidy up the list in the browser.

To get to the comparable set of features in Internet Explorer, click Tools, View Downloads.

Using SmartScreen Filter to avoid phishing sites and dicey downloads

The term *phishing sites* refers to websites designed by scammers to resemble online commerce and banking sites. The scammer's goal is to fool you into visiting the site (often by enticing you to click a link in an email message) and have you fill in sensitive information such as your sign-in credentials, account numbers, and details about your identity.

SmartScreen Filter, introduced with Internet Explorer 7, detects known and suspected phishing sites and does its best to deter you from falling prey. The feature does its detective work with the help of an allow list, a set of rules, and a server-based block list that is continually updated. The initial check is heuristic, looking at the content of the page itself; if all the images are from a bank's website, for example, but the submit button goes to a URL containing an IP address, red flags go up.

If SmartScreen Filter thinks you're headed to a dodgy page, it displays a bold warning before you ever get there. An icon in the address bar identifies the address as an Unsafe Website, and a banner on the warning page itself provides one-click egress.

SmartScreen Filter also steps up to warn you about downloads it considers to be potentially hazardous. Such a warning does not necessarily mean the download is unsafe (the feature bases its judgment on information that Windows users supply to Microsoft, but it is not infallible). But unless you're sure that the download is from a trusted source, you should heed the warning.

To make sure that SmartScreen Filter is on in Edge, click More Actions, Settings, View Advanced Settings. The switch you're looking for is at the bottom of the Advanced Settings pane:

Help protect me from malicious sites and downloads with SmartScreen Filter

 On

To enable SmartScreen Filter in Internet Explorer, click Tools, Safety, Turn On SmartScreen Filter. If the link says "Turn Off . . . ," that means the feature is already enabled.

Making text more readable

Edge and Internet Explorer both provide easy ways to make text and graphics on a webpage larger or smaller. If you're working on a touchscreen or on a device with a precision touchpad, you can zoom in and out with the standard touch gestures. Spread two fingers on a page to make the content larger; bring two fingers together to make it smaller.

With a wheel mouse, you can zoom in or out by holding down the Ctrl key while you roll the wheel forward or back. Zooming with the mouse wheel has the advantage of maintaining the position of whatever object you're pointing to when you begin zooming. Suppose, for example, that you're zooming in to get a better look at a graphic element lying near the right edge of the screen. If you use other zooming methods, the element you care about will eventually drift out of the window. But if you zoom in by pointing to it and rolling the wheel, the element retains its position relative to your mouse pointer as it gets larger.

If a mouse is not at hand, hold down Ctrl and press the Plus Sign to increase magnification; do the same with the Minus Sign to zoom back out. To return to normal (100%) magnification, press Ctrl+0.

Should you forget these shortcuts, you can always go to the menu. In Edge, click More Actions. The Zoom command with its Plus and Minus icons is near the top of the pane. In Internet Explorer, click Tools, and then Zoom.

Using Reading View in Edge

Zooming in is an excellent way to make small text easier on the eyes. But for more improvement in reading comfort, try Reading View in Edge. Introduced in Windows 8 with the modern app version of Internet Explorer, Reading View removes distracting elements from a webpage to let you focus on the text you're actually trying to read. You might find Reading View especially valuable on narrow tablets or phones, where text of interest can easily get crowded out by nonessential elements. Figures 11-12 and 11-13 show the same page in normal display and in Reading View.

In converting a page to Reading View, Edge removes such distractions as ads and navigational display elements, while retaining hyperlinks, source information, and graphics that are integral to the article. Generous amounts of white space, a soft sepia background, and a specially designed font further augment readability. (The background and font size can be customized.)

Reading View also makes some intelligent layout decisions. Notice in Figure 11-13, for example, that the byline and date have been moved from above the title, where they appear in Figure 11-12, to below it, where you would expect to see them in a conventional newspaper or magazine article. Similarly, on wide screens in landscape mode, Reading View is likely to create a multicolumnar display. On narrow screens, it sticks with a single column.

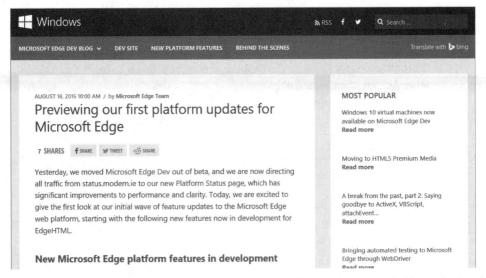

Figure 11-12 In its normal display, the text you want to read might be surrounded by navigational elements and ads.

CHAPTER 11

Previewing our first platform updates for Microsoft Edge

Microsoft Edge Team
Microsoft Edge Dev Blog | August 18, 2015 10:00 am

Yesterday, we moved Microsoft Edge Dev out of beta, and we are now directing all traffic from status.modern.ie to our new Platform Status page, which has significant improvements to performance and clarity. Today, we are excited to give the first look at our initial wave of feature updates to the Microsoft Edge web platform, starting with the following new features now in development for EdgeHTML.

New Microsoft Edge platform features in development

CSS

File APIs

Figure 11-13 In Reading View, the navigational elements have been removed (although hyperlinks are retained), and a generous amount of white space has been added to enhance readability.

To display a page in Reading View, click the Reading View icon, which resembles an open book; it's the first in the set of icons at the right side of the toolbar. If Reading View is not available (because the page is not suitable for that kind of display), the icon will be dim. (The icon might also be dim for a few seconds while Edge analyzes your page to see whether it can be displayed in Reading View.) To switch back to normal view, click the Reading View icon again or click the Back icon.

Reading View is not available in Internet Explorer 11.

Customizations for Reading View appear in two drop-down boxes in the Settings pane (click More Actions, then Settings):

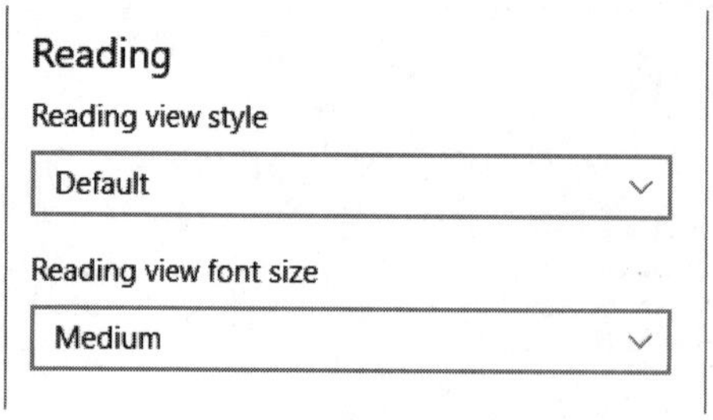

Reading

Reading view style

Default

Reading view font size

Medium

The alternatives to Default for Reading View Style are Light, Medium, and Dark. If you choose Dark, Reading View switches to a reversed format, with white text on a black background, with blue retained for hyperlinks. For Reading View Font Size, your choices are Small, Medium, Large, and Extra Large.

Sharing webpages from Edge

Got something to share? Click the Share icon. Edge responds with a list of installed apps that can receive your offering, as shown in Figure 11-14.

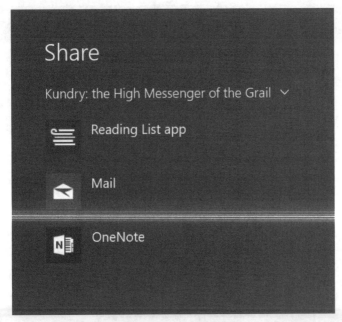

Figure 11-14 Clicking the Share icon reveals a list of programs installed on your system to which you can send a copy of the current page.

The system from which you are sharing may offer a different set of targets—perhaps including Facebook or an RSS reader, for example. If you have previously shared pages to Mail, the addresses of your recent recipients will appear at the top of the list.

At the top of the Share pane you'll find the name of your page, and to the right of that is a small drop-down arrow. Click the arrow if you want to share a screen shot of the page (for example, if you're sending a picture rather than text). Otherwise, Edge will share a link to the current page.

Annotating Edge pages with web notes

The web note feature in Edge lets you draw on, highlight, add text annotations to, and clip sections of webpages that you want to call attention to. Edge turns your webpage into a static graphic image on which you can draw with your fingers or a stylus (on a touchscreen) or use the mouse on a nontouch monitor. After you've marked up a page, you can email it, send it to your OneNote notebooks (or other sharing target), or simply save it to your own favorites or reading list. Figure 11-15 shows an example of a page with a red encirclement and some yellow highlighting.

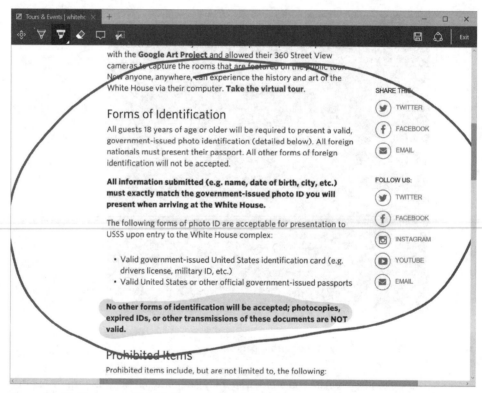

Figure 11-15 The pen and highlighter are two of the tools you can use to create web notes.

To begin creating a web note, click Make A Web Note, the icon to the left of Share near the right edge of the toolbar. Edge opens a set of drawing tools for your use, shown next:

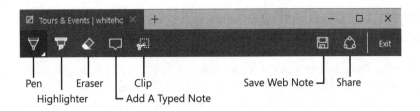

Click the drop-down arrows on the Pen and Highlighter tools to reveal size and color options. If your stylus or mouse goes astray, you can use the Eraser tool and try again. To get rid of all the marks you've made, you can click the drop-down arrow on the Eraser tool and choose Clear All Ink. (Alternatively, you can exit drawing mode and then come back for another go.)

To add a text box to the page, click Add A Typed Note, and then click to indicate where you want the text to go. To copy a snippet to the Clipboard, click the Clip tool, then select the area you want to copy.

The Save Web Note tool, on the right side of the toolbar, offers OneNote, Favorites, and Reading List as destinations. If you save to your favorites or the reading list, you'll be able to pull the page back up at any time and review your annotations. The Share icon presents the usual set of sharing choices (see the previous section).

Inside OUT

Use a web note to freeze a webpage

Website content tends to be ephemeral. If you need to capture the current state of a rapidly changing webpage, grab it with a web note and save it to your reading list, favorites, or OneNote. If you don't care to annotate it, you can simply click Make A Web Note and then click Share. There are many other ways to take screen shots, but this one is right at hand as you browse, and it captures the entire page, not just what you see in the confines of your screen. When you reopen your web note from wherever you put it, you can quickly switch back to the "live" version of the site by means of the Go To Original Page link that appears atop the web note.

CHAPTER 11

Managing and troubleshooting add-ons in Internet Explorer

The Toolbars And Extensions section of the Manage Add-Ons dialog box, shown in Figure 11-16, provides information about whatever ActiveX controls, browser helper objects, and other add-ons you have installed in Internet Explorer. You can inspect version numbers, see how many times an add-on has been used or blocked, and view details of the performance impact of any add-on. More important, you can disable an add-on completely, either as a troubleshooting step or as a way to improve the performance and reliability of Internet Explorer.

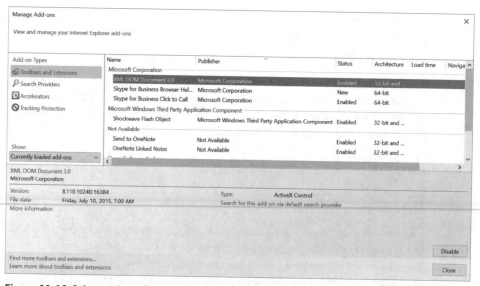

Figure 11-16 Select an item from the list of installed add-ons to enable or disable it. You can view a summary of details about the item in the pane below the list.

When you select an item in the list of add-ons, you can see more details about it in the pane below, including the publisher's name, the version number and file date (if available), and the add-on type. Buttons in the lower right corner let you disable or enable the add-on.

If you're ready to be completely overloaded with information, double-click an add-on's name in the list. If the selected add-on is an ActiveX control, you see an information-rich dialog box like the one shown next:

In the large box here, the asterisk—the wildcard character for "all"—indicates that you have approved the add-on to run on all sites. If you're particularly cautious, you might want the option to approve websites on a site-by-site basis. In that case, click the Remove All Sites button. From that point forward, whenever you visit a site that uses that ActiveX control, Internet Explorer will request your permission to run it.

Privacy and security issues

In Windows 10, you can eliminate most security concerns by browsing whenever possible in Edge. Because the new browser runs in a sandboxed environment, what happens in Edge stays in Edge, so to speak. That is to say, nothing that you do in Edge is going to damage your system by exploiting a third-party add-on. Privacy issues, on the other hand, will always accompany our visits to the web, in part because privacy choices are a matter of personal preference, involving tradeoffs between convenience and the desire to be left alone. We discuss those tradeoffs and the settings by which they're implemented in the following sections.

CHAPTER 11

Allowing or not allowing your browser to save sign-in credentials

Both Edge and Internet Explorer will happily store user IDs and passwords in a secure location, simplifying their reuse. The data is saved in a "vault," a folder to which your user account does not have direct access.

Saving credentials is an optional feature. It can save you time and trouble when you're revisiting sites—shopping sites, for example—that require you to sign in to an account. But if you think that someone else might be sitting down at your computer and going to those same sites without your permission, you might want to forego the convenience. To turn credential saving on or off in Edge, click More Actions, Settings, View Advanced Settings, and then put this switch in whichever position you favor:

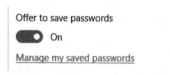

The Manage My Saved Passwords link below the switch produces a list of all the credentials that Edge has collected, with a handy X next to each in case you want to remove particular items. If you click an entry in this list, Edge provides the URL, user name, and encrypted password in a dialog box similar to this:

URL

https://www.amazon.com/

Username

patelrajeshm@outlook.com   ×

Password

•••••••••

Save

You can modify the user name or password in this dialog box, but for your security, Edge will not show you (or anyone else using your computer) the current password. (You can, however, inspect passwords by means of Credential Manager, discussed in a moment.)

To reach the comparable setting in Internet Explorer, click Tools, Internet Options. Go to the Content tab of the Internet Options dialog box and click Settings in the AutoComplete section. The option to save passwords (and be prompted for approval each time Internet Explorer finds new credentials to save) appears in the AutoComplete Settings dialog box, along with numerous similar options:

Viewing and deleting credentials with Credential Manager

The Manage Passwords button in the AutoComplete Settings dialog box takes you to Credential Manager, a destination you can also reach by searching for Credential Manager in Control Panel. The Web Credentials section of Credential Manager displays a list of user names and passwords saved by either Edge or Internet Explorer. Clicking an item reveals details, as shown in Figure 11-17.

CHAPTER 11

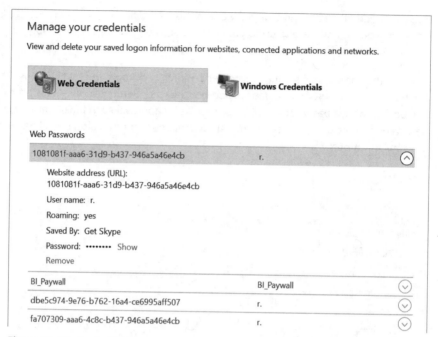

Figure 11-17 Credential Manager, a part of Control Panel, lists all web credentials saved by either browser.

The Remove link here provides a way to clean out credentials you no longer need. The Show link lets you see the password you saved, but for your security it requires you to reenter the password by which you sign in to Windows.

Blocking pop-ups

Windows that pop up unexpectedly while you're browsing aren't usually malicious, but they can be annoying. Both browsers offer the ability to suppress them.

In Edge, visit the Advanced Settings pane and make sure that Block Pop-Ups is set to On. It's only an on-off switch; there are no further options here, but when you encounter a site that requires a blocked pop-up, you will have the option to add it to a safe-sites list.

To shut down pop-ups in Internet Explorer, click Tools, Internet Options, go to the Privacy tab, and select Turn On Pop-up Blocker. For fine-tuning, click Settings to get to the following dialog box:

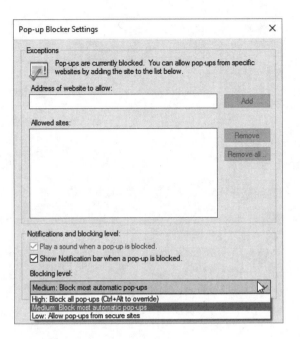

The pop-up blocker defaults to a medium level of scrutiny, which means that it blocks "most" pop-ups. The low and high alternatives let you accept pop-ups only from secure sites (those to which you connect via an HTTPS URL) or accept no pop-ups from any site.

The top of this dialog box is devoted to a safe-sites list. You can build it manually by copying URLs to the Address Of Website To Allow box and clicking Add. Or you can build it as you go; when you come to a site that requires a pop-up, you can choose to have the blocker ignore that site in the future.

Clearing your browser history and other personal information

Your browser keeps a copy of webpages, images, and media you've viewed recently. This cached information—combined with cookies, saved form data, and saved passwords (although these are saved to generally inaccessible locations)—might give another person who has access to your computer more information than you might want him or her to have.

To wipe away most of your online trail in Edge, click More Actions, Settings, and then click Choose What To Clear. These steps take you to the set of check boxes shown in Figure 11-18. To get to the comparable location in Internet Explorer, click Tools, Safety, Delete Browsing History.

CHAPTER 11

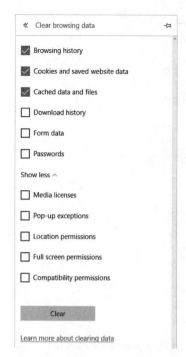

Figure 11-18 The options under Clear Browsing Data in Edge, and the corresponding choices in Internet Explorer, let you specify which elements of your history you want to erase.

The most important of these choices are as follows:

- **Browsing History.** This is simply a list of sites you've been to, whether you went to them directly or followed another site's hyperlinks, since you last cleared your history.

- **Cookies And Saved Website Data.** A *cookie* is a small text file that enables a website to store persistent information on your hard disk. Cookies, particularly first-party cookies, are generally benign and more often than not useful. Note that removing cookies via this option does not block their arrival in the future. (To do that, see "Blocking cookies and sending do-not-track requests" later in this chapter.)

- **Cached Data And Files.** These are local copies of pages and media content from sites that you visit. The browser "caches" this data to speed up its display on subsequent visits.

- **Download History.** This is the list that appears on the History tab of the Hub. Deleting this history here (or clicking Clear All in the Hub—the actions are equivalent) does not remove the downloads themselves, which remain where you put them.

- **Form Data.** Your browser stores some information—for example, your shipping or email address—that you use to fill out forms, simplifying reuse. You can erase its memory here.

- **Passwords.** As mentioned earlier (see "Allowing or not allowing your browser to save sign-in credentials"), there are pros and cons associated with caching passwords. If you change your mind after you've allowed the browser to store these credentials, you can erase the data here.

Squelching history temporarily with InPrivate browsing

If you want to cover your tracks only for a particular browsing session, don't bother fussing with history settings or clearance. Simply open an InPrivate window. In Edge, click More Actions, New InPrivate Window. In Internet Explorer, press Ctrl+Shift+P or click Tools, Safety, InPrivate Browsing. When you subsequently close the InPrivate session, any data the browser has stored (session cookies and other temporary files) is deleted.

Be aware that browsing privately is not the same as browsing anonymously. Sites you visit can record your IP address, and your network administrator or Internet service provider can see which sites you connect to and can capture any unencrypted information that you transmit or receive.

During an Internet Explorer InPrivate session, toolbars and extensions are disabled by default. If you want them enabled, click Tools, open the Internet Options dialog box, and go to the Privacy tab. Then clear the Disable Toolbars And Extensions When InPrivate Browsing Starts check box.

Blocking cookies and sending do-not-track requests

Cookies—small bits of information that websites store on your hard disk—come in two flavors. First-party cookies are used by the site that you are currently visiting, generally for such purposes as personalizing your experience with the site, storing shopping-cart information, and so on. Third-party cookies are used by a site other than the one you're visiting—such as an advertiser on the site you're currently visiting.

Cookies do not carry executable code (they're text files) and can't be used to spread viruses or malware; they can't scurry around your hard disk reading your address book and financial records, for example. A cookie can provide a website only with information that you supply while visiting the site. The information a cookie gathers can be read only by pages in the same domain as the one that created the cookie.

Nevertheless, privacy concerns arise when advertisers and web-analytics companies begin to correlate the information from third-party cookies to build a profile of your activities. Because it's not always obvious who's sending you a cookie and what purposes that cookie serves, some people are understandably wary about allowing cookies on their systems.

Both browsers allow you to block either all cookies or third-party cookies. In Edge, click More Actions, Settings, View Advanced Settings. Then open the drop-down list below the Cookies heading. You'll see the following simple set of choices:

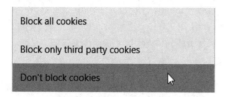

In Internet Explorer, click Tools, Internet Options. On the Privacy tab, click Advanced. In the Advanced Privacy Settings dialog box, shown in Figure 11-19, you can express your preferences separately for first-party and third-party cookies. In addition to accepting or blocking cookies, you can ask to be prompted each time a first or third party wants to deliver or update a cookie. You are likely to find this choice more trouble than it's worth. In addition, you can also choose to allow all session cookies—cookies that are deleted at the end of your browsing session.

Figure 11-19 It's hard to think of a reason for blocking first-party cookies while allowing cookies from third parties, but Internet Explorer will let you do it.

In a separate dialog box (click Sites on the Privacy tab of the Internet Options dialog box), you can block individual domains from serving cookies or allow them to.

Suppressing unwanted data collection by sending do-not-track requests

Manually blocking cookies is a tedious and error-prone process. A better way to request that advertisers refrain from collecting and storing personal data from your browser is by sending do-not-track requests.

The do-not-track (DNT) standard, introduced first with Firefox in 2011, is now included with most modern browsers. If DNT is enabled, when you visit a site, the browser sends a header requesting that the site refrain from passing information about you to third parties. This is not a guarantee that the site will honor your request (and it's possible that you will still receive third-party cookies), but DNT has found widespread acceptance among mainstream advertisers.

In Windows 8, the option to send do-not-track requests was turned on by default (included with Internet Explorer's "express settings"). This provoked controversy and resistance from both competing browsers and the advertising industry because the standard, as codified by the World Wide Web Consortium (W3C), stipulates that DNT requests result from an active decision by end users. Microsoft reversed its position on the matter, and in both Edge and Internet Explorer, DNT is initially turned off. To turn it on in Edge, click More Actions, Settings, View Advanced Settings and set Send Do Not Track Requests to On. In Internet Explorer, click Tools, Safety, Turn On Do Not Track Requests.

Configuring security zones in Internet Explorer

Internet Explorer uses a system of "security zones" to let you configure security settings differently for different categories of websites. The zones are called Internet, Local Intranet, Trusted Sites, and Restricted Sites, and you can configure them by going to the Security tab of the Internet Options dialog box, shown in Figure 11-20.

The four zones are intended to be used as follows. The Restricted Sites zone, designed for sites that you trust the least (or explicitly distrust), has the highest security settings—that is, the maximum in safeguards. The Trusted Sites zone has, by default, a medium level of protection, blocking the download of unsigned ActiveX controls and prompting for permission before downloading other material considered potentially unsafe. The Internet Zone—with medium-high settings—is reserved for all nonintranet sites that you have not assigned to the Trusted Sites or Restricted Sites zone. The Intranet Zone, with low security settings, is populated with intranet sites that you have not explicitly moved to Trusted Sites or Restricted Sites, sites that bypass your proxy server, and all network servers accessed via a UNC path (*server_name*).

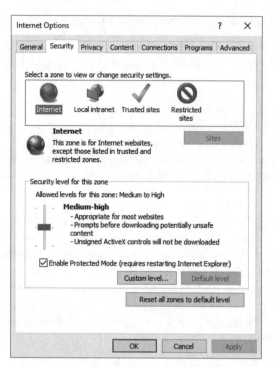

Figure 11-20 Use this dialog box to add sites to specific zones in Internet Explorer or to modify the security settings associated with a zone.

To add sites to a zone, select the zone and click Sites. To change the security settings for a zone, adjust the slider or click Custom Level.

Unless you use your computer exclusively as a game machine, learning to manage your "stuff"—your documents, programs, and communications—is probably the single most critical computing skill you need to acquire. Because the continual growth in storage capacity encourages a corresponding increase in digital retentiveness, keeping track of files, media items, and other documents is more crucial than ever.

The redesigned File Explorer (in Windows 7 it was known as Windows Explorer) is rich with organizational power tools, including live-icon previews of file contents (for applications and document types that support this capability), a preview pane that allows you to peek inside a file's contents without actually opening it, and a details pane that displays file properties and lets you add descriptive tags to files. In this chapter, we dive deeply into this rich feature set and explain how Windows 10 can help you organize your data files.

Organizing is just the first step to a well-ordered documentary life, of course. Finding things again when you need them is every bit as crucial. Windows 10 incorporates a powerful indexing service and search engine that can help you find what you need quickly and with a minimum of effort wherever it may reside.

Exploring File Explorer

You can't become a Windows expert without mastering File Explorer. This general-purpose tool is used throughout Windows for general file-management tasks, for opening and saving files in Windows programs, and even in parts of the Windows shell. The more you understand about how File Explorer works, the more effective you'll be at speeding through tasks without unnecessary delays. Because it's vital to know your way around, we'll begin this chapter with a short tour.

Figure 12-1 shows the major landmarks in a typical File Explorer display.

Figure 12-1 File Explorer includes the navigation and display elements shown here, some of which can be customized.

Inside OUT

Use a keyboard shortcut to open File Explorer

You can find File Explorer in a variety of places in Windows 10, but if you're handy with the keyboard, don't bother hunting for it. Press Windows key+E to get there directly.

If you've used any of the recent versions of Microsoft Office, or if you're coming to Windows 10 by way of Windows 8, then you won't be startled to see the ribbon atop File Explorer. If, by any chance, this aspect of the user interface is new to you, the only thing you need to know is that it replaces the old system of drop-down and cascading menus with a set of top-level tabs—Home, Share, and View in the example shown in Figure 12-1. When you click a tab, an appropriate set of options appears below it:

You'll notice that the various commands under a tab are organized into groups—Clipboard, Organize, New, Open, and Select on the Home tab, for example. More important points to note are the following:

- The command bar from Windows 7 days is gone. The ribbon itself provides the context-specific commands that used to appear on the command bar.

- When certain items are selected in the contents pane, an additional tab appears at the right side of the ribbon, with commands relevant to the context. If you select a picture folder, for example, or one or more picture files in any folder, a Manage tab bearing picture-related commands appears:

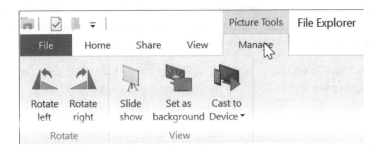

- The ribbon can be minimized or not, according to your preference. If the ribbon is minimized, as it is in Figure 12-1, the commands appear only when a tab is selected. If it's not minimized, they're always visible. To switch from one view to the other, right-click the ribbon.

- Most of what's on the ribbon is also available on the menus that appear when you right-click files or folders. If you ever become impatient when trying to find a command on the ribbon, simply right-click and look there. Microsoft adopted the ribbon to reduce the number of cascading submenus that we all used to have to traverse. But sometimes the old ways seem simpler; it's your choice.

To the left of the ribbon tabs, displayed in blue, is the File menu. There you will find commands for opening a new File Explorer window; for opening Windows PowerShell and the command prompt (Cmd.exe), with and without administrative privileges; a list of recently used folders for quick navigation; and more.

CHAPTER 12

Inside OUT

Use the keyboard instead of the mouse (if you prefer)

Hardcore keyboard users will appreciate that any command on the ribbon can be accessed and applied without the mouse. Press Alt, then notice the letters and numbers that appear under the ribbon tabs and the Quick Access Toolbar. Press one of those letters—H for Home, for example—and the appropriate tab itself appears, adorned with its own set of shortcut letters. Follow the shortcuts to your destination.

The design of the ribbon—its purpose—is to put the commands you use most often front and center, easy to find. A secondary benefit is that it makes less frequently used commands easier to discover. Here are a few gems that merit your attention:

- The Copy Path command, on the Home tab, puts the path of the current folder or file on the Clipboard. This is handy for sending someone a link to a network share via email. (As an alternative, you can click in the address bar and press Ctrl+C, or you can press Shift as you right-click, and then click Copy As Path on the shortcut menu.)

- The Move To and Copy To commands, also on the Home tab, drop down a list of likely targets (recently used folders) for your move and copy operations.

- The Zip command, on the Share tab, instantly creates a Zip (compressed) file from the current selection, thereby providing an alternative to the time-honored approach of right-clicking and choosing Send To, Compressed (Zipped) Folder. (See "Using compressed (zipped) folders" later in this chapter.)

- On the View tab, you'll find handy commands for showing or not showing files and folders with the Hidden attribute. Another command nearby lets you assign the Hidden attribute to the current selection.

Customizing the Quick Access Toolbar

As its name implies, the Quick Access Toolbar—that set of icons in the upper left corner of File Explorer, above the ribbon—puts commonly used functions close at hand (or close to your mouse pointer). If you'd like those items a few centimeters closer, you can move the Quick Access Toolbar below the ribbon by clicking the arrow at the end to display the menu shown here:

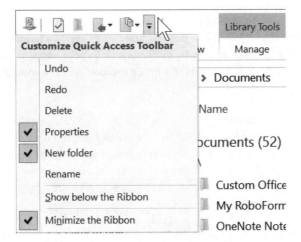

This menu also lets you change the items that appear on the Quick Access Toolbar. Here, for example, we've set up the toolbar to offer Properties and New Folder. Any command on the ribbon in File Explorer can be added to the Quick Access Toolbar—not just the few that are shown in the preceding illustration. To add a command, right-click it and then click Add To Quick Access Toolbar, as we've done here with the Move To and Copy To commands. To remove it, right-click it on the Quick Access Toolbar and then click Remove From Quick Access Toolbar.

Navigating in File Explorer

In its default arrangement, File Explorer displays the navigation pane with a handful of starting points for navigating through files on your computer and on your network:

NOTE

On a Windows 10 device that is joined to a domain, you cannot create a homegroup, but you can join one that has been created by someone else on your home network. In that case, the Homegroup node will be available in File Explorer only if a homegroup is available for you to join.

Displaying the navigation pane is optional (to remove it, click the View tab, open the Navigation Pane drop-down menu, and clear the Navigation Pane check box), but unless you need every bit of available screen space for the contents pane (perhaps with the addition of the preview pane or details pane), you'll probably find it convenient to keep the navigation pane in view. It helps you with navigation, of course, but it also serves as a handy drop target when you're moving or copying files or folders.

The Quick Access node at the top of the navigation pane is new in Windows 10. When it's selected, File Explorer displays a collection of recently used folders and another of recently used files. Windows makes some intelligent choices about what to display under Quick Access, but you can customize this to suit your needs. In the Frequent Folders section, you'll find some folders marked with pins and others without one. The pinned folders always appear under Quick Access (unless you unpin them). The unpinned folders are ones that you have recently worked with, and these folders are replaced by others if you begin to use them less frequently. You can unpin a pinned folder by right-clicking it and then clicking Unpin From Quick Access. And you can make any folder anywhere a permanent resident of Quick Access by right-clicking it and then clicking Pin To Quick Access.

The Recent Files section of Quick Access contains files that you have recently worked with, sorted with the most recently used at the top. By right-clicking a file name and clicking Open File Location, you can go directly to the folder in which the file resides. If you find that you don't need to see a particular file (and want to make room for another), you can right-click that file and then click Remove From Quick Access.

Quick Access is an extremely handy navigational tool because it gathers together the stuff you're most likely to be concerned with, regardless of where that stuff is actually stored. But if you don't need it, or you're not keen on having passersby see what you've been working on, you can suppress either or both the Frequent Folders section or the Recent Files section. To do this, click the View tab and then click Options. On the General tab of the Folder Options dialog box, you'll find the check boxes you need in the Privacy section. (If you just want to cover your immediate tracks without changing the overall behavior of File Explorer, it's probably simpler to click Clear in the Privacy section.)

The OneDrive node is also new in the Windows 10 File Explorer. Note that a click here does not take you to the cloud. Instead it opens the folder %UserProfile%\OneDrive, which stores local copies of documents that you have synced with OneDrive. (For more details about One-Drive, see Appendix C, "OneDrive and other cloud services.")

By clicking the View tab and then opening the Navigation Pane drop-down menu, you can avail yourself of three additional options related to this pane:

- **Expand To Open Folder.** By default, selecting a folder in the contents pane has no effect on the navigation pane. If you select Expand To Open Folder, File Explorer opens the parent folder of the folder you select in the contents pane, making it easier to see the parentage and neighborhood of the selected item.

- **Show Libraries.** If you choose to directly manage files stored in libraries (see "Working with libraries" later in this chapter), you might want to include them in your navigation pane. If you select the Show Libraries option, all of your libraries—those that Windows provides and any that you create yourself—appear in a node in the navigation pane. If you want to see only particular libraries, click the Libraries node heading, and then right-click each library you want to remove and click Don't Show In Navigation Pane. To restore a library to this node, use the Show In Navigation Pane command. Both commands are also in the Manage group on the Libraries tab.

- **Show All Folders.** For the most inclusive navigation pane, select Show All Folders. The resulting tree will include, in addition to your libraries, your profile folders (click your user name in the navigation pane to expand this item), any media folders on your network to which you have access (these will appear directly under This PC), Control Panel, and the Recycle Bin. (For more about your profile folders, see the next section.)

What's what and where in a user profile

A *user profile* contains all the settings and files for a user's desktop environment. In addition to personal documents and media files, this profile includes the user's own registry settings, cookies, browser favorites, and user data and settings for installed programs.

By default, each user who signs in to a computer has a local user profile, which is created when the user signs in for the first time. Local user profiles are stored in %SystemDrive%\Users. Each user's profile is stored in a subfolder where the user account name is the folder name (for example, C:\Users\Katy). The entire path for the current user's profile is accessible via another commonly used environment variable, %UserProfile%. If you have File Explorer's navigation pane set to show all folders, you can see the subfolders of your profile by clicking your user name in the navigation pane.

Here's a rundown of the major profile folders. Because apps can add their own data to the profile, your system might have some additional profile folders.

- **Contacts.** This folder first appeared in Windows Vista and was designed to store contact information used by Windows Mail. It is not used by any programs included in Windows 10 and is maintained for compatibility purposes with third-party personal information management programs.

- **Desktop.** This folder contains items that appear on the user's desktop, including files and shortcuts. (A Public counterpart also contributes items to the desktop.) A link to this location appears in the Quick Access section of the navigation pane.

- **Documents.** Most applications use this folder as the default location for storing user documents.

- **Downloads.** This folder, which was introduced in Windows Vista, is the default location for storing items downloaded from websites. A link to this location appears by default in the Quick Access section of the navigation pane.

- **Favorites.** Internet Explorer favorites are saved in this folder by default. To open it quickly in File Explorer, type the shortcut **shell:favorites** in the address bar.

- **Links.** This folder contains shortcuts that appear under the Quick Access heading in the navigation pane. You can create shortcuts here directly, but it's easier to drag items from a file list or the address bar directly to the navigation pane.

- **Music.** This folder is the default location for ripped CD tracks. Most third-party music programs store downloaded tracks in a subfolder here.

- **Pictures.** If you transfer images from external devices (such as digital cameras) or save images from external locations, they end up here.

- **Saved Games.** This folder is the default storage location for apps that can save a game in progress.

- **Searches.** This folder stores saved search specifications, allowing you to reuse previous searches.

- **Videos.** Video files that you download from external services or from external devices are saved here by default.

Application data

The hidden AppData folder, introduced in Windows Vista, is used extensively by programs as a way to store user data and settings in a place where they'll be protected from accidental change or deletion. This folder contains application-specific data—customized dictionaries and templates for a word processor, junk sender lists for an email client, custom toolbar settings, and so on. It's organized into three subfolders, named Local, LocalLow, and Roaming. The Roaming folder (which is also accessible via the environment variable %AppData%) is for data that is made available to a roaming profile (a profile stored on a network server; the server makes the profile available to any network computer where the user signs in). The Local folder (which is also accessible via the system variable %LocalAppData%) is for data that should not roam. The LocalLow folder is used only for Internet Explorer Protected Mode data.

Subfolders under AppData\Local include the following:

- **Microsoft\Windows\History.** This hidden folder contains the user's Internet Explorer browsing history. You can open it directly by using the shortcut **shell:history**.

- **Temp.** This folder contains temporary files created by applications. The %Temp% variable points to AppData\Local\Temp.

Subfolders under AppData\Roaming\Microsoft\Windows include the following:

- **Libraries.** You'll find files that define the contents of default and custom libraries here.

- **Network Shortcuts.** This folder contains shortcuts to network shares that appear in the This PC folder. The folder is not hidden; you can add your own shortcuts here, although it is easier to right-click in This PC and choose Add A Network Location.

- **SendTo.** This folder contains shortcuts to some of the folders and applications that appear on the Send To submenu. Send To is a command that appears when you right-click a file or folder in File Explorer (or on the desktop). The SendTo folder is not hidden. You can add your own items to the Send To menu by creating shortcuts here. Type **shell:sendto** in the address bar to open this folder and add or delete shortcuts.

Inside OUT

Expand the Send To menu

Normally, the Send To menu displays a limited selection of items, including the Desktop and your Documents library as well as any removable storage devices and mapped network drives. To see an expanded Send To menu that includes all folders in your user profile, hold down Shift and then choose Send To from the shortcut menu. The list expands to include your profile folders:

Common profiles

Windows creates a local user profile for each user account, storing the profiles in subfolders of %SystemDrive%\Users with folder names that match the account names. In addition to these user profiles, the operating system creates two others:

- **Public.** The Public profile contains a group of folders that mirror those in your user profile. You can see the Public Documents, Public Music, Public Pictures, and Public Videos folders in their matching libraries. The advantage of these folders is that other users can save files to these locations from different user accounts on the same computer or from across the network.

- **Default.** When a user signs in to a computer for the first time (and her account is not set up to use a roaming profile or mandatory profile), Windows creates a new local profile by copying the contents of the Default profile to a new folder and giving it the user's name. Note that the Default folder is hidden, and you must approve a User Account Control (UAC) consent dialog box to add files to it. You can configure the Default profile the way you want new users' initial view of Windows to appear. Note, however, that some of the customizations that you make to the Default profile might not be copied to profiles for new users. For more information about this topic, see the series of articles by Windows MVP Mitch Tulloch at *w7io.com/21101*.

CAUTION

In the unlikely event that Windows is unable to access your user profile when you sign in, the system might create a temporary user profile in %SystemDrive%\Users\Temp, warning you at sign-in that it has done so. Any changes you make to this temporary profile (including any files you save in its data folders) will be deleted when you sign out.

Working with libraries

A *library* is a virtual folder that aggregates the contents of multiple folders stored on your computer or on your network. You can sort, filter, group, search, arrange, and share the data in a library as if it were in a single location. Windows 10 gives you several by default: Documents, Music, Pictures, Saved Pictures, and Videos. You can create additional libraries to suit your storage needs, and you can customize any library by changing or adding to the physical folders that make up that library.

The important things to understand about libraries are the following:

- A library can encompass multiple folders on multiple disks.

- Libraries are automatically indexed for fast searching, provided their component folders are indexed. Thus, for example, you can open a library, enter a search term in its search box, and quickly pull up all matching documents, even if they're located on far-flung corners of your storage empire.

- Library files are automatically backed up by the Windows 10 File History feature.

Here are some usage scenarios for libraries:

- **Large digital media collections.** You keep your favorite music in the Music folder on your notebook so that you have it available when you leave home. The bulk of your collection, including large high-definition movie files and albums you don't listen to regularly, are stored on an external hard drive. By arranging content on the external drive into Music, Pictures, and Videos folders and then adding those folders to the corresponding libraries, you have full access to your entire collection when you're home and connected to the external drive.

- **Workgroup projects.** You and some coworkers are collaborating on a project. Your drafts are stored in a subfolder of the Documents folder on your local hard disk. You also need access to shared graphics on a network file server, and final drafts from you and your coworkers will be saved in another shared network folder. By adding the local Drafts folder and the two network folders to a custom library, you can search and browse through all those files from one virtual location.

- **Homegroup projects.** At the end of every year, you create a holiday newsletter to send to friends and family. You create a custom library that includes one local folder where you copy photos that will go in the newsletter. You also save the draft of the newsletter there. With two clicks, you can share the custom library with your homegroup so that other family members can add their own files and photos to the project.

- **School-related or work-related projects.** You keep documents, notes, spreadsheets, and other files organized in subfolders, one for each client or project you're working on. Adding those subfolders to a custom library allows you to quickly browse a single subfolder or search through all folders at once. Searching for proposals, contracts, or homework assignments can help you find a document you did for a previous project, adapt it for a new project, and save it quickly in the correct subfolder.

Figure 12-2 illustrates a library search. Here we've created a custom library called School and searched for the term *tulip*. File Explorer returns four items—two Word files, a webpage, and a JPEG image—stored in four different locations. We could, of course, have searched globally, but the search results would likely have included extraneous material not related to schoolwork.

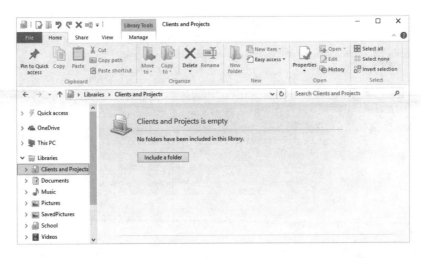

Figure 12-2 The custom library shown here includes four folders on two local drives. Search results cover all four locations.

To create a new library, click the Libraries heading in the navigation pane, and then click New Item, Library on the Home tab. (Alternatively, right-click Libraries in the navigation pane, and then click New, Library.) Give the new library a descriptive name and then press Enter. Your newly created library appears in the navigation pane. Click the Include A Folder button to populate the library.

Using the Include Folder dialog box, select the folder you want to use as the default location for saving files in this library and then click Include Folder. That opens the library and lists the contents of the folder you just selected.

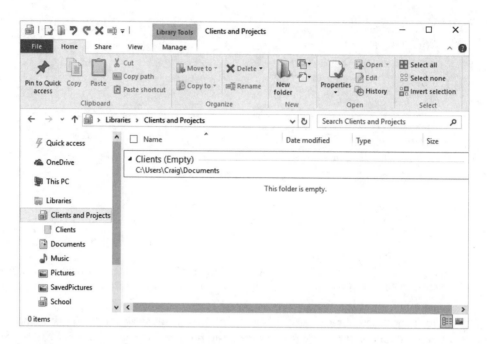

To add more folders to the library, click the Manage tab. Then click Manage Library to get to the Library Locations dialog box:

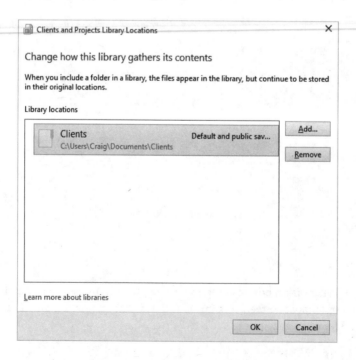

In this dialog box, you can delete folders as well as add them, of course, and you can also change the library's default save folder. The default save folder is important for applications that expect to save their documents in particular places—a music service, for example, that expects to save downloaded songs in a certain folder within the Music library. It's also the folder that File Explorer will use if you drag a file to the library's heading in the navigation pane.

What locations can you add to a library? The most important consideration is that the folder must be indexed so that it can be included in searches. Folders and network shares in any of the following locations are eligible for inclusion:

- The system drive.

- An additional volume on an internal local drive formatted using NTFS or FAT32.

- An external USB or IEEE 1394 (FireWire) hard drive, formatted using NTFS or FAT32.

- A USB flash drive, if the device appears in the navigation pane, under the This PC heading.

- A shared network folder that is indexed using Windows Search; this includes any shared folder from another computer in your homegroup.

- A shared network folder that has been made available offline and is therefore available in your local index.

> **For more details on how to manage the search index, see "Configuring search and indexing options" later in this chapter.**

To delete a library, simply right-click it in the navigation pane and click Delete. The library is gone, but its component folders and their contents remain.

Inside OUT

Open a file or folder location from a library

Because libraries are virtual folders, it's sometimes difficult to perform operations directly on their contents. If you want to see a file or folder in its actual location in File Explorer, right-click and choose Open File Location or Open Folder Location.

Using compressed (zipped) folders

Depending on the file type, you can dramatically reduce the amount of disk space used by one or more files by compressing those files into a zipped folder. Don't be fooled by the name: a zipped folder (also known as a Zip file or archive) is actually a single file, compressed using the industry-standard Zip format and saved with the .zip file name extension. Any version of Windows can open a file saved in this format, as can other modern operating systems. The format is also accessible with the help of many third-party utilities. Thus, zipped folders are an ideal way to compress large files in order to send them in email or transfer them across a network, including the Internet.

> ### TROUBLESHOOTING
>
> *Your application can't open zipped files*
>
> **File Explorer compresses and decompresses files in zipped folders on the fly, displaying the contents of an archive in a window that closely resembles a folder. But most applications do not support this format. Thus, to view a WordPad document stored in a zipped folder, you need to double-click the zipped folder in File Explorer to display its contents and then double-click the file. If you try the same task using WordPad's Open command, you'll open the binary Zip file itself and display its unreadable contents. (If you want to edit a file stored in a Zip file, be sure to extract it to a local or network folder first.)**

To create a new archive using zipped folders, follow these steps:

1. In File Explorer, display the folder in which you want the new archive to reside.

2. Right-click any empty space in the folder, and then click New, Compressed (Zipped) Folder.

3. Name the folder.

To add files and folders to your archive, drag and drop them onto the zipped folder icon in File Explorer (or double-click to open the zipped folder in its own window and then drag items into it). You can also use the Clipboard to copy and paste items. To remove an item from the zipped folder, double-click the folder to display its contents, right-click the item, and then click Delete.

You can also create a compressed folder from the current selection by clicking Zip on the Share tab in File Explorer. Windows creates an archive file with the same name as the selected object. Use the Rename command (or press F2) to replace the default name with a more descriptive one.

To extract individual files or folders from a zipped folder, open it in File Explorer and then drag the items you want to extract to a new location, or use the Clipboard to copy and paste. To extract all items from a zipped folder to a specific location, right-click the zipped folder icon and then click Extract All, or open the zipped folder in File Explorer and click Extract All on the Extract tab on the ribbon.

Inside OUT

Add password protection to zipped folders

When creating a new archive, you no longer have the option to add a password to protect the file from casual snoops (that feature disappeared with Windows 7). If you need password protection, you can use a third-party program. You have many choices, including the venerable WinZip (*winzip.com*), which costs $30 per copy. An attractive freeware alternative is 7-Zip (*7-zip.org*), which supports a huge number of compression formats, and also allows you to secure compressed files using 256-bit Advanced Encryption Standard (AES) encryption. It integrates neatly into File Explorer.

Displaying or suppressing check boxes

File Explorer offers two modes of file and folder selection—with and without check boxes. You can switch between them by means of the Item Check Boxes command on the View tab.

With check boxes on, you can select multiple items that are not adjacent to one another simply by selecting each one in turn; no need to hold down the Ctrl key. In any case, though, Ctrl-selecting and Shift-selecting work as they always have, with or without check boxes.

Arranging data in File Explorer

You can adjust the display of any individual folder's contents in File Explorer by means of options in the Layout section of the View tab. As Figure 12-3 shows, your choices are numerous: icons in various sizes, Tiles, List, Details, and Content. Display options are folder-specific and persistent.

Figure 12-3 The View tab provides a large set of options for displaying content in File Explorer.

CHAPTER 12

You can get a look at each display option by hovering the mouse over it on the View tab. File Explorer gives you a preview of each choice, making it easier for you to decide.

The range of options for the various icon views is larger than it looks. Although there are four discrete choices available on the View tab—small, medium, large, and extra large—the actual number of sizes is 76. You can cycle smoothly through all 76 sizes by choosing one of them, holding down the Ctrl key, and turning the wheel on your mouse. With each step, you'll see the icons grow or shrink (although at some of the smaller sizes the change is barely perceptible).

Content view, introduced in Windows 7, is intended primarily for use with search results. In the case of documents, it shows a fairly lengthy snippet of text with the matching search items highlighted.

List view displays file names only. If you have a large number of items in the folder you're working with, the list snakes; that is, you read down the first column, then up to the top of the second, and so on. Details view provides a multicolumn tabulation of your files. The column headings vary by folder type, but you can tailor them in any case. To add or remove a column heading, put your folder in Details view, click the View tab, click anywhere in the row of headings, and then click Add Columns. (Alternatively, right-click anywhere in the row of column headings.) If the list of column headings that appears doesn't include the one you want, click Choose Columns (at the bottom of the list). As Figure 12-4 shows, the Choose Details dialog box that appears next provides you with a wealth of choices. In fact, Figure 12-4 shows only the first 15 choices in a vast array of possibilities.

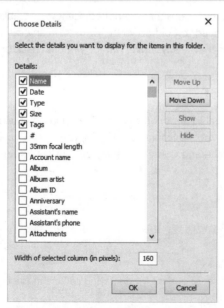

Figure 12-4 Use this dialog box to select which headings are displayed in Details view.

In the Choose Details dialog box, you can also use the Move Up and Move Down buttons to change the order in which column headings appear. (You can also change the column order in File Explorer by dragging headings with the mouse.)

As you'll discover momentarily (see "Sorting, filtering, and grouping" later in this chapter), headings in Details view are important for sorting data as well as simply displaying it.

Inside OUT

Change display settings in Open and Save dialog boxes

In many programs, you can change display settings in common file-management dialog boxes, although you will not find a View tab there. To switch between an icon view and Details view (or to make any other comparable switch), right-click an open space within the dialog box (you might have to enlarge the dialog box first), then click View.

Initially, all folders intended for the storage of user data (including those you create) are assigned one of five folder templates. These templates define the default headings that File Explorer considers appropriate for the content type. These headings are used atop columns in Details view and are available on the Sort By menu in all other views. The logic is straightforward: you'll probably want to sort a folder full of MP3 tracks by track number, but that column would be superfluous in a folder full of Microsoft Word documents. And the Date Taken column is extremely useful for filtering digital photos, but it isn't much use with any other kinds of data.

Table 12-1 lists the default column headings available in each of these five templates. It also lists additional headings that are not included by default but might be useful for each template.

Table 12-1 Standard folder templates

Template	Default headings	Additional headings
General Items	Name, Date Modified, Type, Size	Date Created, Authors, Tags, Title
Documents	Name, Date Modified, Type, Size	Date Created, Authors, Categories, Tags, Title
Pictures	Name, Date, Tags, Size, Rating (in libraries); Name, Date, Type, Size, Tags (in folders)	Date Created, Date Taken, Dimensions, Rating
Music	Name, [Track] #, Contributing Artists, Album	Type, Size, Date Created, Date Modified, Album Artist, Bit Rate, Genre, Length, Protected, Rating, Year
Videos	Name, Date, Type, Size, Length	Date Created, Date Modified, Media Created, Dimensions

Inside OUT

Customize folder templates

Not sure what folder "type" you're in? Right-click a blank space in the folder and then click Customize This Folder, or tap the Alt key to reveal the menu bar, and then choose View, Customize This Folder. (If this option isn't available, you're viewing a system folder whose template can't be changed.) On the Customize tab of the properties dialog box for the selected folder, look at the selection in the Optimize This Folder For drop-down list, which shows the folder type that's currently in effect.

Sorting, filtering, and grouping

Regardless of the view settings you've chosen for a folder, you can adjust the way its contents are displayed at any time by changing the sort order, filtering the contents by one or more properties to include only selected items, and grouping and arranging the contents by a particular heading. In any view, these options are available by right-clicking anywhere in the contents pane and choosing a Sort By or Group By option. In most cases, however, these actions are easier to accomplish by switching to Details view and using the column headings, which is also the preferred way to filter.

Sorting a folder's contents   To sort a folder in Details view, click the heading that you want to use as a sort key. For example, to sort by Date Modified, click the Date Modified heading. Click again on the same heading to reverse the sort order. The current sort order is indicated by an up arrow or down arrow above the heading to indicate whether the sort is in ascending or descending order.

In all other views, right-click any empty space in the contents pane and select a value from the Sort By menu. A bullet next to Ascending or Descending indicates the current sort order; choose the other option to reverse the sort order.

Filtering folder contents   In Details view only, you can use headings to filter the contents of a folder. If you rest your pointer on a heading, a drop-down arrow appears at the right. Clicking the arrow reveals a set of filter check boxes appropriate for that heading. In some cases (the Tags heading, for example, as shown in Figure 12-5), the filter list is built on the fly from the contents of the current file list.

Select any check box to add that item to the filter list; clear the check box for an item to remove it from the filter. After you filter the list in Details view, you can switch to any other view and the filter will persist. (Look in the address bar to see the specific filter applied, and click the previous breadcrumb to remove all filtering without switching back to Details view.)

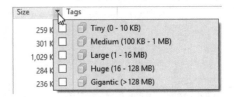

Figure 12-5 When you click the drop-down arrow next to a column heading, a set of filtering options appropriate for the heading appears.

If you filter by Size, you get a set of choices based on the file sizes that Windows deems appropriate given the current folder contents, as shown here:

A filter can use multiple check boxes and multiple headings. So, for example, you could filter a picture folder based on ratings as well as a "date taken" value, resulting in a file list like this one:

When a folder is filtered, check marks appear to the right of headings used for filtering (see the Rating and Date headings in the preceding illustration). The values on which you have filtered appear in the address bar.

When you select multiple check boxes in the same heading, File Explorer displays items that match any of the selected check boxes. When you select filtering check boxes from two or more separate headings, however, File Explorer displays only items that satisfy the criteria applied to each heading (in Boolean terms, it uses the conjunction AND between the headings).

CHAPTER 12

Inside OUT

Use the date navigator to zoom through time

If you click a date heading, the filter options display a date navigator like the one shown next, with common date groupings available at the bottom of the list. You can also click Select A Date Or Date Range and use the calendar to filter the file list that way.

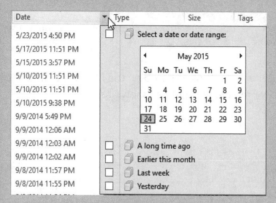

The date navigator is much more powerful than it looks at first glance. Use the calendar to zoom in or out and narrow or expand your view of the contents of a folder or a search. Initially, the calendar shows the current month, with today's date highlighted. Click the month heading to zoom out to a display showing the current year as a heading with the current month highlighted. You can then drag or hold down Ctrl and click to select multiple months, as shown here:

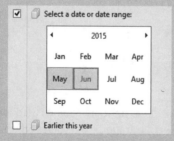

Click the year to zoom out again to show the current decade. Click once more to show the current century. In any calendar view, you can use the arrows to the left and right of the column heading to move through the calendar a month, year, decade, or century at a time. To zoom back in, click any month, year, decade, or century on the calendar control. This technique is especially valuable with folders or search results containing hundreds or thousands of files and folders.

Grouping folder contents   If sorting and filtering don't give you enough ways to organize or locate files, try grouping. Grouping generates a display comparable to the one shown in Figure 12-6. Here we have grouped a set of picture files by their tags.

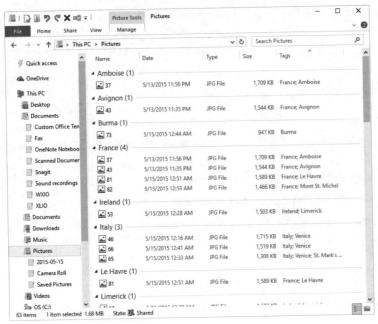

Figure 12-6 You can group items in any view. Here we have grouped some pictures by tag in Details view.

When you group items, File Explorer collects all the items that have some common property, displaying each group under a heading that can be expanded or collapsed in most views. List view offers a particularly interesting perspective, with each group of results appearing under a column heading. The grouped arrangement is saved as part of the custom view settings for that folder; the next time you open the folder, it will still be grouped.

To group items in a File Explorer window, open the View tab, click Group By, and then click the property you want to use. File Explorer displays a dot before the selected property. You can remove the grouping by returning to Group By and choosing None.

Inside OUT

Zip through File Explorer with keyboard shortcuts

Pressing Ctrl+N in File Explorer opens a new window on the same folder. Ctrl+W closes the current window. (These keyboard shortcuts function the same way in Internet Explorer.) The following additional keyboard shortcuts work in File Explorer:

- **Alt+Up Arrow** Go up one level.
- **Alt+Right Arrow** Go forward.
- **Alt+Left Arrow** Go back.
- **Alt+D** Move the focus to the address bar and select the current path.
- **F4** Move the insertion point to the address bar and display the contents of the drop-down list of previous addresses.
- **Alt+Enter** Show properties of the selected file.
- **Tab** Cycle through the following elements: navigation pane, file list, column headings, address bar, search box.
- **F11** Switch in and out of full-screen mode.
- **Ctrl+Shift+N** Create a new subfolder in the current folder.
- **Ctrl+Shift+E** Expand the navigation pane to the current folder.

Managing file properties and metadata

Every file you view in File Explorer has a handful of properties that describe the file itself: the file name and file name extension (which in turn defines the file type), the file's size, the date and time it was created and last modified, and any file system attributes. These properties are stored in the file system itself and are used for basic browsing and searching.

In addition to these basic file properties, many data file formats can store custom metadata. These additional properties can be added by a device or by software; in some cases, they can be modified by the user. When you take a digital picture, your camera or smartphone might add the device make and model, exposure time, ISO speed, and other details to the file when it's saved. When you rip a CD using Windows Media Player, it retrieves details about the artist and album from the Windows Metadata service and adds them to the MP3 or WMA files. Microsoft Word automatically adds your name to the Author field in a document you create; you can fill in additional properties such as keywords and comments and save them with the file.

Inside OUT

Rate your favorite digital media files

For digital photos, music, and other media files, you'll notice that the Rating field is available in the details pane. Instead of providing a box to enter free-form text or a number, this field shows five stars, all of which are shown in gray initially. You can rate any file on a scale of one to five stars by clicking the appropriate star in the details pane. Adding ratings is a great way to filter large media collections so that they show only the entries you've previously rated highly. Ratings are also useful in playlists and screen savers.

The details pane, which you can display by clicking Details Pane on the View tab, displays a thumbnail of the selected file (if a thumbnail is available), plus quite a few properties. In the following illustration from a subfolder in the Pictures library, you can see the date the photo was taken, the make of the camera, the dimensions of the picture, the exposure settings, and quite a bit more.

001
JPG File

Date taken:	3/12/2015 4:39 PM
Tags:	Add a tag
Rating:	☆ ☆ ☆ ☆ ☆
Dimensions:	3456 x 5184
Size:	7.92 MB
Title:	Add a title
Authors:	Add an author
Comments:	Add comments
Availability:	Available offline
Camera maker:	Canon
Camera model:	Canon EOS REBEL T5i
Subject:	Specify the subject
F-stop:	f/10
Exposure time:	1/250 sec.
ISO speed:	ISO-100
Exposure bias:	0 step
Focal length:	33 mm
Metering mode:	Pattern
Flash mode:	No flash, compulsory
Date created:	4/10/2015 12:30 AM
Date modified:	3/12/2015 4:39 PM

The properties displayed in the details pane might not be everything the operating system knows about the selected file, however. For the complete list, right-click the item and click Properties (or select the item and press Alt+Enter). Then click Details in the properties dialog box.

Figure 12-7 shows a side-by-side comparison of the properties dialog box and the details pane for a music track. Note that the properties dialog box includes such exotica as Period, Mood, Beats-Per-Minute, and Initial Key.

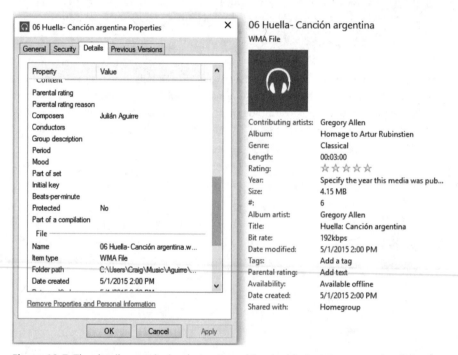

Figure 12-7 The details pane is simple to use and invaluable, but the properties dialog box might offer a more exhaustive set of properties.

In either place, the details pane or the properties dialog box, you can edit many (but not all) of the item's properties. Some properties, such as file size, are calculated by the file system or are otherwise fixed and cannot be directly modified. But you can edit custom metadata if the format of the underlying file allows you to do so.

To enter or change a property's value, simply click and type. If you add two or more words or phrases to a field that accepts multiple entries (such as Tags or Authors), use semicolons to separate them. Press Enter or click Save to add the new or changed properties to the file.

You can edit properties for multiple files at one time. This is especially useful when you're correcting an error in an album or artist name; just select all the songs in the album's folder. When more than one file is selected, you'll note that some properties in the details pane (such as track numbers and song titles) change to indicate that the specified field contains multiple values. A change you make to any field will be written to all of the files in your selection.

Metadata is saved within the file itself, using industry-standard data storage formats. Software developers who need to create a custom file format can make its metadata available to Windows by using an add-in called a property handler, which opens the file format to read and write its properties. Because metadata is saved within the file itself, the properties you edit in File Explorer or a Windows program are fully portable. This means

- You can move files to other computers, even those running other operating systems, without losing the files' tags and other metadata.

- You can edit a file in an application other than the one in which it was created without losing any of the file's properties (assuming the other application properly adheres to the file format's standard for reading and writing metadata).

- A file's properties are visible to anyone who has read access to the file.

You can edit custom properties (including tags) only in files saved using a format that accommodates embedded metadata. For digital image files, Windows supports the JPEG, GIF, and TIFF formats, but you cannot save metadata in bitmap images and graphics files saved in PNG format because these formats were not developed with metadata in mind. Among music file formats, MP3, WMA, and FLAC fully support a wide range of properties designed to make it easy to manage a music collection; files saved in the uncompressed WAV (.wav) format do not support any custom tags. Plain text and Rich Text Format (.rtf) files do not support custom metadata; files saved in Word formats expose a rich set of additional properties, as do all other native file formats from Microsoft Office programs.

In some cases, you'll find that you're unable to view or edit metadata in a file even though the underlying format supports metadata. In that case, the culprit is a missing property handler. In some cases, you can lose data in this situation if you're not careful. This might happen, for example, if you create a file using WordPad and save it in the Office Open XML Document format. If you then open that file using Word, you can add properties such as author name, title, and comments. When you save the file, the file name extension (.docx) remains unchanged. However, if you reopen the document in WordPad, you'll see an information bar at the top of the document warning you that the program does not support all the features of the file format.

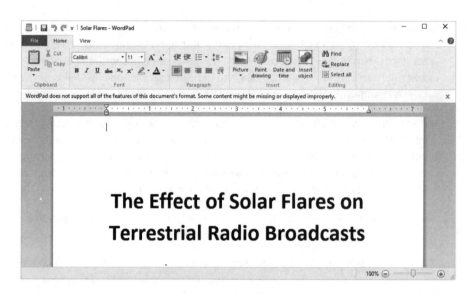

If you make some changes and attempt to save the document under the same name or a different name, you'll see the following stern warning:

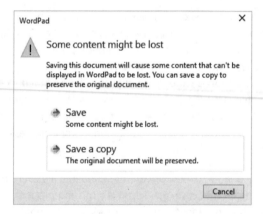

Believe that warning. If you choose the Save option, any custom properties you saved in an earlier version of the file will be stripped out permanently.

Inside OUT

Remove personal metadata for privacy's sake

Metadata within a file can tell a lot about you. Cameras record data about when a picture was taken and what camera or smartphone was used. Microsoft Office automatically adds author and company information to documents and spreadsheets. With user-created tags, you can add personal and business details that might be useful on a local copy but are unwise to disclose to the wider world.

To scrub a file of unwanted metadata, select one or more files in File Explorer, click the Home tab, click Properties, and then click Remove Properties. This opens the Remove Properties dialog box, an example of which is shown here:

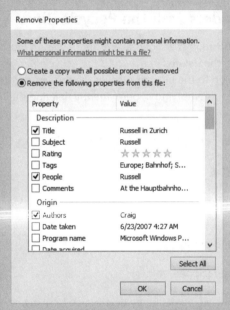

At this point, you have two choices. The default option creates a copy of your file (using the original file name with the word Copy appended to it) and removes all properties that can be changed, based on the file type. The second option, Remove The Following Properties From This File, allows you to select the check boxes next to individual properties and permanently remove those properties from the file when you click OK. (If no check box is visible, that property is not editable.)

Of course, common sense should prevail when it comes to issues of privacy. This option zeroes out metadata, but it does nothing with the contents of the file itself. You'll need to be vigilant to ensure that a digital photo doesn't contain potentially revealing information in the image itself or that sensitive personal or business details aren't saved within a document's contents.

Recovering lost, damaged, and deleted files and folders

It takes only a fraction of a second to wipe out a week's worth of work. You might accidentally delete a folder full of files or, worse, overwrite an entire group of files with changes that can't be undone. Whatever the cause of your misfortune, Windows includes tools that offer hope for recovery. If a file is simply lost, try searching for it (see "Using Windows Search" later in this chapter). For accidental deletions, your first stop should be the Recycle Bin, a Windows institution since 1995. If you don't find what you're looking for in the Recycle Bin, your next recourse is a considerably more powerful recovery tool called File History.

> ➤ For information about File History, see "Using File History to protect files and folders" in
> Chapter 16, "Backup, restore, and recovery."

Recovering files and folders with the Recycle Bin

The Recycle Bin provides protection against accidental erasure of files. In most cases, when you delete one or more files or folders, the deleted items go to the Recycle Bin, not into the ether. If you change your mind, you can go to the bin and recover the thrown-out items. Eventually, when the bin fills up, Windows begins emptying it, permanently deleting the files that have been there the longest.

The following kinds of deletions do not go to the Recycle Bin:

- Files stored on removable disks

- Files stored on network drives, even when that volume is on a computer that has its own Recycle Bin

- Files deleted from a command prompt

- Files deleted from compressed (zipped) folders

You can bypass the Recycle Bin yourself, permanently deleting an item, by holding down the Shift key while you delete the item. You might want to do this if you need to get rid of some very large files and you're sure you'll never want those files back. Skipping the Recycle Bin in this case will reclaim some disk space.

You can also turn off the Recycle Bin's services permanently, as we explain in the following section.

Changing Recycle Bin settings

To see and adjust the amount of space currently used by the Recycle Bin for each drive that it protects, right-click the Recycle Bin icon on your desktop and then click Properties. In the Recycle Bin Properties dialog box (shown in Figure 12-8), you can select a drive and enter a different value in the Custom Size box. Windows ordinarily allocates up to 10 percent of a disk's space for recycling. (When the bin is full, the oldest items give way to the newest.) If you think that amount of space is excessive, enter a lower value.

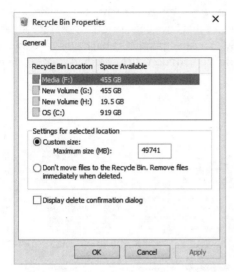

Figure 12-8 You can use the Recycle Bin Properties dialog box to alter the amount of space devoted to the bin—or to turn the feature off for selected drives.

NOTE

If you don't see a Recycle Bin icon on your desktop, it's probably hidden. To make it visible, type desktop icons in the Windows search box. Next, in the search results, click Show Or Hide Common Icons On The Desktop. Then, in the Desktop Icon Settings dialog box, select the Recycle Bin check box and click OK. If you use the Show All Folders option in File Explorer, you'll have access to the Recycle Bin from the bottom of the navigation pane.

If you'd rather do without the Recycle Bin for a particular drive, select the drive in the Recycle Bin Properties dialog box and then select Don't Move Files To The Recycle Bin. Remove Files Immediately When Deleted. This action is equivalent to setting the maximum capacity to 0.

Whether the Recycle Bin is enabled or disabled, Windows normally displays a confirmation prompt when you delete something. If that prompt annoys you, clear the Display Delete Confirmation Dialog check box.

CHAPTER 12

Restoring files and folders

When you open the Recycle Bin, Windows displays the names of recently deleted items in an ordinary File Explorer window. In Details view (see Figure 12-9), you can see when each item was deleted and which folder it was deleted from. You can use the column headings to sort the folder—for example, to display the items that have been deleted most recently at the top, with earlier deletions below. Alternatively, you can organize the bin by disk and folder by clicking the Original Location heading. If these methods don't help you find what you're hoping to restore, use the search box.

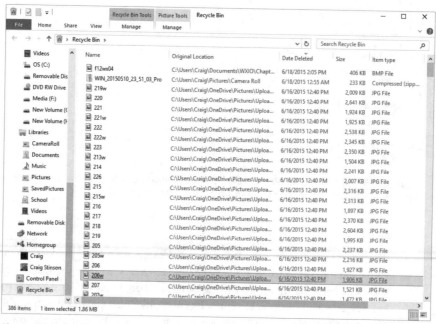

Figure 12-9 Sorting the Recycle Bin in Details view can help you find what you need to restore; so can the search box.

Note that deleted folders are shown only as folders; you don't see the names of items contained within the folders. If you restore a deleted folder, however, Windows re-creates the folder and its contents.

The Restore commands on the Manage tab (Restore All Items and Restore The Selected Items) puts items back in the folders from which they were deleted. If a folder doesn't currently exist, Windows asks your permission to re-create it. Note that if your Recycle Bin contains hundreds or thousands of deleted files dating back weeks or months, Restore All Items can create chaos. That command is most useful if you recently emptied the Recycle Bin and all of its current contents are visible.

If you want, you can restore a file or folder to a different location. Select the item, click the Home tab, click Move To, and then choose a new location. Or, simplest of all, you can drag the item out of the Recycle Bin and put it where you want it.

Purging the Recycle Bin

A deleted file sitting in your Recycle Bin takes up as much space as it did before it was deleted. If you're deleting files to free up space for new programs and documents, transferring them to the Recycle Bin won't help. You need to remove them permanently. The safest way to do this is to move the items to another storage medium—a different hard disk or a removable disk, for example.

If you're sure you'll never need a particular file again, however, you can delete it in the normal way, and then purge it from the Recycle Bin. Display the Recycle Bin, select the item, and then press Delete.

To empty the Recycle Bin entirely, click Empty Recycle Bin on the Manage tab.

Relocating personal data folders

Although the organizational scheme that Windows has adopted for personal data folders—the visible subfolders of %UserProfile%—is suitable for many users, the scheme has one potential defect: it combines data and system files on the same physical volume. For a variety of reasons, some users prefer to separate their documents and other profile data. These reasons might include the following:

- Large collections of data, in particular digital media files, have a way of overwhelming the available space on system volumes, eventually necessitating their removal and relocation to a separate, larger volume.

- Separating data from system files makes restoration easier in the event of system corruption (for example, by malware).

- Separation reduces the size and time devoted to image backups, encouraging their regular use.

- Separation can make it easier, when the time comes, to upgrade the operating system.

On a large system volume, it might not be a problem to keep data files and system files together on the same disk. But if you have installed Windows on a solid state drive—an excellent strategy for performance—the space on your system drive is likely to be at a premium. It's a good idea to keep at least 20 percent of your system drive free. If you find your space shrinking below that threshold, you should probably consider relocating some of your personal data folders.

Inside OUT

Get industrial-strength file management with Robocopy and RichCopy

Dragging files between folders in File Explorer is fine for some tasks, but when it comes to heavy-duty file management you might want a better tool. If you're willing to do a little typing in exchange for power and flexibility that you can't get with File Explorer, get to know Robocopy.

Robocopy (the name is short for Robust File Copy) was introduced with the Windows Server 2003 Resource Kit and is included in Windows 10. Its many strengths include the ability to copy all NTFS file attributes and to mirror the contents of an entire folder hierarchy across local volumes or over a network. If you use the right combination of options, you can recover from interruptions such as network outages by resuming a copy operation from the point of failure after the connection is restored.

The Robocopy syntax takes some getting used to. If you're familiar with the standard Copy and Xcopy commands, you'll have to unlearn their syntax and get used to Robocopy's unconventional ways. The key difference is that Robocopy is designed to work with two directories (folders) at a time, and the file specification is a secondary parameter. For details, type **robocopy /?** at a command prompt.

If you aren't keen on the idea of using a command-line tool, check out RichCopy, a graphical copy utility written by Microsoft engineer Ken Tamaru. You can read about RichCopy and download the bits at *bit.ly/richcopy*.

The easiest, safest way to accomplish this goal is to store personal data in folders on a separate volume, and then include those folders in your libraries. (For information about using libraries, see "Working with libraries" earlier in this chapter.) This approach leaves you with a default set of profile folders, which you can still use when it's convenient to do so, but it keeps the bulk of your personal information in a separate place.

Not everyone loves libraries, however, and there's no requirement to love them. You can still move some or all of your profile subfolders in Windows 10, just as you could in earlier versions. To relocate a user profile folder by editing its properties, follow these steps:

1.   In the navigation pane, click your account name (you might need to display all folders first) to open the root folder of your profile.

2.   Right-click a folder that you want to relocate, and choose Properties. (Or select the folder, and then click Properties on the Home tab.)

3. On the Location tab of the properties dialog box, enter the address that you want to relocate the folder to. For example, to move the Downloads folder from C:\Users\Craig\Downloads to F:\Users\Craig\Downloads, you could simply replace the C with an F at the beginning of the path.

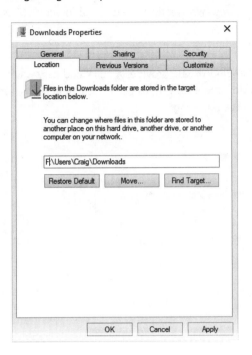

4. Click OK. Windows asks permission to create the target folder if it doesn't already exist. Click Yes. A Move Folder dialog box similar to this one appears:

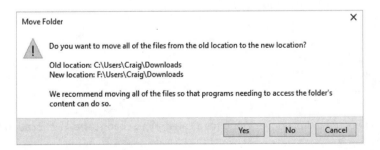

5. Unless you have some good reason not to move the existing files from the original location to the new one, click Yes.

    It's really not a good idea *not* to click Yes in this dialog box. First, it's difficult to imagine why you would want some of your personal documents in a given category on one disk and the rest on another. (If you want to keep your existing files separate from those you save in the future, move the old files to a subfolder in the new location instead of leaving them in the old location.) Second, because %UserProfile% is a system-generated folder, not an ordinary data folder that corresponds to a fixed disk location, leaving some files behind will give you two identically named subfolders in %UserProfile%.

Using Save locations

Save locations, a new feature in Windows 10, provides a quick and easy way to see which disks Windows will use to save new documents in various categories. At Settings, System, Storage, you will see a display similar to the following:

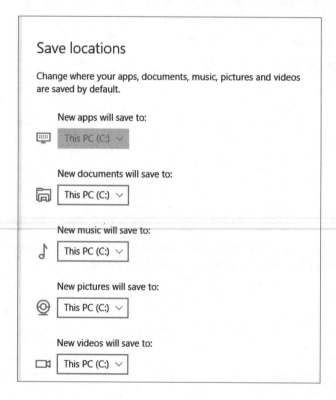

You can open the drop-down menu for a category to change the save location for that category.

Using Windows Search

Perhaps more than any other feature in Windows, the search tools have the potential to change the way you work. If your filing philosophy involves the digital equivalent of throwing everything into a giant shoebox, you'll be startled at how easy it is to find what you're looking for. Even if you consider yourself an extremely well-organized Windows user, we predict that you'll find ways to integrate the new search tools into your everyday routine.

Searching everywhere

If you're accustomed to the way that search worked in Windows 7 or Windows 8.1, the difference you're likely to notice first is that Windows 10 takes a "search everywhere" approach. Internet searching is tightly integrated with file searching, and both are integrated with your personal assistant, Cortana.

When you begin typing into the search box on your taskbar (it's located directly to the right of the Start menu button), Cortana (assuming you have enabled her) pops up and checks to see if you're making a request that she can handle—such as "remind me to call Russell at 8 this evening." If you enter what appears to be a search term, Cortana steps aside, and Windows Search presents a categorized list of possible hits, comparable to the one shown in Figure 12-10.

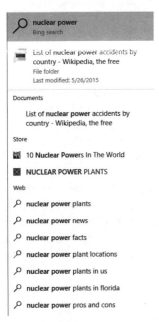

Figure 12-10 Windows Search searches everywhere, both locally and on the web.

In this example, our search term was "nuclear power," and Windows has returned a number of items. The Bing search item at the top of the list represents the search tool's judgment about what we're most likely looking for—in this case, a general web search through our default web search service. Immediately below that, however, is a folder and a document, both found in our local file resources. As it happens, both relate to the same item, a file and supporting documents downloaded from Wikipedia. Below that are a couple of items of possible interest in the Windows Store. And finally, the search tool gives us a set of more specific web searches.

At the bottom of the search results pane, not shown in Figure 12-10, are two handy buttons, labeled My Stuff and Web:

These buttons let you restrict your search to local resources or the Internet. If you click My Stuff, the search tool gives you an expanded results pane, again categorized. (In this example, the results were organized into Documents, OneDrive, Folders, and Photos.)

The results pane is sorted by default according to relevance—the system's judgment about what you're most likely to want. You can use a drop-down list to switch from relevance to most recent. A second drop-down list lets you filter the results pane according to type—Documents, Folders, Apps, Settings, Photos, Videos, Music.

Finally, in case the My Stuff hits don't include what you're looking for, there's a handy Search The Web button that redirects your inquiry to the Internet.

This "search everywhere" approach is ideal when you're not exactly sure whether you want a local item or something from the web. When you know you want a local file, as you'll see momentarily, it's typically quicker to search within File Explorer.

Configuring search and indexing options

At its heart, Windows Search relies on a speedy, powerful, and well-behaved indexing service that does a fine job of keeping track of files and folders by name, by properties, and (in supported formats) by contents. All of those details are kept in the search index, a database that keeps track of indexed file names, properties, and the contents of files. As a rule, when you do most common types of searches, Windows checks the index first and returns whatever results it finds there.

NOTE

The search index is stored by default in %ProgramData%\Microsoft\Search\Data. Default permissions for this folder are set to allow access only to the System account and to members of the Administrators group. This folder contains no user-editable files, and we recommend that you leave its contents undisturbed.

Inside OUT

When do searches skip the index?

Although we focus mostly on indexed searches in this section, Windows 10 actually includes two search engines. The second engine is informally known as *grep* search (the name comes from an old UNIX command derived from the full name *global | regular expression | print*). Windows Search uses the index whenever you use the search box on the taskbar, in libraries, and in locations that are part of a homegroup. In those circumstances, search looks only in the index and ignores any subfolders that are excluded from the index.

Windows uses the grep search engine if you begin your search from the This PC folder, from the root of any local drive (including the system drive), or from a local file folder. Grep searches include the contents of all subfolders within the search scope regardless of whether they're included in the search index. For a more detailed examination of nonindexed searches, see "Advanced search tools and techniques" later in this chapter.

To build the index that makes its magic possible, Windows Search uses several separate processes. The index is constructed dynamically by the Windows Search service, SearchIndexer.exe. The indexer crawls through all locations that are prescribed to be indexed, converting the content of documents (in supported formats) into plain text and then storing the text and metadata for quick retrieval.

The Windows Search service begins running shortly after you start a new Windows session. From that point on, it runs in the background at all times, creating the initial index and updating it as new files are added and existing ones are changed or deleted. Protocol handlers do the work of cracking open different data stores to add items to the index. Property handlers allow Windows Search to extract the values of properties from items and store them properly in the index. Filters extract the contents of supported file types so that you can do full-text searches for those items.

Which files and folders are in the index?

Indexing every 0 and 1 on your hard disk would be an exhausting task—and ultimately point-less. When you search for a snippet of text, you're almost always looking for something you wrote, copied, or saved, and you don't want the results to include random program files that happen to have the same snippet embedded in the midst of a blob of code. So the default set-tings for the indexer make some reasonable inclusions and exclusions.

Certain locations are specifically included. These include your user profile (but not the AppData folder), the contents of the Start menu, and your browser history. Offline files stored in the client-side cache (CSC) are automatically included in your local index. You can explicitly add other folders to the index, but Windows 10 eliminates the need to do that. Instead, just add the folder to a library; when you do so, Windows automatically adds that folder to the list of indexed locations and begins indexing its contents without requiring any additional steps on your part.

CAUTION

Data from Microsoft Outlook 2010 and subsequent versions is not stored in the index. The ability to find messages using Windows Search was removed because these recent versions of Outlook provide their own search tools. For more information, see *support.microsoft.com/en-us/kb/2385524*.

To see which folders are currently being indexed, open the Indexing Options dialog box. You can get there in various ways, including by entering **Indexing Options** in the search box on the taskbar. As Figure 12-11 shows, the Indexing Options dialog box initially shows the top level of folders that are included in the index.

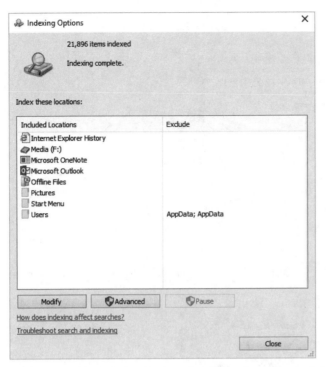

Figure 12-11 The Indexing Options dialog box shows the top level of locations that are included in the index. Subfolders (for example, all the profile subfolders of Users) are not shown here.

To get more information about what's being indexed, click Modify. Figure 12-12 shows the elaborate dialog box that results.

CAUTION

We strongly recommend that you not try to manage locations manually using the Indexed Locations dialog box. If you add a folder to a library and then remove it from the list of indexed locations, the folder will remain in the navigation pane under the associated library, but none of its contents will be visible in the library itself.

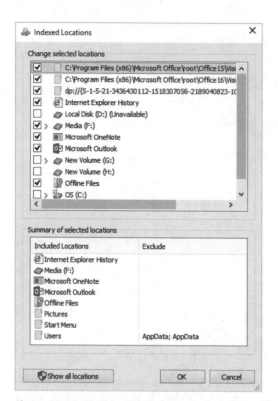

Figure 12-12 Clicking Modify lets you see in more detail which locations are being indexed. Adding a folder to a library automatically selects the corresponding check box here.

In its default view, the Indexed Locations list shows only locations that are accessible to your user account. To see (and manage) locations from other user profiles, click Show All Locations. As the User Account Control (UAC) shield icon makes clear, you'll need to be signed in as an administrator (or provide an administrator's credentials) to continue.

Within that list of indexed locations, the Windows Search service records the file name and properties (size, date modified, and so on) of any file or folder. Files marked as System and Hidden are indexed but are displayed in search results only when you change File Explorer settings to show those file types. Metadata for common music, image, and video file formats is included in the index by default. The indexer also includes the contents of a file and its custom properties if the file format has an associated property handler and filter. Some of the more common file formats supported by filters included with Windows 10 are shown in Table 12-2.

Table 12-2 Some file formats that support content indexing

File format	Extension
HTML	.ascx, .asp, .aspx, .css, .hhc, .hta, .htm, .html, .htt, .htw, .htx, .odc, .shtm, .shtml, .sor, .srf, .stm, .wdp, .vcproj
MIME	.mht, .mhtml
Office	.doc, .dot, .pot, .pps, .ppt, .xlb, .xlc, .xls, .xlt
Plain text	.a, .ans, .asc, .asm, .asx, .bas, .bat, .bcp, .c, .cc, .cls, .cmd, .cpp, .cs, .csa, .csv, .cxx, .dbs, .def, .dic, .dos, .dsp, .dsw, .ext, .faq, .fky, .h, .hpp, .hxx, .i, .ibq, .ics, .idl, .idq, .inc, .inf, .ini, .inl, .inx, .jav, .java, .js, .kci, .lgn, .lst, .m3u, .mak, .mk, .odh, .odl, .pl, .prc, .rc, .rc2, .rct, .reg, .rgs, .rul, .s, .scc, .sol, .sql, .tab, .tdl, .tlh, .tli, .trg, .txt, .udf, .usr, .vbs, .viw, .vspcc, .vsscc, .vssscc, .wri, .wtx
XML (xmlfilt.dll)	.csproj, .user, .vbproj, .vcproj, .xml, .xsd, .xsl, .xslt
Favorites	.url
Journal file	.jnt
Rich Text Format	.rtf
WordPad	.docx, .odt
XML Paper Specification	.dwfx, .easmx, .edrwx, .eprtx, .jtx, .xmlps

Inside OUT

Add text from faxes to the search index

Picture file types are not included in the list of formats in Table 12-2 because images by definition consist of colored pixels rather than words, and they thus contain no content to index. But one image format is a noteworthy exception to that rule. If you use a device or service to receive pages sent from a remote fax machine, the received faxes are saved using Tagged Image File Format (TIFF), but the original document usually consists of at least some text. Windows includes code that can perform optical character recognition on received faxes saved as TIFF files and include the recognized text in the search index. To enable this feature, open Control Panel and click Turn Windows Features On Or Off (under the Programs And Features heading). In the Windows Features dialog box, select Windows TIFF IFilter and then click OK.

To see which file formats support indexing, open the Indexing Options dialog box and click the Advanced button (you'll need to supply an administrator's credentials to do so, although elevation is silent if your sign-in account is a member of the Administrators group). On the File Types tab of the Advanced Options dialog box (see Figure 12-13), you will find a long list of file name extensions. By default, the check box next to every item in this list is selected, meaning that all of the listed file types are included in the index. As we describe later, not all of them support content indexing, however.

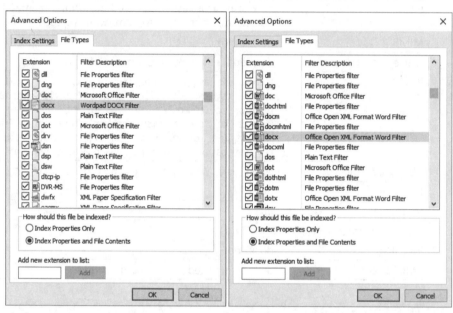

Figure 12-13 Installing Microsoft Office adds a slew of new indexing filters, as shown on the right.

The list of formats on the File Types tab on your computer might include more file types if you've installed Windows programs that include custom property handlers and filters, such as those installed with recent versions of Microsoft Office. Figure 12-13, for example, shows a side-by-side view of common Word document formats before and after installing Microsoft Office 365. The original list includes a generic Microsoft Office filter for .doc and .dot files as well as a WordPad filter for .docx files. After installing Office, the Office Open XML Format Word Filter takes over content indexing and also adds support for additional document and template formats. Any file with one of these extensions that is stored in an indexed location has its full contents added to the index, courtesy of the new filters.

Each of the file types in this list can be indexed in one of two manners by using the option buttons below the list—Index Properties Only or Index Properties And File Contents. The latter option is selected by default for any file type that has a registered filter, and the name of the associated filter is listed in the Filter Description column. If you don't need to search content in a file type that has a filter and would normally be indexed, you can save some processing overhead by selecting the file type and choosing Index Properties Only. If you need content indexing where none is currently provided, you can try switching a file from Index Properties

Only to Index Properties And File Contents. In that case, the indexer will use the Plain Text fil-ter—which might or might not yield satisfactory results.

Windows Search does not index the content of files that are saved without a file name exten-sion, nor does it index contents of files that are protected by Information Rights Management (IRM) or digital rights management (DRM).

A handful of locations are specifically excluded from indexing. Even if you manually specify that you want your system drive (normally C) to be included in the index, the following files and folders will be excluded:

- The entire contents of the \Windows folder and all its subfolders (the Windows.old folder that is created by an upgrade installation of Windows 10 is also excluded)

- \$Recycle.Bin (the hidden folder that contains deleted files for all user accounts)

- \Users\Default and all of its subfolders (this is the user profile template used to create a profile for a new user)

- The entire contents of the \Program Files and \Program Files (x86) folders and all of their subfolders

- The \ProgramData folder (except the subfolder that contains shortcuts for the shared Start menu)

Monitoring the index, and tuning indexer performance

The status message at the top of the Indexing Options dialog box offers real-time updates on what the indexer is doing at the moment. "Indexing complete" means there are no pending tasks. The status message lists the number of items (files, folders, and so on) that are currently in the index.

"Indexing paused" means the service has temporarily stopped all indexing tasks; you'll see this message if you check the indexer status shortly after you start the computer because the default setting for the Windows Search service is Automatic (Delayed Start).

If indexing tasks are currently under way, the status message will display an increase or decrease in the number of items indexed as new, changed, and deleted files are processed. The indexer is designed to throttle itself whenever it detects that the system is working on other, presumably more important tasks. As a result, you'll most likely be told that "Indexing speed is reduced due to user activity" when you first check.

That message indicates that the indexing service has backed off in response to your activity and is operating at a fraction of its normal speed. If the number of files to be indexed is big enough (if you copied a folder full of several thousand documents, for instance), you'll see the indexing speed pick up dramatically after you keep your hands off the keyboard and mouse for a minute or so.

The exact speed of indexing depends on a variety of factors, starting with the speed of your CPU and storage subsystem and including as well the number, size, and complexity of documents and whether their full contents are being indexed. Unfortunately, the status message in the Indexing Options dialog box doesn't include a progress bar and doesn't indicate how many files are yet to be indexed, so there's no easy way to tell whether the current task is barely under way or nearly complete. If you haven't recently added any new folders to the index but have simply been changing a few files in the course of normal work, the index should stay close to complete (assuming you've ever had a complete index).

Some websites for performance-obsessed Windows users complain about the performance hit that Windows Search causes; some even recommend disabling the Windows Search service to improve overall system performance. We recommend that you leave it running. In our experience, the Windows Search service uses only a small percentage of available CPU resources even at its busiest. The indexing service is specifically designed to back off when you use your computer for other activities, switching to low-priority input/output (I/O) and allowing foreground I/O tasks, such as opening the Start menu, to execute first. When Windows 10 first builds its index, or if you copy a large number of files to the system at once, indexing can take a long time and cause some spikes in CPU and disk activity, but you shouldn't notice any impact on performance.

File Explorer accesses the index directly, so even if the indexer is busy processing new and changed files it shouldn't affect the speed of a search operation. In normal operation, retrieving search results from even a very large index should take no more than a few seconds.

Other index maintenance tasks

The Indexing Options dialog box is also your gateway to buttons and check boxes that let you rebuild a corrupted index, change the location where the index stores its data, add folders to the index, change how the index deals with particular file types, and so on. To perform any of these maintenance tasks, display the Index Settings tab of the Advanced Options dialog box, shown in Figure 12-14.

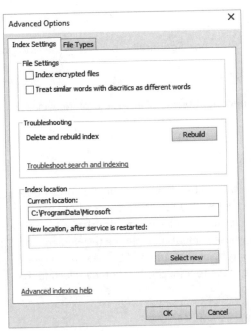

Figure 12-14 You can use this dialog box to rebuild an index that has stopped functioning properly.

It's not supposed to happen, but if your index stops working properly (or if you just performed major file maintenance and you want to give the index a fresh start), click Rebuild in the Troubleshooting area. Then give your system time to re-create the index. Be aware that rebuilding the index might take a considerable amount of time.

For security reasons, the contents of encrypted files are not included in the index by default. (Properties such as the name, date, and size of such files are indexed.) If you use Encrypting File System and you need those files indexed, select Index Encrypted Files in the File Settings area. This limitation does not apply to drives protected with BitLocker Drive Encryption.

By default, the index files live in subfolders of %ProgramData%\Microsoft\Search. If you install a faster hard disk on your computer, you might be able to improve search performance by moving the index files to the new disk. (Note that the index must reside on a fixed disk.) Simply type or paste the full path of the folder you want to use in the Current Location box. (The path must not be greater than 128 characters in length.) Be prepared to restart your computer and wait while the index is rebuilt.

Although this option sounds like an appealing performance tweak, we recommend you think twice before trying it. The actual difference in performance is likely to be minor, and you can expect to encounter problems reestablishing the index if you have to restore your system drive from a backup and you don't also restore the volume containing the index.

CHAPTER 12

Basic search techniques

You can search wherever you see a search box. Specifically, that means the following:

- From the search box on the taskbar

- From the search box in the upper right corner of any File Explorer window

- From Settings or Control Panel

- From a common file dialog box

When you type in the search box on the taskbar, in a library, or in a homegroup location, the list of results is drawn from the search index. The list includes files whose names or properties contain the specified text; for files in formats that include appropriate property handlers and filters, the results will include items whose contents contain the text you entered. The scope of the search depends on your starting point. From the taskbar search box, you'll search the entire index, but you can restrict the scope to a specific location by selecting that location in File Explorer and using its search box.

The following rules govern how searches work:

- Whatever text you type must appear at the beginning of a word, not in the middle. Thus, entering **des** returns items containing the words *des*ire, *des*tination, and *des*troy but not un*des*irable or sad*des*t. (You can override this behavior by using wildcard characters, as we explain in "Advanced search tools and techniques" later in this chapter.)

- Search terms are not case-sensitive. Thus, entering **Bott** returns items with Ed Bott as a tag or property, but the results also include files containing the words *bott*om and *bott*le.

- By default, searches ignore accents, umlauts, and other diacritical marks. If you routinely need to be able to distinguish, say, Händel from Handel, open the Indexing Options dialog box, click Advanced (you'll need administrative credentials), and then select Treat Similar Words With Diacritics As Different Words.

- To search for an exact phrase, enclose the phrase within quotation marks. Otherwise, you search for each word individually.

Searching from the taskbar

The search box on the taskbar has a multiple personality. Its primary role is to help you find shortcuts to applications on the All Apps menu and tasks in Settings or Control Panel. When you type a search term that matches an item in any of those locations, the results appear almost instantaneously. But this box also offers access to everything else in the search index:

websites in your history folder; saved favorites; any shared network folders that are included in any of your libraries; and, of course, files and folders in your file system.

The search box (here and elsewhere) is a "word wheel"—which means that the search begins as soon as you start typing, and each new character you type refines the results. If you type the letters *m* and *e* into the search box on the taskbar, you'll see results for Windows Media Player as well as the Windows Memory Diagnostic. You'll also see various Settings items (Media Streaming Options, Messaging Privacy Settings, and so on), folders and documents that begin with those two characters, and a smattering of websites.

Because the word wheel action is snappy and the taskbar search is optimized to find items on the Start menu, typing a few characters here can be a great alternative to hunting up a program shortcut from the All Apps section of the Start menu. Typing **media** into the search box, for example, produces a list like this:

The scope of a search from the taskbar covers the entire index, including document files, folders, Internet shortcuts, objects on a Microsoft OneNote page, and more. Results, as we noted earlier, are ranked by relevance and categorized.

The results pane lists only a few hits for each of the categories. The category headings, however, are links, and clicking a link brings up a more complete list. Here, for example, is what you might see if you click the Settings link in the previous example:

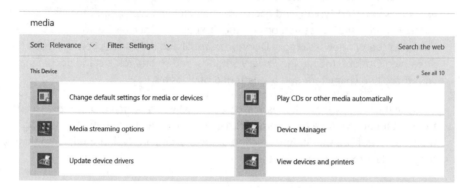

Even this is not complete, however. Clicking the See All link at the right side of this display adds four more items to the result set.

Inside OUT

You can search for programs that aren't on the Start menu

Searching from the taskbar's search box can be a good way to run a program that isn't on the Start menu—such as Registry Editor or an .msc console. (To run an .msc console, type the full name, including the .msc extension.) The taskbar's search looks for executables in system folders that are not ordinarily indexed. Because the search engine's word-wheel feature works only with indexed locations, however, you need to type the full name before it appears in the search results. You also need to identify the program by the full name of its executable file, rather than its friendly title. Typing **Registry Editor** in the search box gets you nothing (unless you happen to have created a shortcut and saved it under that name). Typing **regedit** summons the program.

Searching from File Explorer

When you know that what you're looking for is stored in a library folder somewhere, it's more efficient to search for it from File Explorer. Select the likely parent folder in the navigation pane (or select Libraries if you're not sure which library folder it's in), then begin typing in the File Explorer search box.

Search results for indexed folders appear so quickly that you may have a substantial number of hits before you type the second or third character in the search string. At this point, Windows may simplify your task by recalling earlier search strings and presenting you with a list of possible completions:

Inside OUT

See all files in a folder and its subfolders

If you have opened File Explorer to a particular folder and you want to avoid the tedium of opening subfolders to view their contents, try using the wildcard character that's been around as long as Microsoft has been making operating systems. Entering an asterisk (*) in the search box immediately returns all files in the current folder and all its subfolders. Assuming the list is of manageable size, you can then group, filter, sort, or otherwise rearrange the items within the folder to find exactly what you're looking for.

Once you have a set of search hits, a contextual Search tab appears on the ribbon, offering you a wealth of options to refine and re-search:

The options in the Refine group let you narrow the search by date range, size range, and kind. The Kind list includes such things as Document, Picture, Music, Folder—and many more. The Other Properties list is context-specific. In a music folder, for example, this list will offer Album,

Artists, Genre, Length, Folder Path, Year, Rating, and Title; in a Pictures folder, you'll see Date Taken, Tags, Type, Name, Folder Path, and Rating.

If you find you've initiated your search from the wrong location, try Search Again In, in the Location group of the Search tab. Or just switch to a different node in the navigation pane and start again.

Inside OUT

Search from a common dialog box

Like the search box in File Explorer, the search box in a common Open or Save As dialog box takes as its default scope the current folder and its subfolders. Searching from a dialog box might not sound all that nifty at first. After all, if you're trying to open a file and you don't know exactly where it is, you can always hunt for it from a File Explorer folder and then double-click it when the Windows Search engine ferrets it out. But searching from a dialog box can be quite useful if you're already in the dialog box and find yourself confronted by too many files.

Advanced search tools and techniques

For search needs that go beyond the options presented on the Search tab, Windows offers the Advanced Query Syntax (AQS). AQS is the official name for the set of rules that Windows Search follows when interpreting what you type in the search box. (You'll find detailed documentation of AQS at *w7io.com/0903*.)

NOTE

You can use any of these search formulations in the File Explorer search box but not in taskbar searches.

In addition to keywords, AQS supports the following types of search parameters, which can be combined using search operators:

- **Kinds of items.** Folders, documents, pictures, music, and so on

- **Data stores.** Specific databases and locations containing indexed items

- **File properties.** Size, date, tags, and so on

The most basic query typically begins with a keyword (or a portion of a word) typed in the search box. Assuming that you begin typing in a location that supports indexed searches (the taskbar search box or your Documents library, for example), the list of search results will include any item in that location containing any indexed word (in its name or properties or content) that begins with the letters you type. You can then narrow the search by using additional parameters. In every case, these consist of a word that AQS recognizes as a property or other index operator, followed by a colon and the value for that operator.

The value that immediately follows the colon can take several forms. If you want a loose (partial) match, just type a word or the beginning of a word. Thus, **type:Word** will turn up files of the type Microsoft Word Document, Microsoft Word 97 – 2003 Document, Microsoft Word 97 – 2003 Template, Microsoft Word Macro-Enabled Document, and so on. To specify a strict (exact) match, use an equal sign and, if necessary, quotation marks, as in this example: **type:="Microsoft Word Document"**.

You can also use Boolean operators (AND, OR, and NOT) and parentheses to combine criteria. If you have fond memories of MS-DOS, you'll welcome using * and ? as wildcards, and you can dramatically change the behavior of a search by means of the innocuous-looking tilde (~) character (which forces Windows to perform a strict character search in indexed locations; see the discussion later in this section).

> ➤ Of course, all of these techniques become much more useful when you're able to reuse your carefully crafted search criteria, as we explain in "Saving searches and clearing search history" at the end of this chapter.

Searching by item type or kind

To search for files with a particular file name extension, you can simply enter the extension in the search box, like this:

```
*.ext
```

(Note that this method of searching does not work for .exe or .msc files.) The results will include files that incorporate the extension in their contents as well as in their file names—which might or might not be what you want. You will get a more focused search by using the ext: operator, including an asterisk wildcard and a period like this:

```
ext:*.txt
```

NOTE
As with many properties, you have more than one way to specify an exact file name extension. In addition to ext:, you can use fileext:, extension:, or fileextension:.

File name extensions are useful for some searches, but you'll get even better results using two different search properties: Type and Kind. The Type property limits your search based on the value found in the Type field for a given object. Thus, to look for files saved in any Microsoft Excel format, type this term in the search box:

```
type:excel
```

To find any music file saved in MP3 format, type this text in the search box:

```
type:mp3
```

To constrain your search to groups of related file types, use the Kind property. Table 12-3 lists many (but not all) of the options available with this search term.

Table 12-3 Limiting items in search results by kind

Kind syntax	Returns as search results
kind:=calendar kind:=appointment kind:=meeting	Appointments and meetings stored in iCalendar and vCalendar files
kind:=communication	Email messages and attachments that you have saved as files
kind:=contact kind:=person	vCard files, Windows Contact files
kind:=doc kind:=document	Text files, Microsoft Office documents, Adobe Acrobat documents, HTML and XML files, and other document formats
kind:=folder	File folders, search folders, compressed (Zip) files, and cabinet files
kind:=link	Shortcuts to programs and files, Internet shortcuts
kind:=music kind:=song	Groove Music or Windows Media Player playlists and audio files in supported formats, including MP3, WMA, FLAC, and WAV
kind:=pic kind:=picture	Picture files in any indexed format, including JPEG, GIF, bitmap, PNG, as well as icons and shortcuts to image files
kind:=program	Windows and MS-DOS applications, batch and VBScript files, saved registration entries, Windows Installer packages, and program shortcuts
kind:=video	Movie files and clips in any indexed format

Changing the scope of a search

You can specify a folder or library location by using folder:, under:, in:, or path:. Thus, **folder:documents** restricts the scope of the search to your Documents library, and **in:videos mackie** finds all files in the Videos library that contain *Mackie* in the file name or any property.

Searching for item properties

You can search on the basis of any property recognized by the file system. (The list of available properties for files is identical to the ones we discuss in "Arranging data in File Explorer" earlier in this chapter.) To see the whole list of available properties, right-click any column heading in File Explorer and then click More. The Choose Details dialog box that appears enumerates the available properties.

When you enter text in the search box, Windows searches file names, all properties, and indexed content, returning items where it finds a match with that value. That often generates more search results than you want. To find all documents of which Jean is the author, omitting documents that include the word Jean in their file names or content, you would type **author:jean** in the search box. (To eliminate documents authored by Jeanne, Jeannette, or Jeanelle, add an equal sign and enclose jean in quotation marks: **author:="jean"**.)

When searching on the basis of dates, you can use long or short forms, as you please. For example, the search values

`modified:6/15/15`

and

`modified:06/15/2015`

are equivalent.

To search for dates before or after a particular date, use the less-than (<) and greater-than (>) operators. For example:

`modified:>11/16/12`

would search for dates later than November 16, 2012. Use the same two operators to specify file sizes below and above some value.

Use two periods to search for items within a range of dates. To find files modified in September or October 2014, type this search term in the Start menu search box:

`modified:9/1/2014 .. 10/31/2014`

You can also use ranges to search by file size. The search filters suggest some common ranges and even group them into neat little buckets like the ones shown here, so you can type **size:** and then click Medium to find files in the range 100 KB to 1 MB.

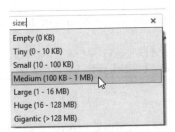

Again, don't be fooled into thinking that this list represents the full selection of available sizes. You can specify an exact size range, using operators such as >, >=, <, and <=, or you can use the "." operator. For example, **size:0 MB..1 MB** is the same as **size:<=1 MB**. You can specify values using bytes, KB, MB, or GB.

CHAPTER 12

Inside OUT

Make your searches flexible

You don't need to enter a precise date as part of a search term. Instead, Windows Search recognizes "fuzzy" date qualifiers like *today*, *yesterday*, *this week*, and *last month*. This technique lets you create saved searches that you can use to quickly open a window showing only the files you've worked on this week or last week. A search that uses dates picked from the calendar wouldn't be nearly as useful next month for identifying current projects, but one built using these relative dates will continue to be useful indefinitely.

Using multiple criteria for complex searches

You can use the Boolean operators AND, OR, and NOT to combine or negate criteria in the search box. These operators need to be spelled in capital letters (or they will be treated as ordinary text). In place of the AND operator, you can use a plus sign (+), and in place of the NOT operator, you can use a minus sign (–). You can also use parentheses to group criteria; items in parentheses separated by a space use an implicit AND operator. Table 12-4 provides some examples of combined criteria.

Table 12-4 Some examples of complex search values

This search value	Returns
Siechert AND Bott	Items in which at least one indexed element (property, file name, or an entire word within its contents) begins with or equals Siechert and another element in the same item begins with or equals Bott
title:("report" NOT draft)	Items in which the Title property contains the word report and does not contain a word that begins with draft
tag:tax AND author:Doug	Items authored by Doug that include Tax in the Tags field
tag:tax AND author:(Doug OR Craig) AND modified:<1/1/14	Items authored by Doug or Craig, last modified before January 1, 2014, with Tax in the Tags field

NOTE

When you use multiple criteria based on different properties, an AND conjunction is assumed unless you specify otherwise. The search value **tag:Ed Author:Carl** is equivalent to the search value **tag:Ed AND Author:Carl**.

Using wildcards and character-mode searches

File-search wildcards can be traced back to the dawn of Microsoft operating systems, well before the Windows era. In Windows 10, two of these venerable operators are alive and well:

- ***** The asterisk (also known as a star) operator can be placed anywhere in the search string and will match zero, one, or any other number of characters. In indexed searches, which treat your keyword as a prefix, this operator is always implied at the end; thus, a search for **voice** will turn up *voice*, *voices*, and *voice-over*. Add an asterisk at the beginning of the search term (***voice**), and your search will also turn up any item containing *invoice* or *invoices*. You can put an asterisk in the middle of a search term as well, which is useful for searching through folders full of data files that use a standard naming convention. If your invoices all start with INV, followed by an invoice number, followed by the date (INV-0038-20140227, for example), you can produce a quick list of all 2014 invoices by searching for **INV*2014***.

- **?** The question mark is a more focused wildcard. In index searches, it matches exactly one character in the exact position where it's placed. Using the naming scheme defined in the previous item, you could use the search term **filename:INV-????-2014*** to locate any file in the current location that has a 2014 date stamp and an invoice number (between hyphens) that is exactly four characters long.

To force Windows Search to use strict character matches in an indexed location, type a tilde (~) as the first character in the search box, followed immediately by your term. If you open your Documents library and type **~??v** in the search box, you'll find any document whose file name contains any word that has a *v* in the third position, such as *saved, level,* and, of course, *invoice*. This technique does not match on file contents.

Searching nonindexed locations

In both the previous examples, we described the behavior of searches in indexed locations, such as a library or a folder within a library. In other locations, the grep search engine kicks in. By default, anything you enter in one of these locations is treated as a character search that can match all or any part of a word. Thus, if you open a data folder that is not in a library and enter the search term **voice**, you'll get back *voices* and *voice-over* and *invoice*. The behavior of wildcards varies slightly as well. In a grep search, **??voice** matches *invoice* but not *voice*. In an indexed search, the wildcards at the beginning of the term are ignored in favor of loose matches. (Extra question marks at the end of a search term are ignored completely.)

When Windows does a grep search of the folder's contents, a green progress bar traversing your address bar warns you that the search is likely to be slow. While the search is still under way, you can click the Search tab and refine the search.

By default, when searching nonindexed locations, Windows looks at file names and basic properties (date modified and size) only. You can change this behavior so that Windows searches the contents of files that include a property handler and filter. To do this, click the Search tab, click Advanced Options, and then click File Contents. Be aware that this can add significantly to your search times.

Inside OUT

Search shared remote folders

When you connect to a shared folder on a networked computer, the search engine can detect whether Windows Search is running and whether the location you've accessed is already part of the remote index. If it is, great! Your query gets handed off to the remote search engine, which runs it on the other machine and returns its results to your computer. Note that for an indexed search of a shared folder, that folder must be included in the list of indexed locations on the remote computer, and the remote computer must be running version 4.0 or later of Windows Search. All versions of Windows released since 2008 are supported.

Saving searches and clearing search history

After you have completed a search and displayed its results in File Explorer, you can save the search parameters for later reuse. Click Save Search on the Search tab. The saved search is stored, by default, in %UserProfile%\Searches. You can reexecute the search at any time, against the current state of the index, by clicking it in the navigation pane or Searches folder.

When you save a search, you are saving its specification (technically, a persistedQuery), not its current results. If you're interested in the XML data that defines the search, right-click the saved search in your Searches folder, choose Open With, and choose Notepad or WordPad.

Recent searches are also included in a history list. To see what you have searched for, click in the search box in File Explorer, click the Search tab, and then click Recent Searches. If the list of recent searches gets unwieldy or you want to cover your tracks, click Clear Search History at the bottom of this list.

TROUBLESHOOTING

Your search returns unexpected results

If Windows Search does not perform as expected, try typing **fix search** in the taskbar search box. Then click Find And Fix Problems With Windows Search. The troubleshooter that appears automatically finds and fixes any problems that it can detect. If it finds none, it leads you through a series of steps to identify and resolve your problem.

PART 3

System maintenance and troubleshooting

Hardware

It's probably only a slight exaggeration to say that no two computers are alike. Motherboards, storage devices and controllers, video and network adapters, and peripherals of all shapes and sizes combine to create a nearly infinite number of possible computer configurations.

The good news for anyone using Windows 10 is that most of these devices should just work. For most common hardware upgrades, Windows detects the device automatically and installs a driver so that you can use the device and its full array of features. This chapter covers those installations as well as devices that need to be added manually, those that have optional configuration steps, and of course troubleshooting devices.

In this chapter, we cover the nerve center of hardware, Device Manager, with an explanation of how drivers work. We also explain how to set up specific device configurations, including multiple monitors, Bluetooth adapters, and printers.

Adding, configuring, and removing hardware devices

Since its introduction in Windows 95, Plug and Play technology has evolved tremendously. Early incarnations of this technology were notoriously unreliable, leading some users to dismiss the feature as "plug and pray." As this now-mature technology enters its third decade, however, hardware and software standards have converged to make most device configuration tasks completely automatic.

Any computer that was certified as compatible with Windows 7 or later supports the Plug and Play device standard, which handles virtually all the work of configuring computer hardware and attached devices. A Plug and Play device identifies itself to Windows by using unique identifiers in a well-organized hierarchy, listing its required resources (including drivers), and allowing software to configure it.

Plug and Play devices can interact with the operating system, with both sides of the conversation responding to device notification and power management events. A Plug and Play driver can load automatically when Windows detects that a device has been plugged in, and it can suspend and resume operation properly along with the system.

> **NOTE**
> Although it's still possible to find older devices that require non–Plug and Play inputs, such as scanners, plotters, and similar peripherals that connect to serial and parallel ports, these legacy devices are becoming increasingly rare. If you own this type of device, we recommend retiring it if possible and replacing it with a supported modern alternative. If you have no choice but to keep it around, look for a community of fellow owners of that device; they're the most likely to be able to help you with configuration issues.

Installing a new Plug and Play device

When you install a Plug and Play device for the first time, Windows reads the Plug and Play identification tag in the hardware's BIOS or firmware. It then compares that ID tag with a master list of corresponding tags drawn from all the Setup Information files in the %SystemRoot%\ Inf folder. If it finds a signed driver with a matching tag, it installs the correct driver file (or files) and makes other necessary system modifications with no intervention required from you. If everything goes as expected, the only subtle indication you might see is a progress dialog box (typically minimized) that displays a green bar over its taskbar icon and then vanishes when its work is complete.

> **NOTE**
> Any user can plug in a new device and begin using it if a driver for that device is included with Windows 10 or is available via Windows Update. Installing a new driver that is downloaded from a third-party site and is digitally signed by a third party rather than by Microsoft requires an administrator's credentials.

If Windows detects a Plug and Play device (after you've plugged it into a USB port, for instance) but cannot locate a digitally signed driver that matches the device, it doesn't provide any warning notification. Instead, a stub for the device is installed as it awaits the arrival of a proper driver. These partially installed devices appear in Device Manager, under the Other Devices heading, with a yellow exclamation point over the device name, as in Figure 13-1.

CHAPTER 13

Figure 13-1 If Windows 10 can't find drivers for a new Plug and Play device, it adds a yellow exclamation point to the Device Manager listings and files the devices under the Other Devices heading.

TROUBLESHOOTING

Drivers for built-in devices are missing

Device Manager might show some devices in the Other Devices category, with a yellow exclamation point indicating that the correct drivers are missing, after a clean installation of Windows 10. This usually occurs on a PC where some low-level devices built into the motherboard aren't recognized during Windows 10 setup. The usual cure for this sort of problem is to check with the device manufacturer to see whether drivers are available for download; pay special attention to chipset drivers, which add the necessary entries to the Windows Plug and Play database to allow the correct built-in drivers to be installed.

When Windows Update can't find a signed driver (and, thankfully, those occasions are becoming rarer as the Windows ecosystem matures), you need to manually install a device driver, a topic we cover in more detail later in this chapter.

The built-in Windows drivers are perfectly adequate for many device classes. Some devices, especially complex ones like scanners and all-in-one printers, might require utility software and additional drivers to enable the full range of features for that device.

How device drivers and hardware work together

Before Windows can work with any piece of hardware, it requires a compatible, properly con-figured device driver. Drivers are compact control programs that hook directly into Windows and handle the essential tasks of communicating your instructions to a hardware device and then relaying data back to you. After you set up a hardware device, its driver loads automati-cally and runs as part of the operating system, without requiring any further intervention on your part.

Many of the individual technologies used in Windows 10 devices use minidriver models, where the device driver is made up of two parts. Typically, Microsoft writes a general class driver that handles tasks that are common to devices in that category. The device manufacturer can then write device-specific code to enable custom features.

Windows 10, even more than its recent predecessors, includes a surprisingly comprehensive library of class drivers that allow most devices to function properly without requiring any additional software. There are class drivers for pieces of hardware that are, these days, typically integrated into a larger system: audio devices, network adapters, webcams, and display adapt-ers, for example. Windows 10 also includes drivers for external add-ons (wired and wireless) including printers, monitors, keyboards, scanners, mice and other pointing devices, smart-phones, and removable storage devices.

This core library is copied during Windows setup to a protected system folder, %SystemRoot%\System32\DriverStore. (Driver files and associated elements are stored in the FileRepository subfolder.) Anyone who signs in to the computer can read and execute files from this location, but only an installation program working with authorization from a member of the Adminis-trators group can create or modify files and folders there.

You can add new drivers to the driver store in a variety of ways, including the following:

- Windows Update offers drivers when it detects that you're running a device that is com-patible with that driver but is currently using an older version. (You can also search for the most recent driver via Windows Update when installing a new device.)

- A Windows cumulative update may refresh the driver store with new and updated drivers.

- As an administrator, you can add signed third-party drivers to the driver store by run-ning an installer program. All drivers added to the driver store in this fashion are saved in their own subfolder within the FileRepository folder, along with some supporting files created by Windows 10 that allow the drivers to be reinstalled if necessary.

Any driver that has been added to the store is considered to be trusted and can be installed without prompts or administrator credentials. All drivers, new or updated, that are copied here from Microsoft servers are certified to be fully compatible with Windows 10 and are digitally signed by Microsoft.

Inside OUT

Copy the FileRepository folder before a clean reinstall

If you're planning a clean reinstall of Windows 10 using bootable installation media rather than the Reset function, consider copying the FileRepository folder from %SystemRoot%\System32\DriverStore to removable media, such as a USB flash drive. After your clean install is complete, you can quickly reinstall any custom drivers by using the Update Driver option from Device Manager and specifying that saved folder as the location for the new driver files.

A Windows hardware driver package must include a Setup Information file (with the extension .inf). This is a text file that contains detailed information about the device to be installed, including the names of its driver files, the locations where they are to be installed, any required registry settings, and version information. All devices with drivers in the DriverStore folder include Setup Information files in the %SystemRoot%\Inf folder.

Although the Setup Information file is a crucial part of the driver installation process, you don't work with it directly. Instead, this file supplies instructions that the operating system uses during Plug and Play detection, when you use a setup program to install a device, or when you manually install a driver update.

CAUTION

The syntax of Setup Information files is complex, and the intricacies of .inf files can trip up even experienced software developers. If you find that a driver setup routine isn't working properly, you might be tempted to try editing the Setup Information file to work around the hang-up. Trust us: that approach is almost certain to fail. In fact, by tinkering with .inf files to install a driver that is not certified to be compatible with your hardware, you run the risk of corrupting registry settings and making your system unstable.

When Windows completes the installation of a driver package, it performs all the tasks specified by the Setup Information file and copies the driver files themselves to %SystemRoot%\System32\Drivers.

Inside OUT

For Windows 10, signed drivers only

Beginning with the release of Windows 10, all new kernel-mode drivers must be submitted to Microsoft and digitally signed by the Windows Hardware Developer Center Dashboard portal. (Kernel-mode drivers run at the same level of privilege as Windows itself, as opposed to user-mode drivers, which run in the context of the currently signed-in user and cannot cause the system to crash.) Additionally, beginning 90 days after the release of Windows 10, any new drivers submitted to Microsoft must be signed by a valid Extended Validation Code Signing Certificate—a higher-cost option that provides extra assurance about the identity of a software publisher.

The net effect of these changes is to make it extremely difficult for malware to be delivered as part of a driver update. Drivers that were properly signed under the previous rules and were released before those two Windows 10 milestones will continue to work, but Windows 10 will not load new kernel-mode drivers unless they are signed by that Microsoft-controlled portal.

Driver signing establishes an initial threshold of trust, but by itself it's not necessarily an indicator of quality. For that you need to look at the signature a little more closely.

The highest level of quality is found with drivers that have passed compatibility and reliability tests for that category of device, as defined in Microsoft's Hardware Lab Kit. Those devices earn the right to use the Windows logo and can be included on Microsoft's Certified Products List.

Hardware developers who simply want to deliver a signed driver to their customers can submit the driver to Microsoft and "attest" to its quality rather than submitting actual test results. The Attested Signing Service signature is different from the one for a logo-certified device, but Windows 10 treats them the same, allowing either type of signed driver to be installed with no prompts by any user.

In the distant past, users could change default settings to allow installation of unsigned drivers and even completely eliminate warnings about the accompanying security risks. Those options are available by changing advanced startup settings in Windows 10, but they require disabling Secure Boot and fundamentally undermine the device's security. As a result, we strongly recommend against using them.

Getting useful information from Device Manager

The more you know about individual hardware devices and their associated driver versions, the more likely you are to make short work of troubleshooting problems or configuring advanced features for a device. In every case, your starting point is Device Manager, a graphical utility that provides detailed information about all installed hardware, along with controls that you can use to configure devices, assign resources, and set advanced options.

> **NOTE**
>
> In Windows 10, Device Manager also includes categories that don't represent actual hardware—print queues, for example, or anything under the Software Devices heading. In this section, we focus only on physical hardware devices and their associated drivers.

To open Device Manager (Devmgmt.msc), type **device** in the search box and then click its entry from the top of the results list. Power users can click the Device Manager shortcut on the Quick Access menu that appears when you right-click the Start button or press Windows key+X. (Device Manager is also available as a snap-in under the System Tools heading in the fully stocked Computer Management console.)

As Figure 13-2 shows, Device Manager is organized as a hierarchical list that inventories every piece of hardware within or connected to your computer. The default view shows devices by type.

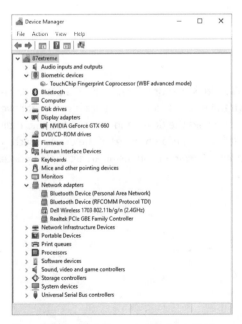

Figure 13-2 Click the arrow to the left of any category in Device Manager to see individual devices within that category.

To view information about a specific device, double-click its entry in Device Manager's list of installed devices. Each device has its own multitabbed properties dialog box. Most hardware devices include a selection of tabs, including General and Driver. The General tab lists basic facts about the device, including the device name and type, the name of its manufacturer, and its current status, as in the example in Figure 13-3.

Figure 13-3 The General tab supplies basic information about a device and indicates whether it is currently functioning properly.

The Driver tab, shown in Figure 13-4, lists version information about the currently installed driver for the selected device. Although the information shown here is sparse, it covers the essentials. You can tell at a glance who supplied the driver and you can see who digitally signed it; you can also determine the date and version number of the driver, which is important when considering whether you should download and install an available update.

Figure 13-4 The Driver tab, which is available for every installed device, offers valuable information and tools for managing installed drivers.

Clicking the Driver Details button on the Driver tab leads to another dialog box that lists the names and locations of all files associated with that device and its drivers. Selecting any file name from this list displays details for that file in the lower portion of the dialog box. (We'll get to the other buttons in the next section.)

Click the Details tab for a potentially overwhelming amount of additional information, arranged in a dialog box that allows you to see one property and its associated value at a time. You can see the full list of properties by clicking the arrow to the right of the current entry in the Property box; Figure 13-5 shows the typically dense result.

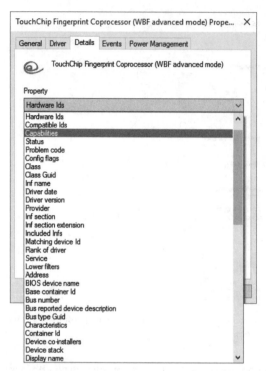

Figure 13-5 Most of the device properties you can select from this list return obscure details, but a few are useful for troubleshooting purposes.

Choosing a property tucks the list away and displays the value associated with that property, as in the example shown here, which lists the Plug and Play IDs associated with the selected device.

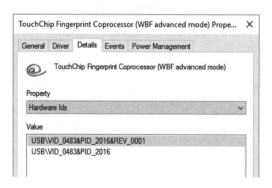

TROUBLESHOOTING

Device Manager shows an unknown device

Most modern hardware built for Windows 7 or later just works with Windows 10. But occasionally you might find mysterious entries under the Other Devices heading in Device Manager, with few or no details, no associated drivers, and no clue about what to do next. This problem is most likely to appear after you perform a clean install of Windows 10 on a device originally designed for another operating system, but it's also possible for the issue to occur with older external hardware.

You can often get important clues by opening the properties dialog box for the device and looking on the Details tab. The Hardware IDs property, in particular, can be invaluable. The string VID_ followed by a number is a Vendor ID code; PID_ is a Product ID code. Use your favorite search engine to look on the web for a combination of those two values. For best results, limit the scope of your search to **site:catalog.update. microsoft.com**.

In addition to this basic information, the properties dialog box for a given device can include any number of custom tabs. The USB hub built into the motherboard of the PC shown in Figure 13-6, for example, adds a custom tab (Power) that allows you to view how much power is available for devices connected to ports on a particular USB hub (although it might take some further sleuthing and some trial and error to figure out which of the PC's physical ports are associated with that hub).

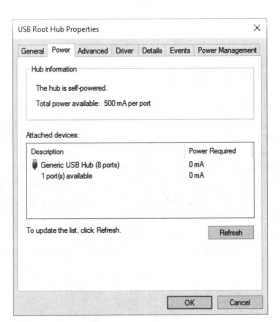

Figure 13-6 Yes, the properties dialog box for this USB hub includes separate tabs for Power and Power Management.

By design, the information displayed in Device Manager is dynamic. When you add, remove, or reconfigure a device, the information stored here changes as well.

Enabling and disabling devices

Any device listed in Device Manager can be disabled temporarily. You might choose this option if you're certain you won't need an installed device under normal conditions but you want to keep it available just in case. On a desktop PC with a permanent wired Ethernet connection, for example, you can keep a Wi-Fi adapter installed but disabled. That configuration gives you the option to enable the device and use the wireless adapter to connect to a mobile hotspot when the wired network goes out of service.

Right-click any active entry in Device Manager to see the Disable menu. To identify any device that is currently disabled, look for the black, downward-pointing arrow over its icon in Device Manager, as shown here. To turn a disabled device back on, right-click its entry in Device Manager and then click Enable.

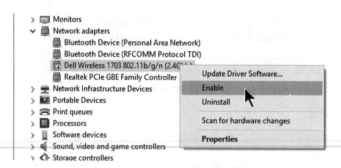

Adjusting advanced device settings

As we mentioned earlier, some devices include specialized tabs in the properties dialog box available from Device Manager. Controls on these additional tabs allow you to change advanced settings and properties for devices. For example:

- Network cards, modems, input devices, and USB hubs often include a Power Management tab that allows you to control whether the device can force the computer to wake up from Sleep mode. This option is useful if you have fax capabilities (yes, some businesses still use faxes) enabled for a modem or if you use the Remote Desktop feature over the Internet on a machine that isn't always running at full power. On both portable and desktop computers, you can also use this option to allow Windows to turn off a device to save power.

- The Volumes tab for a disk drive contains no information when you first display the properties dialog box for that device. Click the Populate button to read the volume information for the selected disk, as shown in Figure 13-7, and click the Properties button to check the disk for errors, run the Defrag utility, or perform other maintenance tasks. Although you can perform these same tasks by right-clicking a drive icon in File Explorer, this option might be useful in situations where you have multiple hard disks installed and you suspect that one of those disks is having mechanical problems. Using this option allows you to quickly see which physical disk a given volume is stored on.

Figure 13-7   After you click the Populate button, the Volumes tab lists volumes on the selected drive and gives you full access to troubleshooting and maintenance tools.

CAUTION

DVD drives offer an option to change the DVD region, which controls which discs can be played on that drive. The DVD Region setting actually increments a counter on the physical drive itself, and that counter can be changed only a limited number of times. Be extremely careful with this setting, or you might end up losing the capability to play any regionally encoded DVDs in your collection.

- When working with network cards, you can often choose from a plethora of settings on an Advanced tab, as shown in the following example. Randomly tinkering with these settings is almost always counterproductive; however, you might be able to solve specific performance or connectivity problems by adjusting settings as directed by the device manufacturer or a Microsoft Support article.

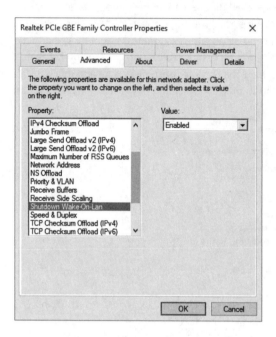

Updating and uninstalling drivers

If you're having a hardware problem that you suspect is caused by a device driver, your first stop should be Device Manager. Open the properties dialog box for the device, and use the following buttons on the Driver tab to perform maintenance tasks:

- **Update Driver.** This choice opens the Update Driver Software dialog box, which we describe in the next section.

- **Roll Back Driver.** This option uninstalls the most recently updated driver and rolls back your system configuration to the previously installed driver. This option is available from Safe Mode if you need to remove a driver that is causing blue-screen (Stop) errors. Unlike System Restore, this option affects only the selected device. If you have never updated the selected driver, this option is unavailable.

- **Uninstall.** This button completely removes driver files and registry settings for the selected device and, if you select the appropriate option, completely removes the associated driver files as well. Use this capability to remove a driver that you suspect was incorrectly installed and then reinstall the original driver or install an updated driver.

Inside OUT
Create a safety net before tinkering with drivers

When you install a new hardware driver, Windows automatically attempts to create a new System Restore checkpoint. That doesn't mean it will be successful, especially if a problem with your System Restore settings has caused this utility to suspend operations temporarily. To make certain that you can roll back your changes if necessary, set a new System Restore checkpoint manually before making any kind of hardware configuration change. (For more details, see "Rolling back to a previous restore point" in Chapter 16, "Backup, restore, and recovery.")

Disabling automatic driver updates

Microsoft uses the Windows Update mechanism to deliver drivers for many devices. This feature allows you to plug in a new device with relative confidence that it will work without extra effort on your part. It also allows you to automatically receive updated drivers, which typically fix reliability, stability, and compatibility problems.

The dark side of driver updates is that they can occasionally cause a previously functional device to act up or even shut down. For that reason, some cautious Windows users prefer to disable automatic driver updates. To find this well-hidden option, type **device installation** in the search box and click the top result, Change Device Installation Settings. That opens the dialog box shown in Figure 13-8, which is set by default to Yes, Do This Automatically. When you change the setting to No, a group of additional options, previously hidden, appears.

Selecting the Never Install Driver Software From Windows Update offers some assurance that an unexpected driver update won't clobber your working setup. It does, of course, impose an additional maintenance burden, as you have to manually monitor devices for driver updates and apply them using the techniques we describe in the remainder of this section.

CHAPTER 13

The final option in the dialog box, which is selected by default, allows Windows Update to retrieve icons and support information for devices, allowing a more accurate depiction of installed devices in the Devices And Printers window, which we describe in the next section.

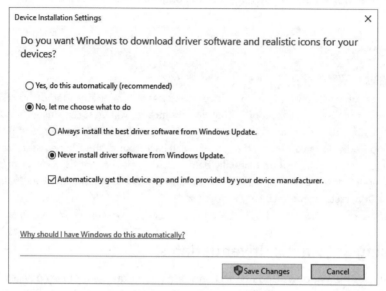

Figure 13-8 If you're willing to accept the burden of manually checking for driver updates in exchange for the assurance of not being inconvenienced by a defective driver update, use these settings.

Updating a device driver manually

Microsoft and third-party device manufacturers frequently issue upgrades to device drivers. In some cases, the updates enable new features; in other cases, the newer version swats a bug that might or might not affect you. New Microsoft-signed drivers are often (but not always) delivered through Windows Update. Other drivers are available only by downloading them from the device manufacturer's website. Kernel-mode drivers must still be digitally signed before they can be installed.

If the new driver includes a setup program, run it first so that the proper files are copied to your system. Then start the update process from Device Manager by selecting the entry for the device you want to upgrade and clicking the Update Driver button on the toolbar or the Update Driver option on the right-click shortcut menu. (You can also click Update Driver on the Driver tab of the properties dialog box for the device.)

That action opens the dialog box shown in Figure 13-9.

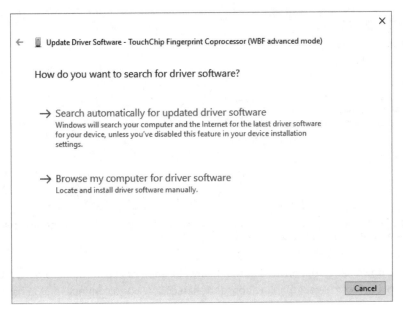

Figure 13-9 When manually updating a driver, try the automatic option first unless you want to select a specific driver you previously downloaded.

Click Search Automatically For Updated Driver Software if you want to look in local removable media and check Windows Update. Click Browse My Computer For Driver Software if you want to enter the location of a downloaded driver package or choose from a list of available drivers in the driver store. Clicking the latter option opens a dialog box like the one shown in Figure 13-10, with two options for manually selecting a driver.

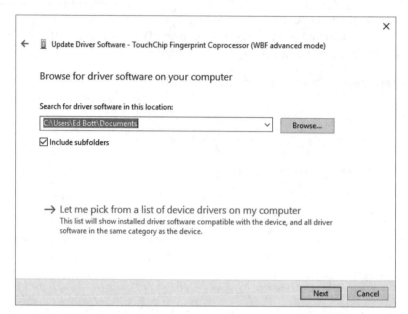

Figure 13-10 If you've downloaded a driver package that doesn't include an installer, select its location here to allow the update to proceed.

If you've downloaded the driver files to a known location or copied them to removable storage, click Browse to select that location, and then click Next to continue. (If you have a copy of the FileRepository folder from a previous Windows installation on the same hardware, you can choose that location.) With the Include Subfolders option selected, as it is by default, the driver update software will do a thorough search of the specified location, looking for a Setup Information file for the selected device; if it finds a match, it installs the specified driver software automatically.

Use the second option, Let Me Pick From A List Of Device Drivers On My Computer, if you know the driver software you need is already in the local driver store. In general, choosing this option presents a single driver for you to choose. If you need to install an alternative driver version that isn't listed, clear the Show Compatible Hardware check box, as we've done in Figure 13-11, and then choose a driver from an expanded list of all matching devices in the device category.

CHAPTER 13

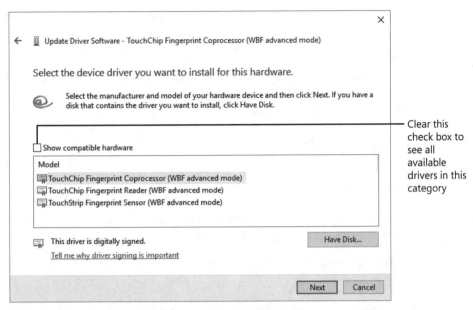

Figure 13-11 Clear the check box here only if you are certain that Plug and Play has selected the wrong driver and you want to manually install a different driver.

Inside OUT

Make sure that update is really an update

How do you know whether a downloaded version is newer than the currently installed driver on your system? A good set of release notes should provide this information and is the preferred option for determining version information. In the absence of documentation, file dates offer some clues, but they are not always reliable. A better indicator is to inspect the properties of the driver files themselves. After unzipping the downloaded driver files to a folder on a local or network drive, right-click any file with a .dll or .sys extension and choose Properties. On the Version tab, you should be able to find details about the specific driver version, which you can compare with the driver details shown in Device Manager.

Rolling back to a previous driver version

Unfortunately, updated drivers can sometimes cause new problems that are worse than the woes they were intended to fix. This is especially true if you're experimenting with prerelease versions of new drivers. If your troubleshooting leads you to suspect that a newly installed driver is the cause of recent crashes or system instability, consider removing that driver and rolling your system configuration back to the previously installed driver.

To do this, open Device Manager and double-click the entry for the device you want to roll back. Then go to the Driver tab and click Roll Back Driver. The procedure that follows is straightforward and self-explanatory.

Uninstalling a driver

There are at least three circumstances under which you might want to completely remove a device driver from your system:

- You're no longer using the device, and you want to prevent the previously installed drivers from loading or using any resources.

- You've determined that the drivers available for the device are not stable enough to use on your system.

- The currently installed driver is not working correctly, and you want to reinstall it from scratch.

Inside OUT

Manage Plug and Play drivers

Removing and reinstalling the driver for a Plug and Play device requires a little extra effort. Because these drivers are loaded and unloaded dynamically, you can remove the driver only if the device in question is plugged in. Use the Uninstall button to remove the driver before unplugging the device. To reinstall the device driver without unplugging the device, open Device Manager and choose Action, Scan For Hardware Changes.

To remove a driver permanently, open Device Manager, right-click the entry for the device in question, and click Uninstall. (If the entry for the device in question is already open, click the Driver tab and click Uninstall.) Click OK when prompted to confirm that you want to remove the driver, and Windows removes the files and registry settings completely. You can now unplug the device.

If you installed the driver files from a downloaded file, the Confirm Device Uninstall dialog box includes a check box (shown in Figure 13-12) that allows you to remove the files from the driver store as well. This prevents a troublesome driver from being inadvertently reinstalled when you reinsert the device or restart the computer.

Figure 13-12 Be sure to select this check box if you want to prevent a troublesome driver from being inadvertently reinstalled.

Note that you can't delete driver software that is included with Windows 10.

Troubleshooting sporadic hardware errors

When your computer acts unpredictably, chances are good that defective hardware or a buggy device driver is at fault.

In those circumstances, using a powerful troubleshooting tool called Driver Verifier Manager (Verifier.exe) is a terrific way to identify flawed device drivers. Instead of your computer locking up at a most inopportune time with a misleading Blue Screen of Death (BSOD), Driver Verifier stops your computer predictably at startup with a BSOD that accurately explains the true problem. Although this doesn't sound like a huge improvement (your system still won't work, after all), Driver Verifier Manager performs a critical troubleshooting step: identifying the problem. You can then correct the problem by removing or replacing the offending driver. (If you're satisfied that the driver really is okay despite Driver Verifier Manager's warning, you can turn off Driver Verifier for all drivers or for a specific driver. Any driver that Driver Verifier chokes on should be regarded with suspicion, but some legitimate drivers bend the rules without causing problems.)

Driver Verifier works at startup to thoroughly exercise each driver. It performs many of the same tests that are run as part of the Windows certification and signing process, such as checking for the way the driver accesses memory.

Beware: If Driver Verifier Manager finds a nonconforming driver—even one that doesn't seem to be causing any problems—it will prevent your system from starting. Use Driver Verifier only if you're having problems. In other words, if it ain't broke . . .

To begin working with Driver Verifier Manager, open an elevated Command Prompt window and type **verifier**. In the Driver Verifier Manager dialog box, shown here, select **Create Standard Settings**. (If you want to assess current conditions before proceeding, select the last option, Display Information About The Currently Verified Drivers.)

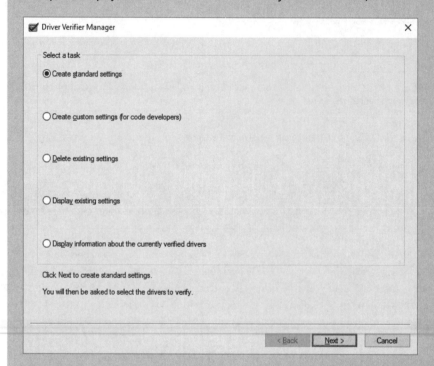

When you click Next, you get a list of all currently installed drivers that match the conditions you specified. Note that the list might contain a mix of hardware drivers and some file-system filter drivers, such as those used by antivirus programs, CD-burning software, and other low-level system utilities.

At this point, you have two choices:

- Go through the list and make a note of all drivers identified and then click Cancel. No changes are made to your system configuration; all you've done is gather a list of suspicious drivers, which you can then try to remove or disable manually.

- Click Finish to complete the wizard and restart your computer. Don't choose this option unless you're prepared to deal with the consequences, as explained in the remainder of this sidebar.

If your computer stops with a blue screen when you next sign in, you've identified a problem driver. The error message includes the name of the offending driver and an error code.

Driver Verifier has been included with every version of Windows since Windows 2000 and is included with Windows 10. For information about using Verifier, see the Microsoft Support article 244617, "Using Driver Verifier to identify issues with Windows drivers for advanced users," at *support.microsoft.com/kb/244617*. To resolve the problem, boot into Safe Mode (press F8 during startup) and disable or uninstall the problem driver. You'll then want to check with the device vendor to get a working driver that you can install.

To disable Driver Verifier so that it no longer performs verification checks at startup, run Driver Verifier Manager again and select Delete Existing Settings in the initial dialog box. Alternatively, at a command prompt, type **verifier /reset**. (If you haven't yet solved the driver problem, of course, you'll be stopped at a BSOD, unable to disable Driver Verifier. In that case, boot into Safe Mode and then disable Driver Verifier.)

You can configure Driver Verifier so that it checks only certain drivers. To do that, open Driver Verifier Manager, select Create Standard Settings, click Next, and select the last option, Select Driver Names From A List. This option lets you exempt a particular driver from Driver Verifier's scrutiny—such as one that Driver Verifier flags but you are certain is not the cause of your problem.

Fine-tuning hardware and printer settings

In Windows 7, Microsoft introduced the Devices And Printers folder. It lives on in Windows 10, within the classic Control Panel, under the Hardware And Sound category, where it offers a slightly old-fashioned look at installed devices you're likely to interact with. Figure 13-13 shows Devices And Printers with its two namesake categories expanded. Note the photo icons, which are downloaded automatically as part of the driver installation for some devices and add a touch of realism to the contents of this folder.

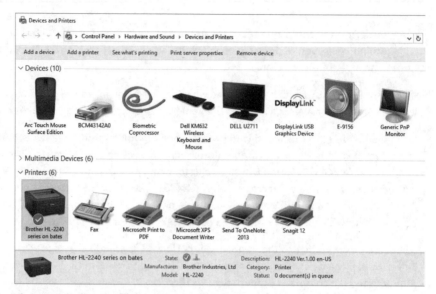

Figure 13-13 **The Devices And Printers folder looks spiffier than Device Manager, but it doesn't allow you to do much with devices.**

Double-click any item here to see an abbreviated properties dialog box, which contains a shortcut to the more complete properties dialog box from Device Manager. Shortcut menus are available for some devices, such as monitors, keyboards, and mice. The shortcut menu for the Microsoft Arc Touch Mouse shown here includes commands that open settings for it and other input devices.

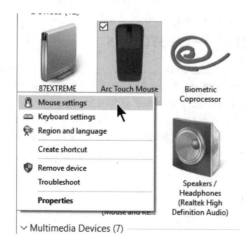

Three commands are common to all of these context menus: Create Shortcut, Troubleshoot, and Properties. Devices that aren't working properly are flagged with yellow exclamation points, with the same familiar symbol added to that device's Troubleshoot command.

The shortcut menus for storage devices allow you to browse files stored on that drive. Right-click the icon for your computer itself and you'll find a rich assortment of options, including System Properties, Network Settings, Bluetooth Settings, and Power Options.

The Create Shortcut command plants a shortcut on your desktop, which makes the device's context menu accessible outside Devices And Printers. If you create a shortcut to the entry for your computer, for example, you can right-click that shortcut to go straight to such places as Sound Settings or Power Options.

The Properties command provides an alternative route to the dialog boxes that have traditionally been provided by Device Manager.

Printers and print queues

To install a modern printer that plugs into a USB port on the PC where you plan to use it, just connect the device. Plug and Play does the rest of the work. (See "Installing a new Plug and Play device" earlier in this chapter.)

NOTE
Although it's possible that there are still some non–Plug and Play printers out there, connecting to creaky parallel ports on PCs from the late Cretaceous period, we are happy to bid those devices adieu, and we urge you to do the same. We don't cover manual connection options for legacy devices in this book.

Wireless printers that connect over Wi-Fi or by using Bluetooth also support Plug and Play. Follow the manufacturer's instructions to complete the wireless connection, or skip ahead a few pages to our explanation of the Add A Printer option.

➤ **You can share a printer for use by other users on the same local network. The simplest way is using the HomeGroup feature, which we describe in "Sharing files, digital media, and printers in a homegroup" in Chapter 5, "Networking essentials." On business networks, the procedure is more formal; see "Sharing a printer" in Chapter 20, "Advanced networking."**

To configure a printer or work with documents in a print queue, double-click the printer's icon in the Devices And Printers folder. Depending on the type of printer, you will see either a simple printer-queue dialog box or a more elaborate display, like the one shown in Figure 13-14. Note that it includes printer settings, configuration options, and links to webpages where the maker of the device is eager to sell you accessories and supplies such as ink and toner cartridges.

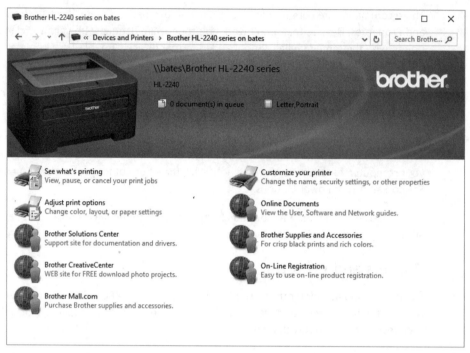

Figure 13-14 Despite the fancy formatting, the available controls here are no different from those you'd see by right-clicking the printer icon and using its shortcut menu.

For a multifunction device, this page might include options to scan documents and photos using the built-in scanner, and to download software and obtain support information from the manufacturer.

The display, with a photo of the actual printer model to reassure you that you're in the right place, might be dramatic, but the available controls for the network-connected printer shown in the Devices And Printers folder are no different from those you would see if you right-click the printer icon and use its shortcut menu.

The top part of the display provides status information. In Figure 13-14, for example, you can see that the Brother HL-2240 series laser printer is set to print in portrait mode on letter-size paper and currently has no print jobs waiting. The options below let you see and manage documents in the print queue or adjust print options (switch from portrait to landscape, for example, or feed an envelope by using a different paper tray). If the Customize Your Printer option is available, click it to open a dialog box where you can manage the general device settings available for this class of device, as shown in Figure 13-15.

Figure 13-15 Change the name of the printer and check its currently available features here. Also consider printing a test page before you tackle a big job, just to be on the safe side.

Printers aren't exactly like snowflakes, but there are far too many variations in hardware and software design for us to offer more than the most general advice: get to know your printer by inspecting these settings, and don't be afraid to read the manual.

To make a wireless or networked printer available locally, click Add A Printer on the Devices And Printers toolbar. If the planets are properly aligned, the autodiscovery software might locate your printer and walk you through setting it up. If you're not so lucky, click The Printer I Want Isn't Listed to open the manual options shown in Figure 13-16.

Among the "other options" available on this page in the Add Printer Wizard, you can connect to a network printer using its Universal Naming Convention (UNC) name. The printer in Figure 13-14 earlier, for example, was connected to a printer on a server named Bates, making its UNC address \\BATES\Brother HL-2240 Series. You can also use an IP address for a device that has a permanently assigned address, and enlist the help of a wizard to connect a wireless or Bluetooth printer.

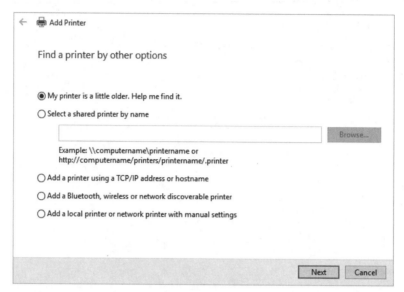

Figure 13-16 The Add Printer Wizard offers numerous paths to connect to a printer, even one that's "a little older."

Inside OUT

Find a printer's TCP/IP address or host name

Often the easiest way to determine the TCP/IP address or host name for a printer is to use the printer's control panel to print a configuration page, which usually includes this information.

One of the simplest ways to connect to a shared network printer doesn't involve any wizards at all. Just use File Explorer to browse to the network computer, where you should see an entry for any shared printer available to you. Double-click that icon to begin the process of connecting to that printer. Because Windows requires a local copy of the network printer's driver, you'll need an administrator's credentials, and you are likely to see a dialog box similar to the following, with a bright yellow banner that means "Proceed with caution."

If you're confident that the shared network printer is safe and trustworthy, click Install Driver. In a moment, you'll receive a success message and be given the opportunity to make the new printer your default.

Inside OUT

Use a compatible driver

If you can't find a driver that's specifically designed for your printer, you might be able to get away with another driver. Check the hardware documentation to find out whether the printer emulates a more popular model, such as a Hewlett-Packard Laser-Jet. If so, choose that printer driver, and then print some test documents after completing setup. You might lose access to some advanced features available with your model of printer, but this strategy should allow you to perform basic printing tasks.

Keyboards, mice, touchpads, and pens

Windows 10 supports a wide range of input devices. Most wired keyboards and mice configure themselves automatically at startup. Bluetooth devices need to be paired first (a topic we cover a bit later in this chapter). For a wireless device that uses a USB-connected radio transceiver, you might need to go through an initial pairing process.

When an external keyboard and mouse are installed, you'll find some basic customization abilities available for generic keyboard and mouse functions in the classic Control Panel. Enter **keyboard** or **mouse** in the search box to see the corresponding shortcuts for these two groups of options, as shown in Figure 13-17. Both of these dialog boxes include a Hardware tab with details about the device and its installed driver.

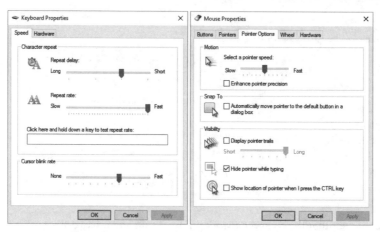

Figure 13-17 Windows 10 includes basic support for keyboards and mice; check the Hardware tab in either of these dialog boxes to get more device details.

You'll find some additional mouse configuration options in Settings, under the Devices heading. (See "Taming your mouse or other pointing device" in Chapter 4, "Personalizing Windows 10.") The Mouse & Touchpad Settings page offers only minimal options when a basic mouse or pointing device is attached.

But the Touchpad heading expands tremendously when a *precision touchpad* is included as part of a mobile device. All members of the Surface family that are capable of running Windows 10 support this input standard, as do some portable PCs from other manufacturers (typically premium models intended for a business audience). The precision touchpad driver supports a wide range of gestures and additional settings, including options to disable the touchpad completely or when a mouse is attached. Figure 13-18 shows just a few of these options—the list continues for another full screen.

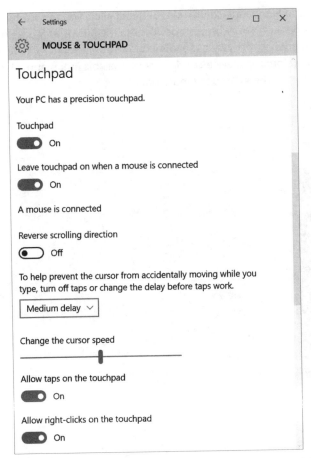

Figure 13-18 A precision touchpad offers a dramatically richer set of options for a pointing device. This dialog box is from the Microsoft Surface 3 running Windows 10.

The most useful options with a precision touchpad expand tapping and dragging options, allowing a two-finger tap to serve as a right-click substitute, for example, or to double-tap and then drag a window. Default gestures include a two-finger scroll and a three-finger swipe that shows Task View when swiping up and minimizes the current window when swiping down.

If your device doesn't include precision touchpad support, you might still have access to a broader range of touchpad behaviors. Devices that include a Synaptics ClickPad, for example, have access to many of the same gestures through a utility that hooks into the Mouse Properties dialog box.

Some third-party mice include separate control modules that allow you to customize the behavior of the pointing device. Many Microsoft devices use the Microsoft Mouse And Keyboard Center utility, with options that vary depending on the device model. Figure 13-19 shows one of the highly customized, device-specific pages available in this app. (Remarkably, this app even gets the color of the Arc Touch Mouse right.)

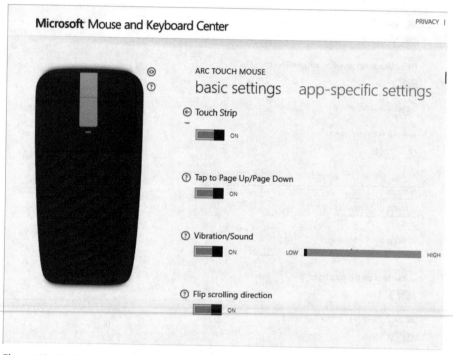

Figure 13-19 This control software, the Microsoft Mouse And Keyboard Center, is capable of identifying a specific device and even noting its color. These options aren't available for generic mice.

For devices that include a pen, you'll find a few configuration options on the Pen page, under the Devices heading in Settings. If you're having trouble getting the pen's input to register properly when you tap, try running the Calibrate utility, which is available via a button on the Tablet PC Settings page in Control Panel. (Search for **calibrate** and you'll find this otherwise well-hidden option.)

Displays

Of all hardware categories in the modern PC world, the display category is the most mature, with any display capable of configuring itself as soon as it's connected.

In general, you'll need to visit the Display pages in Settings only when something goes wrong, which isn't often.

Here are the three display settings you need to pay attention to:

- **Resolution.** Every display has a native resolution, one where the number of physical pixels matches the number of pixels Windows wants to show. Configuring the display at a non-native resolution generally results in a subpar viewing experience, often with a blurry, stretched display. That's probably why you have to take an extra step and go to the Advanced Display Settings page to see and change resolution. Figure 13-20 shows a 27-inch high-resolution monitor running at its native resolution of 2560 x 1440 pixels, as indicated by the word "(Recommended)" in the label.

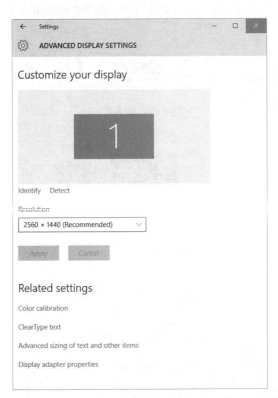

Figure 13-20 The "(Recommended)" after this option indicates that it's the native resolution and most likely the correct choice.

- **Scaling.** On high-resolution monitors, you can increase the apparent size of apps and text. Scaling the display is a necessity when using a high resolution on a relatively small screen. Full HD (1920 x 1080) might look great on a 24-inch desktop monitor, but on an

11-inch display, actually seeing those icons and reading the accompanying text labels would require superhuman vision at 100 percent scaling. On a system with a single display, you can adjust the scaling by using a slider below the thumbnail of the current monitor on the Display page in Settings.

➤ We cover scaling in "Making text easier to read" in Chapter 4.

- **Multiple displays.** When you attach a second (or third or fourth) display to Windows 10, the Display page in Settings changes. Thumbnails in the preview pane (Figure 13-21) show each display at its relative size (in terms of resolution), and you can drag the displays to either side of one another (or even stack one on top of the other). You can also adjust the alignment of the two displays to match their actual physical alignment, with the goal of having your mouse pointer move naturally between displays without a jarring shift when crossing the bezels.

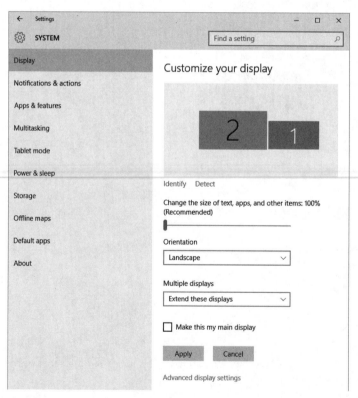

Figure 13-21 With two monitors, you can arrange each so that it matches the physical layout. Pick a display and click Make This My Main Display to control how the taskbar behaves.

CHAPTER 13

Bluetooth devices

Bluetooth is one of those rare standards that passes the "it just works" tests consistently. These days virtually every portable device supports Bluetooth for wirelessly connecting headsets and pairing fitness devices. Many desktop PCs include Bluetooth support as well, for connecting keyboards and mice.

Before you can use one Bluetooth device with another, you have to pair it, a process that generally involves making the external device discoverable, switching to the Bluetooth tab in Settings, and then following some instructions. Figure 13-22 shows a Surface pen, made discoverable by holding down a special button combination for several seconds. Tapping Pair completes the connection and makes the device usable with Windows 10, running in this example on a Surface 3 tablet.

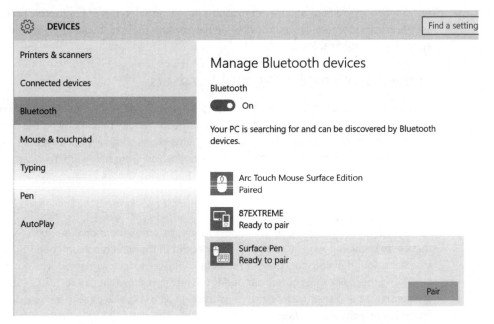

Figure 13-22 Before using a Bluetooth device, it must be paired with a Windows 10 PC.

One sure-fire indication that the Bluetooth Settings page in Figure 13-22 is on a mobile device is the presence of an on-off switch for the Bluetooth adapter. Desktop PCs don't normally allow Bluetooth to be disabled, a wise precaution given that doing so could render the keyboard and mouse—and thus the entire PC—unusable.

USB devices

Universal serial bus, more commonly known as USB, is one of the oldest and most reliable Plug and Play standards in the world. Through the years, the USB standard has progressed from version 1.1 to 2.0 to 3.0, with the latest jump making a monumental difference in the speed of data transfer between USB-connected devices. The new USB 3.1 standard is probably the greatest evolution of all, offering the ability to power full-size laptops, transfer data at blistering speeds, and even drive high-resolution displays.

Confusingly, a new USB Type-C connector is arriving at the same time as USB 3.1 begins to appear in high-end computing machinery. The USB Type-C connector is reversible (no more flipping the USB plug three times until you find the right orientation). These new connectors are compatible with older USB devices, but only with an adapter.

All USB devices are Plug and Play compatible. Knowing the types of connectors and the highest standard supported on your device can help ensure that you avoid compatibility hassles and carry the right cables.

Speakers, microphones, and headsets

Windows 10 supports a broad array of high-quality audio outputs, capable of delivering multi-channel surround sound to sophisticated home theater setups or just driving the tiny speakers on a laptop. As with other hardware subsystems, most of this capability is built into the Windows core drivers and doesn't require custom drivers from hardware manufacturers.

A few useful built-in capabilities are buried deep in the configuration dialog boxes of the Windows 10 audio subsystem.

The first allows you to test your surround-sound (or stereo) audio configuration to confirm that every speaker is working properly. Enter **audio** in the search box and open the Playback tab of the Sound dialog box. Choose the default playback device (marked with a green check mark) and then click Configure. That opens the test app shown in Figure 13-23. Pick your speaker layout and then click Test to cycle through all the speakers, with a visual display showing which one should be playing.

Windows 10 also allows you to designate a playback device, typically a headset, for use as the default communications device, as shown in Figure 13-24. After making that designation, you can change playback behavior so that other sounds automatically reduce their volume when your communication device is in use and the sound of, say, loud music would interfere with your communication.

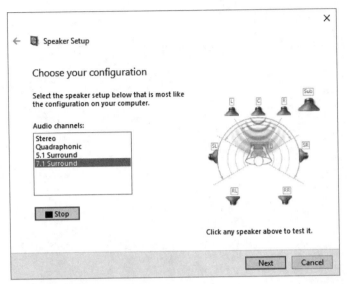

Figure 13-23 This speaker setup test allows you to confirm that you haven't accidentally wired the right speakers to left and vice versa.

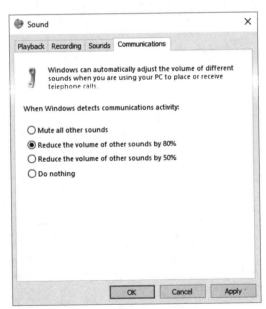

Figure 13-24 This well-hidden option allows you to reduce other sounds (music and notifications, for example) when Windows detects that you're trying to communicate.

Managing disks and drives

When you get right down to it, storage defines what you can and can't do with Windows. A big hard disk (or two or three) makes it possible for you to download and store an enormous amount of digital music, photos, and video; manage large-scale, data-intensive projects; and keep your entire collection of digital resources safely backed up.

Using today's gigantic disks effectively, however, often entails partitioning them intelligently so that separate volumes can be assigned distinct purposes. For a variety of reasons, we recommend, for example, that you keep your operating system and personal data on separate volumes, that (if possible) you make a full image backup of the volume on which the Windows system files are stored, and that you make regular and frequent backups of your valuable data. All of this requires some planning and some familiarity both with disk-management concepts and with management tools that Windows 10 provides.

➤ **For more information, see Chapter 12, "Organizing and searching for files," and Chapter 16, "Backup, restore, and recovery."**

In this chapter, we'll look at the disk-management tools provided by Windows 10 and survey some of the scenarios under which you might find these tools of use.

The Windows 10 disk-management tools

The principal disk-management tool in Windows 10 is the Disk Management console (Diskmgmt.msc). For those who need to incorporate disk-management tasks in scripts (as well as for those who simply prefer carrying out administrative tasks at the command prompt), Windows also provides a powerful command-line program called DiskPart. Everything you can do with Disk Management you can also do by using DiskPart; you just have to work harder and more carefully. Accessing Windows Management Instrumentation (WMI) through Windows PowerShell provides another method for managing disks. This method offers capabilities that are not available with the Disk Management console or DiskPart, and it has the additional advantage of custom programmability, which can be useful when you need to perform disk-management operations repeatedly on different computers.

Knowing when to use which tool is the secret of disk wizardry in Windows 10. Disk Management, for example, is ideal for shrinking and expanding volumes, while the Clean command in DiskPart makes short work of preparing a disk to be formatted for a new role. That command has no counterpart in Disk Management.

Running Disk Management

To run Disk Management, type **diskmgmt.msc** at a command prompt, or press Windows key+X and then click Disk Management. You need administrative credentials to run Disk Management. Figure 14-1 illustrates the Disk Management console.

Figure 14-1 Use the Disk Management console to gather information about and manage hard disks and removable disks.

Disk Management provides a wealth of information about physical disks and the volumes, partitions, and logical drives in place on those disks. You can use this utility to perform the following disk-related tasks:

- Check the size, file system, status, and other properties of disks and volumes

- Create, format, and delete partitions, logical drives, and dynamic volumes

- Assign drive letters to hard disk volumes, removable disk drives, and optical drives

- Create mounted drives

- Convert basic disks to dynamic disks and vice versa

- Create spanned and striped volumes

- Extend or shrink partitions

Disk Management displays information in two panes. In its default arrangement, the upper pane lists each volume on your system and provides information about the volume's type, status, capacity, available free space, and so on. You can carry out commands on a volume by right-clicking in the first column of this pane (the column labeled Volume) and choosing a command.

In the lower pane, each row represents one physical device. In the headings at the left of each row, you see the name by which the device is known to the operating system (Disk 0, Disk 1, and so on), along with its type, size, and status. To the right are areas that display information about the volumes of each device. Note that these areas are not by default drawn to scale. To change the scaling used by Disk Management, click View, then Settings. You'll find various options on the Scaling tab of the Settings dialog box.

Right-clicking a heading at the left in the lower pane displays commands pertinent to an entire storage device. Right-clicking an area representing a volume provides a menu of actions applicable to that volume.

Managing disks from the command prompt

To use DiskPart, start by running Cmd.exe with elevated privileges. You can do that by pressing Windows key+X and then clicking Command Prompt (Admin).

> ➤ **For more information about the command prompt, see Chapter 21, "Working with Command Prompt and Windows PowerShell."**

When you run DiskPart, it opens a console window and dumps you at the DISKPART> prompt. If you type **help** and press Enter, you see a screen that lists all available commands, like the one shown next.

Even if you don't prefer the command line and don't intend to write disk-management scripts, you should know about DiskPart because, if you ever find yourself needing to manage hard disks from the Windows Recovery Environment (Windows RE), you will have access to DiskPart but you won't have access to the Disk Management console. (Windows RE is a special environment that you can use for system-recovery purposes if a major hardware or software problem prevents you from starting Windows.)

Windows also includes a second command-line tool for file-system and disk management, called Fsutil. This utility allows you to find files by security identifier (SID), change the short name of a file, and perform other esoteric tasks.

CAUTION

Fsutil and DiskPart are not for the faint of heart or casual experimentation. Both are intended primarily to be incorporated into scripts rather than for interactive use. DiskPart in particular is dense and cryptic, with a complex structure that requires you to list and select objects before you act on them. For more details about DiskPart, see Microsoft Support article 300415, "A Description of the DiskPart Command-Line Utility" (*w7io.com/2501*). Although this article dates from Windows XP days and some of the comparisons it makes between DiskPart and the Disk Management console are out of date, its tutorial information about the syntax and usage of DiskPart is still accurate.

Understanding disk-management terminology

The current version of Disk Management has simplified somewhat the arcane language of disk administration. Nevertheless, it's still important to have a bit of the vocabulary under your belt. The following terms and concepts are the most important:

- **Volume.** A volume is a disk or subdivision of a disk that is formatted and available for storage. If a volume is assigned a drive letter, it appears as a separate entity in File Explorer. A hard disk can have one or more volumes.

- **Mounted drive.** A mounted drive is a volume that is mapped to an empty folder on an NTFS-formatted disk. A mounted drive does not get a drive letter and does not appear separately in File Explorer. Instead, it behaves as though it were a subfolder on another volume.

- **Format.** To format a disk is to prepare it for storage by using a particular file system (such as NTFS).

- **File system.** A file system is a method for organizing folders (directories) and files on a storage medium. Windows 10 supports the following file systems: FAT (File Allocation Table), NTFS, exFAT (Extended File Allocation Table; optimized for use with flash drives), CDFS (Compact Disc File System; also sometimes identified as ISO-9660), and UDF (Universal Disk Format). Windows 10 does not currently support the new Resilient File System (ReFS, for short) but this support is likely to arrive in a future update.

- **Basic disk and dynamic disk.** The two principal types of hard-disk organization in Windows are called basic and dynamic:

  - A basic disk can be subdivided into as many as four partitions. (Disks that have been initialized using a GUID Partition Table can have more than four.) All volumes on a basic disk must be simple volumes. When you use Disk Management to create new simple volumes, the first three partitions it creates are primary partitions. The fourth is created as an extended partition using all remaining unallocated space on the disk. An extended partition can be organized into as many as 2,000 logical disks. In use, a logical disk behaves exactly like a primary partition.

  - A dynamic disk offers organizational options not available on a basic disk. In addition to simple volumes, dynamic disks can contain spanned or striped volumes. These last two volume types combine space from multiple disks.

- **Simple volume.** A simple volume is a volume contained entirely within a single physical device. On a basic disk, a simple volume is also known as a partition.

- **Spanned volume.** A spanned volume is a volume that combines space from physically separate disks, making the combination appear and function as though it were a single storage medium.

- **Striped volume.** A striped volume is a volume in which data is stored in 64-KB strips across physically separate disks to improve performance.

- **MBR and GPT disks.** MBR (master boot record) and GPT (GUID Partition Table) are terms describing alternative methods for maintaining the information regarding a disk's subdivisions. GPT disks support larger volumes (up to 18 exabytes) and more partitions (as many as 128 on a basic disk). You can convert a disk from MBR to GPT (or vice versa) only before a disk has been partitioned for the first time (or after all partitions have been removed). GPT is required on drives that contain the Windows partition on UEFI-based systems,

- **Active partition, boot partition, and system partition.** The active partition is the one from which an x86-based computer starts after you power it up. The first physical hard disk attached to the system (Disk 0) must include an active partition. The boot partition is the partition where the Windows system files are located. The system partition is the partition that contains the bootstrap files that Windows uses to start your system and display the boot menu.

Setting up a new hard disk

Whether you're installing Windows on a brand new hard disk or simply adding a new disk to an existing system, it's a good idea to consider how you want to use the new storage space before you begin creating volumes. If your goal is to set up a large space for backup or media storage, for example, you might want to devote the entire disk to a single volume. On the other hand, if your plan is to establish two or more separate volumes—perhaps one for each family member on a shared home computer—decide how many gigabytes you want to assign to each partition. You can change your mind later (see "Managing existing disks and volumes" later in this chapter), but it's easiest to adjust the number of volumes on a disk and their relative sizes before you've put a lot of data on the platter.

Installing Windows on a new disk

When you run the Windows 10 setup program on a computer with a single, raw hard disk, you are presented with a screen identifying the disk and its size. If you want to create a single volume encompassing the entire disk, you can click Next to proceed. Otherwise, you can click New, and then in the same screen you can choose the size of the volume you want to create for your Windows installation.

If you decide not to use the entire disk for Windows, you can create additional volumes from within the Setup program. But there's no particular need to do this. After you install Windows, you can use Disk Management to create one or more additional volumes in the unallocated space remaining on the disk.

➤ **For more information about setting up Windows, see Chapter 2, "Installing, configuring, and deploying Windows 10."**

Adding a new disk to an existing Windows installation

In the graphical view pane of Disk Management, a brand new hard disk, whether internal or external, appears like this:

To make this disk available for storage, you need to create one or more volumes, assign drive letters, label the volumes (if you don't want them to be identified in File Explorer as simply "New Volume"), and format the new volumes. You can carry out all of these steps from the New Simple Volume Wizard.

Specifying volume capacity

To begin, right-click anywhere in the area marked Unallocated and then click New Simple Volume. The New Simple Volume Wizard appears. Click Next to get past the welcome page. On the Specify Volume Size page, you're shown the maximum and minimum amounts of space you can devote to the new volume:

```
New Simple Volume Wizard                                      ✕

  Specify Volume Size
     Choose a volume size that is between the maximum and minimum sizes.


     Maximum disk space in MB:        953867

     Minimum disk space in MB:        8

     Simple volume size in MB:        953867  ▲▼



                              < Back    Next >      Cancel
```

The wizard doesn't give you the option of designating volume space as a percentage of unallocated space, so if your goal is to create two or more volumes of equal size, you might want to do a bit of arithmetic before going on. In this example, if you wanted to split the disk into two equal partitions, you would enter 466933 in the Simple Volume Size In MB box.

Assigning a drive letter

After you have specified the volume size in megabytes and clicked Next, you are given the opportunity to assign a drive letter to the new volume. Note that the letters A and B, which used to be reserved for floppy disks, are no longer reserved:

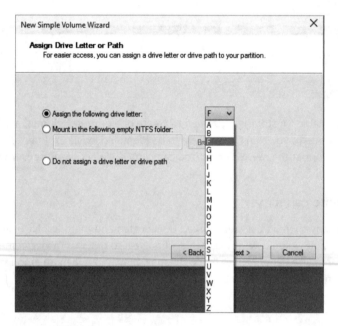

Formatting the new volume

The Format Partition page, which follows the Assign Drive Letter Or Path page, gives you a chance to do just that, but it does not require that you do so. If you prefer to wait, you can always do the formatting later (right-click the area for the volume in the graphical view pane of Disk Management and then click Format). Figure 14-2 illustrates the Format Partition page.

Your choices are as follows:

- **File System.** For hard disk volumes larger than 4 GB (4,096 MB), your only options are NTFS (the default) and exFAT. If you are formatting removable media such as USB flash drives or a writable optical disc, other file systems are available. For more information, see "Choosing a file system" later in this chapter.

- **Allocation Unit Size.** The allocation unit size (also known as the cluster size) is the smallest space that can be allocated to a file. The Default option, in which Windows selects the appropriate cluster size based on volume size, is the best choice here.

- **Volume Label.** The volume label identifies the drive in File Explorer's Computer window. The default label is "New Volume." It's a good idea to give your new volume a name that describes its purpose.

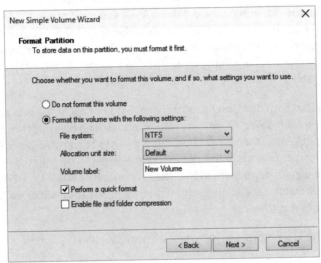

Figure 14-2 The Format Partition page lets you specify your new volume's file system, allocation unit size, and volume label.

Select the Perform A Quick Format check box if you want Disk Management to skip the sometimes lengthy process of checking the disk media. Select Enable File And Folder Compression if you want all data on the new volume to use NTFS compression. (This option, which you can also apply later, is available only on NTFS volumes. For more information, see "Increase storage space with NTFS compression" later in this chapter.)

The wizard's final page gives you one more chance to review your specifications. You should actually take a moment to read this display before you click Finish.

After Disk Management has done its work and disk formatting is complete, a dark blue bar appears over the new volume in the console's graphical view pane:

Disk 1		
Basic 931.51 GB Online	**Music (F:)** 455.99 GB NTFS Healthy (Primary Partition)	475.52 GB Unallocated

If your disk still has unallocated space (as the disk in this example does), you can add another volume by right-clicking that part of the display and then clicking New Simple Volume again.

Choosing a file system

Whether you're setting up a new disk or reformatting an existing one, the process of formatting entails choosing a file system. The choices available to you depend on the type of media you are formatting. With hard disks, the only options made available by Disk Management are NTFS and exFAT. If you want to format a hard disk in FAT32, you need to use the Format command with the /FS switch at the command prompt. (Type **format /?** at the command prompt for details.) The only good reason to do this, however, is for the sake of compatibility with devices running non-Microsoft operating systems that don't natively support NTFS. (See "The Advantages of NTFS" later in this chapter.)

If you're formatting a USB flash drive, on the other hand, FAT32 or exFAT is a reasonable choice. Because NTFS is a journaling file system, reading and writing files on NTFS disks involves more disk input/output than similar operations on FAT32 and exFAT disks. Flash drives can perform a finite number of reads and writes before they need to be replaced—hence, they may have a longer life expectancy under FAT32 or exFAT than under NTFS. On UEFI systems, FAT32 is required for bootable installation media. (For more information about exFAT, see "exFAT vs. FAT32" later in this chapter.)

Choosing the right UDF version for optical media

If you're formatting a writable CD or DVD disc, your choices are various flavors of the Universal Disk Format (UDF). UDF, a successor to the Compact Disk File System (CDFS), is an evolving specification. Windows 10 can format discs using version 1.50, 2.00, 2.01, or 2.50. (Windows 10 can also use—but not format—discs using the latest version, which is 2.60.) Which to choose? It depends on whether you want the CDs or DVDs that you generate to be readable on systems running earlier versions of Windows or Windows Server 2003. The differences are as follows:

- **Version 1.50.** Can be read on systems running Windows 2000 and later.

- **Version 2.00 or 2.01.** Cannot be read on Windows 2000. Can be read on Windows XP Service Pack 3 and later. Note that version 2.01 is a minor revision of version 2.00. There is no reason to prefer version 2.00.

- **Version 2.50.** Can be read only on computers running Windows Vista or later.

All of these variants are afforded read/write support by Windows 10.

Choosing between UDF and mastered optical media

You do not have to format a CD or DVD (using one of the compatible UDF flavors) to store files on it. You can burn files to optical media by copying files to a temporary folder and transferring them en masse to the CD or DVD. Using UDF is somewhat more convenient because it allows you to read and write CD or DVD files as though they were stored on a USB flash drive or floppy disk. But the older method, sometimes called Mastered or ISO, offers greater compatibility with computers running other operating systems, and it's the only method that allows you to burn audio files and play them back on consumer audio devices.

The advantages of NTFS

NTFS offers a number of important advantages over the earlier FAT and FAT32 file systems:

- **Security.** On an NTFS volume, you can restrict access to files and folders by using permissions. (For information about using NTFS permissions, see "What are ACLs?" in Chapter 6, "Managing user accounts, passwords, and credentials.") You can add an extra layer of protection by encrypting files if your edition of Windows 10 supports it. On a FAT or FAT32 drive, anyone with physical access to your computer can access any files stored on that drive.

- **Reliability.** Because NTFS is a journaling file system, an NTFS volume can recover from disk errors more readily than a FAT32 volume. NTFS uses log files to keep track of all disk activity. In the event of a system crash, Windows 10 can use this journal to repair file-system errors automatically when the system is restarted. In addition, NTFS can dynamically remap clusters that contain bad sectors and mark those clusters as bad so that the operating system no longer uses them. FAT and FAT32 drives are more vulnerable to disk errors.

- **Expandability.** Using NTFS-formatted volumes, you can expand storage on existing volumes without having to back up, repartition, reformat, and restore.

- **Efficiency.** On partitions greater than 8 GB, NTFS volumes manage space more efficiently than FAT32. The maximum partition size for a FAT32 drive created by Windows 10 is 32 GB; by contrast, you can create a single NTFS volume of up to 16 terabytes (16,384 GB) using default settings, and by tweaking cluster sizes you can ratchet the maximum volume size up to 256 terabytes.

- **Optimized storage of small files.** Files on the order of a hundred bytes or less can be stored entirely within the Master File Table (MFT) record, rather than requiring a minimum allocation unit outside the MFT. This results in greater storage efficiency for small files.

CHAPTER 14

exFAT vs. FAT32

Microsoft introduced the Extended FAT (exFAT) file system first with Windows Embedded CE 6.0, an operating system designed for industrial controllers and consumer electronics devices. Subsequently, exFAT was made available in Windows Vista Service Pack 1 (SP1). Its principal advantage over FAT32 is scalability. The exFAT file system removes the 32-GB volume and 4-GB file-size limitations of FAT32. It also handles more than 1,000 files per directory. Its principal disadvantage is limited backward compatibility. Some non-PC consumer electronics devices may be able to read earlier FAT systems but not exFAT.

If you're formatting a flash drive and you expect to store large video files on it, exFAT might be a good choice for the file system. And if you're planning to take that flash drive to a photo kiosk at your local convenience store, FAT32 is definitely the way to go.

Inside OUT

Formatting does not remove a volume's data

Whatever formatting options you choose, you are warned that the action of formatting a volume makes that volume's data inaccessible. That's true. Whatever data is there when you format will no longer be available to you by normal means after you format. Unless you use the /P switch, the data remains in some form, however. If you're really concerned about covering your tracks, either use the format /P:x (where x represents the number of passes) or wipe the disk after you format it by using the command-line program Cipher.exe, with the /W switch. (Type **cipher /?** at the command prompt for details.) For information about other ways to clean a disk, see "Permanently wiping all data from a disk" later in this chapter.

Managing existing disks and volumes

No matter how well you plan, your approach to deploying storage resources is likely to change over time. Disk Management can help you adjust to changing requirements. You can expand volumes (assuming space is available), shrink volumes, reformat, relabel, assign new drive letters, and more. We'll consider these options next.

Extending a volume

Disk Management will be happy to make an NTFS volume larger for you, provided unallocated space is available on the same or another hard disk. To accomplish the expansion, right-click the volume you want to expand and then click Extend Volume. Click Next to move past the Extend Volume Wizard's welcome page. The Select Disks page, shown in Figure 14-3, appears.

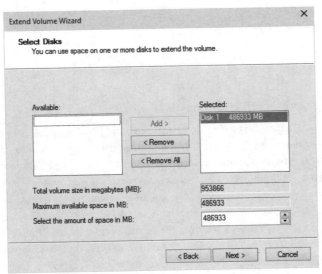

Figure 14-3 The Extend Volume Wizard lets you extend a volume into unallocated space on the same or another hard disk with free space.

The Selected list, on the right side of this dialog box, initially shows the disk whose volume you intend to extend. The Maximum Available Space In MB box shows you how much larger you can make the volume, assuming you want to confine your expansion to the current disk. The Select The Amount Of Space In MB box, initially set to equal the maximum available space, is where you declare the number of megabytes you want to add to the volume, and the Total Volume Size In Megabytes (MB) box shows you how big your volume is about to become. When you're ready to continue, click Next, review your orders on the ensuing page, and then click Finish. If your volume resided on a basic disk to begin with, it will remain basic after the expansion—provided that the space into which you expanded was contiguous with the original volume. Note that no separate formatting step is required; the new territory acquires the same formatting as the original.

Volume extension is subject to the following limitations:

- Only NTFS-formatted volumes can be extended.

- A logical drive can be extended only within the extended partition that contains it.

- The system and boot partitions can be extended only into contiguous unallocated space.

- You cannot extend a striped volume.

Inside OUT

Increase storage space with NTFS compression

If you're thinking of expanding a partition because you're short of space, consider compressing your files and folders instead. You can compress individual files, particular folders, or entire volumes. Items compressed in this manner are decompressed on the fly when you open them and compressed again when they are closed. You won't achieve huge savings in storage space this way—less than you would get by using compressed (zipped) folders—but the convenience of NTFS is high and the cost, in terms of performance, is virtually unnoticeable. To compress a volume, open This PC in File Explorer, right-click the volume, click Properties, and then, on the General tab of the properties dialog box, select Compress This Drive To Save Disk Space. To compress a particular folder or file, right-click it in File Explorer, click Properties, and then click Advanced on the General tab of the properties dialog box. In the Advanced Attributes dialog box, select Compress Contents To Save Disk Space. Note that this form of compression is available only on NTFS volumes and that NTFS compression is incompatible with encryption that uses the Encrypting File System. You can have one or the other, but not both.

Shrinking a volume

Provided that space is available, you can shrink an NTFS-formatted volume to make more space available for other volumes. To do this, right-click the volume in either the volume list or graphical view pane and then click Shrink Volume. Disk Management responds by analyzing the disk, and then it reports the amount of shrinkage possible, as shown next:

Shrink F: ✕

Total size before shrink in MB: 466933

Size of available shrink space in MB: 463811

Enter the amount of space to shrink in MB: 463811

Total size after shrink in MB: 3122

ⓘ You cannot shrink a volume beyond the point where any unmovable files are located.
See the "defrag" event in the Application log for detailed information about the
operation when it has completed.

See "Shrink a basic volume" in Disk Management help for more information

                                                    Shrink   Cancel

Enter the number of megabytes by which you want to reduce your volume, and then click
Shrink. Disk Management defragments the disk, moving all its data to a contiguous block, and
then performs the shrink.

Be aware that page files and volume shadow copy files cannot be moved during the defragmentation process. This means that you might not have as much room to shrink as you would
like. Microsoft also advises that the amount by which you can shrink a volume is "transient"
and depends on what is happening on the volume at the time. In other words, if you are trying
to eliminate, say, 10 GB from the volume, and Disk Management can manage only 7, take the
7 and then try for more later.

Deleting a volume

Deleting a volume is easy—and irreversible. All data is lost in the process, so be sure you have
backed up or no longer need whatever the volume currently contains. Then right-click the
volume and click Delete Volume. The volume reverts to unallocated space, and if it happens to
have been the last volume on a dynamic disk, the disk itself is converted to basic.

Converting a FAT32 disk to NTFS

To convert a FAT or FAT32 disk to NTFS, use the command-line Convert utility. The essential
syntax is

```
convert d: /fs:ntfs
```

where d is the drive letter you want to convert. For information about optional parameters,
type **convert /?** at the command prompt.

CHAPTER 14

The Convert utility can do its work within Windows if the drive to be converted is not in use. However, if you want to convert the system volume or a volume that holds a page file, you might see an error message when you run Convert. In that case, you must schedule the conversion to occur the next time you start Windows. After you restart the computer, you'll see a prompt that warns you that the conversion is about to begin. You have 10 seconds to cancel the conversion. If you allow it to proceed, Windows will run the Chkdsk utility and perform the conversion automatically. During this process, your computer will restart twice.

Assigning or changing a volume label

In Windows 10, as in previous versions of Windows, you can assign a descriptive text label to any volume. Assigning a label is purely optional, but it's a good practice, especially if you have a multiboot system or if you've set up separate volumes to keep your data organized. You can use Data as the label for your data drive, Music for the drive that holds your collection of digital tunes, and so on.

You can enter a volume label when you format a new volume, or you can do it at any time afterward by right-clicking a volume (in Disk Management or in File Explorer), clicking Properties, and entering text in the edit field near the top of the General tab.

Assigning and changing drive letters

You can assign one and only one letter to a volume. For all but the following volumes, you can change or remove the drive letter at any time:

- The boot volume

- The system volume

- Any volume on which the page (swap) file is stored

To change a drive-letter assignment, right-click the volume in Disk Management and then click Change Drive Letter And Paths. (You can do this in either the upper or lower pane.) To replace an existing drive letter, select it and click Change. To assign a drive letter to a volume that currently has none, click Add. Select an available drive letter from the Assign The Following Drive Letter list, and then click OK twice.

TROUBLESHOOTING

The drive letter for my card reader has disappeared

Windows 10 does not display empty drives by default. If your computer has a set of drives for memory cards, you may be accustomed to seeing those drives listed in File Explorer whether the drives are empty or not. If you want to make the empty drives visible, open File Explorer, click the View tab, and then select Hidden Items.

Mapping a volume to an NTFS folder

In addition to (or in place of) a drive letter, you can assign one or more paths to NTFS folders to a volume. Assigning a drive path creates a mounted volume (also known as a mounted drive, mounted folder, or volume mount point). A mounted volume appears as a folder within an NTFS-formatted volume that has a drive letter assigned to it. Besides allowing you to sidestep the limitation of 26 drive letters, mounted volumes offer these advantages:

- You can extend storage space on an existing volume that's running low on free space. For instance, if your digital music collection has outgrown your drive C, you can create a subfolder of your Music folder and call it, say, More Music. Then you can assign a drive path from a new volume to the More Music folder—in effect increasing the size of your original Music folder. The More Music folder in this example will appear to be part of the original Music folder but will actually reside on the new volume.

- You can make commonly used files available in multiple locations. Say you have an enormous collection of clip art that you store on drive X, and each user has a subfolder in his or her Documents folder where desktop publishing files are stored. In each of those personal folders, you can create a subfolder called Clip Art and assign that folder's path to volume X. That way, the entire clip art collection is always available from any user's desktop publishing folder, and no one has to worry about creating shortcuts to X or changing drive letters while they work.

To create a mounted volume, follow these steps:

1. In Disk Management, right-click the volume you want to change (you can do this in either the graphical view pane or the volume list pane), and then click Change Drive Letter And Paths.

2. Click Add to open the Add Drive Letter Or Path dialog box.

3. Select Mount In The Following Empty NTFS Folder. (This is the only option available if the volume already has a drive letter assigned.)

4. Click Browse. The Browse For Drive Path dialog box that appears shows only NTFS volumes, and the OK button is enabled only if you select an empty folder or click New Folder to create one.

5. Click OK to add the selected location in the Add Drive Letter Or Path dialog box, and then click OK to create the drive path.

You can manage files and subfolders in a mounted volume just as though it were a regular folder. In File Explorer, the folder icon will be marked by a shortcut arrow. If you right-click the

CHAPTER 14

folder icon and then click Properties, the General tab will reveal that the folder is actually a mounted volume, as shown next.

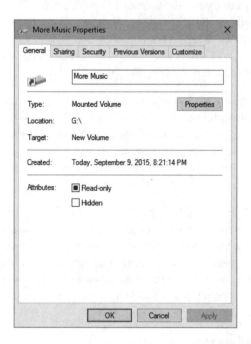

And, as Figure 14-4 shows, if you click the Properties button within that properties dialog box, you'll see more details about the drive to which the folder is mapped.

If you use the Dir command in a Command Prompt window to display a folder directory, a mounted volume is identified as <JUNCTION> (for junction point, yet another name for a mounted volume), whereas ordinary folders are identified as <DIR> (for directory, the MS-DOS term for a folder).

CAUTION

When creating mounted volumes, avoid establishing loops in the structure of a drive—for example, by creating a drive path from drive X that points to a folder on drive D and then creating a drive path on drive D that points to a folder on drive X. Windows allows you to do this, but it's invariably a bad idea, because an application that opens subfolders (such as a search) can go into an endless loop.

To see a list of all the mounted drives on your system, click View, Drive Paths in Disk Management. A dialog box like the one shown in Figure 14-5 appears. Note that you can remove a drive path from this dialog box; if you do so, the folder remains in the same spot it was previously located, but it reverts to being a regular, empty folder.

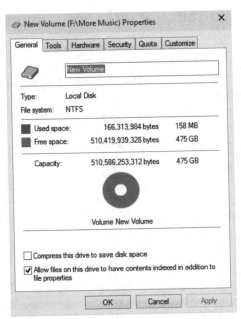

Figure 14-4 The properties dialog box for a mounted drive identifies the volume that actually holds its files.

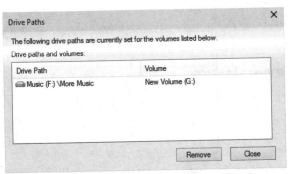

Figure 14-5 This dialog box lists all the mounted drives on a system and shows the volume label, if any, of each mounted drive.

> For instructions on how to make a USB flash drive bootable so that you can use it to install Windows 10, see "Making bootable media" in Chapter 2. For details on how to mount an ISO file so you can run the setup program without requiring external media, see "Upgrade directly from an ISO file," also in Chapter 2.

Checking the properties and status of disks and volumes

You can check the properties of any drive—including the volume label, file system, and amount of free space available—by right-clicking the drive in File Explorer's This PC folder and then clicking Properties. You can see the same details and more in Disk Management. Most of the crucial information is visible in the volume list, the tabular pane that appears by default at the top of the Disk Management window. Slightly less information is available in the graphical view at the bottom of the window. Of particular interest is information about the status of a disk or volume. Figure 14-6 shows where to look for this information.

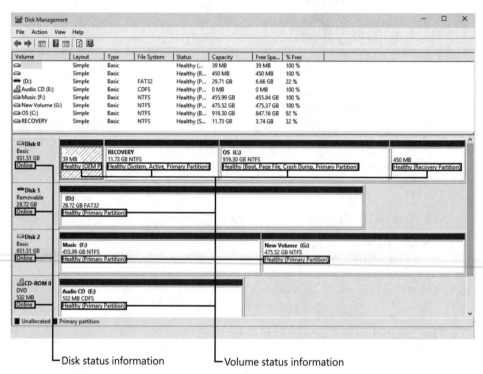

Figure 14-6 Disk Management displays information about the status of each disk and volume.

Under normal circumstances, the status information displayed here should report that each disk is online and each volume is healthy. Table 14-1 lists all possible disk status messages you might see on a system running Windows 10, along with suggested actions for resolving possible errors.

Table 14-1 Disk status messages

Status	Description	Action required
Online	The disk is configured correctly and has no known problems.	None.
Online (Errors)	The operating system encountered errors when reading or writing data from a region of the disk. (This status message appears on dynamic disks only.)	Right-click the disk, and then click Reactivate Disk to return its status to Online. If errors continue to occur, check for damage to the disk.
Offline	The disk was once available but is not currently accessible. The disk might be physically damaged, or it might be disconnected. (This status message appears on dynamic disks only.)	Check the physical connections between the disk and the power supply or disk controller. After repairing connections, right-click the disk and then click Reactivate Disk to return its status to Online. If the damage cannot be repaired, delete all volumes, right-click the disk, and then click Remove Disk.
Foreign	The disk was originally installed on another computer and has not yet been set up for use on your computer. (This status message appears on dynamic disks only.)	Right-click the disk, and then click Import Foreign Disks.
Unreadable	All or part of the disk might be physically damaged, or (in the case of a dynamic disk) the dynamic disk database might be corrupted.	Restart the computer. If the problem persists, right-click the disk and then click Rescan Disks. If the status is still Unreadable, some data on the disk might be recoverable with third-party utilities.
Missing	The disk is corrupted, disconnected, or not powered on. (This status message appears on dynamic disks only.)	After you reconnect or power on the missing disk, right-click the disk and click Reactivate Disk to return its status to Online.
Not Initialized	The disk does not contain a valid signature. It might have been prepared on a system running a non-Microsoft operating system, such as Unix or Linux, or the drive might be brand new.	If the disk is used by another operating system, do nothing. To prepare a new disk for use with Windows 10, right-click the disk and click Initialize Disk.
No Media	A disc is not inserted in the drive. (This status message appears only on removable media drives, such as CD and DVD drives.)	Insert a disc in the drive, and then click Action, Rescan Disks.

Table 14-2 describes volume status messages you're likely to see.

CHAPTER 14

Table 14-2 Volume status messages

Status	Description	Action required
Healthy	The volume is properly formatted and has no known problems.	None.
Healthy (At Risk)	Windows encountered errors when reading from or writing to the underlying disk. Such errors are often caused by bad blocks on the disk. After encountering an error anywhere on the disk, Disk Management marks all volumes on that disk as Healthy (At Risk). (This status message appears on dynamic disks only.)	Right-click the disk, and then click Reactivate Disk. Persistent errors often indicate a failing disk. Back up all data, and run a thorough diagnostic check using the hardware manufacturer's software; if necessary, replace the disk.
Healthy (Unknown Partition)	Windows does not recognize the partition; this occurs with some partitions created by another operating system or by a computer manufacturer that uses a partition to store system files. You cannot format or access data on an unknown partition.	If you're certain the partition is unnecessary, use Disk Management to delete it and create a new partition in the free space created.
Initializing	Disk Management cannot determine the disk status because the disk is initializing. (This status message appears on dynamic disks only.)	Wait. The drive status should appear in a few seconds.
Failed	The dynamic disk is damaged or the file system is corrupted.	To repair a failed dynamic volume, check to see whether the disk is online. (If not, right-click the disk, and then click Reactivate Disk.) Right-click the volume, and then click Reactivate Volume. If the failed volume is on a basic disk, be sure that the disk is properly connected.
Unknown	The boot sector for the volume is corrupted, and you can no longer access data. This condition might be caused by a virus.	Use an up-to-date virus-scanning program to check for the presence of a boot-sector virus.

Permanently wiping all data from a disk

Formatting a volume results in a root folder that appears to be empty. However, as we mentioned earlier in this chapter, someone with data-recovery tools might be able to restore deleted files even after you format the volume. If you're discarding or recycling an old computer or hard disk, you don't want to risk the possibility of it landing in the hands of someone who might search it for recoverable data that can be used for identity theft or other nefarious purposes.

If your old disk is headed for the dumpster, you can ensure that the data can't be recovered by removing the disk drive from the computer and physically destroying the disk. Using tools as varied as a power saw, drill, torch, or sledge hammer, you can render the disk inoperable. Although this method is effective, it has several disadvantages: it takes time, considerable physical effort, and has all the usual risks associated with tools. (Be sure you're wearing safety goggles.) Perhaps most important, you're left with a disk that can't be sold or donated to someone who can use it.

As we mentioned earlier, the Format command (with the /P switch) and the Cipher command (with the /W switch) can be used to overwrite everything on a disk, but these tools are impractical for cleaning the system partition.

A better solution is to use a third-party disk-wiping tool. A free one that we like is Darik's Boot And Nuke (DBAN), which you can download from *www.dban.org*. DBAN is a bootable disk that securely wipes a computer's hard disks. If you're worried that DBAN or another purported disk-wiping utility might surreptitiously steal your data before destroying it, remove your concerns by disconnecting your computer from your network before using the program.

If your disk contains highly sensitive material and you want to be absolutely sure its data can't be recovered, search for a utility that conforms to the United States Department of Defense DoD 5220.22-M standard for clearing and sanitizing media. This standard requires each sector to be overwritten with different characters several times, thus defeating even the most sensitive data-recovery tools. Programs that meet the standard include Active@ KillDisk (*www.killdisk.com*) and BCWipe (*www.jetico.com*).

Working with virtual hard disks

Disk Management can create virtual hard disks in the VHD format used by the Windows 10 Hyper-V Manager program. A .vhd file encapsulates all the characteristics of a simple disk volume in a single file. Once created, initialized, and formatted, it appears as a disk drive in File Explorer and Disk Management, but you can copy it, back it up, and do anything else with it that you might do with an ordinary file.

> ➤ For more information about Hyper-V Manager, see Chapter 22, "Running virtual machines with Hyper-V."

To create a virtual hard disk, open Disk Management and click Action, Create VHD. Disk Management responds with the Create And Attach Virtual Hard Disk dialog box:

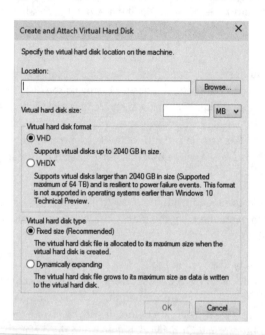

Specify a file name with a fully qualified path. It's easiest to do this with the help of the Browse button, but note that the file cannot be stored in your %SystemRoot% (usually C:\Windows) folder. If you want the disk to expand in size as you add files to it, select Dynamically Expanding. Otherwise, select Fixed Size (Recommended). Either way, you must also specify a size (that's an initial size if you select Dynamically Expanding). The minimum size is 3 MB; the maximum is the amount of free space available on your (real) disk.

New in Windows 10 is the option to create a virtual hard disk in either of two formats. The VHD format supports disks up to 2 TB, which can be used on systems running Windows 7, Windows 8 or 8.1, or Windows 10. The VHDX format supports much larger disks, up to 64 TB, but is not supported by earlier versions of Windows. The VHDX format was introduced with Windows Server 2012, and the option to create gigantic virtual disks is perhaps primarily of interest to server administrators. VHD is still the default format in Windows 10. However, because metadata in VHDX disks continuously tracks changes (a service not provided in VHD), they are, as the dialog box indicates, more resilient to power failures. For that reason, you might prefer the newer format even if your size requirements are well under 2 TB. Provided that you don't require interoperability with Windows 7 or Windows 8 or 8.1, we don't know of a good reason not to prefer VHDX.

After you have finished with the Create And Attach Virtual Hard Disk dialog box, Disk Management adds the new virtual disk to its graphical view pane as an unknown, uninitialized disk with unallocated space:

Right-click the area at the left side of this display (with the disk number), and then click Initialize Disk. The Initialize Disk dialog box that appears gives you the option of setting up a disk with a master boot record or a GUID Partition Table:

Select MBR (Master Boot Record) unless you're working with a very large disk. After completing these steps, you can follow the procedures described earlier in this chapter to create one or more volumes on the new disk. After you have created a volume, formatted it, and assigned it a drive letter, the disk appears like any other in Disk Management and File Explorer.

To remove a virtual hard disk, right-click the disk-number box at the left side of Disk Management's graphical view pane, and then click Detach VHD. Disk Management informs you that deleting the disk will make it unavailable until you reattach it. The dialog box also reminds you of the location of the file that encapsulated your virtual hard disk.

To reattach a deleted virtual disk, click Action, Attach VHD in Disk Management. Then type or browse to the location of the VHD or VHDX file. (It will be identified in File Explorer as Hard Disk Image File.)

Checking disks for errors

Errors in disk media and in the file system can cause a wide range of problems, from an inability to open or save files to blue-screen errors and widespread data corruption. Windows is capable of recovering automatically from many disk errors, especially on drives formatted with NTFS.

To perform a thorough inspection for errors, you can run the Windows Check Disk utility (Chkdsk.exe). Two versions of this utility are available—a graphical version that performs basic disk-checking functions, and a command-line version that provides a much more extensive set of customization options.

To check for errors on a local disk, follow these steps:

1. In File Explorer, open This PC, right-click the icon belonging to the drive you want to check, and then click Properties.

2. On the Tools tab, click Check. (If you're using a standard account, you'll need to supply credentials for an account in the Administrators group to execute this utility.) Unless Windows is already aware of problems with the selected disk, you are likely to see a message similar to the following:

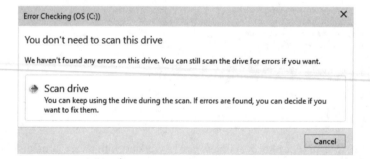

3. If you want to go ahead and check the disk, click Scan Drive. Windows will perform an exhaustive check of the entire disk. If there are bad sectors, Windows will locate them and recover readable information where it can.

The command-line version of Check Disk gives you considerably more options. It also allows you to set up regular disk-checking operations using Task Scheduler (as described in "Using Task Scheduler" in Chapter 19, "Automating tasks and activities"). To run this command in its simplest form, open a Command Prompt window using the Run As Administrator option, and then type **chkdsk** at the prompt. This command runs Chkdsk in read-only mode, displaying the status of the current drive but not making any changes. If you add a drive letter after the command (*chkdsk d:*, for instance), the report applies to that drive.

To see descriptions of the command-line switches available with the chkdsk command, type **chkdsk /?**. Here is a partial list of the available switches:

- **/F** Instructs Chkdsk to fix any errors it detects. This is the most commonly used switch. The disk must be locked. If Chkdsk cannot lock the drive, it offers to check the drive the next time you restart the computer or to dismount the volume you want to check before proceeding. Dismounting is a drastic step; it invalidates all current file handles on the affected volume and can result in loss of data. You should decline the offer. When you do, Chkdsk will make you a second offer—to check the disk the next time you restart your system. You should accept this option. (If you're trying to check the system drive, the only option you're given is to schedule a check at the next startup.)

- **/V** On FAT32 volumes, /V displays verbose output, listing the name of every file in every directory as the disk check proceeds. On NTFS volumes, this switch displays cleanup messages (if any).

- **/R** Identifies bad sectors and recovers information from those sectors if possible. The disk must be locked. Be aware that this is a time-consuming and uninterruptible process.

The following switches are valid only on NTFS volumes:

- **/I** Performs a simpler check of index entries (stage 2 in the Chkdsk process), reducing the amount of time required.

- **/C** Skips the checking of cycles within the folder structure, reducing the amount of time required.

- **/X** Forces the volume to dismount, if necessary, and invalidates all open file handles. This option is intended for server administrators. Because of the potential for data loss, it should be avoided.

- **/L[:size]** Changes the size of the file that logs NTFS transactions. If you omit the size parameter, this switch displays the current size. This option is intended for server administrators. Because of the potential for data loss, it also should be avoided in normal use.

- **/B** Reevaluates bad clusters.

CHAPTER 14

Optimizing disks for better performance

On a relatively new system with a speedy processor and plenty of physical memory, hard disk performance is the single biggest bottleneck in everyday operation. Even with a zippy hard disk, it takes time to load large data files into memory so that you can work with them. The problem is especially noticeable with movies, video clips, DVD-burning projects, databases, ISO image files, and virtual hard disks, which can easily take up multiple gigabytes, sometimes in a single file.

On a freshly formatted disk, files load fairly quickly, but performance can degrade over time because of disk fragmentation. To understand how fragmentation works, it helps to understand the basic structure of a hard disk. The process of formatting a disk divides it into sectors, each of which contains space for 512 bytes of data. The file system combines groups of sectors into clusters, which are the smallest units of space available for holding a single file or part of a file.

On any NTFS volume greater than 2 GB in size, the cluster size is 4 KB. Thus, when you save a 200-MB video clip, Windows divides the file into roughly 50,000 pieces. When you save this file for the first time on a freshly formatted, completely empty hard disk, Windows writes it in contiguous clusters. Because all the clusters that hold individual pieces of the file are physically adjacent to one another, the mechanical components of the hard disk can work very efficiently, scooping up data in one smooth operation. As a bonus, the hard disk's onboard cache and the Windows disk cache are able to anticipate the need for data and fetch nearby clusters that are likely to contain other parts of the file, which can then be retrieved from fast cached memory rather than from the relatively slow disk.

Unfortunately, hard disks don't stay neatly organized for long. When you add data to an existing file, the file system has to allocate more clusters for storage, typically in a different physical location on the disk. As you delete files, you create gaps in the once-tidy arrangement of contiguously stored files. As you save new files, especially large ones, the file system uses all these bits of free space, scattering the new files over the hard disk in many noncontiguous pieces. The resulting inefficiency in storage is called fragmentation; each time you open or save a file on a badly fragmented disk, disk performance suffers, sometimes dramatically, because the disk heads have to spend extra time moving from cluster to cluster before they can begin reading or writing data.

The Optimize Drives service in Windows 10 runs as a low-priority background task that defragments your disks at regularly scheduled intervals. By default, the program kicks off once a week in the middle of the night, without requiring any attention from you. If you would like a different schedule, or if you want to optimize certain disks and not others, type **dfrgui** at a command prompt. The Optimize Drives dialog box appears:

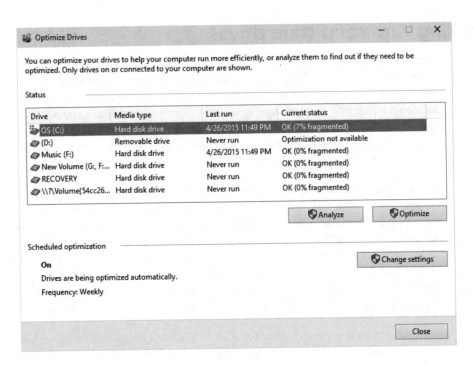

Here you can analyze the fragmentation level of particular disks, optimize a disk ad hoc, or reconfigure the system's background defragmentation schedule. To reconfigure, click Change Settings. The frequency options are Daily, Weekly, and Monthly:

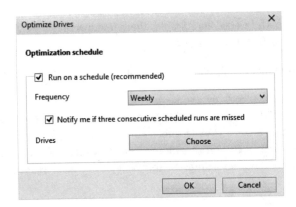

By clicking the Choose button, you can turn optimization on or off for particular drives.

Working with solid state drives

Many newer computers are equipped with a solid state drive (SSD), which is a chunk of flash memory instead of a spinning magnetic disk coupled with an onboard disk controller and the requisite power and data connectors. Such drives can provide improved performance, increased battery life, better durability, reduced likelihood of damage caused by drops and shocks, faster startup times, and reductions in noise, heat, and vibration. These benefits come at a price: SSDs typically cost more and have less storage capacity than current hard disk drive (HDD) models, although the gap is closing.

Conventional hard disk drives are typically the biggest performance bottleneck in any computing environment. If you can speed up disk activity, especially reads, the effects on system startup and application launch times can be breathtaking. On our test platform, which has a conventional hard disk and a solid state drive configured for dual booting, the total boot time when using the SSD is less than half the time (about 30 seconds) than when booting from the HDD. Close examination of log files created by the Windows System Assessment Tool (WinSAT), which are stored in %SystemRoot%\Performance\WinSAT\DataStore, shows radically higher throughput and faster times in the DiskMetrics section of the SSD-based system.

Although the underlying technology in SSDs and HDDs is completely different, for the most part the devices are treated identically by Windows, and you don't need to concern yourself with the differences. Behind the scenes, Windows does several things differently on SSDs, including the following:

- SuperFetch, ReadyBoost, ReadyBoot, and ReadyDrive, features designed to overcome hard disk bottlenecks, are unnecessary and are disabled by default on most SSDs. (Windows analyzes disk performance and disables these features only on SSDs that are fast enough to make these features superfluous.)

- When creating a partition on an SSD, Windows properly aligns the partition for best performance.

- Windows 10 supports the TRIM command. SSDs have to erase blocks of data before those blocks can be reused; they can't write directly over deleted data as rotating disks can. The TRIM command makes this process more efficient by reclaiming deleted space in the background. You can find more details in this Wikipedia article: *wikipedia.org/wiki/Trim_(computing)*.

Optimizing solid state drives

If your system includes one or more SSDs and you have read that defragmentation is inappropriate with such drives, you might be startled to see something akin to the following in the Optimize Drives dialog box:

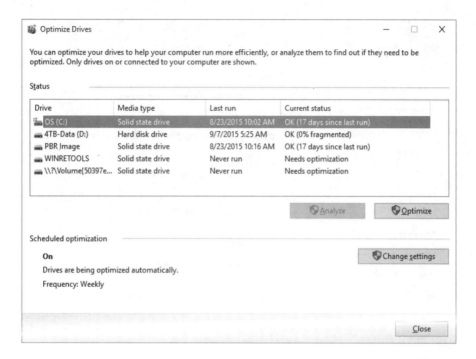

Rest assured that the optimization that Windows performs automatically at (by default) weekly intervals is retrimming, not defragmenting. (See the comments about the TRIM command in the preceding section.) For an interesting discussion of the application of TRIM to SSDs and the issues in general surrounding optimization with such drives, see Scott Hanselman's blog post at *bit.ly/defrag-ssd*.

That blog post includes a quotation from an unnamed Microsoft spokesperson indicating that Windows *does* defragment SSDs once a month provided that System Restore is enabled. This is done to improve performance of the System Restore process on drives that have become fragmented. In our view, there is no good reason to interfere with this optimization.

Monitoring disk usage

The Windows 10 Storage page lets you see at a glance how your various storage assets are being consumed. Go to Settings, System, click on Storage in the list of subsections at the left, and you will be presented with a display comparable to the following:

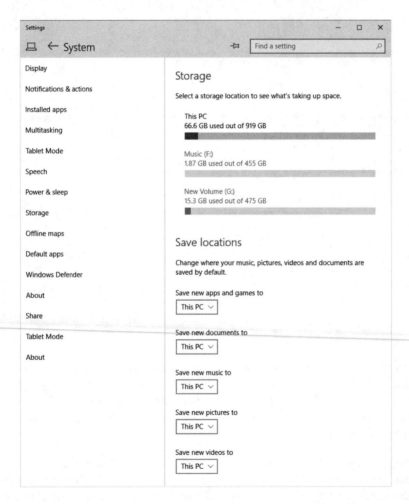

This initial display shows a bar graph for each volume, letting you see at a glance how much storage is in use and how much remains. The controls below the bar graphs provide an easy way to change the default storage locations for various categories of files—documents, music, pictures, and so on.

➤ For a detailed discussion of how this feature works, see "Managing disk space" in Chapter 15, "System maintenance and performance."

Changing default save locations

In the Save Locations section of the initial Storage Sense display, you'll find a set of drop-down lists for various categories of files—apps and games, documents, music, pictures, and videos. These controls let you change the locations where new items are saved by default. All of these categories, except for apps and games, represent libraries, and changing the default storage location simply adds a new location to the library. Opening the Save New Music To list and switching from This PC to Music (F:), for example, expands the Music Library to include drive F, as Figure 14-7 shows.

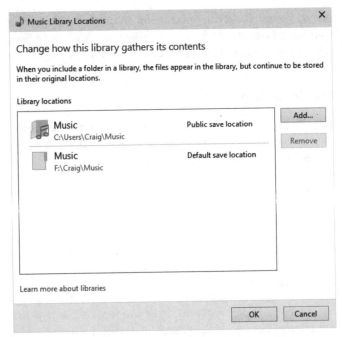

Figure 14-7 Changing the default save location for a file type expands the library, if any, associated with that file type.

Note that if the volume to which you redirect new saves does not already include an appropriate folder for the selected document type, Windows creates the folder. In Figure 14-7, for example, the folder F:\Craig\Music did not exist before we changed the default save location for music. Also note that the previous save folder (in this case, C:\Users\Craig\Music) becomes a public save location. If you subsequently change the default save location again, the

CHAPTER 14

previous save location remains in the library (and, of course, the folder and its contents also remain). You can change the library locations by using the Manage command in File Explorer.

➤ **For information about libraries, see "Working with libraries" in Chapter 12.**

Using Storage Spaces

Storage Spaces is a technology introduced with the server editions of Windows in 2012 and with Windows 8 and Windows 8.1. The technology allows you to aggregate collections of disks into "storage pools" and then create virtualized disks ("storage spaces") within those pools. For example, you could take two 3-TB disks (Serial-Attached SCSI, Serial ATA, or USB) and use Storage Spaces to create from them a single 6-TB virtualized disk.

You can also use Storage Spaces to establish resiliency for critical data. For example, using your two 3-TB disks, you could create a mirrored storage space in which each file saved on one of the physical disks is mirrored on the other; if one of the physical disks fails, your data is preserved.

Three types of resiliency are available:

- **Two-way mirror.** The system writes two copies of your data. You can lose one physical disk without data loss. A minimum of two physical disks is required. The amount of storage available is half of the total storage pool.

- **Three-way mirror.** The system writes three copies of your data. You can lose two physical disks without data loss. A minimum of three physical disks is required, and the amount of storage available is one-third of the storage pool.

- **Parity.** The system stripes data across physical disks while also maintaining parity information that allows it to protect and recover your data more efficiently in the event of drive failure. A minimum of three drives is required.

Simple (nonresilient) storage spaces are recommended if you require a large virtual disk in preference to separate physical disks. You might make this choice, for example, if you have a very large media collection and several older (hence smaller) disks that are not currently in service. Simple storage spaces are also a good choice for space-intensive operations (video editing, for example) that do not require resiliency. Files in a simple storage space are striped across physical disks, resulting in better performance.

Use parity for maximum resiliency, but note that write performance is degraded by the requirement for the system to calculate and store parity information. This choice might be ideal for archival storage.

Note the following:

- You can create a storage space only on freshly formatted blank disks. Storage Spaces will erase all data on the physical components of a pool (with due warning to you, of course) before setting up the storage space, and such erased data cannot be recovered via the Recycle Bin or other data-recovery tools.

- Storage spaces should not be used as a substitute for backups. They do not protect you against theft, fire, or other comparable adversities.

To set up a storage space, type **storage spaces** in the search box. (Or you can go to Control Panel and search for it there.) Click Create A New Pool And Storage Space and respond to the UAC prompt. A display comparable to the one shown next appears.

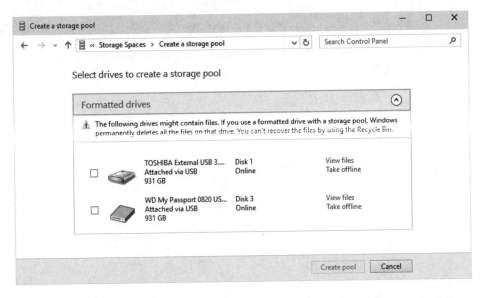

After noting the warning about the erasure of existing data on the available drives, select the drives you want to use, and then click Create Pool. The Create A Storage Space window appears, as shown next.

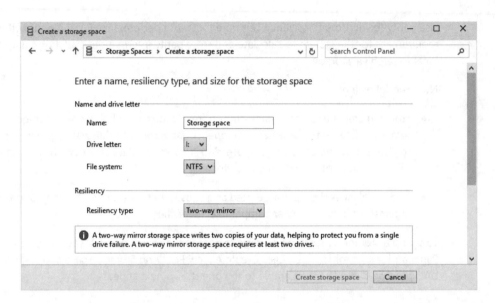

Choose a drive letter, file system, and resiliency type, and then click Create Storage Space.

For much more information about Storage Spaces, see *bit.ly/storage-spaces* and *bit.ly/storage-spaces-faq*.

System maintenance and performance

Expectations for how a Windows 10 device should perform are defined by a host of factors. Among them is your threshold of patience, but for big jobs, such as converting and editing video files, time is literally money. For those tasks it's worth spending a little effort tweaking and tuning to shave a few minutes off the time needed to complete them.

For the most part, Windows 10 works acceptably out of the box. Yes, it's possible to improve performance for some tasks, but we don't believe there is a secret formula, magic bullet, or special MakeRocketShipGoFast registry value that will suddenly send your system zooming into warp speed. Our formula for getting great performance out of a Windows PC is much more prosaic: start with quality parts, make sure everything has the right drivers and is up to date, and then look at ways to speed you through your workday and make games go faster.

We also know that performance problems can crop up unexpectedly. This chapter covers a number of tools that you can use to establish a performance baseline and identify the cause of performance issues. Our goal in this chapter is to help you measure performance accurately and to understand the routine maintenance tasks that can keep a system running smoothly and prevent performance problems from occurring in the first place.

We begin with the single most important maintenance tool of them all: Windows Update.

Keeping Windows up to date

In Windows 10, the Windows Update service delivers security fixes, performance and reliability improvements, and updated device drivers, just as its predecessors have done for two decades. But this release also assigns a crucial new role to this core Windows feature. In the "Windows as a Service" model, Windows Update delivers regular upgrades to Windows 10, with new and improved features alongside the bug fixes.

Windows Update and its associated services, such as the Background Intelligent Transfer Service (BITS), should run automatically, with little or no attention required from you. We strongly suggest checking in at regular intervals to confirm that updates are being delivered as expected and that the various Windows Update services are working properly.

Inside OUT

Don't fear automatic updates

Over the past decade, Microsoft and other software companies, large and small, have occasionally delivered updates that caused new problems. Among conservative IT pros and Windows experts, it became practically dogma to stand out of the line of fire when updates were first released. Historically, problematic updates are usually identified within the first week or two and either pulled or fixed, making it safe to deploy them after a suitable delay.

So why are things different this time around? Are monthly updates in Windows 10 more trustworthy than their predecessors? The crucial difference is the introduction of the Windows Insider program, which allows a large group of early adopters to test updates in the Fast and Slow Insider tracks before updates are released to the general population.

Yes, it's still possible for a seemingly innocuous update to cause problems for some users, but the risk is much lower now because those updates will have been tested more fully than ever before. For truly mission-critical systems, where any downtime could be disastrous and a conservative approach is imperative, consider upgrading to Windows Enterprise edition, where the Long Term Servicing Branch is available.

One major change in the servicing model for Windows is likely to dismay traditionalists who want the option to sort through updates at their leisure, accepting some, delaying others, and rejecting still others.

In recent years most newly discovered vulnerabilities in Windows have been patched quickly—usually before they became widespread problems. In fact, many of the worst outbreaks were based on vulnerabilities that had been patched months or years earlier. Windows users who installed the updates promptly were able to avoid infection, whereas those who failed to keep their systems updated fell victim. With Windows 10, Microsoft has taken additional steps to ensure that more systems are updated quickly—namely by installing updates automatically in many cases.

Windows 10 has no supported mechanism for consumers and small businesses to skip individual updates, although it's possible to choose the installation time for the next batch of updates, which has the practical effect of postponing updates for several days.

The level of control you have over how and when updates are installed depends on which edition of Windows you have and on settings controlled by your network administrator:

- With Windows 10 Home, new features, bug fixes, and security updates are pushed to your computer automatically. You don't need to take any additional action aside from observing the occasional reminders to restart your computer. (When Windows does require a restart, you can control when it occurs, as shown next.) As a result, Windows 10 Home systems are always up to date; users who want to skip or postpone certain updates do not have that option. In Microsoft parlance, this servicing "ring" is called the Current Branch.

● Users of Windows 10 Pro can use the default settings and receive Current Branch servicing. An additional option, not available in Windows 10 Home, allows you to select Defer Upgrades from the Windows Update Advanced Options page. This option shifts update delivery to the Current Branch for Business; security updates arrive through Windows Update when they are released, but feature upgrades are delayed several months, until they have been thoroughly tested by users in the Insider preview program and by the general public in the Current Branch. Administrators can use an update manager, Windows Update for Business, to deploy this policy throughout a network.

● Organizations that deploy Windows 10 Enterprise get the same servicing options as Windows 10 Pro: they can receive all features, fixes, and security updates immediately via Windows Update and Current Branch, or they can configure updates with Current Branch for Business to receive them under the direction of an administrator using Windows Update for Business. Enterprises also have the option to manage updates using Windows Server Update Services (WSUS). One additional option is available: the Long Term Servicing Branch. Like Current Branch for Business, this option allows system administrators to control when updates are installed using Windows Update for Business or WSUS. But they can also opt to install only security updates, without installing any new features.

● Windows 10 Education, which most closely resembles Windows 10 Enterprise in terms of features, has the same update servicing options as Windows 10 Pro.

➤ **For a full discussion of how Microsoft delivers security updates, see "Staying on top of security updates" in Chapter 7, "Securing Windows 10 devices."**

The tools for managing updates are no longer in the old-style Control Panel. Search for **Windows Update** and the following results, all included as part of the modern Settings app, should appear at the top of the results list:

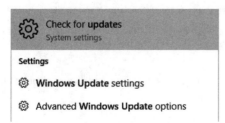

CHAPTER 15

Click or tap Check For Updates to open the Windows Update page in Settings. A list of available updates appears at the top of the page. If the updates have been installed and require a restart, you see a suggested restart time similar to the one shown in Figure 15-1.

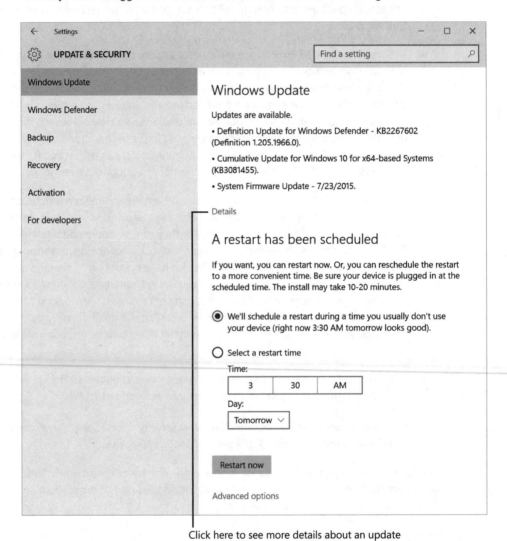

Click here to see more details about an update

Figure 15-1 In Windows 10, updates are installed automatically. If one or more updates requires a restart, you can adjust the suggested time to one that's more convenient.

If the suggested time is inconvenient, click Select A Restart Time and then choose an alternative time and day from the respective controls.

You also have the option of restarting manually. This option is ideal if you know you're going to be away from the PC for a meeting or lunch break that will last longer than the few minutes it takes to install a batch of updates. Save your existing work and close any open files, then click Restart Now. Be sure to wait for all open apps to close before you head out the door. It's highly annoying (and a big drag on productivity) to come back from a meeting and discover that the restart hasn't taken place because a dialog box was open, waiting for your okay.

In previous Windows versions, you had a wide range of configuration options for Windows Update. In Windows 10, the Advanced Options list contains the three items shown in Figure 15-2.

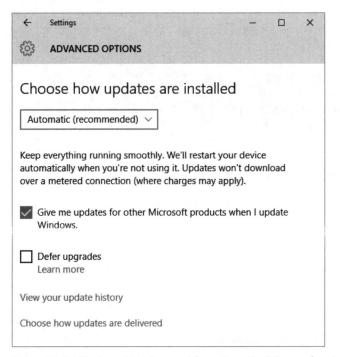

Figure 15-2 Windows 10 is designed for automatic delivery of updates, with only a few configuration options available.

As we noted earlier, the default Windows Update settings allow Windows 10 to install updates and restart automatically if necessary. You can exert slightly more control over the process by changing the Choose How Updates Are Installed option to Notify To Schedule Restart. You can't delay the restart indefinitely, however. If you haven't responded to the notification within six days, the system restarts automatically, typically overnight.

CHAPTER 15

The first check box in the middle of the page allows you to expand the scope of Windows Update to include other Microsoft products, such as perpetual-license versions of Microsoft Office. A second check box allows you to defer large upgrades while still allowing important security updates to be installed. This option is especially useful if you're traveling and can't afford the bandwidth or the time required to install a major upgrade package.

Two other options are available via subtle links at the bottom of the Advanced Options page.

Click Choose How Updates Are Delivered to open the page shown in Figure 15-3. This peer-to-peer feature, which is new in Windows 10, allows you to share updates with devices on your local network rather than requiring a connection to Microsoft's update servers. In a small office or lab, this can significantly reduce the amount of data you download through your Internet connection. The last option allows you to share updates over the Internet at large, using Microsoft's peer-to-peer service.

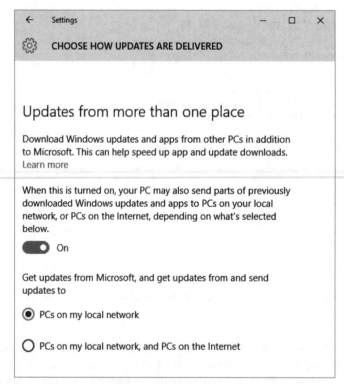

Figure 15-3 Enabling this peer-to-peer option can speed up installation of large updates on a small network, reducing the demands on your Internet connection.

Clicking the View Your Update History link shown in Figure 15-2 reveals a list that includes the name of each installed Windows update, the date on which it was installed, and a link that includes the update's KB number.

Most of the options for Windows Update have been moved to the modern Windows 10 Settings app. Clicking the Uninstall Updates option on the View Your Update History page reveals a noteworthy exception, as shown in Figure 15-4. This list, which uses the old-style Control Panel interface, displays all updates that have been installed for Windows and other Microsoft products using Windows Update.

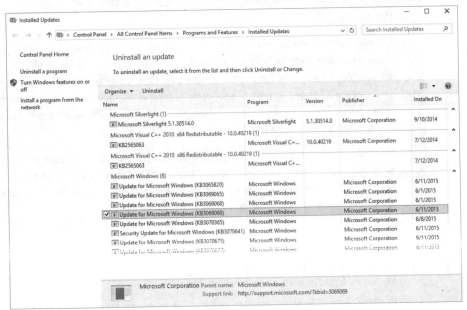

Figure 15-4 If an update is causing problems, you can select it from this list and use the Uninstall option to remove it for troubleshooting purposes.

From this page, you can confirm that a particular update has been installed by referring to its KB number in the list of installed items. A support link at the bottom of the page lets you see details about the selected update. The Uninstall option appears above the list and allows you to remove an update. This option should be a last resort for troubleshooting and used only when you suspect that a recently installed update is causing serious performance or reliability issues.

CHAPTER 15

Inside OUT

Other software needs updates, too

On a typical Windows PC, it's not unusual to find many apps, services, plug-ins, and utilities that also update themselves automatically. Microsoft Edge and Internet Explorer include Adobe's Flash Player, for example, which is updated automatically through Windows Update. Third-party browsers that support Flash-based content require separate updates for the Flash Player plug-in. Likewise, it's crucial to ensure that Oracle's Java, which is regularly targeted by malware writers, has the most recent security updates.

Other programs and features you're likely to use on a PC running Windows 10 also require updates. This list includes Microsoft Office and Office 365 and offline content for the Maps app. Apps acquired from the Windows Store automatically update themselves as well. Many third-party programs and services, including web browsers and cloud-based file-storage services, include their own updaters, which typically run in the background or as scheduled tasks.

In general, it's a good idea to allow these updaters to run. Studies have shown repeatedly that most malware arrives through exploits that target vulnerabilities for which security patches have long been available. Keeping all installed software up to date is an excellent way to avoid being a victim.

TROUBLESHOOTING

Windows Update is stuck in a reboot loop

In some cases, Windows Update can get stuck in a loop, unable to complete the installation of one or more updates and continually repeating the unsuccessful update process each time you restart.

The solution? Reset Windows Update completely, removing content from the update cache and starting with fresh downloads. In most cases, that's enough to get things unstuck.

Microsoft has created a help resource for diagnosing and fixing Windows Update problems, which is available at *support.microsoft.com/kb/971058*. At the time we wrote this chapter, the automated Fix-It tool on that page was not yet compatible with Windows 10. As an alternative, you can follow the manual instructions on that page, which involve stopping several services, removing the folder containing updates in progress, and reregistering a list of system files.

Mastering Task Manager

The easiest way to open Task Manager is with its keyboard shortcut, Ctrl+Shift+Esc. (You can also press Ctrl+Alt+Delete and then click or tap Task Manager.) Task Manager's instant accessibility is its most endearing trait, especially when something appears to have gone awry. Its executable file, Taskmgr.exe, runs at a Base Priority of High, allowing it to kick into action even when another program running at Normal priority is refusing to surrender control. When you need to stop an application (or process) that doesn't respond to the usual measures, or if your system suddenly slows down and you want to know who's eating your processor cycles, Task Manager is your best friend.

If you're upgrading from Windows 7, you're in for a treat. The new Task Manager debuted in Windows 8, and in our humble opinion it is awesome. We'll repeat that keyboard shortcut, Ctrl+Shift+Esc, because we think every Windows user should memorize it. Pressing that combination opens Task Manager using the simple view shown in Figure 15-5.

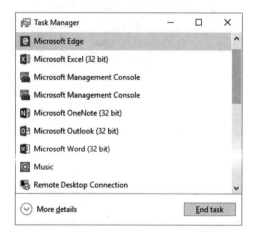

Figure 15-5 In its Fewer Details view, Task Manager shows only apps that were started by the current user, with the option to end a task that is nonresponsive.

The short list shows only processes that were started by and can be directly controlled by the current user account. If a program has hung, you'll see "Not responding" after its entry in the list, and you can use the End Task button to kill the app and start fresh.

Click More Details to see Task Manager in all its multitabbed, information-rich glory. Figure 15-6 shows this dramatically expanded display, with the Processes tab selected.

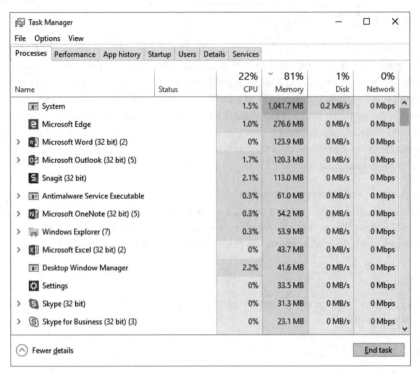

Figure 15-6 In the More Details view, Task Manager includes a much longer list of running processes, with real-time performance information for each one.

Although the list of running apps in Figure 15-6 looks similar to the one in the simpler view, scrolling down reveals a much longer list, grouped into three categories: Apps, Background Processes, and Windows Processes. Processes that have multiple child windows have an arrow at their left, allowing you to expand the entry and see the titles of Microsoft Office document windows, Skype sessions, and the like.

You can end a task in the Apps group with minimal consequences (you'll lose any unsaved work); however, attempting to end a task in the Windows Processes group is equivalent to pulling the plug on Windows, as the following stern warning message makes clear:

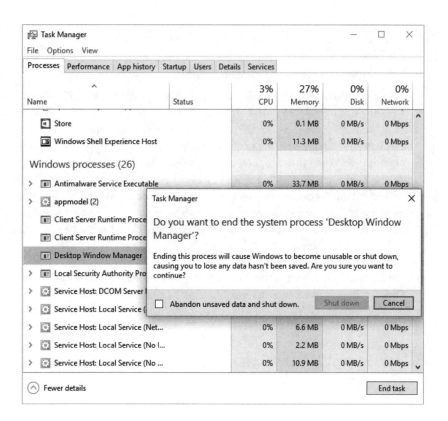

In the More Details view the totals at the top of each of the four performance-related headings show total resource use for that category. You can click any column heading to sort by that value, making it possible to see at a glance which program is hogging the CPU or using more memory than its fair share. (We discuss performance monitoring strategies in more detail later in this chapter.)

Inside OUT

Why is the System process using so much memory?

Any experienced Windows user who has tracked per-process memory usage in previous versions of Windows might be startled to see the System process using far more RAM than it seemingly should (look back at Figure 15-6 for an example). Relax. That's not a bug; it's a feature, specifically a new memory-management subsystem that improves performance by compressing memory pages for processes you haven't used recently. If the system needs the memory, it will reclaim it quickly by flushing those compressed pages to disk.

Inside OUT

Restart Explorer.exe to fix shell-related problems

In the expanded view of Task Manager, you'll find an entry for Windows Explorer under the Name heading on the Processes tab. If you have multiple File Explorer windows open, each of them will be listed as a child task under that heading. Occasionally, for any of a variety of reasons, the main Windows shell process (Explorer.exe) can become unresponsive. When that happens, clicking the taskbar or Start button does nothing, and the search box is unusable as well. The cure? Open Task Manager, select Windows Explorer on the Processes tab (it might be in any of the three groups), and look in the lower right corner, where the button normally labeled End Task now reads Restart. Click this button to close all existing instances of Explorer.exe and restart the Windows shell.

When you right-click any item in the Processes list, you'll see several choices on a shortcut menu. Click Go To Details to jump to Task Manager's Details tab.

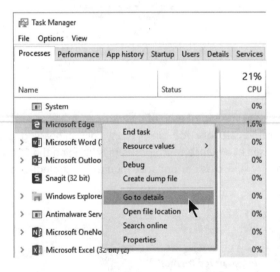

Windows veterans will feel right at home on the Details tab, which is a dense, data-rich list that was the default view in Task Manager in Windows 7 and earlier editions. It shows the executable file for the original process, along with technical details like those shown in Figure 15-7.

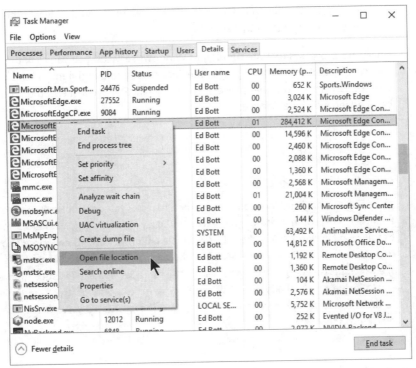

Figure 15-7 To show an executable file in its parent folder, select the item on the Details tab and then use the Open File Location option on the shortcut menu.

As with the Processes tab, right-clicking any entry on this list displays a shortcut menu with some technical options. The four at the bottom of the menu are most useful for troubleshooting:

- Click Open File Location to locate the file responsible for the running process. Often, just knowing which folder this file appears in is enough to help ease your mind about a process with a name and description that don't provide useful details.

- Click Search Online to open a browser window and pass the name and description of the selected executable file to the default search engine. This is a useful way to get additional information about a mysterious file, but beware of information from unknown and untrusted sources—the search results occasionally lead to scam sites bent on convincing you to buy bogus security software.

- The Properties menu choice leads directly to the properties dialog box for the associated executable file, where the Details tab includes copyright information and other relevant data drawn from the file itself. That information can help you decide whether a file is legitimate or needs further investigation.

- Finally, for processes that are running as Windows services, you can click the Go To Service(s) option, which takes you to the Services tab and highlights all the individual services associated with that process. For an instance of Svchost.exe, the list might number a dozen individual services.

Inside OUT

Get to know the Process ID column

The default arrangement of columns on the Processes tab does not include the Process Identifier (PID) column, although you can add it by right-clicking any visible column heading and clicking PID in the list of available columns. The PID column is shown by default on the Details and Services tabs, where it's extremely useful in enabling you to see which processes are running as part of the same Svchost.exe instance. To find out what's inside a particularly busy Svchost process, make a note of its PID and then switch to the Services tab and sort by the PID column. The associated services will appear in a block using that PID.

As was true with its predecessors, Task Manager's Details tab includes the option to display many more columns than the handful that are shown by default. To add or remove columns, right-click any visible column heading and then click Select Columns. That action opens the dialog box shown in Figure 15-8.

The list of available columns is overwhelming and highly technical. Some provide interesting information you can't find elsewhere, though. For example, on a device running 64-bit Windows 10, the Platform column lets you sort 32-bit and 64-bit processes quickly, while the Elevated column distinguishes processes that are running with full administrative privileges (usually in the context of the SYSTEM account). If you're experiencing issues with display corruption, show the GDI Objects column and then sort its values in descending order to locate processes that might be to blame.

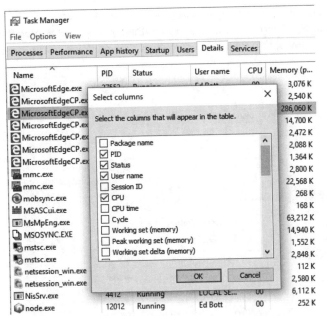

Figure 15-8 If you're comfortable interpreting technical information about resources associated with a running process, you can add columns to the Details tab in Task Manager.

Managing startup programs and services

One of the most common performance problems occurs when Windows automatically loads an excessive number of programs at startup. The result, especially on systems with limited resources, can be unpleasant: startup takes an unnecessarily long time, applications that you never use steal memory from programs you use frequently, and the page file, which swaps programs and data from memory to disk when RAM fills up, gets more of a workout than it should. Some programs, such as antivirus utilities, need to start up automatically. But in many cases, you're better served by running programs when you need them and closing them when they're not needed.

Overcrowded startups are often a "feature" on computer systems sold in retail outlets, where Windows is preinstalled along with a heaping helping of applications. In some cases, the bundled programs are welcome, but a free software program is no bargain if it takes up memory and you never use it.

CHAPTER 15

Task Manager's Startup tab, shown in Figure 15-9, lets you see at a glance which programs are starting automatically. Using the Disable button or the equivalent option on the shortcut menu, you can disable any option that you determine is slowing down your system.

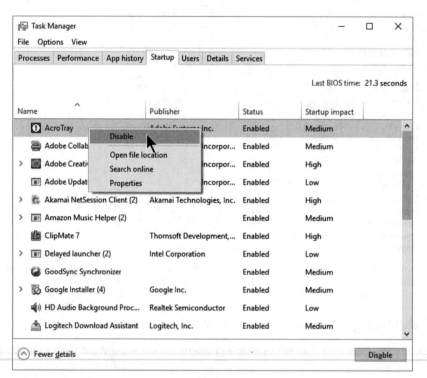

Figure 15-9 The Startup tab in Task Manager shows all programs that start automatically with Windows, with an easy option to disable those you prefer to start manually.

By default, the Startup tab shows only a gross measurement of the effect of a program on startup time. This value is displayed under the Startup Impact heading as High, Medium, or Low. To discover more details about the precise impact of an app that runs at startup, right-click the column headings on the Startup tab and add the two columns shown next—Disk I/O At Startup and CPU At Startup—which quantify just how much disk activity and CPU usage occur when the program starts.

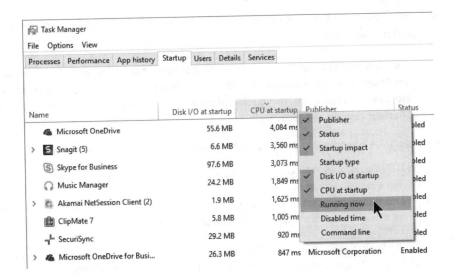

Managing disk space

At the dawn of the Windows 10 era, several long-term trends have converged to make data storage more of a performance issue than it has been in years.

For many years, the trend with conventional hard disks was simple: more storage space at a lower cost per gigabyte. Each new Windows version required more space than its predecessor, but the accompanying new generation of hardware meant there was plenty of room for system files and data.

The advent of solid state drives (SSDs) and flash memory changed all that. SSDs are dramatically faster than conventional hard disks. They're also more reliable than hard disks because they have no moving parts. But SSDs are far more expensive per gigabyte than conventional hard disks, causing PC makers to choose smaller default disks for new PCs. Couple that trend with the arrival of small, cheap tablets that run Windows 10 with 32 GB of total storage or less and you have a recipe for chronic space shortage.

On a desktop PC, you have the option to expand storage by replacing the primary drive with one that's faster, larger, or both; on most full-size desktop PCs, you can also install additional drives to make room for extra data files. Many portable devices, on the other hand, provide built-in primary storage that is soldered to the system board and can't be replaced. For some portable devices, the option to expand storage using inexpensive removable media is available. Microsoft's Surface Pro 3, for example, includes a slot that accepts up to 128 GB of removable storage in the form of a MicroSD card, which can be treated as dedicated storage and used for File History.

> ➤ For a full discussion of the ins and outs of managing hard drives and SSDs in Windows 10, see Chapter 14, "Managing disks and drives." For a discussion of how to use removable storage for backup, see "Using File History to protect files and folders" in Chapter 16, "Backup, restore, and recovery."

Managing storage on a Windows 10 device involves two separate challenges:

- Setting default file locations to make best use of available storage, and

- Performing occasional maintenance to ensure that useful space (especially on the system drive) isn't being wasted with unnecessary files.

For an overview of how much total storage is available and what's in use on a Windows 10 device, open Settings, System, and then click or tap Storage to see a page like the one shown in Figure 15-10. This example shows a desktop PC with a 500-GB SSD used as the system drive (C) and a much larger (3-TB) hard drive configured as drive D.

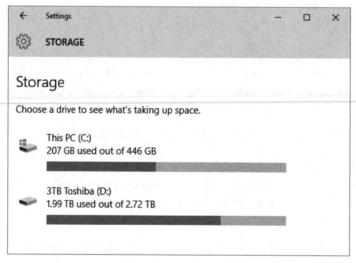

Figure 15-10 The Storage page in Settings shows all available disks, with an indication of how much space is currently in use on each one.

Inside OUT

Why is actual storage capacity lower than advertised disk sizes?

When you use Microsoft's built-in disk utilities to view the storage capacity of a disk, the capacity is reported by using the binary system (base 2) of measurement: 1 KB is 1,024 bytes, 1 MB is 1,024 KB, 1 GB is 1,024 MB, and so on. Thus, measured in binary terms, 1 GB is calculated as 1,073,741,824 bytes. But the makers of storage devices and the PC makers who build SSDs and hard disks into their products typically advertise storage using the convenient metric that 1 GB is equal to 1 billion bytes. That difference is why a system advertised with 32 GB of storage displays only about 28 GB when detailed in Disk Management and other Windows tools. Fortunately, those same tools also report the number of bytes of storage, which allows more accurate comparisons with the advertised space.

With small portable devices, you can accomplish the same goal, on a smaller scale, by installing an expansion card. Figure 15-11, for example, shows a Surface Pro 3 with a 128-GB SSD as the system drive and a 128-GB Micro SDXC card used for data storage.

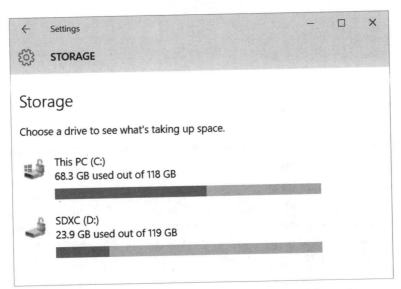

Figure 15-11 Adding a removable Micro SDXC card doubled the total storage capacity of this Windows 10 PC.

CHAPTER 15

Regardless of how many drives are available, you can see which types of files are using that space. Open Storage in Settings and click any drive to show a breakdown of storage space in use, color coded by file type as in Figure 15-12.

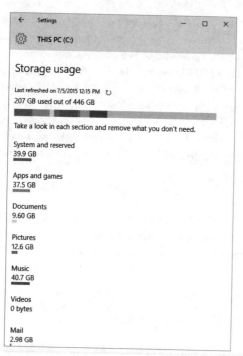

Figure 15-12 This is just the start of a long list that displays a detailed breakdown of how much space is in use, grouped by type of file.

Click or tap any category to see more details about what's in it. Here are some examples of what you'll find in each category:

- **System And Reserved.** This category is typically large and includes files that are essential to the operation of the system. The actual amounts of storage in use depend on the type of device and how much memory it contains. Figure 15-13, for example, shows the breakdown for this category on a Windows 10 desktop PC with 16 GB of RAM (note in particular the large hibernation file).

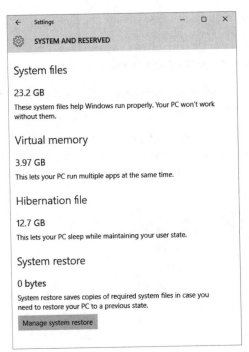

Figure 15-13 The System And Reserved category shows how much space is in use by Windows, space reserved for virtual memory, and hibernation files.

- **Apps And Games.** This category includes default apps as well as those you have downloaded from the Windows Store.

  In theory, you can relocate apps to a secondary drive, such as a MicroSD card, preserving space on the system drive. This feature is not enabled in the initial release of Windows 10 for PCs and tablets, although it works as expected on Windows 10 Mobile.

- **Documents, Pictures, Music, Videos.** These separate categories show how much space is in use in the default save locations for the respective files types. Note that this value is not the total found in the libraries of the same names.

- **Mail.** This value measures the space used by local copies of messages saved using the default mail app. Clicking or tapping the Manage Mail button will take you to the default email app: Mail or Microsoft Outlook, for example.

- **OneDrive.** The total amount of space occupied by local copies of files synced from OneDrive.

- **Desktop.** This total should be small unless you use the desktop as a dumping ground for downloads and other potentially large files.

- **Maps.** If you have a large collection of offline maps, this category can get fairly large.

- **Other Users.** Displays the total amount of space in use for data files from other user accounts, not broken down by file types.

- **Temporary Files.** This category includes files that are managed by Windows but are not typically necessary for the operation of a Windows 10 device. On the system shown in Figure 15-14, it's possible to recover more than 20 GB of storage space with a few clicks.

Figure 15-14 Several of the options in this category allow you to free up large amounts of disk space.

- **Other.** If you have large collections of files that don't slot into the standard categories, you might see a very large Other category. Figure 15-15 shows an example of the types of large files that might show up in this category, including Hyper-V virtual machines and associated VHD files, Windows image backups, and recorded TV programs.

Figure 15-15 Developers and IT pros are likely to have large amounts of space in use for files that don't fit into standard categories and wind up under the Other heading.

As you click to navigate deeper into the categories in the Storage section of Settings, you'll find buttons and links that allow you to manage files contained in that category by using File Explorer.

On systems with multiple drives (including removable media), you can change the default location for specific file types. If you have a large music collection, for example, you might prefer to store MP3 files on an SD card rather than on your main system drive. To make that possible, open the Storage page in Settings and adjust the options under the Save Locations heading, as shown in Figure 15-16.

CHAPTER 15

Figure 15-16 You can change the default location for new files you save in default categories. Existing files remain in their current locations.

When you set the default save location for these categories to a secondary drive, Windows 10 creates folders on the secondary drive, with subfolders that correspond to the category name for each file type within a folder named after your user account name.

You can also examine how much storage is currently available and in use by opening File Explorer, right-clicking a disk icon in This PC, and then clicking Properties. Figure 15-17 shows an example of what you might see.

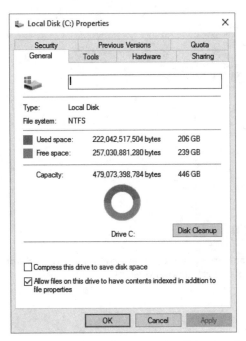

Figure 15-17 Open the properties dialog box for a disk to see the total disk capacity and how much space is in use. Click Disk Cleanup to open the utility of the same name.

Click Disk Cleanup to run the utility of the same name (Cleanmgr.exe). Note that this utility initially opens in standard user mode, allowing you to manage files available to your user account but blocking access to system files. To enable the full range of Disk Cleanup options, click Clean Up System Files and enter the credentials for an administrator account if necessary. That restarts the utility and unlocks access to the full range of cleanup options, as shown in Figure 15-18.

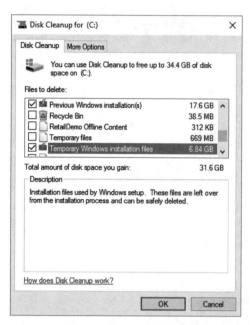

Figure 15-18 When you start Disk Cleanup using administrative credentials, you have the option to remove Windows installation files and previous Windows versions.

CAUTION

It's tempting to obsess over disk space usage and use every trick to create as much free space as possible. That strategy might come back to haunt you, however. If you remove previous Windows installations, for example, you lose the ability to roll back to a previous version to recover from compatibility problems. As a general rule, it's good to keep at least 20 percent of total disk capacity free. That allows enough room to process temporary files properly without affecting performance dramatically. Beyond that baseline, think long and hard before deleting what might be important files.

Power management and battery life

Power management features in Windows 10 can be broadly divided into two groups. Features in the first group apply universally to all Windows devices, even those that are permanently tethered to AC power. Allowing a PC or tablet to sleep or hibernate cuts the amount of power it consumes, which translates into monetary savings for you and a benefit for society at large.

For portable devices, including Ultrabooks, hybrid devices, and tablets, paying attention to power management has additional productivity benefits. Anything you do to extend the battery life of a portable device means you don't have to quit working because your battery has given up the ghost.

On a portable device, a flyout control, visible with a tap of the battery icon in the notification area, shows how much charge your battery is currently holding. If the device is disconnected from AC power, this display offers an estimate of how many hours and minutes you can continue working. If you're plugged in, the display shows how much longer until the battery is fully charged, as in the example in Figure 15-19.

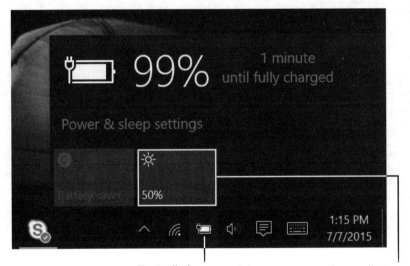

Tap to display power status   Tap to adjust screen brightness

Figure 15-19 Tap the battery icon on a portable device running Windows 10 to display this flyout control, which gives an up-to-date picture of your current battery status.

That battery indicator isn't just a status box, however. It's actually an entry point to multiple settings where you can fine-tune how a portable device uses power.

The screen brightness button, for example, cycles through brightness settings (25 percent, 50 percent, 75 percent, and 100 percent). Lowering the display brightness saves energy but makes the display dimmer and hence possibly more difficult to see well. For watching movies on a long-haul flight in a darkened jumbo jet, the power-saving setting has many advantages.

To adjust additional settings, click or tap Power & Sleep Settings. Figure 15-20 shows the corresponding options on a battery-equipped device—in this case, a Microsoft Surface Pro 3. (Although this option is also available in the Settings app on a desktop PC sans battery, only one option is available in each group, and the Wi-Fi option is missing completely. Other portable PCs may show a slightly different set of options, depending on which power-saving features are supported in hardware.)

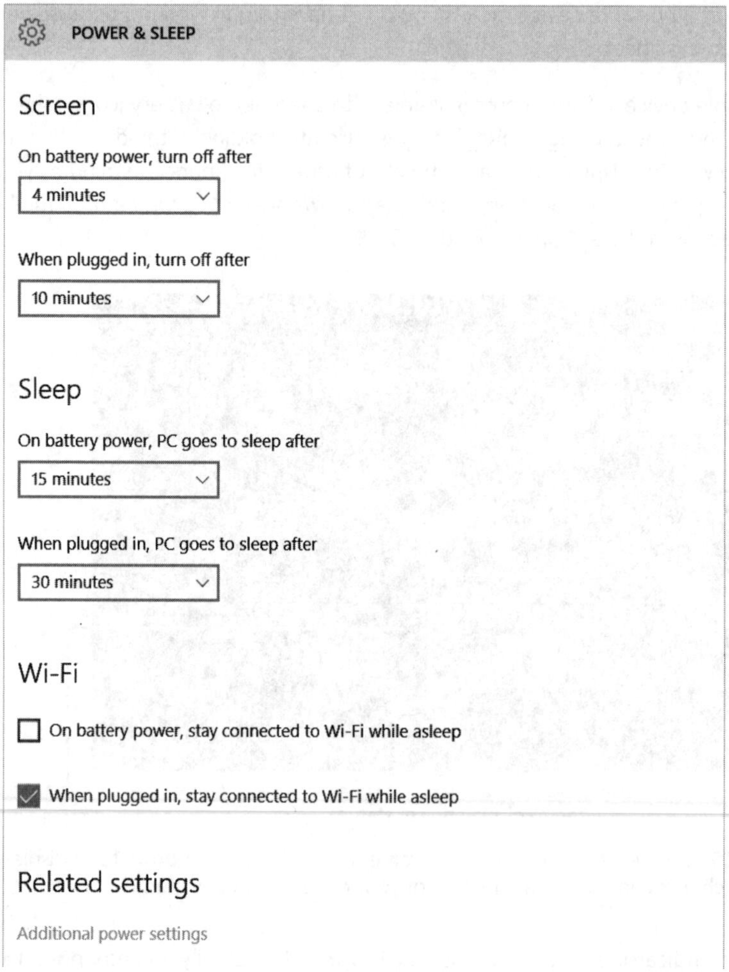

Figure 15-20 On a battery-powered device, you can fine-tune these settings for better performance when the device is plugged in to AC power and better battery life when it's unplugged.

As with several other Windows features, the transition of power-management settings from the traditional Control Panel to the modern Settings app is not yet complete. Clicking the Additional Power Settings link at the bottom of the Power & Sleep page in Settings opens the Power Options page in Control Panel, where you'll find an extensive selection of power settings, some extremely esoteric.

The old-school Power Options in Control Panel, shown in Figure 15-21, is based on power plans, which represent a collection of saved settings. With older versions of Windows, it wasn't uncommon to find at least three power plans, with a hardware maker sometimes defining its own plan as well. In the Windows 10 era, you're likely to find a single Balanced plan that should work for most use cases.

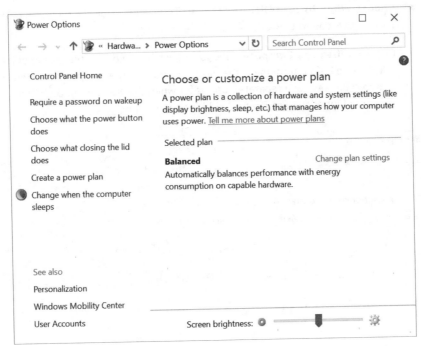

Figure 15-21 Default power options in Windows 10 include a single Balanced power plan. You can create additional plans for special purposes.

Your options here include the following (the list you see on a PC or mobile device will vary based on the capabilities of your hardware):

- **Require A Password On Wakeup.** This is an essential security option for a portable device or one that is in a place where it can be accessed by strangers or coworkers. For a home PC, you might choose the convenience of not requiring a password.

- **Choose What The Power Button Does.** These settings allow you to define whether pressing the power button shuts down the device, puts it to sleep, hibernates the device, turns off the display, or does nothing. If your device has multiple power, sleep, and/or standby buttons, you might see additional options here.

- **Choose What Closing The Lid Does.** This option, available on laptop devices, has the same choices as the previous option.

- **Create A Power Plan.** Click to copy the current settings to a new power plan, which then appears in the list of available plans and can be customized separately.

- **Choose When To Turn Off The Display.** This option, typically found on desktop systems, allows you to blank the screen to save energy.

- **Change When The Computer Sleeps.** Allows you to define the period of inactivity that must elapse before turning off the display or putting the computer to sleep. Battery-powered devices have separate options for when they're running on battery and when they are plugged in. (See Figure 15-22 for an example.)

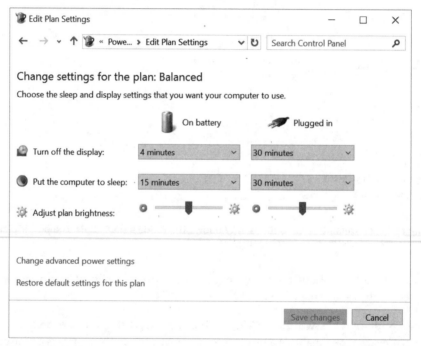

Figure 15-22 To maximize battery life on a portable PC, set the sleep option to the minimum acceptable amount. When the PC is plugged in, you might prefer to set the sleep option to a higher value for the convenience of instant access.

For each option, the choices in the drop-down list range from 1 minute (probably more annoying than most people will accept) to 5 hours (useful if you want the computer to sleep only when you're away for a long time). To disable either option, choose Never from the drop-down list.

If those options aren't sufficient, click the Change Advanced Power Settings option to open the advanced options dialog box shown in Figure 15-23.

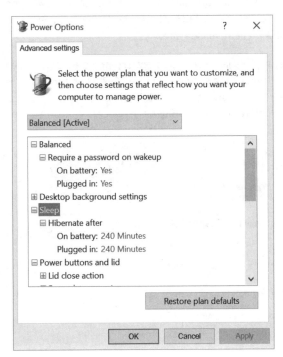

Figure 15-23 These advanced options give you incredibly granular control over power management settings in Windows 10.

Inside OUT

Adjust Hibernate options for maximum battery life

To maximize battery life on a portable device, make use of the Hibernate option, which shifts from Sleep mode at an interval you define. Hibernation saves the current state of the system as well as the contents of memory to a hidden file (Hiberfil.sys), and then shuts down the computer. That effectively cuts power use to zero. Resuming from hibernation is much faster than a cold start, and when you resume you're back where you left off, with apps and files open exactly as they were. To adjust this option, open the Advanced Settings dialog box and change the values in the Hibernate After setting under On Battery. Switching from the default 240 minutes to, say, 30 minutes can significantly extend the battery life of a device that you use intermittently.

A new feature in Windows 10, Battery Saver mode, allows you to apply a group of power-saving settings with a single click or tap. Battery Saver mode, which stops many background processes and limits notifications, kicks in automatically when the battery level drops below a predefined threshold; you can also turn on Battery Saver mode manually, even on a device with a fully charged battery, as a preventive measure.

To change settings for this feature (available only on a battery-powered device), search for **Battery Saver** and open the Settings page shown in Figure 15-24. For aggressive management of battery life, set the threshold higher than the default 20 percent. You can also define exceptions for background operation for critical apps.

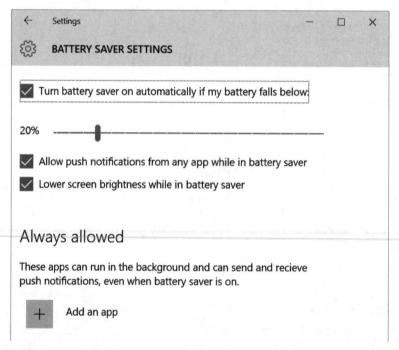

Figure 15-24 By default, your laptop or tablet goes into this aggressive battery-saving mode when your battery drops to 20 percent. You can adjust the settings to be more or less aggressive.

Monitoring and improving system performance

As we noted at the beginning of this chapter, the out-of-the-box performance of a Windows 10 PC should be acceptable, assuming that the device you're using is capable of the work you're asking it to perform. A small tablet with a low-power mobile processor will almost certainly struggle at a processor-intensive task like video processing, for example.

But even a workstation-class PC can perform poorly if you have a problem with a major subsystem or if Windows is configured incorrectly. In our experience, the most common causes of poor performance (in no particular order) are these:

- **Defective hardware.** Memory and disk errors are most obvious when they cause system crashes, but hardware-related problems can also cause performance to drag. Check with your hardware manufacturer to see what diagnostic tools are available.

- **Outdated or flawed device drivers.** PC and device makers are responsible for supplying drivers for the individual hardware components that go into their hardware. If you do a clean install, Windows might install a generic driver instead of one written specifically for that device. We have seen performance problems vanish immediately after a simple driver upgrade. Always be certain you're using the best possible drivers for all system devices. (Don't assume that a newer driver is automatically better than an older one, however; any driver update has the potential to cause new problems.)

- **Inadequate hardware resources.** Windows 10 should perform basic tasks well on even low-end hardware that was designed and built five or more years ago. But more demanding tasks, such as digital media encoding, can push some systems to the breaking point. The performance monitoring tools we identify later in this chapter should help you identify areas where hardware resources are being pushed to the limit.

- **Out-of-control processes or services.** Sometimes, a program or background task that normally runs just fine will spin out of control, consuming up to 100 percent of CPU time or grabbing increasing amounts of memory or other system resources. In the process, of course, performance of all other tasks slows down or grinds to a halt. Knowing how to identify and kill this sort of process or service and prevent it from recurring is a valuable troubleshooting skill.

  ➤ For instructions on how to identify programs that run automatically at startup or when you sign in, see "Managing startup programs and services" earlier in this chapter.

- **Malware.** Viruses, Trojan horse programs, spyware, and other forms of unwanted software can wreak havoc on system performance. Be sure to check for the possibility that malware is present on a system that exhibits otherwise unexplained performance problems.

CHAPTER 15

Windows 10 offers two valuable tools for monitoring the performance of your system in real time. To gain access to these tools, type **resource** in the search box. The two items shown here should appear at the top of the list.

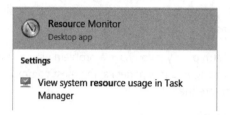

Task Manager has been a mainstay of Windows through many versions. It received a dramatic rewrite in Windows 8, adding detailed performance monitoring tools. For zeroing in on performance issues with even more detail, you can use an advanced tool called Resource Monitor. In combination, these tools allow you to keep an eye on CPU, memory, disk, and network usage, with the ability to isolate troublesome processes. We describe both of these utilities in detail in the following sections.

Monitoring performance with Task Manager

The Performance tab of Task Manager gives you a quick overview of your system's performance as measured in multiple dimensions, including CPU, memory, disk, and network usage. The small thumbnail graphs at the left report current data in real time; clicking any of these thumbnails displays a much larger version, with additional information below the chart. Figure 15-25 shows the performance data for a desktop PC, roughly 30 seconds after opening Task Manager.

The graphs to the right show 60 seconds' worth of data, with updates at one-second intervals. In Figure 15-25, for example, the CPU graph shows a large spike to 100 percent usage (which occurs, ironically, when you open Task Manager), followed by several additional spikes as other activities make demands on the CPU.

Keeping this pane open as you work allows you to see what the impact of a given activity is. For example, you might monitor CPU usage when encoding a video file to see whether the operation pins CPU usage at 100 percent; if so, that might be evidence that you need to upgrade your desktop PC to one with a more powerful CPU that's capable of doing the same work faster, generating less heat and allowing you to do other things while the task completes in the background.

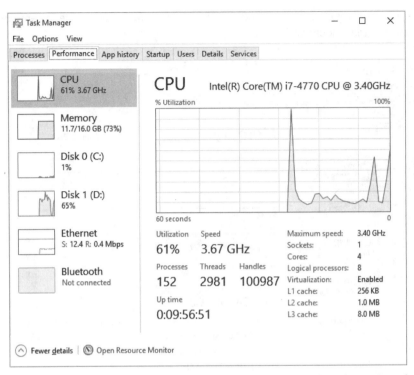

Figure 15-25 The Performance tab of Task Manager gives you a big-picture view of resource usage.

Inside OUT

How long has your PC been running?

Many of the details below the performance graph on the CPU tab in Task Manager are obscure and only of use to developers. You probably don't need to know how many handles are in use by your current workload, for example. But one detail here is interesting as a benchmark of stability. The Up Time measure shows the amount of time that has elapsed, in days, hours, minutes, and seconds, since the machine was last restarted. Thanks to monthly updates that include mandatory restarts, it's unlikely you'll ever see this number go beyond 30 days.

The Memory option offers a snapshot of memory usage, as shown in Figure 15-26. Note that the total amount of memory is visible above the graph, with details about the physical memory itself (number of sticks and slots, for example) below, alongside the amount of RAM in use and the amount available.

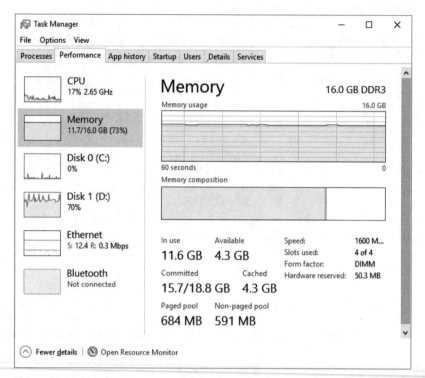

Figure 15-26 Use the Memory option on the Performance tab to see how much of your system's RAM is in use. If the value is at 100 percent, it's time to close some apps to improve performance.

On this page, a detailed Memory Composition bar chart appears below the main graph. At first glance, it appears to be just an alternate view of the main Memory Usage chart, but hover the mouse pointer over any segment to see its real purpose. The ScreenTips that appear over each segment explain what each one represents.

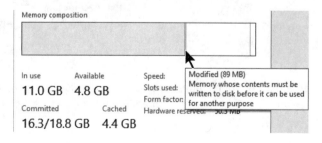

The Disk options, likewise, graph the performance of all nonremovable disks on the current system. Each disk gets its own entry on the left side, with details about the selected disk's performance on the right, as shown in Figure 15-27. The top graph depicts the percentage of time the disk is busy processing read or write requests; the bottom graph shows the disk transfer rate.

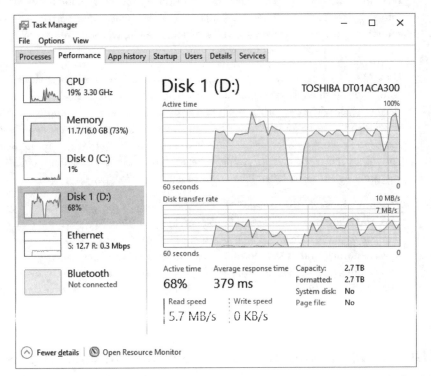

Figure 15-27 The Disk options in Task Manager let you see the throughput of a fixed disk and determine whether a particular activity is causing a bottleneck.

➤ For a discussion of how to use the networking performance information from Task Manager (Ethernet, Wi-Fi, and Bluetooth), see Chapter 5, "Networking essentials."

Inside OUT

What happened to the Windows Experience Index?

Beginning with Windows Vista, Microsoft published a set of numbers purporting to quantify your system's performance in five distinct areas. These numbers were merged into an overall score. In Windows 10, these values are no longer reported on the System Properties page. However, they're still available if you're willing to run the Windows System Assessment Tool (Winsat.exe).

Using WinSAT, as it's known for short, you can run a full performance analysis (type **winsat formal** at an elevated command prompt) or test individual Windows sub-systems (type **winsat –?** for the full syntax). You can also save the output as an XML file or redirect the verbal output of the tests to a text file for subsequent review. To see the most recent set of detailed results, type **winsat query** in a Command Prompt window. This report shows the raw test results instead of the Windows Experience Index scores and provides a more detailed look at your system's performance.

Windows keeps a history of WinSAT performance results that you can use for compari-sons. You'll find them in %SystemRoot%\Performance\WinSAT\DataStore, each one stamped with the date and time it was run. Minor variations in results between WinSAT runs are normal, and usually occur because of other processes and services interfering with resource usage. Keeping even an informal record of detailed results over time can help you determine whether a significant change in test scores is normal or a sign of a problem to be found and fixed.

Using Resource Monitor to pinpoint performance problems

Like the Performance tab in Task Manager, Resource Monitor gives you both instantaneous and recent-history readouts of key performance metrics. Also like Task Manager, Resource Monitor can show you, in excruciating detail, what each process is doing.

To open Resource Monitor, you can search for it from the Start menu or use its command line, **perfmon /res**, from an elevated Command Prompt window. But the fastest way is to click the link at the bottom of the Task Manager Performance tab. This is, in our opinion, the preferred way to use this utility. Start with a quick overview from Task Manager, and if you need more information call on Resource Monitor. (Note that you must supply administrative credentials to run this tool.)

When you first open Resource Monitor, you see the Overview tab shown in Figure 15-28, which provides both detailed tables and charts that summarize performance in four areas.

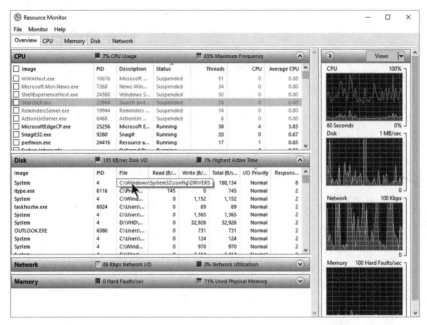

Figure 15-28 Use the check boxes in the top section of Resource Monitor to limit the results to a specific process. ScreenTips show details for files that are truncated in the list below.

Tabs along the top of the Resource Monitor window allow you to switch to a different context and focus on a specific type of resource usage. The basic layout of each tab is similar and consists of a handful of common elements.

One or more tables contain details about the resource featured on that tab. The first table on each tab is called the key table; it contains a list of all processes currently using the selected resource, with a check box to the left of each process that allows you to filter the data displayed in additional tables on the tab. The key table at the top of the Overview tab lists all running processes in a display that is similar to the Processes tab of Task Manager.

Resource Monitor is overkill for most performance troubleshooting tasks. But it shines when you want to see exactly which process or file is responsible for an unexplained burst of activity.

CHAPTER 15

Backup, restore, and recovery

In the Unabridged Edition of Murphy's Law, you'll find an entire chapter of corollaries that apply to computers in general and your important data files in particular. Murphy says, "Anything that can go wrong will go wrong." That's certainly true of hard disks and solid state drives (SSDs), where it's not a matter of whether they'll fail but when. When a hard disk fails catastrophically or an SSD suddenly becomes unreadable, any data files on that device are gone, as are your Windows installation and all your apps and settings.

Even if your hardware never lets you down, human error can wreak havoc with data. You can press the wrong key and inadvertently delete a group of files you meant to move. If you're not paying attention, you might absent-mindedly click the wrong button in a dialog box, saving a new file using the same name as an old one, wiping out a week's worth of work in the process.

Some of the most important new features in Windows 10 let you recover quickly from either type of disaster.

In this chapter, we explain how to use the backup tools included with Windows 10, which allow you to prepare for the inevitable day when you need to restore a lost file (or an entire drive's worth of files). We also explain your options for resetting Windows when the operating system becomes damaged, for whatever reason. And finally, we offer a guide to the venerable but still useful System Restore feature.

An overview of Windows 10 backup and recovery options

Through the years, the backup and recovery tools in Windows have evolved, but their fundamental purpose has not changed. How well you execute your backup strategy will determine how easily you're able to get back to where you were after something goes wrong—or to start over with an absolutely clean slate. When you reach into the recovery toolkit, you're hoping to perform one of the following three operations:

- **Full reset.** If you're selling or giving away a PC or other device running Windows 10, you can reset it to a clean configuration, wiping personal files in preparation for the new owner. Some Windows users prefer this sort of clean install when they just want to get a fresh start, minus any cruft from previous installations.

- **Recovery.** The "stuff happens" category includes catastrophic hardware failure, malware infection, and system corruption, as well as performance or reliability problems that can't easily be identified with normal troubleshooting. The recovery process involves reinstalling Windows from a backup image or a recovery drive.

- **File restore.** When (not if) you accidentally delete or overwrite an important data file or (ouch) an entire folder, library, or drive, you can call on a built-in Windows 10 tool to bring back the missing file. This same feature also lets you find and restore earlier versions of a saved file—an original, uncompressed digital photo, for example, or a Word document that contains a section you deleted and now want to revisit.

For quick access to the full range of options available, use the search box. Figure 16-1 shows the results for the keywords **backup** (left) and **recovery** (right).

Figure 16-1 These two sets of search results provide an excellent overview of your backup and recovery options in Windows 10.

In Windows 10, the primary built-in tool for backing up files is called File History. Its job is to save copies of your local files—every hour, if possible—so that you can find and restore your personal documents, pictures, and other data files when you need them.

Inside OUT

Integrating the cloud into your backup strategy

It's tempting to think of OneDrive and other cloud-based storage services as a primary backup. But that strategy is potentially dangerous as well. Cloud services can fail, and online accounts can be compromised. In either case, if your only backup is in the cloud, you risk losing files. And even when you think you have a backup, it might not be what you expect. Your cloud backups of photos, for example, might be converted to a lower resolution than the original images, meaning that your only copy of a priceless photo is an inferior compressed version.

Having a complete archive of files backed up to the cloud does offer the reassurance that you can recover any or all of those saved files in the event of an accident or natural disaster, such as a fire or flood, that wipes out your primary device and its separate local backup. Given the ubiquity and relatively low cost of online storage services, in fact, it's probably prudent to keep copies of important files in two separate cloud-based services. Just remember that those distant archives are not a replacement for comprehensive local backups on an external storage device or a networked PC.

File History was introduced in Windows 8 and has evolved since. Still, it's designed to be simple and not full featured, which is why Windows 10 also includes the old-style Windows 7 Backup And Restore tool. You'll find both backup solutions on the Backup page in Settings, under the Update & Security heading, as shown in Figure 16-2.

Despite its advanced age, the Windows 7 backup tool can still do one impressive digital magic trick that its newer rivals can't: It can create an image of the system drive that can be restored to an exact copy of the original saved volume, complete with Windows, drivers and utilities, desktop programs, settings, and data files. System image backups were once the gold standard of backup and are still a perfect way to capture a known good state for quick recovery.

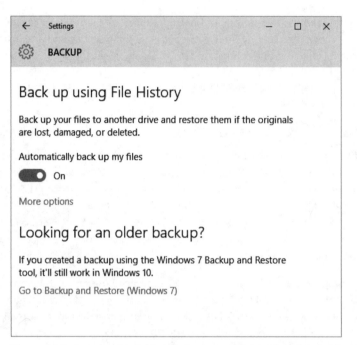

Figure 16-2 Once you've designated an external drive for File History, its controls are deceptively simple. For fine-tuning, click the More Options link.

The disadvantage of a full image backup is that it's fixed at a moment in time and doesn't capture files created, changed, or deleted since the image was created. If your primary data files are located in the cloud or on a separate volume from the system drive, that might not be a problem.

Over the decades, the clean install has taken on almost magical properties among some Windows users. This classic recovery option involves reinstalling Windows from installation media, installing custom drivers, rebuilding connections to network resources, restoring data files, reinstalling apps, and redoing individual preferences. You can still follow that old-school routine, if you're willing to spend the time and energy. But there are faster, easier ways in Windows 10.

In Windows 8, Microsoft formally introduced a "push button reset" feature with two options. Windows 10 simplifies this feature under a single Reset heading, which allows you to reinstall Windows with the option to keep or discard personal data files. This option allows you to reset a misbehaving system on the fly, rolling back with relative ease to a clean, fully updated Windows 10 installation minus any third-party programs or drivers that might be causing problems.

The Recovery page in Settings, which sits alongside Backup in the Update & Security group, gives the Reset option top billing, as shown in Figure 16-3. (The middle option, Go Back To An Earlier Build, is available because this machine is configured to receive preview releases of Windows 10 through the Windows Insider program. If you've upgraded to Windows 10 within the past month, you might see the option to go back to Windows 8.1 or Windows 7 in that middle position.)

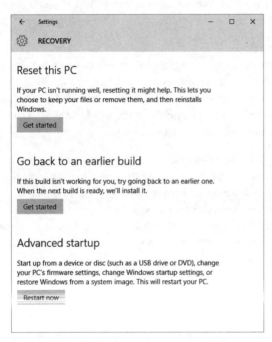

Figure 16-3 All of these recovery options allow you to reinstall Windows to work around performance problems or to get a fresh start.

Windows 10 also includes a built-in option to turn a USB flash drive into a bootable recovery drive. The recovery drive allows you to restore Windows, even after a complete system drive failure.

Inside OUT

Do you need the OEM recovery image?

The Windows 10 Reset feature, in a major change from Windows 8.1, is capable of reinstalling Windows without requiring a recovery partition or any external media. Instead, it uses the existing Windows system files to create a new, clean, side-by-side copy. The result, at least in theory, allows you to recover the sometimes significant disk space used by OEM recovery images.

The OEM image restores the device to its original, factory-installed configuration, complete with custom drivers and utilities as well as bundled (and potentially unwanted) software. Depending on when the machine left the factory, this option is likely to be significantly out of date. Unless you're running short of space for storing data, this partition is worth keeping on any device that's still under warranty.

You can safely remove the OEM recovery image if you are confident that you have a reliable way to restore your system to a clean image (to pass it along to a new owner, for example). Creating your own recovery drive or system image, as we explain in this chapter, fills either bill. Removing the OEM partition might require a trip to the Command Prompt window and some judicious use of the DiskPart utility, as we explain in "Managing disks from the command prompt" in Chapter 14, "Managing disks and drives."

In the remainder of this chapter, we discuss these backup and recovery options in more detail.

Using File History to protect files and folders

As we noted earlier, the File History feature was introduced in Windows 8 as a replacement for the Backup And Restore tool in Windows 7. Although you can delve into advanced settings if you dig deeply enough, File History is designed as a "set it and forget it" feature. After you enable this backup application, it first copies all files in the backup location and then scans the file system at regular intervals (hourly, by default), looking for newly created files and changes to existing files. Copies of each new or changed file are stored on a secondary drive, usually an external device.

You can browse the backed-up files by date and time—or search the entire history—and then restore any or all of those files to their original location or to a different folder.

But first, you have to go through a simple setup process.

Setting up File History

Although the File History feature is installed by default, it's not enabled until you designate a drive to serve as the backup destination. This can be a second internal hard disk or an external storage device, such as an external hard drive, or a network location.

CAUTION

Be sure you specify a File History volume that is on a separate physical drive from the one that contains the files you're backing up. Windows will warn you, sternly, if you try to designate a separate volume on the same physical drive as your system drive. The problem? One sadly common cause of data loss is failure of the drive itself. If the backups and original files are stored on the same drive, a failure wipes everything out. Having backups on a separate physical drive allows them to remain independent.

To turn on File History for the first time, open Settings, and then open the Backup page (under the Update & Security heading). Click Add A Drive to scan for available File History drives. Figure 16-4 shows a system that has a 32-GB external drive available for use as a File History location. Selecting that drive turns on the File History service and begins the hourly backup process.

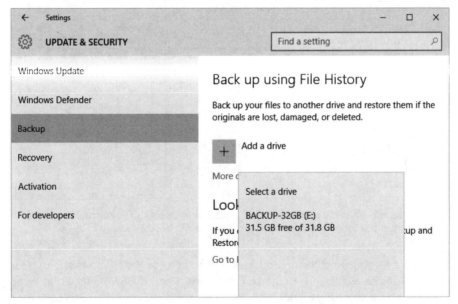

Figure 16-4 Before you can enable File History, you must specify a drive (preferably external) to hold the backed-up files.

When you first enable File History, it creates a full copy of all files in the locations you've des-ignated for backup. That list contains either the default locations or your customized list (we describe how to create a custom backup list in the next section).

The drive you designate as a File History drive must be either an internal or external hard drive (that category includes SSDs). Removable drives, such as USB flash drives, are not eligible. The File History setup wizard will show you only eligible drives when you set up File History for the first time.

In a home or small office that contains multiple computers, you have the option of specify-ing a shared network location as the File History location. This option is available only from the classic Control Panel; when prompted to select a File History drive, click the Add Network Location link below the list of available drives and browse to a network share where you have sufficient permissions. The newly added drive (in *servername**sharename* syntax) shows up in the list, as shown in Figure 16-5.

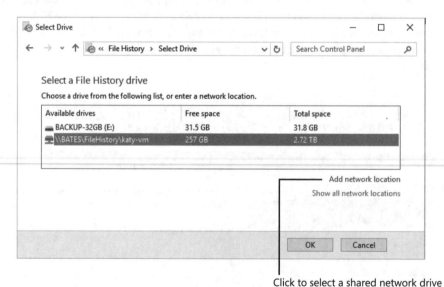

Click to select a shared network drive

Figure 16-5 After you successfully add a network location to File History, its full network path appears in this list of available destinations for saving backup history.

If the drive you select has previously been used as a File History destination, you see one addi-tional choice, as shown in Figure 16-6. After selecting a drive from the list at the top, you can choose an existing backup location. That option is the correct choice if you're reconnecting to a File History drive after successfully restoring Windows 10 and you want your old backups to be available as well.

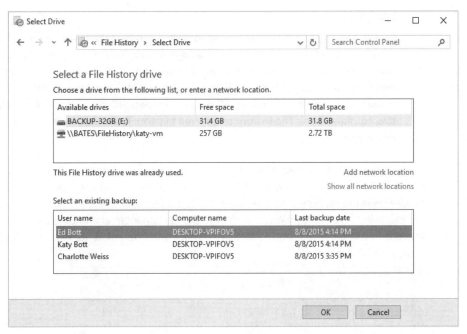

Figure 16-6 If the volume you select in the list above has already been used for File History, you need to select an existing backup from the list below.

There's nothing complicated or proprietary about File History volumes.

- When you use an external drive, Windows creates a FileHistory folder, with a separate subfolder for each user. Thus, on a device that includes multiple user accounts, each user's files can be backed up separately.

- Within each user's private folder are separate subfolders, one for each device backed up. This folder arrangement allows you to use a single external drive to record File History backups on different devices.

- Each individual backup set includes two folders. The Configuration folder contains XML files and, if necessary, index files to allow speedier searches. The Data folder contains backed-up files, which are stored in a hierarchy that matches their original location.

- Backed-up files are not compressed. File names are the same as the original, with a date and time stamp appended (in parentheses) to distinguish different versions. As a result, you can browse a File History drive in File Explorer and use search tools to locate a file or folder without using the File History app.

CHAPTER 16

CAUTION

Files stored on a File History drive are not encrypted by default. Anyone who has physical possession of the drive can freely read any files stored there. If you're concerned about confidential information contained in an external File History drive, we recommend that you encrypt the drive (see "Encrypting with BitLocker and BitLocker To Go" in Chapter 7, "Securing Windows 10 devices," for detailed instructions). As an alternative, consider saving File History to a shared network folder for which you have appropriate permissions.

File History is yet another example of a feature caught in the transition from the classic Windows Control Panel to the new Settings app. The overlap between old interface and new is more pronounced here than elsewhere. From the old Control Panel or the new Settings app, you can select a File History drive or change the backup interval and time period for saving backups. The latter two options, identical in effect but different in appearance, are shown here.

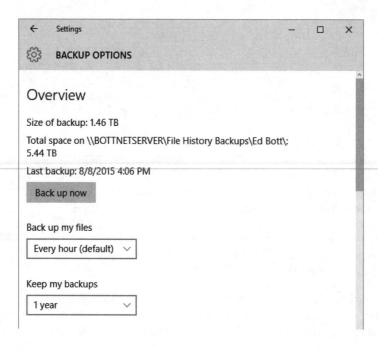

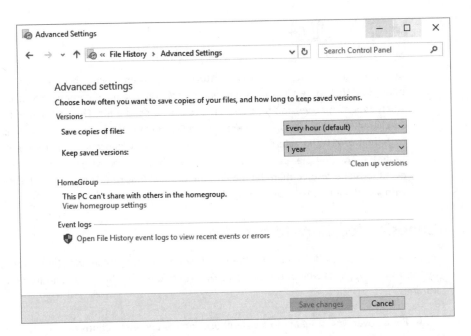

By default, File History checks your designated drives and folders once an hour, saving copies of any new or changed files as part of the operation. You can adjust this setting in either direction, choosing from nine intervals that range from every 10 minutes (if you really hate the idea of ever losing a saved file) to once daily.

File History backups are saved by default forever (you receive a warning when your File History drive is full), although you can alter the Keep Saved Versions setting to 1, 3, 6, or 9 months or 1 or 2 years. The set-it-and-forget-it Until Space Is Needed setting allows File History to automatically jettison old backups to make way for new ones when the drive is full.

As you can see, the options in Settings and Control Panel overlap but aren't identical. As of the initial release of Windows 10, for example, the options to share a File History drive with others in a homegroup and to quickly view File History event logs are available only in the Advanced Settings section of the classic Control Panel.

CHAPTER 16

TROUBLESHOOTING

Some files are missing from File History backups

Because of the unique way that File History organizes and names backed-up files, you might find that some files aren't backed up properly. The most common cause occurs when appending a version date and time to the name of a file. The addition of those 26 characters can cause the file name in the File History folder to exceed the maximum path limit of 260 characters. That situation is most likely to occur when a file is deeply nested inside multiple subfolders. You can spot these errors easily in the File History event logs and resolve them by moving the original files or subfolders to a location with a path name that's sufficiently shorter.

Choosing locations to back up

By default, File History backs up all folders in the current user profile (including those created by third-party apps) as well as the contents of local folders that have been added to custom libraries.

➤ For an overview of what's in a default user profile and instructions on how to work with libraries, see Chapter 12, "Organizing and searching for files."

To manage the list of folders backed up by File History, open the Backup page in Settings (under the Update & Security category) and then click More Options. Scroll down to view the folder list on the Backup Options page, as shown in Figure 16-7.

To remove any folder from this list, select its name and then click or tap Remove. To add a folder from any local drive, click or tap Add A Folder and then select the location using the Select Folder dialog box.

NOTE

Although the OneDrive folder is included by default in the list of folders to be backed up by File History, only files that are synced to the local drive are actually backed up.

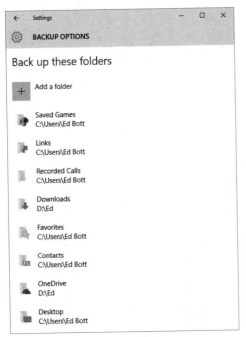

Figure 16-7 Individual profile folders relocated to a separate drive (as with the Downloads and OneDrive folders here) are automatically backed up by File History.

At the end of the list is an Exclude These Folders option, shown in Figure 16-8. It's useful when you want to avoid filling your File History drive with large files that don't require backing up. If you routinely put interesting but ephemeral video files into a subfolder in your Downloads folder, you might choose to exclude that Videos subfolder completely from File History, while leaving the rest of the Downloads folder to be backed up.

When a File History drive fills up, you can either change the settings to remove old backed-up files and make room for new ones or swap in a new drive. If you choose the latter option, click or tap the Stop Using Drive button on the Backup Options page, remove the old drive, and set up the new one.

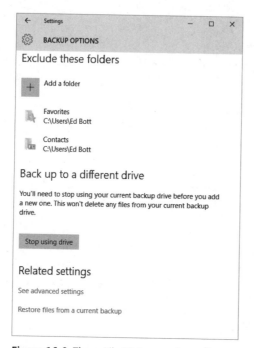

Figure 16-8 These File History options allow you to exclude folders that are part of a folder that would otherwise be backed up. The Stop Using Drive button lets you switch to a new File History drive.

Restoring files and folders

To find and restore a backed-up file, folder, or drive, you can use File Explorer or the File History app (C:\Windows\System32\FileHistory.exe).

The File Explorer option is the simplest way to locate a previous version of a file you've been working on, or to restore the contents of a folder as it existed at a specific date and time in the past.

Details of each previously saved copy are stored on the Previous Versions tab in the properties dialog box for a file, folder, or drive. To view this tab, open File Explorer, right-click the item whose history you want to inspect, and then click Restore Previous Versions. Figure 16-9 shows the history of an Excel spreadsheet with 10 saved versions from the previous week available.

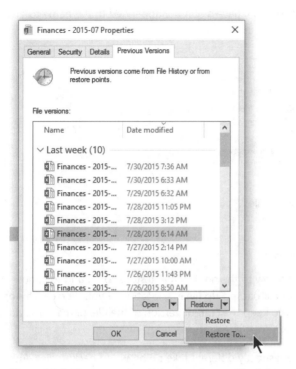

Figure 16-9 The properties dialog box for any file, folder, or drive lists available File History back-ups here. Open the file to see a read-only copy, or use the Restore To option to save a copy of the selected version in a safe location, without disturbing the current version.

From the Previous Versions tab, you can take any of the following actions:

- **Open.** This command works only with files, opening a read-only copy of the document in the application associated with that file type. The file name in the title bar includes the File History date and time stamp. Note that this command has no effect on folders and drives.

- **Open In File History.** Click the arrow to the right of the Open command to choose this option, which displays the current selection (file, folder, or drive) in the File History app. (We describe this app's workings shortly.)

- **Restore.** Click this option to restore the selected version to its original location. If the original file still exists, you'll see the Replace Or Skip Files dialog box, which gives you an opportunity to change your mind or save the new file as a copy in the same location. (If you want to restore a copy without deleting the original, click Compare Info For Both Files and then select the check box for both the original file and the restored previous version. The restored copy will have a number appended to the name to distinguish it from the original.)

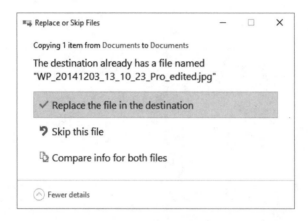

- **Restore To.** Click the arrow to the right of the Restore command to choose this option, which allows you to save a backed-up file in a location of your choice. This option is handy when you want to keep the current version of the file, perhaps to add material to it from the restored file.

The File History app offers a distinctly different take on browsing backup files. Although it resembles File Explorer in some respects, it adds a unique dimension—the ability to choose a set of saved files from a specific date and time to scan, scroll through, or search.

You can start the File History app in several ways:

- From the Settings app, look for Restore Files From A Current Backup, at the bottom of the Backup Options page.

- Using the classic Control Panel, open File History and click Restore Personal Files in the links at the left of the settings.

- From File Explorer, open the Previous Versions tab for a folder and then click Open With File History.

Figure 16-10 shows the File History app, which has an address bar, navigation controls, and a search box along the top, very much like File Explorer. What's different are the time stamp (above the file browsing window) and three controls (below the window) that allow time control without the need for flux capacitors or other imaginary time-machine components.

Address bar

Search box

Folders and libraries
selected for backup

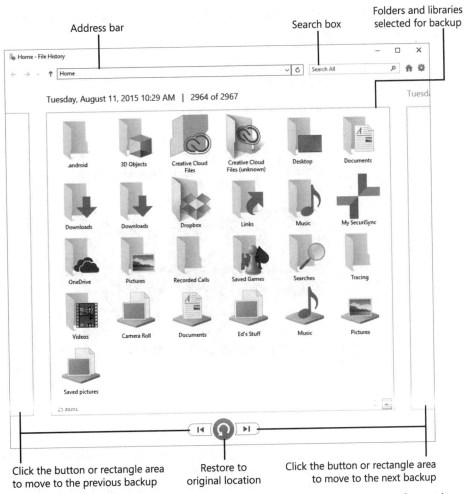

Click the button or rectangle area
to move to the previous backup

Restore to
original location

Click the button or rectangle area
to move to the next backup

Figure 16-10 In its Home view, the File History app shows all files and folders set for regular
backup. Scroll left for older files, right for more recent backups.

As with File Explorer, you can use the search box in the upper right to narrow the results by file
type, keyword, or file contents. Because file names rarely provide enough detail to determine
whether a specific file is the one you're looking for, File History has a preview function. Click
a file to show its contents in the File History window. Figure 16-11 shows one such preview of
a PowerPoint presentation, with the full path and filename in the address bar and a scroll bar
along the right for moving through the document in the preview window.

The option to restore entire folders is especially useful when you're switching to a new PC.
After you complete one last backup on your old PC, plug the File History drive into your new

PC, and then use the big green Restore button to copy your backed-up files to corresponding locations on the new PC.

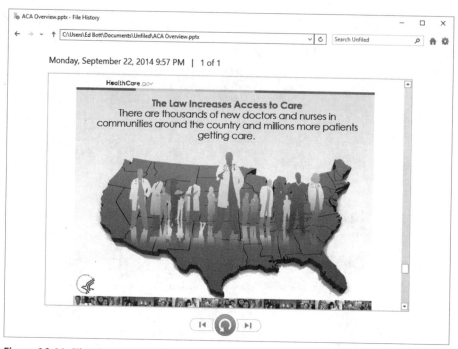

Figure 16-11 File History is capable of previewing most popular file types, including images, PDF files, and Office documents like this PowerPoint presentation.

As with File Explorer, you can change the view of files in the File History browsing window. Two shortcuts in the lower right corner allow you to quickly switch to Details or Large Icons view, although you have a total of eight predefined views, available from the well-hidden shortcut menu shown in Figure 16-12.

Inside OUT

Transfer your File Explorer smarts to File History

There's no need to open a menu or click a tiny icon to change the view in File History. Any of the eight predefined views, from Content through Extra Large Icons, can be invoked with its keyboard shortcut, Ctrl+Shift+*number*. Any number between 1 and 8 works, with Ctrl+Shift+2 switching to Large Icons view and Ctrl+Shift+6 to Details view. These same shortcuts work in File Explorer as well.

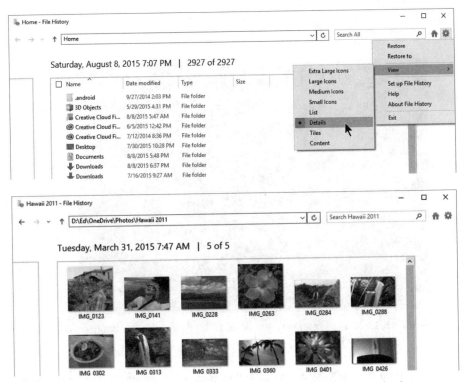

Figure 16-12 The gear icon in the upper right corner of the File History app leads to a menu with eight view settings. Details view (top) and Large Icons (bottom) work the same as in File Explorer.

Using the Reset option to recover from serious problems

One of the signature features of Windows 8 was a feature that turned out to be quietly revolutionary: a way for any user, even those without technical skills, to reset Windows to its original configuration using a Refresh or Reset command.

Windows 10 significantly refines that capability under a single Reset command. The most important change eliminates the need to have a disk-hogging OEM recovery image in a dedicated partition at the end of the hard drive. In Windows 10, that recovery image and its associated partition are no longer required. Instead, Windows 10 accomplishes recovery operations by rebuilding the operating system to a clean state using existing system files.

This push-button reset option has the same effect as a clean install, without the hassles of finding drivers and without wiping out potentially valuable data. The Reset This PC option is at the top of the list on the Recovery page in Settings, as shown earlier in Figure 16-3. It's also the

CHAPTER 16

featured choice on the Troubleshoot menu when you restart in the Windows Recovery Environment, as shown in Figure 16-13.

Figure 16-13 You can reset your Windows 10 PC by starting the Windows Recovery Environment and choosing the top option shown here.

When you reset a PC, Windows 10 and its drivers are restored to the most recent rollup state. The reset PC includes all updates except those installed in the last 28 days, a design that allows recovery to succeed when a freshly installed update is part of the problem.

For PCs sold with Windows 10 already installed, any customized settings and desktop programs installed by the manufacturer are restored with the Windows 10 reset. These customizations are saved in a separate container, which is created as part of the OEM setup process.

All Windows apps included with Windows 10 by default (Photos, Weather, Groove Music, and Mail and Calendar, for example) are restored, along with any Windows apps that were added to the system by the OEM or as part of an enterprise deployment. App updates are downloaded and reinstalled via the Store automatically after recovery.

Windows desktop programs are not restored and must be manually reinstalled. Likewise, any previously purchased Windows apps are discarded and must be reinstalled from the Store.

Resetting a PC isn't something you do accidentally. The process involves multiple confirmations, with many opportunities to bail out if you get cold feet or realize that you need to do just *one* more backup before you irrevocably wipe the disk. The first step offers you the option to keep your personal files or remove everything, as shown in Figure 16-14.

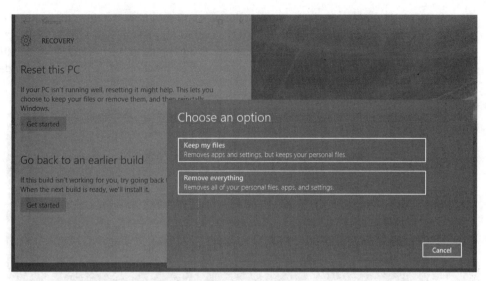

Figure 16-14 The Reset This PC option lets you choose whether to keep files for all user accounts or remove everything and start with a completely clean slate.

The Remove Everything option removes all user data, including user accounts, apps, and personalization settings. This option is useful when you plan to sell or give away an existing PC.

If the system contains multiple volumes that are visible in File Explorer, such as a dedicated data volume or an OEM-created utility partition, you're given the option to wipe all drives clean or just the system drive, as shown in Figure 16-15.

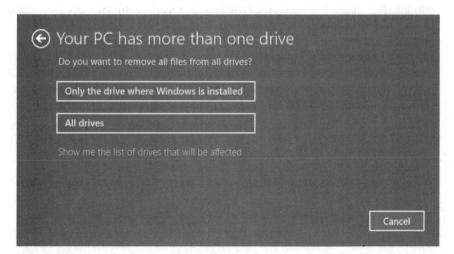

Figure 16-15 If you're resetting a PC because you plan to give it away or sell it, choose the All Drives option here; reset only the Windows system drive if you have a secondary drive that contains valuable data files.

CHAPTER 16

The reset process also includes an option to scrub data from the drive so that it cannot easily be recovered using disk utilities. As the explanatory text in Figure 16-16 makes clear, the
Remove Files And Clean The Drive option can add hours to the process. Note that this option,
while thorough, is not certified to meet any government or industry standards for data
removal.

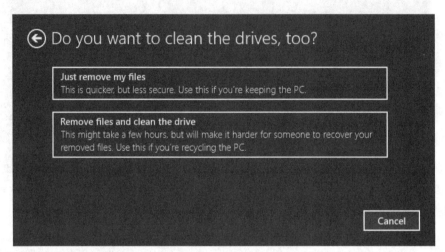

Figure 16-16 Choose the first option if you're resetting a PC for a trusted friend or family member
to use. The second option might be worth the time if your PC was used for work or contained sensitive information.

If you've made it this far through the process, you have only one more confirmation to get
through. That dialog box shows the choices you've made, with one last Cancel option. To
plunge irreversibly ahead, click Reset, shown in Figure 16-17.

The fresh recovery image is applied to the newly cleaned Windows partition, and a new Boot
Configuration Data store is created on the system partition. After the PC restarts, each user
must go through the standard procedures for setting up the PC and creating a new user
account, a process formally known as the out-of-box experience (OOBE) phase.

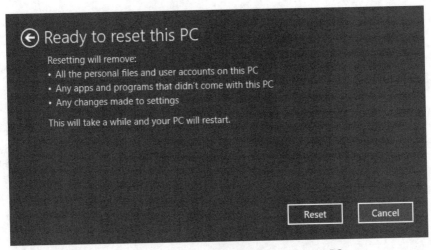

Figure 16-17 This is your last chance to back out when resetting a PC.

The reset option is a tremendous time-saver, but it's not all-powerful. Your attempts to reset Windows can be thwarted by a handful of scenarios:

- If operating system files have been heavily corrupted or infected by malware, the reset process will probably not work.

- If the problem is caused by a cumulative update that is more than 28 days old, the reset might not be able to avoid that problem.

- If a user chooses the wrong language during the OOBE phase on a single-language Windows version (typically sold in developing countries and regions), a complete reinstallation might be required.

If the reset option doesn't work, it might be time for a more drastic solution: reinstalling with the assistance of a recovery drive.

CHAPTER 16

Creating and using a recovery drive

If you upgraded to Windows 10 over an existing copy of Windows 8.1 or Windows 7, the one thing you didn't get out of the deal was a shiny disk. Relax—you don't need it. Windows 10 includes the capability to turn a USB flash drive into a recovery drive that you can use to perform repairs or completely reinstall Windows.

The Recovery Media Creator (C:\Windows\System32\RecoveryDrive.exe) creates a bootable drive that contains the Windows Recovery Environment. If you select the Back Up System Files To The Recovery Drive option, as shown in Figure 16-18, the utility creates a bootable drive that can be used to fully restore Windows, skipping most of the setup process.

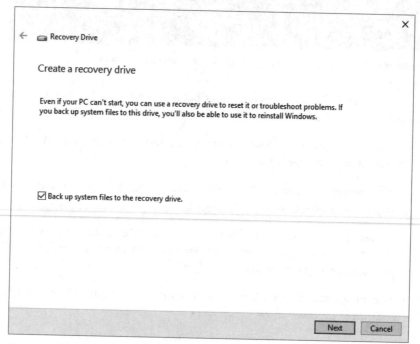

Figure 16-18 You'll typically need a USB flash drive with a capacity of at least 8 GB to create a recovery drive that includes backed-up system files.

Inside OUT

Turn a recovery drive into installation media

The Recovery Media Creator creates a FAT32-formatted drive that's fully capable of booting and installing Windows 10. In fact, you can use that drive as a shortcut to turn an ISO file, such as those available to MSDN subscribers, into a full-fledged Windows installer. Skip the option to back up system files to the recovery drive. Open the newly created recovery drive in one File Explorer window. Double-click the ISO file to mount it as a virtual drive in a separate File Explorer window and then copy the entire contents of the mounted ISO drive by dragging them to the recovery drive, overwriting any existing files. The resulting drive can be used for clean installs on any PC.

To use the recovery drive, configure your PC so that you can boot from the USB flash drive. (That process, which is unique for many machines, might involve tapping a key or pressing a combination of buttons such as Power+Volume Up when restarting.)

If you see the Recover From A Drive option selected as shown here, congratulations—the system recognized your recovery drive and you are (fingers crossed) a few minutes away from being back in business.

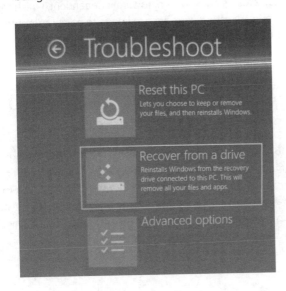

Creating and restoring a system image backup

Windows 10 includes the Windows Backup program (Sdclt.exe) originally released as part of Windows 7. Its feature set is basically the same as its predecessor, and it's included primarily for compatibility with backups created using that older operating system.

If you have a working backup routine based on the Windows 7 Backup program, we don't want to stand in your way. The version included with Windows 10 does all the familiar tasks you depend on, and we suggest you carry on. After all, the best backup program is the one you use.

For Windows 10, there are better backup utilities, but we continue to recommend the Windows Backup program for the one task it does exceptionally well: Use it to make a system image backup that can re-create a complete PC configuration, using a single drive or multiple drives. Restoring that system image creates a perfect copy of the system configuration as it existed on the day that system image was captured.

You don't need to install, update, and activate Windows, reinstall all your applications, and then configure your applications to work the way you like; instead, you boot into the Windows Recovery Environment, choose an image file to restore, and then complete the process by restoring from your latest file backup, which is likely to be more recent than the image. The image files that Windows Backup creates are largely hardware independent, which means that—with some limitations—you can restore your backup image to a new computer of a different brand and type. (Just be prepared to jump through some activation hoops on the new PC.)

Inside OUT

Use a system image to save your custom configuration

The single greatest use for a system image backup is to clean up an OEM configuration, leaving Windows intact, removing unwanted software, and installing your favorite apps. Being able to return to a baseline configuration quickly is a trick that IT pros learned long ago, as a way of deploying Windows in large organizations. By mastering the system image backup feature, you can accomplish the same result even in an environment with a few PCs instead of a thousand.

Creating a system image backup

Type **backup** in the search box to find the Windows 7 Backup And Restore tool, shown in Figure 16-19.

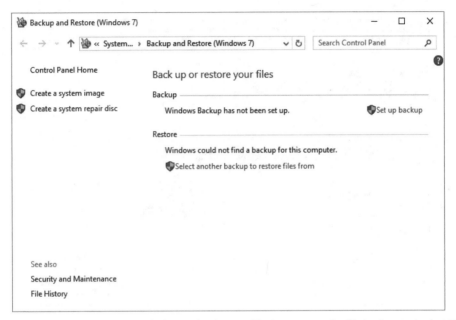

Figure 16-19 The vintage Windows 7 backup tool isn't necessary for file backup tasks, but it's ideal for capturing a complete image of a Windows installation for disaster recovery.

> ## NOTE
> When you first open Windows Backup, a message alerts you that the program has not been set up. You can ignore the Set Up Backup link forever if you simply want to create a system image backup (an excellent idea if you just finished performing a clean installation with all your drivers and programs installed and ready to use). Click the Create A System Image link in the left pane.

Ignore the options in the center of that window and instead click the Create A System Image link at the left side of the window. That opens the efficient Create A System Image Wizard. The first step asks you to define a destination for your system image, as shown in Figure 16-20.

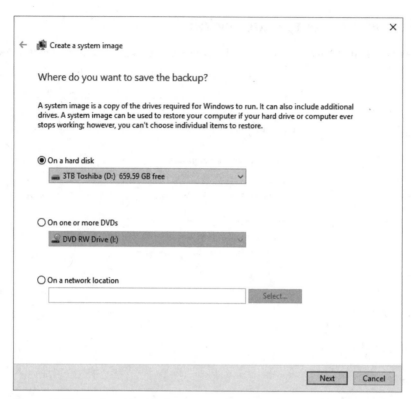

Figure 16-20 The best location for a system image backup is an external hard disk. Avoid the DVD option.

The ideal destination for a system image backup is a local hard disk, internal or external. If the Windows Backup program detects a drive that qualifies, it suggests that destination in the list of hard disks at the top of the dialog box.

The second option lets you choose a DVD writer as the target for the backup operation. You'll need to supply two, three, and maybe more blank discs to store the image backup. Although this option might have made sense in a bygone era, it's downright quaint today. Most new PCs don't even include a DVD drive, making backups stored on that media inconvenient at best and potentially useless. Even when a DVD drive is available, a single corrupted disc in the series can ruin the whole backup.

TROUBLESHOOTING

Windows Backup says your drive is not a valid location

If you try to choose a removable drive that is not a hard drive, such as a USB flash drive or SD card, Windows Backup will return this error message: "The drive is not a valid backup location." In its conventional backup role, Windows Backup can save data files on just about any storage medium. System image backups, however, must be saved on a hard disk, a DVD, or a network location.

When you create a system image backup, the resulting image file stores the complete contents of all selected drives during its first backup. If the backup target is a local (internal or external) hard drive, subsequent backup operations store only new and changed data. Therefore, the subsequent, incremental backup operation typically runs much faster, depending on how much data has been changed or added since the previous image backup operation.

If you choose a shared network folder as the backup destination, you can save only one image backup. Any subsequent image backup wipes out the previous image backup.

Inside OUT

Save multiple image backups on a network

If you specify a shared network folder as the destination for an image backup, beware of the consequences if you try to reuse that location for a subsequent backup of the same computer. If the backup operation fails for any reason, the older backup will be overwritten, but the newer backup will not be usable. In other words, you'll have no backup.

You can avoid this risk by creating a new subfolder in the shared network folder to hold each new image backup. The disadvantage, of course, is that each image file will occupy as much space as the original disk, unlike an incremental image backup on an external hard drive, which stores only the changed data.

If you have multiple hard drives, Windows displays a dialog box like the one shown in Figure 16-21, in which you choose the volumes you want to include in the backup. By default, any volume that contains Windows system files is selected. If other drives are available, you can optionally choose to include them in the image backup as well.

CHAPTER 16

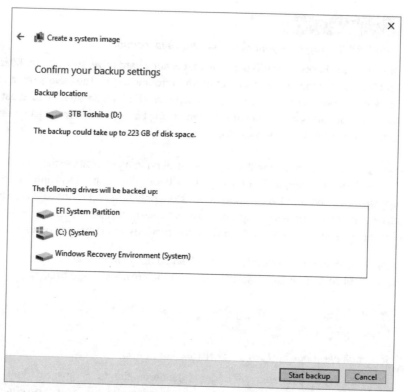

Figure 16-21 The Windows boot volume (indicated by the logo on the drive icon) and other system volumes must be included in a system image. Other volumes, such as a dedicated data drive, are optional.

The disk space requirements for an image-based backup can be substantial, especially on a well-used system that includes lots of user data files. Windows Backup estimates the amount of disk space the image will use (as shown in Figure 16-21) and will warn you if the destination you choose doesn't have sufficient free disk space.

After you confirm your settings, click Start Backup to begin the process of building and saving your image.

System images are stored in virtual hard disk (.vhd) format. Although the data is not compressed, it is compact because the image file does not include the hard drive's unused space and some other unnecessary files, such as hibernation files, page files, and restore points. Incremental system image backups on a local drive are not written to a separate folder. Instead, new and updated files (actually, the changed blocks in those files) are written to the same .vhd file. The older blocks are stored as shadow copies in the .vhd file, allowing you to restore any previous version.

CHAPTER 16

The final step of the image backup process offers to help you create a system repair disc on a writable CD or DVD. This option might be useful for an older PC, but it's redundant if you've already created a recovery drive as described in the previous section.

Restoring a system image backup

The system image capabilities in Windows Backup are intended for creating an emergency recovery kit for a single PC. In that role, they function exceptionally well. If your hard drive fails catastrophically, or if you want to wipe your existing Windows installation and start with a clean custom image you created a few weeks or months ago, you've come to the right place.

Your options (and potential gotchas) become more complex if you want to use these basic image backup and restore tools to work with a complex set of physical disks and partitions, especially if the disk layout has changed from the time you created the original image.

In this chapter, we assume that you have created an image backup of your system disk and want to restore it to a system that is essentially the same (in terms of hardware and disk layout) as the one you started with. In that case, you can restart your computer using a recovery drive or a Windows 10 installation drive and then choose the Repair Your Computer option.

Choose Advanced Options and then select System Image Recovery, as shown in Figure 16-22.

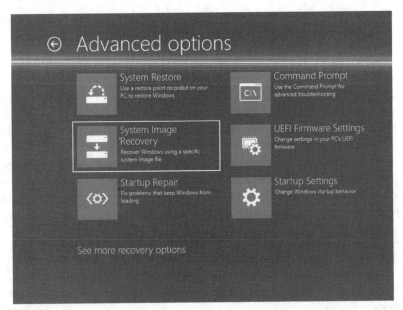

Figure 16-22 Booting into the Windows Recovery Environment allows you to wipe the current device clean and replace its contents with a saved system image backup.

If the backup deities are smiling, you should see the dialog box shown here. Assuming that Windows recognized the drive containing your system image backup, your most recent system image backup should be available in the first (recommended) option.

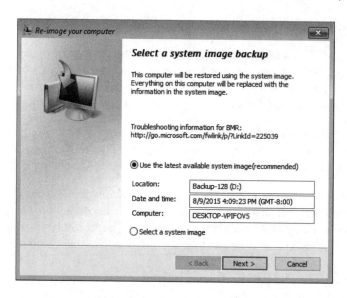

If you're restoring the most recent image backup to the same system on which it was originally created and the backup is stored on an external hard drive attached to the computer, your job is easy. The latest system image should be available for your selection. Verify that the date and time and other details of the image match the one you want to restore, and then click Next to continue.

If the image file you're planning to restore from is on a network share or if you want to use a different image, choose Select A System Image and then click Next. You'll see a dialog box that lists additional image files available on local drives. Select the correct file, and click Next to select an image created on a specific date if more than one is available. If the image file you're looking for is in a shared network folder, click the Advanced button and then click Search For A System Image On The Network. Enter the network location that contains your saved image, along with a user name and password that have authorized access to that location.

Restoring an image backup completely replaces the current contents of each volume in the image file. The restore program offers to format the disk or disks to which it is restoring files before it begins the restore process; if you have multiple drives or volumes and you're nervous about wiping out valuable data files, it offers an option to exclude certain disks from formatting.

The important point to recognize about restoring a system image is that it replaces the current contents of system volumes with the exact contents that existed at the time of the image backup you select. That means your Windows system files and registry will be returned to health (provided the system was in good shape when you performed your most recent backup and that no hardware-related issues have cropped up since then). Whatever programs were installed when you backed up your system will be restored entirely. All other files on the restored disk, including your documents, will also be returned to their prior states, and any changes made after your most recent backup will be lost.

CAUTION

If you keep your documents on the same volume as your system files, restoring a system image is likely to entail the loss of recent work—unless, of course, you have an up-to-date file backup or you have the good fortune to have made an image backup almost immediately before your current troubles began. The same is true if you save documents on a volume separate from your system files but have included that data volume in your image backup. If you have documents that have not been backed up, you can avoid losing recent work by copying them to a disk that will not be affected by the restore process—a USB flash drive, for example, or some other form of removable media. You can use the Command Prompt option in the Windows Recovery Environment to copy these documents. (For details about using the Command Prompt option, see "Working at the Command Prompt" in Chapter 21, "Working with Command Prompt and Windows Powershell.") If you do have a recent file backup, you can restore files after you have restored the image backup and your system is running again.

NOTE

The main hardware limitation for restoring a system image backup is that the target computer must have at least as many hard drives as the source system, and each drive must be at least as big as its corresponding drive in the source system. This means, for example, that you can't restore a system image from a system that has a 500-GB hard drive to a system with a 256-GB SSD, even if the original system had far less than 256 GB of data on its drive. Keep in mind also that on a system with multiple hard drives, the BIOS determines which one is the bootable drive, and this is the one on which Windows will restore the image of your system volume. (You have no choice in the matter, aside from reconnecting the drives or, if your BIOS permits it, selecting a different bootable drive.)

If your new computer meets the space requirements, restoring a system image should work. This is true even when the source and target computers use different disk controllers. Similarly, other differences—such as different graphics cards, audio cards, processors, and so on—shouldn't prevent you from restoring a system image to a different computer, because hardware drivers are isolated from the rest of the image information and are rebuilt as part of the restore process.

CHAPTER 16

> ### TROUBLESHOOTING
>
> **Your backup folders are "empty"**
>
> If you use File Explorer to browse to the folder containing your system image backup, when you rest the mouse pointer over a folder name, the pop-up tip might identify it as an "Empty folder." Alarmed, you right-click the folder and choose Properties, only to find that the folder apparently contains 0 bytes, 0 files, and 0 folders. Don't worry. This is the normal condition when your backups are stored on an NTFS volume because, by default, only the System user account has permission to view the files. (That's a reasonable security and reliability precaution, which prevents you or another user from inadvertently deleting a key backup file.) If you're confident of your ability to work safely with backup files in their native format, the solution is simple: Double-click the folder name. Follow the prompts, including a User Account Control (UAC) consent dialog box, to permanently add your user account to the folder's permissions list, giving you Full Control access to the folder.

Configuring system protection options

The System Restore feature has been part of Windows since the turn of the twenty-first century. It's a relatively minor part of the recovery toolkit now, but it can be useful for quickly undoing recent changes that introduced instability. When System Restore is enabled, the Volume Shadow Copy service takes occasional snapshots of designated local storage volumes. These snapshots occur before Windows Update installs new updates and when supported software installers run. The snapshots can also be created manually—a sensible precaution before making any system-level changes.

System Restore snapshots make note of differences in the details of your system configuration—registry settings, driver files, third-party applications, and so on—allowing you to undo changes and roll back a system configuration to a time when it was known to work correctly.

NOTE

In Windows 7, the volume snapshots created by System Restore also included a record of changes to data files on designated drives, allowing you to restore previous versions of those data files. In Windows 10, this capability has been moved into the File History feature, which we describe in detail earlier in this chapter.

It's worth noting that System Restore monitors all files that it considers system-related, which includes executable files and installers. If you downloaded the latest version of a favorite utility and stored it in your Downloads folder, it would be removed if you rolled back to a System Restore checkpoint from before it was downloaded.

Inside OUT

What's in a restore point?

Restore points in Windows 10 include a full copy of the registry at the time of the snapshot as well as information about changes made to specific files on that volume since the previous snapshot was created. Historically, files are monitored if they include any of 250+ file name extensions specifically designated for monitoring. This list (which cannot be modified) contains many file types that are clearly programs and system files, with extensions such as .exe, .dll, and .vbs. But it also includes other files that you might not think of as system files, including .inf and .ini, and some that are truly head-scratchers, such as .d01 through .d05 and .d32. (Apparently .d06 through .d31 are unmonitored.) The entire list is available at *bit.ly/restore-points-windows*. It's most useful for programmers and system administrators, but you might want to take a look at it if you're curious why System Restore deleted a file.

To check the status of System Protection, open System in Control Panel and click the System Protection link in the left pane. (To go directly to the System Properties dialog box, click Start, type **systempropertiesprotection**, and press Enter.) The resulting dialog box, shown in Figure 16-23, lists all available NTFS-formatted drives (internal and external). The value under Protection Settings indicates whether restore points are being created automatically for each drive.

Using the System Properties dialog box, you can enable or disable automatic monitoring for any local drive. By design, system protection is fully enabled for the system drive and is disabled for all other local drives.

You can also manually create a restore point at any time for all drives that have system protection enabled. Click the Create button at the bottom of the System Protection tab to open the Create A Restore Point dialog box shown in Figure 16-24. Enter a meaningful description (you can't leave the box blank, although you can tap the Spacebar to leave that box effectively blank) and then click Create to enter the descriptive text.

CHAPTER 16

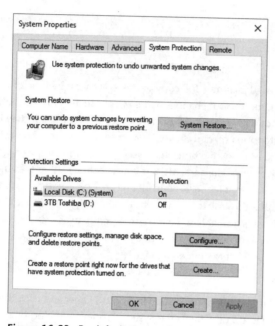

Figure 16-23 By default, System Restore monitors changes to the system drive. Select another drive and click Configure to enable System Protection for that drive.

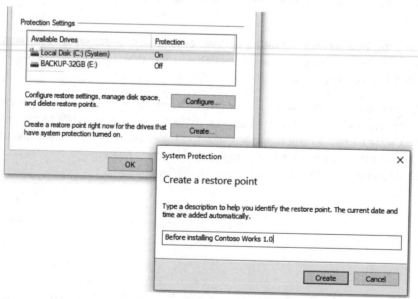

Figure 16-24 When you create a restore point manually, you're required to enter a description that will help you identify it later.

To turn system protection on or to adjust the amount of space it uses, select a drive from the Available Drives list and then click Configure. That opens the dialog box shown in Figure 16-25.

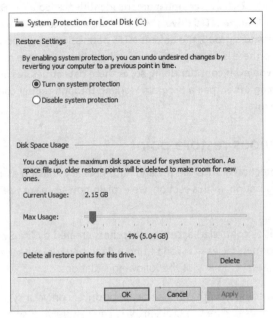

Figure 16-25 Use this slider to adjust the amount of disk space used by System Restore snapshots.

The information under the Disk Space Usage heading shows both the current usage and the maximum amount of space that will be used for snapshots before System Protection begins deleting old restore points to make room for new ones. Microsoft has not yet published its rules for how it reserves space for system protection in Windows 10. In our tests, we typically see this value set to 5 percent of the disk, up to a maximum of 10 GB, on volumes that are larger than 64 GB.

To adjust the maximum amount of disk space available for volume snapshots, click the System Protection tab in the System Properties dialog box, select a drive letter from the list of available drives, click Configure, and move the Max Usage slider to the value you prefer. For drives greater than 64 GB in size, you can choose any value between 1 percent and 100 percent.

If you're concerned about disk space usage and you're confident that you won't need to use any of your currently saved restore points, you can click the Delete button under the Disk Space Usage heading to remove all existing restore points without changing other System Protection settings.

NOTE

The default location for System Restore data is *d*:\System Volume Information, where *d* is the letter of each drive. Each restore point is stored in its own subfolder, under a name that includes a unique 32-character alphanumeric identifier called a GUID. This location cannot be changed. On an NTFS drive, these files are not accessible to users, even those in the Administrators group; the default NTFS permissions grant access only to the System account, and there is no easy way to view these files or to take ownership of them (nor should you even consider doing so, as these data structures are not intended for use by anything other than a program working through tightly controlled application programming interfaces).

Rolling back to a previous restore point

After you configure System Protection, it runs silently and automatically, making as-needed snapshots of your system configuration. In this section, we explain how to make use of those snapshots.

The System Restore utility provides controlled access to snapshots created by the System Protection feature. It can't perform miracles—it won't bring a dead hard drive back to life, unfortunately—but it can be a lifesaver in any of the following situations:

- You install a program that conflicts with other software or drivers on your system. If uninstalling the program doesn't cure the problem, you can restore your system configuration to a point before you installed the program. That should remove any problematic files or registry settings that were left behind by the uninstaller.

- You install one or more updated drivers that cause performance or stability problems. Rather than using the Roll Back Driver command in Device Manager, use System Restore to replace the new, troublesome driver (or drivers) with those that were in place the last time you saved a restore point.

- Your system develops performance or stability problems for no apparent reason. This scenario is especially likely if you share a computer with other family members or coworkers who have administrator accounts and are in the habit of casually installing untested, incompatible software and drivers. If you know the system was working properly on a certain date, you can use a restore point from that date, undoing potentially harmful changes made since then and, if all goes well, returning your system to proper operation.

CAUTION

Don't count on System Restore to protect you from viruses, worms, Trojan horses, and other malware. Use Windows Defender or a reliable and up-to-date third-party anti-virus program.

The quickest way to get to System Restore is to type **rstrui** at a command prompt. You can also click System Restore on the System Protection tab of the System Properties dialog box to find this well-hidden feature.

If you're running under a standard user account, you'll need to enter an administrator's credentials in a UAC dialog box to continue.

When the System Restore wizard appears, it might recommend the most recent restore point. To see a complete list of available restore points, select Choose A Different Restore Point and click Next. That displays a list of recent restore points, as shown in Figure 16-26.

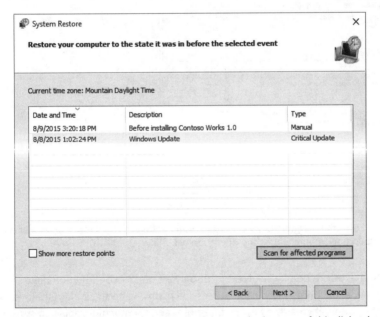

Figure 16-26 You must select the check box at the bottom of this dialog box to see more than the five most recent restore points.

If the restore point you're looking for is older than the oldest entry in the list, select Show More Restore Points to see the full list.

What impact will your choice of restore points have? To see a full list of programs and drivers that will be deleted or restored, select the restore point you're planning to use, and then click Scan For Affected Programs. That displays a dialog box like the one shown in Figure 16-27, highlighting every change you've made since that restore point was created. (Note that this list does not warn you about any executable files that might be deleted from your Desktop, Downloads, or other folders).

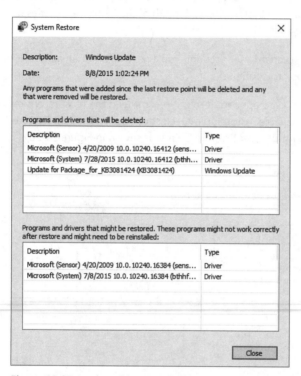

Figure 16-27 Look at this report before using System Restore to roll back to an earlier configuration so that you know what changes the operation will make.

After selecting a restore point, click Next to display a series of confirmation dialog boxes, including the one in Figure 16-28. After successfully convincing the system that, yes, you really want to do this, it creates a new restore point and then begins replacing system files and registry settings with those in the previous restore point you selected. As part of the restore process, your computer will restart and various messages will appear, all counseling you to be patient and not to interfere with the goings-on.

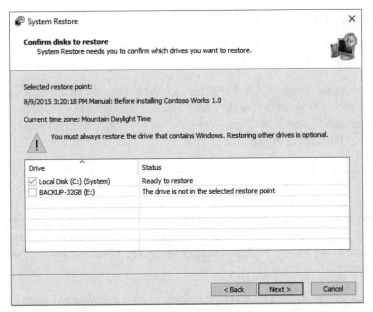

Figure 16-28 Review the descriptions carefully as you prepare to roll back to a previous restore point. After you begin the System Restore operation, it cannot be interrupted.

When System Restore reinstates a previously saved configuration using a restore point, your data files—documents, pictures, music files, and the like—are not tampered with in any way. (The only exception is if you or a program created or saved a file using file name extensions from the list of monitored extensions, as described in the previous section.) Before System Restore begins the process of returning your system to a previous restore point, it creates a new restore point—making it possible for you to return to the present if this time machine doesn't meet your expectations.

When the process is complete, do some testing to see whether the restoration fixed the problem you were encountering. If it has not and you want to return the system to the state it was in before you restored it, retrace your steps to System Restore. At or near the top of the list of available restore points, you will find one labeled Undo: Restore Operation. Choose that one and you're back where you started.

System Restore do's and don'ts

You don't have to be a science-fiction aficionado to appreciate the hazards of time travel. Here are some to be aware of:

- If you create a new user account and then use System Restore to roll back your system configuration to a point before the new account was created, the new user will no longer be able to sign in, and you will receive no warning. (The good news is that the new user's documents will be intact.)

- System Restore does not uninstall programs, although it does remove executable files, dynamic-link libraries (DLLs), and registry entries created by the installer. To avoid having orphaned program shortcuts and files, view the list of programs and drivers that will be affected when you return to the restore point you're about to roll back to. If you don't want the program anymore, uninstall it in the normal way before running the restore operation. If you want to continue using the program, reinstall it after the restore is complete.

- Any changes made to your system configuration using the Windows Recovery Environment are not monitored by System Protection. This can produce unintended consequences if you make major changes to system files and then roll back your system configuration with System Restore.

- Although you can restore your system to a previously saved restore point from the Windows Recovery Environment, you cannot create a new restore point from that location. As a result, you cannot undo a restore operation that you perform by starting from the Windows Recovery Environment. You should use System Restore in this mode only if you are unable to start Windows normally to perform a restore operation.

Troubleshooting

As they say, stuff happens. That might not be exactly how the famous quote goes, but it's certainly true whenever hardware and software are involved.

Although Windows has generally become more stable and reliable over time, it will never be perfect. Apps hang (stop responding) or crash (shut down unexpectedly). Once in a while, a feature of Windows walks off the job without warning. And on rare occasions, the grim BSOD ("blue screen of death," more formally known as a Stop error or bugcheck) arrives, bringing your whole system to a halt.

In a fully debugged, perfect world, such occurrences would never darken your computer screen. But you don't live there, and neither do we. So the prudent course is to prepare for the unexpected. That starts with making regular backups, of course, along with system restore points. But it also entails learning to use the many tools that Windows provides for diagnosing errors and recovering from problems. Those tools are the subject of this chapter.

> ➤ For information about creating regular backups and image backups as well as information about system restore points, see Chapter 16, "Backup, restore, and recovery."

Getting to know your troubleshooting toolkit

As any detective will tell you, solving a mystery requires evidence. If your mystery involves inexplicably slow performance or crashes, you have several places to look for clues.

Built-in troubleshooters

The most obvious first step on the road to resolving performance issues is the aptly named Troubleshooting section in the classic Control Panel. By default, it displays a list of the most commonly used troubleshooters included with Windows 10, as shown in Figure 17-1.

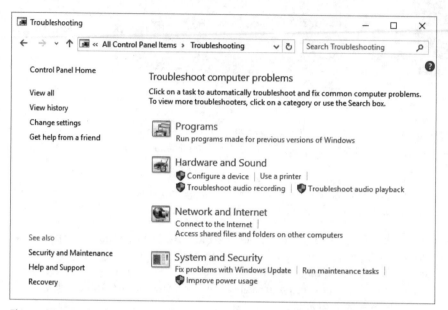

Figure 17-1 Each of the troubleshooters included with Windows 10 launches an interactive problem-solving tool that steps you through diagnosis and resolution of common problems.

Click the View All link on the left of the Troubleshooting page to see an expanded list that includes modules for fixing more esoteric problems, such as issues with search and indexing or with the Background Intelligent Transfer Service.

There's nothing magical about any of these troubleshooters. Their purpose is to ensure that you check the most common causes of problems, including some that might seem obvious (Is the network cable plugged in? Is the printer turned on?). Running a troubleshooter can result in easy fixes for some issues; more importantly, it establishes a baseline for further troubleshooting.

A troubleshooter might lead you through several steps and ask you to check settings or connections. At the end, it displays its results, which include a View Detailed Information link that displays a troubleshooting report similar to the one shown in Figure 17-2.

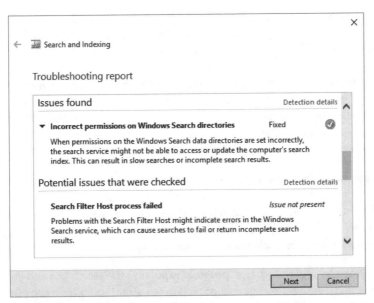

Figure 17-2 The troubleshooting report lists issues and indicates whether they were fixed. Click the Detection Details link to see more granular information about that item.

Inside OUT

Microsoft Fix It provides another self-repair option

Using technology similar to the troubleshooting packs, Microsoft Fix It provides online configuration settings and solutions to a variety of problems. Typically, a Fix It solution allows you to automatically apply a system setting that would otherwise require manual work, such as editing the registry. You can find a full listing of existing Fix It solutions at *support2.microsoft.com/fixit*, although many of the entries there apply only to earlier Windows versions. It's more common to find a new Fix It associated with a Knowledge Base article that identifies a workaround or mitigation for a security or reliability issue before an update is available.

Windows Error Reporting

Often an early indication that something is amiss is an error message informing you that an application is "not responding"—as if you hadn't figured that out already. If the application doesn't come back to life, you kill the process with Task Manager and move on, ideally without losing any data.

While all that's happening, the Windows Error Reporting (WER) service runs continuously in the background, keeping track of software and driver installations (successful and otherwise) as well as crashes, hangs, and other system events that indicate a possible problem with Windows. (In fact, although the service and programs that enable the feature are called Windows Error Reporting, the term you're more likely to see in Windows is *problem reporting*.) Microsoft provides this diagnostic information to the developers of the program that caused the error (including Microsoft developers when the issue occurs with a feature in Windows, Office, or another Microsoft program). The goal, of course, is to improve quality by identifying problems and delivering fixes through Windows Update.

In previous versions, Windows was downright chatty about reporting crashes, successful updates, and minor speed bumps. In Windows 10, most of these problem reports (including diagnostic reports sent after successful upgrades) are completely silent, but each report is logged. You can use the history of problem reports on a system to review events and to see whether any patterns demand additional troubleshooting.

To open the Problem Reports log, type **problem reports** in the search box and then click View All Problem Reports. Figure 17-3 shows a portion of the error history for a computer that was upgraded to Windows 10 in the first month after it was available.

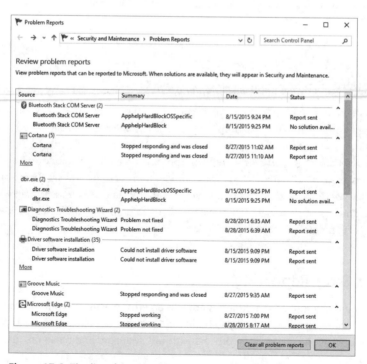

Figure 17-3 The list of saved problem reports displays only the two most recent reports in each group; click More to see earlier reports.

If the words *Solution Available* appear in the Status column for an item, right-click that item and then click View Solution. Note also that the shortcut menu includes commands to group the entries in the list of problem reports by source (the default view, shown in Figure 17-3), summary, date, or status—or you can choose Ungroup to see the entire, uncategorized list. With the list grouped or not, you can sort by any field by clicking the field's column heading.

You can see a more detailed report about any event in this log by double-clicking the event. The Description field is usually written clearly enough to provide potentially useful information. The rest of the details might or might not be meaningful to you, but they could be helpful to a support technician. Some reports include additional details sent in a text file that you can inspect for yourself. In Figure 17-4, for example, a file called WERInternalMetadata.xml captures information about the Windows installation and its memory use. None of this information is personal or linked to your PC.

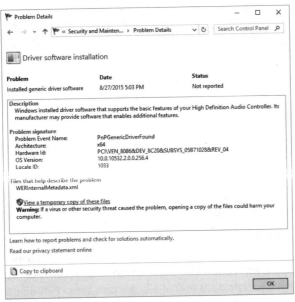

Figure 17-4 You can review the contents of a problem report, including any additional information sent as file attachments, before or after it's sent.

By default, Windows 10 configures your system so that it sends a generous amount of diagnostic and feedback information, including error reports that could inadvertently contain personal information. If you are concerned about data use or privacy, you can dial back the amount of diagnostic information by using the Feedback & Diagnostics page under the Privacy heading in Settings. Figure 17-5 shows the default settings.

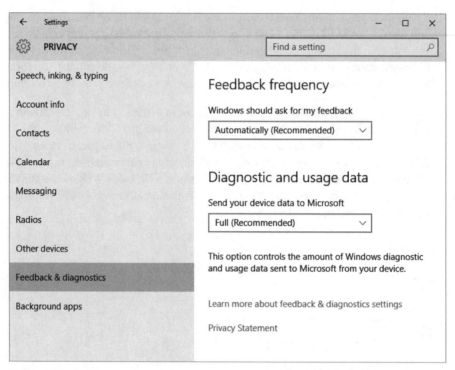

Figure 17-5 If you're concerned about sensitive data leaking out as part of diagnostic reports, consider changing the Diagnostic And Usage Data setting from its default of Full.

The Feedback Frequency setting at the top of this page controls how often Microsoft asks you about your use of features. If you prefer to be left alone, set this to Never.

The second heading, Diagnostic And Usage Data, allows you to specify how much diagnostic information your Windows 10 device sends to Microsoft servers as part of its normal operation. Much of that information is from problem reports, which rarely mean much by themselves but can be tremendously important as part of a larger data set to pinpoint the cause of problems. There are three available settings:

- **Basic.** This level includes data that is fundamental to the operation of Windows and Windows Update. It includes information about the capabilities of your device, what is installed, and whether Windows is operating correctly (which includes sending basic error reports to Microsoft). No personally identifiable information is included.

- **Enhanced.** Along with the data sent with the Basic setting, this setting adds data about how you use Windows (how often you use certain features or apps, for example) and collects enhanced diagnostic information, such as the memory state of your device when a system or app crash occurs. Information sent to Microsoft also includes reliability data for devices, the operating system, and apps.

- **Full (Recommended).** This setting, which is enabled by default, includes the full set of information from the Basic and Enhanced levels and turns on advanced diagnostic features that provide much more detailed error reports. These reports might include system files or memory snapshots that could include the contents of a file or message you were working on when the problem occurred. If a report inadvertently contains personal or sensitive information, Microsoft's privacy policy says the information will not be used to identify, contact, or target advertising to you.

The basic report that Windows Error Reporting transmits typically includes information such as the application name and version, module name and version, exception (error) code, and offset. Hardware reports include Plug and Play IDs, driver versions, and other system details. The likelihood that any of these items will convey personally identifiable information is essentially nil. The process does transmit your IP address to a Microsoft server, but Microsoft's privacy statement asserts that the IP address is used only to generate aggregate statistics and will not be used to identify you.

In work environments, your network administrators will almost certainly disable the sending of advanced error reports that might inadvertently disclose confidential information.

If privacy is a major concern, you should, of course, read Microsoft's privacy statement for this feature, which is available at *bit.ly/win10-feedback-privacy*. Although most people are understandably reluctant to send information to a faceless corporation, remember that this is a two-way street. You're sending information about a problem, and there's a good chance that, in return, you'll receive a solution to the problem, as explained in the next section. (Remember, too, that the engineers who analyze the problem information to develop solutions are not faceless!)

Reliability Monitor

Windows 10 keeps track of a wide range of system events. For a day-by-day inventory of these events, type **reliability** in the search box and then click the top result, View Reliability History. That opens Reliability Monitor, shown in Figure 17-6.

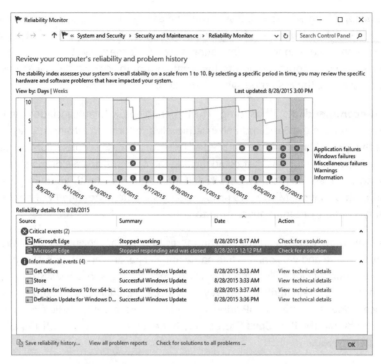

Figure 17-6 Reliability Monitor rates your system's stability on a scale of 1 (wear a crash helmet) through 10 (smooth sailing). This PC has had a rough week.

Each column in the graphical display represents events of a particular day (or week, if you click that option in the upper left corner). Each red X along the first three lines below the graph (the various "Failures" lines) indicates a day on which problems occurred. The "Warnings" line describes minor problems unrelated to system reliability, such as a program whose installation process didn't complete properly. The last line below the graph—the line marked Informa-tion—identifies days on which an app or an update was installed or removed. You can see the details about the events of any day by clicking on the graph for that day. Reliability Monitor retains its system stability records for one year, giving you plenty of history to review.

This history is most useful when you begin experiencing a new problem and are trying to track down its cause. Examine the critical events for the period when the problem began, and see whether they correspond with an informational item, such as a program installation. The align-ment of these events could be mere coincidence, but it could also represent the first appear-ance of a long-term problem. Conjunctions of this sort are worth examining. If you think a new software application has destabilized your system, you can try uninstalling it.

Double-clicking any item exposes its contents, which are filled with technical details that are potentially useful, confusing, or both.

Although the various signatures and details for each such incident by themselves are probably just baffling, they're much more useful in the aggregate. Armed with a collection of similar reports, an engineer can pin down the cause of a problem and deliver a bug fix. If a previously common error suddenly stops appearing in the logs, chances are it was resolved with an update.

Note also that you can click the link in the Action column to take additional steps, such as searching for a solution or viewing the technical details of a particular event.

Event Viewer

Technically, we should probably have included Event Viewer (Eventvwr.msc) in the previous section. It is, after all, just another troubleshooting tool. But we think that this, the most powerful of all the diagnostic tools in Windows 10, deserves its own section in this chapter.

In Windows, an *event* is any occurrence that is potentially noteworthy—to you, to other users, to the operating system, or to an application. Events are recorded by the Windows Event Log service, and their history is preserved in one of several log files, including Application, Security,

CHAPTER 17

Setup, System, and Forwarded Events. Event Viewer, a Microsoft Management Console (MMC) snap-in supplied with Windows, allows you to review and archive these event logs, as well as other logs created by the installation of certain applications and services.

You can examine the history of errors on your system by creating a filtered view of the Application log in Event Viewer. Why would you want to do this? The most likely reasons are to troubleshoot problems that have occurred, to keep an eye on your system to forestall problems, and to watch out for security breaches. If a device has failed, a disk has filled close to capacity, a program has crashed repeatedly, or some other critical difficulty has arisen, the information recorded in the event logs can help you—or a technical support specialist—figure out what's wrong and what corrective steps are required.

To start Event Viewer, find it by searching for **event** and then click Event Viewer or View Event Logs in the search results. Figure 17-7 offers an overview of Event Viewer.

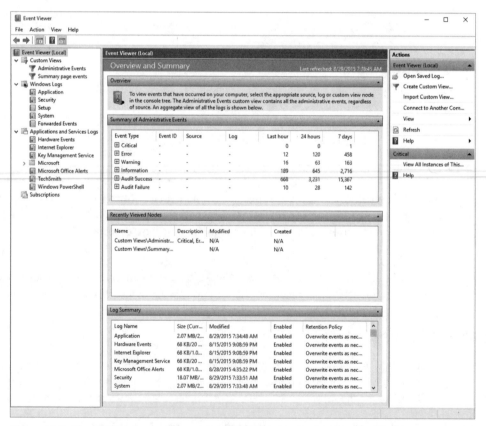

Figure 17-7 Event Viewer's console tree (left) lists available logs and views; the details pane (center) displays information from the selected log or view; the Actions pane (right) provides a menu of tasks relevant to the current selection.

NOTE

Event Viewer requires administrator privileges for full functionality. If you start Event Viewer while signed in as a standard user, it starts without requesting elevation. However, the Security log is unavailable, along with some other features. To get access to all logs, right-click and choose Run As Administrator.

When you select the top-level folder in Event Viewer's console tree, the details pane displays summary information, as shown in Figure 17-7. This view lets you see at a glance whether any significant events that might require your attention have occurred in the past hour, day, or week. You can expand each category to see the sources of events of that event type. Seeing a count of events of various types in various time periods is interesting—but not particularly useful in and of itself. If you see an unusually large number of recent errors from a particular source, for example, you might want to see the full list to determine whether a particular error needs closer examination. Right-click an event type or an event source under Summary Of Administrative Events, and then click View All Instances Of This Event, as shown here.

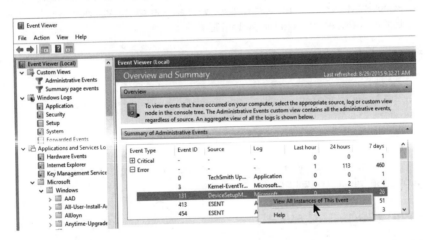

The resulting filtered list of events is drawn from multiple log files, sparing you from having to search in multiple places. Armed with this information, you can quickly scroll through and examine the details of each one, perhaps identifying a pattern or a common factor that will help you find the cause and, eventually, the cure for whatever is causing the event.

Types of events

As a glance at the console tree confirms, events are recorded in one of several logs. The following default logs are visible under the Windows Logs heading:

- **Application.** Application events are generated by applications, including programs you install, programs that are preinstalled with Windows, apps from the Windows Store, and operating system services. Program developers decide which events to record in the Application log and which to record in a program-specific log under Applications And Services Logs.

- **Security.** Security events include sign-in attempts (successful and failed) and attempts to use secured resources, such as an attempt to create, modify, or delete a file.

- **Setup.** Setup events are generated by application installations.

- **System.** System events are generated by Windows itself and by installed features, such as device drivers. If a driver fails to load when you start a Windows session, for example, that event is recorded in the System log.

- **Forwarded Events.** The Forwarded Events log contains events that have been gathered from other computers.

Under the Applications And Services Logs heading, you'll find logs for individual applications and services. The other logs generally record events that are system-wide in nature, but each log in Applications And Services Logs records the events related only to a particular program or feature. The Applications And Services Logs folder contains a Microsoft\Windows folder, which in turn contains a folder for each of hundreds of features that are part of Windows 10. Each of these folders contains one or more logs.

Viewing logs and events

When you select a log or a custom view from the console tree, the details pane shows a list of associated events, in reverse chronological order, with each event occupying a single line. A preview pane below the list displays the contents of the saved event record. Figure 17-8 shows one such listing from the System log.

Each event is classified by severity level (more on that shortly) and has a date and time stamp. The Source column reports the application or Windows feature that generated the event, and each entry has an Event ID—a numerical value that you can use as part of the criteria when filtering for similar events or searching for solutions online. The Task Category column is provided for some events but is blank for many others.

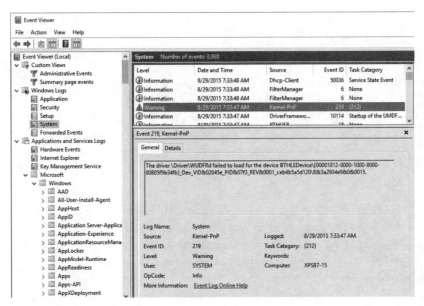

Figure 17-8 All the details you need for an individual event are visible in this preview pane. Double-click an event to see those same details in a separate window.

NOTE

The Windows Event Log service records the date and time each event occurred in Coordinated Universal Time (UTC), and Event Viewer translates those time values into dates and times appropriate for your own time zone.

Events in most log files are classified by severity, with one of three entries in the Level field: Error, Warning, or Information. Error events represent possible loss of data or functionality. Examples of errors include events related to a malfunctioning network adapter and loss of functionality caused by a device or service that doesn't load at startup. Warning events represent less significant or less immediate problems than error events. Examples of warning events include a nearly full disk, a timeout by the network redirector, and data errors on local storage. Other events that Windows logs are identified as information events.

The Security log file uses two different icons to classify events: a key icon identifies Audit Success events, and a lock icon identifies Audit Failure events. Both types of events are classified as Information-level events; "Audit Success" and "Audit Failure" are stored in the Keywords field of the Security log file.

CHAPTER 17

Inside OUT

Export data from Event Viewer

You can save selected events, all events in the current view, or all events in a particular log to a file for archival purposes, for further analysis in a different program, or to share with a technical support specialist. (To select events for exporting, hold down the Ctrl key and click each event you want to include.) The command to export events is on the Action menu, but the command name varies depending on the current view and selection: Save Selected Events, Save Filtered Log File As, Save Events In Custom View As, or Save Events As.

Saving event data in Event Viewer's native (.evtx) format creates a file that you can view only in Event Viewer (or a third-party application capable of reading native event logs). However, Event Viewer can export log data to XML and to tab-delimited or comma-delimited text files, and you can easily import these into database, spreadsheet, or even word-processing programs.

The preview pane shows information about the currently selected event. (Drag the split bar between the list and preview pane up to make the preview pane larger so that you can see more details, or double-click the event to open it in a separate dialog box that includes Next and Previous buttons and an option to copy the event to the Clipboard.)

The information you find in Event Viewer is evidence of things that happened in the past. Like any good detective, you have the task of using those clues to help identify possible issues. One hidden helper, located near the bottom of the Event Properties dialog box, is a link to more information online. Clicking this link opens a webpage that might provide more specific and detailed information about this particular combination of event source and event ID, including further action you might want to take in response to the event.

Filtering the log display

As you can see from a cursory look at your System log, events can pile up quickly, obscuring those generated by a particular source or those that occurred at a particular date and time. Sorting and grouping can help you to find that needle in a haystack, but to get the hay out of the way altogether, use filtering. With filtering, you can select events based on multiple criteria; all other events are hidden from view, making it much easier to focus on the items you currently care about.

To filter the currently displayed log or custom view, click Filter Current Log or Filter Current Custom View in the Actions pane on the right. A dialog box like the one shown in Figure 17-9 appears. To fully appreciate the flexibility of filtering, click the arrow by each filter. You can, for example, filter events from the past hour, 12 hours, day, week, month, or any custom time period you specify. In the Event Sources, Task Category, and Keywords boxes, you can type text to filter on (separate multiple items with commas), but you'll probably find it easier to click the arrow and then click each of the items you want to include in your filtered view. In the Includes/Excludes Event IDs box, you can enter multiple ID numbers and number ranges, separated by commas; to exclude particular event IDs, precede their number with a minus sign.

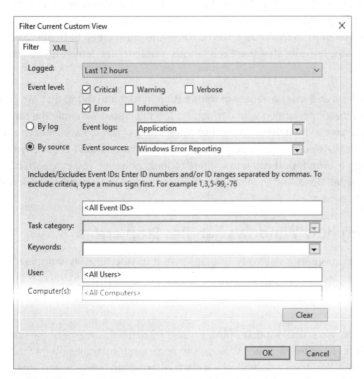

Figure 17-9 If you don't select any Event Level check boxes, Event Viewer includes all levels in the filtered results. Similarly, any other field you leave blank includes all events without regard to the value of that property.

Click OK to see the filtered list. If you want to save your criteria for reuse later, click Save Filter To Custom View in the Actions pane on the right. To restore the unfiltered list, in the Event Viewer window, click Clear Filter.

NOTE

Event Viewer also includes an anemic search capability, which you access by clicking Action, Find. You can perform more precise searches by filtering.

CHAPTER 17

Dealing with Stop errors

If Windows has ever suddenly shut down, you've probably experienced that sinking feeling in the pit of your stomach. When Windows 10 encounters a serious problem that makes it impossible for the operating system to continue running, it does the only thing it can do, just as every one of its predecessors has done in the same circumstances. It shuts down immediately and displays an ominous text message whose technical details begin with the word *STOP*. Because a Stop error typically appears in white letters on a blue background, this type of message is often referred to as a blue-screen error or the Blue Screen of Death (BSOD). When a Stop error appears, it means that there is a serious problem that demands your immediate attention.

Windows 10 collects and saves a variety of information in logs and dump files, which a support engineer or developer armed with debugging tools can use to identify the cause of Stop errors. You don't have to be a developer to use these tools, which are available to anyone via download from *bit.ly/windows-debugging-tools*. (Don't worry; you can't break anything by simply inspecting a .dmp file.) If you know where to look, however, you can learn a lot from these error messages alone, and in many cases you can recover completely by using standard troubleshooting techniques.

Customizing how Windows handles Stop errors

When Windows encounters a serious error that forces it to stop running, it displays a Stop message and then writes debugging information to the page file. When the computer restarts, this information is saved as a crash dump file, which can be used to debug the specific cause of the error.

You can customize two crucial aspects of this process by defining the size of the crash dump files and specifying whether you want Windows to restart automatically after a Stop message appears. By default, Windows automatically restarts after a Stop message and creates a crash dump file optimized for automatic analysis. That's the preferred strategy in response to random, isolated Stop errors. But if you're experiencing chronic Stop errors, you might have more troubleshooting success by changing these settings to collect a more detailed dump file and to stop after a crash.

To make this change, open Settings, type **advanced** in the search box, and then click View Advanced System Settings in the results list. (Or, in the Run or search box, type the undocumented command **systempropertiesadvanced** and press Enter.)

On the Advanced tab of the System Properties dialog box, under Startup And Recovery, click Settings. Adjust the settings under the System Failure heading, as shown in Figure 17-10.

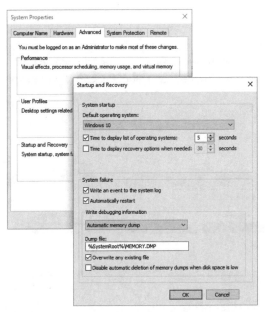

Figure 17-10 By default, Windows keeps a kernel memory dump and restarts automatically after a Stop error. You can pick a larger or smaller dump file here.

If you want Windows to pause at the Stop error message page, clear the Automatically Restart check box and click OK.

From the same dialog box, you can also define the settings for crash dump files. By default, Windows sets this value to Automatic Memory Dump, which saves a kernel memory dump after a crash. This option includes memory allocated to kernel-mode drivers and programs, which are most likely to cause Stop errors. Because this file does not include unallocated memory or memory allocated to user-mode programs, it will usually be smaller in size than the amount of RAM on your system. The exact size varies, but in general you can expect the file to be no larger than one-third the size of installed physical RAM, and much less than that on a system with 16 GB of RAM or more. The crash files are stored in %SystemRoot% using the file name Memory.dmp. (If your system crashes multiple times, each new dump file replaces the previous file.)

If disk space is limited or you're planning to send the crash dump file to a support technician, you might want to consider setting the system to store a small memory dump (commonly called a mini dump). A small memory dump contains just a fraction of the information in a kernel memory dump, but it's often enough to determine the cause of a problem.

CHAPTER 17

What's in a Stop error

The exact text of a Stop error varies according to what caused the error. But the format is predictable. Don't bother copying down the error code from the blue screen itself. Instead, look through Event Viewer for an event with the source BugCheck, as shown in the example in Figure 17-11.

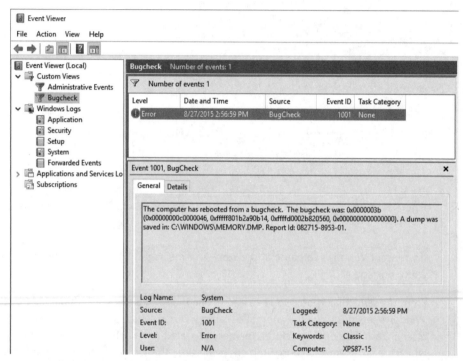

Figure 17-11 Decoding the information in a Stop error can help you find the underlying problem and fix it. Start with the error code—0x0000003b, in this example.

You can gather important details from the bugcheck information, which consists of error number (in hexadecimal notation, as indicated by the 0x at the beginning of the code) and up to four parameters that are specific to the error type.

Windows 10 also displays the information in Reliability Monitor, under the heading Critical Events. Select the day on which the error occurred and double-click the "Shut down unexpectedly" entry for an event with Windows as the source. That displays the bugcheck information in a slightly more readable format than in Event Viewer, as shown next, even using the term *BlueScreen* as the Problem Event Name. (For more information, see "Reliability Monitor," earlier in this chapter.)

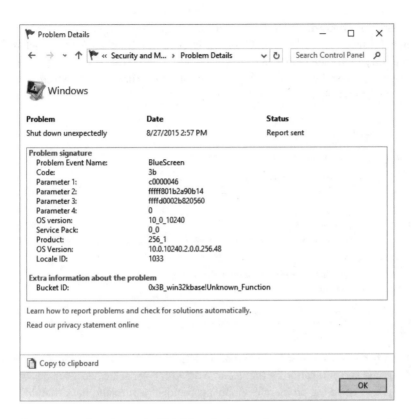

For a comprehensive and official list of what each error code means, see the MSDN "Bug Check Code Reference" at *bit.ly/bugcheck-codes*. A code of 0x00000144, for example, points to problems with a USB 3 controller, whereas 0x0000009F is a driver power state failure. (Our favorite is 0xDEADDEAD, which indicates a manually initiated crash.) In general, you need a debugger or a dedicated analytic tool to get any additional useful information from a memory dump file.

Isolating the cause of a Stop error

If you experience a Stop error, don't panic. Instead, run through the following troubleshooting checklist to isolate the problem and find a solution:

- **Don't rule out hardware problems.** In many cases, software is the victim and not the cause of blue-screen errors. Common hardware failures such as a damaged hard disk or a corrupted SSD, defective physical RAM, an overheated CPU chip, or even a bad cable can result in Stop errors. If the errors seem to happen at random and the message details vary each time, there is a very good chance that you are experiencing hardware problems.

CHAPTER 17

- **Check your memory.** Windows 10 includes a memory diagnostic tool that you can use if you suspect a faulty or failing memory chip. To run this diagnostic procedure, type **memory** in the search box and click Windows Memory Diagnostic in the search results. This tool, shown here, requires a restart to run its full suite of tests, which you can per-form immediately or defer until your next restart.

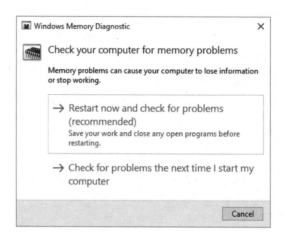

- **Look for a driver name in the error details.** If the error message identifies a specific file name and you can trace that file to a driver for a specific hardware device, you might be able to solve the problem by disabling, removing, or rolling back that driver to an earlier version. The most likely offenders are network interface cards, video adapters, and disk controllers. For more details about managing driver files, see "Updating and uninstalling drivers" in Chapter 13, "Hardware."

- **Ask yourself, "What's new?"** Be suspicious of newly installed hardware and software. If you added a device recently, remove it temporarily and see whether the problem goes away. Take an especially close look at software in the categories that install services or file-system filter drivers—these hook into the core operating system files that manage the file system to perform tasks such as scanning for viruses. This category includes backup programs, multimedia applications, antivirus software, and DVD-burning utilities. You might need to permanently uninstall or update the program to resolve the problem.

- **Search Microsoft Support.** Make a note of the error code and all parameters. Search Microsoft Support using both the full and short formats. For instance, if you're experi-encing a KMODE_EXCEPTION_NOT_HANDLED error, use 0x1E and 0x0000001E as your search keywords.

- **Check your system BIOS or firmware.** Is an update available from the manufacturer of the system or motherboard? Check the BIOS or firmware documentation carefully; resetting all BIOS options to their defaults can sometimes resolve an issue caused by overtweaking.

- **Are you low on system resources?** Stop errors are sometimes the result of a critical shortage of RAM or disk space. If you can start in Safe Mode, check the amount of physical RAM installed and look at the system and boot drives to see how much free disk space is available.

- **Is a crucial system file damaged?** To reinstall a driver, restart your computer, press F8, and start Windows in Safe Mode. In Safe Mode, only core drivers and services are activated. If your system starts in Safe Mode but not normally, you very likely have a problem driver. Try running Device Manager in Safe Mode and uninstalling the most likely suspect. Or run System Restore in Safe Mode. If restoring to a particular day cures the problem, use Reliability Monitor to determine what changes occurred on or shortly after that day.

Troubleshooting with alternative boot options

Before there was Reset, there was Safe Mode.

The recovery and reset options in Windows 10 make some traditional troubleshooting techniques less important than they used to be. Booting into Safe Mode, for example, used to be a mandatory step for recovering from problems. On modern hardware, with UEFI firmware and solid state drives, it's literally impossible to interrupt the boot process to switch into Safe Mode.

If you can start Windows and get to the sign-in screen, you can then hold down Shift and click the Power button in the lower right corner of that screen. Clicking Restart while holding down Shift makes an alternative boot menu available, with some interesting troubleshooting options.

To get to the Startup Settings menu, open Settings, Update & Security, Recovery, and then click Restart Now under Advanced Startup. After restarting, you can tap Troubleshoot, Advanced Options, and finally Startup Settings to reach the blue, full-screen menu shown in Figure 17-12. The nine choices shown there (one additional option is on the next screen) allow you to start Windows in modes that make some forms of troubleshooting easier.

The three choices in the middle enable Safe Mode, which starts Windows using a built-in administrator account, using only services and drivers that are absolutely required to start your system. The operating system runs with a generic video driver, with support for keyboard, mouse, monitor, local storage, and default system services. In Safe Mode, Windows does not

CHAPTER 17

install support for audio devices and nonessential peripherals. USB flash drives, hard disks, keyboard, and mouse are supported. All programs that normally run when you sign in (programs in your Startup folder, for example) are bypassed.

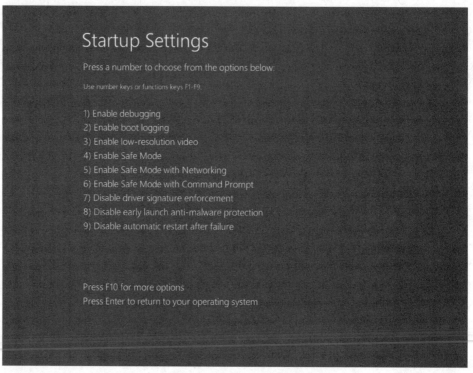

Figure 17-12 The Startup Settings menu lets you boot into Safe Mode to remove a troublesome program or driver that is preventing you from signing in normally.

In Safe Mode, you can access certain essential configuration tools, including Device Manager, System Restore, and Registry Editor. If Windows appears to work properly in Safe Mode, you can safely assume that there's no problem with the basic services. Use Device Manager, Driver Verifier Manager, and Event Viewer to try to figure out where the trouble lies. If you suspect that a newly installed device or program is the cause of the problem, you can remove the offending software while you're running in Safe Mode. Use Device Manager to uninstall or roll back a hardware driver; use Control Panel to remove a desktop program or utility. Then try restarting the system normally to see whether your changes have resolved the problem.

One important troubleshooting tool that is not available in Safe Mode is Backup And Restore. To restore a system image backup, for example, you need to use the Windows Recovery Environment, not Safe Mode.

If you need access to network connections, choose the Safe Mode With Networking option, which loads the base set of Safe Mode files and adds drivers and services required to start Windows networking.

The third Safe Mode option, Safe Mode With Command Prompt, loads the same stripped-down set of services as Safe Mode, but it uses the Windows command interpreter (Cmd.exe) as a shell instead of the graphical Windows Explorer (Explorer.exe, which also serves as the host for File Explorer). This option is unnecessary unless you're having a problem with the Windows graphical interface. The default Safe Mode also provides access to the command line. (Press Windows key+R, and then type **cmd.exe** in the Run dialog box.)

The six additional choices on the Startup Settings menu are of use in specialized circumstances:

- **Enable Debugging.** This choice starts Windows in kernel debug mode and requires a physical connection to another computer running a debugger.

- **Enable Boot Logging.** With this option enabled, Windows creates a log file that lists the names and status of all drivers loaded into memory. To view the contents of this file, look for Ntbtlog.txt in the %SystemRoot% folder. If your system is hanging because of a faulty driver, the last entry in this log file might identify the culprit.

- **Enable Low-Resolution Video.** This option starts the computer in 640 by 480 resolution using the current video driver. Use this option to recover from video problems that are caused not by a faulty driver but by incorrect settings, such as an improper resolution or refresh rate.

- **Disable Driver Signature Enforcement** Use this option if Windows is refusing to start because you installed an unsigned user-mode driver. Windows will start normally, not in Safe Mode. (Note that you cannot disable the requirement for signed kernel-mode drivers.)

- **Disable Early Launch Anti-Malware Protection.** This is one of the core security measures of Windows 10 on a UEFI-equipped machine. Unless you're a security researcher or a driver developer, we can't think of any reason to disable this important security check.

- **Disable Automatic Restart After Failure.** Use this option if you're getting Stop errors (blue-screen crashes) and you want the opportunity to see the crash details on the Stop error screen instead of simply pausing there before restarting.

The second page of the Advanced Boot Options menu includes a single menu choice that starts the Windows Recovery Environment. (We discuss this and other recovery tools in more detail in Chapter 16.)

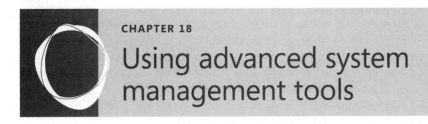

Using advanced system management tools

In this chapter, we look at a handful of programs and management consoles that can help you attain greater mastery over Windows. We start with tools for unearthing details about your system—its hardware, software environment, running programs and services, and so on. In the remainder of the chapter, we discuss the Services console, Registry Editor, and a variety of specialized tools that use the Microsoft Management Console.

Viewing details about your system

For answers to basic questions about your operating system and computer, there's no better place to start than the System application, which displays the current Windows edition and whether it is a 32-bit or 64-bit version; basic system details, including processor type and installed memory; details about the computer name and network membership (domain or workgroup); and the current activation status.

Windows 10 offers two versions of this information. On a tablet or touchscreen-enabled system, you'll probably use the new Settings app, which is pinned to the Start menu by default. Open Settings, tap System, and then tap About to display details like those shown in Figure 18-1.

An alternative display that includes most of the same information is in the old-style Control Panel, shown in Figure 18-2. The simplest way to get to the System settings page in Control Panel is to right-click the Start button (or press Windows key+X) and then click System on the Quick Link menu. If File Explorer is open, right-click This PC and click Properties to reach the same destination.

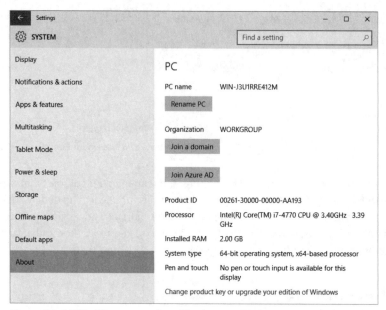

Figure 18-1 This About page, found in the new Settings app, includes basic details about the local PC along with options to change its name and join a corporate network.

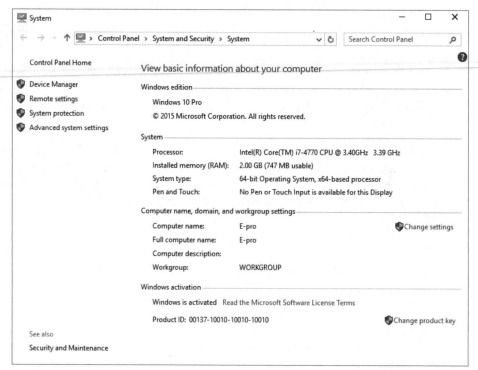

Figure 18-2 The System application in Control Panel provides basic details about your computer's configuration.

For the most exhaustive inventory of system configuration details in a no-frills text format, Windows offers three tools that provide varying levels of technical information, which we describe in the rest of this section.

Systeminfo

Systeminfo.exe is a command-line utility, installed in the Windows\System32 folder, that displays information about your Windows version, BIOS, processor, memory, network configuration, and a few more esoteric items. Figure 18-3 shows sample output.

Figure 18-3 The command-line utility Systeminfo.exe provides an easy way to gather information about all your network computers in a single database.

To run Systeminfo, open a Command Prompt window, type **systeminfo**, and then press Enter. In addition to the list format shown in the figure, Systeminfo offers two formats that are useful if you want to work with the information in another program: Table (fixed-width columns) and CSV (comma-separated values). To use one of these formats, append the /FO switch to the command, along with the Table or Csv parameter. You'll also need to redirect the output to a file. For example, to store comma-delimited information in a file named Info.csv, enter the following command:

```
systeminfo /fo csv > info.csv
```

CHAPTER 18

The /S switch allows you to get system information about another computer on your network. (If your user name and password don't match that of an account on the target computer, you'll also need to use the /U and /P switches to provide the user name and password of an authorized account.) When you've gathered information about all the computers on your network, you can import the file you created into a spreadsheet or database program for tracking and analysis. The following command appends information about a computer named Bates to the original file you created:

```
systeminfo /s Bates /fo csv >> info.csv
```

Windows Management Instrumentation command-line utility

This tool with the extra-long name is better known by the name of its executable, Wmic.exe, which is located in the Windows\System32\Wbem folder. Wmic provides an overwhelming amount of information about hardware, system configuration details, and user accounts. It can be used in either of two ways.

Enter **wmic** from a command prompt and the utility runs in console mode, allowing you to enter commands and view output interactively. Alternatively, you can add global switches or aliases, which constrain the type of output you're looking for, and see the output in a Command Prompt window or redirect it to a file. For example, use the following command to produce a neatly formatted HTML file:

```
wmic qfe list brief /format:htable > %temp%\hotfix.html
```

You can then open that file in a web browser to see a list of all installed updates on the current system. To see the full syntax for Wmic, open a Command Prompt window and type **wmic –?**.

System Information

System Information—often called by the name of its executable, Msinfo32.exe—is a techie's paradise. It displays a wealth of configuration information in a simple tree-and-details arrangement, as shown in Figure 18-4. You can search for specific information, save information, view information about other computers, and even view a list of changes to your system.

To start System Information, type **msinfo32** at a command prompt or in the search box.

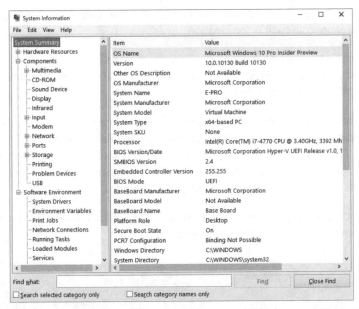

Figure 18-4 System Information is for viewing configuration information only; you can't use it to actually configure settings.

You navigate through System Information much as you would through File Explorer or any of the other Windows management tools that use the Microsoft Management Console (MMC): click a category in the left pane to view its contents in the right pane. To search for specific information, use the Find What box at the bottom of the System Information window. (If the Find bar is not visible, press Ctrl+F, or click Edit and then clear the check box next to Hide Find.)

The Find feature is basic but effective. Here are a couple of things you should know:

- Whenever you type in the Find What box to start a new search, Find begins its search at the top of the search range (the entire namespace unless you select Search Selected Category Only)—not at the current highlight.

- Selecting Search Category Names Only causes the Find feature to look only in the left pane. When this check box is cleared, the text in both panes is searched.

Using the System Information tool, you can preserve your configuration information—which is always helpful when reconstructing a system—in several ways:

- Save the information as an .nfo file. You can subsequently open the file (on the same computer or on a different computer with System Information) to view your saved information. To save information in this format, click File, Save. Saving this way always saves the entire collection of information.

- Save all or part of the information as a plain-text file. To save information as a text file, select the category of interest and click File, Export. To save all the information as a text file, select System Summary before you export.

- You can print all or part of the information. Select the category of interest; click File, Print; and be sure that Selection is selected under Page Range. To print everything, select All under Page Range—and be sure to have lots of paper on hand. Depending on your system configuration and the number of installed applications, your report could top 100 pages. (Even better, consider "printing" to PDF and saving the results.)

Regardless of how you save your information, System Information refreshes (updates) the information immediately before processing the command.

Inside OUT

Save your system information periodically

Saving system configuration information when your computer is working properly can turn out to be very useful when you have problems. Comparing your computer's current configuration with a known good baseline configuration can help you spot possible problem areas. You can open multiple instances of System Information to display the current configuration in one window and a baseline configuration in another. Save the configuration in OneDrive, and you'll be able to retrieve the information even after a hard-disk replacement.

Managing services

A *service* is a specialized program that performs a function to support other programs. Many services operate at a very low level (by interacting directly with hardware, for example) and need to run even when no user is signed in. For this reason, they are often run by the System account (which has elevated privileges) rather than by ordinary user accounts. In this section, you'll learn how to view installed services; start, stop, and configure them; and install or remove them. We'll also take a closer look at some of the services used in Windows 10 and show you how to configure them to your advantage.

For the most complete view of services running on your computer, use the Services console. You can also view running services and perform limited management functions by using Task Manager. In this section, we discuss both tools.

Using the Services console

You manage services with the Services snap-in (Services.msc) for Microsoft Management Console, shown in Figure 18-5. To view this snap-in, type **services** in the search box and then click the Services desktop app at the top of the results list. (You must have administrator privileges to gain full functionality in the Services console. Running it as a standard user, you can view service settings, but you can't start or stop most services, change the startup type, or make any other configuration changes.)

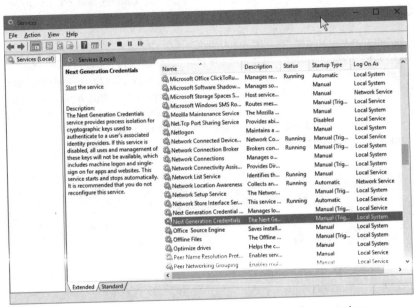

Figure 18-5 Use the Services console to start, stop, and configure services.

The Extended and Standard views in the Services console (selectable by clicking a tab near the bottom of the window) have a single difference: the Extended view provides descriptive information of the selected service in the space at the left edge of the details pane. This space also sometimes includes links for starting, stopping, or pausing the selected service. Unless you need to constrain the console display to a small area of your screen, you'll probably find the Extended view preferable to the Standard view.

The Services console offers plenty of information in its clean display. You can sort the contents of any column by clicking the column title, as you can with similar lists. To sort in reverse order, click the column title again. In addition, you can do the following:

- Start, stop, pause, resume, or restart the selected service, as described in the following section.

- Display the properties dialog box for the selected service, in which you can configure the service and learn more about it.

Most of the essential services are set to start automatically when your computer starts, and the operating system stops them as part of its shutdown process. A handful of services that aren't typically used at startup are set with the Automatic (Delayed Start) option, which starts the associated service two minutes after the rest of startup completes, making the startup process smoother. The Trigger Start option allows Windows to run or stop a service as needed in response to specific events; the File History service, for example, doesn't run unless you enable the File History feature.

But sometimes you might need to manually start or stop a service. For example, you might want to start a seldom-used service on the rare occasion when you need it. (Because running services requires system resources such as memory, running them only when necessary can improve performance.) On the other hand, you might want to stop a service because you're no longer using it. A more common reason for stopping a service is because it isn't working properly. For example, if print jobs get stuck in the print queue, sometimes the best remedy is to stop and then restart the Print Spooler service.

Inside OUT

Pause instead of stopping

If a service allows pausing, try pausing and then continuing the service as your first step instead of stopping the service. Pausing can solve certain problems without canceling jobs in process or resetting connections.

Starting and stopping services

Not all services allow you to change their status. Some prevent stopping and starting altogether, whereas others permit stopping and starting but not pausing and resuming. Some services allow these permissions to only certain users or groups. For example, most services allow only members of the Administrators group to start or stop them. Which status changes are allowed and who has permission to make them are controlled by each service's discretionary access control list (DACL), which is established when the service is created on a computer.

NOTE

In Windows 10, software installers can stop and restart running applications and services by using a feature called Restart Manager (introduced in Windows Vista). A handful of system services are considered critical, however, and cannot be restarted manually or programmatically except as part of a system restart. These critical services include Smss.exe, Csrss.exe, Wininit.exe, Logonui.exe, Lsass.exe, Services.exe, Winlogon.exe, System, Svchost.exe with RPCSS, and Svchost.exe with DCOM/PnP.

To change a service's status, select it in the Services console. Then click the appropriate link in the area to the left of the service list (if you're using the Extended view and the link you need appears there). Alternatively, you can use the Play/Pause/Stop controls on the toolbar or right-click and use the corresponding command.

You can also change a service's status by opening its properties dialog box and then clicking one of the buttons on the General tab. Taking the extra step of opening the properties dialog box to set the status has only one advantage: you can specify start parameters when you start a service by using this method. This is a rare requirement.

Configuring services

To review or modify the way a service starts up or what happens when it doesn't start properly, view its properties dialog box. To do that, simply double-click the service in the Services console. Figure 18-6 shows an example.

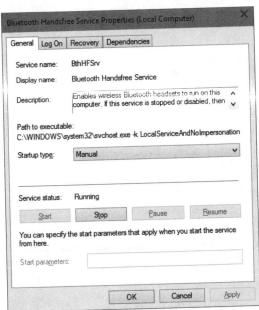

Figure 18-6 Specify a service's startup type on the General tab, where you can also find the actual name of the service (in this case, BthHFSrv) above its display name.

Setting startup options

On the General tab of the properties dialog box (shown in Figure 18-6), you specify the startup type:

- **Automatic (Delayed Start).** The service starts shortly after the computer starts in order to improve startup performance and user experience.

- **Automatic.** The service starts when the computer starts.

- **Manual.** The service doesn't start automatically at startup, but it can be started by a user, program, or dependent service.

- **Disabled.** The service can't be started.

The Trigger Start option cannot be configured manually from the Services console. Instead, you have to use SC (Sc.exe), a command-line program that communicates with the Service Control Manager. If you'd rather not tinker with the arcane syntax of this command, try the free Service Trigger Editor, available from Core Technologies Consulting, at *bit.ly/servicetriggereditor.*

You'll find other startup options on the Log On tab of the properties dialog box, as shown in Figure 18-7.

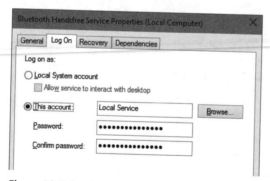

Figure 18-7 On the Log On tab, you specify which user account runs the service.

NOTE

If you specify a sign-in account other than the Local System account, be sure that account has the requisite rights. Go to the Local Security Policy console (at a command prompt, type **secpol.msc**), and then go to Security Settings\Local Policies\User Rights Assignment and assign the Log On As A Service right to the account.

Specifying recovery actions

For a variety of reasons—hardware not operating properly or a network connection being down, for example—a service that's running smoothly might suddenly stop. Settings on the Recovery tab of the properties dialog box allow you to specify what should happen if a service fails. Figure 18-8, for example, shows the default settings for the Windows Firewall service.

Figure 18-8 Use the Recovery tab to specify what should happen if a service fails.

You might want to perform a different action the first time a service fails than on the second or subsequent failures. The Recovery tab enables you to assign a particular response to the first failure, the second failure, and all subsequent failures, from among these options:

- **Take No Action.** The service gives up trying. In most cases, the service places a message in the event log. (Use of the event log depends on how the service was programmed by its developers.)

- **Restart The Service.** The computer waits for the time specified in the Restart Service After box to elapse and then tries to start the service.

- **Run A Program.** The computer runs the program that you specify in the Run Program box. For example, you could specify a program that attempts to resolve the problem or one that alerts you to the situation.

- **Restart The Computer.** Drastic but effective, this option restarts the computer after the time specified in the Restart Computer Options dialog box elapses. In that dialog box, you can also specify a message to be broadcast to other users on your network, warning them of the impending shutdown.

Viewing dependencies

Many services rely on the functions of another service. If you attempt to start a service that depends on other services, Windows first starts the others. If you stop a service upon which others are dependent, Windows also stops those services. Before you either start or stop a service, therefore, it's helpful to know what other services your action might affect. To obtain that information, go to the Dependencies tab of a service's properties dialog box, as in the example shown in Figure 18-9.

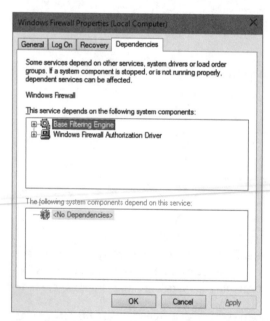

Figure 18-9 The Dependencies tab shows which services depend on other services.

Managing services from Task Manager

Using the Services tab in Windows Task Manager, you can start and stop services and view several important aspects of the services, both running and available, on your computer. You can also use this as a shortcut to the Services console.

To open Task Manager, use any of the following techniques:

- Right-click Start (or press Windows key+X), and then click Task Manager on the Quick Link menu.

- Right-click the taskbar, and then click Task Manager.

- Press Ctrl+Alt+Delete, and then click Task Manager.

- Press Ctrl+Shift+Esc.

The Services tab is shown in Figure 18-10.

Figure 18-10 By sorting on the Status column, you can see which services are running and which are stopped.

To start, stop, or restart a service, right-click its name on the Services tab and then click Start, Stop, or Restart.

Using the Services tab, you can also associate a running service with its process identifier (PID) and then further associate that PID with other programs and services being run under that PID. For example, Figure 18-10 shows several services running with PID 1220. Right-clicking one of the services with PID 1220 gives you two options, one to stop the service and one called Go To Details. Clicking the latter option opens the Details tab in Task Manager with the particular process (typically Svchost.exe) highlighted.

Determining the name of a service

As you view the properties dialog box for different services, you might notice that the service name (shown at the top of the General tab) is often different from the name that appears in the Services console (the display name) and that neither name matches the name of the service's executable file. (Many services run as part of a service group, under Services.exe or Svchost.exe.) The General tab (shown earlier in Figure 18-6) shows all three names.

So how does this affect you? When you work in the Services console, you don't need to know anything other than a service's display name to find it and work with it. But if you use the Net command to start and stop services from a Command Prompt window, you might find using the actual service name more convenient; it is often much shorter than the display name. You'll also need the service name if you're ever forced to work with a service's registry entries, which can be found in the HKLM\System\CurrentControlSet\Services*service* subkey (where *service* is the service name).

And what about the executable name? You might need it if you or a user you support have problems running a service; in such a case, you need to find the executable and check its permissions. Knowing the executable name can also be useful, for example, if you're using Windows Task Manager to determine why your computer seems to be running slowly. Although the Processes tab and the Services tab show the display name (under the Description heading), because of the window size it's sometimes easier to find the more succinct executable name.

Editing the Windows registry

The Windows registry is the central storage location that contains configuration details for hardware, system settings, services, user customizations, applications, and every detail, large and small, that makes Windows work.

> ## NOTE
>
> The registry is the work of many hands, over many years, and capitalization and word spacing are not consistent. With readability as our goal, we have made our own capitalization decisions for this book, and our treatment of names frequently differs from what you see in Registry Editor. No matter. Capitalization is irrelevant. Spelling and spacing must be correct, however.

Although it's convenient to think of the registry as a monolithic database, its contents are actually stored in multiple locations as separate *hive* files, alongside logs and other support files. Some of those hive files are read into memory when the operating system starts; hive files that contain user-specific settings are stored in the user profile and are loaded when a new user signs in.

The Boot Configuration Database (BCD) has its own file on the boot drive. The core hives for Windows—the Security Account Manager (SAM), Security, Software, and System—are securely stored in %SystemRoot%\System32\Config. Two hives that contain settings for local and network services are located in %SystemRoot%\ServiceProfiles\LocalService and %SystemRoot%\ServiceProfiles\NetworkService, respectively. User-specific hives are stored as part of the user profile folder.

The Hardware hive is unique in that it has no associated disk file. This hive, which contains details about your hardware configuration, is completely volatile; that is, Windows 10 creates it anew each time you turn your system on.

NOTE
You can see where the hives of your system physically live by examining the values associated with HKLM\System\CurrentControlSet\Control\HiveList. Windows assigns drive letters after assembling the registry, so these paths do not specify drive letters.

You can't work with hive files directly. Windows 10 is designed in such a way that direct registry edits by end users are generally unnecessary. When you change your configuration by using the Settings app or Control Panel, for example, Windows writes the necessary updates to the registry for you. Likewise, when you install a new piece of hardware or a new program, the setup program makes the required registry changes; you don't need to know the details.

On the other hand, because the designers of Windows couldn't provide a user interface for every conceivable customization you might want to make, sometimes working directly with the registry is the only way to make a change. Even when it's not the only way, it might be the fastest way. Removing or modifying registry entries is occasionally a crucial part of troubleshooting and repair as well. Windows includes a registry editor that you should know how to use—safely. This section tells you how.

CAUTION
Most Microsoft support articles contain a dire warning about the risks associated with editing the registry. We echo those warnings here. An incorrect registry modification can render your system unbootable and in some cases might require a complete reinstall of the operating system. Use Registry Editor at your own risk.

Understanding the Registry Editor hierarchy

Registry Editor (Regedit.exe) offers a unified view of the registry's contents as well as tools for modifying its contents. You won't find this important utility on the All Apps list, however, and it doesn't show up when you type its name in the search box. To start Registry Editor, you must use the name of its executable file, Regedit.exe, or type **regedit** at a command prompt.

Figure 18-11 shows a collapsed view of the Windows 10 registry, as seen through Registry Editor.

Figure 18-11 The registry consists of five root keys, each of which contains many subkeys.

The Computer node appears at the top of the Registry Editor tree listing. Beneath it, as shown here, are five root keys: HKEY_CLASSES_ROOT, HKEY_CURRENT_USER, HKEY_LOCAL_MACHINE, HKEY_USERS, and HKEY_CURRENT_CONFIG. For simplicity's sake and typographical convenience, this book, like many others, abbreviates the root key names as HKCR, HKCU, HKLM, HKU, and HKCC, respectively.

Root keys, sometimes called *predefined keys,* contain subkeys. Registry Editor displays this structure in a hierarchical tree in the left pane. In Figure 18-11, for example, HKLM is open, showing its top-level subkeys.

Subkeys, which we call keys for short, can contain subkeys of their own, which can be expanded as necessary to display additional subkeys. The status bar at the bottom of the Registry Editor window shows the full path of the currently selected key: HKLM\System\ DriverDatabase, in the previous figure.

The contents of HKEY_LOCAL_MACHINE define the workings of Windows itself, and its subkeys map neatly to several of the hives we mentioned at the start of this section. HKEY_USERS contains an entry for every existing user account (including system accounts), each of which uses the security identifier, or SID, for that account.

> ### NOTE
> For a detailed discussion of the relationship between user accounts and SIDs, see "What are security identifiers?" in Chapter 6, "Managing user accounts, passwords, and credentials."

The remaining three predefined keys don't exist, technically. Like the file system in Windows— which uses junctions, symlinks, and other trickery to display a virtual namespace—the registry uses a bit of misdirection (implemented with the REG_LINK data type) to create these convenient representations of keys that are actually stored within HKEY_LOCAL_MACHINE and HKEY_USERS:

- HKEY_CLASSES_ROOT is merged from keys within HKLM\Software\Classes and HKEY_ USERS*sid*_Classes (where *sid* is the security identifier of the currently signed-in user).

- HKEY_CURRENT_USER is a view into the settings for the currently signed-in user account, as stored in HKEY_USERS*sid* (where *sid* is the security identifier of the currently signed-in user).

- HKEY_CURRENT_CONFIG displays the contents of the Hardware Profiles\Current subkey in HKLM\SYSTEM\CurrentControlSet\Hardware Profiles.

Any changes you make to keys and values in these virtual keys have the same effect as though you had edited the actual locations. The HKCR and HKCU keys are generally more convenient to use.

Registry values and data types

Every key contains at least one value. In Registry Editor, that obligatory value is known as the default value. Many keys have additional values. The names, data types, and data associated with values appear in the right pane.

The default value for many keys is not defined. You can therefore think of an empty default value as a placeholder—a slot that could hold data but currently does not.

CHAPTER 18

All values other than the default always include the following three components: name, data type, and data. Figure 18-12, for example, shows customized settings for the current user's lock screen (note the full path to this key in the bottom of the Registry Editor window).

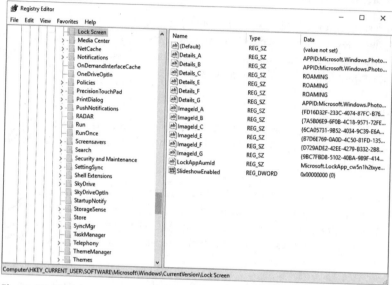

Figure 18-12 Selecting a key on the left displays all of its values on the right.

The SlideshowEnabled value (last in the list) is of data type REG_DWORD. The data associated with this value (on the system used for this figure) is 0x00000000. The prefix 0x denotes a hexadecimal value. Registry Editor displays the decimal equivalent of hexadecimal values in parentheses after the value.

The registry uses the following data types:

- **REG_SZ** The SZ indicates a zero-terminated string. This is a variable-length string that can contain Unicode as well as ANSI characters. When you enter or edit a REG_SZ value, Registry Editor terminates the value with a 00 byte for you.

- **REG_BINARY** The REG_BINARY type contains binary data—0s and 1s.

- **REG_DWORD** This data type is a "double word"—that is, a 32-bit numeric value. Although it can hold any integer from 0 to 232, the registry often uses it for simple Boolean values (0 or 1) because the registry lacks a Boolean data type.

- **REG_QWORD** This data type is a "quadruple word"—a 64-bit numeric value.

- **REG_MULTI_SZ** This data type contains a group of zero-terminated strings assigned to a single value.

- **REG_EXPAND_SZ** This data type is a zero-terminated string containing an unexpanded reference to an environment variable, such as %SystemRoot%. (For information about environment variables, see "Interacting with PowerShell" in Chapter 21, "Working with Command Prompt and Windows PowerShell.") If you need to create a key containing a variable name, use this data type, not REG_SZ.

Internally, the registry also uses REG_LINK, REG_FULL_RESOURCE_DESCRIPTOR, REG_RESOURCE_LIST, REG_RESOURCE_REQUIREMENTS_LIST, and REG_NONE data types. Although you might occasionally see references in technical documentation to these data types, they're not visible or accessible in Registry Editor.

Registry virtualization

One of the longstanding fundamental principles of security in Windows is that it prevents applications running under a standard user's token from writing to system folders in the file system and to machine-wide keys in the registry, while at the same time enabling users with a standard account to run applications without running into "access denied" roadblocks.

Many applications that require administrator-level access are still in use in Windows 10, but standard users can run them without hassle. That's because User Account Control uses registry virtualization to redirect attempts to write to subkeys of HKLM\Software. (Settings in HKLM apply to all users of the computer, and therefore only administrators have write permission.) When an application attempts to write to this hive, Windows writes instead to a per-user location, HKCR\VirtualStore\Machine\Software. Like file virtualization, this is done transparently; the application (and all but the most curious users) never know this is going on behind the scenes.

> **NOTE**
> When an application requests information from HKLM\Software, Windows looks first in the virtualized key if it exists. Therefore, if a value exists in both the VirtualStore hive and in HKLM, the application sees only the one in VirtualStore.

Note that because the virtualized data is stored in a per-user section of the registry, settings made by one user do not affect other users. Running the same application in Windows XP, which doesn't use virtualization and therefore looks only at the actual HKLM hive, presents all users with the same settings. This can lead to confusion by users who are accustomed to sharing an application in Windows XP and find that it works differently in Windows 10.

CHAPTER 18

Inside OUT

Copy virtualized registry entries to other user accounts

The hive that stores virtualized registry data, HKCR\VirtualStore\Machine\Software, can also be found in HKU*sid*_Classes\VirtualStore\Machine\Software, where *sid* is the security identifier of the user who is currently signed in. If you want to make sure that a certain application works identically for a different user, you can copy that application's subkey to the corresponding HKU subkey for the other user.

➤ For more information about UAC and virtualization, see "Preventing unsafe actions with User Account Control" in Chapter 7, "Securing Windows 10 devices."

NOTE

Registry virtualization is an interim solution to application compatibility problems. It was introduced with Windows Vista; at that time, nearly 10 years ago, Microsoft announced its intention to remove the feature from a future version of the operating system. It is still a feature in Windows 10. For more information about registry virtualization, see *w7io.com/22502*.

Backing up and restoring parts of the registry

The two most important things to know about Registry Editor are that it copies your changes immediately into the registry and that it has no Undo command. Registry Editor doesn't wait for you to issue a File, Save command (it has no such command) before making changes in the registry files. And after you have altered some bit of registry data, the original data is gone forever—unless you remember it and restore it yourself or unless you have some form of backup that you can restore. Registry Editor is therefore a tool to be used sparingly and cautiously; it should not be left open when not in use.

Before you make any changes to the registry, consider using System Restore to set a restore point, which includes a snapshot of the registry as it currently exists. This precaution allows you to roll back any ill-advised changes.

➤ For information about using System Restore, see "Rolling back to a previous restore point" in Chapter 16, "Backup, restore, and recovery."

In addition, you can use the Export command in Registry Editor to back up the branch of the registry where you plan to work.

Registry Editor can save all or portions of your registry in any of the four different formats described here:

- **Registration Files.** The Registration Files option creates a .reg file, a text file that can be read and edited in Notepad or a similar program. A .reg file can be merged into the registry of a system running any version of Windows. When you merge a .reg file, its keys and values replace the corresponding keys and values in the registry. Using .reg files allows you to edit your registry "offline" and add your changes to the registry without even opening Registry Editor. You can also use .reg files as an easy way to share registry settings and copy them to other computers.

- **Registry Hive Files.** The Registry Hive File format saves a binary image of a selected portion of the registry. You won't be able to read the resulting file (choose one of the text-file options if that's what you need to do), but if you need to restore the keys you've worked on, you can be confident that this format will do the job correctly.

  Registry hive file is the format of choice if you want to create a backup before working in Registry Editor. That's because when you import a registry hive file, it restores the entire hive to exactly the way it was when you saved it. (The .reg file types, when merged, restore all the saved keys and values to their original locations, which repairs all deletions and edits. But the process does not remove any keys or values that you added.) Note, however, that a registry hive file has the potential to do the greatest damage if you import it to the wrong key; see the caution in the following section.

- **Win9x/NT4 Registration Files.** The Win9x/NT4 Registration Files option also generates a .reg file, but one in an older format used by earlier versions of Windows. The principal difference between the two formats is that the current format uses Unicode and the older format does not. We can't think of a real-world scenario where you would actually want to use this legacy format.

- **Text Files.** The Text Files option, like the Registration Files option, creates a file that can be read in Notepad or another text editor. The principal advantage of this format is that it cannot accidentally (or intentionally) be merged into the registry. Thus, it's a good way to create a record of your registry's state at a particular time. Its disadvantage, relative to the .reg file format, is its size. Text files are considerably larger than corresponding .reg files, and they take longer to create.

To export a registry hive, select a key in the left pane, and then on the File menu, click Export. (Easier yet: right-click a key and click Export.) In the Save As Type list in the Export Registry File dialog box, select one of the four file types. Under Export Range, select Selected Branch. The resulting file includes the selected key and all its subkeys and values.

If you need to restore the exported hive from a registry hive file, select the same key in the left pane of the Registry Editor window, click Import on the File menu, and specify the file. You'll see a confirmation prompt letting you know that your action will overwrite (replace) the current key and all its subkeys. This is your last chance to make sure you're importing the hive into the right location, so take a moment to make sure you've selected the correct key before you click Yes.

CAUTION

Importing a registry hive file replaces the entire content of the selected key with the contents of the file—regardless of its original source. That is, it wipes out everything in the selected key and then adds the keys and values from the file. When you import, be absolutely certain that you've selected the correct key.

If you saved your backup as a .reg file, you use the same process to import it. (As an alternative, you can double-click the .reg file in File Explorer without opening Registry Editor.) Unlike with a registry hive file, however, the complete path to each key and value is stored as part of the file and it always restores to the same location. This approach for recovering from registry editing mishaps is fine if you did not add new values or subkeys to the section of the registry you're working with; it returns existing data to its former state but doesn't alter the data you've added.

TROUBLESHOOTING

You used a registry cleaner and your system is no longer working properly

The registry is often inscrutable and can appear messy. Misguided attempts at cleanup can cause unexpected problems that are nearly impossible to troubleshoot, which explains why Microsoft is so insistent with its warnings that improper changes to the registry can prevent your computer from operating properly or even booting. We've never found a so-called registry cleaner that justifies the risk it inevitably entails. If you find yourself with a misbehaving system after using a registry cleaner, use the Reset option to recover your system and start over. And this time, don't bother to install that unnecessary utility.

Browsing and editing with Registry Editor

Because of the registry's size, looking for a particular key, value, or data item can be daunting. In Registry Editor, the Find command (on the Edit menu; also available by pressing Ctrl+F) works in the forward direction only and does not wrap around when it gets to the end of the registry. If you're not sure where the item you need is located, select the highest level in the left pane before issuing the command. If you have an approximate idea where the item you want is located, you can save time by starting at a node closer to (but still above) the target.

After you have located an item of interest, you can put it on the Favorites list to simplify a return visit. Open the Favorites menu, click Add To Favorites, and supply a friendly name (or accept the default). If you're about to close Registry Editor and know you'll be returning to the same key the next time you open the editor, you can skip the Favorites step because Registry Editor always remembers your last position and returns to that position in the next session.

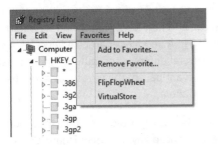

Registry Editor includes a number of time-saving keyboard shortcuts for navigating the registry. To move to the next subkey that starts with a particular letter, simply type that letter when the focus is in the left pane; in the right pane, use the same trick to jump to the next value that begins with that letter. To open a key (revealing its subkeys), press the Right Arrow key. To move up one level in the subkey hierarchy, press the Left Arrow key; a second press collapses the subkeys of the current key. To move to the top of the hierarchy, press Home. To quickly move between the left and right panes, use the Tab key. In the right pane, press F2 to rename a value, and press Enter to open that value and edit its data. Once you get the hang of using these keyboard shortcuts, you'll find it's usually easier to zip through the subkey hierarchy with a combination of arrow keys and letter keys than it is to open outline controls with the mouse.

Changing data

You can change the data associated with a value by selecting a value in the right pane and pressing Enter or by double-clicking the value. Registry Editor pops up an edit window appropriate for the value's data type.

Adding or deleting keys

To add a key, select the new key's parent in the left pane, open the Edit menu, point to New, and click Key. The new key arrives as a generically named outline entry, exactly the way a new folder does in File Explorer. Type a new name. To delete a key, select it and then press Delete.

Adding or deleting values

To add a value, select the parent key, open the Edit menu, and point to New. On the submenu that appears, click the type of value you want to add. A value of the type you select appears in the right pane with a generic name. Type over the generic name, press Enter twice, enter your data, and press Enter once more. To delete a value, select it and press Delete.

CHAPTER 18

Using .reg files to automate registry changes

The .reg files created by the Export command in Registry Editor are plain text, suitable for reading and editing in Notepad or any similar editor. Therefore, they provide an alternative method for editing your registry. You can export a section of the registry, change it offline, and then merge it back into the registry. Or you can add new keys, values, and data to the registry by creating a .reg file from scratch and merging it. A .reg file is particularly useful if you need to make the same changes to the registry of several different computers. You can make and test your changes on one machine, save the relevant part of the registry as a .reg file, and then transport the file to the other machines that require it.

Figure 18-13 shows a .reg file. In this case, the file was exported from the HKCU\Software\Microsoft\Windows\CurrentVersion\Explorer\Advanced key, shown in Figure 18-14.

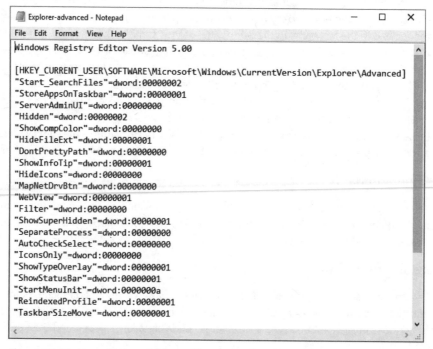

Figure 18-13 A .reg file is a plain-text file suitable for offline editing. This .reg file was exported from the key shown in Figure 18-14.

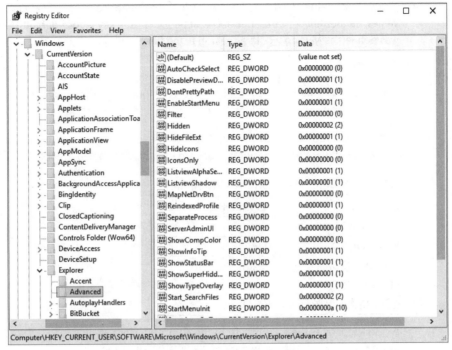

Figure 18-14 This key's name, values, and data are recorded in the .reg file shown in Figure 18-13.

Identifying the elements of a .reg file

As you review the examples shown in the two figures, note the following characteristics of .reg files:

- **Header line.** The file begins with the line "Windows Registry Editor Version 5.00." When you merge a .reg file into the registry, Registry Editor uses this line to verify that the file contains registry data. Version 5 (the version used with Windows 7 and later versions, including Windows 10) generates Unicode text files, which can be used with all supported versions of Windows as well as the now-unsupported Windows XP and Windows 2000.

- **Key names.** Key names are delimited by brackets and must include the full path from the root key to the current subkey. The root key name must not be abbreviated. (Don't use HKCU, for example.) Figure 18-13 shows only one key name, but you can have as many as you please.

- **The default value.** Undefined default values do not appear in .reg files. Defined default values are identified by the special character @. Thus, a key whose default REG_SZ value was defined as MyApp would appear in a .reg file this way:

  `"@"="MyApp"`

- **Value names.** Value names must be enclosed in quotation marks, whether or not they include space characters. Follow the value name with an equal sign.

- **Data types.** REG_SZ values don't get a data type identifier or a colon. The data directly follows the equal sign. Other data types are identified as shown in Table 18-1:

Table 18-1 Data types identified in .reg files

Data type	Identifier
REG_BINARY	hex
REG_DWORD	dword
REG_QWORD	hex(b)
REG_MULTI_SZ	hex(7)
REG_EXPAND_SZ	hex(2)

A colon separates the identifier from the data. Thus, for example, a REG_DWORD value named "Keyname" with value data of 00000000 looks like this:

`"Keyname"=dword:00000000`

- **REG_SZ values.** Ordinary string values must be enclosed in quotation marks. A back-slash character within a string must be written as two backslashes. Thus, for example, the path C:\Program Files\Microsoft Office\ is written like this:

  `"C:\\Program Files\\Microsoft Office\\"`

- **REG_DWORD values.** DWORD values are written as eight hexadecimal digits, without spaces or commas. Do not use the 0x prefix.

- **All other data types.** All other data types—including REG_EXPAND_SZ, REG_MULTI_SZ, and REG_QWORD—appear as comma-delimited lists of hexadecimal bytes (two hex digits, a comma, two more hex digits, and so on). The following is an example of a REG_MULTI_SZ value:

  ```
  "Addins"=hex(7):64,00,3a,00,5c,00,6c,00,6f,00,74,00,00,75,00,73,00,5c,00,\
  31,00,32,00,33,00,5c,00,61,00,64,00,64,00,64,00,69,00,6e,00,73,00,5c,00,\
  64,00,71,00,61,00,75,00,69,00,2e,00,31,00,32,00,61,00,00,00,00,00,00,00,00
  ```

- **Line-continuation characters.** You can use the backslash as a line-continuation character. The REG_MULTI_SZ value just shown, for example, is all one stream of bytes. We've added backslashes and broken the lines for readability, and you can do the same in your .reg files.

- **Line spacing.** You can add blank lines for readability. Registry Editor ignores them.

- **Comments.** To add a comment line to a .reg file, begin the line with a semicolon.

Using a .reg file to delete registry data

.Reg files are most commonly used to modify existing registry data or add new data. But you can also use them to delete existing values and keys.

To delete an existing value, specify a hyphen character (minus sign) as the value's data. For example, to use a .reg file to remove the value ShellState from the key HKCU\Software\Microsoft\Windows\CurrentVersion\Explorer, add the following lines to the .reg file:

```
[HKEY_CURRENT_USER\Software\Microsoft\Windows\CurrentVersion\Explorer]
"ShellState"=-
```

To delete an existing key with all its values and data, insert a hyphen in front of the key name (inside the left bracket). For example, to use a .reg file to remove the key HKCR\.xyz\shell and all its values, add the following to the .reg file:

```
[-HKEY_CLASSES_ROOT\.xyz\shell]
```

Merging a .reg file into the registry

To merge a .reg file into the registry from within Registry Editor, open the File menu and click Import. Registry Editor adds the imported data under the appropriate key names, overwriting existing values where necessary.

The default action for a .reg file is Merge—meaning merge with the registry. Therefore, you can merge a file into the registry by simply double-clicking it in File Explorer and answering the confirmation prompt.

Using Microsoft Management Console

Microsoft Management Console (MMC) is an application that hosts tools for administering computers, networks, and other system components. By itself, MMC performs no administrative services. Rather, it acts as the host for one or more modules, called *snap-ins*, which do the useful work. MMC provides user-interface consistency so that you or the users you support see more or less the same style of application each time you need to carry out some kind of

CHAPTER 18

computer management task. A combination of one or more snap-ins can be saved in a file called a Microsoft Common Console Document or, more commonly, an MMC console.

Creating snap-ins requires expertise in programming. You don't have to be a programmer, however, to make your own custom MMC consoles. All you need to do is run MMC, start with a blank console, and add one or more of the snap-ins available on your system. Alternatively, you can customize some of the MMC consoles supplied by Microsoft or other vendors simply by adding or removing snap-ins. You might, for example, want to combine the Services console with the Event Viewer console, the latter filtered to show only events generated by services. You might also want to include a link to a website that offers details about services and service-related errors. Or perhaps you would like to simplify some of the existing consoles by removing snap-ins that you seldom use.

MMC consoles use, by default, the file-name extension .msc, and .msc files are associated by default with MMC. Thus, you can run any MMC console by double-clicking its file name in a File Explorer window or by entering the file name at a command prompt. Windows 10 includes several predefined consoles; the most commonly used ones, described in Table 18-2, can be easily found by typing their name in the search box.

Inside OUT

Avoiding User Account Control problems with MMC consoles

Consoles can be used to manage all sorts of computer hardware and Windows features: with a console you can modify hard-drive partitions, start and stop services, and install device drivers, for example. In other words, MMC consoles perform the types of tasks that User Account Control (UAC) is designed to restrict. In the hands of someone malicious (or simply careless), consoles have the power to wreak havoc on your computer.

Therefore, when using an MMC console, you're likely to encounter a User Account Control request for permission to continue. If UAC is enabled on your computer, the type of request you get and the restrictions that are imposed depend on your account type and the console you're using. Some consoles, such as Device Manager (Devmgmt.msc), display a message box informing you that the console will run with limitations. (In effect, it works in a read-only mode that allows you to view device information but not make changes.) Others block all use by nonadministrative users. To ensure that you don't run into an "access denied" roadblock when performing administrative tasks while signed in with a standard account, always right-click and then click Run As Administrator.

Table 18-2 Useful predefined consoles

Console name (file name)	Description
Computer Management (Compmgmt.msc)	Includes the functionality of the Task Scheduler, Event Viewer, Shared Folders, Local Users And Groups, Performance Monitor, Device Manager, Disk Management, Services, and WMI Control snap-ins, providing control over a wide range of computer tasks.
Device Manager (Devmgmt.msc)	Uses the Device Manager snap-in to enable administration of all attached hardware devices and their drivers. See Chapter 13 for more information on configuring hardware.
Event Viewer (Eventvwr.msc)	Uses the Event Viewer snap-in to display all types of logged information. See "Event Viewer" in Chapter 17, "Troubleshooting," for details.
Performance Monitor (Perfmon.msc)	Uses the Performance Monitor snap-in to provide a set of monitoring tools far superior to Performance Monitor in earlier Windows versions. See Chapter 15, "System maintenance and performance," for details.
Services (Services.msc)	Uses the Services snap-in to manage services in Windows. For details, see "Managing startup programs and services" in Chapter 15.
Task Scheduler (Taskschd.msc)	Uses the Task Scheduler snap-in for managing tasks that run automatically. For details, see "Using Task Scheduler" in Chapter 19, "Automating tasks and activities."
Windows Firewall With Advanced Security (Wf.msc)	Uses the Windows Firewall With Advanced Security snap-in to configure rules and make other firewall settings. For details, see "Advanced tools for managing Windows Firewall" in Chapter 7.

CHAPTER 19

Automating tasks and activities

If you use your computer very often—and if you're reading this book you probably do—you likely find yourself performing certain ordinary tasks repeatedly. Such tasks might include routine maintenance activities, such as backing up your data or cleaning deadwood from your hard disk, or they might be jobs that require many steps. Computers excel at repetitive actions, and Windows 10 provides several ways to automate such tasks:

- **Task Scheduler.** Probably the most important automation tool at your disposal is Task Scheduler, which lets you set up automated routines that are triggered by events or by a schedule and requires no programming expertise.

- **Batch programs.** A carryover from the earliest days of MS-DOS, batch programming still offers an easy, reliable way to run sequences of tasks. Most Windows programs can be started from a command prompt, which means they can be started from a batch program.

- **Windows Script Host.** This feature allows you to run scripts written in VBScript, JScript, and other languages. Although learning how to use Windows Script Host is more difficult than learning to create batch programs, scripts can interact with the operating system and with other programs in more powerful ways.

- **Windows PowerShell.** Windows PowerShell is a .NET-based command-line shell and scripting language tailored to work with Windows. If you're serious about scripting Windows 10, you'll want to take a look at Windows PowerShell. Chapter 21, "Working with Command Prompt and Windows PowerShell," provides an introduction to this important topic as well as references for further study.

Using Task Scheduler

Task Scheduler is a Microsoft Management Console (MMC) snap-in that supports an extensive set of triggering and scheduling options. You can run programs or scripts at specified times, launch actions when a computer has been idle for a specified period of time, run tasks when particular users sign in or out, and so on. Task Scheduler is also tightly integrated with the

Event Viewer snap-in, making it easy for you to use events (an application crash or a disk-full error, for example) as triggers for tasks.

To launch Task Scheduler, in the search box, type **sched**. In the results list, click Task Scheduler (Desktop App) or Schedule Tasks (Settings). Alternatively, press Windows key+R and type **taskschd.msc** in the Open box.

Figure 19-1 shows a sample of Task Scheduler in its default layout. As you can see, the window is divided into three regions—a console tree on the left, the Actions pane on the right, and, in between, various informative windows in the details pane. The console tree shows you which computer you're working with (the local machine or a network computer) and provides a folder tree of currently defined tasks. You can create your own folders here to organize the tasks that you create yourself, or you can add new tasks to existing folders.

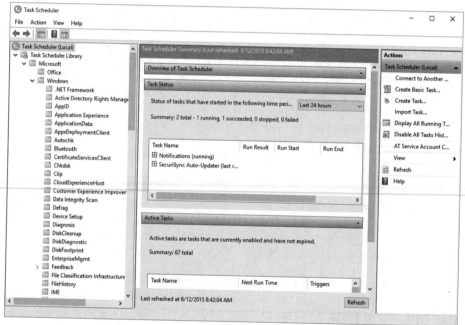

Figure 19-1 Like many other MMC snap-ins, Task Scheduler presents a console tree, the Actions pane, and various informative windows.

The Actions pane provides a menu of things you can do. Some, but not all, of the items here are also available on the menus at the top of the window. If your screen is too crowded with the Actions pane displayed, you can hide—and redisplay—it using the button at the right end of the toolbar, directly below the menu bar.

In the center part of the window, initially you see an overview message (this is a bit of static text; once you've read it, you can hide it by clicking the collapse arrow at the right), a status report of all tasks that have run (or were scheduled to run) during some period of time (by default, the most recent 24 hours), and a summary of all the currently enabled tasks. Entries in the Task Status list have outline controls; click an item's plus sign to see more details.

The Task Status and Active Tasks areas are not updated automatically. To get the latest information, click Refresh at the bottom of the screen, in the Actions pane, or on the Action menu.

If this is your first visit to Task Scheduler, you might be surprised by the number of active tasks that Windows and your applications have already established. To see which tasks managed by Task Scheduler are currently running, click Display All Running Tasks in the Actions pane.

To satisfy your curiosity about what an active task does and how it has been set up, you need to locate it in the console tree. Expand the outline entries as needed, and browse to an item of interest. The entries in the console tree are virtual folders, each of which can contain subfolders or one or more tasks. When you select a folder, the upper part of the details pane lists all tasks stored in the folder. The lower area of the pane, meanwhile, shows a tabbed display of the properties of the selected task. Figure 19-2 shows the Customer Experience Improvement Program folder selected in the console tree, the task named KernelCeipTask selected in the upper area of the details pane, and the General tab of the KernelCeipTask properties displayed in the lower area. (The Actions pane has been hidden in this figure.)

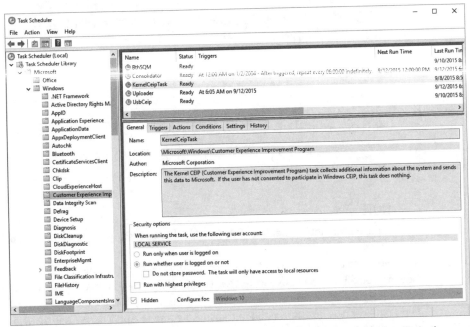

Figure 19-2 Selecting a folder in the console tree produces a list of that folder's tasks in the upper part of the details pane and a properties display in the lower part.

The properties display that appears is read-only. To edit the properties associated with a task, right-click the task name and then click Properties (or double-click the task's entry). That will open a read/write dialog box in a separate window.

With the exception of the History tab, the properties dialog box is identical to the Create Task dialog box, one of the tools you can use to create a new task; we'll explore that dialog box in some detail in the following section, "Creating a task." The History tab allows you to see exactly how, whether, and when a task has run. Figure 19-3 shows the History tab for the ProactiveScan task in the Microsoft\Windows\Chkdsk folder.

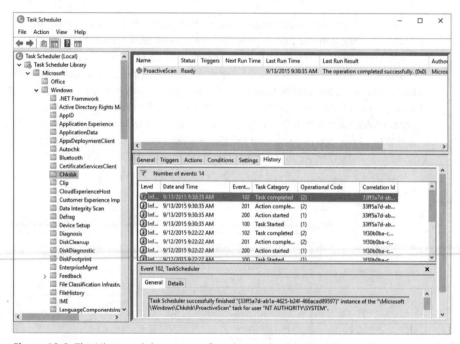

Figure 19-3 The History tab lets you confirm that a scheduled task is running as expected.

NOTE

If the History tab is disabled, click Enable All Tasks History in the Actions pane.

When you display the History tab, the relevant portion of the Event Viewer snap-in snaps in, showing you all the recent events related to the selected task. (Only the top of that pane is visible in Figure 19-3, directly below the properties pane.) This is exactly what you would see if you ran Eventvwr.msc, navigated in the console tree to Applications And Services Logs\ Microsoft\Windows\TaskScheduler\Operational, and filtered the resulting log to show events related to the selected task. (Obviously, if you want this information, it's quicker to find it in the

Task Scheduler console than in the Event Viewer console.) If a task you've set up is not being triggered when you expect it to or not running successfully when it should, you can double-click the appropriate event entry and read whatever details the event log has to offer.

Inside OUT
Use the History tab to troubleshoot tasks

The Windows 10 Task Scheduler maintains an ample history of the events generated by each task. If a task is failing regularly or intermittently, you can review all the causes by scrolling through the History tab on the task's properties display.

Task Scheduler terminology

As you go through the steps to create or edit a task, you'll encounter the following terms:

- **Trigger.** The time at which a task is scheduled to run or the event in response to which a task runs. A task can have multiple triggers.

- **Action.** What the task does. Possible actions include starting a program, sending an email message, and displaying a message on the screen. A task can have multiple actions, in which case the actions occur sequentially in the order in which you assign them.

- **Condition.** An additional requirement that, along with the trigger, must be met for the task to run. For example, a condition might stipulate that the task run only if the computer has been idle for 10 minutes or only if it's running on AC power.

- **Setting.** A property that affects the behavior of a task. With settings, you can do such things as enable a task to run on demand or set retry parameters to be followed if a task fails to run when it's triggered.

Creating a task

You can set up tasks on your own computer or any other computer to which you have access. If you're administering a remote computer, start by selecting the top item in the console tree—the one that says Task Scheduler (Local) if you haven't yet connected to a remote computer. Then click Connect To Another Computer in the Actions pane or on the Action menu.

To begin creating a new task, select the folder in the console tree where you want the task to reside. (If you need to create a new folder for this purpose, right-click the folder's parent in the console tree and click New Folder.)

You can create a new task in the Task Scheduler snap-in by using a wizard or by filling out the Create Task dialog box. The wizard, which you launch by clicking Create Basic Task (in the Actions pane or on the Action menu), is ideal for time-triggered tasks involving a single action. It's also fine for setting up a task to run when you sign in or when Windows starts. For a more complex task definition, you need to work through the Create Task dialog box. Select the folder where you want the task to appear (in the console tree), and then click Create Task in the Actions pane or on the Action menu. Figure 19-4 shows the General tab of the Create Task dialog box.

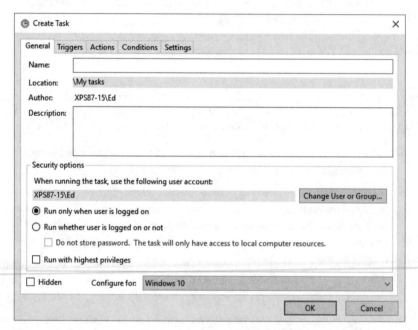

Figure 19-4 On the General tab, type a name for your new task and indicate the security context it should run in.

The one required entry on the General tab is a name for the task; everything else is optional. The task's author is you (you can't change that), and unless you specify otherwise, the task will run in your own security context. If you want it to run in the security context of a different user or group, click Change User Or Group and fill out the ensuing dialog box.

The circumstance under which you're most likely to need to change the security context is when you're setting up tasks to run on another computer. If you intend to run programs with which another user can interact, you should run those in the other user's security context. If you run them in your own, the tasks will run noninteractively (that is, the user will not see them).

Regardless of which user's security context the task is to run in, you have the option of allowing the task to run whether that user is signed in or not. If you select Run Whether User Is Logged On Or Not, you will be prompted for the user's password when you finish creating the task. If you don't happen to have that password, you can select Do Not Store Password. As the text beside this check box indicates, the task will have access to local resources only.

Creating a task to run with elevated privileges

If the task you're setting up is one that would generate a User Account Control (UAC) prompt if it is run interactively, you'll want to select Run With Highest Privileges. If you're setting up a task to run with elevated privileges in the context of a user who does not have administrative credentials, you are asked to supply credentials when you complete the task-setup process.

Creating a hidden task

Windows XP Service Pack 2 introduced the ability to create hidden tasks—tasks that did not ordinarily appear in the Windows XP Scheduled Tasks folder. Such tasks could be created only by means of an application programming interface (API). In Windows 10 and other recent versions of Windows, you can create such tasks without using the API by selecting the Hidden check box. Presumably the reason to do this is to make tasks that you set up for other users less visible (hence, less subject to alteration or deletion) on their target machines.

Note, however, that anyone with administrative credentials can make hidden tasks visible by clicking View, Show Hidden Tasks. And anyone running Task Scheduler can alter or delete tasks at will, regardless of who created them.

Configuring a task to run in a different operating system

If you're setting up a task on a remote computer that's running an operating system other than Windows 10, open the Configure For list and choose appropriately. Note that some applications that create scheduled tasks as part of their installation might configure those tasks for Windows 7, Windows Vista, or Windows XP. These tasks should run properly on Windows 10.

Setting up a task's trigger or triggers

Tasks can be triggered in the following ways:

- On a schedule
- At sign-in
- At startup
- On idle

- On an event

- At task creation or modification

- On connection to a user session

- On disconnection from a user session

- On workstation lock

- On workstation unlock

You can establish zero, one, or several triggers for a task. If you don't set any triggers, you can still run the task on demand (unless you clear the Allow Task To Be Run On Demand check box on the Settings tab of the Create Task dialog box). This gives you a way to test a new task before committing it to a schedule, for example. If you set multiple triggers, the task runs when any one of the triggers occurs.

To set up a trigger, click the Triggers tab in the Create Task dialog box, and then click New. In the New Trigger dialog box (shown in Figure 19-5), choose the type of trigger you want from the Begin The Task list.

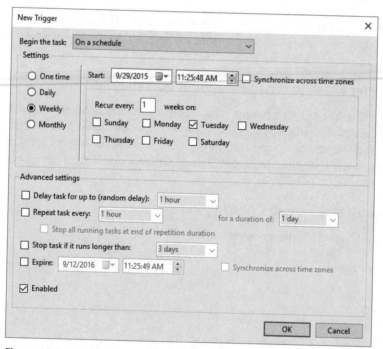

Figure 19-5 A task can have zero, one, or several triggers. Advanced Settings options let you set delay, repeat, and expiration parameters.

Note the Advanced Settings options at the bottom of the dialog box shown in Figure 19-5. These choices—which let you establish delay, repeat, and expiration parameters (among other things)—are not so easy to find when you're reviewing a task that you or someone has already created. They don't appear in the read-only version of a task's properties, and in the read/write version of the properties dialog box, you need to select a trigger (on the Triggers tab) and click Edit to see or change the advanced settings.

Triggering a task on schedule   Time-triggered tasks can be set to run once or to recur at regular intervals. The choices are probably self-explanatory, with the possible exception of the Synchronize Across Time Zones check box. Time triggers are governed by the clock of the machine on which the task is to run, unless you select this check box—in which case, they are based on coordinated universal time (UTC). You might want to go with UTC if you're trying to coordinate time-triggered tasks on multiple machines in multiple time zones.

Triggering a task at sign-in   Sign-in tasks can be set for any user or a specific user or user group. If the user whose sign-in triggers the task is not the user in whose security context the task is running, the task will be noninteractive—in other words, essentially invisible. (The user can note the presence of the task—and terminate it—by running Windows Task Manager, going to the Users tab, and expanding the current user to see a list of running processes.)

Triggering a task at startup   If you set a task to be triggered at startup, the trigger takes effect when you start your own computer (assuming you have Task Scheduler set to configure the local machine) but before you sign in. Therefore, if you intend for the task to run on your own system, be sure to choose Run Whether User Is Logged On Or Not on the General tab of the Create Task dialog box. Otherwise, the task will never run.

If you use the Change User Or Group button on the General tab to specify another user on your domain and you select Run Only When User Is Logged On, the startup-triggered task will run on the remote system when you restart your own, provided the specified user actually is signed in.

Triggering a task on idle   If you set a task to be triggered when your computer is idle, you should also go to the Conditions tab of the Create Task dialog box to specify what you mean by idle. For information about how Task Scheduler defines idleness, see "Starting and running a task only if the computer is idle" later in this chapter.

Note that you need to set an idle trigger on the Triggers tab only if idleness is the only trigger you want to use. If you're setting one or more other triggers but want to ensure that the task starts only when the computer is idle, select Start The Task Only If The Computer Is Idle For on the Conditions tab.

Using an event to trigger a task   Anything that generates an item in an event log can serve as a task trigger. The simplest way to use this feature is to launch Event Viewer (Eventvwr.msc), find the event that you want to use as a trigger, right-click it in Event Viewer, and click Attach

Task To This Event. This action launches the Create Basic Task Wizard, with the trigger portion of the wizard already filled out. The new task appears in a folder called Event Viewer Tasks (newly created for you if it doesn't already exist), and you can modify the task if needed by selecting it there and opening its properties dialog box.

> ➤ For information about events and event logs, see "Event Viewer" in Chapter 17, "Troubleshooting."

It's possible, of course, to create an event-driven task directly in Task Scheduler—by selecting On An Event in the New Trigger dialog box. If you set up the task in this fashion, you need to supply the Log, Source, and Event ID information yourself. It's more trouble to do it this way, and there's no need.

Triggering at task creation or modification   The option to trigger a task at task creation or modification gives you an easy way to run a task the moment you finish setting it up or edit it subsequently. You can use this setting for testing purposes or, by combining it with other triggers, to make a task run immediately as well as subsequently.

Triggering a task at user connection or disconnection   The options On Connection To A User Session and On Disconnect From A User Session give you some flexible ways to run tasks in response to user activities. Option buttons associated with these choices let you specify whether the settings apply to any user or to a particular user or group. Additional options make the trigger apply to remote connections and disconnections or to local connections and disconnections. Setting a trigger to a particular user on the local computer, for example, enables you to run a task in response to that user's connection via Remote Desktop Connection or the Switch User command.

Triggering a task at workstation lock or unlock   Like several other triggering choices, the On Workstation Lock and On Workstation Unlock options can be configured to apply to a particular user or group or to anyone who locks or unlocks the computer.

Setting up a task's action or actions

Besides its name (which you supply on the General tab of the Create Task dialog box), the only other task parameter you must provide is the action or actions the task is supposed to perform. This you do by clicking New on the Actions tab and filling out the rest of the dialog box.

Opening the Start A Program drop-down menu, you will find three choices: Start A Program, Send An E-Mail, and Display A Message. The second and third of these, however, have been deprecated since Windows 8. So leave Action set at Start A Program, and then supply the program (or script) name, optional arguments, and an optional start location.

You can specify one or several actions. Multiple actions are carried out sequentially, with each new action beginning when the previous one is complete.

The Start A Program option can be applied to anything that Windows can execute—a Windows program, a batch program or script, a document associated with a program, or a shortcut. You can use the Browse button to simplify entry of long path specifications, add command-line parameters for your executable on the Add Arguments line, and specify a start-in folder for the executable. If your program needs elevated privileges to run success-fully, be sure that you select Run With Highest Privileges on the General tab of the Create Task dialog box.

Starting and running a task only if the computer is idle

On the Conditions tab of the Create Task dialog box (shown in Figure 19-6), you can require that the computer be idle for a specified period of time before a triggered task can begin. To do this, select Start The Task Only If The Computer Is Idle For, and specify the time period in the field to the right. Other check boxes in the Idle section of the Conditions tab let you spec-ify what should happen if the task starts to run during a required idle period but the computer subsequently becomes active again.

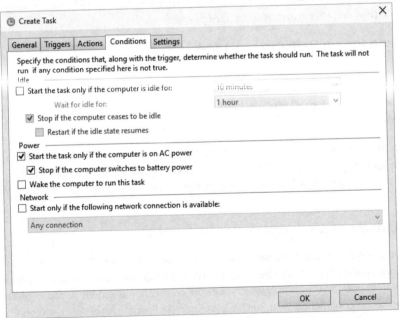

Figure 19-6 You can configure a task to run only when the computer is idle, only when it's running on AC power, or only when it's connected to a network.

Task Scheduler defines idleness as follows:

- If a screen saver is running, the computer is presumed to be idle.

- If a screen saver is not running, the system checks for idleness every 15 minutes, considering the machine to be idle if no keyboard or mouse input has occurred during that interval and if the disk input/output (I/O) and CPU usage figures were 0 percent for 90 percent of that time.

In addition to specifying a required period of idleness, you can tell Windows to wait some period of time after a task has been triggered before beginning to determine whether the computer is idle. Clearly, adjusting the idle parameters is a bit of an art; if you have precise requirements for some reason, you might need to experiment and test to get things just the way you want them.

Requiring AC power

If you're setting up a task to run on a portable computer, consider whether you want the task to begin running while the computer is running on battery power. If you do not, select Start The Task Only If The Computer Is On AC Power in the Power section of the Conditions tab. A second check box below this one lets you specify whether the task, once it begins, should cease if the computer switches to battery power.

Waking the computer to run a task

If it's essential that your task run at some particular time, whether or not the computer is asleep, be sure to select Wake The Computer To Run This Task on the Conditions tab. Once roused, the computer will then perform whatever duties you've assigned, returning to sleep on completion in accordance with whatever power plan is in effect.

If you do not want to disturb your computer's rest, you might want to stipulate that the task run as soon as possible after the machine wakes. You can do that by selecting Run Task As Soon As Possible After A Scheduled Start Is Missed on the Settings tab of the Create Task dialog box.

Requiring a network connection

If your task requires access to network resources, be sure to select Start Only If The Following Network Connection Is Available on the Conditions tab. Then use the drop-down list directly below this check box to specify which network connection is required. You might want to use this option in conjunction with Run Task As Soon As Possible After A Scheduled Start Is Missed, a check box on the Settings tab.

Running a task on demand

You can run a scheduled task on demand as well as in response to various time or event trig-gers. You can turn this feature off for a task by clearing the Allow Task To Be Run On Demand check box on the Settings tab. But unless you're concerned that another user with access to your system might run a task against your wishes, it's hard to imagine why you would want to disallow on-demand execution.

To run a task on demand, assuming you have not disallowed it, locate the task's folder in the console tree, right-click the task in Task Scheduler's upper pane, and then click Run.

Scheduling tasks with the Schtasks command

Task Scheduler provides a friendly and versatile method of creating and managing scheduled tasks. In some instances, however, you might find it easier to manage scheduled tasks from a command prompt. For these occasions, Windows provides the Schtasks command, a replace-ment for the venerable At command that was included with earlier versions of the Windows NT platform. With Schtasks, you can create, modify, delete, end, view, and run scheduled tasks—and, of course, you can incorporate the command in batch programs and scripts.

Tasks created via Schtasks appear in the top-level folder (Task Scheduler Library) in the Task Scheduler console tree, and you can edit, run, or delete them from there as well as from the command prompt.

Schtasks is a rather complex command with lots of command-line switches and other param-eters, but it has only six main variants:

- **Schtasks /Create.** This variant, which you use to create a new scheduled task, is the most complex because of all the available triggering options, conditions, and settings. For details, type **schtasks /create /?** at the command prompt.

- **Schtasks /Change.** This variant allows you to modify an existing task. Among other things, you can change the program that the task runs, the user account under which the task runs, or the password associated with that user account. For details, type **schtasks /change /?** at the command prompt.

- **Schtasks /Delete.** This variant deletes an existing task or, optionally, all tasks on a computer.

- **Schtasks /End.** This variant stops a program that was started by a scheduled task.

- **Schtasks /Query.** This variant displays, with optional verbosity, all scheduled tasks on the local or a remote computer. You can use arguments to restrict the display to particular tasks or tasks running in particular security contexts. For details, type **schtasks /query /?** at the command prompt.

- **Schtasks /Run.** This variant runs a specified task on demand.

A few examples should give you an idea of the power of the Schtasks command. Suppose, for example, that you want to run OneNote 2013 every four hours at 20 minutes past the hour. Assuming the OneNote executable exists at the specified location on your computer, the following command sets you up:

```
schtasks /create /tn "Run OneNote" /tr "%programfiles%\Microsoft Office 15\root\
office15\onenote.exe" /sc hourly /mo 4 /st 00:20:00
```

In this example, the /tn switch specifies the name of the task, /tr specifies the path to the executable program, /sc specifies the schedule type, /mo specifies the interval, and /st specifies the starting time.

The following example creates a task that runs a script on the last Friday of each calendar quarter. (The script isn't included with Windows; it's just an example.)

```
schtasks /create /tn "Quarterly wrap-up" /tr c:\apps\qtrwrap.vbs /sc monthly /mo last
/d fri /m mar,jun,sep,dec
```

By default, tasks scheduled via the Schtasks command run under the user account that's currently signed in. To make them run under a different account, use the /ru switch followed by the account name you want to use; you also need to know the sign-in password for that account. To use the built-in System account, append */ru "System"* to the command. No password is required for the System account, but because only administrators can use Schtasks, this doesn't present a problem.

Automating command sequences with batch programs

A batch program (also commonly called a *batch file*) is a text file that contains a sequence of commands to be executed. You execute the commands by entering the file name at a command prompt. Any action you can take by typing a command at a command prompt can be encapsulated in a batch program.

When you type the name of your batch program at the command prompt (or when you specify it as a task to be executed by Task Scheduler and the appropriate trigger occurs), the command interpreter opens the file and starts reading the statements. It reads the first line, executes the command, and then goes on to the next line. On the surface, this seems to operate just as though you were typing each line yourself at the command prompt. In fact, however, the batch program can be more complicated because the language includes replaceable parameters, conditional and branching statements, the ability to call subroutines, and so on.

Batch programs can also respond to values returned by programs and to the values of environment variables.

Batch programming is a venerable art, having been with us since the earliest days of MS-DOS (long before Windows was so much as a twinkle in Microsoft's eye). These days there are more powerful scripting tools at your disposal. Nevertheless, if you have already invested some time and energy in learning the language of batch programming, that investment can continue to serve you in Windows 10. Your batch programs will run as well as they ever have, and you can execute them in response to events by means of Task Scheduler.

Automating tasks with Windows Script Host

Microsoft Windows Script Host (WSH) provides a way to perform more sophisticated tasks than the simple jobs that batch programs are able to handle. You can control virtually any component of Windows and of many Windows-based programs with WSH scripts.

To run a script, you can type a script name at a command prompt or double-click the script's icon in File Explorer. WSH has two nearly equivalent programs—Wscript.exe and Cscript.exe—that, with the help of a language interpreter dynamic-link library such as Vbscript.dll, execute scripts written in VBScript or another scripting language. (Cscript.exe is a command-line program; Wscript.exe is its graphical counterpart.)

With WSH, the files can be written in several different languages, including VBScript (a scripting language similar to Microsoft Visual Basic) and JScript (a form of JavaScript). All the objects are available to any language, and in most situations you can choose the language with which you are most comfortable. WSH doesn't care what language you use, provided the appropriate interpreter dynamic-link library is available. VBScript and JScript interpreters come with Windows 10; interpreters for Perl, KiXtart (Kix), Python, Rexx, and other languages are available elsewhere.

CHAPTER 20

Advanced networking

For most users of Windows at home or in a small office, HomeGroup and the other networking methods and procedures described in Chapter 5, "Networking essentials," provide all the needed connectivity. In these environments, accessing shared files, media, and printers throughout a local area network is easily achieved.

But there's much more to networking, enough to fill another book the size of this one. In this chapter, we touch upon a few of these more complex features.

We begin with a look at other ways to share resources over a network. While HomeGroup has the advantage of being easy to set up and use, it doesn't allow you to apply resource permissions on a granular level. If you need to provide different types of access to individual users, you can use the procedures in this section. Another limitation of HomeGroup is that it works only with Windows 7 and later versions; if your network includes computers running other operating systems or older versions of Windows, this section is for you.

In this chapter we also look at situations in which accessing shared files and printers is not enough; you want access to an *entire computer*. With Remote Desktop, you can do exactly that, and a section of this chapter is devoted to showing you how.

Networked devices don't always communicate the way they should, so we conclude with a survey of network troubleshooting tools included with Windows and explain sound procedures for using them.

Viewing network status

If you're familiar with earlier Windows versions, you probably know Network And Sharing Center as the place to go for a quick overview of your network connections and the condition of your network. And, if you're experiencing problems with your network, it serves as a launch pad to various diagnostic tools.

➤ For more information, see "Network And Sharing Center" in Chapter 5.

As you've seen with other Control Panel applications, much of the functionality of Network And Sharing Center from previous Windows versions has made the transition to Settings in Windows 10. Take a look by opening Settings, Network & Internet, which is shown in Figure 20-1.

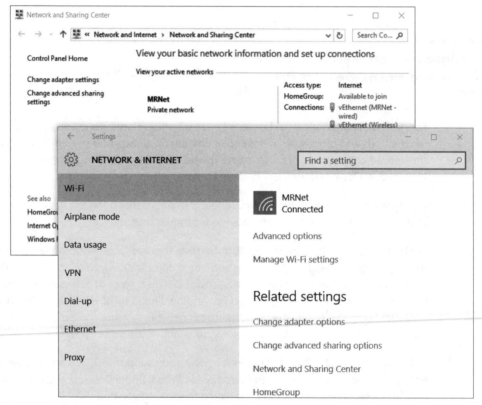

Figure 20-1 Network & Internet in Settings will someday supplant Network And Sharing Center. In the meantime, a link in the Settings app leads to the Control Panel app.

Inside OUT

Easily open Network & Internet or Network And Sharing Center

The quickest way to get to either network settings app is to click or tap the network icon in the notification area of the taskbar. To open Network & Internet in Settings, click the icon and then click Network Settings. To open the Network And Sharing Center in Control Panel, right-click or long tap the network icon in the taskbar and then choose Open Network And Sharing Center.

Sharing resources with other users

The simplest way to share files, digital media, printers, and other resources in a small network is with HomeGroup, a feature we cover in Chapter 5. Convenient as it is, however, HomeGroup isn't appropriate for all networks. First, it's designed for use in a home, where you fully trust everybody. Hence, it has limited abilities for applying different access requirements to various objects and for various users. Second, HomeGroup works only on computers running Windows 7 and later. Computers running earlier versions of Windows or other operating systems must use different methods for sharing and accessing network resources.

These other methods are fully supported in Windows 10 and can be used alongside Home-Group if you want to. The underlying system of share permissions and NTFS permissions for controlling access to objects remains in Windows 10, working much like it has in previous versions of Windows going all the way back to Windows NT in the early '90s.

➤ For more information about HomeGroup, see "Sharing files, digital media, and printers in a homegroup" in Chapter 5.

Understanding sharing and security models in Windows

Much like Windows 7, Windows 10 offers two ways (aside from HomeGroup) to share file resources, whether locally or over the network:

- **Public folder sharing.** When you place files and folders in your Public folder or its subfolders, those files are available to anyone who has a user account on your computer. Each person who signs in has access to his or her own profile folders (Documents, Music, and so on), and *everyone* who signs in has access to the Public folder. (You'll need to dig a bit to find the Public folder, which doesn't appear by default in the left pane of File Explorer. Navigate to C:\Users\Public. If you use the Public folder often, pin it to the Quick Access list in File Explorer.)

  By default, all users with an account on your computer can sign in and create, view, modify, and delete files in the Public folders. The person who creates a file in a Public folder (or copies an item to a Public folder) is the file's owner and has Full Control access. All others who sign in locally have Modify access.

  Settings in Advanced Sharing Settings (accessible from Settings, Network & Internet; see the next section for details), determine whether the contents of your Public folder are made available on your network and whether entering a user name and password is required for access. If you turn on password-protected sharing, only network users who have a user account on your computer (or those who know the user name and password for an account on your computer) can access files in the Public folder. Without password-protected sharing, everyone on your network has access to your Public folder files if you enable network sharing of the Public folder.

CHAPTER 20

You can't select which network users get access, nor can you specify different access levels for different users. Sharing via the Public folder is quick and easy—but it's inflexible.

- **Advanced sharing.** By choosing to share folders or files outside the Public folder, you can specify precisely which user accounts are able to access your shared data, and you can specify the types of privileges those accounts enjoy. You can grant different access privileges to different users. For example, you might enable some users to modify shared files and create new ones, enable other users to read files without changing them, and lock out still other users altogether.

You don't need to decide between sharing the Public folder and sharing specific folders because you can use them both simultaneously. You might find that a mix of sharing styles works best for you; each has its benefits:

- Sharing specific folders is best for files that you want to share with some users but not others—or if you want to grant different levels of access to different users.

- Public folder sharing provides a convenient, logical way to segregate your personal documents, pictures, music, and so on from those that you want to share with everyone who uses your computer or your network.

Configuring your network for sharing

If you plan to share folders and files with other users on your network through options other than those available in the HomeGroup feature, you need to take a few preparatory steps. (If you plan to share only through HomeGroup and with others who use your computer by signing in locally, you can skip these steps. And if your computer is part of a domain, some of these steps—or their equivalent in the domain world—must be done by an administrator on the domain controller. We don't cover those details in this book.)

1. **Be sure that all computers use the same workgroup name.** With versions of Windows newer than Windows XP, this step isn't absolutely necessary, although it does improve network discovery performance. For details, see the sidebar, "Renaming your workgroup."

2. **Be sure that your network's location is set to Private.** This setting provides appropriate security for a network in a home or an office. For details, see "Setting network locations" in Chapter 5.

3. **Be sure that Network Discovery is turned on.** This should happen automatically when you set the network location to Private, but you can confirm the setting—and change it if necessary—in Advanced Sharing Settings, which is shown in Figure 20-2. To open Advanced Sharing Settings, go to Network & Internet or Network And Sharing Center. In either app, click Change Advanced Sharing Options.

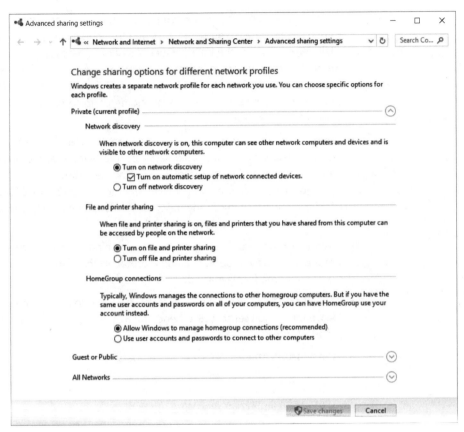

Figure 20-2 After you review settings for the Private profile, click the arrow by All Networks to see additional options.

4. **Select your sharing options.** In Advanced Sharing Settings, make a selection for each of the following network options. You'll find the first two under the Private profile; to view the remaining settings, expand All Networks.

- **File And Printer Sharing.** Turn on this option if you want to share specific files or folders, the Public folder, or printers; it must be turned on if you plan to share any files (other than media streaming) over your network.

  The mere act of turning on file and printer sharing does not expose any of your computer's files or printers to other network users; that occurs only after you make additional sharing settings.

- **HomeGroup Connections.** If you use a homegroup for sharing, it's generally best to use the default setting, Allow Windows To Manage Homegroup Connections (Recommended). With this setting, when a user at a computer that is also part of a homegroup attempts to use a shared resource on your computer, Windows connects using the HomeGroupUser$ account.

When a user connects from a computer that is not a member of the homegroup, Windows first tries to authenticate using that person's sign-in credentials; if that fails, Windows uses the built-in Guest account (if password-protected sharing is off) or prompts for credentials (if password-protected sharing is on). If you select Use User Accounts And Passwords To Connect To Other Computers, homegroup computers work like nonhomegroup computers instead of using the HomeGroupUser$ account.

- **Public Folder Sharing.** If you want to share items in your Public folder with all network users (or, if you enable password-protected sharing, all users who have a user account and password on your computer), turn on Public folder sharing. If you do so, network users will have read/write access to Public folders. With Public folder sharing turned off, anyone who signs in to your computer locally has access to Public folders, but network users do not.

- **Media Streaming.** Turning on media streaming provides access to pictures, music, and video through streaming protocols that can send media to computers or to other media playback devices.

- **File Sharing Connections.** Unless you have very old computers on your network, leave this option set to 128-bit encryption, which has been the standard for most of this century.

- **Password Protected Sharing.** When password-protected sharing is turned on, network users cannot access your shared folders (including Public folders, if shared) or printers unless they can provide the user name and password of a user account on your computer. With this setting enabled, when another user attempts to access a shared resource, Windows sends the user name and password that the person used to sign in to his or her own computer. If that matches the credentials for a local user account on your computer, the user gets immediate access to the shared resource (assuming permissions to use the particular resource have been granted to that user account). If either the user name or the password does not match, Windows asks the user to provide credentials.

  With password-protected sharing turned off, Windows does not require a user name and password from network visitors. Instead, network access is provided by using the Guest account. As we explain in Chapter 6, "Managing user accounts, passwords, and credentials," this account isn't available for interactive use but can handle these tasks in the background.

5. **Configure user accounts.** If you use password-protected sharing, each person who accesses a shared resource on your computer must have a user account on your computer. Use the same user name as that person uses on his or her own computer and the same password as well. If you do that, network users will be able to access shared resources without having to enter their credentials after they've signed in to their own computer.

Renaming your workgroup

A workgroup is identified by a name; all computers in a workgroup must be in the same local area network and subnet, and all must share the same workgroup name. In Windows 10, the workgroup name is largely invisible and irrelevant; when you open the Network folder or look at a network map, Windows displays all computers in the network, regardless of which workgroup they're in. (However, network discovery is faster when all computers are in the same workgroup.) The default name for a workgroup in recent Windows versions is WORKGROUP.

To set the workgroup name, follow these steps:

1. In the search box or in Control Panel, type **workgroup**, and then click Change Workgroup Name.

2. On the Computer Name tab of the System Properties dialog box, click Change, which displays the following dialog box:

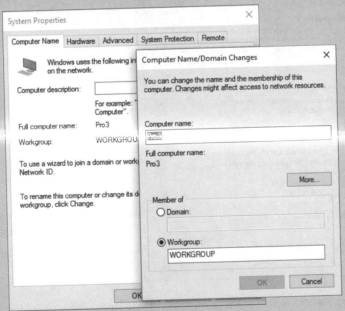

3. In the Computer Name/Domain Changes dialog box, select Workgroup and type the name of the workgroup (15-character maximum; the name can't include any of these characters: ; : < > * + = \ | / ? ,). Then click OK in each dialog box.

4. Restart your computer.

Sharing files and folders from any folder

Whether you plan to share files and folders with other people who share your computer or those who connect to your computer over the network (or both), the process for setting up shared resources is the same as long as the Sharing Wizard is enabled. We recommend that you use the Sharing Wizard even if you normally disdain wizards. It's quick, easy, and certain to make all the correct settings for network shares and NTFS permissions—a sometimes daunting task if undertaken manually. Once you've configured shares with the wizard, you can always dive in and make changes manually if you need to.

To be sure the Sharing Wizard is enabled, open Folder Options. (Type **folder** in the search box and choose File Explorer Options. Or, in File Explorer, click View, Options.) In the dialog box that appears, shown next, click the View tab. Near the bottom of the Advanced Settings list, see that Use Sharing Wizard (Recommended) is selected.

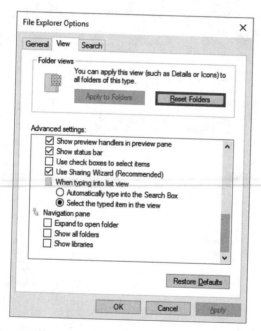

With the Sharing Wizard at the ready, follow these steps to share a folder or files:

1. In File Explorer, select the folders or files you want to share. (You can select multiple objects.)

2. Right-click and choose Share With, Specific People. (Alternatively, click or tap the Share tab and then click Specific People in the Share With box. You might need to click the arrow in the Share With box to display Specific People.) The File Sharing dialog box appears, as shown in Figure 20-3.

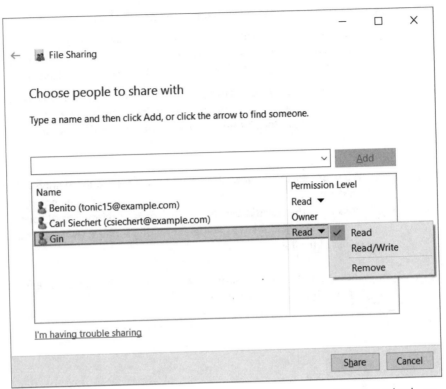

Figure 20-3 For each name in the list, you can click the arrow to set the access level—or remove that account from the list.

3. In the entry box, enter the name or Microsoft account for each user with whom you want to share. You can type a name in the box or click the arrow to display a list of available names; then click Add. Repeat this step for each person you want to add.

   The list includes all users who have an account on your computer, plus Everyone. If you've joined a homegroup, the list also includes any Microsoft accounts that have been linked to user accounts on any PC that is part of the homegroup. Guest is included if password-protected sharing is turned off. If you want to grant access to someone who doesn't appear in the list, click Create A New User, which takes you to User Accounts in Control Panel. (This option appears only if your computer is not joined to a homegroup.)

   ## NOTE
   If you select Everyone and you have password-protected sharing enabled, the user must still have a valid account on your computer. However, if you have turned off password-protected sharing, network users can gain access *only* if you grant permission to Everyone or to Guest.

4. For each user, select a permission level. Your choices are:

   - **Read.** Users with this permission level can view shared files and run shared programs, but they cannot change or delete files. Selecting Read in the Sharing Wizard is equivalent to setting NTFS permissions to Read & Execute.

   - **Read/Write.** Users assigned the Read/Write permission have the same privileges you do as owner: they can view, change, add, and delete files in a shared folder. Selecting Read/Write sets NTFS permissions to Full Control for this user.

   ## NOTE

   You might see other permission levels if you return to the Sharing Wizard after you set up sharing. Contribute indicates Modify permission. Custom indicates NTFS permissions other than Read & Execute, Modify, or Full Control. Mixed appears if you select multiple items and they have different sharing settings. Owner, of course, identifies the owner of the item.

5. Click Share. After a few moments, the wizard displays a page like the one shown in Figure 20-4.

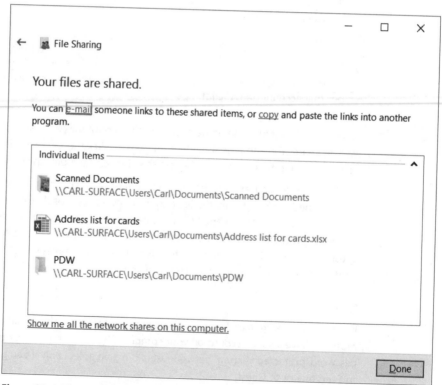

Figure 20-4 The Sharing Wizard displays the network path for each item you've shared.

6.   In the final step of the wizard, you can do any of the following:

- Send an email message to the people with whom you're sharing. The message includes a link to the shared folder or file.

- Copy the network path to the Clipboard. This is handy if you want to send a link via another application, such as a messaging app. (To copy the link for a single item in a list, right-click the share name and choose Copy Link.)

- Double-click a share name to open the shared item.

- Open a search folder that shows all the folders and files you're sharing.

When you're finished with these tasks, click Done.

Creating a share requires privilege elevation, but after a folder has been shared, the share is available to network users no matter who is signed in to your computer—or even when nobody is signed in.

Inside OUT

Use advanced sharing to create shorter network paths

Confusingly, when you share one of your profile folders (or any other subfolder of %SystemDrive%\Users), Windows creates a network share for the Users folder—not for the folder you shared. This isn't a security problem; NTFS permissions prevent network users from seeing any folders or files except the ones you explicitly share. But it does lead to some long Universal Naming Convention (UNC) paths to network shares. For example, sharing the PDW subfolder of Documents (as shown in Figure 20-4) creates the network path \\CARL-SURFACE\Users\Carl\Documents\PDW. If this same folder had been anywhere on your computer outside the Users folder, no matter how deeply nested, the network path would instead be \\CARL-SURFACE\PDW. Other people to whom you granted access wouldn't need to click through a series of folders to find the files in the intended target folder.

Network users, of course, can map a network drive or save a shortcut to your target folder to avoid this problem. But you can work around it from the sharing side too: use advanced sharing to share the folder directly. (Do this after you've used the Sharing Wizard to set up permissions.) For more information, see "Setting advanced sharing properties" following the next section. (And while you're doing that, be sure the share name you create doesn't have spaces. Eliminating them makes it easier to type a share path that works as a link.)

Stopping or changing sharing of a file or folder

If you want to stop sharing a particular shared file or folder, select it in File Explorer and on the Share tab, click Stop Sharing. (Or right-click and choose Share With, Stop Sharing.) Doing so removes access control entries that are not inherited. In addition, the network share is removed; the folder will no longer be visible in another user's Network folder.

To change share permissions, right-click and choose Share With, Specific People. In the File Sharing dialog box (shown earlier in Figure 20-3), you can add users, change permissions, or remove users. (To stop sharing with a particular user, click the arrow by the user's name and choose Remove.)

Setting advanced sharing properties

With Advanced Sharing, you configure network shares independently of NTFS permissions. (For more information about this distinction, see the sidebar "How shared resource permissions and NTFS permissions work together" later in this chapter.) To open Advanced Sharing, right-click a folder, choose Properties, and click the Sharing tab. Or, if the Sharing Wizard is disabled, select a folder in File Explorer and on the ribbon's Share tab (or the right-click Share With menu) choose Advanced Sharing. Both methods display the Sharing tab, which is shown in Figure 20-5.

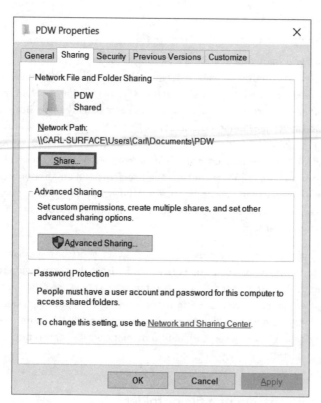

Figure 20-5 The Share button under Network File And Folder Sharing summons the Sharing Wizard, but it's available only when the wizard is enabled.

NOTE

The Sharing tab is part of the properties dialog box for a folder, but not for files. Also, when the Sharing Wizard is disabled, the Advanced Sharing button appears on the ribbon only when you select a single folder. Only the Sharing Wizard is capable of making share settings for files and for multiple objects simultaneously.

To create or modify a network share using advanced settings, follow these steps:

1. On the Sharing tab, click Advanced Sharing to display the Advanced Sharing dialog box.

2. Select Share This Folder, as shown next.

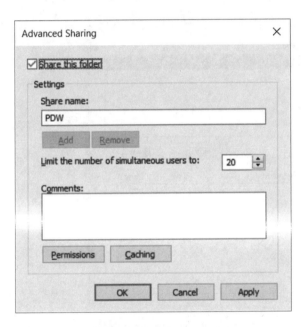

3. Accept or change the proposed share name.

NOTE

If the folder is already shared and you want to add another share name (perhaps with different permissions), click Add and then type the name for the new share.

The share name is the name that other users will see in their own Network folders. Windows initially proposes to use the folder's name as the share name. That's usually a good choice, but you're not obligated to accept it. If you already have a shared folder with that name, you'll need to pick a different name.

4. Type a description of the folder's contents in the Comments box.

Other users will see this description when they inspect the folder's properties dialog box in their Network folder (or use Details view).

5. To limit the number of users who can connect to the shared folder concurrently, specify a number in the box. Windows 10 permits up to 20 concurrent network connections. (If you need to share a resource with more users, you must use Windows Server.)

6. Click Permissions.

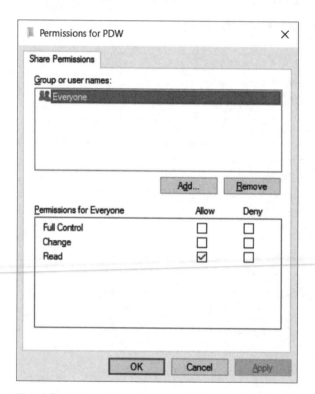

The default shared resource permission associated with a new share is Read access to Everyone.

CAUTION

When you share a folder, you also make that folder's subfolders available on the network. If the access permissions you set for the folder aren't appropriate for any of its subfolders, either reconsider your choice of access permissions or restructure your folders to avoid the problem.

7. In the Group Or User Names list, select the name of the user or group you want to manage.

   The shared resource permissions for the selected user or group appear below in the permissions list.

8. Select Allow, Deny, or neither for each access control entry:

   - **Full Control.** Allows users to create, read, write, rename, and delete files in the folder and its subfolders. In addition, users can change permissions and take ownership of files on NTFS volumes.

   - **Change.** Allows users to read, write, rename, and delete files in the folder and its subfolders but not create new files.

   - **Read.** Allows users to read files but not write to them or delete them.

   If you select neither Allow nor Deny, it is still possible that the user or group can inherit the permission through membership in another group that has the permission. If the user or group doesn't belong to another such group, the user or group is implicitly denied permission.

NOTE

To remove a name from the Group Or User Names list, select it and click Remove. To add a name to the list, click Add to open the Select Users Or Groups dialog box, where you can enter the names of the users and groups you want to add.

CHAPTER 20

How shared resource permissions and NTFS permissions work together

The implementation of shared resource permissions and NTFS permissions is confusingly similar, but it's important to recognize that these are two separate levels of access control. Only connections that successfully pass through both gates are granted access.

Shared resource permissions control *network* access to a particular resource. Shared resource permissions do not affect users who sign in locally. You set shared resource permissions in the Advanced Sharing dialog box, which you access from the Sharing tab of a folder's properties dialog box.

NTFS permissions (also known as discretionary access control lists, DACLs) apply to folders and files on an NTFS-formatted drive. For each user to whom you want to grant access, you can specify exactly what that user is allowed to do: run programs, view folder contents, create new files, change existing files, and so on. You set NTFS permissions on the Security tab of the properties dialog box for a folder or file.

It's important to recognize that the two types of permissions are combined in the most restrictive way. If, for example, a user is granted Read permission on the network share, even if the account has Full Control NTFS permissions on the same folder, the user gets only read access when connecting over the network. In effect, the two sets of permissions act in tandem as "gatekeepers" that winnow out incoming network connections. An account that attempts to connect over the network is examined first by the shared resource permissions gatekeeper. The account is either rejected or allowed to enter with certain permissions. It's then confronted by the NTFS permissions gatekeeper, which might strip away (but not add to) some or all of the permissions granted at the first doorway. In many advanced sharing scenarios, it's common practice to simply configure the shared folder with Full Control permissions for Everyone and then configure NTFS permissions to control access as desired.

In determining the effective permission for a particular account, you must also consider the effect of group membership. Permissions are cumulative; an account that is a member of one or more groups is granted all the permissions granted explicitly to the account as well as all permissions granted to each group of which it's a member. The only exception to this rule is Deny permissions, which take precedence over any conflicting Allow permissions.

Inside OUT

Review and change your sharing and NTFS permissions settings

A tool in File Explorer opens a dialog box that shows NTFS permissions and share permissions in a format that's sometimes easier to decipher than the properties dialog box. Select a single folder or file in File Explorer and then, on the ribbon's Share tab, click Advanced Security. Here, in addition to viewing each type of permission, you can determine the *effective access*, which shows for a specific user or group the cumulative effect of various permissions and group memberships. (On a small network, the easiest way to specify a user on the Effective Access tab is to click Select A User, Advanced, Find Now.)

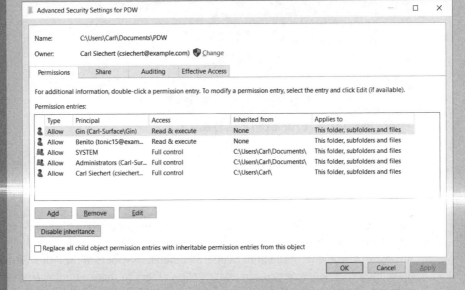

Sharing a printer

Although Windows doesn't have a wizard for sharing a printer over the network, the process is pretty simple. You configure all options for a printer—whether you plan to share it or not—by using the printer's properties dialog box, which you access from Devices And Printers in Control Panel.

To make a printer available to other network users, right-click a printer and click Printer Properties. On the Sharing tab, select Share This Printer and provide a share name, as shown in Figure 20-6.

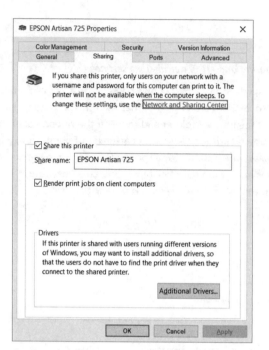

Figure 20-6 The share name can include spaces.

Unlike for shared folders, which maintain separate share permissions and NTFS permissions, a single set of permissions controls access to printers, whether by local users or by network users. (Of course, only printers that have been shared are accessible to network users.)

When you set up a printer, initially all users in the Everyone group have Print permission for documents they create, which provides users access to the printer and the ability to manage their own documents in the print queue. By default, members of the Administrators group also have Manage Printers permission—which allows them to share a printer, change its properties, remove a printer, and change its permissions—and Manage Documents permission, which lets them pause, restart, move, and remove all queued documents. As an administrator, you can view or modify permissions on the Security tab of the printer properties dialog box.

Setting server properties

In addition to setting properties for individual printers by using their properties dialog boxes, you can set other properties by visiting the Print Server Properties dialog box. To get there, select a printer in the Devices And Printers folder, and then click Print Server Properties. You'll find more details in "Fine-tuning hardware and printer settings" in Chapter 13, "Hardware."

The first three tabs control the list of items you see in the properties dialog box for a printer:

- The Forms tab controls the list of forms that you can assign to trays using the Device Settings tab in a printer's properties dialog box. You can create new form definitions and delete any that you create, but you can't delete any of the predefined forms.

- The Ports tab lets you configure the ports that appear on the Ports tab in a printer's properties dialog box.

- The Drivers tab offers a list of all the installed printer drivers and provides a centralized location where you can add, remove, or update drivers.

On the Advanced tab you can specify the location of spool files (you might want to change to a folder on a different drive if, for example, you frequently run out of space on the current drive when you attempt to print large documents) and set notification options.

Inside OUT

Use the Print Management console

Users of Windows 10 Pro and Enterprise editions have a tool that places all print management tasks in one convenient console. Print Management (Printmanagement.msc), shown here, provides a place for managing printers, drivers, queues, and shares. If your edition includes Print Management, you can start it by typing **print** in the search box and then clicking Print Management.

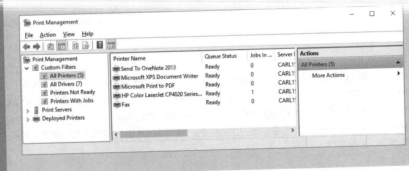

Finding and using shared resources on a Windows network

The Network folder is your gateway to all available network resources, just as This PC is the gateway to resources stored on your own system. The Network folder (shown in Figure 20-7) contains an icon for each computer that Windows discovers on your network; double-click a computer icon to see that computer's shared resources, if any.

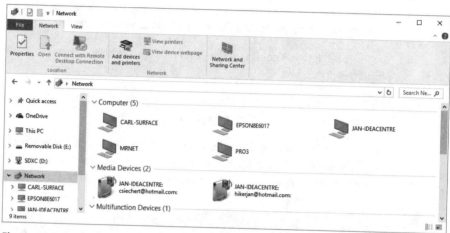

Figure 20-7 The Network folder shows all computers on your network, not just those in your workgroup.

To open a shared folder on another computer, double-click its icon in the Network folder. If you have the proper permissions, this action displays the folder's contents in File Explorer. It's not always that easy, however. If the user account with which you signed in doesn't have permission to view a network computer or resource you select, a dialog box asks you to provide the name of an account (and its password, of course) that has permission. Don't be fooled by the Domain reference below the User Name and Password boxes; in a workgroup, that value refers to the local computer.

Perhaps the trickiest part of using shared folders is fully understanding what permissions have been applied to a folder and which credentials are in use by each network user. It's important to recognize that *all network access is controlled by the computer with the shared resources*; regardless of what operating system runs on the computer attempting to connect to a network share, it must meet the security requirements of the computer where the shared resource is actually located.

Working with mapped network folders

Mapping a network folder makes it appear to applications as though the folder is part of your own computer. Windows assigns a drive letter to the mapped folder, making the folder appear like an additional hard drive. You can still access a mapped folder in the conventional manner by navigating to it through the Network folder. But mapping gives the folder an alias—the assigned drive letter—that provides an alternative means of access.

To map a network folder to a drive letter, follow these steps:

1. Open This PC in File Explorer, and on the ribbon's Computer tab, click Map Network Drive. (Alternatively, after you open a computer in the Network folder, right-click a network share and choose Map Network Drive.)

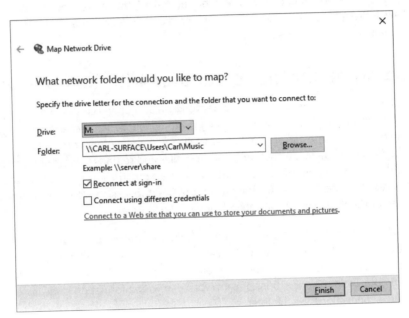

2. Select a drive letter in the Drive box. You can choose any letter that's not already in use.

3. In the Folder box, type the path to the folder you want or, more easily, click Browse and navigate to the folder.

4. Select Reconnect At Sign-In if you want Windows to connect to this shared folder automatically at the start of each session.

5. If your regular sign-in account doesn't have permission to connect to the resource, select Connect Using Different Credentials. (After you click Finish, Windows asks for the user name and password you want to use for this connection.)

6. Click Finish.

In File Explorer, the "drive" appears under This PC.

If you change your mind about mapping a network folder, simply right-click the folder's icon in your This PC folder. Choose Disconnect on the resulting shortcut menu, and the connection will be severed.

CHAPTER 20

Connecting to a network printer

To use a printer that has been shared, open the Network folder in File Explorer and double-click the name of the server to which the printer is attached. If the shared printers on that server are not visible, return to the Network folder, click to select the server, and then, on the ribbon's Network tab, click View Printers. Right-click the printer and choose Connect. Alternatively, from the Devices And Printers folder, click Add A Printer and use the Add Printer Wizard to add a network printer.

Connecting to another computer with Remote Desktop

Sharing computer resources over a network, when properly configured, gives you access to all the files you might need, wherever they're stored. But sometimes even that is not enough. You might need to run a program that is installed only on another computer, or you might need to configure and manage another computer's files and settings in ways that can be done only by sitting down in front of that computer. As it turns out, there is an alternative to direct physical access: Remote Desktop. By using a Remote Desktop session, you can operate a computer by remote control over a local network or over the Internet.

With Remote Desktop, applications run on the remote computer; your computer is effectively used as a dumb terminal. You can use a low-powered computer—an inexpensive laptop or even an old desktop clunker—and enjoy the speed and power of the remote computer. Remote Desktop connections are encrypted, so your information is secure, even if you're making a connection over the Internet.

The basic requirements for using Remote Desktop are pretty simple: you need two computers that are connected via a local area network, the Internet, or a dial-up connection.

NOTE

The computer that you want to control—the one at the remote location—is called the *remote computer*. The computer you want to use to control the remote computer is called the *client computer*.

These are the requirements for the two computers:

- **Remote computer.** You need a computer running Windows 10 Pro, Enterprise, or Education. (Windows 10 Home does not include the software required for hosting Remote Desktop sessions.) The remote computer can also use Windows 8 or 8.1 (Pro or Enterprise editions), Windows 7 (Professional, Enterprise, or Ultimate editions), Windows Vista (Business, Enterprise, or Ultimate editions), Windows XP Professional (or Windows XP Media Center or Tablet PC editions), Windows Home Server, or Windows Server. This computer must have a connection to a local area network or to the Internet. If you're going to connect to this computer over the Internet, its Internet connection must have a known, public IP address. (For ways around this last requirement, see the next section, "Configuring your network for Remote Desktop connections.")

- **Client computer.** You can access Remote Desktop from a computer running any version of Windows or Windows Phone. Remote Desktop client software from Microsoft is also available for iOS, Mac OS X, and Android; third-party apps are available for Linux and other operating systems. To find one, search for "RDP apps." (RDP is short for *Remote Desktop Protocol*, the networking protocol that enables Remote Desktop.)

Configuring your network for Remote Desktop connections

When you enable Remote Desktop on Windows 10 Pro, Enterprise, or Education, the remote computer listens for incoming connections on port 3389. Enabling Remote Desktop also creates an exception in Windows Firewall that allows authenticated traffic on this port.

That makes Remote Desktop easy to use over a local network where no third-party security software is installed. But it doesn't solve the many problems you face when trying to connect to Remote Desktop over the Internet. To connect through the Internet, you must be able to reach the remote computer by using a known public IP address, and you have to get through a router and past any security software in between the two computers. If you're sitting in a hotel room or an airport, connecting to Remote Desktop poses several challenges imposed by firewalls, routers, and IP addresses. The solutions to these issues depend on your specific hardware configuration, but we can offer some general advice.

If the remote computer is connected to the Internet through a router, you need to accomplish two tasks. First, you have to ascertain the router's public IP address. (Depending on your ISP, this public address can change over time. See the following tip for a workaround.) Then you have to configure the router to forward Remote Desktop Protocol traffic it receives on port 3389 to the remote computer.

To find the router's IP address, open its browser-based administration interface and find the status screen. The public IP address is typically labeled as the WAN (wide area network) address; don't use the local area network (LAN) address, which is the private IP address used to forward traffic to computers on your local network.

To make sure RDP traffic reaches your remote PC, look for a "port forwarding" page in the same router administration interface (it's often buried within an advanced configuration section). You'll need to specify the local (private) IP address of the remote computer and tell the router that you want all traffic on port 3389 to be forwarded to that PC instead of being discarded. Figure 20-8 shows this configuration on a Linksys router, allowing incoming Remote Desktop requests to be forwarded to a computer with a local (private) IP address of 192.168.10.25.

CHAPTER 20

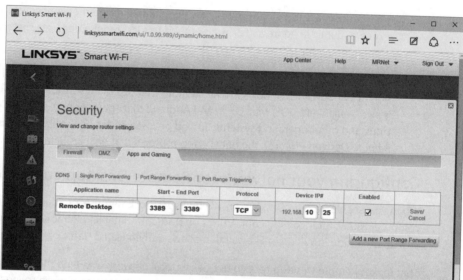

Figure 20-8 Every router has a different configuration interface, but the basic concepts of port forwarding are similar to the one shown here, which will forward traffic on port 3389 to a local PC with the specified private IP address.

Inside OUT

Use dynamic DNS to avoid IP address confusion

Using a bare IP address for Remote Desktop connections is easy but potentially risky. If you forget the public IP address assigned to your computer, you'll be unable to make a connection. Worse, if your ISP decides to change your IP address, you'll be stymied until you discover the new address, which is a challenge if you're away from home. The solution is to use a dynamic DNS service, such as those offered by Dyn (*dyndns.com*), No-IP (*noip.com*), and Duck DNS (*duckdns.org*). (A web search for "dynamic DNS service" will turn up many more options.) Such services map the public IP address on your router to a domain name that doesn't change. Dynamic DNS services typically rely on software installed on your remote computer, which notifies the service provider's domain name servers if your IP address changes. Because the domain name server correlates your domain name with its current IP address, you (or anyone you designate) can always find your computer by using your registered domain name instead of a numeric IP address.

Enabling inbound remote desktop connections

If you intend to connect to a remote computer—whether it's at home while you're away, at work when you're out of the office, or just down the hall—you must first enable Remote Desktop on that computer. To set up a computer running Windows 10 Pro, Enterprise, or Education to accept Remote Desktop connections, follow these steps:

1. Open System in Control Panel. Right-click the Start button and choose System; or, in Control Panel, open System And Security, System.) In the left pane, click Remote Settings. (Or use the undocumented command **systempropertiesremote**.)

2. Under Remote Desktop, select Allow Remote Connections To This Computer, as shown here:

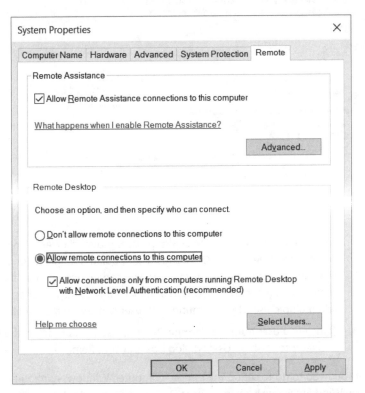

Unless you anticipate that you will need to access your computer from a computer running an ancient version of Remote Desktop Connection, leave Allow Connections Only From Computers Running Remote Desktop With Network Level Authentication (Recommended) selected. This requires Remote Desktop version 6 or later, but all versions of Windows and Windows Server released since 2007 (that is, Windows Vista or later, or Windows Server 2008 or later) meet this requirement. In addition, versions of Remote

Desktop that support Network Level Authentication are available for earlier Windows versions and for other operating systems.

At this point, the current user account and any user account that is a member of the local Administrators group can be used to connect remotely to the computer, provided that the account has a sign-in password. (As a security precaution, accounts that use a blank password cannot be enabled for remote connections.)

3. If you want to change which users can connect remotely, click Select Users. The Remote Desktop Users dialog box appears.

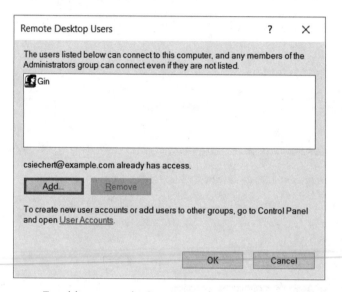

- To add a user to the Remote Desktop Users group, click Add. Then type the user's name in the Select Users Or Groups dialog box that appears (or click Advanced, Find Now to select names from a list). You can type the name of any local user account or, if your computer is in a domain, any domain user account. You can add multiple users by separating each user name with a semicolon.

- To delete a user from the Remote Desktop Users group, select the user's name in the Remote Desktop Users dialog box and click Remove.

That's all you need to do to set up the remote computer. Windows configures rules for Remote Desktop in Windows Firewall when Remote Desktop is enabled, allowing connection requests on port 3389 to be received from any IP address.

If your connection has to pass through a router to get to your computer, be sure you take the additional steps outlined earlier in "Configuring your network for Remote Desktop connections." If you have replaced Windows Firewall with a third-party software firewall, you need to configure it to allow incoming access to TCP port 3389.

Using Remote Desktop Connection

If you've enabled incoming remote connections on your PC at home or in the office and verified that your network and firewall have the welcome mat out (for visitors with suitable credentials only, of course), you're ready to begin using Remote Desktop Connection. In the search box, type **remote** and then click Remote Desktop Connection. A dialog box like the one shown in Figure 20-9 appears. In the Computer box, type the name of the remote computer or its IP address.

Figure 20-9 You can specify the remote computer by name or IP address.

> **NOTE**
>
> After a successful connection to a remote desktop, the name of the remote computer is added to the drop-down list in the Computer box. Thereafter, you can simply select it from the list (if it isn't already selected) instead of typing the name each time.
>
> In addition, if Remote Desktop Connection is pinned to your taskbar or Start menu (or if it's in the Start menu's recently used list), the name of each computer to which you've successfully connected appears on the Jump List. By using the Jump List and saved sign-in credentials, you can bypass this dialog box completely.

> **TROUBLESHOOTING**
>
> *Your firewall blocks outbound access*
>
> If you use a third-party firewall that blocks unknown outbound traffic to the Internet, it prevents your initial attempt to connect to your remote desktop. Configure the firewall to enable Mstsc.exe (the file name of the Remote Desktop Connection program) to make outbound TCP connections on port 3389.

CHAPTER 20

If you're willing to accept the default settings (about which we'll go into great detail shortly), you can click Connect at this point.

If you're signed in to the client computer using an account other than one that's authorized on the remote computer, Windows first displays a request for credentials, as shown here. After you enter your credentials and they're approved, Windows initiates the Remote Desktop Connection session.

The remote computer's sign-in screen then appears on your computer, either in a window or a full-screen display. Enter your password; other sign-in options (that is, PIN, picture password, or biometric sign-in) are not available for a remote connection.

If the account you use for the remote connection is already signed in to the remote computer—or if no one is signed in to the remote computer—the remote computer's desktop then appears on your computer.

If a different user account is signed in to the remote computer, Windows lets you know that you'll be forcing that person to sign out and gives you a chance to cancel the connection. On the other end, the signed-in user sees a similar notification that offers a short time to reject the remote connection before it takes over. It's important to note that only one user at a time can control the desktop of a computer running Windows. Whoever is currently signed in has the final say on whether someone else can sign in.

While you're connected to the remote computer, the local display on that computer (if it's turned on) does not show what you see on the client computer but instead shows the lock screen. A person who has physical access to the remote computer can't see what you're doing (other than the fact that you are signed in remotely).

An alternative client: Remote Desktop universal app

The Remote Desktop Connection program that's included with Windows is a desktop app, and it has changed very little in the past 15 years. A newer alternative, a modern app called Remote Desktop, is available via the Store. Remote Desktop, shown here in a preview release, supports connections to remote computers in much the same way as Remote Desktop Connection, albeit in a streamlined, modern-looking app.

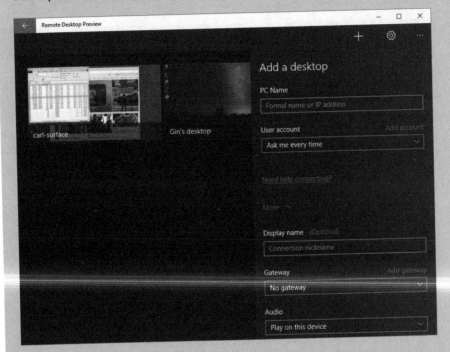

The Remote Desktop modern app also offers several additional features not found in Remote Desktop Connection. Its visual approach shows all your remote connections on the home screen, allowing you to open one with a single click or tap. Within a single window, it allows you to connect to multiple remote desktops simultaneously. (You can use multiple instances of the traditional Remote Desktop Connection app for concurrent connections, but the modern app makes it easier to see and manage multiple sessions.)

In addition, Remote Desktop includes several performance enhancements that optimize your connection quality. And, of course, as a modern app, it's touch friendly.

Don't be confused when looking for this app in the Store. An older version of the Remote Desktop app, designed for Windows 8.1, is still available as well, although it offers a completely different user experience. If you see a hamburger menu in the upper left corner, you have the older one and should seek out the newer, Universal version in the Store.

Changing screen resolutions and display settings

When you connect to a remote computer using Remote Desktop Connection, the remote computer takes over your entire screen. It uses the resolution of the client computer, regardless of the resolution set on the remote computer. Along the top of the screen, in the center, a small title bar appears, as shown next. This title bar, dubbed the *connection bar* in Remote Desktop Connection, lets you switch between your own desktop and the remote desktop. The Minimize, Maximize, and Restore buttons work as they do in other programs.

The pushpin button locks the connection bar in place. If you click the pushpin, the connection bar disappears completely, retracting into the top of the screen. To make the connection bar reappear, "bump" the mouse pointer to the top edge of the screen. To keep the connection bar visible at all times, click the pushpin again. The Close button disconnects the remote computer (but does not sign you out of the remote computer) and closes Remote Desktop Connection. You can pick up where you left off by reopening Remote Desktop Connection and reconnecting or by signing in locally at the remote computer.

Inside OUT

Move the connection bar

If the connection bar covers a part of the screen that you need to see, you can move it instead of hiding it altogether with the pushpin button. Simply slide it left or right.

You might prefer to use less than your full screen resolution for the remote desktop. (This option is especially useful if you have a large monitor and the work you want to do with Remote Desktop is just another task among several.) You must set the resolution—along with a number of other options—before you connect to the remote computer. After you start Remote Desktop Connection, click the Show Options button (shown in Figure 20-9) to expand the dialog box. Then click the Display tab, which is shown in Figure 20-10. You can set the screen resolution to any size that is supported on the client hardware, from 640 by 480 up to the current resolution of the client computer (not the remote computer). Set it to full screen by moving the slider all the way to the right.

Figure 20-10 Screen resolution is determined by the client computer.

Remote Desktop Connection allows the use of multiple monitors, although you should be aware that this feature requires that the remote computer is running Windows 7 or later. To configure the connection for use with more than one monitor, select Use All My Monitors For The Remote Session.

Accessing local resources

While you use Remote Desktop Connection, it's immediately apparent that you have control of the remote computer. You see its desktop, Start menu, and so on. That's terrific if the remote computer has everything you need. But you'll often want to use local resources and information from the client computer as well as from the remote computer. In addition, you might want to move information between the two computers. With Remote Desktop Connection, you can do so easily by clicking Show Options to expand the Remote Desktop Connection dialog box and then adjusting any of the options on the Local Resources tab, shown in Figure 20-11.

Figure 20-11 Configure these Remote Desktop Connection settings before you make the connection—you can't change settings while the connection is active.

The following options are available:

- **Remote Audio.** If your music collection is on the remote PC and you want some tunes at your current location, click Settings and select Play On This Computer. If you want both computers to be silent, choose Do Not Play. After clicking Settings, you can also tell Remote Desktop Connection whether to pay attention to the microphone (or other audio input) on the client computer.

- **Keyboard.** When you press a Windows keyboard shortcut such as Alt+Tab, do you want the shortcut to take effect on the remote machine or on your client computer?

- **Printers.** When this option is selected, your local printers appear in the remote computer's Printers folder. Their entries have "(from *clientcomputername*)" appended to each printer name. To print to a local printer, select its name in the Print dialog box from any application.

- **Clipboard.** When you copy or cut text or graphics on either the remote computer or the local computer, it's saved on the Clipboard in both locations. The Clipboard contents are then available for pasting in documents on either computer. Similarly, you can cut or copy files or folders from a File Explorer window on either computer and paste them into a folder on the other computer. Clear this option if you want to keep the contents of the two Clipboards separate.

The More button leads to additional devices in the Local Devices And Resources category. Smart cards are automatically enabled, and serial ports are disabled by default. Local drives and Plug and Play devices are also disabled by default. They can be enabled individually in this dialog box, as shown in Figure 20-12. These options are most useful if you're expecting to do most or all of your work with the Remote Desktop session in full-screen view and you don't want to continually flip back to your local desktop for file-management tasks.

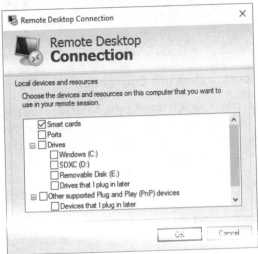

Figure 20-12 You control which (if any) client computer resources are available in the Remote Desktop Connection window.

TROUBLESHOOTING

You receive a security warning when you try to sign in remotely

Remote Desktop Connection considers any connections to local hard drives to be a potential security risk. As a result, you'll see an extra security dialog box ("Do you trust this remote connection?") if you choose to make any local drives or Plug and Play devices available on the remote desktop. If you're comfortable with the configuration you've chosen, click Connect. If you want to adjust the connect settings, click the Details button to expand the dialog box. Then clear the check box for any category of resources.

Inside OUT

Use your pen in Remote Desktop Connection

In addition to keyboard, mouse, and touch input, if your client computer supports the use of a pen or stylus, you can use it in a Remote Desktop session. You won't see pens mentioned on the Local Resources tab because no configuration is required. You'll need to have Windows 10 or Windows Server 2016 on the remote computer and the client computer. This feature allows you to add handwriting and other drawings even if the remote computer has no built-in pen capability. You can use the full pen capabilities of the local computer; for example, pens that vary in line width based on the pressure you apply to the screen can use this feature on remote documents.

Using the keyboard with Remote Desktop Connection

When the Remote Desktop Connection window is active, almost every key you press is passed to the remote computer. Certain key combinations, however, can be processed by the client computer, depending on the setting you make in the Keyboard section of the Local Resources tab of the Remote Desktop Connection dialog box (shown in Figure 20-11). You can specify that the key combinations shown in the first column of Table 20-1 are sent to the remote computer all the time, only when the remote desktop is displayed in full-screen mode, or never.

If you select On This Computer, key combinations from the first column of Table 20-1 are always applied to the client computer. To get the equivalent function on the remote computer, press the key combination shown in the second column. The same is true if you select Only When Using The Full Screen and the remote session is displayed in a window.

If you select On The Remote Computer, key combinations from the first column are applied to the remote computer. Key combinations in the second column are ignored (unless they have some function in the active application on the remote desktop). The same is true if you select Only When Using The Full Screen and the remote session is displayed in full-screen mode. One exception is the Ctrl+Alt+Delete combination, which is always applied to the client computer. Regardless of your Local Resources tab setting, you must press Ctrl+Alt+End to obtain the same result on the remote computer.

Table 20-1 Special keys in Remote Desktop Connection

Key combination for local session	Equivalent key combination for Remote Desktop session	Description
Alt+Tab	Alt+Page Up	Switches between programs
Alt+Shift+Tab	Alt+Page Down	Switches between programs in reverse order
Alt+Esc	Alt+Insert	Cycles through programs in the order they were started
N/A	Ctrl+Alt+Break	Switches the remote desktop between a window and full screen
Ctrl+Alt+Delete	Ctrl+Alt+End	Displays the Windows Security screen
Ctrl+Esc	Alt+Home	Displays the Start menu
Alt+Spacebar	Alt+Del	Displays the Control menu of the active window (does not work when using Remote Desktop in full-screen mode)
Shift+Print Screen	Ctrl+Alt+Plus Sign (on numeric keypad)	Captures a bitmap image of the remote desktop and places it on the remote computer's Clipboard
Alt+Print Screen	Ctrl+Alt+Minus Sign (on numeric keypad)	Captures a bitmap image of the active window and places it on the remote computer's Clipboard

CHAPTER 20

Configuring performance options

When you first use Remote Desktop Connection, you might notice that the remote desktop doesn't display a background. Disabling the background is one of several settings you can make that affect the perceived performance of your remote session. How you set these options depends in large measure on the speed of the connection between the two computers. If you're using a dial-up connection, you should disable as many features as possible to reduce the amount of information that must be transmitted across the wire and keep the mouse and windows movements responsive. On the other hand, if you're connecting to another desktop over a fast local area network, you might as well enable all features to enjoy the full experience of working at the remote computer.

The performance-related options are on the Experience tab of the Remote Desktop Connection dialog box, shown in Figure 20-13. To quickly select an appropriate set of prepackaged options, select the speed of your connection from the list box. Use those settings or select your own options.

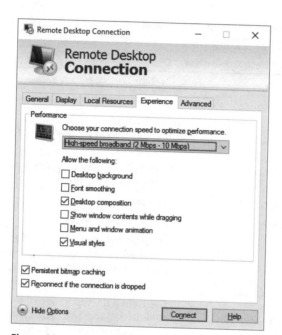

Figure 20-13 Remote Desktop Connection has a default collection of settings for each connection speed.

Saving a Remote Desktop configuration

Changes you make in the expanded Remote Desktop Connection dialog box are automatically saved in a hidden file named Default.rdp (stored in your default save location for documents) and they're used the next time you open Remote Desktop Connection. But you might want to have several different Remote Desktop Connection configurations for connections to different computers. If you have a portable computer, you might want different settings for use with different connections to the same computer (for example, a slow Wi-Fi connection from a hotel versus a fast LAN at your branch office).

You can also save your credentials (user name and password) along with the other settings. To do so, enter your user name under Logon Settings on the General tab and select Allow Me To Save Credentials. You'll be prompted to save the password (in encrypted form, of course) when you sign in. Note that not all remote operating systems allow the use of saved credentials.

To save a configuration, make all your settings, click the General tab, and click Save As.

To reuse a stored configuration at a later time, start Remote Desktop Connection, click Show Options, click Open, and then double-click the stored file. More simply, select it from the Jump

List for Remote Desktop Connection (on the taskbar or Start menu), or double-click the stored file in File Explorer.

Ending a remote session

When you're through with a Remote Desktop Connection session, you can lock, sign out, or disconnect. If the remote computer is running Windows 10, you'll find these options in the usual places where comparable options appear on your local computer: Lock and Sign Out appear when you click the user name at the top of the remote session's Start menu, and Disconnect appears when you click Power on the remote Start menu. For remote machines running earlier Windows versions, these options appear in the lower right corner of the remote session's Start menu. (You must click the arrow to see all the options.)

Locking the computer keeps the remote session connected and all programs running, but it hides everything behind a sign-in screen that requests a password; this is comparable to pressing Windows key+L to lock your computer.

Signing out closes all your programs, exits your user session, and disconnects.

If you disconnect without signing out, your programs continue to run on the remote computer, but the remote connection is ended. The sign-in screen is visible on the remote computer, and it's available for another user. If you sign in later—either locally or through a remote connection—you can pick up right where you left off. As an alternative to the Start menu command, you can disconnect by simply clicking the Close button on the connection bar of the remote session.

Troubleshooting network problems

Network connectivity problems can be a source of great frustration. Fortunately, Windows 10 includes several tools and wizards that can help you identify and solve problems. Even better, Windows has built-in network diagnostic capabilities, so in many cases, if there is a problem with your network connection, Windows knows about it before you do, displays a message, and often solves the problem.

When a network-dependent activity (for example, browsing to a website) fails, Windows works to address the most common network-related issues, such as problems with file-sharing, website access, newly installed network hardware, connecting to a wireless network, and using a third-party firewall.

If you encounter network problems that don't trigger an automatic response from Windows, you should first try to detect and resolve the problem with one of the built-in troubleshooters.

In Network And Sharing Center, click Troubleshoot Problems to display the choices shown in Figure 20-14.

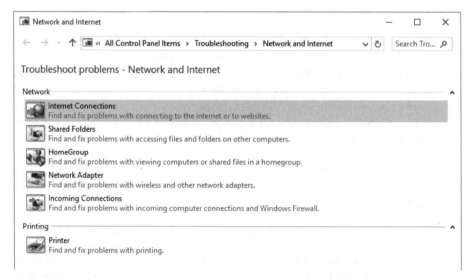

Figure 20-14 Click any of these options to launch a troubleshooter that performs numerous diagnostic and corrective steps.

Inside OUT

Skip the troubleshooting menu

You can bypass Network And Sharing Center and the troubleshooting menu shown in Figure 20-14. Simply right-click the network icon in the notification area and choose Troubleshoot Problems; doing so launches right into a network troubleshooter.

Each of the troubleshooting wizards performs several diagnostic tests, corrects some conditions, suggests actions you can take, and ultimately displays a report that explains the wizard's findings. Sometimes, the problem is as simple as a loose connection.

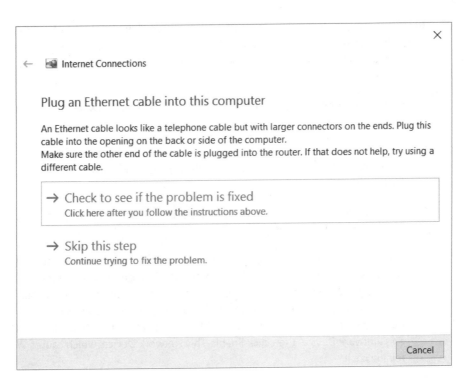

Other situations might point to problems outside your network.

If the diagnostic capabilities leave you at a dead end, you'll find that restarting the affected network hardware often resolves the problem, because the hardware is forced to rediscover the network. The first step in troubleshooting is to isolate the problem. Here is a good general procedure:

1. Isolate the problem. Does it affect all computers on your network, a subset of your network, or only one computer?

2. If it affects all computers, try restarting the Internet device (that is, the cable or DSL modem). If it doesn't have a power switch, unplug it for a few moments and plug it back in.

3. If the problem affects a group of computers, try restarting the router to which those computers are connected.

4. If it affects only a single computer, try repairing the network connection for that computer. In Network And Sharing Center, click Change Adapter Settings. (Alternatively, in Settings, Network & Internet, click Change Adapter Options.) Then, in Network Connections, select the connection and click Diagnose This Connection. If the troubleshooter doesn't resolve the problem, select the connection and click Disable This Network Device; then click Enable This Network Device, which causes Windows to reinitialize it.

Troubleshooting HomeGroup problems

The HomeGroup troubleshooting wizard provides a good example of how these troubleshooters work. If you're having problems seeing shared resources in a homegroup and you didn't have the benefit of the troubleshooter's assistance, you'd need to check the following settings, among others:

- The network location profile must be set to Private.

- In Windows Firewall With Advanced Security, you need to ensure that the following groups of rules are enabled on private networks:
    - Core Networking
    - Network Discovery
    - HomeGroup
    - File/Printer Sharing
    - Windows Media Player
    - Windows Media Player Network Sharing

- The following services must be configured so that they can run:

  - HomeGroup Listener

  - HomeGroup Provider

  - Function Discovery Provider Host

  - Function Discovery Resource Publication

  - Peer Name Resolution Protocol

  - Peer Networking Grouping

  - Peer Networking Identity Manager

Running the HomeGroup troubleshooter—which you can launch from HomeGroup or by right-clicking HomeGroup in File Explorer as well as from the list of troubleshooters shown in Figure 20-14—checks each of these items and more. When you get to the wizard's last window, you can click View Detailed Information to see a troubleshooting report that lists the potential problems that the wizard attempted to identify and fix.

Network troubleshooting tools

When the troubleshooters don't solve the problem, it might be time to dig deeper into the Windows toolbox. Windows contains an assortment of utilities you can use to diagnose, monitor, and repair network connections. Table 20-2 lists some of the more useful networking-related command-line utilities and summarizes how you can use them. To learn more about each utility, including its proper syntax, open a Command Prompt window and type the executable name followed by **/?**.

Table 20-2 Windows network command-line utilities

Utility name	What it's used for
Get MAC Address (Getmac.exe)	Discovers the Media Access Control (MAC) address and lists associated network protocols for all network cards in a computer, either locally or across a network.
Hostname (Hostname.exe)	Displays the host name of the current computer.
IP Configuration Utility (Ipconfig.exe)	Displays all current Transmission Control Protocol/Internet Protocol (TCP/IP) network configuration values, and refreshes Dynamic Host Configuration Protocol (DHCP) and DNS settings.
Name Server Lookup (Nslookup.exe)	Displays information about Domain Name System records for specific IP addresses and/or host names so that you can troubleshoot DNS problems.
Net services commands (Net.exe)	Performs a broad range of network tasks. Type **net** with no parameters to see a full list of available command-line options.

CHAPTER 20

Utility name	What it's used for
Netstat (Netstat.exe)	Displays active TCP connections, ports on which the computer is listening, Ethernet statistics, the IP routing table, and IPv4/IPv6 statistics.
Network Command Shell (Netsh.exe)	Displays or modifies the network configuration of a local or remote computer that is currently running. This command-line scripting utility has a huge number of options, which are fully detailed in Help.
PathPing (Pathping.exe)	Combines the functions of Traceroute and Ping to identify problems at a router or network link.
TCP/IP NetBIOS Information (Nbtstat.exe)	Displays statistics for the NetBIOS over TCP/IP (NetBT) protocol, NetBIOS name tables for both the local computer and remote computers, and the NetBIOS name cache.
TCP/IP Ping (Ping.exe)	Verifies IP-level connectivity to another Internet address by sending Internet Control Message Protocol (ICMP) packets and measuring response time in milliseconds.
TCP/IP Route (Route.exe)	Displays and modifies entries in the local IP routing table.
TCP/IP Traceroute (Tracert.exe)	Determines the path to an Internet address, and lists the time required to reach each hop. It's useful for troubleshooting connectivity problems on specific network segments.

As is the case with other command-line utilities, the Windows PowerShell environment includes cmdlets that offer much of the same functionality along with the scripting capability of PowerShell. (Indeed, one of the commands shown in Table 20-2—Netsh—displays a notice that it might be removed from future versions of Windows. The trend in Windows command-line utilities, certainly, is moving away from Command Prompt toward PowerShell. However, because of the one-off nature of troubleshooting tasks—the topic of this section—our emphasis here is on command-line utilities that run in a Command Prompt window.)

You can get a list that includes many of the more commonly used network-related cmdlets by entering at a PowerShell prompt

```
get-command –module nettcpip, netadapter
```

> ➤ For more information about PowerShell, see "An introduction to Windows PowerShell" in Chapter 21, "Working with Command Prompt and Windows PowerShell." For details about the Net TCP/IP cmdlets, go to *w7io.com/20401*. On that page, you'll also find (using the navigation pane on the left) details about other network-related cmdlets, including those for Network Adapter, Network Connection, and Network Connectivity Status.

Troubleshooting TCP/IP problems

Transmission Control Protocol/Internet Protocol (TCP/IP) is the default communications protocol of the Internet; in Windows 10, it's installed and configured automatically and cannot be removed. Most of the time, your TCP/IP connection should just work, without requiring any manual configuration. When you encounter problems with TCP/IP-based networks, such as an inability to connect with other computers on the same network or difficulty connecting to external websites, the problems might be TCP/IP related. You'll need at least a basic understanding of how this protocol works before you can figure out which tool to use to uncover the root of the problem.

Setting IP addresses

Networks that use the TCP/IP protocol rely on *IP addresses* to route packets of data from point to point. On a TCP/IP network, every computer has a unique IP address for each protocol (that is, TCP/IPv4 and TCP/IPv6) in use on each network adapter. An IPv4 address consists of four 8-bit numbers (each one represented in decimal format by a number from 0 through 255) separated by periods. An IPv6 address consists of eight 16-bit numbers (each one represented in hexadecimal format) separated by colons. In addition to the IP address, each computer's TCP/IP configuration has the following additional settings:

- A *subnet mask*, which tells the network how to distinguish between IP addresses that are part of the same network and those that belong to other networks

- A *default gateway*, which is a computer that routes packets intended for addresses outside the local network

- One or more *Domain Name System (DNS) servers*, which are computers that translate domain names (such as *www.microsoft.com*) into IP addresses

Windows provides several methods for assigning IP addresses to networked computers:

- **Dynamic Host Configuration Protocol (DHCP).** This is the default configuration for Windows 10. A DHCP server maintains a pool of IP addresses for use by network devices. When you connect to a network, the DHCP server assigns an IP address from this pool and sets subnet masks and other configuration details. Many corporate networks use DHCP to avoid the hassle of managing fixed addresses for constantly changing resources; all versions of Windows Server include this capability. Most routers and residential gateways also incorporate DHCP servers that automatically configure computers connected to those devices.

- **Automatic Private IP Addressing (APIPA).** When no DHCP server is available, Windows automatically assigns an IP address in a specific private IP range. (For an explanation of how private IP addresses work, see the sidebar "Public and private IP addresses.") If all computers on a subnet are using APIPA addresses, they can communicate with one another without requiring any additional configuration. APIPA was introduced with Windows 98 and works the same in all versions of Windows released since that time.

- **Static IP Addressing.** By entering an IP address, subnet mask, and other TCP/IP details in a dialog box, you can manually configure a Windows workstation so that its address is always the same. This method takes more time and can cause some configuration headaches, but it allows a high degree of control over network addresses.

  Static IP addresses are useful if you plan to set up a web server, a mail server, a virtual private network (VPN) gateway, or any other computer that needs to be accessible from across the Internet. Even inside a local network, behind a router or firewall, static IP addresses can be useful. For instance, you might want to configure the router so that packets entering your network on a specific port get forwarded to a specific computer. If you use DHCP to assign addresses within the local network, you can't predict what the address of that computer will be on any given day. But by assigning that computer a static IP address that is within the range of addresses assigned by the DHCP server, you can ensure that the computer always has the same address and is thus always reachable.

- **Alternate IP Configuration.** This feature allows you to specify multiple IPv4 addresses for a single network connection (although only one address can be used at a time). This feature is most useful with portable computers that regularly connect to different networks. You can configure the connection to automatically acquire an IP address from an available DHCP server, and you can then assign a static backup address for use if the first configuration isn't successful.

To set a static IP address, follow these steps:

1. In the Network Connections folder, select the connection whose settings you want to change. On the command bar, click Change Settings Of This Connection. (Alternatively, right-click the icon and choose Properties.)

2. In the list of installed network items, select Internet Protocol Version 4 (TCP/IPv4) or Internet Protocol Version 6 (TCP/IPv6), and then click Properties.

3. In the Internet Protocol (TCP/IP) Properties dialog box, select Use The Following IP Address and fill in the blanks. You must supply an IP address, a subnet mask (for IPv6, the length of the subnet prefix, which is usually 64 bits), and a default gateway.

4. Select Use The Following DNS Server Addresses, and then fill in the numeric IP addresses for one or more DNS servers as well. Figure 20-15 shows the dialog box with all fields filled in.

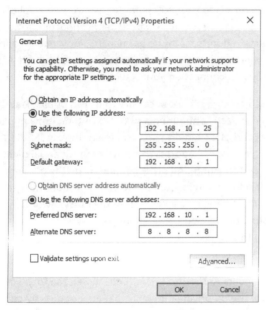

Figure 20-15 When assigning static IP addresses, you must fill in all fields correctly. To avoid making a mistake that could cause you to lose your network connectivity, select Validate Settings Upon Exit.

5. Click OK to save your changes.

Public and private IP addresses

Any computer that is directly connected to the Internet needs a public IP address—one that can be reached by other computers on the Internet—so that information you request (webpages and email, for instance) can be routed back to your computer properly. When you connect to an Internet service provider, you're assigned a public IP address from a block of addresses registered to that ISP. If you use a dial-up connection, your ISP probably assigns a different IP address to your computer (drawn from its pool of available addresses) each time you connect. If you have a persistent connection to your ISP via a DSL or cable modem, your IP address might be permanent—or semipermanent if you turn off your computer when you leave your home or office to travel and your assigned IP address is changed when you reconnect on your return.

On a home or small office network, it's not necessary to have a public IP address for each computer on the network. In fact, configuring a network with multiple public addresses can increase security risks and often requires an extra fee from your ISP. A safer, less costly solution is to assign a single public IP address to a router or residential gateway (or a computer that performs that function). All other computers on the network connect to the Internet through that single address. Each of the computers on the local network has a private IP address that is not directly reachable from the outside world. To communicate with the Internet, the router on the edge of the network uses a technology called Network Address Translation (NAT) to pass packets back and forth between the single public IP address and the multiple private IP addresses on the network.

The Internet Assigned Numbers Authority (IANA) has reserved the following three blocks of the IP address space for use on private networks that are not directly connected to the Internet:

- 10.0.0.0–10.255.255.255
- 172.16.0.0–172.31.255.255
- 192.168.0.0–192.168.255.255

In addition, the Automatic Private IP Addressing feature in all post-1998 Windows versions uses private IP addresses in the range 169.254.0.0 through 169.254.255.255.

Routers and residential gateways that use NAT almost always assign addresses from these private ranges. Linksys routers, for instance, typically assign addresses starting with 192.168.1.x. If you're setting up a small business or a home network that will not be connected to the Internet, or that will be connected through a single proxy server, you can freely use these addresses without concern for conflicts. Just make sure that all the addresses on the network are in the same subnet.

Checking for connection problems

Anytime your network refuses to send and receive data properly, your first troubleshooting step should be to check for problems with the physical connection between the local computer and the rest of the network. Assuming your network connection uses the TCP/IP protocol, the first tool to reach for is the Ping utility. When you use the Ping command with no parameters, Windows sends four echo datagrams—small Internet Control Message Protocol (ICMP) packets—to the address you specify. If the machine at the other end of the connection replies, you know that the network connection between the two points is alive.

To use the Ping command, open a Command Prompt window (Cmd.exe) and type the command **ping *target_name*** (where *target_name* is an IP address or the name of another host machine). The return output looks something like this:

```
C:\>ping www.example.com

Pinging www.example.com [93.184.216.34] with 32 bytes of data:
Reply from 93.184.216.34: bytes=32 time=54ms TTL=51
Reply from 93.184.216.34: bytes=32 time=40ms TTL=51
Reply from 93.184.216.34: bytes=32 time=41ms TTL=51
Reply from 93.184.216.34: bytes=32 time=54ms TTL=51

Ping statistics for 93.184.216.34:
    Packets: Sent = 4, Received = 4, Lost = 0 (0% loss),
Approximate round trip times in milli-seconds:
    Minimum = 40ms, Maximum = 54ms, Average = 47ms
```

If all the packets you send come back properly in roughly the same time, your TCP/IP connection is fine and you can focus your troubleshooting efforts elsewhere. If some packets time out, a "Request timed out" message appears, indicating that your network connection is working but one or more hops between your computer and the target machine are experiencing problems. In that case, repeat the Ping test using the –n switch to send a larger number of packets; **ping –n 30 192.168.1.1**, for example, sends 30 packets to the computer or router at 192.168.1.1.

NOTE

The –n switch is case-sensitive; don't capitalize it.

A high rate of timeouts, also known as *packet loss*, usually means the problems are elsewhere on the network and not on the local machine. (To see the full assortment of switches available for the Ping command, type **ping** with no target specified.)

If every one of your packets returns with the message "Request timed out," the problem might be the TCP/IP connection on your computer or a glitch with another computer on that network. To narrow down the problem, follow these steps, in order, stopping at any point where you encounter an error:

1. Ping your own machine by using any of the following commands:

   ```
   ping ::1
   ping 127.0.0.1
   ping localhost
   ```

   These are standard addresses. The first line is the IPv6 address for your own computer; the second line is the IPv4 address; the third line shows the standard host name. If your local network components are configured correctly, each of these three commands should allow the PC on which the command is run to talk to itself. If you receive an error, TCP/IP is not configured properly on your system. For fix-it details, see "Repairing your TCP/IP configuration" later in this chapter.

2. Ping your computer's IP address.

3. Ping the IP address of another computer on your network.

4. Ping the IP address of your router or the default gateway on your network.

5. Ping the address of each DNS server on your network. (If you don't know these addresses, see the next section for details on how to discover them.)

6. Ping a known host outside your network. Well-known, high-traffic websites are ideal for this step, assuming that they respond to ICMP packets.

7. Use the PathPing command to contact the same host you specified in step 6. This command combines the functionality of the Ping command with the Traceroute utility to identify intermediate destinations on the Internet between your computer and the specified host or server.

Inside OUT

Choose your test site carefully

In some cases, pinging an external website results in a string of "Request timed out" messages, even when you have no trouble reaching those sites. Don't be misled. Some popular sites block all ICMP traffic, including Ping packets, as a routine security measure. Some routers and residential gateways are also configured to block certain types of ICMP traffic. Try pinging several sites before concluding that your Internet connection is broken.

If either of the two final steps in this process fails, your problem might be caused by DNS problems, as described later in this chapter. (For details, see "Resolving DNS issues.") To eliminate this possibility, ping the numeric IP address of a computer outside your network instead. (Of course, if you're having DNS problems, you might have a hard time finding an IP address to ping!) If you can reach a website by using its IP address but not by using its name, DNS problems are indicated.

If you suspect that there's a problem on the Internet between your computer and a distant host or server, use the Traceroute utility (Tracert.exe) to pinpoint the problem. Like the Ping command, this utility works from a command line. You specify the target (a host name or IP address) by using the syntax **tracert _target_name_**, and the utility sends out a series of packets, measuring the time it takes to reach each hop along the route. Timeouts or unusually slow performance indicate a connectivity problem. If the response time from your network to the first hop is much higher than the other hops, you might have a problem with the connection to your Internet service provider (ISP); in that case, a call to your ISP's support line is in order. Problems farther along in the traceroute might indicate congestion or hardware problems in distant parts of the Internet that are out of your ISP's hands. These symptoms might disappear when you check another URL that follows a different path through the Internet.

If your testing produces inconsistent results, rule out the possibility that a firewall program or Network Address Translation (NAT) device (such as a router or residential gateway) is to blame. If you're using Windows Firewall or a third-party firewall program, disable it temporarily. Try bypassing your router and connecting directly to a broadband connection such as a DSL or cable modem. (Use this configuration only for testing and only very briefly because it exposes your computer to various attacks.)

If the Ping test works with the firewall or NAT device out of the picture, you can rule out network problems and conclude that the firewall software or router is misconfigured. After you complete your testing, be sure to enable the firewall and router again!

Diagnosing IP address problems

On most networks, IP addresses are assigned automatically by Dynamic Host Configuration Protocol (DHCP) servers; in some cases, you may need (or prefer) to use static IP addresses, which are fixed numeric addresses. Problems with DHCP servers or clients can cause network connections to stop working, as can incorrectly assigned static IP addresses.

To see details of your current IP configuration, follow these steps:

1. In Settings, Network & Internet, click Change Adapter Options.

2. Double-click the icon for the connection about which you want more information. (Alternatively, you can select the icon and click View Status Of This Connection on the command bar.)

3. Click Details to see the currently assigned IP address, subnet mask, and default gateway for this connection. (If you have IPv4 and IPv6 connectivity, the Network Connection Details dialog box shows information for both.) In the following example, you can tell that the IP address was automatically assigned by the DHCP server in a router; details indicate that DHCP is enabled and the DHCP server address matches that of the router.

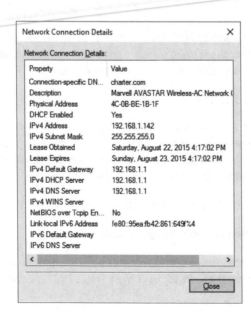

You can also get useful details of your IP configuration by using the IP Configuration utility, Ipconfig.exe, in a Command Prompt window. Used without any parameters, typing **ipconfig** at a command prompt displays the DNS suffix, IPv6 and/or IPv4 address, subnet mask, and default gateway for each network connection. To see exhaustive details about every available network connection, type **ipconfig /all**.

The actual IP address you see might help you solve connection problems:

- If the address is in the format 169.254.*x.y*, your computer is using Automatic Private IP Addressing (APIPA). This means your computer's DHCP client was unable to reach a DHCP server to be assigned an IP address. Check the connection to your network.

- If the address is in one of the blocks of IP addresses reserved for use on private networks (for details, see the sidebar "Public and private IP addresses" earlier in this chapter), make sure that a router or residential gateway is routing your Internet requests to a properly configured public IP address.

- If the address of your computer appears as 0.0.0.0, the network is either disconnected or the static IP address for the connection duplicates an address that already exists on the network.

- Make sure you're using the correct subnet mask for computers on your local network. Compare IP settings on the machine that's having problems with those on other computers on the network. The default gateway and subnet mask should be identical for all network computers. The first one, two, or three sets of numbers in the IP address for each machine should also be identical, depending on the subnet mask. A subnet mask of 255.255.255.0 means the first three IP address numbers of computers on your network must be identical—192.168.0.83 and 192.168.0.223, for instance, can communicate on a network using this subnet mask, but 192.168.1.101 will not be recognized as belonging to the network. The gateway machine must also be a member of the same subnet. (If you use a router, switch, or residential gateway for Internet access, the local address on that device must be part of the same subnet as the machines on your network.)

NOTE

Are you baffled by subnets and other related technical terms? For an excellent overview of these sometimes confusing topics, read Knowledge Base article 164015, "Understanding TCP/IP Addressing and Subnetting Basics" (*w7io.com/1908*), which offers information about IPv4. For comparable details about IPv6, see the "Introduction to IPv6" white paper at TechNet (*w7io.com/1909*).

CHAPTER 20

Repairing your TCP/IP configuration

If you suspect a problem with your TCP/IP configuration, try either of the following repair options:

- **Use the automated repair option.** Right-click the connection icon in Network Connections and click Diagnose.

- **Release and renew your IP address.** Use the **ipconfig /release** command to let go of the DHCP-assigned IPv4 address. Then use **ipconfig /renew** to obtain a new IP address from the DHCP server. To renew an IPv6 address, use **ipconfig /release6** and **ipconfig /renew6**.

NOTE

If these methods don't work, you can use the Netsh utility to restore the TCP/IP stack to its original configuration when Windows was first installed. The utility restores all registry settings relating to the TCP/IP stack to their original settings, which is effectively the same as removing and reinstalling the protocol. The utility records a log of the changes it makes. For details about this drastic, but effective, solution, see Microsoft Knowledge Base article 299357 (*w7io.com/299357*). Another option is to uninstall and reinstall the network adapter, as described in "Enabling and disabling individual devices" in Chapter 13.

Resolving DNS issues

The Domain Name System (DNS) is a crucial part of the Internet. DNS servers translate host names (*www.microsoft.com*, for instance) into numeric IP addresses so that packets can be routed properly over the Internet. If you can use the Ping command to reach a numeric address outside your network but are unable to browse websites by name, the problem is almost certainly related to your DNS configuration.

Here are some questions to ask when you suspect DNS problems:

- **Do your TCP/IP settings point to the right DNS servers?** Inspect the details of your IP configuration, and compare the DNS servers listed there with those recommended by your Internet service provider. (You might need to call your ISP to get these details.)

- **Is your ISP experiencing DNS problems?** A misconfigured DNS server (or one that's offline) can wreak havoc with your attempts to use the Internet. Try pinging each DNS server to see whether it's available. If your ISP has multiple DNS servers and you encounter problems accessing one server, remove that server from your TCP/IP configuration temporarily and use another one instead.

- **Have you installed any "Internet accelerator" utilities?** Many such programs work by editing the Hosts file on your computer to match IP addresses and host (server) names. When Windows finds a host name in the Hosts file, it uses the IP address listed there and doesn't send the request to a DNS server. If the owner of the server changes its DNS records to point to a new IP address, your Hosts file will lead you to the wrong location.

Temporary DNS problems can also be caused by the DNS cache, which Windows maintains for performance reasons. If you suddenly have trouble reaching a specific site on the Internet and you're convinced there's nothing wrong with the site, type this command to clear the DNS cache: **ipconfig /flushdns**.

A more thorough solution is offered by **ipconfig /registerdns**, which renews all DHCP leases (as described in the previous section) *and* reregisters all DNS names.

Inside OUT

Translate names to IP addresses and vice versa

The Nslookup command is a buried treasure in Windows. Use this command-line utility to quickly convert a fully qualified domain name to its IP address. You can tack on a host name to the end of the command line to identify a single address; type **nslookup ftp.microsoft.com**, for instance, to look up the IP address of Microsoft's File Transfer Protocol (FTP) server. Or type **nslookup** to switch into interactive mode. From this prompt, you can enter any domain name to find its IP address. If you need more sophisticated lookup tools, you can find them with the help of any search engine. A good starting point is DNSstuff (*w7io.com/22201*), which offers an impressive collection of online tools for looking up domains, IP addresses, and host names. The site also offers form-based utilities that can translate obfuscated URLs and dotted IP addresses, both of which are widely used by spammers to cover their online tracks.

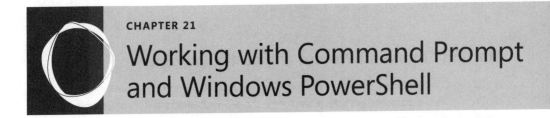

CHAPTER 21

Working with Command Prompt and Windows PowerShell

Windows 10, like all previous versions of Windows, lets you enter commands, run batch pro-grams, and run applications by typing commands in a Command Prompt window. If you're accustomed to performing administrative tasks at the command line, you can go on doing that in Windows 10. But this latest version of Windows, like its most recent predecessors, also includes a more powerful tool for performing administrative tasks at the command line. This newer, more versatile shell is called Windows PowerShell.

This chapter provides only a cursory introduction to the legacy Command Prompt and Windows PowerShell, with an emphasis on the latter. We presume that if you're perusing this chapter, you already have some familiarity with Command Prompt (if not, a quick scan of the bibliosphere will turn up several worthwhile references); we will confine ourselves therefore to a few tips and tricks. If your work calls on you to administer systems through scripts, you will find it worth your while to dive into Windows PowerShell. This chapter provides an overview of this newer, more versatile shell, and points you to additional resources.

Working at the command prompt

To get to the command prompt, run Cmd.exe. You can do this by double-clicking any short-cut for Cmd.exe, but since you like to type, you might find it easiest to press Windows key+R, and then type **cmd.** To open a second or subsequent Command Prompt window when one is already open, you can type **start** in the window that's already running.

Running with elevated privileges

Your activities in a Command Prompt session are subject to the same User Account Control (UAC) restrictions as anything else you do in Windows. If you use Command Prompt to launch a program (for example, Regedit) that requires an administrative token, you will be asked to confirm a UAC prompt before moving on. If you plan to run several such tasks from Command Prompt, you might prefer to run Cmd.exe itself with elevated privileges. To do this, right-click any shortcut for Command Prompt and then click Run As Administrator. Alternatively, type **cmd** in the search box, and then press Ctrl+Shift+Enter. Windows displays the word *Adminis-trator* in the title bar of any Command Prompt window running with elevated privileges.

CHAPTER 21

Starting Command Prompt at a particular folder

If you run Cmd.exe from a shortcut or from %SystemRoot%\System32, the session begins with that folder as the current directory. (*Directory* is the MS-DOS-era term for *folder*, and you will encounter it frequently in command names, help files, and so on.) If you run Cmd from the Start menu, it begins in your %UserProfile% folder. To run a Command Prompt session at a different folder, hold down the Shift key while you right-click the folder in File Explorer. On the shortcut menu, click Open Command Window Here.

Starting Command Prompt and running a command

The /C and /K command-line arguments allow you to start a Command Prompt session and immediately run a command or program. The difference between the two is that **Cmd /C** **commandstring** terminates the Command Prompt session as soon as *commandstring* has finished, whereas **Cmd /K commandstring** keeps the Command Prompt session open after *commandstring* has finished. Note the following:

- You must include either /C or /K if you want to specify a command string as an argument to Cmd. If you type **cmd commandstring**, the command processor simply ignores *commandstring*.

- While *commandstring* is executing, you can't interact with the command processor. To run a command or program and keep the Command Prompt window interface, use the Start command. For example, to run Mybatch.bat and continue issuing commands while the batch program is running, type

```
cmd /k start mybatch.bat
```

- If you include other command-line arguments along with /C or /K, /C or /K must be the last argument before *commandstring*.

Using AutoRun to execute commands when Command Prompt starts

By default, Command Prompt executes on startup whatever it finds in the following two registry values:

- The AutoRun value in HKLM\Software\Microsoft\Command Processor

- The AutoRun value in HKCU\Software\Microsoft\Command Processor

The AutoRun value in HKLM affects all user accounts on the current machine. The AutoRun value in HKCU affects only the current user account. If both values are present, both are executed—HKLM before HKCU. Both AutoRun values are of data type REG_SZ, which means they can contain a single string. To execute a sequence of separate Command Prompt statements, therefore, you must use command symbols or store the sequence as a batch program and then use AutoRun to call the batch program.

You can also use group policy objects to specify startup tasks for Command Prompt.

Editing the command line

When working at a command prompt, you often enter the same command multiple times or enter several similar commands. To assist you with repetitive or corrective tasks, Windows includes a feature that recalls previous commands and allows you to edit them on the current command line. Table 21-1 lists these editing keys and what they do.

Table 21-1 Command-line editing keys

Key	Function
Up Arrow	Recalls the previous command in the command history
Down Arrow	Recalls the next command in the command history
Page Up	Recalls the earliest command used in the session
Page Down	Recalls the most recently used command
Left Arrow	Moves left one character
Right Arrow	Moves right one character
Ctrl+Left Arrow	Moves left one word
Ctrl+Right Arrow	Moves right one word
Home	Moves to the beginning of the line
End	Moves to the end of the line
Esc	Clears the current command
F7	Displays the command history in a scrollable pop-up box
F8	Displays commands that start with the characters currently on the command line
Alt+F7	Clears the command history

Using command symbols

Old-fashioned programs that take all their input from a command line and then run unaided can be useful in a multitasking environment. You can turn them loose to perform complicated processing in the background while you continue to work with other programs in the foreground.

CHAPTER 21

To work better with other programs, many command-line programs follow a set of conventions that control their interaction:

- By default, programs take all of their input as lines of text typed at the keyboard. But input in the same format also can be redirected from a file or any device capable of sending lines of text.

- By default, programs send all of their output to the screen as lines of text. But output in the same format also can be redirected to a file or another line-oriented device, such as a printer.

- Programs set a number (called a *return value*) when they terminate to indicate the results of the program.

When programs are written according to these rules, you can use the symbols listed in Table 21-2 to control a program's input and output or chain programs together.

Table 21-2 Command symbols

Symbol	Function
<	Redirects input
>	Redirects output
>>	Appends redirected output to existing data
|	Pipes output
&	Separates multiple commands in a command line
&&	Runs the command after && only if the command before && is successful
||	Runs the command after || only if the command before || fails
^	Treats the next symbol as a character
(and)	Groups commands

The redirection symbols

Command Prompt sessions in Windows allow you to override the default source for input (the keyboard) or the default destination for output (the screen).

Redirecting output   To redirect output to a file, type the command followed by a greater than sign (>) and the name of the file.

Using two greater than signs (>>) redirects output and appends it to an existing file.

Redirecting input   To redirect input from a file, type the command followed by a less than sign (<) and the name of the file.

Redirecting input and output   You can redirect both input and output in a command line. For example, to use Batch.lst as input to the Sort command and send its output to a file named Sorted.lst, type the following:

```
Sort < batch.lst > sorted.lst
```

Standard output and standard error   Programs can be written to send their output either to the standard output device or to the standard error device. Sometimes programs are written to send different types of output to each device. You can't always tell which is which because, by default, both devices are the screen.

The Type command illustrates the difference. When used with wildcards, the Type command sends the name of each matching file to the standard error device and sends the contents of the file to the standard output device. Because they both go to the screen, you see a nice display with each file name followed by its contents.

However, if you try to redirect output to a file by typing something like this:

```
type *.bat > std.out
```

the file names still appear on your screen because standard error is still directed to the screen. Only the file contents are redirected to Std.out.

Windows allows you to qualify the redirection symbol by preceding it with a number. Use 1> (or simply >) for standard output and 2> for standard error. For example:

```
type *.bat 2> err.out
```

This time the file contents go to the screen and the names are redirected to Err.out.

The pipe symbol

The pipe symbol (|) is used to send, or pipe, the output of one program to a second program as the second program's input. Piping is commonly used with the More utility, which displays multiple screenfuls of output one screenful at a time. For example:

```
help dir | more
```

This command line uses the output of Help as the input for More. The More command filters out the first screenful of Help output, sends it to the screen as its own output, and then waits for a keystroke before sending more filtered output.

Customizing Command Prompt windows

You can customize the appearance of a Command Prompt window in several ways. You can change its size, select a font, and even use eye-pleasing colors. And you can save these settings independently for each shortcut that launches a Command Prompt session so that you can make appropriate settings for different tasks.

To customize a Command Prompt window, you make settings in a properties dialog box that you can reach in any of three ways:

- Right-click a shortcut that opens a Command Prompt window, and then click Properties on the shortcut menu. Changes you make here affect all future Command Prompt sessions launched from this shortcut.

- Click the Control menu icon in a Command Prompt window, and then click Properties on the Control menu. (If Command Prompt is running in full-screen mode, press Alt+Enter to switch to window display.) Changes you make here affect the current session. When you leave the properties dialog box, you'll be given the option of propagating your changes to the shortcut from which this session was launched.

- Click the Control menu icon in a Command Prompt window, and then click Defaults on the Control menu. Changes here do not affect the current session. Instead, they affect all future sessions, except those launched from a shortcut whose properties you have modified.

Setting the window size and position

To change the screen position where a newly launched Command Prompt window appears, open the window's properties dialog box and click the Layout tab.

The dialog box maintains two different sizes—the screen buffer size and the window size. The width for both sizes is specified in columns (characters); the height is specified in rows (text lines).

The screen buffer settings control the size of the "virtual screen," which is the maximum extent of the screen. Standard screen sizes are 80 by 25, 80 by 43, or 80 by 50, but you can set your Command Prompt session to any size you want.

The window size settings control the size of the Command Prompt window on your screen. In most cases, you'll want it to be the same size as the screen buffer. But if your screen is crowded, you can reduce the window size. If you do, scroll bars are added. The window size settings cannot be larger than the screen buffer size settings.

Because you size a window by specifying how many rows and columns of characters it should have, the size of those characters also affects the amount of space the window occupies on your display. For information about changing the character size, see "Selecting a font" below.

Setting the window size and position visually

Rather than guess at the settings for window size and position, you can drag the borders of a Command Prompt window to adjust its size and drag its title bar to adjust its position. To retain the settings for future sessions, click the Control menu icon, click Properties, and click the Layout tab. You'll see the settings that reflect the window's current condition. Click OK to apply these settings.

Selecting a font

Applications in a Command Prompt window can display only one font at a time. Your choice is limited, as you'll see if you click the Font tab in the Command Prompt window's properties dialog box.

Make a selection in the Font list first because your choice here determines the contents of the Size list. If you select the Consolas or Lucida Console font, you'll find point sizes to choose from in the Size list. If you select Raster Fonts, you'll find character widths and height in pixels.

Setting colors

You can set the color of the text and the background of the Command Prompt window. You can also set the color of the text and the background of pop-up windows that originate from the command prompt, such as the command history window.

To set colors, click the Colors tab in the Command Prompt window's properties dialog box. Here you can set separate foreground and background colors for the Command Prompt window and pop-up windows, such as the command history window.

An introduction to Windows PowerShell

Microsoft describes Windows PowerShell as a "task-based command-line shell and scripting language designed especially for system administrators." That means that you can use PowerShell for the same kinds of tasks you're accustomed to performing with Cmd.exe, and you can use its scripting power to automate routine work. If you're a Windows user who occasionally likes to take advantage of the power of text-based command-line tools such as Ipconfig or Netsh, you'll find that PowerShell lets you interact with the operating system in all the old familiar ways—and a good many new ones as well. If you're accustomed to using batch programs, VBScript, or JScript to automate administrative tasks, you can retain your current scripting investment but take advantage of the additional capabilities afforded by PowerShell's object orientation and .NET Framework foundation as your scripting needs grow.

CAUTION

If you use Netsh to configure TCP/IP, you should familiarize yourself with equivalent procedures in PowerShell. In 2015, Microsoft began displaying the following message in response to the **netsh /interface** command: "Microsoft recommends that you transition to Windows PowerShell if you currently use netsh to configure and manage TCP/IP." Type **Get-Command –Module NetTCPIP** at the Windows PowerShell prompt to view a list of commands to manage TCP/IP. As of this writing, **netsh/interface** continues to work, but the message suggests that it might not always.

Among the advantages that PowerShell offers over previous shells and scripting platforms are the following:

CHAPTER 21

- **Integration with the .NET Framework.** Like more traditional development languages, such as C#, PowerShell commands and scripts have access to the vast resources of the .NET Framework.

- **Object orientation and an object-based pipeline.** All PowerShell commands that generate output return .NET Framework objects rather than plain text, eliminating the need for text parsing when the output of one command provides input to a second (that is, when one command is "piped" to another).

- **A consistent, discoverable command model.** All of PowerShell's commands (or "cmdlets," as they are called) use a verb-noun syntax, with a hyphen separating the two components. All cmdlets that read information from the system begin with Get; all those that write information begin with Set. These and other similar consistencies make the language easy to learn and understand. Each cmdlet has a help topic that can be retrieved by typing **get-help *cmdletname*** (where *cmdletname* is the name of a cmdlet). A –Whatif parameter lets you test the effect of a cmdlet before you execute it.

- **Universal scripting capability.** A PowerShell script is a text file, with the extension .ps1, containing PowerShell commands. Any commands that can be used interactively can be incorporated into a script, and scripting structures, such as looping, branching, and variables, can also be used interactively—that is, outside the context of a script.

- **A focus on administrators.** PowerShell includes features of particular interest to system administrators, such as the ability to work with remote computers; access to system resources such as files, folders, registry keys, events, and logs; and the ability to start and stop services.

- **Extensibility.** Developers can extend the PowerShell language by importing modules—packages of PowerShell commands and other items.

The following pages introduce PowerShell. Our discussion focuses primarily on the use of PowerShell as an interactive command shell because PowerShell scripting is itself a book-length subject. For sources of additional information, see "Finding additional PowerShell resources" later in this chapter.

Starting PowerShell

To launch Windows PowerShell, type **power** into the search box; the Windows PowerShell application should appear at or near the top of the results list. Nearby you will also find the 64-bit and 32-bit versions of the Windows PowerShell Integrated Scripting Environment (ISE). The ISE is a multitabbed graphical environment of particular use for developing and debugging scripts.

As Figure 21-1 shows, PowerShell's default appearance differs minimally from that of Cmd.exe. The caption *Windows PowerShell* and the letters *PS* at the beginning of the command prompt may be the only details you notice.

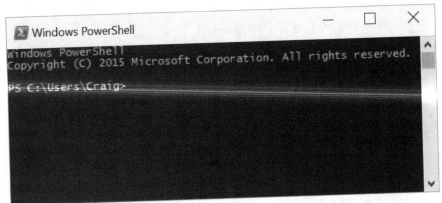

Figure 21-1 An uncustomized (default) PowerShell window looks a lot like Cmd.exe.

Interacting with PowerShell

If you're an old hand at the command prompt but new to PowerShell, the first thing you might want to try is using some of Cmd.exe's familiar internal commands. You'll discover that such items—for example, *dir, cd, md, rd, pushd,* and *popd*—still work in PowerShell. Redirection symbols, such as > to send output to a file and > > to append output to a file, work as well, and you can pipe lengthy output to More, just as you are accustomed to doing in Cmd.exe. PowerShell uses aliases to map Cmd.exe commands to its own cmdlets. Thus, for example, *dir* is an alias for the PowerShell cmdlet *Get-Childitem*; *cd* is an alias for PowerShell's *Set-Location*.

You can create your own aliases to simplify the typing of PowerShell commands that you use often; for details, see "Using and creating aliases" later in this chapter.

Like any other command prompt, PowerShell can be used to launch executables. Typing **regedit**, for example, launches Registry Editor; typing **taskschd** launches Task Scheduler. (Note that PowerShell also lets you work directly with the registry without the use of Registry Editor; for details, see "Working with the registry" later in this chapter.)

Using cmdlets

The core of PowerShell's native vocabulary is a set of cmdlets, each consisting of a verb, followed by a hyphen, followed by a noun—as, for example, *Start-Service*. A cmdlet may be followed by one or more parameters; each parameter is preceded by a space and consists of a hyphen connected to the parameter's name followed by a space and the parameter's value. So, for example,

```
Get-Process -Name iexplore
```

returns information about any currently running processes named iexplore.

With parameters that accept multiple values, you can use a comma to separate the values. For example,

```
Get-Process -Name iexplore, winword, excel
```

would generate information about Word and Excel as well as Internet Explorer.

Many cmdlets use positional parameters. For example, the –Name parameter for *Get-Process* is positional. PowerShell expects it to come first, so you may omit –Name and simply specify the names of the processes in which you're interested.

If you omit both the first positional parameter and its value, PowerShell typically assumes a value of *. So, for example,

```
Get-Process
```

returns information about all running processes, as shown in Figure 21-2.

In some cases, if you omit values for an initial positional parameter, PowerShell will prompt you to supply the parameter. For example, in response to

```
Get-Eventlog
```

PowerShell will do you the courtesy of prompting for the name of an event log. (Event logs are large; it wouldn't be reasonable to ask for all of them at once.)

For information about any particular cmdlet, type **get-help** followed by the cmdlet name.

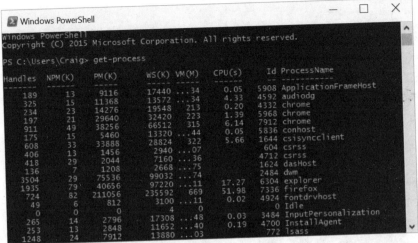

Windows PowerShell

```
Windows PowerShell
Copyright (C) 2015 Microsoft Corporation. All rights reserved.

PS C:\Users\Craig> get-process

Handles  NPM(K)    PM(K)      WS(K) VM(M)   CPU(s)     Id ProcessName
-------  ------    -----      ----- -----   ------     -- -----------
    189      13     9116      17440 ...34     0.05   5908 ApplicationFrameHost
    325      15    11368      13572 ...34     4.33   4592 audiodg
    234      23    14276      19548   213     0.20   4332 chrome
    197      21    29640      32420   223     1.39   5968 chrome
    911      49    38256      66512   315     6.14   7912 chrome
    175      15     5460      13320 ...44     0.05   5836 conhost
    608      33    33888      28824   322     5.66   1644 csisyncclient
    406      13     1456       2940 ...07             604 csrss
    418      29     2044       7160 ...36            4712 csrss
    136       7     1208       2668 ...75            1624 dasHost
   3504      29    75536      99032 ...74            2484 dwm
   1935      79    40656      97220 ...11    17.27   6304 explorer
    724      82   211056     235592   669    51.98   7336 firefox
     49       6      812       3100 ...11     0.02   4924 fontdrvhost
      0       0        0          4     0                0 Idle
    265      14     2796      17308 ..:48     0.03   3484 InputPersonalization
    253      13     2848      11652 ...40     0.19   4700 InstallAgent
   1248      24     7912      13880 ...03             772 lsass
```

Figure 21-2 Typing *Get-Process* without parameters produces information about all running processes.

Using the pipeline

The pipe operator (|) lets you supply the output of one cmdlet as input to another. You can connect as many cmdlets as you please in this manner, as long as each cmdlet to the right of a pipe operator understands the output of the cmdlet to its left. Because PowerShell cmdlets return full-fidelity .NET objects rather than text, a cmdlet to the right of a pipe operator can operate directly on properties or methods of the preceding cmdlet's output.

The following paragraphs provide examples of the use of piping to format, filter, and sort the output from various Get- cmdlets.

Formatting output as a list   The default output from many Get- cmdlets is a table that presents only some of the resultant object's properties (about as many as the width of your display is likely to accommodate). For example, the cmdlet

```
Get-Service
```

generates a three-column display that includes only the Status, Name, and DisplayName properties.

If you pipe the same output to *Format-List*,

```
Get-Service | Format-List
```

PowerShell, no longer constrained by display width, can display more of the object's properties (see Figure 21-3), including in this case such useful items as the dependencies of each service and whether the service can be paused or stopped.

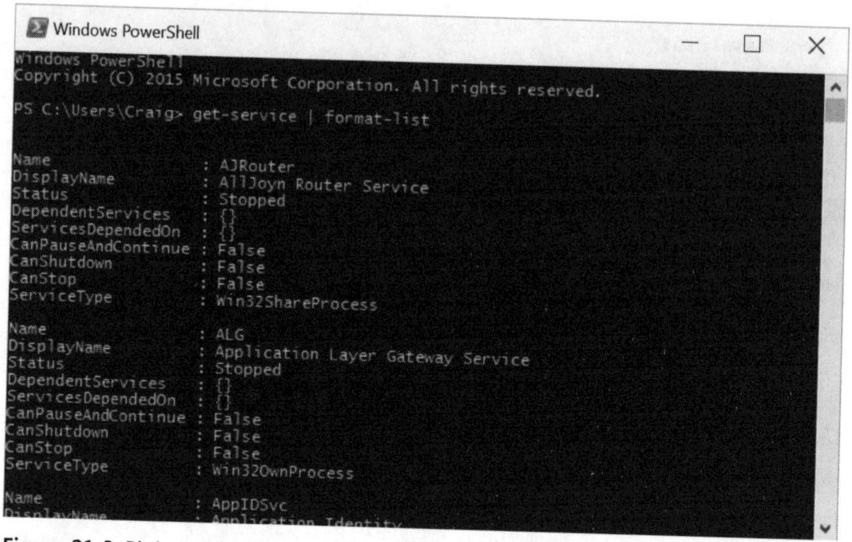

Figure 21-3 Piping a cmdlet to *Format-List* allows you to see more of a resultant object's properties.

In some cases, the *Format-List* cmdlet, with no parameters, is equivalent to *Format-List* –Property *. But this is by no means always the case. For example,

```
Get-Process | Format-List
```

returns four properties for each process: ID, Handles, CPU, and Name. Asking for all properties produces a wealth of additional information.

To generate a list of particular properties, add the –Property parameter to *Format-List* and supply a comma-separated list of the properties you want to see. To see what properties are available for the object returned by a cmdlet, pipe that cmdlet to *Get-Member*:

```
Get-Process | Get-Member -Itemtype property
```

(Omitting the –Itemtype parameter returns methods as well as properties.)

Creating a multicolumn list with *Format-Wide*   By piping a cmdlet to *Format-Wide*, you can generate a multicolumn list displaying a single property, comparable to a List view in File Explorer. Use the –Column parameter to specify the number of columns you want. For example,

```
Get-Childitem hkcu:\appevents\eventlabels | Format-Wide -Column 2
```

generates a two-column list of the subkeys of HKCU:\Appevents\Eventlabels.

Formatting output as a table   Perhaps you want tabular output but with different properties from those that your cmdlet gives you by default. *Format-Table* does the trick. For example,

```
Get-Service | Format-Table -Property name, dependentservices, servicesdependedon
```

generates a table consisting of these three enumerated properties. Note that PowerShell's console output is constrained by your console width, no matter how many properties you ask to see. For results that are too wide to display, redirect output to a file (using the > operator) or try the *Out-Gridview* cmdlet, described next.

Generating an interactive graphical table with *Out-Gridview*   Piping output to *Out-Gridview* generates a graphical tabular display that you can filter, sort, and copy easily into other programs, such as Excel, that accommodate tabular data. For example,

```
Get-Process | Select-Object * | Out-Gridview
```

produces output comparable to that shown in Figure 21-4. Note that in this example, *Get-Process* is piped first to *Select-Object* * because *Out-Gridview*, unlike *Format-Table*, does not include a –Property parameter. *Select-Object* * passes all properties of the object returned by *Get-Process* along the pipeline to *Out-Gridview*.

_NounName	Name	Handles	VM	WS	PM	NPM	Path	Comp
Process	ApplicationFr...	293	2,199,249,801,216	27,189,248	14,331,904	20,528	C:\WINDO...	Micro
Process	audiodg	331	2,199,110,033,408	13,955,072	11,714,560	15,952		
Process	chrome	234	222,879,744	19,996,672	14,618,624	23,464	C:\Program...	Goog
Process	chrome	197	233,340,928	33,521,664	30,523,392	21,888	C:\Program...	Goog
Process	chrome	932	336,797,696	68,988,928	39,989,248	51,920	C:\Program...	Goog
Process	conhost	168	2,199,119,544,320	13,713,408	5,484,544	14,808	C:\WINDO...	Micro
Process	csisyncclient	628	339,951,616	30,035,968	35,225,600	35,112	C:\Program...	Micro
Process	csrss	427	2,199,081,062,400	3,031,040	1,544,192	14,208		
Process	csrss	434	2,199,109,603,328	7,245,824	2,113,536	29,704		
Process	dasHost	136	2,199,047,012,352	2,727,936	1,236,992	7,536		
Process	dwm	4,336	2,199,374,393,344	102,391,...	89,645,056	31,304		
Process	explorer	1,970	2,199,533,977,600	108,212,...	45,109,248	82,880	C:\WINDO...	Micro
Process	firefox	741	688,422,912	234,340,...	209,289,...	85,048	C:\Program...	Mozil
Process	fontdrvhost	49	2,199,085,252,608	3,170,304	831,488	5,976		
Process	Idle	0	65,536	4,096	0	0		
Process	InputPersona...	267	2,199,124,881,408	17,747,968	2,891,776	15,064	C:\Program...	Micro

Figure 21-4 The *Out-Gridview* cmdlet produces a graphical tabular display that you can sort, filter, and copy into a spreadsheet.

You can manipulate the *Out-Gridview* display with techniques comparable to those used by many other programs:

- To sort the display, click a column heading; click a second time to reverse the sort.

- To change the position of a column, drag its heading. You can also rearrange columns by right-clicking any column head, choosing Select Columns, and then using the Move Down and Move Up buttons in the Select Columns dialog box.

- To remove columns from the display, right-click any column heading, click Select Columns, and then use the << button in the Selected Columns dialog box.

- To perform a quick filter, enter text in the line labeled Filter. For example, to limit the display in Figure 21-4 to processes with properties containing the word Microsoft, type **Microsoft** on the Filter line.

- To filter on one or more specific columns, click the Add Criteria button. In the drop-down list that appears, select check boxes for the columns on which you want to filter and then click Add.

Filtering output with *Where-Object*   To filter output from a cmdlet, pipe it to the *Where-Object* cmdlet. With *Where-Object* you encapsulate filtering criteria in a script block, between curly braces. The following example filters output from *Get-Service* so that only services whose status is Stopped are displayed:

```
Get-Service | Where-Object {$_.Status -eq "Stopped"}
```

Sorting output with *Sort-Object*   The *Sort-Object* cmdlet lets you sort the output from a cmdlet on one or more of the resultant object's properties in a variety of useful ways. If you omit the –Property parameter, *Sort-Object* sorts on the default property. For example,

```
Get-Childitem | Sort-Object
```

sorts the contents of the current directory by Name, the default property in this case. To sort on multiple properties, follow –Property with a comma-separated list. *Sort-Object* sorts on the first named property first, sorting items with identical values for the first property by the second property, and so on. Sorts are ascending by default; to sort in descending order, add the parameter –Descending.

By piping *Sort-Object* to *Select-Object* you can do such things as returning the largest or smallest *n* items in a resultant object. For example,

```
Get-Process | Sort-Object -Property WS | Select-Object -Last 10
```

returns the processes with the 10 largest values of the working set (WS) property. Using –First 10 instead of –Last 10 would give you the items with the smallest values.

Piping output to the printer   To redirect output to the default printer, pipe it to *Out-Printer*. To use a nondefault printer, specify its name, in quotation marks, after *Out-Printer*. For example,

```
Get-Content C:\Users\Craig\Documents\Music\Sonata.sib | Out-Printer "Microsoft Print
To PDF"
```

sends the content of C:\Users\Craig\Documents\Music\Sonata.sib to the device named Microsoft Print To PDF.

Using PowerShell features to simplify keyboard entry

PowerShell is a wordy language and doesn't take kindly to misspellings. Fortunately, it includes many features to streamline and simplify the task of formulating acceptable commands.

Using and creating aliases   An alias is an alternative formulation for a cmdlet. As mentioned earlier, PowerShell uses aliases to translate Cmd.exe commands to its own native tongue—for example, *cd* to *Set-Location*. But it includes a great many more simply for your typing convenience; *gsv*, for example, is an alias for *Get-Service*. And you can create aliases of your own.

To see what aliases are currently available (including any that you have created yourself during the current session), type **get-alias**. To see whether an alias is available for a particular cmdlet, pipe *Get-Alias* to *Where-Object*, like this:

```
Get-Alias | Where-Object { $_.definition -eq "Set-Variable" }
```

This particular command string inquires whether an alias is available for the *Set-Variable* cmdlet. If you type this, you'll discover that PowerShell offers two—*sv* and *set*.

To create a new alias, type **set-alias** ***name value***, where *name* is the alias and *value* is a cmdlet, function, executable program, or script. If *name* already exists as an alias, *Set-Alias* redefines it. If *value* is not valid, PowerShell won't bother you with an error message—until you try to use the alias.

Aliases that you create are valid for the current session only. To make them available permanently, include them in your profile. See "Using your profile to customize PowerShell" later in this chapter.

Abbreviating parameter names   Aliases are dandy for cmdlets, but they're no help for parameter names. Fortunately, PowerShell allows you to abbreviate such names. The commands *Get-Process –name iexplore* and *Get-Process –n iexplore* are equivalent. As soon as you've typed enough of a parameter name to let PowerShell recognize it unambiguously, you can give your fingers a rest. And, of course, you can combine aliases with parameter abbreviations to further lighten your load.

Using Tab expansion   As a further convenience, PowerShell lets you complete the names of files, cmdlets, or parameters by pressing Tab. Type part of a name, press Tab, and PowerShell presents the first potential completion. Continue pressing Tab to cycle through all the possibilities. Note, however, that Tab expansion works only with the noun portion of a cmdlet; type the verb and the hyphen, and then you can use Tab expansion for the noun.

Using wildcards and regular expressions   Like all its Windows-shell predecessors, PowerShell supports the * and ? wildcards, the former standing in for any combination of zero or more characters, the latter for any single character. PowerShell also provides a vast panoply of "regular expressions" for matching character strings. For details about regular expressions in PowerShell, type **get-help about_regular_expressions**.

Recalling commands from the command history   PowerShell maintains a history of your recent commands, which makes it easy to reuse (or edit and reuse) a command that you've already entered. To see the history, type **get-history**. Each item in the history is identified by an ID number. Type **invoke-history** *ID* to bring an item to the command line. On the command line, you can edit an item before executing it. With the exception of Alt+F7, the editing keys available in Cmd.exe (see Table 21-1) work the same way in PowerShell.

The number of history items retained in a PowerShell session is defined by the automatic variable $MaximumHistoryCount. By default, that variable is set to 64. If you find you need more, you can assign a larger number to the variable. For example, to double the default for the current session, type **$MaximumHistoryCount = 128**. To change the history size for all sessions, add a variable assignment to your profile. For more information, see "Using your profile to customize PowerShell" later in this chapter.

Using PowerShell providers for access to file system and registry data

PowerShell includes a set of built-in providers that give you access to various kinds of data stores. Providers are .NET Framework–based programs, and their data is exposed in the form of drives, comparable to familiar file-system drives. Thus, for example, you can access a key in the HKLM registry hive with a path structure similar to that of a file-system folder; for example, the path HKLM:\Hardware\ACPI specifies the ACPI key of the Hardware key of the HKLM hive. Or, to use a quite different example, you can use the command *Get-Childitem env:* to get a list of current environment variables and their values.

Table 21-3 lists PowerShell's built-in providers. For more information about providers, type **get-help about_providers**.

Table 21-3 Built-in providers

Provider	Drive	Data store
Alias	Alias	Currently defined aliases
Certificate	Cert X509	Certificates for digital signatures
Environment	Env	Windows environment variables
FileSystem	(varies)	File-system drives, directories, and files
Function	Function	PowerShell functions
Registry	HKLM, HKCU	HKLM and HKCU registry hives
Variable	Variable	PowerShell variables
WSMan	WSMan	WS-Management configuration information

The following paragraphs provide some basic information about working with the file system and registry.

Working with the file system For very simple file-system operations, you might find that familiar Cmd.exe commands are adequate and easier to use than PowerShell cmdlets. The built-in aliases listed in Table 21-4 let you stick with time-honored methods. PowerShell supports the familiar single period (.) and double period (..) symbols for the current and parent directories, and it includes a built-in variable, $Home, that represents your home directory (equivalent to the HomePath environment variable).

Table 21-4 File-system aliases

Alias	PowerShell cmdlet
cd	*Set-Location*
chdir	*Set-Location*
copy	*Copy-Item*
del	*Remove-Item*
dir	*Get-Childitem*
move	*Move-Item*
md, mkdir	*New-Item*
rd, rmdir	*Remove-Item*
type	*Get-Content*

The PowerShell cmdlets, however, include valuable optional parameters:

- **–Confirm and –Whatif.** The –Confirm parameter, used with *Copy-Item*, *Move-Item*, *Remove-Item*, or *Clear-Content*, causes PowerShell to display a confirmation prompt before executing the command. (*Clear-Content* can be used to erase the contents of a

CHAPTER 21

file.) If you use the –Whatif parameter, PowerShell shows you the result of a command without executing it.

- **–Credential.** Use the –Credential parameter to supply security credentials for a command that requires them. Follow –Credential with the name of a user, within double quotation marks. PowerShell will prompt for a password.

- **–Exclude.** The –Exclude parameter allows you to make exceptions. For example, *Copy-Item directory1*.* directory2 –Exclude *.log* copies everything, excluding all .log files, from Directory1 to Directory2.

- **–Recurse.** The –Recurse parameter causes a command to operate on subfolders of a specified path. For example, *Remove-Item x:\garbagefolder*.* –Recurse* deletes everything from X:\Garbagefolder, including files contained within that folder's subfolders.

- **–Include.** The –Include parameter, used in conjunction with –Recurse, allows you to restrict the scope of a command. For example, *Get-Childitem c:\users\craig\documents* –Recurse –Include *.xlsx* restricts a recursive listing of C:\Users\Craig\Documents to files with the extension .xlsx.

- **–Force.** The –Force parameter causes a command to operate on items that are not ordinarily accessible, such as hidden and system files.

For detailed information about using these parameters with *Set-Location, Get-Childitem, Move-Item, Copy-Item, Get-Content, New-Item, Remove-Item,* or *Get-Acl,* type **get-help cmdletname**.

Working with the registry   The built-in registry provider provides drives for two registry hives, HKLM and HKCU. To change the working location to either of these, type **set-location hklm:** or **set-location hkcu:**. Use standard path notation to navigate to particular subkeys, but enclose paths that include spaces in quotation marks; for example, *set-location "hkcu:\control panel\accessibility"*.

To display information about all subkeys of a key, use *Get-Childitem*. For example,

```
Get-Childitem -Path hkcu:\software\microsoft
```

returns information about all the subkeys of HKCU:\Software\Microsoft.

To add a key to the registry, use *New-Item*. For example,

```
New-Item -Path hkcu:\software\mynewkey
```

adds the key mynewkey to HKCU:\Software. To remove this key, type **remove-item –path hkcu:\software\mynewkey**.

To copy a key, use *Copy-Item* and specify the source and destination paths; like this, for example,

```
Copy-Item -Path hkcu:\software\mykey hkcu:\software\copyofmykey
```

To move a key, use *Move-Item*. The command

```
Move-Item -Path hkcu:\software\mykey -Destination hkcu:\software\myrelocatedkey
```

copies all properties and subkeys associated with HKCU:\Software\Mykey to HKCU:\Software\ Myrelocatedkey and deletes HKCU:\Software\Mykey.

To display the security descriptor associated with a key, use *Get-Acl*. To see all the properties of the security descriptor, pipe this to *Format-List –Property* *. For example,

```
Get-Acl -Path hkcu:\software\microsoft | Format-List -Property *
```

generates a display comparable to this:

For more information about working with the registry, type **get-help registry**.

Discovering PowerShell

PowerShell provides plenty of resources to help you learn as you go. You can display help information about any cmdlet by typing **get-help *cmdletname***. For example, to read help about *Get-Help*, type **get-help get-help**. If you omit the first *get,* PowerShell helpfully pipes the help text to More. So, for example, if you type **help get-help**, PowerShell will pause the output after each screenful.

Among the useful parameters for *Get-Help* are the following:

- **–Examples.** To display only the name, synopsis, and examples associated with a particular help text, add the –Examples parameter.

- **–Parameter.** To get help for a particular parameter associated with a cmdlet, include –Parameter. Specify the parameter name in quotation marks.

- **–Detailed.** To get the description, syntax, and parameter details for a cmdlet, as well as a set of examples, use the –Detailed parameter. (Without this parameter, the examples are omitted; with –Examples, the syntax information is omitted.)

- **–Full.** For the works, including information about input and output object types and additional notes, specify –Full.

- **–Online.** For the latest information that Microsoft has, including additions or corrections to the native output of *Get-Help*, specify –Online. The relevant information, from the Microsoft TechNet Script Center, will appear in your browser.

PowerShell includes a compiled HTML (.chm) help file, which you can run from the Jump List that appears on the recent items or pinned items section of your Start menu (or on the taskbar if you pin PowerShell there). But the information made available via the –Online parameter is more current and more accurate than that provided in the .chm file. For the most recent updates visit the "Scripting with Windows PowerShell" page at Microsoft TechNet, *bit.ly/scripting-with-powershell*.

Getting help on conceptual topics

The PowerShell help resources include a number of entries on conceptual topics, such as operators, parameters, variables, and pipelines. These topics all begin with *about*. You can generate a list by typing **get-help about*** or **get-help –category "helpfile"**. To read information about aliases, for example, type **get-help about_aliases**. Note that the TechNet site described in the previous section also includes these conceptual topics.

Finding the right cmdlet to use

The *Get-Command* cmdlet can help you figure out which cmdlet is the right one to use for a given task. Type **get-command** with no arguments to get the names and definitions of all available cmdlets, functions, and aliases. *Get-Command* can also give you information about non-PowerShell executables. If you type **get-command ***, for example, you'll get a huge list including all files in all folders included in your current Path environment variable.

Either global list (with or without the non-PowerShell executables) is likely to be less than useful when you just want to know which cmdlets are available for use with a particular object. To get such a focused list, add the –Noun parameter. For example, type **get-command –noun eventlog** to get a list of the cmdlets that use that noun; you'll be rewarded with the names and definitions of *Clear-Eventlog*, *Get-Eventlog*, *Limit-Eventlog*, *New-Eventlog*, *Remove-Eventlog*, *Show-Eventlog*, and *Write-Eventlog*. You can get a list focused similarly on a particular verb by using the –Verb parameter.

Scripting with PowerShell

A PowerShell script is a text file with the extension .ps1. You can create a script in any plain text editor (Notepad will do fine), or you can use the Integrated Scripting Environment (ISE).

Anything that you do interactively with PowerShell you can also do in a script. The reverse is true as well; you can take lines from a script, including those that involve looping or branching structures, and execute them individually outside the context of a script. For example, if you type

```
For ($i=1; $i -le 5; $i++) { "Hello, World" }
```

at the PowerShell command prompt, PowerShell will perform the familiar greeting five times.

Using PowerShell's history feature, you can easily transfer commands that you have used interactively into a script. That way you can test to see what works and how it works before committing text to a .ps1 file.

For example, the command

```
Get-History | Foreach-Object { $_.commandline } >> c:\scripts\mynewscript.ps1
```

appends the Commandline property from each item in your current history to the file C:\Scripts\Mynewscript.ps1. (If the path doesn't exist, the command returns an error.) Once you have transferred your history to Mynewscript.ps1 in this manner, you can edit it in Notepad by typing **notepad c:\scripts\mynewscript.ps1**.

Running PowerShell scripts

Although files with the extension .ps1 are executable PowerShell scripts, running one is not quite as straightforward as double-clicking a .bat file. In the first place, if you double-click a .ps1 file in File Explorer, you'll get an Open File—Security Warning dialog box, from which the only forward step leads to Notepad. In effect, the default action for a PowerShell script in File Explorer is Edit.

Second, the first time you try to run a script by typing its name at the PowerShell command prompt, you might well see a distressing message displayed in red letters and with possibly unwelcome detail. This means that PowerShell has declined to run your script "because the execution of scripts is disabled on this system." You need to change PowerShell's execution policy.

Third, even after you've cleared the execution-policy hurdle, you might still be rebuffed if you try to run a script stored in the current directory. That's because PowerShell requires a full path specification—even when the item you're running is stored in the current directory. For example, to run Displayprocessor.ps1, which resides in the current directory, you must type **.\displayprocessor**.

Getting and setting the execution policy

PowerShell's power can be used for evil ends. The majority of Windows users will never run PowerShell, but many will have .ps1 files lying about on their system or will download them inadvertently. To protect you from malice, PowerShell disables script execution until you explicitly enable it. Enabling execution requires a change to the execution policy.

Note that your profile script (if you have one) is subject to the same execution policy as any other script. (See "Using your profile to customize PowerShell" later in this chapter.) Therefore, it's pointless to set an execution policy by means of a profile script; that script itself will not run until you've enabled script execution elsewhere.

The following execution policies, listed here from least permissive to most, are available:

- **Restricted.** The default policy. No scripts are allowed to run.

- **AllSigned.** Any script signed by a trusted publisher is allowed to run. PowerShell presents a confirmation prompt before running a script signed by a publisher that you have not designated as "trusted."

- **RemoteSigned.** Scripts from local sources can run. Scripts downloaded from the Internet (including scripts that originated as email or instant-messaging attachments) can run if signed by a trusted publisher.

- **Unrestricted.** All scripts can run, but PowerShell presents a confirmation prompt before running a script from a remote source.

- **Bypass.** All scripts are allowed to run.

Execution policies can be set separately for the following scopes:

- **Process.** Affects the current PowerShell session only. The execution policy is stored in memory and lost at the end of the session.

- **CurrentUser.** The execution policy is stored in a subkey of HKCU and applies to the current user only. The setting is retained between PowerShell sessions.

- **LocalMachine.** The execution policy is stored in a subkey of HKLM and applies to all users at this computer. The setting is retained between PowerShell sessions.

If policies are set at two or more of these scopes, the Process policy takes precedence over the CurrentUser policy, which takes precedence over the LocalMachine policy. Execution policy can also be set via Group Policy, however, and settings made in that manner trump any of the foregoing scopes. (Group Policy settings can be made in either the Computer Configuration or User Configuration node; a Computer Configuration setting trumps any other.)

To see the execution policies in effect at all scopes, type **get-executionpolicy –list**.

To set an execution policy, use *Set-ExecutionPolicy*. To set a policy at the LocalMachine scope, you need to be running PowerShell with administrative privileges.

The default scope for *Set-ExecutionPolicy* is LocalMachine, so if you're planning to apply a policy to all users at your computer, you can omit the –Scope parameter. For example, if you're comfortable disabling all of PowerShell's script-execution security measures, including warning prompts, you can type **set-executionpolicy bypass.** For a slightly more protective environment, type **set-executionpolicy unrestricted**.

To set a policy at the CurrentUser or Process scope, add –Scope followed by CurrentUser or Process. Note that you can also set an execution policy at the Process scope by adding an –executionpolicy argument to a command that launches PowerShell. For example, from a command prompt in Cmd.exe, in PowerShell, or on the Start menu, you could type **power-shell –executionpolicy unrestricted** to launch PowerShell with the Unrestricted execution policy at the Process scope.

To remove an execution policy from a particular scope, set that scope's policy to Undefined. For example, if you have set a Process policy to, say, Bypass, and you would like PowerShell to revert to the policy at the next level of precedence (CurrentUser, if a policy is set there, or LocalMachine, if not), type **set-executionpolicy undefined –scope process**.

Using your profile to customize PowerShell

Your profile is a script that PowerShell executes at the beginning of each session. You can use it to tailor your PowerShell environment to your preferences. Your profile must have the following path and file name:

$Home\Documents\WindowsPowerShell\Profile.ps1

where $Home is a system-generated *PowerShell* variable corresponding to the environment variable UserProfile. You can see where this is on your system by typing **$profile**, and you can edit an existing profile by typing **notepad $profile**. If you have not yet created a profile, you can type the following:

```
if (!(test-path $profile)){New-Item -Type file -Path $profile -Force}
```

PowerShell will create the file for you in the appropriate folder. Then you can type **notepad $profile** to edit the blank file.

You can use your profile to customize PowerShell in a variety of ways. Possibilities to consider include changing the default prompt and creating new aliases.

PowerShell's prompt is derived from a built-in function called Prompt. You can overwrite that function with your own. For example, the function

```
Function prompt {"PS [$env:computername] $(Get-Date) > "}
```

replaces the built-in PowerShell prompt with the letters PS, followed by your computer name, followed by the current date and time. For more information about PowerShell prompts, type **get-help about_prompts**.

To add new aliases to the ones that PowerShell already offers, simply include *Set-Alias* statements in your profile. (See "Using and creating aliases" earlier in this chapter.)

Using the PowerShell ISE

A feature introduced with PowerShell 2.0 allows you to issue commands and work with scripts in a graphical environment. This Integrated Scripting Environment (ISE) includes a command pane, a script pane, and an output pane. The output pane displays the results of any commands you issue in the command pane or any scripts that you run in the script pane.

The ISE supports multiple tabs, so you can open several scripts at once. Click File, New to open a new blank tab (for example, to write a new script) or File, Open to open an existing script in a new tab. To run the current script, click Run/Continue on the Debug menu, press F5, or click the green arrow in the middle of the toolbar. Other commands on the Debug menu allow you to set and remove breakpoints and step through execution.

The ISE offers all the usual amenities of a graphical environment. You can resize and rearrange the panes, for example. You can use the View menu's Zoom commands (or adjust the slider in the lower right corner of the window) to make the text display larger or smaller. And you can easily select and copy text from one pane to another or from the ISE to another application.

The ISE uses its own profile, separate from the one you use to customize PowerShell itself. The path and file name are as follows:

$Home\Documents\WindowsPowerShell\ProfileISE.ps1

and you create the file by typing:

```
if(!(Test-Path $profile)){New-Item -Type file -Path $profile -Force}
```

Finding additional PowerShell resources

This chapter's discussion of PowerShell has barely nicked the surface. For further exploration, we recommend the following:

- *Windows PowerShell 3.0 First Steps*, by Ed Wilson (Microsoft Press, 2013)

- *Windows PowerShell Cookbook*, third edition, by Lee Holmes (O'Reilly Media, 2013)

- "Windows PowerShell Scripting" (part of the Microsoft TechNet Script Center) at *bit.ly/ps-script-center*

- The "Hey, Scripting Guy!" blog at *bit.ly/scripting-guy*

- "Getting Started with Windows PowerShell" (part of the MSDN Script Center) at *bit.ly/get-started-powershell*

Running virtual machines with Hyper-V

Hyper-V allows you to create and run *virtual machines*—effectively, computers within a computer. A console on your computer acts as a monitor for a virtual machine (sometimes called a *VM*), which generally has all the features and capabilities of a standalone computer. The only difference is that a virtual machine is running as a program on a host computer.

Hyper-V has long been a power feature in server editions of Windows, allowing IT managers to use a single server machine to host a variety of server roles, each in its own virtual machine. Beginning with Windows 8, Client Hyper-V is included in Pro and Enterprise editions of Windows, to the great delight of IT professionals, developers, security researchers, and tech enthusiasts. Client Hyper-V has most, but not all, of the features of Hyper-V Server. In Windows 10, Client Hyper-V gains some additional features, such as production checkpoints, better support of older operating systems, and the ability for users to change memory and other settings without first shutting down a virtual machine.

Virtual machines running under Hyper-V are useful in the following situations, among many others:

- People who have programs that work only in older versions of Windows can run them in a virtual machine.

- Developers who need to test their programs in different Windows versions or on different hardware configurations can set up a virtual machine for each target platform.

- Security researchers and curious users who want to test software of unknown provenance or explore potentially dangerous websites can do so safely within the confines of a virtual machine (assuming it's properly isolated from the host and the host network). If a virus or other malware is found, the host machine remains unscathed, and the virtual machine can be rolled back to a safe state.

- Tech enthusiasts who want to test a new beta (prerelease) version of Windows or other software can install it in a virtual machine. This way, they can try software without having to dedicate a physical machine (or worse, upgrading their main system to run an operating system that's not ready for prime time).

- Authors of books like this one can use virtual machines not only to test various setups, but also to capture images of screens that would be impossible to grab using ordinary screen-capture tools (for example, images showing sign-in screens or even Windows setup before Windows itself is fully functional).

To use Hyper-V, your system must meet certain minimum requirements and you might need to enable Hyper-V, as described in the next section. After that is done, you use Hyper-V Manager to create virtual machines. With enough system resources, you can then run one or more virtual machines, each in its own window. Because they function as independent computers, each virtual machine can run a different version of Windows—32-bit or 64-bit, old or new, server or desktop—or even other operating systems that work on PC-compatible hardware.

Setting up Hyper-V

Before you get started with Hyper-V, be sure your computer meets the system requirements. Because each virtual machine uses system resources on a par with a standalone computer, the requirements are somewhat steep:

- **64-bit version of Windows 10 Pro, Enterprise, or Education.** Hyper-V is unavailable on 32-bit versions and is also not part of Windows 10 Home.

- **At least 4 GB of RAM.** With 4 GB, you can probably run up to three virtual machines simultaneously. More machines require more RAM.

- **Copious disk space.** Each virtual machine is stored in files on your hard drive. The size can vary considerably depending on how you configure your virtual machines (for example, the size of the VM's virtual hard disks), how many checkpoints you save, and so on—but expect to use at least 20 GB of disk storage for each virtual machine.

- **CPU with Second Level Address Translation (SLAT) support.** Your computer must have a 64-bit processor that supports SLAT. Most 64-bit processors sold by Intel and AMD in the past few years have this capability.

With those prerequisites in place, you're ready to enable Hyper-V, which is not enabled by default. To do so, open Windows Features, shown in Figure 22-1. (In the search box, type **features** and then click Turn Windows Features On Or Off.)

Inside OUT

Determine whether your computer supports SLAT

A utility from Windows Sysinternals can tell you more than you need to know about your computer's CPU. Download Coreinfo from *bit.ly/sysinternals-coreinfo*. At an elevated command prompt, enter **coreinfo –v** to see results similar to this:

```
Administrator: Command Prompt                                     —

c:\>E:\Data\Downloads\Coreinfo\Coreinfo.exe -v

Coreinfo v3.31 - Dump information on system CPU and memory topology
Copyright (C) 2008-2014 Mark Russinovich
Sysinternals - www.sysinternals.com

Intel(R) Core(TM) i7-2600 CPU @ 3.40GHz
Intel64 Family 6 Model 42 Stepping 7, GenuineIntel
Microcode signature: 00000029
HYPERVISOR          *        Hypervisor is present
VMX                 *        Supports Intel hardware-assisted virtualization
EPT                 *        Supports Intel extended page tables (SLAT)
```

For an Intel processor (as shown here), an asterisk in the EPT line indicates SLAT support; a hyphen in that space indicates that the processor does *not* support SLAT. For an AMD processor, the line to look for is NP. Note that you'll get valid results only if Hyper-V is *not* already running. (But if it's already running, you didn't need to run this diagnostic test anyway, did you?)

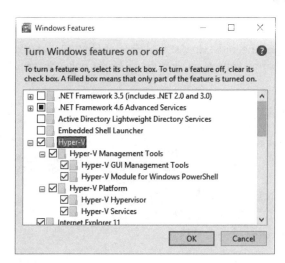

Figure 22-1 To select all the Hyper-V-related entries, simply select the top-level Hyper-V check box.

Click the plus sign by the top-level Hyper-V entry to show all the subentries. If your computer does not fully support Hyper-V, the Hyper-V Platform entry is not available.

Inside OUT

Using Hyper-V on a computer that doesn't support SLAT

Hyper-V Management Tools, the first subentry under Hyper-V, can be installed on any computer running Windows 10. Therefore, even if the Hyper-V Platform entry is dimmed (which means your computer isn't capable of hosting virtual machines), you can use Hyper-V Management Tools to manage virtual machines that are hosted on a different physical computer (in most cases, a computer running Window Server). To create and run virtual machines on your own computer, you must enable Hyper-V Platform.

Select Hyper-V (which also selects all the available subentries) to enable it, and then click OK. After a few moments, Windows asks you to restart your computer.

Alternatively, you can enable Hyper-V by using Windows PowerShell. Use this cmdlet:

```
Enable-WindowsOptionalFeature –Online –FeatureName Microsoft-Hyper-V –All
```

Using Hyper-V Manager

Hyper-V Manager is the program you use to create, run, and manage your virtual machines. When you start Hyper-V Manager, the initial view, shown here, might leave you scratching your head. You're faced with a barren console window, one that has only one available action.

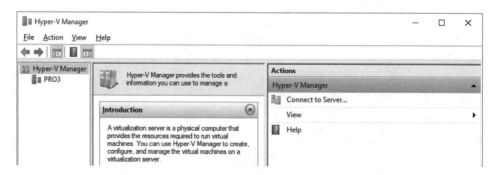

The trick is to select a "server" (in this case, your local computer) in the left pane, the console tree. (On computers that do not have Hyper-V Platform enabled, the only option is to choose the Connect To Server action, which lets you connect to a different computer running Hyper-V Platform.) Lots more information and options then appear, as shown in Figure 22-2.

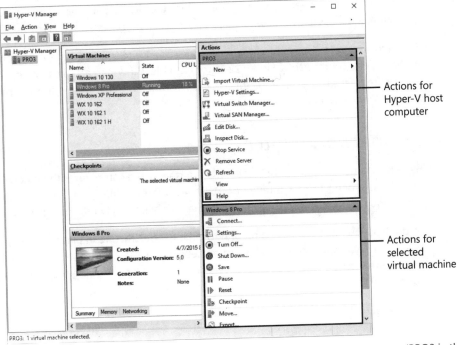

Figure 22-2 When you select a local machine or remote server in the console tree (PRO3 in this example), Hyper-V Manager shows the virtual machines stored on that physical computer.

TROUBLESHOOTING

The name of your computer doesn't appear in the console tree

If your computer's name doesn't appear under Hyper-V Manager in the console tree, then it is not running Hyper-V Platform. Be sure you're running a 64-bit version of Windows 10, and be sure that your computer's processor supports Second Level Address Translation, as described in the previous section. If your computer meets the requirements, then check to be sure that Hyper-V Platform is selected in Windows Features.

When you select a server in the console tree, the center pane lists the virtual machines available on that server and shows a bit of information about the current state of each one. Below that, you'll see a list of checkpoints for the selected virtual machine. (A *checkpoint* captures the configuration and data of a virtual machine at a point in time. For more information, see "Working with checkpoints" later in this chapter.) At the bottom of the center pane, the

Summary, Memory, and Networking tabs show additional details about the selected virtual machine. Here you can see at a glance what IP address has been assigned to the virtual machine, how much memory is in use, and so on. The thumbnail image on the Summary tab also provides a convenient launching method for the virtual machine; double-click it to open a full-size screen in a new window.

As in other console applications, the right pane shows available actions for the items selected in the left and center panes. Figure 22-2, for example, shows the actions that apply to the PRO3 computer (the name of the local computer running Hyper-V) and to the virtual machine named Windows 8 Pro.

Creating a network switch

By default, a new virtual machine is set up as a standalone computer with no network connection. It can't connect to the Internet or to other computers on your network. In this connected world, you'll probably want to give your virtual machines a network connection.

To do that, you must first have a bit of networking infrastructure in place—namely, a virtual switch. A *virtual switch* connects the virtual network adapter in your virtual machine to the physical network adapter in your physical computer, thereby allowing the virtual machine to connect to the outside world.

> NOTE
>
> You can create and manage a virtual switch *after* you set up a virtual machine and then modify your virtual machine to use the virtual switch. Setting up the virtual switch before you set up your virtual machines simply saves a few steps.

To create a virtual switch or make changes to an existing one, in the Actions pane (or on the Action menu) click or tap Virtual Switch Manager. Then select the type of switch you want to create:

- **External.** This is the most common type because it binds the virtual switch to your computer's physical network adapter so you can access your physical network. Assuming your physical network adapter is connected to the Internet, your virtual machines also have Internet access.

- **Internal.** An internal virtual switch can be used only to make a connection among the virtual machines running on your physical computer, and between the virtual machines and your physical computer.

- **Private.** Use a private virtual switch to set up a network that comprises only the virtual machines running on your physical computer. This network is isolated from all physical computers, including the one on which it's installed.

When you click or tap Create Virtual Switch, you're asked for more details, as shown in Figure 22-3. Click OK to complete the switch creation.

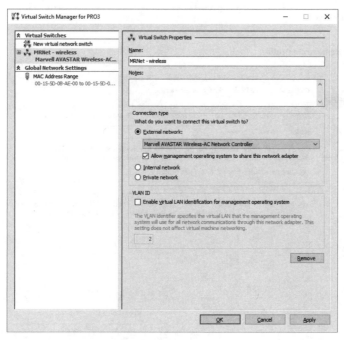

Figure 22-3 If your computer has more than one physical network adapter, specify the one you want to use under External Network.

Creating a virtual machine

With your virtual network switch in place, you're ready to create a new virtual machine. To do that, in the Actions pane, click or tap New, Virtual Machine, which launches the New Virtual Machine Wizard. You navigate through the wizard, which leads you through the process of setting up a virtual machine, by using the Next and Previous buttons or the links along the left side. At any point in the wizard, you can click Finish to create a virtual machine that uses default values for any wizard pages you skip.

Specify name and location

After you step through the Before You Begin page, the wizard asks you to provide a name for your virtual machine. Enter a name or description that'll help you differentiate this virtual machine from others you might create. If you don't like the proposed storage location for the virtual machine files, select the check box and specify another, as shown in Figure 22-4.

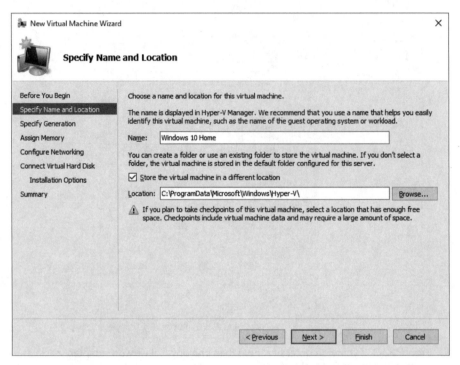

Figure 22-4 For our purposes, the operating system name provides a good name for a virtual machine, but you might have different needs.

The default location is %ProgramData%\Microsoft\Windows\Hyper-V\. (%ProgramData% is an environment variable that is set to C:\ProgramData on a standard Windows installation.) If your computer has a small system drive (common in systems that use a solid state drive for system files and a large hard disk for data files), you might want to store the files elsewhere. Keep in mind that a virtual machine can occupy 10–40 GB or more.

It is possible to move the virtual machine files after you create the machine, but it's not easy. Although some parts of a virtual machine (the virtual hard disk and the paging file, for example) can be moved by changing the settings of the virtual machine, this option isn't available for some of the core files. To completely move a machine at a later time, you can import a virtual machine, copy it, and store it in a different location. You're much better off choosing a suitable location *before* you create the virtual machine.

Specify generation

On the next wizard page, shown here, you select either Generation 1 or Generation 2 for the style of virtual machine you need.

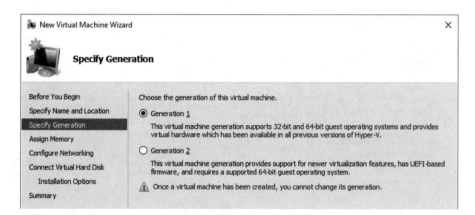

This choice is new to Hyper-V in Windows 10 and offers some tradeoffs between compatibility and features.

Generation 1 supports a wide range of guest operating systems, including most versions of Windows (32-bit and 64-bit) and Linux. The virtual hardware in a generation 1 virtual machine is typical of that found in BIOS-based PCs for many years.

Generation 2 supports only a few guest operating systems: 64-bit versions of Windows 8, Windows 8.1, Windows 10, Windows Server 2012, and Windows Server 2012 R2. In addition, generation 2 removes support for attaching physical DVD drives and other older hardware to a virtual machine. But a generation 2 virtual machine has modern UEFI-based firmware, which enables Secure Boot and booting from a network adapter, SCSI hard drive, or DVD. In addition, generation 2 virtual machines enable new Hyper-V features, such as the ability to adjust memory or add a network adapter while the virtual machine is running.

If you're going to install one of the newer supported operating systems in your virtual machine, select Generation 2 to enable additional features. For an older operating system, you must stick with the default option, Generation 1.

NOTE
If you select Generation 2, you must install the operating system from an ISO file; you can't use a DVD.

CHAPTER 22

Assign memory

On the Assign Memory page, shown in Figure 22-5, you specify the amount of RAM your virtual machine will have.

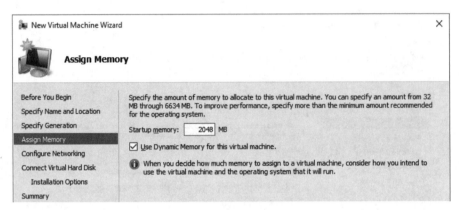

Figure 22-5 The Dynamic Memory option lets you use memory more efficiently when running multiple virtual machines.

If you enable Dynamic Memory, Hyper-V uses memory as a shared resource that can be reallocated as needed among running virtual machines. This way, each machine gets as much
memory as it needs, but it doesn't reserve a fixed amount of memory (which would preclude
other machines from using it).

Therefore, if you plan to run more than one virtual machine at once, we recommend that you
select Dynamic Memory to get the best performance. Then set Startup Memory to at least the
minimum amount required for the operating system you plan to install in this virtual machine.

If you plan to run only one virtual machine, or if you know how much memory your virtual
machine will need to perform its given tasks, you can turn off Dynamic Memory and specify
a fixed amount of memory. This setup works more like a physical computer, in that whatever
memory you specify is the total amount of installed RAM in the virtual machine.

Configure networking

On the next wizard page, shown in Figure 22-6, you specify the virtual network switch where
you want to connect your virtual machine's network adapter. The default option is Not Connected, which results in a virtual machine that's isolated from all other computers (physical and

virtual) and from the Internet. Even to connect to the physical computer on which the virtual machine runs, you must create a virtual network switch and select it here.

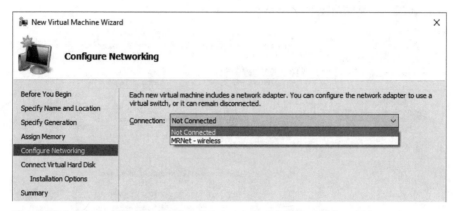

Figure 22-6 Select a virtual network switch to connect to the outside world.

TROUBLESHOOTING

The only available option is Not Connected

Before you can connect to a network, you must create a virtual network switch, as described earlier in "Creating a network switch." Each virtual network switch you create appears in the Connection list.

To determine which type of network switch you're using (External, Internal, or Private), you need to return to the Virtual Switch Manager.

Connect virtual hard disk

On the Connect Virtual Hard Disk page, shown in Figure 22-7, you set up the virtual machine's first virtual hard disk (VHD). (Just like a physical computer, a virtual machine can have multiple hard drives.) A virtual hard disk is actually a file in the VHD or VHDX format. By default, it's created in a subfolder of the virtual machine location you specified earlier. But you can override that default and store the virtual hard disk on any physical disk that's accessible to the host computer running Hyper-V.

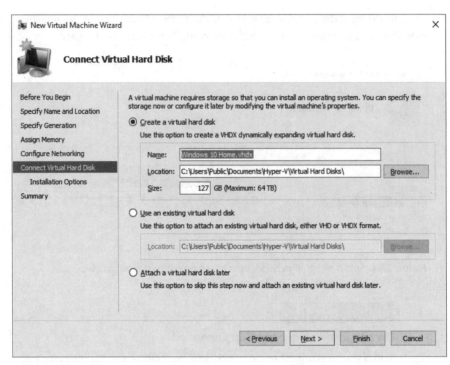

Figure 22-7 With the first option, you create a virtual hard disk. The other options allow you to use an existing virtual hard disk.

In addition to specifying the name and location of your virtual hard disk file, you must specify the disk's capacity in gigabytes. Be sure you create a virtual hard disk that's big enough to store the operating system, programs, and data you plan to use on the virtual machine. Although you don't want to go overboard, don't worry too much about specifying a size that's too big. Because of the way data is stored in a virtual hard disk, the size of the VHDX file roughly corresponds with the amount of disk space in use rather than the size you specify, which is the maximum. However, its dynamically expanding nature also means that the VHDX file can grow to that maximum size; be sure that the physical hard drive where you store it has enough room to accommodate growth.

NOTE

You can change the location later, but it's a multistep process. And it is possible to resize a virtual hard disk after it has been created, but doing so brings some risk of data loss. (For more information, select the virtual hard disk in the Settings window for the virtual machine, and then click Edit.) Therefore, it's best to get it right from the beginning.

If you have an existing virtual hard disk you want to use instead of creating a new one, select the second or third option on this wizard page.

Installation options

Almost done! You use the wizard's next page, shown in Figure 22-8, to specify how and when you want to install an operating system in your new virtual machine.

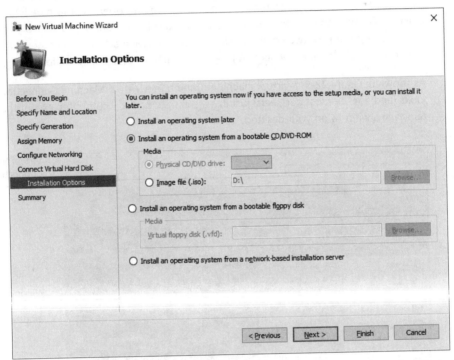

Figure 22-8 If you choose Generation 2 on the Specify Generation page, the options for installing from a CD/DVD drive or floppy disk don't appear because generation 2 virtual machines don't support these types of physical devices.

Like a physical computer, a virtual machine is nothing without an operating system, so installing one should be your first order of business. Select the appropriate option, specify the location of your operating system installation media, and click Next.

This brings you to a Summary page, where you can review your settings before clicking Finish to complete the wizard.

At this point, even though you've specified installation options, you still don't have a working virtual machine. Now back in Hyper-V Manager, double-click the new virtual machine to open it in a Virtual Machine Connection window. Then click or tap the Start button on the toolbar or choose Start on the Action menu. This "powers on" your virtual machine and launches operating system setup from the location you specified in the wizard.

Running a virtual machine

As the final step in creating a virtual machine, described in the previous sections, you double-click the name of a virtual machine in Hyper-V Manager to open the machine in a Virtual Machine Connection window. You then click the Start button on the toolbar to power on the machine. This is one of two common ways to run a virtual machine. (The other is to use the Hyper-V Virtual Machine Connection program, which we describe in the following section.)

As shown in Figure 22-9, a virtual machine running in a Virtual Machine Connection window looks (and, for the most part, acts) just like a separate physical computer, except that it's contained in a window on your desktop.

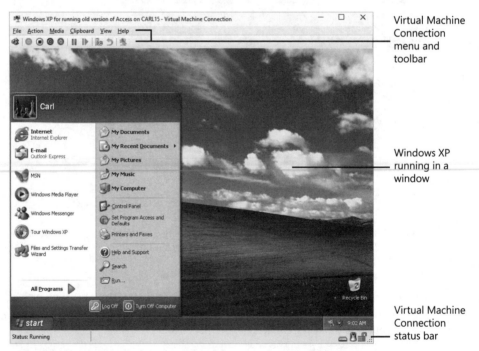

Virtual Machine Connection menu and toolbar

Windows XP running in a window

Virtual Machine Connection status bar

Figure 22-9 For a nostalgic look back—or to run a legacy program that doesn't run properly on newer operating systems—you can run Windows XP in a Virtual Machine Connection window.

You use the toolbar at the top of the window (or the corresponding commands on the Action menu) to operate the virtual machine.

From left to right, the buttons have the following functions:

- **Ctrl+Alt+Del.** Because the Ctrl+Alt+Del key combination is reserved by Windows 10 on your physical computer, when you press it while you're using a virtual machine, the key combination goes to your host computer. There are two ways to mimic the effect of Ctrl+Alt+Del within a virtual machine: Press Ctrl+Alt+End or click or tap this toolbar button.

- **Start.** This button turns on a virtual machine that is off.

- **Turn Off.** This button turns the virtual machine off, but it does so by effectively unplugging the machine. This, of course, is not a graceful way to shut down a computer, and you'll lose any unsaved data.

- **Shut Down.** This is equivalent to using the Shut Down command on the Start menu, and the machine goes through the usual shut-down process. Note that some (usually older) operating systems do not support Shut Down, even with Integration Services enabled. For a virtual machine without this support, use commands within the virtual machine to shut down properly.

- **Save.** This button saves the virtual machine state and then turns it off, much like hibernation on a physical computer. When you next start the virtual machine, you return immediately to where you left off.

- **Pause/Resume.** Pausing a virtual machine stops it temporarily but does not fully release its resources, as the Turn Off, Shut Down, and Save options do.

- **Reset.** Resetting a virtual machine discards any changes and reboots using the last saved version.

- **Checkpoint.** This button creates a checkpoint, which is a snapshot of the virtual machine's state and its data. For more information, see "Working with checkpoints" later in this chapter.

- **Revert.** This button restores the virtual machine to its condition at the previous checkpoint and restarts the virtual machine.

- **Enhanced Session.** On guest operating systems that support it, this button toggles the virtual machine between basic session mode and enhanced session mode. For more information, see the next section, "Using enhanced session mode."

Within the Virtual Machine Connection window, you use the virtual machine just as you would a physical computer, with only a few exceptions:

- When you run an older guest operating system, using a mouse is not as fluid as it is when your guest operating system is Windows 8 or later. That's because once you click inside the virtual machine window, the mouse becomes trapped in that window. To release it, press Ctrl+Alt+Left Arrow.

- Not all of your physical computer's hardware is available in all virtual machines.

  For example, DVD drives are not available in generation 2 virtual machines. (You can, however, mount an ISO image as a DVD drive.) For generation 1 machines, only one virtual machine can use a physical DVD drive at any given time. (To release the DVD drive from one virtual machine so that you can use it in another, use commands on the DVD menu.)

  USB devices, audio devices, and some other local resources work only in enhanced session mode. (For more information, see "Using enhanced session mode.")

CHAPTER 22

Inside OUT

Start a virtual machine automatically

By default, when you open a Virtual Machine Connection window, it opens with the machine turned off. If you want to save yourself the trouble of starting the virtual machine after you open it, you can change a setting for the virtual machine so that it starts automatically. In Hyper-V Manager, select the virtual machine; in the right pane, under the virtual machine name, click Settings; in the Settings dialog box, under Management, select Automatic Start Action and then select an option.

When you close the Virtual Machine Connection window, note that your virtual machine continues to run. By closing the window, all you're doing, in effect, is turning off the monitor. To shut down or turn off the virtual machine, you should use the appropriate buttons on the Virtual Machine Connection window. If that window is closed? You can reopen it by using Hyper-V Manager.

Using enhanced session mode

With previous versions of Hyper-V, access to your physical computer's hardware is quite limited. Your physical computer's screen, keyboard, and mouse could be redirected for use by the virtual machine, but connecting other devices is somewhere between difficult and impossible. Audio playback is not supported. In addition, capabilities for copying files between a virtual machine and its host computer are very limited in older Hyper-V versions. You could overcome some of these limitations (specifically, audio playback and file copying) by using Remote Desktop Connection to connect to a virtual machine, but that requires a working network connection to the virtual machine.

With Windows 10, Hyper-V adds *enhanced session mode*, which solves many of these shortcomings. With enhanced session mode, you can redirect the following resources from your physical computer to a virtual machine in a Virtual Machine Connection window:

- Audio devices

- Printers

- Plug and Play devices

- Clipboard (which allows you to copy and paste files and other information between the virtual machine and your physical computer)

Inside OUT

Determine at a glance whether you're in enhanced session mode

Need a quick way to tell whether your machine is running in enhanced session mode? Look at the speaker icon in the notification area of your virtual machine's taskbar. If it has a red X, that's because no audio device is available, which means you're in basic session mode.

Alas, enhanced session mode comes with its own limitations. First and foremost: enhanced session mode requires a guest operating system that supports it, and there are only a few that do (Windows 8.1, Windows 10, Windows Server 2012 R2). Of less importance, you'll also discover that in enhanced session mode you can't readily change the resolution of the virtual machine's monitor. (For a workaround, see the following tip.)

If your virtual machine is running an operating system that supports enhanced session mode, you can switch between basic and enhanced session mode by clicking or tapping the rightmost button on the Virtual Machine Connection toolbar.

CHAPTER 22

Inside OUT

Change screen resolution for an enhanced mode session

Within an enhanced session mode window, using the normal Windows settings for changing screen resolution leads to this message: "The display settings can't be changed from a remote session." (Enhanced session mode, in effect, uses Remote Desktop Connection to connect to the virtual machine, hence the message about a "remote session.")

If you need to change the screen resolution, switch to basic session mode and then close the Virtual Machine Connection window. In Hyper-V Manager, click Connect to open a new Virtual Machine Connection window, and you'll be greeted by a dialog box in which you can specify the screen resolution, as shown here.

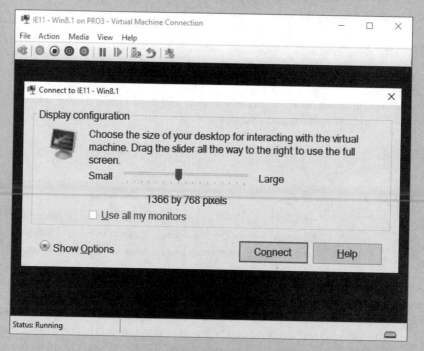

In this same dialog box, clicking Show Options adds a Local Resources tab to the dialog box. On that tab, you specify which local resources—that is, printers, drives, and other devices from the host computer—you want to use within the virtual machine. For more information about these settings, see "Using Remote Desktop Connection" in Chapter 20, "Advanced networking."

You can enable and disable enhanced session mode on a per-server or per-user basis. To view or change either setting, in Hyper-V Manager select the server and then, under the server name in the right pane, click or tap Hyper-V Settings. In the Hyper-V Settings dialog box that appears, you'll find enhanced session mode settings under Server and User.

Inside OUT

Get ready-to-run virtual machines

As part of its support for developers, Microsoft offers fully configured virtual machines that you can download and run. Each one has a different guest operating system with certain software installed. These virtual machines are for testing and evaluation and expire after a limited time, but instructions provided with the virtual machine files explain how to use the files after expiration. You can find these virtual machine files at *bit.ly/virtualmachines*.

Changing settings for a virtual machine

The settings you make when you create a new virtual machine are but a small subset of the settings you can apply to a virtual machine. You can change almost all the settings you make in the New Virtual Machine Wizard plus scores more. You can add virtual devices such as network adapters and hard drives, change the location of some of the files that make up the virtual machine, reconfigure devices at a granular level, and more.

To dive into these settings, in Hyper-V Manager select the name of the virtual machine and then, near the bottom of the Actions pane, click or tap Settings. A dialog box like the one shown in Figure 22-10 appears.

Many settings can be changed even while a machine is running (which is important for virtual machines running critical tasks), especially on generation 2 virtual machines.

CHAPTER 22

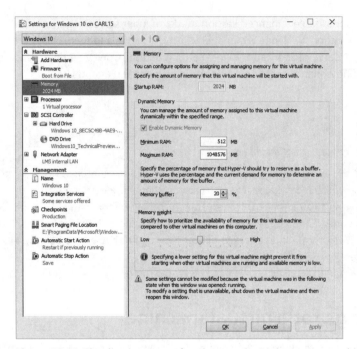

Figure 22-10 The dizzying array of options on the Memory page—which is similar in complexity to many other pages in the Settings dialog box—will make you glad that the New Virtual Machine Wizard asks for only a single number.

Working with checkpoints

A *checkpoint* captures the data and configuration of a running virtual machine—a snapshot in time. Indeed, in earlier versions of Hyper-V, checkpoints were called snapshots. A checkpoint can be restored, allowing you to quickly and easily return your virtual machine to an earlier time—perhaps a time before that misguided software installation.

To capture a checkpoint, simply click or tap the Checkpoint button on the Virtual Machine Connection toolbar. You can provide a descriptive name for the checkpoint, but no other inter-action is required. The checkpoints you collect for a given virtual machine appear in the center of the Hyper-V window, as shown in Figure 22-11. To revert to an earlier checkpoint, select the checkpoint and, in the Actions pane, click or tap Apply.

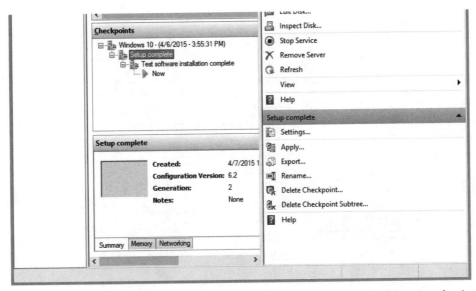

Figure 22-11 When you select a checkpoint in the center pane, a list of applicable actions for that checkpoint appear in the bottom of the Actions pane.

Microsoft engineers have discovered that droves of Hyper-V users use checkpoints as a form of backup. (Although it doesn't provide the full capabilities of a more traditional backup pro- gram—such as the ability to restore individual folders and files—it's convenient and easy.) However, the checkpoint feature as implemented in earlier Hyper-V versions is far from ideal for backup. Because those checkpoints (now called standard checkpoints) include information on the virtual machine state, running applications, and network connections, restoring one often takes you to an unstable condition (for example, the same network connections might not be available).

In response, Client Hyper-V in Windows 10 adds a new type of checkpoint called a *production checkpoint*. A production checkpoint uses the Volume Snapshot Service (VSS) backup tech- nology to save the data and configuration of a running virtual machine but not its state. This provides a much better backup solution, and it is now the default checkpoint in Hyper-V. You can still use standard checkpoints if you prefer; to make the switch, open Settings for a virtual machine and, under Management, click Checkpoints.

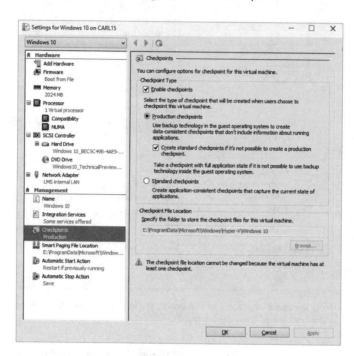

Windows 10 editions at a glance

Microsoft's lineup of Windows 10 editions is refreshingly simple.

Consumers and small businesses that acquire Windows on a new device or as an upgrade have their choice of two and only two editions: Windows 10 Home and Windows 10 Pro.

On corporate networks, you have the option to enable additional features by upgrading to the Enterprise edition. At universities and other institutions of learning, administrators can enable advanced features by upgrading to the Education edition, which is, except for a few small details, roughly equivalent to the Enterprise edition.

That makes a grand total of four editions, of which you are still only likely to encounter two.

Yes, the Windows 10 family also includes Windows 10 Mobile, which runs on smartphones and, at least in theory, on other small devices that have not yet appeared in the market. Sometime in the future, you might encounter embedded versions of Windows 10 for use in specialized machines (such as automated teller machines) and wearables. But our focus in this appendix is on the four versions of Windows 10 designed for use on traditional PCs and PC-like devices such as tablets.

That simple lineup is a stark and welcome improvement over the sometimes confusing assortment of previous Windows editions, and it makes our job in this appendix simple. We start with a recitation of the features you can find in all Windows 10 desktop editions and then, in separate sections, list the additional features available in individual editions.

You can use this information to decide whether to upgrade from Home to Pro when you're shopping for a new PC, for example. You can also use the data in these tables to help decide which PCs on a corporate network should be upgraded to the Enterprise edition using your organization's Volume License agreement.

We start with a brief discussion of hardware configurations. Table A-1 lists technical limits related to CPU and memory support that might affect your purchase or upgrade decision.

Table A-1 Supported hardware configurations in Windows 10

Hardware component	Supported configurations
Number of CPUs/cores	Windows 10 Home: One physical processor, unlimited cores Windows 10 Pro/Enterprise/Education: One or two physical processors, unlimited cores
Addressable memory (RAM)	32-bit (x86) editions: 4 GB maximum (because of 32-bit memory architecture, usable memory is typically 3.5 GB or less) 64-bit (x64) editions: 128 GB for Windows 10 Home, 512 GB for Windows 10 Pro/Enterprise/Education

Features available in all Windows 10 editions

With some minor exceptions, which are noted here, the features listed in Table A-2 are available in all retail editions of Windows 10 sold worldwide, including Windows 10 Home edition.

Table A-2 Features available in all Windows 10 editions

Feature	Description
Core Windows features	
Customizable Start menu and taskbar	Similar in concept to the Windows 7 Start menu, with the additional ability to pin apps as Windows 8–style live tiles.
Windows Update	Provides regular security updates, device drivers, and new features. Business editions have limited options to delay updates.
Fast User Switching	Allows a user to sign in to another user account without requiring the current user to sign out.
Hiberboot and InstantGo	These features, which are supported on most modern devices, allow faster startup as well as low-power, always-on updates even when a device is sleeping.
Settings app	Offers access to many system settings previously available only in Control Panel; uses an interface that scales to devices of different sizes and is especially usable on touch devices.
Virtual desktops	Allows collections of running apps to be arranged on separate virtual desktops, with keyboard shortcuts or gestures for switching between desktops.
Window snap	An upgrade to the classic Aero Snap behavior, with Snap Assist improving the usability of displaying two windows side by side. Allows snapping of up to four windows to any corner or side of a display; also supports multiple displays.
Task View	Quickly switch between running programs with a taskbar button, keyboard shortcuts, or touch gestures.

Feature	Description
Power management	In addition to support for classic Windows power schemes, includes new Battery Saver options for more aggressive control over battery life.
Ease Of Access features	High-contrast themes, Ease Of Access Center, Magnifier, Narrator, and On-Screen Keyboard.
Windows Mobility Center	Central location for managing power, display, network, and other settings on a notebook PC.
Windows PowerShell and Integrated Scripting Environment	Command-line shell and graphical host application for scripting administrative tasks.
Virtual hard drive (VHD) support	Create a new VHD; attach (mount) an existing VHD.
Display	
Touchscreen/pen support	With appropriate hardware and drivers, adds support for touch, multitouch, and pen input.
Tablet Mode and Continuum	Tablet Mode changes the layout of the Start menu, taskbar, and running programs for easier use on handheld touch devices. Continuum allows hybrid devices to switch modes when the keyboard is attached or removed.
Miracast	Allows streaming of audio and video from a Windows 10 device to a Miracast receiver, such as the Microsoft Wireless Display Adapter.
Multimonitor support	With properly configured hardware, extends the main display to include a second (or third, fourth, and so on) monitor.
Cortana and Search	
Windows Search	Indexed search of local files, programs, and settings, with ability to expand search to include cloud-based items and the web.
Cortana	Adds a "personality" and a natural language interface to Windows Search and allows access to an ever-expanding collection of web services.
Speech-based interaction	Allows hands-free activation with the "Hey Cortana" trigger phrase, as well as intelligent and trainable speech recognition.
Interest-based suggestions	Proactive display of news, sports scores, weather forecasts, traffic reports, and more, based on defined interests and linked calendars or other activities.
Intelligent actions	Create reminders, appointments, tasks, and spoken notes from speech or typed input.

Feature	Description
Security and reliability	
Trusted Platform Module (TPM) support	Supports the latest TPM specification for secure storage of system secrets such as encryption keys and configuration information.
Secure Boot and Early Launch Antimalware	On UEFI devices, ensures the integrity of boot files and prevents malicious software from acting before Windows has fully loaded.
Device encryption	Full disk encryption, even on Windows 10 Home devices, when signing in with a Microsoft account. BitLocker administration tools are available only with business editions.
Windows Hello	Biometric sign-in and authentication options enabled through support for compatible fingerprint readers, facial recognition devices, and iris scanners.
Microsoft Passport	Supports authentication to online resources using biometric credentials without transmitting passwords.
User Account Control	Allows the use of standard accounts for day-to-day use; includes Enhanced Protected Mode in Internet Explorer 11.
Security and maintenance notifications	Messages and updates about security and maintenance issues.
Windows Defender	Real-time antivirus and antispyware protection, with free updates.
Windows Firewall	Blocks unsolicited inbound network connections; includes advanced security interface to manage inbound and outbound connections.
System recovery drive/ Windows Recovery Environment	Provides the ability to access a troubleshooting/repair environment at startup without requiring original installation media.
Reset	Allows the user to recover from system corruption or compromise by reinstalling Windows, with options to keep or remove personal files and account information.
File History	Provides the ability to recover changed or deleted files from automatic or manual backups.
System image backup	Includes the capability to create a system image and restore Windows from a previously saved image.
Family safety	For accounts you designate as family members, provides the ability to set time limits on computer usage and block access to specific games, programs, and websites.
Windows Remote Assistance	Allows direct network connections between two Windows PCs for troubleshooting and repair.

Feature	Description
Sideloading of line of business apps	In managed environments, supports deployment of custom Windows apps directly, without requiring access to the Windows Store.
Mobile device management	Allows administrators to manage Windows 10 mobile devices from a management console. This feature is not available in Windows Home edition at launch but will be available later.
Installed apps	
Microsoft Edge	Default web browser for retail editions of Windows 10, updated through Windows Store; supports reading view, PDF viewing, ink comments, and Cortana integration.
Internet Explorer 11	Secondary web browser for Windows 10; provides compatibility with older websites and allows use of ActiveX controls and browser plug-ins.
Mail & Calendar	Allows sending, receiving, and managing email messages, appointments, and meeting invitations; supports industry-standard protocols as well as cloud services from Microsoft, Google, Apple, and Yahoo.
Maps	Online and offline support for maps covering the entire world; supports navigation functions on devices equipped with a GPS.
Photos	Allows viewing and basic editing of photos stored locally or in the cloud.
Alarms & Clock	Displays the current time, with the option to display multiple time zones; also includes stopwatch, alarm, and countdown features.
Calculator	Full-featured calculator that performs basic arithmetic as well as advanced statistical functions; also includes programmer and scientific modes and has the ability to convert units of measurement.
News, Weather, Sports, Money	A suite of information apps powered by MSN and connected via the current Microsoft account
Phone Companion	Manages synchronization with mobile devices, including those running non-Windows operating systems.
Xbox and other games	Allows access to casual games, including a preinstalled modern version of Solitaire; can also stream games from an Xbox One console.
Groove Music	Plays supported audio file formats, including MP3, WMA, AAC, and FLAC; also connects to Microsoft's Groove (previous Xbox Music) subscription service.
Camera	Controls built-in camera (front and back) for taking photos or communicating via programs such as Skype.

APPENDIX A

Feature	Description
Scan	Used to scan documents and send and receive faxes. Requires properly configured scanner, fax modem, or both.
XPS Document Writer and Viewer	Provides the capability to create and view documents using the XML Paper Specification.
Voice Recorder	Creates simple voice memos.
Networking	
Remote Desktop client	Connect via a network to a Remote Desktop host.
SMB network connections	Maximum of 20 simultaneous connections. Because each PC or device requires two Server Message Block (SMB) connections, 10 PCs or devices can be connected at once.
Ability to join a homegroup	Share local resources and access shared resources on other devices running Windows 7 or later versions that are part of the same homegroup.
Microsoft Wi-Fi	Automatically connects to Microsoft-managed Wi-Fi hotspots; requires subscription.

Windows 10 Pro

Windows 10 Pro includes the same core features as Windows 10 Home, with the addition of features that are primarily of interest to business users and corporate network administrators. All of the features listed in Table A-3 are also available in the Enterprise and Education editions.

Table A-3 Features available only in Windows 10 Pro, Enterprise, and Education editions

Feature	Description
Core Windows features	
Client Hyper-V	With proper hardware support, this hypervisor-based virtualization software allows users to create a virtual machine (VM), install Windows or another operating system on the VM, and use it as if it was a separate physical device.
Boot from virtual hard drive (VHD)	Configure a VHD as a boot device.
Language packs	Change the Windows 10 interface to display menus, dialog boxes, and other elements in a user-selected language.
Subsystem for Unix-based Applications	Compatibility subsystem for compiling and running custom Unix-based applications.
Encrypting File System	Enables strong encryption of files and folders on an NTFS-formatted volume.

Feature	Description
Management, security, and networking features	
BitLocker	Allows an entire drive to be encrypted, protecting its contents from unauthorized access if the computer is lost or stolen.
BitLocker To Go	Encrypts data on removable media such as USB flash drives.
Domain join/Group Policy management	Allows the device to join a Windows domain and be managed by using Active Directory and Group Policy.
Enterprise Data Protection	Provides advanced control over data files, including encryption and remote wipe. This feature is not available at launch.
Enterprise Mode Internet Explorer (EMIE)	Using network configuration files, administrators can define compatibility settings for sites accessed using Internet Explorer, including those on corporate intranets, enabling continued use of older web apps that aren't compatible with Microsoft Edge.
Assigned Access	A special configuration mode primarily for use on tablets and task-specific workstations that restricts the ability of a user to run any apps except those on an approved list.
Remote Desktop (server)	Allows remote access to the full Windows experience on the current PC; the connection is made using Remote Desktop Protocol from a client program running on any Windows PC, Mac, or supported mobile device.
Offline Files	Used to synchronize, cache, and index network files locally so that they are available when the computer is disconnected from the network.
Deployment features	
Azure Active Directory support	Allows a Windows 10 device to join Azure Active Directory, with single sign-in to cloud-hosted apps.
Business Store for Windows 10	Using this feature, an organization can provision apps and packaged Windows desktop programs in a restricted area of the Windows Store for installation by employees. This feature is not available at launch.
Windows Update for Business	Allows central management of security updates and new features delivered through Windows Update. The Current Branch for Business enhances stability by delaying delivery of new features until they have been thoroughly tested in the Current Branch.

APPENDIX A

Windows 10 Enterprise and Education

Windows 10 Enterprise edition is available as an upgrade to Volume License customers; it requires an underlying license for Windows 10 Pro. Windows 10 Education edition provides equivalent features for large networks in academic environments and allows upgrades from Windows 10 Home or Pro editions. Table A-4 lists features available only in these editions.

Table A-4 Features available only in Windows 10 Enterprise and Education editions

Feature	Description
Management and security features	
Granular control of user experience	Provides standard Start menu layouts defined by administrators, and prevents users from altering the standard user experience.
AppLocker	Enables administrators of enterprise networks to create an authorized list of programs that users can install and run.
Credential Guard	Supports multifactor authentication using smart cards and biometric information.
Device Guard	Allows organizations to lock down a Windows 10 device so that only approved apps and desktop programs can be installed or run, preventing the installation of most forms of malware and any unauthorized software.
Windows To Go Creator	Allows the installation of Windows 10 Enterprise or Education on certified, high-performance USB drives that can boot and run in secure, self-contained mode, isolated from access by the host PC.
Long Term Servicing Branch	Allows administrators to limit deployment of new features in Windows 10, installing reliability and security updates only; this feature is designed for use in mission-critical environments; available only in Enterprise edition.
Networking	
BranchCache	Increases network responsiveness of applications in environments running on Windows Server 2008 R2 and later.
DirectAccess	Provides secure connections (without a virtual private network, or VPN) between a client PC running Windows 10 and a remote server running Windows Server 2008 R2 or later.
Location-aware printing	Helps domain-joined computers find the correct printer when a user moves between office and home networks.

Help and support resources

We hope this book is helpful. We also know that even if we had unlimited pages and multiple volumes to fill, there's no way we could answer every question or cover every nook and cranny of a product as rich and diverse as Windows 10. And, of course, in the "Windows as a Service" model, Windows 10 continues to evolve with new and reworked features and apps that we weren't able to describe in this edition because they didn't exist when we wrote it.

So we've put together this appendix to serve as a compendium of places where you can go to find help, troubleshooting tips, how-to guides, drivers, utilities, and advice.

Our list starts with official resources, collated and curated by Microsoft, but we also include community-based resources where you are likely to find reliable answers.

Online help

Over the years, what longtime Windows users call "the Help file" has evolved, with the Internet serving as the greatest agent of change. As recently as Windows 7, a Help And Support link on the Start menu led to Compiled HTML Help (.chm) files, readable with a built-in Windows utility (Hh.exe) that acts like a special-purpose browser.

That utility is still included with Windows 10, and you can still find a few .chm files (mostly for third-party products) if you search hard enough, but for Windows 10 itself most help is available online, where it's easily updated without the hassle of having to deliver those updated files to a billion or so PCs.

So for most questions, your first stop should be Microsoft's search engine, Bing, which delivers results directly from Microsoft Help when you ask a question about Windows. Figure B-1 shows one such question, with the answer in a box above all other search results and the source clearly labeled as "Help from Microsoft."

If a specific search doesn't return the official answer you're looking for, you can try browsing through Windows Help online (*windows.com/help*), which contains instructions for common tasks, organized by category, with a search box to help deliver more refined results, as shown in Figure B-2.

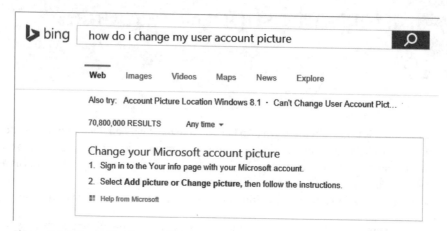

Figure B-1 Microsoft's Bing search engine delivers results directly from its collection of online Help from Microsoft if you ask the right questions.

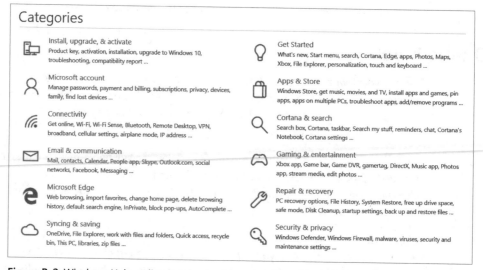

Figure B-2 Windows Help online is organized by category, with each entry shown here leading to a list of topics containing explanations and instructions.

Sometimes, of course, you're not looking for a detailed explanation or step-by-step instructions but simply trying to find a Windows setting without having to dig through menus or dialog boxes. For that type of chore, you have your choice of no fewer than three separate places to start a search.

- **The search box on the taskbar.** Entering a search term (in this case, the word **display**) in the search box on the taskbar returns a short but usually well-focused set of results.

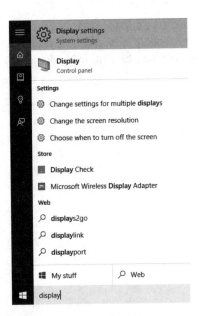

- **The Settings search box.** Click Settings on the Start menu (or use the keyboard short-cut Windows key+I) and enter a word or phrase in the search box in the upper right corner. Note that the top of the results list contains matching entries from the modern Settings app, followed by results from the desktop Control Panel, with the latter identifiable by their unique icons, as shown here:

- **The Control Panel search box.** The classic desktop Control Panel has its own search box in the upper right corner. Entering a word or phrase here returns results exclusively from the All Control Panel Items list, as shown here. Its index does not include options from the modern Settings app.

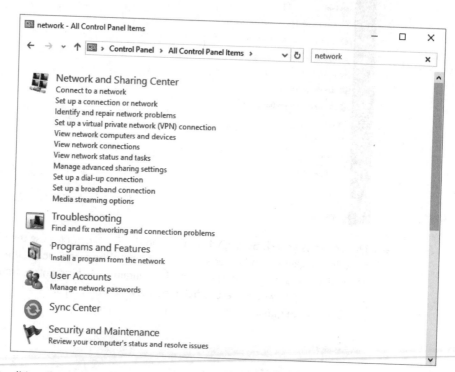

For traditionalists, one bit of help is available on a Windows 10 device, courtesy of a Windows Store app called Get Started. The app, shown in Figure B-3, is installed with Windows 10 and updated through the Windows Store.

The content in the Get Started app is basic, offers an overview of core features, and is aimed primarily at nontechnical users. Most of the readers of this book will probably find little new information there, but it's an excellent resource to suggest to friends, family members, and coworkers who could benefit from it.

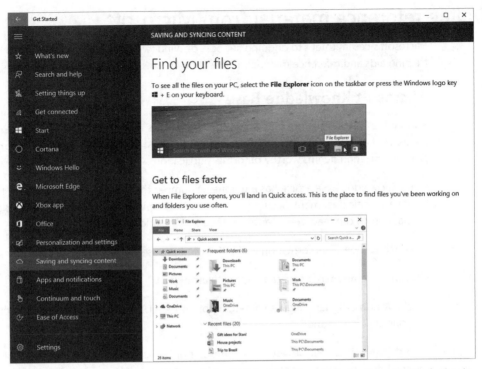

Figure B-3 The Get Started app is installed with Windows 10 and is intended primarily for beginners and nontechnical users.

You can open Get Started directly from the Start menu. An alternative entry point comes via pop-up tips that appear occasionally after you install Windows 10, suggesting that you try out new features. Those tips are designed to be unobtrusive and won't appear if you've already used the feature the tip is intended to introduce. But if you want to eliminate them completely, you'll find a Show Me Tips About Windows switch in Settings, under the System, Notifications & Actions category. Turn that setting off and you won't be bothered by those pop-ups.

➤ An additional source of detailed help in Windows 10 is available through the Troubleshooting section of Control Panel. We cover these guided tools as well as online Fix It resources in Chapter 17, "Troubleshooting."

Online reference material from Microsoft

Microsoft's commitment to ongoing support of Windows 10 includes an enormous library of training aids and reference material. This section lists the most important of these resources.

Microsoft Knowledge Base

Knowledge Base articles are official support documents that provide details about known issues, workarounds, security updates, new features, and anything else that the Microsoft Support organization deems worthy of formal publication.

Every Knowledge Base article has a unique ID number that you can use as a search term to locate a specific document. Security updates, for example, are documented with KB numbers so that IT pros can read details about what a specific update does.

To search for specific information in the Knowledge Base, start with this search term:

site:support.microsoft.com/en-us/kb "windows 10"

If your Windows 10 language is something other than US English, replace *en-us* with the prefix for your regional settings.

Save that search in your browser's Favorites bar or bookmarks and use it as the starting point for any future searches, appending your search terms in the search box. The results list will contain only documents that have been formally published in the Knowledge Base.

Microsoft TechNet

TechNet (*technet.microsoft.com*) is Microsoft's hub for technical information written primarily for IT pros. It includes news, technical articles, and downloads for all Microsoft products.

To focus exclusively on information about Windows 10, visit the Windows 10 TechCenter: *technet.microsoft.com/windows/dn798751*.

The TechNet library for Windows is continually expanding as new technical articles are added. It's worth bookmarking that page and visiting occasionally to see what's new.

Microsoft Virtual Academy

This online learning resource (*microsoftvirtualacademy.com*) is an excellent source of free training on a wide range of topics, including Windows 10. Available content includes prerecorded courses, live events (and archives of previous events), and books, with walk-throughs and demos bringing complex topics to life. New content is added regularly.

Getting technical support

If you can't find an answer in the Knowledge Base, or if a problem seems to be unique to your system configuration, you can turn to Microsoft's support forums for help.

Microsoft Community

For consumer versions of Windows and nontechnical users, start with the Microsoft Community forums at *answers.microsoft.com*. These threaded message boards are organized into categories—choose Windows, then Windows 10 to find the most relevant answers.

It's tempting to start by firing off a question, but a much better strategy is to use the search box in the upper right corner of the page to see whether anyone else has reported a similar issue. After entering the Windows 10 topic area, enter your search term and choose Current Scope from the drop-down list, as shown in Figure B-4. That step ensures that you see only answers that are relevant to Windows 10.

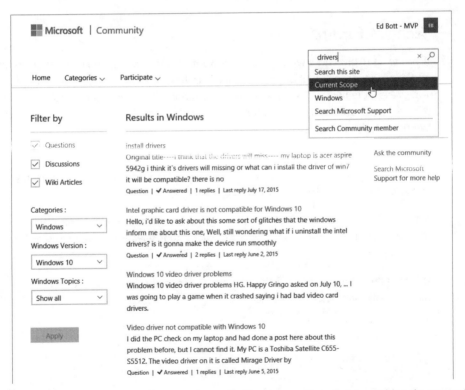

Figure B-4 Use the Current Scope option to limit search results to those matching the categories you selected from the lists on the left side of the Microsoft Community forums.

If your search doesn't turn up the answer you're looking for, click Ask The Community to begin composing a question of your own. (You can use this same form to start a discussion if you want to raise an issue that doesn't require an answer.) When posting to the Community forums, try to be as specific as possible, providing relevant details about your system configuration and hardware as well as any troubleshooting steps you've already tried and their results.

Note that support in these forums is provided by community members as well as Microsoft support personnel. You're also likely to run into an occasional Microsoft MVP (Most Valuable Professional), including one of the authors of this book. There's no guarantee you'll get a satisfactory answer, but we can testify from experience that this route has been successful for many people, including the authors of this book.

To keep track of a discussion, sign in with your Microsoft account and use the notification options at the bottom of any message. You'll receive an email at the address associated with your Microsoft account whenever anyone replies to the message; this is true regardless of whether you started the discussion yourself or found an existing discussion that you want to follow.

TechNet forums

If you're an IT pro and have a question or want to start a discussion with other like-minded and experienced individuals, go to the TechNet forums, *social.technet.microsoft.com/Forums*. Topics available here include a much broader range of Microsoft products and technologies than those covered in the Community forums, with a special emphasis on deploying and using Windows in the enterprise.

The basic rules of these more advanced message boards are similar to those we recommend for the Microsoft Community forums: search first, and ask a new question only if you can't find an existing discussion that addresses your issue.

Search options for the TechNet forums allow you to select multiple forums, shown on the left in Figure B-5, and then find specific topics within that selection by using a search box above the message list.

Use the filtering and sorting options (above the message list) to narrow your search further or make specific answers easier to locate.

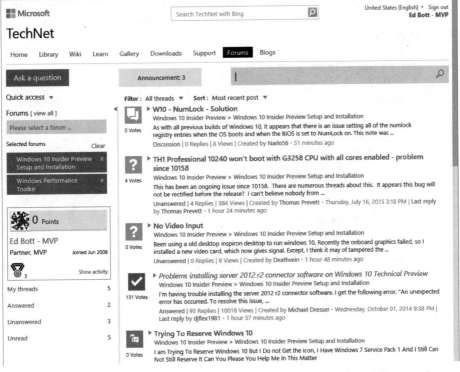

Figure B-5 Choose one or more TechNet forums from the list on the left, and then use the search box at the top of the message list to narrow your results.

Free and paid support from Microsoft

Getting answers from fellow Windows users has the advantage of being free and easily accessible, but sometimes you need formal support from Microsoft engineers.

Microsoft provides free support for security issues. If you suspect you've been infected with malware, for example, you can request and receive support at no charge. Other support options might be covered under a product warranty that's provided if you purchase Windows directly from Microsoft, or you can open a support ticket (called an "incident") for a fee.

To see your support options, you can visit the Microsoft Answer Desk online at *support.microsoft.com/contactus*. Listings on that page direct you to the appropriate technical support resources for different business categories.

As an alternative, use the Contact Support app, which is installed by default with Windows 10. Figure B-6 shows the options available for Windows support, which includes chat and telephone options.

Figure B-6 Use the Contact Support app to chat online or talk with a support representative. Note that some options might require payment.

APPENDIX C

OneDrive and other cloud services

OneDrive, Microsoft's cloud-based file-storage service, is a crucial part of the Windows 10 experience. Every free Microsoft account starts with 15 GB of OneDrive storage. You can expand that storage with paid upgrades to OneDrive or get a massively increased cloud storage allotment with an Office 365 Home or Personal subscription.

That consumer version of OneDrive is separate from OneDrive for Business, which is associated with Office 365 Business and Enterprise subscriptions.

When we began planning this book, a year before Windows 10 was released to the public, we gave OneDrive its own chapter. In that chapter, we planned to explain how to store, sync, and share files between a Windows 10 device and Microsoft's two OneDrive services.

But shortly after releasing the first preview edition of Windows 10, Microsoft made the decision to completely rewrite its OneDrive synchronization client. As we write this appendix, more than a month after Windows 10 was officially released, we still haven't seen that new sync client. Instead, the OneDrive software that was included with the initial release of Windows 10 is essentially the same as what was in Windows 8 more than three years ago.

By the time you read this, that new software will probably be ready, or at least available in a preview release for Windows Insiders. As a result, our coverage here is deliberately general, designed to get you oriented with Microsoft's cloud services.

How OneDrive and OneDrive for Business work

Despite the brand name they share, Microsoft's two cloud-based file-storage services have different origins and different feature sets. Both are designed to allow access to files and folders in a web browser, but there are some big differences in how the two services work.

OneDrive, the consumer service, is designed for personal use, with special views that showcase photo libraries and albums, as well as the ability to store a music collection that can be streamed through Groove Music. OneDrive is the default storage option for Office 365 Home and Personal editions, although nothing prevents you from using it for work. (In fact, the authors, editors, and production professionals who collaborated on this book used OneDrive to exchange and share files.)

Files stored in OneDrive are organized into folders and subfolders just as they would be on a local drive. Figure C-1 shows the contents of a subfolder in the OneDrive Documents folder, as viewed in a web browser. Note the range of options available in the command bar for the selected file, as well as the additional menu choices available with a click.

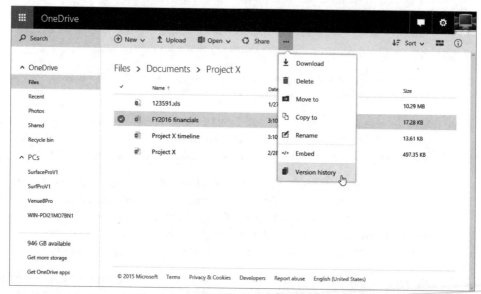

Figure C-1 When using OneDrive in a web browser, you can perform most file-management tasks, with the ability to create, edit, and collaborate on Office documents.

OneDrive for Business offers a similar web-based view, as shown in Figure C-2. Note that subscription settings aren't accessible from the navigation pane on the left. That's because a OneDrive for Business subscription is managed by a company administrator, with additional security and collaboration options appropriate for use in an organization.

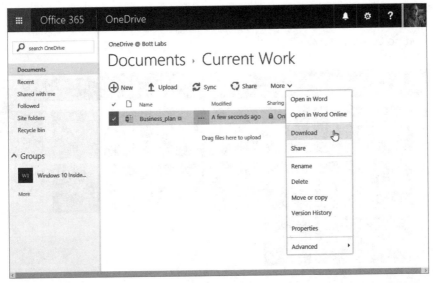

Figure C-2 OneDrive for Business offers a familiar web-based view of files and folders, with options that are more appropriate for collaboration in an organization.

When you sign in with a Microsoft account, OneDrive is just one of several services available. Clicking the menu button on the left (it looks like grid of nine squares and is sometimes referred to as the "waffle" button) displays the full range of options, shown here.

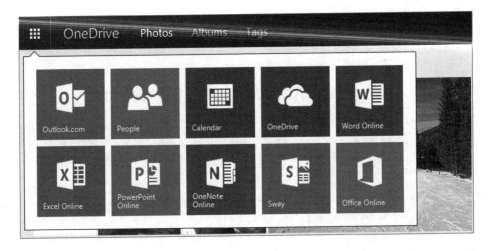

When you sign in to an Office 365 Business or Enterprise account, clicking the waffle-shaped menu button in the same location displays a larger group of options, and the OneDrive icon leads to OneDrive for Business.

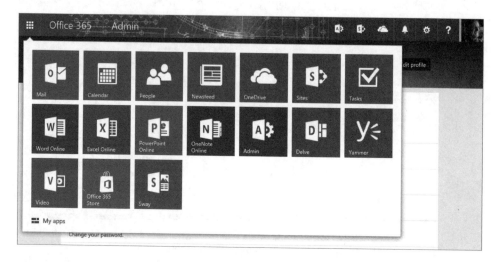

Both services allow subscribers to share files and folders with other people. The consumer edition of OneDrive allows complete control of sharing, letting you make a file, a photo, or an entire folder public. You can also share access by using a link that doesn't require signing in to a Microsoft account.

Sharing options for OneDrive for Business are managed by a company administrator, who might apply restrictions on sharing files with other people, especially in folders that contain confidential company information.

Synchronizing files with Windows 10 devices

The whole point of OneDrive is to allow you to store your files in the cloud and then access those files from anywhere. One option, of course, is through a web browser. But Microsoft has also released platform-specific clients that allow you to browse, open, and synchronize those files on any device.

As we mentioned at the beginning of this chapter, the OneDrive sync client in the initial release of Windows 10 is a stopgap, to be replaced by a new utility that wasn't available at the time we finished this book. Figure C-3 shows the settings for that initial Windows 10 OneDrive client, with the option to choose which files and folders to sync between the cloud and the Windows 10 PC.

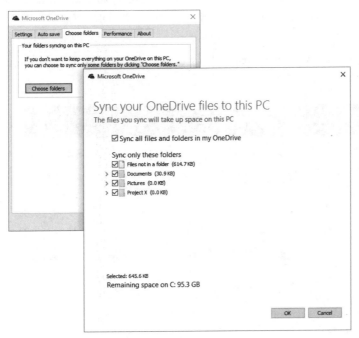

Figure C-3 The OneDrive sync client in the initial release of Windows 10 (July 2015) includes this interface for specifying which folders to sync between the cloud and a local device.

At the initial launch of Windows 10, synchronizing files with OneDrive for Business required a separate piece of client software, included with an Office 365 ProPlus installation. The new sync client will reportedly be able to handle both OneDrive and OneDrive for Business accounts, giving you the option to choose which folders in the cloud are synced to the local device and which are available only from the cloud. That's a crucial feature, especially if you have hundreds of gigabytes of photos, music and video files, and documents on OneDrive. Selective sync is an essential strategy for using OneDrive on devices that have limited local storage, such as laptop PCs, phones, and tablets.

Office 365 and Office Web Apps

Both OneDrive and OneDrive for Business allow you to create, edit, and collaborate on documents created in Office applications and saved in the broadly supported Office document formats.

To create a new Office document online, click New and then choose a file type from the menu, as shown here.

Both versions of OneDrive allow you to view and edit an Office document online, again using only a web browser. The feature set is limited compared with the full Office programs, as shown in the example in Figure C-4, but the Office Online apps maintain document fidelity, preserving features and formatting that might not be available in the web-based apps.

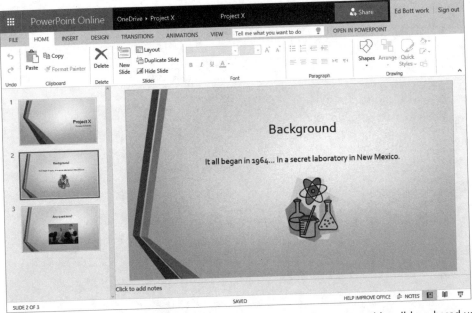

Figure C-4 You can open and edit any Office document in a web browser, with a ribbon-based user interface that's consistent with the full Office desktop apps.

Index to troubleshooting topics

Index

About the authors

Ed Bott is an award-winning author and technology journalist who has been researching and writing about Windows and PC technology, in print and on the Internet, for more than two decades. He has written more than 30 books, all on Windows and Microsoft Office, which in turn have been translated into dozens of languages and read worldwide. You can catch up with Ed's latest opinions and get hands-on advice at *The Ed Bott Report* on ZDNet (*zdnet.com/blog/bott*). You can also follow his lively and occasionally irreverent Twitter feed (@edbott). Ed and his wife, Judy, live in northern New Mexico with two English springer spaniels, Mackie and Lucy, who were adopted with the help of English Springer Rescue America (*springerrescue.org*). Both of those lucky dogs make cameo appearances in this book.

Carl Siechert began his writing career at age eight as editor of the *Mesita Road News*, a neighborhood newsletter that reached a peak worldwide circulation of 43 during its eight-year run. Following several years as an estimator and production manager in a commercial printing business, Carl returned to writing with the formation of Siechert & Wood Professional Documentation, a Pasadena, California, firm that specializes in writing and producing product documentation for the personal computer industry. Carl is a coauthor of more than 20 books, covering operating systems from MS-DOS 3.0 to Windows 10 and productivity applications from Microsoft Works 3 to Office 2013. In a convergence of new and old technology, Carl's company now operates a popular website for hobby machinists, *littlemachineshop.com*. Carl hiked the Pacific Crest Trail from Mexico to Canada in 1977 and would rather be hiking right now. He and his wife, Jan, live in Southern California.

Craig Stinson, an industry journalist since 1981, was editor of *Softalk for the IBM Personal Computer*, one of the earliest IBM-PC magazines. He is the author or coauthor of numerous books about Windows and Microsoft Excel. Craig is an amateur musician and reformed music critic, having reviewed classical music for various newspapers and trade publications, including *Billboard*, the *Boston Globe*, the *Christian Science Monitor*, and *Musical America*. He lives in Bloomington, Indiana.

Now that you've read the book...

Tell us what you think!

Was it useful?
Did it teach you what you wanted to learn?
Was there room for improvement?

Let us know at http://aka.ms/tellpress

Your feedback goes directly to the staff at Microsoft Press,
and we read every one of your responses. Thanks in advance!

WITHDRAWN

THE QUEST FOR VALUE

THE QUEST FOR VALUE

The EVA™ Management Guide

G. Bennett Stewart, III

HarperBusiness
A Division of HarperCollins*Publishers*

Chapter 13 was originally published in modified form in *Cash Flow* magazine.

The excerpt in chapter 13 from *Barbarians at the Gate* by Byran Burroughs and John Helyer is reprinted by permission of HarperCollins *Publishers*, Inc., © 1990 by Byran Burroughs and John Helyer.

Library of Congress Cataloging-in-Publication Data

Stewart, G. Bennett.
    The quest for value: the EVA^{TM} management guide/G. Bennett Stewart III.
      p. cm.
    ISBN 0-88730-418-4
    1. Corporations—Valuation.   2. Cash flow.   I. Title.
    HG4028.V3S84   1990
    658.15'54—dc20   90-20299
                                      CIP

Printed in the United States of America

94 95 CC/HC 9 8 7

For my family,
Judy, "GB," Charlotte, and Elizabeth,
with love and gratitude

Contents

Exhibits

Preface

It is a pleasure to reach the stage in life when I can feel content to write prefaces to books instead of laboring to write the books. One reason is the confidence that my partner, Bennett Stewart, will say what I would like to say about almost any subject in corporate finance, only more so. But lest you think that this was all his idea or, worse, someone else's, permit me the opportunity to reflect on an accomplishment of which I am particularly proud. It is the practical development of the concept of free cash flow (FCF), which is the very foundation upon which corporate values stand. The origins of my FCF valuation framework have deep roots in both the academy and our consulting experiences.

The Academic Background

The theory underlying FCF was first set forth in the seminal article, "Dividend Policy, Growth and the Valuation of Shares," *Journal of Business,* October 1961, by Professors Franco Modigliani and Merton H. Miller. M&M, as they became known, asked and answered the question "what measures of corporate performance does the market capitalize" in arriving at a firm's market value. They considered four alternatives: earnings, cash flow, dividends, and investment opportunities. Initially, their conclusions shocked me: all four. How could that be? Because, under the conditions they presented, all four are identical!

I had the good fortune to study directly under Merton Miller while attending the University of Chicago's Graduate School of Business. As I read the M&M article, I asked myself how dividends and earnings could be the same? How could earnings and cash flow be the same? And what were investment opportunities? I wondered if investment included research and development outlays. Did accounting depreciation lives matter, or was it only economic considerations? Could advertising and promotion outlays be deemed to have a longer life if the firm were Coca-Cola as compared with, say, Al's Hardware Store?

My invention of the concept of free cash flow while I was associated with the Chase Manhattan Bank in the late 1960s was an attempt at understanding more fully the issues raised in the M&M article, especially as they concerned corporate finance strategies and communicating them to senior managements.

Before elaborating upon that experience, however, an explanation of the equivalence of dividend, earnings, cash flow, and investment opportunities is in order. The M&M article employs higher forms of mathematics to demonstrate the proof, but it boils down to this: FCF is cash from operations that is available or attributable to both lenders and shareholders. In other words, it is the cash that is "free" for distribution to investors after *all* investments have been financed. Thus, when it is discounted to a present value at the firm's cost of capital, FCF is the foundation of any firm's market value. Since the M&M article is simplified to an all-equity-financed firm, FCF is also equal to dividends. And if earnings are not reinvested, FCF can equal earnings too. Of course, the value of investment opportunities is contained within the present value of expected future FCF. Thus, there can be an equivalence between these competing measures, but it does not always hold. Adjusting the M&M model to account for the complexity encountered in practice became one of my life's great challenges.

As I came to understand it, the principal implication of the paper is that a firm's value is based on the timing and risk of future cash receipts and disbursements. For the purpose of valuation there really are no such things as a balance sheet and an income statement. Rather, it is the model of the corner grocery store, in which the surest indicator of success is a cigar box lid rising with net cash collections. If that is the case, and I am thoroughly convinced it is, it means also that bookkeeping entries that have no effect on cash have no effect on value. Those entries include goodwill amortization, deferred taxes, LIFO reserve, and other accounting provisions which distort FCF measures of performance.

The opposite is true as well. When a firm consistently collects cash that the accountants refuse to record as income, there is another distortion of value. Time-Warner and Pitney Bowes make the point perfectly. Some of their most important assets are actually recorded as liabilities. The specific issue concerns unearned income items, magazine subscriptions payable, and advanced billings net. In the case of Time-Warner, this semipermanent financing has a minimum average life of 6 to 12 months. For Pitney Bowes, it is one-month deposits on postage meters. These are cash receipts that are used to finance growth, yet the cash is free of tax until the products are shipped. These items are in the hundreds of millions of dollars and have been growing rapidly for both firms over long periods of time. As long as the backlog of business does not shrink in size, these "liabilities" will continue as a cash source indefinitely. The accounting model, in contrast, records these cash benefits as revenues only sometime in the future as taxable income. That practice makes no sense if FCF is the measure of value.

The ultimate importance of FCF versus mere accounting results can best be appreciated with cash outlays that alternatively can be expensed or capitalized. Those who believe that accounting earnings measures are paramount in valuing a firm—examples include the bottom-line net profit after tax provision, the per-share figure, and return on equity—would capitalize cash outlays whenever possible to boost reported results. FCF proponents, in contrast, expense such cash items because expensing often reduces taxes paid. I call this the Benjamin Franklin valuation principle: "A penny saved is a penny earned." That is, if the firm still has the money, its value is greater than if the money is in the hands of the tax collector.

Before leaving the theory of finance, let me say that I also owe a debt of gratitude to Milton Friedman, under whom I also studied at the University of Chicago. He made me see that unfettered markets operate rationally. Friedman's legacy was to encourage me to search out the truth in market behavior, to look for what is real, even when market practices on the surface appear to be unaccountably irrational. My later development of the lead-steer concept of the stock market (about which you will learn more in this volume) owes much to Friedman's influence.

The Anecdotes

As I left the University of Chicago in 1964 to join the Chase Manhattan Bank, these thoughts were on my mind. After passing through the credit-training program, I began to discuss them with clients of the bank. It was frustrating, I confess, to discover how emotionally charged these issues could become when addressed one by one. After all, the 1960s were the go-go era of conglomeration, when poolings mergers to boost earnings per share were all the rage, despite the fact that my model saw no value to purely diversifying acquisitions. The final stimulus to develop my concept of FCF came from something else, however. It occurred in 1968 when I visited the chief executive of an exceedingly small high-technology firm in Silicon Valley. He observed that his price/earnings ratio was an astronomic 88 but that the much larger, more stable, and far more successful Hewlett Packard commanded a P/E ratio of only 31! "Who wants to become big and successful," he asked, "if by doing so my multiple will drop so dramatically?" Admittedly, I was puzzled. But, again, the culprit was a distortion caused by accounting convention. Small high-technology firms spend a very large fraction of revenues on research and development, which is expensed. Thus, bottom-line net profit is trivial and the P/E is enormous. As the firm grows in size, it will likely spend a smaller fraction of its revenues on R&D and thus accounting earnings will increase much more rapidly than revenues—and thereby drive the P/E down to a more "normal" level. What I was able to show with the FCF model, however, was that despite these misleading accounting consequences, additional value was likely to be created all along the way.

I have Harry Abplanalp, my first boss at Chase, to thank for suggesting to me the idea of presenting a two-day forum to senior management as a means of getting across an integrated approach to valuation and financial planning issues. He saw that all of the main topics in corporate finance and valuation are so highly inter-related that only a thorough immersion in this new approach might have a chance of changing the minds of experienced business executives. The public two-day forum ultimately proved to be so successful that I have continued this practice for more than 20 years. For the past eight years, my partner, Bennett Stewart, has shared the speaking with me. It is a relief to draft a disciple with younger lungs to the cause.

The first such two-day program was held in Chicago in January 1969. It was there and then that my byline was born: "Earnings per Share Don't Count; It's Free Cash Flow That Really Matters." (Some years later the chairman of Union Carbide presented me with a tie clip engraved with that slogan, and I have worn it faithfully every day since!) One of the attendees at that inaugural two-day session was J. B. Fuqua, the innovative head of Fuqua Industries. I shall never forget his comment at the conclusion of the program: "But Joel, anything else is just tea leaf reading."

Another early attendee was Herman Schaeffer, former executive vice president, Pepsico. Afterward, he asked me to bring the program in-house by addressing the company's entire senior management in a private two-day program. That occurred in the fall of 1969, and it is a service I continue to render (though now I am able to cover in one day what once took two). I would estimate that I have addressed over 500 companies worldwide in such sessions, and I look forward to many more. The challenge always is to stimulate the thinking of the senior management team about how the stock market actually operates and what the team must do to improve its company's share value. I am deeply indebted to Herman for getting me started down that path.

The early successes persuaded me to put my ideas down on paper. The conceptual foundation of free cash flow was first documented in working papers I wrote during the period 1967 to

1971, and it was first published in 1972 in the *Wall Street Journal*. The FCF valuation model appeared in 1973 and 1974 in a series of articles published biweekly in the *Financial Times* (London) from 1973 through 1976, in a lengthy formal description in the *Financial Analysts Journal* in 1974, and in 1975 in a book, *Measuring Corporate Performance*. It was also included in *Analytical Methods in Financial Planning*, a compendium first published in March 1974.

Since those early days, when I was a lone voice crying in the wilderness, many others have joined me in promoting the FCF model. Al Rappaport of Northwestern University's Business School was the first academic to adopt it. More recently, McKinsey & Co. also has embraced it as a planning technique. I welcome their interest as confirmation that my original work in translating the best of academic financial theory to business practice is taking an ever-firmer hold in corporate America.

In many ways the accomplishment of which I am most proud, however, is the *Journal of Applied Corporate Finance*, a quarterly review that is produced by my firm on behalf of the Continental Bank. I started it in 1981 (as the *Chase Financial Quarterly*) in order to promote a continuing dialogue between financial scholars and business practitioners on such topics as performance measurement, valuation, restructurings, dividend policy, financial communication, risk management, mergers and acquisitions, and incentive compensation, in short, the field of finance as it concerns the senior decision maker. After 10 years of publication under the sure editorial hand of my colleague Donald Chew, the *Journal*'s popularity and reputation have exceeded my greatest expectations.

It is gratifying, too, that many people have begun to use my term "free cash flow," though they frequently define it in ways that deviate from my original intent. Several investment analysts, for example, subtract only "necessary" reinvestment from cash receipts to arrive at a sort of discretionary FCF. Professor Michael Jensen of Harvard Business School also is in this camp when he discusses the tendency of companies to waste their "surplus" cash flow. Others subtract dividends as well to obtain an even stricter definition of discretionary cash. Unfortunately, these approaches are indicative more of debt service capability than of value. Only when FCF is defined as distributable cash from operations over a firm's life do we have all expected net returns from all current and expected future investment, which is the underpinning of any firm's market value.

Both Bennett Stewart and I see this book as a continuation of a journey that I first embarked upon over 25 years ago. The message we bring is not new, but it is not as well understood or as widely practiced even today as it should be. It is my hope that this book will convince the reader that markets are smart, that key investors who are influential in the valuation process do focus on FCF and will respond positively to improved communication of fundamentals, and that the signals and performance improvements derived from new techniques in financial management, incentive compensation, and financial structuring can enhance value.

Joel M. Stern
Managing Partner
Stern Stewart & Co.

Acknowledgments

Being a great believer in the benefits of debt, it is wonderful to be indebted to the many people who helped to make this book possible. But if they expect anything more than a brief mention in this section, I am afraid they will be sorely disappointed. As my father has taught me from a very early age, "Ben, I would rather owe it to you than cheat you out of it." That principle has guided me throughout my life, and it has never failed me.

On a slightly more serious vein, I must begin by thanking my partner, Joel M. Stern, for hiring me out of the University of Chicago Graduate School of Business in 1976 and then giving me the opportunity to apply what I had learned. He has been a constant source of intellectual stimulation over the 14 years that we have been together. I am proud to be part of the fine tradition he pioneered: translating the best of academic corporate finance to the needs of the business practitioner. I look forward to many more years together as his partner in our mutual and rather more personal quest for value.

I must thank, too, the financial scholars whose research substantiates much of what I have attempted to say in this book. Though there are far too many of them to name individually, I have drawn a special inspiration from the papers written by Franco Modigliani and Merton Miller on the subject of valuation and by Michael Jensen on the productive role of debt and financial restructurings.

I also want to thank all of my colleagues at Stern Stewart & Co. for their loyal support throughout. In particular, I must express gratitude to my partner, David Glassman, for his fine series of investigations of financial restructurings over the past 5 years. I have learned much from his patient explanations. Others, including Donald Chew, Patrick Finegan, and William Fallon, provided useful input on the text, if nothing else, by expurgating some of my more outlandish opinions. Carolyn Peet did a splendid job, as always, of keeping my normal business affairs running smoothly while I was consumed in the hellfires of the book.

One junior member of our squad also stands out for a special citation. Richard Rosson has been an untiring researcher for me on subjects great and small. Almost all of the graphs and tables, and many of the cases in the book, derive from his long hours at the workstation. I thank him most of all for the many nights he stopped by my apartment to discuss the latest round of his findings. I know that my son, "GB," appreciated those house calls because they gave him the perfect pretext to stay up well beyond his bedtime.

The statistical analysis for the Stern Stewart Performance 1000 was performed with the assistance of Thomas Hahn, of THK Associates, 863 Waller Street, San Francisco, California 94117, a former colleague. Tom is an accomplished econometrician and an author of several important finance papers. I am grateful for the hours he spent with me on the phone, hashing out the statistical errata. He has produced a very fine product, one that I would hope to continue for many years to come.

I would be remiss if I did not mention the contribution of another of my mentors at the Chase Manhattan Bank, Dennis Soter. For almost five years I worked with him on a variety of highly stimulating consulting engagements. Whether he realizes it or not, Dennis helped to crystallize in my mind a number of the planning concepts presented in the book. I thank him for that and wish him well, along with other colleagues from those halcyon Chase days who also influenced my thinking, including Hugh Morrison, Joe Kelley, Frank Altieri, Joe Willett, and Henry Higbie.

I also want to mention that Martha Jewett, my editor at HarperCollins, has been a nearly constant source of irritation over the past year and a half. Thank you, Martha. Without your gentle prodding I am sure that I never would have finished this lengthy tome.

Finally, I want to thank my family from the bottom of my heart for the sacrifice they made on behalf of this book. My darling Judy, I promise never again to subject you to this agony. Next time, I will get a two-year contract and a much bigger up-front advance.

1

Introduction

It is easy to forget why senior management's most important job must be to maximize its firm's current market value. If nothing else, a greater value rewards the shareholders who, after all, are the owners of the enterprise. But, and this really is much more important, society at large benefits too. A quest for value directs scarce resources to their most promising uses and most productive users. The more effectively resources are deployed and managed, the more robust economic growth and the rate of improvement in our standard of living will be. Adam Smith's invisible hand is at work when the investor's private gain turns into a public virtue. Although there are exceptions to this rule, most of the time there is a happy harmony between creating stock market value and enhancing the quality of life.

In many companies the all-important quest for value is being confounded by a hopelessly obsolete financial management system. The wrong financial goals, performance measures, and valuation procedures are emphasized. Managers are improperly and in many cases inadequately rewarded for their efforts. Balance sheets are but dully structured when surgical sharpness often is needed. These shortcomings cry out for approaches to financial management so profoundly different from current ones that nothing less than a revolution in thinking is called for.

Abandon Earnings Per Share

First of all, the myth that increasing earnings, earnings per share, or return on equity is the way to attract Wall Street must be abandoned. Many senior executives believe that the market wants earnings, and wants them now, despite the fact that not one shred of convincing evidence to substantiate that outlandish claim has ever been produced. To satisfy Wall Street's alleged craving for reported profits, many top managers feel compelled to conjure up earnings through time-consuming and ethics-corroding accounting legerdemain. Expenses that should be deducted to save taxes are deferred. Valuable acquisitions are avoided if a large amount of goodwill must be amortized. R&D and market-building outlays get short shrift. The execution of dying businesses is postponed. And perhaps worst of all, lusty earnings growth is sustained by overinvesting in mature businesses.

Arrayed against the earnings myth and these harmful practices is an overwhelming body of established academic research. It shows that accounting measures of performance are only coincidentally related to stock prices and are not the primary movers and shakers. What truly determines stock prices, the evidence proves, is the cash, adjusted for time and risk, that investors can expect to get back over the life of the business. What the market wants is *not* earnings now, but *value* now. The question is: How can discounted cash flow, which truly is at the heart of market valuation, become the driving and integrating force behind the financial management system?

Economic Value Added: A True Measure of Corporate Success

The answer, for the most part, is actually quite straightforward: Management should focus on maximizing a measure called economic value added (EVA), which is operating profits less the cost of all of the capital employed to produce those earnings. EVA will increase if operating profits can be made to grow without tying up any more capital, if new capital can be invested in projects that will earn more than the full cost of the capital and if capital can be diverted or liquidated from business activities that do not provide adequate returns. It will be reduced if management fritters away funds on projects that earn less than the cost of capital or passes over projects likely to earn more than the cost of capital. It just so happens that EVA is the only performance measure that is entirely consistent with the standard capital budgeting rule: Accept all positive and reject all negative net present value investments. (Earnings per share, on the other hand, will increase so long as new capital investments earn anything more than the after-tax cost of borrowing, which is hardly an acceptable return.)

The most important reason to adopt EVA as the main corporate financial goal, however, is that it is the only measure to tie directly to intrinsic market value. Discounting the EVA to be generated by an individual capital project, for instance, automatically results in its net present value. (The cost of the new capital employed to finance the project is explicitly subtracted in the very calculation of EVA.) The capital budgeting prescription to accept positive NPV projects can be restated as follows: Accept all investment opportunities which will produce a positive discounted EVA. It is one and the same thing.

Carrying this concept to a higher level, projecting and discounting EVA for an entire company automatically sums the net present value of all of the firm's past and projected capital investment projects. The sum accounts for the company's market value premium to capital employed (which is simply the total of all investments the company has made to date). A company for which projected EVA discounts to, say, $100 million, and which currently employs $500 million of capital, has an intrinsic market value of $600 million. This relation tells us that if its EVA is expected to be positive, a company has added value to the out-of-pocket cost of the resources drawn into the firm; if EVA is projected to be negative, value has been destroyed. EVA, in short, is the fuel that fires up a premium in the stock market value of any company or accounts for its discount. That is EVA's greatest significance, and it is a property that sets EVA above every other financial performance measure, including cash flow.

Abandon Cash Flow!

However important cash flow may be as a measure of value, it is virtually useless as a measure of performance. So long as management invests in rewarding projects—those with returns above the cost of capital—the more investment that is made, and therefore the more negative the immediate net cash flow from operations, the more valuable the company will be. It is only when it is considered over the life of the business, and not in any given year, that cash flow becomes significant.

EVA, on the other hand, is both a measure of value and a measure of performance. As a matter of fact, it is the only measure that can link forward-looking valuation and capital budgeting procedures with the manner in which performance subsequently can be evaluated. The conclusion is inescapable but perhaps shocking: Abandon the practice of discounting cash flow, and discount EVA instead. The valuations will be the same, that's true, but comprehension and communications will be dramatically strengthened.

For those reasons and more, EVA is the right measure to use for setting goals, evaluating performance, determining bonuses, communicating with investors, and for capital budgeting and valuations of all sorts. EVA is the bedrock upon which a new and completely integrated financial management system can be constructed, a system which in this book goes by the name "value planning."

Making Managers into Owners

The second major initiative is to revitalize and redirect managerial incentives. Here again, EVA is key. For although operating people can do countless individual things to create value, all the things eventually must fall into one of the categories measured by EVA. Giving managers a bonus that is a share of EVA is the right way to motivate them to create value and make them think and behave more like owners.

The EVA bonus plan works much like the plan designed for Michael Eisner when he took the helm at Disney. CEO Eisner was to receive 2% of Disney's profits above a predetermined required return on capital. The bonus was not tied to an explicit strategic plan or negotiated financial result. It simply rewarded Eisner to create value by increasing Disney's residual income and left him free to choose the most appropriate means to that end.

In 1989, Eisner was one of the most highly paid executives in America, earning almost $9 million from his cash bonus plan alone. Far from representing a cost to shareholders, the payment was but a share in the discretionary value that he created. Over the period from September 1984 to September 1989, Eisner was able to increase Disney's market value by $15.4 billion while investing just $3.2 billion in new capital, a spread of $12.2 billion. His bonus shrinks to insignificance in comparison with the value left over for the shareholders (and in relation to the income of other entertainment powerhouses, such as Stephen Spielberg). Ironically, with well-designed bonus plans such as Eisner's, the higher the bonus that is paid, the better it is for the shareholders.

Despite the widely publicized success of Eisner's scheme, most companies persist in basing bonuses on the attainment of planned levels of performance, which is a catastrophic mistake. Make budgets the targets for determining bonuses, and the opportunity for fruitful collaboration vanishes and is replaced by an endless series of negotiations in which managers have every incentive to sandbag the potential for their businesses instead of reaching for the stars and to manage earnings and the expectations of the corporate office instead of maximizing value. The use of budgets for bonuses is a vestige of an archaic accounting model that emphasizes earnings over cash flow, control over delegation, variances instead of vision, and questions instead of answers. That model must go.

The new system turns the time-worn practice on its head. It liberates manacled managers from the tyranny of the budget-setting process. For instead of having budgets drive their bonuses, bonuses—or rather the ownership imperative—drive their budgets.

As depicted in exhibit 1.1, the goal is to move from a system requiring a continuous negotiation of financial targets to one that requires a one-time setting of the bonus parameters. The most effective way to do this is, in essence, the Michael Eisner plan: Give managers throughout the company a bonus that is a share of the level and increase in the level of the EVA of their operation (and of sister units and overarching groups with which their units interrelate). By fixing their share of EVA in advance—and not changing it in light of subsequent performance—the managers will be given a tremendous personal incentive to devise and execute extremely aggressive plans. In this case, just achieving planned performance levels can produce extraordinary bonuses for them; performance in relation to the plan itself is not used in any way to determine their reward. Thus, if bonuses drive the budgets, instead of the other way around, better and altogether more aggressive plans and performances are likely to be forthcoming from the key operating people.

A corollary to providing managers with the incentive of ownership is to delegate to managers the autonomy needed to maximize the value of the operation. Decentralizing decision making

Exhibit 1.1   The New Bonus System

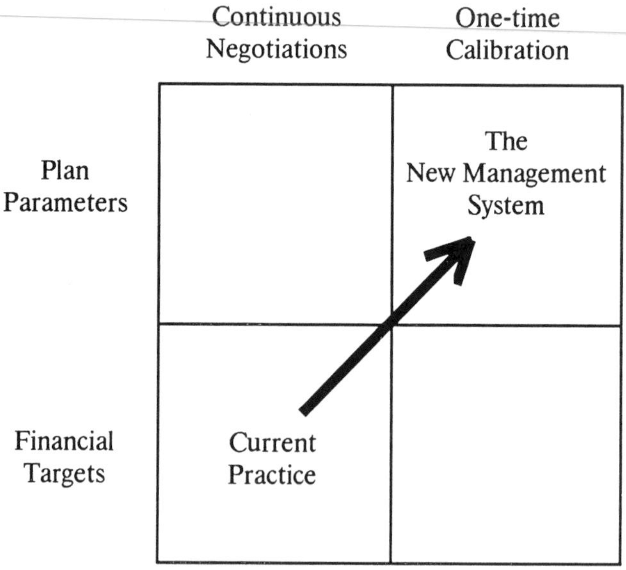

	Continuous Negotiations	One-time Calibration
Plan Parameters		The New Management System
Financial Targets	Current Practice	

along with incentives has become all the more imperative as the pace of new product development and the fragmentation of markets have accelerated and as computing power has proliferated. Recognizing these trends, the new financial model emphasizes management by motivation and not by mandate, by empowerment and not by punishment.

Delegating autonomy to operating unit managers is not without risk, however. There is the danger that, once they are freed from corporate shackles, empire building will take priority over value building. To guard against the dark side of delegation, unit managers should face the prospect of suffering meaningful monetary losses if the financial performances of their units are unacceptable. In other words, the quid pro quo for being granted greater autonomy and the possibility of an unlimited reward for success must be the risk of some loss for poor or even just mediocre performance. Ultimately, both a carrot and a stick are needed to make managers truly behave more like owners. This book shows how to simulate for managers the thrill of victory and the agony of defeat that are central to the illusion of ownership.

Amplifying managers' risk-reward profile is one of the reasons why LBOs have so often succeeded in creating value (even in cases when not all of the LBO debt has been repaid). Managers are required to put down money for an equity stake that is recovered only when and if the LBO debt has been substantially repaid but which can return many times the initial investment if the restructuring is successful. Faced with this stark choice between success or failure, most people will choose to succeed. The question is: How can the terrific incentives of LBOs be replicated without actually undergoing an LBO?

One way that I have devised is to sell managers a very large number of in-the-money stock options with a rising exercise price. A company with a current stock price of, say, $30, could set the initial strike price on a special option at $27, a 10% discount to current value, and then sell the options to its managers for $3, or the in-the-money amount. The $27 exercise price will rise thereafter at a rate to reflect the cost of capital (less a discount for dividends on the shares and the risk and the illiquidity of the options), a rate of, say, 10% per annum.

In contrast to ordinary options, which are more compensation than incentive, these special options are in the money rather than at the money, are bought and not merely granted, and will not begin to dilute the common equity value unless and until the shareholders realize a return above the rate at which the exercise price grows. In view of those assurances, a board of directors can feel comfortable about selling a relatively small cadre of senior managers a very large number of the options and using them aggressively as a tool to increase management ownership.

As far as the managers are concerned, the options give them qualitatively the same incentive as a bonus plan that pays them to improve EVA. The charge for the use of capital that is subtracted from EVA shows up as the interest that accrues on the option's exercise price. To come out ahead with the options, the managers must increase the firm's value faster than the cost of capital accrues, a result which depends upon increasing the EVA within the firm.

Though the message is the same, it is transmitted far more powerfully through the special options than it might be by an EVA bonus plan. For one thing, any improvement in EVA that investors think is sustainable will be capitalized with a multiple into the value of the shares. These performance-related share value gains, in turn, will be amplified by the 10-to-1 leveraging built into the option. A mere 10% increase in the market value of the company's shares (above accrued interest) will double the value of the managers' investment. If they acquire a sufficient number of the options, the managers have a shot at becoming wealthy. Alternatively, they could lose their initial investment. A mere 10% decline in share value (again in relation to accrued interest) will wipe the investment out.

The exaggerated payoff profile duplicates the pressures and rewards associated with an LBO. Indeed, the special options effectively shrink the typical leverage and ownership structure of an LBO down to a size that fits just the management and without forcing shareholders to sell their equity. The shareholders can continue to reap the benefits of owning stock in a healthy, publicly traded company while management feels the agony and the ecstasy of a buy-out.

As with an actual LBO, the urgency for managers will be to create value—and to create it now. Confronted with that challenge and opportunity, managers may be more inclined to reach for the potentially most powerful initiative: financial restructuring.

Financial Restructuring

The last of the three great imperatives to be discussed in this book is financial restructuring. Partnership or subchapter S conversions, spin-offs, divestitures, joint ventures, public stock offerings of a subsidiary's shares, ESOPs, recapitalizations and leveraged buy-outs are among the many maneuvers to alter the ownership of a firm's assets and its equity, which is the most fundamental definition of financial restructuring. All of the maneuvers champion a change in the right-hand side of a firm's balance sheet without, at least initially, altering the left-hand, or business side, of the ledger. The great mystery is how merely changing the financial or ownership structure can enhance the value of assets residing on the other side of the balance sheet.

Consider a spin-off, a classic and superficially innocuous financial restructuring technique. A spin-off refers to a particular type of transaction in which a company gives its own shareholders all (or virtually all) of the common shares of one of its subsidiary units. In the immediate aftermath of a spin-off, the same group of shareholders will own the same body of assets as before, but through two common stock certificates instead of one. For them, it is a non-event, and yet the effect on market value is often immediate and significant.

Broad-based academic research shows that when a company first announces the intention to spin off a subsidiary unit, its stock price almost always increases in value. On the surface, the market's favorable response is hard to fathom; it is much like cutting a slice from a pie, putting it onto a separate plate, and then saying there is more pie than before. Just as that statement defies the laws of physics, so a spin-off appears incapable of increasing a company's market value.

To answer the riddle, some people say that spin-offs increase value because investors are better able to grasp the actual value of the unit once it is separated from its parent. The parent's common stock price rise, so this faulty explanation goes, is in reaction to a change in the perception of value and not to a change in value per se. That claim, however, cannot be reconciled to the fact that the parent company's stock price rises when the intention to spin off is first announced, a time well before the spin-off becomes effective and new information on the unit is disclosed.

In June 1987, IC Industries (now renamed Whitman Corporation) announced its intention to spin off the Illinois Central Gulf Railroad. The common shares of IC Industries, the parent company, climbed in value at *that* time, despite the fact that the spin-off did not become effective until December 1988, after various tax and regulatory hurdles were surmounted. Why, then, would the parent's value rise a year and a half before new information on the railroad was made available to the public if the new information was the reason why the value was changing? Obviously impossible.

As confounding as the favorable stock price reaction is, it is now possible to demonstrate convincingly that, in some 10 to 15 key ways, financial restructurings such as spin-offs do change the way corporations are run and do create new, enduring values. Senior executives and their planning and finance associates should be intimately familiar with the restructuring rationales and their potential applications; if the stock market evidence is any indication, they are at least the equal of any of the latest planning paradigms at improving corporate performance. Needless to say, all of them are covered in detail in this "slim" volume.

The aggressive use of debt neatly illustrates the benefits that arise from using many different types of financial restructurings. In the right circumstances, a debt-financed recapitalization can create value in five ways. The most obvious of the five is the tax benefit of substituting debt for equity. But it is far more than just that.

The obligation to repay debt will remove the almost irresistible temptation to overinvest surplus cash flow in undeserving basic businesses or make overpriced acquisitions. Value is created because the market expects there will be fewer mistakes in allocating capital once capital becomes scarcer. The risk of unproductive reinvestment of surplus cash flow has proved to be most acute in mature, cash-rich companies. It is, ironically, a disease that afflicts the healthy as much as if not more than the infirm, a fact which makes the cure all the harder to swallow for managers involuntarily subjected to the strong debt discipline.

The third reason to use debt aggressively is that it makes it easier to concentrate ownership in the hands of the people best able to affect value: the managers and employees. For a business worth $100 million it would cost the insiders $10 million to obtain a 10% stake if the firm were financed entirely with equity. But if the same concern borrowed $80 million to make a special distribution to its shareholders, the insiders would have to come up with only $2 million to obtain a 10% interest (ignoring any premium to the equity that might arise). By leaving less equity to support a given level of assets, the aggressive use of debt facilitates the process of making the doers into the owners, an important benefit.

The fourth reason debt is advantageous is that the desire to repay it frequently stimulates the sale of assets or businesses. To the extent that another company or management team is better positioned to maximize the value, a profitable exchange can be arranged: The buyer pays the seller a large part of, if not more than all of, the extra value that the buyer expects to create, a tangible reward for finding a better business fit. Moreover, once rid of extraneous assets, management will find itself in a position to lavish attention and scarce resources upon the assets that remain, thereby elevating their value and garnering a reward for an improved focus.

The last reason is largely psychological. Debt creates an illusion of financial distress, even for what may be fundamentally healthy businesses, and thereby precipitates painful but necessary changes. A renewed sense of urgency to create value supplants bureaucratic complacency; a dedication to cash flow replaces a common concern with reported profits; and Darwinian selection suppresses the all-too-human tendency to support weak lines of business that should be put out of their misery.

For many people, debt's illusion is all too real. Popular opinion construes an LBO to be a failure if all of its debt cannot be repaid. In some respects, the sentiment is correct. Creditors and equity investors, including management, will lose out, at least to some extent. But whatever may be their magnitude, these back-end sacrifices almost always are offset by the up-front premium realized by the original shareholders. So long as the total value of the firm's assets (or, what is the same thing, of all of the firm's debt and equity) is greater after the LBO than it was before (or, more accurately, than it would have been in the absence of the LBO), the LBO has succeeded at enhancing the allocation and management of scarce resources. That, and not whether the debt is fully repaid, is the true measure of social desirability. Judged by that criterion, an overwhelming majority of LBOs and recapitalizations, poor Robert Campeau's included, have been astonishingly successful at creating value. There simply is no good reason why they should be subjected to regulation.

But rather than concern ourselves with inscrutable political issues, the more important question for top management is how best to harness the power of financial restructurings while, as in the case of atomic energy, avoiding its excesses. Many companies in the 1980s made the mistake of restructuring bluntly, taking on a whopping debt at the corporate level and thereby gambling all their assets against all the debt. Not only did such a strategy expose the firm to the risk of a financial meltdown in the event things did not materialize as planned, it was insensitive to the particular strategic challenges facing the individual business units. It also failed to involve local personnel as fully as would be desirable. As depicted in exhibit 1.2, two changes from traditional corporate practice may be advisable.

The first is to "decentralize" capital structure. Rather than hold all financing at headquarters and maintain an undifferentiated corporate capital structure, debt and equity should be pushed down selectively into the business units: debt for the mature, cash-rich operations, equity for the promising new ventures. The goal is to replicate internally the disciplinary and incentive effects that external capital markets have to offer while sidestepping the risk of having all the corporate eggs in one financial basket.

The second recommendation is to wind up the capital structure like a spring to propel the creation of value. Instead of maintaining a relatively fixed blend of debt and equity in the capital structure, which is the traditional "static" policy, companies should use debt "dynamically" by borrowing heavily with the objective of paying the debt down—the sooner the better. As the

Exhibit 1.2   The New Capital Structure Strategy

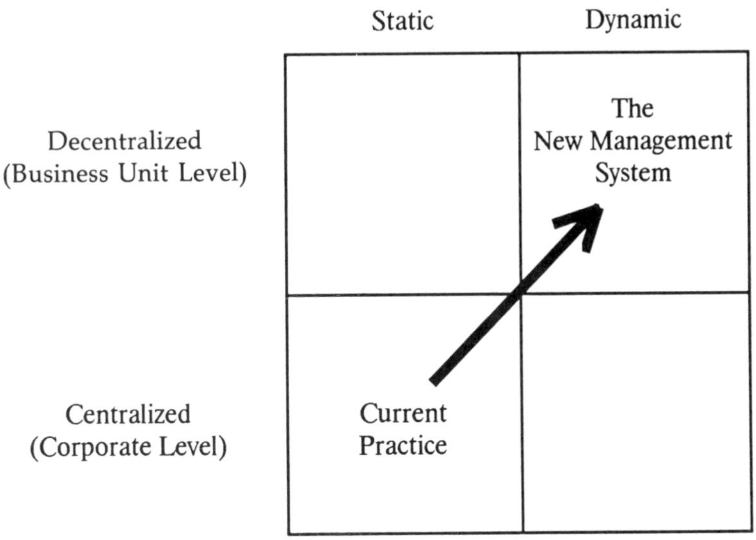

	Static	Dynamic
Decentralized (Business Unit Level)		The New Management System
Centralized (Corporate Level)	Current Practice	

debt unwinds to be replaced by equity, additional value often will be created as a result.

A new restructuring technique that I propose, one that combines the dynamic and decentralized use of debt, is an internal LBO. Surplus cash-generating units can borrow to distribute substantial amounts of cash to their corporate parent, concentrate a significant equity stake in the hands of the unit's management and employees, and instill a sense of urgency by setting up a demanding debt repayment schedule. In many ways the most important consequence is to capitalize a challenging, multiyear cash flow budget into a debt burden that must be repaid and then to free the unit managers to devise and carry out aggressive plans to pay down the debt and maximize the residual value. Management by exception now takes on a new meaning: So long as the debt is being serviced, there is no need for the parent to get involved, for the unit's business plan is being accomplished.

Unlike an outright sale or an ordinary LBO, an internal LBO of a business unit leaves the original corporate parent in place as a significant owner of the unit's equity. Its upside potential is preserved for the parent company's shareholders rather than being lost to some other company or a third-party financier. In essence, then, an internal LBO is just a very sophisticated and powerful incentive compensation scheme for the unit's managers, one that also rewards residual income, or EVA.

Equity, too, can be used in a manner that is both dynamic and decentralized. Most of the time common stock is used as nothing more than a patient and passive source of funds for the parent. But that overlooks some other very important roles that equity can play. A company with a publicly traded equity can reward managers and employees for efforts that create value while preserving cash within the firm. Moreover, the trading value of common stock is a constant source of feedback alerting managers to impending problems or new opportunities. And on the occasions when management has to raise equity from the outside, it forces them to expose their investment plans to the scrutiny of informed investors, and thereby to pass a market test. Investors, for their part, may be willing to pay more for the opportunity to invest in the shares of a unique and promising outfit. All these advantages to equity are denied to individual business units if just the parent company raises it, however. The alternative is to capitalize promising new ventures within a firm with their own common stock, to work some of it into the hands of their key managers and employees, and then possibly to take some of the shares public, a process I refer to as venture capitalization.

In the end, a decentralized and dynamic capital structure divides a company in two. On the one side are the mature, stable, cash-surplus units which, like mushrooms, flourish best in the darkness of debt. There are many reasons to think that internal LBOs are the best way for them to be structured. On the other side are the fledgling ventures and rapidly growing lines of business. In such cases financial leverage would snuff out the value that is glimmering in the eyes of entrepreneurs. A decentralization of equity alone through, say, a partial public stock offering, or better if it can be done, completely internally, is advisable. The trick is to keep the flame of a start-up flickering under the protective umbrella of a larger infrastructure.

In addition to progressing toward more refined and fluid capital structures, one other change should distinguish the 1990s from the 1980s. Top management should begin to financially restructure willingly rather than reluctantly. The evidence shows that companies that have restructured voluntarily (such as FMC) ended up with greater integrity, a more favorable reputation, and a superior stock market performance in comparison with those in which a third party set the agenda (such as Interco). Now with the fall of the house of Drexel, the implosion of the junk bond market, and higher obstacles to takeovers, the opportunity to embrace the power of financial restructuring has never been greater.

The three great imperatives—planning for value through EVA, making managers into owners, and the surgical structuring of balance sheets—shall inform and guide our forthcoming quest for value.

Plan of the Book

The book is divided into four main parts. The first, consisting of chapters 2 through 9, covers value planning. Our quest is launched with a debunking of market myths (chapter 2). The most widely shared misconception centers on the primacy of accounting results, most notably, earnings per share, as determinants of share value. All but the most hardened accounting enthusiast must succumb to the logic and evidence marshalled against these false gods.

"Market Reality" (chapter 3) unveils the fundamental but invisible economic forces that truly account for market value. The competition for capital—earning an adequate rate of return in relation to the cost of capital—is shown to be a primary influence on stock price levels. The chapter concludes with a description of how to estimate the true cash-to-cash rate of return being earned in a business. A powerful beacon to illuminate the performance of any enterprise, this return measures the productivity of capital employed without regard to financing methods, and it is purged of distortions that arise from accrual bookkeeping entries, from the conservative bias of accounting, and from the tendency to understate investment by writing off the unsuccessful ones.

Chapter 4 ("The EVA Financial Management System") leads to the holy grail, for it shows why economic value added must be adopted as the paramount corporate financial goal and how to use it as the foundation for the new and entirely more fruitful financial management system.

The actual link between EVA and value is firmly established in chapter 5 ("The Stern Stewart Performance 1000"). Though it may be confused with a road rally by its title, The Stern Stewart Performance 1000 ranks prominent U.S. companies by the market value that they have added to the capital at their disposal. Of great import, evidence is presented that the market value premium is directly related to the level and change in the level of EVA that each company has produced. Here is a proof that adopting the goal of increasing EVA will build a premium into the value of a company.

Chapter 6 ("Making Managers into Owners") describes how EVA can be the basis for a bonus system that stimulates managers to behave more like committed proprietors than mere hired hands. Like Disneyland, the approach taken in this chapter tricks the senses into believing the impossible. By operation of a magical bonus system, managers are persuaded that they have the risk and reward of an ownership stake in their unit without actually owning a share at all.

The next chapter, "Valuation Concepts," sets the scaffolding under corporate value. Six factors are shown to account for intrinsic market valuations. Four of the six are subject to management control; the other two are due to exogenous market forces over which management has little influence. The tax benefit of debt financing and its effect on the cost of capital are investigated with the perspicacity of a Sherlock Holmes. Common objections expressed to the use of debt are evaluated, and found to be sorely wanting.

In chapter 8, "The Valuation Contest," Wal-Mart, the world's greatest retailer and nearly most value-adding company, is the subject of a case study that illustrates three equivalent valuation procedures and their important planning implications. Pitting a young upstart contender against the reigning valuation champion, the Wal-Mart contest culminates with the ringing declaration that the practice of discounting cash flow for capital budgeting and valuations be abandoned in favor of discounting EVA instead.

The last chapter in the value-planning section covers the pricing and structuring of acquisitions. Twelve common acquisition pitfalls are discussed before the actual requirements for value-adding business combinations are revealed. Two case studies highlight one winning and one losing acquisition. The first is the mutually satisfying purchase of Saga, a food services company, by Marriott. A Bronx cheer is reserved for the highly disappointing acquisition of the Signal Companies by Allied Corporation, at the time the largest industrial merger in the United States— possibly its only favorable distinction.

The next part of the book addresses financial policy issues from a *static* perspective. It is assumed throughout that a company's financial affairs should be structured to serve the needs of the business and that over time a reasonably fixed blend between debt and equity should be maintained. Within that context, chapter 10 ("Financial Planning") describes how to tailor a financial strategy to support the most value-adding business plan. A system for predicting the bond rating associated with alternative capital structures is presented, and it forms the basis for assessing important financial planning trade-offs.

Next as fodder for the gristmill are the financing instruments that might be employed to fill in the cash flow gaps in a company's financial plan (chapter 11). After rumination over preferred stock, common stock, convertibles, and junk bonds, hardly any are found to survive the investment bankers' inflated claims.

The last panel in the financial planning triptych is the cost of capital (chapter 12). Two approaches to this unglamorous but necessary task are presented. One is the result of weighting the individual costs of debt and equity, and the other is the product of a fundamental assessment of business risk in comparison with a profile of publicly traded business peers.

The third part of the book will rouse the sentiments, for it clearly will be the most controversial. Here finance turns dynamic and becomes an engine of exceptional value creation. The first of two chapters (chapter 13, "Financial Restructuring") discusses the real reasons why financial restructurings are capable of increasing market value while at the same time dispensing with the many specious claims advanced by traditional financial advisors and the press. The aggressive use of debt, which is the most misunderstood restructuring method, is the subject of an intense evaluation. Case studies resound from virtually every page in a cannonade so steady and convincing that even the most fortified critic must surrender to the appeal of financial restructurings. This formidable chapter clears the field for the next.

Once the smoke has cleared, a three-step plan to revitalize corporate performance is unveiled in chapter 14 ("Remaking the Public Corporation from Within"). Making managers into own-ers and the dynamic and decentralized use of debt and equity are the three legs that support a powerful new corporate form, one that combines the best of public ownership, LBOs, and venture capital.

The Quest for Value concludes with a recipe to revive the Camp-bell Soup Company (chapter 15). Blending together almost all of the ingredients discussed throughout the book, this culminating case study concocts a hypothetical value planning and financial restructuring exercise around the real-life circumstances of the Campbell Soup Company.

The Quest for Value is not a journey for the faint of heart. Courage will be required to challenge popular myths and misconceptions; the will to fight for change must be summoned; and endurance to get through this magnum opus will be needed. But the rewards for those who complete the odyssey will be bountiful. Welcome aboard.

PART I

Value Planning

2

Market Myths

Introduction

The quest for value is often complicated by a failure to understand how share prices are set. I regularly encounter senior executives and board members who believe that stock prices are set by some vague combination of earnings, growth rates, returns, book values, cash flows, dividends, and trading volumes. (In one particularly memorable meeting I was harangued for several hours by an elderly gentleman who claimed that mysterious forces—the so-called gnomes of Wall Street—controlled the market. His "voodoo valuation" framework will not be formally rebutted in this book.)

Confusion over what it is that investors really want can make it difficult for top management to reach sensible decisions regarding business strategies, acquisitions and divestitures, accounting methods, financial structure, dividend policy, and most important of all (let's be honest), bonus plans. As the competition for scarce capital grows ever fiercer, the cost of ignorance is escalating. It is high time management learns the answer to the question: What is the engine that drives share prices?

In Search of Value: The Accounting Model versus the Economic Model

Right away there are two competing answers. The traditional accounting model of valuation contends that Wall Street sets share prices by capitalizing a company's earnings per share (EPS) at an appropriate price/earnings multiple (P/E). If, for example, a company typically sells at 10 times earnings, and EPS is now $1, the accounting model would predict a $10 share price. But, should earnings fall to $0.80 per share, then—however temporary the downturn—the company's shares are expected to fall to $8.

The appeal of this accounting model is its simplicity and apparent precision. Its shortcoming is an utter lack of realism: The accounting model assumes, in effect, that P/E multiples never change. But P/E multiples change all the time—in the wake of acquisitions and divestitures, changes in financial structure and accounting policies, and new investment opportunities. P/E multiples, in short, adjust to changes in the quality of a company's earnings. And that makes EPS a very unreliable measure of value.

A competing explanation—the economic model of value to which I subscribe—holds that share prices are determined by smart investors who care about just two things: the cash to be generated over the life of a business and the risk of the cash receipts.

Because most companies' earnings and cash flow move together most of the time, it can be difficult to say for sure whether stock prices truly result from capitalizing earnings or from discounting cash flow. To sort out this potentially misleading correlation, academic researchers have studied how share prices react to events that cause a company's earnings and its cash flow to depart from one another. (An anecdotal example of a case in which earnings severely misrepresented cash flow appears in exhibit 2.1.)

Exhibit 2.1 Just Say No: RJR Joins the Cash Flow Generation

Just how damaging an addiction to earnings can be is illustrated by the case of RJR, the tobacco giant. As reported in *The Wall Street Journal,* RJR puffed up its sales and earnings for several years prior to its LBO by loading cigarette inventories on its distributors. Dealers were encouraged to purchase billions of surplus cigarettes just before semiannual price increases were put into effect. (Company officials estimated that there were a staggering 18 billion excess cigarettes on dealers' shelves as of January 1, 1989.) As a result, RJR was able to report higher sales and earnings. But, in so doing, management forfeited future sales at higher prices, accelerated the payment of excise taxes, and turned off smokers with cigarettes that had turned stale.

Within months of the LBO, RJR announced it would discontinue this harmful practice cold turkey; it slashed cigarette shipments 29% in the third quarter and 17% in the fourth quarter of 1989 compared to year-earlier levels. Though the accounting symptoms look bad (reported profits will be reduced by about $170 million in each quarter), the vital signs of corporate health are restored right away.

"This is a very positive development for the company as far as cash flow is concerned," noted Kurt von der Hayden, RJR's CFO. "I view it as a very positive contribution to our debt service."

Because RJR offered extended-payment terms to induce its dealers to load inventories, cash flow will not be hurt by the shipment drop. But excise taxes will be postponed, production and distribution can become more efficient, and fresher cigarettes may help to stem a further loss of market share to Philip Morris.

A former senior RJR officer said that management had been aware of the problem but couldn't withdraw from the practice because it feared the impact on earnings would have outraged Wall Street. James W. Johnston, the head of the RJR Tobacco Company, stated, "Here is probably the clearest, most positive statement of what we can accomplish by being private for a while."

For shame! What about the evidence that the stock market really responds to the generation of cash and not to illusory accounting profits? As my colleague Joel Stern puts it, "Run your public company as if it were privately held, and you will be making the right decision for your public stockholders." And maybe you won't be vulnerable to its being taken private at twice the current stock price (RJR traded for $55 a share before being taken private for $110 a share.)

Kick the earnings habit. Join the cash flow generation.

The Accounting Model versus the Economic Model: Some Evidence

The accounting model relies on two distinct financial statements—an income statement and balance sheet—whereas the economic model uses only one: sources and uses of cash. Because earnings are emphasized in the accounting model, whether a cash outlay is expensed on the income statement or is capitalized on the balance sheet makes a great deal of difference. In the economic model, where cash outlays are recorded makes no difference at all—unless it affects taxes. This conflict is highlighted when a company is permitted to choose between alternative accounting methods.

LIFO versus FIFO

Switching from FIFO (first in, first out) to LIFO (last in, first out) inventory costing in times of rising prices decreases a company's reported earnings because the most recently acquired and, hence, most costly inventory is expensed first. But, in so doing, it saves taxes, leaving more cash to accumulate in the cigar box.

Now we have an important question: Does the market focus on the decline in earnings or the increase in cash? Following the empirical tradition of the Chicago School, let's find out what investors actually do to stock prices instead of asking them what they might do.

Professor Shyam Sunder demonstrated that companies switching to LIFO experienced on average a 5% increase in share price on the date the intended change was first announced. An analysis performed by a second group of researchers revealed that the share price gain was in direct proportion to the present value of the taxes to be saved by making the switch. Taken together, these studies provide powerful evidence that share prices are dictated by cash generation, not book earnings.

These findings also prove that a company adopting LIFO will sell for a higher multiple of its earnings than if it used FIFO. The higher multiple is consistent with the higher quality of LIFO earnings; inventory-holding gains are purged from income, and there are the tax savings besides.

And if, as this research suggests, a company's share price depends upon the quality as well as the quantity of its earnings, then the accounting model of value collapses. It collapses because a company's P/E multiple is not a primary *cause* of its stock price, as the model seems to suggest, but a consequence of it. The accounting model cannot answer the question: What determines a company's stock price in the first place?

In the LIFO-FIFO example, earnings go down while cash goes up. Let us now examine a second accounting choice, one in which earnings go down but there is no change in cash.

The Amortization of Goodwill.   When the purchase method is used to account for an acquisition, any premium paid over the estimated fair value of the seller's assets is assigned to goodwill and amortized against earnings over a period not to exceed 40 years. Because it is a non-cash, non-tax-deductible expense, the amortization of goodwill per se is of no consequence in the economic model of valuation. In the accounting framework, by contrast, it matters because it reduces reported earnings.

With pooling of interests accounting, by contrast, buyers merely add the book value of the sellers' assets to their own book value. No goodwill is recorded or amortized, and that usually makes the acquisitor's subsequent reported earnings and return on equity look much better than if purchase accounting had been employed.

Now, if the amortization of goodwill were the only difference between pooling and purchase, I might consider a preference for pooling accounting to be harmless. But, sellers will often take only cash or buyers are unwilling to issue equity, thereby ruling out pooling transactions. Avoiding a sensible transaction merely because it must be recorded under purchase rules is the height of folly.

Sad to say, it was apparently just this foolish thinking that stalled the disposition of some of Beatrice's last remaining properties. The press has reported on more than one occasion that interested suitors balked at purchasing Beatrice units because of a concern over how the market would react to the enormous goodwill they would be forced to record. H. J. Heinz, for one, canned a bid in part over just such a concern with goodwill.

Now, if Don Kelly, Beatrice's CEO at that time, was asking too high a price—one that the potential buyers could not justify by the likely future generation of cash—then that would have been a good reason for them to step back. But if, as the press suggested, the potential buyers walked away from value-adding acquisitions merely because it would have required the recognition and amortization of goodwill, then they let the accounting tail wag their business dog (and I can only shake my head in wonder).

As these cases suggest, it is important to know whether investors are fooled by the cosmetic differences between purchase and pooling, or if instead they penetrate accounting fictions to focus on real economic value. To find out which answer is correct, let us once again trust our eyes and not our ears. Let's look over the shoulders of researchers who have carefully studied the share prices of acquiring companies.

Hai Hong, Gershon Mandelker, and Robert Kaplan, while associated with Carnegie-Mellon's business school, examined the share prices of a large sample of U.S. companies making acquisitions during the 1960s. They divided all the acquisitors into two camps: those electing purchase and those using pooling. Over the interval covered by their study, it was much easier to qualify an acquisition for pooling than it is now. Most acquisitions could be recorded by using either purchase or pooling, with the choice largely up to management. Thus, if it were true that investors were concerned with the recognition and amortization of goodwill, the stock prices of purchase acquisitors should have underperformed the pooling acquisitors. And yet, no significant difference in stock returns could be detected.

This evidence supports the view that accounting entries that do not affect cash do not affect value. It also proves that what matters in an acquisition is only how much cash (and cash-equivalent value) is paid out to consummate the transaction relative to how much cash is likely to flow in afterward, and not how the transaction is recorded by accountants. (The earnings/cash flow controversy posed by acquisitions does not end with the amortization of goodwill. See exhibit 2.2 for a discussion of a related conflict.)

The studies I have cited (along with many other tests of share price behavior too numerous to review here) offer persuasive evidence that share prices are determined by expected cash generation and not by reported earnings. A company's earnings ex-

---

Exhibit 2.2 Earnings or Cash Flow?

On May 9, 1989, my colleague Joel Stern and I corralled a group of respected money managers and deal-doers—experienced, pragmatic, market-focused people—and we asked these insiders how the stock market works. I have to thank Donald Chew, one of my partners at Stern Stewart and the editor of *The Continental Bank Journal of Applied Corporate Finance,* for furnishing this excerpt from the full transcript of the day's proceedings:

STEWART: Dick [that's Dick Fredericks, general partner of Montgomery Securities and its senior bank analyst], let me see if I can pose the question in this way. There are times when a company has to choose between two accounting methods which have different consequences for earnings and cash flow. That is, the one method will increase reported earnings but, by so doing, it will also increase corporate taxes paid and thereby reduce corporate cash flow.

To make the dilemma more concrete, an acquisition takes place and it is a purchase acquisition—one where it's possible to assign part of the purchase price to assets that can be expensed against both book and tax earnings to reduce the tax liability of the firm. The alternative would be to put the premium into goodwill, which will be amortized against earnings over a much longer period of time. In doing so, you will increase reported earnings, but also increase the tax liability and thus reduce corporate cash flow.

Thus, it becomes a question that senior management wrestles with. Is it really earnings that matters to the market, or is it cash flow? Which one would you choose?

FREDERICKS: Cash flow.

LAFFERTY [John Lafferty, executive vice president and director of quantitative research with Stein Roe & Farnham, which manages $17 billion in assets]: I agree, it's cash flow that matters in this kind of case. But for most companies, changes in earnings and cash flow tend to track each other fairly closely.

STERN: Well, I think it's important to focus on this issue because so many firms refused to switch to LIFO inventory accounting during the high-inflation period not long ago. They refused to do so because it would have reduced their reported earnings, even while conserving tremendous amounts of cash.

FERENBACH [Carl Ferenbach, former head of M&A for Merrill Lynch and presently one of the partners of Berkshire Partners, which has done over 30 buy-outs]: But, Joel, in today's world, managements

Exhibit 2.2   continued

> pay a price for persisting in those policies. Today, if you try to maximize earnings per share at the expense of cash flow, you are inviting some other company that does look at cash flow to come along and take you out. Because they are looking at the underlying economics.
>
> BRUNIE [Charles Brunie, chairman of Oppenheimer Capital which manages $17 billion in assets]: I agree.

plain its share price only to the extent that earnings reflect cash. Otherwise, earnings are misleading and should be abandoned as the basis for making decisions (and, as I shall argue later, for determining bonuses).

More Troubles with Earnings

Is R&D an Expenditure or an Expense?

Another problem with earnings as a measure of value is improper accounting for research and development. Accountants are required to expense R&D outlays as if the potential R&D contribution to value is always exhausted in the period incurred. But common sense says otherwise.

Why would Merck, the spectacularly successful pharmaceutical company, spend more than 10% of its sales each year on R&D if it did not expect a substantial return to follow? In fact, Merck is looking for a long-term payoff from such spending, and so are its investors. The company's shares sell for a multiple of over 20 times reported earnings and nearly 10 times accounting book value. Merck's earnings and book value apparently understate the company's value by a wide margin. Expensing R&D is one of the reasons why.

Although the payoff from any one of its projects is unpredictable, Merck's overall R&D spending is almost certain to bear fruit. Like any capital expenditure that is expected to create an enduring value, Merck's R&D should be capitalized onto the balance sheet and then amortized against earnings over the period of projected payoff from its successful R&D efforts. Such accounting would lead Merck to report both a higher book value and higher current earnings, thereby making the company's actual P/E and price-to-book multiples more understandable.

The accountants' cavalier dismissal of R&D is what accounts in part for the sky-high share price multiples enjoyed by the many small, rapidly growing high-tech Silicon Valley and Route 128 firms. As in Merck's case, their stock prices capitalize an expected future payoff from their R&D, whereas their earnings are charged with an immediate expense. It is especially ironic to note that, following the acquisitions of R&D-intensive companies, the accountants will agree to record as goodwill for the buyer the R&D they had previously expensed for the seller. Thus, according to the accountants, R&D can be an asset if acquired but not if it is home-grown. (Again, I shake my head in wonder.)

What possible justification could there be for writing off R&D as an immediate expense when it is so obviously capitalized in stock market values? My answer is that the accountants are in bed with the bankers.

Accountants Take Downers, Too

To protect their loans, bankers prefer to lend against assets that retain value even if the borrower must be liquidated. Such "tangible" assets include receivables, inventories, and property, plant and equipment—assets that have a use to others. But because an insolvent company is unlikely to recover much value from its prior R&D investments (if it did, why is it going bankrupt?), lenders are reluctant to lend against it. Their accounting pals accommodate their desire for concreteness by expensing "intangibles" like R&D.

Accountants, to be sure, do not accept my contention that they are the unwitting slaves of the bankers. They explain their overzealous pen strokes as an adherence to the "principle of conservatism," a slogan that in practice means, "when in doubt, debit." You might have more appreciation for the poor accountants' cynical bent if I told you that accountants are much more likely to be sued for overstating earnings than for understating them. So perhaps their conservatism is more pragmatic than principled.

The key question remains: Are the investors who set share prices knee-jerk conservatives or hard-headed realists when it comes to R&D? Do they consider R&D a cost to be expensed or an expenditure to be capitalized?

Stock prices provide the answer that economic realism prevails. (The academic evidence to support that is reviewed later in this chapter.) R&D outlays should be capitalized and amortized over their projected lives—not because they always do create value, but because they are expected to.

Full Cost versus Successful Efforts

One objection that might be raised to capitalizing R&D is that it may leave assets on a company's books that no longer have any value. What if the R&D fails to pay off? Should not at least the unsuccessful R&D outlays be expensed? I say no. Full-cost accounting is the only proper way to assess a company's rate of return.

The issue of successful-efforts versus full-cost accounting is best illustrated by oil companies. With successful-efforts accounting, an oil company capitalizes only the costs associated with actually finding oil; all drilling expenditures that fail to discover economic quantities of oil are immediately expensed. Such a policy reduces earnings early on, but it causes a permanent reduction in assets that eventually leads to the overstatement of future rates of return.

With full-cost accounting, by contrast, an oil company capitalizes all drilling outlays onto its balance sheet and then amortizes them over the lives of the successful wells. If you believe (as I do) that part of the cost associated with finding oil is that unsuccessful wells have to be drilled (if not, why are they drilled in the first place?), then full-cost accounting must be employed to properly measure an oil company's capital investment and thus its true rate of return.

The misuse of successful-efforts accounting is not limited to oil companies, though. Any company that writes off an unsuccessful investment will subsequently overstate the rate of return its investors have realized. Such an overstatement may tempt management to overinvest in businesses that really are not as profitable as they seem to be on paper.

Citibank illustrates the point. In 1987, Citibank took a $3 billion charge to earnings to establish a reserve for the eventual charge-off of LDC loans. Now Citibank sleeps better, for in the years after the charge-off, loan losses are charged against the reserve, never to touch earnings. And, with $3 billion of equity erased with an accounting stroke of the pen, Citibank's accounting return on equity has rebounded quite smartly. Management may wonder why, with such an improved return, the bank still sells for such a lowly multiple. One reason is that while Citibank has employed successful-efforts accounting, the market uses full cost to judge rates of return.

To overcome such distortions, the economic model of accounting for value would reverse unusual write-offs by taking the charges off the income statement and adding them back to the balance sheet. In that way a company's rate of return would rise only if there were a genuine improvement in the generation of cash from operations after the write-off.

Abraham Briloff, an accounting professor at NYU, is one who has fallen into the trap of advocating successful-efforts accounting. For example, in a book titled *Unaccountable Accounting,* he chastised United Technologies for not writing down the goodwill associated with its acquisition of Mostek, a semiconductor company. He argued that, in light of the severe operating problems that materialized at Mostek in the years after the acquisition, the goodwill on UT's books clearly overstated Mostek's value to UT's stockholders and should be written off just as if it were an unsuccessful drilling expenditure.

I am afraid that Briloff labors under the mistaken belief that a company's balance sheet somehow attempts to represent its market value. He and, it seems, the entire accounting profession apparently have forgotten one of the first principles of economics: Sunk costs are irrelevant.

Burn the Books

As any first-year economics student knows, the cash already invested in a project is an irrecoverable sunk cost that is irrelevant to computing value. Market values are determined not by the cash that has gone into the acquisition of assets, but by the cash flow that can subsequently be gotten out of them. Therefore, a company's book value simply cannot be a measure of its market value (as Briloff seems to assume).

Rather, a company's balance sheet can at best be a measure of "capital"—that is, the amount of cash deposited by (debt as well as equity) investors in the company. Whether such capital translates into value depends on management's success in earning a high enough discounted cash flow rate of return on that capital. That is the question that, although critical to the economic model of value, no balance sheet can answer. This judgment is best left to the stock market.

Briloff's singling out Mostek's goodwill but not, for example, its plant or its inventories for write-down, also is puzzling. If future free cash flow is what determines value, it does not matter through which accounts cash passes on its way in and out of a company. That some cash may now or in the future take up residence in a bin labeled "plant" or "inventories" or "goodwill" makes no difference except to keep the accountants occupied and the bankers pacified. Briloff's concern over the book value of goodwill misses the mark because the real issue is not the value of individual assets, but the value of the collective cash flows to be derived from Mostek's semiconductor business over time, a judgment best left to the stock market.

In the economic model, the value of a company is an ever-unfolding journey for its cash, not one-night stands that voyeuristic accountants can take snapshots of. The book value of assets simply is not an accurate picture of the value of a business, and it should not be construed to that purpose.

A company's book value should be used only to measure its capital, which, simply put, is the cash deposited in a company over its life, much like a savings account. Whether the cash deposited into a company's capital account actually translates into market value is a topic taken up in earnest in the Chase Manhattan Bank parable presented in the next chapter.

The Deferred Tax Chameleon

The inadequacy of conventional accounting statements is further exposed by this question: Is the deferred tax reserve appearing on a company's balance sheet debt or equity? Clearly the accountants cannot decide; that's why they stick it in the no-man's-land between debt and equity. My answer to the question is uncomfortably close to the accountants' hedged position. I too say, "It depends."

Pity the pessimistic lenders, for they must consider the deferred tax reserve to be a debt-like liability. Bankers realize that if a company's condition deteriorates, the company probably will not be able to replace the assets that give rise to the deferral of taxes. Moreover, should the assets be sold to secure debt repayment, the company may be obligated to pay a recapture of the past deferred tax benefit. In either event, the deferred tax reserve is quite rightly considered by creditors to be a quasi-liability that uses up a company's capacity to borrow.

But if you divorce yourself from the downright depressing company of lenders and take up with the more genial society of shareholders, you will discover that the entire character of the deferred tax reserve changes right before your eyes. For as long as a company remains a viable going concern—an assumption taken for granted in the stock market valuation of most companies—the assets that give rise to the deferral of taxes will continue to be replenished. Because the shareholders in a going concern do not expect it ever to be repaid, the company's deferred tax reserve is properly considered to be the equivalent of common equity and thus a meaningless accounting segregation from net worth.

Furthermore, if the deferred tax reserve is properly considered to be a part of shareholders' equity, then, to be consistent, the year-to-year change in the reserve ought to be added back to reported profits. That way taxes are taken as an expense only when paid, not when provided for by the accountants.

An analogy can be drawn to the Individual Retirement Accounts (IRAs) many people opened some years back. If you are accounting for yours properly, you must consider only part of the funds in your account to be true equity. An accountant would insist that you set aside a deferred tax reserve because eventually you will have to pay taxes when you withdraw the funds from the account. Do you expect to earn a return from that part of your account that is the deferred tax reserve, or do you consider that to be a free loan from the government?

Of course, you expect to earn a return on the entire balance in your account. Nonetheless, I have heard otherwise level-headed corporate executives suggest that their corporate deferred tax reserve ought to be considered a free advance from the government. But, just as you do, corporations should expect to earn a return on all cash invested, no matter what the accountants may call it.

Steal This Book

Permit me one final accounting irony. No doubt the cash you parted with to buy this book has been expensed by your company's accountants. I wish they had had the charity (if not the wisdom) to capitalize it. They insult me by assuming that, when you put this book down for the last time, you will forget everything you've read.

Where They Ought to Be

The accountants, then, are stuck between a rock and a hard place. They can prepare financial statements either for creditors or for stockholders—that is, either for judging a company's debt capacity or its stock market value. But they simply cannot do both at once. It should be clear by now that the lenders won this debate: The accountants take the position that a company is more dead than alive.

Managers must stop making business decisions with financial statements that assume their company is one day away from bankruptcy. To make realistic judgments of performance and value, accounting statements must be recast from the liquidating perspective of a lender to the going-concern perspective of shareholders. The balance sheet must be reinterpreted as the cash invested in a capital account, and not as the value of "assets." To do this, all of the investments a company makes in R&D, along with bookkeeping provisions that squirrel away cash from operations (for deferred tax reserve, warranty reserve, bad debt reserve, inventory obsolescence reserve, deferred income reserve, and so on), must be taken out of earnings and put back into equity capital. (The topic is discussed in numbing detail in a later chapter.)

Earnings per Share Do Not Count

Although EPS suffers from the same shortcomings as earnings, it is such a popular measure of corporate performance that it warrants further attention.

Consider an acquisition in which a company selling for a high P/E multiple buys a firm selling for a low P/E ratio by exchanging shares. Because fewer of the high P/E shares are needed to retire all the outstanding low P/E shares, the buyer's EPS will always increase. Many think that is good news for the buyer's shareholders, yet it will happen even if the combination produces no synergies.

To see how really silly a preoccupation with EPS is, reverse the transaction so that now the low P/E firm buys the high-multiple company through a share exchange. This time the buyer's EPS must always decrease; a greater number of low-multiple shares will have to be issued to retire all the high-multiple ones. Many think such EPS dilution signals bad news for the buying company's shareholders and advise that it be avoided at all cost.

But regardless of which company buys or which sells, the merged company will be the same, with the same assets, prospects, risks, earnings, and value. Can the transaction really be desirable if it is consummated in one direction but not in the other? Of course not. Yet that is what accounting EPS suggests.

Let's take an example. Assuming that two companies each currently earn $1 a share and have 1,000 shares outstanding, and that one firm sells for 20 times earnings while the other sells at 10 times its earnings, the facts are as shown in exhibit 2.3.

To make it simple, assume that there are no synergies and that

Exhibit 2.3   The EPS Acquisition Fallacy

	Hi*	Lo†	Hi Buys Lo	Lo Buys Hi
No. shares	1,000	1,000	1,500*	3,000†
Total earnings	$1,000	$1,000	$2,000	$2,000
Total value	$20,000	$10,000	$30,000	$30,000
Share price	$20.00	$10.00	$20.00	$10.00
EPS	$1.00	$1.00	$1.33	$0.66
P/E ratio	20	10	15	15

*Hi must issue 500 shares at $20 to retire all 1,000 of Lo's $10 shares.

†Lo must issue 2,000 shares at $10 to retire all 1,000 of Hi's $20 shares.

the buyers pay precisely market price for the seller's shares. With fair value paid for value acquired, these transactions have all the excitement of kissing your sister. A proponent of the economic model would expect the acquisitor's stock price to sit still.

Yet, when Hi buys Lo, EPS increases to $1.33; and when Lo buys Hi, EPS falls to $0.66. Preoccupied with EPS, accounting enthusiasts may see a good deal and a bad deal when in fact the two transactions are the same: Lo-Hi is just Hi-Lo with a two-for-one stock split.

EPS does not matter because, in the wake of an acquisition, a company's P/E multiple will change to reflect a deterioration or improvement in the overall quality of its earnings. In our example, observe that no matter which firm buys and which sells, the combined company will have a P/E multiple of 15 (the consolidated value of $30,000 divided by the consolidated earnings of $2,000). Hi's 20 P/E must fall, and Lo's 10 P/E must rise.

Hi must give up part of its P/E multiple to acquire relatively more current earnings from Lo, and Lo must surrender part of its current earnings to purchase Hi's more promising future growth prospects and a higher multiple. P/E counters EPS, rendering it a meaningless measure of an acquisition's merits.

In the economic model, what does matter is the exchange of value, and not the exchange of earnings so popular with accounting enthusiasts. If a buyer receives from a seller a value greater than it gives, the difference (which I call *net value added*) will accrue to the benefit of the buyer's shareholders. (In many cases the benefit will show up as an increase in the value of the buyer's shares immediately after the deal is announced.)

Now if this seems a simple and sensible way to judge an acquisition's merits, please note that it has nothing to do with EPS. If a prospective acquisition promises to generate a positive net value added for the buyer, but the accountants inform us that EPS will be diluted, then I conclude that the acquisitor will sell for a higher P/E multiple, that's all. Once again, a company's P/E multiple is not the cause of its stock price, but a consequence of it. Let's take an example.

I once advised a large telecommunications company on an acquisition in which EPS dilution was a potential stumbling block. Our client was thinking about buying a company engaged in a rapidly growing and potentially highly profitable business—one that appeared to have an excellent strategic fit with its own capabilities and business plan. I was enthusiastic about the transaction because I saw a prospect for the value created through the combination to be shared by both the buyer and the seller. (The candidate was a unit of another company.)

The chairman, too, was enthusiastic until he saw how much the deal would dilute EPS. He pointed out that the P/E multiple the company would have to pay was much higher than its own, so that the acquisition would lead to a substantial dilution in EPS.

I remarked that the target had far brighter growth prospects than it, so that, when the new business was added to its more mature operations, he could expect his company to command a higher P/E multiple. He said: "You mean it's like adding high-octane gas to low-octane gas; our octane rating will increase."

"Right," I said. "The candidate has supercharged earnings, and when you add them to your underpowered earnings, your pro forma earnings power will take off. Your multiple will climb, and that will counter the dilution in EPS."

"Then we are in big trouble," he said. "My compensation plan is tied to EPS. We are rewarding just the quantity of earnings. But you're telling me that the quality of our earnings matters, too. So what should we do?"

"Well, you could change your incentive compensation plan," I said, "and then make the acquisition."

Which is what the company did. And on the date of the announcement of the transaction, the seller's stock price increased, our client's price increased, and a key competitor's stock price plunged. Now that is what I call a successful acquisition. The seller wins. The buyer wins. And the competition gets clobbered.

I warn you, however, that my definition of a successful acquisition is different from that of many investment bankers. For them, successful acquisitions are all those that happen.

That's No Reason to Spin Off

A spin-off is a pro rata distribution of the shares of a subsidiary unit to the shareholders of the parent. It is simply the reverse of a stock-for-stock acquisition, and it is subject to the same accounting quirks. This time, though, instead of acquiring a lower-multiple company to boost EPS, the accounting enthusiast will recommend spinning one off to boost the parent company's P/E multiple.

Referring again to the example presented above, suppose Hi did acquire Lo to form Hi-Lo, a company that sells for a P/E multiple of 15, an even blend of Hi's 20 multiple and Lo's 10 multiple. Now why not spin off Lo to leave behind a company that sells for Hi's P/E of 20? Is this really advisable? I don't think so, but for a definitive answer you will have to ask an investment banker whose finger is on the pulse of the market.

Seriously, though, the increase in P/E cannot by itself benefit Hi-Lo's shareholders. They are still stuck with their pro rata share of the low-multiple business after it is spun off. The spin-off merely takes Lo's earnings from Hi-Lo into a separate company where they are capitalized at Lo's multiple of 10. Thus, the increase in multiple that attaches to Hi's earnings is offset by the diminished multiple the market places on Lo's share of the consolidated profits. No matter how the accounting pie is sliced, it's still the same pie.

Just such a spin-off was used to undo R. J. Reynolds' acquisition of Sea Land, a containerized shipping operation whose P/E multiple was even lower than that of Reynolds. Several years after acquiring it, Reynolds' management decided to spin off Sea Land to its shareholders and was quite pleased to note that as a result Reynolds' P/E multiple jumped from 7.5 to 9.5. But that increase in multiple just reversed the decline suffered when Reynolds first acquired Sea Land, no doubt to increase EPS.

So what we have described here is an investment banker's fantasy, an infinite deal generator: Have Hi multiple acquire Lo multiple in an exchange of shares to improve Hi's EPS (never mind, please, the collapse in P/E), and then, after a respectable period elapses, spin off shares in Lo to improve the multiple (never mind what happens to EPS); and then have Hi reacquire Lo to improve Hi's EPS . . . and, well, you get the idea (and the investment bankers get the fees).

Now please don't get the idea that I oppose spin-offs. As a matter of fact, I believe that spin-offs have been one of the most neglected tools of corporate finance. But the merits of a spin-off and other financial restructurings simply cannot be judged by the accounting model of value.

The Problem with Earnings Growth

Earnings growth also is a misleading indicator of performance. Although it is true that companies that sell for the highest stock price multiples are rapidly growing, rapid growth is no guarantee of a high multiple.

To see why, consider a situation in which two companies, X and Y, have the same earnings and are expected to grow at the same rate. At this point, we would be forced to conclude that both companies would sell for the same share price and P/E multiple because, as far as we can tell, they are identical.

Suppose now that X must invest more capital than Y to sustain its growth. In this case, Y will command a higher share price and P/E multiple because it earns a higher rate of return on the new capital it invests. X merely spends its way to the growth that Y achieves through a more efficient use of capital.

I had an opportunity, while completing the Chase Manhattan Bank's credit training program in 1976, to analyze W. T. Grant's financial performance over the period leading up to the eventual liquidation of the company in 1975. Grant's management decided in the late 1960s to embark on an aggressive growth strategy to shift their stores from depressed inner-city locations to more

attractive suburban ones. Besides the brick and mortar investment, this strategy also entailed a large initial outlay for the new
stores' inventories. To build volume, store managers were compensated to generate more sales.

Not surprisingly, credit approval became quite lax. This plan
led to impressive sales and reported earnings gains for a time, but
with the pile-up of receivables and inventories, it also resulted in
a cash flow problem. In fact, with poor and declining rates of
return on capital, Grant's free cash flow was negative for each
year from 1968 to 1975. And, despite this need for new capital,
dividends were maintained at 30% of earnings and not a penny
of new equity was raised. Growth was financed with new debt,
commercial paper, and leases. By 1974 the grim reaper was at the
company's door.

W. T. Grant's management apparently forgot one important
principle: Growth without a commitment to careful capital management—earning an acceptable rate of return—is a sure formula
for disaster. Their bankers forgot something, too. Risky expan-
sions should be financed with equity, not with debt.

In sum, rapid growth can be a misleading indicator of added
value because it can be generated simply by pouring capital into
a business. Earning an acceptable rate of return is essential to
creating value. Growth adds to value only when it is accompanied
by an adequate rate of return. If returns are low, growth actually
reduces value. (Just ask Saatchi & Saatchi.)

The Role of Lead Steers

How can it be true, as I claim, that the cash generated over the
life of a business (adjusted for risk) is what determines share
prices when most investors seem to be preoccupied with such
traditional accounting measures as earnings, EPS, and earnings
growth? The answer is that prices in the stock market, like all
other prices, are set "at the margin" by the smartest money in the
game, leaving the majority of investors as mere price-takers. The
concept of marginal pricing—one of the most difficult in all economics to grasp—can be illustrated by the metaphor of the lead
steers made popular by Joel Stern. He says, "If you want to know

where a herd of cattle is heading, you need not interview every steer in the herd, just the lead steer."

The stock market works in very much the same way. Although millions of people invest in the stock market, a relative handful of prominent investors account for the great majority of trades. For example, about 55% of the volume on the NYSE consists of block trades of 10,000 shares or more, and over two-thirds of all volume is attributable to trades of 5,000 shares or more. The importance of small, unsophisticated investors has been exaggerated in the press and, I'm afraid, in the minds of many senior executives.

The price of oil is set in just this way, too. When I pull my car into a gas station, I may feel in some way responsible for determining the price of oil. But, no, I am just a price-taker. Be it cash or credit, the price is posted, and I can take or leave it. I realize now that the price of oil is set by professional oil traders who compete with each other to get the price right before the other traders do.

But even this characterization is not really accurate. The astute traders I just tipped my hat to must in turn bow to the economic forces of supply and demand. They cannot make oil depart from the price that will clear the market—the one that will leave no excess supply or unsatisfied demand. You see, even the lead steers do not really lead. They too must follow the will of economic forces.

My point is this: Let's not confuse the process by which prices are set in the market with the economic forces that truly set market prices. The question that needs to be answered is not *who* sets stock prices, but *what* sets stock prices. The answer lies within the economic model of valuation.

A Lead Steer Up Close

Getting a lead steer to reveal his true investment strategy is about as easy as getting a magician to disclose the secret to his tricks. Each prefers that you enjoy the performance without figuring out how it is done. As one particularly astute investor (who wishes to remain anonymous) put it to me: "Why should I popularize my approach—that's my edge."

But there are some who will draw the curtain back for a tantalizing peek at their magic. What they reveal goes far beyond a myopic preoccupation with next quarter's EPS. Consider, as but one example, O. Mason Hawkins, president of Southeastern Asset Management, Inc. (SAM), an investment management firm located in Memphis, Tennessee. Since hanging out a shingle in 1975, Hawkins has never had a down year, and only once has he underperformed the S&P 500—and this with a billion dollars under active management. According to CDA Investment Technologies (a firm which evaluates portfolio management), SAM was the fifth best money manager for the five years ending June 30, 1988, with an annualized return of 19.7% versus 14.4% for the market.

Here is some straight bull from Mr. Hawkins:

> Our investment philosophy is based on the approach of trying to buy stocks at a significant discount from what we appraise their private market value to be. There are several ways to do that.
>
> The first method is to determine what the free cash flow is and can be in the coming business cycle under normalized conditions. Then we buy the company at a very reasonable multiple of that free cash flow.
>
> Another way is liquidating value; we simply add up all the assets on the balance sheet, subtracting all the liabilities, and adjust for things like understated inventories or real estate, overfunded or underfunded pensions, overdepreciated plant and equipment, and trademarks, franchises, and brand names. We come up with a net value for what the company could be liquidated for on the courthouse steps, if it came to that, and buy the company at a significant discount.
>
> We also take sales in the marketplace, arm's-length transactions between competent businessmen, and compare what they will pay for businesses versus the market value of the company we are looking at.
>
> We talk with management, we talk with suppliers, we talk with competitors. However, we reach most of our conclusions by looking at the numbers and analyzing them.
>
> Next comes the qualitative things, because we don't want to own stocks just because they are cheap . . . We are interested in companies whose insiders, management members and board members, have a vested interest in the company and who are

adding to that position. We are looking for a partner rather than an adversary in the executive office.

The Daily News, April 29, 1986

We're trying to avoid a situation like Phillips Petroleum, where management was virtually willing to destroy the company in order to maintain their positions.

Pensions and Investment Age, February 17, 1986

We'd rather get with a guy who pays himself $100,000 a year and can make millions on his stock than someone . . . who's making a million dollars a year and has a couple hundred shares of his stock.

Investor's Daily, November 1, 1985

Mason practices what he preaches. He sold 60% of his firm to employees and then invested the proceeds in a mutual fund that the employees manage. Hawkins admits, though, that having his mother-in-law's money in the fund is his greatest motivation to perform well.

Mason Hawkins's record and philosophy are typical of the lead-steer investors who truly set stock prices: They think like businessmen, not like accountants. Perhaps surprisingly, many of the lead steers have no formal association or identity with Wall Street; they prefer the anonymity and perspective that is gained by distancing themselves from The Street. You can't find them. They find you (exhibit 2.4 and exhibit 2.5).

Dividends Do Not Matter

At this point I will make a bold statement. Not only do earnings and earnings growth not matter: Dividends do not matter either.

In the economic model, paying dividends is an admission of failure—management's failure—to find enough attractive investment opportunities to use all available cash. Companies are valued for what they do, not for what they do not do. By paying dividends, management has less money available to fund growth. The value of profitable investment opportunities forgone is subtracted from share price.

If management chooses to raise debt or equity to replace the

Exhibit 2.4   More Bull

One of the reasons why corporate managers do not accept the fact that the stock market is sophisticated is because they confuse the roles of buy- and sell-side security analysts. Sell-side analysts are the ones who write reports for public consumption and work for brokerage firms. They really are in the business of stimulating trading volume, not the business of setting stock prices. A number of them are quite talented, but many sell-side analysts just turn out advertising copy to help brokers promote stocks to an uninformed retail clientele. As a group, almost all the reports they write recommend buying or holding shares. That makes it difficult to understand why the stocks they follow ever fall in value. That they seem preoccupied with earnings per share is only further testimony to their lack of influence in setting stock prices.

But buy-side securities analysts are another matter. They work for the big-money players who are serious about maximizing the return on their portfolios in a very competitive business. The research they perform and the recommendations they make are for private eyes only. And although it is not published, their analysis goes far beyond a myopic and rather childish preoccupation with near-term earnings, the popular myth.

To truly understand the market, though, it is necessary to go beyond even buy-side analysts to the real decision makers, the money managers themselves. Just how they think is one of the world's great secrets. In this business, information and knowledge are the only differentiating factors.

One lead-steer money manager who has spoken publicly, though guardedly, is Michael Steinhardt. As Jack Schwager reports in his fascinating book, *Market Wizards,* Steinhardt Partners has achieved, in the 21 years since its inception, a compounded rate of return of over 30% per annum versus 8.9% for the S&P 500 over that period. A $1,000 investment with Steinhardt in 1967 would have grown to over $93,000 by the spring of 1988 (and that's after subtracting the 20% of profits that Steinhardt charges as an incentive fee). The same $1,000 invested in the S&P 500 would have grown to just $6,400. Equally impressive, Steinhardt has recorded only two losing years while compiling his record. Clearly, his investment philosophy ought to be of interest to any CEO who is interested in understanding the lead steers.

> The word "trading" is not the way I think of things. I may be a trader in the sense that the frequency of my transactions is relatively high, but the word "investing" would apply just as much, if not more. . . . The

bulk of what I do is for a much longer duration and for more complex reasons. For example, when I went long in the debt markets in 1981, I held onto that position for 2½ years.

I look for situations where I have a variant perception, an idea that tells me a stock should be selling for something other than it is. If my perception of value is different than the market's, I am just as liable to go short a stock as long. For example, I was short Genentech for two years because I believed, rightly as it turned out, that the heart drug, TPA, would never be as successful as others did. I had a variant perception. [Genentech went from a high of $65 to below $15 over this period.]

One of the allures of this business is that sometimes the greatest ignoramus can do well. That is unfortunate because it creates the impression that you don't need any professionalism to do well, and that is a great trap. So the major advice I would give is: Recognize that this [picking stocks] is a very competitive business, and that when you decide to buy or sell a stock, you are competing with people who have devoted a good portion of their lives to this same endeavor. In many instances, these professionals are on the opposite sides of your trades, and they are going to beat you.

Good trading is a peculiar balance between the conviction to follow your ideas and the flexibility to recognize when you have made a mistake. You need to believe in something, but at the same time, you are going to be wrong a considerable number of times. The balance between confidence and humility is best learned through extensive experience and mistakes. There should be a respect for the person on the other side of the trade. Always ask yourself: Why does he want to sell? What does he know that I don't? Finally, you have to be intellectually honest with yourself and others. In my judgment, all great traders are seekers of truth.

Standing almost diametrically opposed to Steinhardt's intuitive, quick-witted command of fundamental values is the Alpha Factory run by the highly numerical Barr Rosenberg. Formerly a professor of finance, econometrics and economics at Berkeley, he is now the driving genius behind Rosenberg Institutional Equity Management (RIEM). In the brief period since its founding in 1987, RIEM has attracted nearly $7 billion in assets for management from blue chip clients like the Rockefeller Foundation, AT&T, and GM. The firm's objective for each client is to outperform a designated benchmark portfolio by 4% per annum within a close risk tolerance, an objective met handily for each of the past 4 years. What's their secret? To remove all human judgment and to stick strictly to the numbers.

REIM's process is anything but routine, and the amount of data it ingests is staggering. REIM focuses on uncovering undervalued stocks

Exhibit 2.4   continued

in a universe of 3,500 securities. Their computers are programmed to classify a company into no fewer than 150 categories and compare it, for example, with similar businesses in any industry; each of the company's operations is broken down and the segments compared with those of comparable business operations at other companies. These segment valuations are adjusted for variables such as taxes, capital structure and pension funding considerations that affect the whole company.

Finally, a single valuation for each of the 3,500 companies is derived. The difference between REIM's valuation and the market price is its profit opportunity, or "alpha." Stocks with large profit opportunities are bought.

What happens when the lead steers lock horns? Steinhardt and Rosenberg, for example, obviously have contrasting investing approaches—one intuitive and perceptive, the other quantitative and logical; one left-, the other right-brained; Dr. McCoy and Mr. Spock—and yet there is only one market price for every company. Which one is the lead steer? Are you ready for a shock? Neither one is, but both are! Actually, no one individual is a lead steer; only the market is. Let me try to explain the paradox.

The stock price of a company is constantly pushed and pulled by people with variant perceptions. Trading prices balance the information put into the market in a way that no one observer, be it a Steinhardt or a Rosenberg, can fully comprehend. That is what an economist means when he or she says that prices are set at the margin. Pricing at the margin makes the market smarter than any one of its individual players. Is that a hard concept to swallow? Let me try an analogy. No one person is smart enough to make a pencil. But pencils exist.

People can readily accept the everyday miracle of a pencil but somehow refuse to swallow the notion that the stock market could be as miraculous, as intelligent. Out of all the millions of investors, no one individual contributes more than an infinitesimal part of all the knowledge embodied in stock prices. The market is smarter than them all, and it is guided as if by an invisible hand to the intrinsic value of companies. The stock market, like the making of pencils, works by a miraculous decentralization, by dividing and conquering.

The first bit of knowledge put into stock prices comes from people expert at discerning values within an industry. Their understanding of how competing companies are likely to fare gives them an edge in picking winners and losers within a given industry group.

Jesse Meyers, for instance, the publisher and owner of *Beverage Digest,* would be one force, though not the only one, for valuing soft drink companies. Among his many coups, Meyers scooped the industry by correctly predicting that Coke would change the formula for the world's best-selling soft drink. "Jesse is really good," said Emanual Goldman, an analyst who at the time followed the industry for Montgomery Securities, Inc. in San Francisco. "He has been associated with the soft drink business for time immemorial, he digs and he knows a lot of people." Meyer's clue that the Coke formula would change was an inconspicuous message sent to its bottlers. "In the memo they told the bottlers they were about to put a 100th anniversary logo on their packages. That was inconsistent with anything Chairman Goizueta, who won't let anybody look back at the past, had ever done. After seeing that memo, I started to talk to all the people I could reach." After Jesse published his prediction, Coke was forced the next week to confirm his suspicion. Now, that is a lead steer in action.

The next powerful pull comes from the portfolio managers who worry about the relative values of different industry sectors. Should oil or chemical stocks be bought would be a question up their alley. As to whether Exxon would be preferrable to Amoco would be a question delegated to others.

Market-timers are next to weigh in. These macroeconomic thinkers try to get a handle on the direction of broad aggregates such as the GNP and the level of interest rates. They decide whether it is timely to move into stocks, or bonds, or cash, or a hedge like gold.

The last force are the international players, investors like George Soros and John Templeton who compare growth rates, interest rates, inflation rates, exchange rates, and valuation multiples across countries. Their buying and selling maintains a parity in the value of markets throughout the world.

Mario Gabelli is a perfect example of an analyst who focuses upon individual stock picking, disdaining the broader view. As the head of Gamco investors, Gabelli has chalked up a 5-year record through year-end 1988 that is unmatched by any of the other investment advisors tracked by CDA Investment Technologies.

Gabelli has never wavered from his bottom-up stock-picking orientation. Indeed, when he sits down with the other panel members for the annual *Barron's* roundtable, he says that he dozes through the first two hours. "During the first hour, they talk about the world," he notes, "and then for another hour, the stock market." Only when they get down to discussing actual stocks, Gabelli says, does he join in.

"What Makes Mario Run"
Institutional Investor
March 1989

Exhibit 2.4   continued

> When all is said and done, it is possible to pick out some obscure company operating out of Canton, Ohio, and compare it with some equally unknown firm from Birmingham, England, and find that their common shares are properly valued vis-à-vis one another. And yet, no one may have made that comparison directly. In a decentralized market, the actions of the individual lead steers impound into stock prices an intelligence that supersedes what any one of them could divine.
>
> An implication of a decentralized stock market is that it is nearly a useless exercise for a company to survey investors to identify what actions will be most appreciated in the market. No one of the lead steers actually sets the price; all of them together do so in a way no one individual (including, certainly, the interviewer) could ever comprehend.

dividend, then current shareholders' interests are diluted by introducing new claims on future cash flow. Such a policy makes a company incur transactions costs for unnecessary financings and forces investors to pay taxes on dividends that might otherwise be deferred as capital gains. So why pay dividends?

What if a company has exhausted its investment opportunities? Then it certainly would be better to pay dividends rather than make unrewarding investments. In most cases, however, it would be even better to use the funds to buy back stock. Then only will the investors who choose to sell be taxed, and they will be taxed only on the gain realized after the basis in their shares is applied against the proceeds from the sale. Even when the tax rate on capital gains is the same as it is for dividends, so long as the tax basis in the shares is not zero, investors will pay a lower tax on a capital gain. The Tax Reform Act of 1986 did not make dividends attractive; it only made them less unattractive than before.

Moreover, if paying any dividends at all is thought to be advisable, then borrowing to pay them all at once is probably even better. One benefit is the corporate income taxes saved when debt replaces equity, and yet no additional tax burden is placed on investors. Shareholders will just pay in advance the discounted present value of the taxes they otherwise would have paid over

---

Exhibit 2.5   The *Lead* Lead Steers

How can the view of absolute market sophistication I am proposing be reconciled with the fact that some investors, Steinhardt, Rosenberg, and Gabelli among them, earn extraordinary rates of return over long periods of time? That is a good question.

The answer first came to me as I read Bill James' *Baseball Digest* (1984 edition), a compendium of erudite baseball analysis that columnist George F. Will has called "the most important scientific treatise since Newton's *Principia*. (Will is a die-hard Chicago Cubs fan.) Bill was the first to study the game of baseball statistically, in a way much the same as the academic researchers have studied stock prices. He, too, has undone many heartfelt myths, and he is unloved by romantics who believe in clutch hitters, winning streaks, stolen bases score runs and win games and believe that Freddy Lynn was a good batter.

In the 1984 *Digest*, Bill drew a diagram of baseball playing ability as a normal, or bell-shaped curve (I won't reveal where I plot).

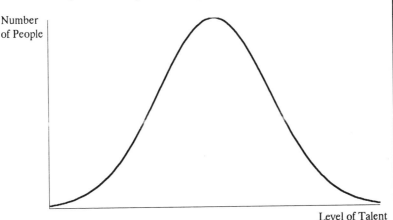

Exhibit 2.5   continued

Who would you expect to play baseball in the major leagues? Those exceptional athletes at the extreme right end of the distribution. If you blow up that right tail, it looks like this.

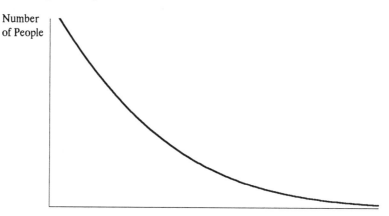

Bill James collected data on the number of games won by pitchers in the American League in 1983.

# of Wins	# of Pitchers	# of Wins	# of Pitchers
0	46	13	6
1	25	14	4
2	20	15	3
3	12	16	2
4	10	17	2
5	14	18	1
6	8	19	1
7	16	20	1
8	8	21	1
9	11	22	1
10	6	23	0
11	9	24	1
12	6		

Bill plotted the number of games won. It looks remarkably like the right end of a normal distribution, doesn't it?

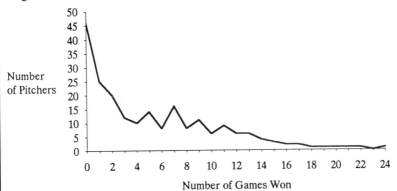

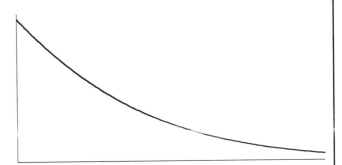

The Far Right End of a Normal Distribution

No one planned for it to work that way, but it works that way nevertheless. That's the fascinating thing about markets of all kinds: They are guided to an economic answer without any one individual knowing why or how, as if an overarching intelligence were at work.

The pitchers who won no games are marginal players in the big leagues. They are barely hanging on to a contract. Their salaries are low because they are replaceable by other, essentially equally qualified players, and because their alternative career opportunity is not that great. (They might end up as a bartender at Cheers, for example.) But what caliber athlete are they, exactly? They are phenomenal, of course. If I ever faced one of them in a hitter-pitcher confrontation, I would die.

But there are a few more gifted than the gifted. There are the

Exhibit 2.5   continued

20-game winners. Their extra little bit of talent is enough to set them apart from the very elite company that they keep. They earn phenomenal salaries because they are irreplaceable in what they do. And though they do win more frequently than the others, these stars would be hard pressed to explain exactly why.

What is the analogy to stock picking? I hope it is obvious. Of all the people who might engage in selecting stocks, the ones who survive the cutoff in a competitive business are the exceptionally gifted individuals at the tail end of the distribution. That is what makes the market sophisticated. As in the big leagues, the game is played at the highest level of which humans are capable. Most of us could not beat them.

The second part of the analogy is that stock prices are set "at the margin" by the players on the borderline. As with the marginal big-league pitcher, these lead steers would strike out any casual investor in the game. From the perspective of 99% of the population, stock prices impound more knowledge than any of us could bring to the table. Though the lead steers are only the marginal professional investors in the stock market, their income is high because the lead steers are very talented people. Their alternative livelihood is very good. Too bad they must play against one another.

But with prices set at the margin by the lead steers, there is room for a select group of *lead* lead steers, the 20-game winners in the stock market, the Mario Gabellis, John Templetons, Warren Buffetts, and Peter Lynches of the world. The exceptional portfolio return they earn is the reward the market confers on them for seeing the truth only a little more clearly than their competitors. Steinhardt admits as much. "Having [traded] for as long as I have gives me the opportunity to be 51% right rather than 50% right. Actually, it is more than a 1% edge, but it is not a big advantage like being right 80% of the time, or anything approaching that."

The fact that only a tiny handful of exceedingly astute investors can consistently outperform the market indicates that stock prices essentially represent true intrinsic values. From the perspective of anyone who is not a *lead* lead steer, the market is as sophisticated as humans are capable of making it. Corporate managers should accept that stock prices represent intrinsic value, for none but the very, very best investors can see even the slightest departures from this judgment, and even then, not regularly.

a period of time. Moreover, it will probably reassure investors to know that the tendency of cash-rich companies to overinvest in their undeserving basic businesses and to make overpriced acquisitions will be reined in by the obligation to service debt first. And it may also bring about the transfer of a more significant equity stake into the hands of key managers and employees, thereby heightening their incentives to add value.

But I am getting ahead of the story at hand. I will discuss the benefits of such financial restructurings in greater detail later on in this book. For now, let me summarize the discussion thus far by saying that, depending upon where a company's cash flow is in relation to its investment needs, it makes sense either to pay no dividends at all or to pay them all at once. The middle of the road is the most reckless place to drive a company's dividend policy.

But the corporate perspective on this question certainly is not all that matters. What about investors? Do they want dividends?

Granted some may need cash for consumption and thus may require a dividend. But they can create their own dividends by selling or borrowing against some of their shares or, better yet, by adding income-yielding bonds and preferred stocks to a non-dividend-paying common stock portfolio. Investors who need cash do not need to get it from every component of their portfolio.

Even so, the payment of dividends actually taking place is out of all proportion to the consumption needs of investors. Most get reinvested in the market, but only after the brokers' turnstile has been ticked. Besides, if a cash yield is so desirable, why have deep-discount bonds, which pay no cash return at all, become so popular? Much like a non-dividend-paying common stock, the return on such bonds is entirely in the form of expected price appreciation.

Does paying a dividend make a stock less risky to own? Some argue that a bird in the hand (a dividend) is worth two in the bush (capital gains). But the retort is not that dividends not paid will show up as capital gains for sure, but that dividends that are paid are capital gains lost for sure. Stock prices fall by the amount of any dividends paid, never to be recouped. Paying certain dividends out of uncertain earnings cannot make earnings, or common shares, any less risky. It can only make the residual capital gain that much riskier.

It is true that some investors are precluded by law or by policy from buying the common shares of companies that do not pay at least a nominal dividend. Will the share prices of companies that pay no dividends be penalized by not appealing to this group? Absolutely not. Once again, share prices are not set by a polling technique in which every investor has a vote on value. Prices in the stock market are set at the margin. So long as there is a sufficient number of investors with sufficient wealth who are not seeking dividends, companies that pay few or no dividends have no cause for concern. Their stocks will sell for their fair value.

This issue reminds me of an exchange I once heard during a debate between Newt Gingrich and Pat Schroeder. Ms. Schroeder was doubting the sincerity of Gingrich's hard-line stance against the Russians in view of the fact that Gingrich had voted against the grain embargo. Newt replied that he had voted to strike down the embargo because it hurt U.S. farmers more than Soviet consumers. Grain, Newt noted, is priced in a global market. Forbidding Russian purchases of U.S. grain just led the Russians to purchase more Argentinian and Common Market grain for just pennies more a bushel. The U.S. farmers, by contrast, suffered costly dislocations. They had to hustle to find buyers to make up for the loss of the Russians. In any market where prices are set at the margin, prohibiting a certain group of buyers from lining up with a certain group of suppliers will not change price (except to the extent it leads to economic inefficiencies, such as extra transportation and search costs, which are a deadweight loss for everyone). By the same token, investors who cannot or will not buy the shares of companies that pay no dividends may be harming themselves, but certainly not the companies they shun.

How can the view that I am articulating for investors—namely, that dividends do not matter—be reconciled with the fact that dividend announcements often have a pronounced effect on stock prices? Managements and boards of directors apparently have conditioned investors to associate dividend increases with a healthy outlook and dividend cuts with impending catastrophe. For example, in 1983, Bethlehem Steel halved the dividend and the stock price collapsed. At the same time, management disclosed its intention to close basic steelmaking at the Lackawanna mill, a decision that would trigger the payment of $1 billion in unfunded vested pension benefits.

Bethlehem's stock price would have collapsed no matter what had happened to the dividend. But in light of the company's need for cash, cutting the dividend made sense. And thus, there is just a correlation, but not a true causal relationship, between dividend announcements and share prices. Radical changes in dividend policy simply tend to coincide with the release of other important news to the market.

The Evidence on Dividends

Finally, and most decisively, let us once again turn to definitive academic research to answer the question.

The most important empirical study on dividends appeared in the prestigious *Journal of Financial Economics* in 1974. Although it has been updated and retested on several occasions, the fundamental findings have withstood the test of time. The study, performed by Professors Fischer Black and Myron Scholes, tested whether the total returns achieved during the period 1936 to 1966 from 25 carefully constructed portfolios depended upon the dividend yield or dividend payout ratios of the underlying stocks. Their analysis revealed that the return to investors was explained by the level of risk and was not at all affected by how the return was divided between dividends and capital gains. They found that, within a given risk category, some stocks paid no dividends, some paid modest dividends, and some paid a lot of dividends, but all experienced the same overall rate of return over a period of time.

Black and Scholes concluded that investors will do best by assuming that dividends do not matter and by ignoring both payout and yield in choosing their stocks (i.e., they should worry about risk, diversification, taxes, and value, but not dividends per se). Their advice to corporate managers is no less important than it is to investors: Do not formulate dividend policy in an attempt to influence shareholders' returns. Instead, set dividend policy in the context of the company's own investment needs and financing options, and then carefully explain it to investors.

The Myth of Market Myopia

It is easy to imagine that the pressure put on money managers to perform each quarter will force them to ignore the long-term payoffs from farsighted business decisions and instead focus only on near-term results. Here is the popular view of a myopic stock market as articulated by Donald N. Frey, the former CEO of Bell & Howell:

> When the typical institutional portfolio in the U.S. has an annual turnover rate of 50% and some smaller ones have turnover rates of more than 200%, it is no surprise that American business is hobbled compared with foreign rivals. . . . Playing the market the way our money managers do ignores two critical factors: the time required to bring a product from development to market and the time required to redirect resources from a maturing business to a new one. . . . The pressure for short-term results puts unnecessary hurdles in the way of sound management. Investors' expectations for simultaneously high dividends on stocks, high interest rates on bonds, and rapid growth in the price of securities force managers to forgo many of their most promising ventures. Ultimately, these pressures rob consumers of future products, workers of future jobs, and investors of future profits.

Frey is joined in this view by Andrew C. Sigler, chairman and CEO of Champion International Corporation, a large paper products company:

> The only pressure I have on me is short-term pressure. I announce that we're going to spend half a billion dollars at Courtland, Alabama, with a hell of a payout from redoing a mill and my stock goes down two points. So I finally caved in and announced I'm going to buy back some stock, which makes no sense. If the economy is supposedly run by corporations and corporations are supposed to invest and be competitive, buying back your own stock, if you have alternatives, makes no sense. But you can't fight it. The share price today is refined constantly by that proverbial young man looking at a CRT screen. There's an assigned P-E ratio based on what I did last quarter and what I'll do next quarter.

Now in one sense, Frey and Sigler are right. Because rates of interest have been quite high this past decade, especially in real terms, distant payoffs are more heavily discounted by investors. Projects must pay off more quickly and handsomely in order to pass muster. That is just a fact of life with which all projects must contend.

After all, the amount of capital available for companies to invest is limited. It is constrained in the aggregate to an amount equal to just what individuals throughout the world choose to save. High real interest rates are the result of too many promising projects chasing too little savings. A high rate of interest is the market's way of attracting more savings on the one hand and discouraging less rewarding capital projects on the other in order to strike a balance between the available supply of and demand for capital.

For management to ignore this obvious market signal is to misallocate capital, destroy wealth and welfare, and attract raiders like bees to honey. Frey and Sigler seem not to understand that capital budgeting is the process of deciding which projects ought not to be funded so that other, even more promising ones can be.

But their allegations go farther still. They claim our economic system is fundamentally flawed because of the tendency of investors—mainly professional money managers—to be unduly shortsighted. If it were true that stock prices failed to reflect the true value of insightful investment decisions, then regulations preventing hostile corporate takeovers (a fate, I might add, that eventually befell Bell & Howell) might be in order.

Unfortunately—at least for those who believe in greater market regulation—their claims are refuted by both logic and observations of share prices. Economic logic says that a company's stock price should depend on the cash expected to be generated over the entire life of the business—otherwise, there are large profit opportunities for long-term investors. The simple fact that stocks trade at multiples of current earnings is prima facie evidence of the stock market's extended time horizon, for a stock selling at a multiple of, say, just 10 times earnings, would have to be held for 10 years for the earnings to recoup just the principal paid and be held indefinitely for an appropriate return on investment to be earned.

Moreover, differences in P/E ratios indicate that the market responds to the relative prospects for profitable growth. If all the market cared about was near-term earnings, wouldn't all companies sell for the same P/E ratio? But it is precisely those companies whose prospects for long-run growth and profitability are brightest that sell for the highest P/E multiples, and that is a strong sign of market sophistication.

The CEOs also go astray when they accuse institutional investors of impatience. The long-term nature of pension and life insurance liabilities suggests that most of the large institutional investors accused of a short-term mentality actually would be better off investing in risky stocks that promise a higher long-term payoff than more conservative investments are apt to provide.

And, apparently, the institutions do just that. A study undertaken by the SEC's economics staff shows that institutional investors own a far larger percentage of the shares of R&D-intensive companies than of more mature, blue chip stocks. Far from indicating shortsightedness, this ownership pattern reveals patience and, indeed, a positive appetite for long-run payoffs.

But even if it is true that money managers are evaluated each quarter—and no doubt many are—it still does not logically follow that share price movements each quarter are dictated by that quarter's results. In fact, because share prices are forward looking, share price movements from quarter to quarter must be determined by the change in outlook extending beyond that quarter into the indefinite future. For if share price movements did respond myopically to quarterly results, a simple trading rule would exist: Just buy depressed stocks (the most recent earnings understate the long-term outlook) and sell short overpriced ones (current earnings overstate long-term value) and you will outperform the market over a period of time. But such a simple investment rule does not work.

Most fundamentally, does the frenetic trading activity that Frey in particular disparages arise from a short-term horizon on the part of U.S. investors? And does trading activity motivated by a quick payoff depress the value of companies investing for the long term? Not at all.

For every buyer there must be a seller and for every seller a buyer. If both buyers and sellers were equally shortsighted, trading per se would have no effect on value. For if the seller is selling because of an unwarranted concern over a near-term earnings problem, is the buyer buying because of an unjustified enthusiasm over near-term earnings prospects? Trading volume simply does not affect the level of stock prices (a theme to which I will return shortly). Consider another simple example. Have you ever heard the expression, "The market fell yesterday in a great wave of selling?" For example, on October 19, 1987, the Dow fell 508.32 points with an all-time record $21 billion worth of selling volume. That account of the market decline sounds right at first blush, but because sellers must sell to buyers it would be equally accurate to say, "The market fell 508.32 points in a great wave of buying." Although both statements are correct, they could be used on another occasion to explain why the market *rises,* and therefore neither statement can be the reason why the market rises or falls.

The real reason why the market rises or falls is simply that the lead steers decide that intrinsic value has changed. When that happens, trading volume may surge as investors adjust their portfolios to accommodate a new market value. It may seem as if the trading volume is what causes a change in value when, in fact, it is the trading volume that results from a change in value.

The increase in trading volume this past decade probably is best explained as a consequence of the deregulation of brokerage commissions in May 1976 and the automation of the brokerage industry, both of which have made the United States the low-cost producer of trades worldwide. Lower trading costs mean more trades, and more trades mean that even more information is being digested by market participants and actively impounded into stock market values. The growing demands placed on management to invest capital wisely actually are the result of an increasingly efficient and sophisticated capital market. They are not, as the CEOs assert, some new-found institutional focus on the short term at the expense of the long term. But, again, don't take my word for it, nor the words of Frey or Sigler, for that matter. Let's consult the academic experts who have no axe to grind.

The Evidence on Market Myopia

Definitive evidence proving the market's farsightedness comes from research performed by John McConnell of Purdue University and Chris Muscarella of Southern Methodist University. They examined share price reactions to announcements of capital spending plans (like Mr. Sigler's Courtland project), including R&D outlays. Because of the lag between making an investment and realizing its payoff, the immediate effect of an increase in a company's capital spending would be to reduce both its earnings and cash flow—a result Mr. Sigler is convinced leads inevitably to a markdown in a company's stock price.

Indeed, if the market were dominated by the callow, computer-driven automations familiar to Mr. Sigler, then share prices would be expected to decline with almost any planned capital-spending increase, no matter how significant might be the long-term payoff. If, however, the projects to be undertaken are generally sound—ones in which discounted cash flows over the lives of the investments offer promising returns—and if the market is dominated by astute, forward-looking lead steers, then share prices should rise despite any negative near-term accounting consequences. The converse would be true for an announced decrease in capital spending.

McConnell and Muscarella's evaluation of 547 capital-spending announcements made by 285 different companies over the period 1975 to 1981 reveals a statistically significant share price appreciation for companies announcing an increase in capital spending and a decrease in share price for firms announcing reductions.

Their findings do not imply that every single capital-spending increase was greeted favorably (Sigler's Courtland project, for example, was not), only that most were. When in early 1984 Federal Express announced Zapmail, a service designed to pre-empt fax machines, the company's stock fell in price nearly $10 a share, from the mid-$40s to the mid-$30s. Several years later, the project was called off in the wake of a widespread proliferation of fax machines, and Federal's stock price rose by nearly $8 a share. Investors heaved a sigh of relief to learn that no more money would be poured into a black hole. The point, though, is that Federal Express's share price fell initially not because the market was unable to visualize the long-run payoff from the Zapmail project, but because it saw the consequences so clearly.

Will Sigler's Courtland project suffer a similar fate? Only time will tell. For now, Sigler is free to rail against the stock market and protest that spending half a billion dollars to redo a paper mill is the world's best use for that scarce capital (despite the fact that his stock price fell when the project was first announced and rose when, by repurchasing shares, he freed up funds for other companies to invest). Essentially, then, we have one man's opinion arrayed against the collective wisdom of market investors who, in moving stock prices, are putting their money where their mouth is.

The R&D Issue. Returning to the research of McConnell and Muscarella, let me mention that they also discovered that share prices reacted no differently to announcements of stepped-up R&D that was to be immediately expensed against earnings than they did in cases of new capital expenditures to be added to the balance sheet. Here is the proof that R&D is a capital expenditure, not an expense, and should be capitalized onto a company's books just like any other capital expenditure that is intended to create an enduring value.

They also found that 111 capital-spending announcements made by 72 public utilities over the same time period had, as expected, no discernible impact on share prices. The explanation here is that regulators constrain public utilities to charging prices intended to provide only a zero net present value for new capital projects.

The McConnell-Muscarella study provides impressive evidence that, far from being myopic, the market:

- Factors into stock prices a realistic estimate of the long-run payoff from management's current investment decisions.
- Is able to distinguish value-adding from value-neutral opportunities.

- Does not care whether the accountants expense or capitalize value-building outlays.

The burden of proof lies on those who think otherwise.

Supply and Demand

Mr. Frey's aforementioned concern about excessive trading volume is particularly confusing to me because I have met with many CEOs who are concerned that their stock prices are depressed because of insufficient trading activity, a view to which I also cannot subscribe.

Both misconceptions hinge on the belief that share prices are set by a relationship between supply and demand and that management, accordingly, can (and should) market its common stock in much the same fashion as any other consumer product. After all, if the number of common shares outstanding is fixed, would not advertising in concert with frequent analysts' presentations spark demand for the shares and thereby raise share prices through a surge in volume?

Don Carter, former chairman and chief executive officer of The Carter Organization, at one time the world's largest proxy solicitation and corporate governance firm, was (quite predictably) a proponent of the supply-demand model of stock price behavior. "Every company," he asserts,

> has a shareholder family and that family consists of many components: mom and pop shareholders, institutional shareholders, management holdings, and speculative holdings. We identify those holders and generate two-way communication by mail or visit, to learn why they own their stock. Their answer will help us in our search for new investors with similar motives. Our job is to make sure that those who are in the stock stay in it, and those who are not—come in and join the party. When you have more buyers than sellers, the stock price will rise—period. It's still supply and demand that determines stock price.

Bell South has in the past adopted this Madison Avenue approach to Wall Street. For some time, hardly a week would pass without a full-page advertisement appearing in *The Wall Street*

Journal touting the company's investment appeal. After the reader was informed of a little-known fact—namely, that rapid growth in population in the southeastern part of the United States is expected to continue—Bell South would let us know that it was preeminently positioned to benefit from this trend. We were then advised to call our broker and purchase its shares.

To repeat our opening question: Will such a campaign increase share price? It will not, because it simply is not true that the supply of a company's shares is fixed. Instead, supply is perfectly flexible by virtue of options and short-selling. The lead steers can combine call options on Bell South stock with less risky T-bills to create a position equivalent to owning Bell South stock, but without owning Bell South stock directly. Or they could sell Bell South shares short—that is, shares they do not own. When this happens, the total number of shares owned by all investors will exceed the number of shares that have been issued by the company, with the difference being accounted for by the short sales. Would you be surprised to learn that Bell South has had one of the largest short positions of any stock on the Big Board?

Another, though admittedly less precise, approach to re-creating the unique investment opportunity that Bell South claims it represents would be for investors to purchase certain proportions of the shares of other regional telephone companies, such as Bell Atlantic, along with, say, Wal-Mart and Food Lion—retailers who, like Bell South, are benefiting from the burgeoning growth of the southeast.

Through these and other actions, sophisticated investors can create an artificial supply of a company's shares or close proxies for those shares in order to offset any surge in demand a PR campaign might generate. And the evidence on this issue reveals that efforts to promote a company's appeal to investors lead to an increase in trading volume, but not in stock price, thereby benefiting brokers (and maybe Don Carter), but not shareholders.

An elegant indictment of trading volume comes from Warren Buffett, the highly regarded chairman of Berkshire Hathaway:

> One of the ironies of the stock market is the emphasis on activity. Brokers, using terms such as "marketability" and "liquidity," sing the praises of companies with high share turnover . . . But

investors should understand that what is good for the croupier is not good for the customer. A hyperactive market is the pickpocket of enterprise.

Flexibility in the demand for a company's shares also makes trading volume an unimportant determinant of value. Investors for the most part are not interested in buying shares of stock in only a single company. To diversify risk, an investor holds a portfolio of stocks. The attributes that an investor wants a portfolio to exhibit—in terms of income, risk, potential for capital appreciation, exposure to the business cycle, and so on—can be obtained by selecting shares from among a wide variety of easily substitutable companies. When shares are purchased to play a role in a portfolio, the shares of stocks in individual companies will be priced much like undifferentiated commodities. Advertising will serve to raise only volume, not price.

The Evidence on Supply and Demand

Fortunately, this important issue has also been the subject of expert academic research. A test conducted by Professor Myron Scholes as part of his doctoral dissertation at the University of Chicago provides strong evidence that share prices are determined by intrinsic values and not by an interaction between supply and demand.

Scholes's ingenious study examined secondary offerings when already issued shares of a company's common stock are sold by investors who own them. Because no new shares are sold, a secondary offering by itself should not affect the intrinsic cash flow value of a company. And yet, a supply-demand enthusiast would predict that, given a downward-sloping demand schedule, additional shares could be sold only at a discount from market price. Presumably, the greater the number of shares unleashed on the market, the greater would be the discount required to induce investors to take up the shares. Another implication of the supply-demand view is that the price decline would likely be temporary. After the surplus supply of shares was absorbed into the market, a more normal share value should return.

Secondary offerings thus provide a very clear test of whether intrinsic value or supply and demand best explains how individual company's share prices are set.

Professor Scholes did find that secondary offerings reduced share price (an average of 2% measured against the market), but the price decline was unrelated to the size of the offering. It is reasonable to assume that secondary issues are timed by sellers to occur when the sellers believe the shares are overvalued. Scholes concluded, therefore, that the price decline was caused by the adverse connotation associated with the decision to sell, and not the temporary overhang of supply.

He obtained further support for this interpretation by dividing the sellers into various groups. The largest price decline was associated with sales by management (as when Charles Schwab sold large blocks of Bank of America stock shortly before a more devastating decline in share price), the next largest by venture capitalists and by others close to the company, and little, if any, price decline was detected following large-block sales by third-party institutions. Scholes's study showed that the quality of information rather than the quantity of shares traded is what determines the depth of the price discount.

Scholes traced the price decline several months after the offering and found that it persisted, though not in every case, as some shares recovered in value and others fell further. But as a statistical statement, the price decline apparently was in response to some likely fundamental decline in the company's prospective economic performance.

Scholes's research offers convincing and reassuring evidence that stock prices are set by the lead steers' appraisal of intrinsic values (i.e., the prospect for cash generation and risk), and not by supply and demand.[1]

His research findings imply that the objective of investor relations should be to revise expectations rather than to stimulate demand. To increase share price, management must convince the

---

[1]Lest the case be overstated, I add that supply and demand do play a role in determining share values, but only in the aggregate. The intersection of the aggregate demand for capital relative to worldwide supply determines the underlying level of real interest rates and hence, indirectly, the value of all stock markets. But it is only in setting the value of the market as a whole, and not for any single company, that supply and demand operate.

right investors—the lead steers—to pay more, and not simply convince more investors in the herd to buy. It is unfortunate that most of what passes for investor relations is retail as opposed to wholesale in orientation, aims to inform the herd and not the lead steers, and stimulates volume instead of price.

In Conclusion

Earnings, earnings per share, and earnings growth are misleading measures of corporate performance. Earnings are diminished by bookkeeping entries that have nothing to do with recurring cash flow, and are charged with such value-building capital outlays as R&D, all in an attempt to placate lenders' desire to assess liquidation value. EPS at best measures only the quantity of earnings, but the quality of earnings reflected in the P/E multiple matters, too. Rapid earnings growth can be manufactured by pouring capital into substandard projects; earning an adequate rate of return is far more important than growing rapidly.

Many investors are fooled by accounting shenanigans, but the investors who matter are not. Stock prices are not set through a polling technique whereby all investors have an equal vote. They are set rather by a select group of lead steers who look through misleading accounting results to arrive at true values. The rest of the herd, though blissfully ignorant of why the price is right, is well protected by the informed judgments of the lead steers.

The best research on the subject shows that paying dividends does not enhance the total return received by investors over a period of time. But paying dividends may deprive worthwhile projects of capital or may force the company and investors to incur unnecessary transactions costs. And because boards of directors usually are loathe to cut the dividend except in the most dire circumstances, dividends become an additional and unnecessary fixed cost of running the business. Returning excess cash through periodic share repurchases, or a large, one-time, special dividend (with future dividends suspended to support the repayment of debt), is likely to be more rewarding than paying out a stream of dividends over a period of time.

Although it is fashionable to think so, the market is not myopic. The investors who set stock prices take into account the likely payoff from a capital project, no matter how distant, but discount it for the additional investment, risk, and time involved in getting there. On the occasions when a company's stock price responds unfavorably to a new capital project, it probably is not because the market is unable to visualize the eventual payoff. The real reason is that the market predicts that the long-run return will be inadequate, and its judgment will prove to be right more often than not. The record shows conclusively that betting against the market is simply not rewarding.

Stimulating investors' demand for shares will increase share volume, but not share price; it will benefit brokers, but not shareholders. Lead steers head off a stampeding herd of investors by selling shares short or buying puts, thereby providing an artificial supply of shares to siphon off any temporary surge in demand. To increase share price through more effective financial communication, management needs to convince the right investors that the company is worth more, not just persuade more investors to buy the stock.

Despite the impressive evidence assembled in the academic community in support of an economic model of value, many companies still forsake truly rational decisions in deference to an earnings totem. How many senior managers of publicly traded companies, for example, relish the thought of switching to LIFO to save taxes, gladly ignore goodwill amortization when an acquisition is contemplated, and care not a whit about the hit to earnings suffered when capital spending is increased? Not many, I suspect. They have been hypnotized by the cant of the popular press, sell-side security analysts, and many investment bankers and accountants into believing the myth that the market wants earnings, and wants them now. To make matters much worse, their incentive compensation often is tied to near-term earnings and earnings-related measures, so that they cannot afford to let their common sense be their guide.

What is the answer? Senior managers and boards of directors must be educated about how the stock market really works, and their compensation schemes must be changed accordingly.

3

Market Reality

Introduction

In chapter 1, I discussed market myths: popular but mistaken accounts of how share prices are set. In this chapter, I describe market reality: the fundamental but unseen forces that truly determine stock prices. The reality of the stock market is that all managers and all companies are essentially in the same business, the business of putting scarce capital to its most promising uses. To increase their company's stock price, managers must beat their capital competitors. They must earn rates of return on capital that exceed the return offered by other, equally risky companies that also are hungry for funds. If they do, they will add value to the capital placed at their disposal. If they do not, capital will have been misallocated or mismanaged and the company will sell for a stock market value that discounts the sum total of the resources employed. The Chase Manhattan Bank parable illustrates the competition for capital that drives stock prices.

The Chase Manhattan Bank Parable

A decade ago, at a time when I was associated with it, Chase Manhattan Bank paid a 5% rate of interest on savings accounts while Merrill Lynch offered 15% on virtually equally risky money market accounts. It did not take a rocket scientist to figure that 15 was a lot better than 5. Many people stormed into the bank, withdrew their life's savings, and marched down the street to Merrill Lynch. Economists politely labeled this aggressive behavior "disintermediation." In practice, it meant that billions of dollars abandoned the banking system in search of a higher return.

The stock market works in essentially the same way. If the rate of return a company earns is not up to snuff with the return offered by other, equally risky investment alternatives, disintermediation will take place. But this time it will be a disintermediation of value. The tendency of value to flow from low- to high-return companies is expressed by the fundamental principle of valuation:

$$\frac{\text{Corporate return}}{\text{Investors' required return}} = \frac{\text{market value}}{\text{capital}}$$

Or, in symbols:

$$\frac{r}{c^*} = \frac{\text{market value}}{\text{capital}}$$

The principle states that the relation between the rate of return r that a company earns within its businesses and its required return c^* is what drives a company's market value to a premium or discount to the level of its capital employed. (Signifying the cutoff rate or cost of capital, c^* is required by a company's investors because it is a return available to them by investing in other, comparably risky companies.) Before discussing the principle further, it is necessary to define "capital."

Capital

Capital is a measure of all the cash that has been deposited into a company over its life without regard to the financing source, accounting name, or business purpose, much as if the company were just a savings account. It does not matter whether the investment is financed with debt or equity, it does not matter whether it is employed in working capital or in fixed assets. Cash is cash, and the question is how well does management manage it.

Capital employed can be estimated by taking the standard accounting book value for a company's net assets and then grossing it up three ways:

- To convert from accrual to cash accounting (by adding accounting reserves that are formed by recurring, non-cash-bookkeeping provisions such as the deferred tax reserve)
- To convert from the liquidating perspective of lenders to the going-concern perspective of shareholders (as by capitalizing R&D outlays and market-building expenditures)
- To convert from successful-efforts to full-cost accounting (as by adding back cumulative unusual losses, less gains, after taxes)

These adjustments produce a more accurate measure of the capital base upon which a company's rate of return must be earned than is represented by conventional accounting book value. I will illustrate the calculation of capital and rate of return a little later on. For now, let's return to the parable.

The Parable Revisited

Recall that, when Chase offered a 5% return and Merrill Lynch provided 15%, the disparity induced a flow of funds, or disintermediation. By the same token, a company that produces a 5% return on its capital when its capital competitors offer investors the prospect of a 15% rate of return also will be faced with a disintermediation, but this time, a disintermediation of value. For every dollar of capital invested, only 33 cents of the dollar will now appear in the market's valuation of the firm, and value will have been lost:

$$\frac{\text{Corporate return } r}{\text{Investors' required return } c^*} = \frac{\text{market value}}{\text{capital}}$$

$$\frac{5\%}{15\%} = \frac{\$0.33}{\$1.00}$$

Flipping the coin, if Chase had offered to pay a 30% yield on savings accounts (including the monetary value of toasters, microwave ovens, and other such baubles that banks tend to give away) at a time when Merrill offered 15%, the bank would have been overwhelmed with new deposits. In the same way, a company that earns a 30% return within its businesses when its capital competitors offers just 15% will also experience a great infusion, but this time, an infusion of value. For every dollar invested, two dollars will appear in the stock market's valuation of the firm, and value will have been created.

$$\frac{\text{Corporate return } r}{\text{Investors' required return } c^*} = \frac{\text{market value}}{\text{capital}}$$

$$\frac{30\%}{15\%} = \frac{\$2.00}{\$1.00}$$

The message of the Chase parable is that earning an attractive rate of return, one in excess of the cost of capital, is a prerequisite for enhancing its shareholder wealth.

An Illustration

Six factors are needed to fully account for a company's market value (see chapter 5). But two factors—the relation between the rate of return and the cost of capital—are so important that together they often account for a large portion of a company's market value. Consider, for example, the fundamental principle of market valuation for the food processing industry (a group of 34 food companies tracked in the Standard & Poor's Industry Survey) plotted in exhibit 3.1, with supporting data in exhibit 3.2. The horizontal axis plots "rate of return per unit of risk," the ratio of r to c^*; it indicates the fraction or multiple of the cost of capital that each company has earned on average over the past 5 years. (The rate of return is measured on all capital employed after taxes but before non-cash-bookkeeping entries; the cost of capital is the weighted average cost of the debt and equity capital.)

The r to c^* index is graphed against the ratio of actual market value to capital employed. The strong upward-sloping relation indicates that the higher the rate of return in relation to the cost of capital, the greater the premium built into the market value of the shares. Put aside the differences in their lines of business, market shares, advertising effectiveness, and product innovations—none explain the stock prices of these food companies as well or as readily as their relative rates of return per unit of risk. Research performed by Stern Stewart & Co. demonstrates that this relation between corporate returns and required returns accounts for the share price premiums or discounts for countless industry groups worldwide. The reason for this is best expressed by exhibits 3.3 and 3.4: respectively a company's investment opportunity schedule and the market's risk-reward trade-off.

Exhibit 3.1   The Food Processing Industry

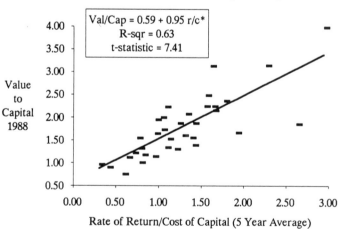

Val/Cap = 0.59 + 0.95 r/c*
R-sqr = 0.63
t-statistic = 7.41

Value to Capital 1988

Rate of Return/Cost of Capital (5 Year Average)

Exhibit 3.2 Rate of Return per Risk in the Food Processing Business
(Dollars in Millions)

		(1)=(2)/(3)	(2)	(3)	(4)=(5)/(6)	(5)	(6)
		1-5 Year Average			Value/ Capital	Value	Capital
	Company	r/c*	r	c*	1988	1988	1988
1	Kellogg Co	2.94x	34.9%	11.9%	3.98x	$8,064.4	$2,026.3
2	Tyson Foods Inc	2.62	25.1	9.6	1.86	1,306.3	703.5
3	Lance Inc	2.26	28.7	12.7	3.14	575.1	183.0
4	ConAgra Inc	1.91	20.0	10.5	1.66	2,945.2	1,769.9
5	General Mills Inc	1.77	18.9	10.7	2.36	4,953.7	2,097.7
6	Dean Foods Co	1.64	20.2	12.3	2.15	843.2	391.8
7	H.J. Heinz Co	1.63	19.8	12.2	2.24	6,947.6	3,096.3
8	J.M. Smucker Co	1.61	22.4	14.0	3.13	407.6	130.2
9	Ralston Purina Co	1.55	16.2	10.4	2.48	7,160.0	2,889.6
10	Flowers Industries Inc	1.54	16.7	10.9	2.24	784.3	349.8
11	Holly Farms Corp	1.41	16.6	11.8	1.87	1,100.8	588.6
12	Pioneer Hi-Bred Intl	1.40	16.8	12.0	1.39	1,142.6	824.4
13	Hershey Foods Corp	1.38	16.7	12.1	1.55	2,631.1	1,697.0
14	Quaker Oats Co	1.32	15.4	11.7	2.07	4,933.2	2,379.7
15	Campbell Soup Co	1.28	15.6	12.2	1.60	4,568.4	2,850.5
16	Sara Lee Corp	1.22	14.5	11.8	1.87	6,006.5	3,218.4
17	Savannah Foods & Inds	1.19	11.9	10.0	1.30	317.7	244.7
18	McCormick & Co	1.11	13.2	11.9	1.52	865.6	568.9
19	Smithfield Foods Inc	1.08	10.9	10.1	1.34	202.3	151.5
20	Gerber Products Co	1.07	13.5	12.6	2.23	1,337.4	600.8
21	Hormel & Co	1.03	13.0	12.5	1.73	835.3	483.4
22	CPC International Inc	1.03	12.4	12.1	1.99	5,164.2	2,592.0
23	Universal Foods Corp	0.96	11.4	11.9	1.95	687.4	352.9
24	Borden Inc	0.95	11.1	11.6	1.64	5,796.0	3,534.3
25	Curtice-Burns Food	0.93	8.6	9.2	1.14	353.1	310.9
26	Archer-Daniels-Midland	0.81	11.8	14.6	1.17	3,735.3	3,192.0
27	Intl Multifoods Corp	0.78	8.2	10.6	1.00	586.4	583.9
28	Pilgrims Pride Corp	0.77	7.3	9.5	1.31	280.9	214.7
29	Castle & Cooke Inc	0.75	8.1	10.8	1.54	2,483.8	1,608.1
30	IBP Inc	0.70	8.9	12.8	1.21	1,017.2	840.5
31	United Brands	0.63	7.5	12.0	1.12	1,320.8	1,182.7
32	American Maize	0.58	6.9	11.9	0.75	290.2	386.0
33	Dekalb Genetics Corp	0.41	5.4	13.2	0.89	176.8	198.0
34	Thorn Apple Valley Inc	0.31	3.1	10.1	0.96	70.1	73.2

Value in 1988 is market value of equity plus book value of net liabilities.
Capital is 1988 net operating assets (adjusted).
Average r's and c*'s are the arithmetic averages over 5 years (or years for which data is available).

The Investment Opportunity Schedule

In exhibit 3.3 a company's potential new capital investment projects are ranked according to their prospective rates of return. Investment I comprises the additional funds that might be committed to build up working capital and acquire new long-term assets organized into projects (or strategies, if you prefer a grander aggregation). The rate of return r on the proposed investments is measured in relevant cash flow terms along lines I will describe a little later. The downward-sloping schedule indicates that the most attractive investment opportunities are taken first and the least attractive ones last.

Assuming that all projects entail roughly the same risk, there is a single rate c^* beneath which new projects should not be accepted. As a cutoff rate or cost of capital, c^* is not a cash cost. Rather, it is an opportunity cost that is equal to the rate of return investors could expect to earn by investing in the stocks and bonds of other companies of comparable risk. Management should reject projects providing a return less than c^* because the company's investors could do better elsewhere.

Exhibit 3.3 The Investment Opportunity Schedule

Rate of Return (r)

Cost of Capital (c*)

Prospective Investment (I)

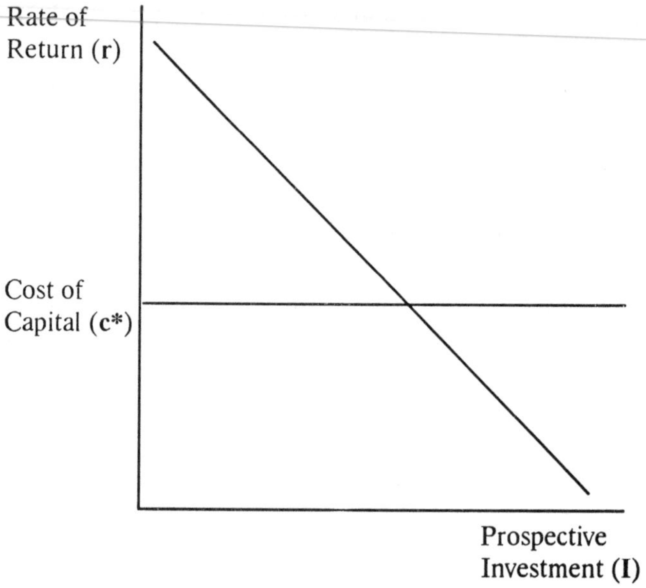

c^* also represents the rate of return that some other company, quite possibly outside the company's industry or home country, is capable of earning on a new investment in its business. For if not one company anywhere could invest funds to cover its cost of capital, investors would be forced to accept a lower return if they still wanted to invest. Interest rates in general would have to fall to the point at which some company somewhere would be able to earn at least its cost of capital. Thus, c^* is an opportunity cost in a second way: It is the rate of return that some alternative, or marginal, project also up for consideration promises to earn. To be acceptable, any one project must beat the return offered by that hypothetical alternative project in order for the world at large to be better off.

Accepting a project likely to earn an r less than c^* now has an even more important consequence than merely eroding shareholders' wealth. It also means that capital is misallocated, the greatest sin to which corporate management can fall prey. When capital is misallocated, whether intentionally or not, it is taken away from an even more worthwhile investment project. Economic growth and the standard of living will suffer worldwide. The objective of maximizing value is justifiable mainly on the ground that it promotes the greatest good for the greatest number of people and not just shareholders.

No matter which interpretation you prefer, cost of capital can be used to divide projects and, in the aggregate, companies, industries, and even countries, into three categories:

Group 1 Projects return more than the cost of capital. Because management can earn a greater return by investing capital inside the company than investors could by investing in the market, value is created. The common shares of group 1 companies sell at high P/E ratios and at premiums to their economic book values (a measure of the true cash invested and at risk in the business).

Group 2 Projects break even in economic terms. The return earned just covers the cost of capital, so that no value is created over and above the capital invested. The common shares of group 2 companies sell at modest P/Es and at their economic book values.

Group 3   Projects, a favorite of many large, mature companies with cash to burn, return less than their cost of capital. Because the return earned on the capital invested within the company is less than investors could earn elsewhere, an economic, or opportunity, loss is suffered and value is destroyed. The common shares of group 3 companies sell at low P/Es and beneath their economic book values.

There is a biological analogy. Group 1 projects add muscle; a company grows in size and strength. Group 2 projects add fat; a company gets bigger but not better. Group 3 projects are tumorous; they sap the strength of the corporate body.

Incidentally, there is no guarantee that a group 3 company will go bankrupt. A company could in theory go on forever earning a rate of return that, though short of recovering the full cost of capital, is sufficient to cover the after-tax cost of whatever money it borrows. With positive accounting earnings, this unfortunate company could continue to invest, grow earnings per share, and seemingly prosper all the while, when in reality it destroys value with each additional breath that it takes. Culling the herd of such capital misallocators was one of the useful functions served by the corporate raiders in the 1980s.

The Risk-Reward Trade-off

Exhibit 3.4 shows the relationship between the risk investors bear and the expected rewards. The reward for investing is the total rate of return obtained through a combination of cash yield and cash-equivalent price appreciation. Risk is the variability or uncertainty in the prospective return. Even when they take no risk, investors can still expect to earn some return just because there is a time value to money. At any moment such a risk-free rate of return R_f is indicated by the prevailing yield on U.S. government bonds. If held to maturity, U.S. government bonds guarantee investors a nominal return without subjecting their principal to a risk of default. Risk-free government bonds generally provide

Exhibit 3.4   The Risk-Reward Tradeoff

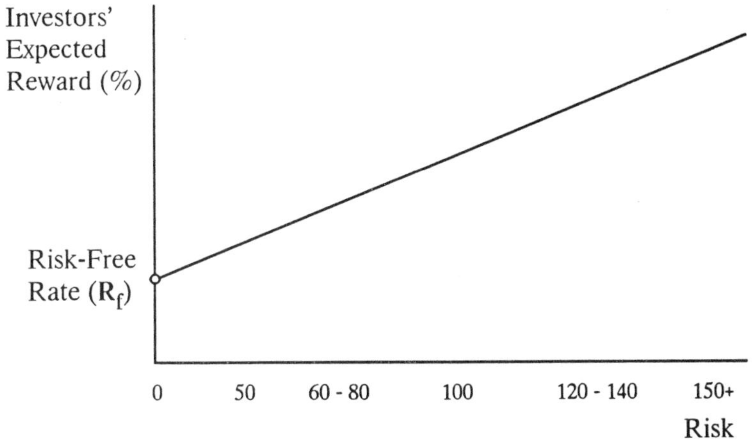

about a 3% real rate of return plus a premium to offset the expected rate of inflation.

To move beyond such riskless bonds, 100 can be used as an index to represent the degree of risk entailed in holding a broad common stock portfolio such as the S&P 500. That way, the risk of all individual equity investments can be positioned on a risk map that progresses from left to right. For example, it is around a risk score of 50 that public utilities tend to cluster. They are regulated to earn steady rates of return, and as a result, their common shares are only about half as risky as the average common stock investment.

Food companies tend to plot between 60 and 80 on the risk map, with food wholesalers such as SuperValu around 60 and food processors such as General Mills and Quaker Oats that take trademark risk closer to 80. In general, however, food stocks are less risky than the market because people tend to eat quite regularly. Around 100 are the consumer products giants such as Proctor & Gamble and Johnson & Johnson. It seems anything that people put in their mouths or wipe with anywhere plots around there. 120 to 140 is the domain of the cyclical stocks—the steel, cement, aluminum, automotive, chemical, textile, machine tool, and tire and rubber companies, for example.

From 150 on up are the airlines, hotel and motel chains, and construction, leisure time and photographic companies—businesses in which many of the costs are fixed and revenues are strongly tied to the economy, making profits highly dependent on the stage of the business cycle. The risk score can be as high as 200 to 300 for companies developing new technologies but without current products to sell and for firms in or near bankruptcy much like Chrysler in the early 80s—firms whose stocks behave more like options.

The upward slope of the line stretching beyond the risk-free yield indicates that, because they bear more risk, investors *ought* to expect to earn a greater return. I emphasize the word "ought" because, without the prospect of earning a greater reward, who would bother to buy riskier stocks? One of the greatest achievements in all financial academic research has been to prove that such a risk-reward trade-off does in fact exist in the stock market.

Comprehensive studies of actual share price data stretching back to 1925 show that in diversified portfolios of stocks (where forecasting errors cancel) and over sufficiently long periods of time (long enough for the long-term upward trend in the stock market to dominate its inherent near-term variability), investors have indeed been rewarded linearly for bearing additional risk. Risk and reward do in fact go hand-in-hand.[1]

A Casino in Reverse.   The risk-reward trade-off study shows that the stock market works much like a gambling casino, although just in reverse. A casino loses many individual bets, but it always wins more than it loses because it establishes the odds in its favor, places many bets, and is in the game for the long haul. The risk in buying the common shares of casino operators is not knowing how many people will walk through their front doors, and not what happens on their gaming tables.

A casual observer who is unaware of that may be tempted to think casinos are exciting because some gamblers enjoy exhilarating winning streaks while others lose fortunes. Observing the anguish and ecstasy of gamblers in a casino may be fun, but it diverts attention from the central fact: The casino always wins

[1]Fischer Black, Michael Jensen, and Myron Scholes, "The Capital Asset Pricing Model: Some Empirical Tests," *Studies in the Theory of Capital Markets* (New York: Praeger Publishers, 1972), 79–124.

and the gamblers always lose. There is no real excitement in a casino, just a predictable transfer of wealth.

The stock market works much like a casino but with one important difference. This time the gamblers win. The odds favor investors to win appropriate returns because the entry price on common shares is set at a level that discounts the value of likely future cash flows. Although individual stocks do over- and underperform investors' expectations, investing in a broad portfolio of stocks essentially guarantees that a return will be earned *over the long haul* to compensate for the degree of risk borne over the short term.

The Patience Premium. Now I know that you are thinking this sounds too easy. If investors are always rewarded for bearing additional risk, as indeed the evidence shows is the case, why wouldn't everyone invest in common stocks instead of bonds, and risky common stocks at that, and earn higher returns?

The reason is that an investor in stocks must often wait longer to earn a return that is higher than that provided by bonds, like as much as about 20 years longer, and the riskier the investment the longer the wait is likely to be. The return for risk really is a premium for patience.

With that in mind, The Vanguard Group of Valley Forge, Pennsylvania, rightly admonishes investors to "Take stock of time when investing in stocks." To support its case, Vanguard computed rates of return provided by an investment in the S&P 500 over the period from 1950 to 1980. As portrayed in exhibit 3.5 research shows that the return from common stocks was highly variable and uncertain over single-year intervals. The highest return garnered from the market in any one year was a positive 52.3% and the lowest was a negative 26.3%. But once the time horizon for investing was stretched out to even just 5 years, a remarkable central tendency began to appear. The cumulative return began to converge in accordance with a statistical phenomenon known as a regression toward the mean.

Notice that the highest cumulative annual return over 5 years was a positive 20.1%, whereas the lowest was only a negative 2.4%. In fact, the data show that extending the time horizon to 15 or 20 years leaves little risk to investing in the

Exhibit 3.5   Regression toward the Mean

Range of Annual Return on Common Stocks
for Various Time Period 1951-81

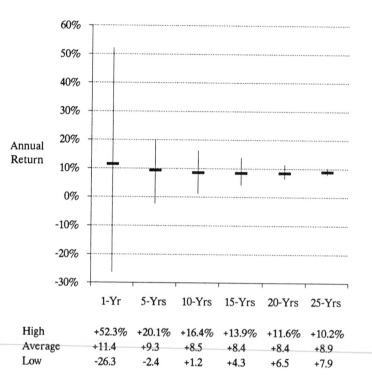

	1-Yr	5-Yrs	10-Yrs	15-Yrs	20-Yrs	25-Yrs
High	+52.3%	+20.1%	+16.4%	+13.9%	+11.6%	+10.2%
Average	+11.4	+9.3	+8.5	+8.4	+8.4	+8.9
Low	-26.3	-2.4	+1.2	+4.3	+6.5	+7.9

Source: The Vanguard Group of Investment Companies.

stock market. There is only the return sought by investors to compensate for risk. The Vanguard Group concludes: "Over the long haul, annual market swings tend to cancel each other out, making common stock investing prudent for even the cautious investor."

The risk-reward trade-off can now be presented in another way. Invest in "risk-free" bonds, and the result will be a steady if unexceptional return over a period of time (as represented by the R_f line in exhibit 3.6). Invest in common stocks, and over the short term there is a great uncertainty over the potential return, but over the long run the return will narrow to the reward that investors expect in order to compensate them for risk.

Exhibit 3.6 The Patience Premium

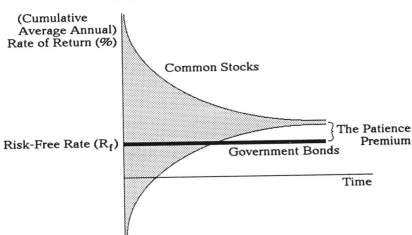

The Market Is a Fair Game. The importance of the risk-reward trade-off can hardly be overstated. For one thing, it is one more bit of evidence that the market is dominated by sophisticated, lead-steer investors. The "average" investor in the market would be incapable of doing so, but lead steers are able to set stock prices in such a way that all investors get what they bargained for: a portfolio return that fairly compensates them for the risk that they take. The fact that the market is a fair game over the long haul may be the strongest evidence to prove that it is run by "sophisticated" investors.

The Definitive Evidence. But the risk-reward test makes an even stronger statement than that. It proves that share prices are the result of discounting projected cash flows. I will state that one more time in case you missed it: *The risk-reward trade-off is proof that share prices are set by discounting cash flows, and not by capitalizing earnings.*

The observed risk-return trade-off falls right out of the mechanics of projecting and discounting cash flow to a present value. For the greater the risk in the future cash flows, the higher the rate used to discount them to a present value, the lower the current stock price becomes, and thus the higher the return for investors as the company's cash flows subsequently unfold and are paid out. Discounting cash flows is the only valuation procedure that can account for the fact that investment risk is rewarded with a higher cash return over a period of time and therefore *must* be the basis by which share prices are set.

Having never noticed a trading halt in a stock as market makers quickly recompute cash flow forecasts, you may be excused for being skeptical about this evidence. However, whether or not lead steers, to say nothing of the investing public at large, literally discount cash flows is unimportant. What is important is that the risk-reward test demonstrates conclusively that share prices behave *as if* all investors employed a discounted cash flow approach.

It is like suggesting to Minnesota Fats, the famous pool player, that he is a brilliant physicist. He might protest that he could hardly be considered such, having failed to graduate from high school. Nevertheless, to sink a pool ball in the pocket, Mr. Fats must put the right momentum and spin on the ball and properly calculate the angles of incidence and reflection. Minnesota again demurs, claiming that it is only his instinct for the game gained through years and years of practical experience that enables him to sink pool balls so reliably in the pockets. Although he is right in what he says, it is still true that his pool play can be modeled by a few simple laws of physics discovered by Sir Isaac Newton. Moreover, every time he sinks the ball in the pocket it is only because his instinct for the shot conformed to the laws of nature. So he really is a fabulous applied physicist.[2]

Its just the same in the stock market. Lead-steer investors, with their years of experience and sound business instincts, reach conclusions about value that are consistent with discounting projected cash flows, even though most do not explicitly employ such a technique, nor would many of them recognize it if they saw it.

The Cost of Capital Unveiled.   The final important application of the risk-return trade-off is to estimate the required return for creating value. By measuring where a company (or project) plots along the risk map (going from left to right) and drawing

[2]Adapted from an example in Milton Friedman, *Essays in Positive Economics* (Chicago: University of Chicago Press, 1966).

a line northward and westward along the risk-reward trade-off, we get an intersection that is the cost of capital c^* (exhibit 3.7). It is equal to the return investors could expect to earn by buying a portfolio of companies of similar risk; in short, it is the return offered by a firm's capital competitors.

Exhibit 3.7 The Foundations of the Economic Model of Value

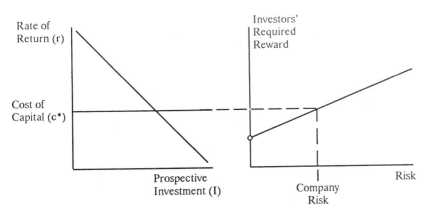

An interaction between two simple diagrams—one portraying the menu of investment opportunities available within a single company and the other showing the returns available to investors in the capital market relative to risk—is what truly drives stock prices. For readers who seek the assurance of academic support for my intuitively obvious propositions, I offer the two diagrams in exhibit 3.7 as the intellectual and empirical underpinnings for the Chase Manhattan parable (i.e., the tendency of value to flow from low- to high-return companies).

A Practical Digression: How to Measure the Rate of Return

(High-level general-manager types can skip this section without much loss of continuity; on the other hand, it is required reading for all accountants, please.)

The Chase parable, by illustrating the critical importance of earning an attractive rate of return, raises this question: What is the best way to measure a company's rate of return?

ROE Is Not All It's Cracked Up to Be

One candidate that may leap immediately to mind is the standard accounting return on common equity, which is computed by dividing bottom-line net income available to the common stockholders by bottom-line accounting equity capital:

$$\text{ROE} = \frac{\text{Income Available to Common}}{\text{Common Equity}}$$

Although it has the virtues of being easy to compute and being widely understood, ROE suffers from such severe distortions that I strongly recommend against using it.

Accounting Distortions. For one thing, ROE is based upon the same accounting earnings I roundly criticized in chapter 2. Reported accounting earnings are distorted by, among other things, the choice of LIFO or FIFO for inventory costing and purchase or pooling for acquisitions, the expensing of R&D, the use of successful efforts instead of full cost to account for risky investments, and accrual bookkeeping entries that bury in reserves the cash flows a company recurringly generates from its operations.

Financing Distortions. Another problem is that ROE reacts to changes in the mix of debt and equity that a company employs and in the rate of interest it pays on its debts. That makes it difficult to tell whether ROE rises or falls for operating or financial reasons. With ROE as its goal, management may be tempted to accept truly substandard projects that happen to be financed with debt and pass by very good ones if they must be financed with equity.

An Explosive Concoction

The Liquigas fallacy illustrates why a mixture of operating and financing decisions is an explosive concoction. As reported in a now famous Harvard Business School case, in one year the management of Liquigas would employ debt to finance the company's expansion and, accordingly, required all projects to return more than just the after-tax cost of borrowing funds. The logic for the decision-making criteria was that all such projects would increase EPS and ROE. Not surprisingly, many low-return projects were accepted in those years. By the next year, the company had become so highly leveraged that management was forced to raise equity. All projects up for review were required to cover the full cost of equity (once again to prevent dilution in EPS and ROE), which made it difficult for even very attractive projects to pass muster.

The moral of the Liquigas fallacy is not to associate sources with the uses of funds. Such association distorts the desirability of undertaking a project by mixing operating and financing decisions. Instead, all projects should be thought of as being financed with a target blend of debt and equity no matter how they might specifically be financed. That way, each investment stands or falls on its own merits.

To be consistent with this commendable capital budgeting procedure, subsequent performance should be measured and evaluated in a manner that clearly distinguishes operating and financing decisions. Unfortunately, comparing the rate of return on equity against the cost of equity does not (or at least, does not without great difficulty). Comparing the rate of return on total capital with the weighted average cost of debt and equity capital does.

The Rate of Return on Total Capital

In place of ROE, the rate of return on total capital is the return that should be used to assess corporate performance. Computed by dividing a firm's net operating profits after taxes (NOPAT) by the total capital employed in operations, it is a savings account equivalent, after-tax, cash-on-cash yield earned in the business. It measures the productivity of capital employed without regard to the method of financing, and it is free from accounting distortions that arise from accrual bookkeeping entries, from the conservative bias of accounting statements, and from the tendency to understate capital by writing off unsuccessful efforts. It may be compared directly to the company's overall cost of capital to indicate whether value is being created or destroyed.

$$r = \frac{NOPAT}{capital}$$

Capital is the sum of all cash that has been invested in a company's net assets over its life and without regard to financing form, accounting name, or business purpose—much as if the company were a savings account. NOPAT is the profits derived from the company's operations after taxes but before financing costs and non-cash-bookkeeping entries. As such, NOPAT also is the total pool of profits available to provide a cash return to all financial providers of capital to the firm.

The one non-cash charge that is subtracted from NOPAT is depreciation. Indeed, the "net" in NOPAT stands for "net of depreciation." Depreciation is subtracted because it is a true economic expense. The assets consumed in the business must be replenished before investors achieve a return on their investment. Another way to see this is to observe that a company, when it leases assets, must pay a rent that covers the depreciation the lessor suffers on the lessee's behalf (plus interest). Thus, the economic charge of depreciation does have a cash-equivalent cost. To be consistent with NOPAT, capital is charged with the accumulated depreciation suffered by the assets.

The rate of return on capital may be computed from either a financing or an operating perspective. The financing perspective, because it builds up to the rate of return on capital from the standard return on equity, is the most intuitive place to start.

The Rate of Return from a *Financing* Perspective

Step 1: Deleverage the Rate of Return. The first adjustment to the standard ROE formula removes the effect of gearing up the capital structure with debt. To do so, add all interest-bearing debt (and the present value of noncapitalized leases[3]) to common equity and the interest expense on the debt (including the imputed interest in rents) to bottom-line accounting profits:

$$r = \frac{\text{NOPAT}}{\text{capital}}$$

where   NOPAT
          = Income available to common
          + Interest expense after taxes

Capital
= Common equity
+ Debt

When interest expense, net of the taxes saved by deducting it, is backed out of bottom-line profits, the result is the earnings that would have been reported had all of the company's capital requirements been financed solely with common equity. Thus, the NOPAT return on capital is what the return on equity would be assuming that only common equity financing had been employed. It is a return purged of the consequences of financial leverage.

This does not mean that leverage is unimportant for assessing performance. Debt does shelter operating profits from being fully taxes. This benefit, however, is incorporated into c^*, the weighted average cost of capital, but by assuming that a target capital structure, not each year's actual financing proportions, is employed. That way, the temptation to improperly associate sources and uses of funds is avoided, but at the same time the tax benefit of debt is properly taken into account. (This is brought out more fully in chapter 7, on valuation.)

To illustrate this important principle, suppose that a company

---

[3]Although some leases need not be capitalized for accounting purposes, so long as management intends to employ a leased asset in the business on a relatively permanent basis, the lease should be capitalized and treated as a debt and asset equivalent.

has $10,000 of capital, all equity-financed, and that it produces $1,000 of bottom-line profits (exhibit 3.8). Without any leverage, the $1,000 of bottom-line profits is also NOPAT, and the rates of return on equity and total capital are the same, in this case 10%.

Exhibit 3.8   All Equity-Financed

	All Equity
Sales	$16,667
Operating expenses	15,000
Net operating profit	$ 1,667
Interest expense	0
Net profit before taxes	$ 1,667
Taxes @ 40%	667
Net profit after taxes (NPAT)	$ 1,000
Debt	0
Equity	$10,000
Capital	$10,000
NPAT	$ 1,000
Equity	$10,000
ROE	10.0%
NPAT	$ 1,000
Interest expense	0
(Taxes saved)	0
NOPAT	$ 1,000
Capital	$10,000
r	10%

Now suppose the company borrows $5,000 at 6% (thereby incurring a $300 annual interest charge) to retire common equity (exhibit 3.9). No longer are bottom-line profits equal to NOPAT, and no longer is the return on equity equal to the return on the capital employed in the business. To compute NOPAT, the $820 of bottom-line accounting profits is increased by the interest expense of $300, net of the $120 in taxes saved by deducting it.[4]

---

[4]Note that the corporate income tax decreased from $667 to $547, a difference explained by multiplying the $300 interest expense by the 40% marginal income tax rate. In the

Exhibit 3.9 Debt- and Equity-Financed

	All Equity	$5,000 Debt
Sales	$16,667	$16,667
Operating expenses	15,000	15,000
Net operating profit	$ 1,667	$ 1,667
Interest expense	0	300
Net profit before taxes	$ 1,667	$ 1,367
Taxes @ 40%	667	547
Net profit after taxes	$ 1,000	$ 820
Debt	0	$ 5,000
Equity	$10,000	$ 5,000
Capital	$10,000	$10,000
NPAT	$ 1,000	$ 820
Equity	$10,000	$ 5,000
ROE	10.0%	16.4 %
NPAT	$ 1,000	$ 820
Interest expense	0	300
(Taxes saved)	0	(120)
NOPAT	$ 1,000	$ 1,000
Capital	$10,000	$10,000
r	10%	10 %

Despite the leverage, the underlying NOPAT profits remain unchanged, as does the NOPAT return on capital. The return on equity is another matter. It has increased profoundly even though the company's underlying operating performance has not changed.

The example illustrates that the NOPAT to capital rate of return, unlike the ROE, is completely unaffected by a change in the mix of debt and equity a company chooses to employ. What matters is simply the productivity of capital employed in the business, no matter the financial form in which the capital has been obtained. Moreover, with after-tax interest on the debts added to profits, the return is insulated from changes in the level of interest rates too (although such changes will affect the cost of

economic model, the benefit of not paying this tax shows up as a reduction in the overall cost of capital, not as an addition to NOPAT.

capital). Because the effect of financial structure is entirely eliminated, this rate of return is a much clearer measure of operating
performance than the standard return on equity, and it is one that
can justifiably be compared year by year for an individual company and among companies in the same year. Projects, including
acquisitions, that happen to be financed with debt will look no
better with this return as a performance measure, nor will those
financed with equity appear any worse.

Step 2: Eliminate Other Financing Distortions. The next
step to improve the rate of return is to eliminate other financing
distortions. This is accomplished by adding the equity provided
by preferred stockholders and minority investors to capital and
by bringing the income diverted to these equity sources back into
NOPAT:

$$r = \frac{\text{NOPAT}}{\text{capital}}$$

where   NOPAT

    = Income available to common

    + Preferred dividend

    + Minority interest provision

    + Interest expense after taxes

Capital

    = Common equity

    + Preferred stock

    + Minority interest

    + All debt

Observe that, for every component of capital, there is corresponding entry in the calculation of NOPAT. NOPAT is the sum
of the returns attributable to all the providers of funds to the
company. In this way the NOPAT return is completely unaffected by the financial composition of capital.

Step 3: Eliminate Accounting Distortions. The next, and
final, step is to eliminate accounting distortions from the rate of
return by adding equity equivalent reserves to capital and the
periodic change in such reserves to NOPAT.

$$r = \frac{\text{NOPAT}}{\text{capital}}$$

where   NOPAT   Capital

NOPAT	Capital
= Income available to common	= Common equity
+ Increase in equity equivalents	+ Equity equivalents
Adjusted net income	Adjusted common equity
+ Preferred dividend	+ Preferred stock
+ Minority interest provision	+ Minority interest
+ Interest expense after tax	+ All debt

Equity equivalents (EEs) gross up the standard accounting book value into something I call economic book value, which is a truer measure of the cash that investors have put at risk in the firm and upon which they expect their returns to accrue. Furthermore, it is a standard better than conventional book value for judging a company's market valuation. Only if its stock market value exceeds the economic book value of its common equity (which includes the equity equivalent reserves) is a company truly adding value to the funds shareholders have placed at its disposal.

EEs eliminate accounting distortions by converting from accrual to cash accounting, from a pessimistic lenders' to a realistic shareholders' perspective, and from successful-efforts to full-cost accounting. EEs add back to capital such items as the deferred income tax reserve, the LIFO inventory valuation reserve, the cumulative amortization of goodwill, a capitalization of R&D and other market-building outlays, and cumulative unusual write-offs (less gains) after taxes. (See the appendix to this chapter for a more complete description.) Bringing these items into capital by no means guarantees that they will be included in the company's market value, however. Only if an adequate return is subsequently earned on them will they carry over into stock market value, a question that no balance sheet (or single-period rate of return, for that matter) can ever answer.

In addition to correcting the balance sheet, EEs serve to eliminate the ways in which accountants distort the measurement of a firm's true economic profits. Adding the change in EEs to reported earnings brings back into NOPAT the recurring cash flows and value buildups that the accountants have left to accumulate elsewhere. With the add-backs, NOPAT records the actual timing of cash receipts and disbursements, includes economic holding gains, is normalized to exclude nonrecurring gains and losses, and dodges an unrealistic immediate charge-off of such value-building outlays as R&D and up-front market development expenditures.

By adjusting capital and NOPAT for equity equivalents in the manner I have prescribed, the rate of return is made an even more accurate indication of the true yield actually being earned in the business—an important advantage. At some point a trade-off exists between achieving a more accurate return and additional complexity. Just how far to go is a decision that deserves careful consideration.

I confess that I do not expect these recommendations to be adopted by the Financial Accounting Standards Board anytime soon. Rather, I would like to think that corporate managers will adopt them (as modified for their particular circumstances) for the purpose of internal performance assessment and goal setting, competitor analysis, acquisition screening, communicating with lead steers, and as the basis for determining bonus awards. But as for influencing financial book reporting, it probably will not happen. The accountants are too much the slaves of the bankers and too much the captives of their own professional cynicism.

The Rate of Return from an Operating Perspective

Reflecting the great duality in the universe (to say nothing of the miracle of double-entry bookkeeping), there is another, entirely equivalent way to compute the rate of return on capital. From an operating perspective, capital can be defined as net working capital (NWC) plus net fixed assets (NFA). Net working capital, in turn, is current assets net of NIBCLS (pronounced "nib ik culs," they are little Stephen Spielberg creatures that cover your floor in the dark of night and eat the socks you are missing). Actually, NIBCLS stands, boringly, for non-interest-bearing current liabilities, which are accounts such as accounts payable and accrued expenses, that arise as spontaneous sources of financing in the natural course of business and which offset the need to raise permanent capital. The rationale for excluding them from capital is that the financing costs associated with paying suppliers and employees with some delay are incorporated in the cost of goods sold, and nothing is to be gained by extracting them from earnings. Net fixed assets consist of net property, plant and equipment, goodwill, and other long-term capital necessary to run the business.

To obtain the same measure of capital as the financing approach produces, adjustments must be made to assets for certain equity equivalent reserves (e.g., by adding the LIFO reserve to inventories, the bad-debt reserve to receivables, the cumulative amortization of goodwill to goodwill, and the balance of capitalized intangibles to net fixed assets, and so on). Moreover, if the present value of noncapitalized leases is treated as a debt equivalent, it must also be considered the equivalent of a net fixed asset.

From an operating perspective, NOPAT is, quite literally, net operating profits after taxes. Start with sales as a proxy for operating cash receipts and then subtract, first, recurring cash economic operating expenses, including depreciation. That leaves net operating profits, or trading profits, as Europeans prefer to say. Next, take away taxes, but the taxes payable in cash on the net operating profits. Such "cash operating taxes" can be approximated by taking the accounting provision for taxes, subtracting the deferred taxes that were not paid, and then grossing up for the additional taxes that would have been paid had interest expense not sheltered operating profits from being fully taxed. NOPAT is what's left.

$$r = \frac{\text{NOPAT}}{\text{capital}}$$

where   NOPAT   Capital
             = Sales   = Net working capital
             − Operating expenses   + Net fixed assets
             − Taxes

The Great Equivalence

There is a sequence of events that ties together the operating and financing approaches (see exhibit 3.10). First, a company raises a mix of debt and equity [capital defined from the financing perspective (1)] and then invests those funds in its business [in net working capital and net fixed assets comprising capital viewed from an operating perspective (2)]. Next, the business begins to generate sales and incur genuine operating expenses and taxes [resulting in NOPAT from the operating side (3)], which, in turn, constitutes a pool of cash that is available for distribution to all financiers (4). That is, it is available to provide cash returns (after taxes) to the prior-claim financiers (lenders, minority investors, and preferred stockholders) to be buried in some accounting reserve or to accrue as bottom-line accounting profits whose meaning is quite obscure to me. The point, though, is that what the business earns on the one hand must be the total cash available to reward

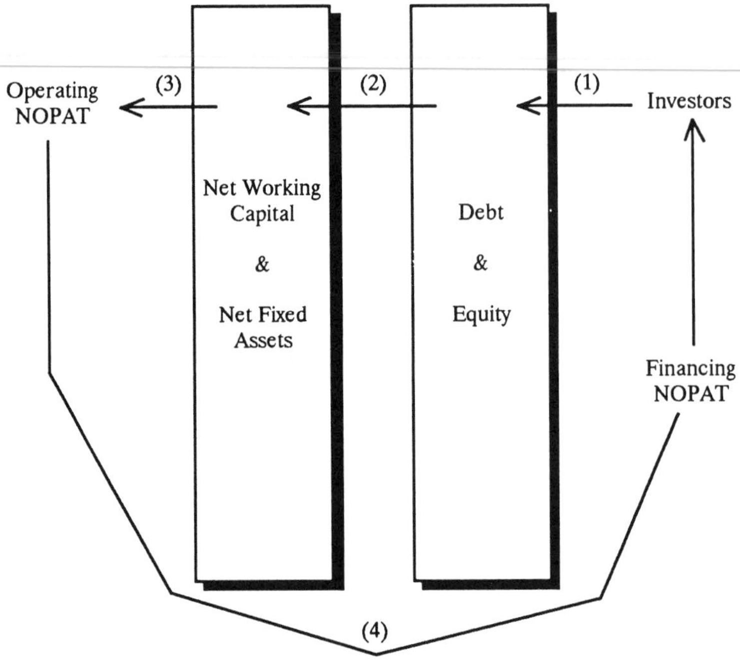

Exhibit 3.10   The Equivalence of Operations and Finance

investors on the other. The equivalence, true by definition because sources and uses of cash must balance, is the reason why the value of all investors' claims can be determined by discounting NOPAT, a topic we take up in chapter 7.

Once operations are separated from finance in this way, a powerful message is delivered: If management can be successful at managing the business, the investors in the business will be well taken care of.

A Calculation of NOPAT and Capital for Wal-Mart

The calculations of NOPAT and capital will be illustrated for Wal-Mart, the discount retailer.

The Accounting Presentation

The conventional accounting balance sheet for Wal-Mart at year-end 1987 and 1988 (FYE January 31, the following year) is presented in exhibit 3.11, and the income statement for the year 1988 appears in exhibit 3.12. Both exhibits deserve your close scrutiny. Of course, all of the really useful information is buried in the footnotes to the financial statements. The footnotes are where the equity equivalent reserves are to be found, as the following excerpts from Wal-Mart's annual report (FYE January 31, 1989) illustrate.

Find It in the Footnotes

Footnote 1 Inventories are stated principally at cost (last-in, first-out), which is not in excess of market. *Conclusion: The LIFO reserve should be added back to inventories and to common equity, and the change taken into profits.*

Footnote 2 Replacement cost for inventories would be $291,-329,000 greater in 1988 and $202,796,000 greater in 1987. *Conclusion: Here is the LIFO reserve to add to capital. Furthermore, the $88,533,000 increase in LIFO reserve ($291,329,000 less $202,796,000) will add to income and reduce the cost of goods sold.*

Exhibit 3.11 Wal-Mart Stores
Balance Sheet

January 31 ($ in thousands)	1987	1988
ASSETS		
Operating Cash	$ 11,325	$ 12,553
Net Accts Receivable	222,845	241,291
Net Inventory	2,651,760	3,351,366
Other Current Assets	19,214	25,776
Total Current Assets	2,905,144	3,630,986
Land	209,211	278,054
Plant & Equipment	2,475,554	3,113,363
Gross Property Plant & Equipment	2,684,765	3,391,417
Accumulated Depreciation	(539,914)	(729,464)
Net Property Plant & Equipment	2,144,851	2,661,953
Goodwill	47,034	41,036
Other Assets	34,775	25,689
Total Assets	$ 5,131,804	$ 6,359,664
	===========	===========
LIABILITIES & NET WORTH		
Short-Term Debt	$ 104,382	$ 19,000
Current Portion LTD	18,544	21,349
Accounts Payable	1,099,958	1,389,726
Accrued Expenses	400,103	514,672
Income Taxes Payable	120,773	121,158
Total Current Liabilities	1,743,760	2,065,905
Senior Long-Term Debt	185,672	184,439
Capitalized Lease Obligations	866,972	1,009,046
Total Liabilities	2,796,404	3,259,390
Deferred Income Taxes	78,135	92,365
Common Stock	56,511	56,559
Addtl Paid in Capital	170,439	174,278
Retained Earnings	2,030,315	2,777,072
Common Equity	$ 2,257,265	$ 3,007,909
Total Liabilities & Net Worth	$ 5,131,804	$ 6,359,664
	===========	===========

Exhibit 3.12   Wal-Mart Stores
Income Statement

Feb-Jan ($ in thousands)	1988
Net Sales	$ 20,649,004
Cost of Goods Sold	15,843,203
Depreciation	207,631
Gross Profit	4,598,170
Selling Gen & Admin	3,267,863
Goodwill Amortization	5,998
Net Operating Profit	1,324,309
Interest Expense	135,681
Other Income	(136,840)
Income Before Taxes	1,325,468
Income Tax Provision	488,246
Income Avail to Common	$ 837,222

Footnote 4 Deferred tax expense results from timing differences in the recognition of revenue and expense for tax and financial reporting purposes with respect to the following:

Depreciation	$30,632,000
Capital leases	(7,741,000)
Other	(8,661,000)
Total	$14,230,000

Conclusion: Because Wal-Mart's deferred income tax arises from ongoing timing differences that are related to its business (the deferred income tax reserve on the balance sheet rose steadily from $740,000 in 1979 to $92,365,000 by 1988), the deferred income tax reserve should be included in capital *and the change taken into earnings and as a reduction in tax expense.*

Footnote 8 Aggregate minimum rentals at January 31, 1989, under noncancelable operating leases, are as follows:

1989	$ 155,108,000
1990	153,271,000
1991	149,572,000
1992	147,537,000
1993	144,872,000
Thereafter	$1,814,784,000

Conclusion: The minimum rents for operating leases should be discounted to a present value and treated as a debt and asset equivalent. Moreover, the after-tax interest component of the rents should be added back to earnings and extracted from rent expense.

Although in theory all of the noncancelable operating lease payments should be discounted to a present value, in practice minimum rents projected for just the first 5 years are discounted. Some companies do not disclose minimum rents beyond the fifth year. Thus, to be consistent, it is ignored in our computations. The discount rate should in general be the rate the company pays on secured indebtedness. Again, to be practical, a discount rate of 10% has been chosen for all companies. The present value of noncancelable operating leases is $598,636,000, an amount to be added to capital.

	Minimum Rent	PV Factor	Present Value
1989	$155,108,000	0.953	$147,890,000
1990	153,271,000	0.867	132,853,000
1991	149,572,000	0.788	117,861,000
1992	147,537,000	0.716	105,688,000
1993	144,872,000	0.651	94,345,000
Total			$598,636,000

To estimate the interest component of rents, 10% cost of money is applied to the average of the present value of the leases at the beginning and at the end of the year. The present value of the non-cancelable leases as of the beginning of the year was $504,526,000, thus making the average over the year $551,581,000. The estimated interest component of rents is 10% times $551,581,000, or $55,-158,100.

Footnote 9 On June 29, 1987, Wal-Mart acquired Super Saver Warehouse Club, Inc. The acquisition was accounted for as a purchase. The excess of cost over fair value of the net assets acquired, that is, goodwill, was $50,034,000, and it is being amortized on a straight-line basis over 10 years. *Conclusion: The amortization of goodwill should be added to income and removed from operating expense, and the cumulative amortization of goodwill should be added to equity capital and to the goodwill remaining on the balance sheet.*

It is important to understand the reason why certain adjustments will not be made. For example, other reserves, such as for bad debts, were not reported and were deemed to be insignificant. Also, Wal-Mart does not have a significant R&D expense, nor has it recorded any material write-offs, or unusual gains, over the past 10 years. Adjustments to convert to successful-efforts accounting thus appear to be inconsequential. Wal-Mart expenses the cost associated with opening new stores during the first month of operation (prior to that, they are accumulated in prepaid expense). Ideally, these up-front expenses would be capitalized as part of the investment in the stores, instead of being immediately expensed, but Wal-Mart did not provide sufficient information to do that.

Wal-Mart's Capital

The Operating Approach. From the operating perspective, presented in exhibit 3.13, the major adjustments to net assets are to add the LIFO reserve to inventory, the present value (PV) of noncapitalized leases to net property, plant, and equipment, and

Exhibit 3.13   Wal-Mart Stores
Capital/Operating Approach

January 31 ($ in thousands)	1987	1988
Operating Cash	$ 11,325	$ 12,553
Net Accts Receivable	222,845	241,291
Net Inventory	2,651,760	3,351,366
LIFO Reserve	202,796	291,329
Other Current Assets	19,214	25,776
Adjusted Current Assets	3,107,940	3,922,315
Accounts Payable	1,099,958	1,389,726
Accrued Expenses	400,103	514,672
Income Taxes Payable	120,773	121,158
NIBCLs	1,620,834	2,025,556
Net Working Capital	1,487,106	1,896,759
Net Property Plant & Equipment	2,144,851	2,661,953
PV of Non-Cap Leases	504,526	598,636
Adj Property Plant & Equipment	2,649,377	3,260,589
Goodwill	47,034	41,036
Accum Goodwill Amort	3,000	8,998
Gross Goodwill	50,034	50,034
Other Assets	34,775	25,689
Capital	$ 4,221,292	$ 5,233,071

the cumulative amortization of goodwill to goodwill—thereby restoring it to the original $50,034,000 balance. The NIBCLs that are netted from current assets to compute net working capital are accounts payable, accrued expenses, and income taxes payable. Capital is $5,233,071M, consisting of net working capital of $1,896,759M and Net fixed assets of $3,336,312M.

The Financing Approach.   From the financing perspective, (exhibit 3.14), the major adjustments are to add the PV of the

Exhibit 3.14   Wal-Mart Stores
Capital/Financing Approach

January 31 ($ in thousands)	1987	1988
Short-Term Debt	$ 104,382	$ 19,000
Current Portion LTD	18,544	21,349
Senior Long-Term Debt	185,672	184,439
Capitalized Lease Obligations	866,972	1,009,046
PV of Non-Cap Leases	504,526	598,636
Total Debt & Leases	1,680,096	1,832,470
Common Equity	2,257,265	3,007,909
Deferred Income Taxes	78,135	92,365
LIFO Reserve	202,796	291,329
Accum Goodwill Amort	3,000	8,998
Equity Equivalents	283,931	392,692
Adjusted Common Equity	2,541,196	3,400,601
Capital	$ 4,221,292	$ 5,233,071
Increase in Capital(I)		$ 1,011,779

noncapitalized leases to all other interest-bearing debt and to add equity equivalents, consisting of the deferred income tax reserve, LIFO reserve, and cumulative goodwill amortization, to common equity capital. The economic book value of common equity, including those reserves, is $3,400,601M (or $6.01 per share), in contrast to the reported book value of $3,007,909M (or $5.32 per share). Only if Wal-Mart sells for a stock price above $6.01 has it truly enriched its shareholders. Without any preferred stock or minority investors, the sum of all debt, common equity, and common equity equivalents is capital, once again totaling $5,233,071M.

Capital Investment.   The year-to-year change in capital is investment or *I.* For Wal-Mart, *I* is $1,011,779,000 in 1988. From the operating perspective, *I* represents the cash committed to build up net working capital plus the expenditures to acquire fixed assets (net of depreciation that is added to the accumulated depreciation account) and to finance acquisitions. With depreciation netted away, I is the investment for growth. From the financing perspective, I is net new debt and equity capital (i.e., net of distributions of cash to investors).

Wal-Mart's NOPAT

The Financing Approach.   From the financing perspective, shown in exhibit 3.15, the accountants' bottom-line profits of $837,222,000 is the economists' starting line. The change in equity equivalent reserves is added, bringing into earnings $108,-761,000 of recurring cash flows and value changes that Wal-Mart's accountants have relegated to reserves on and off the balance sheet.

Exhibit 3.15   Wal-Mart Stores
NOPAT/Financing Approach

Feb-Jan ($ in thousands)	1988
Income Available to Common	$ 837,222
Incr Deferred Taxes	14,230
Incr LIFO Reserve	88,533
Goodwill Amortization	5,998
Increase in Equity Equivalents	108,761
Adj Income Available to Common	945,983
Interest Expense	135,681
Interest Exp Non-Cap Leases	55,158
Adjusted Interest Expense	190,839
Tax Benefit of Interest Expense	(72,519)
Interest Expense After Taxes	118,320
NOPAT	$ 1,064,305

The next step is to deleverage the profits by adding back interest expense after taxes. Interest of $190,839M includes the $55,158M imputed interest on the leases. At an estimated 38% percent marginal income tax rate (federal, state, and local), interest expense reduced Wal-Mart's tax bill by $72,519M. Thus, the effective after-tax cost of Wal-Mart's explicit and implicit debt was $118,320M.

Once the effects of accounting and financial distortions are removed from bottom-line profits, NOPAT of $1,064,305M emerges as a measure of the true economic earnings of the business.

The Operating Approach.   The source of the NOPAT profits is revealed by the operating approach shown in exhibit 3.16. Starting from the top with sales, the first step is to remove operating expenses, including depreciation. Observe that the goodwill amortization of $5,998M that was reported as an expense on Wal-Mart's P&L statement (exhibit 3.15) is nowhere to be found here. Non-cash-bookkeeping entries are ignored. The interest component of leases is subtracted from operating expenses in order to eliminate implicit financing charges. The increase in the LIFO reserve also comes out of operating expenses, in effect converting the cost of goods sold from LIFO to FIFO while retaining LIFO's tax benefit. With these adjustments, Wal-Mart actually delivers net operating profits of $1,474,000M instead of the $1,324,309M the company reports.

Interest expense, because it is a financing charge, is ignored, but the other, presumably operating, income of $136,840M that Wal-Mart reports does add in, and it gives rise to $1,610,840M of pretax economic profits, or net operating profit before taxes (NOPBT).

In the final step, an estimate of the taxes payable in cash on these operating profits, or $546,535M, is subtracted, leaving NOPAT of $1,064,305M, just the same result as was produced by the financing approach. Now that is a miracle of modern finance.

Exhibit 3.16   Wal-Mart Stores
NOPAT/Operating Approach

Feb-Jan ($ in thousands)	1988
Net Sales	$ 20,649,004
Cost of Goods Sold	15,843,203
Depreciation	207,631
Selling General & Administrative	3,267,863
(Interest Exp Non-Cap Leases)	(55,158)
(Incr) LIFO Reserve	(88,533)
Operating Expenses	·19,175,004
Adj Net Oper Profit	1,474,000
Other Income	136,840
NOPBT	1,610,840
Cash Operating Taxes	546,535
NOPAT	$ 1,064,305

Analysis of Taxes

Feb-Jan ($ in thousands)	1988
Income Tax Provision	$ 488,246
Less Incr Def Taxes	14,230
Plus Tax Savings From Interest Expense:	72,519
Cash Operating Taxes	$ 546,535

Cash Operating Taxes

The last item to explain is the computation of the $546,535M in cash operating taxes. I have dubbed this the least interesting calculation in all of corporate finance (although you probably were hoping that you have been through *that* already).

Start with the accounting income tax provision of $488,246M, a number lifted from the company's very own income statement. Subtract the year-to-year increase in the deferred income tax reserve. This difference is the taxes that were provided for by the accountants, but which actually were not due to be paid that year. Taking it away leaves only the taxes that actually were paid. Last, taxes paid is grossed up to account for the additional taxes that would have been paid had the interest expense (on the debt and leases) in that year not served to shelter the operating profits from a full dose of corporate income taxation. Recall that the tax benefit of interest previously was shown to be $72,519M.

The result of these three steps produces $546,535M for cash operating taxes, just the figure we were looking for. Voila.

A Summary

A summary of the NOPAT and capital calculation for Wal-Mart is depicted in exhibit 3.17. It illustrates once again the important equivalence between the financial sources and operating uses of capital and between the NOPAT that is earned in the business and the cash that is available to reward all of the company's financiers.

Wal-Mart's Rate of Return. At long last, the NOPAT to capital rate of return can be computed. Wal-Mart's r is 25.2% on beginning capital.

NOPAT	$1,064,305M
Beginning capital	$4,221,292M
r	25.2%

Beginning capital is used because it is assumed that new capital investment requires a full year to become fully productive.

Exhibit 3.17 A Summary of Wal-Mart's NOPAT and Capital

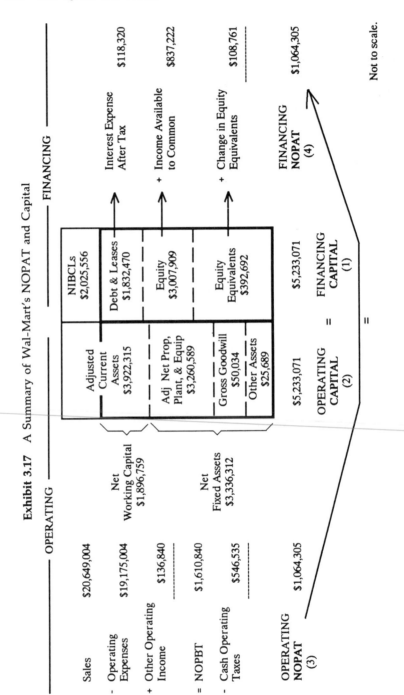

Not to scale.

Incidentally, the conventional rate of return on beginning common equity is 37.1%, the result of leveraging up the rate of return earned in the business.

Net Income available to common	$837,222M
Beginning common equity	$2,257,265M
ROE	37.1%

Rate of Return Analysis.   The rate of return for Wal-Mart, or for any company for that matter, can be broken down into three components reflecting operating profit margin (OPM), the turnover of capital (TO), and the effective cash tax rate on operating income (CTR) as shown in exhibit 3.18.

Exhibit 3.18   Wal-Mart's Rate of Return Components
(Dollar Amounts in Millions)

$$r = \frac{NOPAT}{capital}$$

$$r = OPM \times TO \times (1 - CTR)$$

$$r = \frac{NOPBT}{sales} \times \frac{sales}{capital} \times 1 - \frac{cash\ operating\ taxes}{NOPBT}$$

$$r = \frac{\$1,611}{\$20,649} \times \frac{\$20,649}{\$4,221} \times 1 - \frac{\$547}{\$1,611}$$

$$25.2\% = 7.8\% \times 4.9x \times 1 - 34\%$$

$$25.2\% = 7.8\% \times 4.9x \times 66\%$$

The operating profit margin (OPM) is the ratio of pretax economic earnings, or NOPBT, to sales. For Wal-Mart, it is 7.8%. In other words, for every dollar of sales, 7.8 cents made its way through the income statement to contribute to pretax economic profits. The turnover of capital (TO) is the ratio of sales to beginning capital. For Wal-Mart it is 4.9. Every single dollar of capital turned into $4.90 of sales over the year. Capital turnover itself can be analyzed as a function of the efficiency of working capital management and of net fixed assets.

The effective cash tax rate (CTR) is the taxes payable in cash on operating profits expressed as a percent of those pretax operating profits. It is the rate at which NOPBT would disappear as an immediate cash tax liability in the absence of debt financing. The effective cash tax rate for Wal-Mart is 34%, which reflects about a 38% marginal corporate income tax rate reduced by the benefit of accelerated versus straight-line depreciation and by the use of LIFO taxes, but FIFO cost of goods sold when NOPAT is computed, among other things.

It is a mathematical truism that multiplying the three components together will always yield the NOPAT to capital rate of return, in this case, 25.2%. A word of warning before you get too intoxicated with the beauty of the components. What determines a company's value, and what should matter for performance measurement and goal setting, is the overall rate of return and not the individual components. Some companies, like Wal-Mart, earn very attractive returns and sell for attractive market multiples with rapid turnover ratios compensating for narrow margins. Other, more capital-intensive companies, such as Brown Forman Distillers, also earn attractive returns and sell for lofty valuations, but they do so by producing very wide profit margins to make up for very slow capital turns. (In Brown Forman's case, it is a question of storing spirits for many years before they can be sold.) An attempt to improve one of the components, say profit margin, may only lead to an unforeseen reduction in one of the elements going into the turnover ratio, let's say, thereby potentially reducing the overall rate of return. In asking the baritones to sing louder, the sopranos may be drowned out, and the company chorus put off-key. Assessing the impact on the overall rate of return, or better, on value, is the right way to approach business decisions, and not through an explicit concern over those components per se.

The components are useful, it is true, but only as a way of better understanding the causes of poor or exceptional performance in relation to business peers and of judging the reasonableness of projections that anticipate a dramatic change in the overall rate of return. But unlike the rate of return, which can be compared with an absolute standard of performance, namely, the cost of capital, the components have meaning only insofar as they may be compared against prior levels and relative to those of business peers.

For example, in its 1988 fiscal year, K-Mart, a direct competitor to Wal-Mart, earned only a 13.0% rate of return on capital, broken down as shown in exhibit 3.19.

Exhibit 3.19 K-Mart's Rate of Return Components
(Dollar Amounts in Millions)

$$r = \frac{\text{NOPAT}}{\text{capital}}$$

$$r = \text{OPM} \times \text{TO} \times (1 - \text{CTR})$$

$$13.0\% = 6.8\% \times 2.8X \times (1 - 32\%)$$

$$13.0\% = 6.8\% \times 2.8X \times 68\%$$

K-Mart's unfavorable comparison with Wal-Mart is due to a 1% lower operating profit margin and a significantly slower turnover of capital. The effective cash operating tax rate is essentially the same. K-Mart's slower capital turnover can be traced to differences in working capital management and fixed asset utilization rates. The ratio of net working capital to sales, for example, is 14.7% for K-Mart versus only 9.2% for Wal-Mart. In a subsequent chapter, the business factors that account for these financial distinctions will be discussed.

Wal-Mart's Rate of Return and Market Valuation. Wal-Mart's rate of return of 25.2% is twice its weighted average cost of capital of 12.6% for the year 1988. (Trust me on this, I will show you how to perform this calculation later on.) And yet Wal-Mart sells for a market value that is nearly 4 times the economic book value of its capital employed.

	Economic Book Value	*Fair Market Value*
All debt and leases	$1,832,466M	$ 1,832,466M
Common equity and EEs	3,400,601M	17,748,245M
Capital	$5,233,067M	$19,580,711M

In the absence of quoted prices, the market value of Wal-Mart's debt and leases is assumed to be the same as its accounting book value. But although the economic book value of Wal-Mart's common equity (including EEs) is $3,400,601M, the fair market value is estimated to be $17,748,245M, a result produced by multiplying Wal-Mart's 565,591M shares outstanding by the $31.38 stock price prevailing at the end of its 1988 fiscal year. The "fair" market value of Wal-Mart's capital thus amounts to 3.7 times its economic book value ($19,580,711M/$5,233,067M). Why it is that Wal-Mart should sell for so large a premium will become clearer in the next chapter when the company's extraordinary growth rate is taken into account.

Summary

Warren Buffett, chairman of Berkshire Hathaway, epitomizes the thinking behind the economic model of value. He believes that his primary responsibility as a CEO is to be an effective steward of his shareholders' funds, not a manager dedicated to any one particular business:

> "I'm in the capital allocation business," he says. "My job is to figure out which businesses to invest in, with whom, and at what price. I'm not like a steel executive who can think only about how to invest best in steel. I've got a bigger canvas, simply because I have spent my life looking at companies from Abbott Labs and going through to Zenith."
>
> "Leaders of the Most Admired"
> *Fortune*
> January 29, 1990

To satisfy astute investors who think like Buffet, a company must earn a rate of return that exceeds its cost of capital. Those that do so will add value to the capital they employ and will sell for premium stock prices. Those that do not will have misallocated or mismanaged capital and will sell for stock market values that discount their capital employed.

Although it is easy to compute and is relatively widely understood, the rate of return on equity is a flawed measure of performance. It is distorted by accounting conventions that make financial statements more useful for lenders than for shareholders. It also mixes operating and financing decisions in a flagrant contradiction of a fundamental principle of corporate finance. With ROE as its goal, management may be tempted to accept truly substandard projects that happen to be financed with debt and to pass by very good ones if they must be financed with equity.

In its place, the rate of return on total capital should be the measure employed to assess corporate performance. Computed by dividing NOPAT by the capital employed in operations, it is a savings account equivalent, after-tax cash-on-cash yield earned in the business. It measures the productivity of capital employed without regard to the method of financing, and it is free from accounting distortions that arise from accrual bookkeeping entries, from the conservative bias of accounting statements, and from the tendency to understate capital by writing off unsuccessful efforts.

The cost of capital is the minimum rate of return that must be earned in order to add value to capital. It is not a cash cost, though. Rather, it is an opportunity cost equal to the total rate of return that a company's investors could expect to earn by investing in the stocks and bonds of other companies of comparable riskiness. From the perspective of a company's investors, who can invest in anything ranging from essentially default-free government bonds to corporate bonds, high-yield bonds, common stocks, venture capital funds, and, ultimately, options, the cost of capital is driven by the proven trade-off between risk and expected reward.

For corporate managers the cost of capital can be defined perhaps more meaningfully as the rate of return that some alternative, or marginal, project also up for consideration promises to earn. To be acceptable, any one project must beat the return offered by that hypothetical alternative in order for the world at large to be better off. Although it may be difficult to visualize, it is nonetheless true that it is the competition for capital at the margin that drives stock prices, and not the trench warfare against business competitors per se.

The competition for capital is the essence of the economic framework, but it is only a snapshot. In reality, corporate performance is dynamic, and that adds another dimension to our quest for value.

APPENDIX
EQUITY EQUIVALENTS

Equity equivalent reserves gross up the standard accounting book value for common equity to its economic book value. Only if a company's stock market value exceeds its economic book value is the company truly adding value to the funds placed at its disposal.

In computing the rate of return, equity equivalents are added to capital and the period-to-period change is taken into NOPAT. These adjustments turn capital into a more accurate measure of the base upon which investors expect their returns to accrue and make NOPAT a more realistic measure of the actual cash yield generated for investors from recurring business activities.

A list of equity equivalents and their effect on capital and NOPAT is presented in the following table. It is followed by a discussion of each of the equity equivalent reserves.

Add to Capital: Equity Equivalents	Add to NOPAT: Increase in Equity Equivalents
Deferred tax reserve	Increase in deferred tax reserve
LIFO reserve	Increase in LIFO reserve
Cumulative goodwill amortization	Goodwill amortization
Unrecorded goodwill	
(Net) capitalized intangibles	Increase in (net) capitalized intangibles
Full-cost reserve	Increase in full-cost reserve
Cumulative unusual loss (Gain) AT	Unusual loss (gain) AT
Other reserves, such as: Bad debt reserve Inventory obsolescence reserve Warranty reserve Deferred income reserve	Increase in other reserves

EE # 1: Deferred Income Tax Reserve

One of the most prevalent and significant of the equity equivalents is the reserve for deferred income taxes. It stores the cumulative difference between the accounting provision for taxes and the taxes actually paid. So long as the company replenishes the assets that give rise to the deferral of taxes (an assumption investors take for granted in the valuation of going-concern businesses), the deferred tax reserve will never be repaid but instead constitutes the equivalent of permanent equity. Moreover, by adding back the increase in the deferred tax reserve to earnings, NOPAT is charged only with the taxes that actually are paid instead of the accounting tax provision. This renders a much clearer reading of the true cash-on-cash yield actually being earned in the business.

EE # 2: The LIFO Reserve

In the economic model, income and capital are measured *as if* the company's inventories were sold for their end-of-period prices and immediately repurchased, with any gain booked into periodic profits and the cumulative gain appearing as a revaluation reserve on the balance sheet. This gain belongs in profits because the rate of return is to be compared with a cost of capital that includes a premium for inflation. This is still cash accounting, but cash accounting assuming a simultaneous sale and purchase of inventories, an approach identical with that taken by investors who consider unrealized capital gains as part of their total return.

To save taxes, a company is well advised to elect LIFO for inventory costing in times of rising prices. But by expensing the most recently acquired goods first, LIFO accumulates costs from many prior periods in inventory. Inventory and equity are outdated and understated. Thus, there is a need to mark the LIFO inventories to current value.

FIFO, by contrast, expenses first in, first out, leaving inventories on the balance sheet valued at the most recent prices. There is no need to adjust the FIFO value of inventories, since it is a good approximation of current replacement cost.

The LIFO reserve is the difference between the LIFO and FIFO value of the inventory. It is a measure of the extent to which the LIFO inventories are understated in value. It is almost always reported in the footnotes to the financial statements if a company uses LIFO. Adding the LIFO reserve to capital as an equity equivalent converts inventories from a LIFO to a FIFO basis of valuation, a better approximation of current replacement cost. Moreover, adding the increase in the LIFO reserve to NOPAT brings into earnings the unrealized gain attributable to holding inventories that appreciated in value.

The periodic change in the LIFO reserve may also be thought of as the difference between LIFO and FIFO cost of goods sold. Adding such a change to reported profits converts from the cost of goods sold expense of LIFO to that of FIFO, but while retaining LIFO's tax benefit. Thus, the overall effect of treating the LIFO reserve as an equity equivalent is to produce a FIFO balance sheet and income statement but to preserve the LIFO tax charge.

Now a switch from FIFO to LIFO in a period of rising prices will bring about a clear improvement in rate of return measured in this way because the LIFO tax benefit will shine through. A second advantage of this approach is that rates of return computed for LIFO and FIFO companies are directly comparable.

EE # 3: Cumulative Goodwill Amortization

Another equity equivalent arises from the accounting for acquisitions. The accountants' insistence that goodwill be amortized against earnings over a period not to exceed 40 years depresses reported earnings in a way that stops many a management from consummating sensible acquisitions. To make the noncash, non-tax-deductible amortization of goodwill the nonissue it really is, it should be added back to reported earnings. And, to be consistent, the cumulative goodwill amortization must be added back to equity capital and to goodwill remaining on the books. By unamortizing the goodwill in this way the rate of return will more properly reflect the true cash-on-cash yield that is of interest to shareholders.

EE # 4: Unrecorded Goodwill

A potentially more serious measurement problem arises when goodwill is not recognized at all. This happens when acquisitions are accounted for by using the pooling of interests technique. In this case, the cost recognized on the buying company's books is merely the seller's accounting book value. From the standpoint of the buying company's shareholders, however, the true cost of an acquisition is the market value of the securities offered to consummate the deal as of the transaction date. The acquirer, after all, could have issued an identical package of securities for cash and then used the cash as the medium of exchange. The difference between book value acquired and the often much higher market value of the securities offered is unrecorded goodwill.

Let's take an example. Suppose A will acquire B in an exchange of shares. Assume that the book value of B's equity is $50 million. B earns an attractive return, however, and thus sells for $75 million, a 50% premium to its (accounting) book value. Suppose A offers to pay a 33% premium over market value to acquire B, or $100 million, by swapping 10 million of its own shares having a current quoted price of $10 per share to acquire all of B's shares. Under pooling of interests accounting, A would acquire the net assets of B at a cost of $50 million and would record an equal increment to its equity capital. Of course, the number of A's shares outstanding would increase by 10 million, so pooling implies new common stock is issued at $5 ($100 million/10 million shares) when it is quoted in the market at $10. Had the same acquisition been accounted for as a purchase, the fair market value of the common shares issued ($100 million, or $10 per share) would be added to equity and the net assets acquired would be recorded at their book value of $50 million (assuming no write-up), leaving the difference of $50 million as goodwill.

Because pooling often understates the true cost of making an acquisition, rates of return are overstated. When Security Pacific Bank acquired the Rainier Bank in a pooling, for example, the value of the shares exchanged was 3 times Rainier's book value. Security Pacific is showing on its books 3 times the rate of return it is actually earning from the acquisition. Lead-steer investors were not fooled, however. Security Pacific's stock price fell sharply when the acquisition was announced.

To record the true cost of a pooling-of-interest acquisition, and thereby more accurately measure the rate of return the acquirer is earning, unrecorded goodwill is added both to goodwill and to equity capital as an equity equivalent that does not amortize, thus making the treatment of purchase and pooling acquisitions entirely equivalent.[5]

EE # 5: Intangibles

R&D outlays should be capitalized onto the balance sheet as an equity equivalent and then amortized into earnings over the anticipated

---

[5]The one exception is a true pooling acquisition in which there is a merger of equals, say a SmithKline Beecham combination. In such cases where neither party really acquires the other, pooling can make sense as an accounting method. But when one party acquires another and simply uses stock to finance the acquisition, the more common occurrence, pooling should be converted to purchase accounting.

payoff period for the successful projects. The result of capitalizing and amortizing R&D is a (net) capitalized R&D intangible that counts as an equity equivalent reserve. By adding the change in the (net) capitalized R&D intangible to NOPAT, the R&D expense of the period is replaced with the amortization of the capitalized R&D. Once a company reaches a steady-state growth, the two will equal one another and there will be no effect on NOPAT. But the (net) capitalized R&D intangible will be a recurring addition to capital that will bring the rate of return down from illusory accounting heights to truer economic levels.

With the same principle in mind, new product development and up-front marketing costs incurred to capture an initial market share also should be capitalized and amortized over the lives of successful new products. For example, the cost of designing and promoting Infiniti and Lexus, the new luxury cars from Japan, should be capitalized on Nissan's and Toyota's books instead of being expensed. Closer to home, the hundreds of millions of dollars that Gillette spent to develop and market the new spring-suspended Sensor razor, all of which has been written off by the company's accountants, also should be considered a form of capital investment. Moreover, like public utilities which capitalize interest into the cost of the plants they build until they are put into service, Gillette also should add the time value of money to the protracted investment it already has made in the development of Sensor. Though the accountants think so, that the payoff from these projects is uncertain is not the issue. The up-front cash outlays should be capitalized because management's strategy, if successful, anticipates and requires a payoff over an extended period of time.

EE # 6: Successful Efforts to Full Cost

Natural resource companies that follow successful-efforts accounting overstate their rates of return and ought to restate to full-cost accounting. But the issue of converting successful efforts to full cost extends to any firm that makes risky investments it subsequently has to write off. In other words, it applies to all companies.

Investors capitalize the earnings that can be expected from a firm's ongoing business activities. NOPAT therefore should be normalized to exclude nonrecurring gains and losses, such as restructuring charges and gains and losses on dispositions of assets. To be consistent, though (and this is where corporate practice falls down), the cumulative unusual losses, less gains, after taxes must be added back to capital. This converts disposals and divestitures from successful efforts to full (cash) cost accounting. The economic model recognizes that part of the capital required to generate successful products and services and acquisitions is the investment in unsuccessful ones. To carry only the capital associated with the winners leads to an over-statement of the true rate of return that actually has been earned in a risky business.

EE # 7: Other Equity Equivalent Reserves

Precautionary reserves obscure the actual timing of cash receipts and disbursements. Reserves for bad debts, inventory obsolescence, war-ranties, and deferred income should be considered to be equity equiva-lents if they are a recurring part of the business and will grow along with the general level of business activity. If they are more episodic in nature, it may be appropriate to leave them as offsets to capital (i.e., as NIBCLS).

It may be useful to review the workings of reserve accounts and how they affect NOPAT. By taking the change in such reserves into NOPAT, the accounting provision is replaced with the actual cash charge of the period. Take the warranty reserve, for example. In any given year the provision for warranty expense, that is, the charge that reduces accounting profits, is added to the warranty reserve (credit warranty reserve and debit earnings, say the accountants). The war-ranty reserve decreases whenever cash is expended to satisfy a war-ranty claim (debit warranty reserve and credit cash, quoth the raven). In general, the warranty reserve increases with the passage of time because, given their conservative bent, accountants are inclined to debit earnings more often than they will feel obliged to credit cash. The warranty reserve thus becomes a buffer to absorb swings in the actual cash loss experience year by year, a valued tool of earnings management. The lead steers are not so easily fooled, however. In computing NOPAT, they bring the change in the warranty reserve into earnings. The change adds back the warranty expense to profits, canceling out the bookkeeping entry, and substitutes the actual cash cost of satisfying warranties. Thus, NOPAT reflects the actual timing of the warranty charges as they are incurred, and not the accounting bookkeeping entry.

4

The EVA Financial Management System

Introduction

To win the competition for capital and build a premium-valued company, an attractive rate of return surely must be earned. But aspiring to earn a high return is not enough. In fact, it may send the wrong signals to operating people. To maximize its rate of return, an already highly profitable unit may pass by truly attractive investment opportunities. Units earning inadequate returns may seek still more capital in the hope of spending their way back to a better return. Stars will be starved, the dogs fed. In both cases, capital is misallocated. Rate of return may be a perfectly good way to evaluate whether an individual project should be accepted or rejected, but as a performance measure for an entire company or business unit, it is flawed.

The one performance measure to account properly for all of the ways in which corporate value may be added or lost is economic value added (EVA). EVA is a residual income measure that subtracts the cost of capital from the operating profits generated in the business. Operating people can do countless individual things to create value, but they must all eventually fall into one of the three categories measured by EVA. EVA will increase if operating profits can be made to grow without tying up any more capital, if new capital is invested in *any and all* projects that earn more

118

than the full cost of capital, and if capital is diverted or liquidated from business activities that do not cover their cost of capital. EVA's most important advantage, however, is that it is the only performance measure to tie directly to the intrinsic market value of a company. It is the fuel that lights up a premium in the stock market value of any company (or accounts for its discount). Accordingly, it is the measure I recommend for goal setting, capital budgeting, performance assessment, incentive compensation, and communication with the lead steers. In other words, I am advocating that EVA be used as the basis for implementing a new and completely integrated financial management system. The reason for choosing EVA, and not earnings, earnings growth, rate of return, or even cash flow, is illustrated by comparing three archetypal companies.

Profitability First

First, consider just two companies which, for lack of imagination, I shall call X and Y. Suppose that both earned $1,000 of NOPAT this past year and that their earnings are expected to grow at a 10% clip for as far the eye can see:

	X	Y
NOPAT	$1,000	$1,000
Growth rate	10%	10%

If they are the same in every other way, too, except that X must invest a lot more capital each year than Y to sustain its growth, for which company, X or Y, would you pay a higher value?

I hope you said Y, although many years go I asked the treasurer of a large oil company this question, and he said "X, because X has more investment opportunities." Apparently as the company's treasurer he cared only about the challenge of getting more money into the firm, not whether any cash ever came out again.

The investment rate is one way to quantify X's greater capital intensity. Computed by dividing the net new capital invested in

a business in a year, or I, by the NOPAT profits the business earns
that year, it is a ratio of uses to sources of funds that shows the
rate at which operating profits are plowed back to support
growth. Suppose that company X's investment rate is 100% but
Y's is just 80%:

	X	Y
NOPAT	$1,000	$1,000
Growth rate	10%	10%
I/NOPAT	100%	80%

A premium value for company Y can now be justified by computing a measure of capital efficiency. Dividing the increase in
NOPAT by the corresponding increase in capital produces a measure of the bang obtained from the buck invested. With earnings
growing 10% from a $1,000 base, both companies project NOPAT
to increase by $100 next year. But although X must commit all its
earnings, or $1,000, to incremental capital expenditures, Y needs
to invest only 80% of its earnings, or $800, to grow as fast:

	X	Y
NOPAT	$1,000	$1,000
Growth rate	10%	10%
I/NOPAT	100%	80%
$\dfrac{\text{Increase in NOPAT}}{\text{Increase in capital}}$	$\dfrac{\$100}{\$1,000}$	$\dfrac{\$100}{\$800}$
r	10%	12.5%

It should now be evident that the real reason Y is more valuable
than X is that it earns a higher rate of return on its invested
capital: an r of 12.5% for Y versus just 10% for X. But is Y also
more valuable because it pays more dividends? Not necessarily.

Though company X earns $1,000 and invests $1,000 back into
its business, and thus appears to be incapable of paying a dividend, it still could finance a dividend by borrowing or by raising

new preferred or common stock, and it could persist with such a policy indefinitely. Although it cannot be determined for sure that Y pays more dividends than X, it is nevertheless certain that Y is more valuable than X. The inescapable conclusion: Dividends are a misleading indicator of a company's true performance.

It is a company's ability to pay dividends that is critical to the creation of value, but actually paying dividends is unimportant. The ability to pay dividends is indicated by the rate of return a company earns. That is one sure measure of corporate success that, unlike dividends, cannot be financially manipulated.

The example proves that earnings growth, too, is a deceptive measure of value. For, if both X and Y will grow at the same rate but Y clearly is more valuable, earnings growth must be a false god to worship. Earnings growth is deceptive because it is always just the result of multiplying the rate of return a company earns on its new investments by its investment spending rate:

	Growth rate	=	r	$\times$	I/NOPAT
X	10%	=	10.0%	$\times$	100%
Y	10%	=	12.5%	$\times$	80%

Company X shows that it is possible to manufacture rapid earnings growth merely by pumping more capital into low-return projects. Earning a high rate of return on invested capital must be the paramount objective of any company, one far more important to achieve than growing rapidly.

Before a final verdict is rendered, there is one more measure yet to testify on Y's behalf. It is free cash flow, or NOPAT less the net new capital invested for growth (I):

	X	Y
NOPAT	$1,000	$1,000
Increase in capital (I)	$1,000	$ 800
FCF	$ 0	$ 200

Both X and Y start with NOPAT of $1,000, but X, by investing all that it earns, leaves zero free cash. Y, being more efficient, needs to invest just 80% of its earnings and thus generates surplus operating cash flow of $200. Y's extra free cash flow is a measure of its value because it is cash available to make interest payments on its debt (after taxes), to retire debt, to pay dividends, to buy back shares, or to accumulate as a portfolio of marketable securities. Y is more valuable than X because it can provide its investors with a greater cash reward to compensate them for risk.

Now there are three equivalent statements to justify setting Y above X:

1. Y can grow at the same rate as X, but it needs to invest less capital to grow.
2. Y earns a higher rate of return on its invested capital.
3. Y generates more free cash flow while it grows as a means of rewarding its investors for the risks that they take.

The bad news for the accounting enthusiasts is that current earnings, earnings growth, and even dividends have been shown to be unreliable measures of value. So far, earning a high rate of return and generating more free cash have gone hand in hand as the only true measures of corporate performance and value. But now its time for the curveball: company Z.

The Curveball

Like X and Y, company Z earns a NOPAT of $1,000. But it invests $2,000 back into its business. Company Z spends not only what it earns, it spends more than it earns, not unlike my personal situation at this time. I say this to my wife, Judy. "My dear, we cannot go on like a company Z, a negative free cash flow household, spending beyond our means year after year." But she is a clever woman. She says to me: "Bennett, what about the tax benefit of debt financing you keep talking about." I haven't had the heart to tell her that our favorite deduction has been phased out at the personal level.

If company Z has anything like our personal spending habits, it must have a whopping financing problem. For, with a negative FCF, it must raise some combination of debt and equity to finance expansion. And what's worse, with a negative FCF, any dividends or interest Z pays must just be refinanced each year, too. Given that Z has a negative and Y has a positive free cash flow, which company would you pay more to own, Y or Z?

	X	Y	Z
NOPAT	$1,000	$1,000	$1,000
Increase in capital (*I*)	$1,000	$ 800	$2,000
FCF	$ 0	$ 200	−$1,000

Many of my commercial banking friends say they prefer company Y. Bankers love companies that generate cash to repay their loans. But I did not ask which company had the greater debt capacity; I asked which had the greater value. The answer must be: It depends. It depends on the rate of return Z can earn on the additional capital it puts back into its business. After all, Z could be just a company Y that uncovers another $1,200 capital project.

Suppose that Z will earn a 12.5% return on its new capital investment, just like Y, and that all three companies have the same weighted average cost of capital, or c^*, of 10%. Thus, X is a group 2 company that earns just its cost of capital, and should sell at a value close to its economic book value, and Y and Z are group 1 companies that return more than their cost of capital, and thus should sell for premium stock market values. Now, which company, Y or Z, will command the greater value? They earn identical rates of return, but Z has a negative and Y a positive FCF.

The answer must now be Z, because it can invest in even more value-adding group 1 projects than Y can. Although its rate of return is the same as Y's, Z can earn that same superior return on each of the units of capital it invests. Investing more such capital units to earn the same spread as Y produces an even greater net present value for company Z.

Z will also grow more rapidly. By investing more capital to earn the same return as Y, it must grow even faster. Indeed, if Z continues to invest $2 for every $1 that it earns, it will grow at the stupendous rate of 25% per annum:

$$\text{Growth rate} = r \times I/\text{NOPAT}$$

$$25\% = 12.5\% \times 200\%$$

The rest of the chart for Z can now be completed. Please review my calculations.

	X	Y	Z
NOPAT	$ 1,000	$ 1,000	$1,000
Growth rate	10%	10%	25%
I/NOPAT	100%	80%	200%
Increase in NOPAT	$ 100	$ 100	$250
Increase in capital (I)	$ 1,000	$ 800	$2,000
r		10%	12.5%	12.5%
NOPAT	$ 1,000	$ 1,000	$1,000
Increase in capital (I)	$ 1,000	$ 800	$2,000
FCF	$ 0	$ 200	$-1,000

Excuse me. I almost left you with the wrong impression. Z is not more valuable than Y because it grows more rapidly. It is more valuable solely because it invests in even more group 1 projects. Its more rapid growth just happens to be a natural by-product of its more aggressive capital spending program but is not in and of itself what really adds to Z's value. The comparison of X to Y had put to rest the myth that growth is important.

There is a T-shirt that runs around Central Park that reads: "Happiness is a positive cash flow." I have been meaning to stop her to say, "Excuse me, young lady, but your shirt is not quite correct. It should read, on the front, 'Happiness is a negative cash flow,' and on the back, 'so long as the returns are attractive.'" I have not worked up the nerve to point out the flaw in her shirt. I just cannot imagine where the conversation goes from there. To tell the truth, I cannot catch her. She runs too fast.

Returning to more mundane thoughts, compare X to Y, and profitability emerges as far more important than growth. Compare Y to Z, and investing even more capital in attractive projects is yet another important dimension of corporate success. This means, unfortunately, that after having carried us this far, even rate of return and free cash flow stumble just short of the goal line. They too cannot be employed as reliable measures of corporate performance. For although Z earns the same return as Y and has a negative free cash flow, it is more valuable. A company that tried to maximize its return and current cash flow would cease investing and growing, and would soon liquidate. Granted, cash flow is important. Actually, it is all-important. But it is important only when it is considered over the entire life of the business and discounted to a present value, and not in any one year. The simple but sad truth is that, despite all the recent kowtowing to it, cash flow cannot and should not be used as a measure of performance.

But if earnings, growth, dividends, returns, and cash flow are flawed, does no measure matter? Must we be valuation nihilists? Before addressing that burning philosophical question, let's now take a closer look at our hypothetical X, Y, Z companies and actual companies that look just like them.

Roll the Camera: The Three Archetypal Companies in Motion

Company X. The trailing history year (1989) and first five projected years (1990 to 1994) for company X are presented in exhibit 4.1. Observe, please, that NOPAT starts at $1,000 and compounds at a 10% rate. Capital, the sum of net working capital and net fixed assets (as adjusted for certain equity equivalent reserves), commences with an opening balance of $10,000 but then it too compounds at 10% thereafter.

The year-to-year increase in capital, (yes, just the simple arithmetic change) is *I,* or net capital investment. *I* is the capital invested in the business over and above depreciation, and hence for growth. When the NOPAT earned on the income statement is charged with the injection of capital made onto the company's balance sheet, what's left over is free cash flow. In every year, it is just zero. Spending what it earns, X is a model of Yankee self-sufficiency.

But the best measure of X's performance (so far) is the rate of return it earns on capital employed. The ratio of NOPAT to the opening balance of capital is a flat 10% across the board. (The

Exhibit 4.1   Projected Performance of Companies X, Y, and Z

FINANSEER (data in millions)	History 1988	History 1989	Forecast 1990	Forecast 1991	Forecast 1992	Forecast 1993	Forecast 1994
COMPANY X							
1 NOPAT		$1,000	$1,100	$1,210	$1,331	$1,464	$1,611
2 Capital	10,000	11,000	12,100	13,310	14,641	16,105	17,716
3 Increase in Capital(I)		1,000	1,100	1,210	1,331	1,464	1,611
4 Free Cash Flow		0	0	0	0	0	0
5 Invest Rate (I/NOPAT)		100%	100%	100%	100%	100%	100%
6 NOPAT/Beg Capital r		10.0%	10.0%	10.0%	10.0%	10.0%	10.0%
7 Wtd Avg Cap Cost c*		10.0%	10.0%	10.0%	10.0%	10.0%	10.0%
8 Index r/c*		1.00x	1.00x	1.00x	1.00x	1.00x	1.00x
COMPANY Y							
1 NOPAT		$1,000	$1,100	$1,210	$1,331	$1,464	$1,611
2 Capital	8,000	8,800	9,680	10,648	11,713	12,884	14,173
3 Increase in Capital(I)		800	880	968	1,065	1,171	1,288
4 Free Cash Flow		200	220	242	266	293	322
5 Invest Rate (I/NOPAT)		80%	80%	80%	80%	80%	80%

6 NOPAT/Beg Capital	r	12.5%	12.5%	12.5%	12.5%	12.5%	12.5%
7 Wtd Avg Cap Cost	c*	10.0%	10.0%	10.0%	10.0%	10.0%	10.0%
8 Index	r/c*	1.25x	1.25x	1.25x	1.25x	1.25x	1.25x

COMPANY Z

1 NOPAT			$1,000	$1,250	$1,563	$1,953	$2,442	$3,052
2 Capital		8,000	10,000	12,500	15,625	19,532	24,415	30,519
3 Increase in Capital(I)			2,000	2,500	3,125	3,906	4,883	6,104
4 Free Cash Flow			(1,000)	(1,250)	(1,563)	(1,953)	(2,442)	(3,052)
5 Invest Rate (I/NOPAT)			200%	200%	200%	200%	200%	200%
6 NOPAT/Beg Capital	r		12.5%	12.5%	12.5%	12.5%	12.5%	12.5%
7 Wtd Avg Cap Cost	c*		10.0%	10.0%	10.0%	10.0%	10.0%	10.0%
8 Index	r/c*		1.25x	1.25x	1.25x	1.25x	1.25x	1.25x

opening capital balance is used here because it is assumed that it takes a full year for capital investment to begin to contribute to earnings.) As I had advertised, X grows its NOPAT earnings 10% a year by earning a 10% rate of return and then shoveling all of the return back into its business.

Company Y.   Company Y is spread in the middle section of exhibit 4.1. It shows a stream of NOPAT identical with that generated by X, $1,000 compounding at 10%. But, being more efficient, Y's new capital investment year by year can be less in order to achieve the same growth. Indeed, take the change in Y's capital account as a charge against NOPAT, and this time what's left is a positive and growing free cash flow, one hallmark of a Y company. But the most important difference between X and Y is the rate of return. For Y, r is 12.5% across the board. The numbers bear out that, by virtue of earning a higher rate of return, Y can grow at X's 10% rate by investing only four-fifths of its NOPAT back into the business.

Company Z.   The last classic company is Z (bottom section, exhibit 4.1). Starting from the same $1,000 base, NOPAT grows at the spectacular rate of 25% per annum. By the end of 5 years, profits reach almost twice the levels achieved by X and Y. The cost of supporting this lofty growth is a feverishly compounding capital account. Capital expands so rapidly, in fact, that taking the year-to-year change as a charge to NOPAT produces a negative free cash flow that becomes progressively more negative with each passing year. Z simply must raise some mix of debt and new equity to finance its growth and thereby dilute its current stockholders' claim on future cash flow. How can that be advisable?

So long as the new capital invested will earn a rate of return that more than covers the combined cost of the new debt and equity to be raised, Z's current shareholders will be better off with the prospect of owning a smaller share of a larger pie than holding onto a larger share of a smaller pie. Dilution in ownership or in earnings is just not the issue (control concerns aside). Earning an r in excess of c^*—now that is absolutely essential.

Apparently Z's new projects do more than make up for the cost of carving in new investors. Its NOPAT to beginning capital rate of return is 12.5% each year, more than covering the 10% cost incurred to attract new capital. Despite, or rather, because of its deficit free cash flow, Z creates the most value because it plans to pump the most capital into positive net present value projects.

Before showing some actual X, Y, and Z companies, two more types must be introduced to complete the categorization of corporate performance.

Company X-Minus. Some companies consistently manage to earn less than their cost of capital. I call them X-Minuses, the minus meaning they lose part of the value of every dollar they spend and sell at discounts to their economic book value.

Company Pre-Z. The last type of company looks deceptively like an X-Minus, but, in reality, it holds the potential to create the greatest value of them all. A Pre-Z is a firm that is poised at the vanguard of a terrific new business opportunity, so terrific, in fact, that the company has forgotten about making any money anytime soon. The financial clues to suggest that a company is a Pre-Z (and not an X-Minus) is an astounding rate of growth, an extremely negative free cash flow, and a supercharged market value. Presumably such a company would not be able to tap the external markets it does for vast amounts of new funds unless astute investors believed a distant but meaningful payoff was to come. Although not all of them fulfill their destiny, the Pre-Zs that do become real Z companies.

Some Examples

The extent to which actual companies look like one of the five basic companies I have described is remarkable. In a subsequent chapter, I will show how essentially every one of a sample of 1,000 companies can be assigned to one of these five groups. For now, let's focus on five companies that fall clearly into one of the categories (exhibit 4.2 spreads their results for some recent years, and is summarized in exhibit 4.3).

Exhibit 4.2 Ten-Year Performance of Five Archetypal Companies

UNITED TECHNOLOGIES CORP X-

FINANSEER (Data in Millions)		1979	1980	1981	1982	1983	1984	1985	1986	1987	1988	10-Year Summary
1 Sales		$9,053.3	$12,324.0	$13,667.7	$13,577.1	$14,669.2	$16,331.7	$14,991.6	$15,669.1	$17,170.2	$18,282.6	8.1%
2 Sales Growth		44.5%	36.1%	10.9%	-0.7%	8.0%	11.3%	-8.2%	4.5%	9.6%	6.5%	12.3%
3 NOPAT		843.7	817.8	929.4	729.8	944.9	1,044.7	726.5	148.6	965.4	910.8	0.9%
4 Capital		5,325.3	6,049.9	6,588.6	7,150.8	7,668.3	8,814.7	8,299.5	9,234.8	9,596.5	10,269.4	7.6%
5 Incr in Capital (I)		1,699.4	724.6	538.6	562.3	517.5	1,146.4	(515.2)	935.3	361.7	672.9	6,643.5
6 Free Cash Flow		(855.7)	93.2	390.8	167.5	427.4	(101.7)	1,241.7	(786.7)	603.7	237.9	1,418.1
7 I/NOPAT		201%	89%	58%	77%	55%	110%	-71%	629%	38%	74%	82%
8 NOPAT/Beg Capital	r	23.3%	15.4%	15.4%	11.1%	13.2%	13.6%	8.2%	1.8%	10.5%	9.5%	12.2%
9 Wtd Avg Cap Cost	c*	14.5%	15.9%	17.8%	17.3%	16.1%	17.1%	15.7%	13.0%	14.1%	14.4%	15.6%
10 Index	r/c*	1.61	0.97	0.86	0.64	0.82	0.80	0.52	0.14	0.74	0.66	0.78
11 Market Value		$4,160.2	$5,198.0	$4,365.3	$5,476.8	$6,495.2	$7,071.7	$7,399.9	$9,079.2	$7,235.7	$8,357.7	$6,484.0
12 Capital		5,325.3	6,049.9	6,588.6	7,150.8	7,668.3	8,814.7	8,299.5	9,234.8	9,596.5	10,269.4	7,899.8
13 Value/Capital		0.78	0.86	0.66	0.77	0.85	0.80	0.89	0.98	0.75	0.81	0.82

SPX CORP X

FINANSEER (Data in Millions)	1979	1980	1981	1982	1983	1984	1985	1986	1987	1988	10-Year Summary
1 Sales	$279.4	$257.9	$304.2	$366.0	$424.6	$500.1	$624.5	$665.8	$774.2	$877.7	13.6%
2 Sales Growth	14.0%	-7.7%	18.0%	20.3%	16.0%	17.8%	24.9%	6.6%	16.3%	13.4%	14.0%
3 NOPAT	24.9	26.1	28.3	36.0	35.9	43.6	52.4	49.4	54.2	71.8	12.5%
4 Capital	145.0	171.0	197.7	241.7	261.1	306.6	459.8	486.5	513.5	659.2	18.3%

NOXELL Y

		1979	1980	1981	1982	1983	1984	1985	1986	1987	1988	10-Year Summary
5	Incr in Capital (I)	18.5	25.9	26.8	44.0	19.3	45.6	153.1	26.7	27.1	145.7	532.7
6	Free Cash Flow	6.3	0.2	1.5	(8.0)	16.6	(2.0)	(100.8)	22.7	27.1	(73.8)	(110.0)
7	I/NOPAT	75%	99%	95%	122%	54%	105%	292%	54%	50%	203%	126%
8	NOPAT/Beg Capital r	19.6%	18.0%	16.6%	18.2%	14.9%	16.7%	17.1%	10.8%	11.1%	14.0%	15.7%
9	Wtd Avg Cap Cost c*	14.0%	16.0%	17.9%	17.3%	16.2%	17.5%	15.2%	12.5%	12.7%	13.3%	15.3%
10	Index r/c*	1.41	1.12	0.92	1.05	0.92	0.96	1.12	0.86	0.88	1.05	1.03
11	Market Value	$139.5	$135.1	$131.1	$285.3	$332.4	$338.1	$481.0	$457.8	$494.4	$704.1	$354.9
12	Capital	145.0	171.0	197.7	241.7	261.1	306.6	459.8	486.5	513.5	659.2	344.2
13	Value/Capital	0.96	0.79	0.92	1.18	1.27	1.10	1.05	0.94	0.96	1.07	1.03

FINANSEER
(Data in Millions)

		1979	1980	1981	1982	1983	1984	1985	1986	1987	1988	10-Year Summary
1	Sales	$179.7	$204.2	$233.1	$261.9	$304.3	$349.5	$382.1	$438.8	$489.5	$521.6	12.6%
2	Sales Growth	14.9%	13.6%	14.2%	12.3%	16.2%	14.9%	9.3%	14.8%	11.5%	6.6%	12.8%
3	NOPAT	14.1	17.5	20.2	22.5	26.7	33.0	35.9	40.4	48.6	56.2	16.7%
4	Capital	64.7	77.9	88.8	99.7	110.7	140.7	138.8	156.2	174.0	191.7	12.8%
5	Incr in Capital (I)	6.9	13.2	10.8	10.9	11.0	30.0	(1.9)	17.5	17.8	17.7	133.9
6	Free Cash Flow	7.2	4.3	9.3	11.5	15.7	3.0	37.8	22.9	30.7	38.5	181.0
7	I/NOPAT	49%	76%	54%	49%	41%	91%	-5%	43%	37%	31%	43%
8	NOPAT/Beg Capital r	24.3%	27.0%	25.9%	25.3%	26.8%	29.8%	25.5%	29.1%	31.1%	32.3%	27.7%
9	Wtd Avg Cap Cost c*	13.5%	15.5%	17.6%	17.0%	15.4%	16.6%	15.3%	14.5%	14.7%	14.4%	15.5%
10	Index r/c*	1.80	1.74	1.47	1.49	1.74	1.79	1.66	2.01	2.11	2.24	1.80
11	Market Value	$98.9	$110.1	$147.2	$240.1	$355.2	$439.1	$552.7	$792.3	$788.4	$687.1	$421.1
12	Capital	64.7	77.9	88.8	99.7	110.7	140.7	138.8	156.2	174.0	191.7	124.3
13	Value/Capital	1.53	1.41	1.66	2.41	3.21	3.12	3.98	5.07	4.53	3.58	3.39

Exhibit 4.2   continued

NOVELL
Z

FINANSEER (Nov-Oct) (Data in Millions)		1986	1987	1988	1989	3-Year Summary
1 Sales		$81.5	$182.8	$281.2	$421.9	51.9%
2 Sales Growth			124.2%	53.8%	50.1%	76.0%
3 NOPAT		11.6	28.3	50.1	79.3	67.4%
4 Capital		38.0	95.1	174.6	250.5	62.3%
5 Incr in Capital (I)		28.6	57.1	79.5	75.9	212.5
6 Free Cash Flow		(17.0)	(28.8)	(29.4)	3.4	(54.8)
7 I/NOPAT		246%	202%	159%	96%	135%
8 NOPAT/Beg Capital	r	122.9%	74.4%	52.6%	45.4%	57.5%
9 Wtd Avg Cap Cost	c*	15.5%	16.4%	15.7%	13.4%	15.2%
10 Index	r/c*	7.94	4.53	3.34	3.39	3.79
11 Market Value		$286.4	$622.4	$824.5	$972.3	$806.4
12 Capital		38.0	95.1	174.6	250.5	173.4
13 Value/Capital		7.54	6.54	4.72	3.88	4.65

McCAW CELLULAR COMM
Pre-Z

FINANSEER (Data in Millions)		1986	1987	1988	2-Year Summary
1 Sales		$17.9	$150.1	$310.8	107.1%
2 Sales Growth			740.9%	107.1%	424.0%
3 NOPAT			(107.7)	(93.3)	infinite
4 Capital		441.6	822.4	1,538.0	87.0%
5 Incr in Capital (I)			380.8	715.5	1,096.3
6 Free Cash Flow			(488.5)	(808.9)	(1,297.4)
7 I/NOPAT			infinite	infinite	infinite
8 NOPAT/Beg Capital	r		-24.4%	-11.3%	-17.9%
9 Wtd Avg Cap Cost	c*		8.1%	9.3%	8.7%
10 Index	r/c*		(3.00)	(1.22)	(2.05)
11 Market Value			$2,504.2	$4,986.2	$3,745.2
12 Capital			822.4	1,538.0	1,180.2
13 Value/Capital			3.04	3.24	3.17

Exhibit 4.3 Archetypal Companies
Ten-Year Average (1979–1988)

Type	Company	(1) r	(2) r / c*	(3) Value / Capital	(4) I / NOPAT	(5) Capital Growth
X-Minus	United Technologies	12.2 %	0.8x	0.8x	82%	8%
X	SPX	15.7 %	1.0x	1.0x	126%	18%
Y	Noxell	27.7 %	1.8x	3.4x	43%	13%
Z	Novell	57.5 %	3.8x	4.7x	135%	62%
Pre-Z	McCaw Cellular	−17.9 %	−2.1x	3.2x	Infinite	87%

Novell's data are averaged over 1987 to 1989 (Nov–Oct fiscal year).

McCaw Cellular data are averaged over 1987 to 1988.

X-Minus: United Technologies

United Technologies (UT) is at the bottom of the heap, an X-Minus company. The last time UT earned its cost of capital was in 1979. As a result, it may be the only company in America longing for the return of Jimmy Carter. For the past 10 years on average, UT earned only about 80% of its cost of capital and sold for a market value that was only about 80% of the (economic) book value of its capital employed. In the face of such poor returns, it is a shame that UT nearly doubled its capital base over this period. An additional $5 billion was subjected to a 20% loss in value.

X: SPX

SPX, a manufacturer of auto parts for the original equipment manufacturer (OEM) and replacement markets, is a break-even X company almost by definition, given its business. Though the company's sales and profits tripled over the past 10 years, on average SPX earned its cost of capital and sold for just its economic book value. It has been able to sustain its lusty growth rate only by investing more than it earned, thereby going more deeply into debt. In 1989, the company split in two, separating the lower-returning OEM business from the more profitable replacement parts operation (a transaction that is reviewed, incidentally, in chapter 14). Time will tell whether two Xs can make a Y.

Y: Noxell

Noxell makes and markets Cover Girl, Clarion Cosmetics, Noxema, and, . . . Lestoil?! (That's chess jargon for a questionable but possibly brilliant move.) Before male readers get too excited about buying stock in the company for which Christie Brinkley works, I should mention that the company was acquired by Procter & Gamble in November 1989. The numbers show what a delicious company it is. Though its sales and capital grew more slowly than SPX's did, Noxell's average rate of return has been almost double its cost of capital over time, and it has had a market value that is a billowy 3.4 times its capital employed. As is typical of a Y company also, Noxell has invested far less than it has earned (only about 43%), giving rise to a superb positive free cash flow—another indication of its comparatively greater value versus SPX. From what I see, there is no need to gloss over this company's performance.

Z: Novell

Novell, the world's leader in systems that connect PCs together in local area networks (LANs), is a lightning-quick Z Company. Sales burst from $180 to $420 million in 2 brief years, a growth rate of better than 50% per annum. With a 60% share of the market for LANs, Novell has earned a striking rate of return, averaging 57.5%, almost 4 times the cost of capital. But its return alone cannot account for a market value that has averaged nearly 5 times its economic book value. After all, Novell's rate of return actually has been precipitously falling year by year. The phenomenal market value premium has much to do with Novell's aggressive rate of investment. Capital has grown at the rate of 62% per annum on average, way outpacing Noxell, the Y company. As a result, Novell has had to weather negative free cash flows by plowing $1.35 back into its business for every $1 earned. The difference has been financed by raising common stock and convertible debentures. Given the tremendous returns they anticipate from the new investments, current shareholders have been only too happy to be diluted.

Pre-Z: McCaw Cellular

McCaw Cellular, the largest cellular phone company in the United States, is still on the verge of realizing a return from its investments. As for any Pre-Z company, the financial data for McCaw Cellular is essentially meaningless, except that the company sells for a market value that is 3.2 times the level of capital employed. The best thing for me to do is let Chairman McCaw speak for himself.

> During the last six years we have challenged conventional wisdom by investing heavily in an unproven industry which many people viewed as highly speculative. We committed early to the industry and throughout this period paid what were then record prices for cellular properties. During this period we also challenged conventional wisdom by making use of financial leverage and by emphasizing growth in shareholder value through long-term growth in operating cash flow rather than short-term book earnings. By following this strategy, in a very short time we have been able to position McCaw as the largest participant in this rapidly emerging industry.
>
> Our continued enthusiasm for the business, like our early willingness to commit decisively, is not based so much upon the industry's current results but instead upon our belief in what the industry will become as it continues to evolve. We believe that cellular technology will help to gradually transform the way we and future generations will think about communications as well as the way in which we work and live.
>
> Letter to Shareholders
> Craig O. McCaw
> Chairman and Chief Executive Officer
> McCaw Cellular Communications, Inc.
> 1987 Annual Report

Craig McCaw may be building the next IBM. Fortunately, he is not letting accounting numbers or a deficit free cash flow stand in his way.

A summary of the five classic categories of corporate performance is presented in exhibit 4.4.

Exhibit 4.4   Characteristics of the Five Classic Companies

Pre-Z Prospective Value Added	Z Aggressive Value Added	Y Conservative Value Added	X Neutral Value Added	X-Minus Negative Value Added
Explosive growth	Rapid growth	Moderate growth	Slow growth	Slow growth
−FCF	−FCF	+FCF	?FCF	?FCF
and chaotic returns (group 1)	soaring but risky returns (group 1)	healthy returns (group 1)	"break-even" returns (group 2)	inadequate returns (group 3)
Stellar multiples	High multiples	Moderate multiples	Unitary multiples	Depressed multiples
McCaw Cellular	Novell	Noxell	SPX	United Technologies

The five archetypal companies illustrate why it is vitally important for any business to earn at least its cost of capital, and hopefully more, and why, once an attractive return is being earned, aggressive investment carries value even higher. They also show why rate of return and free cash flow cannot be used as reliable measures of corporate performance. The representative Z company, Novell, enjoyed a tremendous market valuation in spite of its negative free cash flow, a rapidly tumbling rate of return, and no dividends. So if earnings, growth, dividends, returns and cash flow do not matter, what does?

All About EVA: The Heart and Soul of "Value Planning"

Economic value added (EVA) is the one measure that properly accounts for all the complex trade-offs involved in creating value. It is computed by taking the spread between the rate of return on capital r and the cost of capital c^* and then multiplying by the economic book value of the capital committed to the business:

$$\text{EVA} = (r - c^*) \times \text{capital}$$
$$\text{EVA} = (\text{rate of return} - \text{cost of capital}) \times \text{capital}$$

If, for example, NOPAT is $250, capital is $1,000, and c^* is 15%, then r is 25% (NOPAT/capital) and EVA is $100.

$$\text{EVA} = (r - c^*) \times \text{capital}$$
$$\$100 = (25\% - 15\%) \times \$1,000$$

Although in any given business there are countless individual things that people can do to create value, eventually they all must fall into one of the three categories measured by an increase in EVA. EVA will rise if operating efficiency is enhanced, if value-adding new investments are undertaken, and if capital is withdrawn from uneconomic activities. To be more specific, EVA increases when:

1. The rate of return earned on the existing base of capital improves; that is, more operating profits are generated without tying up any more funds in the business.

2. Additional capital is invested in projects that return more than the cost of obtaining the new capital.

3. Capital is liquidated from, or further investment is curtailed in, substandard operations where inadequate returns are being earned.

These are the only ways in which value can be created, and EVA captures them all.

EVA can be thought of in a second, and perhaps, more meaningful way by multiplying through by capital:

$$\text{EVA} = (r - c^*) \times \text{capital}$$
$$= r \times \text{capital} - c^* \times \text{capital}$$

$$\text{EVA} = \text{NOPAT} - c^* \times \text{capital}$$
$$= \text{operating profits} - \text{a capital charge}$$

EVA is residual income, or operating profits less a charge for the use of capital. With EVA as a performance measure, a company is, in effect, charged by its investors for the use of capital through a line of credit that bears interest at a rate of c^*. EVA is the difference between the profits the company derives from its operations and the charge for capital incurred through the use of its credit line.

Our preceding example can be presented in this alternative format. Recall that, with an r of 25%, c^* of 15%, and capital employed of $1,000, EVA was $100.

Formerly

$$EVA = (r - c^*) \times capital$$
$$\$100 = (25\% - 15\%) \times \$1,000$$

Now

$$EVA = NOPAT - c^* \times capital$$
$$\$100 = \$250 - 15\% \times \$1,000$$

$$NOPAT = r \times capital = 25\% \times \$1,000 = \$250$$

The three EVA strategies can now be stated more directly as follows:

1. To improve operating profits without tying up any more capital
2. To draw down more capital on the line of credit so long as the additional profits management earns by investing the funds in its business more than covers the charge for the additional capital
3. To free up capital and pay down the line of credit so long as any earnings lost is more than offset by a savings on the capital charge.

Those who are sophisticated enough to understand the accounting for a line of credit have all they need to know about how to create value (see exhibit 4.5 for some simple numerical examples).

Exhibit 4.5   Simple Numerical Examples of Value-Creating Strategies

Base Case

Start with NOPAT of $250, capital of $1,000, and c^* of 15%. r is 25%, and EVA is $100.

$$EVA = (r - c^*) \times capital$$
$$\$100 = (25\% - 15\%) \times \$1,000$$

or

$$EVA = NOPAT - c^* \times capital$$
$$\$100 = \$250 - 15\% \times \$1,000$$

Value-Creating Strategy 1: Improve Operating Efficiency

Widen NOPAT profits from $250 to $300, the result, say, of achieving greater administrative or production efficiencies. Then r increases from 25% to 30%, and EVA climbs to $150:

$$EVA = (r - c^*) \times capital$$
$$\$150 = (30\% - 15\%) \times \$1,000$$

or

$$EVA = NOPAT - c^* \times capital$$
$$\$150 = \$300 - 15\% \times \$1,000$$

Value-Creating Strategy 2: Achieve Profitable Growth

A proposed new project requires a $1,000 investment and is expected to earn a 20% rate of return, thereby adding $200 to sustainable NOPAT. Taking it on would increase EVA, even though the consolidated rate of return would fall to 22.5% (the average of 20% and 25%).

$$EVA = (r - c^*) \times capital$$
$$\$150 = (22.5\% - 15\%) \times \$2,000$$

or

$$EVA = NOPAT - c^* \times capital$$
$$\$150 = \$450 - 15\% \times \$2,000$$

Maximizing EVA is more important than maximizing return. The project should be accepted.

Value-Creating Strategy 3: Rationalize and Exit Unrewarding Businesses

3a: Liquidate Unproductive Capital

$333 of excess working capital can be withdrawn from the business without affecting NOPAT. Withdrawing it would increase the rate of return to 37.5% [$250/($1,000 − $333)] and EVA to $150.

Exhibit 4.5   continued

$$EVA = (r - c^*) \times capital$$
$$\$150 = (37.5\% - 15\%) \times \$667$$

or

$$EVA = NOPAT - c^* \times capital$$
$$\$150 = \$250 - 15\% \times \$667$$

See exhibit 4.6 for an illustrative analysis of a liquidation strategy and exhibit 4.7 for a review of Warner-Lambert's 1985 rationalization plan.

3b: Curtail Investment in Unrewarding Projects

Start with a completely different case. Suppose a company earns a NOPAT of only $50 on $1,000 of capital. With a return of only 5%, EVA is a deficit $100.

$$EVA = (r - c^*) \times capital$$
$$-\$100 = (5\% - 15\%) \times \$1,000$$

or

$$EVA = NOPAT - c^* \times capital$$
$$-\$100 = \$50 - 15\% \times \$1,000$$

A project that requires $1,000 of new capital is undertaken. It earns a 13% rate of return, and thereby adds $130 to sustainable NOPAT. EVA declines, even as the consolidated rate of return increases to 9% (the average of 13% and 5%).

$$EVA = (r - c^*) \times capital$$
$$-\$120 = (9\% - 15\%) \times \$2,000$$

or

$$EVA = NOPAT - c^* \times capital$$
$$-\$120 = \$180 - 15\% \times \$2,000$$

Though the overall return will nearly double as a result, accepting the project will impoverish shareholders, and it should be rejected. Turning off the spigot on such unrewarding investments is the last way to create value.

Exhibit 4.6 The EVAnalysis of a Rationalization Plan

The analysis of the stock market merits of downsizing strategy is much the same as that for any capital investment. But instead of investing capital to produce an acceptable incremental return, capital is withdrawn when it earns an inadequate rate of return. What's important, however, is to measure the rate of return from liquidating an asset or selling a business on the net exit proceeds, and not on book value, as the following example illustrates.

A Plant-Closing Example

Suppose that an inefficient plant could be shuttered and its production partly transferred to another facility within the company. (The example would apply to a contemplated reduction in working capital or a sale or liquidation of an entire line of business equally as well as to the closing of an individual facility.) The sale of the plant and liquidation of working capital will bring in net proceeds of $500 (after taxes and other winding-up expenses). Assume also that closing the plant means the permanent loss of $25 in NOPAT (the plant itself was making $40, say, but transferring production elsewhere will recover $15). Given these facts, closing the plant and withdrawing the cash are advisable even though the company's sales, market share, employment, and profits may diminish. Such an action will improve EVA, and value.

	(1) Original	—	(2) Liquidated	=	(3) Residual
NOPAT	$ 250		$ 25		$ 225
Capital	$1,000		$ 500		$ 500
r	25%		5%		45%
c^*	15%		15%		15%
$r - c^*$	10%		−10%		30%
× Capital	$1,000		$ 500		$ 500
EVA	$ 100		−$50		$ 150

By subtracting the incremental NOPAT lost and the net cash proceeds gained as a result of liquidating the plant, the residual operation that emerges from the original consolidated company is more valuable. EVA increases because capital is to be withdrawn from an uneconomic activity.

Exhibit 4.6   continued

Rationalize or Invest?
It's One and the Same Question

The best way to see this is to start with the residual operation, the rationalized business which by itself generates $150 in EVA (column 3). Moving from right to left this time, the liquidation strategy (in column 2) now turns into a potential investment opportunity. This new project entails investing $500 to reacquire the inefficient plant and build up its working capital and shifting some production into the decrepit facility, all for the benefit of generating an additional $25 in NOPAT, on net. Put in this way, it is unlikely anyone would accept such a plan. That's good, because rejecting this new project is just the same as deciding to rationalize the existing company.

The rate of return from liquidating an asset or selling a business is measured by taking the resulting reduction in economic earnings (as a proxy for long-run cash flow, which is what I really mean to use) and dividing by the net exit proceeds, *and not book value.* Book value is irrelevant because the investment the company makes to keep the plant running is the exit proceeds forgone. As an irrecoverable sunk cost, book value is meaningless in any economic analysis, and it should be ignored.

In the example, the return is a sacrifice of $25 in sustainable NOPAT divided by $500 in net liquidation proceeds, or 5%. This return can be compared against the cost of capital just as for any other capital project. If it is less than the cost of capital, the project should be rejected (i.e., the capital should be liquidated because the capital has a higher valued use elsewhere). If the return is greater than the cost of capital, the project should be accepted (i.e., the capital should *not* be liquidated). EVA shows the same thing, scaled to the size of the project. This is all very straightforward and commonsensical—until the accountant walks into the room.

Another Accounting Nightmare

One reason why many companies are reluctant to rationalize their operations is the adverse near-term accounting consequence. A consolidation can lead to an immediate book loss, even in situations where there is a clear and present economic gain.

Suppose, to continue the example, that the liquidated assets had a book value of $600. Upon realizing $500 of net liquidation proceeds, the accountants will reduce assets by $600 and book a loss of $100 for the difference.

Accounting Treatment	
Net proceeds	$ 500
Less book value charge-off	600
Gain/(loss)	$(100)

Managers preoccupied with accounting results abhor having to book a loss. So great is their loathing they may even forestall a sensible rationalization program, protesting a concern over how The Street will react. But the evidence on share price behavior strongly suggests such fears are misplaced. The market is driven by investors who are concerned with long-term economic consequences. The response of the lead steers will be to the economic value added by the decision, not to the non-cash-bookkeeping loss.

The best way to evaluate the market's likely reaction to a proposed rationalization is to use cash accounting before computing EVA. Cash accounting gives more sensible signals to managers who are faced with the opportunity to rationalize and focus. With cash accounting, the net exit proceeds reduce capital. It's that simple. Unlike conventional accounting, there is no immediate recognition of loss (or gain, for that matter) in the calculation of NOPAT. Cash accounting thus focuses attention on whether the up-front exit proceeds are worth more than the ongoing cash flows that will be forfeited as a result of the liquidation or sale of an asset, the basis for a true economic decision.

In the example, cash accounting would reduce capital by the net exit proceeds of $500. It is as if the accountants had simply debited cash for the $500 proceeds and credited the capital account for $500.

Cash (Economic) Treatment	
Original capital	$1,000
Less net proceeds	500
Ending cash capital	$ 500

Very clean. No messy gains or losses to obscure the pure and simple question: Are the up-front exit proceeds worth more or less than the ongoing cash flows that will be forfeited? With cash accounting, the capital base is reduced in such a way that the answer to the question will flow in unadulterated by non-cash-bookkeeping blather.

These same cash accounting consequences can be gotten by

Exhibit 4.6   continued

manipulating the regular accounting statements. The noncash loss ($100 in this case) is backed out of the income statement and put back onto the balance sheet. Thus, there is no loss as a result of the decision to rationalize, and the balance sheet is restored from $400 to $500.

Revised Accounting Treatment	
Original capital	$1,000
Less book value charge-off	600
Ending book capital	$ 400
Add back accounting loss (gain)	100
Ending cash capital	$ 500

In effect, the $100 add-back represents an investment made in the decision to rationalize. This is a more important decision for the subsequent financial statements to evaluate than whether the original funds spent to acquire the plant have paid off. The answer to that question is by this time obvious and irrelevant.

Another benefit to using cash accounting is to prevent the overstatement of subsequent rates of return and EVA. Ordinarily in the years following a large accounting write-off, the accounting return will be inflated because the loss collapses the book value of equity. But that is only because the accountants have taken a book loss without a cash consequence. A company can seem to improve its return and sell at a greater premium to book if it writes down its assets with pen strokes. But are the resulting figures a very good way to judge its performance?

Accounting for Gains

The cash-accounting treatment for gains is perfectly symmetrical to that for losses. Suppose, for example, that the plant and working capital assets to be liquidated had a book value of $100 instead of $600. This time, accountants would book a gain of $400.

	Loss	Gain
Net proceeds	$ 500	$ 500
Less book value charge-off	600	100
Gain/(loss)	$(100)	$ 400

From a cash perspective, no gain would be recognized, however. As before, the capital account would be credited for the $500 cash proceeds.

Cash (Economic) Treatment		
	Loss	Gain
Original capital	$1,000	$1,000
Less net proceeds	500	500
Ending cash capital	$ 500	$ 500

Much as with the loss situation, the cash consequences can be obtained by subtracting the accounting gain from book capital.

Revised Accounting Treatment		
	Loss	Gain
Original capital	$1,000	$1,000
Less book value charge-off	600	100
Ending book capital	$ 400	$ 900
Add back accounting loss (gain)	100	(400)
Ending cash capital	$ 500	$ 500

Accounting Gains and Losses Are Irrelevant

Observe that, no matter whether a $400 accounting gain or a $100 accounting loss was recognized, the economic analysis is identical (of course, the tax consequences of recognizing a gain or loss must be factored in). Because mere accounting bookkeeping entries have no bearing on cash flow, gains and losses must be ignored. Management should employ cash accounting instead, followed by a rigorous analysis of the potential for economic value added.

What Happens to the Proceeds?

What happens to the $500 in net proceeds from liquidating the plant? What does the company do with this money, and does the choice affect the analysis? It does not affect the analysis because it is assumed that the exit proceeds earn the cost of capital and therefore have no bearing on EVA. This assumption is employed in any economic value analysis because the company could always use the proceeds to retire its debt and buy back its stock in target capital structure proportions

Exhibit 4.6   continued

and thereby earn its cost of capital by retiring those investors' claims on future cash flows.

If the company chooses to invest the proceeds instead of paying them out, this should be viewed as two independent decisions: to liquidate and pay out the funds and then to issue new debt and equity to finance the new venture. Each of the options should stand or fall on its own merits. To associate sources and uses of funds is the first deadly sin of value mismanagement.

Summary

The decision to rationalize is really the same as the decision to reject an unrewarding capital project. The capital project in question is one which calls for investing the net exit proceeds for a return equal to the subsequent cash flow forgone. If the return from this project is less than the cost of capital, management should rationalize the business, no matter what the impact might be on near-term accounting profits.

To account for a downsizing properly, cash accounting should be employed. With such a system, mere bookkeeping losses or gains are ignored. Instead, the net exit proceeds are charged against capital. If adopted for internal performance assessment, EVA with cash accounting will make it more likely that managers will go for the economic benefit and let the irrelevant accounting chips fall where they may.

Exhibit 4.7   Warner-Lambert Takes the Plunge

In 1985, Warner-Lambert, a maker of pharmaceuticals and consumer products, initiated a bold plan to restructure and streamline. The company announced, on November 26, that it would dispose of its barely profitable high-tech health equipment operations, consolidate facilities, and implement a voluntary early-retirement incentive plan. A large percentage of the anticipated sale proceeds were earmarked to buy back stock.

The Charge-off

The company's big bath triggered a special charge of $654 million ($553 million after taxes, or $7.10 a share). The write-down produced the first full-year deficit in the company's history, a loss of $315 million. The market "punished" Warner-Lambert for showing a bookkeeping loss by sending its stock price up 10%, from $40 to $44 a share, a market value increase of approximately $300 million. Where accountants saw a loss, lead steers recognized a gain.

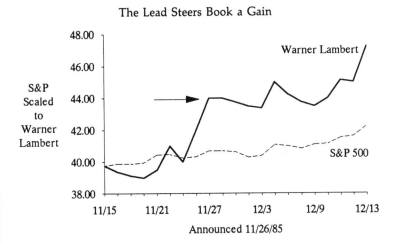

The Lead Steers Book a Gain

Announced 11/26/85

The High-Tech Sell-off

Cost containment by hospitals had put a severe pinch on the profit margins at Warner-Lambert's Deseret Medical, IMED, and Reichert Scientific Instruments units. Their sales were plunging; profits were just above breakeven; depreciation was not being replaced.

Results of Divested Operations

	1985*	1984	1983
Sales	$368	$ 476	$486
Profit before R&D	$ 33	$ 35	$ 45
R&D	28	37	30
Profit after R&D	$ 5	−$2	$ 15
Identifiable Assets	$800	$ 822	$853
Capital Expenditures	$ 20	$ 31	$ 40
Depreciation	$ 32	$ 43	$ 42

*1985 results include sales and profits through October 1985, when the decision to divest became effective. Thereafter, the profits were taken against the charge to earnings for nonrecurring items. Identifiable assets is a very good guess on my part.

Source: 1985 Annual Report, Segment Data.

Exhibit 4.7 continued

Rather than attempt a valiant but certain to be ill-fated turnaround, management wisely decided to sell "to companies whose comprehensive product lines and distribution systems are specifically dedicated to the hospital market."

The Economic Analysis

An economic analysis reveals the benefit of that decision. In the 1985 annual report, Warner-Lambert reduced the assets of its high-tech units from approximately $800 million to $279 million, the level of anticipated net realizable values as determined by independent investment bankers. Let us suppose that, in the absence of a sale, the units' aggregate pretax, but after R&D expense, operating profits could be restored to as much as $25 million a year, or a NOPAT of $15 million, assuming a 40% tax rate. The decision to sell for $279 million amounts to an EVA savings of $25 million a year.

EVAnalysis

Estimated NOPAT	$15
Estimated net liquidation proceeds	$279
r	5.4%
c^*	12.3%
$r - c^*$	-6.9%
$\times$ Net liquidation proceeds	$279
EVA	$-\$25$

The Year After

The year after the write-off (1986), Warner-Lambert surprised shareholders with a net nonrecurring pretax gain of $8.4 million which hid more than it revealed. The gain actually was the combination of realizing $196.4 million more on the sale of the health technologies properties than had been anticipated (making the annual EVA savings from the dispositions more like $43.5 million than $25 million), offset by a $188 million charge to close, consolidate, and upgrade still more facilities, to centralize worldwide R&D, and to expand the voluntary early-retirement incentive, reorganization, and other programs. Awash in a gain after its "big bath," Warner-Lambert continued its aggressive rationalization program.

The Financial Consequences

NOPAT and capital have been computed for Warner-Lambert in two ways.[1] The unadjusted results show what NOPAT and capital would have been assuming that the nonrecurring charges and gains had been taken into income as occurs on the conventional accounting statements. The cash results add back the unusual losses (less unusual gains) after taxes to NOPAT, and the cumulative unusual losses (less cumulative unusual gains) after taxes to capital (see exhibit 4.6 for a description of cash accounting).

	1984	1985	1986	1987	1988
Unadjusted NOPAT	$ 361.3	$ −237.0	$ 346.1	$ 418.3	$ 461.7
Plus unusual loss (gain) after tax	0.0	553.3	−48.0	0.0	0.0
NOPAT	$ 361.3	$ 316.3	$ 298.1	$ 418.3	$ 461.7
Unadjusted capital	$ 2615.4	$ 2145.3	$ 1874.6	$2113.0	$2404.3
Plus cum unusual loss (gain) after tax	152.3	705.6	657.6	657.6	657.6
Capital	$ 2767.7	$ 2850.9	$ 2532.2	$2770.6	$3061.9
Unadjusted r	14.1 %	−9.1 %	16.1 %	22.3 %	21.9 %
r	13.3 %	11.4 %	10.5 %	16.5 %	16.7 %
c^*	15.3 %	13.8 %	11.5 %	12.2 %	12.3 %
$r − c^*$	−2.0 %	−2.4 %	−1.0 %	4.3 %	4.4 %
× Beginning capital	$ 2715.4	$ 2767.7	$ 2850.0	$2532.2	$2770.6
EVA	−$55.3	−$64.6	−$29.7	$ 109.9	$ 120.9

The unadjusted NOPAT to capital rate of return shows a large loss in 1985 (−9.1%) followed by exaggerated increases thereafter. These are the distortions of successful-efforts accounting. The cash return, by contrast, has been normalized to exclude nonrecurring losses and gains and to capitalize the full cost of the restructuring effort. It is more indicative of the true profitability of the business and the efficacy of the restructuring. It too improved handsomely in 1987 and 1988,

[1] In both cases, the company's bad debt provision, the amortization of goodwill, operating leases, and R&D were capitalized. The capitalized R&D was straight-line-amortized over 5 years.

Exhibit 4.7   continued

a genuine testimony to the wisdom of the rationalization. The best internal performance measure, however, is EVA, which progressed from significantly negative to strongly positive over this period, hand in hand with the company's growing market value versus the S&P 500.

A Shrinking Company Expands Value

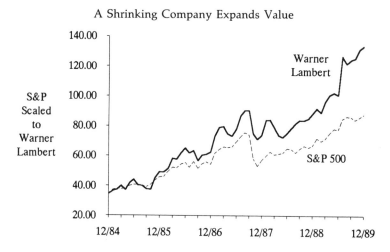

Summary

Warner-Lambert accomplished a successful divestiture and streamlining program beginning in late 1985. As embarrassing as booking an accounting loss may have been, the economic loss had already been registered in the company's market value, and the disposed properties simply were worth more to others. Thus, receiving the sale proceeds was worthwhile relative to giving up the future cash flows of these businesses, an annual economic value added of $25 million or more. The rationalization of production and personnel, although initially costly, was an investment that eventually paid off. Rather than expense charges that have an enduring benefit, in the economic model they are capitalized. Cash accounting procedures produce rates of return that are more indicative of the real merits of a downsizing strategy than conventional accounting measures. In the final analysis, however, it is the improvement in EVA that is most significant in driving up the value of a company that dramatically restructures its business portfolio.

The X,Y,Z Challenge

If EVA is truly worth its salt as a performance measure, it ought to handle the challenge of setting apart companies X, Y, and Z. Let's see. (Refer to exhibit 4.8 for a complete spread.)

	X	Y	Z
$(r - c^*)$	10% − 10%	12.5% − 10%	12.5% − 10%
× Inc in cap (I)	$1,000	$800	$2,000
Incremental EVA	$ 0	$ 20	$ 50

Multiplying the new capital invested in 1990 by the spread between r and c^* gives the incremental EVA generated by growth. Rising from X through Z, EVA goes hand in hand with the cre-

Exhibit 4.8   EVA for Companies X, Y, and Z

FINANSEER (data in millions)	History 1989	Forecast 1990	Forecast 1991	Forecast 1992	Forecast 1993	Forecast 1994
COMPANY X						
1 NOPAT/Beg Capital r	10.0%	10.0%	10.0%	10.0%	10.0%	10.0%
2 Wtd Avg Cap Cost c*	10.0%	10.0%	10.0%	10.0%	10.0%	10.0%
3 Spread r - c*	0.0%	0.0%	0.0%	0.0%	0.0%	0.0%
4 x Beginning Capital	$10,000	$11,000	$12,100	$13,310	$14,641	$16,105
5 Economic Value Added (EVA)	$0	$0	$0	$0	$0	$0
6 Increase in EVA		$0	$0	$0	$0	$0
COMPANY Y						
1 NOPAT/Beg Capital r	12.5%	12.5%	12.5%	12.5%	12.5%	12.5%
2 Wtd Avg Cap Cost c*	10.0%	10.0%	10.0%	10.0%	10.0%	10.0%
3 Spread r - c*	2.5%	2.5%	2.5%	2.5%	2.5%	2.5%
4 x Beginning Capital	$8,000	$8,800	$9,680	$10,648	$11,713	$12,884
5 Economic Value Added (EVA)	$200	$220	$242	$266	$293	$322
6 Increase in EVA		$20	$22	$24	$27	$29
COMPANY Z						
1 NOPAT/Beg Capital r	12.5%	12.5%	12.5%	12.5%	12.5%	12.5%
2 Wtd Avg Cap Cost c*	10.0%	10.0%	10.0%	10.0%	10.0%	10.0%
3 Spread r - c*	2.5%	2.5%	2.5%	2.5%	2.5%	2.5%
4 x Beginning Capital	$8,000	$10,000	$12,500	$15,625	$19,532	$24,415
5 Economic Value Added (EVA)	$200	$250	$313	$391	$488	$610
6 Increase in EVA		$50	$63	$78	$97	$122

ation of value. No other measure can do that. We are definitely onto something here.

The Basketball Analogy.   EVA shows that an X company is much like a basketball player who scores lots of baskets (i.e., generates lots of earnings) only because he takes many shots (i.e., invests lots of capital). X's shooting percentage (i.e., rate of return) is quite ordinary, and the team would do just as well if he passed off the ball to other, equally capable players instead of hogging so many of the shots for himself. X thinks it can keep pace with the big boys, but in reality it is just a big zero.

Y scores the same number of baskets as X does (i.e., produces the same earnings), but it does so while taking far fewer shots at the basket (invests less capital). Y's shooting percentage is impressive. If only Y would take more shots at the basket.

Z is the Michael Jordan of the corporate league. It enjoys the same shooting percentage advantage as Y does, but it takes far more shots at the basket (i.e., pumps more capital into the business). Give Z the MVC—that's right, the Most Valuable Company award.

One more basketball player is still on the court, X-Minus. X-Minus has a poor shooting percentage but makes up for it by taking many shots at the basket. It reminds me of Gulf + Western while Charles Bludhorn was on his acquisition binge, and Saatchi & Saatchi more recently.

Suppose, for example, that X-Minus earns only a 7.5% rate of return but persists in investing $2,000 for every $1,000 of NOPAT. Its growth rate will be twice 7.5%, or 15%, a rate of expansion that handily surpasses both X's and Y's. Although scoring lots of points is their apparent forte, they dig deeper holes for their teams with every shot they take. Take their shooting percentage r of 7.5%, less their capital competitors' shooting percentage c^* of 10%, and multiply by the number of shots they take by pumping capital into the business, or $2,000. EVA, sadly, is a negative $50.

That's just great. Bench those gunners until they figure out how to really help the team. For X-Minus, value could be created if only by turning off the investment spigot on its unrewarding capital projects.

The Clincher. To my mind, EVA really needs no more sub-stantiation as a performance measure, but there is a clincher. EVA *ties directly to the intrinsic market value of any company.* When it is projected and discounted to a present value, EVA accounts for the market value that management adds to, or subtracts from, the capital it has employed.

$$MVA = \text{market value} - \text{capital}$$
$$MVA = \text{present value of all future EVA}$$

MVA, market value added, is the absolute dollar spread between a company's market value and its capital. Unlike a rate of return which reflects the outcome of one period, MVA is a cumulative measure of corporate performance. It represents the stock market's assessment as of a particular time of the net present value of all a company's past and projected capital projects. It reflects how successfully a company has invested capital in the past and how successful it is likely to be at investing new capital in the future. Maximizing MVA should be the primary objective for any com-pany that is concerned about its shareholders' welfare.

A company's EVA is the fuel that fires up its MVA. EVA, because it is defined to be operating profits net of a capital charge, implicitly subtracts the cost of the existing capital and new capi-tal investment when it is projected and discounted to a present value. What's left over from the operating cash flow is the net present value of all capital projects, past and future. Thus, EVA is the internal measure which leads to the external consequence of building a premium (or discount) into the market value of a company (exhibit 4.9).

With EVA and MVA as corresponding internal and external measures of corporate performance, let us turn to a review of the five classic companies. (Exhibit 4.10 presents a detailed spread over the past 10 years.)

Arranging the companies from X-Minus to Pre-Z in exhibit 4.11 also ranks them in ascending order of the total market value they have added to the capital they have employed (column 5). That should come as no surprise by this point.

Market value added has been computed each year in exhibit

Exhibit 4.9   The Relationship Between EVA and MVA

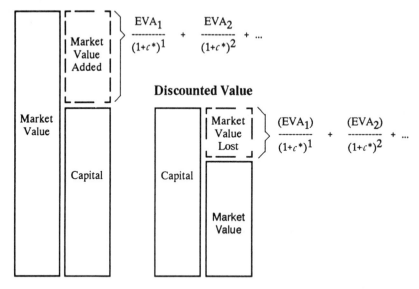

4.10 by taking each company's spread between its year-end share price and the underlying per share economic book value of its common equity and multiplying by the number of common shares outstanding (net of those in treasury). Observe how market value added goes hand in hand with the level and change in the level of economic value added, with the exception of McCaw Cellular, whose EVA is yet to come.

- United Technologies, the X-Minus representative, has a negative EVA, becoming progressively more negative, and a negative MVA, becoming somewhat more negative (although, as often happens, the market anticipated some of the damage).

- SPX, the X, has essentially a zero EVA, and accordingly sells for essentially no premium to capital. It is an unregulated public utility.

- Noxell, the Y, has a positive and gently sloping EVA, accounting for a similar trend in its MVA (though the pace did pick up in the most recent years).

- Novell, our class Z company, is noteworthy in that its MVA rocketed as its rate of return plummeted. Judged by return

Exhibit 4.10 EVA and MVA for Five Archetypal Companies

UNITED TECHNOLOGIES CORP
X-

FINANSEER (Data in Millions)	1979	1980	1981	1982	1983	1984	1985	1986	1987	1988	10-Year Summary
1 NOPAT/Beg Capital r	23.3%	15.4%	15.4%	11.1%	13.2%	13.6%	8.2%	1.8%	10.5%	9.5%	12.2%
2 Wtd Avg Cap Cost c*	14.5%	15.9%	17.8%	17.3%	16.1%	17.1%	15.7%	13.0%	14.1%	14.4%	15.6%
3 Spread r - c*	8.8%	-0.5%	-2.4%	-6.2%	-2.9%	-3.5%	-7.5%	-11.2%	-3.6%	-4.9%	-3.4%
4 x Beginning Capital	$3,625.9	$5,325.3	$6,049.9	$6,588.6	$7,150.8	$7,668.3	$8,814.7	$8,299.5	$9,234.8	$9,596.5	$7,235.4
5 Economic Value Added (EVA)	$319.0	($26.8)	($146.9)	($410.7)	($205.0)	($268.1)	($657.4)	($932.8)	($335.8)	($470.1)	($313.5)
6 Share Price	$21.50	$30.50	$30.88	$28.31	$36.25	$36.25	$43.75	$46.00	$33.88	$41.13	7.5%
7 "Economic" Book Value/Shr	35.33	40.25	42.30	43.73	46.06	50.61	51.07	47.19	51.98	55.74	5.2%
8 Price - Book	($13.83)	($9.75)	($21.43)	($15.41)	($9.81)	($14.36)	($7.32)	($1.19)	($18.10)	($14.62)	($12.58)
9 x No. Shares Outst'g	84.2	87.3	103.8	108.6	119.6	121.4	122.9	130.4	130.4	130.8	113.9
10 Market Value Added (MVA)	($1,165.1)	($851.9)	($2,223.3)	($1,674.0)	($1,173.1)	($1,743.0)	($899.6)	($155.6)	($2,360.8)	($1,911.7)	($1,415.8)

SPX CORP
X

FINANSEER (Data in Millions)	1979	1980	1981	1982	1983	1984	1985	1986	1987	1988	10-Year Summary
1 NOPAT/Beg Capital r	19.6%	18.0%	16.6%	18.2%	14.9%	16.7%	17.1%	10.8%	11.1%	14.0%	15.7%
2 Wtd Avg Cap Cost c*	14.0%	16.0%	17.9%	17.3%	16.2%	17.5%	15.2%	12.5%	12.7%	13.3%	15.3%

Exhibit 4.10 continued

FINANSEER

(Data in Millions)	1979	1980	1981	1982	1983	1984	1985	1986	1987	1988	10-Year Summary
3 Spread r - c*	5.7%	2.0%	-1.4%	0.9%	-1.3%	-0.8%	1.9%	-1.7%	-1.5%	0.7%	0.4%
4 x Beginning Capital	$126.5	$145.0	$171.0	$197.7	$241.7	$261.1	$306.6	$459.8	$486.5	$513.5	$290.9
5 Economic Value Added (EVA)	$7.2	$2.9	($2.3)	$1.7	($3.1)	($2.0)	$5.7	($8.0)	($7.5)	$3.6	($0.2)
6 Share Price	$13.44	$12.13	$16.13	$22.31	$26.63	$25.88	$27.75	$26.13	$29.75	$38.63	12.4%
7 "Economic" Book Value/Shr	14.01	15.85	17.84	18.73	20.79	23.30	26.02	28.46	31.31	35.01	10.7%
8 Price - Book	($0.57)	($3.72)	($1.71)	$3.58	$5.83	$2.57	$1.73	($2.33)	($1.56)	$3.61	$0.74
9 x No. Shares Outst'g	9.6	9.6	9.7	12.2	12.2	12.2	12.3	12.3	12.3	12.4	11.5
10 Market Value Added (MVA)	($5.5)	($35.9)	($16.6)	$43.6	$71.3	$31.5	$21.2	($28.7)	($19.1)	$44.9	$10.7

NOXELL Y

FINANSEER

(Data in Millions)	1979	1980	1981	1982	1983	1984	1985	1986	1987	1988	10-Year Summary
1 NOPAT/Beg Capital r	24.3%	27.0%	25.9%	25.3%	26.8%	29.8%	25.5%	29.1%	31.1%	32.3%	27.7%
2 Wtd Avg Cap Cost c*	13.5%	15.5%	17.6%	17.0%	15.4%	16.6%	15.3%	14.5%	14.7%	14.4%	15.5%
3 Spread r - c*	10.8%	11.5%	8.3%	8.3%	11.3%	13.2%	10.2%	14.7%	16.3%	17.9%	12.2%
4 x Beginning Capital	$57.8	$64.7	$77.9	$88.8	$99.7	$110.7	$140.7	$138.8	$156.2	$174.0	$110.9
5 Economic Value Added (EVA)	$6.2	$7.4	$6.4	$7.4	$11.3	$14.6	$14.3	$20.3	$25.5	$31.1	$14.5
6 Share Price	$2.69	$2.97	$3.98	$6.41	$9.44	$11.34	$14.81	$21.00	$21.25	$19.25	24.5%
7 "Economic" Book Value/Shr	1.83	2.14	2.49	2.86	3.34	3.81	4.47	5.14	6.06	7.00	16.1%
8 Price - Book	$0.86	$0.83	$1.49	$3.54	$6.10	$7.53	$10.35	$15.86	$15.19	$12.25	$7.40
9 x No. Shares Outst'g	39.7	39.0	39.1	39.6	40.1	39.6	40.0	40.1	40.4	40.4	39.8
10 Market Value Added (MVA)	$34.2	$32.2	$58.4	$140.4	$244.5	$298.4	$413.9	$636.1	$614.4	$495.4	$296.8

NOVELL, INC.

FINANSEER (Nov-Oct) (Data in Millions)	Z				3-Year
	1986	1987	1988	1989	Summary
1 NOPAT/Beg Capital r	122.9%	74.4%	52.6%	45.4%	57.5%
2 Wtd Avg Cap Cost c*	15.5%	16.4%	15.7%	13.4%	15.2%
3 Spread r - c*	107.4%	58.0%	36.9%	32.0%	42.3%
4 x Beginning Capital	$9.4	$38.0	$95.1	$174.6	$102.6
5 Economic Value Added (EVA)	$10.1	$22.0	$35.1	$55.8	$37.7
6 Share Price	$12.88	$24.00	$30.00	$31.00	13.7%
7 "Economic" Book Value/Shr	1.84	4.27	6.16	9.09	46.0%
8 Price - Book	$11.04	$19.73	$23.84	$21.91	$21.83
9 x No. Shares Outst'g	22.5	26.7	27.3	33.0	29.0
10 Market Value Added (MVA)	$248.4	$527.3	$649.9	$721.8	$633.0

McCAW CELLULAR COMM
Pre-Z

FINANSEER (Data in Millions)				2-Year
	1986	1987	1988	Summary
1 NOPAT/Beg Capital r		-24.4%	-11.3%	-17.9%
2 Wtd Avg Cap Cost c*		8.1%	9.3%	8.7%
3 Spread r - c*		-32.5%	-20.6%	-26.6%
4 x Beginning Capital		$441.6	$822.4	$632.0
5 Economic Value Added (EVA)		($143.7)	($169.7)	($156.7)
6 Share Price		$16.13	$27.00	67.4%
7 "Economic" Book Value/Shr		1.14	0.82	-28.1%
8 Price - Book		$14.99	$26.18	$20.59
9 x No. Shares Outst'g		112.2	131.7	122.0
10 Market Value Added (MVA)		$1,681.8	$3,448.2	$2,565.0

Exhibit 4.11   Archetypal Companies
Ten-Year Average (1979–1988)

		(1)	(2)	(3) Avg Capital	(4) Avg EVA	(5) Avg EVA
Type	Company	r	$r - c^*$			
X-Minus	United Technologies	12.2 %	−3.4 %	$7235.4	$−313.5	$−1415.8
X	SPX	15.7 %	0.4 %	$ 290.9	$ −0.2	$ 10.7
Y	Noxell	27.7 %	12.2 %	$ 110.9	$ 14.5	$ 296.8
Z	Novell	57.5 %	42.3 %	$ 102.6	$ 37.7	$ 633.0
Pre-Z	McCaw Cellular	−17.9 %	−26.6 %	$ 632.0	$−156.7	$ 2565.0

Novell's data are averaged over 1987 to 1989 (Nov–Oct fiscal year).

McCaw Cellular data are averaged over 1987 to 1988.

alone, Novell collapsed. But EVA tells an entirely different story. EVA shows a stirring improvement every year. Novell's incremental growth is value adding, but there is no way to know that without looking at EVA.

The lead steers somehow are getting the message, though. Novell's market value added steadily climbed in the face of its declining returns, moving up in line with the growing EVA. Market value added almost tripled over 3 years, from $250 million in 1986 to $720 million by 1989, even as the ratio of price to book value fell in half, from a multiple of 7.0× ($12.88/$1.84) to just 3.4× ($31.00/$9.09).

Novell sold for its highest market value premium when its return was lowest and its ratios of r to c^* and price to book were lowest. But ratios do not matter. Creating value is what matters.

• McCaw, the Pre-Z, sells for a huge premium to its capital, all on the come. By agreeing to pay a $2.5 billion market value premium for McCaw's common shares, investors are signaling their confidence in McCaw's eventual ability to generate great internal rates of return on a growing base of capital. Now, who was it who said the market ignored the prospect of distant payoffs?

The Retailer Roundup

The relationship between EVA and MVA is perhaps even more meaningful when it is assessed for companies within a given industry group. For instance, in exhibit 4.12 I have identified a group of five retailers which nicely span all three of the archetypal X,Y,Z categories (see exhibit 4.13 for year-by-year details).

Kroger and K-Mart

- Kroger and K-Mart are classic X companies earning commodity returns and generally selling for commodity market values.

- Kroger performed a leveraged recapitalization in 1988, paying out a whopping $3.8 billion ($3.2 billion in cash and the remainder in junior debentures), all debt-financed. Net worth plunged to a deficit $2.9 billion, and leverage soared from a total debt to total capital ratio of 55% the year before to 145% (including the present value of minimum operating leases over 5 years).

- All of the company's conventional accounting measures of performance and value went haywire, another indication of why they must be abandoned by corporate America. Kroger's earnings per share dove from $2.99 the year before the recapitalization to $0.24 in 1988. With a nega-

Exhibit 4.12 Archetypal Retailers
Ten-Year Average (1979–1988)
(Dollars in Millions)

Type	Company	(1) r	(2) $r - c^*$	(3) Avg Capital	(4) Avg EVA	(5) Avg MVA
X	Kroger	11.5%	1.4%	$2,558.6	$ 24.8	$ 406.3
X	K-Mart	11.2%	−0.3%	$6,705.2	$−22.5	$ 266.3
Y	Melville	20.7%	9.0%	$1,358.1	$ 112.4	$1,059.0
Z	Food Lion	22.1%	9.5%	$ 280.0	$ 24.5	$1,048.1
Z	Wal-Mart	23.6%	11.1%	$1,600.1	$ 185.1	$5,861.8

Exhibit 4.13 EVA & MVA Relations for Five Retailers

KROGER CO
Retail
X

FINANSEER (Data in Millions)	1979	1980	1981	1982	1983	1984	1985	1986	1987	1988	10-Year Summary
1 NOPAT/Beg Capital r	12.5%	13.7%	15.1%	12.3%	14.6%	10.3%	10.4%	6.4%	9.0%	10.2%	11.5%
2 Wtd Avg Cap Cost c*	9.3%	10.8%	12.4%	11.8%	10.5%	11.5%	10.0%	7.5%	9.1%	8.2%	10.1%
3 Spread r - c*	3.3%	3.0%	2.7%	0.6%	4.2%	-1.1%	0.4%	-1.1%	-0.1%	1.9%	1.4%
4 x Beginning Capital	$1,240.4	$1,491.3	$1,661.1	$1,921.3	$2,361.4	$3,094.3	$3,097.9	$3,551.7	$3,321.2	$3,845.4	$2,558.6
5 Economic Value Added (EVA)	$40.4	$44.5	$44.8	$10.7	$98.2	($34.3)	$12.3	($39.0)	($4.4)	$74.7	$24.8
6 Share Price	$9.50	$10.88	$13.00	$19.69	$18.50	$19.63	$23.94	$29.88	$24.75	$8.88	-0.8%
7 "Economic" Book Value/Shr	13.27	15.37	18.05	19.75	16.68	18.20	19.77	19.57	19.99	(27.10)	-208.3%
8 Price - Book	($3.77)	($4.50)	($5.05)	($0.06)	$1.82	$1.43	$4.17	$10.30	$4.76	$35.98	$4.51
9 x No. Shares Outst'g	55.2	55.5	56.0	56.0	89.5	90.2	87.4	84.1	78.6	80.9	73.3
10 Market Value Added (MVA)	($208.1)	($249.8)	($282.5)	($3.4)	$162.6	$128.6	$364.4	$866.1	$374.0	$2,910.8	$406.3

KMART CORP
Retail
X

FINANSEER (Feb-Jan) (Data in Millions)	1979	1980	1981	1982	1983	1984	1985	1986	1987	1988	10-Year Summary
1 NOPAT/Beg Capital r	13.9%	11.2%	10.2%	7.5%	11.9%	11.3%	10.2%	11.2%	11.7%	13.0%	11.2%
2 Wtd Avg Cap Cost c*	9.8%	11.2%	12.8%	12.2%	11.1%	12.0%	12.1%	10.4%	11.4%	12.1%	11.5%

	1979	1980	1981	1982	1983	1984	1985	1986	1987	1988	10-Year Summary
3 Spread r - c*	4.1%	0.0%	-2.6%	-4.7%	0.8%	-0.7%	-1.9%	0.8%	0.3%	0.8%	-0.3%
4 x Beginning Capital	$3,933.9	$4,604.3	$5,186.4	$5,929.5	$5,970.7	$6,289.5	$7,915.8	$8,451.7	$9,002.4	$9,767.7	$6,705.2
5 Economic Value Added (EVA)	$161.1	($1.3)	($135.2)	($280.1)	$49.2	($41.6)	($151.9)	$66.8	$28.3	$79.9	($22.5)
6 Share Price	$15.83	$11.92	$10.50	$14.67	$22.17	$23.50	$23.58	$29.25	$29.75	$35.13	9.3%
7 "Economic" Book Value/Shr	13.20	14.65	16.01	16.91	18.80	20.54	21.03	23.96	26.97	30.92	9.9%
8 Price - Book	$2.64	($2.73)	($5.51)	($2.24)	$3.37	$2.96	$2.55	$5.29	$2.78	$4.21	$1.33
9 x No. Shares Outst'g	184.3	185.1	186.0	186.7	188.9	187.5	189.0	200.3	199.7	199.4	190.7
10 Market Value Added (MVA)	$485.9	($505.2)	($1,025.5)	($418.1)	$635.9	$554.4	$482.2	$1,059.6	$555.1	$838.9	$266.3

MELVILLE CORP
Retail
Y

FINANSEER
(Data in Millions)

	1979	1980	1981	1982	1983	1984	1985	1986	1987	1988	10-Year Summary
1 NOPAT/Beg Capital r	23.2%	22.7%	23.8%	19.9%	20.1%	19.0%	18.7%	18.9%	19.4%	20.8%	20.7%
2 Wtd Avg Cap Cost c*	9.6%	11.3%	13.0%	12.4%	11.1%	12.1%	11.4%	10.7%	12.5%	13.1%	11.7%
3 Spread r - c*	13.6%	11.5%	10.8%	7.5%	9.0%	7.0%	7.3%	8.2%	6.9%	7.7%	9.0%
4 x Beginning Capital	$608.6	$689.4	$603.7	$1,068.2	$1,275.8	$1,469.9	$1,684.8	$1,779.7	$1,960.3	$2,240.6	$1,358.1
5 Economic Value Added (EVA)	$83.0	$78.9	$37.0	$80.0	$115.2	$102.7	$122.6	$146.8	$135.5	$172.0	$112.4
6 Share Price	$6.88	$8.69	$9.44	$17.69	$17.44	$18.63	$25.25	$27.00	$26.50	$37.19	20.6%
7 "Economic" Book Value/Shr	4.45	5.28	6.24	7.20	8.43	9.64	10.90	12.49	14.34	16.71	15.8%
8 Price - Book	$2.43	$3.41	$3.20	$10.49	$9.01	$8.98	$14.35	$14.51	$12.16	$20.48	$9.90
9 x No. Shares Outst'g	100.1	102.4	103.6	104.2	104.9	105.7	108.1	108.5	108.7	109.0	105.5
10 Market Value Added (MVA)	$242.8	$349.4	$331.3	$1,092.7	$945.5	$949.6	$1,550.9	$1,573.8	$1,321.7	$2,232.0	$1,059.0

Exhibit 4.13 continued

FOOD LION INC
Retail
Z

FINANSEER (Data in Millions)	1979	1980	1981	1982	1983	1984	1985	1986	1987	1988	10-Year Summary
1 NOPAT/Beg Capital r	30.7%	27.4%	25.0%	18.9%	18.0%	17.9%	22.4%	20.3%	19.8%	20.5%	22.1%
2 Wtd Avg Cap Cost c*	11.7%	13.4%	15.3%	14.4%	12.7%	13.5%	12.8%	11.1%	10.7%	10.8%	12.6%
3 Spread r - c*	19.1%	13.9%	9.8%	4.5%	5.3%	4.3%	9.6%	9.2%	9.1%	9.7%	9.5%
4 x Beginning Capital	$56.2	$76.8	$100.2	$131.0	$205.2	$266.3	$270.7	$393.4	$540.9	$759.0	$280.0
5 Economic Value Added (EVA)	$10.7	$10.7	$9.8	$6.0	$10.9	$11.6	$26.1	$36.1	$49.4	$73.9	$24.5
6 Share Price	$0.59	$0.61	$1.06	$2.19	$1.71	$2.42	$3.63	$5.56	$12.00	$9.38	36.0%
7 "Economic" Book Value/Shr	0.16	0.22	0.29	0.35	0.44	0.58	0.73	0.93	1.17	1.51	28.1%
8 Price - Book	$0.43	$0.39	$0.77	$1.84	$1.27	$1.84	$2.90	$4.63	$10.83	$7.86	$3.28
9 x No. Shares Outst'g	309.0	309.7	312.2	313.3	315.0	318.2	319.4	321.0	321.7	321.9	316.1
10 Market Value Added (MVA)	$131.9	$121.0	$239.8	$576.1	$399.1	$585.9	$925.0	$1,487.9	$3,482.9	$2,531.7	$1,048.1

WAL-MART STORES
Retail
Z

FINANSEER (Feb-Jan) (Data in Millions)	1979	1980	1981	1982	1983	1984	1985	1986	1987	1988	10-Year Summary
1 NOPAT/Beg Capital r	24.2%	23.8%	25.3%	20.4%	23.4%	24.2%	21.5%	23.2%	24.8%	25.2%	23.6%
2 Wtd Avg Cap Cost c*	10.8%	12.4%	13.9%	13.5%	12.3%	13.6%	12.9%	11.0%	11.7%	12.6%	12.5%
3 Spread r - c*	13.4%	11.4%	11.3%	6.9%	11.1%	10.6%	8.7%	12.3%	13.1%	12.6%	11.1%
4 x Beginning Capital	$274.7	$382.5	$528.2	$860.2	$1,068.5	$1,312.7	$1,876.7	$2,362.1	$3,114.4	$4,221.3	$1,600.1
5 Economic Value Added (EVA)	$36.9	$43.5	$59.9	$59.4	$118.4	$139.3	$162.9	$289.6	$407.5	$533.7	$185.1
6 Share Price	$1.09	$1.89	$2.66	$6.23	$9.75	$9.47	$15.94	$23.25	$26.00	$31.38	45.3%
7 "Economic" Book Value/Shr	0.42	0.60	0.81	1.13	1.58	2.04	2.62	3.40	4.50	6.01	34.3%
8 Price - Book	$0.66	$1.29	$1.85	$5.10	$8.17	$7.43	$13.32	$19.85	$21.50	$25.36	$10.45
9 x No. Shares Outst'g	483.9	517.5	518.7	537.7	559.7	560.9	562.1	564.4	565.1	565.6	543.5

tive net worth, the accounting return on equity cannot even be computed. In spite of these misleading signs of ill health, Kroger's MVA increased by about $2.5 billion in comparison with the year before. The other economic measures came sailing through, too. The rate of return on total capital r was not affected by the recapitalization of debt for equity per se. But the spread between r and c^* did widen, in part because the aggressive use of debt drove down the after-tax cost of capital. The improvement in return and EVA during 1988 is, however, only a harbinger of much better things to come, as Kroger is undertaking an extensive downsizing and deintegration program to restore its focus and boost profitability.

• Kroger's recap illustrates an important point. The aggressive use of debt is a recommended financial strategy for many X companies or X-like units of large companies. For without the prospect for creating value through new investments and growth, an X company can dedicate its cash flows to debt service without impairing its intrinsic market value. Moreover, the drive to pay down debt may point the X company toward its most important market mandate: become profitable before growing.

  Investors recognize that the characteristics that made Kroger a logical candidate for leverage apply with equal force to K-Mart. The possibility of a recapitalization is the reason why K-Mart has sold for even as much of a premium over book capital as it has in recent years. The company's returns and EVA certainly do not warrant it.

Melville

• Melville is a successful operator of 13 specialty retail divisions, and it is a classic Y company. Melville is a model of controlled, profitable growth. Its rate of return handsomely exceeds its cost of capital; the company has enjoyed strong positive free cash flow in all but one year; and a positive and growing EVA has driven its market value to an ever greater premium to its (economic) book value. If you have but one life to live, work for a Y company. It is a pleasant, aristocratic existence, I find.

Food Lion and Wal-Mart

- The contrast between Kroger and Food Lion (the former Food Town grocery chain that, when its name was lost to another company, selected Food Lion as a replacement because only two letters on its store fronts had to be replaced), and between K-Mart and Wal-Mart is positively striking. How two sets of companies, each set operating in the same business, can perform so divergently, is an amazing story I will not tell here. But one cannot look at the performance of Food Lion and, in particular, Wal-Mart, both classic Z companies, without a sense of awe and wonder in light of what mere mortals in their businesses are able to accomplish.

  By the end of 1988, Wal-Mart had added $14.3 billion in value to the capital resources drawn into the firm, a change of nearly $14 billion since the end of 1979. This occurred, incidentally, despite, or rather because of, the fact that Wal-Mart has had a negative free cash flow in 8 of the past 10 years. EVA at the end of 1988 was $534 million, a change of almost incomprehensible magnitude since 1979. I venture to say that Wal-Mart is one of the world's greatest companies. For, without brilliant scientific talent, without a brand name franchise, without addicting its consumers, without high technology, and without a long, prestigious history behind it, Wal-Mart is very nearly the most value-adding company in the United States. Wal-Mart's success is the result of good management, plain and simple.

- Wal-Mart is also inspiring because, although retailing in the aggregate is a slow-growth business, by being more efficient, by creating a comparative advantage, and by taking market share away from others, Wal-Mart has proved the potential for a company in almost any business to create exceptional value. All it takes is great management. Woolworth supports this hypothesis, too.

Woolworth: The High-Plains Drifter

A final retail example illustrates the potential for climbing back from the depths of X-Minus to the high plains of Y. Woolworth, under the leadership of Chairman Harold E. Sells, adopted a bold but necessary plan to reverse the company's sagging fortunes in 1982.

> The company's achievements in 1988 continued to reflect the vitality of the strategies it has pursued with ever increasing success since undertaking a major corporate restructuring some six years ago. The strategies adopted at that time targeted rapid expansion of specialty store operations by internal development and acquisitions as well as improved productivity in general merchandise operations. Since then, revenues and profits have consistently trended upwards and at the close of 1988, attained their highest levels ever.
>
> The vigorous push into specialty retailing, coupled with the renovation and remerchandising of a substantial number of larger general merchandise stores, were underwritten by $1.2 billion in capital expenditures since 1983—more than half of which was spent in the last two years alone. A record 1,154 new stores were opened in 1988, virtually all through the expansion of existing specialty formats and the development and acquisition of new ones. This achievement, unprecedented in retail annals, is clear and unequivocal evidence that the new Woolworth will cede the high ground in specialty retailing to no one.
>
> Woolworth 1988 annual report

Woolworth's financial results bear tribute to a remarkable turnaround (exhibit 4.14). Starting with a very negative EVA in 1981 and 1982, Woolworth's progress was first registered by an EVA that became progressively less negative as rates of return improved on an essentially flat capital base. By 1986, the company's returns were once again above the cost of capital. The floodgates on new capital spending were opened, which sent EVA surging to over $70 million by 1988. The company's market value added followed a pattern quite similar to that of EVA, though tending to anticipate EVA progress by one year. In a turnaround situation like Woolworth's, investors will want to be convinced

Exhibit 4.14 Woolworth Corp. X → Y

FINANSEER
(Feb-Jan)
(Data in Millions)

	1979	1980	1981	1982	1983	1984	1985	1986	1987	1988	10-Year Summary
1 NOPAT/Beg Capital r	11.4%	11.0%	7.2%	2.7%	8.4%	9.0%	10.1%	11.8%	13.1%	14.5%	9.9%
2 Wtd Avg Cap Cost c*	8.8%	10.3%	12.0%	11.5%	10.3%	11.3%	10.8%	9.5%	11.5%	12.1%	10.8%
3 Spread r - c*	2.6%	0.7%	-4.8%	-8.8%	-1.9%	-2.4%	-0.8%	2.3%	1.6%	2.3%	-0.9%
4 x Beginning Capital	$2,655.9	$2,931.0	$3,323.3	$3,346.8	$2,361.8	$2,415.5	$2,393.6	$2,481.4	$2,755.6	$3,128.5	$2,779.3
5 Economic Value Added (EVA)	$69.6	$20.2	($158.1)	($294.9)	($45.6)	($57.3)	($18.4)	$56.2	$45.3	$73.1	($31.0)
6 Share Price	$12.56	$12.38	$9.00	$12.94	$17.56	$18.50	$30.00	$38.63	$34.50	$51.75	17.0%
7 "Economic" Book Value/Shr	24.25	26.62	26.33	18.66	18.66	18.92	21.09	24.73	29.26	32.28	3.2%
8 Price - Book	($11.69)	($14.25)	($17.33)	($5.72)	($1.09)	($0.42)	$8.91	$13.89	$5.24	$19.47	($0.30)
9 x No. Shares Outst'g	59.3	60.0	60.7	61.3	63.0	62.9	64.1	65.5	64.3	64.0	62.5
10 Market Value Added (MVA)	($693.5)	($854.8)	($1,051.0)	($350.5)	($68.8)	($26.6)	$570.8	$909.7	$336.7	$1,245.9	$1.8

the improvement is real and sustainable before projecting the reversal too far ahead.

Woolworth illustrates the potential for moving up-category, from X-Minus back into Y. It is rare, however, for a company that has fallen from a Z to ever move back to that category again. As a matter of fact, there is a tendency for all companies to progress through a life cycle from Pre-Z to Z and then Y, at which point they can stay at Y almost indefinitely, growing profitably along with the population or GNP (Coca-Cola would be a good example), or they can fall down into X (IBM, recently) or X-Minus (the railroads, textiles, tire and rubber companies, etc.), depending upon barriers to entry, the intensity of competitor rivalry, and the sort of stuff that Michael Porter writes about in his lengthy tomes and I will not bother to rehash here. As for economic life cycles of companies, I will have more to say in the chapter on valuation.

Standardization

Despite EVA's advantages as a performance measure, there is one shortcoming to its use. Unlike growth rates or rates of return, it is more difficult to compare among companies or business units of different sizes. But this deficiency is easily rectified. EVA can be standardized to reflect a common level of capital employed.

To illustrate, all of the dollar results for the six retailers have been scaled to the assumption that each company started with $100 of capital 5 years ago, that is, at the beginning of the 1984 fiscal year. To do this, each year's financial results are divided by the capital outstanding at the end of fiscal 1983, and then multiplied by $100. The results are given in exhibit 4.15.

In each year standardized EVA is computed by taking the spread between that year's rate of return and cost of capital (which are unaffected by the scaling) and multiplying by the standardized capital outstanding at the beginning of the year. Thus, the standardized EVA in the first year of the analysis, in this case 1984, always will be equal to the spread between that year's r and c^* times $100.

$$\text{Standardized 1984 EVA} = 1984 \, (r - c^*) \times \$100$$

Exhibit 4.15   Standardized EVA-MVA for Six Retailing Companies

K MART CORP
Retail
X

FINANSEER (Feb-Jan) (Scaled to Beginning Capital)	1984	1985	1986	1987	1988	5-year Summary
1 Sales	$338.7	$360.1	$382.4	$411.3	$438.1	6.6%
2 Sales Growth	13.4%	6.3%	6.2%	7.6%	6.5%	8.0%
3 Capital	$125.9	$134.4	$143.1	$155.3	$166.9	7.3%
4 NOPAT/Beg Capital r	11.3%	10.2%	11.2%	11.7%	13.0%	11.5%
5 Wtd Avg Cap Cost c*	12.0%	12.1%	10.4%	11.4%	12.1%	11.6%
6 Spread r-c*	-0.7%	-1.9%	0.8%	0.3%	0.8%	-0.1%
7 x Beginning Capital	$100.0	$125.9	$134.4	$143.1	$155.3	$131.7
8 Economic Value Added	($0.7)	($2.4)	$1.1	$0.4	$1.3	($0.1)
9 Year End Share Price	$23.50	$23.58	$29.25	$29.75	$35.13	10.6%
10 Adj Book Value Per Shr	20.54	21.03	23.96	26.97	30.92	10.8%
11 Price - Adj Book	$2.96	$2.55	$5.29	$2.78	$4.21	$3.56
12 x No. Shares Outst'g	2.4	2.4	2.5	2.5	2.5	2.5
13 Market Value Added	$7.0	$6.1	$13.4	$7.0	$10.6	$8.8

KROGER CO
Retail
X

FINANSEER (Scaled to Beginning Capital)	1984	1985	1986	1987	1988	5-year Summary
1 Sales	$514.6	$553.5	$553.4	$570.8	$615.8	4.6%
2 Sales Growth	4.5%	7.5%	0.0%	3.1%	7.9%	4.6%
3 Capital	$100.1	$114.8	$107.3	$124.3	$125.9	5.9%
4 NOPAT/Beg Capital r	10.3%	10.4%	6.4%	9.0%	10.2%	9.3%
5 Wtd Avg Cap Cost c*	11.5%	10.0%	7.5%	9.1%	8.2%	9.3%
6 Spread r-c*	-1.1%	0.4%	-1.1%	-0.1%	1.9%	0.0%
7 x Beginning Capital	$100.0	$100.1	$114.8	$107.3	$124.3	$109.3
8 Economic Value Added	($1.1)	$0.4	($1.3)	($0.1)	$2.4	$0.1
9 Year End Share Price	$19.63	$23.94	$29.88	$24.75	$8.88	-18.0%
10 Adj Book Value Per Shr	18.20	19.77	19.57	19.99	(27.10)	-210.5%
11 Price - Adj Book	$1.43	$4.17	$10.30	$4.76	$35.98	$11.33
12 x No. Shares Outst'g	2.9	2.8	2.7	2.6	2.6	2.7
13 Market Value Added	$4.2	$11.7	$28.0	$12.1	$94.0	$30.0

WOOLWORTH CORP
Retail
X-->Y

FINANSEER
(Feb-Jan)

(Scaled to Beginning Capital)		1984	1985	1986	1987	1988	5-year Summary
1	Sales	$237.5	$246.6	$269.1	$295.3	$334.8	9.0%
2	Sales Growth	5.2%	3.9%	9.1%	9.7%	13.4%	8.2%
3	Capital	$99.1	$102.7	$114.1	$129.5	$150.1	11.0%
4	NOPAT/Beg Capital r	9.0%	10.1%	11.8%	13.1%	14.5%	11.7%
5	Wtd Avg Cap Cost c*	11.3%	10.8%	9.5%	11.5%	12.1%	11.0%
6	Spread r-c*	-2.4%	-0.8%	2.3%	1.6%	2.3%	0.6%
7	x Beginning Capital	$100.0	$99.1	$102.7	$114.1	$129.5	$109.1
8	Economic Value Added	($2.4)	($0.7)	$2.3	$1.9	$3.0	$0.8
9	Year End Share Price	$18.50	$30.00	$38.63	$34.50	$51.75	29.3%
10	Adj Book Value Per Shr	18.92	21.09	24.73	29.26	32.28	14.3%
11	Price - Adj Book	($0.42)	$8.91	$13.89	$5.24	$19.47	$9.42
12	x No. Shares Outst'g	2.6	2.7	2.7	2.7	2.7	2.7
13	Market Value Added	($1.1)	$23.9	$38.0	$14.1	$52.0	$25.4

MELVILLE CORP
Retail
Y

FINANSEER

(Scaled to Beginning Capital)		1984	1985	1986	1987	1988	5-year Summary
1	Sales	$300.9	$324.8	$358.0	$403.4	$461.2	11.3%
2	Sales Growth	12.8%	7.9%	10.2%	12.7%	14.3%	11.6%
3	Capital	$114.6	$121.1	$133.3	$152.4	$179.0	11.8%
4	NOPAT/Beg Capital r	19.0%	18.7%	18.9%	19.4%	20.8%	19.4%
5	Wtd Avg Cap Cost c*	12.1%	11.4%	10.7%	12.5%	13.1%	12.0%
6	Spread r-c*	7.0%	7.3%	8.2%	6.9%	7.7%	7.4%
7	x Beginning Capital	$100.0	$114.6	$121.1	$133.3	$152.4	$124.3
8	Economic Value Added	$7.0	$8.4	$10.0	$9.2	$11.7	$9.3
9	Year End Share Price	$18.63	$25.25	$27.00	$26.50	$37.19	18.9%
10	Adj Book Value Per Shr	9.64	10.90	12.49	14.34	16.71	14.7%
11	Price - Adj Book	$8.98	$14.35	$14.51	$12.16	$20.48	$14.09
12	x No. Shares Outst'g	6.3	6.4	6.4	6.5	6.5	6.4
13	Market Value Added	$56.4	$92.0	$93.4	$78.5	$132.5	$90.6

Exhibit 4.15   continued

FOOD LION INC
Retail
Z

FINANSEER						5-year
(Scaled to Beginning Capital)	1984	1985	1986	1987	1988	Summary
1 Sales	$552.6	$701.5	$904.9	$1,110.5	$1,434.2	26.9%
2 Sales Growth	25.3%	27.0%	29.0%	22.7%	29.2%	26.6%
3 Capital	$101.9	$147.7	$203.4	$285.3	$382.0	39.2%
4 NOPAT/Beg Capital r	17.9%	22.4%	20.3%	19.8%	20.5%	20.2%
5 Wtd Avg Cap Cost c*	13.5%	12.8%	11.1%	10.7%	10.8%	11.8%
6 Spread r-c*	4.3%	9.6%	9.2%	9.1%	9.7%	8.4%
7 x Beginning Capital	$100.0	$101.9	$147.7	$203.4	$285.3	$167.7
8 Economic Value Added	$4.5	$9.8	$13.5	$18.4	$27.8	$14.7
9 Year End Share Price	$2.42	$3.63	$5.56	$12.00	$9.38	40.3%
10 Adj Book Value Per Shr	0.58	0.73	0.93	1.17	1.51	27.3%
11 Price - Adj Book	$1.84	$2.90	$4.63	$10.83	$7.86	$5.61
12 x No. Shares Outst'g	117.3	117.7	118.5	118.8	118.8	118.1
13 Market Value Added	$216.2	$341.3	$549.1	$1,285.2	$934.3	$665.3

WAL-MART STORES
Retail
Z

FINANSEER (Feb-Jan)						5-year
(Scaled to Beginning Capital)	1984	1985	1986	1987	1988	Summary
1 Sales	$487.5	$643.6	$907.0	$1,215.5	$1,572.7	34.0%
2 Sales Growth	37.2%	32.0%	40.9%	34.0%	29.4%	34.7%
3 Capital	$143.0	$179.9	$237.2	$321.5	$398.6	29.2%
4 NOPAT/Beg Capital r	24.2%	21.5%	23.2%	24.8%	25.2%	23.8%
5 Wtd Avg Cap Cost c*	13.6%	12.9%	11.0%	11.7%	12.6%	12.3%
6 Spread r-c*	10.6%	8.7%	12.3%	13.1%	12.6%	11.5%
7 x Beginning Capital	$100.0	$143.0	$179.9	$237.2	$321.5	$196.3
8 Economic Value Added	$10.6	$12.4	$22.1	$31.1	$40.7	$23.4
9 Year End Share Price	$9.47	$15.94	$23.25	$26.00	$31.38	34.9%
10 Adj Book Value Per Shr	2.04	2.62	3.40	4.50	6.01	31.1%
11 Price - Adj Book	$7.43	$13.32	$19.85	$21.50	$25.36	$17.49
12 x No. Shares Outst'g	29.9	29.9	30.0	30.1	30.2	30.0
13 Market Value Added	$222.1	$398.9	$596.8	$647.4	$764.3	$525.9

Wal-Mart, for example, had a standardized EVA of $10.6 in 1984 because its rate of return that year was 10.6% above its prevailing cost of capital.

$$
\begin{aligned}
\text{Standardized 1984 EVA} &= 1984 \ (r - c^*) \times \$100 \\
&= (24.2\% - 13.6\%) \times \$100 \\
&= \$10.6\% \times \$100 \\
&= \$10.6
\end{aligned}
$$

So for the first year of the 5-year historical record, standardized EVA measures just the spread of the rate of return versus the cost of capital. To begin with, it is no more revealing than $r - c^*$. But in subsequent years standardized EVA will increase if there is an improvement in the rate of return on capital versus the cost of capital, if new capital is invested productively, or if capital is withdrawn from uneconomic activities. It is a three-dimensional measure of corporate performance packed into one.

Wal-Mart's standardized EVA, for example, grew to $40.7 by 1988, a change of $30.1 over 4 years.

$$
\begin{aligned}
\text{Standardized} \\
\text{1988 EVA} &= 1988 \ (r - c^*) \times 1988 \text{ standardized capital} \\
&= (25.2\% - 12.6\%) \times \$321.5 \\
&= 12.6\% \times \$321.5 \\
&= \$40.7
\end{aligned}
$$

The increase from $10.6 to $40.7 stands out among the retailers. The analysis of the beginning and ending EVA just performed for Wal-Mart is repeated here for the others.

Company	Standardized 1984 EVA	ΔEVA	Standardized 1988 EVA
K-Mart	$(11.3\% - 12.0\%) \times \$100$ $-0.7\% \times \$100$ $-\$0.7$	$+\$2.0=$	$(13.0\% - 12.1\%) \times \$155.3$ $0.8\% \times \$155.3$ $\$1.3$
Kroger	$(10.3\% - 11.5\%) \times \$100$ $-1.1\% \times \$100$ $-\$1.1$	$+\$3.5=$	$(10.2\% - 8.2\%) \times \$124.3$ $1.9\% \times \$124.3$ $\$2.4$
Woolworth	$(9.0\% - 11.3\%) \times \$100$ $-2.4\% \times \$100$ $-\$2.4$	$+\$5.4=$	$(14.5\% - 12.1\%) \times \$129.5$ $2.3\% \times \$129.5$ $\$3.0$

Company	Standardized 1984 EVA	ΔEVA	Standardized 1988 EVA
Melville	(19.0% − 12.1%) × $100 7.0% × $100 $7.0	+ $4.7 =	(20.8% − 13.1%) × $152.4 7.7% × $152.4 $11.7
Food Lion	(17.9% − 13.5%) × $100 4.4% × $100 $4.4	+ $23.4 =	(20.5% − 10.8%) × $285.3 9.7% × $285.3 $27.8
Wal-Mart	(24.2% − 13.6%) × $100 10.6% × $100 $10.6	+ $30.1 =	(25.2% − 12.6%) × $321.5 12.6% × $321.5 $40.7

Shortcomings and distinctions show up all the more clearly when EVA is standardized in this way. For example, in absolute-dollar terms, K-Mart ended 1988 with an EVA of $79.9 million and Melville finished with $172.0 million, only slightly more than twice as much. The difference is as small as it is only because K-Mart employs more than 4 times the amount of capital that Melville does. In standardized terms, Melville closed 1988 with 9 times the EVA of K-Mart, $11.7 versus $1.3.

The comparison of Woolworth and K-Mart also is revealing. In absolute terms, both companies have shown essentially the same reversal of EVA from 1984 to 1988, from about − $50 million to + $75 million. But when it is standardized, the true significance of the change in EVA becomes apparent. Relative to their capital bases, the change in EVA for K-Mart has been rather immaterial, and it is pronounced for Woolworth.

Absolute EVA	1984	1988
K-Mart	− $41.6 million	$79.9 million
Woolworth	− $57.3 million	$73.1 million

Standardized EVA	1984	1988
K-Mart	− $0.7	$1.3
Woolworth	− $2.4	$3.0

Thus, to reiterate, the level of standardized EVA by the end of an historical period of, say, 5 years and the change in getting there are measures that can be used to evaluate the performance of companies within an industry, as I have illustrated for this group of retailers, or for individual business units within a company in three important dimensions and without the distraction of size.

Market value added also can be standardized and then related to the scaled version of EVA. In exhibit 4.15 the retailers' MVA has been standardized by dividing the number of shares outstanding by the capital outstanding at the end of 1984, and multiplying by 100.[2] It shows, for example, that, as of the end of 1984, Wal-Mart had added $222.1 of market value to each $100 of capital employed at that time and that, by the end of 1988, it had added $764.3 in value, a change of $542.2. In theory, the change in standardized MVA will mirror or anticipate the capitalized value of a change in standardized EVA. This predicted relationship is essentially borne out in the following table, in which the change in standardized MVA from the end of 1984 to the end of 1988 is set beside the contemporaneous change in standardized EVA.

Company	Change in EVA	Change in MVA
K-Mart	$ 2.0	$ 4
Kroger	$ 3.5	$ 90
Woolworth	$ 5.4	$ 53
Melville	$ 4.7	$ 76
Food Lion	$ 23.5	$719
Wal-Mart	$ 30.1	$542

Kroger and Food Lion stand out because the change in their MVAs anticipates subsequent changes in their EVAs. For Kroger, $82 out of the $90 increase in its standardized MVA occurred in 1988 as the company performed its leveraged recapitalization. The bulk of the EVA benefits are to follow. In Food Lion's case investors look forward to an even greater relative increase in its

[2]MVA is scaled to the capital outstanding at the end of 1984, as opposed to the end of 1983. The reason for this discrepancy is that rates of return and EVA are measured on capital at the *beginning* of the year but MVA is measured on the basis of capital outstanding at the *end* of a given year. That's a policy decision I have made in order to measure as accurately as possible rates of return and EVA, given that it takes time for capital investment to become fully productive.

EVA than is likely to occur at even so remarkable a company as Wal-Mart. Food Lion is smaller and is riding on a greater growth trajectory than Wal-Mart at the present time. In that respect, their relative size and stage in life cycle do matter.

In the next chapter the relation between standardized EVA and MVA will be extended to a sample of nearly 1,000 American companies. Not only does this examination provide useful benchmarks for corporate performance; it proves that EVA accounts for MVA in practice as well as in theory. Before doing that, however, I need to cement EVA even more firmly into a practical valuation framework.

The EVA Valuation Formula

EVA's tie to value can be rearranged to come up with a formal valuation framework, as follows.

Start with:

MVA = market value — capital

MVA = present value of all future EVA

Therefore:

market value = capital + present value of all future EVA

It says that the stock market valuation of a company is equal to the capital the company currently has invested plus a premium, possibly less a discount, for its EVA projected and discounted to a present value.

Businesses capable of earning more than their cost of capital produce positive EVAs and build premiums into their market values. Conversely, businesses whose returns fall short of the cost of capital generate negative EVAs and thus discount the value of the capital they employ. Thus, *maximizing the present value of EVA amounts to exactly the same thing as maximizing intrinsic market value.*

Many specialty retailers, such as The Limited and Toys 'R' Us (and maybe Woolworth), earn rates of return that more than compensate their investors for risk. By aggressively investing new capital to support growth, they produce a positive and rapidly growing pool of EVA that accounts for their premium stock market valuations.

On the other hand, take a steel company. In fact, you can take a steel company as far as I am concerned. Many steel companies are unable to earn returns sufficient to cover their cost of capital. They produce negative EVAs and market values that discount the capital employed. This sends a subtle hint that the market wishes no more such steel plants just now. (See exhibit 4.16, The Meaning of EVA Valuations.)

EVA Valuation Identical to Free Cash Flow Valuation.
This EVA valuation procedure is not some far-fetched new theory of valuation; it is just a rearrangement of discounted cash flow. In fact, it is a mathematical truism that, for a given forecast, the value determined by discounting projected EVA and adding it to the current capital balance will equal the value computed by discounting the anticipated future free cash flow to a present value. (This essential principle is demonstrated in chapter 7 with a numerical example.)

Abandon Discounted Cash Flow.
You may think this heresy, but *I strongly recommend that corporate management stop using discounted cash flow for the purposes of capital budgeting and valuations and use the EVA valuation procedure instead.* The reasons for my preference will be more apparent as the book progresses. For now, suffice it to say that the main reason for advocating the use of EVA is that people will for the first time be able to see clearly the connection between their operating and strategic investment decisions and the retrospective appraisal of their performances. No other measure can do that, not even free cash flow.

The End (or the Beginning) of the Quest for Value

The unicorn is penned, the grail discovered. Rest, good knight, for victory is ours! Here at last is the one performance measure to properly account for the creation of value. Every company's most important goal must be to increase its EVA. Let that be your

---

Exhibit 4.16 The Meaning of EVA Valuations

Awhile back a senior management group told me that they had just completed a sensational acquisition. Apparently they were going to build a new steel facility for $100 million but found a company trading in the stock market for just $50 million that possessed an asset almost identical to the one they intended to construct. (Incidentally, their target really was worth only $50 million, based upon discounting the free cash flow it could be expected to generate.) But our unfortunate friends concluded that they could pay $75 million to acquire this firm, a 50% premium to market value, and save themselves $25 million relative to the cost of building anew.

"That's true," I said. "Relative to losing $50 million, losing $25 million is not so bad. But what convinced you that you wanted to be in the steel business in the first place? All that you have done is find the cheapest way to lose money."

In any group 3 business, assets dedicated to the business can be acquired in the stock market at a discount from their reproduction cost. But that does not mean a rewarding acquisition can be made as a result. The replacement cost of the assets is irrelevant because the buyer is acquiring not assets, but the cash flow that the assets can be expected to generate.

It reminds me of statements made in the early 1980s about oil companies. "It's cheaper to acquire oil on Wall Street than it is to drill for oil," was a popular line said as if it somehow cast doubt upon the market's valuation of oil companies' shares. What it really meant was that, based upon prevailing if not forecast oil prices, the lead steers judged the marginal oil drilling projects to be unrewarding group 3 investments. It made sense, therefore, for oil companies to go prowling for other oil companies instead of drilling, if they needed to acquire more reserves.

But instead of responding to this obvious market signal, many oil companies, flush with cash, could not resist the temptation to keep drilling aggressively. Many plotted extensive drilling programs, arguing, you may recall, that oil would sell for $90 a barrel by the end of the decade. It seems their extrapolation of a short-term price bubble proved a bit high. Of course, hindsight is the exact science (although Milton Friedman did predict in 1974 that the OPEC cartel would last only 5 to 10 years, arguing that the forces of conservation, new discoveries, the possible development of substitutes, and ultimately cheating among the members of the cartel itself would eventually restore oil to the discipline of marginal pricing).

With this as a backdrop, Boone Pickens made his run at Gulf Oil, proposing to create value in two ways. Boone intended to convert Gulf into a petroleum royalty trust, a pass-through vehicle for tax purposes much like a partnership. To avoid all tax, a royalty trust is obligated to pay out 95% of its income to investors. Gulf objected to the plan, protesting that paying out the cash to save taxes would deny the company the opportunity to carry out its aggressive drilling plan. But that was the second reason Boone thought he could create value.

In sum, the EVA valuation framework shows that the market, in paying for the value of future free cash flow, may be justified in paying far more or less than the amount of capital a company currently has employed in its business. EVA is what accounts for the difference in value between the cash management has already put or is about to put into the business and the present value of the free cash flow that subsequently can be gotten out of the business. Thus, when market value is less than the cost of replacement assets, incremental EVA is negative. Management should plan an orderly retreat, not a new attack.

quest. Forget about earnings, earnings per share, earnings growth, rate of return, dividends, and even cash flow. All of them are fundamentally flawed measures of performance and value. EVA is all that really matters.

First, EVA matters, because, when accompanied by cash accounting, it properly measures all three ways in which a company can create value: by raising the efficiency of its current operations, by achieving profitable growth, and by paring uneconomic activities in which the immediate exit proceeds more than make up for the subsequent cash flow forgone.

EVA is most important, however, because it is the fuel that fires a premium in the market value of any company (or accounts for its discount). When projected and discounted to a present value, EVA represents the net present value of all past and projected capital projects. Thus, setting the internal goal of maximizing EVA and EVA growth will lead to the external consequence of building a premium-valued company, one whose stock market value exceeds the capital resources drawn into the firm.

EVA will yield the same value as discounting free cash flow, an important identity. But it is better than discounting cash flow because it clearly connects forward-looking valuation procedures with the subsequent evaluation of performance. No other measure can do that.

My recommendation is this: Use EVA as the basis for setting goals, allocating capital, evaluating performance, determining bonuses, and communicating with the lead steers in the stock market. Decision making will be more effective; communication will be enhanced; and bonuses will be more rewarding for all concerned if maximizing EVA and EVA growth is adopted as the paramount corporate objective.

In chapter 5, I present evidence that proves the critical importance of EVA in the valuation process and a ranking of nearly 1,000 prominent companies according to the market value they have added to the capital they have employed.

5

The Stern Stewart
Performance 1000

Everybody loves a winner. But what makes a winner in the corporate sweepstakes? All of the most popular rankings focus on size, be it measured in sales, assets, or market value. But size is not a very reliable indicator of how well a corporation has fulfilled its basic mission—maximizing shareholder value.

Two companies ranked side by side in the 1989 *Business Week 1,000* provide a nice illustration of the fallacy of equating corporate size with success. Number six on the list was General Motors, with an equity capitalization of $25.63 billion (as of March 17, 1989). Number seven, in a virtual tie, was Merck, with $25.59 billion of equity value. Now, I grant that GM has had to contend with Herculean challenges over the past decade. And it is possible that the company may yet be able to recover some of its past luster. But, to rank GM so high on this prestigious list—and next to Merck, the immensely successful pharmaceutical giant—must strike most observers as misleading, given the relative performance of the two companies over the past 10 years.

After inspecting the *Business Week* survey, I was overwhelmed by a sense of the need for a ranking procedure that would properly recognize corporate excellence—one that would elevate Merck to its rightful standing at the very pinnacle of corporate America while also making clear the seriousness of GM's failure to deliver value to its shareholders. Not finding anywhere a ranking to my satisfaction, I decided to commission on my own. I am pleased to present the findings of the first annual *Stern Stewart Performance 1000.* [1]

Market Value Added: A Better Measure of Corporate Success

I decided to rank companies according to how much value they have added to, or subtracted from, their shareholders' investment. Market value added, or MVA, is the difference between a company's fair market value, as reflected primarily in its stock price, and the economic book value of capital employed.[2] Stated as a simple formula,

$$\text{Market value added} = \text{market value} - \text{capital}$$

If, for example, a company has a market value of $25 billion but has invested $40 billion of capital, then its market value added is a *negative* $15 billion. But if this same company had invested only $5 billion of capital, then it would have added $20 billion in value to the capital resources put at its disposal by investors.

MVA can be thought of as the stock market's assessment, at any given point in time, of the *net* present value of all a company's past and projected capital investment projects. It reflects how successfully a company has invested capital in the past and how successful investors expect it to be in investing capital in the future. Maximizing MVA should be the objective of any company that professes to be concerned about maximizing its owners' wealth.

[1] Though starting with the same 1,000 companies as *Business Week,* I ended up with only 900 industrial and service companies after making several modifications. Utilities and financial institutions were deleted because their accounting makes it difficult to generate strictly comparable data for certain measures. Once this was done, the list was rounded out to an even 900 companies by adding other firms which *Business Week* included in industry surveys during 1988. For the 1989 ranking, I plan to expand the list to encompass an even 1,000 companies.

[2] A company's economic book value, let me say at the outset, is likely to be considerably larger than the accounting book value presented in the annual report; besides conventional book equity, it also includes equity equivalent reserves to provide a more accurate measure of shareholders' total cash investment in the company. See the definition of capital in the glossary for a more explicit description of the reserves added to make accounting into economic book value.

Unlike *Business Week,* which uses the market value of *equity* alone as the basis for its rankings, I focused instead on the market value of companies' total debt and equity capitalization in relation to the capital employed in net assets. After all, managers are really managers of assets, not of equity. Moreover, rates of return computed on a more broadly-based definition of capital serve to eliminate distortions that arise from capital structure differences as well as certain accounting bookkeeping entries. The complete MVA ranking begins on page 749. It should be reviewed with the glossary on page 741.

A Quick Look at Warner-Lambert

To illustrate the Stern Stewart ranking method, let us take the case of Warner-Lambert (which was ranked number 49 on our list). As of year-end 1988, Warner-Lambert had added almost $3 billion to the capital resources employed within the firm.

$$\text{Market value added} = \text{market value} - \text{capital}$$
$$\$2.862B = \$5.924B - \$3.062B$$

That $2.862 billion represents the amount by which the market value of its total debt and equity capital as of December 31, 1988 (almost $6 billion) exceeded the total historical investment (including retained earnings) by debt as well as equity investors.

For most companies, MVA can also be computed by multiplying the number of shares outstanding by the spread between stock price and economic book value per share.[3] (GM is an exception because of the special E and H classes of stock it has issued.) For example, Warner-Lambert's $2.862 billion MVA can also be accounted for by multiplying its $42.22 spread by its 67.8 million shares outstanding.

$$
\begin{aligned}
\text{MVA} &= \text{no. shrs} \times (\text{price} - \text{economic book}) \\
&= 67{,}796M \times (\$78.38 - \$36.16) \\
\$2.862B &= 67{,}796M \times \$42.22
\end{aligned}
$$

Exhibit 5.1 presents a detailed illustration of the calculations involved.

[3]See note 2.

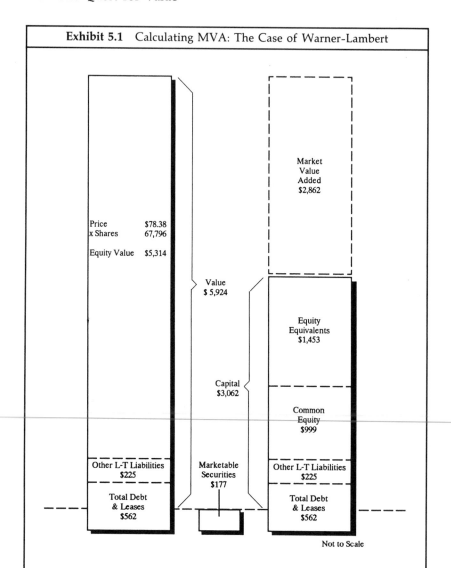

Exhibit 5.1   Calculating MVA: The Case of Warner-Lambert

Price	$78.38
x Shares	67,796

Equity Value $5,314

Market Value Added $2,862

Value $5,924

Capital $3,062

Equity Equivalents $1,453

Common Equity $999

Other L-T Liabilities $225

Marketable Securities $177

Total Debt & Leases $562

Other L-T Liabilities $225

Total Debt & Leases $562

Not to Scale

By the end of 1988, Warner-Lambert had added $2.862 billion in value to the capital it has employed, the difference between an estimated market value of $5.924 billion and capital of $3.062 billion.

Capital is the sum of all cash invested or retained within the firm to build its business. For Warner-Lambert, it consists of all debt and leases ($562 million, including the present value at 10% of the minimum rents over the next five years), other long-term liabilities ($225 million), common equity ($999 million), and equity equivalent reserves ($1.453 billion), less marketable securities ($177 million). Marketable securities are subtracted from capital (and from market value) in order to focus on the performance of the company's operations.

To estimate Warner-Lambert's market value, the book value of debt and other long-term liabilities less marketable securities is added to the actual market value of common equity. Book value was used to approximate the market value of all items except common equity due to the absence of broad availability of quoted prices. The actual market value of the common equity of $5,314 million is the year-end 1988 share price of $78 ⅜ times the 67,796,000 shares outstanding (net of those in treasury).

Because the book value of the net liabilities is reflected in both market value and capital, MVA also can be computed as the spread

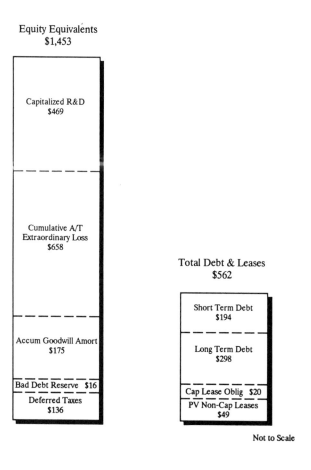

Equity Equivalents
$1,453

Capitalized R&D
$469

Cumulative A/T
Extraordinary Loss
$658

Total Debt & Leases
$562

Short Term Debt
$194

Long Term Debt
$298

Accum Goodwill Amort
$175

Bad Debt Reserve $16
Deferred Taxes
$136

Cap Lease Oblig $20
PV Non-Cap Leases
$49

Not to Scale

Exhibit 5.1   continued

between the market value and the economic book value of just the common equity capital alone. The economic book value of Warner-Lambert's common equity is the reported book value of $999 million plus the $1.453 billion in equity equivalents, for a total of $2.452 billion.

$$\text{MVA} = \text{equity market value} - \text{economic book value}$$
$$\$2.862\text{B} = \$5.314\text{B} - \$2.452\text{B}$$

Taking this simplification one step further, the number of shares outstanding can be factored away from both the market value and economic book value of common equity. In other words, Warner-Lambert's MVA can be expressed as the spread between the share price and the economic book value per share, times the number of shares outstanding:

$$\text{MVA} = \text{no. shrs} \times (\text{price} - \text{economic book})$$
$$= 67,796\text{M} \times (\$78.38 - \$36.16)$$
$$\$2.862\text{B} = 67,796\text{M} \times (\$42.22)$$

No matter how MVA is computed, it is assumed that changes in value of the debt and marketable securities generally are far less significant than are changes in the value of the common equity. For the average company this is probably a reasonable assumption, though it may not be true of very highly leveraged companies, such as FMC (number 191).

But rather than dwell on the shortcomings to this ranking (which are fairly modest in the aggregate) what is noteworthy is that by adding equity equivalents to capital, MVA has been adjusted for many distortions that may tend to overstate the value created by capital intensive, acquisitive, high-tech, or risky businesses. For example, in Warner-Lambert's case, the equity equivalent reserves capitalize the company's R&D expense; cumulate unusual losses, less gains, after taxes and the amortization of goodwill; and add back the bad debt reserve and the deferred income tax reserve.

The calculation of the net capitalized R&D investment for Warner-Lambert is shown in the Calculation of Equivalents. Each year's R&D expense is straight line amortized over 5 years, including the year in which it is spent. The amortization of the R&D is cumulated and subtracted from the cumulative R&D expense to measure the investment in net capitalized R&D. By the end of 1988, it was $469 million,

Calculation of Equivalents for Warner–Lambert
(Dollars in Millions)

				Capitalized R&D					
	1980	1981	1982	1983	1984	1985	1986	1987	1988
R&D Expense	$102.9	$114.8	$145.4	$175.0	$194.9	$208.2	$202.3	$231.8	$259.4
Yearly Amortization*									
1980	20.6	20.6	20.6	20.6	20.6				
1981		23.0	23.0	23.0	23.0	23.0			
1982			29.1	29.1	29.1	29.1	29.1		
1983				35.0	35.0	35.0	35.0	35.0	
1984					39.0	39.0	39.0	39.0	39.0
1985						41.6	41.6	41.6	41.6
1986							40.5	40.5	40.5
1987								46.4	46.4
1988									51.9
TOTAL	20.6	43.5	72.6	107.6	146.6	167.7	185.2	202.4	219.3
Cumulative R&D Expense	102.9	217.7	363.1	538.1	733.0	941.2	1,143.5	1,375.3	1,634.7
Less Cumulative Amortization	20.6	64.1	136.8	244.4	391.0	558.6	743.8	946.2	1,165.5
Capitalized R&D	NA	NA	NA	NA	$342.0	$382.6	$399.7	$429.1	$469.1

*Straight-line amortization over five years.

Calculation of Equivalents for Warner-Lambert, continued
(Dollars in Millions)

Cum A/T Extra Loss

	1984	1985	1986	1987	1988
A/T Extra Loss (Gain)	$ 0.0	$ 553.3	($48.0)	$ 0.0	$ 0.0
Cum A/T Loss (Gain)	$ 152.3	$ 705.6	$ 657.6	$ 657.6	$ 657.6

Cum Goodwill Amortization

	1984	1985	1986	1987	1988
Goodwill Amortization	$ 25.7	$ 21.9	$ 1.4	$ 2.4	$ 5.8
Cum Goodwill Amortization	$ 143.6	$ 165.5	$ 166.9	$ 169.3	$ 175.1

Warner-Lambert

1988 Balance Sheet
(Dollars in Millions)

Assets		Liabilities & Net Worth	
Marketable Securities	$ 177	Short-Term Debt	$ 187
Net Accts Receivable	525	Current Portion LTD	7
Net Inventory	381	Accounts Payable	298
Other Current Assets	181	Income Taxes Payable	136
Total Current Assets	1,265	Other Current Liabs	397
		Total Current Liabs	1,025
Net Prop Plant & Equip	1,053	Senior Long-Term Debt	298
Goodwill	149	Capital Lease Oblig	20
Other Assets	237	Other LT Liabilities	225
		Total Liabilities	1,569
		Deferred Income Taxes	136
		Common Equity	999
Total Assets	$2,703	Total Liab & Net Worth	$2,703

1988 Capital
(Dollars in Millions)

Operating Approach

Net Accts Receivable	$ 525
Bad Debt Reserve	16
Net Inventory	381
Other Current Assets	181
Current Oper Assets	1,103
Accounts Payable	298
Income Taxes Payable	136
Other Current Liabs	397
NIBCLs	831
Net Working Capital	272
Net Prop Plant & Equip	1,053
PV of Non-Cap Leases	49
Adj Prop Plant & Equip	1,102
Goodwill	149
Accum Goodwill Amort	175
Adjusted Goodwill	324
Capitalized R&D	469
Cum A/T Extra. Loss	658
Other Assets	237
Capital	$3,062

Financing Approach

Short-Term Debt	$ 187
Current Portion LTD	7
Senior Long-Term Debt	298
Capital Lease Oblig	20
PV of Non-Cap Leases	49
Total Debt & Leases	562
Other LT Liabilities	225
Common Equity	999
Capitalized R&D	469
Cum A/T Extra. Loss	658
Accum Goodwill Amort	175
Bad Debt Reserve	16
Deferred Income Taxes	136
Equity Equivalents	1,453
Common Equity Capital	2,451
Total Capital	3,238
Less:	
Marketable Securities	177
Capital	$3,062

Exhibit 5.1   continued

or about 15% of capital. If this had not been considered to be an equity equivalent form of capital, Warner-Lambert's MVA would be $3.331 billion instead of $2.862 billion, an overstatement.

The exhibit on page 186 shows the cumulation of after-tax unusual losses, less gains. For the ten years leading up through 1983, Warner-Lambert had recorded net cumulative after-tax unusual losses of $152 million. In 1985, the company took a charge of $654 million pre-tax, or $553 million after-tax, to write down certain health technologies businesses to estimated realizable value. Unusual losses cumulated to $705 million, representing an investment in failed strategies. The next year, Warner-Lambert booked a pre-tax gain of $8.4 million, or $48 million after tax, as the actual sale value of the health tech properties exceeded expectations. The investment in unsuccessful efforts was thereby reduced to $658 million on net by the end of 1988, an amount that represented over 20% of capital and a necessary reduction in the measure of the market value added to the capital entrusted to the firm.

The bottom panel presents the cumulation of goodwill amortization, a non-cash, non-tax deductible charge. Up through 1983, Warner-Lambert had amortized $118 million in goodwill. In 1984, $26 million of goodwill was charged to earnings, bringing the cumulative amortization to $144 million. Repeating the same procedure the total goodwill amortization summed to $175 million by the end of 1988, an amount which is added to capital and thus subtracted from MVA.

The other equity equivalents, for bad debt reserve and the deferred income tax reserve, are lifted directly from the company's balance sheet and the footnotes to the financial statements. These reserves, like the others, make capital a more meaningful base upon which to measure the creation or destruction of value.

To close the loop, Warner-Lambert's 1988 balance sheet, and the complete calculation of capital from operating and financing perspectives, are presented in the table on page 187.

A Tale of Two Companies

As of the end of 1988, General Motors had reduced the value of its shareholders' investment by nearly $20 billion.[4]

General Motors	(1) Value	(2) Capital	(3)=(1)−(2) MVA
1988	$56.6	$76.5	−$19.9
1978	14.0	20.6	−6.5
Change	42.6	55.9	−13.3

At that point, GM's MVA was the lowest of the 900 industrial and service companies covered by this survey. It also ranked lowest in terms of the *change* in MVA over the 10-year period from 1978 to 1988. During that time GM's MVA fell by a staggering $13.3 billion.

Merck, by contrast, moved up from *Business Week*'s number 7 to Stern Stewart's number 2. By the end of 1988, the company had added almost $19 billion to its shareholders' wealth, trailing only IBM (and this is even after the book value of

[4]The calculations of MVA for GM is complicated by the fact that GM partially financed the acquisitions of EDS and Hughes by issuing special E and H classes of common stock. The market value of these two special common stock issues has been included in GM's market value because the assets of EDS and Hughes are part of GM's capital. The E and H shares, on net, account for $5.2 billion of GM's lost value. Here is the data for 1988:

	Value	Capital	MVA
E shares	$2.499B	$ 1.857B	$ 0.641B
H shares	4.803B	10.610B	−5.807B
Total	7.302B	12.467B	−5.166B

Even setting aside the net value lost on the E and H shares, GM still lost $8.1 billion on its ordinary common shares.

In accordance with FASB No. 94, GM began to consolidate GMAC, its financing arm, as of 1988. In order to make the results comparable for the full ten years covered by the survey, however, GMAC was deconsolidated. This has no bearing one way or another on MVA. It does, however, improve the accuracy and consistency with which GM's rate of return on capital is measured.

Merck's capital base is expanded to include its sizable R&D expenditures).[5]

Merck	(1) Value	(2) Capital	(3)=(1)−(2) MVA
1988	$22.7	$4.1	$18.6
1978	5.1	1.9	3.2
Change	17.6	2.2	15.3

Merck's *increase* in MVA, over the ten-year period since 1978 was also second among all American corporations, amounting to an astonishing $15.3 billion. I extend my congratulations to this remarkable company.

As the numbers above also show, over the 10-year period from 1978 to 1988, GM's total market value increased by $42.6 billion (or roughly fourfold, from $14.0 to 56.6 billion). In this respect management was very successful at increasing "long-run" value. The important lesson here, however, is that the increase in total value, even when considered over a long time period, is an incomplete guide to judging corporate performance. Any company can maximize its *total* value simply by spending as much money as possible (both by retaining most of its earnings and raising new capital). But that, of course, is hardly a useful prescription for capital budgeting. The effective corporate use of investor capital can be measured only according to *net* present values—that is, the increase in value minus the amount of new capital drawn into or retained by the firm. It's what's left over that counts, and in the stock market that is reflected in MVA. Over the period 1978–1988, GM invested an additional $55.9 billion of capital (over and above depreciation) to produce only $42.6 billion in additional value, thus reducing MVA by $13.3 billion.

Fortunately, Merck more than recovered GM's value lost,

[5]To eliminate the distortions encountered when a hard-assets-intensive business like GM's is compared with a research-intensive business such as Merck's, capital for all companies has been computed by capitalizing each year's R&D expense and amortizing it on a straight-line basis over 5 years (5 years was somewhat arbitrarily chosen to represent the typical payoff period for a successful R&D investment). Over the 10-year period from 1978 to 1988, the increase in the net capitalized R&D asset for Merck was $856.2 million, or about 40% of the $2.2 billion increase in all capital.

proving again the benefits of holding a diversified portfolio of stocks. True, Merck created far less of an increase in its "long-run" total value than did GM, only $17.6 billion worth. But it did so by investing a pittance: just $2.2 billion, including capitalized R&D. What was left over was $15.3 billion in added value for shareholders and society.

More Silver Bullets

I am afraid that GM was not the only company subject to rough handling by our survey. Many of the very large companies at the top of the *Business Week* list placed far below their accustomed premier positions in our market value added ranking (as the short list below suggests).

	Business Week **Rank**	*Stern Stewart* **Rank**
IBM	1	1
Exxon	2	11
GE	3	3
AT&T	4	77
Philip Morris	5	5
GM	6	900
Merck	7	2
Ford	8	899
Du Pont	9	850
Amoco	10	730

Moving Up the Ladder

Changes in MVA over a period of time are likely to be as useful as the levels of MVA (if not more so) in assessing a company's performance. An increasing MVA is the reward bestowed on a company that is producing (or promises to produce) higher rates of return on capital than the cost of capital. A decreasing MVA is the punishment visited on firms that have fallen short of expectations or that have committed capital to new investments the market doesn't expect will earn their cost of capital. Another important advantage to using the *change* in MVA as a measure of corporate performance is that it is less susceptible to any remaining accounting distortions in measuring capital—especially those caused by inflation—than is the raw level of MVA at a point in time.

Economic value added, or EVA, is the *internal* measure of operating performance that best reflects the success of companies in adding value to their shareholders' investments. As such, it is strongly related to *both* the level and changes in the level of MVA over time. EVA is the residual income left over from operating profits after the cost of capital has been earned. Stated as a formula,

$$EVA = (\text{rate of return} - \text{cost of capital}) \times \text{capital}$$
$$EVA = (\quad r \quad - \quad c^* \quad) \times \text{capital}$$

EVA can also be thought of as the economic earnings that are capitalized by the market in arriving at a company's MVA. In theory, a company's market value added at any point in time is equal to the discounted present value of all the EVA, or residual income, it is expected to generate *in the future.* Thus, a company expected to earn precisely its cost of capital, and nothing more, will sell at a market value equal to capital; and thus its MVA will be zero. Companies earning less than the cost of capital, and therefore producing negative EVAs, can be expected to sell at discounts to book capital and have negative MVAs. Companies whose investments exceed the cost of capital are rewarded by the stock market with positive MVAs; and in such cases, the more investment (or the higher the growth rate), the larger the MVA.

A company's EVA, and thus its MVA, can be increased in three different ways: (1) by increasing the efficiency of existing operations, and thus the spread between r and c^*; (2) by increasing the amount of capital invested in projects with positive spreads between r and c^*; or (3) by withdrawing capital from operations where r is less than c^*. (The latter, incidentally, helps explain why the market response to large stock repurchases was so consistently positive throughout the 1980s.) As with MVA, moreover, the *change* in EVA is a measure of performance that is less subject to accounting biases.

Because the stock market tends to be forward looking, current changes in MVA often anticipate *subsequent* changes in EVA; and thus we should not expect to find a precise correspondence between concurrent changes in EVA and MVA. But, to the extent they are not anticipated by the market, changes in EVA will be reflected in contemporaneous changes in MVA.

The general relationship between MVA and EVA is illustrated by three companies at the top of the ranking.

Rank/Company	1/IBM	4/Wal-Mart	5/Philip Morris
MVA 1988	$ 20.3	$14.3	$ 13.9
ΔMVA since 1983	−25.9	9.9	10.6
ΔMVA since 1978	−7.1	14.2	11.8
EVA 1988	−1.78	0.53	−0.14
ΔEVA since 1983	−4.77	0.42	−0.54
ΔEVA since 1978	−3.77	0.52	−0.40

$ in billions

By the end of 1988, IBM's MVA, though still the largest in our survey, had fallen precipitously in line with a simultaneous and largely unanticipated plunge in its EVA. Though IBM had a negative EVA for the year 1988, investors apparently expect IBM's future EVA to increase to a level that will justify $20.3 billion of MVA (which, once again, can be thought of as the capitalized value of expected future EVA). Only time will tell if such expectations are borne out.

In contrast to IBM, Wal-Mart has steadily built its MVA over the past ten years. The principal reason for this strong market reception is that, over this period, Wal-Mart has generated a positive and steadily growing EVA. And, with its MVA pegged at $14.3 billion at the end of 1988, investors apparently expect large increases in EVA to continue at Wal-Mart for many years to come.

Philip Morris has recorded a positive and increasing MVA, but has not yet produced the EVA to justify it. In this case, the increase in MVA is best interpreted as the harbinger of EVA to come, the payoff that has yet to materialize from the recent acquisition of Kraft and the increase in market share relative to RJR.

Up, Up, and Away

What will it take for a company to move up in the *Stern Stewart Performance 1000?* Will more growth, higher returns, or paying dividends help?

Growth Per Se Does Not Matter

Growth—and this includes growth in earnings per share— will increase MVA *only* if it is the result of making investments that earn more than the cost of capital. Consider these three companies:

Rank/Company	4/Wal-Mart	854/James River	893/United Tech
g	32 %	32 %	6 %
r	25.2 %	13.1 %	9.5 %
MVA	$14.3	−$0.4	−$1.9
ΔMVA since 1983	9.9	−0.7	−0.7
Value	19.6	4.4	8.4
Capital	5.2	4.7	10.3

g = Compound average annual growth rate in capital 1983–88

r = 1988 rate of return on capital

- Wal-Mart's growth helped build a premium-valued company because it was accompanied by a very attractive rate of return.
- James River, a paper company, created no MVA despite the fact that it expanded its capital base as rapidly as did Wal-mart, mostly as the result of a string of acquisitions. Because its rate of return barely met its cost of capital, James River's rapid expansion failed to generate any EVA. In theory James River would have sold for the same stock price at the end of 1988 if it had not grown at all.

- The growth of United Technologies has actually reduced its market value. Investors could have earned higher returns elsewhere with the funds UT chose to invest.

Undertaking all positive net present value projects and rejecting negative net present value ones—the standard capital budgeting rule—is also the prescription for maximizing MVA. Once that's done, growth will take care of itself.

Returns Do Not Matter

What about maximizing *rates* of return? Will that increase a company's MVA? Not necessarily. Maximizing rate of return, it is true, will maximize the *ratio of* market value to capital. But ratios do not matter. What matters is creating absolute dollar amounts of surplus value over and above the material resources drawn into the firm. The cases of IBM, Apple, and Microsoft help to make this point clear.

Rank/Company	1/IBM	40/Apple	67/Microsoft
r	9.7 %	71.5 %	90.8 %
Value/Capital	1.3	3.2	7.4
MVA	$20.3	$ 3.3	$ 2.4
Value	80.7	4.7	2.8
Capital	60.4	1.5	0.4

Top-ranked IBM, though it sold for only a 30% premium to capital, has created over $20 billion of surplus value. Microsoft, Bill Gates's super-software company, sold for over seven times capital but has created just $2.8 billion in surplus value. Microsoft, which earns over a 90% rate of return on capital, uses what little capital it does employ far more efficiently than does IBM. But it is unlikely that Microsoft will ever have the opportunity to become as large and profitable a force in the marketplace as has IBM. Apple too earns a stupendous rate of return and sells at a huge multiple to the level of capital it has employed; but it has not come close to creating the surplus value of a company the size of Big Blue. Once again, undertaking *all* positive net present value projects, no matter how close their rates of return may be to the cost of capital, will maximize a company's MVA.

Dividends Do Not Matter

Will paying a dividend increase MVA? Actually, neither paying nor cutting a dividend will change MVA, in and of itself. So long as a company's stock price falls by the amount of the dividend paid (as the evidence shows to be the case, on average and in the aggregate), the market value and book value of common equity capital fall together, leaving MVA unaffected.[6] Only if the change in dividend policy signals or triggers a change in some fundamental operating or investment policy will MVA be affected. The same goes for share repurchases and leveraged recapitalizations.

The Industry Ranking

Using the 59 industry groups defined in the *Business Week* survey, we added the MVAs and EVAs for all companies in each industry grouping to produce industry totals. As presented in exhibit 5.2, pharmaceutical companies topped the list with a total market value added of $64 billion; $49 billion of that value added has come since 1978. The drug companies as a group earned a 21.6% rate of return on capital in 1987, and an EVA of $2.7 billion, up $1.8 billion since 1978. Only the Medellin cartel may be more profitable.

Here are a few random observations on these industrial rankings:

- Perhaps surprising, discount and fashion retailing companies have been the second largest shareholder benefactor as a group, with Wal-Mart, The Limited, and Toys 'R' Us leading the charge.

[6]MVA is unavoidably distorted, however, for companies that either spin off or dividend shares in subsidiary units to their shareholders. Coca-Cola, for example, gave its shareholders 51% of the shares in Columbia Pictures as a dividend at the end of 1987. To the extent that Columbia Pictures at the time had a market value in excess of its economic book value, Coca-Cola has lost that bit of MVA in our calculation.

Exhibit 5.2 Industry Rankings

1988 MVA Rank	Industry	Industry	Market Value Added (MVA) 1988	Change from 1983	1978	Economic Value Added (EVA) 1988	Change from 1983	1978	Profitability (1988) Return On Cap r (%)	Wtd Avg Cost Cap c* (%)	r to c*	Value to Capital	Size (1988) Value	Capital	5-Year Growth in Cap (Avg %)
1	26	Drugs & Research	64,255	45,168	49,337	2,764	1,496	1,829	21.6	13.5	1.60	2.69	102,379	38,125	9.4
2	14	Discount & Fashion Retailing	42,417	23,000	34,980	771	321	95	13.2	12.1	1.08	1.26	207,519	165,101	13.5
3	20	Food Processing	39,076	30,369	36,986	1,932	1,656	1,320	16.8	11.7	1.43	1.91	81,927	42,852	11.2
4	43	Computers & Peripherals	35,480	28,452	-4,420	-320	-2,608	-3,675	13.1	13.4	0.98	1.29	157,972	122,492	13.4
5	48	Publishing	34,950	15,989	28,892	432	431	142	14.3	12.8	1.12	2.13	65,947	30,997	19.8
6	6	Conglomerates	32,819	21,671	42,130	-2,818	5,721	-2,755	9.9	12.0	0.82	1.20	200,925	168,105	7.9
7	11	Tobacco	30,813	26,025	29,777	730	681	274	13.1	11.4	1.15	1.63	79,945	49,131	17.5
8	28	Medical Products	30,658	16,134	22,896	944	487	705	16.8	13.2	1.27	2.04	60,229	29,571	17.7
9	9	Beverages	24,406	18,372	19,676	1,086	660	611	15.6	11.1	1.41	1.94	50,446	26,040	16.0
10	5	Chemicals	21,819	20,670	24,543	2,036	6,658	910	15.3	13.2	1.16	1.21	126,312	104,493	6.0
11	47	Broadcasting	21,000	13,032	8,880	-559	-464	-681	7.9	10.1	0.78	1.71	50,525	29,525	39.3
12	54	Telephone Equip. & Service	15,847	3,922	6,986	-964	-240	-596	5.4	10.5	0.52	1.69	38,951	23,105	13.9
13	10	Personal Care	15,765	8,714	8,084	601	280	41	14.3	11.8	1.22	1.66	39,794	24,029	11.6
14	51	Pollution Control	13,101	8,005	9,739	286	247	214	19.5	14.0	1.39	2.80	20,375	7,273	32.7
15	21	Food Retailing	12,478	4,681	8,927	334	169	345	11.9	10.1	1.18	1.56	34,868	22,390	19.4
16	32	Entertainment	12,333	9,423	9,635	-232	899	12	11.5	13.3	0.86	1.79	27,928	15,595	21.0
17	44	Software	11,025	1,036	2,056	712	426	-197	20.6	14.0	1.47	1.74	25,912	14,887	28.7
18	41	Other Metals	10,058	3,016	4,902	518	1,550	765	20.8	13.2	1.57	2.25	18,120	8,062	2.7
19	23	Oil & Gas	9,336	60,671	28,080	-11,075	9,043	-8,743	7.4	11.4	0.64	1.03	285,857	276,521	3.3
20	15	Electrical Products	8,384	4,834	8,945	100	790	43	14.3	13.7	1.04	1.43	27,678	19,294	9.8
21	35	General Manufacturing	8,141	5,441	7,771	1	568	-163	13.2	13.2	1.00	1.54	23,296	15,156	14.5
22	31	Eating Places	7,229	2,548	5,246	201	188	141	13.0	11.2	1.16	1.57	19,855	12,626	16.0
23	33	Hotel & Motel	7,222	3,854	6,082	123	101	103	11.6	10.4	1.12	1.66	18,204	10,982	12.0
24	34	Other Leisure	6,048	926	303	46	221	-682	12.5	12.4	1.01	1.18	40,360	34,312	17.8
25	18	Semiconductors	5,417	-5,958	3,503	-595	-225	-716	11.5	16.3	0.70	1.41	18,695	13,278	14.7
26	55	Telephone Companies	5,269	5,994	5,419	-7,380	3,736	-5,376	7.3	10.8	0.68	1.02	231,252	225,982	5.5
27	42	Business Machines	5,145	2,805	4,045	68	8	-55	14.6	13.6	1.08	1.71	12,366	7,221	20.1
28	7	Apparel	4,684	2,463	3,170	90	11	-112	13.4	12.5	1.07	1.43	15,684	10,990	19.3
29	29	Building Materials	4,507	3,861	5,960	-7	939	-138	12.1	12.2	1.00	1.20	27,144	22,637	8.1
30	50	Industrial Distn Services	4,478	841	3,121	180	338	115	16.9	13.5	1.25	1.73	10,595	6,118	11.6

Exhibit 5.2   continued

1988 MVA Rank	Industry		Market Value Added (MVA)			Economic Value Added (EVA)			Profitability (1988)				Size (1988)		5-Year Growth in Cap (Avg %)
			1988	Change from 1983	1978	1988	Change from 1983	1978	Return On Cap r (%)	Wtd Avg Cost Cap c* (%)	r to c*	Value to Capital	Value	Capital	
31	24	Petroleum Services	3,624	-5,442	-4,874	-1,579	-599	-2,125	3.9	14.2	0.27	1.22	19,906	16,282	1.1
32	53	Other Services	3,342	1,209	1,059	79	87	4	14.8	12.6	1.17	1.70	8,148	4,806	31.8
33	13	Paper Containers	3,145	2,625	2,485	432	588	306	18.5	13.1	1.41	1.34	12,523	9,378	13.4
34	8	Appliances & Furnishings	3,087	1,778	3,166	-61	170	-32	13.5	14.2	0.95	1.33	12,393	9,306	16.1
35	27	Health Care Services	2,966	-2,610	1,802	-583	-830	-661	7.5	10.9	0.69	1.16	20,942	17,977	11.9
36	16	Electronics	2,823	-4,502	2,255	-279	-34	-302	12.2	14.0	0.87	1.16	20,325	17,502	14.0
37	19	Food Distribution	2,784	1,409	2,700	97	85	69	13.3	11.1	1.20	1.48	8,575	5,791	19.0
38	25	Drug Distribution	2,685	414	2,201	-43	-74	-57	11.2	11.8	0.94	1.40	9,331	6,646	17.1
39	37	Special Machinery	2,581	7,620	3,610	-635	3,360	-1,150	10.9	13.5	0.81	1.08	30,713	28,132	2.1
40	46	Paper	2,446	2,713	5,135	695	2,090	716	14.9	13.0	1.14	1.06	43,276	40,830	13.4
41	30	Construction & R.E.	2,415	1,086	955	-327	-194	-278	6.1	10.6	0.58	1.28	10,929	8,513	20.2
42	49	Construct & Eng. Services	2,306	3,157	2,829	-1,468	-484	-1,971	-3.9	13.0	-0.30	1.29	10,136	7,830	-1.7
43	59	Trucking & Shipping	2,211	770	2,017	-86	-54	-210	11.2	12.8	0.88	1.32	9,105	6,894	13.7
44	52	Printing & Advertising	1,920	1,154	1,658	28	7	8	14.3	13.5	1.06	1.48	5,902	3,981	19.4
45	58	Transportation Services	1,625	-390	1,704	-1,062	-778	-1,042	4.9	10.7	0.46	1.07	24,013	22,388	23.1
46	36	Machine & Hand Tools	1,513	178	1,555	-205	283	-273	10.0	13.5	0.74	1.24	7,757	6,243	7.2
47	3	Auto Parts & Equipment	1,310	229	2,129	-1,020	-377	-1,185	6.6	12.9	0.51	1.07	18,996	17,686	15.4
48	56	Airline	1,228	-769	3,084	-1,439	-428	-1,523	6.3	10.3	0.62	1.03	39,469	38,241	20.6
49	12	Glass, Metal & Plastics	642	755	764	-85	-15	-95	9.2	13.1	0.70	1.28	2,972	2,330	12.8
50	38	Textiles	610	379	775	-23	-1	14	11.5	12.0	0.96	1.10	6,637	6,026	24.1
51	17	Instruments	579	-1,347	-172	-1,267	-676	-1,338	3.6	13.2	0.27	1.04	13,900	13,321	8.4
52	45	Forest Products	432	230	112	-42	1,285	-299	13.1	13.3	0.98	1.02	18,955	18,523	5.6
53	4	Tire & Rubber	284	993	2,004	-201	-79	-155	9.2	12.0	0.77	1.04	7,631	7,347	3.0
54	22	Coal	-588	164	99	-139	170	-40	10.0	13.8	0.72	0.86	3,508	4,096	19.0
55	39	Aluminum	-1,465	780	1,088	792	3,380	991	17.7	12.9	1.37	0.91	15,567	17,032	5.2
56	40	Steel	-1,585	878	3,232	-19	3,317	356	14.6	14.8	0.99	0.91	16,781	18,367	5.5
57	1	Aerospace	-3,385	-3,319	-1,884	-1,185	-124	-1,643	10.5	13.4	0.78	0.93	42,010	45,396	10.8
58	57	Railroads	-3,968	5,471	3,522	-4,758	-5,521	-3,161	4.5	13.0	0.35	0.93	49,895	53,864	1.5
59	2	Cars & Trucks	-28,224	-20,582	-8,962	-541	562	-3,887	13.3	13.8	0.96	0.77	92,959	121,183	17.4
		All	551,513	328,087	461,698	-24,929	39,204	-35,184	10.9	12.2	0.89	1.26	2704314	2152802	9.8

- Far from a discount, the sixth-ranked conglomerates sold at a premium to the value that their EVA performance would seem to justify, at least as of the end of 1988. But, with the RJR LBO underway at that time, investors may well have been betting that all large diversified companies ("LDCs," I call them) would soon be broken up by the takeover machinery, and their underlying values released to more productive owners.

- Almost as profitable as drugs are the software companies (#17), another business that encapsulates the fruits of brilliant minds in its products. In view of the fact that the capital employed in software companies has been growing at 29% per annum over the past five years versus only 9% for the pharmaceuticals, it may not be too long before the encoders catch up with the decoders.

- Oil and gas companies (#19) and telephone companies (#26) represent the largest clusters of capital and value in the survey. These vital industries deliver tremendous value to their customers but leave little, if any, premium on the table for their shareholders. Unbridled competition in the one and strict regulation of the other pushes value to the consumer.

- The most efficient creators of value are the pollution control companies (#14). They have created $20 billion in value with just $7 billion in capital. Theirs is a dirty and arduous task, fraught with risk, and not many will volunteer to do it.

- The industries bringing up the rear are transportation-related and basic resources, companies at the very cutting edge of the industrial revolution—of the last century, that is.

The XYZ Ranking

All 900 companies in the ranking have also been assigned to one of five categories according to their operating rates of return and growth rates. The five categories are as follows:

- An "X-Minus" company earned a rate of return on capital that was at least 2.5% less than its cost of capital, on average, over the five years 1984–1988 (for example, United Technologies, #893).

- An "X" company earned an average return within plus or minus 2.5% of its cost of capital (James River, #854).
- A "Y" company earned a return at least 2.5% more than its cost of capital, but could manage an average growth rate in its capital that was not more than 25% per annum (Bristol-Myers, #9).
- A "Z" company also earned at least 2.5% more than its cost of capital but expanded capital at a rate above 25% per annum (Wal-Mart, #4).
- A "Pre-Z" company earned at least 2.5% less than its cost of capital, but exhibited such explosive capital growth (at least 25% per annum on average) that management and the market must be hoping for a payoff to materialize down the road (McCaw Cellular, #36).

In some cases the categories to which companies were originally assigned were changed in light of recent performance, upgraded in the case of "turnarounds" or downgraded for "fallen angels." Johnson & Johnson (#8), for example, initially considered to be an X company because its five-year average rate of return r was only 1.9% above its cost of capital c^*, was upgraded to a Y as a result of the significant improvement in the spread over its cost of capital in the most recent two years. J&J, it seems, was a Y masquerading as an X.

Johnson & Johnson's Turnaround: $(r - c^*)$ Spread				
1984	1985	1986	1987	1988
0.4%	0.9%	−6.3%	7.1%	7.4%

Subaru of America (#772) went in the opposite direction. Classified a Y company initially because it returned nearly 25% more than its cost of capital on average, Subaru was reduced to an X-Minus in view of its recent kamikaze dive.

The Fall of Subaru: ($r - c^*$) Spread				
1984	1985	1986	1987	1988
43.1%	52.3%	75.7%	−21.2%	−26.8%

In order for a company to be reclassified, the most recent two-year trend in rates of return had to be statistically significant (at an 80% confidence level) considering the inherent variability in returns over the five-year period.

Though this simple grading system works well overall, it is not without its flaws. For instance, Chrysler, #897, is classified as a Z company based upon its historical profitability and growth. Ford, #899, is also misclassified as a Y company. It appears very doubtful that either company will do as well over the next five years as they have in the recent past. They are angels not yet fallen from grace. But, even admitting to inaccuracies such as these, it is remarkable how well this simple classification system performs, as we shall now see.

The XYZs of Value Creation

To examine the relation between the relative performance and market value of the five XYZ categories, the 900 companies were sifted into a usable, representative sample using the following procedure:

- First, a company had to have at least five complete years of financial data through 1988. Use of this criterion alone eliminated 152 of the original 900 companies, leaving 748.

- Second, very large companies were deleted because they would reduce the significance of the results for the typical firm. All companies whose market value or capital in 1988 exceeded $20 billion were stricken. This cast out 17 giants, including Ford and GM, but not Chrysler. (So we threw out Chrysler, too, for good measure, but really because it was so wrongfully classified.) This left 730 companies.

- Last, companies were excused if the volatility of their rates of return made it difficult to determine to which XYZ category they should be assigned. Humana, for example, although earning an average rate of return that was more than 2.5% above its cost of capital, experienced such variability in its rate of return that we could not confidently characterize it as either a Y or an X.

Humana: ($r - c^*$ Spread)				
1984	1985	1986	1987	1988
3.4%	4.5%	−1.6%	5.7%	1.3%

Ninety-two such equivocators were expelled for this reason, leaving 638 stalwarts to enter the analysis.

The 638 survivors of this winnowing process were distributed over the five categories as follows:

X-Minus	199	31%
X	236	37%
Y	125	20%
Z	53	8%
Pre-Z	25	4%
Total	638	100%

The disturbing revelation here is that only about one-third of the companies in the sample—the Ys and Zs—are in the business of creating *surplus* value for their shareholders. Fully two-thirds—the X-Minus and X companies—do not.

Comparing Internal and External Performance Measures

At this point, then, the EVAs and the MVAs of all the companies in each category were added together to come up with totals for all five performance categories. To allow for meaningful comparisons, the consolidated financial results for each category were standardized by dividing through by an initial level of capital, and multiplying by $100. While ignoring the absolute dollar amounts of value created by the companies in each of the categories, this standardization enabled us to project an image of the "average company," if you will, for each of the five categories.

The results of our analysis (summarized in exhibit 5.3 for 1988 and presented in detail in exhibit 5.4) suggest that the XYZ classification is a very powerful quantitative tool for evaluating the performance and value of this large set of companies. Without regard to industry, and without explicitly considering such factors as quality of management, market share, sustainable competitive advantage, and the like, stock market values are explained to a remarkable extent by dividing all companies into these five categories based solely on growth rates and operating rates of return. Moving down both panels in exhibit 5.3 from categories X-Minus through Z, the standardized market value premium in column 6 rises hand in hand with standardized EVA in column 1. (The Pre-Zs, understandably, resist classification and remain in a world of their own.) The strength of this correspondence between EVA—the internal measure of performance—and in MVA—the external market's assessment of that performance—is persuasive evidence in support of the economic model of valuation.

A Closer Look at the EVAs: Distinguishing Between Profitability and Growth

As stated earlier, there are two dimensions of corporate performance that are captured in the calculation of EVA: profitability and growth. One key insight here is that whether growth adds value depends critically on whether rates of return r exceed the cost of capital c^*.

To illustrate this principle, the standardized capital measure appearing in column 4 of exhibit 5.3 is the simple result of compounding an assumed initial $100 capital balance for four years at the *actual* average annual growth rate in capital (over the period 1984–88) that appears in column 5. The Z companies, for example, compounded $100 of starting capital to $350 using a growth rate of 36.8% per annum over the intervening four years. The X and the Y companies grew their capital at the same rate of

Exhibit 5.3 The XYZ Scheme:
Performance and Valuation as of 1988

| | | Panel A: Internal Performance | | | | Panel B: External Performance | | | |
| | (1) | (2) | (3) | (4) | (5) | (6) | (7) | (8) | (9) |
Type	EVA	r	r/c*	Beg. Capital	Capital Growth	MVA	Market Value	Value/ Capital	Ending Capital
X Minus	$ −7.5	5.7%	0.5×	$112	2.9%	$ 1	$111	1.0×	$109
X	0.6	12.7%	1.0×	160	12.5%	47	212	1.3×	165
Y	11.3	19.7%	1.6×	160	12.5%	170	334	2.0×	164
Z	41.0	25.3%	1.9×	350	36.8%	519	847	2.6×	328
Pre-Z	−29.8	4.1%	0.4×	427	43.8%	69	475	1.2×	406
Total	$ −1.9	11.1%	0.9%	$141	9.0%	$ 51	$195	1.4×	$144

Panel A's results are scaled to the capital outstanding at the beginning of 1984 and in Panel B results are scaled to the capital outstanding at end of 1984. The reason for this discrepancy is that rates of return and EVA in Panel A are measured on beginning of the year capital, but MVA in Panel B is measured on end of year capital. Thus, column 5 reports the capital in place at the beginning of 1988 relative to $100 at the beginning of 1984 whereas column 9 is the capital in place at the end of 1988 relative to $100 at the end of 1984. All results are for the year or end of year 1988, Panel A scaled to capital = $100 as of 1983; Panel B scaled to capital = $100 as of 1984.

Exhibit 5.4 Five Standardized Composite Companies

Internal Performance

(A) Beginning Capital, $

	1984	1985	1986	1987	1988	1989
X-Minus	100	105	110	113	112	114
X	100	111	126	141	160	183
Y	100	111	130	146	160	180
Z	100	140	220	263	350	453
Pre-Z	100	143	243	340	427	483
Total	100	109	121	132	141	155

(B) Rate of Return, %

	1984	1985	1986	1987	1988
X-Minus	7.1	4.9	2.6	5.3	5.7
X	11.1	10.3	9.8	11.6	12.7
Y	18.4	18.1	16.1	18.2	19.7
Z	27.5	24.9	24.5	24.8	25.3
Pre-Z	6.3	5.6	4.6	1.9	4.1
Total	10.3	9.0	7.7	9.9	11.1

(C) r/c*

	1984	1985	1986	1987	1988
X-Minus	0.4	0.3	0.2	0.4	0.5
X	0.7	0.8	0.9	1.0	1.0
Y	1.2	1.3	1.4	1.5	1.6
Z	1.7	1.6	2.0	1.9	1.9
Pre-Z	0.5	0.4	0.4	0.2	0.4
Total	0.7	0.6	0.7	0.8	0.9

(D) EVA, $

	1984	1985	1986	1987	1988
X-Minus	-9.3	-10.2	-10.0	-7.7	-7.5
X	-3.8	-3.7	-1.9	-0.4	0.6
Y	3.5	4.6	6.1	8.6	11.3
Z	11.2	13.6	24.1	30.6	41.0
Pre-Z	-7.5	-11.3	-15.0	-29.5	-29.8
Total	-5.4	-5.7	-4.7	-2.8	-1.9

Exhibit 5.4 continued

External Performance

(E) Ending Capital, $

	1984	1985	1986	1987	1988
X-Minus	100	105	109	109	109
X	100	112	126	143	165
Y	100	115	132	146	164
Z	100	140	185	250	328
Pre-Z	100	159	276	348	406
Total	100	110	122	132	144

(F) Market Value, $

	1984	1985	1986	1987	1988
X-Minus	85	100	106	104	111
X	113	144	170	183	212
Y	167	227	289	309	334
Z	305	470	653	759	847
Pre-Z	116	194	345	416	475
Total	111	141	167	176	195

(G) Value/Capital

	1984	1985	1986	1987	1988
X-Minus	0.9	1.0	1.0	1.0	1.0
X	1.1	1.3	1.3	1.3	1.3
Y	1.7	2.0	2.2	2.1	2.0
Z	3.0	3.3	3.5	3.0	2.6
Pre-Z	1.2	1.2	1.3	1.2	1.2
Total	1.1	1.3	1.4	1.3	1.4

(H) MVA, $

	1984	1985	1986	1987	1988
X-Minus	-15	-5	-3	-5	1
X	13	31	44	40	47
Y	67	113	157	163	170
Z	205	329	468	509	519
Pre-Z	16	35	69	68	69
Total	11	30	45	44	51

12.5%—but with vastly different consequences for shareholders, as we shall see.

The composite rate of return achieved in the year 1988 is reported in column 2, and its relation to the cost of capital appears in column 3. In that year, the X-Minus companies as a group earned only half their cost of capital, the X companies earned just their cost of capital, and the Y and Z companies earned on the order of one-and-a-half to two times their required rates of return.

The 1988 EVAs reported in column 1 of exhibit 5.3 are calculated by multiplying the "standardized" capital employed at the beginning of the year by the spread between the rate of return and the cost of capital for each category of firms. The calculations of EVA, both for 1984 and 1988, are shown below for each of the performance categories (except for the wild and woolly Pre-Zs).

Type	Standardized 1984 EVA $(r - c^*) \times \$100$	ΔEVA	Standardized 1988 EVA $(r - c^*) \times$ std. cap
X-Minus	$(7.1\% - 16.4\%) \times \$100$ $(-9.3\%) \times \$100$ $\$-9.3$	$+\$1.8=$	$(5.7\% - 12.4\%) \times \$112$ $(-6.7\%) \times \$112$ $\$-7.5$
X	$(11.1\% - 14.9\%) \times \$100$ $(-3.8\%) \times \$100$ $\$-3.8$	$+\$4.4=$	$(12.7\% - 12.3\%) \times \$160$ $(0.4\%) \times \$160$ $\$0.6$
Y	$(18.4\% - 14.9\%) \times \$100$ $(3.5\%) \times \$100$ $\$3.5$	$+\$7.8=$	$(19.7\% - 12.6\%) \times \$160$ $(7.1\%) \times \$160$ $\$11.3$
Z	$(27.5\% - 16.3\%) \times \$100$ $(11.2\%) \times \$100$ $\$11.2$	$+\$29.8=$	$(25.3\% - 13.6\%) \times \$350$ $(11.7\%) \times \$350$ $\$41.0$

In the case of 1984, the standardized EVA is simply the spread between that year's rate of return r and cost of capital c^* multiplied by $\$100$. For example, the Z companies as a group had an initial standardized EVA of $\$11.2$, which simply reflects the fact that their average rate of return was 11.2% above the prevailing cost of capital in that year. Using our method, the first (or base) year in the EVA calculation thus reflects only the comparison of rates of return to the cost of capital, while effectively ignoring the growth dimension of performance.

By 1988, however, the Z companies' standardized EVA increased sharply to $41.0, a change of $29.8 over four years. One of the contributors to this increase in EVA was the significant growth in capital by this group of companies. Although the Zs failed to make any real progress in widening the spread between their rate of return and cost of capital (it increased only from 11.2% to 11.7%), they were distinguished from the other performance categories by the fact that the large return spread they maintained was earned on a 1988 capital base that was three-and-a-half times as large as the 1984 base level. In short, the performance of the Zs was truly outstanding, combining extraordinary growth with superior rates of return; and the changes in their EVAs (and MVAs) shows it.

By contrast, the X-Minus companies barely increased their capital employed (which, in light of their rates of return, undoubtedly came as a relief to their shareholders). Their EVAs remained depressingly negative over the five-year period covered by this survey. (And, had they achieved higher rates in growth in capital spending while earning the same substandard rates of return, EVA would have been still more negative.) Their ability to achieve a modest improvement in EVA between 1984 and 1988 can be attributed almost entirely to a reduction in interest rates that in turn reduced the general corporate cost of capital over that period.

In the comparison of X to Y companies, differences in rate of return rather than growth are largely responsible for the differences in EVA. Though the X and Y companies grew at roughly the same rate over this period, only the Y companies had positive and rapidly improving EVAs—a distinction that, as we will see below, is reflected in the relative market valuations of these two groups. But, here again, the X companies did increase their EVA somewhat, as their profitability increased slightly and interest rates eased.

Compare Y to Z, and the importance of aggressively investing capital in high-returning projects becomes clear. By the end of four years, the Z companies as a group had invested new capital at twice the rate of the Ys. Combined with their outstanding profitability, the Z companies' exceptional growth made them exceptionally valuable.

The Link of EVA to External Performance: A Closer Look at MVA

It is worth restating the principal finding of the analysis: namely, MVA marches in lockstep with EVA, thus confirming the usefulness of EVA as a measure of corporate performance. (For habitual skeptics, an even more striking relation will be demonstrated a little later.)

To allow comparison among the five different performance categories, we had to standardize our calculations of MVA in a manner similar to that used in standardizing the EVA calculations just described. To compute a standardized MVA, we simply began with a standardized capital measure (again, using the arbitrarily chosen base year of 1984) and multiplied by the spread between the value to capital (V/C) ratio and 1, as follows:

Standardized MVA $=$ (V/C $-$ 1) $\times$ standardized capital

As in the EVA calculation, standardized capital in the base year is assumed to be $100. Thus, in all the 1984 calculations, standardized MVA is nothing more than the percentage market value premium over (or discount to) economic book value. The Z companies, for instance, sold at the end of 1984 for a market value that was slightly more than 3 times the level of capital employed (as shown in exhibit 5.3). Specifically, the standardized MVA in the 1984 base year was $205, which reflects a 205% market value premium over economic book at which the shares of Z companies were then trading.

$$
\begin{aligned}
\text{Standardized 1984 MVA} &= 1984 \ (V/C-1) \times \$100 \\
&= (3.05-1) \times \$100 \\
&= \$205
\end{aligned}
$$

Four years later (that is, by the end of 1988) the standardized MVA for the Z companies was $519, or more than 2.5 times greater than it was in 1984.

Standardized
1988 MVA = 1988 (V/C−1) × 1988 standardized capital
= (2.58−1) × $328
= $519

The fallacy of focusing on ratios rather than absolute dollar amounts becomes apparent once again. Even though the value-to-capital multiple shrank from 3.0 to 2.6, over the period from 1984 to 1988 the Z companies created $314 of market value in excess of the new capital they invested ($519 − $205). Creating value is what matters, not maximizing ratios.

The analysis of beginning and ending MVA is repeated below for the other categories (excepting, again, the Pre-Zs). As shown there, just as the Z companies generated the greatest change in their EVAs, they also produced the largest increment to MVA because they invested the most capital and sold for the highest multiples to capital (see column 8 in exhibit 5.3).

Type	Standardized 1984 MVA	ΔMVA	Standardized 1988 MVA
	(V/C − 1) × $100		(V/C − 1) × std. cap
X-Minus	(0.85 − 1) × $100		(1.01 − 1) × $109
	$−15	+$16=	$1
X	(1.13 − 1) × $100		(1.28 − 1) × $165
	$13	+$34=	$47
Y	(1.67 − 1) × $100		(2.04 − 1) × $164
	$67	+$103=	$170
Z	(3.05 − 1) × $100		(2.58 − 1) × $328
	$205	+$314=	$519

And, although the Xs and Ys expanded capital at virtually identical rates, only the Ys added substantially to their market value. Curiously, though, the Xs did increase their MVA somewhat. That is because, as we saw earlier, even the Xs produced some increase in their EVA over the period.

A Clearer Correlation. The strong relationship between performance and value is perhaps clearest when the *change* in EVA is paired with the *change* in MVA over a given period of time.

Type	Change in EVA	Change in MVA
X-Minus	$1.8	$16
X	4.4	34
Y	7.8	103
Z	29.8	314
Pre-Z	−22.3	53

Excepting once again the Pre-Zs, the change in MVA is close to being 10 times the change in EVA for all categories of profitability. Just as the MVA theoretically is equal to the *capitalized* value of all future EVA, so the change in MVA should be equivalent to the capitalized value of the change in EVA. (A little later on, the change-to-change relation will be established even more forcefully.)

The Empire Builders (Or Why Growth for Growth's Sake Does Not Reward Shareholders)

The comparison of the X group of companies to the Y group shows that despite equal growth, there was a marked difference in value. This should not come as a surprise because, in theory, the growth rate of an X company should not affect its market value added at all. With capital earning only what it costs, there is no economic value added, one way or another.

To test this fundamental proposition even more carefully, the X companies were separated into three groups according to the compound average growth rate in their ending capital from 1983 to 1988:

1. growth greater than 15% per annum on average
2. growth between 5% and 15% per annum and
3. growth less than 5% per annum

There were 104 rapidly growing X companies (labelled X FSTs), 106 moderately growing ones (X MODs), and 26 slow growers (X SLOs). The differences in market value added (see exhibit 5.5) among the three X groups are not statistically meaningful. This is suggestive evidence that the growth rate for X companies is irrelevant.

After five years of relentless expansion, the X FSTs have more than double the market value of the X SLOs (see column 7), to say nothing of the much greater level of EPS. Thus, it is true that these empire-building companies have successfully increased their long-run value. But such increases have conferred no benefit on their shareholders. In their all-consuming drive to grow, the X FSTs have consumed so much capital (column 8) that they produced virtually no more market value added than the other less ambitious X companies.

The irrelevance of growth for X companies also is borne out by relating the *change* in EVA to the *change* in MVA over the four-year period from 1984 to 1988.

Type	Change in EVA	Change in MVA
X SLO	$ 14.3	$51
X MOD	4.0	21
X FST	−1.2	32
X	4.4	34

If anything, it appears that the wisest strategy was that adopted by the managers of the slow-growing X companies. By holding back on growth and focusing instead upon improving their profitability, they increased their EVA and MVA the most over the four-year period.

That is not to say that the rapidly growing X companies are worse than the others. But nor should they be construed to be better just because they are growing faster. The point is that rapidly growing X companies should not expect the stock market to reward them for their aggressive expansion efforts. And, if they should happen not to grow as fast, other companies are likely to step into the breach, absorb the capital they free up, and use it to bring other, equally-valued products and services to

Exhibit 5.5 Why Growth Per Se Doesn't Matter

		Panel A: Internal Performance					Panel B: External Performance		
	(1)	(2)	(3)	(4)	(5)	(6)	(7)	(8)	(9)
Type	EVA	r	r/c*	Beg. Capital	Capital Growth	MVA	Market Value	Value/ Capital	Ending Capital
X SLO	$ 2.3	15.0 %	1.2×	$ 95	0.6 %	$46	$149	1.4×	$103
X MOD	0.7	13.1 %	1.0×	141	7.4 %	41	184	1.3×	143
X FST	−0.9	11.5 %	1.0×	255	19.9 %	62	310	1.3×	248
X	0.6	12.7 %	1.0×	165	10.5 %	47	212	1.3×	165

All results are for year or end of year 1988. Panel A scaled to capital=$100 as of 1983; Panel B to capital=$100 as of 1984.

consumers and producers. There simply is no compelling reason for any one X company to grow more rapidly. They are the marginal players in the capital competition game.

This is why X companies often make such excellent candidates for LBOs and other leveraged recapitalizations. By forgoing growth, no value is lost. And if paying down debt brings about operating efficiencies, wealth increases on net.

An Anomaly.   You may have noticed that the X, and in particular, the X-Minus companies, sell for market values that EVA seems inadequate to justify. The X-Minus companies, though earning returns short of those required by the market, nonetheless sell at par, and the X companies sell for a slight premium without a premium return.

Turnaround potential and takeover value are probably the reasons for these apparent deviations from our economic model of value. When a company's rate of return falls to or below its cost of capital, management may be changed, strategies altered, and resources reallocated away from an industry suffering from overcapacity. Corrective forces tend to swing a company and its industry back to an equilibrium in which the marginal project earns the cost of capital.

Moreover, should a hapless X or X-Minus company be unable to reverse its misfortunes, it may be taken over by astute investors or aggressive managers—and the market knows it. Also, because growth potential is not contributing to their value, these companies are ideal candidates, as I already mentioned, for leveraged payouts of cash to investors. A premium may be built into their stock market values in anticipation of just such a transaction.

Not all X and X-Minus companies, however, have market values that seem to defy the laws of gravity. Some have sunk to depressed values despite the buoyant forces in the market. The last 50 companies on our ranking, for example—those falling in the #850 to #900 range—do sell at substantial discounts to the level of capital invested.

Why are their values resistant to improvement? Many are strongly unionized—the auto companies, steel companies, the rails, and the airlines, for example. The unions have extracted considerable value from the shareholders of these companies, and they are not apt to give it back anytime soon. Others seem to be impervious to takeover, either due to sheer size (Sears #872), or the chairman's expressed determination to fight a hostile bid (IT&T #891, and Champion International #879), or a national security umbrella (McDonnell Douglas #887, General Dynamics #888, and United Technologies, #893). Lastly, a fair number of them are high-tech companies that got caught in the crossfires of rapid and withering change (e.g., National Semiconductor #853, Tektronix #860, Advanced Micro Devices #861, Data General #866, Wang Laboratories #869, Xerox #880, and Control Data #883).

But, to come back to my earlier point, other than the last 50 to 100 or so companies on the ranking, the X and X-Minus firms sell more for their potential rather than actual performance.

Summing Up the Case for XYZ

Our analysis suggests, in short, that the XYZ paradigm proves to be an effective way to rank the performance and value of companies irrespective of industry. Stock market values can be explained to a remarkable extent by dividing all companies into just five categories. The most critical part of the classification scheme is to separate those companies earning more than their cost of capital from those that are not. For those that are not, relative rates of growth had an imperceptible bearing on their market values. For those that are, growth matters a great deal. This evidence is entirely consistent with the proposition that EVA accounts for the premium or discount built into the market value of a company's shares.

More Evidence on the Correlation Between EVA and MVA (Or, Why Beat Around the Bush?)

The best way to prove the significance of EVA is to correlate EVA directly to MVA, without resort to an XYZ categorization.

In performing this kind of analysis, we excluded Pre-Zs from the sample, thus leaving us with 613 companies. Data for the remaining companies were individually standardized to start with $100 of capital in the manner I have already described. The companies were ranked according to their average 1987–1988 EVA and assigned from highest to lowest into 25 groups of 25 companies each (actually, the bottom group only had 13 companies). The final output was the average EVA and MVA for each of the 25 groups.

The same procedure was then repeated using *changes* in EVA and MVA between the periods 1984–85 and 1987–88 as the basis for the ranking.

As shown in exhibit 5.6 and as plotted in exhibits 5.7 and 5.8, there is a striking relationship between both the levels of EVA

Exhibit 5.6   The Relationship Between EVA and MVA

	Level to Level		Change to Change	
	(1)	(2)	(3) 84–85 EVA to 87–88 EVA	(4) 84–85 MVA to 87–88 MVA
	87–88 EVA	88 MVA		
1.	$ 131.1	$1203.2	$ 112.1	$ 736.9
2.	30.6	552.1	22.6	192.1
3.	20.6	335.9	16.0	131.4
4.	14.0	265.7	12.8	78.6
5.	10.5	215.0	10.6	88.5
6.	8.0	122.1	9.1	76.3
7.	6.2	119.3	7.9	63.0
8.	4.9	97.9	6.9	42.1
9.	3.9	143.1	6.0	46.8
10.	2.8	96.5	5.0	53.8
11.	1.6	64.5	4.1	43.5
12.	0.8	54.7	3.3	38.2
13.	−0.3	46.8	2.5	11.4
14.	−1.3	49.2	1.9	13.3
15.	−2.2	25.8	1.3	23.3
16.	−2.3	15.3	0.6	16.5
17.	−4.1	23.2	0.0	31.1
18.	−5.1	18.3	−0.9	3.6
19.	−6.0	25.2	−1.8	6.9
20.	−7.2	52.7	−2.9	6.1
21.	−8.8	15.0	−4.3	−2.1
22.	−11.0	1.1	−6.0	−5.1
23.	−13.5	−8.6	−9.6	−7.2
24.	−18.7	2.0	−14.7	−34.3
25.	−37.7	1.2	−38.0	−112.9

and MVA—and, even more pronounced, between *changes* in these levels. For the groups of companies with negative EVA, the correlation is less evident. Until EVA becomes positive, market values are decoupled, in effect, from current internal measures of performance. Instead, the potential for liquidation, recovery, recapitalization, or takeover sets a floor on market value. But, once the EVA turns positive, there is a very high correspondence between the level of EVA and the level of market value added (as reflected in the upward-sloping line in exhibit 5.7).

The relation between EVA and MVA becomes even clearer when *changes* in the levels of EVA and MVA are plotted (as shown in exhibit 5.8). Here is strong visual evidence that adopting the goal of maximizing EVA and EVA growth will in fact build a premium into the market value of any company.[7]

Exhibit 5.7   MVA vs. EVA: Averages by Groups of 25

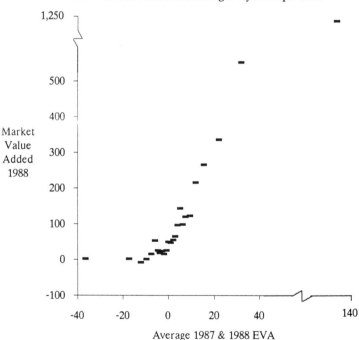

Average 1987 & 1988 EVA

[7]For those who are statistically inclined the R-squared of the change-to-change relation is 97%; the t-statistic is 28.

Exhibit 5.8   Changes in MVA vs. Changes in EVA: Averages by Groups of 25

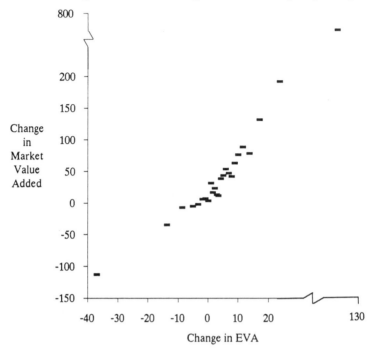

Corporate Uses of the Stern Stewart 1000

Setting Performance Goals and Valuation Expectations

The table below has been constructed by lifting roughly every fifth group from the table in exhibit 5.6 in order to isolate key "break points" in performance and value. It can also be used to target expectations for future performance.

Rank	Percentile	Change in EVA	Change in MVA
1.	100th	$ 112.1	$ 736.9
5.	80th	10.6	88.5
10.	60th	5.0	53.8
12.5	50th	2.8	24.8
15.	40th	1.3	23.3
20.	20th	−2.9	6.1
25.	0th	−38.0	−112.9

To illustrate, a company wishing its performance to qualify for the top 20th percentile of American companies would have to increase its standardized EVA by $10.6 over a four-year period. This means, for example, that a company that currently employs $1 billion of capital would have to *increase* its EVA by $106 million over four years to move into the top 20%. The right-hand column indicates the payoff in terms of expected market recognition from achieving a given level of performance. To continue the example from above, if our $1 billion company is successful in increasing its EVA by $106 million, then it can expect to have added another $885 million to its value in excess of the additional capital invested over the period.

The Retailer Review

Another potential application of this research is to evaluate the performance of companies or individual business units against the results for our performance categories (at least the X through Z categories). Such results could also be held up as future goals as well.

To illustrate such an application, we have scaled the results for the six retailers introduced in chapter 4 and then assigned them to appropriate performance categories (see exhibit 5.9).

Exhibit 5.9   The Retailer Performance Review

	Panel A: Internal Performance				Panel B: External Performance			
	(1)	(2)	(3)	(4) Capital	(5)	(6)	(7)	(8) Value/
Company	EVA	r	r/c*	Growth	MVA	Value	Capital	Capital
X	$ 0.6	12.7%	1.0×	12.5%	$ 47	$ 212	$165	1.3×
K-Mart	1.3	13.0%	1.0×	11.6%	11	143	132	1.1×
Kroger	2.4	10.2%	1.2×	5.5%	94	220	126	1.7×
Woolworth	3.0	14.5%	1.2×	6.8%	52	204	152	1.3×
Y	11.3	19.7%	1.6×	12.5%	170	334	164	2.0×
Melville	11.7	20.8%	1.6×	11.0%	133	289	156	1.8×
Z	41.0	25.3%	1.9×	36.8%	519	847	328	2.6×
Wal-Mart	40.7	25.2%	2.0×	34.0%	764	1,043	279	3.7×
Food Lion	27.8	20.5%	1.9×	30.0%	935	1,310	375	3.5×

All results are for year or end of year 1988. Panel A scaled to capital = $100 as of 1983; Panel B to capital = $100 as of 1984.

Here are some observations that come out of this exercise:

- K-Mart's results make it look just like a classic X company except for the fact that its market valuation is a little lower. This valuation probably reflects the fact that it is directly in the expansion path of Wal-Mart.

- Kroger's 1988 leveraged recapitalization has driven down its cost of capital, and raised its EVA and market value above the level typical of an X company.

- Woolworth's EVA and MVA show it to be in the process of heaving off the shackles of an X company and putting on the wings of a Y (nevertheless, for the XYZ analysis, Woolworth was considered an X based upon its average performance over the past five years).

- Melville appears to be a classic Y company in almost every respect.

- Wal-Mart's internal performance is the epitome of the Z company. It does sell for significantly higher market value, though. Many of the Z companies are driven by technology or fads that can fade fast, whereas Wal-Mart operates in the retailing arena with advantages that are more likely to withstand the force of competition for a longer time.

- Food Lion's historical rate of return, growth rate, and EVA are shy of the typical Z company. Yet, the company sells for a market valuation that is well above that of the typical Z, for some of the same reasons as does Wal-Mart. Another reason is that, though its performance comes up short of the typical Z company, Food Lion performs clear leagues ahead of any other grocery store chain. "Perhaps Food Lion will become the Wal-Mart of grocery stores," say investors.

Changes in the retailers' MVAs from 1984 to 1988 reflect contemporaneous changes in their EVA as well as current developments expected to affect future EVA.

Type	Change in EVA	Change in MVA
X	$ 4.4	$ 34
K-Mart	2.0	4
Kroger	3.5	90
Woolworth	5.4	53
Y	7.8	103
Melville	4.7	76
Z	29.8	314
Wal-Mart	30.1	542
Food Lion	23.5	719

Summary

The new Stern Stewart Performance 1000 ranks prominent American companies according to the market value they have added to their shareholders' cumulative investment. It is the single most reliable measure of a company's past performance, as well as a useful predictor of future performance.

Any ranking based on sheer size, including total equity capitalization, can lead to assessments radically different from rankings using the measure of market value added. Most notable was the case of General Motors, which tumbled from number 6 on *Business Week*'s 1988 ranking of the 1,000 most valuable American companies to dead last in the market value added sweepstakes. But others were subject to much the same rough handling. Ford fell from number 8 to number 899, just behind GM; Du Pont from number 9 to number 850; and Amoco from number 10 to number 730.

The one company to hold its own was IBM, which stood at the top of both 1988 lists. IBM's direction is less certain. The juggernaut's MVA fell by over $7 billion over the ten-year period since 1978, and by a whopping $25.9 billion since 1983. Merck ranked number 2 in MVA, and also claimed second prize for improving MVA, adding a remarkable $15.3 billion since 1978.

MVA increases when a company lives up to its anticipated potential for creating value, develops new value-enhancing investment opportunities, or shuts down unprofitable operations. MVA decreases when a company's performance falls short of expectations or when it commits capital to new investment that fails (or is expected to fail) to earn the cost of capital. Merck and General Motors exemplify these two divergent paths.

The best internal guide to the enhancement of MVA is economic value added, or EVA. EVA is the residual income (or economic profit) that remains after subtracting the cost of capital from operating profits. It is the fuel that fires up MVA. In theory, market value added at any point in time is equal to the discounted present value of all the EVA that a company can be expected to generate in the future.

There is suggestive evidence that increasing EVA is indeed the key to building a premium-valued company, one whose stock market value exceeds the capital resources committed to the firm. The theory and the evidence all point to the same fundamental conclusion: Increasing EVA should be adopted as the paramount objective of any company that professes to be concerned about maximizing its shareholders' wealth.

The Stern Stewart Annual Review, which includes the Stern Stewart Performance 1000, a comprehensive booklet of corporate performance analysis, broken down by industry, including an analysis of creditworthiness and cost of capital, is available for a fee from Stern Stewart & Co. 450 Park Avenue, 5th Floor, New York, NY, 10022, (212) 751-3900. The year-end 1989 corporate survey, which reviews corporate performances and financial conditions throughout the decade of the 1980s, can be obtained from this office.

6

Making Managers into Owners

Introduction

Making managers into owners is a proven and potent way to create value. To be sure, ownership must go beyond the merely monetary. It is first and foremost a question of attitude. Pride in one's work, sensible risk taking, and, above all, accepting responsibility for the success or failure of the enterprise are among the attitudes that separate owners from mere hired hands. But most people will turn their heads the other way unless there is also the prospect of a corresponding financial reward. The philosophy I am advocating is value sharing: making everyone a meaningful partner in the process of adding to value.

The issue of ownership is broad. At the level of rank-and-file employees, it encompasses gain-sharing and profit-sharing plans, ESOPs, and the like, all of which are important scaffolding to the overall structure of ownership and all of which certainly warrant improvement over current practice. Though I recognize the need to address ownership in the broadest terms, in this chapter I will confine the discussion to the question of how to make managers into owners. The ways to do this range from the simulated to the realistic, the conventional to the more radical.

A realistic approach works equity into the hands of management people and provides a mechanism for cashing out the value that those people have created over a reasonable period of time (some of the realistic methods are described in chapter 13, "Financial Restructuring," and chapter 14, "Remaking the Public Corporation from Within"). The equity may be stock in the overall parent or a phantom stock representing ownership in a business unit.[1] As a general rule, the more realistic the ownership method, the more precise and powerful the incentive is apt to be. But then again, such methods are more radical, and not everyone will consider them to be suitable.

The simulated approaches reward managers for increasing performance measures that are as close as possible to the creation of value on an annual basis, *with the restriction that no stock market or projected data be required.* I impose this limitation as a practical matter and as one of the things that separates a simulated from a realistic plan.

Introducing Economic Value Added

By this point, one thing should be clear: The best practical periodic performance measure is economic value added (EVA). With EVA as a performance measure, the parent company in effect acts as a bank that advances capital to its units through a line of credit that bears interest at a rate equal to the cost of capital c^*. EVA is the difference between the profits each unit derives from its operations (NOPAT) and the charge for capital each unit incurs through the use of its credit line.

$$\text{EVA} = \text{NOPAT} - c^* \times \text{capital}$$
$$= \text{operating profits} - \text{a capital charge}$$

To compute EVA in practice, operating profits for each line of business and for the consolidated company are tracked quarterly, if not monthly. A capital charge is computed by taking the aver-

---

[1]This really should not be as alien a concept as it seems to be. After all, every private company that has an ESOP is required by law to have an independent appraisal as the basis for establishing a value for the shares employees receive when they leave. There is no reason why appraised valuations also could not be used as the basis for structuring a phantom equity plan for managers of units within large public companies.

age level of net assets employed (i.e., capital) over that quarter or that month and multiplying by an appropriate periodic cost of capital set at the beginning of the year. EVA is the difference, cumulated over the year. It's that simple most of the time (see exhibit 6.1 and exhibit 6.2 for qualifications).

The Three Key Incentives

The bonus plan, too, is simplicity itself. Managers are rewarded for increasing EVA relative to target, and they are penalized for falling short (more on this later). With EVA to guide them, operating managers have three important incentives that are either absent from or distorted by many other measures:

1. To improve operating profits without tying up any more capital
2. To draw down more capital on the line of credit so long as the additional profits management earns by investing the capital cover the charge for the additional capital
3. To free up capital and pay down the line of credit so long as any earnings lost are more than offset by savings on the capital charge

EVA Drives Value

Besides providing all of the right incentives, another important advantage to using EVA is that it is the one and only internal measure of corporate performance to tie directly to value. It is the fuel that fires a premium (or accounts for the discount) in the market's valuation of any business. No other measure can make the connection between performance and value as clear as EVA can.

The Ends or the Means?

Despite all of its advantages, some may object to the use of EVA as a bonus measure and prefer instead to compensate managers for attaining goals set forth in a strategic plan. Perhaps an analogy can best differentiate the means and the ends approaches.

Exhibit 6.1   Better Late than Never

The one time the EVA calculation might transcend the elegant simplicity of line of credit accounting is when a strategic investment is made, one in which the full payoff is expected to materialize down the road. One way to handle such investments for the purpose of computing EVA and determining bonuses is to use public utility accounting: Part or all of the strategic investment is held back from the capital base that is subject to the capital charge, is instead stored in a suspense account that bears interest at a rate equal to the cost of capital, and is brought into capital as the expected payoff materializes. In this way, management will not be deterred from making sensible strategic investments, but neither will it be excused from eventually earning an acceptable return on capital. In practice, public utility accounting should be used selectively, for certain major strategic projects, and only with the prior approval of the compensation committee of the board.

Acquisitions provide good examples of the problem that is posed by strategic investments in general. Suppose, for example, a company pays 16 times earnings for a target that was selling for a 12 multiple, justifying the premium with synergies and future growth potential. Even if the buyer's judgment about the eventual payoff is absolutely correct, the immediate yield on the purchase price, which is just the inverse of the multiple paid, is only 6.25% ($\frac{1}{16}$), hardly an acceptable rate of return. With any reasonable capital charge rate, EVA will suffer, at least initially, and that may dissuade managers from pursuing a perfectly acceptable acquisition.

In such a case I would recommend that the purchase price be divided in two for the purpose of computing EVA. One part would reflect the value of the target's current earnings power, and the residual would be the premium paid for synergies and growth that are on the come. For example, if the operating profits of the acquired company are running at, say, $150 million and the cost of capital is 15%, then $1 billion ($150 million/15%) of the purchase price enters the capital base right away. The capital charge at 15% on $1 billion is $150 million, which cancels the operating profits and produces neither a reward nor a deterrent to the takeover, at least initially. If, to continue the preceding example, 16 times the earnings of $150 million were paid, or $2.4 billion, the $1.4 billion residual over the $1 billion embedded value would be carried in a suspense account bearing interest at 15%, and it would amortize with interest into the capital base over the period in which the synergies and value-adding growth are expected to materialize. The amortization schedule for the suspense account would be the subject of a negotiation between the board and senior management or between senior management and unit management, depending on the impetus for the transaction and the parties responsible for making the acquisition payoff afterward. Because it is an added complication and requires some negotiation, the use of public utility accounting should be kept to a minimum—restricted to just those sizable significant strategic acquisitions and internal investments which can make a real difference in the long run.

Exhibit 6.2 Inflated Expectations

I remember calling on a company several years after it had gone to the expense of installing a sophisticated inflation-adjusted accounting system to track performance and determine bonuses. The chief planning officer admitted to me that it wasn't working. There was total confusion. He told me about a memorable meeting early on in the implementation process in which they had tried to explain to key operating people the difference between real and nominal assets. After listening to the planners' earnest presentation for over two hours, one of the operators threw his hands up in exasperation and said, "Listen, let me tell you something: All of my assets are real."

A little forethought could have saved them a lot of needless anxiety. All it takes is to recognize that value is created at the margin, by looking forward, not by looking backward at the distortions created by past inflation. A company could rip up its balance sheet and toss it away, and that should not affect decisions pertaining to the enhancement of value. That's what economists mean when they say, "Sunk costs are irrelevant."

And so it is that none of the three EVA incentives is affected by past inflation or the current balance sheet. Making more money, investing cash productively, and withdrawing cash from substandard activities—not one depends upon the current accounting basis for assets. As a result, in any country where the rate of inflation over time is less than 10%, accounting for inflation is a needless complexity to the issue of motivating managers to create value through EVA.

Suppose you wanted to induce people to lose weight. One way, a means approach, would be to reward the poor souls for adhering to a regimented exercise program and diet. Better though, to weigh them periodically and to pay them if they lose weight, leaving them free to choose between diet and exercise. It's just the same with EVA, which is a scale that can be used to weigh a business's value and reward a positive change without being an inflexible harness on initiative or ability to respond to changes.

Should one reward the means or reward the ends is the question. Perhaps some of each. But the greater a manager's control over resources, the broader his or her decision-making mandate and the more volatile the markets served, the more the bonus should be tilted toward rewarding the ends and not the means, the end being to create value.

In sum, EVA is an all-encompassing measure of the value management adds to the capital it chooses to employ. Tying bonuses to improvements in EVA forges a clear and powerful link between managerial pay and rewards for the company's stockholders. That is the first critical requirement in making managers into owners.

The Real Thing

Coca-Cola uses EVA as the foundation of its planning and reward system.

> To ensure that Coke's operations managers think like the top brass about the cost of money, [Chairman Roberto] Goizueta insists they use a calculation he calls "economic value added." He defines that as after-tax operating profits minus the cost of capital employed to produce those earnings. In recent years each of Coke's 19 division presidents has had to present annual three year projections of the "economic value" he expects to add to the corporation. Says Goizueta: "adding economic value to the company is the key to rewarding shareholders in the 1990s."
>
> "Leaders of the Most Admired"
> *Fortune*
> January 29, 1990

Coke's fabulous results testify to the benefit of focusing management's attention upon EVA.

Applied Power

Applied Power is another successful EVA case history. The company is led by its forceful chairman and CEO, Richard Sim. Dick appeared full-face on the front cover of the firm's 1988 annual report above the bold statement: "We have a goal of building a world class company . . . worth $50 per share by the end of 1992." At the time, Applied Power's shares traded for only about $17.50.

Dick decided to play a trick on me once. I met with Dick and several of his management colleagues at the Waldorf Astoria Hotel in New York. At the conclusion of our breakfast meeting, several of the company's important institutional investors were to join Dick in his suite. As I arose to greet the lead steers, Dick suddenly grabbed me by the collar and began to shout: "I am telling you the $50 share goal is in the bag. In fact," he said as he went into a crouch, "I am beginning to think it is a slam dunk." As he finished his proclamation in full view of the stunned steers, he uncorked for a mock dunk uncomfortably near my head. As unrealistic as his goal may seem, Dick has a way of making people believe he may just do it.

One reason is the incentive compensation program the company has adopted. In a separate section of the 1988 Annual Report, Robert T. Foote, Vice President and Chief Financial Officer, described their plan:

> While the Company recognizes that earnings per share is a widely used financial performance measure in the United States, we believe measures that compare cash and cash equivalent returns on operating capital to the minimum return expected by both equity and debt investors more effectively help management guide the performance of the Company. We use a concept called Economic Value Added (EVA) as one of the fundamental measures for a multitude of analyses. Economic Value Added by our definition is the difference between our economic return and the minimum required by all investors, times capital employed, as shown in the following formula:

$$EVA = (R - C) \times TC$$
$$R = \text{Economic Rate of Return}$$
$$C = \text{Cost of Capital}$$
$$TC = \text{Total Capital}$$

We use the Economic Value Added concept to measure our annual operating performance, to evaluate annual business plans, to create measures for management incentive bonuses, and to judge the merits of major capital investments.

Applied Power presented the results generated by their program in the same special section of the report to shareholders. EVA in just 2 years improved from slightly negative to clearly positive:

	Years Ended August 31			
	1989*	1988	1987	1986
Net operating profit after taxes	$ 25.6	$19.1	$ 9.5	$ 5.4
Beginning operating capital	$153.9	$99.9	$67.2	$ 55.6
Economic return	16.7%	19.1%	14.1%	9.8%
Cost of capital	11.1%	12.0%	13.5%	10.9%
Economic value added	$ 8.6	$ 7.1	$ 0.4	−$0.6

*The 1989 data were added to the table presented in the 1988 annual report in order to present a more complete record of the company's performance.

Applied Power's common stock performance has closely tracked the improvement in the company's EVA (exhibit 6.3). From August 6, 1987, when the company first went public, through October 13, 1989, Applied Power provided a 56.9% compound average annual return for investors (dividends and price appreciation) versus only 6.6% for the S&P 500. Said differently, a dollar invested in Applied Power at the initial listing cumulated to $2.75 compared to just $1.16 for the S&P 500.

As important as it is, the company's incentive compensation system is just one strand in a broad organizational fabric chairman Dick Sim intends to weave.

One objective I have is the creation of a corporate culture with the values required for a sustainable long term growth. Certain intrin-

Exhibit 6.3 A Result of EVA: Applied Power Stock Price Performance since IPO

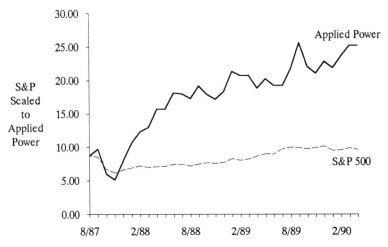

sic characteristics endure from generation to generation—characteristics that are always associated with achievement: hard work, persistence, intelligence, belief.

We endorse these lessons from the past as the foundation for adding other values. One of these is called MERITOCRACY.

I first read the word in the *Sunday Observer* in Britain when I was 13 years old. I thought it was a wonderful word. It said to me, "work hard and the world will reward you." An ideal, yes, but it has guided me since that day. We are striving to make Applied Power a Meritocracy: an ideal business environment in which we continually recognize results created by people with merit.

We offer a concept I call high performance employment. Simply put, we reward people who perform and we will not tolerate consistent lack of performance. Our objective is to achieve world class productivity at all levels of the Company. We select and retain only those employees whose added value fits our business needs. The rewards for delivering high levels are two fold: the pride of being at the leading edge and the financial rewards derived from increased shareholder value.

Richard G. Sim
Chairman and CEO
Applied Power
Chairman's Report
1989 Annual Report

I would be hard pressed to improve upon Dick's statement. That is why I decided to let him do the talking. But if I might be permitted the liberty of reading between the lines, he is saying that making people into owners must be more than a question of incentive compensation alone, of providing just a financial reward. The people must become involved as owners in the fullest sense of the word; they must be dedicated to personal excellence and the quality of product or service, responsive to their customers' needs, willing to take sensible entrepreneurial risks, and above all, committed to the success of the enterprise. Then they will be true owners and not just hired hands. But Dick also suggests, and this is the important point, that these ideals are little more than platitudes to most adult people unless the potential for earning a significant financial reward backs them up (exhibit 6.4).

Exhibit 6.4   High-Performance Employment

Dick Sim is a believer in demanding high performance and responsiveness to incentives as a condition of employment, and I must say that I agree with him. As much as I believe in the incentive of ownership, I realize that it, too, has its limitations. Sometimes it is necessary to replace managers who, for one reason or another, are not performing well and will not respond to incentives and bring in new, more capable, more aggressive ones, and then give *them* the incentive. The benefits of adopting a high-performance employment philosophy finds a supporting voice in Bill James, as evidenced by this excerpt from his engaging *1984 Baseball Digest.*

> Poor organizations virtually always act as if they believed that talent was in short supply. They believe that there is a magic in "proven" major league talent. Why do teams keep playing people like Rick Manning, like Charlie Moore, like Hubie Brooks? Why do they give those players regular jobs, and suffer with them for years and years after they have shown themselves to be below-average players? Because they believe talent to be in short supply.
>
> I would say that if you look at any successful manager, with very few exceptions you'll find a manager who is not afraid to make changes. You'll find a manager who is not afraid to look at a kid who has not proven what he can do in the major leagues, and say, "This kid can help me."

Unsuccessful organizations have good excuses for their timidity; they say things like "minor league batting records don't mean anything" and "young pitchers will break your heart." But what it comes down to is, they have no confidence in their own judgment, their ability to solve a problem. They look at their lineup and when they consider the possibility of making a change, they see themselves as teetering on the brink of an abyss.

A Whitey Herzog, a Billy Martin, a Dick Williams, a Bobby Cox, or an Earl Weaver doesn't see it that way. The confidence that a good manager has in his ability to draw useful talent from alternative sources puts him in a position of strength when dealing with a player. He can say, "If you don't want to do this the way we need to have it done, we'll try somebody else." He can say that, and mean it. The lack of confidence in his options places a John McNamara or a Bill Virdon in a position of weakness, which he must cover with an autocratic veneer.

Making managers who will not respond to ownership into owners will not generate an incentive. That's true. But who said they had to stay in the lineup.

Infinity Goes Both Ways

Evaluating performance with EVA as Applied Power and Coca-Cola do is one element of my recommended plan. Equally important is a payoff schedule that provides the prospect of unlimited rewards for success and a genuine penalty for failure. The potential bonus for improving EVA should not be capped because, far from being an expense, such bonuses simply provide management with a share of the discretionary value they create for investors. But to be fair, and to provide an incentive of another sort, managers should be penalized if they fail to deliver satisfactory levels of EVA.

Unfortunately, the typical payoff profile from an American incentive compensation system falls well short of this ideal. Many times it looks something like exhibit 6.5. An improving performance goes left to right on the x axis, and the bonus earned as a percent of salary progresses upward along the y axis. As depicted, a typical plan provides no bonus until some minimum target level of performance is achieved; then there is a bonus that increases with performance until a cap is reached. Sad to say, this typical payoff profile is much like communism. There is no risk.

There is no exceptional reward. There are just two perverse incentives.

Exhibit 6.5 The Typical Payoff Profile

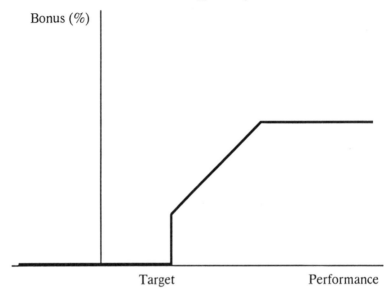

Once it becomes obvious that performance over a whole year will fall short of the target, it might as well fall very short of the target. With no downside penalty, there may be a temptation to concentrate losses in a single year—to clear the decks to set the stage for better bonuses in the following years. Here is the motivation for the big-bath school of accounting.

On the other hand, if things are going very well, why bother? Once the bonus reaches the cap, deferring profits (or improving their golf swing) will probably become more important priorities for managers than a drive for even more value. Now I am a very simple-minded person. I like straight lines the best. I suggest that the potential bonus award be extended upward ad infinitum and downward ad nauseam (exhibit 6.6). People say to me, "Bennett, I was with you up until that last point. What's this ad nauseam stuff?"

Value can fall just as well as it can rise. If the intent is to make managers behave like owners, which is a more radical proposition than it may seem to be on the surface, then they should face the

Exhibit 6.6 Infinity Goes in Both Directions

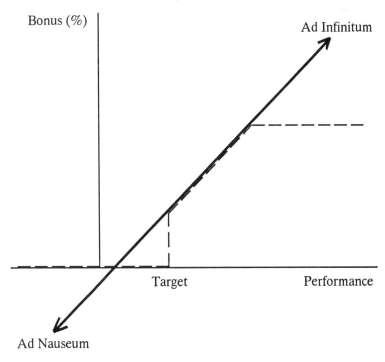

risks as well as the rewards of ownership. But not even I am so Draconian as to suggest that managers be obliged to give back part of their salaries. Rather, the potential for suffering a negative bonus is made possible because the annual bonus awards are not fully paid out but instead are banked forward and put at risk, with their full payout contingent upon continued successful performance. Here is how it works.

Bank the Bonuses

Suppose a manager has a nice round salary of $100,000 and it is agreed that hitting the target for EVA should produce a 25% bonus. The EVA target, incidentally, could be positive or negative depending upon the outlook for the business when the plan is first instituted; making EVA less negative is as valid a way to

create value as is making it more positive (exhibit 6.7). Suppose
the manager does hit the target and that a 25% bonus is earned.

Salary	$100
Bonus earned, %	25%
Bonus earned, $	$ 25

Exhibit 6.7   The Target Bonus

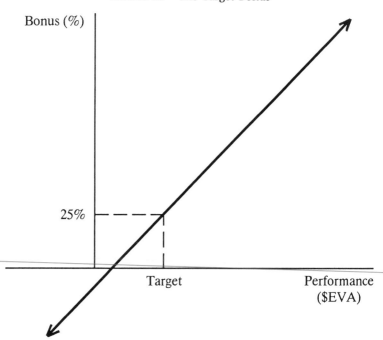

Before any payout, the $25,000 bonus must pass through a bank
account that starts with an opening balance, in this case $50,000.
The opening balance is a hypothetical carryforward from prior
years that permits the target bonus to be fully paid out even in
the first year of the plan, as will soon become obvious. This
opening balance can arise in one of three ways.

First, the $50,000 opening balance may come from nowhere at
all. It may be just a part of the formula that determines the bonus
but is unfunded in any real way. Second, it may be contributed
by the plan participants themselves and put at risk, subject to
forfeiture. Making managers buy into, instead of merely participate in, their bonus plans would seem to be an effective way to

get their attention (if not their resignation). That's because a true incentive involves providing a potentially unlimited reward for success *and* a genuine penalty for failure. Both the thrill of victory and the agony of defeat are important motivators. Faced with this stark choice, most people will choose to succeed. You can count on it.

The third approach is the most popular. The company loans the $50,000 to the participant's bank account and amortizes it over 5 years. Then in each of the first 5 years of the plan, $10,000 of bonus that would otherwise be paid is instead retained to pay off the loan. By the end of the 5 years, $50,000 of equity will have accumulated in the account to replace the $50,000 of debt that has been amortized. This approach replicates an LBO whereby management builds personal wealth as equity replaces debt in the capital structure. It also is less onerous than requiring people to come up with money they may not have. To the extent management buys into the plan, either all at once or over time, the payoff schedule should move and tilt upward. It is only fair to compensate for additional risk while providing an even greater incentive for success.

Continuing with the example, add the $25,000 bonus earned to the $50,000 starting balance and $75,000 is available for payout. In this illustrative plan, one-third is paid out and two-thirds is banked forward. The payout could be more attenuated if the business is highly cyclical or if it takes a long period of time to demonstrate that value has been created; or it could be more compressed if the business is relatively stable. In practice, though, a 3-year payout seems to be a reasonably good compromise.

Salary	$ 100
Bonus earned, %	25%
Bonus earned, $	$ 25
Beginning bank	50
Available for payout	$ 75
Payout ratio	1/3
Bonus paid	$ 25
Banked forward	50

Observe that, by design of the plan, the bonus actually paid and the bonus earned are the same in a year in which the manager hits target. So excuse me if I mislead you because, even though all bonuses pass through the bank, in reality, a normal or target bonus is fully paid out; it is only the exceptional part of the exceptional bonuses that will be banked forward and placed at risk.

With $25,000 paid out, $50,000 is banked forward as the next year's opening balance, and the process repeats. Suppose the manager handsomely exceeds the EVA target in the next year. There are two possibilities. First, the manager has produced an increase in EVA that is a harbinger of a sustainable gain in the value of the business. The second possibility is that it arises from good fortune, a cyclical peak, or even a shortsighted business decision. Rather than assume the worst, and place an arbitrary cap on the bonus, assume the best and bank the bonus forward until it is possible to discover its true meaning (exhibit 6.8).

Suppose the exceptional performance equates to a bonus that

Exhibit 6.8   A Boom Bonus

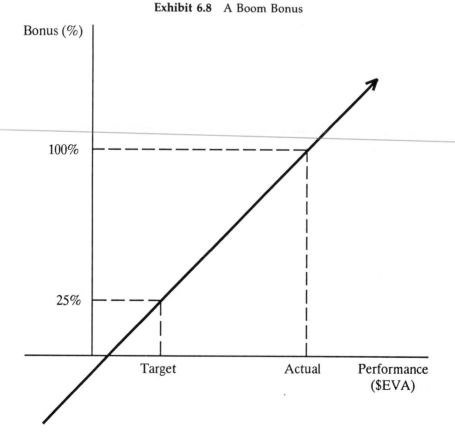

is 100% of salary. It's possible—again, the sky is the theoretical limit although in practice competition is the real constraint. Add the 100% of salary bonus to the $50,000 opening bank balance and a $150,000 pool is available for payout. Pay out one-third, or $50,000, and bank forward $100,000. Thus, in a good year, the manager is rewarded much like a shareholder who enjoys rising cash dividends and capital appreciation; there is increase in the cash bonus paid out and in the bank balance carried forward.

	Target Year	*Good Year*
Salary	$ 100	$ 100
Bonus earned, %	25%	100%
Bonus earned, $	$ 25	$ 100
Beginning bank	50	50
Available for payout	$ 75	$ 150
Payout ratio	1/3	1/3
Bonus paid	$ 25	$ 50
Banked forward	50	100

Suppose the following year's EVA falls well short of target, so much so, in fact, that it equates to a bonus that is a *negative* 50% of salary (exhibit 6.9). Taking 50% of salary away from the opening bank balance leaves only $50,000. Pay out a third, or $16,666, and bank forward $33,333. Thus in a poor year, and again like a shareholder who suffers dividend cuts and capital losses, the penalty is a shrunken cash distribution and a depletion in the bank balance which must be replenished before a full normal bonus could once again be expected.

	Target Year	*Good Year*	*Bad Year*
Salary	$ 100	$ 100	$ 100
Bonus earned, %	25%	100%	−50%
Bonus earned, $	$ 25	$ 100	$ −50
Beginning bank	50	50	100
Available for payout	$ 75	$ 150	$ 50
Payout ratio	1/3	1/3	1/3
Bonus paid	$ 25	$ 50	$16⅔
Banked forward	50	100	33⅓

Exhibit 6.9   A Bust Bonus

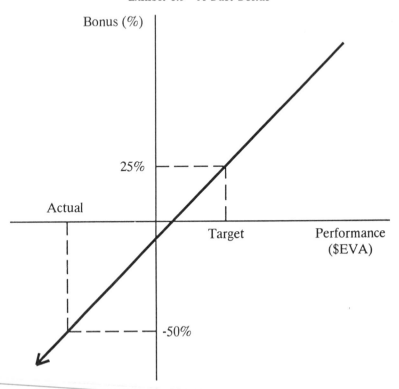

It may seem curious to pay any bonus at all in a year when the manager apparently performed horribly. But that is the quid pro quo for the year before, when the manager performed exceptionally well and received an unexceptional cash bonus. The banking system smooths out the ups and downs of the business cycle and extends forward managers' time horizon for decision making.

It also makes it unnecessary to have both long- and short-term bonus plans. Managers who do participate in both types of plans must decide whether to work for the long run or the short run on a given day. One ingenious fellow told me that he solved this dilemma by working in the morning for the short run and in the afternoon switching his attention over to the long term. Even managers who take the two plans seriously almost always end up working mostly for the short-run plan because it provides the most immediate and typically most generous payoff.

Lord Keynes observed that in the long run we are all dead. To which Milton Friedman responded that the long run is but a series of short runs added together. And so it is with a bonus plan that banks bonuses forward. The long-run bonus is just a partial payout of the value created over a series of short-run periods. The EVA plan is both a long- and a short-term plan at the same time. *There is a need for only this one plan.* Keep it simple.

Combining the two plans is beneficial also because all of the potential bonus payoffs can be added together and concentrated in the one plan. Massing the upside potential in one bonus plan, rather than spreading it over several, is a more efficient way to use bonus dollars to motivate management. As far as I can tell, the pervasive use of multiple-incentive compensation schemes must be due to the marketing ingenuity of the traditional compensation consulting firms, for there is not a convincing economic rationale for the practice.

Another advantage to the bonus bank is that it puts a golden handcuff on solid performers and concrete boots on the poor ones. If individuals perform consistently above expectations, equity will build up in their accounts. They will not be penalized if they leave in a normal retirement sequence. But if they leave the company peremptorily, a provision can be made for them to sacrifice part or all of the equity that has accumulated in the account (particularly if they go to competitors).

Someone who performs poorly for several years in a row, on the other hand, may end up with a very negative bank account. Realizing that the possibility for a cash bonus is slim anytime soon, he or she may conclude that it is best to seek other gainful employment. It is hard to imagine the company wanting to stand in the way.

Thus, the use of a bonus bank smooths out the bumps and grinds of business cycles, extends a manager's time horizon forward, makes meaningless the common distinction drawn between a long- and a short-term bonus plan, encourages good performers to stay and poor ones to go, and emulates the cash yield and cash equivalent price appreciation that would be derived from owning a common equity stake in the business. It's the next best thing to actually owning equity (exhibit 6.10).

Exhibit 6.10   Separate Bonuses from Budgets

The way targets for performance are set and revised can make or break an incentive compensation system. Unfortunately, most companies make the mistake of using the budgets negotiated with unit managers as benchmarks against which the managers' performances are to be judged and their bonuses determined. A typical scheme might have a bonus begin when, say, 80% of budgeted profits are achieved and peak when profits exceed 120% of the budget.

But no matter how it is specifically implemented, I believe that *the whole notion of using the budget as a bonus benchmark is a mistake.* For one thing, it encourages the unit managers to sandbag their budgets in order to qualify for comfortable bonuses with minimal effort. With so much money riding on the budget, moreover, budgeting is likely to deteriorate into an adversarial negotiation instead of being a constructive and collaborative planning effort.

Another problem with using budgets as benchmarks is that it discourages managers from ever performing way above their plan. Performing too far above budget may call into question their integrity when they negotiated it in the first place. Here is a classic Catch-22 situation: How can a manager spectacularly outperform the budget when the budget expresses what the manager has committed to do? Unit managers also may fear that if they perform exceptionally well, the next budget they face will demand more of the same high level of performance but without the prospect for a correspondingly heightened reward. Not knowing in advance how subsequent goals might be revised in light of their actual performance, risk-averse managers may be tempted to run their operations conservatively rather than entrepreneurially. This dysfunctional feedback of actual performance to subsequent targets is so well known to economists that it goes by the name of the the Russian Quota Problem.[2]

When a new plant comes on stream, it is difficult to know what its true productive capacity is, a problem particularly acute in the Soviet Union because of the absence of effective competition. During an initial shakeout period, a Soviet plant manager has an incentive to suppress the mill's output so that an easy-to-reach quota will be established by the central bureaucracy. Thereafter, the Russian plant manager can effortlessly meet personal quotas for mill production and vodka consumption. Though the well-documented Russian experi-

---

[2] I wish to thank Bruce Jurin, one of my former colleagues, for pointing this out to me.

ence admittedly is extreme, it exists to a less-pronounced but nevertheless significant degree in capitalistic countries too, and not just for mills but for entire businesses.

What is the answer? I believe it is to decouple the means from the ends. *Instead of having budgets drive bonuses, the bonus system ought to drive the budgets.* LBOs do just that, by the way. In fact, I believe that one of the chief reasons why LBOs improve corporate performance is because they free hitherto manacled managers from the tyranny of the budget process, for their main incentive becomes to pay down debt and earn out their equity. Bob Kidder, CEO of Duracell, the battery company and a successful KKR LBO in the making, admitted during a roundtable conference in which I participated in early 1990 that many of his key lieutenants were setting their budgets *upward* because they wanted to make as much of a contribution as possible to the serious financial task at hand. I can tell you that the jaws of the other CEOs attending the session fell palpably with this revelation. But that is the benefit of letting the bonus drive the budget, rather than the other way around.

But putting LBOs aside, there is another, less radical, way to separate bonuses from the budget. In the system I am recommending, bonuses should be determined by comparing performance versus some absolute benchmark that is not the budget but which is linked to value and to investor expectations and is revised in a predictable way. Then managers will have the incentive to devise and prosecute aggressive plans without the fear that those plans will be used to second-guess or even to punish their exceptional efforts.

Of course, once the budget is divorced from the bonus, a new way must be found to measure performance and set and revise targets. The new measure, I have argued, should be economic value added because it provides all of the right incentives at the margin and ties directly to creating value. And instead of *negotiating* an EVA target, the target for EVA should be set and revised from year to year according to a predetermined *formula.* Although at first blush that may seem a concept difficult to swallow—that the board and senior corporate managers should surrender their right to negotiate performance expectations with subordinates—I believe that on balance the use of a formula to set targets brings about benefits that far exceed the loss in flexibility. Let's take an example.

One formula to revise targets, useful in practice, is an "adaptive expectations" model:

Exhibit 6.10　continued

$$\text{Target}(t+1) = \text{target}(t) + B\% [\text{actual}(t) - \text{target}(t)]$$

Don't be put off by all the brackets. The formula is simpler than it appears at first glance. It says that the EVA target for the next year (i.e., $t+1$) is the EVA target for the prior year (year t) plus some percent (B) of the difference between the prior year's actual performance and the target for that year (a difference which, incidentally, is the basis for determining the bonus award in that year).

Suppose, for instance, that an initial target for EVA of $10 is set. (All the targets are set and performance is measured in standardized EVA terms; thus, an initial target EVA of $10 calls for a 10% spread to be earned over the cost of capital in the first year, applicable obviously to a very profitable business.)

$$\text{Target}(1) = \$10$$

Suppose that management comes forth with a budget to produce $12 of EVA (again in standardized terms), something more than the target, and then goes about achieving it. (Observe, please, the possibility of adopting a budget that shoots for an exceptional bonus.) With actual performance exceeding target by a handsome margin, a rich bonus would be earned and added to the managers' bank accounts. But at the same time the target for the next year would be revised to accommodate the demonstrated higher level of performance.

$$\text{Target}(t+1) = \text{target}(t) + B\% [\text{actual}(t) - \text{target}(t)]$$
$$\text{Target}(1+1) = \text{target}(1) + B\% [\text{actual}(1) - \text{target}(1)]$$
$$\text{Target}(2) = \$10 + B\% [\$12 - \$10]$$

B, or beta, ranges from 0 to 100% and is the pace at which the target is revised in light of actual prior performance. For instance, if B is set to 0, the target never changes. Next year's target always equals last year's target. There is no adaptation of expectations in light of actual performance. In the example, the target for the second year would remain at the $10 level established for the first year.

$$\text{Target}(t+1) = \text{target}(t) + 0\% [\text{actual}(t) - \text{target}(t)]$$
$$\text{Target}(t+1) = \text{target}(t)$$
$$\text{Target}(2) = \$10$$

In certain classic group 2, X businesses, this may be a very effective approach, for any effort that succeeds at improving performance will translate into an incremental value to investors and an enduring bonus for managers. Without revising expectations at all, this version of the formula completely solves the dysfunctional feedback problem. But in solving one problem others may be created. Managers may be reluctant to leave the unit once it becomes exceptionally profitable, even if their talents are best deployed elsewhere (though they could be bought out), and they may be tempted to pass by worthwhile but risky investment opportunities.

Therefore, consider the extreme opposite. With B set to 100%, the target for the next year is always the actual performance of the prior year.

$$Target(t+1) = target(t) + 100\%[actual(t) - target(t)]$$
$$Target(t+1) = actual(t)$$
$$Target(2) = \$12$$

Thus, if performance exceeds target in a year, the next year's target immediately leaps up to that higher level. As a result, in order to continue to earn an exceptional bonus, management must continue to increase the unit's performance over time. Although that is an appealing requirement in theory, in practice it can lead to the dysfunctional feedback problem because managers will quickly realize that any increase in performance is automatically backed out of their subsequent bonuses.

Between the two extremes of never and instantaneously changing targets is a reasonable compromise. For example, if B is set to 50%, then half of any deviation from target is incorporated into expectations for the next year.

$$Target(t+1) = target(t) + 50\%[actual(t) - target(t)]$$
$$Target\ (2) = \$10 + 50\%[\$12 - \$10]$$
$$Target\ (2) = \$11$$

Now a sustainable increase in performance in one year will continue to be rewarded thereafter, but at a decreasing rate. The target in each ensuing year will march a half step closer to the actual performance and produce an exceptional though diminishing bonus that will eventually evaporate. Thus, in the short term there is no negative feedback

Exhibit 6.10   continued

to penalize a sustained improvement in performance, but in the longer term, performance must continue to improve if exceptional bonuses are to continue. That sounds about right, doesn't it?[3]

It may be, but I will mention a variation. For a publicly traded company, or, for that matter, any business in which there is a good way to establish its market value, a projection of EVA can be derived which equates to that value. The projected EVAs for the next 3 years, say, can be used as initial targets for those years, though they too could be revised according to an "adaptive expectations" formula. With that approach, the EVA targets can anticipate new developments and strategic actions which a simple period-to-period formula may miss. Explicitly linked to value, the targets may have more credibility with the board of directors too. The additional accuracy and salability, however, is purchased at the expense of additional

[3]It may be, but I, for one, cannot resist the temptation to tinker with the formula. For example, B could be 33% if actual performance exceeds target and 66% if it falls short of target. With a slower uptick for improvements, and a faster drop down, the system may be viewed as fairer to manager participants. In comparison with a uniform B of 50%, there will be a greater reward for a sustained increase in performance and less of an ongoing penalty for any shortfall.

The formula also could build in an expectation for improved performance by adding a constant:

$$\text{Target}(t+1) = \text{target}(t) + B\% \, [\text{actual}(t) - \text{target}(t)] + \text{drift}$$

Entering a positive value for drift is a way to force the target to march up and become ever more challenging with the passage of time. (Alternatively, drift could be negative if it is anticipated that a more intensively competitive market is evolving.) If, for example, drift is set to $1 (in standardized EVA terms) and $B\%$ is set to 0, then the target will steadily rise by $1 a year, in our example from $10 initially to $11 in the next year (as shown below), $7 thereafter, etc.

$$\text{Target}(t+1) = \text{target}(t) + B\% \, [\text{actual}(t) - \text{target}(t)] + \text{drift}$$
$$\text{With } B = 0\% \text{ and drift} = \$1,$$
$$\text{Target}(t+1) = \text{target}(t) + \$1$$
$$\text{Target}(2) = \$10 + \$1$$
$$\text{Target}(2) = \$11$$

Using the compromise version of the formula, in any one year the target may move up by more or less than $1 depending upon where actual performance came out versus target in the year before. But unless managers increase the actual performance by at least $1 per period, their bonus will eventually fall below its expected level.

$$\text{With } B = 50\% \text{ and drift} = \$1,$$
$$\text{Target}(t+1) = \text{target}(t) + 50\% \, [\text{actual}(t) - \text{target}(t)] + \$1$$
$$\text{Target}(2) = \$10 + 50\% \, (\$12 - \$10) + \$1$$
$$\text{Target}(2) = \$12$$

complexity. Thus, if management is willing to go to the trouble of projecting and valuing financial data, it may make sense to go the next step and make managers into actual owners of common stock in their unit (see chapters 13 and 14).

For those for whom the additional accuracy of projections is not worth the salt, my colleague David Glassman has devised what may be the simplest and most elegant, but still theoretically sound approach, one that in practice has met with great enthusiasm among operating people. David recommends abandoning the concept of a target entirely and instead basing the bonus on a percent of the annual change in EVA and a percent of the level of EVA (but only if EVA is positive), as follows:

$$\text{Bonus} = \text{M1\%} \times \text{change in EVA} + \text{M2\%} \times \text{EVA}$$

where M1 = a percent of the change in EVA, no matter whether the change is positive or negative

M2 = a percent of EVA, if EVA is positive, and 0% if EVA is negative.

M1 is greater than M2 to provide a powerful incentive to continue to improve performance (and a powerful penalty if performance falls). For example, M1 might be 10% and M2 5%:

$$\text{Bonus} = 10\% \times \text{change in EVA} + 5\% \times \text{EVA}$$

If a manager improves the EVA of a unit, there is an immediate and substantial reward coming through from the first term. But as important, and this solves the negative feedback problem, there is an enduring reward coming from the second term. An increase in EVA, if sustainable, will take up residence in the ongoing level of EVA and thereby produce a bonus extending into subsequent years to reward an increase in performance occurring in one year. Of course, if EVA falls, there also is both an immediate and sustained penalty.

The managers of a business that currently has a negative EVA will be rewarded for an increase in EVA only until EVA turns positive. M2 is zero so long as EVA is underwater, because there is no sense in penalizing people for sunk causes. In such a case M1 will be greater than otherwise, since all of the weight must be put on the effort to turn the business around and restore its economic viability. In practice, M1 and M2 are set in accordance with the fundamentals of the business and the targeted levels of compensation for the participating managers.

Exhibit 6.10   continued

No matter how well it is designed, a formula will at times produce performance expectations and bonus levels that are obviously unrealistic in light of a windfall change in business conditions and or a wellspring change in business strategy. To allow for this possibility, a provision can be made to allow the board to override the targets and payouts that are produced by formula. To preserve the credibility of the bonus system, however, resetting should be kept to a minimum. The board, and senior management, should guard against letting the bonus system lapse into a series of capricious negotiations or shapeless qualitative assessments of performance.

A Review

I believe that the pervasive use of budgets as the benchmarks for bonus awards, and not Wall Street, is to blame for the conservative, short-term focus that pervades the ranks of American managers. One way to set managers free from the tyranny of budget negotiations is an LBO. Another is to use EVA as the performance measure and to revise the EVA targets according to a formula. With their targets completely predictable from one year to the next, and intentionally lagging improvements in performance, managers can map out and prosecute a long-term strategy to create value and be confident that they will be amply rewarded if they are successful. When bonuses are divorced from their budgets and strategies, managers are apt to devise and carry out more realistic if not more aggressive plans. What more could be asked of any incentive compensation system?

Summary

Ownership must engage at a visceral level as much as at the merely monetary one. But emotion swells when people participate in the fruits of their labors. It is a positive feedback, a reward for a job well done, and a necessary stimulus, in most cases.

The most powerful way to make managers into owners is to provide them with equity in the units they manage and a means of cashing out the value they have created over a reasonable time frame. But realistic plans such as these are more radical than some will accept, at least initially. Besides, owning equity begs the question: Now that I have the incentive, what must I do to create value? Hence there is the need for a simulated approach to making managers into owners, even when a realistic plan is employed.

The simulated approach focuses management attention on EVA, the wellspring of all corporate values. With EVA as their goal, managers are provided with three explicit directives to help them enhance value and with a framework that clearly links their prospective operating and strategic decisions with subsequent evaluation of their performance. No other performance measure can do that, not even cash flow.

There are six specific elements to the simulated approach to making managers behave like owners:

First	There should be only one cash bonus plan, and not a short- and a long-term plan. Mass the payoff.
Second	Long-range goals, resource allocation decisions, and operating performance should all be evaluated in terms of EVA.
Third	EVA targets should be decoupled from the budgetary and strategic planning processes and should be revised according to some predetermined formula.
Fourth	The potential bonus should be unlimited in both directions.
Fifth	The exceptional parts of exceptional bonuses should be banked forward with their full payout contingent upon continued successful performance.
Sixth	Managers should be encouraged to buy into and not merely participate in the plan as the quid pro quo for aggressively amplifying their reward for success.

7

Valuation Concepts

Introduction

Valuation is the essence of planning. Without some method of simulating how alternative business strategies and financial structures are likely to affect a company's stock market value, decision making can easily deteriorate into endless subjective debates. Of course, judgment seasoned by experience must play a role. But judgment shaped by a projection of the likely costs and benefits, risks and rewards is likely to lead to the selection of business strategies and financial structures that will be more highly regarded by the market than those chosen by companies that rely upon instinct alone or which place the attainment of seemingly laudable business goals above all else.

Besides helping management to select strategy and structure, a valuation framework can place a value on an entire consolidated company and its individual business units and also on acquisition and divestiture candidates.

The Consolidated Company

A corporate valuation can show whether a company currently is trading for fair value and thus whether it is in need of improved communication with its investors, whether it is advisable to raise or retire equity at current prices, and whether an overall restructuring needs to be considered.

For private companies, a periodic valuation is essential to determine the value of shares for an ESOP and possibly for the purpose of cashing out management incentives. An outside appraisal can also help management to get a sense of its progress in creating value as a reality check on the success or failure of current strategies and structures. Without a public quote to provide informative feedback, a private company may in some respects need a technique to simulate value even more than a public one. Of course, public companies have private companies, too—their individual business units, that is.

Individual Business Units

As for individual business units, a valuation framework can show which ones are creating value and which are not, which may be candidates for sale and which for restructuring. In one recent engagement, for example, we discovered that the performance of 30% of the company's businesses could account for 200% percent of the company's total market value. Hard to fathom? The other 70% of its businesses were destroying 100% of its market value. Not that it was losing money, mind you. Money just kept pouring into businesses that never ultimately earned their cost of capital, and substantial value was being lost in that way. This admittedly is an extreme case, but I find that the phenomenon is present in almost all companies to a greater or lesser extent.

Valuation can also be employed to isolate pockets of competitive advantage or comparative weaknesses within what appear to be integrated business units and thereby sharpen the allocation of resources to either capitalize upon a strength or rectify or dispose of a weakness. Further, a valuation framework can teach operating people what they must really accomplish to increase the value of their unit. Giving key managers an education in the fundamentals of valuation expedites decision making and facilitates communication throughout the company.

Acquisitions

Finally, a valuation framework can help management determine how much is too much to pay for an acquisition candidate. Overpaying is one of the quickest ways for an acquirer to reduce its own market value and increase the probability that someday it will be on the wrong end of an acquisition. The evidence is overwhelming that the best acquisitions are made by companies that know when to say when. Pricing acquisitions is so important it is the subject of an entire chapter later in the book.

Valuation can be used in reverse too. Stock prices convey the distilled wisdom of astute investors concerning a company's prospects and risks. Thus, a valuation framework can be used to develop a set of projections which equate to a company's actual market value. These projections can, in turn, be used to set breakeven goals—performance which, if met at a minimum, guarantees investors will receive the return they expect from their investments. Acquisitions can be priced in that way, too, particularly when the seller has a firm asking price.

M&M's Are Not Just Candies

With all of this riding, it is unfortunate that most managers labor to create value without a thorough grounding in the valuable lessons set forth many years ago in a path-breaking paper written by Professors Merton Miller of the University of Chicago and Franco Modigliani of MIT ("M&M"). M&M presented the original "economic" models of corporate valuation in 1961. In their revolutionary paper, "Dividend Policy, Growth, and the Valuation of Shares,"[1] M&M derived intrinsic valuation formulas by ingeniously applying long-standing microeconomic principles of price formation and market arbitrage. They liberated valuation from the tyranny of the accounting model, from P/E multiples and earnings per share, and from the view that the level of a company's dividend payments somehow fundamentally determined its value. To this day the propositions M&M set forth are

[1]Merton Miller and Franco Modigliani, "Dividend Policy, Growth, and the Valuation of Shares," *Journal of Business* (October 1961) 34: 411–433.

considered by almost all serious academic researchers to be the definitive statements on corporate valuation.

M&M developed three distinct valuation procedures and showed how each would yield an identical value for a given set of projections. At this time, only one of the three methods— discounted cash flow—is at all widely understood and practiced. The other two remain little known despite having didactic and practical advantages. I intend to change that. In this chapter I shall introduce just one of M&M's three valuation methods, leaving the other two to the next chapter, in which valuation applications are discussed.

To Begin With

All of the M&M procedures predict a company's total market value V: the market value of its entire debt D and equity E capitalization:

$$V = D + E$$

For an individual business unit or a private company, total value is probably what matters, but for traded companies share prices may be of greater interest. To obtain a share price P for an individual company, the market value of current debt (and other claims senior to the common stockholders) is subtracted from total value, and then the resulting common equity value is divided by the number of common shares outstanding N:

$$E = V - D \qquad P = E/N$$

This approach follows the reasoning of leading investors like Warren Buffett of Berkshire Hathaway. When valuing a company, they do not look at earnings per share, cash flow per share, or anything per share. Instead, they recognize that common shares are best understood as shares in the value of a business enterprise. They acquire stakes in companies that sell at a discount from what they believe to be the true per share value of the underlying operations. The fundamental question, in other words, is not how to value common shares, but how to value businesses. There are three ways. Here is the first.

The Value-Driver Model

Corporate values actually arise from six essential factors. Four of them are under management's control through policies and performance. Two are market-determined. Taken together, they describe the magnitude, riskiness, growth, quality, duration, and financing of future free cash flow. And they show how much of a company's overall value comes from its current operations, from the tax benefit of debt financing, and from the value of its forward plan. As a conceptual simplification of discounted cash flow, the value-driver model is useful for explaining the fundamentals of valuation to senior managers and key operating people more than as a practical procedure for valuation.

The Value of Current Operations

In the context of this value-driver model, let's begin by defining the intrinsic market value of a company's current operations, limited to the assets already in place.

To measure the value contributed by just the current business activities, new investment will temporarily be limited to an amount that just replaces the depreciation incurred on existing assets. Any value to be derived by investing more than depreciation, that is, to grow, will appear in the third component: the value of the forward plan. Turning off the spigot on investment beyond depreciation makes two convenient things happen:

- First, the company's NOPAT will cease to grow; without any "net" new investment, it will be frozen at its current level.
- Second, the current NOPAT becomes the free cash flow available for distribution to the firm's debt and equity investors in each and every future year.

Thus, the value of a company's existing operations can be obtained by capitalizing current NOPAT as a perpetuity (that's an annuity that goes on forever) at a rate of interest c that compensates investors for bearing business risk.

$$V = D + E = \frac{\text{NOPAT}}{c}$$

This first valuation component recalls the valuation of Consol Bonds, bonds so named because they were first issued by the British government in 1814 to consolidate debts incurred in the Napoleonic Wars. What makes Consols unusual is that the principal value of the bonds is never to be repaid; in return, Consols promise to pay interest forever. That way, British taxpayers can show their eternal gratitude for victory at Waterloo.

Suppose a Consol offers to pay £10 in each future year, and long-term interest rates in Great Britain are 10%. Such a Consol bond would trade for £100:

$$£100 = \frac{£10}{10\%}$$

By paying £100 now for the right to receive a £10 check in the mail in each and every future year, Consol investors will always earn 10% on their money. Even though the British government never intends to repay their principal, investors can always recover their principal by selling the bonds to the next poor soul who decides to buy. If Consuls are any indication, the market (dating back as far as 1814!) is perfectly willing to convert a perpetual future stream of cash flow to an equivalent present value. And so it is with equities too.

The British invented Consols—bonds paying no principal, only interest—many years ago. Americans, on the other hand, became enamoured of deep-discount bonds only in the past decade. They are the opposite of Consols: deep-discount bonds pay no interest, only a deferred principal. My favorite financing instrument combines features from both. I call them deep-discount consol bonds, and they pay neither principal nor interest. Some claim that I have invented nothing new. They point to Brazil, Mexico, and Argentina as among the original issuers of such bonds.

An Example.   Let's take an example. Suppose that a company's net operating profits are $1,667 (a number I chose at random), it employs no debt whatsoever, only common equity, and the corporate income tax rate is 40%. Its P&L statement would run as follows:

	No Debt
Net operating profit (NOP)	$1,667
Interest expense	0
Net profit before Taxes	$1,667
Tax (40%)	667
Net profit after Taxes	$1,000

Bottom-line profits (NPAT) are conveniently $1,000. And so is NOPAT. NOPAT comprises the profits that a company will report as its bottom line *if* it employed only common equity to finance its business (so that no financing charges appear on its income statement) and *if* the accountants record the actual timing of cash receipts and disbursements (which I assume is happening in this case). Then, in those limiting circumstances, a company's reported profits will equal its NOPAT.

Assume that the only investment this company makes in a year is an amount equal to the depreciation that is subtracted from NOPAT. Its business will not expand, and NOPAT will not grow. Moreover, the gross plant account will rise by an amount just equal to the depreciation that is added to the accumulated depreciation account. With no change in the balance sheet on net, what is earned on the income statement is available for payout. And with no debt outstanding, the full $1,000 of NOPAT is paid out to the common stockholders in each and every year, just like a Consol bond. Assuming the company's stockholders require 10% to compensate for the risk in the business (in reality c's are usually higher than this in recent years, but let's keep it simple), the total value of this company's current operations is $10,000:

$$V = D+E = \frac{NOPAT}{c}$$

$$\$10{,}000 = D+E = \frac{\$1{,}000}{10\%}$$

With no debt, all of the company's $10,000 value must fall into the hands of the common stockholders. Assuming 1,000 common shares are outstanding, the stock price is $10 per share ($10,000 common equity value/1,000 common shares).

An Accounting Representation of an Economic Valuation. If desired, the value of this company could be expressed in the terms of an accounting model of value. With earnings per share of $1 ($1,000 of bottom line profits/1,000 common shares), the common shares apparently sell for a P/E multiple of 10:

$$\text{Share price} = \text{EPS} \times \text{P/E ratio}$$
$$\$10 = \$1 \times 10$$

Bear in mind, please, that this company sells for 10 times earnings because its shares are worth $10; it does not have a $10 share price because it sells for 10 times its earnings. To say so is to confuse cause with consequence. The accounting model may be a convenient way to represent and compare corporate values, but it does not explain what creates value in the first place. For that we need an economic model, and this one is not finished yet.

The Tax Benefit of Debt Financing

There are five ways in which debt can improve a company's performance and increase its intrinsic value. Eventually I will tell you about all five of them (in chapter 13, on financial restructuring), but for now I will concentrate on one of debt's most controversial powers: its ability to save taxes.

The tax benefit of debt actually is quite straightforward to describe. Start with the notion that all of the capital that a company employs has a cost associated with its use, if nothing else—

an opportunity cost equal to the rate of return investors could expect to earn by investing in other stocks and bonds of equal risk. Even a company such as Apple Computer, which traditionally borrowed no money and paid no dividends, had a cost of capital. Indeed, it was quite a high one given the risk in its business, although the company had no explicit cash costs to pay. Unless Apple earned some minimum acceptable return in its business, the company's shares would sell at a discount from their book value, and value would be lost.

Now here is the tax benefit of debt. Substitute debt for equity. Notice I said *substitute* debt for equity. Then the overall amount of capital used in the business will not change. The return required to compensate investors for bearing the risk in the business will not change. But the implicit cost of equity is replaced, at least partially, by an explicit cash cost on debt which is tax-deductible. The IRS will believe that the company now has a new cost which in fact it had all along. The present value of the corporate income taxes saved when debt replaces equity adds to the intrinsic value of the common shares.

A Leveraged Recapitalization.   The value of debt is best illustrated by engineering a swap of debt for equity. I propose to swap debt for equity, rather than to use debt to fund a new investment, because only in that way can the benefit of debt per se be isolated from a change in the value of the business. Incidentally, this example was devised by my partner, Joel Stern, in 1965. Remarkably, it took about 15 years for people to begin to apply its lessons in earnest, but then Joel has always been considered more a prophet than a practitioner. Now perhaps people will take his provocative messages more seriously.

Assume $5,000 is borrowed at 6% interest. (The rate is admittedly low by today's standards, but then so is 10% low for c. The point is that some spread exists between the rate to borrow money and the rate to capitalize risky business profits, and the example is realistic in that way.) The $5,000 proceeds are used to buy back 500 shares of our hypothetical company's stock for $10 each, leaving just 500, or half, of the original 1,000 shares outstanding. Assuming that net operating profits (NOP) are unaf-

fected by a mere financial recapitalization, and so remain $1,667, what happens to income? Bottom-line profits (NPAT) will fall from $1,000 to $820.

	No Debt	$5,000 Debt
Net operating profit (NOP)	$1,667	$1,667
Interest expense	0	300
Net profit before taxes	$1,667	$1,367
Tax (40%)	667	547
Net profit after taxes	$1,000	$ 820

Question: What is NOPAT now that the company has borrowed $5,000 and incurred $300 of interest expense (6% on $5,000). Think about this one before you answer, please.

NOPAT still is $1,000! NOPAT is a measure of profits from operations and as such is unaffected by leverage. With operations and operating profits assumed to be identical in both cases, NOPAT must be the same too. A financial restructuring per se has no impact on the profitability (or riskiness) of the current business (unless, as I will argue later, the pressure to cover interest payments spurs management to operate more efficiently, but for now I will ignore such incentive effects and will concentrate solely on debt's tax benefit). To compute NOPAT for the leveraged firm, start with the bottom-line profits of $820 and add the interest expense of $300, net of the $120 of taxes saved by deducting it. It is $180, or interest expense after taxes, that separates bottom-line profits from the NOPAT profits.

	No Debt		$5,000 Debt
Net operating profit	$1,667		$1,667
Interest expense	0		300
Net profit before taxes	$1,667		$1,367
Tax (40%)	667	—$120—	547
Net profit after taxes	$1,000	= $180 +	$ 820

More to the point, to place a value on the entire company, the income attributable to the debt and equity investors should be combined into one all-encompassing stream. Common equity investors are entitled to the bottom-line profits (coming either as a dividend or as a capital gain that relates to the retained earnings). The creditors collect income in an amount equal to the interest expense the company incurs. Economists refer to the sum of these two streams as a company's total return. The total return is the return available to all of a firm's investors. It is a measure of the combined value of the entire debt and equity capitalization V:

	No Debt		$5,000 Debt
Net profit after taxes	$ 1,000		$ 820
Interest	$ 0		$ 300
Total return	$ 1,000	+ $120 =	$ 1,120

Notice that the total return with debt exceeds the total return without debt; the value of the company with debt must therefore exceed the value of the company without debt.

The source of the additional value is the $120 of taxes saved when debt is substituted for equity. The company was going to pay $667 in taxes when it was financed with common equity but will pay only $547 in taxes with debt in the picture. Debt creates value by sheltering a company's operating profits from being fully taxed. Period.

Where the Value Comes From.   The $1,120 total return with debt arises from the $1,000 of NOPAT coming out of the business and the $120 corporate income tax benefit. It is paid, first, to the lenders in an amount of $300, leaving $820 for the shareholders. By definition, the sources and uses of the total return must be equal:

Sources
Total return = NOPAT + tax savings
$1,120   = $1,000 + $120

Uses
Total return = return to creditors + return to shareholders
$1,120   = $300 + $820

One approach to value a company would be to capitalize the total return as it divides into the returns payable to the debt and equity investors, a "uses" approach. For example, the $300 of interest allocated to the creditors, when capitalized (divided) by the 6% interest rate on the debt, accounts for the debt's $5,000 value. Similarly, the value of the common equity could be determined by capitalizing the $820 of bottom-line profits at a rate that reflects the risk borne by the shareholders. A dividend discount model is a variation of this approach, one that values just that part of bottom-line profits expected to be paid out over time to the common stockholders.

I advise against these valuation approaches for three reasons. First, it is difficult to estimate accurately the return required by the shareholders (i.e., the cost of equity) because the financial leverage shareholders face may change year by year. Second, it mixes operating and financing results and thereby obscures the true sources of value. Third, it may suggest that a company's value depends on paying dividends, a myth that M&M took great pains to show was false.

A better method, one that I advocate, capitalizes the total return as it arises within the company from business profits and tax savings. It captures the combined value of the debt and the equity, postponing a separation of their values to a subsequent step. As before, NOPAT should be capitalized at c, the rate that compensates investors for bearing the risk in the business:

$$V = D+E = \frac{\text{NOPAT}}{c}$$

$$\$10{,}000 = D+E = \frac{\$1{,}000}{10\%}$$

In other words, contained within the value of a leveraged company is the value of the unleveraged business, still $10,000 in this case.

Assuming that the company replaces the $5,000 debt as it comes due and maintains a constant level of debt in its capital structure against the constant level of net assets (which, it is assumed, also are being replaced as they depreciate), the $120 tax savings will be realized in every future year. Thus, it too should be capitalized as a perpetuity that goes on forever but at a rate that reflects its specific risk, a risk that is different, indeed lower, than that embodied in NOPAT.

Notice that the $120 tax benefit will exist as long as the company earns as little as $300 of net operating profits. In the absence of debt, a $120 tax would be imposed on $300 of profit. But with $5,000 of debt brought into the picture, interest at a 6% rate will fully shelter that $300 of profits from being taxed at all. With any further decline in profits, however, the company will no longer realize the full $120 tax benefit (although that probably would be the least of its concerns). Evidently the risk entailed in saving taxes is just the same as the risk of covering the interest payments, and, accordingly, the 6% borrowing rate b on the debt is appropriate to discount the tax savings to a present value:

$$V = D+E = \frac{\text{NOPAT}}{c} + \frac{\text{tax savings}}{b}$$

$$= D+E = \frac{\$1,000}{10\%} + \frac{\$120}{6\%}$$

$$\$12,000 = D+E = \$10,000 + \$2,000$$

$2,000 is the present value of the taxes not paid when $5,000 of debt is substituted for $5,000 of equity, making the total value of the company, from business and tax sources, equal to $12,000. With $5,000 worth of cash flow allocated to service the debt, the value of the cash flows available to the equity investors must be the residual, or $7,000:

$$V = D + E$$
$$\$12,000 = \$5,000 + \$7,000$$

With only 500 common shares remaining out of the original 1,000, the equity is now valued at $14 per share, a 40% increase over the former $10 share value! Not bad for a day's work.

Take It to the Limit. Shoot for the stars for a moment. How would the value of the tax benefit to debt financing be maximized? By using 100% debt you say? 100% of what I ask? The answer is to borrow until the interest expense on the debt just equals the company's underlying net operating profits, without regard to the degree of leverage that brings into the balance sheet. Then the company's operating profits will be fully sheltered from taxation and the company will effectively convert from a corporation into a partnership.

As a flow-through vehicle, a partnership incurs no tax liability. Instead, the investors in a partnership are taxed directly on their share of partnership income whether distributed or not. With the personal income tax rate now beneath the corporate rate for the first time in memory, the logic of siting income-producing assets in a partnership is compelling. Why put assets in a corporation where earnings are taxed once at 34% and twice if distributed when the same assets housed in a partnership would have their earnings taxed just once at 28%?

The favorable tax attributes of a partnership can be obtained by aggressively leveraging a corporation and using the proceeds to retire equity. Then interest expense will largely shelter the company's operating profits from the corporate income tax. Instead, the operating profits will mostly flow through directly to the holders of the company's bonds to be taxed just once and just at their rate, much like a partnership. Approaching a 1:1 interest coverage ratio admittedly leaves a company perched on a knife's edge, but the idea is to dream awhile about taking the tax benefit of debt to the limit.

Besides, aggressive investors seem to know all too well how to maximize debt's tax benefit. By highly leveraging their targets, they are able to capitalize the value of pretax profits instead of after-tax profits:

> "Accountants just assume taxes have to be paid," says Mario J. Gabelli, a money manager, buyout specialist, and aficionado of

cash flow analysis long before it was fashionable. "But you don't have to pay taxes."

How so? Remember you're an owner-investor, not a passive shareholder, and you have control of the cash. You don't care about profit. So you take on a bundle of debt and devote the cash flow more towards servicing the debt than to producing taxable profits. And as you pay down the debt, your equity in the company automatically grows.

"The Savviest Investors Are Going with the (Cash) Flow"
Business Week
September 7, 1987

Less Is More. I frequently encounter chief financial officers who, though they may grudgingly acknowledge some tax advantage to debt, argue against the use of debt because their companies apparently do not need to borrow. They point out that their businesses already generate more cash than they can productively reinvest and conclude that, for them, borrowing money is unnecessary. I think this view is mistaken. To take full advantage of the tax benefit of debt and thereby maximize share value, *a company should borrow if it is able to, and not because it needs to; it should borrow money if it can, not because it must.* Indeed I will go further and say the *less* a company needs to raise capital to finance expansion the *more* money it ought to borrow.

It is precisely the companies that need to raise new capital that should shun debt and prefer equity to preserve their financing flexibility. Continuously funding new product development has been so much more important than saving taxes to Apple Computer, as an example, that the company quite rightly borrowed no money at all. Equity supported Apple's growth. It is ironic but true that the more a company needs money to finance a wealth of attractive new investment opportunities, the less money it should borrow.

But when a company can productively reinvest less than it earns, and thus has a surplus cash flow that makes it easy to service debt, new debt should aggressively be raised to take advantage of the tax shelter it provides. That is recommended even if the borrowing proceeds are used merely to retire shares or to pay a special dividend.

A leveraged buy-out carries the premise to its logical extreme.

The classic LBO candidate is eminently bankable precisely because it generates a steady stream of surplus cash flow to repay
debt. Apparently Will Rogers was right in observing that "bankers lend money to their friends, and to those who don't need it."
Of course, Voltaire went him one better. He said that if a banker
jumped out a window, you should follow him, because money
would probably be at the bottom.

Again, my recommendation is to borrow money if you can, not
because you must. Neglecting debt's tax benefit is one sure way
for a strong surplus cash generator to attract the attention of
unwanted suitors.

A Mystery Wrapped in an Enigma inside a Puzzle.   There
is a striking paradox to the use of debt. The more debt replaces
equity in a company's capital structure, the higher becomes the
cost of its debt and the higher becomes the cost of its equity, too.
The irony is that, as its leverage increases, a company's debt
becomes riskier and its equity becomes riskier—and I still say it
is a sensible thing to do.

The resolution of the paradox lies in correcting an improper
comparison. The cost of the debt should not be compared with
what it was prior to leveraging up, nor the cost of the equity with
what it was before. Rather, the cost of the debt raised should be
compared with the cost of the equity it replaces. Then, no matter
how high the rate of interest on the debt becomes, it must always
cost less than the equity it replaces because its cost is subsidized
by a corporate tax savings. Junk bonds, in short, should not be
thought of as expensive debt financing. Junk bonds are an inexpensive form of equity.

Look Before You Leap.   What if you take my advice and aggressively leverage your firm with debt, but then subsequently
are unable to repay the debt as it comes due? You may be thinking that my advice is gratuitous because I will not be around to
suffer the adverse consequences. True, but let's play out the
scenario.

In fact, to make the example more concrete, I propose to consider the plight of RJR, the largest LBO so far but not, if I am
right, the largest LBO there will ever be. Suppose RJR is unable

to pay its contractual interest and principal payments. What recourse will the lenders have?

Sell the Assets?   The first thing they might think to do is to throw the company into bankruptcy and proceed to liquidate its assets. But will it ever make sense to sell the assets that turn out Winston cigarettes, Oreo cookies, and Ritz crackers? The cash flow generated by those established consumer products has a value so far in excess of the realizable value of the machinery that produces it that it is inconceivable RJR will ever be physically liquidated.

Besides, the subordinated bondholders, who are the first to feel pain if there is a shortfall in profitability, realize that in a liquidation the senior lenders have first claim on the proceeds and are secured by the assets. For junk holders, liquidation probably will erase any chance they have of recovering their principal. Their only hope of recovering their investment is the continued operation one way or another of the businesses that make up RJR.

That will not always be the case, however. Sometimes it will pay to liquidate the assets. All attempts by Sandy Sigoloff (the turnaround champion who prefers the moniker Ming the Merciless) to sell the seven B. Altman stores acquired by the troubled and highly leveraged L. J. Hooker, even at liquidation value, failed. All but the Cincinnati store, which anchors a Hooker megamall, were closed and liquidated. All of the Altman jobs—about 2,000, many of the workers near retirement age—were eliminated. No doubt, that is a wrenching loss, but it is one that must be faced when, in open auction, no one is willing to pay more than liquidation value. The market spoke: The resources tied up in Altman's have a greater value to society when deployed elsewhere.

Sell the Businesses?   Assuming that a sale of the company's assets will not bring in a premium, the second thought to occur to the lenders may be to sell the businesses that make up RJR. Although that is a possibility, it may not improve matters for the subordinated lenders. The sale of a business merely discounts the cash likely to flow in over time to an up-front lump of cash. It is unlikely that a sale will make possible the repayment of more debt than would eventually occur with continued ownership of a business, particularly if it already is well managed and synergistically situated.

Of course, if a business is not positioned or managed as well as it might be, then a sale would be advisable in any event. And with that in mind, RJR is proceeding to divest some of its food and international units that apparently are worth more to others. But, as in RJR's case, such sales mostly happen soon after an LBO and not in response to a subsequent inability to service debt.

Shoot the Managers? So far, it seems that selling RJR's assets and its businesses will not help. What about replacing management? It is possible that the reason debt is not being serviced is the fault of management. If so, replacing management may be an appropriate step toward recovery, painful as it may be.

When a company operates with a high leverage ratio, its debt holders will be enfranchised with the right to vote a change in management when the company is not performing as well as was initially expected, and management's performance and business strategy probably ought to be called into question. It may not be pleasant for management to live under such a dangling sword, but then, the question on the table is how to create value for shareholders, not how to make management comfortable.

But what if RJR's management performs as well as could be expected under the circumstances? In other words, suppose that no one else could manage the assets any more effectively than they are being managed. Then getting rid of management will only make matters worse. So, if selling assets, selling businesses, or replacing management is not the answer, what is?

Reverse the Recapitalization! The only recourse available to creditors is to reverse the recapitalization. The adage, "Owe a banker a little, and he controls you; owe a banker a lot, and you control him," applies. If borrowing debt to retire equity is what winds up such a transaction, then issuing equity to retire debt will unwind it, and then life will go on.

Michael Milken probably was the first to fully appreciate the power of using such *dynamic* capital structures. His thesis rejected the common wisdom that a company should attempt to maintain a target capital structure that prudently balanced the tax benefit of debt against a need for ongoing financial flexibility. Milken argued that for many mature companies a more valuable strategy would be to borrow well above what might ordinarily be considered a prudent leverage ratio, if only temporarily, and then to work like the dickens to pay down the debt out of a more efficient operation, and failing that, by reversing the recapitalization.

What made *dynamic* capital structures work in practice was the creation of a public market for junk bonds. That way, if a company's fortunes soured so that its junk bonds began to trade at a discount from their original par value, the holders of such bonds would be able to recognize the merits of swapping their discounted debt for a more valuable package of debt and equity, and life would go on.

> In 1985, holders of 79% of the $230 million of debt of Oak Industries chose to accept an exchange offer of the same principal amount of new debt securities, common stock and warrants rather than bankruptcy. The new securities ranked senior to, carried a lower coupon, and matured sooner than the existing securities and provided that the interest payments could be made in either cash or shares of common stock. Such features gave Oak the time and flexibility it needed to restructure, while providing the bondholders with a means to continue to receive interest.
>
> 1989 High Yield Market Report
> Drexel Burnham Lambert

Leaseway Transportation, a June 1987 LBO, is a more recent example. Over 50% of Leaseway's business is to haul GM cars from factories to dealers and appliances and other stuff for Sears. Having its wagon hitched to those two sorry mules, Leaseway found itself unable to meet its scheduled debt payments after its LBO. The company's $193 million in senior debt began to trade at between 20% and 30% of par value. As of November 1989, Leaseway is proposing to pay back its commercial back lenders in full (with the proceeds of a new commercial loan), contingent on getting the senior bondholders to agree to swap their bonds for new debentures, with lower face amount and lower cash interest, *plus a controlling equity interest in the firm.* Here, then, is a reverse recapitalization: swapping debt for equity but leaving the assets, the business, and the managers in place.

One final example comes from the netherworld of casinos and high rollers. Merv Griffin overpaid by a long shot when he acquired Resorts International for $915 million, putting up $50 million of his own capital. A year after the deal was signed, the company was valued at just $536 million, a 40% loss. Using a little-known provision of the bankruptcy code known as an instantaneous bankruptcy, Resorts quickly restructured its liabilities without protracted legal costs. All the parties to the restructuring agreed in advance how the shrunken pie would be sliced and jointly submitted a plan to the bankruptcy courts for swift approval. Merv Griffin, who had owned 100% of the equity, came away with just 22%, and that was after agreeing to inject another $30 million into the company. He did, however, reserve the right to appoint a majority of the board, and he would continue running the company. The bondholders agreed to exchange debt securities with a face value of $865 million for a package of new debt securities with a face value of just $400 million, *plus 78% of the equity in the reorganized company,* believed to be worth $100 million. Resorts is yet another reverse recapitalization, and it illustrates another way to do it.

Debt, Where Is Thy Sting?   In the past, a company unable to meet its debt obligations in a timely manner was at a significant risk of liquidation, and at the very least, protracted legal expenses and business disruptions. A dishonorable discharge of incumbent management almost certainly was called for too. But if the cases I have cited are any indication, the traditional remedies no longer apply. What's different?

One difference is where debt begins. If debt begins conservatively, at just, say, 30% of total capital, then fully 70% of the company's total value must be lost before the firm becomes insolvent. In that case, management should not be replaced, but skinned, and the company's assets should be sold at auction.

But when a company takes on debt that is, say, 90% of a fully capitalized value, an inability to fully service the debt, particularly the subordinated debt at the bottom of the pile, is not so portentous. A fundamentally healthy and well-managed business may still be squirming underneath the mountain of debt. If so, replacing management or selling assets will not increase the value of the bonds. Neither will protracted argumentation in front of a bankruptcy judge. But stretching out the debt, or converting it into equity, will increase the bonds' value if it gives the company a chance to realize the operating cash flow that is the foundation of its intrinsic value.

In some respects Michael Milken's true genius lay not in creating a new way to raise capital, but in a better way to get out of trouble (for corporations, that is). It is the change in the back end of leveraged transactions that justifies raising more debt at the front end. As the adverse consequences of leverage have been mitigated through financial innovations, the optimal level of debt for almost every company has increased.

My conclusion: So long as a company remains as well managed and its business units as synergistically situated as is possible, it has little to fear from a towering leverage ratio, even if its business fortunes deteriorate. That is yet another manifestation of the principle that operating considerations must always be kept separate from and held to be superior to financial considerations.

Here We Go Again?   Some have expressed concern over the aggressive corporate use of debt by drawing parallels to the risky loans commercial banks made to Third World countries (or to the Savings and Loan crisis). Scratch beneath the surface and the truth is far different from this popularly held view. As I see it, an LBO actually is the precise opposite of such Third World lending.

Through those loans the commercial banks committed new funds to uneconomic projects. It did not matter that the funds were advanced in the form of debt. The Third World loans destroyed value not because they were loans, but because the projects they financed did not pan out. With LBOs, in contrast, no new money enters the target on the day of the transaction. For RJR, it's true that $25 billion of cash came in from the lenders, but then, $25 billion of cash was paid out to the shareholders. No new money was invested in the business and put at risk that day.

Power to the People.   It is what happens *after* the LBO that is important. To retire debt, RJR will have to pay out $25 billion of cash that otherwise would have accumulated within the firm for no good purpose. By forcing companies to disgorge cash to creditors that management may be reluctant to part with, LBOs actually *increase* the overall liquidity of our capital markets and make more funds available to other more promising projects. The political problem is that it is easier to see the harm done to a company that is forced to pay out cash than it is to visualize the greater good that the cash does when it is invested elsewhere. But, to conclude, LBO loans are the precise opposite of Third World loans. Foreign loans put new capital at risk; LBOs pull cash out.

How Debt Affects the Cost of Capital

Our analysis seems to favor debt so clearly that it is almost frightening. Have we missed something? What about the increase in risk to the shareholders? Doesn't c go up with debt? Actually c does not increase, though y, the cost of equity, does. (y symbolizes the cost of equity because it is the last letter in the last word.) But the increasing risk to shareholders is not a good reason not to borrow money, as we shall see.

c does not change because it is the return investors require to compensate for the difficulty encountered in accurately forecasting NOPAT, and NOPAT is unaffected by leverage. c reflects the risk in the business no matter how the business is financed. Here is another manifestation of the principle to keep operations separate from finance. It applies to keeping the risks apart, too.

The cost of the common equity y, however, does increase with debt. The reason for this is best seen in light of what happens to the P/E ratio of a company that borrows money. There are three possibilities: The P/E multiple could go up, go down, or remain the same.

The P/E Isn't What It Used to Be. Here is your one and only clue. With debt, a company incurs a fixed interest expense to be paid out of uncertain operating profits, making bottom-line profits more volatile, and hence risker, over a business cycle, than before. Would you be willing to pay a higher or a lower multiple for riskier earnings? I don't know about you, but the lead steers discount a riskier stream of earnings at a higher rate and, therefore, will pay a lower P/E multiple. Let's see if our numbers bear this out.

With only equity financing, recall that our hypothetical company had a value of $10 a share, had earnings per share of $1, and sold for 10 times earnings:

Without Debt
Share price = EPS × P/E ratio
$10   = $1 × 10

Recall also that, by raising $5,000 of debt to retire one-half of the common shares, the company's stock price was increased from $10 to $14. The P part of its P/E multiple goes up because of the tax benefit of debt financing you may have heard about. The question at hand is whether the E part of the multiple—the earnings per share—rises more or less quickly than the stock price.

Interest on the debt makes bottom-line profits fall from $1,000 to $820, but, with only 500 of the original 1,000 common shares outstanding, earnings per share goes from $1.00 up to $1.64 ($820 of earnings/500 shares). Earnings per share (EPS) climb even faster than the stock price, and the P/E multiple falls from 10 to 8.5 ($14 share price/$1.64 EPS):

With Debt
Share price = EPS × P/E ratio
$14   = $1.64 × 8.5

Which would you rather have: a higher stock price or a higher P/E multiple? With debt, they go in opposite directions.

For many years the Coca-Cola Company sold for a higher P/E multiple than Pepsi. Part of the reason was Coke's greater profitability. But a large part was due to Coke's traditional (though since abandoned) policy of being debt free, whereas Pepsi used debt as an integral part of its capital structure. As a result of the company's use of debt, Pepsi stock sold for a higher price than it otherwise would, but a lower P/E. Since then, Coke too has caught the debt wave. It's the real thing.

The decline in P/E multiple is consistent with the greater risk and hence return expected by shareholders. The inverse of the P/E multiple is the earnings yield. When a company is without exceptional growth opportunities (as assumed for our company thus far) and has earnings normalized for the stage of the business cycle and nonrecurring gains and losses (an heroic assumption that I also now make but is almost never met with in practice), then and only then is the inverse of the price/earnings multiple an indication of the rate of return shareholders expect to earn on their investment (i.e., the cost of equity capital y).

Without debt, the shareholders stood to earn a yield of 10% on the price paid for the shares, the inverse of the 10 multiple:

$$\text{Yield} = \frac{\text{EPS}}{P} = \frac{1}{P/E}$$

$$10\% = \frac{\$1}{\$10} = \frac{1}{10}$$

The yield for shareholders is c because, absent debt, the required return for shareholders compensates solely for the risk in the business.

With debt, the yield investors expect to earn climbs to 11.7%, the inverse of the 8.5 multiple.

$$\text{Yield} = \frac{\text{EPS}}{P} = \frac{1}{P/E}$$

$$11.7\% = \frac{\$1.64}{\$14.00} = \frac{1}{8.5}$$

The tax benefit of debt financing is so compelling that, even after they pay a higher price for their shares, shareholders can expect to earn a higher return consistent with the greater risk they face. Weep not for the shareholders.

Besides, nothing can force shareholders to take the higher risk if they choose not to. Recall that, as a result of the recapitalization, shareholders received $5,000 in cash from the repurchase of their shares. What have they done with that money? They could have invested it in a well-diversified portfolio of stocks and bonds, thereby potentially bringing down the overall risk in their portfolio. In fact, to make the case perfectly comparable, they could have invested it in the bonds that their own company issued to finance the repurchase of their shares. Then, holding a portfolio consisting of the company's common stock and its bonds, they would own the same representative slice of NOPAT as before, bear the same overall risk as before, but receive a higher reward due to the corporate income taxes saved. Not a bad deal.

In sum, a fear of imposing additional risk on shareholders simply is not a very good reason to avoid the use of debt.

The Financial Risk Premium in the Cost of Equity.   To be technical for a moment, leverage causes the cost of equity y and, hence, the yield on the shares to rise because investors add a financial risk premium (FRP) to the underlying cost of capital for business risk:

$$y \quad = \quad c \quad + \quad \text{FRP}$$
$$11.7\% \ = \ 10.0\% \ + \ 1.7\%$$

The financial risk premium compensates investors for suffering the additional variability over the business cycle in bottom-line earnings and hence in stock price. A little later I will show you why 1.7% is the right financial risk premium. For now, just take my word for it.

I can tell you, though, that it is *not* due to an increasing risk of bankruptcy. The potential for bankruptcy is better thought of as a deadweight reduction in value than a risk that enters the cost of capital. Such a reduction in value arises from, among other things, the explicit costs of retaining attorneys, bankers, and other professionals to negotiate a settlement, the diversion of management attention from pressing operating matters, a loss of consumer confidence and goodwill, and perhaps most important, the dissipation of potentially valuable investment opportunities. As a first, and rough, approximation, an "optimal" capital structure (if there is such a thing) is one that strikes a balance between the tax benefit of debt and the potential deadweight losses from bankruptcy. I will have more to say on this subject in chapter 10, "Financial Planning."

Touchdown!   It is time now to articulate the second term in the economic model of valuation. You may recall that the present value tax benefit of debt financing for our hypothetical company is $2,000, a value that accrues to the benefit of stockholders. It was computed by taking the annual tax savings ($120) and capitalizing (dividing) by the cost of borrowed funds (6%):

Formerly

				(1)		(2)
V	$=$	$D + E$	$=$	$\dfrac{\text{NOPAT}}{c}$	$+$	$\dfrac{\text{Tax savings}}{b}$
	$=$	$D + E$	$=$	$\dfrac{\$1{,}000}{10\%}$	$+$	$\dfrac{\$120}{6\%}$
$\$12{,}000$	$=$	$D + E$	$=$	$\$10{,}000$	$+$	$\$2{,}000$

Now

				(1)		(2)
V	$=$	$D + E$	$=$	$\dfrac{\text{NOPAT}}{c}$	$+$	tD
	$=$	$D + E$	$=$	$\dfrac{\$1{,}000}{10\%}$	$+$	$40\% \times \$5{,}000$
$\$12{,}000$	$=$	$D + E$	$=$	$\$10{,}000$	$+$	$\$2{,}000$

In symbols, the $2,000 tax benefit of debt is simply tD. t is the corporate marginal income tax rate (the rate at which incurring interest as an expense, while holding the business profits constant, saves taxes), and D is the *target* level of debt employed to finance the currently held assets. Since D represents the present value of the stream of interest payments on the debt (assuming that D is like a Consol bond that never amortizes), multiplying D by t gives the present value of a perpetual stream of taxes saved by deducting interest on the debt. Thus, the second term in the economic model is the corporate equivalent of throwing the bomb: tD. Go for it.

The Weighted Average Cost of Capital c*. Another way to express the tax benefit of debt financing is to incorporate tD into the cost of capital and thereby drive c, the cost of capital for business risk, down to c^* (pronounced "c star"), the weighted average cost of the debt and equity capital:

Formerly

				(1)		(2)
V	$=$	$D + E$	$=$	$\dfrac{\text{NOPAT}}{c}$	$+$	tD
	$=$	$D + E$	$=$	$\dfrac{\$1,000}{10\%}$	$+$	$40\% \times \$5,000$
$\$12,000$	$=$	$D + E$	$=$	$\$10,000$	$+$	$\$2,000$

Now

V	$=$	$D + E$	$=$	$\dfrac{\text{NOPAT}}{c^*}$
$\$12,000$	$=$	$D + E$	$=$	$\dfrac{\$1,000}{8\frac{1}{3}\%}$

By equating values, c^* must be $8\frac{1}{3}\%$. It incorporates a $1\frac{2}{3}\%$ discount for taxes saved from the 10% cost of capital in the absence of debt financing.

The Financing Approach.   The conventional financing approach to compute c^* is to weight the individual after-tax costs of debt and equity by the proportions they represent in a company's target capital structure:

	(1) After-Tax Cost	(2) Weight	(3)=(1)×(2) Weighted Cost
Debt	$(1-t)b$	D/TC	
Equity	y	E/TC	
			$\overline{}$ c^*

The after-tax cost of debt is represented by $(1-t)b$, where t is the corporate marginal income tax rate (40%) and b is the rate that must be paid to borrow new permanent debt capital (6% in our example):

$$(1 - t)b = (1 - 40\%)6\% = 3.6\%$$

Recall that incurring $5,000 of debt reduced bottom-line profits from $1,000 to $820, or by $180, an amount that is 3.6% of the debt raised. Thus, $(1-t)b$ represents as a percent what is the explicit cash cost of making interest payments on the debt, after taxes. Y, the cost of equity, is 11.7%, a combination of the cost of capital for business risk and a financial risk premium (still to be explained).

Debt is $5,000; equity is $7,000; and total capital (TC) is $12,-000. The proportions of debt and equity are $5/12$ and $7/12$, together accounting for all capital employed. Plugging these elements into the table, the weighted average cost of capital c^* is shown to be $8\frac{1}{3}\%$, just as I advertised it to be:

	(1) After-Tax Cost	(2) Weight	(3)=(1)×(2) Weighted Cost
Debt	3.6%	$5/12$	1.50%
Equity	11.7%	$7/12$	6.83%
c^*			8.33%

With the tax benefit of debt, our company can afford to earn a lower overall return on its total capital ($8\frac{1}{3}\%$ vs. 10%). Its NOPAT will still be sufficient to make interest payments on the debt with enough left over to provide an 11.7% return on equity, a return that will just adequately compensate shareholders for the combined business and financial risks they face. The hurdle rate for accepting new projects is now $8\frac{1}{3}\%$, assuming that the projects also are financed in the proportion of $5/12$ debt and $7/12$ equity.

The Operating Approach. c^* can also be expressed as a combination of c and the tax benefit of debt:

$$c^* = c \left(1 - \frac{tD}{TC}\right)$$

$$8\tfrac{1}{3}\% = 10\% \left(1 - \frac{\$2{,}000}{\$12{,}000}\right)$$

The operating approach states that c^*, the weighted average cost of debt and equity, begins with c, the required return for the risk in the business. According to the conservation of risk principle, leverage can neither create nor destroy business risk; it can only pass risk around at a cost. Because together they own the company, the debt and equity investors must collectively bear its business risk. Using low-risk debt creates higher-risk equity in a way that the changes in risk for the components cancel in the aggregate. c^* starts with c.

But then the business risk the company's investors collectively must bear is mitigated to the extent that the use of debt saves taxes, a benefit that reads as "1 less the tax benefit of debt financing tD per unit of total capital TC." With debt a company effectively gets another financier for free. The government provides financing in the form of sacrificed tax revenues. tD, the present value of the financing provided by the government, offsets the need to raise debt and equity capital to finance the business.

The government provides $2,000 of financing for our hypothetical company through the present value of tax savings tD while $12,000 of total capital is committed overall. $2,000 divided by $12,000, or one-sixth, of the company's financing costs are paid by the government in the form of sacrificed tax revenues. The remainder, or just five-sixths of the financing costs, must be borne by the debt and equity investors. Five-sixths times 10%, the required return for the risk in the business, is the weighted average cost of capital of $8\tfrac{1}{3}\%$. Isn't that nifty?

The Message.   This formula actually delivers a powerful message: The true benefit of debt financing is not the leveraging up of earnings per share for the shareholders. Although it is true that raising lower-cost debt to retire higher-cost equity does increase EPS, the increase is required to compensate the equity investors

for the additional financial risk they face as a result of the leverage. Value is created only because interest expense is tax-
deductible, and not because debt bears a lower rate than the cost
of equity.

A Restatement.   Factor t away from tD, and the formula becomes even more meaningful:

$$c^* = c(1 - t\frac{D}{TC})$$

It shows that two key elements actually determine hurdle rates
for companies, individual business units within companies, and
acquisition candidates:

- The perceived risk in the business c
- The tax benefit associated with the use of debt, expressed as
  a *target* ratio of debt to total capital (D/TC)

When practical, management should assign hurdle rates to individual business units and investment opportunities (including
acquisitions) that reflect their specific business risks and capital
structures. If such distinctions are not made, low-risk, high-debt-
capacity businesses will be penalized and high-risk, low-debt-
capacity business will be subsidized. Capital will be misallocated;
value will be destroyed (see chapter 10 for a determination of
debt capacity and chapter 12 for assessing business risk).

Great Expectations.   To illustrate, suppose that a public utility, flush with cash and the hopeful expectations of a young man
at his first dance, courts an electronics company for acquisition.
What cost of capital c^* should the utility employ to discount the
cash flow of the electronics company? Let's break the question
into two parts. First, whose c should be used: the public utility's
c or the electronics company's c?

The public utility should use the c of the electronics company
to discount the electronics company's cash flow. The utility's
managers should act as agents for their own shareholders, who
might otherwise invest directly in the electronics company and

bear that risk. Said differently, the cost of capital is determined by the risk of the use to which funds are put, and not the financing source. Though the public utility is the one to raise the funds for the acquisition, the funds will be used to acquire an electronics company. To conclude, a buyer must seek compensation for the risk in the seller's business.

The second question concerns the appropriate leverage ratio to employ: Should it be the public utility's or the electronics company's target capital structure? Suppose, for example, that the public utility has a total debt to total capital ratio of 75% and that the electronics company has traditionally employed no debt but, in light of the practice of similarly situated and comparably risky electronics firms, could justifiably support a 25% debt ratio. When computing c^*, should we use the utility's 75% ratio, the electronics firm's own debt-free policy, or the electronic firm's potential 25% debt ratio?

The cost of capital should reflect the capital structure the buyer will employ as a target to finance the seller's assets. The correct answer is 25%. This suggests a possible financial synergy to consider when making an acquisition. A buyer can afford to pay a premium over the current value of a target if the buyer more fully utilizes the seller's true debt capacity or if, as many conglomerates claimed, the combination itself creates additional debt capacity.

Although it may be true that the offsetting business cycles of the units comprising a conglomerate's portfolio make for a more bankable whole, the judgment that history renders is that conglomerates suffer from so many other disadvantages that the species is about to die out. For strategic business buyers, I conclude that the tax benefit of a greater use of debt should be invoked only after an acquisition is justified on the grounds of operating synergies, or if it is used in a dynamic manner as described in chapter 13.

Charting the Stars.   All companies and business units have four costs of capital. They are charted for our hypothetical company in exhibit 7.1. Increasing from left to right is leverage, measured as the ratio of debt to equity. Plotted north-south is the cost of capital as a percent.

Exhibit 7.1 The Four Costs of Capital

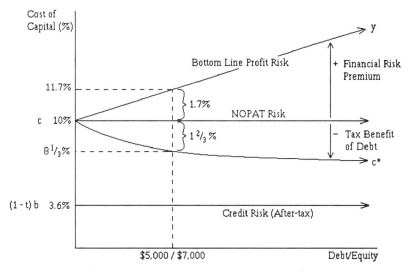

The North Star c

c, the one cost of capital that truly is independent of leverage, plots at a flat 10%. c reflects the difficulty investors will have in accurately forecasting NOPAT. In the same way that NOPAT is a measure of operating profits before financing costs, c is unaffected by capital structure. c is the required return for the risk in the business no matter how the business is financed.

The Cost of Equity y

The cost of equity y reflects the difficulty investors will have in accurately forecasting bottom line profits. y starts at c because, in the absence of debt, the only risk the shareholders take is the risk in the business. Bottom-line profits and NOPAT are one and the same.

But as leverage works into the capital structure, a wedge of fixed interest payments is interjected between operating profits and bottom-line profits, making the bottom-line profits over a business cycle more volatile, and hence, riskier, than the underlying operating profits. A financial risk premium is added on top of the cost of capital for business risk.

$$y = c + \text{FRP}$$
$$11.7\% = 10.0\% + 1.7\%$$

In our example, with $5,000 of debt and $7,000 of equity, the cost of equity is 11.7%, including a 1.7% premium for financial risk on top of c. It's time I come clean with the FRP:

$$
\begin{aligned}
\text{FRP} &= (1 - t) & (c-b) & \quad (D/E) \\
&= (1 - 40\%) \, (10\% - 6\%) \, (\$5,000/\$7,000) \\
1.7\% &= (60\%) & (4\%) & \quad (5/7)
\end{aligned}
$$

If you are a frustrated physicist, you must be feeling goose bumps right now. Have you ever seen such a beautiful formula? It states that the premium shareholders require to compensate for financial risk is the after-tax spread between business risk and financial risk multiplied by the debt/equity leverage. A company borrows funds at a risk reflected in its borrowing rate b and invests the proceeds in business projects with risk of c, so c minus b is the risk not taken by the lenders but instead passed to the shareholders, but after taxes and in proportion to the debt to equity leverage. Makes sense, right? It just falls out of the conservation of risk principle, in case you care to derive it.

The Cost of Borrowing b

Hovering at the bottom of the chart is the 3.6% after-tax cost of borrowing debt capital. It reflects the risk to the company of paying on the one hand and to the lenders of receiving on the other hand the interest after tax. Notice how each cost of capital has an income stream with which it is associated: c reflects NOPAT risk; y reflects bottom-line profit risk; and $(1-t)b$ reflects credit risk.

c Star

Combine the cost of debt and the cost of equity, while putting an ever greater emphasis on the cost of debt as leverage increases, and c^*, the weighted average cost of capital, plots as c, the cost of capital for business risk less the tax benefit of debt financing. With \$5,000 of debt and \$7,000 of equity, c^* is $8\frac{1}{3}\%$, incorporating a $1\frac{2}{3}\%$ tax benefit in debt financing.

Of the four costs of capital, only c^* truly matters. The other costs are just means to an end, that end being to know c^*. c^* is the rate to discount operating cash flow to a present value, the hurdle rate to qualify new investment projects, and a benchmark to judge the adequacy of the rate of return earned on total capital.

A Cost-of-Capital Simulation.   What if management now wishes to test the effect of increasing the target leverage from a debt to equity ratio of 5 to 7 to 1 to 1? To determine the new c^* from a financing approach, a new cost of equity must be computed first to account for the increasing financial risks that the shareholders would face:

$$\begin{aligned}
FRP &= (1-t) & (c-b) & \quad (D/E) \\
&= (1-40\%) \; (10\%-6\%) & (1/1) \\
2.4\% &= (60\%) & (4\%) & \quad (1/1)
\end{aligned}$$

The financial risk premium will rise from 1.7% to 2.4%; the cost of equity will rise from 11.7% to 12.4%; and the P/E multiple will fall yet again, from 8.5 to 8.1 ($\frac{1}{12.4}\%$).

Reality check? Do your investment bankers compute the prospective dilution in your P/E multiple as they propose to finance your acquisition entirely with debt? Of course not. But they should. Or you should. Otherwise you might think any increase in earnings per share will increase stock price. It won't. Caveat emptor.

$$y = c + FRP$$
$$12.4\% = 10.0\% + 2.4\%$$

With a debt to equity ratio of 1 to 1, debt and equity each make up 50% of capital. The new weighted average cost of capital c is an even 8%:

Financing Approach

	(1) After-Tax Cost	(2) Weight	(3)=(1)×(2) Weighted Cost
Debt	3.6%	50%	1.80%
Equity	12.4%	50%	6.20%
c^*			8.00%

But there is an even more direct way to calculate c^*, and speed is now of the essence.

Operating Approach

$$c^* = c\left(1 - t\frac{D}{TC}\right)$$
$$c^* = 10\%\ (1 - 40\% \times 50\%)$$
$$8\% = 10\%\ (1 - 20\%)$$

With a tax rate of 40% and a target ratio of total debt to total capital of 50%, 20% of c is paid by the government and c^* is 8%. This conclusion follows logically from the fact that the debt and equity investors must share the risk in the business, so that the only result of any real consequence arising from a change in capital structure is the tax benefit of debt.

The Cost of Debt and the Cost of Capital

In the foregoing calculations the borrowing rate was assumed to remain at 6% even as target leverage was increased. Indeed, in the cost-of-capital plot, the cost of borrowing money is dead level, suggesting the creditors are insensitive to the additional risk they bear as leverage is stoked up. Although the assumption clearly is unrealistic, it does not affect any of our conclusions.

In truth, as leverage increases, bondholders run a greater risk of not being fully repaid, and they demand a higher interest rate to compensate. But, so long as the bondholders are taking a greater risk, less of the risk in the business will be passed on to the shareholders. As the spread between business risk and credit risk contracts, c minus b narrows, and the financial risk premium will not rise as quickly as was originally suggested. In practice, the lines tracing the cost of debt and equity bend toward c, but, according to the conservation of risk principle, their mutual attraction just cancels out in the calculation of the overall cost of capital.

Suppose, for example, that as leverage increases from a debt to equity target of 5 to 7 to 1 to 1, the cost of borrowed funds increases by 50 basis points, from 6% to 6.5%, or from 3.6% to 3.9% after taxes. With a greater proportion of the firm's overall business risk in the laps of the lenders, the financial risk premium for shareholders will be only 2.1% instead of 2.4% as in our preceding calculation, the cost of equity will be 12.1% instead of 12.4%, but c^* remains 8%:

$$
\begin{aligned}
\text{FRP} &= (1-t) & (c-b) & \quad (D/E) \\
&= (1-40\%) \ (10\%-6.5\%) \ (1/1) \\
2.1\% &= (60\%) & (3.5\%) & \quad (1/1) \\
y &= c & + \text{FRP} \\
12.1\% &= 10.0\% + 2.1\%
\end{aligned}
$$

	(1) After-Tax Cost	(2) Weight	(3)=(1)×(2) Weighted Cost
Debt	3.9%	50%	1.95%
Equity	12.1%	50%	6.05%
c^*			8.00%

Now isn't this everything you ever wanted to know about the cost of capital? Probably not, actually. You may want to know how to estimate the cost of capital for real-life situations. In chapter 12 I will discuss how to use capital market data to estimate the costs of capital.

A Recap of a Recap.   Thus far, the value of the leveraged company has been shown to be the value of the underlying unleveraged business plus the tax benefit of debt financing:

$$
\begin{array}{ccc}
& (1) & (2) \\
& Current & Tax\ Benefit \\
& Operations & of\ Debt
\end{array}
$$

$$
V = D + E = \frac{\text{NOPAT}}{c} + tD
$$

or

$$
V = D + E = \frac{\text{NOPAT}}{c^*}
$$

It's time now to complete the value-driver model of value.

The Value of the Forward Plan

The third and final component calculates the value that investors are willing to pay today for the right to participate in the company's forward business plan. It capitalizes the fruits of undertaking new group 1 investment projects, ones in which the internal rates of return exceed those available to the company's investors. It can be shown numerically, graphically, and algebraically.

To be numeric for a moment, suppose that a company's management can invest $1,000 in a new project that over its life will earn a 25% cash flow rate of return r but that, by purchasing an equally risky portfolio of stocks and bonds, the company's investors could invest such funds to earn only a 10% total return c^*. The investment is the same; the risk is the same; but performance is different. A wealth index compounds the rates of return on the two investment alternatives into the future:

	Wealth Index by Future Year		
	1	2	3
The company: $1,000 at $r = 25\%$	$1,250	$1,563	$1,953
The market: $1,000 at $c^* = 10\%$	$1,100	$1,210	$1,331
Economic value added (EVA)	$ 150	$ 353	$ 622

The difference in the rate of wealth accumulation is EVA, a measure of the proprietary ability of management to outperform their capital competitors, and to add value to the new capital invested. The present value of EVA generated by all new investments is one way to arrive at the third component in the valuation model.

It can also be portrayed graphically as a widening gap (exhibit 7.2). Starting from a position of equal wealth, management is able to grow value within the company at a 25% rate whereas, out in the market and taking equivalent risk, investors can compound their wealth at just a 10% pace. The widening gap in wealth is economic value added.

EVA is projected to grow for just a finite period of time T (pronounced "Big T"). T, the last factor in the model, is the finite time horizon, in years, over which investors expect management can initiate new, value-adding projects. Beyond T, competition is expected to become so intense that only group 2 projects remain, ones in which r just equals c^*. The wealth indices proceed in parallel beyond T as value is created within the firm at a rate that is freely available to investors through the market (T is investi-

Exhibit 7.2   The Widening Gap between Corporate and Investor Wealth

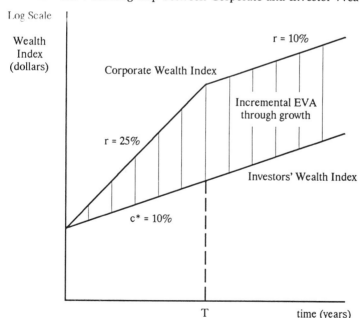

gated in greater detail below). The present value of the gap in value over the entire life of the business is the third component in the valuation.

And now, finally and formally, the third component can be represented algebraically:

(1)	(2)	(3)
Current	Tax Benefit	Forward
Operations	of Debt	Plan

$$V \;=\; D + E \;=\; \frac{\text{NOPAT}}{c} \;+\; tD \;+\; \frac{I(r - c^*)\, T}{c^*(1 + c^*)}$$

The third term takes the spread between the internal rate of return the company is projected to earn on new investment projects r and investors' required return for bearing risk c^* and multiplies it by the normal dollar amount of capital to be invested each year in new projects I. This incremental annual EVA is multiplied by the finite period of years T, over which it is likely to expand, and then it is capitalized as a perpetuity and fully discounted to a present value at c^*.[2] If you are interested, the derivation is in M&M's 1961 paper. Later on I will show you that it works, and I am hoping that may satisfy the curiosity of all but the most hardened cynics. Some observations on the third term are in order.

- The hurdle rate for the new investment projects is c^*, not c, because it is assumed that the new projects also will be financed by using a target blend of debt and equity. Thus, communicating management's target capital structure to the market assumes even greater importance when a company has a cornucopia stuffed full of potential group 1 projects.
- Prospective investment or I may be negative for a time, reflecting the cash proceeds from liquidating underperforming

[2]As a technical matter, because the new investment takes place in the first forecast year but the return on the new investment does not begin until the year after that (assuming a one-year delay between investing capital and beginning to realize its return), the third term is discounted one more year by c^* (i.e., divided by $1 + c^*$) to fully convert it to a present value.

assets. So long as the rate of return measured on the net cash proceeds is less than the cost of capital, value will be added by disinvesting capital and repatriating the funds to the market.

- It is possible for the value of the forward plan—the entire third term—to be negative. If over a period of time management has demonstrated the uncanny ability and willingness to invest in group 3 projects—ones in which r is less than c^*—investors may see fit to discount value out of a justifiable fear that such unrewarding investments will continue to be made. For such companies value could be created merely by turning off the investment spigot. Debt, in such circumstances, plays a role beyond just saving taxes. The obligation to repay it assures investors that the company will be unable to finance any more group 3 projects.

- Any company that sells for a high P/E multiple owes that to the perception that the third term is a big contributor to its value. The prospect of investing lots of capital in high-return projects for a sustained period of time is what it takes for any company to sell for a high multiple to its current earnings.

The Time Horizon T

Competition sooner or later drives rates of return on new projects down to the cost of capital. New entrants and the development of substitutes are the twin forces that undermine the profitability of even the best-managed companies. Not that the exceptional profits simply vanish into thin air. Rather, they are passed to consumers in the form of higher quality and lower prices. What starts out as a producer surplus ends up as a consumer surplus.

Irresistible economic forces drag companies through the stages of Pre-Z, to Z, to Y, to X, at which point the ability to create value through growth is exhausted (there may be a temporary overshooting into X-Minus, though). Once X is reached, a company has attained its "competitive equilibrium."

Introducing Big T. The projected length of time that it will take for a business to progress from its current state to a fully competitive equilibrium is its time horizon T. In theory, T grows smaller with each passing year. As a company's prospective investment opportunities are undertaken and come to fruition, value flows from the last valuation term into the first, from potential future value into current earnings power, all the while bringing the P/E multiple down, until at last there are no more group 1 projects. Though the company may continue to grow in size, the prospect of its growth will no longer add to its current value.

When the value of the forward plan becomes a flat tire, all value will reside in just the first two valuation components. Then, though its total value may never have been as great, a company will sell for a P/E multiple that just inverts its weighted average cost of capital c^*. Therefore, to the extent that a company trades for a P/E multiple that is above this commodity multiple, the market believes it still has value-adding growth prospects ahead of it. In a moment we will see how well this rule applies to computer manufacturers.

Countdown to an LBO.   Once the end of T is reached, the company will be just as valuable if the spigot is turned off on any investments above depreciation. Actually, it may be more valuable if it harvests its business and uses the cash flow to pay down the debt taken on in an LBO. Thus, I call T the countdown to an LBO. The duration of T ranges anywhere from 0 to 30 years, depending upon both the general business climate and conditions specific to individual companies and the industries within which they compete.

The Big Picture.   A country's macroeconomic and political outlooks affect the time horizons of all companies operating in that country to a greater or lesser extent and cannot be ignored in the valuation of any one company. In the United States, for example, time horizons were quite long, and P/E multiples as a result were quite high across the board in the 1960s (exhibit 7.3) because a climate very favorable to business expansion and profitability existed: The United States was dominant in the world economy; there was an absence of stifling regulations; free trade was widely practiced; low and stable interest rates, inflation rates, and exchange rates prevailed; a gold standard anchored currencies to a stalwart measure of value; economic growth was buoy-

Exhibit 7.3 S&P 500 Price/Earnings Ratio
High and Low Quarters, 1960–1989

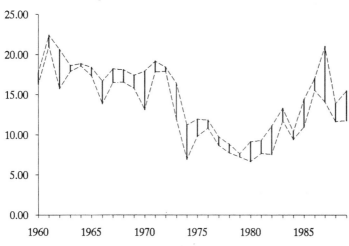

ant and predictable. In such an environment investors extrapolated corporate profits many years into the future.

With the 1970s the environment turned hostile, and P/E multiples collapsed along with investors' confidence. The full cost of Lyndon Johnson's simultaneous guns and butter programs finally began to be felt; taxes were increased; as inflation veered "out of control" (4% to 5% per annum was thought to be excessive) President Nixon imposed wage and price controls in August 1971; the gold standard was abandoned and floating exchange rates were substituted for fixed ones; oil prices were hiked by a foreign cartel; regulations proliferated; and protectionist sentiment began to build as the first real competition of the post–World War II era arrived on our shores. As globalization of the world economy exposed pockets of comparative underperformance, tariffs and quotas were slapped on autos, textiles, and steel, undermining long-run competitiveness and misallocating capital. Forecasting became impossible; risk management was a growth industry. Need I say more? People fled investments and turned to speculation. Real estate, gold and other precious metals, antique cars, works of art all enjoyed their day in the sun as hedges against uncertainty and inflation, and common stocks suffered. The P/E multiple for the S&P 500, a barometer of general investor confidence, crashed from the high teens to well under ten.

During the Reagan years, some of the harmful regulations of the 1970s were dismantled, marginal tax rates were cut to spur productivity, the fear of takeover and LBOs produced a more efficient utilization of resources, and the United States reasserted itself in the world, forcing even communist countries to acknowledge the failings of their system. Confidence soared along with the longest peacetime expansion in U.S. history. As investors lengthened their time horizons once again, the P/E multiple for the S&P 500 recovered to the mid-teens. The valuation of a given company must incorporate the general level of investor confidence at the time. *T* is how this works into the economic valuation model.

Micro Factors.   *T* also depends on factors specific to individual companies and industries, such as the cyclicity and growth of demand; economies of scale; the level of differentiation established through exceptional scientific, marketing, or service skills; the relative strengths of customers, suppliers and competitors; convergent technologies or businesses; and fixed-cost intensity, regulations, and of course, the quality and depth of management.

The Product Life Cycle Is Where It Begins.   The force of competition is easiest to visualize for individual products. The pattern in the price and profitability of hand-held calculators provides a vivid example of the power of competitive market forces. Hewlett Packard's and Texas Instrument's first calculators of the early 1970s cost over $500 and did little more than add, subtract, multiply, and divide. Nowadays a calculator with the same capabilities costs a pittance—so little, in fact, that if one lay on a street, it would go untouched by passersby. After all, its battery may be run down or the previous owner may have been the victim of a contagious disease. Calculators have become commodities produced in the Far East at little expense. Their only remaining value added comes from slapping names with cachet on their faces. Pierre Cardin calculators, whose main appeal seems to be that the punch of a button emits a pleasing fragrance, now proliferate. Big T has arrived, for all but the French salons (and a few persistent differentiators).

A Company Life Cycle

Kodak gives an example of the power of competitive forces operating at the level of an entire business. For many years, until strong direct competition emerged from Fuji, Kodak enjoyed an almost exclusive international franchise to manufacture and distribute film. It was a classic Y company, and it was a comfortable place to work. A vast bureaucracy grew up to fine-tune the workings of the great yellow empire. But then the advent of VCRs created another popular photographic recording medium in which Kodak faced a whole new set of competitors and different distribution channels. A more dramatic change may be in wings, though. Advances in digital technology make it likely that cameras eventually will store bits of data to represent the color of the image, much as a compact disk now records music in a digital format. Kodak, in other words, will no longer be in the film business; it will be in the information storage and retrieval business. The competitors that may unseat Kodak for good are not Fuji, but Sony, 3M, and others. The bureaucracy would prefer life to go on as before. But Kodak will never be the same again.

In 1973, Federal Express created a new industry—overnight package delivery—and after a rough start-up quickly became a sensational Z company. But with every passing year since, Federal has had to face increasingly powerful competitive threats from all sides. In an attempt to deter the proliferation of fax machines, for example, Federal embarked upon a costly diversionary tactic, Zap Mail, a fax service that foundered. Fax machines now are commonplace, and they compete at the margin for Federal's business. Federal also has been confronted by ever stiffer direct competition in the United States as the post office and UPS have awakened to the opportunity. Overseas expansion has not been nearly as profitable for Federal Express as its core U.S. operations have been. For one thing, Federal ran up against an established and astute competitor in DHL. For another, the cost of obtaining routes to build an international network proved to be so expensive that Federal decided instead to pay a premium to acquire Tiger International, which had an established international network. All in all, as Federal has grown and the overnight delivery business has matured, both direct and indirect competition have pushed incremental rates of return closer and closer to the cost of capital.

Thus, despite its head start, Federal is destined to become an X company in 5 years or less. Federal does not have the prospect for achieving meaningful differentiation or a sustained cost advantage over its competitors. Once demand ceases to grow as rapidly as it once did, cutthroat competition will drive returns down to the cost of capital, if not below it, until a shakeout occurs.

Industry Life Cycle

Like Kodak, the commercial banks in this country were undone by indirect competitors more than by other commercial banks. The advent of commercial paper, NOW accounts, junk bonds, General Electric Credit Corporation, and the invasion by foreign banks eroded the profitability of the commercial banking franchise. Government regulations originally designed to protect the banks now impede efforts to improve profitability. It is the fortunate money center bank that sells for over 7 times earnings these days.

The Big Eight, excuse me Seven, I mean Six, accounting firms also are running into waves of stiffening competition. Despite enjoying high barriers to entry, differentiation, long-standing client relationships, and gentlemanly rivalry, the audit function has become a commodity. Prices have fallen, and where they have not, compelling services are loaded on top to compete. Consolidation has begun. The end of Big T has arrived.

Easy Come, Easy Go

Shocking evidence is mounting that computer manufacturers also are approaching the end of *T*. That does not include the microcomputer upstarts like Compaq just yet; just the mainframe and minicomputer producers.

> If you want to raise an eyebrow, tell a computer executive that the industry is maturing. Suggest that after 40 years of non-stop buying, the best customers have so much equipment they can't keep spending at historic rates. Note that amazing reductions in the

price of raw computing power mean that demand must rise at least 20% a year just to keep the industry from shrinking. List some facts: Revenue growth is slowing, products are getting more standardized, margins are under pressure, consolidation is accelerating.

"Is the Computer Business Maturing?"
Business Week
March 6, 1989

To confirm this trend, I asked my associate Richard Rosson to study the price/earnings (P/E) multiples over the period from 1970 to 1988 for a sample of 11 old-line mainframe and minicomputer manufacturers (see exhibit 7.4). The companies in the sample are:

- Amdahl
- Cray Research
- Control Data
- Data General
- Digital Equipment
- Hewlett Packard
- Honeywell
- IBM
- NCR
- Prime Computer
- Unisys

I realize that Honeywell no longer makes mainframes, but then that's part of the point. The average P/E multiple for the group was standardized by dividing by the P/E multiple for the S&P 500 (column 3). P/E multiples over 100 and less than 0 were eliminated because they reflect accounting distortions. The average of the standardized P/E multiples for the group exhibits a downward trend, with the exception of a couple of years leading up to 1980.

Since 1980, the computer multiples have foundered vis-à-vis the market multiple, coinciding with the extraordinary success of the personal computer and workstations. Open architectures are driving more profitable proprietary hardware and software from the market. By the end of 1988, the average P/E multiple for the group essentially matched that of the market. *T* is finished. La-

ments Barton Biggs, chairman of Morgan Stanley Asset Management and a longtime fan of IBM, "Computers have really become
just a commodity business. Maybe IBM is just another cyclical
company making a piece of industrial machinery with a high
obsolescence factor."[3]

Exhibit 7.4   The Decline and Fall of the Mainframe

	(1)=(2)/(3) Average Standardized P/E	(2) Average Computer P/E	(3) S&P 500 P/E
1970	2.09×	35.5×	18.0×
1971	2.66	47.6	17.9
1972	2.58	47.5	18.4
1973	2.37	28.3	12.0
1974	1.64	12.6	7.7
1975	1.75	19.8	11.3
1976	1.60	17.3	10.8
1977	1.87	16.3	8.7
1978	2.10	16.4	7.8
1979	2.00	14.5	7.3
1980	2.48	22.7	9.2
1981	1.73	13.8	8.0
1982	1.48	16.5	11.1
1983	1.51	17.8	11.8
1984	1.38	13.9	10.1
1985	1.46	21.1	14.5
1986	1.17	19.6	16.7
1987	1.15	16.2	14.1
1988	1.03	12.0	11.7

To quantify the downward trend, the standardized P/E multiple was regressed against itself, with a lag of one year:

$$\text{P/E multiple } (t) = a + b \times \text{P/E multiple } (t-1)$$
$$\text{P/E multiple } (t) = 0.31 + 0.80 \times \text{P/E multiple } (t-1)$$
$$R\text{-squared} = 56\%$$
$$t\text{-statistic} = 4.54$$

[3]"IBM at $97: A Screaming Buy or a Sucker's Bet?" *Fortune,* January 1, 1990.

With a beta coefficient of 0.80, the industry P/E multiple (relative to the market) in any given year tended to be only 80% of its level the year before, a clear indication of a progression toward a competitive equilibrium in which no more than the cost of capital will be earned by the surviving companies. The current P/E multiple for this computer group predicts that, in the decade of the 90s, the challenge for them will shift from growth to cost containment, product rationalization, and consolidation. LBO IBM, anyone?

A Qualification. It is conceivable that some companies may beat the Grim Reaper. Coca-Cola and Pepsi, for example, have such a dominant share of the soft drink market worldwide it is difficult to imagine any direct competitors or substitutes dethroning them. Their advertising is mutually reinforcing; their product offerings are perfectly complementary; in effect, they are one company sharing the spoils of an extremely profitable business.

Having taken a 6.3% stake in the company, Warren Buffett has signaled his confidence that Coca-Cola has a franchise whose profitability will endure over the ages. When the market judges a company to have an infinite T on a certain core business, the question turns to how fast the business can grow while maintaining its extraordinary profitability, instead of how long its profitability will last. The last valuation term thus becomes:

$$
V \;=\; D + E \;=\; \underset{(1)}{\frac{\text{NOPAT}}{c}} \;+\; \underset{(2)}{tD} \;+\; \underset{(3)}{\frac{I(r - c^{*})}{(c^{*} - g)(1 + c^{*})}}
$$

T goes; and in discounting projected EVA, c^* is reduced by g, the long-run sustainable growth rate,[4] which eventually must, in a given business, be limited by either economic growth or population growth. The formula works because the continued growth in the business offsets the discounting process. The effective discount rate thus is c^* net of g, but without the limiting factor of a finite time horizon.

[4] The real growth rate must be increased by the expected rate of inflation since that is in the discount factor c^*.

Great caution should be exercised before this version of the model is used to value a company. At one time a good case could be made that the profitability of IBM's mainframes, Kodak's film business, or Campbell's soup lines would be impervious to assault by market forces. Such has not proved to be the case. In the end, which version to use is a matter of judgment and an unavoidable risk to investing in stocks.

Some Guidelines.   Rules of thumb are dangerous, and they should not be applied mechanically. But some guidelines may be of value in estimating T. Exhibit 7.5 sets forth typical T's for various types of industry configurations. The ranges also depend upon the general economic and political outlook as represented by the contrast between the 1960s and the 1970s.

The growth rate of the markets that a company serves and the sheer size of the company (as a proxy for entrepreneurship vs. statism) are important overlays on exhibit 7.5. Slower growth and larger size generally make for lower T's.

In the final analysis, however, the quality of management can overwhelm all other considerations in determining T. Astute managers can overcome almost any structural adversity and build valuable businesses. Warren Buffett, for example, made Berkshire Hathaway a stellar stock market performer starting from a textile company! Or consider Harold Sells, who inherited a decrepit Woolworth and then turned it into a star athlete. Where once T was meaningless for Woolworth, it is again meaningful.

Exhibit 7.5 T Table
(in Years)

	Pessimistic Times (1970s)	Optimistic Times (1960s)
1. Undifferentiated commodity businesses; highly cyclical, fixed-cost-intensive businesses	0	0–3
2. Exceptional scientific, marketing, or service differentiation; profound economies of scale	5–20	15–30
3. Supportive regulations; cartels	5–7	7–12
4. Generic businesses (all others)	3–5	5–7

A Recapitulation

Our first of three valuation frameworks is complete. The value-driver model presents the six essential factors that collectively account for the intrinsic value of any company, business unit, or acquisition candidate. These four are under the control of management:

NOPAT The net operating profits after taxes (but before financing costs and non-cash-bookkeeping entries) expected on average and over a business cycle from currently held assets

tD The tax benefit of debt associated with management's target capital structure

I The amount of new capital invested for growth in a normal year of the investment cycle

r The after-tax rate of return (in relevant cash flow terms) expected from new capital investments

The value-driver model tells us that, to enhance value, management must:

- Increase the sustainable level of fundamental profits derived from the company's current business operations (NOPAT)
- Sensibly adopt a target capital structure that employs greater proportions of debt than currently is being employed (as discussed in chapter 10, on financial planning, and chapters 13 and 14, on financial restructuring)
- Identify ways to step up capital spending in businesses where attractive returns can be earned
- Withdraw capital from businesses in which inadequate returns are being earned on the potential net exit proceeds

These may sound like the motivations that come from increasing EVA. They are! EVA ties directly to the creation of value, a fact that will become even clearer in the next chapter.

The factors beyond management's control are:

c　The cost of capital for business risk, c is the return required by lead steers to compensate for the risk in forecasting NOPAT. When it is combined with the tax benefit of target debt financing, c is driven down to c^*, the weighted average cost of debt and equity capital.

T　The future period of time, in years, over which investors expect management will have attractive investment opportunities. Beyond T, competition is expected to become so intense that the returns on new projects just cover the cost of capital.

It is very difficult for management to influence c and T. The cost of capital is determined by the return expectations of investors who hold diversified portfolios. Managers' attempts to diversify risk will be largely redundant with their investors' efforts, and more expensive too. c will be reduced only if a company can stabilize the return it earns over the business cycle in a way that shareholders could not duplicate through portfolio diversity. This is so rare an opportunity that, in general, working on c is not a worthwhile corporate objective.

Though a company's T is mostly set by the irresistible advance of competitive market forces, unforeseeable technological developments, and the limitations of size, I suppose that great managers can make and extend a T in any business. Truly great managers, like 20-game–winning pitchers, are rare.

An Illustration

To illustrate the mechanics of the value-driver model, the intrinsic market value of the hypothetical X,Y,Z companies is computed in exhibit 7.6. For simplicity, the three components of value have been collapsed into two by incorporating the tax benefit of debt financing tD into the cost of capital used to discount NOPAT. In order to value a company at any particular time, NOPAT and I must be projected for the year ahead and normalized for the stage of the business cycle.

Exhibit 7.6 Value-Driver Model

	X	Y	Z
Operating Characteristics			
NOPAT	$1,000	$1,000	$1,000
$-I$	$-1,000$	-800	$-2,000$
FCF	$\$\ 0$	$\$\ 200$	$-\$1,000$
$g = r \times \dfrac{I}{\text{NOPAT}}$	$10.0\% = 10.0\% \times \dfrac{\$1,000}{\$1,000}$	$10.0\% = 12.5\% \times \dfrac{\$800}{\$1,000}$	$25.0\% = 12.5\% \times \dfrac{\$2,000}{\$1,000}$

Valuation

1. Project next year's NOPAT and I

	X	Y	Z
Next year's NOPAT = this year's NOPAT $\times (1 + g)$	$\$1,100 = \$1,000 \times (1 + 10\%)$	$\$1,100 = \$1,000 \times (1 + 10\%)$	$\$1,250 = \$1,000 \times (1 + 25\%)$
Next year's I = next year's NOPAT $\times \dfrac{I}{\text{NOPAT}}$	$\$1,100 = \$1,100 \times 100\%$	$\$880 = \$1,100 \times 80\%$	$\$2,500 = \$1,250 \times 200\%$

2. Cost of capital and investors' confidence horizon

$$c^* = 10\%, \quad T = 5 \text{ years}$$

3. Valuation

$$V = \frac{\text{NOPAT}}{c^*} + \frac{I\,(r - c^*)\,T}{c^*\,(1 + c^*)}$$

	X	Y	Z
	$\dfrac{\$1,100}{10\%} + \dfrac{\$1,100\,(10\% - 10\%)\,5}{10\%\,(1-10\%)}$	$\dfrac{\$1,100}{10\%} + \dfrac{\$880\,(12.5\% - 10.0\%)\,5}{10\%\,(1+10\%)}$	$\dfrac{\$1,250}{10\%} + \dfrac{\$2,500\,(12.5\% - 10.0\%)\,5}{10\%\,(1-10\%)}$
	$\$11,000 + \$0$	$\$11,000 + \$1,000$	$\$12,500 + \$2,841$
	$\$11,000$	$\$12,000$	$\$15,341$

4. Correct to midyear discounting

$$V = V \times (1 + c^*)^{0.5}$$

	X	Y	Z
	$\$11,536 = \$11,000 \times (1+10\%)^{0.5}$	$\$12,586 = \$12,000 \times (1+10\%)^{0.5}$	$\$16,090 = \$15,341 \times (1+10\%)^{0.5}$

Next Year's Normalized NOPAT

X and Y expect NOPAT to be $1,100 in the first forecast year ($1,000 trailing NOPAT compounding at 10%), and Z expects NOPAT to be $1,250 ($1,000 compounding at 25%).

Next Year's Normalized Investment

I is $1,100 for X (100% of NOPAT), $880 for Y (80% of NOPAT), and $2,500 for Z (200% of NOPAT).

To make matters simple, assume that c^* is 10% and T is 5 years for all three companies, recognizing that in practice Z is likely to be riskier and have a higher cost of capital but also, typically, a longer time horizon.

X derives all of its value from the first valuation component, the capitalization of its expected NOPAT. The market will not pay a premium to participate in a commodity forward plan, one in which the capital employed will earn only what it costs. With r the same as c^* for X, its I, T, growth, and the entire forward plan are completely irrelevant to value. Depressing, isn't it?

Y pulls down the same value from its capitalized NOPAT but gets a modest boost from its ability to initiate some group 1 projects over the next 5 years.

Z has the greatest value of them all. The value of its capitalized NOPAT is higher than that of the others because it captures the payoff from investments made in the year before. An investor in Z buys into a company that is pregnant with the potential payoff from its recent prior investments. Z also has a higher value because it has the greatest opportunity to invest in new, group 1 projects.

The values determined by a straightforward application of the formula are imprecise because they are discounted from year-end, when cash flow takes place on average halfway through the year. To account for the time value of money properly, the components of value are grossed up for a half-year's interest earned at the cost of capital. Once that is done, the predicted values are $11,536 for X, $12,586 for Y, and $16,090 for Z.

This approach is appealing because it brings into sharp focus the factors that drive a company's value and shows how much value is embedded in current operations and how much is banked on the forward plan. This simple illustration informs us that X's main challenge is to boost its profitability, Y's is to uncover even more such attractive investment opportunities, and Z's is to live up to its potential. But it cannot depart from the assumptions of smooth growth, level returns, and normalized starting points. Unfortunately, the real world just isn't that simple.

Summary

Any company's market value can be represented as the sum of three components:

- A capitalization of current operating profits (NOPAT) at a rate that compensates investors for bearing business risks c
- The tax benefit of the debt that will be employed in management's *target* capital structure tD
- The present value of the economic value added by new capital projects I $(r-c^*)$ that are available until new entrants and substitutes compete away the exceptional profit potential T

An understanding of how the value of a company and its individual business units divides into these three components, and how it is changing over time, often will raise important planning and policy issues for management.

One such issue, for example, is how much debt to employ in the company's capital structure. The negatives of too much debt are well known. What is less well understood are the benefits. When debt substitutes for equity, one benefit is that the implicit cost of equity is replaced, at least partially, by an explicit cost of debt which is tax-deductible. The present value of the corporate income taxes saved will add into the company's share value, a benefit that can also be reflected as a reduction in the overall, or weighted average, cost of capital. A company's optimal *target* capital structure thus is one in which the tax benefit of any additional debt would just be offset by the cost of giving up more financial flexibility. The optimal level of debt may be higher than is commonly supposed.

For one thing, the tax benefit of debt is realized no matter how high the rate of interest on the debt gets to be and no matter how high the financial risk to the shareholders becomes as a result. Nor does it depend upon whether the company actually needs to borrow. In fact, the less a company needs to access capital, because its supply of group 1 projects has been exhausted, the more advantage there is likely to be to borrowing aggressively, if only to buy back stock.

Indeed, companies or business units for which the third term in the valuation expression has expired may benefit from dropping all pretense of a *target* capital structure. Instead, debt should be used aggressively to drive greater operating efficiencies into the firm, to force the discharge of surplus cash flow, and to draft more managers and employees into the ranks of owners. The act of leveraging to towering heights, and then paying it down, is a process that unto itself has a value that supersedes the mere tax benefit of debt financing. Moreover, so long as a company remains as well managed and its business units as synergistically situated as is possible, it has little to fear from a towering leverage ratio, even if its business fortunes deteriorate. The lenders' only recourse must be to accept a swift reversal of the original recapitalization, for any other action will only make them worse off. Such a *dynamic* use of debt is explored more fully in chapters 13 and 14.

Integral to valuation is the cost of capital. All companies and all individual business units within companies have four costs of capital:

- c, the cost of capital for business risk, is the required return investors will have for the difficulty encountered in accurately forecasting NOPAT. c is what the cost of equity would be in the absence of debt financing.

- y, the cost of equity, reflects the difficulty investors will encounter in their attempts to accurately forecast the bottom-line profits that are available to shareholders. It is equal to c plus a premium to compensate shareholders for the risk of leverage.

- $(1-t)b$ is the after-tax borrowing rate on debt. t is the corporate marginal income tax rate, the rate at which additional interest expense reduces tax. b is the rate the company would have to pay to raise new permanent debt capital.

- c^*, the weighted average cost of capital, can be computed from a financing approach by weighting the after-tax costs of debt and equity in the proportions employed in management's *target* capital structure. Better, though, is the operating approach, which reduces the required return for business risk by the tax benefit that arises from debt in management's *target* capital structure.

Of the four costs of capital, c^* is the one that really matters. It is the one to use to discount operating free cash flow to a present value; it is the rate new projects must hurdle to be acceptable; and it is the benchmark to judge actual rates of return on capital. In view of its importance, c^* should, when practicable, be established for individual business units and capital projects to account for their specific business risks and ability to support debt. Otherwise, low-risk, high-debt-capacity business units are apt to subsidize high-risk, low-debt-capacity units.

In the next chapter our attention turns to practical ways to value companies, business units, and alternative strategies and structures.

8

The Valuation Contest

Introduction

Altogether, there are three entirely equivalent methods for valuing corporate performance. The value-driver model breaks value
into six factors that describe the magnitude, riskiness, growth,
quality, duration, and financing of future free cash flow. It shows
how much of a company's overall value comes from its current
operations, from the tax benefit of debt, and from the value of
its forward plan. It clarifies the importance of capital structure
and the cost of capital to the valuation process in a way that no
other model can. Too bad, though, there's a problem with it. It
just is not a practical method of valuation, for it assumes steady
growth and steady returns from normalized values and it over-
simplifies the actual mathematics of discounting cash flow. Other
than that, it has everything going for it.

Fortunately, there are two valuation procedures that, although
in theory identical to the value-driver model, have the advantage
of being able to convert a specific, year-by-year forecast into an
estimate of value. Unfortunately, it is my opinion that corporate
practitioners, for reasons I intend to make perfectly clear in this
chapter, have chosen to use the wrong one of the two. Before
turning to the valuation contest, an introduction to the two oppo-
nents may be helpful.

Discounted Cash Flow. The most popular valuation procedure is just capital budgeting taken to a grander level. A company's free cash flow from operations is forecast over the entire life of the business and is discounted to a present value at a rate that reflects risk. Although discounting cash flow produces perfectly acceptable valuations, I recommend that it be abandoned, for a far better approach exists.

The Economic Value Added to Capital. Although it yields the same answer for a given forecast that discounting cash flow yields, the EVA approach has the advantage of showing how much value is being added to the capital employed in each year of the forecast. Also, it is the only method that can clearly connect prospective capital budgeting and strategic investment decisions with the way in which actual operating performance could subsequently be evaluated. For those reasons, I strongly urge that the EVA procedure be employed for all valuations. Let's meet the teetering world champ first and then turn to the promising young contender.

The Free Cash Flow Model

The mom and pop running the corner grocery store may not know much about accounting, but they know the value of their business. What matters to the corner grocers is the cash they can withdraw from their cigar box with the passage of time. Without even thinking about it, mom and pop value their store by discounting to a present value (PV) the free cash flow (FCF) they expect it to generate over the life of the business:

Value = PV of all future FCF

FCF is the cash flow generated by a company's operations that is free, or net, of the cash invested for growth. To compute it, imagine that all of a company's cash operating receipts are deposited in a cigar box and that all of its cash operating outlays are taken out, regardless of whether they are recorded by the accountants as expenses on the income statement or as expenditures on the balance sheet. What's left over in the cigar box is FCF. It is what the mom and pop running the corner grocery store knew all along determined the value of their business.

A free cash flow statement begins with sales as a proxy for cash operating receipts, then takes away, first, the cash operating outlays ordinarily recorded as expenses on the income statement, including taxes.[1] This leaves NOPAT as a resting place partway down the FCF statement:

$$\text{Sales} - \text{operating expenses} - \text{taxes} = \text{NOPAT}$$

Next, the use of cash to build up assets on the balance sheet is taken away. Outlays for working capital and fixed asset expansion, including acquisitions, are subtracted. FCF is what's left over.

$$\text{NOPAT} - \text{increase in working capital} - \text{fixed capital expenditures} = \text{free cash flow (FCF)}$$

The expenditures for working capital and fixed assets taken together are termed investment I. I can be computed by taking the period-to-period change in capital employed. With this definition of investment, FCF reduces to NOPAT $- I$.

$$\text{FCF} = \text{NOPAT} - I$$

In practice, NOPAT and I are measured net of depreciation. Subtracting depreciation makes NOPAT sustainable and I represent capital expenditures above and beyond capital maintenance requirements, and thus I equals capital spent to grow. Mom and pop groceries should not be concerned with those adjustments, however, because with both NOPAT and I net of the same depreciation charge, FCF still registers the cash passing through their cigar box.

---

[1] The taxes owing, in cash, on the operating profits. In practice, such "cash operating taxes" can be estimated by taking the accounting provision for taxes, subtracting the deferred taxes the company did not actually pay that year, and then adding the additional taxes that would have been paid had interest expense not served to shelter operating profits from being fully taxed.

The Other Side of the Coin

Do mom and pop know something that many corporate managers have forgotten? Mom and pop know that their sources and uses of cash must balance. As a result, the free cash flow generated or required by a company's operations *must* be equal to the sum of all the cash transactions with all the providers of capital to the company. This identity justifies the FCF valuation method, for it says that, in discounting projected operating cash flow to a present value, the cash rewards for all of the investors are being discounted, too.

Operating FCF

$$FCF = NOPAT - I$$

Financing FCF

$$FCF = \begin{array}{ll} \text{interest expense} & - \text{ new debt} \\ + \text{ dividends} & - \text{ new equity} \\ - \text{ interest income} & + \text{ new marketable securities} \end{array}$$

A business that invests less than it earns generates a positive FCF. That pool of surplus cash from operations is available to make interest payments (after taxes), retire debt, pay dividends, buy back shares, or accumulate a marketable securities portfolio. A business that invests more than it earns produces a deficit FCF. A negative operating cash flow must be financed by liquidating marketable securities or raising new debt and equity in amounts that exceed any financial distributions made in that year. The important equality between operating and financing FCF for Wal-Mart is shown in exhibit 8.1.

In view of this identity, a procedure of discounting operating free cash flow at the weighted average cost of capital *must* be the same as discounting all of the cash flowing back and forth between a company and its investors at a rate that reflects the combined debt and equity risk. This irrefutable equivalence is the

Exhibit 8.1   Wal-Mart Stores (Dollars in Millions)

FINANSEER (Feb-Jan)	1987	1988
Operating FCF		
NOPAT	$771.9	$1,064.3
- I	1,106.8	1,011.8
FCF	($334.9)	$52.5
Financing FCF		
Interest Expense AT	$89.2	$118.3
- Net New Debt	485.0	152.4
Dividends	67.7	90.5
- Net New Equity	6.9	3.9
FCF	($334.9)	$52.5

reason why discounting operating cash flow must be the way in which a company's debt and equity claims are valued. It only makes common sense.

Forecast Interval

The FCF valuation procedure seems to require forecasts of cash flow over the indefinite future life of a company. In fact, that is not necessary. A simplification can be invoked after T is reached. Once a company has exhausted all of its attractive investment opportunities, additional investment may increase the company's size but not its per share value. As a result, new investment (over and above depreciation) can be ignored. Turning off the investment spigot has two important consequences: NOPAT will cease to grow and FCF will equal NOPAT as an annual cash payment distributable to all capital investors. Thus, the value of a company's FCF beyond T is the same as capitalizing the NOPAT earnings in the year just after T as a perpetuity and then discounting it to the present.

FCF Valuation Illustration

The FCF valuation methodology will be illustrated first with company Y. Later on the values of X and Z also will be shown. The key operating characteristics for Y are:

- NOPAT is $1,000 for the year 1989 (which is assumed to be the most recent historical period).

- Y grows at 10% by virtue of earning a 12.5% return and investing 80% of NOPAT back into the business (exhibit 8.2).

The simple trend forecast that arises from extrapolating these smooth assumptions is plotted in exhibit 8.3. It shows NOPAT growing at a 10% rate from a base of $1,000 and I, the (net) capital investment, absorbing 80% of NOPAT each year. What is left over, FCF, grows along with NOPAT at a 10% rate. This pattern is followed through 1994, when T is reached by assumption. Beyond T, competition forces the rate of return to be earned on *new* capital investment to fall to the cost of capital of 10%. If the new capital investment earns only what it costs, it will not contribute to present value. For the purpose of valuation, the spigot is turned off on any investment above depreciation beyond 1994. Thus, NOPAT ceases to grow and FCF equals NOPAT each year in perpetuity. The total value of company Y is the present value of all future FCF (as represented by the vertical lines).

Value is calculated in two steps. First, the FCF generated over the group 1 growth period up through T is discounted to present

	Hist.	Projected		
	1989	1990	1991	1992
Sales	$16,667	$18,333	$20,167	$22,184
Sales growth g	10%	10%	10%	10%
NOPBT	1,667	1,833	2,017	2,218
% to sales (OPM)	10%	10%	10%	10%
NOPAT	1,000	1,100	1,210	1,331
Cash tax rate (CTR)	40%	40%	40%	40%
Change net work'g cap	333	367	403	444
% to incr sales (IWC)	20%	20%	20%	20%
Change net fixed assets	467	513	565	621
% to incr sales (IFA)	28%	28%	28%	28%
I	$800	$880	$968	$1,065
FCF	$200	$220	$242	$266
I/NOPAT	80%	80%	80%	80%
Incr NOPAT/incr cap	12.5%	12.5%	12.5%	12.5%
g	10%	10%	10%	10%

Exhibit 8.2 A Simple Sales-Driven Forecast

Y's FCF forecast could be generated by making assumptions for profit margin, capital turnover and sales growth.

Growth Rate

To begin with, suppose Y's revenues in 1989 are $16,667 and grow thereafter at a 10% rate g.

Profit Margin and Tax Rate

Suppose the operating profit margin (OPM) is 10% and the effective cash tax rate on operating profits (CTR) is 40%. Then in 1989 NOPAT is $1,000 and in 1990 it is $1,100, a 10% growth rate that continues in line with sales.

Turnover of Capital

Suppose incremental (net) working capital (IWC) and incremental (net) fixed assets (IFA) are 20% and 28% of incremental sales, respectively. Then, to support the $1,833 increase in sales anticipated for

1991, incremental capital will be $880 in 1990, 10% above the $800 level of the year before, and will continue to grow along with sales.

$$\text{Incr capital } I = \text{increase in sales} \times (\text{IWC} + \text{IFA})$$
$$= \text{sales} \times g \times (\text{IWC} + \text{IFA})$$
$$= \$18{,}333 \times 10\% \times (20\% + 28\%)$$
$$\$880 = \$1{,}833 \times 48\%$$

Free Cash Flow

FCF, the difference between NOPAT and I, also grows at the same 10% rate as sales. Thus, with the assumption that sales growth rate g, profit margin (OPM), tax rate (CTR), and turnover ratios (IWC and IFA) are constant, NOPAT, I, and FCF will all grow at a constant rate along with sales. In fact, the five sales-driven forecast assumptions can be combined to account directly for the profitability and investment measures of the economic model.

Value-Driver Model

$$g = r \times \frac{I}{\text{NOPAT}}$$

$$10\% = 12.5\% \times 80\%$$

Sales-Driven FCF Model

$$g = \frac{\text{OPM} \times (1 - \text{CTR})}{\text{IWC} + \text{IFA}} \times \frac{g \times (\text{IWC} + \text{IFA})}{\text{OPM} \times (1 - \text{CTR})}$$

$$= \frac{10\% \times (1 - 40\%)}{20\% + 28\%} \times \frac{10\% \times (20\% + 24\%)}{10\% \times (1 - 40\%)}$$

$$10\% = 12.5\% \times 80\%$$

By substitution of different values for g, OPM, IWC and IFA, and CTR, a revised incremental rate of return r, investment spending rate (I/NOPAT), and growth rate are predicted and easily valued. The combination should produce an incremental rate of return r that exceeds c^*, or else growth will reduce value, not increase it. In practice, however, all these rigidly uniform assumptions are relaxed to estimate the precise value of a given FCF projection.

Exhibit 8.3   FCF Valuation of Company Y

NOPAT	$1,100	$1,210	$1,331	$1,464	$1,611	$1,772	$1,772	$1,772	$1,772	$1,772	...
- I		880	968	1,065	1,171	1,288	0	0	0	0	0	...
= FCF		220	242	266	293	322	1,772	1,772	1,772	1,772	1,772	
x PV Factor at 10%^{A}		.953	.867	.788	.716	.651	6.512^B					
= PV of FCF		210	+210	+210	+210	+210+11,538	=	12,587	=	Value		
								8,800	=	Capital		
								1.43	=	Value/Capital		

^{A}FCF discounted from mid-year.
^{B}PV of $1 in perpetuity beginning in 1995.

value at the company's 10% cost of capital (using midyear discounting for improved accuracy) and then the NOPAT achieved in the first year beyond T, or $1772, is capitalized as a perpetuity and discounted to present value.[2]

The factor to present-value each $1 of NOPAT in perpetuity is 6.512. It is calculated, first, by estimating the value of a perpetual payment of $1:

[2]NOPAT grows for 1 year beyond T because a 1-year delay between making a capital investment and seeing its return show up in earnings is assumed. Thus, the investment made in T will grow NOPAT in $T + 1$.

$$\text{Perpetual value} = \frac{\text{annual payment}}{\text{cost of capital}}$$

$$\$10 = \frac{\$1}{10\%}$$

By paying $10 for the right to receive $1 each year forever, investors will receive an annual 10% yield on their money, and they can always recoup their principal by selling the claim on all future payments. Thus, each $1 of NOPAT beginning in 1995 is worth $10 as of 1994.

Next, the $10 perpetual value is discounted from 1994 to its present value. The PV Factor for 1994 is 0.6512. Multiplying that by 10, the overall PV factor for the perpetuity is 6.5123, a number which automatically capitalizes each dollar of NOPAT earnings as a perpetuity and discounts the resulting perpetual value to current worth.

By adding together the present values of all future FCFs, a value V of $12,586 is determined for Y. This represents a 43% premium over the $8,800 of capital employed at the end of 1989. In other words, every $1 invested in the business has been transformed into $1.43 of value. Not coincidentally, the FCF valuation of Y produces the same value as does the value-driver model, $12,586:

			$(1)\&(2)$ Current Operations		(3) Forward Plan
V	$=$	$D+E$	$=$	$\dfrac{\text{NOPAT}}{c^*}$ $+$	$\dfrac{I(r-c^*)T}{c^*(1+c^*)}$
V	$=$	$D+E$	$=$	$\dfrac{\$1,100}{10\%}$ $+$	$\dfrac{\$880(12.5\%-10\%)5}{10\%(1+10\%)}$
$\$12,000$			$=$	$\$11,000$ $+$	$\$1,000$

$\underline{\quad586\quad}$ adjustment for midyear discounting
$\$12,586$

Amazing, is it not! In valuing FCF, it really is the six factors that matter, and the six factors do nothing less than project the magnitude, riskiness, growth, quality, duration, and financing of future free cash flow.

The FCF Valuation of X and Z. The same procedure has been employed to value X and Z in exhibits 8.4 and 8.5. X, like Y, grows NOPAT at 10%, but it must invest every penny it earns to do so. FCF is zero all the way up until *T* is reached in 1994. Thereafter, the investment spigot is turned off and X is shunted into economic liquidation. NOPAT ceases to grow, and it becomes the FCF available for perpetual payout to investors. Without producing any FCF over its growth stage, X's $11,537 value is attributable solely to its capitalizing its projected NOPAT

Exhibit 8.4   FCF Valuation of Company X

	1989	1990	1991	1992	1993	1994	1995	1996	1997	1998	
NOPAT	$1,100	$1,210	$1,331	$1,464	$1,611	$1,772	$1,772	$1,772	$1,772	$1,772	...
- I	1,100	1,210	1,331	1,464	1,611	0	0	0	0	0	...
= FCF	0	0	0	0	0	1,772	1,772	1,772	1,772	1,772	
x PV Factor at 10%[A]	.953	.867	.788	.716	.651	6.512[B]					
= PV of FCF	0	+0	+0	+0	+0+11,538	= 11,538 = Value					
							11,000 = Capital				
							1.05 = Value/Capital				

[A]FCF discounted from mid-year.
[B]PV of $1 in perpetuity beginning in 1995.

beyond T as a perpetuity and discounting it all the way back to a present value.

To tell the truth, though, X reached the end of T long ago. It has nothing better than group 2 projects anymore. Therefore, its value could be computed by turning off the investment spigot right away and capitalizing the NOPAT in the first project year ($1,100) as a perpetuity. That, of course, is just the way the value-driver model sees things.

			(1)&(2) Current Operations		*(3)* Forward Plan
V	$=$	$D + E$	$= \dfrac{\text{NOPAT}}{c^*}$	$+$	$\dfrac{I(r - c^*)T}{c^*(1 + c^*)}$
V	$=$	$D + E$	$= \dfrac{\$1,100}{10\%}$	$+$	$\dfrac{\$1,100(10\% - 10\%)5}{10\% (1 + 10\%)}$
$11,000			$= \$11,000$	$+$	$0

$\underline{537}$ adjustment for midyear discounting
$11,537

This is absolutely critical to see. Value is the same no matter whether X invests and grows (as the FCF model supposes) or immediately turns off the investment spigot and harvests its current cash flow (as the value-driver model assumes). Therein lies the secret of LBOs. For if the prospect of growth adds nothing to present value, the investment spigot might as well be turned off and FCF be dedicated to service debt.

Z's projection is shown in exhibit 8.5. NOPAT compounds at the phenomenal rate of 25% per annum and reaches $3,815 by the time T arrives, a level more than twice that attained by X or Y. The capital invested to support the growth makes FCF more negative with each passing year until, at last, T is abruptly reached, the investment spigot is turned off, and NOPAT is frozen into perpetuity. The key valuation question is whether the eventual NOPAT payoff will more than compensate for the deficit FCF that investors are being asked to finance all along the way. The answer depends upon whether the rate of return on investment exceeds the cost of capital, an issue explicitly addressed in the value-driver model.

				(1)&(2) Current Operations		(3) Forward Plan

$$V \;=\; D + E \;=\; \frac{\text{NOPAT}}{c^*} \;+\; \frac{I(r - c^*)T}{c^*(1 + c^*)}$$

$$V \;=\; D + E \;=\; \frac{\$1{,}250}{10\%} \;+\; \frac{\$2{,}500(12.5\% - 10\%)5}{10\%(1+10\%)}$$

$$\$15{,}341 \;=\; \$12{,}500 \;+\; \$2{,}841$$

$$\underline{749} \quad \text{adjustment for midyear discounting}$$
$$\$16{,}090$$

The Emperor Has No Clothes.   Now I have an admission to make. The value of Z produced by discounting FCF, $17,022, and the value determined by the value-driver model, $16,090, are not the same. Don't panic. The last term of the value-driver model only approximates the actual mathematics of discounting FCF, that's all. The approximation is precise only when the projected growth rate and the discount rate are exactly the same (as it is for X and Y). Growth then cancels discounting, and T years worth of investment results can be summed together in the last term. But other than that, it is just an approximation to the correct answer given by discounting FCF. The value-driver model can be used only to represent value, not actually to compute it. Before turning to the valuation of a real company, in fact, one of the world's greatest companies—Wal-Mart—the contender to dethrone discounted cash flow will be introduced.

The EVA Valuation

In this corner we have the EVA valuation method, the one that I have all my money riding on. I prefer it because it shows how much value has been and will be created (or destroyed) by the allocation and management of capital. And since all companies

Exhibit 8.5 FCF Valuation of Company Z

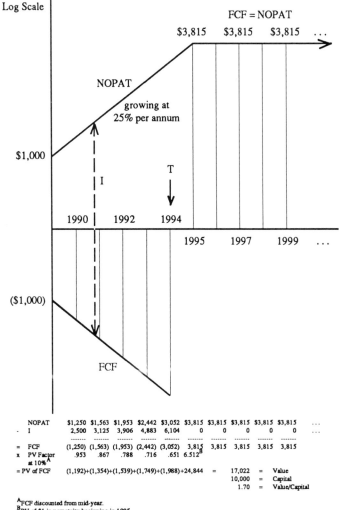

NOPAT	$1,250	$1,563	$1,953	$2,442	$3,052	$3,815	$3,815	$3,815	$3,815	$3,815	...
- I	2,500	3,125	3,906	4,883	6,104	0	0	0	0	0	...
= FCF	(1,250)	(1,563)	(1,953)	(2,442)	(3,052)	3,815	3,815	3,815	3,815	3,815	
x PV Factor at 10%[A]	.953	.867	.788	.716	.651	6.512[B]					
= PV of FCF	(1,192)+(1,354)+(1,539)+(1,749)+(1,988)+24,844					=	17,022	=	Value		
							10,000	=	Capital		
							1.70	=	Value/Capital		

[A] FCF discounted from mid-year.
[B] PV of $1 in perpetuity beginning in 1995.

are really in the business of allocating and managing capital, this method is the winner just on the strength of the conceptual distinction alone. But don't take my word for it. In just a couple of minutes, there will be a real donnybrook to decide the contest. But first, let's put the EVA model through its paces.

When it is projected and discounted to a present value, EVA accounts for the market value that management has added to or subtracted from the capital it has employed:

$$\text{Value} = \text{capital} + \text{PV of all future EVA}$$

The EVA approach is entirely equivalent to a procedure for discounting FCF, but it makes clear that the quality, and not the current level, of FCF is what truly matters.

EVA Valuation Illustration

Once again, the value of company Y will be established first, but this time by discounting its EVA. Y's EVA forecast is presented in exhibit 8.6. The rate of return on beginning capital is a steady 12.5% across the board, and it exceeds the 10% cost of capital by 2.5% each year. Applying this constant spread to the opening capital balance produces an EVA that is positive and growing at 10%, the rate of capital formation. This pattern of EVA growth continues through 1994, when it is assumed that T is reached. After that, new capital investment will earn a return identical to the cost of capital. EVA will not change; it will remain frozen at $354. The present value of the $354 of EVA as a perpetuity is estimated by using the 6.512 multiple used in the FCF procedure.

The present value of all future EVA, $3,356, is the premium value created over the mere commodity value of capital. Adding it to the capital outstanding at the end of the last history period (as adjusted for the time value of a half year's interest earned at the cost of capital[3]) yields a value identical to the FCF approach. As I said, there is not going to be a difference in the tale of the tape. Both the champ and the contender are equally adept at flexing their valuation muscles (exhibit 8.7).

The EVA Valuation of X and Z

The EVA valuation of X is a lark because there is nothing to do (exhibit 8.8). With projected rates of return equal to required returns, there is no value added to capital. X is worth current capital employed (plus an adjustment for the time value of money), and no more.

Z creates a handsome premium in its forward plan, the result of discounting a positive and rapidly compounding EVA (exhibit

[3]The capital in place at the end of 1989, the last history year, is grossed up to reflect a half year's interest earned at the cost of capital: $9,230 = $8,800 × (1 + 10%). This adjustment arises from the justifiable use of midyear discounting of projected cash flows.

Exhibit 8.6 EVA Valuation of Company Y

	1990	1991	1992	1993	1994	1995
NOPAT	$1,100	$1,210	$1,331	$1,464	$1,611	$1,772
Beg capital	8,800	9,680	10,648	11,713	12,884	14,173
r	12.5%	12.5%	12.5%	12.5%	12.5%	12.5%
c^*	10.0%	10.0%	10.0%	10.0%	10.0%	10.0%
Spread	2.5%	2.5%	2.5%	2.5%	2.5%	2.5%
Beg capital	$8,800	$9,680	$10,648	$11,713	$12,884	$14,173
EVA	$220	$242	$266	$293	$322	$354
PV factor at 10%	0.9535	0.8668	0.7880	0.7164	0.6512	6.5123
PV of EVA	$210	$210	$210	$210	$210	$2,306
Cum PV of EVA	$210	$420	$630	$840	$1,050	$3,356
Capital*						$9,230
Value						$12,586

*Capital in place at the beginning of 1990 is grossed up to reflect the time value of money by adding a half year's interest earned at the cost of capital:
$9,230 = $8,800 \times (1 + 10\%)^{0.5}$.

Exhibit 8.7 Capital Budgeting Exercise

The EVA valuation method can be used to evaluate individual capital projects as well as to evaluate whole companies. Because EVA is a residual income measure that subtracts the cost of capital from operating profits, discounting EVA produces the same net present value answer as discounting projected cash flows and subtracting the up-front investment.

Consider a simple project in which $2,000 of capital is invested in two equal stages, $1,000 up front and $1,000 at the end of the first year. The project rings up $250 of NOPAT in the first year and $500 thereafter. Once the project reaches steady state in the second year, the only investment made is depreciation, which is subtracted from NOPAT. Discounting operating cash flow (at a cost of capital of 10%, of course) and capitalizing terminal FCF as a perpetuity yields a net present value of $2,863. That represents the value created after the investment is recovered (hence the word "net" in net present value). The project appears to be a winner. (Did you think for a moment I would show you a loser?)

FCF Approach	0	1	2
NOPAT	$ 0	$ 250	$ 500
− I	1,000	1,000	0
FCF	$−1,000	$ −750	$ 500
× PV factor at 10%	1.0	.9091	9.091
Net present value, $2,863	$−1,000	$ −682	$4,545

An alternative approach is to compute the project's EVA year by year and discount it to a present value. In the following table, capital accumulates as the investments are made. EVA is computed by subtracting a 10% charge for the use of capital outstanding at the *beginning* of the year against each year's anticipated NOPAT. The present value of EVA is just the net present value of the capital project, $2,863.

EVA Approach	0	1	2
NOPAT	$0	$250	$500
Capital	$1,000	$2,000	$2,000
Beg capital	0	1,000	2,000
× c*	10%	10%	10%
Capital charge	$0	$100	$200

Exhibit 8.6 continued			
EVA Approach	0	1	2
EVA	$0	$150	$300
× PV factor	1.0	.9091	9.091
Net present value, $2,863	$0	$136	$2,727

Thus, the classic capital budgeting rule to accept all positive NPV projects can be restated: Accept all projects that have positive discounted EVAs. It is one and the same thing. But by stating the project acceptance criteria in EVA terms, rather than in terms of discounted cash flow, operating and planning people can clearly connect the way in which individual projects are evaluated and the manner in which subsequent performance will be evaluated. It's EVA ahead and EVA behind. The champ is bloodied now; chalk up another round for the challenger.

8.9). The increase in Z's EVA shows that the company is adding to its value all along the way. By contrast, anyone looking at Z's negative FCF would be hard pressed to know whether value was being created until the end of *T*, when the spigot on investment is turned off and cash flow turns positive. But even then it would be impossible to know whether value had been created in the forward plan until all the cash flows had been discounted to a present value. Give this round to the challenger.

EVA, in effect, assumes that no further investment is made after any given year and captures the increment to value generated to that point. That is reasonable because, though Z as a company has a negative FCF over the entire forecast period, each of the individual capital projects undertaken year by year is paying off relatively quickly in that Z's NOPAT is forecast to grow year by year. Thus, EVA turns the value of an entire company into the valuation of a series of individual projects as the projects unfold. The FCF technique, on the other hand, treats corporate valuation as one large and protracted capital budgeting exercise, and that is not as meaningful an analytical device for planning purposes.

Another reason to prefer the EVA method is that, unlike discounting FCF, it is immediately obvious why Z is more valuable than is Y and why Y is more valuable than X. The level and growth in EVA are immediate distinctions. With FCF, it is not obvious at all. Give another round to the challenger.

Exhibit 8.8 EVA Valuation of Company X

	1990	1991	1992	1993	1994	1995
NOPAT	$1,100	$1,210	$1,331	$1,464	$1,611	$1,772
Beg capital	11,000	12,100	13,310	14,641	16,105	17,716
r	10.0%	10.0%	10.0%	10.0%	10.0%	10.0%
c^*	10.0%	10.0%	10.0%	10.0%	10.0%	10.0%
Spread	0.0%	0.0%	0.0%	0.0%	0.0%	0.0%
Beg capital	$11,000	$12,100	$13,310	$14,641	$16,105	$17,716
EVA	$0	$0	$0	$0	$0	$0
PV factor at 10%	0.9535	0.8668	0.7880	0.7164	0.6512	6.5123
PV of EVA	$0	$0	$0	$0	$0	$0
Cum PV of EVA	$0	$0	$0	$0	$0	$0
Capital*	$11,537					
Value	$11,537					

*Capital in place at the beginning of 1990 is grossed up to reflect the time value of money by adding a half year's interest earned at the cost of capital:
$11,537 = $11,000 \times (1 + 10\%)^{0.5}$.

Exhibit 8.9   EVA Valuation of Company Z

	1990	1991	1992	1993	1994	1995
NOPAT	$1,250	$1,563	$1,953	$2,442	$3,052	$3,815
Beg capital	10,000	12,500	15,625	19,532	24,415	30,519
r	12.5%	12.5%	12.5%	12.5%	12.5%	12.5%
c^*	10.0%	10.0%	10.0%	10.0%	10.0%	10.0%
Spread	2.5%	2.5%	2.5%	2.5%	2.5%	2.5%
Beg capital	$10,000	$12,500	$15,625	$19,532	$24,415	$30,519
EVA	$250	$313	$391	$488	$610	$763
PV factor at 10%	0.9535	0.8668	0.7880	0.7164	0.6512	6.5123
PV of EVA	$238	$271	$308	$350	$398	$4,969
Cum PV of EVA	$238	$509	$817	$1,167	$1,565	$6,534
Capital*						$10,488
Value						$17,022

*Capital in place at the beginning of 1990 is grossed up to reflect the time value of money by adding a half year's interest earned at the cost of capital: $10,488 = $10,000 \times (1 + 10\%)^{0.5}$.

The Valuation of Wal-Mart

Enough hypotheticals, already. It is about time to value a real company, don't you think? I selected Wal-Mart in part because there is something of value to value there. Another reason Wal-Mart is interesting is that its market value approximately divides evenly between the capitalized value of its current NOPAT and the value of its forward plan. That makes it clear where its 22.4 P/E ratio comes from. It does not come from a low cost of capital; it does not come from The Street. It comes from the expectation that Wal-Mart can invest lots of capital in high-return projects for a long period of time. Before placing a value on Wal-Mart, however, a brief review of operations and historical performance is in order.

Operations

Wal-Mart, founded by the legendary Sam Walton, operates an expanding chain of retail stores in 25 southeast and central states. By January 31, 1989, the company had 1,259 Wal-Mart stores and 105 Sam's Wholesale Clubs, and another 155 Wal-Mart stores and 20 to 25 Sam's Wholesale Club units were slated to open during the year ending January 31, 1990. The company's tremendous success can be attributed to a number of interrelated factors.

1. Stores are located in sparsely populated towns in which Wal-Mart can be the dominant retailer of basic hard goods and apparel. The average community served has a population of 15,000.

2. Wal-Mart builds stores in concentric circles around its 16 distribution centers, always keeping its stores within a 450-mile radius.

3. The company has established an unambiguous reputation for everyday low prices by living up to its slogan, "Always the low price on the brands you trust. Always."

4. Operating expenses are the lowest in the industry, the result of high volume, just-in-time inventory management, extensive coordination with vendors, an experienced private

truck fleet, bar-coded checkout counters, highly trained and motivated personnel, and the timely flow of information through a private satellite network, among many other things.

5. Wal-Mart is people-sensitive. Customers are called guests and are treated as such. Employees are referred to as associates, and they participate in extensive formal training and incentive programs including the stretch incentive bonus plans for nonmanager associates, store management bonuses, shrinkage savings incentives, and company-wide profit sharing.

6. Entrepreneurship and personal growth are encouraged. Assistant managers and department managers develop as merchants through "store within a store," a management system whereby each Wal-Mart store is typically broken down into 34 separate departments that are run by individual managers. That gives up-and-coming associates the chance to try out their own merchandising concepts and to develop confidence in their business judgment. Above all, it encourages them to think like owners at a very decentralized level.

Historical Performance Review

A summary of Wal-Mart's and K-Mart's performance from 1980 to 1989 (FYE January 31 the following year) is presented in exhibit 8.10 (1989 is estimated from the *Value Line* report on Wal-Mart dated December 1, 1989). Sales for 1989 are estimated to be $25.9 billion. Though K-Mart is still larger, it is only a matter of time before Wal-Mart blows by it. Wal-Mart's sales growth for the past 10 years has been in excess of 35% per annum on average. In recent years, however, as the company has grown larger, the growth rate has slowed:

	Sales Growth, %
Past 10 years	35.5
Past 3 years	29.5
Past 1 year	25.4

Exhibit 8.10 Wal-Mart Stores: Summary of Performance
(Dollars in Millions)

FINANSEER (Feb-Jan)	History 1980	History 1981	History 1982	History 1983	History 1984	History 1985	History 1986	History 1987	History 1988	History 1989	10-Year Summary
Operating Results											Growth/Avg
1 Operating Sales	$1,643.2	$2,445.0	$3,376.3	$4,666.9	$6,400.8	$8,451.5	$11,909.0	$15,959.2	$20,649.0	$25,892.2	35.8%
2 Sales Growth	31.6%	48.8%	38.1%	38.2%	37.2%	32.0%	40.9%	34.0%	29.4%	25.4%	35.6%
3 NOPBT	$143.4	$212.1	$291.6	$426.6	$571.2	$701.5	$979.5	$1,279.8	$1,610.8	$2,025.4	34.2%
4 Pct. of Sales	8.7%	8.7%	8.6%	9.1%	8.9%	8.3%	8.2%	8.0%	7.8%	7.8%	8.4%
5 NOPAT	$90.9	$133.5	$175.2	$249.9	$317.6	$404.4	$548.5	$771.9	$1,064.3	$1,308.1	34.5%
6 Oper. Cash Tax Rate	36.6%	37.1%	39.9%	41.4%	44.4%	42.4%	44.0%	39.7%	33.9%	35.4%	39.5%
7 Capital	$528.2	$860.2	$1,068.5	$1,312.7	$1,876.7	$2,362.1	$3,114.4	$4,221.3	$5,233.1	$6,676.9	32.6%
8 Sales/Beg Capital	4.3x	4.6x	3.9x	4.4x	4.9x	4.5x	5.0x	5.1x	4.9x	4.9x	4.7x
9 PPE Expenditures	$87.6	$183.8	$188.4	$264.6	$352.7	$560.5	$626.1	$740.9	$818.8	$1,222.5	34.0%
10 Net Working Cap/Sales	14.7%	16.4%	13.7%	10.4%	11.7%	9.2%	8.6%	9.3%	9.2%	9.1%	11.2%
Free Cash Flow											Cumulative
11 NOPAT	$90.9	$133.5	$175.2	$249.9	$317.6	$404.4	$548.5	$771.9	$1,064.3	$1,308.1	$5,064.3
12 Increase in Capital(I)	145.7	331.9	208.3	244.2	564.0	485.4	752.3	1,106.9	1,011.8	1,443.8	6,294.3
13 Free Cash Flow	(54.8)	(198.4)	(33.1)	5.7	(246.4)	(81.0)	(203.8)	(334.9)	52.5	(135.8)	($1,230.0)
14 Invest Rate (I/NOPAT)	160.3%	248.6%	118.9%	97.7%	177.6%	120.0%	137.2%	143.4%	95.1%	110.4%	124.3%

Internal Performance

												Average
15	NOPAT/Beg Capital r	23.8%	25.3%	20.4%	23.4%	24.2%	21.5%	23.2%	24.8%	25.2%	25.0%	23.7%
16	Wtd Avg Cap Cost c*	12.4%	13.9%	13.5%	12.3%	13.6%	12.9%	11.0%	11.7%	12.6%	12.2%	12.6%
17	Spread r-c*	11.4%	11.3%	6.9%	11.1%	10.6%	8.7%	12.3%	13.1%	12.6%	12.8%	11.1%
18	x Beginning Capital	$382.5	$528.2	$860.2	$1,068.5	$1,312.7	$1,876.7	$2,362.1	$3,114.4	$4,221.3	$5,233.1	$2,096.0
19	Economic Value Added	43.5	59.9	59.4	118.4	139.3	162.9	289.6	407.5	533.7	671.7	248.6
20	Change in EVA	6.5	16.4	(0.6)	59.0	21.0	23.6	126.7	117.9	126.1	138.1	63.5

External Performance

												Growth/Avg
21	Year End Share Price	$1.89	$2.66	$6.23	$9.75	$9.47	$15.94	$23.25	$26.00	$31.38	$44.88	42.2%
22	Adj Book Value Per Shr	0.60	0.81	1.13	1.58	2.04	2.62	3.40	4.50	6.01	7.87	33.0%
23	Price - Adj Book	$1.29	$1.85	$5.10	$8.17	$7.43	$13.32	$19.85	$21.50	$25.36	$37.00	$14.09
24	x No. Shares Outst'g	517.5	518.7	537.7	559.7	560.9	562.1	564.4	565.1	565.6	566.0	551.8
25	Market Value Added	$665.8	$958.9	$2,744.6	$4,572.7	$4,168.4	$7,488.2	$11,202.1	$12,151.7	$14,344.8	$20,942.3	$7,923.9
26	Change in MVA	344.8	293.1	1,785.7	1,828.1	(404.2)	3,319.8	3,713.9	949.6	2,193.1	6,597.4	2,062.1

Exhibit 8.10 continued

FINANSEER (Feb-Jan)	History 1980	History 1981	History 1982	History 1983	History 1984	History 1985	History 1986	History 1987	History 1988	History 1989	10-Year Summary
Operating Results											Growth/Avg
1 Operating Sales	$14,342.6	$16,678.6	$16,941.6	$18,789.1	$21,303.3	$22,645.0	$24,046.0	$25,864.0	$27,550.0	$29,793.0	8.5%
2 Sales Growth	11.5%	16.3%	1.6%	10.9%	13.4%	6.3%	6.2%	7.6%	6.5%	8.1%	8.8%
3 NOPBT	$807.1	$758.0	$782.5	$1,216.7	$1,199.1	$1,294.4	$1,548.9	$1,707.7	$1,860.0	$1,766.0	9.1%
4 Pct. of Sales	5.6%	4.5%	4.6%	6.5%	5.6%	5.7%	6.4%	6.6%	6.8%	5.9%	5.8%
5 NOPAT	$513.4	$526.6	$445.1	$709.6	$711.2	$804.3	$944.9	$1,053.7	$1,265.7	$1,012.8	7.8%
6 Oper. Cash Tax Rate	36.4%	30.5%	43.1%	41.7%	40.7%	37.9%	39.0%	38.3%	32.0%	42.6%	38.2%
7 Capital	$5,186.4	$5,929.5	$5,970.7	$6,289.5	$7,915.8	$8,451.7	$9,002.4	$9,767.7	$10,496.3	$12,621.1	10.4%
8 Sales/Beg Capital	3.1x	3.2x	2.9x	3.1x	3.4x	2.9x	2.8x	2.9x	2.8x	2.8x	3.0x
9 PPE Expenditures	$622.6	$584.6	$389.7	$390.0	$897.9	$765.3	$423.7	$659.3	$716.6	$734.8	1.9%
10 Net Working Cap/Sales	12.3%	12.4%	11.4%	11.2%	13.8%	12.7%	13.5%	14.3%	14.7%	17.6%	13.4%

Free Cash Flow

											Cumulative
11 NOPAT	$513.4	$526.6	$445.1	$709.6	$711.2	$804.3	$944.9	$1,053.7	$1,265.7	$1,012.8	$7,987.3
12 Increase in Capital(I)	582.1	743.2	41.2	318.8	1,626.3	535.9	550.7	765.3	728.6	2,124.8	8,016.9
13 Free Cash Flow	(68.7)	(216.5)	403.9	390.8	(915.1)	268.4	394.2	288.4	537.1	(1,112.0)	($29.5)
14 Invest Rate (I/NOPAT)	113.4%	141.1%	9.2%	44.9%	228.7%	66.6%	58.3%	72.6%	57.6%	209.8%	100.4%

Internal Performance

											Average
15 NOPAT/Beg Capital r	11.2%	10.2%	7.5%	11.9%	11.3%	10.2%	11.2%	11.7%	13.0%	9.6%	10.8%
16 Wtd Avg Cap Cost c^*	11.2%	12.8%	12.2%	11.1%	12.0%	12.1%	10.4%	11.4%	12.1%	12.1%	11.7%
17 Spread $r-c^*$	0.0%	-2.6%	-4.7%	0.8%	-0.7%	-1.9%	0.8%	0.3%	0.8%	-2.5%	-1.0%
18 x Beginning Capital	$4,604.3	$5,186.4	$5,929.5	$5,970.7	$6,289.5	$7,915.8	$8,451.7	$9,002.4	$9,767.7	$10,496.3	$7,361.4
19 Economic Value Added	(1.3)	(135.2)	(280.1)	49.2	(41.6)	(151.9)	66.8	28.3	79.9	(261.5)	(64.7)
20 Change in EVA	(162.4)	(133.8)	(144.9)	329.3	(90.8)	(110.3)	218.7	(38.4)	51.6	(341.4)	(42.2)

External Performance

											Growth/Avg
21 Year End Share Price	$11.92	$10.50	$14.67	$22.17	$23.50	$23.58	$29.25	$29.75	$35.13	$35.00	12.7%
22 Adj Book Value Per Shr	14.65	16.01	16.91	18.80	20.54	21.03	23.96	26.97	30.92	32.61	9.3%
23 Price - Adj Book	($2.73)	($5.51)	($2.24)	$3.37	$2.96	$2.55	$5.29	$2.78	$4.21	$2.39	$1.31
24 x No. Shares Outst'g	185.1	186.0	186.7	188.9	187.5	189.0	200.3	199.7	199.4	200.0	192.3
25 Market Value Added	($505.2)	($1,025.5)	($418.1)	$635.9	$554.4	$482.2	$1,059.6	$555.1	$838.9	$478.9	265.6
26 Change in MVA	(991.1)	(520.3)	607.3	1,054.0	(81.4)	(72.3)	577.4	(504.5)	283.8	(360.0)	-0.7

Wal-Mart's operating profit margin has been slipping since 1983—from over 9% to under 8%. Still, it compares favorably with K-Mart's 6% to 7% operating profit margin over the past 5 years. Wal-Mart, like most other retailers, benefited greatly from the reduced corporate income tax rate enacted at the end of 1986. The company's effective cash operating income tax rate has fallen from something above 40% to around 35%. Wal-Mart really shines, however, in its ability to manage its assets. Capital is turning over nearly 5 times a year, in comparison with only about 3 times for K-Mart. In particular, the ratio of (net) working capital to sales has declined from near 15% in the early 1980s to around 9% at present. K-Mart's working capital ratio, on the other hand, is stuck at 14% to 15% of sales. Wal-Mart's declining profit margin can now be seen in a new light: It was an intentional investment made to build volume and install new technology in order to improve the turnover rate of capital in a self-fueling drive for ever greater efficiency.

FCF has been negative in 8 of the last 10 years. On average, for every dollar of NOPAT earned, $1.25 was pumped back into the business. The NOPAT to capital rate of return has not been under 20% over the 10-year period, and it has been close to 25% for the past 3 years running. The rate of return typically has exceeded the cost of capital by 12% to 13%, a spread which, when multiplied by a rapidly compounding capital account, has produced a positive and exploding EVA. MVA, the external measure, has increased in line with EVA, from $666 million to $20.9 billion by the end of the 1989 fiscal year!

With its rapid growth, high returns, negative FCF, and sky-high market valuation, Wal-Mart has been a classic Z company. But I predict that it is on the cusp of becoming a Y company as it enters the 1990s, as we shall soon see.

The Projections

For the purposes of this illustration, I decided to employ a relatively straightforward, top-down, sales-driven forecast, one that ties in to *Value Line* expectations in the short term and my sense of the company's economic destiny in the longer term. There probably are better ways to forecast Wal-Mart, ways that would examine the rate of new store openings, account for the economics of the company's expansion into new areas of the country, the likely success of new retailing formats, and so forth. If I were that ambitious, I would be a securities analyst. Because my main concern is with the technique of valuing a forecast, rather than forecast preparation (which deserves a book unto itself), I decided to keep it simple. Besides, that way I can blame *Value Line* for any errors. (Actually, I find the *Value Line* forecasts to be extremely useful for the most part.)

Raymond Cohen, *Value Line* analyst for Wal-Mart, expects sales for the 1990 fiscal year to be $32.4 billion, a 25.3% growth from 1989's estimated $25.9 billion in sales. He also projects sales to reach $57.4 billion within the period 1992–94. Centering that expectation on 1993 gives a sales growth rate of 21% per annum over the 3-year period from 1990 to 1993.

My projections hit Cohen's prognostications on the nose in 1990 and in 1993, as follows:

Aggregate Sales Forecast		
	Sales	Growth
1989	$ 25.9	25.3%
1990	$ 32.4	25.1%
1991	$ 39.5	22.0%
1992	$ 47.8	21.0%
1993	$ 57.4	20.0%
1994	$ 68.3	19.0%
2010	$342.5	5.0%

The aggregate sales growth is projected to decline 1% a year after 1991 until it reaches a 5% rate in the year 2008 and beyond. The reason for this declining growth rate is simple. There is only so much stuff that can be sold in the world. Even with growth slowing, Wal-Mart's total sales are projected to be $342.5 billion in the year 2010! (See exhibit 8.11 for complete sales projections.)

The forecast for Wal-Mart's aggregate sales was divided into two components. The first component is same-store sales, the

Exhibit 8.11 Wal-Mart Stores
Sales Projections
(Dollars in Millions)

	Total Sales	Growth	Same Stores Sales	Growth	Incr Sales	Growth
History						
1979	$1,248.2	38.6%				
1980	1,643.2	31.6				
1981	2,445.0	48.8				
1982	3,376.3	38.1				
1983	4,666.9	38.2				
1984	6,400.8	37.2				
1985	8,451.5	32.0				
1986	11,909.0	40.9				
1987	15,959.2	34.0				
1988	20,649.0	29.4				
1989	25,892.2	25.4	$25,892.2		$0.0	
Forecast						
1990	$32,400.0	25.1%	$28,740.3	11.0%	$3,659.7	
1991	39,528.0	22.0	31,758.1	10.5	7,769.9	112.3%
1992	47,828.9	21.0	34,933.9	10.0	12,895.0	66.0
1993	57,394.7	20.0	38,252.6	9.5	19,142.1	48.4
1994	68,299.6	19.0	41,695.3	9.0	26,604.3	39.0
1995	80,593.6	18.0	45,239.4	8.5	35,354.2	32.9
1996	94,294.5	17.0	48,858.6	8.0	45,435.9	28.5
1997	109,381.6	16.0	52,523.0	7.5	56,858.6	25.1
1998	125,788.8	15.0	56,199.6	7.0	69,589.3	22.4
1999	143,399.3	14.0	59,852.5	6.5	83,546.7	20.1
2000	162,041.2	13.0	63,443.7	6.0	98,597.5	18.0
2001	181,486.1	12.0	67,250.3	6.0	114,235.8	15.9
2002	201,449.6	11.0	71,285.3	6.0	130,164.3	13.9
2003	221,594.6	10.0	75,562.4	6.0	146,032.1	12.2
2004	241,538.1	9.0	80,096.2	6.0	161,441.9	10.6
2005	260,861.1	8.0	84,902.0	6.0	175,959.2	9.0
2006	279,121.4	7.0	89,996.1	6.0	189,125.3	7.5
2007	295,868.7	6.0	95,395.8	6.0	200,472.8	6.0
2008	310,662.1	5.0	100,165.6	5.0	210,496.5	5.0
2009	326,195.2	5.0	105,173.9	5.0	221,021.3	5.0
2010	342,505.0	5.0	110,432.6	5.0	232,072.4	5.0

sales derived from the stores already in place as of the end of 1989. Historically, this was running at 11% to 12% per annum.

Same-Store Sales	
	Growth Rate, %
1987	13
1988	11
1989	12
1990E	11

Source: 1987–1988 Wal-Mart Annual Report; 1989 *Value Line* estimate

One reason the growth rate persisted in staying in the range of 11% to 12% is that new stores were added into the same-store category after they became 1 year old. But if the stores in the same-store category are limited to just those in place by the end of 1989, a declining sales growth rate can be expected, as follows:

Same-Store Sales				
	Same Stores		**Incremental**	
	Sales	**Growth**	**Sales**	Growth
1989	$ 25.9			
1990	$ 28.7	11.0%	$ 3.7	N.A.
1991	$ 31.8	10.5%	$ 7.8	112.3%
1992	$ 34.9	10.0%	$ 12.9	66.0%
1993	$ 38.3	9.5%	$ 19.1	48.4%
1994	$ 41.7	9.0%	$ 26.6	39.0%
2010	$110.4	5.0%	$232.1	5.0%

The true same-store sales growth rate is projected to decline 0.5% each year until it reaches 6% by the year 2000. At that point, it holds at a 6% rate until 2008, when consolidated sales are forecast to be growing at only 5%. (Again, see exhibit 8.11 for a complete run down.) Subtracting the same-store sales forecast from the aggregate sales forecast produces incremental sales—the sales from adding new stores in the same territories, from opening stores in new regions of the country (Wal-Mart is now beginning its push into the northeast and west), and adding new retailing formats. Though starting small, incremental sales quickly surpass core sales. (The two are projected to cross in 1997.) Incremental sales are projected to be two-thirds of all sales by the year 2010 ($232.1 billion/$342.5 billion).

Drawing a distinction between incremental and same-store sales is important because the profitability of the two is expected to be different (see exhibit 8.12) The capital that supports same-store sales is projected to earn a 25% rate of return initially, which is in line with the company's recent historical perform-ance. The capital invested to support incremental sales, on the other hand, is projected to earn only a 20% rate of return.

It is reasonable to expect that Wal-Mart already has picked the most favorable locations for its stores in the southeast, south-west, and midwest regions it dominates. Any additional stores added there will not be as profitable as the ones already opened. (If not, why did Wal-Mart open the existing stores first?) In addition, a large portion of the incremental sales will come from a push into the northeast and west, areas which are more heavily populated in general. They are therefore somewhat less suscepti-ble to Wal-Mart's niche marketing strategy, and they are already served by other discount retailers such as K-Mart and Sears. Again, it is unlikely that expanding into those regions will be as profitable as the existing base of business.

That is not to say *un* profitable. A 20% rate of return after taxes on capital employed is still well above the company's cost of capital (estimated to be 12% at the time of the valuation), and the expectation for incremental growth accounts for a large part of the company's current market value. After 10 years have passed, that is, beginning in the year 2000, rates of return in general are projected to decline as the irresistible march of competition be-gins to be felt. As the markets Wal-Mart serves grow increasingly saturated, as competitors begin to emulate the company's suc-cessful formula, as the new stores that Wal-Mart opens start to cannibalize sales in its existing stores, rates of return will come down. This must be projected as a matter of faith in the way competitive free markets operate. T is inevitable. The big ques-tion is when will it arrive.

The projected rates of return break down into expectations for

Exhibit 8.12 Wal-Mart Stores: Profitability Assumptions

	Return on Capital, %		(OPM) NOPBT/Sales, %		(TO) Sales/Beg Capital		(CTR) Cash Tax Rate, %
	Same Stores	Incremental	Same Stores	Incremental	Same Stores	Incremental	
History							
1979	24.2		8.5		4.5×		37.4
1980	23.8		8.7		4.3		36.6
1981	25.3		8.7		4.6		37.1
1982	20.4		8.6		3.9		39.9
1983	23.4		9.1		4.4		41.4
1984	24.2		8.9		4.9		44.4
1985	21.5		8.3		4.5		42.4
1986	23.2		8.2		5.0		44.0
1987	24.8		8.0		5.1		39.7
1988	25.2		7.8		4.9		33.9
1989	25.0		7.8		4.9		35.4
Forecast							
1990	25.0	20.0	7.8	6.9	4.9	4.5	35.0
1991	25.0	20.0	7.8	6.9	4.9	4.5	35.0
1992	25.0	20.0	7.8	6.9	4.9	4.5	35.0
1993	25.0	20.0	7.8	6.9	4.9	4.5	35.0
1994	25.0	20.0	7.8	6.9	4.9	4.5	35.0

Exhibit 8.12 continued

	Return on Capital, %		(OPM) NOPBT/Sales, %		(TO) Sales/Beg Capital		(CTR) Cash Tax Rate, %
	Same Stores	Incremental	Same Stores	Incremental	Same Stores	Incremental	
1995	25.0	20.0	7.8	6.9	4.9	4.5	35.0
1996	25.0	20.0	7.8	6.9	4.9	4.5	35.0
1997	25.0	20.0	7.8	6.9	4.9	4.5	35.0
1998	25.0	20.0	7.8	6.9	4.9	4.5	35.0
1999	25.0	20.0	7.8	6.9	4.9	4.5	35.0
2000	24.5	19.5	7.8	6.8	4.9	4.4	35.0
2001	24.0	19.0	7.7	6.7	4.8	4.3	35.0
2002	23.5	18.5	7.6	6.6	4.8	4.3	35.0
2003	23.0	18.0	7.5	6.5	4.7	4.2	35.0
2004	22.5	17.5	7.4	6.5	4.7	4.2	35.0
2005	22.0	17.0	7.4	6.4	4.6	4.1	35.0
2006	21.5	16.5	7.3	6.3	4.6	4.1	35.0
2007	21.0	16.0	7.2	6.2	4.5	4.0	35.0
2008	20.7	15.7	7.1	6.1	4.5	3.9	35.0
2009	20.3	15.3	7.1	6.0	4.4	3.9	35.0
2010	20.0	15.0	7.0	6.0	4.4×	3.9×	35.0

operating profit margins (OPM), capital turnover ratios (TO), and cash tax rates on operating profits (CTR). For example, the initial 25% return on core sales arises from a 7.8% operating profit margin times a 4.9 turnover ratio on working and fixed capital times 1 less the effective cash tax rate on operating profits of 35%, all in line with the performance of the recent past (see exhibit 8.12). The profit margin and turnover ratio have been shrunk proportionately to produce the 20% rate of return for incremental sales.

Return	OPM NOPBT/Sales	TO Sales/Capital	CTR Cash Oper Taxes /NOPBT
25%	7.8%	4.9×	35%
20%	6.9%	4.5×	35%

Operating profits and capital were computed by applying the margins and turnover ratios to the projected sales in each category. The projected overall return on capital declines steadily over the forecast period as the lower incremental returns weigh in and as the end of the T horizon starts to phase in (exhibit 8.13).

The Valuation

In exhibit 8.14, a value is placed upon Wal-Mart by using both the FCF and the EVA methods. On the left-hand side, each year's FCF is discounted to a present value at Wal-Mart's 12% weighted average cost of capital. At the end of 20 years, NOPAT is valued as a perpetuity. The present value of all the cash to be cast off over the life of the business is $27.5 billion. The value of marketable securities is added and the market value of debt and leases is subtracted, leaving the common stockholders with a $25.2 billion pie to carve up. Dividing by the 566 million shares that are outstanding gives—drum roll, please—an intrinsic per common equity value of $44.53. Close, but not perfect. Wal-Mart was selling for $42.63 at the close of business on January 31, 1990, the hypothetical date of this valuation. Not bad for a rookie, eh?

Notice, incidentally, that FCF in column 3 is strictly positive in

Exhibit 8.13 Wal-Mart Stores Overall Projection Results
Dollars in Millions

	Sales	Sales Growth	NOPBT	(OPM) NOPBT/ Sales	NOPAT	(CTR) Cash Tax Rate	Capital	Sales/Beg. Capital (TO)	Return on Capital
History									
1979	$1,248.2		$106.4	8.5%	$66.6	37.4%	$382.5	4.5x	24.2%
1980	1,643.2	31.6%	143.4	8.7	90.9	36.6	528.2	4.3	23.8
1981	2,445.0	48.8	212.1	8.7	133.5	37.1	860.2	4.6	25.3
1982	3,376.3	38.1	291.6	8.6	175.2	39.9	1,068.5	3.9	20.4
1983	4,666.9	38.2	426.6	9.1	249.9	41.4	1,312.7	4.4	23.4
1984	6,400.8	37.2	571.2	8.9	317.6	44.4	1,876.7	4.9	24.2
1985	8,451.5	32.0	701.6	8.3	404.4	42.4	2,362.1	4.5	21.5
1986	11,909.0	40.9	979.5	8.2	548.5	44.0	3,114.4	5.0	23.2
1987	15,959.2	34.0	1,279.8	8.0	771.9	39.7	4,221.3	5.1	24.8
1988	20,649.0	29.4	1,610.8	7.8	1,064.3	33.9	5,233.1	4.9	25.2
1989	25,892.2	25.4	2,025.4	7.8	1,308.2	35.4	6,676.9	4.9	25.0
Forecast									
1990	$32,400.0	25.1%	$2,504.6	7.7%	$1,628.0	35.0%	$8,212.7	4.9x	24.4%
1991	39,528.0	22.0	3,024.7	7.7	1,966.0	35.0	10,009.0	4.8	23.9
1992	47,828.9	21.0	3,627.2	7.6	2,357.7	35.0	12,086.0	4.8	23.6
1993	57,394.7	20.0	4,318.3	7.5	2,806.9	35.0	14,460.9	4.7	23.2
1994	68,299.6	19.0	5,102.9	7.5	3,316.9	35.0	17,145.1	4.7	22.9

1995	80,593.6	18.0	5,984.4	7.4	3,889.9	35.0	20,143.3	4.7	22.7
1996	94,294.5	17.0	6,963.6	7.4	4,526.4	35.0	23,451.4	4.7	22.5
1997	109,381.6	16.0	8,038.9	7.3	5,225.3	35.0	27,055.3	4.7	22.3
1998	125,788.8	15.0	9,205.5	7.3	5,983.5	35.0	30,929.5	4.6	22.1
1999	143,399.3	14.0	10,454.8	7.3	6,795.6	35.0	35,449.2	4.6	22.0
2000	162,041.2	13.0	11,639.1	7.2	7,565.4	35.0	40,266.7	4.6	21.3
2001	181,486.1	12.0	12,846.0	7.1	8,349.9	35.0	45,329.4	4.5	20.7
2002	201,449.6	11.0	14,053.7	7.0	9,134.9	35.0	50,569.3	4.4	20.2
2003	221,594.6	10.0	15,238.4	6.9	9,905.0	35.0	55,904.2	4.4	19.6
2004	241,538.1	9.0	16,374.3	6.8	10,643.3	35.0	61,238.4	4.3	19.0
2005	260,861.1	8.0	17,434.6	6.7	11,332.5	35.0	66,465.0	4.3	18.5
2006	279,121.4	7.0	18,392.8	6.6	11,955.3	35.0	71,468.3	4.2	18.0
2007	295,868.7	6.0	19,223.4	6.5	12,495.2	35.0	75,779.1	4.1	17.5
2008	310,662.1	5.0	19,991.2	6.4	12,994.3	35.0	80,365.8	4.1	17.1
2009	326,195.2	5.0	20,785.8	6.4	13,510.8	35.0	85,247.9	4.1	16.8
2010	342,505.0	5.0	21,607.6	6.3	14,044.9	35.0		4.0	16.5

Exhibit 8.14 Wal-Mart Stores: FCF and EVA Valuations

Free Cash Flow Valuation
(Data in Millions)

FINANSEER (Feb-Jan)

Year	1 NOPAT	2 Investment	3=1-2 FCF	4 P.V. Factor	5=3x4 Present Value of FCF
1990	$ 1,628.0	$ 1,535.8	$ 92.2	0.945	$ 87.2
1991	1,966.0	1,796.3	169.7	0.844	143.2
1992	2,357.7	2,077.0	280.6	0.753	211.4
1993	2,806.9	2,374.8	432.1	0.673	290.6
1994	3,316.9	2,684.2	632.7	0.601	379.9
1995	3,889.9	2,998.2	891.7	0.536	478.1
1996	4,526.3	3,308.1	1,218.2	0.479	583.2
1997	5,225.3	3,603.9	1,621.4	0.427	693.0
1998	5,983.5	3,874.2	2,109.3	0.382	805.0
1999	6,795.5	4,519.7	2,275.9	0.341	775.5
2000	7,565.4	4,817.6	2,747.9	0.304	836.0
2001	8,349.9	5,062.6	3,287.2	0.272	892.9
2002	9,134.8	5,239.9	3,894.9	0.243	944.6
2003	9,905.0	5,334.9	4,570.1	0.217	989.6
2004	10,643.2	5,334.2	5,308.9	0.193	1,026.5
2005	11,332.4	5,226.6	6,105.8	0.173	1,054.1
2006	11,955.3	5,003.3	6,951.9	0.154	1,071.5
2007	12,495.1	4,310.8	8,184.3	0.138	1,126.3
2008	12,994.2	4,586.8	8,407.5	0.123	1,033.1
2009	13,510.6	4,882.1	8,628.5	0.110	946.6
2010 & Beyond	14,331.3	0.0	14,331.3	0.914	13,102.5
C.	14,331.3		B. 14,331.3	B. 0.914	13,102.5

Economic Value Added Valuation
(Data in Millions)

Year	1 Return on Capital R	2 Wtd Avg Cap Cost C*	3 = 1-2 Perform Spread R-C*	4 Beg Capital	5 = 3x4 EVA	6 P.V. Factor	7 = 5 x 6 A. Present Value of EVA
1990	24.38%	12.00%	12.38%	$ 6,676.9	$ 826.8	0.945	$ 781.2
1991	23.94	12.00	11.94	8,212.7	980.5	0.844	827.2
1992	23.56	12.00	11.56	10,009.0	1,156.6	0.753	871.2
1993	23.22	12.00	11.22	12,086.0	1,356.5	0.673	912.4
1994	22.94	12.00	10.94	14,460.9	1,581.6	0.601	949.8
1995	22.69	12.00	10.69	17,145.1	1,832.5	0.536	982.5
1996	22.47	12.00	10.47	20,143.3	2,109.1	0.479	1,009.7
1997	22.28	12.00	10.28	23,451.4	2,411.1	0.427	1,030.6
1998	22.12	12.00	10.12	27,055.3	2,736.9	0.382	1,044.5
1999	21.97	12.00	9.97	30,929.5	3,084.0	0.341	1,050.9
2000	21.34	12.00	9.34	35,449.2	3,311.5	0.304	1,007.5
2001	20.74	12.00	8.74	40,266.7	3,517.9	0.272	955.6
2002	20.15	12.00	8.15	45,329.4	3,695.3	0.243	896.2
2003	19.59	12.00	7.59	50,569.3	3,836.7	0.217	830.8
2004	19.04	12.00	7.04	55,904.2	3,934.7	0.193	760.8
2005	18.51	12.00	6.51	61,238.4	3,983.8	0.173	687.7
2006	17.99	12.00	5.99	66,465.0	3,979.5	0.154	613.4
2007	17.48	12.00	5.48	71,468.3	3,918.9	0.138	539.3
2008	17.15	12.00	5.15	75,779.1	3,900.7	0.123	479.3
2009	16.81	12.00	4.81	80,365.8	3,866.7	0.110	424.2
2010 & Beyond	16.81	12.00	4.81	85,247.9	4,101.6	0.914	B. 3,749.7
Premium (Discount)				Premium (Discount) Capital			A. $ 20,404.7
							C. 7,066.2

Exhibit 8.14 continued

Intrinsic Operating Value	$ 27,470.8
Marketable Securities	9.4
Intrinsic Total Value	$ 27,480.2
Total Debt & Leases	2,281.1
Intrinsic Common Equity Value	$ 25,199.1
Number of Shares Outstanding	566
Intrinsic Share Value	$ 44.53

A. Cash flow discounted from mid-year.
B. Present value of $1 in perpetuity beginning in 2010.
C. NOPAT increases by $ 820.7 based on a return of 16.8% on 2009 investment of $ 4,882.1 .

Intrinsic Operating Value	$ 27,470.8
Marketable Securities	9.4
Intrinsic Total Value	$ 27,480.2
Total Debt & Leases	2,281.1
Intrinsic Common Equity Value	$ 25,199.1
Number of Shares Outstanding	566
Intrinsic Share Value	$ 44.53

A. EVA discounted from mid-year.
B. Present value of $1 in perpetuity beginning in 2010.
C. Beginning capital of $ 6,676.9 adjusted for mid-year discounting by multiplying by $(1+C^*)^{**}.5$, where $C^* = 12.0\%$ in the first forecast period.

the forecast years, whereas it was mostly negative in the past. If I am right, Wal-Mart is at present right on the verge of switching from a Z to a Y company. Wal-Mart has become so large and so profitable that even its phenomenal rate of expansion will not be able to absorb all available internal cash flow. Indeed, by 1995 Wal-Mart will be generating approximately $1 billion a year more than it can productively reinvest, and the surplus builds at a frightening pace thereafter. This will pose a series of very interesting financial planning questions in about 4 to 5 years. Perhaps they will be addressed in the next installment of this book. For now, let's take a look at the EVA valuation.

A positive and growing EVA, when discounted to present value, accounts for a staggering $20.4 billion in market value added to the capital installed by the end 1989 (adjusted for a half year's interest, naturally). This is a performance worthy of awe and admiration. A hearty round of applause, at least. Add that premium to capital and the predicted intrinsic value of the company's operations, $27.471 billion, matches the FCF valuation to the penny.[4]

The Fifteenth Round

A couple of important differences between the FCF and the EVA methods are now apparent. For one thing, the process of projecting and discounting EVA to estimate value automatically has produced a series of EVA targets for management to achieve in order to justify the valuation—a particularly useful feature, incidentally, when negotiating an earn-out type of acquisition. The EVA goals to achieve drop out of the valuation process itself. Now that is a thunderous punch in favor of the challenger. Take a look, for example, at column 5 in the EVA valuation report (exhibit 8.14). Those are the EVA targets that must be achieved to justify Wal-Mart's current stock price. In Wal-Mart's case I would say that if those targets are achieved, there should be quite rich bonuses all around.

Tarry awhile in column 5, please. Notice EVA rising in the face

---

[4]Both of these valuation reports were generated by FINANSEER, Stern Stewart & Co.'s financial spreading and forecasting package for value planning and financial structuring. Information is available by calling Stern Stewart & Co., (212) 751-3900.

of a declining overall rate of return. Though the return in column 1 declines from 24% to under 17%, EVA steadily rises *until the year 2005 or so, when* T *is reached.* After 2005, the company's continued growth in size no longer adds to its net present value. In theory, therefore, at that time the investment spigot above depreciation could be turned off without impairing the company's current market value. Let's do just that, and see what happens.

In exhibit 8.15, Wal-Mart is valued by using the same set of projections, but truncated for the years after 2005. *The valuation is the same* as it was when 4 more years of growth were projected. This is an important finding, for it means that, in only 16 years' time, Wal-Mart will become a prime candidate for an LBO. Look, I realize it will be a big transaction, but by that time Boesky and Milken may be back in action. Seriously, though, if the investment spigot could be turned off without impairing the company's value, as this suggests, there would be almost $12 billion of FCF coming in each year to pay off the debts.

Though my initial projection stretched out over 20 years, only the first 16 years were really necessary. That Wal-Mart's *T* is 16 years was apparent by inspecting its projected EVA and discovering the point at which additional growth no longer added to EVA. FCF was no help at all in this regard, I might add. Wal-Mart's FCF continued to increase in each of the years after 2005.

Back to ringside. I am afraid that the cumulative toll of body blows has been too much for the reigning champ to withstand. The FCF method must be dethroned. Make way for the new king of value planning: EVA.

The Value-Driver Model

Now that Wal-Mart's value has been determined by discounting EVA and FCF, the value-driver model can be used to *represent* it. For example, exhibit 8.16 shows that almost half of Wal-Mart's total intrinsic market value is accounted for by capitalizing the $1.628 billion projected 1990 NOPAT by the 12% weighted average cost of capital and that the other half comes from the forward plan. It is generous of the market, don't you think, to pay $12.3 billion in anticipation of the residual income to be generated by stores that have not yet been opened, in locations that manage-

Exhibit 8.15 Wal-Mart Stores: Truncated FCF and EVA Valuations

Free Cash Flow Valuation
(Data in Millions)

FINANSEER (Feb-Jan)

Year	1 NOPAT	2 Investment	3=1-2 FCF	4 P.V. Factor	5=3x4 Present Value of FCF
1990	$ 1,628.0	$ 1,535.8	$ 92.2	0.945	$ 87.2
1991	1,966.0	1,796.3	169.7	0.844	143.2
1992	2,357.7	2,077.0	280.6	0.753	211.4
1993	2,806.9	2,374.8	432.1	0.673	290.6
1994	3,316.9	2,684.2	632.7	0.601	379.9
1995	3,889.9	2,998.2	891.7	0.536	478.1
1996	4,526.3	3,308.1	1,218.2	0.479	583.2
1997	5,225.3	3,603.9	1,621.4	0.427	693.0
1998	5,983.5	3,874.2	2,109.3	0.382	805.0
1999	6,795.5	4,519.7	2,275.9	0.341	775.5
2000	7,565.4	4,817.6	2,747.9	0.304	836.0
2001	8,349.9	5,062.6	3,287.2	0.272	892.9
2002	9,134.8	5,239.9	3,894.9	0.243	944.6
2003	9,905.0	5,334.9	4,570.1	0.217	989.6
2004	10,643.2	5,334.2	5,308.9	0.193	1,026.5
2005	11,332.4	5,226.6	6,105.8	0.173	1,054.1
2006 & Beyond	11,955.3	0.0	11,955.3	1.439	17,198.9
	C.			B.	

Economic Value Added Valuation
(Data in Millions)

Year	1 Return on Capital R	2 Wtd Avg Cap Cost C*	3 = 1-2 Perform Spread R-C*	4 Beg Capital	5 = 3x4 EVA	6 P.V. Factor	7 = 5 x 6 A. Present Value of EVA
1990	24.38%	12.00%	12.38%	$ 6,676.9	$ 826.8	0.945	$ 781.2
1991	23.94	12.00	11.94	8,212.7	980.5	0.844	827.2
1992	23.56	12.00	11.56	10,009.0	1,156.6	0.753	871.2
1993	23.22	12.00	11.22	12,086.0	1,356.5	0.673	912.4
1994	22.94	12.00	10.94	14,460.9	1,581.6	0.601	949.8
1995	22.69	12.00	10.69	17,145.1	1,832.5	0.536	982.5
1996	22.47	12.00	10.47	20,143.3	2,109.1	0.479	1,009.7
1997	22.28	12.00	10.28	23,451.4	2,411.1	0.427	1,030.6
1998	22.12	12.00	10.12	27,055.3	2,736.9	0.382	1,044.5
1999	21.97	12.00	9.97	30,929.5	3,084.0	0.341	1,050.9
2000	21.34	12.00	9.34	35,449.2	3,311.5	0.304	1,007.5
2001	20.74	12.00	8.74	40,266.7	3,517.9	0.272	955.6
2002	20.15	12.00	8.15	45,329.4	3,695.3	0.243	896.2
2003	19.59	12.00	7.59	50,569.3	3,836.7	0.217	830.8
2004	19.04	12.00	7.04	55,904.2	3,934.7	0.193	760.8
2005	18.51	12.00	6.51	61,238.4	3,983.8	0.173	687.7
2006 & Beyond	17.99	12.00	5.99	66,465.0	3,979.5	1.439	5,724.9
							B.

C. $ 20,323.5

Premium (Discount) Capital C. 7,066.2

Exhibit 8.15 continued

Intrinsic Operating Value	$ 27,389.6
Marketable Securities	9.4
Intrinsic Total Value	$ 27,399.0
Total Debt & Leases	2,281.1
Intrinsic Common Equity Value	$ 25,117.9
Number of Shares Outstanding	566
Intrinsic Share Value	$ 44.39

A. Cash flow discounted from mid-year.
B. Present value of $1 in perpetuity beginning in 2006.
C. NOPAT perpetuity value set by user.

Intrinsic Operating Value	$ 27,389.6
Marketable Securities	9.4
Intrinsic Total Value	$ 27,399.0
Total Debt & Leases	2,281.1
Intrinsic Common Equity Value	$ 25,117.9
Number of Shares Outstanding	566
Intrinsic Share Value	$ 44.39

A. EVA discounted from mid-year.
B. Present value of $1 in perpetuity beginning in 2006.
C. Beginning capital of $ 6,676.9 adjusted for mid-year discounting by multiplying by (1+C*)**.5, where C* = 12.0% in the first forecast period.

Exhibit 8.16   Wal-Mart Stores: Value-Driver Valuation (Dollars in Millions)

Value of Current Operations	+	Value of the Forward Plan	=	Value

$$\frac{\text{Next Period NOPAT}}{c^*} + \frac{I^A \times (r - c^*) \times T}{c^* \times (1 + c^*)} = V$$

$$\frac{\$1,628.0}{12.0\%} + \frac{\$1,500.9 \times (18.9\% - 12.0\%) \times 16}{12.0\% \times (1 + 12.0\%)} = V$$

$13,566.7	+	$12,314.1	=	$25,880.8
Adj for Mid-Year Discounting[B]				$ 1,508.9
Intrinsic Operating Value				$27,389.6
Marketable Securities				9.4
Intrinsic Total Value				$27,399.0
Total Debt & Leases				2,281.1
Intrinsic Common Equity Value				$25,117.9
Number of Shares Outstanding				566
Intrinsic Share Value				$ 44.39

A.   Annualized new investment in working capital and fixed assets, net of depreciation. Estimated by dividing present value of projected net capital additions by T.

B.   Adjustment converts value to middle-of-year.

ment has not even identified, over the next 16 years? Whosoever sayeth that the market is shortsighted apparently has not thought through the valuation of Wal-Mart.

In the forward-plan component, the annualized, normalized level of current investment, or I, is estimated by discounting all of the projected year-by-year investment of capital to a present value at the 12% cost of capital and then dividing through by 16, the number of years in the forecast. I comes to approximately $1.5 billion. T is 16 years, for reasons already discussed, and the cost of capital is 12%. The rate of return is a plug that makes the expression equate to the value determined by using the other practical methods. It is almost 19%, and is an approximation of the average internal rate of return projected to be earned on all new capital investments.

Casting valuations in the terms of the value-driver model can help managers to identify the units which may be ideal candidates for LBOs or PPOs (partial public stock offerings). Business units for which the strategy component is negligible or negative qualify for the aggressive use of debt, for there is little value to lose with the loss of financing flexibility. Ventures for which the strategic growth term is a large contributor are candidates for public offerings. Public offerings may accelerate their growth by giving them a direct access to the capital markets and by helping them to attract, retain, and motivate key employees through stock options and other stock-market-based compensation.

In Wal-Mart's case neither restructuring really applies. The company has too much value on the come to justify the aggressive use of debt right now. Moreover, the company's exceptional strategic value is really a corporate asset and is not attributable to any one isolatable unit. Sorry, investment bankers, but there's no good restructuring deal here right now.

Summary

The valuation contest pitted the upstart EVA valuation framework against the tried and true discounted cash flow method. From my ringside seat, I give the EVA framework a unanimous decision over the reigning champ. The procedure of discounting free cash flow does yield an accurate value, but it fails to provide any meaningful measures to assess progress in creating value or useful benchmarks to judge performance. The cash flow perform-ance of one company simply cannot be meaningfully compared with another.

The EVA valuation approach, on the other hand, provides a clear basis for reviewing performance after a new capital project has been accepted or a new strategy has been implemented; namely, has it increased EVA over a reasonable period of time? In addition, the Stern Stewart 1000 ranks prominent companies over 10 years according to EVA and standardized for size differ-ences, further facilitating the use of EVA as a management tool. EVA points to three fundamental ways to create value. The bene-fit of those strategies is not immediately obvious if value is couched in terms of discounted cash flows. Finally, because EVA reflects the value management adds to the capital placed at its disposal, it is an ideal performance measure for determining ap-propriate levels of executive bonuses but cash flow is not. In view of those advantages, I recommend that discounted cash flow be abandoned in favor of the EVA procedure for valuation and capital budgeting.

9

Acquisitions Pricing and Planning

Introduction

Acquisitions all too frequently reduce the share prices of the acquiring company. Sometimes this occurs because the buyer's acquisition criteria make no sense. More often, however, the buyer simply overpays for the benefits that are likely to arise from the combination, leaving sellers with an attractive gain and buyers with a loss.

The consequences of overpaying can be more catastrophic than many managers realize. Overpriced acquisitions make it more likely that the acquirer itself will be acquired someday. A 1988 study entitled "Do Bad Bidders Become Good Targets?"[1] presented evidence that if a company's share price fell after it announced an acquisition, it was later more likely to become a takeover target itself than was a company that announced a deal that lifted its stock price. What's more, the probability of being taken over was shown to be higher the more adverse the market's initial reaction to a preceding acquisition. This finding, incidentally, is one of several powerful proofs that the initial market reaction to an acquisition is a reliable measure of the long-run

[1]Kenneth Lehn and Mark Mitchell, chief economist and senior research scholar of the SEC, respectively.

351

merits of the transaction. To protect the interests of shareholders and managers alike, acquisitive companies will want to quantify the likely value to be derived from an acquisition and then pay something less, or walk away.

Common Acquisition Fallacies

Acquisitions often are made for silly reasons. Here are a bunch:

1. *EPS.* Does an increase in EPS guarantee a successful acquisition, and does EPS dilution signify a poor one? Absolutely not. The proposition is preposterous, and it is refuted by an overwhelming body of share price data. P/E ratios change in the wake of acquisitions to reflect a change in quality of pro forma earnings and in long-term cash flow prospects, thereby rendering near-term EPS effects completely misleading as a guide to merger value. EPS must be abandoned as the basis for judging the desirability of undertaking acquisitions.

2. *Earnings growth.* Acquisitions undertaken merely to fuel growth will not create value unless an adequate return is earned on the capital employed. Ask Saatchi & Saatchi.

3. *Why not (buy) the best?* Buying the best (performing) company is no guarantee of a successful acquisition. The best companies sell at the highest share prices, making them expensive acquisition candidates. Only if the buyer can outperform the forward plan already reflected in the seller's share price will the acquisition create value for the buyer's shareholders. More often than not, buying poor performers with plenty of room for improvement is a better strategy.

For example, many securities analysts claim that one of the best acquisitions ever was ConAgra's acquisition of Banquet Foods from RCA in 1980. Why RCA was in the food business to begin with no serious analyst has been able to defend (unless it was because Banquet Foods made TV dinners and that "fit" with NBC, one of RCA's units). ConAgra acquired Banquet Foods for about $50 million, less than half what RCA had paid for it 10 years earlier, and proceeded to add tremendous value to it. Under RCA's stewardship, Banquet Foods had introduced one new product, and it failed (at least the company knew when to quit).

Under ConAgra's management, by contrast, Banquet Foods introduced over 100 new products, many of which have been quite successful. Banquet now has a stranglehold on what marketers call the value side of the frozen dinner business: not top quality, but good enough and cheap. Analysts hold the acquisition in high regard because it created such a tremendous value for the buying company's shareholders.

Buying undermanaged and underperforming companies, and then fixing them up, has been a very successful strategy for ConAgra over the decade of the 1980s, one that has reaped astronomical returns for shareholders (exhibit 9.1.) The acquisition of Banquet Foods was just the first in a long string of acquisitions that has taken ConAgra from an undifferentiated (and nearly bankrupt) producer of feed, flour, and poultry to a value-added food-processing powerhouse (exhibit 9.2).

4. *What price glory?* Using an acquisition to attain seemingly laudable business objectives is itself no guarantee of a successful acquisition. Beating business competitors may not be sufficient; management must outperform its capital competitors to increase share price. An adequate return must be earned on the value paid; else, value will be destroyed for the buyer's shareholders and it is likely the buyer itself will become the target someday.

5. *Buying bargain companies.* By attempting to buy undervalued companies, ones whose trading values are thought to be below their true intrinsic values, management competes directly with

Exhibit 9.1 ConAgra: Buying Losers Makes a Winner

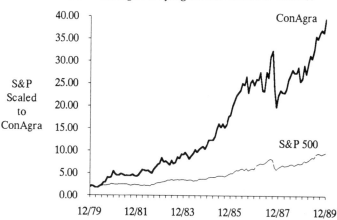

Exhibit 9.2   A Contrarian Acquisition Strategy

ConAgra's Chairman Mike Harper prefers to buy companies at the bottom of their cycles and with room for improvement. After each acquisition, he makes sure top-notch management is in place, gives it a terrific incentive, and then has the good sense to leave it alone. Frequently, additional acquisitions are made in the same business line to establish a dominant position and to achieve economies of scale. Five of Harper's most significant transactions were Banquet Foods, Armour Foods, Del Monte Frozen Foods, Monfort of Colorado, and SIPCO.

Banquet Foods—Frozen dinners, 1980.
$45 million cash, $17 million of Banquet straight preferred stock.

   This is the one that got it going. Banquet had not introduced a new product in 12 years, and its tonnage shipped had fallen 30% in the 2 years preceding the acquisition. The vital signs were quickly slipping away when ConAgra stepped into the breech. Harper brought in the president of Campbell's Swanson frozen foods division to run it. He, in turn, eliminated unprofitable product lines, improved quality, repositioned products, and introduced many successful offerings. Operating profits tripled in 3 years.

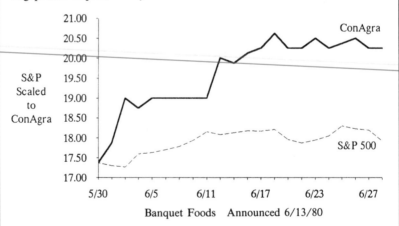

Banquet Foods   Announced 6/13/80

Armour Foods—Processed meats, dairy, frozen foods, 1983.
$182 million in stock.

   The Armour unit of Greyhound was stuck with uneconomic wage scales, unworkable rules, and an unprofitable business. Before ConAgra would agree to acquire it, Greyhound closed some of Armour's plants to eliminate the union. Under Greyhound, Armour had been emphasizing production and market share at the expense of profits.

ConAgra reorganized Armour into five groups, and managers were told to focus on the market rather than the factory. Sales dropped, but profits took off, except in the processed meats unit, which remained a problem. Armour also brought ConAgra an established premium frozen dinner line, Armour Dinner Classics, to complement Banquet Foods. Last, the Armour Star brand had untapped potential as a label for value-added chicken products which ConAgra can supply.

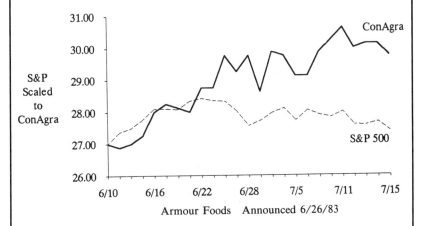

Armour Foods   Announced 6/26/83

Del Monte Frozen Foods—Morton, Chun King, and Patio frozen foods, 1986.
$64 million in cash.

This acquisition added three more brands to ConAgra's frozen foods menu (the brands were struggling, incidentally, because of intense competition from Banquet), and provided much needed distribution and manufacturing capacity in the east.

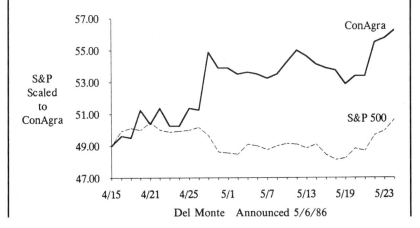

Del Monte   Announced 5/6/86

Monfort of Colorado—Beef and lamb producer and marketer, 1987.
$365 million in stock.

Coming close on the heels of the acquisition of Ernest J. Miller
($400 million sales), a producer of premium boxed beef for western
U.S. markets, Monfort ($1.8 billion sales) made ConAgra into the
nation's third largest beef producer virtually overnight at a time when
the meat-packing industry was undergoing a dramatic consolidation.
Monfort added significantly to ConAgra's nationwide refrigerated
and frozen foods distribution network, which is supported by more
than 1200 trucks, and thereby furthered the economies of scale at that
end of the business. For Monfort, the merger brought marketing
expertise to the beef business, financial security during lean years in
the cycle, and a tax-free transaction that enabled the Monfort family
and the other shareholders to diversify their risks.

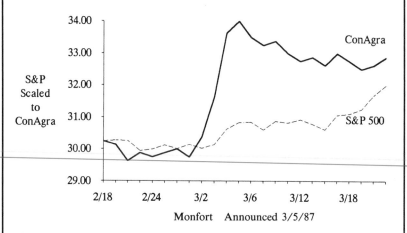

Monfort   Announced 3/5/87

50% of SIPCO (Swift Independent Packing Co.)—Beef, pork, and
lamb processing, 1987.
$51.5 million in cash.

As the next step in beefing up its meat business, ConAgra purchased
a 50% interest in Swift for $51.5 million, a stake that securities analysts
at the time estimated to be worth $100 to $400 million, and obtained an
option to acquire the remaining 50% within 4 years. Swift had gone
private in an LBO less than 2 years earlier, and it subsequently experienced difficulties in meeting scheduled debt payments. Sensing the
seller's vulnerability, ConAgra pounced with its offer. With annual
sales of $4 billion, Swift put ConAgra in an even better position to

compete with the beef powerhouses: IBP, a unit of Occidental Petroleum, and Excel Corporation, a unit of Cargill, Inc. Together, the big three control 70% of the market for boxed beef, with ConAgra holding down the number 2 position, close behind IBP. By adding a valuable, recognizable retail label—Swift—to ConAgra's Armour brand, there was a potential for reaping economies of scale. It also brought on board significant pork-slaughtering capabilities which ConAgra was lacking. In the aftermath of the purchase, SIPCO was able to achieve operating efficiencies in administration and distribution.

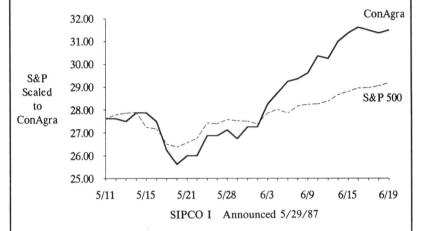

SIPCO I   Announced 5/29/87

The Other 50% of SIPCO 1989.
$51.5 million in cash.

Just to show that ConAgra's management is fallible, when the decision to acquire the remaining half of SIPCO was announced, ConAgra's shares slipped in price. Flourishing supplies of pork and poultry were keeping a lid on beef prices at the retail level at a time when the beef available for slaughter had fallen in number. The combination pinched the profits of the meat-packers and beef processors at just the time ConAgra elected to exercise its option. With 2 years left on the option, perhaps they should have waited a little longer.

In addition to these five major transactions, ConAgra over the years has acquired United Agri Products (agricultural chemicals), Country Pride Foods (broilers), Peavey Company (flour milling and grain trading), 50% of Lamb Weston (frozen potatoes), 45% of Trident Seafoods, eight U.S. flour mills from International Multifoods Corporation, and Cook Family Foods (smoked hams), among others. All things considered, ConAgra's acquisition track record may be the best in America (if not the world, for all I know).

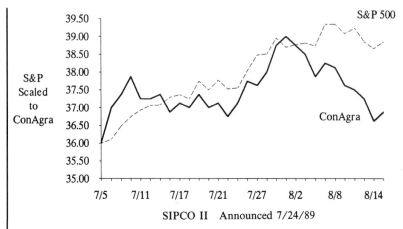

SIPCO II   Announced 7/24/89

ConAgra's success is attributable to many things, among them, an exacting financial standard—a 20% return on equity is an unequivocal goal for each business unit—and a decentralized management system.

> A key to ConAgra's enduring success is our management philosophy inherent in the "independent operating company" concept. Our businesses are independent operating companies with strong management teams who are truly responsible for decisions and results. Yet they gain strength and opportunity by drawing on the power of our family of companies. ConAgra independent operating companies work individually and together to grow their businesses and build a better, more successful ConAgra.
>
> ConAgra Fiscal 1986 Annual Report

Another secret to the company's success is a reasoned approach to a goal of earnings growth, a policy which is articulated each year in the annual report and apparently is appreciated by the securities analysts who follow the company:

> The cyclical nature of some of our basic food businesses does not always permit quarter-to-quarter, or sometimes, year-to-year, increases in reported earnings. However, ConAgra expects to increase trend line earnings—what ConAgra would earn with average or normal industry conditions—more than 14% a year from the 1973 base.
>
> Statement of Objectives and Results
> ConAgra Fiscal 1989 Annual Report

By setting the objective of improving the fundamental earnings power over the long haul, ConAgra's management is able to divorce itself from the myopic preoccupation with the regular growth in reported earnings that so hobbles many American companies. That can give ConAgra a big advantage in acquiring companies during the down phases of their commodity cycles or for which a protracted payoff is anticipated.

As important to ConAgra's success as the acquisitions that have been consummated has been the willingness to walk away from overpriced ones, even when they represented excellent strategic business fits—a policy again much appreciated by the analysts.

> Management has rigid financial standards relating to acquisitions. If another company bids up the price to a point where it jeopardizes ConAgra's earnings growth and return standards, management will back away as they did last year (1988) when attempting to buy Holly Farms. [Tyson "won" the acquisition instead.] We believe that ConAgra is one of a very few food companies where acquisition activity can have a materially positive impact on near and long term prospects.
>
> ConAgra Company Report
> Paine Webber, Inc
> March 19, 1990

One last thing about ConAgra's strategy should be obvious by now. All its acquisitions pertain to food and connect to one another in meaningful ways. There are real and realistic synergies possible in the combinations. That most basic requirement for acquisition success is too often neglected in practice.

sophisticated investors whose full-time profession is to seek out such bargains. How likely is it that corporate managers who only occasionally play this game will out-fox the foxes on Wall Street? Not likely, or at least, not something to bet the ranch on. Even if an undervalued company is spotted, management is well advised not to acquire for that reason alone, but instead to buy a minority interest in the company or, better yet, buy call options on the company's stock.

Shortly after Du Pont acquired Conoco in 1981, Edward G. Jefferson, Du Pont's chairman at the time, justified the purchase partly on the grounds that oil properties, and Conoco in particular, were undervalued:

> The first obvious reason [to acquire Conoco] is it's an opportunity to obtain a strong natural resource position at a substantial discount. If you look at, say, Herold's [John S. Herold, Inc., oil ana-

lysts] valuation of the Conoco assets, they showed around $160 a
share. [We paid] roughly $88 a share.

Fortune

Didn't you know there are free lunches everywhere? Herold
based his valuation on the assumption that oil would be selling
at $90 a barrel by the end of the 1980s. But the lead steers valuing
Conoco in the stock market were more astute about the eventual
direction of oil prices. Did it make sense for Du Point to bet $6.8
billion on a hunch about oil prices, particularly when any of the
company's investors could make that same bet at a huge discount
to the price that Du Pont paid?

6. *Diversification.* Using an acquisition to diversify risk does not
by itself create value, because investors can obtain the same benefits for free. Investors can diversify risk within their portfolios
by purchasing the shares of countercyclical companies. Thus, any
premium that a company pays over the market value that investors would have to pay for diversification is equivalent to making
charitable contributions to random passersby.

Another reason Chairman Jefferson of Du Pont cited to justify
the Conoco acquisition was to reduce the oil price risk to the
company's chemical operations: "If prices are rising at the crude-
oil level, then it becomes difficult to raise the prices of [Du Pont's]
downstream products [which use oil as a raw material]. As soon
as you have a crude-oil position you're insulated from that. The
fact that you lost a little downstream is protected by what you
have upstream." It's true that Du Pont did insulate itself from a
risk by acquiring Conoco. Du Pont will never run the risk of
paying anything less than about $70 a barrel for their oil, given
the price that was paid for Conoco's reserves.

Seriously though, if Du Pont transfers Conoco's oil to its chemical operations at market value—the only economically defensible
price—then the profits of neither its chemical nor its oil operation
will be any better combined than apart, no matter what happens to
the price of oil. That the two together produce more stable profits
than either considered individually is a benefit, that's true. But it's
a benefit available to investors merely by combining shares of Du
Pont and Conoco in their own portfolios. Any premium paid for
that reason is, by definition, a loss for investors.

With two silly reasons as the primary impetus for the transaction, Du Pont's acquisition of Conoco ranks as one of the worst of the 1980s. Du Pont's stock price fell by almost 15% versus the S&P 500 in the period surrounding the acquisition, a market value loss of nearly $1.2 billion (see exhibit 9.3).

Often when the term "diversification" is employed, a more precise definition of the motive is "capital reallocation": funds that cannot be productively employed within a company's existing lines of business are reinvested in others where the prospect of earning an adequate return is thought to be better. Although conceptually it is more justifiable than mere diversification, reallocating capital must always be compared with the simple alternative of paying out excess cash to creditors and shareholders.

7. *Buying bargain assets.* It is true that certain assets can be obtained on Wall Street for less than their current replacement value. Does this discrepancy ensure that a successful acquisition could be made? No. The value of an asset is at most equal to the present value of the cash flow it can be expected to generate when employed in a business. For example, buying a poorly run airline to acquire airplanes at a discount to current cost makes sense only if the buyer can operate those planes more efficiently than the seller or can sell the planes to someone else who will.

8. *Buying management.* The strength of the target's management is likely to be factored into the target's share price. Moreover, in the absence of powerful incentives, nothing can force bought management to work hard for the buyer (particularly after it is made wealthy). To be safe, before acquiring management, think about hiring management.

When the Kennecott Copper Company paid an enormous premium to buy Carborundum, an abrasives manufacturer with no tie to Kennecott's business, Kennecott argued that the acquisition of a talented and experienced management team would be one of the primary benefits. Within months of the acquisition, however, the top echelon of Carborundum management moved on, but the discount on Kennecott's share value stayed. This set in motion an attempted hostile takeover of Kennecott by Roland Berner, the chairman of Curtiss Wright. I remember vividly attending the annual meeting at the Plaza Hotel in New York and watching Roland Berner and Kennecott's chairman wrestle for control of

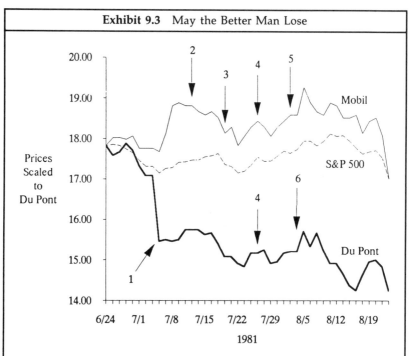

Exhibit 9.3   May the Better Man Lose

Du Pont's acquisition of Conoco was hotly contested by Mobil. The two suitors' stock price movements provide strong and consistent indications that Du Pont was overpaying and that Mobil would have been a more synergistic merger partner. As the events chronicled below suggest, every time it seemed as if Du Pont would be the one to take over Conoco, both companies' stock prices would decline. And when it appeared that Mobil would succeed, both companies' stock prices would rise. In the end Mobil lost the opportunity for a value-adding combination, and its stock price returned to normal. Du Pont overpaid by about $1.2 billion.

1. 7/6/81 Du Pont bids $6.9 billion for Conoco.
2. 7/13/81 Mobil signals interest in bidding.
3. 7/20/81 Conoco's board rejects Mobil's offer.
4. 7/27/81 Mobil and Du Pont sweeten their offers.
5. 8/3/81 Mobil enriches its offer yet again.
6. 8/4/81 Du Pont apparently wins control of Conoco.

the podium and the company. Kennecott prevailed in a very close proxy fight, only to be acquired several years later by SOHIO. I relate this bit of personal experience only to emphasize that over-paying for acquisitions can lead to all sorts of nasty consequences.

9. *Buying cash flow.* Paying a premium just to acquire a steady source of cash flow is a sure way to reduce stock price. Money is a commodity, and it is always available, though at a price. Internalizing the cost of capital does not avoid the cost. Stock price will suffer unless an adequate return is earned on capital, no matter what its source.

10. *Buying earnings.* Buying a steady source of earnings, possibly to obscure the accounting cost of a major investment, does not make sense. The available evidence is that sophisticated investors are able to penetrate accounting cosmetics to see the real value.

For example, about to embark on the costly and ill-fated development of video disk technology, RCA decided in 1979 to acquire CIT, the consumer finance company. Concerned about the adverse impact of the R&D expense on reported profits, and wanting to lock up financing for its risky venture, CIT was acquired for no other reason than to obtain a steady source of cash and earnings.

> What RCA has wanted, the analysts say, is to acquire a big supplier of steady, dependable earnings that also brings in some available cash to support RCA's more volatile operations. CIT, with its big commercial finance subsidiary, would provide that steady support.
>
> "RCA and CIT Confirm Talks on Merger,
> Prompting Finance Firm's Stock to Leap"
> *The Wall Street Journal*
> July 3, 1979

Analysts were uniformly unimpressed with the transaction. "An acquisition like this generates as much excitement as a financing, which, in effect, is what it really is," opined Chuck Ryan, a vice president of Merrill Lynch & Co. Excitement is one thing, stock price is another. RCA's share value shrank by over $100 million vis-à-vis the market as the intended acquisition was announced.

RCA's acquisition of CIT is much like a fellow who, seeing a brute coming at him, punches himself in the nose saying, "Don't bother to hit me, I already did it myself." Out of fear that investors would knock down the company's stock price if they got wind of the accounting and cash flow impact of the R&D venture, RCA decided to overpay on an acquisition, thereby reducing its share value and getting a worrisome discount behind it.

Ironically, RCA's CEO at the time decided to buy CIT for cash in order to avoid diluting earnings per share. Odd, don't you think, to pay cash to acquire cash and to pay a premium price for it at that? But that is the tangled thinking that traps people who make acquisitions for silly reasons. Sometimes one silly reason leads to another.

11. *Scarcity value.* Buyers sometimes agree to pay exorbitant prices for companies that are held to be unique. But a target's exclusivity does not explain why a given buyer should pay a premium. It explains instead why that particular seller is in a position to extract a premium from any buyer. Whether a buyer can afford to pay the premium that a unique seller is able to command depends upon whether it is best able to capitalize upon the seller's proprietary assets. A seller's scarcity value, in other words, is not a reason for a buyer to buy; it is a reason for a seller to sell. There is no such thing as a scarcity value; there is only a scarcity cost.

12. *Making them look good at our expense.* Occasionally, buyers' efforts to raise their targets' profits work to reduce their own. In effect, the buyer subsidizes the seller without increasing profits overall, or at least not by much. Paying a premium to capture the profit that targets gain at the buyers' expense is a certain way to destroy value.

United Airlines pursued a much ballyhooed full-travel-service strategy under chairman Richard Ferris. Starting from a base that included the airline and Westin Hotels, United acquired Hertz rental cars and Hilton International in order to offer comprehensive fly-drive-sleep travel packages. United's stock took it square on the chin when both acquisitions were unveiled. United's travel packages moved neither customers nor money managers.

> Travel packages aren't new, money managers noted. They're currently offered to vacationers and business travelers by agents and airlines that don't own car rental companies or hotels. *UAL's pur-*

chase of Hertz and Hilton might deprive it of some business from their competitors, they add.

"UAL's Effort to Be a Full Travel Company Has
Some Trying to Tally the Price of Success"
The Wall Street Journal
February 13, 1987

Though tying Hertz and Hilton into the airline may have stimulated more traffic for the newly acquired units, it probably caused other car rental agencies and hotel chains to throw business to airlines other than United. What was gained with the one hand was lost with the other. Besides, the other airlines were able to match the convenience and fares of United's travel packages by coordinating their marketing efforts with independent car rental agencies and hotels. "You don't have to go out and buy a car company to give bonus miles for doing business with them," said a spokesman for American Airlines.[2] Delta, for example, established marketing affiliations with such companies as Hyatt, Marriott, National Car Rental, and Alamo.

In light of those alternatives, United's management should have measured the value of making acquisitions for the purpose of offering integrated travel services in relation to what could have been accomplished just by contracting with other companies. Buyers often unwittingly pay too high a price because, through paying acquisition premiums, they give away the value of benefits that could be shared by contracting.

What Makes Acquisitions Successful?

I define a successful acquisition as one in which both the buyer's and the seller's stock prices will increase (frequently right as the acquisition is first announced) because the value created as a result of the combination is shared by the two parties. If the value added by the merger exceeds the premium offered, the buyer's stock price will rise. But if little or no value is created, or if the value created is more than given away to the selling shareholders, then the buyer's stock price will suffer. Stock market data certify that the difference between the combined value added and the

---

[2]"Full Service Just Didn't Fly with Public, Travel Agents," *The Wall Street Journal,* June 11, 1987.

premium paid, or net value added, is the driving force behind the stock price movements of acquiring firms.

Several examples of win-win transactions, in which buying as well as selling shareholders clearly benefited, can be cited: Capital Cities' acquisition of ABC, Triangle Industries' purchase of National and American Can, Ralston Purina's purchase of Eveready Battery from Union Carbide, and Wells Fargo's takeover of Crocker Bank are but a few. The announcements of those transactions led to immediate, substantial share gains for both the buying and selling companies. It can be argued that it is too soon to judge whether the acquisitions will be successful. Of course that is true, but then hindsight is an exact science. The real issue is this: At the time the decision to acquire was made, did the transaction hold the likelihood of creating more value than the buyer paid?

It can also be argued that the market is unable to digest all the relevant information pertinent to judging an acquisition, so that the immediate price reaction should be ignored. That argument, like the last one, is correct in the sense that the market is merely sophisticated, not omniscient. (Sometimes the market just has no idea how bad an acquisition will turn out to be.) But the initial market reaction, although often wrong in retrospect, does represent knowledgeable investors' unbiased estimate of the intrinsic value of an acquisition based on publicly available information. Academic researchers have shown that investors cannot earn exceptional stock market returns by buying shares in companies whose stock prices fall when an acquisition is announced or by selling short the companies whose stock prices rise. Betting against the market's initial judgment of an acquisition's merits is unlikely to be rewarding.

How to Analyze Acquisitions

The proper technique for analyzing whether an acquisition will improve the buyer's share value actually is quite simple. If you will get more value than you give up, your stock price will benefit by that difference, per share. Sounds obvious, does it not? But please notice that it has nothing to do with earnings per share.

Net Value Added (Lost).   To be somewhat more formal, the difference between total value received (by the buyer from the seller) and the total value paid (by the buyer to the seller) is something I call net value added (NVA). It is the engine that drives acquirers' share prices. When divided by the pro forma number of shares outstanding, NVA determines the change in the buyer's share price following an acquisition (exhibit 9.4).

Net value added = total value received — total value paid

Total value received is the intrinsic value of the seller's business (when fused with the buyer's) plus any value conferred on the buyer's operations as a result of merging with the seller. The techniques for computing this are just the same as those I outlined in chapters 7 and 8, that is, projecting and discounting free cash flow (or, better, EVA) to a present value. Total value paid is all cash used to compensate the selling shareholders (no matter whether it resides on the buyer's or seller's books), all debt issued (net of retirements), all of the buyer's equity issued (at current market prices), plus the market value of all seller liabilities assumed by the buyer.

An Exchange of Value.   A benefit of the net value added acquisition pricing framework is that it focuses on the exchange of value instead of on the exchange of earnings so popular with accounting enthusiasts. Let's say that an acquisition will contribute a positive net value added to the buyer but the accountants estimate that EPS will be diluted as a result of the acquisition. Then the buyer will end up selling for a higher P/E multiple, that's all. A true believer in the economic model of valuation will not even bother to compute the EPS consequences of an acquisition. I don't. It just doesn't matter.

Separation of Operating from Financing Decisions.   Another benefit of this framework is that it properly isolates the operating issues from the financing decisions. Suppose, for example, that a buyer judged the total value received from a prospective seller to be $200 million, whereas the total value paid by the buyer was to be $150 million, all in the form of 15 million newly

Exhibit 9.4 Net Value Added or Lost Drives Acquirer's Stock Prices

"Win-Win"

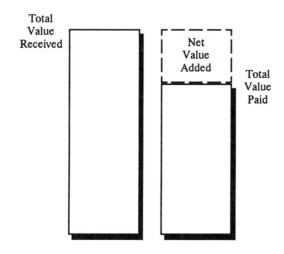

"Win-Lose"

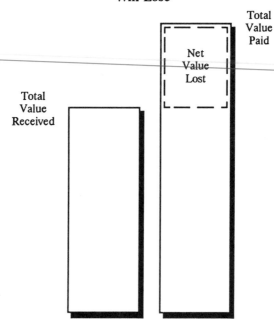

issued shares currently selling for $10 each. The difference between the total value received and the total value paid, or net value added of $50 million ($200 − $150), would accrue to the benefit of the buyer's shareholders no matter what the immediate impact on EPS happened to be.

Now suppose that $50 million of preferred stock and $100 million of common shares are issued (10 million shares at $10 each) to consummate this same transaction. Net value added is still $50 million, yet EPS will increase because fewer shares are issued. The addition to EPS, however, will be offset by a lower P/E multiple. A lower multiple is warranted because the buyer's shareholders will not ignore the increased financial risk they bear when prior-claim preferred stock is substituted for common stock. The new structure is no more valuable than the first, but you wouldn't know it by looking at EPS. Just concentrate on the exchange of value and let EPS fall where it will. In other words, separate the operating from the financing decisions.

The Two Components of NVA. Breaking net value added into two components provides more insight into the actual requirements for a successful acquisition. Total value received can be expressed as the seller's true intrinsic value as an independent entity plus the present value of all benefits, or synergies, expected to be realized through the combination. The total value paid (for a publicly traded company) can be divided into the seller's actual (preoffer) market value plus the premium paid for control.

Total value received = stand-alone value + synergy value

Total value paid = actual market value + premium

By subtraction:

Net value added = (stand-alone value − actual value
+ (synergy value − premium)

Two potential sources of value added for the buyer can now be identified: First, can an undervalued company whose true worth is not fully reflected in its current market value be acquired? Possibly, but not likely, given the overwhelming evidence on market sophistication. It is better to assume that potential targets are fairly valued (absent any leak about the buyer's intentions), in which case the first term is for naught.

That leaves the second term as the sole reliable source of a win-win transaction: The perceived value of all synergies must exceed the premium paid for control. Thus, two things are necessary for an acquisition to be truly successful: (1) There must be some true commercial significance, that is, value must be created through the combination that investors could not duplicate merely by holding both the buyer's and seller's shares in their portfolios, and (2) the premium negotiated must preserve some of the added value for the buyer. This suggests that an incremental approach to identifying acquisition candidates may be the most fruitful. Ignore whether the acquisition candidate itself is fairly valued (that is the market's job) and ignore accounting consequences. Simply evaluate the unique improvements in value that will come about as a result of the combination and pay something less as a premium. Of course, when buying a private company, there is no getting around placing a value on the seller as an independent entity. The intrinsic value of the seller, however, does establish a theoretical floor value beneath which a private seller is better off holding on.

If other potential purchasers are rational and go through a similar pricing calculus, the premium that a seller will be able to exact will reflect the value created by merging with the second highest value-adding buyer. If so, only the most value-adding merger partner could afford to pay the premium and still create value for its shareholders. It is not a question of being a good merger partner; it is a question of being the best merger partner. Of course, if acquirers behave irrationally, as they frequently do (after all, if the world were rational, men would ride sidesaddle), an acquisition can be won over a more logical merger partner— but only if the buying company is willing to suffer a reduction in share price. Thus, a wide-open market for acquisition candidates provides a structure of rewards and penalties encouraging corporate assets to move into the hands of managers and companies best able to maximize their value.

For details of the Marriott-Saga win-win acquisition, see exhibit 9.5, and for those of a win-lose acquisition—of Signal by Allied—see exhibit 9.6.

Exhibit 9.5   A Win-Win Acquisition: Marriott Acquires Saga

Introduction

Marriott's purchase of Saga is a good example of a win-win transaction. The value created by the combination was split between the two parties. When the acquisition was first announced on May 7, 1986, the buyer's as well as the seller's stock soared.

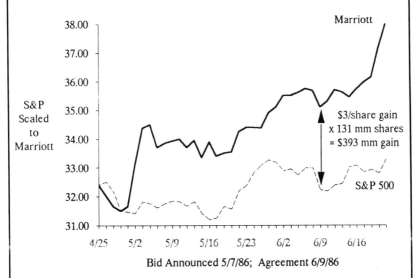

Bid Announced 5/7/86; Agreement 6/9/86

By the time the acquisition terms were settled (June 9, 1986), Marriott's common stock had gained about $3 a share versus the S&P 500 for a total gain in value of almost $400 million (given that Marriott has 131 million shares outstanding). Needless to say, the Saga shareholders benefited as well. Marriott paid them a premium over market that was worth approximately $130 million in the aggregate. Thus, the value of the transaction to the buying and selling shareholders together was almost $530 million. That is a measure of the value that investors expected Mariott to realize from the prospective synergies.

EPS Dilution Does Not Count

Saga was selling for around $28 a share when Marriott offered to pay $34. But to win the Saga board's approval, and to deter other suitors, Marriott eventually increased the offer to $39.50.

"I'm a little surprised that Marriott went that high," said Joseph J. Doyle, a senior vice president at Smith Barney Harris Upham & Co. "It's not their style to pay so much that future earnings are diluted." Mr. Doyle projected that Marriott's earnings per share next year will be diluted by about 3% because of the Saga purchase.

"Saga Endorses Sweetened Bid from Marriott"
The Wall Street Journal
June 10, 1986

In spite of the potential dilution, however, Marriott's common shares responded to the economics of the transaction and appreciated about 8% in value over the time the acquisition was in the works. With an 8% higher share price but 3% lower pro forma earnings, Marriott's P/E multiple increased by 11%, again showing why EPS movements are a misguiding guide to the merits of a transaction.

The Rationale

Concluding in 1984 that contract food services were a largely untapped growth opportunity (85% of the institutional food service market was self-operated at the time), Marriott acquired two food service companies (Service Systems and Gladieux) in 1985, thereby tripling the volume of its activities in that field. Integration of the two acquisitions was swift. Administrative costs were slashed, and profit margins were improved. Having won its spurs with the two smaller acquisitions, Marriott launched an unsolicited offer to acquire Saga in mid-1986.

Prospective Synergies

By that time, Marriott was the number three contract food service company in America, trailing only second-ranked Saga and the industry leader, Philadelphia-based ARA Services Inc. Bringing Saga together with Marriott would create the largest food service concern in America and give Marriott the management depth and marketing clout it needed to make significant inroads into the vast realm of the food services market that still was self-operated.

Whereas normally one thinks of the acquirer adding to the value of the acquired company, in this case the target brought more to the table than the buyer. Saga was considered to be the premier food service company in both the education and health care sectors (the largest and most rapidly growing sectors of the contract food service business, respectively). Its accounts were the largest and most prestigious and its client retention rate the highest in the industry. James M.

Meyer, research director for Janney Montgomery Scott, said he believed Marriott's reputation would be helped by acquiring Saga, making it easier for the company to "sign national contracts with major customers."[3] In terms of creating value, it does not matter in which direction the benefits flow, as long as the benefits are real and realizable.

Another big plus for Marriott was that Saga's restaurant operations, which contributed half of the company's overall profits, could be sold to other parties in a better position than Marriott to realize their full potential values. For example, on August 5, 1986, less than 2 months after Saga's board had given its approval to the acquisition, Marriott announced the sale of four of Saga's restaurants—Black Angus, Grandy's, Velvet Turtle, and Spectrum Foods—to an investor group headed by Anwar Soliman, the former head of W. R. Grace's restaurant group. Then, on December 3, 1986, just 4 months later, Marriott disclosed it was selling all 20 of its Cattle Company restaurants to Ground Round, a unit of Hanson Trust PLC of Britain. With quick turnarounds like those, Marriott obviously had done its homework by identifying and perhaps sounding out logical buyers before making its first move. Prices for the individual transactions were not disclosed, but, all told, Marriott recovered about one-half of the $700 million purchase price by selling Saga's restaurants and administrative facilities.

As with the two small acquisitions, Saga's operations and support staffs could be quickly combined with Marriott's and restructured. Significant margin improvement could be expected through administrative savings, elimination of duplicate facilities, and procurement economics.

The Net Value Added

Marriott's and Saga's stock price movements indicate that investors placed a $526 million value on the prospective synergies. Of that, $133 million, or 25%, was transferred to the Saga shareholders via the premium over market that Marriott paid for their shares. The balance, or $393 million, was the net value added for the benefit of the Marriott shareholders; it accounted for the $3 a share appreciation vis-à-vis the market. If Saga's board had evaluated the transaction in those terms, perhaps it would have held out for an even higher price.

[3]"Saga Stock Soars Amid Signs Marriott's Offer of $34 a Share Will Be Rejected," *The Wall Street Journal,* May 9, 1986.

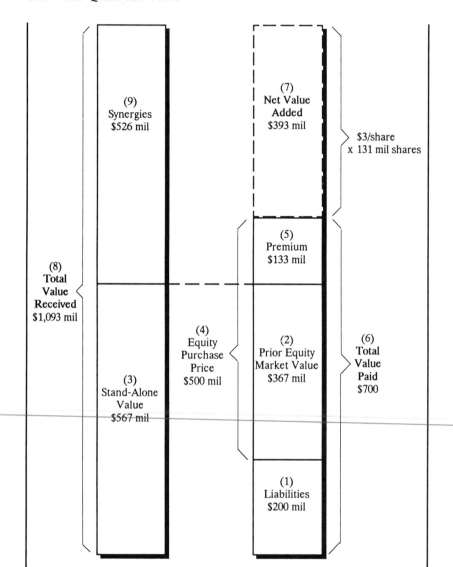

Here is how to read the valuation messages contained within the stock price entrails. Start in the lower right-hand corner of the chart above (labeled item #1). It shows the $200 million in Saga liabilities that Marriott assumed. Prior to Marriott's first offer, Saga was trading for $27⅞. With 12.7 million shares outstanding, Saga's market capitalization prior to the acquisition (item #2) was $367 million (12.7 million shares × $27⅞). This, plus the $200 million in liabilities, implies a total stand-alone value of $567 million for Saga which, assuming that the company was fairly valued in the market, should be equal to the present value of its projected free cash flow (or EVA) in the absence of a takeover (item #3).

In the end, Marriott paid $39.50 for each of Saga's 12.7 million shares, a total equity purchase price of $500 million (item #4). That represents a $133 million premium over the preexisting market value (item # 5), and it raises the total value paid, including the assumed liabilities, to $700 million (item # 6). Marriott's stock price shot up by about $3 a share versus the market. Multiplying that share price gain by the 131 million Marriott shares outstanding indicates that the net value added for Marriott's shareholders is $393 million (item #7). In view of the gain, the total value received (item #8) apparently is $1,093 million. That, in turn, represents a $526 million premium over Saga's stand-alone value, a premium that is attributable to the anticipated value of the synergies (item #9).

Acquisition Pricing

In pricing acquisitions, the entrail reading is reversed. Instead of working back from share price movements to synergies, a quantification of the value of potential synergies can be used to predict the likely share price reaction to a proposed acquisition. The challenge is to estimate the total value received by the buyer from the seller either in the aggregate including the synergies or by taking the value of the synergies separately simulated as an addition to the seller's stand-alone value. No matter how it is done, the total value received represents the most that could be paid for the target without reducing the acquirer's share value.

Acquisition Benefits

Determining the value of acquisition benefits is most clearly identified by the value-driver model of valuation (though it is most accurately simulated by projecting and discounting FCF, or better, EVA, to a present value):

$$\text{Value} = \frac{\text{NOPAT}}{c} + tD + \frac{I(r-c^*)T}{c^*(1+c^*)}$$

1. *Operating benefits.* Operating benefits encompass synergies which will increase net operating profits (NOPAT) or which en-

---

Exhibit 9.6   A Win-Lose Acquisition:
Allied Acquires Signal

Introduction

In contrast to the warm reception showered upon Marriott's acquisition of Saga, the stock market reacted very unfavorably to Allied's proposed merger with the Signal Companies. In this win-lose transaction, Allied paid far more than the value that lead steers thought likely to be created by the combination, leaving the selling shareholders with an attractive gain and the buying shareholders with wounds to lick.

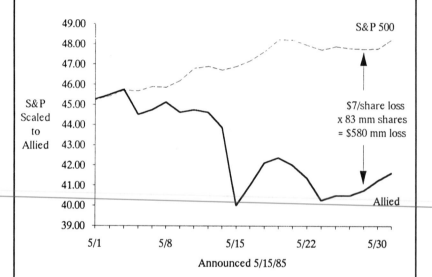

Announced 5/15/85

The acquisition sent Allied's shares reeling down about $7 apiece relative to the S&P 500, a loss in value of approximately $600 million overall (Allied had about 83 million shares outstanding at the time). The Signal shareholders, on the other hand, walked away with an almost $1.1 billion premium. The difference between the seller's gain and the buyer's loss is a net gain of only about $500 million. That is the perceived value of the synergies to be produced by the combination, a rather negligible gain in relation to the combined market values of Allied and Signal.

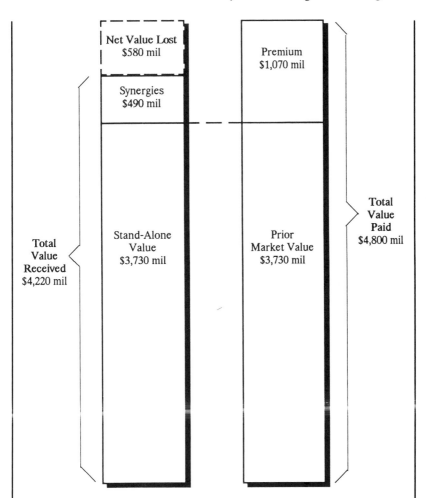

A reporter for *The New York Times* tried to dismiss Allied's initial share price reaction summarily:

> Traders attached no special significance to the decline in Allied [stock price], explaining that buyers' stocks almost always decline because of trading practices.
>
> "$5 Billion Allied Deal for Signal"
> *The New York Times*
> May 16, 1985

Oh, really! Apparently the traders were asleep at the switch during Marriott's and ConAgra's acquisitions, for in those cases they forgot to hold down the buyer's share prices with their usual trading practices. Again, broad-based research shows that the immediate stock price reaction is an unbiased measure of the long-run merits of a merger. It should not be cavalierly dismissed as an irrelevant and meaningless measure of an acquisition's merits, as the *Times* writer seems to suggest.

Allied's acquisition of Signal failed to win over investors for two principal reasons: (1) There were very few real and realizable synergies to be exploited as a result of the combination. The management of Allied seemed hopelessly preoccupied with many of the silly justifications I outlined at the beginning of this chapter, and which I will review in a moment, and (2) Allied paid too much. No matter how convincing the rationale may seem to be, it is very difficult to justify paying over a $1 billion premium for a $3.7 billion market capitalization company.

Growth for Growth's Sake

It is easy to see how management could be seduced by the sheer size and apparent significance of the combination. The $5 billion transaction represented the largest industrial merger in history to that point. It would produce a massive $16.7 billion sales entity and make Allied into one of the 20 largest industrial concerns in the United States. In the quest for value, however, size per se is unimportant.

What Price Glory?

Edward L. Hennessy, Jr., chairman and CEO of Allied, made a statement at the time that betrayed a willingness to pay almost any price to fulfill a fundamental business goal. He called the acquisition "key" to Allied's bid to transform itself into a high-technology concern focused on aerospace, automotive parts, and advanced materials.[4] Allied was primarily a chemical and electronics concern, whereas Signal was largely an automotive and aerospace company. The merger would more than double Allied's aerospace annual sales to $4.5 billion, boost its automotive sales to about $3 billion from $2 billion, and increase Allied's combined R&D and engineering budgets to more than $1 billion from almost $600 million.[5] Although the fit between the two companies appeared good on the surface, in reality the busi-

---

[4]"Allied-Signal Merger Yields Few Benefits," *The Wall Street Journal,* December 29, 1986.
[5]"Allied and Signal Say Staff Cuts Likely as Concerns Begin Merging Operations," *The Wall Street Journal,* September 19, 1985.

nesses failed to mesh at the molecular, or operational, level, at which real synergies can be produced. "Allied-Signal is still a collection of bits and pieces," said Paul Nesbit, aerospace industry analyst with Prudential-Bache Securities Inc., more than a year after the merger had become effective.[6]

At the time, however, even many of the securities analysts were taken in by the superficial potential for cross-fertilization among the many units. (Given Allied's stock price reaction, however, the lead steers were not paying attention to those gullible chaps.) John Simon, an analyst at Seidler Amdec Securities Inc., said he saw particularly strong benefits between operations of Signal's Garret Corporation and Allied's Bendix Company. "Together the combined companies will have more contact [with customers] with a variety of products," Mr. Simon said. "If they can set up a good communication system, they should be able to come up with new products and sales opportunities."[7]

What a pipe dream!

Signal's Garret is dominant in the business of making aircraft auxiliary power units, smaller jet engines, and turbo props. Allied's Bendix makes electronic systems and other parts. So where are the synergies again? To the extent an attempt is made to force cross-marketing between these units, without market power or distributional synergies to exploit, it can be safely predicted that both units' profits will suffer. Besides, if the marketing synergies between the two are so obvious and easily achieved, why did it take the acquisition to get them going? Why wouldn't Garret and Bendix already have worked out a contract to coordinate their marketing efforts? Very difficult, you say? Precisely the point.

Despite the glamour of the acquisition and the superficial fit, Hennessy ironically failed to achieve one of his most important strategic objectives: to become a prime defense contractor. Both Allied and Signal deal mainly in parts and electronics that do not qualify them for lead roles with the Pentagon.

> While praising the Signal purchase, Mr. Hennessy also acknowledges that the deal hasn't fulfilled his vision of transforming Allied into one of the world's premier aerospace concerns. As a result, he says he is likely to set his sights soon on another aerospace target. "I want

[6]"Allied-Signal Merger Yields Few Benefits," *The Wall Street Journal,* December 29, 1986.
[7]"Merged Allied, Signal Is Seen Needing Time to Forge Major Aerospace Force," *The Wall Street Journal,* May 17, 1985.

to be a prime contractor by the end of the decade," declares Mr. Hennessy.

"Allied-Signal Merger Yields Few Benefits"
The Wall Street Journal
December 29, 1986

Charitably, that did not happen.

Scarcity Value

In pursuit of the grand vision, Hennessy was mulling the acquisition of the Hughes Aircraft Company when he stumbled across the opportunity to acquire Signal. Recognizing that the opportunities to become a player in the aero-electronics big leagues were dwindling, Hennessy apparently felt justified in bidding top dollar for a "scarce property."

Why Not the Best?

"Signal has great technology, particularly in aerospace, automotive and electronics," according to Mr. Hennessy.[8] Maybe it has. But the value of that technology will already be factored into Signal's stock price. The question is, why will the two companies' R&D efforts combined be more effective than they are considered individually? Hennessy made a valiant but ultimately unpersuasive effort to explain that in his letter to shareholders.

One of the benefits of our merger with Signal is that the complementary nature of our key businesses offers us myriad opportunities to pool our scientific knowledge and expertise in the development of innovative proprietary products for our customers.

Shareholders' Letter
Allied Signal 1985 Annual Report

Things really haven't worked out that way after all.

The Accounting Consequences

The counter side to improving EPS is improving the P/E multiple. Hennessy apparently was willing to issue shares and dilute EPS because he thought it necessary to obtain the premium P/E multiple associated with a high-tech company. But companies do not sell for high multiples of earnings just because they are high-tech; the typical high-tech company sells for a high multiple because it can earn an

---

[8]"Allied Corp., Signal Cos. Propose $5 Billion Merger," *The Wall Street Journal,* May 16, 1985.

attractive rate of return in a rapidly expanding business. Those are the true requirements for a high multiple. Thus, there is no sex appeal, or multiple to be gained, in overpaying for an acquisition that lacks synergy, no matter how much high technology is involved. Once again, a concern over either EPOS or the P/E multiple is a very poor way to conceive of the merits of an acquisition, as this one profusely illustrates.

Postmortem

Allied's initial adverse stock market reaction underestimated the problems the acquisition subsequently posed. Ever since the merger, Allied's common shares have substantially underperformed the market.

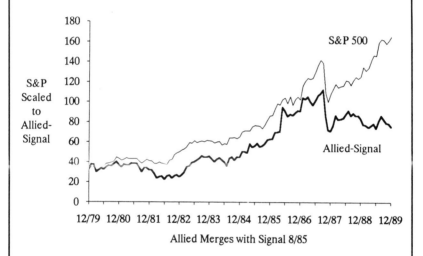

Allied Merges with Signal 8/85

In this respect the market could be accused of being myopic. The lead steers could not have imagined just how unrewarding the acquisition would turn out to be. Whereas initially the market foresaw the prospect of nearly $500 million worth of synergies, in the final analysis it seems that the merger produced diseconomies of scale. A strong case could now be made that Allied-Signal, if serious about creating value, should give up its high-tech, multidisciplinary theme and split into smaller, more focused units.

able the combined company to invest more (I) in attractive (group 1) projects, to earn higher returns (r) in the process, and for a longer period of time (T), or which permit the withdrawal of capital (reducing I) from unproductive activities where inadequate rates of return are being earned (such as surplus working capital, redundant facilities, or business units worth more to others).

Because c, the cost of capital for business risk, is determined by investors who are already well diversified in their portfolios, it is very difficult, if not impossible, to benefit from a lower cost of capital in an acquisition. A buyer should employ the seller's cost of capital in its valuation of the seller's business, because the buyer must compensate its investors for the risk being acquired.

2. *Financial benefits.* Borrowing against the seller's unused debt capacity or against an increase in consolidated debt capacity adds value. The increase in the tax shield of interest expense (tD) lowers the weighted average cost of capital. The value a buyer derives by borrowing against its own assets to undertake an acquisition, on the other hand, should not be treated as a benefit of the transaction. This value is always available to the buyer without an acquisition, if only by borrowing to retire shares. Thus, a recapitalization of the buyer in the course of an acquisition should not be considered an incremental benefit. (Of course, EPS and ROE as performance measures fail to make this subtle but important distinction.)

A merger also may save transaction costs through economies of scale in raising capital. At the same time, the costs of hiring the professionals needed to evaluate and close a deal, including investment bankers, lawyers, accountants, and Stern Stewart & Co., should be counted as an offset.

3. *Tax benefits.* The tax benefits derived from expensing the stepped-up basis of assets acquired or from the use of otherwise forfeited tax deductions or credits (NOLs, AMTs, FTCs, etc.), net of any tax recapture, will enhance cash flows.

The present value of all foreseeable operating, financial, and tax benefits, when weighted by the likelihood of their occurring, is the value added in the transaction. When divided by the number of seller shares outstanding, it represents the maximum price premium above the seller's stand-alone value that can be offered without diluting the buyer's share price.

Summary

For an acquisition to be successful in the stock market, it is necessary (1) that value be created (i.e., that the combination have some operating, financial, or tax benefit that shareholders cannot duplicate) and (2) that management be successful in negotiating a premium that does not exceed the amount of value created. When both conditions occur, the stock price of the buyer as well as of the seller can increase—right away. That is the hallmark of a successful acquisition.

Too often, acquisitions result in an erosion of the buying company's shareholders' wealth. That occurs when management, preoccupied with achieving accounting or business objectives, gives scant attention to the exchange of value driving stock prices. Paying unjustified premiums is tantamount to making charitable contributions to random passersby, never to be recouped by the buying company no matter how long the acquisition is held. To avoid such overpayments, management should identify potential benefits and then estimate the value that influential investors will place on them.

PART II

Static Finance

10

Financial Planning

Introduction

A financial plan can be static or dynamic. A *dynamic* financial structuring strategy makes business the servant of finance. Debt is employed aggressively, and preferably at a decentralized level, to pressure operations to become more efficient, to commit operations to pay out surplus cash, to draft managers and employees more significantly into the ranks of owners, and to save taxes. That strategy is discussed in chapter 13 and 14.

A *static* financial structuring strategy, which is the topic of this chapter, makes finance serve the business. A financial plan is tailored to anticipate and accommodate the cash flows generated or required by the most valuable business plan. There is an emphasis on maintaining an ample reserve of financial liquidity to weather business compressions and take advantage of fleeting investment opportunities.

Another difference is that instead of aiming to repay debt, which is the main thrust of the dynamic approach, the essence of the static planning philosophy is setting and adhering to a relatively fixed blend of debt and equity in the capital structure. The capital structure target should be the one that most effectively balances the tax and signaling benefits of debt financing against the company's ongoing need for financing flexibility.

In practice, this trade-off is best thought of in terms of a bond-rating objective. Moody's and Standard & Poor's bond ratings are a convenient scale to quantify the default risk to which a company is willing to be exposed. In general, the more accessibility a company needs to the capital markets to finance its growth and the more the company's broad stakeholder constituencies depend upon its continued financial strength, the less default risk the company can afford to take and the higher its bond rating ought to be, all other things being equal.

Once the bond-rating objective is established, the next step is to determine the capital structure that will bring it about. Proprietary research conducted by Stern Stewart & Co. shows that a company's bond rating is determined primarily by five factors that reflect track record, profitability, business risk, and leverage, measured in several ways. These five factors, when weighted by coefficients that are the same for all companies, sum to a score of financial strength corresponding to a bond rating. Thus, given a firm's operating attributes and other aspects of its financial structure, it is now possible to predict with a reasonable degree of accuracy the ratio of debt to capital that will produce a desired bond rating. This debt to capital ratio should be considered to be the company's target and a measure of the firm's "debt capacity."

In addition to setting debt policy, a comprehensive financial plan must provide the firm with adequate sources of liquidity, select an appropriate dividend policy, anticipate share issuances or retirements, and identify attractive financing instruments. All those policies should be mutually consistent with one another and, once set, be communicated to investors.

Sources and Uses of FCF

A free cash flow statement is a good place to begin our discussion because it establishes the connection between a company's business plan and its optimal financing strategy.

From the operating perspective, FCF is equal to all cash operating receipts less all cash operating disbursements (or NOPAT less the net new capital invested in the business).

$$FCF = NOPAT - I$$

From the financing side of the equation, FCF is equal to the net cash transactions with all providers of capital to the company, that is, the explicit cash financing charges (i.e., interest and dividends) less net new debt and equity funding.[1]

$$FCF = Interest - \begin{matrix} New \\ Debt \end{matrix} + Dividends - \begin{matrix} New \\ Equity \end{matrix}$$

Given that operating and financing FCF must balance, the question is this: In what sequence is it logical for the projected cash flow to be determined?

Business Planning First

The operating side of FCF should be determined first, for it will be the result of maximizing the firm's business values. The quality of operations management will be reflected in a series of projected NOPATs. The commitment of fresh capital to growth opportunities in which the rate of return is expected to surpass the required return, if not immediately, then eventually, is represented by the projected *I*'s. Combining the best budget to generate cash from operations with the best investment strategy to build value will dictate that a certain level of FCF will be forthcoming, which could be either positive or negative.

$$Operations\ \&\ Strategy = The\ Business\ Plan$$
$$NOPAT - I = FCF$$

So long as management maximizes operating efficiency and undertakes all value-adding group 1 projects (and nothing but group 1 projects), financial policies should be subordinated to business decisions. The financial plan should anticipate and accommodate the FCF generated or required by the most valuable business plan.

To begin with, then, a series of projections that show operating

---

[1]"Net" here refers to net of taxes, to net of the retirement of debt and equity, and to net of the change in marketable securities and of investment income.

profits and investment needs under a variety of planning scenarios should be prepared. The economic assumptions used in
constructing the scenarios should range from optimistic to pessimistic. The scenarios also should simulate the capital that might
be needed to finance unusual investment opportunities such as
acquisitions. Once done, a financial strategy should be tailored to
the FCF that arises from the operating scenarios, thereby ensuring
that the company has financial reserves adequate to withstand
adverse economic conditions and to capitalize on fleeting opportunities.

Debt Financing Strategy Is Next

Three policies appear on the financial side of FCF: debt policy,
dividend policy, and external equity policy (which is the firm's
posture on the question of raising or retiring equity).[2]

The Financial Plan	=	Debt policy	+ Dividend policy	+ External equity policy
FCF	= Interest −	New debt	+ Dividends	− New equity

Of the three, the policy for debt should be determined before
the others because it is the only one that can be shown logically
and empirically to have a long-lasting positive influence on share
value.[3] Be forewarned that the decision to next set the corporate
debt strategy implies that the policies with respect to dividends
and raising or retiring equity will have to bend to accommodate
it.

While there are a variety of ways to express debt policy, for our
purposes it will be specified as a target ratio of total debt to total
capital.[4] Putting the policy in terms of a ratio of debt to capital

[2]Paying interest expense is not a policy; it is a necessity. Besides, the interest component
of cash flow is determined once debt policy is set.
[3]This strict order of debt preference may be inverted for private companies in which
dividend policy and equity constraints may be more important.
[4]Total debt and total capital should include the present value of noncapitalized leases as
well as the explicit debt financing.

accommodates growth in the business and avoids the temptation to associate sources and uses of financing. It also facilitates the calculation of the weighted average cost of capital, for the weights employed will reflect this same target capital structure mix.

The Debt-Equity Trade-off

On the one hand, debt is cheaper than equity because of the tax-deductibility of interest. But debt should be used to the greatest practical extent for another reason too. Raising debt exudes confidence. Investors take it as a sign that management is reasonably certain the interest on the new debt can be covered. Raising equity conveys doubt. Investors suspect that management is attempting to shore up the firm's financial resources for rough times ahead by selling overvalued shares. As a result, announcements of new equity issues frequently depress a company's share price—an average decline of 3% or so—according to a broad-based academic study.[5] Disclosures of new bond issues, it has been found, typically have a neutral effect on stock price. Thus, the more leverage a company employs, the more growth it will be able to finance without having to alarm its investors by announcing the decision to raise new equity.

Too great a reliance on debt, however, also is unwise. It can lead to overly restrictive loan covenants, disqualification from the shelf registration of securities, a lockout from the commercial paper and swap markets, a loss of confidence by customers, suppliers, and employees, a diversion of scarce management time, missed investment opportunities, the forced sale of equity at depressed prices, and, ultimately, a loss of control through bankruptcy. Terrifying, isn't it?

Coleco Industries illustrates the dark side of using too much debt. Once the fabulously successful maker of Cabbage Patch Dolls, Coleco stumbled in 1987 and needed a $40 million loan to build inventories for Christmas. The banks said no, and so Coleco

---

[5] Paul Asquith and David Mullins, "Equity Issues and Offering Dilution," *Journal of Financial Economics* 15 (1986): 61–89.

had to go. It was liquidated, and kids everywhere mourned as the grinches stole Christmas. A company as promising, yet risky, as Coleco needed a lot of financing flexibility, or at least, more than it had.

Thus, in the end, a company's target capital structure should exploit the tax and signaling benefits of debt while holding financial risk at a manageable level and preserving liquidity. Financial risk may be considered to be manageable when the firm and its creditors are reasonably well protected against general economic downturns, changes in industry conditions, and specific company problems that might depress earnings. There probably are many ways to define it, but liquidity may be deemed to be adequate when the company can quickly and surely access funds sufficient to consummate a major strategic acquisition.

Bond Ratings and Target Capital Structure

It is useful to classify financial risk and liquidity in terms of bond ratings because the ratings are a widely recognized measure of creditworthiness. Furthermore, relating financial posture to a particular bond rating makes it easy to determine the availability and cost of funds in both the public and private debt markets.

Bonds are rated by Moody's, Standard & Poor's, Duff & Phelps, and Fitch. Each of the agencies claims to use a unique set of criteria, but their ratings are similar enough in practice that the Standard & Poor's nomenclature can be used to describe bond ratings in general. Bond ratings range from AAA, the designation of gilt-edged quality, all the way to CCC, suggesting that entombment is imminent. Beneath AAA are the AA-rated companies that, although also held in very high regard, possess slightly more long-term risk than the top rating. The next category, A, contains the largest group of rated companies. Although A is a good rating, it implies that there may be an impairment of timely debt service in the future. Just below A are the BBB-rated issues, the lowest of the investment-grade bonds. Beneath BBB are speculative, high-yielding junk bonds with ratings of BB and B. Most bonds rated in the lower categories are subordinated; that is, they are paid only after all senior debt obligations are satisfied.

The Risk of Default

The likelihood of default is directly related to a company's bond rating. Moody's examined the default experience of 3,042 issuers over the 20-year period from 1970 through 1989. Their study confirmed other earlier research by showing that "progressively lower-rated companies are much more likely to default on their obligations to bondholders."[6] Some of their findings are summarized in exhibit 10.1.

Exhibit 10.1	Average Cumulative Default Rates (1970–1989)			
	Time Period Covered (in Years)			
	3	5	10	15
AAA	0.0 %	0.2 %	0.7 %	1.7 %
AA	0.1	0.5	1.3	1.9
A	0.2	0.5	1.3	2.4
BBB	0.9	1.7	3.9	6.1
BB	5.5	8.9	14.3	18.0
B	15.9	21.1	26.4	28.7

Each cell in exhibit 10.1 states the cumulative probability that the companies with a given rating were unable to meet a scheduled principal or interest payment over a subsequent 3-, 5-, 10-, and 15-year period. For example, the figure 28.7 in the lower right-hand corner of the table indicates that nearly three out of ten of all companies that were rated B at a given time defaulted on their bonds within an ensuing 15-year period. There is a reason why they are called junk bonds, after all.

The results presented in exhibit 10.1 confirm that the risk of default increases as the rating grade worsens. Bond ratings indeed are a useful categorization of a company's potential exposure to credit risk. That should be obvious, but it is nice to have the

[6]"Corporate Bond Defaults and Default Rates, 1970–1989." *Moody's Special Report,* April 1990. Moody's Investor Service. Copyright 1990; reproduced by permission.

proof. As I read the table, Moody's findings also indicate that *there is no meaningful risk or difference in risk of default among the top three categories.* The risk of default for even just the A-rated companies over a subsequent 15-year period is less than 3%! In view of that finding, companies with an AAA or AA rating should give serious consideration to leveraging up their balance sheets to reduce their bond rating to no more than A. There will be an imperceptible change in their credit risks but a pronounced reduction in their overall costs of capital.

It is with a BBB rating that the risk of default becomes noticeable for the first time, though it is still rather small, I dare say. If history repeats itself, a company rated BBB has a chance of defaulting that is under 4%, or under 1 in 25, anytime over the next 10 years. It is slightly higher than 6%, or 1 in 16, over the next 15 years. Although those probabilities are more than twice the chances that the A- or AA-rated companies take, it still is rather negligible, don't you think? Besides, default does not necessarily mean bankruptcy. It may mean a few delayed payments, quickly resumed, a restructuring of debt, or one of many other possibilities shy of a liquidation. What it always means is embarrassment and bad press, and that has a cost, that's true. But the cost should be assessed by the impact on the business, and not how red-faced one might feel.

Choosing to *maintain* a target bond rating less than BBB is clearly risky. The likelihood of default increases appreciably as the rating falls below investment grade, the term used to connote a rating of BBB or better. Furthermore, companies with lower than a BBB rating are ineligible for shelf registrations of debt, a financing procedure that can be significantly less expensive than the traditional underwriting route. Also, in times of tight credit, companies of marginal creditworthiness can find themselves literally locked out of the market because investors will settle for nothing less than topflight bonds. For all these reasons, it probably does not make sense to adopt a target rating less than a medium BBB grade, unless the assets being financed generate tremendous levels of steady cash flow (e.g., McCaw Cellular, or MCI, which financed their growth by relying extensively on bonds rated less than investment grade) or in circumstances in which the senior managers also are significant owners.

Interest Rate is Irrelevant

The significance of bond ratings to the likelihood of default has not been missed by the investors in the bond market. Rates of interest on issues of similar maturity generally increase as bond ratings decrease, as the data in exhibit 10.2 for the year 1988 illustrate.

Exhibit 10.2	Bond Ratings and Borrowing Rates (1988 Average)			
Long-Term Government Bond Rate	AAA	AA	A	BBB
8.96%	9.36%	9.62%	9.99%	10.66%

Sources: *Federal Reserve Bulletin* and *Moody's Bond Record.*

As interesting as this progression may be as a confirmation of the significance of bond ratings as measures of credit risk, it does not imply that interest rates should be a factor in selecting a target capital structure. Though a company that adopts a more aggressive leverage target will have to pay a higher rate of interest on the money it borrows, it will also have less equity in its capital structure. So long as the interest on the debt shelters operating profits from being fully taxed, the more debt, the lower the overall weighted average cost of capital will be, and that is what is important. The optimal capital structure trade-off simply cannot be properly evaluated in terms of an effect on the interest rate paid on one of the components of capital. That is an irrelevant consideration, and it ought to be ignored.

More Is Less

The appropriate bond-rating objective does depend, however, on a company's need for capital, but inversely. A company with an abundance of prospective group 1 projects and negative FCF certainly has an appetite for new capital. But precisely because it does require continuous access to funding, such a company should restrain its borrowing and rely more extensively on equity. A higher rather than lower bond rating is advisable in these circumstances. Novell and Cypress Semiconductor, which have many attractive, albeit high-risk, investment opportunities and negative FCF quite sensibly do not borrow. As a matter of fact, they do just the opposite. Cypress, as an example, has raised common equity and invested most of the proceeds in rather low risk marketable securities as a means of deleveraging its business risk and securing a reserve to prefund its future investment needs.

But the less a company needs capital, either because it generates positive FCF or has only group 2 or group 3 projects to finance (whose absence will not be missed and, in fact, may be appreciated), the less important it is to have a high bond rating and the more capital should be borrowed, as a general rule.

Stakeholders

Another consideration in selecting a bond-rating objective is how it might affect the company's stakeholders. A customer who buys a product that requires replacement parts and service, a manager who dedicates his or her career to a company in which the skills gained are not transferable, a supplier that invests in specialized assets for the company's benefit, all have an interest in the sponsor's ongoing financial strength. As a result, a company that is more likely to wind up in financial distress may have to discount its product prices, pay more to its employees, and receive poorer terms from its suppliers and distributors.[7] But, again, based upon the historical record, the stakeholders would appear to have little basis for concern for companies rated A or higher, and even BBB-rated companies impose little additional risk on these broader constituencies.

Introducing The Stern Stewart & Co. Bond Rating System

Once a bond-rating objective has been determined, the question becomes how much debt a company can borrow. The answer is

[7]This section draws upon the article, "Financing Corporate Growth," by Bradford Cornell and Alan F. Shapiro, *The Journal of Applied Corporate Finance*, Summer 1988, vol. 1, no. 2.

facilitated by a financial analysis of all industrial and service companies with rated debt obligations conducted each year by my colleagues at Stern Stewart & Co. This analysis employs a powerful statistical technique, multiple discriminant analysis, to identify the quantifiable factors that are best able to assign companies to their bond-rating categories. Each year the same five factors among the many bonds analyzed emerge as the most important in determining a company's creditworthiness and debt capacity.

1. *Size.* Company size, as measured by total assets, has been found to be the single most important indicator of debt capacity. Being large is a measure of a company's track record and durability. It proves that a company has survived many business cycles and therefore manufactures products or provides services of enduring value. Larger companies also tend to have greater depth to their managements, more diversification of risk, and better access to financial markets. And, to be quite frank, larger companies, because they have a greater number of stakeholders, are better able to marshal political sentiment for their survival. (Witness the tariff protection given to U.S. Steel and the bailouts of Chrysler and Continental Illinois Bank.) Thus, while size per se probably is unimportant, a company's size does convey reliable information about many significant aspects of credit quality.

2. *Risk-adjusted return.* The second most important factor, the risk-adjusted rate of return, is a combined measure of the level and stability of a company's cash-flow-generating ability. It is computed by taking the trailing 5-year average rate of return on total capital and then subtracting one standard deviation in the return. The higher it is, the greater is a company's ability to generate cash to service debt even in the down years of a business cycle.

The rate of return used in this calculation encompasses the earnings generated by all of a company's assets, both operating and passive. It is computed by taking total profits after taxes (TPAT), and dividing by total capital employed. TPAT is the NOPAT earned in the business plus passive (e.g., marketable securities) income after taxes. Similarly, total capital is the capital tied up in the business (net working capital and net fixed assets) plus passive investments. The TPAT to total capital rate of return, and not the return on net business assets alone, is used because bondholders as general creditors can look to all of the firm's assets for repayment, and are exposed to all of the firm's risks.

3. *Ratio of long-term debt to total capital.* Leverage, as measured by the 3-year average ratio of long-term debt to total capital, is a proxy for management's target capital structure. The more leverage a company chooses to use, the more difficult it is to service debt, all other things being equal.

Short-term debt is left out of debt in the leverage ratio because it is not subject to the long-term business risks that enter into a bond-rating assessment. (Including short-term debt was found to actually reduce the statistical significance of the rating predictions.) Long-term debt and total capital do include the present value of noncapitalized operating leases (over the next 5 years) in order to assess all of the long-term-debt-like obligations (again, the statistical analysis proved that including the leases added to the overall accuracy of the model's predictions).

4. *Ratio of adjusted total liabilities to net worth.* The ratio of total liabilities to net worth brings into the picture other liabilities besides long-term debt that might look to net worth as a protective cushion in bankruptcy. Total liabilities includes, for example, all short-term debt, all trade financing, and, if the pension plan is in deficit, the unfunded accumulated benefits (pretax). If the pension plan has a surplus, on the other hand, total liabilities is unchanged, but net worth is increased by the after-tax value of the overfunded portion. Incidentally, the statistical analysis indicated that no improvement in the accuracy of the predictions was gained by substituting tangible net worth for stated net worth in this ratio. Unlike the long-term debt to total capital ratio, which is taken as a 3-year average, this ratio is computed by using only the most recent year's data in order to provide a sensitive barometer of imminent bankruptcy risk.

5. *Ratio of investments and advances to unconsolidated subsidiaries to total capital.* The equity invested in a subsidiary protects the debt on the subsidiary's books and should not be counted a second time as creating debt capacity for the parent. The greater this double-leverage ratio, the lower the bond rating is apt to be. The ratio is computed for just the most recent year.

Those five factors, which collectively measure a company's

size, profitability, business risk, and debt and debt-like financing both on and off its balance sheet, explain about 70% of the bond ratings covered by the survey. When the ratings this system predicts differ from the actual ratings, they almost never miss by more than one grade, and there is reason to believe that the predicted ratings are often more accurate than the actual ones. The agencies are loathe to revise bond ratings until long after a company's true creditworthiness has changed. A change in the rating is an acknowledgment that the original credit assessment was in error. The agencies understandably wish to minimize such occurrences.

Perhaps it is surprising that interest coverage, or debt to cash flow, is not among the five factors in the Bond Rating System. Not that covering interest or servicing principal payments is unimportant. Both of them most certainly are important. But once a company's profitability and leverage have been considered, interest and cash flow coverage, among many other ratios, become redundant.

A Survey of the Bond Rating Factors

The average values for the five bond rating factors are presented in exhibit 10.3 for the year 1988 (given the inevitable delays in gathering and analyzing the data, the 1989 results are available only as of August 1990). As the rating becomes progressively lower, it is clear that asset size and the risk-adjusted return fall off and the leverage ratios rise. The importance of investments to capital, or double leverage, is not apparent across categories. It

Exhibit 10.3 Bond Rating Factors for 1988

	AAA	AA	A	BBB	BB	B
Total assets ($B)	$27.2	$13.4	$4.8	$4.4	$1.7	$1.1
Risk-adjusted return	12.1%	10.7%	6.7%	2.5%	−3.9%	−2.6%
LT debt/total capital	12.5%	17.4%	26.9%	35.9%	35.5%	52.3%
Adj tot liab/ net worth	0.8×	1.0×	1.2×	1.8×	2.8×	5.1×
Investments/ total capital	6.3%	7.7%	6.4%	8.1%	6.5%	3.0%

serves to modify the rating of individual companies within categories.

It should now be apparent why credit risk is so high for companies with less than investment grade bonds. For one thing, the BB- and B-rated companies as a group had negative risk-adjusted returns. Over a given 5-year period, there will be individual years in which many of them will lose money from operations, that is, before they even begin to make interest payments. As if that were not enough, to compound their misery, these hapless companies have by far the highest leverage ratios of the surveyed firms.

A Bond-Rating Scoring Illustration

The five bond rating factors, when multiplied by coefficients that are the same for all companies, sum to a score of financial strength that corresponds to a predicted bond rating.[8] In exhibit 10.4 the scoring method is illustrated for ConAgra as of the close of its 1989 fiscal year (FYE May 31, 1989). The overall bond rating score of 3.65 correctly predicts ConAgra to have a solid A rating for its senior debt obligations.

Before multiplying by the coefficient for size, it is necessary to take the natural log of the assets (expressed in millions of dollars). Taking the natural log has the effect of squeezing down differences in raw size (and encourages learning how to use a neglected function key on the HP 12C calculator). As a company doubles in size, for example, the natural log increases only linearly.

Assets ($ millions)	1,000	2,000	4,000
Natural log of assets	6.91	7.60	8.29
Difference		0.69	0.69

The difference in the log of the assets is in essence a measure of the number of years it would take for a company to grow at a constant rate from one size to the next. The natural log thus transforms assets from a measure of sheer size to a measure of track record, which is what really matters.

[8]The Bond Rating Scoring System is a proprietary service of Stern Stewart & Co. It is presented as one of the reports within FINANSEER™, the firm's PC software system for financial spreading, forecasting, value planning, and financial structuring.

Exhibit 10.4 Bond Rating Score for ConAgra

	Value	×	Coefficient	=	Score	
Total assets	8.4*		.5320		4.45	BBB
Risk-adj return	14.7%†		.0958		1.41	AAA
LTD/total capital	40.3%‡		−.0458		−1.85	BB
Adj total liabs/NW	3.1×§		−.0939		−0.30	BB
Invest & adv/tot cap	7.4%		−.0077		−0.06	AAA
Senior debt score					3.65	A

Bond Rating Score Scale

B	BB	BBB	A	AA	AAA

|- - - - - - - -|- - - - - - - -|- - - - - - - -|- - - - - - - -|- - - - - - - -|- - - - - - - -|

| −2.1 | 0.0 | 1.5 | 2.8 | 4.1 | 5.2 | 6.2 |

*The natural log of FYE 1988 total assets, expressed in millions of dollars (i.e., natural log of $4,278 million).

†The rates of return (TPAT/total capital) for the years 1985 to 1989 were 17.8%, 16.2%, 24.9%, 15.0%, and 19.1%. The average return is 18.6%; the standard deviation is 3.9%; and the difference is the risk-adjusted return of 14.7%.

‡The long term debt to total capital ratios for the three FYE, 1987 to 1989 were 40.2%, 40.8%, 39.9%, an average of 40.3%. ConAgra has a policy of being completely out of short-term debt by the end of its fiscal year. However, in 1989, ConAgra had $331.0 million of short-term borrowings on its books, the result of a pooling of interests merger. The short-term debt was more than offset by $476.5 million in marketable securities outstanding, an unusually high level. Thus, to make the company's capital structure in 1989 consistent with that of the prior years, total capital was reduced by the amount of the incidental short term debt of $331 million before computing the ratio of long term debt to total capital.

§ConAgra reported total liabilities of $3,211.6 million as of FYE 1989. This figure is reduced by the incidental short term debt of $331.0 million and is increased by the present value of noncancelable leases over 5 years, or $234.1 million, for a net total liabilities of $3,114.7. The reported net worth of $958.2 is increased by $33.0 million, the after-tax amount by which the pension plan was overfunded (the plan was overfunded $53.2 million pretax, or $33.0 million after taxes, assuming a 38% marginal corporate income tax rate), for a total net worth of $991.2. Thus, the adjusted total liabilities to net worth ratio is 3.1× ($3,114.7/$991.2).

The ratings appearing in the farthest right column of exhibit 10.4 are the categories that would be assigned to each of Con Agra's factors if they were viewed in isolation. For example, with assets of $4.3 billion, ConAgra's size most closely resembles that of a typical BBB-rated company (confirm this by interpolating the table presented in exhibit 10.3). ConAgra is able to qualify as an A-rated company only because AAA profitability overcomes its relatively small size and rather high leverage.

The Bond-Rating Trade-off

As ConAgra well illustrates, the individual considerations that enter into an assessment of a company's creditworthiness can offset one another in a way that mere mortals might find difficult to discern. This trade-off is even more apparent across the sample of companies presented exhibit 10.5. Both General Electric and Bristol-Myers, for example, are AAA-rated companies, though their qualifications for the top slot are very different. Bristol-Myers is but one-eighth the size of GE (although the logs of their assets, which is what really matters, differ by only 2.09; see columns 4 and 5). Bristol-Myers' superior risk-adjusted profitability (column 8) and more conservative financial structure (columns 8, 9, and 10), however, make up the difference. The overall scores calculated for the two companies are virtually identical (column 1), and they correctly predict the AAA rating both are accorded.

As hard as it may be to fathom, the credit risks of the gigantic Mobil Corporation ($38.4 billion in assets) and the relatively Lilliputian W. W. Grainger, Inc. ($936 million) are judged to be the same. Their bond rating scores (and actual bond ratings) are neck and neck because Grainger shines in every way that Mobil is lacking.

Comparing companies in different categories also can be revealing. Even though their risk-adjusted rates of return are almost the same, Westinghouse is rated AA and FMC is rated BB, a full three grades lower. FMC is only a quarter of Westinghouse's size, but the chief difference between them is leverage. Whereas Westinghouse has maintained a reasonably conserva-

Exhibit 10.5   The Bond Rating Tradeoff

Company	(1) Debt Score 1988	(2) Predicted Bond Rating	(3) S&P Bond Rating	(4) Assets	(5) Log Assets	(6) Average Total Return	(7) Std Dev Total Return	(8) Risk Adj Return	(9) Avg LTD/ Tot Cap	(10) Liab/ NW	(11) Inv & Adv/ Tot Cap
AAA											
General Electric	5.71	AAA	AAA	$41,924	10.64	12.3%	1.0%	11.3%	17.8%	1.09x	15.8%
Bristol-Myers	5.92	AAA	AAA	5,190	8.55	19.9	1.0	18.9	8.5	0.48	0.0
AA											
Mobil Corp	4.42	AA	AA	38,484	10.56	5.7	3.7	1.9	25.9	1.25	9.7
Westinghouse Electric	4.63	AA	AA	10,527	9.26	9.4	2.6	6.8	14.5	2.02	12.7
Wal-Mart Stores	4.85	AA	AA	6,360	8.76	22.8	1.6	21.2	37.4	1.28	0.0
Kimberly-Clark	4.81	AA	AA	4,268	8.36	15.2	0.7	14.5	19.1	0.88	7.9
Pitney-Bowes	4.40	AA	AA	2,332	7.75	14.7	2.0	12.7	15.9	0.65	18.7
Grainger Inc	4.61	AA	AA	936	6.84	14.2	1.6	12.6	4.3	0.44	0.0
Premier Industrial	4.42	AA	AA	278	5.63	19.3	2.1	17.2	3.9	0.24	2.5
A											
AMR Corp	3.14	A	A	9,722	9.18	10.0	2.0	8.0	50.4	2.14	0.0
ConAgra Inc	3.73	A	A	4,278	8.36	18.6	3.9	14.7	38.4	3.48	6.4
Intel Corp	3.46	A	A	3,550	8.17	9.3	9.6	-0.3	15.2	0.72	12.4
Corning Glass	3.85	A	A	2,898	7.97	9.6	1.6	8.0	18.8	0.78	29.4
Stanley Works	3.34	A	A	1,405	7.25	11.4	1.0	10.4	31.1	0.97	0.0
Standard Register	3.44	A	A	444	6.10	14.6	2.0	12.6	21.0	0.51	0.0

Exhibit 10.5 continued

Company	(1) Debt Score 1988	(2) Predicted Bond Rating	(3) S&P Bond Rating	(4) Assets	(5) Log Assets	(6) Average Total Return	(7) Std Dev Total Return	(8) Risk Adj Return	(9) Avg LTD/ Tot Cap	(10) Liab/ NW	(11) Inv & Adv/ Tot Cap
BBB											
Burlington Northern	2.21	BBB	BBB	6,330	8.75	5.8	7.6	-1.9	39.4	4.97	0.0
Nat'l Medical Enterpri	2.51	BBB	BBB	3,877	8.26	10.4	1.9	8.5	53.7	2.62	0.0
Phelps Dodge	2.08	BBB	BBB	2,755	7.92	7.1	14.2	-7.1	29.8	0.59	4.4
Int'l Minerals	1.90	BBB	BBB	1,794	7.49	3.6	6.6	-3.0	34.4	0.75	19.2
U.S. Shoe Corp	1.84	BBB	BBB	1,111	7.01	8.5	2.6	5.9	49.7	1.91	0.0
Wendy's	2.17	BBB	BBB	765	6.64	10.2	7.0	3.2	34.3	0.85	2.5
Cincinnati Milacron	1.97	BBB	BBB	692	6.54	2.3	4.7	-2.4	24.4	1.60	1.7
BB											
FMC Corp	0.42	BB	BB	2,749	7.92	10.1	3.8	6.3	74.8	10.00	4.0
B											
Turner	-1.40	B	B	1,859	7.53	3.4	11.2	-7.9	81.0	10.00	1.6
Ideal Basic	-1.80	B	B	335	5.82	-4.9	8.6	-14.0	49.9	13.50	0.0

tive financial posture, FMC performed a leveraged recapitalization in 1986.

One implication of the trade-off among the various factors is that an attempt to determine the debt capacity of a company or its individual business units in terms of a single measure, such as interest coverage or debt to cash flow, is insufficient to capture the rich complexity involved in assessing creditworthiness properly. Five factors (plus a bit of judgment) are really necessary.

Predicting Subordinated Rating

There is a notable scarcity of firms with senior debt rated in the bottom categories of exhibit 10.5. That's because most of the lower-rated issues are subordinated debentures. The rating agencies as a general rule consider subordinated debt to be about one full grade lower in quality than the rating assigned to the senior debt for the same company. Our analysis confirmed this rule of thumb in that, to predict subordinated ratings, the Bond Rating Scoring System downshifts a company's senior debt score by a constant 1.59 (which is about the range of a single bond-rating grade), and then interpolates the result on the same scale as is used for the senior debts.

The approach is illustrated in exhibit 10.6. Stone Container, for example, has issued subordinated debentures rated weak BB. Weighting the five factors in the usual manner produces a score of 2.07, which would qualify Stone's senior debt for a middling BBB rating. Subtracting the constant 1.59 from its senior score of 2.07 leaves 0.48, a score which, when interpolated on the same scale, correctly predicts a rating of weak BB for the Stone's subordinated bonds, roughly one grade less than its predicted senior debt rating.

A Simulation

One of the more important applications of the Bond Rating Scoring System is to help management select a target debt policy. Suppose, for example, that ConAgra's management wanted to investigate the consequences of reducing the company's bond

Exhibit 10.6 Subordinated Bond Ratings

	(1)	(2)	(3)	(4)	(5)	(6)	(7)	(8)	(9)	(10)	(11)	(12)
Company	Senior Debt Score	Sub Debt Score	Predicted Sub Debt Rating	S&P Sub Debt Rating	Assets	Log Assets	Average Total Return	Std Dev Total Return	Risk Adj Return	Average LTD/ Tot Cap	Liab/ NW	Inv & Adv/ Tot Cap
BBB												
Penn Central Corp	3.62	2.04	BBB	BBB-	$2,400	7.78	4.9%	2.4%	2.5%	10.7%	0.37x	30.7%
Ecolab Inc	3.12	1.53	BBB	BBB	943	6.85	14.6	4.2	10.3	30.2	1.31	1.3
Rohr Industries	3.19	1.60	BBB	BBB	883	6.78	15.6	5.4	10.3	28.0	1.34	0.0
BB												
Santa Fe Southern	2.41	0.82	BB	BB-	6,824	8.83	3.5	4.8	-1.3	29.7	8.50	1.0
Reynolds Metals Co	2.11	0.52	BB	BB+	5,032	8.52	5.6	11.1	-5.5	35.8	1.43	16.1
Wang Labs	2.52	0.93	BB	BB+	2,838	7.95	7.2	7.5	-0.3	33.2	1.03	7.6
Stone Container	2.07	0.48	BB	BB-	2,395	7.78	13.0	8.1	4.9	52.6	1.21	2.7
Pittston Co	1.96	0.37	BB	BB+	992	6.90	-0.1	4.1	-4.1	25.1	1.41	4.8
Caesars World	1.87	0.28	BB	BB-	831	6.72	10.3	4.4	6.0	42.0	3.76	0.0
Home Depot	2.30	0.71	BB	BB-	699	6.55	15.0	5.7	9.2	42.6	1.25	0.0
Ohio Mattress	2.38	0.79	BB	BB+	542	6.30	23.2	16.8	6.4	32.5	1.02	0.0
Thermo Electron	2.00	0.41	BB	BB-	490	6.19	7.4	1.7	5.7	37.0	1.61	0.0
Hexcel Corp	2.11	0.52	BB	BB-	312	5.74	10.4	2.0	8.4	35.3	1.47	0.0
B												
Bally Manufacturing	1.16	-0.42	B	B+	2,867	7.96	5.4	1.8	3.5	64.9	4.25	4.9
Service Merchandise	1.03	-0.56	B	B+	1,711	7.44	8.6	3.7	4.9	66.5	3.78	0.0
Carter Hawley Hale	0.61	-0.98	B	B-	1,674	7.42	5.3	2.5	2.9	58.3	10.00	0.5
Cooper Cos	0.94	-0.65	B	B-	1,138	7.04	9.5	10.2	-0.7	41.9	8.36	4.5
Anchor Glass	0.37	-1.20	B	B	773	6.65	18.7	10.5	8.2	66.0	9.90	0.0
Ramada Inc	0.72	-0.87	B	B-	705	6.56	4.3	0.9	3.4	61.2	2.24	10.5
Blount Inc	0.88	-0.70	B	B+	613	6.42	6.1	9.8	-3.7	41.1	3.04	0.8
Multimedia	-0.50	-2.10	B	B-	405	6.00	19.3	5.0	14.3	90.0	10.00	0.3
Lionel Corp	0.44	-1.10	B	B	232	5.45	7.8	3.0	4.7	58.3	2.56	0.0
Fay's Drug	0.85	-0.74	B	B+	166	5.11	9.8	2.6	7.2	50.9	2.44	0.0

rating from its traditional strong A to, say, strong BBB to weak A. For that purpose the procedure can be used in reverse. Instead of entering given leverage factors into the model, the leverage factors can be re-increased until the score corresponding to the desired bond rating is reached (exhibit 10.7).

The bond-rating scale indicates that a score of 2.80 would put a company right on the border separating a strong BBB and a weak A rating. Holding ConAgra's operating attributes constant (i.e., its size, risk-adjusted return, and the ratio of investments to total capital), the bond score solves for 2.80 when long-term debt steps up from its historical average level of 40.3% to 55.4% of total capital and, correspondingly, when the adjusted total liabilities increase from 3.1 to 5.0 times net worth. Thus, the scoring model suggests that ConAgra could use 15% more debt in its capital structure over time than it has in the past and still retain

Exhibit 10.7 Simulated Bond Rating Score for ConAgra

	Value	×	Coefficient	=	Score	
Total assets	8.4*		.5320		4.45	BBB
Risk-adj return	14.7%*		.0958		1.41	AAA
LTD/total capital	55.4%†		−.0458		−2.54	B
Adj total liabs/NW	5.0†		−.0939		−0.47	B
Invest & adv/tot cap	7.4%*		−.0077		−0.06	AAA
Senior debt score					2.80	BBB/A

Bond Rating Score Scale

B	BB	BBB	A	AA	AAA

$$|-------+-------+-------+-------+-------+-------+-------|$$

| −2.1 | 0.0 | 1.5 | 2.8 | 4.1 | 5.2 | 6.2 |

*Held constant.

†Simulated as follows: ConAgra's FYE 1989 total capital, excluding the incidental short-term debt, is $1,990.2 million. To increase the leverage ratio from 39.9% to 55.4% of total capital would require long-term debt to increase and equity to decrease by $307.9 million [(55.4% − 39.9%) × $1,990.2]. This change takes the net total liabilities from $3,114.7 million to $3,422.6 million and reduces the prior total net worth from $991.2 million to $683.3 million, thereby producing an adjusted liabilities to worth ratio of 5.0× ($3,422.6/$683.3).

the financial flexibility associated with a borderline A- to BBB-rated company.

Expressing a Ratio of Target Debt to Capital

Knowing now how much additional leverage is available as a result of reducing its bond rating, ConAgra's management would be in a better position to decide whether the benefits are worth the loss in financing flexibility. Suppose that, after due consideration, ConAgra's management does decide to adopt a bond rating that straddles BBB and A. Then the last step is to convert the long-term debt ratio used in the bond score to a target for total debt, that is, a ratio that also includes the company's expected utilization of short-term debt over time. Even though it is not *explicitly* considered in the bond score, short-term debt is incorporated into the debt target because it is an integral part of most companies' ongoing capitalization. (Short-term debt does enter the calculation *implicitly* via the liabilities to worth ratio.)

ConAgra actually is a bit unusual in that, as a matter of corporate discipline, management has adopted the policy of paying off all of its short-term borrowings by the end of the fiscal year (short-term borrowings are used extensively over the course of the year to finance seasonal requirements). Thus, the short-term debt that ConAgra does show on its books at year end is just the current portion of its long-term debt (or the unintentional result of the accounting for pooling-of-interests mergers). Over the past 3 years, the current portion of long-term debt has averaged 1.5% of ConAgra's total capital. Assuming such a policy continues, the 55.4% long-term debt ratio derived from the bond-rating simulation is equivalent to adopting a 57% target for total debt to total capital. The short-term debt adjustment admittedly is not significant for ConAgra, but for most companies it adds about 5% to overall leverage.

In any event, it is pretty silly to be as precise as saying 57% when establishing a policy objective. Suffice it to say that Con-

Agra has employed a target total debt to total capital ratio of 40% in the past and may adopt a future policy goal of financing 55% of fiscal year-end permanent capital with debt and leases, an increase of 15% as the scoring model suggested. Whichever capital structure objective management chooses, it should be communicated to the market as the prospective target, and it should serve as the basis for computing the company's weighted average cost of capital, a procedure illustrated in chapter 12.

Let Debt Drive Equity

Once a company's debt strategy has been determined in the foregoing manner, it should be followed. In many cases management borrows only when there is a clear and present need to raise funds for a new project. A more proactive financing policy—one which is apt to minimize the cost of capital and maximize share price—is to adhere to a predetermined leverage objective even if it means borrowing money the company does not presently need. Management should not be lulled into letting FCF determine debt policy; instead, it should borrow against the debt capacity that is created by its new investments. Of course, such a policy raises the question of what to do with any excess cash that is raised.

Suppose, for example, that a firm projects its NOPAT to cumulate to $1 billion over the next 5 years and that the level of investment above and beyond depreciation, including sensible strategic acquisitions, is likely to use up, say, only $600 million over that time. This difference is a positive $400 million in FCF from operations.

Budget	&	Strategy	=	The Business Plan
NOPAT	−	*I*	=	FCF
$1,000	−	$600	=	$400

Suppose that management has decided to adopt a target total debt to total capital ratio of, say, 60% in order to qualify for a particular bond-rating objective. Although, with a positive FCF, the company clearly does not need to borrow, it should nevertheless raise $360 million of debt (above and beyond refinancing any debt that is amortized), which is 60% of the $600 million investment.

The Financial Plan	=			Debt policy	+	Dividend policy	+	External equity policy
FCF	=	Interest	−	New debt	+	Dividends	−	New equity
$400M	=		−	$360M	+	?	−	?

The funds are borrowed not because they are needed, but in order to maintain the company's leverage target in the face of the growth of capital employed in the business. But with $360 million of net new borrowings, plus $400 million of surplus operating cash flow, the company now must find something to do with all the money left over after interest expense is met.

Equity Dispositions

There are several possibilities. First, dividends could be paid. Given the tax benefit of debt, it generally will be better to borrow if only to pay dividends than not to pay dividends and not borrow as a result. Second, excess cash could be used to repurchase common shares. In either case—paying dividends or buying shares—the distribution of cash does not reward investors (their reward is the firm's economic earnings, or NOPAT, regardless of whether it is paid out or retained); instead, it returns part of their capital to them. Moreover, once the company's business plan and debt policy are set, the payment of dividends cannot change the overall cash flow that might be distributed to the company's common shareholders. Paying dividends simply trades off dollar for dollar with the company's ability to buy back stock from the pool of surplus cash flow.

   In our example, $760 million, net of interest, is available for payout from operations and new borrowings. If the company chooses not to pay a dividend, then the entire $760 million (net of interest) will be available to buy back shares.[9]

No Dividends

The Financial Plan	=			Debt policy	+	Dividend policy	+	External equity policy
FCF	=	Interest	−	New debt	+	Dividends	−	New equity
$400M	=		−	$360M	+	$0	−	($760M) (less interest)

Alternatively, if the company pays $300 million in dividends, only $460 million, less interest, is available to retire shares.

Pay Dividends

The Financial Plan	=			Debt policy	+	Dividend policy	+	External equity policy
FCF	=	Interest	−	New debt	+	Dividends	−	New equity
$400M	=		−	$360M	+	$300M	−	($460M) (less interest)

By virtue of the unshakable mathematical balance between sources and uses of cash flow, it should not be surprising that the most reputable and carefully conducted academic research on the subject concludes that the level of dividend payments does not affect the total return earned by investors (through dividends and price appreciation).[10] Both logic and evidence suggest that dividend policy be treated as *the* residual decision, subordinated to undertaking attractive investments, to adhering to a sensible debt policy, and to minimizing the costs of raising equity capital. Thus, even in circumstances in which a company has the cash flow and debt capacity to support the payment of dividends, it may be advisable to follow a policy of using the cash to buy back stock instead. Dividends are treated by boards of directors as fixed costs

[9]A share buy-back is indicated by a negative new equity issue.
[10]Fischer Black and Myron Scholes, "The Effects of Dividend Yield and Dividend Policy on Common Stock Prices and Returns," *Journal of Financial Economics* Vol. I, 1 (May 1974): 1.

that reduce financing flexibility. Share repurchases can be performed when and if the company has surplus liquidity available. In addition, the tax treatment of dividends also generally is less favorable than share repurchases in which investors can apply their basis to reduce the proceeds subject to taxation (see exhibit 10.8).

A third outlet for surplus cash is to invest it in a portfolio of marketable securities, preferably those for which the corporate tax treatment is advantageous vis-à-vis the personal tax treatment (e.g., preferred stock or high-dividend-yielding common shares). After investing surplus cash in, say, common stocks, the value of the portfolio could be tapped at a later date by selling or borrowing against the shares, or perhaps better yet, by issuing exchangeables—that is, convertibles that have the option of converting in shares of stock in a company other than the issuer.

Some managers may think there is another way to use surplus funds. If excess cash is available, they ask, why not find a way to spend it, possibly through an acquisition. That is a line of reasoning that is to be avoided at all costs, for it frequently leads to inadequate rates of return being earned. To counter this inclination, a company can make a special cash distribution to pay out at once the cash flow it might otherwise be tempted to invest. Of course, that entails the dynamic use of debt, a topic reserved for chapters 13 and 14.

No matter which route is chosen, carefully communicating dividend policy and equity financing strategy to investors will be important.

On the Other Hand

Now let's consider the financial planning consequences for a company that has a negative FCF. Suppose a firm projects a cumulative NOPAT of $400 million over 5 years and cumulative investment needs of $600 million over the same time frame, giving rise to a deficit $200 million in FCF.

Operations	&	strategy	=	The Business Plan
NOPAT	−	I	=	FCF
$400M	−	$600M	=	−$200M

Exhibit 10.8 A Dividend Cut Creates Value

Usually when a company stops paying dividends, its stock price falls like a rock. Not so with Litton Industries, because its dividend cut was accompanied by good news.

On May 24, 1985, Litton Industries' board announced the intention to completely eliminate the company's common dividend, which had been running at the rate of $2 a share, a payout of between 20% and 25% of earnings. If Litton's board had sanctioned that move alone, the company's stock price probably would have collapsed. But the board also authorized the purchase of as much as 35.8% of Litton's shares by issuing a package of debt securities with a face value of $87.60. That good news overwhelmed the bad, and the company's common stock rose in price from $70 to nearly $90 a share in a flat market.

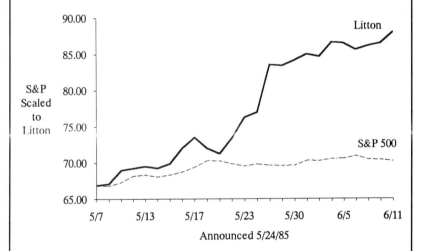

Exchanging the new debt securities for common shares increased Litton's debt to capital ratio from 10% to over 60%. The rating agencies responded by downgrading the company's bonds from strong A to weak A. Still, the stock market reacted favorably, and that is what really matters.

Eliminating the dividend reconfigured the financial side of the company's FCF. In the following table results are averaged for the 4 years before and after 1985, the year of the restructuring.

Free cash flow had been positive for the period leading up to the restructuring, mostly because Litton was in the process of shedding

Litton Industries
Free Cash Flow

FINANSEER (Data in Millions) (Aug-Jul)	Average 1981-84	1985	Average 1986-89
Operating Approach			
NOPAT	$208.0	$237.2	$199.6
- I	87.1	141.7	333.6
Free Cash Flow	$120.9	$95.5	($134.1)
Financing Approach			
Net Int Exp AT	($58.0)	($63.6)	$37.5
- Net New Debt	(164.8)	1,162.4	137.9
- Incr in Other Liabs	67.2	51.6	90.2
Preferred Dividends	4.2	0.8	0.8
- Net New Pfd Stock	(3.0)	0.0	0.0
Common Dividends	64.9	62.7	0.0
- Net New Common Stock	(9.2)	(1,309.5)	(55.7)
Free Cash Flow	$120.9	$95.5	($134.1)
Financial Policies			
Total Debt/Total Capital	13%	49%	43%
Dividend Payout Ratio	23%	21%	0%
Marketable Securities	$1,271.9	$1,563.9	$1,238.6

assets and thereby reducing its I, on net, to limit its activities to (just) defense electronics, industrial automation, and natural resource exploration technology. In the subsequent 4-year period, Litton's FCF turned slightly negative as growth resumed.

On the financial side, net interest expense in the years leading up to the restructuring was negative because the interest expense was more than offset by income from a large marketable securities portfolio (in excess of $1 billion). Net new debt financing also was negative because the positive FCF was used to retire debt and build up the securities portfolio (which is treated as an offset to the debt outstanding). Common dividends running at the rate of $65 million a year served as another outlet for surplus cash.

In 1985, Litton exchanged $1.3 billion of debt for equity, an action which, by itself, had no overall effect on FCF. It was a purely financial transaction with the changes in debt and equity entering the financial side of FCF with opposite signs.

In the years since the restructuring, Litton increased its net debt (by drawing down on its portfolio). Common dividends disappeared entirely and were replaced by share repurchases (indicated by a negative entry for net new common stock). By continuing to raise net debt to retire equity, Litton managed to keep its debt in the range of 40% to 50% of total capital employed.

Satisfied with the shift in its financial policy, Litton's board announced, on February 3, 1990, a new program to buy back 2.5 million, or approximately 10% of its outstanding shares through open-market purchases. A Litton spokesman said its board authorized the program because it believes the stock buy-back is "more beneficial to shareholders than a cash dividend because it increases the value of their ownership in the company."[11]

---

[11]"Litton Authorizes Buy-Back," *The Wall Street Journal,* March 23, 1990.

Suppose that, in order to maintain adequate financial flexibility, management decides that debt shall be limited to 10% of total capital. Then in view of the company's business plan and its debt policy, management can hardly avoid raising equity capital. Though $60 million can be borrowed against the $600 million investment to help defray the overall financing requirements, management still will have to tap the equity markets in an amount of $140 million plus the interest on indebtedness (and any dividends).

The Financial Plan	=			Debt policy	+	Dividend policy	+	External equity policy
FCF	=	Interest	−	New debt	+	Dividends	−	New equity
−$200M	=		−	$60M	+	?	−	$140M (plus interest and dividends)

Because any dividends the board chooses to pay will simply add dollar for dollar to the equity need, it seems senseless for this company to pay dividends. It will only have to recapture with one hand the cash it released with the other.

Knowing that new equity will have to be raised, perhaps the best policy would be to raise at once the equity needed for the foreseeable future, that is, over the next 3 years or so. That will maximize the company's financing flexibility and will sidestep the temptation to time the issuance of equity at some future date when management suspects the shares are overvalued. In any event, management must choose among a variety of equity and equity-like financing instruments, which is the subject of the next chapter.

Summary

A static financial plan is the servant of the business. It anticipates and accommodates the business plan's every desire, with the assumption that the managers are maximizing the cash they can generate from the currently held assets and undertake all available group 1 projects and nothing but group 1 projects. If that is so, the first step in financial planning must be business planning. Forecasts reflecting the cash generated or required under a variety of scenarios for profitability and investment needs should be prepared.

Debt-financing policy, expressed as a target debt to capital ratio, comes next. Five factors collectively determine a company's bond rating and financing flexibility: its size, profitability, business risk, and debt and debt-like financing both on and off the balance sheet. Holding the firm's operating attributes and other aspects of its financial structure constant, the Bond Rating Scoring System can help management get a fix on the leverage ratio that will produce the desired bond-rating objective.

Once leverage policy is established, management should not let the corporate cash flow lead it astray from the proper pursuit of the debt strategy. A company should borrow against growth in its capital base even if it does not need the money and thereby subordinate dividend and equity policy to the capital structure objective. Of them all, dividend policy should be treated as *the* purely residual decision subservient to three more important considerations: undertaking all value-adding projects, maintaining a prudent level of debt, and minimizing the transactions costs of raising equity capital. There are many reasons to expect that a share repurchase, investment in a portfolio of marketable securities, or even a one-time cash distribution may be preferable to committing to pay a steady stream of dividends.

A company with a sustained deficit FCF will almost surely be unable to finance all of its growth needs with debt and retained earnings. Inevitably, it will have to raise some form of equity, a discussion that spills over into the next chapter, on financing instruments.

11

Financing Instruments

Introduction

In spite of the many "brilliant" new financing instruments devised in the 1980s, there really is nothing new under the sun. Four forms—debt, preferred stock, convertibles, and common equity—are the basic elements that make up the financing spectrum. They will be the subject of discussion in this chapter.

To be valuable, a financial instrument must do something that lead-steer investors cannot do for themselves. In markets dominated by astute investors, using financial instruments to shift business risk or to speculate on interest rates, for example, is not likely to be a worthwhile pursuit. What will add value is when a financing instrument:

- Saves taxes
- Reduces transactions costs
- Mitigates bankruptcy risk
- Makes it more likely that attractive investment opportunities will not be missed (or less likely that unattractive investments will be undertaken)
- Appeals to an unsatisfied investor clientele

In this regard, financing instruments, much like investment opportunities, can be ranked according to whether they are likely to create or destroy value. Debt adds to value; preferred stock leaves value unchanged; and convertibles reduce value. Junk bonds, which are in many respects the exact opposite of convertibles, may be the best instrument of all, for they combine the tax, incentive, and disciplinary benefits of debt with the forgiveness and flexibility of equity.

Debt Financing: A Group 1 Financing Instrument

It has already been shown that debt is a value-adding financing instrument, if only because the interest payments on debt are tax-deductible whereas dividend payments are not. (Through financial restructuring there can be at least four other benefits to the aggressive use of debt financing, which are discussed in chapter 13.)

Preferred Stock: A Group 2 Financing Instrument

Preferred stock is a group 2 financing instrument because, unlike the interest on debt, preferred dividends are not tax-deductible. This makes preferred relatively more expensive than debt, but not expensive in absolute terms (i.e., when compared against other forms of equity financing).

The true cost of preferred stock can be illustrated by examining the income statement for a company, initially all-equity-financed, that substitutes $5,000 of preferred stock bearing, say, a 6% dividend yield, for common shares:

	All Equity	$5,000 of Preferred
Net operating profits	$1,667	$1,667
Interest expense	0	0
Net profit before taxes	$1,667	$1,667
Taxes at 40%	667	667
Net profits after taxes	$1,000	$1,000
Preferred dividends	0	300
Net Income avail to common	$1,000	$ 700

The total return available to the preferred and common investors always sums to the NOPAT of $1,000. Accordingly, the impact on the common stock price of raising preferred stock should be the same as if common shares had been issued: no impact at all. Preferred, in short, is a group 2 financing instrument.

The time to use preferred is if a company has first exhausted its debt capacity and is unwilling to raise common stock. If, for example, management feels its common shares are undervalued for a proprietary reason it cannot disclose, then raising preferred stock would be preferable to carving in new common shareholders (or bypassing an attractive project). Another reason to issue preferred stock would be to raise equity while preserving existing ownership interests. It is advisable to raise preferred when a company is in a non-tax-paying position, so that there is no tax benefit to debt financing.

Fixed versus Floating Rates

The preferred should take on as many attributes of common equity as possible so that it performs the financial function of equity: to provide a cushion to protect lenders against business risk and thereby expand the issuer's debt capacity. To do that, a preferred stock issue should be very long-lived, if not perpetual, so that it serves as a permanent cushion to protect creditors. To raise preferred stock that quickly amortizes would seem to be the height of folly, for it would bring none of the tax benefits of debt financing while providing little of the permanence of equity.

To be consistent, the dividend rate on the preferred should float along with rates of interest in the marketplace, so that management will never have an incentive to call in the issue. If, instead, the rate is fixed, management may be compelled to call in the preferred if rates should decline. A fixed-rate preferred is contrary to the objective of creating a permanent equity instrument, and it forces the company to incur unnecessary refinancing costs.

It is widely held that fixed-rate instruments are preferable to floating ones because the variability of income available to common shareholders is reduced. That is true only if the gains and losses taking place on the balance sheet are ignored. With rates fixed, the market value of the preferred floats as interest rates fluctuate; with rates floating along with current rates, on the other hand, the market value of the preferred is fixed. Thus, if accountants marked the preferreds to their market value at the end of each year (as they should) and recorded the change in value as a gain or loss on the income statement, it would become apparent that the cost of fixed-rate financing is floating and the cost of floating-rate financing is fixed in terms of the effect on market value. Thus, fixed-rate instruments are far riskier than floating ones and, indeed, represent a form of speculation.

Admittedly, there is a danger, however, to an excessive reliance on floating-rate debt. When monetary policy is tightened to wring inflation out of the economy, as happened in the early 1980s with Paul Volker at the monetary helm, there may be a spike in real interest rates and a slowdown in economic growth that most adversely affects capital goods producers. In the long run such policies are likely to produce lower inflation and interest rates, and perhaps even more rapid economic growth (as it did), but the near-term consequences can be devastating (witness the case of International Harvester).

A fixed-rate instrument insulates a company against the risk of such a short-term spike in interest rates; floating rates hedge longer-term rate movements. In the end, it is sensible to have as much floating-rate funding as the company can comfortably withstand, given its true economic (as opposed to accounting) exposure to interest rates. Interest rate sensitivity can be determined through a procedure of regressing cash flow from operations against, say, quarterly interest rate movements.

Despite this admonition against an exclusive reliance on floating-rate funding, it still may make sense to raise only floating-rate money (in order to minimize transactions costs) and to control exposure to interest rate risk by following a policy of buying puts (which are the right, but not the obligation, to sell bonds at a fixed price) in the financial futures markets. Then if rates spike and the value of bonds fall, the puts can be sold or exercised for a profit, thereby enabling the company to pay its interest.

Another strategy for controlling risk exposure, while minimizing transactions costs, is the issuing of floaters whose rates adjust according to a moving average of interest rates. Such instruments smooth out near-term rate spikes while eventually giving the company the benefit of longer-term movements in rates.

Speculation

The other side of the fixed versus floating controversy is speculation. Corporate treasurers will often lock in rates with long-term fixed-rate bonds when rates are thought to have bottomed and will rely on short-term, floating-rate bank or commercial paper financing when it is believed rates are likely to fall. Thus, the selection of fixed or floating rates, as described, can be a means of speculating on interest rate movements.

> Says Roger Matthews, assistant treasurer of Allied-Signal: "If you can predict when rates go up or down, you should use fixed- or floating-rate financing accordingly. We actively manage our liability side, look at the mix of floating- and fixed-rate debt, then make our financing decisions based on our forecasts."
> "Dow and Many Others Make the Yield Curve Profitable"
> *Corporate Finance*
> February 1990

Hmmm. If you could predict when rates go up or down, you wouldn't have to labor as an assistant treasurer for a living. Seriously, though, for a bond's issuer to benefit from rate movements, the bond's purchaser must lose; corporations as issuers of securities play a zero-sum game against investors in such securities. How likely is it that corporate treasurers who only occasionally raise capital will be better able to predict rate movements than full-time professionals who manage bond funds, pension funds, insurance portfolios, and so on? It turns out there are lead steers in the bond market too. Besides, if speculation were the objective, it probably would be far more cost-effective to buy and sell interest rate options and futures than to attempt to time the issuance of fixed- or floating-rate debt. Good luck.

Alberic Braas and Charles N. Bralver, of Oliver, Wyman & Company, provide evidence that 40 large trading room operations made no consistent profit whatsoever by holding speculative positions. Their sole sources of reliable profits were retaining part of the bid-ask spread and in having market power over smaller, less well-informed dealers and their business customers. The evidence shows that speculation does not pay even for the big boys, much less the small fries.[1]

Convertibles: A Group 3 Financing Instrument

Many people think that convertible subordinated debentures (CVTs) are attractive financing instruments for two reasons:

1. CVTs are less expensive than straight debt.
2. CVTs represent an opportunity to sell common at a premium to the current stock price.

If these indeed represented genuine advantages to issuing CVTs, it might reasonably be asked why any company would ever employ any other financing instrument. Why, for example, would companies ever raise common at its current price when, by issuing a convertible, the common could have been sold at a premium price?

CVTs are less expensive than straight debt only if the holder's ability to convert into equity is ignored. In fact, since risk and expected reward go hand in hand, convertibles must be more expensive than straight debt because part of the return from owning convertibles is dependent upon an uncertain appreciation in share price. If the cash yield of the convertible were its only cost, then raising common equity would have to be judged preferable to raising convertibles in any event, because the common's dividend yield would almost always be less than the coupon yield paid on the convertible.

It is true that CVTs enable a company to sell common at a premium to the current price. But by the time actual conversion takes place, the common shares will sell for a price still higher

[1]Alberic Braas and Charles N. Bralver (Oliver, Wyman & Company), "An Analysis of Trading Profits: How Most Trading Rooms Really Make Money," *The Continental Bank Journal of Applied Corporate Finance,* vol. 2, no. 4, Winter 1990.

than the original conversion price. Thus, convertibles grant the holder a valuable option to purchase, for a fixed price, common shares that are apt to sell for a much higher price by the time they are converted or called. The fact that the conversion price is above the current stock price is irrelevant; the option is merely an out-of-the-money option, one with no immediate exercise value.

The illusory appeal of convertibles is strongest for risky companies. To see why, compare the financing costs for two companies, one low and the other high in risk.[2] Assume that the low-risk company can raise straight debt at 12% and the high-risk company is required to pay 16% on a straight junk bond issue. Suppose each company considers making the bonds convertible into its common shares at a 15% premium to the current share price. Because the upside potential is greatest for it, the high-risk company will be accorded the best rate break. For example, adding the conversion feature may bring the rate for the high-risk company from 16% to 11%. For the low-risk company, the quote may drop only from 12% to 11%. Thus, it is especially tempting for high-risk companies to conclude that convertibles represent an attractive financing instrument, but such favorable terms of trade really are an illusion. The illusion results from the fact that high-risk companies, by adding a conversion feature to their bonds, surrender more upside potential than low-risk firms.

By such sleight-of-hand, convertibles may appear to be attractive, particularly for the many small, rapidly growing, high-tech (i.e., risky) companies that typically issue them. Upon close scrutiny, however, the advertised benefits prove misleading. So far, all I have tried to prove is that CVTs are not the bargain financing instruments they popularly are alleged to be. I have not proved that convertibles are unattractive. There are, however, three reasons why convertibles are inherently poor financing instruments.

Bad Reason #1

First, CVTs complicate a company's financial planning. Suppose, for example, that the issuing company performs well. With a high stock price, the CVT is apt to convert to common just when the

---

[2]Michael Brennan, "The Case for Convertibles," *Issues in Corporate Finance*, pp. 102–111.

interest expense on the convertible could be used to shelter operating profits from taxation. Alternatively, if the company performs poorly, conversion will not take place, and the CVT holders will insist upon timely principal and interest payments. With CVTs, then, companies get equity when they need debt and debt when they need equity. A CVT has been designed to end up always at the wrong place on a company's balance sheet.

This result is precisely what investors mean when they say, "With convertibles, we have upside potential and downside protection." The attractive investment features of convertibles are precisely the financial planning disadvantages to the issuer. Thus, it is easy to understand why convertibles are bought but not why they are sold.

Bad Reason #2

The second problem with CVTs is that they frequently are called too late by management, giving convertible holders a free ride at the expense of common investors. A call feature enables management to redeem the convertible by offering to pay a fixed redemption price. The investor in the CVT can choose to accept the cash payment or, as usually happens, to convert into the common. So long as the CVT exchanges into shares whose value exceeds the redemption price, it is more sensible for the investor to convert, if only subsequently to sell the stock for its cash value.

It makes sense for management to call the shares as soon as a profitable exchange can be arranged. The longer convertibles remain outstanding, the more income the CVT holders receive relative to that paid on the common. (If the yield were better on the common, then voluntary conversion would already have taken place.) Another way of describing the benefit of an early call is that it denies the CVT holder protection should the stock price fall. Taking away this option and saving income are compelling reasons to call as soon as a profitable exchange can be arranged. By calling early, management ensures that the reduction in the CVT's value accrues to the common shareholders.

A profitable exchange can be arranged as soon as the conversion value of the CVT (the number of shares into which it converts, termed the conversion ratio, multiplied by the current share price) is at least equal to the redemption price. The risk of calling the CVT just at this breakeven price is that the stock price may suddenly plummet over the 30 days that generally elapse between the offer and its expiration date (termed the notice period). In such a case, management would be forced to redeem the bonds for cash and thereby incur an unnecessary underwriting cost. Calculations performed by Jonathon Ingersoll indicate that, even for a very risky company (for which the likelihood of a dramatic plunge in stock price is great and for which underwriting costs are quite steep), convertibles should be called when the share price is no more than 12% above the breakeven price.[3] Investment bankers usually recommend calling when the share price is about 15% to 20% above the breakeven price. Nevertheless, Ingersoll's analysis of CVTs revealed that companies typically called convertibles when their stock price was 40% to 45% above breakeven! CVT holders were given a free ride at the expense of common investors.

Although we can only speculate on why management fails to call convertibles sooner, it is possible that a preoccupation with return on equity or primary EPS deters calling, even when it obviously is in the interest of common shareholders.

Bad Reason #3

To make matters even worse, it is quite common for a company calling its CVTs to retain an underwriter to purchase and convert any securities tendered for cash rather than stock. This ensures conversion will take place even if the stock price should plummet. Not only is this insurance regarded as superfluous by traders (because the cash redemption price generally is 40% to 45% below the market value of the underlying stock); it generally adds another 0.7% to 1.0% to the cost of a convertible.

To summarize, then: the advertising for a convertible's benefits is misleading, convertibles complicate financial planning, management generally waits too long to call, and conversion insurance is both expensive and superfluous.

[3]Jonathon Ingersoll, "An Examination of Corporate Call Policies on Convertible Securities," *The Journal of Finance,* May 1977, pp. 463–478.

The coup de grace, however, is delivered by the research of Wayne Mikkelson and Larry Dann.[4] After studying all 537 primary public offerings of convertibles over the period 1970 through 1979, they selected a sample of 132 issues made by 124 different firms for further scrutiny. Their research shows that the stock price of companies issuing CVTs tends to fall by about 2.5% relative to the market on the date a convertible issue is announced and to fall a further 1.5% when the CVT finally is issued. CVTs, in short, are group 3 financing instruments.

Debt with Warrants

The apparent advantages of convertibles are in many respects just the benefits of adopting a target capital structure, that is, the decision to use a mix of debt and equity over time. Convertibles can seem to be attractive when compared against debt individually or against equity individually. But to be fair, a convertible should be compared against a blend of debt and equity. In fact, to be more precise, a convertible actually is a combination of a straight subordinated debenture and a warrant, a package that may actually be more appealing than a convertible.

American Airlines, Insilco, Intel, and MCI, among others, have in the past issued units of debt with warrants. This combination replicates the apparent advantages of convertibles while avoiding many of the genuine disadvantages. A warrant is the right, but not the obligation, to buy shares of common stock from the company at an exercise price that is set at a premium over the current stock price. Although the interest rate on the debt component of the package will match the rate payable on straight debt, this same rate expressed as a percent of the total proceeds will be less than that on straight debt alone. Thus, all the illusory benefits of convertibles are recreated, but without the complications.

If after issuing such a package the company should perform well, the warrant feature may be exercised, thereby bringing in fresh equity to help finance expansion. The interest paid on the debt component, however, will continue to shelter operating

[4]Larry Y. Dann and Wayne Mikkelson, "Convertible Debt Issuance, Capital Structure Change and Financing-Related Information: Some New Evidence," *The Journal of Financial Economics* June 1984, pp. 157–186.

profits from tax. Should the company go bankrupt, the warrants are subordinated even to common stockholders, thereby representing "super equity." Thus, there is greater financing flexibility than there is with convertibles. An additional benefit is that if the warrant is called, only the value represented by the warrant is at risk in the call, and not the entire value of the package.

Most important, however, is the favorable tax treatment of issuing debt with warrants in comparison with convertibles.[5] For tax purposes, part of the value of the package is ascribed to the warrants, and that gives rise to an original issue discount (OID) on the debt component of the package. So long as the package is sold at par, the OID is precisely equal to the value assigned to the warrant. If the warrant subsequently elapses unexercised, the basis in the warrant goes untaxed. But in any event, the amortization of the OID still is deductible as interest expense over the life of the bond. With an actual convertible, by contrast, only the cash interest is deductible, and not an accretion to par. For that reason debt with warrants can be more attractive than issuing convertibles.

An initial value for the warrants could be established by distributing the warrants as a tax-free dividend to shareholders. Shareholders could sell their warrants immediately, in which case they would be required to pay capital gains taxes on the proceeds. (The tax basis on the stock is divided according to the relative market value of the stock and the warrant itself.) In this case, shareholders receive a modest additional dividend taxed at a capital gains rate (a distinction which may once again come back in vogue). Alternatively, shareholders could hold on to the warrant for subsequent exercise or sale.

Once a trading market for them is established, the warrants could be combined with debt at any time without their value having to be debated by investment bankers. Although no one, to my knowledge, has yet followed this integrated scheme, Warner Communications at one time distributed warrants to its investors as dividends to establish their value in a trading market and then used warrants of identical terms to finance acquisitions.

[5]E. Philip Jones and Scott P. Mason, "Equity-Linked Debt," *Midland Corporate Finance Journal,* Winter 1986, pp. 46–58.

Junk Bonds

As attractive an alternative as debt with warrants appears to be, an even better approach turns the entire concept of a convertible on its head. In order to benefit the issuer instead of the investor, a straight subordinated debenture should be alloyed with a put warrant rather than a a call warrant.

A *call warrant* is what gives the investor the right to buy stock from the issuer at a fixed price. It is the conversion feature implicit in every convertible. A *put warrant* is its opposite; it gives the *issuer* the right to force an investor to buy common shares from the company at a fixed price. The fixed price is set sufficiently beneath the current stock price that the likelihood of the put being exercised anytime soon is slight. But in the event the issuer's fortunes turn sour down the road, so that repaying the debt would be too onerous a burden, the issuer can pull the rip cord and parachute to safety by forcing the debt part of the package to be surrendered in exchange for a set number of common shares.

In much the same way that investors are willing to accept a below-market rate on a convertible because they are given a valuable option to convert when it is in their interest to do so, they will demand a premium rate of interest from a debt with a put warrant package in order to compensate for the added risk. A company should be willing to pay the interest rate premium because it is a small and tax-deductible price for the right to force debt into equity when it is most needed. Debt with put warrants, because the warrants insulate a company from the risk of bankruptcy, dramatically expands debt capacity and financing flexibility.

Of course, what I have been describing is essentially the same thing as a junk bond, which is just a subordinated debenture in which the issuer has the implicit as opposed to explicit right to put the bond into watered-down common stock in the event the company's cash flow or overall value is lacking.[6] Now that is a truly beautiful financing instrument: premium-rate debt with an implicit and nondetachable put warrant. As far as I can tell, junk

---

[6] The right to force conversion into equity is implicit in junk bonds rather than contractual in order to qualify as debt within the meaning of the tax code.

bonds are simply convertibles that have been designed to benefit the issuer instead of the investor. Why they should be the cause of regulatory frenzy is beyond my ken. They are the perfect device to combine the discipline, leverage, and tax deduction of debt with the forgiveness and financial flexibility of equity. It is an oriental and an occidental financing instrument rolled into one. Yin and Yang with one face.

Summary

Financing instruments, like investment projects, can be categorized according to their likely impact on share value. Debt adds value because taxes are saved. Preferred stock, by contrast, cannot enhance the total return generated on behalf of all investors, and accordingly it has a neutral effect on share value. While not absolutely attractive like debt, preferred can make sense when debt capacity is exhausted and when management is unwilling to raise common shares. To fulfill the role of equity, the preferred stock should be nonredeemable and should have a floating rate.

Floating rates, far from being risky, hedge against long-term movements in interest rates. Moreover, floaters save transactions costs because there never is an incentive to call them in. Fixed-rate debt, by contrast, hedges against spikes in interest rates. An equivalent hedging of sudden rate changes, however, may be obtained by purchasing put options in the financial futures market.

Convertibles are a group 3 financing instrument: Their advertised benefits are illusory; they complicate financial planning; and their call feature damages value when exercised. The apparent benefits of convertibles, with none of their genuine disadvantages, can be recreated by a package of debt with detachable warrants. Expensing the value assigned to the warrant for tax purposes makes debt with warrants more attractive than issuing convertibles.

Junk bonds are the best financing instrument of them all, for they combine the tax, disciplinary, and incentive benefits of debt with the forgiveness and flexibility of equity. Too bad the regulators don't see it this way, at least for now.

12

The Cost of Capital

Introduction

The cost of capital is the minimum acceptable return on investment. It is an invisible dividing line between good and bad corporate performance, a cutoff rate that must be earned in order to create value. For the corporate practitioner, it should be used in four ways:

1. As the discount rate to bring projected free cash flows (or EVAs) to their present value
2. As the hurdle rate for accepting new projects
3. As the capital charge rate in the calculation of economic value added
4. As the benchmark for assessing rates of return on capital employed

Even when it seems to be, a company's cost of capital is not really a cash cost. It is an opportunity cost, one that is equal to the total return that a company's investors could expect to earn by investing in a portfolio of stocks and bonds of comparable risk. The cost of capital, in other words, is driven by the proven trade-off between risk and reward. The more risk a company asks its investors to bear, the greater its rate of return must be before value is created and the higher its cost of capital. Accept this elegant theory, and two grimy questions remain: (1) How can risk be measured? and (2) How can the expected return corresponding to a given risk level be priced out? Before this chapter is through, there will be two answers to these two tough questions.

The Four Costs of Capital

To begin with, all companies and all business units within companies actually have four costs of capital with which to contend.

1. The cost of capital for business risk c is the return investors require to compensate them for the inherent cyclicity of NOPAT. In practice, it can be estimated by adding a premium for business risk to the prevailing risk-free rate on long-term government bonds.

2. The cost of borrowing is the required return for credit risk; that is, for the risk in meeting contractual interest and principal payments on debt. It is indicated by the after-tax yield to maturity on the firm's long-term debt obligations; in symbols, it is $(1-t)b$. The tax rate t should be the marginal corporate income tax rate, and the borrowing rate b should be the replacement cost of debt. The embedded cost of debt is irrelevant because funds no longer can be obtained at those rates.

3. The cost of equity y is the return investors require to compensate them for the variability of bottom-line profits. Paying fixed interest payments out of uncertain operating profits makes bottom-line profits more variable, and hence riskier, than the operating profits. The cost of equity is thus the cost of capital for business risk c plus a financial risk premium (FRP). It can be estimated by adding a premium for both business and financial risk to the prevailing risk-free rate.

4. The weighted average cost of capital c^* is the blended cost of the firm's debt and equity. It is the rate to discount operating cash flows to their present value, to rank capital in-

vestment projects, and to judge returns on capital employed. In other words, it is *the* cost of capital. The other costs are useful only insofar as they serve as a means to calculate c^*.

Defining c^*

Much as NOPAT and capital, the weighted average cost of capital too can be defined from an operating and a financing perspective. From an operating perspective, c^* boils down to the cost of capital for business risk less a discount for the tax benefit of debt financing (a concept developed in chapter 7, on valuation):

$$c^* = c \left(1 - \frac{tD}{\text{capital}}\right)$$

Between them, a firm's debt and equity investors must bear the risk in its business, so c^* begins with c. But the use of debt shelters operating profits from tax and thereby lowers the effective cost of capital by the proportion of tD per dollar of total capital employed.

Separating t from tD yields a still more telling expression:

$$c^* = c \left(1 - t\frac{\text{debt}}{\text{capital}}\right)$$

This version says that two things actually drive hurdle rates: the required return for the risk of the business and the tax benefit of debt associated with the target capital structure (expressed as a ratio of debt to total capital). To determine the cost of capital in this manner, then, operating characteristics that account for a firm's underlying business risk must be evaluated and then the benefit of the firm's debt policy must be explicitly factored in. As a result of recent research, this approach is now a reality.

From the financing perspective, on the other hand, c^* is computed by weighting the individual costs of debt and equity by the proportions each financing form represents in the target capital structure:

	(1) After-Tax Cost	(2) Target Percent	(3) = (1) × (2) Weighted Cost
Debt	$(1-t)b$	Debt/capital	$(1-t)b \times D/\text{cap}$
Equity	y	Equity/capital	$y \times E/\text{cap}$
Weighted average cost of capital c^*		=	Sum of weighted costs

Viewed this way, the cost of capital is the return that must be earned on total capital in order to have funds sufficient to pay interest after taxes on the debt and have enough left over to provide an acceptable return on the equity. The two methods, equivalent in theory, come very close in practice. Let's see how cost of capital can be computed from the more traditional financing approach before turning to the avant-garde operating technique.

The Cost of Debt

The easiest to verify is the cost of debt. It is the rate that a company would have to pay in the current market to obtain *new* long-term debt capital. The best indication of this is the prevailing yield to maturity on the firm's own outstanding and publicly traded debt. In the absence of a quote for its bonds, a company's borrowing rate could be approximated by the rate currently being paid by a sample of companies with the same bond rating. (*Moody's Bond Record* or the Standard & Poor's *Bond Guide* provide this information.) The company's bond rating, in turn, could be estimated from the Bond Rating Scoring System of chapter 10.

The Cost of Equity

A company's cost of equity is more abstract because it is not a readily observable cash-to-cash yield. Rather, it is an opportunity cost equal to the total return that a company's investors could expect to earn from alternative investments of comparable risk.

Investors have a wide spectrum of investment alternatives available to them; they range from relatively risk-free government bonds on the low end up through various grades of corporate bonds and preferred stocks to convertibles and common stocks and then to venture capital, LBO funds, and stock options on the high end. As investors take on more and more risk, they must be offered the prospect of receiving a progressively greater reward (exhibit 12.1). That being so, once a company's common shares are positioned on the risk map, drawing a line upward and then leftward along the risk-return trade-off indicates the return required to compensate for risk; that is, it is the cost of equity capital.

To make this theory operational, the slope of the line governing the trade-off between risk and expected reward must be known. The question, in other words, is how much compensation do investors require over and above the return provided by government bonds to compensate them for bearing the risk of investing in the stock market in general, a spread referred to as the market risk premium (MRP) (exhibit 12.2). The track record of stocks and bonds over the past 55 years is a good indication.

Exhibit 12.1   The Risk-Reward Trade-off

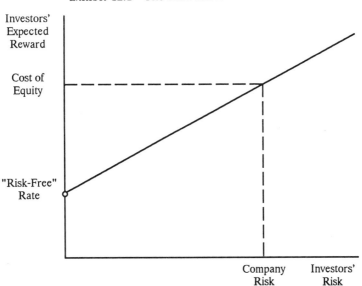

Exhibit 12.2   The Market Risk Premium

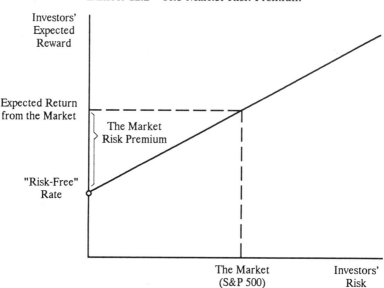

The Market Risk Premium

To assess the historical trade-off of risk for return, researchers have examined a data base maintained at the University of Chicago's Center for Research in Security Prices.[1] This file contains extensive price and income information from 1925 to the present for virtually every publicly traded security in the United States. Rates of return from both cash yield and price change were computed for each year from 1925 to 1989 for the Standard and Poor's 500 ("stocks") and 20-year U.S. Treasury Bonds ("bonds"). The results of this comprehensive study are displayed in exhibits 12.3 and 12.4.

Exhibit 12.3 plots the annual rates of return produced by stocks and bonds. It makes the obvious point that investors in common stocks faced a far greater risk, or variability, in their rate of return than did bondholders. The question is: Were shareholders compensated for bearing this additional risk? But of course they were.

Exhibit 12.4 shows that a dollar invested in stocks in 1925 grew

[1]*Stocks, Bonds, Bills and Inflation 1925–1989,* Ibbotson Associates, Chicago, 1990.

Exhibit 12.3   The Risk-Reward Trade-off

Volatility of Common Stocks vs. L-T Govt Bonds 1926-1989

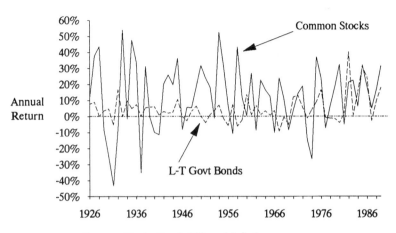

Source: Stocks Bonds Bills and Inflation
(Ibbotson Associates, Chicago, 1990).

Exhibit 12.4   The Risk-Reward Trade-off

Performance of Common Stocks vs. L-T Govt Bonds 1925-1989
Initial Investment of $1 at the end of 1925

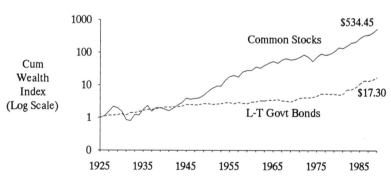

Source: Stocks Bonds Bills and Inflation
(Ibbotson Associates, Chicago, 1990).

to a resounding $534.45 by year-end 1989, equivalent to a thumpingly good compound annual rate of return of about 10.3%. A dollar invested in bonds in 1925, on the other hand, accumulated to a paltry $17.30, a measly 4.5% annualized return. The evidence is conclusive. Over this long time frame, common stock investors indeed were compensated for bearing risk—to the tune of about a 6% premium over the return on bonds. Assuming that this historical record is a guide to the future, at any particular time the return expected from the stock market as a whole can be estimated by adding a 6% market risk premium to the prevailing risk-free rate of interest:

$$\text{Expected stock market return} = \text{risk-free rate} + \text{MRP}$$
$$R_m = R_f + 6\%$$

Is there any fundamental reason why market risk premium should be 6%? Not that I can figure. The question is a little like asking why did God make pi the number 3.14159 . . . Don't ask. Just memorize it, and then head out to recess.

Measuring Risk

In practice, the 6% market risk premium must be scaled up or down to reflect the risk of a particular company. A measure of relative investment risk has been developed as a result of extensive academic research dating back as far as the 1960s. This risk index RI, or beta, has gained wide acceptance over the intervening years. Merrill Lynch, for example, regularly computes risk indexes for the common stocks of essentially all publicly traded companies as part of an on-going Security Risk Evaluation Service. The technique Merrill employs follows the approach sanctioned by the path-breaking academic researchers in the field. Briefly, it involves computing a given company's monthly common stock returns from dividend yield and price change for each month over the past 5 years and then regressing them against corresponding monthly returns for the S&P 500:

$$\text{Company return} = a + b \ (\text{S\&P 500 return}) + c$$

The *b,* or beta, that falls out of the regression equation is the company's risk index. A beta of 1.0 tells us that the company's common share returns generally matched the amplitude of the swings in the market as a whole and hence entail essentially the same degree of riskiness. A beta greater than 1 means that the company's common shares typically exaggerated market movements and, accordingly, are judged by investors to be riskier than investing in the market overall. A beta less than 1 shows that the company's common shares dampened market movements and thus are considered less risky than the typical common equity share. The beta, in short, is the position of a company's common shares on the risk map, with a beta of 0 representing risk-free government bonds and a beta of 1 the stock market in general (see exhibit 12.5). For the ABCs of the beta regression, see exhibit 12.6.

Exhibit 12.5   Beta Measures Investors' Risk

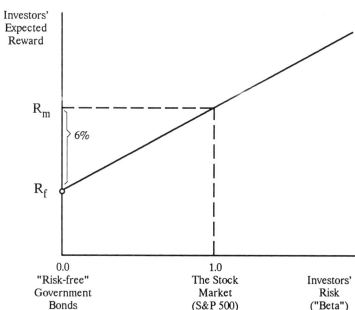

Exhibit 12.6   The ABCs of the Beta Regression

The beta coefficient is all that is needed to measure the cost of capital, but the other results in the regression of stock returns versus the market also are interesting. For example, *a,* or alpha, is the stock's average monthly rate of return relative to the S&P 500; that is, it is the stock's trend. An alpha greater than zero, for instance, indicates that the company's shares tended to rise in relation to the market; an alpha less than zero shows that the stock underperformed the market. Merrill Lynch presents each firm's alpha alongside its beta in the Security Risk Evaluation Service.

Tests have proved that alphas exhibit no serial correlation, or tendency to repeat. That is, a stock that outperformed the market over a given period (i. e., had a positive alpha) is no more (or less) likely to outperform the market (i. e., persist in positive alpha) in a subsequent period than a stock that previously had underperformed the market (i. e., had a negative alpha). This finding alone exposes the shortcomings of technical analysis: The message of the serious research is that the pattern of past stock prices cannot be used to predict future movements.

Here is another startling fact. The alphas for all shares, when weighted by market value, must by definition sum to zero. For any one investor consistently to outperform the market, all other investors as a group must underperform it because together they *are* the market. A famous study conducted by Professor Michael Jensen demonstrated that mutual fund managers, both individually and collectively, were unable to consistently beat the market after accounting for risk.[2] This finding demonstrates the limited value of additional fundamental research as well as the appeal of index funds. Index funds attempt simply to match the market. They thereby guarantee that half of all other investment portfolios will be beaten over any given period of time and more than half will be beaten after accounting for transactions costs.

The *c* in the regression is the part of each month's rate of return that cannot be attributed to movements in the market or the historical trend in return. The *c*'s exhibit a random, and hence unpredictable, pattern from month to month and cumulate to zero over time.

When stock portfolios of as few as 15 companies are constructed, most of the idiosyncratic monthly movements (i.e., the *c*'s) in the

[2]Michael C. Jensen, "The Performance of Mutual Funds in the Period 1945–1964," *Journal of Finance,* vol. 23 (May 1968) pp. 389–416.

individual shares cancel out. Moreover, because historical trends in return cannot be relied upon to continue (i.e., the expected alpha also is zero), the risk of holding a well-diversified portfolio is attributable entirely to unpredictable movements in the market as a whole.

$$\text{Portfolio return} = a + b \text{ (S\&P 500 return)} + c$$
$$\text{Portfolio return} = b \text{ (S\&P 500 return)}$$

In other words, the expected rate of return on a portfolio is simply the beta of the portfolio (which is the sum of the betas of the individual shares in the portfolio weighted by their representation in the portfolio's total market value) multiplied by whatever the return on the market turns out to be. For instance, if the stock market produces a 5% return over some period of time, a portfolio of common stocks with a weighted average beta of 1.5 is very likely to produce a return of 7.5%, or 1.5 × 5%. The more diversified the portfolio, the more likely the actual portfolio return is to track this predicted return and the less necessary it is to look up the prices of the individual shares that make up the portfolio. That is the real benefit of diversification, then. There is no need ever to turn to the last section of *The Wall Street Journal.*

It is in this sense that the risk index, or beta, is the relevant measure of risk for investors; it measures the extent to which adding an individual company's shares to an already well-diversified portfolio will amplify or dampen the expected variability in the portfolio's return and hence change the overall expected rate of return. The risk index, then, does not measure the total risk entailed in purchasing a single company's shares; it measures only that portion of the risk which cannot be eliminated through diversification. One implication is that operating managers, because they experience total risk, are apt to be poor judges of the risk that matters to investors, and hence of the cost of capital. Another is that corporate diversification is redundant to personal portfolio diversification.

Calculating the Cost of Equity Capital

Multiplying the 6% market risk premium by a company's risk index, or beta, scales the premium to the risk of that particular company's common shares. The company's cost of equity, in turn, is the risk-free rate prevailing on long-term government bonds plus the appropriately scaled risk premium.

$$
\begin{array}{llll}
\text{Cost of} & = & \text{Risk-free} & + \text{Risk index} \times \text{Market risk} \\
\text{equity} & & \text{rate} & \text{premium} \\
y & = & R_f & + \text{RI} \quad \times \quad 6\%
\end{array}
$$

Don't be put off by the formula. It is just an algebraic way of tracing out the risk-reward trade-off for a given company under given market conditions.

ConAgra's Cost of Capital: The Financing Approach

To illustrate the financing approach, let's calculate the cost of capital for ConAgra as of the end of the company's 1989 fiscal year (May 31, 1989).

The Cost of Equity

At the time, long-term U.S. government bonds were yielding 8.8% to maturity (source: *The Wall Street Journal*). ConAgra's beta, the result of regressing the firm's common stock returns vis-à-vis the S&P 500, was 1.12, indicating a stock price that was 12% more volatile than the market as a whole over the prior 5-year period (source: Merrill Lynch Security Risk Evaluation Service). Given these parameters, ConAgra's cost of equity was 15.5% (see exhibit 12.7).

$$
\begin{array}{llllll}
\text{Cost of equity} & = & R_f & + & \text{RI} & \times & 6\% \\
y & = & 8.8\% & + & 1.12 & \times & 6\% \\
15.5\% & = & 8.8\% & + & & 6.7\%
\end{array}
$$

In other words, investors in ConAgra's common stock were expecting to realize a 15.5% return over time through a combination of cash dividends and cash-equivalent stock price appreciation. Since ConAgra's dividend yield at the time was running at 2.2%,

Exhibit 12.7   ConAgra's Cost of Equity

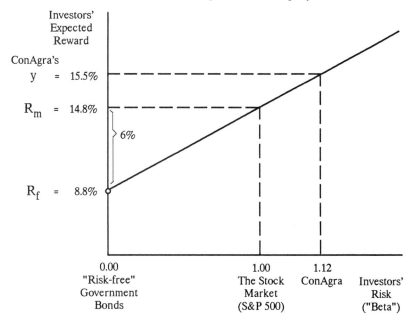

share price appreciation of 13.3% would be expected to make up the difference.

The Cost of Debt

ConAgra does not have publicly traded debt whose yield would indicate the company's marginal cost of debt financing. However, the Bond Rating Scoring System and the company's actual bond rating positioned ConAgra as an A-rated credit (chapter 10). Thus, ConAgra's borrowing rate may be closely approximated by the yield to maturity prevailing on publicly traded bonds issued by a large sample of A-rated companies. At the time, the average A-rated long-term bond was yielding an even 10% (source: *Moody's Bond Record*), a 1.2% spread over the 8.8% rate prevailing on government bonds to compensate for credit risk. Assuming a 38% corporate marginal income tax rate, ConAgra's after-tax cost of borrowing funds thus is 6.2%.

$$(1 - t) \times b = (1 - 38\%) \times 10\% = 6.2\%$$

The Weighted Average Cost of Capital

ConAgra traditionally has financed about 40% of its total capital with debt, leaving 60% to be supported by equity sources (as reported in chapter 10). The weighted average cost of capital, then, is 11.8%

	(1) After-Tax Cost	(2) Target Percent	(3) = (1) × (2) Weighted Cost
Debt	6.2%	40%	2.5%
Equity	15.5%	60%	9.3%
Weighted average cost of capital c^*		=	11.8%

If ConAgra's new projects produce a return that is 11.8% of the incremental capital employed, NOPAT will be sufficient to cover the after-tax cost of the incremental debt financing and still leave enough to drop to the bottom line to produce a 15.5% return to the equity retained or raised to finance the projects, a return which should be acceptable to investors to compensate for the combined business and financial risks that investors face.

This procedure solves for the correct cost of capital in the event that the proportions of debt and equity to be employed in the future mirror those of the past. If a change in target leverage is contemplated, however, c^* can be simulated only by first computing c, the cost of capital for business risk. Merely applying new capital structure proportions to the established costs of debt and equity ignores the fact that these costs will change as leverage changes. If target leverage is increased, for example, the cost of equity (to say nothing of the cost of debt) will go up.

The Cost of Capital for Business Risk

On the other hand, c, will not change as leverage is altered because it reflects the risk in the assets regardless of how the assets are financed. It can be determined by plugging given information into the operating formula:

$$c^* = c \left(1 - t\frac{\text{debt}}{\text{capital}}\right)$$

For ConAgra, c^*, the weighted average cost of capital, is 11.8%; t, the corporate marginal tax rate, is 38%; and the target debt to capital ratio is 40%, the historical proportion of debt employed as a percent of all capital. Thus, c must be 13.9%.

$$11.8\% = c \ (1 - 38\% \times 40\%)$$
$$11.8\% = 13.9\% \ (1 - 15.2\%)$$

The Business Risk Index

In theory, ConAgra's c of 13.9% is what the firm's cost of equity would be in the absence of debt financing. Like the cost of equity, ConAgra's c can be thought of as a risk premium on top of the risk-free rate, with the difference that the premium compensates investors for bearing just the firm's business risk.

Cost of capital for business risk	=	Risk-free rate	+	Business risk premium
13.9%	=	8.8%	+	5.1%

The business risk premium solves for 5.1%, given the firm's c and the prevailing risk-free rate. This 5.1% premium, in turn, can be interpreted as the 6% market risk premium multiplied by a business risk index (BRI) of 0.85 (see exhibit 12.8).

Cost of capital for business risk	=	Risk-free rate	+	Business risk premium
13.9%	=	8.8%	+	5.1%
	=	R_f	+	BRI × MRP
13.9%	=	8.8%	+	0.85 × 6%

The BRI is what ConAgra's beta would have been if ConAgra had been debt-free. The difference between ConAgra's actual

Exhibit 12.8   The Business Risk Index (BRI)

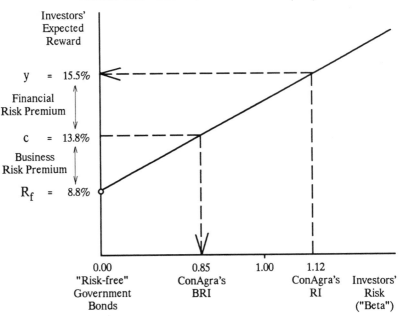

beta of 1.12 and this unleveraged beta of 0.85 is attributable to the risk associated with the company's use of debt. In other words, ConAgra's decision to use financial leverage increased the variability of its bottom-line profits and its stock market returns, pushed the company's common shares farther out on the risk map, and thereby increased the firm's actual beta and the corresponding return that its shareholders have required.

Because they eliminate the effect of capital structure differences, unleveraged betas for companies operating within a given line of business more tightly cluster than the firms' actual betas. Nevertheless, the variation among even the unleveraged betas of business peers still can be significant. Much of the intraindustry difference in business risk can be explained, however, as the result of differences in four key risk factors. Before turning to this fundamental analysis of business risk, let's close the loop on ConAgra's cost of capital from the financing approach.

The Four Costs of Capital

The result of the analysis thus far, ConAgra's four costs of capital are plotted in exhibit 12.9

- c, the cost of capital for business risk, is 13.9%, irrespective of the level of debt behind the assets.
- y, the cost of equity capital, is 15.5%, reflecting a 1.6% premium over c to compensate shareholders for financial risk due to leverage.
- $(1-t)b$, the after-tax cost of borrowing, is 6.2%.
- c^*, the weighted average cost of capital, is 11.8%, or 2.1% less than c because of the tax benefit of debt.

The Prospective Cost of Capital

Now that ConAgra's c has been established, its c^* can be simulated by varying the target capital structure in the operating for-

Exhibit 12.9   ConAgra's Four Costs of Capital

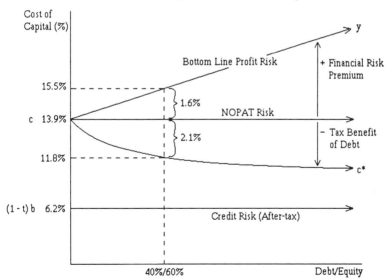

mula. This procedure automatically accounts for the transfer of risk between bondholders and shareholders because collectively they must bear the risk of the business.

Recall that ConAgra could retain the financing flexibility associated with a borderline A/BBB bond rating by increasing its target debt-to-capital ratio from 40% to 55% (from chapter 10), a policy that could be implemented by, say, raising debt to retire common shares (or acquiring Beatrice). If adopted, this would reduce ConAgra's overall cost of capital from 11.8% to 11.0% (see exhibit 12.10).

$$c^* = c(1 - t\frac{\text{debt}}{\text{capital}})$$

$$= 13.9\%(1 - 38\% \times 55\%)$$

$$11.0\% = 13.9\%(1 - 20.9\%)$$

Assuming that the loss in financing flexibility does not impair ConAgra's continued productive growth (actually, a case could be made that increasing leverage might increase the firm's ability to grow), value would be created as a result of making this switch

Exhibit 12.10   The Prospective Weighted Average Cost of Capital

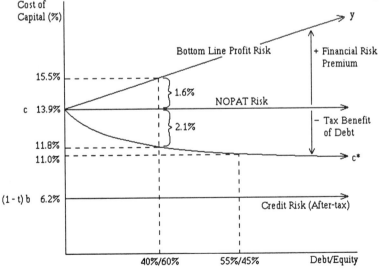

in capital structure policy. The reduced cost of capital will discount any given set of operating projections to a greater present value.

The Operating Approach to the Cost of Capital

The financing approach is a good way to determine the cost of capital for publicly traded companies. But it cannot be used for private companies or individual business units that do not have the share price data necessary to compute a beta. But do not despair. The cost of capital also can be determined by directly estimating c, the cost of capital for business risk, and then explicitly incorporating the tax benefit of debt. This operating approach, the result of extensive research performed by Stern Stewart & Co., examines the characteristics that account for a company's underlying business risk.

The Research

In order to isolate the underlying operating characteristics that account for business risk, a sample of over 1,000 publicly traded, nonfinancial companies in the United States and Canada was analyzed. The firms that were selected participated principally in a single industry group, and they had a stock market value over $30 million and at least 6 years of financial data.[3]

The unleveraged beta, or business risk index (BRI), was computed for each of these companies by subtracting the contribution of leverage from each firm's actual beta. Whereas the average beta is 1.00, the average unleveraged beta, or business risk index, is 0.86, a shift attributable to eliminating capital structure risk. Once this was done, all of the companies were organized into 42

[3]Companies engaged in the electric utilities and gas utilities industry groups have been excluded from the analysis because some required data were not available for these firms. The risk indexes for these regulated companies exhibited little variation relative to the variation observed in other industries. Hence, a reasonable risk index estimate for these firms is just the industry average.

broad industry categories, and an average business risk index was calculated for each group (see exhibit 12.11).

Research and development laboratories topped the business risk list; the average BRI for the group is nearly 1.7. Hot on the heels of the scientists are the specialty retailers, distributors who are constantly discovering innovative and risky ways to hawk their wares. Their typical BRI is in the vicinity of 1.5. Next in line are the semiconductor companies and their primary customers, the office equipment or computer companies, the paragons of U.S. scientific achievement. They are followed by the apogee of U.S. culture—home building and recreational vehicles—which are notoriously cyclical undertakings.

At the very bottom of the risk list are the precious metals producers. Because the value of precious metals frequently moves inversely with the standard of living worldwide, these firms have the lowest business risk index of the lot. With a BRI of not more than 0.6, their returns tend to dampen movements in common stock portfolios. The telephone companies have regulation to thank for insulating them from risk (and the prospect of an exceptional reward). Their typical business risk index is around 0.7. Right beside them in risk are the food, beverage, and tobacco companies and the construction companies (whose operating returns are stabilized by long-term contracts). Apparently it is life's basic necessities that entail the least risk: food, shelter, the phone, gold earrings, and diamond rings.

Most of the BRIs fall within a band from 0.8 to 1.2, a span that would account for only a 2.4% difference in the cost of capital for business risk (0.4 $\times$ 6%, the market risk premium). The difference in business risk within industries, however, often is more significant than it is between these broad industry groups, as we are about to see.

After the companies were herded into these broad business sectors, the next step was to explain the differences in risk among companies operating in the same industry. For example, whereas the average BRI for office equipment companies is 1.34, IBM's BRI is only 1.06, much less than the industry average, and the BRI of Apple Computer is 1.56, well above the norm. As a matter of fact, some of the office equipment companies have risk indexes below 1.00 and others have indexes close to 2.00, a spread that

Exhibit 12.11 Industry Average Risk Indexes

	Industry	(1) Business Risk Index	(2) Fin. Risk Index	(3) = (1)+(2) Risk Index
1	Services, R&D	1.69	0.11	1.80
2	Distribution, apparel	1.54	0.11	1.65
3	Semiconductors	1.52	0.19	1.71
4	Office equipment	1.34	0.12	1.46
5	Home building and rec. vehicles	1.31	0.12	1.43
6	Services, pollution	1.23	0.27	1.50
7	Services, software	1.22	0.07	1.29
8	Instruments	1.17	0.12	1.29
9	Electronics, elec. mach.	1.15	0.11	1.26
10	Drugs	1.14	0.10	1.24
11	Toys, school, and sporting goods	1.10	0.18	1.28
12	Medical supply	1.10	0.11	1.21
13	Consumer durables	1.08	0.17	1.25
14	Distribution, other	1.08	0.15	1.23
15	Textile and apparel	1.05	0.14	1.19
16	Machinery and tools	1.05	0.12	1.17
17	Producers of trans. equip.	1.03	0.13	1.16
18	Services, other	1.02	0.12	1.14
19	Restaurants	1.01	0.13	1.14
20	Forest products and paper	1.01	0.20	1.21
21	Iron and steel	0.99	0.51	1.50
22	Distribution, hardware	0.99	0.12	1.11
23	Chemicals	0.98	0.11	1.09
24	Department stores	0.98	0.16	1.14
25	Printing and publishing	0.98	0.11	1.09
26	Transportation	0.96	0.16	1.12
27	Misc. manufacturing	0.96	0.14	1.10
28	Hospitals	0.95	0.29	1.24
29	Aerospace and defense	0.94	0.11	1.05
30	Personal care	0.92	0.05	0.97
31	Mining and metals	0.92	0.17	1.09
32	Media	0.89	0.17	1.06
33	Construction materials	0.88	0.14	1.02
34	Air transport	0.87	0.21	1.08
35	Hotels and casinos	0.87	0.26	1.13
36	Food and drug distribution	0.86	0.17	1.03

Exhibit 12.11 continued

	Industry	(1) Business Risk Index	(2) Fin. Risk Index	(3)= (1)+(2) Risk Index
37	Fabricated metals	0.81	0.10	0.91
38	Energy	0.81	0.13	0.94
39	Construction	0.73	0.05	0.78
40	Food, beverage, tobacco	0.72	0.09	0.81
41	Telephones	0.67	0.14	0.81
42	Precious metals	0.59	0.02	0.61

would account for as much as a 6% difference in the cost of capital for companies ostensibly operating in the same line of business. The research attempted to identify causal, quantifiable factors that would account for such differences in business risk between business peers. Altogether, four risk factors encompassing 18 individual risk measures were found to be highly statistically significant:

1. *Operating risk.* The first set of ratios gauges the variability in returns on capital earned over a business cycle. The greater the fluctuations in return compared with those of business peers, the greater the business risk index was found to be.

2. *Strategic risk.* The more a company is expected to create value in the future, the greater is its risk; investors fear that the value of the future investment opportunities may not be fully realized. The research showed that as a company's rate of return and its growth rate increase—typical signs of a high P/E multiple—risk rises relative to business peers.

3. *Asset management.* There are four components to asset management: working capital management, plant intensity, plant newness, and useful plant life.
   - Maintaining low and stable levels of working capital relative to business competitors demonstrates a superior budgeting and control capability and thus is a sign of lower than average risk.

- Plant-intensive companies were found to be less risky than labor-intensive companies, possibly because the substitution of capital for labor reflects a dominant, low-cost production capability.
- The newer the plant, the less risky it is deemed to be. Older plants are apt to have higher marginal operating costs than newer ones and hence will be closed first and opened last over a business cycle, thereby increasing the variability in returns.
- A related characteristic is useful plant life. Having to frequently replace important assets exposes the company to risk. In contrast, longer-lived assets convey a sense of operating stability and reduce the perception of business risk.

4. *Size and diversity.* Larger companies take less risk per decision made, and generally have a longer track record, than smaller ones. Moreover, geographic diversification of income makes performance less dependent on any one country's economic cycle, thereby reducing risk.

A more detailed description of the individual risk measures is provided in exhibit 12.12.

The factors there readily suggest why IBM has a lower cost of capital than its business peers. First and foremost, IBM's rates of return are much more stable than the roller-coaster results of a Wang, DEC, or Apple. Second, IBM's profitability and growth rate are lower than for many of its competitors. Because IBM is a more established company, investors in Big Blue have less riding on expectations for the future than they have with, say, a Compaq Computer or Sun Microsystems. Third, almost every aspect of IBM's assets and asset management is superior to the industry average, including very stable levels of working capital in relation to sales and a prominent and durable fixed-asset position. Finally, IBM is the largest and most diversified of the bunch, characteristics that also reduce risk. A detailed comparison of business risk for IBM and Apple Computer is articulated in exhibit 12.15. Business risk summaries for the two firms appear in exhibits 12.16 and 12.17, and supporting measures are reported in exhibits 12.18 and 12.19.

Exhibit 12.12   Business Risk Measures

Risk Characteristic	Definition	Log Transform
Factor 1. Operating Risk		
1. Variation in pretax return	Standard deviation in the ratio of NOPBT to capital over trailing 5 years	Yes
2. Variation in after-tax return	Standard deviation in the ratio of NOPAT to capital over trailing 5 years	Yes
3. Variation in total gross return	Standard deviation in the ratio of total COPAT to total gross capital over trailing 5 years	Yes
	Note: Total COPAT = NOPAT + depreciation + nonoperating income after taxes; total gross capital = capital + accumulated depreciation + nonoperating capital	
4. Variation in operating cash flow return	Standard deviation in the ratio of net operating cash flow to gross permanent capital over trailing 5 years	Yes
	Note: Net operating cash flow = NOPAT + depreciation − change in net working capital; gross permanent capital = capital + accumulated depreciation − net working capital	
5. Variation in capital growth rate	Standard deviation of the annual growth rate in capital over trailing 5 years	Yes

Exhibit 12.12 continued

Risk Characteristic	Definition	Log Transform
Factor 2. Strategic Risk		
Profitability and Growth		
Profitability		
6. Pretax return	Trailing 5-year average of NOPBT/capital	No
7. After-tax return	Trailing 5-year average of NOPAT/capital	No
8. Total gross return	Trailing 5-year average of total COPAT/total gross capital	No
Growth		
9. Net sales growth rate	Average annual compound growth rate of net sales over trailing 5 years	No
10. Internal capital growth rate	Average annual compound growth rate of internal capital over trailing 5 years	No
	Note: Internal capital excludes from capital changes that resulted from significant acquisitions and divestitures	
Factor 3. Asset Risk		
Working Capital and Fixed-Asset Management		
Working Capital Management		
11. Accounts receivable days on hand	365 × (Trailing 5-year average of average Net Accounts Receivable/Sales)	Yes
12. Inventory days on hand	365 × (Trailing 5-year average of average Net Inventory/Cost of Goods Sold)	Yes

Exhibit 12.12 continued

Risk Characteristic	Definition	Log Transform
13. Net working capital variation index	Trailing 5-year standard deviation/mean of net working capital to sales ratio	No
Fixed-Asset Management		
14. Weighted average asset life	Trailing 5-year average of the months on hand of PP&E, receivables, and inventory weighted by the share each represents to the sum of PP&E, inventories, and receivables	Yes
15. Plant newness	Trailing 5-year average of net plant/gross plant (which is the percent of facilities and equipment not yet depreciated)	No
16. Plant life	Trailing 5-year average of gross PP&E/depreciation (which is the average useful life, in years, of facilities and equipment)	No
Factor 4. Size and Diversity		
17. Size	Total capital in the most recent year	Yes
18. International diversity	The 3-year average of NOPBT derived from foreign sources/total NOPBT	Yes

ConAgra's Cost of Capital: The Operating Approach

To illustrate the operating method, let's estimate ConAgra's cost of capital a second time and see how close it comes to the result derived from the financing approach. A summary of ConAgra's business risk analysis appears in exhibit 12.13, and supporting measures are presented in exhibit 12.14.

ConAgra's business activities fall almost entirely within the standard industrial classification (SIC) codes associated with the food, beverage, and tobacco group. As a result, ConAgra initially is assigned the average BRI for this business sector, which is 0.72. Depending upon how ConAgra's operating characteristics stack up against its peers, however, this initial BRI will be adjusted up or down.

For each of the four business risk factors, a standard value is

Exhibit 12.13 ConAgra's Business Risk Index (Based on 5 Years Ended 1988)

```
FINANSEER
Business Risk Report
--------------------

Industry Risk
-------------
                              Business                    Contrib to
Industry Segment              Risk Index      Weight      Risk Index
----------------              ----------      ------      ----------

Food/Beverage/Tobacco            .72          100.0%         .72


Adjustments For:
----------------
                                 (1)           (2)       (3)=(1)x(2)
                              Standard                    Contrib to
Number    Risk Factor          Value         Weight      Risk Index
--------  ---------------     ----------      ------      ----------

1         OPERATING RISK         .47           .37           .17

2         STRATEGIC RISK         .90           .20           .18

3         ASSET RISK           -2.71          -.07           .19

4         SIZE AND DIVERSITY     .61          -.05          -.03

                                                         ----------

   Overall Adjustment                                        .51
 x Industry Std Dev in BRI                                   .18

 = Adjustment to Industry Avg BRI                            .09
 + Industry Avg BRI                                          .72

 = Predicted Business Risk Index (BRI)                       .81
                                                         ==========
```

Exhibit 12.14   ConAgra's Business Risk Measures

FINANSEER Business Risk Report	1 Raw Value	2 Adj Value	3 Average Industry Value	4=3-2 Deviat'n from Avg	5 Standard Deviat'n	6=4/5 Standard Value(Pctile)
OPERATING RISK (Var in:) ==========================						.47 (67%)
NOPBT/Capital	7.3	2.0	1.6	.4	.9	.43 (66%)
NOPAT/Capital	4.8	1.6	1.3	.3	.8	.30 (61%)
Tot COPAT/Tot Grs Capital	3.7	1.3	.9	.4	.8	.47 (68%)
Net Oper Cash Flow/Capital	8.2	2.1	1.9	.2	.8	.32 (62%)
Capital Growth	15.3	2.7	2.4	.3	.7	.42 (66%)
STRATEGIC RISK ==========================						.90 (81%)
Profitability (5 Year Avg) --------------------------						
NOPBT/Capital	29.6	29.6	24.7	4.9	14.5	.34 (63%)
NOPAT/Capital	20.0	20.0	15.0	4.9	8.7	.57 (71%)
Tot COPAT/Tot Grs Capital	20.0	20.0	14.6	5.4	5.9	.91 (81%)
Growth (Compound 5 Years) --------------------------						
Net Sales	28.0	28.0	11.5	16.5	17.2	.96 (83%)
Internal Capital	16.1	16.1	8.1	8.0	11.8	.68 (75%)
ASSET RISK ==========================						-2.71 (0%)
Work Cap Mgmt (5 Year Avg) --------------------------						.51 (69%)
Accts Rec Days on Hand	29.5	3.4	3.4	-.1	.4	-.13 (44%)
Inventory Days on Hand	46.5	3.8	4.1	-.3	.8	-.34 (36%)
Var. Net Work Cap/Sales	.2	.2	.3	-.1	.3	-.43 (33%)
Fixed Assets (5 Year Avg) --------------------------						
Intensity: Wtd Asset Life	41.5	3.7	4.5	-.8	.4	-1.84 (3%)
Newness: Nt Plant/Gr Plant	.6	.6	.6	.0	.1	.23 (59%)
Life: Gr Plant/Depr,Depl	13.8	13.8	15.5	-1.8	4.6	-.39 (34%)
SIZE & DIVERSITY ==========================						.61 (72%)
Total Capital	$2,321.2	14.7	13.1	1.6	1.6	1.00 (84%)
% Foreign Income	.0	-4.0	-1.4	-2.6	3.5	-.75 (22%)

computed. It is the number of standard deviations that ConAgra is away from the industry average (see column 1 of exhibit 12.13). If the standard value is zero, for example, ConAgra's results precisely matched the industry norm for that factor. If it is, say, $+1$, ConAgra is above the average for the industry by 1 standard deviation, and vice versa. These standard values, when multiplied by given coefficients, adjust the industry average business risk index to reflect ConAgra's specific business risk.

Operating Risk

ConAgra's standard value for operating risk is 0.47, an indication that the variations in rate of return and capital growth rate are slightly greater than for the typical competitor. To be more precise, a standard value of 0.47 puts ConAgra at the 67th percentile of the distribution. In other words, two-thirds of the peer companies are less risky than ConAgra and only one-third are more so (see the upper right-hand corner of exhibit 12.14). ConAgra could be expected to have a somewhat higher cost of capital than its peers as result.

Altogether, five individual measures enter into the operating risk factor, combined in a formula proprietary to Stern Stewart & Co. (though it is readily accessible through its PC software system, FINANSEER ™). To relate but one of the measures, the standard deviation in ConAgra's NOPAT to capital rate of return over the trailing 5 years is 4.8% in comparison with only 3.7% for the peer group. (The five measures that drive this factor are compared with the corresponding industry average in the first section of exhibit 12.14, though only after being transformed into logarithms to improve conformity to a normal distribution.)

Returning to exhibit 12.13, ConAgra's standard value for the operating risk factor, 0.47, is multiplied by 0.37, a weight that comes from the statistical analysis and which is the same for all companies. The result, 0.17, is an adjustment to the industry business risk index which will be the subject of more elaboration a little later on.

Strategic Risk

ConAgra's strategic risk is even higher than its operating risk. The standard value for this factor is 0.90, putting ConAgra all the way up at the 81st percentile in this category. To relate but two of the five measures that enter this assessment, over the trailing 5 years ConAgra managed to generate a NOPAT to capital rate of return that averaged 20% against its peers 15%, and its sales grew at an average rate of 28% versus an industry average of only 11.5%. Though ConAgra's exceptional profitability and growth make it an especially valuable company, with a P/E multiple well above the industry average, it also introduces a risk that the enviable track record of the past may not be sustained in the future. This perception is apt to elevate the rate of return investors would seek from ConAgra. As before, the standard value is multiplied by a given weight, further gearing up the adjustments to the firm's risk index.

Asset Risk

The asset risk category comes next. In this case, a higher standard value works to reduce risk rather than to increase it: Better assets and asset management are favorable risk measures. Thus, there is a negative weight associated with this factor.

In this category, ConAgra presents investors with an unusually unappealing combination of characteristics. Though the quality of its working capital management and the relative youthfulness of its plant are somewhat better than the norm, the lack of plant intensity and the shortness of plant life are negative-asset features that tilt the overall judgment to a standard value of −2.71, corresponding to the 0th percentile. Not a company in the industry is apt to be as risky in terms of a lack of reliance on and durability of plant. Fortunately for ConAgra, the research proved that the weight attached to this factor is much less significant than it is for the first two factors. As a result, the multiplication of the very negative asset risk factor by the slightly negative weight produces an increment to risk that is of a magnitude comparable to the contribution of the first two factors.

Size and Diversity

The last factor, size and diversity, is the only one in which Con-Agra offers its investors a degree of comfort. The company's large size overwhelms a dependence on domestic income sources to produce an overall impression of resiliency. The standard value, 0.61, puts ConAgra in the 71st percentile in this category. Too bad, though, that the weight attached to this factor is quite low. Not much reduction in risk is due to that favorable perception.

Bringing It All Together

Adding the four adjustments—three up, one down—produces an overall adjustment of 0.51. That is the number of standard deviations that ConAgra's BRI is predicted to be away from the industry average. Within the food, beverage, and tobacco industry, the BRIs for the public companies in the research sample were distributed about the average of 0.72 with a standard deviation of only 0.18. This standard deviation is rather small (the standard deviation in the BRI among the office equipment companies, for instance, was 0.36, or twice as large), indicating that the BRIs were so tightly clustered that even high-risk food, beverage, and tobacco companies did not depart much from the industry average.

To predict ConAgra's BRI, then, the overall adjustment factor of 0.51 is multiplied by 0.18, the standard deviation in BRI within the industry, and the result, 0.09, is added to the average industry BRI of 0.72. Thus, ConAgra is predicted to have a BRI, or un-leveraged beta, of 0.81.

From the financing approach, recall, the BRI underlying the cost of capital was shown to be 0.85. The operating approach has generated a business risk index remarkably close to that derived directly from stock market data. Admittedly the results do not always match that closely for public companies. But when there is a discrepancy, the operating approach may yield the more accurate answer because it is less subject to measurement errors that may afflict a beta estimated for any one company.

At this point the BRI of 0.81 predicted for ConAgra can be used to compute the company's cost of capital for business risk. It solves to 13.7%.

Cost of capital for business risk		Risk-free rate	+	Business risk premium
c	$=$	R_f	+	BRI × MRP
	$=$	8.8%	+	0.81 × 6%
13.7%	$=$	8.8%	+	4.9%
10.8%	$=$	13.7%(1 − 20.9%)		

The last step is to incorporate the tax benefit of debt financing assuming, say, a target debt to capital ratio of 55% is employed.

$$c^* = c(1 - t\frac{\text{debt}}{\text{capital}})$$

$$= 13.7\%(1 - 38\% \times 55\%)$$

Thus, the operating approach estimates a weighted average cost of capital of 10.8% versus an even 11% from the financing approach, an inconsequential discrepancy. Though the operating approach has been illustrated for a publicly traded company, the technique is most useful in practice to estimate the cost of capital for private companies or for individual business units for which share price data to compute a beta do not exist.

Exhibit 12.15   The Business Risk of IBM versus Apple

Both IBM and Apple have concentrated all of their capital in the office equipment industry, an industry for which the average business risk index is 1.34. That is where the similarities begin and end.

Operating Risk

For the operating risk factor, for instance, IBM has a standard value of −0.80 and Apple has +0.40 (exhibits 12.16 and 12.17). The standard value is the number of standard deviations a company's results are away from the industry average. The standard values indicate that IBM's returns and growth are more predictable and Apple's are somewhat less predictable than for the typical office equipment company, a difference that is evident from an inspection of the NOPAT/capital rates of return over the past 5 years.

Rates of Return

	1984	1985	1986	1987	1988
IBM	34.9 %	27.2 %	15.6 %	15.4 %	10.1 %
Apple	30.0	21.2	47.4	58.5	71.5

To quantify the obvious disparity in risk, the standard deviation in the rate of return for IBM is 10.2% and that for Apple is 20.5%, or twice as large.

The variability in rates of return within industry groups generally is log normally distributed. On the low end, the variability in return cannot be less than zero; a company with a perfectly stable rate of return would have a standard deviation of just 0. But on the upside there almost always are some companies within an industry that exhibit extremely high variability in their returns. As a result, a plot of the variability in returns typically stretches out from left to right, as depicted in exhibit 12.20. Taking the log of these raw numbers compresses the distribution so that it will tend to plot as the well-known bell-shaped curve that lends itself to statistical analysis.

The natural logarithm of Apple's 20.5% standard deviation in return is 3.0 (see the first and second columns of the second line in the top section of exhibit 12.19). The average deviation in return among all firms in the industry is 11.0%, which translates into a logarithmic value of 2.4 (the third column). Thus, Apple's return variations exceed the norm by 9.5% (20.5 less 11.0), or by 0.6 in logarithmic terms (3.0 minus 2.4) (the fourth column). The logarithmic difference of 0.6, when divided by the 0.9 logarithmic standard deviation in this measure within the office equipment industry (the fifth column), produces a standard value of 0.68 (the sixth column), the number of standard deviations Apple is away from the norm for the industry. A standard value of 0.68 corresponds to the 75th percentile (the sixth column) on a cumulative normal probability distribution. In other words, fully 75% of the office equipment companies exhibited less and only 25% exhibited more variability in their returns than Apple.

This measure is but one of five that enters an assessment of operating risk. By analyzing a variety of related measures, the noise, or bias, that results from relying on just one measure is minimized. The operating risk factor actually is gauged by the variability in a pretax return, an after-tax return, a gross cash flow return, a cash flow return–generated net of working capital swings (called net operating cash generation), and the rate of capital growth over the trailing 5 years.

Combining the relative variability in all of these measures produces an aggregate assessment of operating risk. (The precise formula to do this is proprietary to Stern Stewart & Co.) The overall judgment of operating risk is summarized by the +0.40 standard value for Apple and −0.75 for IBM. These standard values, which appear in the first column of exhibits 12.16 and 12.17, are multiplied by a weight to produce an adjustment to the business risk index. The weights, which are the same for all companies, are the product of the statistical analysis. In recognition of its relatively stable returns, IBM's risk index is reduced and Apple's is increased slightly.

Strategic Risk

Apple's risk in maintaining its profitability and growth is well above the industry average; on balance, IBM's strategic risk is about par for the course. Not only is Apple's average NOPAT/capital rate of return far greater than IBM's (45.7% versus 20.6%); Apple is growing far faster too. Sales grew from $983 million in 1983 to $4.071 billion by 1988, a compound annual growth rate of 32.9%. By contrast, IBM's revenues increased at an average annual rate of just 8.2%. All things considered for this factor, Apple is a demonstrably more speculative investment than IBM, warranting yet another upward adjustment to its risk.

Unlike the operating risk measures, there is no need to use logarithms to assess the rate of return and growth rate measures that make up that factor. Without making any adjustments to the raw data, the distributions across an industry group naturally tend to be normally distributed.

Asset Risk

Asset risk is judged by combining six individual risk measures evenly divided into measures pertaining to working capital and fixed assets.

Asset Risk Factors
(Standard Deviations from Industry Average)

	IBM	Apple
Total-asset risk	3.88 (−)	−4.43 (+)
Working capital risk	0.24 (−)	1.19 (−)
Receivables days	0.10 (+)	−1.06 (−)
Inventories days	0.03 (+)	−1.78 (−)
Var net work cap/sales	−0.61 (−)	0.98 (+)
Fixed-asset risk		
Intensity	1.69 (−)	−2.17 (+)
Newness	−0.54 (+)	−1.16 (+)
Life	1.33 (−)	−1.33 (+)

The values for these factors and variables are derived in exhibits 12.17 and 12.18. They are presented here in summary form expressed as deviations from average industry values. The plus or minus sign after each measure indicates the direction of the risk adjustment it causes.

Working Capital Risk

As far as its working capital attributes are concerned, IBM is generally close to the industry average. Apple, on the other hand, maintains levels of inventories and receivables that are quite a bit lower than those of the average industry competitor, a sign of lower risk. Countering this impression is the ratio of working capital in relation to sales. It has been highly volatile at Apple, suggesting that management is less able to schedule production in line with sales expectations or is speculating periodically by hoarding raw materials—with upward implications for risk in either event. Still, the superior management of the level of inventories and receivables dominates the variability, and Apple emerges with a working capital management factor that is a positive 1.19. (Note that the signs of the standard values switch: A positive value for working capital management is used to signify superior risk characteristics, whereas a negative standard deviation for receivables and inventory represents levels lower than the norm, and thus less risk.)

Fixed Asset Risk

Though it conveys more stability overall in working capital than IBM, in all characteristics of fixed-asset risk, Apple appears to be riskier than the average industry participant. Fixed-asset intensity is measured by the weighted average asset life, an indicator calculated by weighting months on hand of receivables, inventory, and plant by their relative magnitudes. The more long-lasting the fixed assets and the greater the capital commitment to plant relative to shorter-term working capital assets, the greater the fixed-asset intensity and the lower the perceived risk. The weighted average asset life for IBM is 68 months (way above the industry average), but for Apple it is just 10 months (far below norm).

Both IBM's and Apple's plants are older than those of the average industry participant. The youthfulness of plant is reflected in the ratio of net plant to gross plant. The higher the ratio, the more recently the assets have been acquired, and vice versa. In this respect IBM and Apple are similar to one another but short of the industry. The plant newness ratio for both companies is near 0.5, indicating that fully 50% of the original gross book value of plant and equipment had been depreciated by year-end 1988. The industry, by contrast, had depreciated only 40% on average.

There is a sharp difference between IBM's and Apple's useful plant life. The ratio of gross plant divided by depreciation is the average number of years over which assets are being depreciated. For IBM it is 11.2 years, and for Apple just 4.5 years. The longer asset life suggests that IBM is a relatively less risky investment.

Taken together, working capital management, plant intensity, plant newness, and plant life produce an overall impression of asset risk for Apple that is much higher than it is for IBM. Apple's standard value of -4.43 reflects an unusually unattractive mix of asset risk characteristics, and it adds significantly to the firm's risk profile with investors. IBM's standard value of $+3.88$, on the other hand, reflects outstanding asset qualities and produces a significant downward adjustment in the perception of its risk.

Size and Diversity

The last and least important factor is assessment of size and diversity. Both firms are larger and derive more of their operating income from foreign sources than their business peers, thereby reducing their investors' perceptions of risk—only somewhat more so for IBM.

Bringing It All Together

Each of the four risk factors adds substantially to the risk index of Apple. For IBM, all the factors serve to diminish the risk score. In the end, IBM's business risk index is predicted to be just 1.06, whereas it is estimated to be 1.56 for Apple. This appraisal of the fundamental determinants of business risk is confirmed by stock market risk. Apple's stock price has been one of the most volatile on the NASDAQ market, whereas IBM is widely regarded as a stable blue chip stock suitable for widows and orphans.

The predicted business risk indices for IBM and Apple can be used to compute the underlying cost of capital for business risk c.

Cost of capital for business risk	$=$	Risk-free rate	$+$	Business risk premium
c	$=$	R_f	$+$	BRI × MRP
		For IBM		
c	$=$	8.8%	$+$	1.06 × 6%
15.2%	$=$	8.8%	$+$	6.4%
		For Apple		
c	$=$	8.8%	$+$	1.56 × 6%
18.2%	$=$	8.8%	$+$	9.4%

There is a full 3% difference in the underlying cost of capital. In view of the fact that Apple focuses almost all its efforts on personal computers, the difference in risk and required return could perhaps more justifiably be interpreted as reflecting a difference between personal computers and mainframes, the segment in which IBM is dominant. If so, even IBM would have to seek a higher return from its personal computer product line, for in this market segment it competes against the likes of Apple Computer for capital.

Now that c has been determined, the weighted average cost of capital c^* could be calculated for IBM and Apple by incorporating the tax benefit of debt associated with their target capital structures.

Exhibit 12.16   IBM's Business Risk Index (Based on 5 Years Ended 1988)

```
FINANSEER
Business Risk Report
--------------------
```

Industry Risk

Industry Segment	Business Risk Index	Weight	Contrib to Risk Index
Office Equipment	1.34	100.0%	1.34

Adjustments For:

Number	Risk Factor	(1) Standard Value	(2) Weight	(3)=(1)x(2) Contrib to Risk Index
1	OPERATING RISK	-.75	.37	-.28
2	STRATEGIC RISK	-.14	.20	-.03
3	ASSET RISK	3.88	-.07	-.28
4	SIZE AND DIVERSITY	3.52	-.05	-.19

Overall Adjustment	-.77
x Industry Std Dev in BRI	.36
= Adjustment to Industry Avg BRI	-.28
+ Industry Avg BRI	1.34
= Predicted Business Risk Index (BRI)	1.06

Exhibit 12.17 IBM's Business Risk Measures

FINANSEER Business Risk Report	1 Raw Value	2 Adj Value	3 Average Industry Value	4=3-2 Deviat'n from Avg	5 Standard Deviat'n	6=4/5 Standard Value(Pctile)
OPERATING RISK (Var in:)						-.75 (22%)
========================						
NOPBT/Capital	13.4	2.6	2.7	-.1	.9	-.17 (43%)
NOPAT/Capital	10.2	2.3	2.4	-.1	.9	-.11 (45%)
Tot COPAT/Tot Grs Capital	6.6	1.9	2.1	-.2	.9	-.18 (42%)
Net Oper Cash Flow/Capital	5.7	1.7	3.1	-1.4	1.0	-1.45 (7%)
Capital Growth	10.8	2.4	3.5	-1.1	.8	-1.27 (10%)
STRATEGIC RISK						-.14 (44%)
==========================						
Profitability (5 Year Avg)						

NOPBT/Capital	31.5	31.5	23.5	8.0	22.0	.36 (64%)
NOPAT/Capital	20.6	20.6	14.4	6.2	16.7	.37 (64%)
Tot COPAT/Tot Grs Capital	18.9	18.9	16.3	2.6	11.0	.24 (59%)
Growth (Compound 5 Years)						

Net Sales	8.2	8.2	28.1	-19.9	26.7	-.75 (22%)
Internal Capital	15.6	15.6	24.1	-8.5	25.8	-.33 (37%)
ASSET RISK						3.88 (99%)
==========================						
Work Cap Mgmt (5 Year Avg)						.24 (59%)

Accts Rec Days on Hand	84.1	4.4	4.4	.0	.4	.10 (53%)
Inventory Days on Hand	157.1	5.1	5.0	.0	.4	.03 (51%)
Var. Net Work Cap/Sales	.2	.2	.3	-.1	.1	-.61 (27%)
Fixed Assets (5 Year Avg)						

Intensity: Wtd Asset Life	68.1	4.2	3.4	.9	.5	1.69 (95%)
Newness: Nt Plant/Gr Plant	.5	.5	.6	-.1	.1	-.54 (29%)
Life: Gr Plant/Depr,Depl	11.2	11.2	7.8	3.3	2.5	1.33 (90%)
SIZE & DIVERSITY						3.52 (99%)
==========================						
Total Capital	53,384.0	17.8	12.3	5.5	1.5	3.77 (99%)
% Foreign Income	30.0	3.4	.6	2.8	3.5	.81 (79%)

Exhibit 12.18   Apple Computer's Business Risk Index
(Based on 5 Years Ended 1988)

```
FINANSEER
Business Risk Report
--------------------

Industry Risk
-------------
```

| | Business | | Contrib to |
Industry Segment	Risk Index	Weight	Risk Index
Office Equipment	1.34	100.0%	1.34

```
Adjustments For:
----------------
```

| | | (1)
Standard | (2) | (3)=(1)x(2)
Contrib to |
Number	Risk Factor	Value	Weight	Risk Index
1	OPERATING RISK	.40	.37	.15
2	STRATEGIC RISK	1.14	.20	.23
3	ASSET RISK	-4.43	-.07	.32
4	SIZE AND DIVERSITY	1.62	-.05	-.09

```
                                                           ---------

   Overall Adjustment                                         .61
 x Industry Std Dev in BRI                                    .36

 = Adjustment to Industry Avg BRI                             .22
 + Industry Avg BRI                                          1.34

 = Predicted Business Risk Index (BRI)                       1.56
                                                          =========
```

Exhibit 12.19 Apple Computer's Business Risk Measures

FINANSEER Business Risk Report	1 Raw Value	2 Adj Value	3 Average Industry Value	4=3-2 Deviat'n from Avg	5 Standard Deviat'n	6=4/5 Standard Value(Pctile)
OPERATING RISK (Var in:)						.40 (65%)
NOPBT/Capital	28.3	3.3	2.7	.6	.9	.70 (75%)
NOPAT/Capital	20.5	3.0	2.4	.6	.9	.68 (75%)
Tot COPAT/Tot Grs Capital	8.4	2.1	2.1	.1	.9	.08 (53%)
Net Oper Cash Flow/Capital	24.9	3.2	3.1	.1	1.0	.08 (53%)
Capital Growth	33.9	3.5	3.5	.1	.8	.08 (53%)
STRATEGIC RISK						1.14 (87%)
Profitability (5 Year Avg)						
NOPBT/Capital	63.0	63.0	23.5	39.4	22.0	1.79 (96%)
NOPAT/Capital	45.7	45.7	14.4	31.3	16.7	1.88 (96%)
Tot COPAT/Tot Grs Capital	31.4	31.4	16.3	15.0	11.0	1.37 (91%)
Growth (Compound 5 Years)						
Net Sales	32.9	32.9	28.1	4.7	26.7	.18 (57%)
Internal Capital	28.8	28.8	24.1	4.7	25.8	.18 (57%)
ASSET RISK						-4.43 (0%)
Work Cap Mgmt (5 Year Avg)						1.19 (88%)
Accts Rec Days on Hand	54.0	4.0	4.4	-.4	.4	-1.06 (14%)
Inventory Days on Hand	76.0	4.3	5.0	-.7	.4	-1.78 (3%)
Var. Net Work Cap/Sales	.4	.4	.3	.1	.1	.98 (83%)
Fixed Assets (5 Year Avg)						
Intensity: Wtd Asset Life	9.7	2.3	3.4	-1.1	.5	-2.17 (1%)
Newness: Nt Plant/Gr Plant	.5	.5	.6	-.1	.1	-1.16 (12%)
Life: Gr Plant/Depr,Depl	4.5	4.5	7.8	-3.3	2.5	-1.33 (9%)
SIZE & DIVERSITY						1.62 (94%)
Total Capital	2,028.5	14.5	12.3	2.2	1.5	1.52 (93%)
% Foreign Income	46.0	3.8	.6	3.2	3.5	.94 (82%)

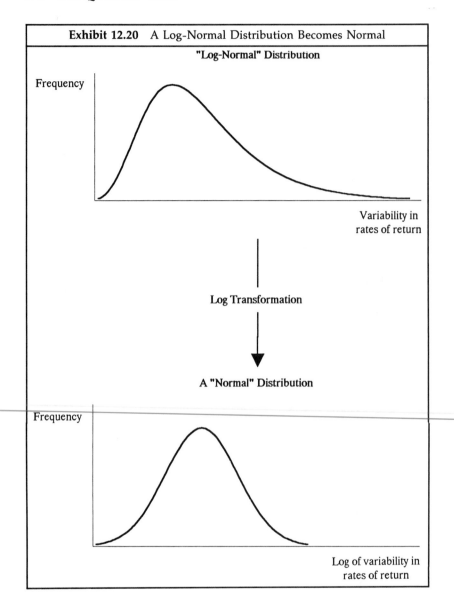

Exhibit 12.20   A Log-Normal Distribution Becomes Normal

"Log-Normal" Distribution

Frequency

Variability in
rates of return

Log Transformation

A "Normal" Distribution

Frequency

Log of variability in
rates of return

Summary

Capital will not work for free; a cost must be paid to use it. There is good reason for this insistence, however. Capital is scarce; it is limited in the aggregate to the amount that people worldwide choose to save. For any one company to invest capital, then, it must deny another company the opportunity to use it. The return that investors could expect to earn from the alternative use of funds is the cost of capital that any one company must earn in order to create value. Earning the cost of capital thus is not a mere financial matter to be ranked alongside or, worse, be subordinate to other corporate concerns, as many managers seem to think. It is *the* market mandate.

The weighted average cost of debt and equity capital is the one to use as the benchmark for evaluating rates of return and new capital projects and as the discount rate to value operating cash flows. It can be calculated, from the financing side of the balance sheet, by using target capital structure proportions to weight the individual costs of debt and equity capital or, from the operating perspective, by explicitly evaluating the factors that create business risk and then incorporating a discount for the tax benefit of debt. The available techniques are powerful enough to measure accurately the cost of capital for fully consolidated, publicly traded companies, for private companies, and for individual business units.

PART III

Dynamic Finance

13

Financial Restructuring

Introduction

Without question, the restructuring boom of the 1980s richly rewarded the dealmakers. But, in the same way that many investors rightly ask their stockbrokers, but where are our yachts? you may be wondering whether the financial restructurings of the past decade have benefited broader constituencies, including shareholders, managers, employees, and our economy at large. Did the "raiders," as the pejorative label suggests, pillage companies solely for their personal enrichment leaving a weakened economy in their wake, or did they instead promote improvements in corporate performance and increases in market values for all to share? If raiders and LBOs were a force for good, is it possible to learn from them any lessons about how to more effectively structure a company?

Those and other questions prompted David Glassman, one of my partner colleagues at Stern Stewart & Co., and I to undertake a comprehensive review of some 300 financial restructuring transactions completed in the past decade. Our single most important discovery was that, in the vast majority of cases, financial restructurings did lead to sustained increases in both market values and operating performance. Although initially skeptical of such financial alchemy, and even more reluctant to embrace the explanations proffered by many investment bankers, we eventually became convinced that there were genuine economic explanations to account for the impressive restructuring benefits. (The most important of these "motives" to restructure are presented in the left-hand column of exhibit 13.1.)

Our explanations are fundamentally different from many of

Exhibit 13.1 The Motives and Methods of Financial Restructuring

Motives	Methods
Strengthen incentives	*Vertical restructurings* change the configuration of assets and activities within a given line of business through:
Achieve a better business fit	
Improve focus	
Cure reinvestment risk	
Eliminate cross-subsidies	• Sale and lease-back
Channel cash to promising opportunities	• Securitized financing
	• Franchising
Achieve a higher-valued use for assets	• Subcontracting
	• Vertical deintegration
Introduce explicit transfer prices	*Horizontal restructurings* can increase a business unit's value in three ways:
Instill a sense of urgency and entrepreneurism	
Express management's commitment and confidence	• Promoting growth through acquisitions, joint ventures, or offering a subsidiary's shares to the public
Subject decisions to a market test	
Syndicate excessive business risks	• Separating a business unit from the firm through a sale, spin-off, split-off or partial liquidation
Create unique pure plays for investors	
Increase debt capacity	• Undertaking an internal leveraged recapitalization
Save taxes	*Corporate restructurings* change the ownership structure of the parent company through:
	• New forms of debt or equity
	• Conversion to partnership, trust, or subchapter S
	• Share repurchases
	• Leveraged ESOPs
	• Leveraged cash-out or leveraged buy-out
	• Strategic merger or complete sale
	• Complete liquidation or split-up

the popular accounts of the restructuring wave. Some see it as the result of unrestrained avarice; others see it as proof that equity investors fail to appreciate the inherent values of certain companies; and still others see it as an unwarranted reaping of a short-term financial gain at the expense of long-run business values. But in view of the strong evidence on market efficiency, and based upon our own evaluations of their far-reaching consequences, we are convinced that most of the time financial restructurings do change the way corporations are run and do create new, enduring values.

Our research has also uncovered some 20 or so recurring methods of financial restructuring. These tax-driven techniques are keys to unlocking value trapped within a firm. For convenience, we grouped them into the categories of vertical, horizontal, and corporate restructurings. They are outlined in the right-hand column of exhibit 13.1.

Restructuring in any of these ways is no guarantee of a higher stock price, however. Our research uncovered numerous examples of companies whose financial maneuverings brought them little if any improvement in market value. Many were ultimately taken over. In such cases, the methods that management chose to use had failed to effectively address the real reasons to restructure the firm. There were form without function and method without motive. A better understanding of the real objectives and concerns of financial restructuring may have helped those hapless firms to craft a more effective restructuring strategy and to implement it before an outsider began to set the agenda. To illustrate our financial restructuring framework, we will examine what is perhaps the most controversial method of restructuring, namely, the aggressive use of leverage.

Why Leverage Matters

The leverage ratios of many U.S. companies increased dramatically over the past decade as the result of leveraged buy-outs, share repurchases, recapitalizations, debt-financed acquisitions, and the proliferation of junk bonds. Has the leveraging strengthened or sapped the competitiveness of U.S. companies? Felix

Rohatyn, senior partner at Lazard Freres, was one of the first to articulate the naysayers' viewpoint:

> This [the high degree of leverage in LBOs] has two consequences, both highly speculative. First, it bets the company on a combination of continued growth and lower interest rates, with no margin for error. Second, it substitutes debt for permanent capital, which is exactly the opposite of what our national investment objectives ought to be.
>
> "On a Buyout Binge and a Takeover Tear"
> *The Wall Street Journal*
> May 18, 1984

To the contrary, I believe that there are five reasons why the aggressive use of debt has, on net, been a positive force—a catalyst for many U.S. companies to increase their productivity and market value:

- Debt saves taxes.
- Debt cures the risk of an unproductive reinvestment of surplus cash flow.
- Debt strengthens the incentives for success and the penalties for failure.
- Debt forces the sales of underperforming or unrelated assets or businesses.
- Debt creates a compulsion to perform well, to focus on cash flow rather than reported earnings, and to eliminate wasteful cross-subsidies between units.

The truth is, I love debt. (Some say I like it more than I like sex. That is untrue, although I admit I do like debt very much.) I remain firm in my affection for leverage despite the current upheaval in the junk bond market and the bankruptcy of a few prominent LBOs. Here's why.

I. Tax Benefits

First of all, debt is a less expensive form of financing than equity because interest expense is tax-deductible whereas dividend payments are not. When debt is substituted for equity, the overall amount of capital used in a business will not change nor will the total rate of return needed to compensate investors for bearing the firm's business risk. But the implicit cost of equity is replaced in part by the explicit tax-deductible cash cost of debt. The present value of the corporate income taxes saved when debt displaces equity will add to a company's intrinsic market value. (A fuller exposition of debt's tax benefit was presented in chapter 7.)

There continues to be a benefit to debt financing, and hence a reduction in the overall, or weighted average, cost of capital even when the interest rate that must be paid on the debt rises. However high the rate on debt may become, the implied interest rate on the equity it replaces must be higher still because equity is riskier to own and its cost is not subsidized by a corporate tax savings.

But however important saving taxes might be in making debt more attractive than equity, it alone cannot account for the great increase in leverage this past decade. If anything, the reduction in the corporate tax rate would reduce the incentive to embrace debt as a tax shelter. There are at least four more reasons why some companies can benefit from using debt aggressively.

II. Cure Reinvestment Risk

A second good reason to borrow money is to repay it! The obligation to pay back debt removes from management the temptation to invest surplus cash in substandard projects or overpriced acquisitions. Like Ulysses lashed to the mast, management will be tied to its debts. Then, though the siren calls of investment opportunities may beckon, the company ship will row assuredly onward and avoid the fate of the many failed projects that litter the shore. Repaying debt need not entirely preclude growth, but when the cash flow that a company internally generates is dedicated to debt service, expansion must be financed with new capital. That will subject management's investment plans to the discipline of passing a market test.

The risk of an unproductive reinvestment of cash flow has proved to be most acute in mature companies that have sound profitability and little growth potential but insist upon growing rapidly anyway. Fears that surplus cash flow will be squandered is one reason why investors mark down the values of cash-flow-rich companies below the inherent value of the cash flow they generate. That produces a gap in value that raiders can exploit. Their aggressive use of debt has an unintended consequence: when all surplus cash flow is dedicated to debt service, value is created by alleviating a reinvestment risk discount.

The Drunken Sailor Syndrome.   The Standard Oil Company of Ohio (SOHIO) provides a good example of reinvestment risk. SOHIO for many years was a sleepy regional refiner and marketer of oil. After it found extensive oil reserves on the Alaskan North Slope, it became an enormously profitable cash cow in the early 1980s. Curiously, SOHIO traded at a very low P/E multiple even though it earned a very high return on equity and sold for the highest premium over book value of any of the major oil companies at that time. How can these contradictory indicators be reconciled?

The company's high return on equity and premium to book resulted from its remarkably successful prior investments. The low P/E multiple, in contrast, signaled that the market lacked confidence in SOHIO's ability to reinvest its stupendous cash flow in attractive new projects. In fact, it reflected a downright fear that the flood of cash from the North Slope would be wasted in SOHIO's basic businesses or unsound acquisitions.

SOHIO justified investors' fears by choosing both downhill paths. Like a drunken sailor on shore leave, management splurged on costly oil exploration forays (of which the dry-as-a-prune Mukluk well is but one prominent example), bought extensive mining reserves at inflated prices, and made the exceedingly expensive ($1.77 billion) and highly suspect acquisition of Kennecott, the copper company. The results of SOHIO's capital investments were so poor that British Petroleum, then SOHIO's part owner, let SOHIO's chairman go and brought in a new team to reverse the company's misfortunes.

But why single out SOHIO when almost all the major oil companies made similar blunders with surplus cash: Exxon with its office systems venture and Reliance Electric acquisition, Mobil with Montgomery Ward, ARCO with Anaconda, AMOCO with Cypress Minerals, and so on. As these failures suggest, corporate executives are not immune to the all-too-human tendency to spend money when you get your hands on it.

Nevertheless, it is a fundamental corporate finance tenet that the wisdom of making an investment should *not* depend on whether the funds come from inside or outside the company. Even when a company uses internal cash flow to finance its growth, those funds could just as well have been repatriated to investors and then explicitly raised. Internalizing the cost of capital does not avoid it. As a practical matter, however, the inclination to invest is more highly related to the availability of cash than it is to the availability of attractive uses.

Why is the textbook lesson so widely ignored? The answer lies in reasons of great importance to management and of grave concern to investors. Foremost among them, most bonus plans reward managers at all levels for increasing profits. Investing beyond the point of no return in order to grow profits is the result. It is also true that a large and growing company commands more power and prestige (and before junk bond financing became available was perhaps less vulnerable to being taken over) than a small or contracting one. Moreover, a large diversified company is more stable than one reliant on a single business and can justify a corporate bureaucracy with no direct operating responsibility or accountability. And, as Harvard's Professor Michael Jensen has observed,[1] middle-level managers are inclined to root for expansion because it creates more lucrative senior management positions to be filled. For all those reasons, most companies prefer to reinvest cash flow than to pay it out. Here's but one example.

Burning a Hole in Their Pockets.   A year and a half before its LBO, the management of RJR's Nabisco baking unit devised a plan costing $2.8 billion to completely revamp and modernize its quite antiquated baking facilities. The capital campaign was to finance the latest state-of-the-art technology and make Nabisco the lowest-cost producer worldwide. All that is well and good. But, as was reported by *The Wall Street Journal* (March 14, 1989), the annual cost savings resulting from fewer cracked crackers and more accurate package stuffing was estimated to be a walloping

---

[1]"How to Detect a Prime Takeover Target," *The New York Times,* March 9, 1986.

$148 million, yielding a pitiful 5% pretax return on the proposed investment. John Greeniaus, the head of the baking unit, is now working feverishly under KKR to scale back the capital budget to a still robust $600 million program. He admitted to the *WSJ* reporters that the original colossal investment was just a "wish list" drawn up when RJR was looking "frantically" for ways to spend its tobacco cash. Holy mackerel! Why didn't they just pay it out instead?

Ford's Follies.   Another good case in point is Ford, which, in the wake of a Herculean turnaround effort and a string of record profits, has been rewarded in the stock market with a P/E multiple of only 5. One reason for this penny ante valuation is that, with a large number of new Japanese plants due to come on line, Ford's earnings probably are at a cyclical peak. Another reason is that Ford's management refused to pay out the $10 to $15 billion worth of surplus cash that the company generated this past decade, announcing instead it would use the windfall to diversify. Oh, no!

> Where will Ford pounce? The stock markets buzz almost daily with rumors about takeover plays by Ford, which openly says it wants to buy companies to offset the auto industry's cyclical swings. In recent months, Boeing, Lockheed, and Singer have been rumored targets.
>
> "Can Ford Stay on Top?"
> *Business Week*
> September 28, 1987

It is easy to envision the benefits diversification may bring to Ford's senior managers and employees (to say nothing of its investment bankers), but is diversification really in the best interest of its shareholders and our economy? Was it not the company's dependence upon the auto market in the early 1980s that forced management to streamline production and to innovate in order to survive—and that is the cause of their present success?

By making survival less dependent on the ability to compete in the auto industry, diversification will dampen the company's drive to make painful, necessary adjustments should hard times come again. The company will hold a balanced portfolio, a code word for waste, and the market knows it. Perhaps Ford can justify buying an electronics or aerospace concern to obtain technology. In light of how unsuccessful the acquisition of Hughes has been for General Motors, however, would it not be more efficient to license the technology, or form a joint venture, if that is the motivation? Most fundamentally, would Ford be making acquisitions if it had to raise the cash, or is the mere availability of cash prompting its use?

Since the time that I first wrote the preceding speculative passages, Ford has indeed succumbed to the perils of reinvestment risk by acquiring Associates, a commercial finance company, from Gulf + Western (since renamed Paramount) and money-losing Jaguar for $2.5 billion, a price no analyst feels will ever be justified (unless it is because Ford has underutilized repair facilities to service Jaguar's cars). Ford's stock price suffered vis-à-vis the market just upon the first hint that Jaguar would be a target, and fell precipitously upon the announcement of the Associates transaction (exhibit 13.2). That Ford's stock did not fall farther than it did on each occasion just shows that the company's stock price already had incorporated a reinvestment risk discount. Investors are not that stupid.

They Deserve a Buffetting. Warren Buffett, the highly regarded chairman of Berkshire Hathaway, states the reinvestment risk problem in typically eloquent and witty style in his company's 1984 annual report:

> Many corporations that show consistently good returns have, indeed, employed a large portion of their retained earnings on an economically unattractive, even disastrous, basis. Their marvelous core businesses camouflage repeated failures in capital allocation elsewhere (usually involving high-priced acquisitions). The managers at fault periodically report on the lessons they have learned from the latest disappointment. They then usually seek out future lessons. (Failure seems to go to their heads.)
>
> In such cases, shareholders would be far better off if the earnings were retained to expand only the high-return business, with the balance paid in dividends or used to repurchase stock (an action that increases the owner's interest in the exceptional business while sparing them participation in the subpar businesses). Man-

Exhibit 13.2   Ford Acquisitions

Ford to Acquire Jaguar

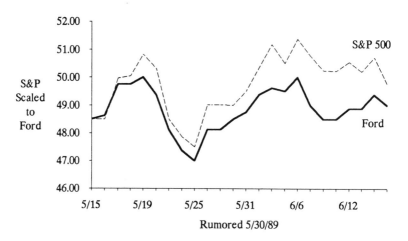

Rumored 5/30/89

Ford Acquires Associates

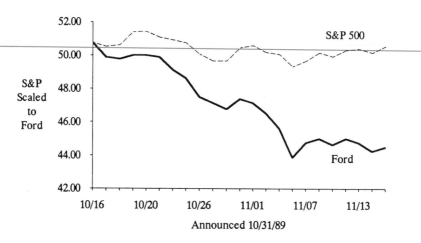

Announced 10/31/89

agers of high-return businesses who consistently employ much of the cash thrown off by those businesses in other ventures with low returns should be held to account for those allocation decisions, regardless of how profitable the overall enterprise is.

As Buffett observes, reinvestment risk is, ironically, more a disease of the healthy than of the infirm. The cockiness and cash that accompany success are breeding grounds for a subsequent misallocation of capital.

Markets versus Managers.   Corporate managers can respond to Buffett by saying that, although mistakes will be made, they are in a better position than their shareholders to judge how to reinvest cash flow. In comparison with most investors, that may be true. But the evidence shows the stock market to be dominated by sophisticated lead steers. As hard as the notion may be to accept, there is reason to believe that, on average and over time, the lead steers in the stock market will be better at the job of allocating capital to promising new uses than corporate managers will be, and not because they are any smarter. It is a question of a better perspective and different incentives.

To take but one example, how could Fred Hartley, the one-time chairman of Union Oil Company, know in 1983 that drilling aggressively for more oil (or investing in a synfuels project that would break even only if the price of oil exceeded $70 a barrel) was the most productive use of society's scarce resources at that time? Impossible, obviously. The resources released by not drilling for oil would be invested somewhere else, in activities with which Mr. Hartley had no relevant experience—developing a next generation of computer chips or software, a biotechnology advance, or who knows what. As complex as such resource allocation trade-offs are to assess, it is precisely such judgments that are made every day by portfolio managers when they decide which companies' shares to buy and which to sell. Moreover, the advent of powerful microcomputers, extensive databases, and a growing body of business school graduates well versed in powerful analytical methods has only enhanced the market's ability to make accurate and rapid-fire evaluations.

Corporate managers, it must be admitted, labor under an inflated and parochial sense of the importance of their products or industry relative to competing alternatives, dogmatic optimism in the face of justifiable market skepticism, a preoccupation with eliminating risks that investors can diversify away, and, perhaps most important, a denial of the strong evidence showing that stock prices tend to be an accurate barometer of a company's intrinsic value (meaning that its upside potential is offset by an honest assessment of its downside risk). For all those reasons, the wave of restructurings in the 1980s had more to do with the *increasing* sophistication of capital markets worldwide, and not the alleged lack of it. In view of the fact that the pricing of securities is becoming ever more sophisticated and global, the wave of financial restructurings can be safely predicted to not only continue but to accelerate (so long as the politicians let it).

There are five ways in which responsible management can return control of discretionary cash flow to the market and shed a discount on value that is caused by the market's perception of reinvestment risk. All five can be illustrated with examples drawn from the oil industry.

Repurchase Shares.   The most flexible way to discharge surplus cash is to repurchase common shares in the open market over time. Exxon did that. Responding aggressively to overcapacity in the oil industry, Exxon cut its employment, refinery capacity, and service stations by a third from 1980 to 1986. Having had a fling with failed diversification efforts (Exxon Enterprises and the ill-fated acquisition of Reliance Electric, now an LBO), Exxon rightly chose to use the cash generated by its retrenchment to buy back common stock on the open market, over $15 billion worth (from June 1983 through December 1989), thereby earning accolades from *Business Week* (August 19, 1985):

> In effect, Exxon has sent a message to its stockholders and the public: "Our industry is shrinking, at least for the present, and we think we should shrink a bit along with it. So we are returning some capital to our shareholders. They, not Exxon management, will decide how this money should be reinvested in the U.S. economy." That is good for the economy.

Exxon's share return (dividend and price appreciation) since the buy-back plan was first announced has bettered the share return produced by both Unocal and Phillips, where restructuring was forced upon management by a raider (exhibit 13.3). Both companies had announced aggressive expansion plans despite declining fundamentals in the oil business, a "damn the facts, full speed ahead" approach guaranteed to put them "in harm's way."

Leveraged Share Repurchases. The second way to cure reinvestment risk, then, is to buy back stock aggressively and finance the purchase with debt. In that way the retirement of stock that might have occurred over time is forcefully discounted to the present. A leveraged buy-out is just a leveraged share repurchase carried to an extreme and will yield the same benefits, only perhaps more so. A leveraged ESOP, which commits a company to pay back debt by purchasing its shares for the benefits of employees, also has elements of curing reinvestment risk, only perhaps less so.

Boone Pickens's threats prodded Unocal and Phillips to use corporate debt and leveraged ESOPs to finance a wholesale stock buy-back, restructurings that, though short of an LBO, did have the effect of forcing recalcitrant managers to discharge cash that they otherwise would have devoted to unrewarding drilling projects or costly diversification.

Exhibit 13.3 Exxon Corporation:
Stock Performance versus Oil Competitors

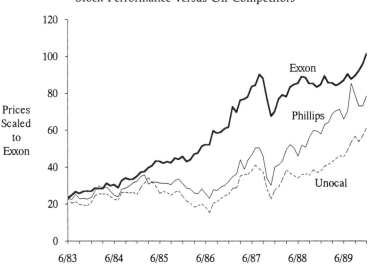

Such leverage admittedly left Unocal and Phillips less able to withstand or capitalize on changing fortunes in the oil industry—one reason why our evidence shows that companies that voluntarily restructure almost always outperform those that restructured at gunpoint. *Business Week* concurred:

> Exxon's program of stock buyback makes a lot more sense than scrambling around to buy new properties. If the oil business comes back, Exxon, tighter and richer, will be in far better shape to benefit than many oil companies now overloaded with debt.

Partnerships.   The third way to give investors control over the reinvestment of cash flow is to house qualifying assets in a partnership. Because the investors in a partnership must pay taxes on their shares of the partnership's earnings, whether distributed or not, they usually insist that the partnership distribute all available cash flow. Thus, in addition to saving taxes, partnerships are ideal vehicles for curing reinvestment risk. On August 25, 1985, the board of Mesa Petroleum announced a plan to convert the corporation to a partnership. It explained the rationale for this move in a shareholders' prospectus:

> Historically, the Company has paid out little of its cash flow as dividends and has been committed to a policy of replacing its annual production of oil and gas reserves through exploration and development and through acquisitions. The Company has paid relatively low amounts of federal income taxes because of deductions resulting from its expenditures. In recent years, however, the Company has significantly reduced its exploration and development expenditures in response to industry conditions, which will result in the Company's paying substantial federal income taxes if it continues its business as presently conducted.
>
> In view of the limited reinvestment opportunities available to the Company, the Board of Directors believes that the interests of stockholders will be better served if a substantial portion of its available cash flow is distributed directly to its owners. To distribute substantially greater cash flow more efficiently, the Board of Directors believes that the partnership form is preferable to the corporate form.

Mesa's stock price soared from $14 to $18 over the period surrounding the announcement (exhibit 13.4). Although the voice of

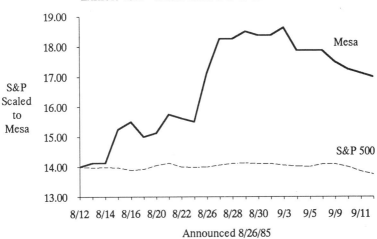

Exhibit 13.4 Mesa Converts to an MLP

the market is all that really matters, analysts also saw the wisdom
of the change:

> Properties appear to be worth full value in partnership form be-
> cause the owners have control of the reinvestment as the partner-
> ship pays out most of its cash flow. Avoidance of the corporate tax
> and a higher basis for cost depletion add to the appeal of newly
> formed partnerships.
>
> > Donaldson Lufkin & Jenrette Securities Corporation
> > *Research Bulletin*
> > September 30, 1985

> We anticipate that future capital expenditures, while rather lim-
> ited, will have a relatively high rate of return because of the
> selectivity available to management. Outstanding debt should be
> reduced sharply over the next few years from both internal cash
> flow and the issue of additional units.
>
> > L. F. Rothschild, Underberg, Towbin
> > Company Research
> > September 25, 1985

Although partnerships normally pay out all available cash
flow, this does not preclude them from expanding. Indeed, after
becoming a partnership, Mesa aggressively sought acquisitions,
starting with Diamond Shamrock, and later Newmont Mining,
usually by offering to swap new partnership units for a target's

outstanding shares. Such expansion is not precluded, but it must pass a market test.

Leveraged Acquisitions.   Professor Michael Jensen of Harvard University has noted that debt-financed mergers also can assure investors that surplus cash flow will not be wasted. After a highly leveraged acquisition is completed, the consolidated entity will dedicate the cash flows of the buyer and seller to repay debt. The result is much the same as if each of the firms had borrowed to buy back its own stock and had then agreed to merge through a stock-for-stock swap. A highly leveraged acquisition milks two cash cows at once. SOCAL's acquisition of Gulf Oil provides a good example, with Boone Pickens again playing the protagonist. Pickens's threats to acquire Gulf and convert it to a royalty trust (a device similar to a partnership) prompted management to seek a white knight. SOCAL responded to the plea by paying $13.2 billion, all financed with debt, to acquire Gulf. Before the merger, SOCAL's leverage ratio (total debt to total debt and equity capital) was 10% and Gulf's was 20%. Afterward, the newly combined entity emerged with a consolidated leverage ratio of 40%, a debt burden both companies worked to pay off. In the period surrounding the takeover, the combined market value of SOCAL and Gulf rose over $5 billion compared to a portfolio of oil stocks. This remarkable increase in value is attributable to three things:

1. The value of operating synergies: the textbook benefits derived from consolidation, rationalization, economies of scale, and so on.

2. The tax benefit of substituting SOCAL's debt for Gulf's equity.

3. Investors, knowing it would be used to retire debt, would be more inclined to fully value the future cash generated by both companies.

Now that the debt has been substantially paid down, SOCAL (since renamed Chevron) is again rumored to be a takeover target. Is it not obvious what they should do now?

Dividends.   The last method that commits a company to distribute surplus cash is to begin to pay or to increase dividends.

Because most companies' boards are reluctant to cut dividends once they have been raised, an increase in dividends usually is interpreted by the market as a lasting commitment to pay out a greater portion of future cash flow to shareholders. Arco, for example, increased its dividend as part of an overall restructuring announced in May 1985. Capital spending was cut 25%; annual operating expenses were to be reduced by $500 million; and refining and marketing operations east of the Mississippi were put up for sale, thereby freeing up cash for Arco to buy back 25% of its stock for $4 billion and increase the dividend by 33%. Although Arco took a $1.3 billion write-down of its eastern refining and marketing assets, investors reacted favorably; they sent Arco's stock price rocketing from about $50 to $62.50 as the plan was first announced, a gain in market value of $2.8 billion (exhibit 13.5).

Though increasing dividends as part of an overall restructuring did increase Arco's market value, increasing dividends usually is less desirable than the other available methods for distributing surplus cash. For one thing, it is generally not as tax-effective. Of greater importance, though, the obligation to pay dividends is not as compelling as servicing debt (a topic I return to later).

Partial Public Offerings.   Offering to sell shares of stock in a subsidiary unit to the public stands in contrast to the methods

Exhibit 13.5   Arco Initiates Restructing Plan

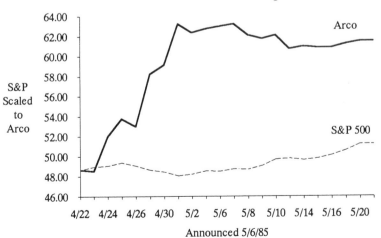

Announced 5/6/85

that pay out surplus cash to investors. A partial public offering (PPO) commits fresh cash to a specific, and presumably appealing, use. Investors know that the new cash raised by a PPO will be used within the unit, unlike a stock offering by the parent company, in which the funds raised must flow through a pachinko machine of competing internal uses with no assurance they will ever reach the firm's most promising ventures.

In addition to channeling cash directly to a business where it is likely to do the most good, creating a publicly traded stock for a subsidiary (with the parent retaining a major stake) may also increase value by:

- Promoting autonomy and entrepreneurism within the unit
- Enabling the unit to attract, retain, and motivate key executives through stock options and other equity-linked compensation devices
- Making it possible for an ESOP that will acquire stock in the unit to be formed
- Providing a market test for the unit's future investment plans
- Syndicating business risks so that the parent will be more inclined to support the unit's promising but risky projects
- Giving the unit access to even more capital outside the parent company's usual capital budgeting process
- Creating for the unit a currency to consummate tax-free acquisitions
- Freeing up a unique pure play for investors

A classic example of a fruitful PPO, one that capitalized upon a number of those benefits, comes from McKesson Corporation, a $6 billion distributor of drugs, beverages, and chemicals that sold a 16.7% stake in its Armor All subsidiary to the public. Upon the announcement of the intended offering on July 24, 1986, McKesson's stock surged from $60 to $66 a share, a 10% gain in value and a strong market endorsement of the merits of the financial restructuring (exhibit 13.6).

Armor All, a marketer of a silicon-based car spray cleaner and protectant, was a relatively small ($90 million in sales), rapidly

Exhibit 13.6 McKesson Spins Off Armor All: Proposes IPO of 16.7%

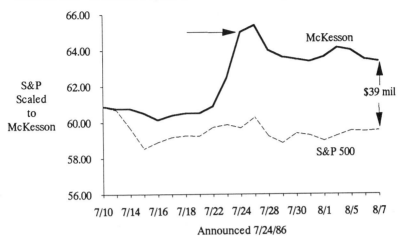

growing (20% per annum, compared to 10% for McKesson), highly profitable unit. Aggressive growth through geographic expansion, new product development, and clever marketing were the ingredients needed to realize its full value. For the parent, McKesson, a company embroiled in highly competitive, cost-competitive, and more mature distribution businesses, the success factors were quite different.

Neil Harlan, McKesson's chairman, said the decision to take Armor All partially public reflects in part that Armor All is "different than most of our operations. It is heavily marketing driven and entrepreneurial in nature." (*The Wall Street Journal,* July 25, 1986.)

With greater accessibility to capital (to say nothing of the heightened incentives for its managers), Armor All stepped up its growth through new product development (a new car wax, car wash, and an all-purpose cleaner in a spray bottle were added), pushed aggressively into Europe and Japan, and acquired Borden's car-care division, an action that alone caused Armor All's market value at the time to climb 5% from $22 to $23 a share (exhibit 13.7). The McKesson case suggests that a PPO can be most beneficial when the parent and the subsidiary are in businesses with markedly different cultures, success factors, and growth opportunities.

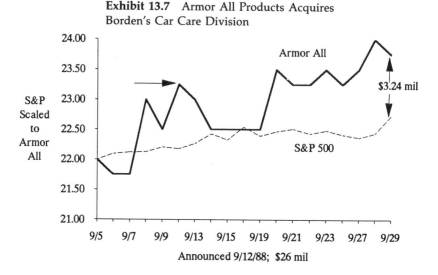

Exhibit 13.7   Armor All Products Acquires Borden's Car Care Division

PPOs Are the Most Misapplied Method of Financial Restructuring.   But even when such conditions are met, PPOs are no panacea. In fact, we have found them to be the most frequently abused method of financial restructuring. For one thing, taking a unit public introduces costs that must be weighed against the potential benefits, including:

- The costs of being public will be duplicated.
- Transactions between parent and the newly public subsidiary must be structured to be fair and at arm's length (see exhibit 13.8).
- An independent board must be solicited, and minority shareholders' interests must be preserved.
- Transactions costs for raising debt and equity through the subsidiary will in general be higher than they would be if the parent raised the funds.
- If the parent winds up owning less than 80%, it can no longer consolidate the subsidiary for tax purposes.
- Proprietary information may be disclosed (exhibit 13.9).

In some cases investors judged that the potential benefits could not overcome these costs, and the parent's stock price suffered as

---

Exhibit 13.8 Look at It My Way

As far as PPOs are concerned, McKesson has tasted the bitter as well as the sweet.

Happy with the results of taking Armor All partially public, McKesson repeated the formula with PCS, its prescription-filling subsidiary, by taking it about 16% public in October 1986. PCS management was thought likely to benefit from the split-off, according to Stephen B. Reid, an analyst for Wedbush, Noble, Cooke, Inc., in Los Angeles. "Becoming a semi-public company will give them a little more freedom to operate," he said. "In a big conglomerate like McKesson, unit managers can feel just like another pea in a pod."

But now McKesson is having second thoughts. The problem began when insurers tried to cut health care costs. PCS, acting in its own interest, responded with plans that cut reimbursements to independent pharmacists. But independent pharmacists are also McKesson's mainstay customers.

Tired of contending with conflicts of interest and the rights of minority investors, McKesson undid the PPO of PCS, offering on December 22, 1989 to buy back the 14% of PCS it did not already own for $30.5 million.

It would stretch the truth to suggest that the market correctly anticipated the unfolding of these events. But when McKesson first announced its intention to take PCS public, its share value barely budged, a striking contrast to the toasty reception accorded Armor All's initial launch.

---

a result of taking the unit public. On other occasions, PPOs failed to create value simply because they were used for the wrong reasons, such as the following.

Fund the Parent?

Some companies use PPOs to fund the parent instead of the subsidiary (exhibit 13.10). Though the unit is the one to raise capital by issuing new shares, the proceeds are handed over to the parent through a special large dividend made prior to the offering.

PPOs that indirectly fund the parent in this way miss the mark. PPOs are supposed to channel cash directly into sectors of a company with promising growth opportunities. A PPO that gives

---

Exhibit 13.9   I've Got a Secret

The cost of disclosing proprietary information is illustrated by Kinetic Concepts (KC), a manufacturer and lessor of rotating hospital beds. KC, private since its founding in the 1970s, grew rapidly in the 1980s, in part by taking market share from Hillenbrand, its main competitor. Because the market for the specialized hospital beds is difficult to track, Hillenbrand apparently was unaware of the significant inroads KC was making.

In 1988, KC went public at an initial offering price of $10.50 a share. To satisfy SEC filing requirements, KC's prospectus recounted the company's business activities in vivid detail. Shocked at what it disclosed, Hillenbrand replaced the management of its specialty bed unit, cut prices, and stepped up the pace of new product development. KC's earnings, which had been growing more than 100% a year, leveled off. In response, the company's shares plummeted in value and began to sell for only about $5.00.

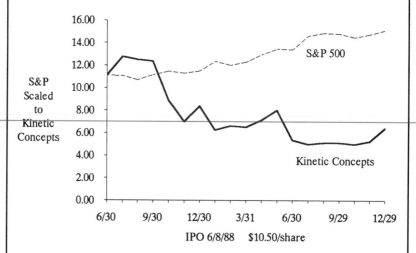

Without the public offering, KC might have enjoyed many more years of profitable growth before its prime competitor woke up to the challenge its progress posed. Going public was costly in this important respect.

Exhibit 13.10	Method without Motive, Form without Function

What better company than Occidental Petroleum ("Oxy") to illustrate how to misuse a PPO?

Oxy, under Chairman Armand Hammer (who must be played by George Burns in real life), has suffered from an extreme case of reinvestment risk. During the 1980s, for example, Oxy had been one of the most acquisitive companies on the face of the earth, purchasing Iowa Beef Processors in 1981 for $800 million, Cities Service ($3.8

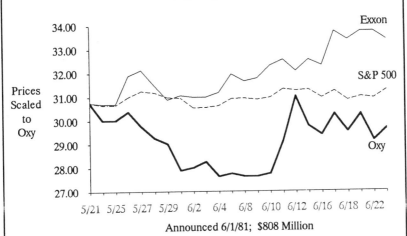

Oxy Acquires Iowa Beef

Announced 6/1/81; $808 Million

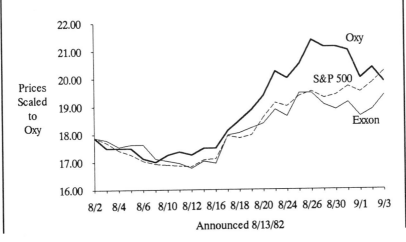

Oxy Acquires Cities Service

Announced 8/13/82

Exhibit 13.10   continued

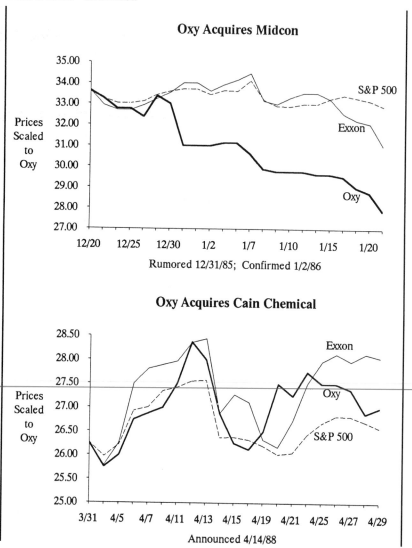

Oxy Acquires Midcon

Prices Scaled to Oxy

Rumored 12/31/85; Confirmed 1/2/86

Oxy Acquires Cain Chemical

Prices Scaled to Oxy

Announced 4/14/88

billion), Midcon ($3 billion), Diamond Shamrock's chemical opera-
tions, and Cain Chemical ($1.2 billion), to name just the larger ones.
Oxy's stock bombed almost every time an acquisition salvo was fired.

Frustrated by Hammer's philosophy of growth at any cost, investors' only recourse was to hold Oxy's stock price essentially flat over
a decade in which the stock market nearly tripled in value.

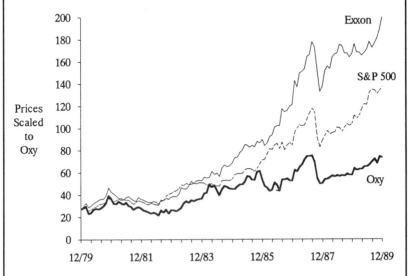

In light of the company's wanton spending habits, investors understandably ran for cover when Oxy announced its intention to sell $1.1
billion of common stock in March 1987: Oxy's shares fell in price
from $34 to $31, and the offering eventually was placed at $30.50.

Oxy Issues Common Stock

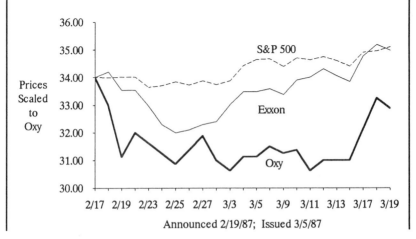

Announced 2/19/87; Issued 3/5/87

Exhibit 13.10   continued

Shell-shocked shareholders figured the more ammunition Oxy got its hands on, the worse off they would become. That is the main reason why the Oxy's PPO of its Iowa Beef Processors (IBP) unit was flawed. Instead of funneling cash to IBP (not that IBP richly deserved the cash, either), the PPO funded Oxy, a direct contradiction to the real purpose of this restructuring technique. Though IBP did receive about $400 million in proceeds from selling shares to the public, prior to the offering Oxy had IBP borrow $950 million to pay a special dividend in like amount. Thus, the net effects of the PPO were to raise equity for the parent and encumber the subsidiary unit with debt.

This maneuver, effective August 21, 1987, was all the more puzzling because Oxy had raised equity in a public offering of its own shares only 5 months earlier. Surely if the objective was to raise cash for Oxy, just upping the parent's own public stock flotation would have made more sense than this convoluted financing strategy. And if the intention was to sever an unrelated business from Oxy, an outright sale or tax-free spin-off would have been preferable. The decision to take IBP partially public remains as inscrutable as Armand Hammer himself.

A second problem was that Oxy sold a 49% interest in IBP. By owning less than 80%, Oxy could no longer consolidate IBP for tax purposes. Dividends received from IBP became taxable to Oxy (after the 70% exclusion) and thereby subjected IBP's earnings to triple taxation (once to IBP, twice to Oxy, and thrice if paid out to Oxy's shareholders). Moreover, had Oxy retained more than 80%, it could have engineered a tax-free spin-off as a graceful way to exit an unrelated business. As it was, should Oxy ever sell its remaining shares in IBP, any gain would be subject to a corporate capital gains tax (and the proceeds would flow to a questionable steward of shareholders' interests).

Oxy's PPO of IBP is a prime example of a restructuring that had form without function, method without motive. It should come as no surprise that Oxy's stock price plummeted as it was announced.

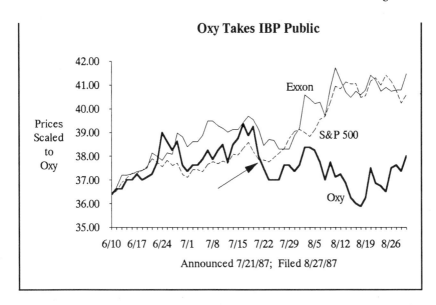

Oxy Takes IBP Public

Prices Scaled to Oxy

Exxon
S&P 500
Oxy

6/10 6/17 6/24 7/1 7/8 7/15 7/22 7/29 8/5 8/12 8/19 8/26

Announced 7/21/87; Filed 8/27/87

the parent cash loses the appeal of such precise targeting. Moreover, if the objective is to raise equity for the parent, it would almost certainly be cheaper to sell more of the parent company's common shares to the public. The one exception to this rule would be private companies that need capital but want to avoid taking the parent company public (exhibit 13.11).

Unearth Hidden Values?

Other companies try to use PPOs to highlight the value of a business unit buried within the overall company. To do so assumes that price-setting investors cannot add 1 and 1 to get 2. An overwhelming body of academic evidence proves that the sophisticated lead-steer investors who set stock prices determine a company's market value by summing the net worth of all its pieces, no matter how obscure they might be. Besides, if management is concerned that the market is overlooking the true value of one of its units, a better strategy, before incurring the expense of taking it public might be to voluntarily disclose all of the information that the unit would be obligated to provide if it actually were to go public. The disdain investment bankers will shower upon such a strategy is but one measure of its true value.

Exhibit 13.11   Going Public to Stay Private

Sam Johnson, the fourth-generation scion of the Johnson Wax family, took public one of his company's individual business units, Johnson Worldwide Associates, Inc. (JWA), a leisure products group, to provide liquidity in the event of an estate tax burden. "What I'm trying to do is build this protection in the company, so that if someone dies, there will be enough liquid assets that could be sold to handle the estate taxes to keep the wax company private," explains Johnson. "I call it going public to stay private."[2]

Going public has not taken away Johnson's control over the leisure products business, however. Even after two public offerings, family-related parties still own 35% of JWA's publicly traded class A shares and, more important, retain a whopping 92% of the closely held class B shares, which confer super voting rights and the right to elect 75% of the board of directors. Family members and trusts can convert their class B holdings into the traded class A shares should they need to raise cash for estate or other reasons.

[2]"Sam Johnson Is 'Going Public to Stay Private,'" *Business Week*, December 5, 1988.

Increase Earnings per Share

~~One of the most popular, and wrongheaded, justifications for~~ PPOs is to enhance earnings per share (EPS). When compared with issuing the parent company's stock to fund expansion, issuing the stock of a subsidiary that will sell for a P/E multiple higher than the parent's will improve the parent's earnings per share. This irrefutable mathematical consequence is of no real value to the parent company's stockholders for one simple reason. The act of carving new investors into a promising subsidiary dilutes the parent shareholders' claim on the earnings of the high-multiple business. As a result, the parent's shares will sell for a P/E multiple that is lower than it would be if the parent itself had raised an equivalent amount of common stock. Replacing an issue of parent shares with high-multiple subsidiary stock is tantamount to swapping a part of the parent's P/E multiple for more EPS, an action which, by itself, makes no sense at all and cannot reward the parent company's shareholders with a higher share value. Its sole appeal will be to corporate managers whose bonuses are wrongly based upon growth in EPS.

Spin-offs Are the Most Neglected Method of Financial Restructuring.   Even when a PPO does resolve genuine restructuring concerns and increases the parent company's value, a PPO is not always the most desirable restructuring technique. A tax-free spin-off would often be even better (exhibit 13.12).

Though taking Armor All partially public did increase McKesson's share value by 10%, it probably would have been preferable to spin it off through a tax-free distribution of Armor All's shares to McKesson's shareholders. As with the PPO, a spin-off would have given Armor All the benefits of being public—autonomy, access to capital, incentives, and so on—but the problems of contending with a minority interest would have been avoided and taxes would have been minimized. Without any ongoing operational, technological, managerial, financial, or tax synergies between the parent and subsidiary (as certainly would appear to be the case with McKesson and Armor All), a spin-off must be preferable to a PPO.

Corporate managers nevertheless are reluctant to spin off business units, particularly star performers like Armor All, because no accounting gain can be recognized upon its disposition and the parent can no longer consolidate the subsidiary's financial results—clearly the worst of both worlds for those thrilled by the upward march of accounting numbers. Only if the senior corporate managers can be made to own a significant equity stake in the parent company will they be inclined to see the appeal of a spin-off through the eyes of their shareholders, a theme we address in the next major section of this chapter.

So Long, Boston Consulting.   The restructuring examples of this section refute a planning paradigm popularized many years ago by The Boston Consulting Group. According to this now widely discredited theory, a company's mature "cash cow" units were supposed to fund the growth of promising new businesses ("question marks"), and thereby make them tomorrow's highly performing "stars." The mangy "dogs" were to be put to sleep. By making a company self-funding and self-perpetuating, this

---

Exhibit 13.12   Spin-offs: The Most Neglected Method
of Financial Restructuring

A tax-free spin-off is often preferable to a PPO, but it finds fewer supporters in senior corporate ranks. A spin-off is the pro rata distribution of shares in a subsidiary unit to the shareholders of the parent. If the parent is public, a spin-off will turn the subsidiary into a separate publicly traded company. No cash changes hands; no values are set; and no taxes are imposed. The same body of shareholders will own the same collection of assets in the same proportions as before, but through common shares in two companies instead of one.

If it qualifies, the spin-off is free from tax on either the distributing parent corporation or the recipient shareholders (see exhibit 13.13). Shareholders allocate their tax basis in the parent's shares to the parent and the spun-off unit in proportion to their respective market values on the day the spin-off first becomes effective. For example, suppose a shareholder has a $5 tax basis in shares of stock in a company that spins off a unit. If on the first day it trades, the spun-off unit closes at $5 and the parent closes at $20, then one-fifth ($5/$25) of the tax basis, or $1, moves over to the spun-off shares, and four-fifths, or $4, of the tax basis remains with the original parent shares. No immediate tax is imposed, however. If the investor subsequently chooses to sell either one of the shares, gain will be calculated vis-à-vis the apportioned tax basis. For corporate tax purposes, the existing net tax basis of the subsidiary's assets is transferred to the spun-off company. The quid pro quo for tax-free corporate treatment is that no step-up in the tax basis of the assets transferred is allowed.

One of the quirks of a spin-off is that the parent company will not recognize an accounting gain or loss. On the historical balance sheet, all of the subsidiary's individual assets and liabilities reduce to a single line reading, "net assets of a discontinued operation." For example, if the unit's assets are $100 and liabilities $40, all those entries collapse into net assets of $60. On the historical income statement, all individual items of revenue and expense congregate on a single line reading, "net income (loss) from a discontinued operation." That's looking back. The spin-off itself wipes the slate clean of the subsidiary's net assets and reduces retained earnings in like amount. Continuing with the preceding example, net assets of $60 is credited, thereby canceling the account, and retained earnings is debited the same $60, thereby reducing the parent's equity by the book value of equity in the unit distributed. The accounting for a spin-off is the same as if a dividend in the amount of the book value of the subsidiary's equity had been paid to the parent's shareholders. But, to repeat, a spin-off, unlike a divestiture, denies the parent company the joy of recognizing an accounting gain and saves it from the trauma of booking a loss. Accounting enthusiasts understandably favor spinning off losers and selling winners. Cash flow devotees, on the other hand, will spin off winners and sell losers, at least as far as minimizing taxes is concerned.

A spin-off, like a PPO, creates a publicly traded stock and all the attendant benefits and costs. But in contrasts to a PPO, it can prevent the parent from meddling, minimize taxes, and avoid the conflicts of interests with minority investors. In the course of our research, almost every time we found a PPO succeed at increasing a company's market value, we concluded that a tax-free spin-off would have been even better. For that reason, we say that a spin-off is the most neglected technique of financial restructuring, and a PPO the most misapplied.

approach to corporate planning initially held great appeal to corporate managers because it circumvented the monitoring processes of the capital markets. (Plus it justified enthroning an aristocratic bureaucracy to oversee the whole process.) In reality, the poorly performing dogs ate the cash and chewed up good managers and the question marks were starved for funds, were overmanaged, or got acquired for obscene premiums. The cash cows soon lost all motivation to be milked for the benefit of others. The bureaucracy equivocated and promised better results next time.

Robert D. Kennedy, the chairman of Union Carbide, is one who has lived through the failings of BCG's *Animal Farm* approach to corporate development:

> "All that stuff about balancing the cash generators and the cash users sounded great on paper. But it never worked. When corporate management gets into the business of allocating resources between businesses crying for cash, it makes mistakes." The investment community, he says, is "a better sorter-outer."
>
> "Learning to Live with Leverage"
> *Business Week*
> November 7, 1988

Our analysis of stock prices confirms the wisdom of Mr. Kennedy's observation. Financial restructurings that severed the

---

Exhibit 13.13　How to Qualify for a Tax-Free Spin-off

The IRS uses six primary criteria to determine whether a spin-off qualifies as tax-free within section 355 of the tax code. In brief, they are:

1. *In control.* The parent must own at least 80% of the stock in the subsidiary unit in order to be "in control."

2. *Substantive distribution.* The parent must dispose of substantially all of its interest in the subsidiary (at least 80%). A company cannot distribute, say, 25% of the stock in a subsidiary as a tax-free spin-off. Think of it this way: The parent must be in control going in and out of control coming out, much like what happens during college fraternity parties.

To gain IRS blessing in a spin-off in which the parent retains some equity interest up to 20%, the parent must agree that its directors and officers will not serve in the same capacity for the subsidiary, that it will dispose of the retained stock within 5 years, and that it will vote the retained stock in the same proportions as the other stockholders.

3. *Active businesses.* Both the parent and subsidiary must consist primarily of active businesses (not passive investments) which had not been acquired in taxable transaction during the past 5 years.

4. *Valid business purpose.* There must be some valid business objective to qualify the transaction. Acceptable reasons include, among others, enhancing accessibility to financing, allowing the market to better evaluate the parent, and providing more effective incentives.

5. *Not a device to avoid taxes.* A company cannot spin off a subsidiary just prior to a prearranged sale as a means of avoiding a corporate capital gains tax.

6. *Continuity of interest.* The same body of shareholders should own shares of stock in the parent and subsidiary in proportions that are the same afterward as before. Technically, this means a spun-off unit, and its parent cannot contemplate issuing new voting common shares for a safe-harbor period of a year following the spin-off.

---

link between mature cash cows and promising growth opportunities increased market values. Our conclusion: Let the cows pass their cash directly to investors, and let the question marks depend directly on the market for their funding. Such a roundabout route is the most direct way to assure that value will be maximized.

III. Concentrate Equity

The third reason to use debt aggressively is that the more debt a company uses, the less equity it employs! A debt-financed recapitalization can dramatically strengthen incentives by concentrating the common shares in fewer hands. This increases the incentive for shareholders to monitor their investments closely and for management and employees, if they are given equity or an equity-like stake, to perform exceptionally well.

Investor Incentives. The reason why concentrating equity benefits investors is first cousin to the theory that won James Buchanan the Nobel prize in economics. Mr. Buchanan wanted to understand why Congress passed laws that did not meet with general approval. The reason, he speculated, was that special interest groups lobby legislators to pass laws that provide their narrow constituencies benefits at the expense of all taxpayers. When the benefits are concentrated and costs are diffused, he believed our democratic system of government lacks a safeguard to stop a minority from exploiting the majority.

A similar conflict exists in broadly held firms, but this time between management and shareholders. Suppose that, in an understandable search for job security, prestige, stability, community recognition, and so forth, management makes decisions that fail to maximize shareholders' wealth. Although all shareholders would benefit from better management, the costs of waging a proxy fight or otherwise rallying investors would be borne selectively. Given the uneven distribution of costs and benefits, it may not make sense for an investor or small group of investors to shoulder the costs of opposing management. But if debt were raised to retire shares, the equity of the firm would be concentrated in fewer investors' hands. With the cost of the value lost through mismanagement now more forcefully registered on each share, shareholders have greater impetus to monitor the company's performance, and that gives management a greater incentive to perform.

To illustrate, suppose that a company starts with 10 million common shares, selling at $10 each for a total market value of

$100 million, and no debt. Assume that misguided management policies reduce value by $20 million, or $2 a share, so that the shares would trade for $12 if the company were properly managed. Even this 20% discount might not rouse shareholders to action. But if management could be induced, for example, to borrow $50 million to retire 5 million common shares in the open market, the $20 million of lost value would be spread over only 5 million remaining shares. The result—a $4 a share discount— would now be a full 40% of value, a gap which might indeed incite a shareholder revolt. Management, alert to the greater incentive that investors have to monitor their performance, would have to be more attentive to creating value for shareholders and less preoccupied with pursuing its own agenda.

Shortly after Sir James Goldsmith prompted Goodyear to buy back 48% of its stock, Robert E. Mercer, chairman and chief executive officer, said that Goodyear "will be more attuned to the stock price than before."[3] Goodyear reversed its wasteful diversification program, selling its aerospace unit to Loral and its oil reserves to Exxon for hefty premiums. Goodyear now concentrates on improving the value of its core tire and rubber operations.

A leveraged buy-out carries even further the benefit of investor concentration. In these transactions, a voiceless herd of stockholders is replaced by a small group of vocal lead steers—sophisticated debt and equity players—who act quickly and surely to change strategies, restructure liabilities, or replace management if such action is called for. One reason an LBO creates value is that it powerfully realigns management with the expressed interests of the company's owners.

> Properly handled, an LBO should also bring about better management. Mr. Magowan, chairman and chief executive officer, thinks it has at Safeway. He now, in effect, is working for one owner, Henry Kravis, not thousands of shareholders [Safeway was taken private in a KKR-sponsored LBO].
>
> "There's a big difference from what a corporate management gets from its board of directors and shareholders and the type

[3]"Goodyear Tire and Rubber Sees Proceeds from Asset Sales Exceeding $3 Billion," *The Wall Street Journal,* January 19, 1987.

of supervision we get from our little narrow band of directors and owners. KKR has never told us how to run the business, but they have to approve our plans and our financial budget. It's very intense. If we're off our plan, they ask the right questions. I don't think corporate boards put management under that type of scrutiny.

"Also, they are the owners. If a corporate board wants management to do something it doesn't have the same credibility as 90% owners who have their own money involved."

"Business World: Safeway's LBO Is Three Years Old and Doing Fine"
The Wall Street Journal
December 5, 1989

Contrast Magowan's cooperative attitude with General Motor's snuffy response when the California and New York public employee pension funds dared to ask for "more, sir"—more performance, more value, and more cooperation with owners in selecting a successor to Roger Smith. GM's board of directors acknowledged no obligation to two of the company's major owners:

> Some guy wants to know how they select management, and the inference is that this board, which is an outstanding board, doesn't know how to do it, one director carped. Are [fund managers] going to be consultants now?
>
> Corporate governance, which includes the selection of officers, is the board's responsibility (an excerpt from the board's official response as disclosed to the press).

"Can GM's Big Investors Get It to Change Lanes?"
Business Week
January 22, 1990

No one is questioning the board's competence. The issue is its will and its incentive to oversee the profound restructuring of General Motors that probably is necessary for the company to survive.

> A truth has become nearly self-evident: Detroit's Big Three are staring death in the face. . . .
>
> Mr. Stempel, a GM employee man and boy, has ruled out radical change. But that is exactly what is needed. To save his firm, Mr.

Stempel must break it up. He should sell off EDS and Hughes, the costly high-tech distractions which have contributed little to cars. He should dismember GM's car division into two or three independent companies, freeing them to compete with one another and to handle their own designs. Such talk is shocking only to bureaucrats, who don't understand America's carmaking tradition.

"Detroit under Siege"
The Economist
April 14, 1990

Please, oh please, let the owners take charge. Or, perhaps even better, make the managers and employees into owners, our next topic.

Incentives for Management and Employees.

Debt, by reducing the amount of equity needed to support a company's assets, makes it even easier for insiders to become significant owners of the enterprise for which they work. To illustrate, suppose that managers and employees as a group were willing to stake $1 million of their own money to purchase common stock in their company. Assume that the company's operations are worth $100 million. Then if the company were financed entirely with equity, the insiders could acquire only a 1% interest with the $1 million they are willing to gamble. But if the company borrowed $80 million to retire common shares, a $1 million investment would bring the insiders a 5% share in the remaining equity.

The substitution of debt for equity thus makes it possible for managers and employees to risk an amount equal to just 1% of the assets and to reap 5% of the payoff from improved asset management. Corporate leverage, by amplifying the reward derived from a more productive use of resources, multiplies the insiders' incentive to perform to the fullest of their capabilities, and with the interests of shareholders put first and foremost. This suggests that combining corporate leverage with an increasing ownership stake for management and employees ought to be an extremely potent way for a company to raise its value. It is.

A "compensation risk map" will take us one step at a time toward just such a full-blown leveraged recapitalization. Moving left to right, from low risk to high risk, creates value by strengthening incentives and a company's capacity to use debt.

Compensation Risk Map

Debt-like				**Equity-like**
Wage	Lower Wage	Lower Wage	Lower Wage	Lower Wage
Defined Benefit Pension	X	X	X	X

Interest Expense (Creditors)

	Gain Sharing	Gain Sharing	Gain Sharing	Gain Sharing
		ESOP	ESOP	ESOP
			Leveraged Equity Purchase Plan	Leveraged Equity Purchase Plan
				Leveraged Cash-Out

No Guts—No Glory. The most secure, debt-like approach to compensation (on the far left of the map) would be to pay a wage and provide a defined benefit pension (along with other perquisites), a no guts and no glory scheme that clearly separates compensation from the success of the business. Employees are treated as bondholders and naturally adopt the risk-averse mentality of creditors as they go about their appointed tasks. Worse yet, because wage payments and vested pension benefits are paid either prior to or equal to the repayment of debt, such a compensation scheme robs a company of its full debt capacity.

Gain Sharing. To move one notch outward on the risk map, reduce wages (if not immediately, then over time), eliminate the defined benefit pension (and other contractual retirement benefits), and make up the shortfall with nondiscretionary performance-related bonuses. For example, take an employee earning $50,000—$45,000 in wages and $5,000 in pension and other defined benefit contributions—and offer instead to pay a $40,000 wage and a bonus that is targeted to be $10,000 assuming no change in performance, but which will be more or less depending upon actual performance. The bonus, for example, might reasonably be as high as $25,000 in times of exceptional performance, and nothing at all in bad times.

The new compensation mix has a value equivalent to the original one, but it works more like a convertible security: one part provides the employee with the fixed return of a bond; the other, like equity, is tied to the success of the firm. It also pays the employer a double dividend, because:

- Employees are given an incentive to improve the company's performance.
- The company's capacity to borrow is increased.

Unlike wages, which are paid no matter what, bonuses shrink when a company's performance slips. More cash is available to repay debt just when the money is most needed. In the example, $10,000 per employee, or 20% of payroll, would be forfeited in favor of creditors in lean years. By convincing employees to give up part of their compensation in a downturn in exchange for a greater reward when things go well, a company effectively creates equity on its income statement to compensate lenders for a greater leveraging of its balance sheet. Even though most widely followed leverage statistics fail to reflect this change, any bank worth its salt would be willing to lend more to a company that restructured its compensation package in this way.

Eliminating a defined benefit pension and the usual speculative funding strategy that goes along with it are two more ways for a company to strengthen its capacity to support debt. By law, a company's pension obligation is a senior claim against the firm. It must be funded either out of the company's ongoing cash flow over time, or in the event of bankruptcy, by satisfying a claim filed by the Pension Benefit Guarantee Corporation that ranks alongside other senior claimants.[4] A defined benefit pension, because it is a debt-like promise to pay employees, reduces the amount of debt that a company can explicitly borrow. It is only recently that the accountants have caught up with this long-standing economic reality.

To make matters worse, almost all companies invest their pension assets in a portfolio of common stocks in the hope of earning a higher return over time than safer bonds would provide. Such a strategy can minimize the out-of-pocket cost of providing a pension, but it is not without risk. What if, ask the always pessimistic bankers, the stock market crashes just as the company's operations falter and the company tilts toward bankruptcy? Then the creditors get hit with a double whammy. The now enlarged unfunded pension liability barges onto the company's books as a senior claim just when the value of the company's assets are dwindling. When companies follow such a speculative pension funding policy, the bankers' only recourse is to restrict the amount of funds they will lend. Abandoning the defined benefit pension plan, or at the very least investing more of the pension fund assets in safe bonds,[5] will expand a company's capacity to borrow.

The additional debt that making these changes in compensation will support is valuable because it enables a company to shelter even more of its operating profits from tax. It also makes possible an even further consolidation of equity in the hands of fewer investors and insiders, plus other benefits yet to be described.

[4]Technically, the PBGC can file a claim having the status of a tax lien, senior to all but secured creditors, to cover any unfunded pension liability in an amount up to a third of the company's net worth. An unsatisfied claim, if any, ranks with other senior creditors.

[5]With a risk-reward trade-off built into the pricing of capital investments, an investment in bonds is expected to yield a lower return over time than an investment in riskier equities would. As a result, a company that switches its pension fund from equities to bonds will have to make greater cash contributions to the fund and thereby reduce its earnings, earnings per share, and return on equity. But its stock price will not suffer as a result, because investing the pension fund in bonds will reduce risk for the company's stockholders as well as for its creditors. A lower cost of equity will offset the lower return on equity the new policy engenders, and there will be no change in value, except that, if the company can borrow more as a result of adopting a more conservative pension investment policy, the tax (and other) benefits of debt financing can increase the company's value. (See A.F. Ehrbar, "How to Slash Your Company's Tax Bill," *Fortune*, February 23, 1981.)

To the extent possible, bonuses should be at least partially based on rewarding the performance attained at a decentralized level—business unit by business unit, plant by plant, shift by shift, person by person—and not according to the results achieved by the company overall. Only that will forge a direct link between pay and performance. If bonuses are based solely on corporate-wide results, the link between pay and performance is so tenuous that only companies with a strong corporate culture, homogeneous businesses, participative management, and effective two-way communication with their employees will derive any incentive as a result.

One of my former employers had a profit-sharing plan in which I participated. One day, while deciding just how expensive a restaurant to patronize with one of our important new clients, I decided to compute my share of this large firm's worldwide profit. When my HP 12C calculator ran out of zeros to the right of the decimal point, I decided to take our guest to a very plush restaurant that day. Needless to say, that is not the kind of sharing plan I am recommending to motivate managers or employees.

The only exception to this rule is when a company's activities are so intertwined that maximizing performance at a decentralized level may work against the collaboration necessary to maximize the value of the whole. But even then, the bonus should combine a participation in the consolidated result with rewarding individual performance to the greatest practical extent. Admittedly, moving compensation to the right on the risk map increases the risk employees must bear. It is important to recognize, however, that there can be no incentive without risk. And, over time, the breed of individual who finds such a package appealing will be drawn to the firm (for an example, see exhibit 13.14).

ESOPs.   Let's turn the compensation amplifier up another notch by introducing an employee stock ownership plan (ESOP), possibly in exchange for an even further reduction in wages and other contractual benefits. Making employees into owners through an ESOP differs from a cash bonus plan in four important ways.

1. ESOPs give employees a share in the value of their company as distinct from a share in its current profits. To be more precise, an ESOP gives

---

Exhibit 13.14 Moving Out on the Risk Map

WTD is a maverick lumber company that has pushed almost all of its operating costs far out on the risk map and substituted fixed financial charges in their place. Bruce Engel, the company's founder, built WTD into the fourth largest lumber company in the United States in just 7 years by rigorously applying three main principles. Engel's first principle flies right in the face of time-honored industry practice. Most lumber companies arrange to purchase logs under 3-year, fixed-price contracts. Not WTD.

> The Company does not speculate in long-term timber contracts which tie up capital and lock companies into raw material costs they may not be able to recover. Instead we buy the majority of our timber on the open market. In most cases, logs acquired are converted and sold within 30 days. This "just-in-time" strategy minimizes our inventory carrying costs.
>
> Because logs represent the single largest production cost, open market procurement is the foundation of a variable cost structure that has made WTD a low-cost manufacturer. When lumber prices are high, we generate healthy margins, even though our log prices may be higher than those of companies with long-term timber contracts. When lumber prices fall, open market log prices generally fall with them. As a result, we should be able to maintain acceptable margins even during the worst of times.
>
> WTD 1988 Annual Report

Engel's first principle is simple: Variable operating costs make for stable profits, and more debt capacity.

Engel's second principle is to increase productivity through employee incentive plans:

> When our employees win big for themselves, the company wins. That's what WTD is all about.
>
> WTD 1988 Annual Report

One reason Engel feels strongly making WTD win big is that he and his wife, Teri, who serves as WTD's vice president for internal affairs and secretary, own nearly 45% of WTD's common stock. The principle of making managers into owners works most effectively when it begins at the top.

A decentralized management structure holds each mill accountable for the profitability of its own operations. Managers are rewarded with monthly bonus payments based upon the earnings of their mills. Weekly bonus compensation encourages hourly workers to increase

Exhibit 13.14   continued

their per shift production by rewarding them for productivity, regular attendance, and safety. Production bonuses average about $3 per hour, though employees at some mills earn substantially more. In addition, Engel customarily passes out $50 bills as "one-shot" bonuses to workers who have exceeded their weekly quotas. There is no limit set on the size of the bonus payments. In return, there are no pension, retirement, savings, or similar benefit plans.[6] All compensation is geared toward variable costs and incentives related to performance.

But WTD does not lose sight of the bigger picture in a narrow-minded pursuit of decentralization. WTD weds the advantages of highly motivated independent lumber mills with the economies of scale of a larger operation. For example, the company markets, distributes, and arranges shipping for all of its mills through a single wholly owned subsidiary, TreeSource. It coordinates the production capabilities of the individual mills to meet a broad range of customer needs. Unlike most sales people, TreeSource representatives do not work on commission. They, too, share in WTD's monthly bonus system, which rewards cooperation in meeting the company's goals for profitability.

Engel's third principle is to use financial leverage aggressively to acquire new production capacity at low capital costs. Engel started WTD in 1981 by taking over a bankrupt lumber mill, assuming its $2 million in debts. He invested $3,000 of his own capital to make it work. By the end of fiscal 1989 (April 30), he had bootstrapped his way into 30 mills in all, using debt aggressively all along the way.

WTD's variable operating cost structure—from the open market purchase of logs and the just-in-time inventory management system to the substitution of cash bonuses and profit sharing for fixed wages and retirement plans—is what enables WTD to use cheap debt capital to a degree that others in the industry cannot prudently match.

WTD's Long-Term Debt/Total Capitalization
(Fiscal Year-End April 30)

1983	1984	1985	1986	1987	1988	1989
100%	93%	79%	69%	66%	70%	69%

[6]Effective May 1, 1989, WTD added a 401(k) retirement savings plan, in which the company makes a matching contribution. Because the company match is tied to the bonus earnings levels achieved by the production workers, this too is a variable operating cost.

Paying no cash dividends also increases WTD's capacity to borrow. Engel has declared that he has no intentions to pay a dividend for the foreseeable future, with good reason. "It's still too early, given our growth opportunities, to pay a dividend," he has said. "A lot of institutional investors would take a dividend as a sign we were slowing down."

Engel's three principles are paying off in a tough business. WTD's rate of return on capital employed[7] has run consistently ahead of WTD's own (weighted average) cost of capital.[8] WTD's 10% cost of capital is low by industry standards, but that is because WTD's variable cost structure stabilizes operating profits, thereby making the firm less risky than its peers, and because the aggressive use of debt saves taxes. Of greater significance than the hefty return, WTD has created a growing pool of residual income, or economic value added; that is, operating profits left over after the cost of capital is recovered.

WTD Economic Value Added (Fiscal Year-End April 30)			
	1987	1988	1989
Sales	$176.2	$293.7	$359.6
Growth	na	66.7%	22.4%
Rate of return	24.5%	14.6%	15.6%
Cost of capital	10.0%	10.0%	10.0%
Spread	14.5%	4.6%	5.6%
Capital	$ 24.6	$ 85.7	$113.0
Economic value added	$ 3.6	$ 3.9	$ 17.6

WTD's common shares have sold for multiples of their economic book value, an indication that the company has added value to the capital placed at its disposal.

[7]WTD's rate of return has been estimated by taking net operating profits after taxes but before financing costs and accrual bookkeeping entries, or NOPAT, and dividing by the capital invested in net operating assets as of the beginning of the year. [8]The cost of capital is an estimate of the minimum rate of return that debt and equity investors combined are seeking to compensate for risk. Although our calculations reveal that WTD's weighted average cost of debt and equity capital did change over this period, because of changes in the general level of interest rates, 10% was chosen as an approximate average cost of capital in order to provide a stationary benchmark against which to judge the company's performance over this time frame.

Exhibit 13.14   continued

	1987	1988	1989
Stock price	$12.13	$16.25	$9.38
Economic book value	3.77	5.13	6.84
Stock price / book value	3.2×	3.2×	1.4×
Stock price — book value	$8.36	$11.15	$2.54
× Shares outstanding	6,267	6,267	6,302
Market value added	$52.4	$70.3	$16.0

Bruce Engel built a premium-valued company by adopting three mutually reinforcing principles. By moving almost all of WTD's operating costs far out on the risk map, Engel has created incentives, debt capacity, and value. His formula looks to be a winner, one that other companies may see fit to emulate.[9]

[9]WTD was severely tested during its 1990 fiscal year, and the outlook for 1991 is more of the same as lumber companies find it difficult to pass on an increase in the cost of timber that is due to growing conservationist pressures. With its operating profit margins pinched, WTD is considering radical action to remain profitable. That is another benefit of aggressive debt financing.

workers a share in the company's value as of the date of their retirement, presumably many years in the future. Changing the employees' focus from maximizing near-term performance to long-run value may be beneficial.

On the other hand, it might not be. Most senior managers, to say nothing of the poor journeyman laborer, have difficulty understanding how value is created (hence the need for this lengthy book). Owning restricted stock via an ESOP may be too abstract to motivate rank-and file-employees unless, again, it is made an integral part of the company's corporate culture. The available evidence strongly suggests that a participative style of management and strong two-way communication are prerequisites to a successful ESOP, no matter what the potential financial reward may appear to be.

2. ESOP incentives accumulate with the passage of time. The number of shares an employee owns via the ESOP increases with each year's allocation, making the employee's monetary, and quite possibly emotional, stake in the firm grow with the passage of time. Cash bonus plans, by contrast, are unchanging. No investment carries over from one year to the next.

Even so, an ESOP still may provide little incentive if the value of the shares accumulating in the account is small relative to the employee's overall net worth. That is one reason why, as a general rule, ESOPs are effective motivators only when they are used aggressively. Otherwise, the ESOP will be lost in the din of employees' total compensation and the encouraging messages it sends will not be heard. The successes of Avis, HealthTrust, and Weirton Steel, in the wake of their 100% employee-owned LBOs, are testimony to the potential benefits of using ESOPs aggressively.

3. An ESOP can increase a company's debt capacity even more effectively than a cash bonus plan can because it is self-financing. By law, the cash that a company contributes to its ESOP must be used to purchase common shares (or equivalents) in the sponsoring corporation.[10] An ESOP makes cash boomerang: What goes out the front door as a compensation expense returns through the back door as new equity available to pay down debt. Substituting an ESOP for other cash-consuming forms of compensation will add powerfully to a company's capacity to borrow and acquire shares.

But beyond the benefit of making it easier to concentrate shares in the hands of employees, borrowing through an ESOP has fewer benefits than is popularly believed. Much has been made of the fact that, whereas corporate debt is amortized from a company's after-tax cash flow, ESOP debt is repaid from cash contributions that are tax-deductible. This apparent tax benefit is an illusion, however. It arises from erroneously associating the benefit of deducting the ESOP contribution with the repayment of debt when, in fact, the tax deduction arises from incurring a compensation expense: the granting of valuable common shares to employees. Despite appearances, it simply is not cheaper to amortize debt through the ESOP than it is through the company itself.

Not only is the ESOP's debt principal not really tax-deductible; the interest on the ESOP debt is not tax-deductible, either. In

---

[10]Even if a company chooses to contribute common shares directly to the ESOP, the result is the same as if cash were first contributed to the ESOP and then used to buy company stock. With a leveraged ESOP, it still is true that contributions to the ESOP finance new equity and expand debt capacity. It's just that the debt capacity is used in advance to repurchase the company's shares.

effect, the ESOP's interest expense simulates the *expected* risk-adjusted increase in the market value of the shares from the time that they are first acquired by the ESOP until they are allocated to the employees and become a compensation expense of the sponsor. The interest on the ESOP's debt is deductible only because it is part of the compensation expense represented by the ESOP, and not because it is a financing charge. Though an ESOP conceptually expands a company's capacity to borrow and buy shares, there is no tax benefit to the additional debt capacity. (See exhibit 13.15 for a further exposition.)

4. Congress has granted ESOPs special tax breaks that are not available to other bonus and retirement plans, among them (exhibit 13.16):

- Commercial banks can exclude from their taxable income one-half of the interest earned on a loan to an ESOP provided the ESOP owns at least 50% of the sponsor's stock. ESOPs that qualify can borrow at favorable rates.

- A company can tax-deduct dividends paid to the ESOP if the ESOP uses the dividends to pay down debt or passes them through to the employee beneficiaries.

- The owners of private companies can sell their shares to an ESOP and defer paying a tax on any gain, provided the ESOP owns at least 30% of the company stock after the sale.

- A company can tax-deduct contributions to an ESOP of up to 25% of covered compensation, or $60,000, whichever is less, versus only 15% of compensation up to a maximum of $30,000 for an ordinary stock bonus plan.

- If an ESOP pays more than fair market value to acquire shares, the sponsor can tax-deduct the premium without incurring an offsetting expense (so long as the price that the ESOP pays is defensible). This unofficial tax benefit is most potent when an ESOP is used so aggressively that it undermines the value of the very shares that the ESOP purchases. (See exhibit 13.15 for a further elaboration.)

The bottom line on ESOPs is that revitalized incentives and special tax benefits team up to make ESOPs particularly attractive

Exhibit 13.15   An ESOP in Slow Motion

The best way to understand a leveraged ESOP is to film it fast and play it back slowly. In fast motion, an ESOP is an up-front, debt-financed purchase of shares in the sponsoring company followed by the allocation of those shares to the accounts of employees as cash contributions from the sponsor repay the ESOP's debt. Got that? Now for the slow motion.

A Stock Bonus Plan

The first freeze frame slows down an ESOP to its most elemental component: a stock bonus plan. A stock bonus plan entails giving employees shares of employer common stock as a form of compensation (though without subjecting them to a current tax, a benefit common to all qualified retirement plans). A stock bonus plan, in turn, amounts to much the same thing as:

1. Compensating the employees with cash (which is a tax-deductible corporate expense)
2. Requiring the employees to use that cash to purchase shares of common stock in the company from the company

The second step, forcing employees to purchase company shares, is what creates debt capacity. The company, in effect, has the right to put its common shares back to its employees: Cash that otherwise would leave the firm as a compensation expense instead returns through the back door to purchase equity. By preserving cash in this way, a stock bonus plan, when it substitutes for other cash-consuming forms of compensation, leaves more funds available to service debt, thereby enhancing debt capacity.

To illustrate, suppose that employees earning $50,000 a year—$45,000 in wages and $5,000 in pension and other defined benefit contributions—are persuaded to take instead a $40,000 wage and $10,000 worth of company shares each year. If the firm employs, say, 1,000 such people, then an additional $10,000,000 (1,000 employees times $10,000 per employee) will be available each year to service debt. The larger a company's payroll is in relation to its market value, the more pronounced this potential benefit is likely to be. And it does not require an ESOP in particular. An aggressive stock bonus plan in lieu of cash compensation would suffice to obtain the benefit of extra debt capacity.

The foregoing compensation restructuring example assumed a *full*

Exhibit 13.15   continued

reduction in wages and other benefits in exchange for stock bonus grants. Seldom is it the case, however, that employees can be convinced to give up wages and other tangible benefits in exchange for stock ownership, at least all at once. More frequently, the stock bonus plan or ESOP is a benefit added on top of existing compensation, a situation in which there is *no reduction* in existing compensation.

For example, suppose that the employees retain the original $50,-000 compensation package but in addition will participate in a stock bonus plan granting them $10,000 worth of company shares each year. Although this plan is more expensive, there still is an increase in debt capacity because the stock bonus plan contributions are tax-deductible. Assuming a 40% corporate marginal income tax rate, the company will reduce its tax bill by $4,000 for each $10,000 of stock it grants to the employees. The taxes saved are cash available to service more debt than before.

It is crucial to observe, however, that the shareholders are not ahead by $4,000. The shareholders are behind by $6,000, the after-tax cost of the new shares granted to the employees. The shareholders will benefit only if the debt that an additional $4,000 of cash flow will support plus the incentives created by handing $10,000 worth of shares to the employees each year is worth more than $6,000, a doubtful proposition at best.

Fortunately, "no reduction in compensation" may be too literal and myopic an interpretation of what actually happens when a new stock bonus plan or ESOP is initiated. At some point, employees are likely to realize that valuable common shares are accumulating in their account. Eventually, competition in the labor market may force them to give up some of their tangible compensation in exchange for on-going stock grants. As to just how long it might take for a partial reduction in compensation to occur, there is no certain answer.

Suppose that eventually a compromise is reached and the employees' original $50,000 compensation package is replaced by $45,000 in tangible rewards and $10,000 in company stock for a total of $55,000, or 10% more overall. This package has much to offer both the company and its employees. True, the company does incur an additional expense of $5,000, or $3,000 after taxes. But $7,000 of extra cash will be available to service debt (the $5,000 reduction in cash compensation plus an additional $2,000 of taxes saved). Furthermore, the company has gotten the employees to put $5,000 of their former tangible compensation at risk. Preserving the income they otherwise would have earned may be an even greater incentive for employees than the prospect of upside potential. The added risk the employees bear in this plan is one reason why they may be justified in earning a total compensation that is 10% greater than it was before.

The *partial reduction* plan indicates how common ground might be found for a win-win restructuring of compensation, a compromise whereby all parties—employees, managers, customers, and, yes, even the neglected shareholders—can come out ahead. The trick is to use the additional debt capacity and to capitalize upon the heightened incentives in order to overcome the additional compensation cost of the plan.

A stock bonus plan is at the heart of an ESOP. What makes an ESOP different, and more confusing, is combining a stock bonus plan with leverage. Next slide, please.

Forming a Leveraged ESOP

A leveraged ESOP is essentially an ordinary stock bonus plan coupled with an up-front, debt-financed share repurchase. There are, however, some crucial accounting and valuation differences.

If a company did borrow to buy back some of its common shares at the same time it instituted a stock bonus plan for its employees, a procedure I refer to as a synthetic ESOP, the accountants initially would record the debt incurred as a liability and would reduce common equity in an equal and offsetting amount. The common shares acquired in the buy-back would be held in the company's treasury, thereby canceling outstanding shares for the purpose of computing earnings per share (EPS). Over time, however, the treasury shares would be reissued to the employees via the stock bonus plan, thereby building back up the company's common equity and shares outstanding.

Accounting for the formation of an ESOP that borrows to buy company shares off the market resembles that for a synthetic ESOP, but with one crucial difference. What is the same is that the ESOP's debt is recorded as a liability of the sponsor and the company's common equity is reduced by a negating entry in a contra account. The difference is that the common shares that the ESOP holds are *not* taken into the company's treasury. Instead, they remain outstanding for the purpose of computing EPS.

This bizarre and misleading accounting treatment is dictated by the accountant's motto: If you can hit a company once or hit it twice, then hit it twice, just in case. On the one hand, the accountants consider the ESOP's debt to be the company's debt, and they record it as a liability. But with the other hand, they deny that the company's shares held by the ESOP are the company's property. The accountants' doubly conservative and wholly inconsistent interpretation sometimes

Exhibit 13.15   continued

stops companies from using ESOPs even when they make sense on economic grounds. That should not happen in this day and age.

The reason why accountants consider the shares the ESOP holds to be outstanding is that they anticipate that the shares will be handed over to the employees in the future. But that is jumping the gun, don't you think? With a synthetic ESOP, by contrast, though the shares the company initially buys in also will be allocated via the stock bonus plan, the shares will become outstanding for the purpose of computing EPS only as they are turned over to the employees. The accounting for a synthetic ESOP is the appropriate way to account for an actual ESOP, for they amount to essentially the same thing.

In the next roll of the camera, after the ESOP has been formed, the sponsor will make a series of tax-deductible cash contributions to the ESOP, which will use the cash to service its debt, thereby triggering the release of shares of an equivalent book value to the accounts of the employees (with vesting over a 3- to 7-year period of plan participation).

Don't Be Sapped by an ESOP

When it is described in this way, an ESOP appears to give the sponsor the advantage of tax-deducting the repayment of debt. (Recall that, as the ESOP repays its debt from company cash contributions, the liability carried on the sponsor's books is written down by the accountants.) Much has been made of the fact that, whereas corporate debt is amortized from a company's after-tax cash flow, ESOP debt is repaid from cash contributions that are tax-deductible. The financial press, commercial and investment bankers, and many others have made statements to the effect:

> The trusts have some very appealing tax advantages. . . . Companies can deduct the cash they give their ESOPs to pay off the principal and interest on the loan.
>
> "The Foolish Rush to ESOPs"
> *Fortune*
> September 25, 1989

Absolutely not. It simply is not true that the sponsor gets a tax deduction for repaying principal and interest on the ESOP loan. To see why, let's rewind the film and play back an economic interpretation of an ESOP, exposing the action in slow-motion frames. An ESOP is the same as:

1. Compensating employees with cash (which is a tax-deductible operating expense)

2. Compelling the employees to use that cash to purchase shares of stock in the company, this time from the ESOP (which then holds the shares in trust for the employees)
3. Instructing the ESOP to use the cash obtained from selling shares to pay down its debt (a non-tax-deductible financial flow)

Put this way, it should be clear that the sponsor does not enjoy a tax deduction for repaying debt. A company's contributions to its ESOP are tax-deductible because they are a real compensation expense of the firm. The fact that the compensation is converted into company stock makes it no less real, nor does the fact that the company's obligation to repurchase those shares is deferred until employees retire. From the perspective of shareholders who own stock in the company before the ESOP is formed, the company must plan to buy back the shares the ESOP will give the employees (and to recoup the cost of dividends paid in the meantime) in order for them to be as well off as they would be without the ESOP. (Private companies actually are obligated to buy back shares from retiring employees; for public companies, doing so is a question of comparability.) The *expected* present value cost to repurchase the shares from employees as they retire (plus the cost of the interim dividends), no matter how distant the buy-back might be, is, by definition, the current value of the shares. As with a more straightforward stock bonus plan, the company must derive sufficient benefits from the ESOP to more than offset the cost of the shares the ESOP gives to the employees, or else there will be a dilution in the company's value.

The operation of a synthetic ESOP dispels once and for all the myth of debt deductibility, for it replicates all of an actual ESOP's illusory tax benefits but without borrowing through an ESOP at all. With a synthetic ESOP, recall, a company initially borrows to retire its shares. Then it institutes a stock bonus plan and realizes a tax deduction as it subsequently grants valuable shares to its employees. The cash conserved by this move is applied to retire the company's debt. Thus, without borrowing through an ESOP, the company reaps a tax deduction as its debt is repaid by issuing shares to employees. Despite appearances, it simply is not cheaper to amortize debt through an ESOP than it is through the company itself.

A Double-Barreled Blast at Leverage

Returning now to the main action in our slow-motion ESOP, as the ESOP debt is retired, the accounting entries made when the ESOP was first formed are reversed. Company debt is pared as the ESOP loan is extinguished. Net worth is written up by the book value of the

Exhibit 13.15   continued

common shares allocated to employees—a value that matches the debt retired.

An ESOP thus takes a double-barreled blast at leverage, making a company's debt go down and its equity go up. Equity goes up as employees acquire stock in the company. Debt goes down as the proceeds from selling shares to the employees repays the debt. Here is the balance sheet manifestation of the increase in debt capacity that arises from using a stock bonus plan in lieu of cash compensation. The two-fisted unleveraging of a leveraged ESOP is perhaps its greatest advantage as a tool of corporate finance: A company's ability to quickly recover from a debt-financed share repurchase is dramatically strengthened by its use.

It is worth stressing again, however, that corporate debt capacity expands because of the stock bonus plan element of an ESOP, and not because of an ESOP per se. Moreover, the additional debt capacity that an ESOP creates is without a tax benefit, for the interest on the debt the ESOP borrows is not really tax-deductible! Before showing why, we need to discuss one other important difference between a regular and a synthetic ESOP.

A Share Fixation

A second crucial difference between a synthetic ESOP and a real one is the price paid for the shares. With a stock bonus plan, shares are acquired each year at prevailing market value. A given cash contribution to the plan will purchase a variable number of shares depending upon the value of the shares at the time.

By contrast, a company acquires shares from its ESOP at book value, that is, at the price the ESOP originally paid for the shares. Thus, in the years after an ESOP is formed, a given cash contribution to the ESOP will acquire a given number of shares for the employees. The actual value of the shares could be far more or far less than the accrued book cost, depending upon how well the company performs after the ESOP is first formed.

For that reason, a leveraged ESOP gives the employees a greater incentive than does a stock bonus plan (if only they knew), because if the company's market value increases, they will be doubly rewarded. Not only will the shares already allocated to their accounts appreciate in value but all of the shares that the ESOP has yet to allocate to the employees will be worth more too. Just sticking around to collect more of the appreciated shares can be rewarding. Of course, if the company performs poorly, it will be burdened with paying book value for shares that are worth less than that.

ESOP Debt's Interest Not Tax-Deductible

Technically, the sponsor acquires shares from its ESOP at original book value plus accrued interest. Accrued interest is part of the cost of the shares because it represents the *expected* risk-adjusted appreciation in the market value of the shares from the time the shares are first acquired by the ESOP until they are allocated to the employees. Considering interest to be part of the cost of the shares has a startling implication: There is no tax benefit to the ESOP's debt financing. All of the contributions the sponsor makes to the ESOP, including those to pay interest, are really compensation expenses and not financing charges. Therefore, though an ESOP conceptually expands a company's capacity to borrow and buy shares, there is no tax benefit to the additional debt capacity.

Once again a comparison to a synthetic ESOP is helpful. A synthetic ESOP produces a tax deduction for compensation expense that is expected to be the same as an actual ESOP but, in addition, allows the deduction of interest on debt incurred to buy back stock. To illustrate, suppose that a company borrows $1,000 at 10% interest and buys back 100 of its shares for $10 each. After 1 year has passed, the company gives employees 100 shares that are worth, say, $11 each, for a total compensation expense of $1,100. The $11 share value at that time represents a 10% appreciation over the former $10 a share value, a gain that is equal, let us say, to the return investors expected to compensate them for risk. The $1,100 of cash conserved by giving employees stock in lieu of tangible compensation repays the debt—principal and interest. With this synthetic ESOP, the company gets to tax-deduct $1,200—an $1,100 compensation expense and $100 of interest on the debt.

Suppose instead that this same company formed a regular ESOP which borrowed $1,000 at 10% and used the proceeds to acquire 100 shares for $10 each. After a year has gone by, the company contributes $1,100 to the ESOP: $1,000 for principal and $100 for interest. The ESOP allocates to the accounts of the employees all 100 shares which, as before, are worth $11 each, or $1,100 in total. This time the company is able to deduct only the $1,100 it contributes to the ESOP, an amount which represents the actual (and expected) value of the shares at that time and a bona fide compensation expense. But the interest on the ESOP debt is not separately tax-deductible to the sponsor, because it is an expense of the trust and not of the company. An ESOP thus creates the illusion of leverage without introducing the tax benefit of debt. A synthetic ESOP actually has a superior tax treatment in this regard (though there are other tax advantages to regular ESOPs that are not enjoyed by synthetic ones).

Exhibit 13.15   continued

Tax-Deducting an Overvaluation of the Shares

Besides leveraging the incentives for employees, fixing the value of the shares the ESOP purchases can save taxes if the ESOP pays more than market value for the shares. For example, suppose that an ESOP pays shareholders $13 million to acquire shares that are really worth only $2.2 million. (The reason for these odd numbers will become apparent with an example to follow.) Though it will cost the shareholders only $2.2 million for the ESOP to give the shares to the employees, the tax authorities will permit the sponsor to deduct the ESOP's $13 million purchase price as an expense. Tax-deducting the overvaluation of the shares produces a value that shareholders and employees can split.

The tax deduction aside, it may seem that the shareholders will lose if the company subsequently must pay the ESOP $13 million to acquire shares that are worth only $2.2 million. But that is not so, for the shareholders were the beneficiaries of the overpayment in the first place. They were the ones to receive $13 million from the ESOP in exchange for shares worth only $2.2 million. Conversely, the shareholders do not benefit from selling shares to the ESOP for a premium to their true value. The shareholders' premium is financed by debt that the sponsor must repay, so on net it is just a wash for them. In reality, the only benefit for the shareholders is tax-deducting the overvaluation of the shares, and not the overvaluation of the shares per se.

There are two ways in which the ESOP can pay more than fair value for the shares that it acquires and thereby make it possible for the sponsor to reap this special tax subsidy. First, the ESOP can simply overpay. An outright overpayment is easiest to disguise in private companies for which no quoted price exists or in public companies that sell to their ESOPs convertible preferred stock in which the trade-off of yield and conversion value is debatable.

A more clever approach is to reduce the value of the ESOP's shares by the very act of forming the ESOP itself. Assuming that there are no offsetting wage or benefit concessions, and ignoring any of the other benefits that might be derived from forming an ESOP, a company's common equity value would be expected to fall by the after-tax present value of the cash the company must contribute to the ESOP. The tax authorities, however, for the most part ignore the fact that setting up a leveraged ESOP may in and of itself diminish the intrinsic value of the common shares that the ESOP purchases. As the company makes cash contributions to the ESOP to acquire the shares for the benefit of employees, it will be able to deduct as a compensation expense the ESOP's cost basis in the shares instead of the true value. The more shares the ESOP buys and the higher the price it pays, the more costly the ESOP will be to the company. As a result, the greater will be the reduction in the shares' value compared to what the ESOP paid for them and the greater will be the tax benefit from deducting an overvaluation of the shares. An ESOP-financed LBO carries this benefit to its logical extreme.

For instance, consider a company whose value is $10 million based upon discounting the likely free cash flow from its operations. Initially, it is all equity-financed and has outstanding 1 million common shares selling for $10 each. The shareholders agree to sell all of their shares to a newly formed leveraged ESOP for $13 a share, or $13 million in total, a 30% premium. If there is no change in the operating performance of the company as a result of the LBO and no reduction in the compensation plans that were in place before the LBO, and assuming a 40% corporate marginal income tax rate, what will be the value of the company's common shares immediately after the ESOP-financed LBO is performed? According to the accountants, it is a negative $3 million, because the accountants will record a $13 million liability and will reduce common equity by $13 million also.

The accountants are wrong again, however, for the entries they make ignore the fact that the contributions to the ESOP are tax-deductible. Given the facts, the shares held by the ESOP will be worth $2.2 million, which is the original $10 million corporate value less the $7.8 million *after-tax* cost of paying off the ESOP's $13 million debt. (This assumes that the company's pretax profits are sufficient to fully cover the contributions necessary to pay off the principal and interest on the ESOP's debt.) Thus, without changing the company's operating performance or altering employee compensation, an ESOP-financed LBO produces a 30% premium for the shareholders and entitles the employees to receive valuable shares of stock in the company. That is the magic of the special tax subsidy for deducting an overvaluation of the shares.

As a matter of fact, the shareholders' $3 million gain can be explained directly as a consequence of tax-deducting the overvaluation of the shares less the after-tax cost of granting valuable shares to the employees:

Exhibit 13.15 continued

Shareholders'

gain (loss) = tax benefit of overvaluation — after-tax cost of employee
compensation
$$= t \times \text{overvaluation} - (1 - t) \text{ (ESOP share value)}$$
$$= 40\% \times (\$13\text{M} - \$2.2\text{M}) - (1 - 40\%) (\$2.2\text{M})$$
$$= 40\% \times (\$10.8\text{M}) - (60\%) (\$2.2\text{M})$$
$$\$3\text{M} = \$4.32\text{M} - \$1.32\text{M}$$

The ESOP's tax basis in the shares it acquires is $13 million. But after taking into account the expense of diverting corporate cash flow to the ESOP, the value of those shares is reduced to just $2.2 million. This difference, or $10.8 million, is an overvaluation of the shares that is tax-deductible at a 40% rate, saving the company $4.32 million in taxes. This special tax subsidy is offset by the expense of granting common shares worth $2.2 million to the employees. The cost to the company and to the shareholders of giving employees shares that are worth $2.2 million is $1.32 million after deducting $2.2 million as compensation expense for tax purposes. Netting the after-tax cost and the benefit produces a $3 million gain for the shareholders, a premium that was reflected in the LBO tender offer.

Unfortunately, shareholders will not always come out ahead, even when there is a substantial subsidy for deducting overvalued shares. As a matter of fact, it is possible for the shareholders to receive a 30% premium upon selling fully half of their shares to the ESOP and to be worse off than before. Suppose, for example, that the facts are the same as in the preceding example, but this time the ESOP borrows $6.5 million to pay $13 a share for just 500,000 shares, or one-half of 1 million shares that are outstanding. This time the company's $10 million value is reduced by $3.9 million, the after-tax cost of the cash that must be contributed to the ESOP to pay off the $6.5 million debt, leaving $6.1 million in value, or $6.10 a share. Once the smoke has cleared, the shareholders will have received $13 a share for the 500,-000 shares they sold to the ESOP and will retain 500,000 shares worth $6.10 each, a total value of $9.55 million, which is a loss of 4.5%. The employees are clear winners, however, for they wind up with 500,000 shares worth $6.10 each, or $3.05 million.

The shareholders lose in this transaction because the value of the tax subsidy is surpassed by the after-tax cost of compensating the employees.

Shareholders'
gain (loss) = tax benefit of overvaluation − after-tax cost of employee
compensation

$$= t \times \text{overvaluation} - (1-t) \text{ (ESOP share value)}$$
$$= 40\% \times (\$6.5M - \$3.05M) - (1-40\%) (\$3.05M)$$
$$= 40\% \times (\$3.45M) - (60\%) (\$3.05M)$$
$$-\$0.45M = \$1.38M - \$1.83M$$

Because the ESOP purchased only half of the company's shares, it is not as costly as it was when all of the shares were acquired for the benefit of the employees. As a result, the shares retain more of the value that the ESOP paid, thereby reducing the overvaluation of the shares and increasing the value of the shares that the ESOP will give to the employees. As a matter of fact, though the employees will be granted only half as many shares with this plan as with the LBO, the total value of the shares they will receive is greater, $3.05 million versus $2.2 million! Confronted with a shrinking tax subsidy and a rising compensation expense, the shareholders lose. Unless wage concessions or the other benefits of the ESOP recover this loss, the shareholders would be better off without the ESOP.

Comparing the two transactions—the LBO and the 50% buy-back —it is easy to see why an ESOP should be used aggressively or not at all. The irony is that, beyond a certain point, the more shares an ESOP acquires, the less value will be conveyed to the employees and the more value will be produced for the shareholders. Thus, an ESOP-financed LBO can add most to shareholders' wealth because it most significantly undermines the value of the shares that the ESOP purchases, thereby maximizing the tax subsidy from deducting over-valued shares and minimizing the value of the shares transferred to the employees. Moreover, it also has the greatest potential to convince employees to make concessions and to create an incentive for them to perform, for they will become the sole owners of the company.

As appealing as it might be, an ESOP-financed LBO is practical only when the sponsor can contribute cash to the ESOP sufficient to pay down the debt. Even when operating cash flow is up to the task, tax law limits the level of tax-deductible contributions a company can make to an ESOP. Here again, Congress has been generous. In comparison with a stock bonus plan in which qualifying cash contributions can be no more than 15% of wages, or $30,000 per employee, whichever is less, a company is allowed to contribute to an ESOP as much as 25% of wages and up to $60,000 per employee. Thus, if 25% of payroll summed over a period of as long as, say, 10 to 15 years, is more than the takeover value of a company, an ESOP-financed LBO may be possible.

Exhibit 13.15   continued

Building upon the previous example, to pay a 30% premium to LBO a company with a $10 million market value, an ESOP would have to borrow $13 million. To pay off the principal on $13 million of debt over 10 years, the sponsor would have to contribute $1.3 million each year to the ESOP. Because contributions to the ESOP to repay principal are limited to no more than 25% of payroll (contributions to repay interest are not constrained), payroll would have to be at least $5.2 million ($1.3 million/0.25), or slightly more than half of current market value ($5.2 million/$10 million).

With this constraint in mind, exhibit 13.17 presents the industry groupings of The Stern Stewart Performance 1000 ranked according to the 1988 ratio of the annual labor expense to the market value of common equity. (Be forewarned that Compustat broke out labor expense for only 160 companies of the 900 industrial and service companies covered in our survey.) The higher the ratio, the more cash a company is allowed to contribute to the ESOP to buy out the shareholders at a premium to the current market value. The industries topping the list are transportation, steel, textiles, and machine tool companies, among others—labor-intensive, fiercely competitive businesses, a number of which have or are about to use ESOPs aggressively (e.g., United Airlines). The bottom of the list is dominated by profitable, capital-intensive companies, for which ESOPs probably make little sense. Out of 47 industries, 15, or almost one-third, passed the 50% threshold in the ratio of labor expense to equity market value necessary to perform an LBO financed with an ESOP. LBO GM with an ESOP, anyone?

Valuing An ESOP Company

To value the common shares of a company that has an ESOP, the projected contributions to the ESOP to service principal and interest on the ESOP debt should be treated as a tax-deductible compensation expense that reduces NOPAT. To determine the value of the common equity, the ESOP debt should *not* be subtracted from the discounted value of the free cash flow. The ESOP debt is repaid by the cash contributions to the ESOP which are netted from NOPAT, so to subtract the ESOP debt would double-count the cost. The resulting equity value should be divided by all of the shares outstanding, including those held by the ESOP. In the final analysis, the accountants are correct in leaving outstanding the common shares held by the ESOP, for they will have the same value as any other shares. It is really the ESOP debt that is not outstanding, for it is to be repaid out of future compensation expenses, but try explaining that to your banker.

Exhibit 13.16 ESOP Tax Benefits

Congress has seen fit to grant a number of generous tax breaks to companies that form ESOPs. The following discussion is current as of April 1, 1990.

First of all, a commercial bank may exclude from its taxable income one-half of the interest attributable to a loan made to an ESOP, provided that:

1. The ESOP holds shares that represent more than 50% of the vote and value of all common equity investors.
2. All voting rights are passed through to employees.
3. The term of the ESOP loan is 15 years or less.

An ESOP that qualifies can borrow at favorable rates (usually less than 85% of prime) to prepurchase shares in the sponsoring corporation (a leveraged ESOP). The net present value of this benefit is worth about $3.60 for every $100 borrowed by the ESOP.[11]

Second, as a result of the Tax Reform Act of 1986, a company can deduct from its taxable income any dividends the ESOP collects on unallocated shares and uses to repay debt, a loophole sizable enough to drive a truck through. To see why, let's devise a slightly illegal scam (one of my favorite pastimes).

Suppose that an ESOP borrows $10 million at 10 percent and uses the proceeds to purchase a special class of preferred stock from the sponsor company. The company invests the proceeds, uses it to pay down its debt, or whatever. The preferred is a little unusual (and just slightly illegal for ESOP purposes) because it promises to pay just a special one-time dividend of $11 million at the end of 1 year, and nothing more.

At the end of the year, the intrepid corporate sponsor pays the special $11 million dividend to the ESOP, which in turn pays off its entire debt with accrued interest. Because the dividend has been used to repay the ESOP's debt, the company is entitled to tax-deduct the full $11 million—principal and interest. Now that the ESOP loan has been fully extinguished, the trustee is obligated to allocate all of the preferred shares to the accounts of its employees. But, surprise! The preferred shares are now worthless! The scam generates the company an $11 million tax deduction without incurring an expense. The ESOP just serves as a tax-deductible conduit for retiring debt.

[11]The benefit is calculated by discounting the after-tax interest expense saved to a present value at the borrowing rate, assuming that the ESOP debt amortizes evenly over 10 years, that the ESOP borrows at 8.5% versus 10% for the company, and that the marginal corporate income tax rate is 38%.

Exhibit 13.16 continued

   This would be a great deal if it were legal, but it isn't (the ESOP can hold only common stock or preferred stock that converts into common stock), though the next best thing is. Sell a convertible preferred stock issue to the ESOP and instruct the ESOP to use the dividends on the unallocated shares to repay its indebtedness. The sponsor will receive a tax deduction for those dividends, but, as before, the dividends are without cost to the company because they extinguish debt. The after-tax value of this perfectly legal and congressionally endorsed tax dodge is on the order of $11.40 for every $100 of ESOP debt used to purchase convertible preferred shares.[12]

   Using a convertible preferred also makes sense on grounds other than saving taxes. An inherent problem with an ESOP is that it forces employees to invest a large portion of their retirement wealth in the stock of one company: their employer. A convertible preferred, because it enjoys a fixed, preferred yield and a liquidation preference when compared with the company's common stock, will hold more of its value in the event the company performs poorly. Being convertible, however, it still is possible for employees to participate in exceptional upside gains, thereby preserving the incentive of equity ownership. For these reasons alone, to say nothing of the tax benefit, a company would be well advised to structure an ESOP to acquire convertible preferred stock.

   Third, the sponsor also can tax-deduct dividends paid on allocated shares that the ESOP passes through to the employee beneficiaries. Of course, doing so imposes a tax on the employees that they would avoid if the dividends were retained by the ESOP and used instead to purchase additional company shares on their behalf (an act which also would increase debt capacity). On the other hand, passing on the dividend gives the employees an immediate, tangible reward, thereby making the abstraction of share ownership somewhat more concrete (plus it does save corporate taxes). The net tax benefit of passing dividends to employees is between about $1.50 and $2.80 (depending on how long the benefit is projected to last) for every $100 of ESOP debt used to purchase convertible preferred shares.[13]

---

[12]The benefit is the present value of the taxes saved by deducting the dividends that are paid on the convertible preferred shares until they are allocated to the accounts of the employees. It is assumed that the preferred stock is allocated evenly over 10 years as the debt is repaid, that it bears a 9% yield, that the marginal corporate income tax rate is 38%, and that the discount rate is 15%, an estimated cost of equity.

[13]The benefit is the present value of the taxes the sponsor saves by deducting the dividends less the tax imposed on the employee beneficiaries. It is assumed that

Tax-deductible dividends, no matter in which manner they arise, are not an unalloyed blessing. They can lead to one of life's most unpleasant experiences: a minimum tax liability. By law, one-half of the difference between taxable income (after certain adjustments) and reported income is a tax preference item subject to a minimum tax of 20%. Deductible for tax but not book purposes, ESOP dividends give rise to just such a tax preference and a potential minimum tax assessment. The Lord giveth and the Lord taketh away.

Fourth, one of the most generous of an ESOP's tax benefits is reserved for the owners of private companies. They are entitled to sell shares to an ESOP, and to defer paying a tax on any gain, provided that:

1. The selling shareholder has held the shares for at least 3 years prior to the sale.
2. The ESOP owns at least 30% of the sponsor's common stock after the sale.
3. The selling shareholder reinvests the proceeds in qualifying domestic securities.

This tax code provision enables the owners of private corporations to cash out and diversify their accumulated wealth, without incurring a current tax, while providing for the eventual transfer of the shares to company employees, a nifty benefit to be sure.

Private companies also can establish ESOPs for employees of individual subsidiary units within the overall company, a benefit that is generally denied to public firms. The ESOP trustee uses cash contributed by a subsidiary of the company to acquire shares of common stock in that subsidiary (either existing shares held by the parent or new shares issued by the subsidiary) and allocates those shares to the employees of just that unit, thereby giving them an incentive to improve the performance and value of a business over which they have a direct influence.

A public company, on the other hand, cannot use the stock of a wholly owned subsidiary in an ESOP, a restriction that makes it more difficult for a public company to forge a link between pay and performance as strong as that available to employees of private firms. A public company can establish an ESOP for a subsidiary unit only if the unit itself is partially publicly traded or if the unit is not partially

---

the convertible preferred stock has a 9% yield and is allocated evenly over 10 years, that there is a 10% differential between the corporate and the personal marginal income tax rate (38% vs. 28%), and that the discount rate is 15%.

Exhibit 13.16   continued

publicly traded but the parent owns less than 80% and meets certain other conditions.

In summary, an ESOP can reduce borrowing costs (but only if the ESOP owns more than 50%), can save taxes from deducting dividends (a largely unqualified benefit), and can avoid an immediate capital gains tax on the sale of stock in a private company to an ESOP (provided the ESOP controls more than 30% of the company's stock).

restructuring devices when used aggressively in companies whose market value is low in relation to payroll. (See exhibit 13.18 for an economic analysis of the decision to implement on ESOP.)

Exhibit 13.17   Stern Stewart & Co. Performance 1000
Industry Groupings Ranked by Labor Expense/Equity Value
(Dollars in Millions)

Rank	Industry	Labor Expense/ Equity	Labor Expense	Equity Value	No of Cos
1	Auto Parts & Equipment	133%	$910.3	$684.8	1
2	Airlines	129	16,527.4	12,855.9	10
3	Trucking & Shipping	119	3,466.0	2,917.2	5
4	Instruments	118	3,732.6	3,158.0	2
5	Aerospace	105	19,012.3	18,029.1	5
6	Printing & Advertising	96	1,651.3	1,724.3	3
7	Cars & Trucks	94	58,155.4	61,907.5	3
8	Steel	87	4,647.3	5,331.2	7
9	Tire & Rubber	85	3,141.2	3,708.9	3
10	Other Services	77	813.3	1,057.6	3
11	Textiles	71	1,315.4	1,862.9	2
12	Transportation Services	68	2,354.2	3,456.2	2
13	Construct. & Eng. Services	65	105.1	162.2	1
14	Electronics	60	2,659.8	4,447.0	1
15	Machine & Hand Tools	56	478.4	848.0	2
16	Special Machinery	46	4,821.5	10,449.8	3
17	Aluminum	46	1,339.2	2,903.0	1
18	Appliances & Furnishings	46	884.2	1,926.4	2
19	Discount & Fashion Retailing	45	5,130.2	11,515.7	4
20	Railroads	41	10,134.9	24,993.7	6

Rank	Industry	Labor Expense/ Equity	Labor Expense	Equity Value	No of Cos
21	Forest Products	35%	$2,843.9	$8,090.8	3
22	Other Leisure	35	6,220.9	17,792.3	3
23	Building Materials	35	1,801.4	5,199.1	5
24	Conglomerates	35	23,297.8	67,478.0	4
25	Food Retailing	34	867.0	2,528.5	1
26	Apparel	32	209.8	650.8	1
27	Paper Containers	32	612.8	1,936.8	3
28	Paper	30	6,262.8	21,096.5	8
29	Electrical Products	26	2,079.3	7,881.1	2
30	Business Machines	26	717.7	2,764.3	3
31	Chemicals	25	9,100.8	36,372.2	9
32	Telephone Equip. & Services	25	135.6	547.1	1
33	Food Processing	24	4,920.9	20,599.4	7
34	Beverages	23	2,244.7	9,660.7	2
35	Telephone Companies	22	8,632.4	39,834.4	3
36	General Manufacturing	22	556.0	2,585.2	2
37	Publishing	21	4,209.6	19,945.3	9
38	Hotel & Motel	19	169.5	908.1	1
39	Medical Products	19	2,663.6	14,295.8	2
40	Computers & Peripherals	18	669.8	3,689.6	1
41	Industrial Distn Services	17	270.7	1,559.2	2
42	Semiconductors	17	986.1	5,771.4	2
43	Eating Places	14	1,330.4	9,553.7	3
44	Petroleum Services	13	98.1	779.2	1
45	Oil & Gas	12	14,118.7	122,544.9	11
46	Drugs & Research	9	3,548.7	40,402.2	3
47	Broadcasting	4	13.3	377.3	1
48	Construction & R.E.	0	0.0	736.1	1
49	Personal Care				0
50	Tobacco				0
51	Glass, Metal & Plastics				0
52	Food Distribution				0
53	Coal				0
54	Drug Distribution				0
55	Health Care Services				0
56	Entertainment				0
57	Other Metals				0
58	Software				0
59	Pollution Control				0

Exhibit 13.18   To ESOP or Not to ESOP?
The Economic Calculus

The decision to use an ESOP can be treated like any other project subject to capital budgeting analysis. The question is whether the present value of the benefits exceeds the present value of the costs.

The Cost of Forming an ESOP

The cost side of the equation is straightforward. It is the net cash outflow the ESOP triggers; it is the cash the sponsor must contribute to the ESOP to service ESOP's debt less any cash conserved as the result of any wage or benefit concessions.

Although correct, putting the cost in this way obscures an equality which can vastly simplify the calculation of an ESOP's cost. The key insight is that a company's employees can be compensated only if their employer pays for it. A simple proposition, it is true, but it means that *the net present value cost to the employer must be equal to the net present value of the compensation that the employees receive.* The link that connects and equates the employer's cost and the employees' compensation is the ESOP loan.

The ESOP Loan

Cost to the employer   =   compensation to employees

(PV of the employer's   =   (PV of shares to be
cash contributions)   allocated to employees)

On the one hand, the ESOP loan measures the sponsor's cost, for the employer is obligated to contribute cash adequate to service the ESOP's loan. Because the ESOP's sources and uses of cash must balance, the discounted present value of the employer's cash contributions to the ESOP must be equal to the initial ESOP loan.

On the other hand, the ESOP's loan proceeds are used to purchase shares that will be allocated to the employees. So long as the ESOP pays fair market value for the shares it will turn over to the employees, the initial ESOP loan balance must be equal to the *expected* present value of the compensation the ESOP provides to the employees. If the ESOP pays more than fair market value for the shares, there is (1) an equal reduction in the cost to the employer and compensation to the employee and (2) a tax benefit. The sponsor will get a tax deduction without incurring a compensation expense to the extent of the over-payment.

But in the absence of overpaying for the shares, both the present value of the cost incurred by the employer and the compensation of the employees are measured by the initial ESOP loan balance. *There is no need to project and discount cash flow or share prices in order to determine the company's cost and the employees' compensation. Both are identical to the ESOP loan.*

In practice, both the cost and compensation sides of the equation will be reduced to the extent that the ESOP uses dividends on unallocated shares to repay its indebtedness. Using dividends to repay debt offsets dollar-for-dollar the cash the employer must contribute to the ESOP in order to meet a given debt repayment schedule, thereby reducing the cost. And, because dividends are part of the expected return on the shares that eventually will be allocated to the employees, if dividends are used to repay debt, the employees lose the value of the dividends and thereby reduce the present value of their compensation. Thus it is necessary to subtract the present value of the dividends on the unallocated shares that will be dedicated to debt service from the initial ESOP loan. What's left over is a measure of the present value of all of the cash the sponsor will have to contribute to the ESOP and of the present value of the shares that will be handed over to the employees, net of the diverted dividends.

The cost and the compensation of an ESOP also are reduced to the extent of wage or benefit concessions. The employer saves, and the employees suffer, when wages or benefits are compressed. In summary, both the net present value cost to the employer and the compensation to the employees can be expressed as:

The ESOP loan (1)
  — Overpayment for the shares (2)
  — PV of dividends on unallocated shares that are applied to debt service (3)
  = PV of the employer's cash contributions to the ESOP (4)
  — PV of wage and benefit concessions (5)
  = Net PV Cost to the employer and compensation to the employees (6)

The Benefit from Forming an ESOP

The more daunting task is to quantify the likely benefits to be derived from forming an ESOP, which include, in rough order of increasing difficulty:

- More an offset to the cost of an ESOP than a benefit are the taxes saved by deducting the net additional cost of the ESOP (i.e., from

Exhibit 13.18   continued

> deducting item #6 in the foregoing table, which is the before-tax
> cost to the sponsor).
>
> - The borrowing rate benefit is the net present value of the interest
>   saved, after taxes, by borrowing through the ESOP versus the
>   company itself.
> - The present value of the taxes saved by diverting dividends to
>   repay debt.
> - The present value of the taxes the sponsor saves by passing
>   through dividends to the employees, less the taxes imposed on
>   the employees as a result.
> - The benefit from tax-deducting the extent to which the ESOP
>   pays more than fair market value for the shares that it acquires.
> - The benefit to private investors of deferring the tax on any gain
>   upon the sale of shares to the ESOP.
> - The benefit from curing reinvestment risk. And, let's not forget:
> - Strengthened employee incentives.
>
> Only if the present value of these benefits exceeds the net present
> value cost to the employer will forming an ESOP reward the com-
> pany's shareholders. Not surprisingly, when ESOPs have been used
> defensively, that is, for the purpose of locking up stock in the hands
> of friendly employees and without an obvious concern for the true
> economic issues involved, the sponsor's stock price typically has suf-
> fered.
>
> ESOPs have produced bonanzas for shareholders and employees
> most frequently when they have been used to finance LBOs, for it is
> then that the potential benefits of an ESOP really shine.

The Empire Strikes Back: Leveraged Recapitalizations.
The next step out the risk map, actually something of a great leap,
is a leveraged cash-out or leveraged recapitalization, the single
most powerful weapon in the restructuring arsenal. Many companies have used a recap as a defensive restructuring strategy, a
reluctant response to an unwanted suitor. Union Carbide, for
instance, repudiated a hostile offer by undertaking a recapitalization that snared the raider's booty for its shareholders and forced
the raider to turn back his assault (exhibit 13.19).

Exhibit 13.19   The Best Defense Is a Good Offense

Union Carbide escaped the clutches of a hostile raider by undergoing a leveraged recapitalization. In the process it proved that the best way for a company to defend against a takeover is to create the greatest possible value for shareholders.

The notorious Bhopal, India, chemical plant accident in December 1984 was just the last straw on the camel's back. For years Union Carbide had been falling behind as major oil companies and foreign chemical producers moved onto its turf. Instead of standing and fighting, Carbide retreated while surrendering half of its market share, branching off into new businesses that management knew nothing about, and pouring resources into wasteful overhead. The years of neglect finally took a toll on the company's financial results. Over the period from 1982 through 1985, Union Carbide's rate of return on capital employed never exceeded 6%, and its stock sold for a sharp discount from its book value.

Robert Kennedy, who became Carbide's chairman in the wake of the restructuring, looked back upon the company's bleak condition in the mid-1980s:

> We had people who would talk about those country boys up in Midland, Michigan [Dow Chemical] who were taking scandalous risks with 50 percent debt. And we watched them go right by us in sales, quality of earnings and quality of returns to their shareholders.
>
> There was a general consensus we weren't making it. The market continued to undervalue our corporation. We were selling at 70% of book value. We thought the market didn't understand. The fact is the market understood very well. We were undervalued because we had not realized the intrinsic value of the businesses we were in. Our weaknesses started to show.
>
> "Endgame for a Corporate Moonwalker"
> *Forbes*
> May 18, 1987

Samuel Heyman, chairman of GAF, was acutely aware of Carbide's predicament. But for him, the company's operating and financial weaknesses presented opportunities. He planned to take over Union Carbide in a highly leveraged acquisition and to sell its parts for a profit.

On August 13, 1985, GAF filed a 13-D statement with the SEC that disclosed the acquisition of a 5% interest. Union Carbide's common shares, which for the first 6 months of 1985 had traded for around $40 a share, rose to $55 a share over the 2-month period in which GAF

Exhibit 13.19 continued

had accumulated the shares, and they gained a further 6% in value on the very day GAF revealed its 5% stake.

GAF's gain was even more impressive and meaningful. On the day the 13-D was filed, GAF's market value skyrocketed upwards nearly 11% (refer, please, to the table and the plot of GAF's stock price in exhibit 13.20). Apparently investors believed that GAF would earn an extraordinarily attractive return on its investment even after paying Carbide shareholders a handsome premium. That is a tangible indication of the value that raiders snare by restructuring their prey and which their targets often neglect to capture for themselves.

On December 9, 1985, GAF made an unsolicited $68 a share cash offer for all Union Carbide shares (a total of $4.13 billion). On the day the offer was made, GAF's shares surged again, climbing over 26% in value from $23 to nearly $29 a share, a remarkable gain for a prospective buyer (#1). Now more than ever it appeared that the raider would be able to reap the full value of an undermanaged and underperforming company.

But that was not to be the case. Carbide's ensuing defense was a classic in the history of takeover battles, for it was the first time that an all-cash tender offer for all shares was defeated. Instead of falling victim to the hostile offer, Union Carbide's board decided to turn the technique of the raider to its own best advantage. The theme that emerged in constructing a defense was to enhance shareholder value and beat Heyman at his own game. "Whatever Heyman bid, we could use our assets to give shareholders more," said Neil Anderson, partner, Sullivan & Cromwell, the law firm that advised the board throughout.[14]

On December 15, Carbide responded with an offer to buy back 35% of its stock for $85 a share (a $2 billion distribution in total). Although not enough to win, the offer was an indication that Carbide was not about to give up without a fight. GAF's shares plunged 10% in value as its takeover looked something less than a fait accompli (#2).

GAF returned with a higher offer of $74 a share, or $4.5 billion for all shares, on December 26. Over the period leading up to the revised offer, GAF's shares more than reversed the losses, gaining 17% in value from $29 to $34 a share (#3), another indication of the prospective raider gains.

The coup de grace was issued by Union Carbide, however, on January 2, 1986. Carbide struck with a decisive leveraged recapitaliza-

[14]"Outside Directors Led the Carbide Defense That Fended Off GAF," *The Wall Street Journal,* January 13, 1986.

tion: It offered to pay $85 a share to buy back 55% of its shares and to distribute the proceeds above book value from the sale of its crown jewel consumer products division (through a special warrant). The total cash distribution was approximately equal to the $4.5 billion in cash GAF was offering for all shares, but it left the existing Carbide shareholders in place as owners, an important advantage.

Six days later, on January 8, 1986, GAF abandoned its quarry. GAF's stock, which sold for almost $35 in the heyday of its bid, plummeted to under $25 a share (#4 and #5). The raider's loss was the target's gain, however. In early 1986, just prior to the distribution of proceeds to its shareholders, Carbide's shares climbed over $100, a 150% gain from their $40 value prior to GAF's involvement.

> Carbide made the decision that unrecognized value in the company should go to the shareholders [instead of GAF, the raider]. I think it is laudable, said Robert Pirie, president, Rothschild, Inc., investment bankers.
>
> "Outside Directors Led the Carbide Defense That Fended Off GAF"
> *The Wall Street Journal*
> January 13, 1986

Carbide was successful in its defense because the company realized that delivering value to its investors is what gets votes in the marketplace. Often corporate managers do not realize that they are playing a zero-sum game against hostile suitors. But Union Carbide's and GAF's countervailing stock price movements demonstrate that the target's share gains are the raider's value lost, and vice versa. The more value a company can create through its own financial restructuring, and the sooner the better, the less value there is to entice a third party to enter the fray or stay in the contest and the more value will be preserved for the company's own shareholders. In the restructuring game, management is well advised by the maxim: The best defense is a good offense: Never let the opponent take the field.

But a recap is too potent a weapon to hold back for mere parrying thrusts; it is most effective when initiated by management as an offensive strike. The history of recaps thus far offers encouraging proof of the maxim that the best defense is a good offense: Never let your opponent get on the field. In our analysis of all significant leveraged recaps performed from 1986 (when they began in earnest) through the end of 1989, we have discov-

Exhibit 13.20   Union Carbide versus GAF: Bid for Control

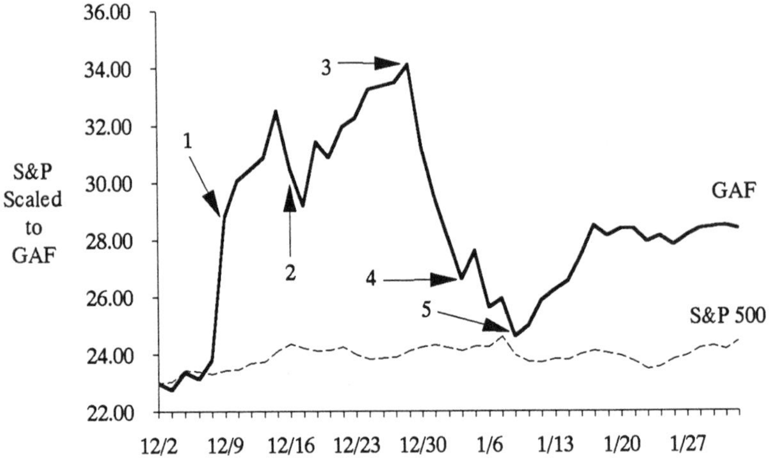

#	Date	Event	% Gain Union Carbide	% Gain GAF
	8/13/85	GAF discloses acquisition of 5% interest in Union Carbide	5.9%	10.6%
	9/2/85	GAF increases interest to 9.9%	(3.1)	3.0
1.	12/9/85	GAF offers $68/share ($4.13 billion) for Union Carbide	2.2	26.3
2.	12/15/85	Carbide makes $2 billion exchange offer for 35% of its stock. Offer valued at $85/share.	1.8	(10.2)
3.	12/26/85	GAF increases offer to $74/share.	0.9	2.6
4.	1/2/86	Carbide revises offer to include 55% of stock at $85/share. Also announces it will sell consumer products business. GAF increases offer to $78/share.	5.8	(6.4)
5.	1/8/86	GAF abandons its bid.	(1.5)%	(3.6)%
		Total Gains (8/12/85 - 1/9/86)	47.6 %	68.8 %

ered not a single instance of a case in which a management-initiated recapitalization was overturned by a subsequent hostile bid (exhibit 13.21). Not a single instance. Moreover, the common stock price performance subsequent to the recap has proved to be better for the management-initiated recaps than for those which overcame a hostile bid. Managers seem to be overestimating the risks and underestimating the rewards of initiating a first-strike recap. For a highly successful management-initiated recapitalization, see exhibit 13.22.

Exhibit 13.21   Survey of Leveraged Recapitalizations

A survey of all significant leveraged recapitalizations since 1984 is presented here. For this purpose, a recapitalization is defined as an actual or proposed payout to shareholders that was at least 50% of the firm's preexisting stock market capitalization and left control in the hands of the public shareholders afterward. All of the recaps were divided into one of these three categories:

Defensive	Undertaken in response to a hostile offer
Precautionary	Undertaken in response to strong indications of an impending hostile offer
Proactive	A management-initiated transaction

Our survey identified 14 proactive, 5 precautionary, and 27 defensive recapitalizations of substance. The recapitalizations also were divided into those that were successful (i.e., the proposed restructuring was implemented) and those that failed (i.e., a third party acquired the company instead).

Our most important discovery was that there was not a single instance of a management-initiated leveraged recapitalization that failed to go through. All 14 proposals initiated by insiders proceeded to implementation. Moreover, this group's subsequent stock market performance has been superior to that of companies whose recapitalizations were undertaken to fend off a hostile takeover attempt.

Exhibit 13.21   continued

Medians	(1) Gain Following Successful Recap	(2) Gain Relative to S&P 500	(3) Est. Recap Premium	(4) Tender Offer Premium Hostile	(5) Management & Employee Ownership Before	(6) After
Proactive/precautionary—						
Successful	42.2%	0.9%	21%	NA	5.3%	15.7%
Defensive—						
Successful	(4.9%)	(33.7%)	34%	47%	4.1%	4.5%

Column 1 contains the total rate of return on the stub shares for the median company (i.e., the one in the middle of the pack) from the effective date of the recapitalization through the end of 1989. The median rate of return less the return on the S&P 500 over the same time frame appears in column 2.

Since the recapitalizations, the median proactive and preemptive company had about a 40% to 50% per annum appreciation on its common shares, a return in the vicinity of that produced by the S&P 500. (The *average* rate of return has been well above the return for the median company, 77% and 98%, for the proactive and preemptive companies, respectively.) The aftermarket performance of the proactive and preemptive recapitalizations indicates the transactions were fairly priced on average. Management paid as much of a premium as could be justified by the improvement in the company's operating performance after the recapitalization.

The stub shares arising out of the typical defensive recapitalization, by contrast, have fallen in value since the opening bell. There appear to be two principal reasons for this disappointing performance. First, companies on the run had to pony up a higher premium out of the starting gate. The estimated recapitalization premium (in column 3) compares the value of all of the cash, securities, and stock distributed plus the initial value of the stub shares to the company's share value prior to the recapitalization. The proactive and precautionary companies produced about a 20% premium for their shareholders right off the bat. The defensive ones produced a whopping 34% premium because they had to be competitive with hostile takeover premiums typically on the order of 47% (column 4).

The second reason the defensive structures were unsuccessful is that they failed to increase the incentive for the insiders to perform to their utmost. Management and employee ownership before and after the recapitalizations are presented in columns 5 and 6. The proactive and precautionary companies increased the insiders' stake by a factor of 2½ to 4 times. Operating in the heat of battle, the defensive companies could not afford the luxury of addressing the all-important ownership imperative.

PROACTIVE

	14
SUCCESSFUL	1989 Holiday (II) Butler Manufacturing Sealed Air 1988 Quantum Chemical Franklin Electric INCO Tyler Shoney's Inc. 1987 The Topps Company Carson Pirie Scott 1986 Colt Industries FMC 1985 Holly Corporation 1984 Teledyne
UNSUCCESSFUL	

Exhibit 13.21   continued

It's a shame that the performance of a select few defensive recapitalizations give a bad name to recapitalizations in general, for the management-initiated ones have met with great success. Not a one has been overturned by an outsider, and the subsequent returns have been perfectly acceptable. In some cases they have been stellar, even after giving shareholders an attractive up-front premium.

	PRECAUTIONARY	*DEFENSIVE*

SUCCESSFUL	**3**
	
	1989 Interlake
	
	1988 Optical Coating Labs
	
	1987 Holiday (I)
		18
		
		1989 Service Merchandise
		        Triad Systems
		        Whittaker
		1988 Kroger
		        Interco
		
		1987 Allegis (UAL)
		        USG
		        Santa Fe Southern Pacific
		        Newmont Mining
		        Harcourt Brace
		        GenCorp
		1986 Carter Hawley Hale
		        Goodyear
		        Owens Corning
		1985 Union Carbide
		        Unocal
		        Multimedia
		1984 Phillips Petroleum

UNSUCCESSFUL	**2**
	
	1986 Anderson Clayton
	        Rexnord
		9
		
		1989 Shaklee
		1988 American Standard
		        IU International
		        Koppers
		        Kraft
		        Macmillan
		        Moore McCormack
		        Pillsbury
		1987 Telex

Exhibit 13.22	The Leveraged Recapitalization of Shoney's, Inc.

Shoney's, Inc. is a restaurant operator with outlets primarily in the south and midwest. It was one of at least eight large companies to perform a leveraged recapitalization in 1988. Far from being a response to a hostile offer, the recapitalization resulted from management's decision to switch from rapid expansion of restaurant outlets to one of profitably managing the existing portfolio, a downshifting of gears necessitated by the maturing of the food service market in the United States.

Shoney's common stock was trading at $24.50 per share when, on March 7, 1988, the board of directors announced the intention to distribute a $20 dividend: $16 in cash and $4 through a subordinated debenture. The debt-financed payout reduced Shoney's net worth from $300 million to a *negative* $400 million.

As part of the transaction, incentives were strengthened well down into the ranks. Senior management and the board realized that, when faced with the prospect of slower growth, the company's middle-level managers may have abandoned ship. To keep the crew in place and highly motivated, shares subject to stock options (excluding the chairman's) were increased from 3% to 19% of the total shares outstanding on a fully diluted basis, and the options were allocated to individuals as far down as divisional directors.

Background

Shoney's chain of full-service family restaurants serve breakfast, salad bar, steak, seafood, chicken, and sandwiches. By the time of the recapitalization, the company operated 652 restaurants and franchised an additional 815. Founded in 1959 by Ray Danner, the current chairman, Shoney's went public in 1969. The company grew rapidly through the 1970s and into the mid 80s. Then, over the period 1984 to 1987, the engine of growth ran out of steam. To illustrate this progression, the company's financial performance has been divided into three periods:

1. 1971–80, a period of rapid growth and strong profitability in a burgeoning business.
2. 1981–83, high profitability but somewhat slower growth.
3. 1984–87, profitability holds despite a leveling off of expansion opportunities.

Exhibit 13.22   continued

Shoney's, Inc.
Historical Summary of Performance
(Dollars in Millions)

	Growth I 1971–80	Growth II 1981–83	Maturity 1984–87
Performance Summary			
Sales (last year)	$216	$393	$690
Growth rate (avg annual)	30%	22%	21%
Free cash flow (cum)	($17)	($35)	$39
Investment rate	130%	150%	70%
Economic Value Added			
Return on capital	22.0%	20.1%	19.5%
Cost of capital	14.3	14.9	13.6
Spread	7.7%	5.2%	5.9%
Capital (cumulative)	$289	$344	$928
Economic value added	$22	$18	$55
Average annual EVA	2	6	14
Market value added			
Stock price (last year)	$4.47	$14.10	$21.63
Economic book value	1.98	4.37	8.96
Spread	$2.49	$9.73	$12.67
Common shares outstanding	31.5	33.7	36.3
Market value added	$78.6	$327.9	$460.0
Increase in MVA	$77.2	$249.5	$132.1
Total shareholder return			
Avg Shoney's return	24.6%	47.6%	12.0%
Avg S&P 500 Return	8.4	12.3	15.1

Growth I (1971–80)

From 1971 to 1980, sales increased from $21 million to $216 million, an average growth rate of 30% per annum. Shoney's rate of return on capital averaged 22% over this period, well above the cost of capital. EVA was positive and rapidly expanding. With growth outstripping its rate of return, Shoney's weathered a negative free cash flow during this time.

Shoney's stock market performance was exceptional in this period:

$77 million was added to the market value of capital employed over the decade. Total returns for shareholders averaged 24.6% per annum in comparison with only 8.4% for the S&P 500.

Growth II (1981–83)

The second growth phase, from 1981 to 1983, was much like the first, though not quite as fast-paced. Revenues grew relatively more slowly, but, at 22% per annum, the rate was still quite robust. The return on capital averaged 20% instead of 22%. EVA continued to rise. Free cash flow remained negative. Despite the relative slowdown, returns to shareholders were very good. Shoney's MVA quadrupled, from $78 million in 1980 to $328 million in 1983. An investor in Shoney's shares from 1981 to 1983 was rewarded with returns averaging 47.6% per annum versus 12.3% for the S&P 500.

Financial Consequences

In light of the company's profitable expansion opportunities over these two growth periods, too great a reliance on debt would have been ill-advised. Maintaining financial flexibility was important in order to be in a position to realize the full potential value of the market opportunity. Free cash flow was negative in 10 of the 13 years and totaled negative $52 million for the total time frame. Shoney's financed the deficit through a prudent mix of debt and equity. The ratio of debt to total capital increased from 8% in 1971 to only 27% by the end of 1983.

Maturity (1984–87)

Over the 1971–83 period Shoney's was a classic Z company exhibiting rapid growth, high returns, negative free cash flow, and exceptional stock market performance, but by 1984–87 Shoney's had become a Y company with X-like growth opportunities at the margin. The transition to maturity was due not so much to any failure on the part of Shoney's as it was to an industry phenomenon. First of all, growth in food service sales nationwide had begun to decline for the first time. In 1985, for example, real restaurant sales growth was only 1.75%, half the rate in 1984.[15] In 1986, McDonalds' sales were flat to slightly higher in restaurants open at least one year and Burger King's were off 2%. In the first 9 months of 1986, Wendy's unit sales volume dropped 10%, precipitating the sale or closing of 164 restaurants. Unfavorable demographics is partly to blame for the slowdown.

---

[15]*Restaurant Business.*

Exhibit 13.22   continued

Young people, the engine of away-from-home dining, began to dwindle in number.

Another problem was that restaurants continued to proliferate, outstripping demand. The total number of eating outlets in the United States surged from 295,000 in 1983 to 354,000 in 1986, a growth rate of 6% per annum.[16] Ironically, continued economic growth was partly to blame for the overcapacity. Recessions ordinarily can be counted on to weed out less-efficient operators, thereby curbing overcapacity. But with the protracted economic expansion of the 1980s, saturation became a serious problem. Sales per restaurant flattened, and the intense bidding for increasingly scarce new locations made growth more expensive. Returns suffered across the board.

Shoney's was not immune to these unfavorable trends. Same-store sales at Shoney's flagship chain of restaurants increased only 2.5% per annum from 1984 to 1987 versus 9.1% per annum from 1978 to 1983. Shoney's was able to keep its overall growth percolating only by introducing new dining concepts, focusing on new market niches, avoiding oversaturated areas of the market, and making a significant acquisition of another restaurant chain for the first time.

Overall, the company's rate of return on capital declined only modestly, but free cash flow turned decisively positive for the first time. The surplus cash flow drove down the company's total debt to just 8% of total capital.

Shoney's evolution into a Y company slowed its stock market performance. Market value added continued to expand, but more slowly than previously. The average annual increase in MVA was $33 million versus $83 million for the prior 3 years. The total return to shareholders 1984–87 was less than the overall market, an average of 12% for Shoney's versus 15.1% for the S&P 500.

The Recapitalization (1988)

By early 1988, Shoney's had produced 115 consecutive quarters of consecutive growth in revenues and operating income relative to the previous year's quarter. Extending this record was becoming increasingly difficult, as management admitted in this public disclosure:

> As the restaurant industry matures . . . and as labor markets tighten, management has concluded that the restaurant industry environment is not sufficiently attractive to justify continued aggressive expansion. Therefore, opening increasing numbers of new restaurants, while in

[16]The Restaurant Consulting Group, Evanston, Ill.

accordance with past practices and within the company's financial capability, is no longer considered to be in the best interests of shareholders.

The Board is increasingly concerned with the amount of management time devoted to aggressive expansion as opposed to focusing on quality of existing operations . . .

Proxy Statement
May 25, 1988

The change in market conditions and in the company's operating strategy preceded and, in fact, made inevitable the financial restructuring. Rather than let momentum carry it unthinkingly into overinvesting in its undeserving basic business, and rather than pursuing illogical and ill-fated diversification, Shoney's management is to be congratulated for a mature, reasoned, and appropriate response to the market reality that confronted it. In announcing the recapitalization, Shoney's CEO at the time, J. Mitchell Boyd, said "This plan is an important step in our transition from a growth company to a mature company in a highly competitive industry." (Press Release, March 7, 1988.)

As the company's business strategy changed, the appropriate financial and incentive structures changed too. The discipline instilled by debt, and the potential rewards from equity ownership, are especially effective in promoting a back-to-basics focus, one that has little tolerance for sloppy cost controls, pricey acquisitions, and unproductive assets.

Strengthening management incentive was an especially important element of the recapitalization plan. The curtailment of new restaurant openings put the brakes on advancement opportunities for the more junior employees. To retain the key middle-management corps, Shoney's broadened its stock option program to sweep deep layers of managers powerfully into the ranks of owners. For employees other than officers and directors, the number of shares subject to options increased from 701,000 (1.9% of fully diluted shares) to 5 million (11.2%) as part of the recapitalization plan. Overall, insiders other than directors and the CEO increased their equity position from 4.7% (fully diluted) to 20.9%.

Results to Date

The restructuring has been a boon to Shoney's shareholders. Just prior to the recapitalization, Shoney's shares traded at $24.50. The common shares closed out 1989 at $11⅞, and that's after the $20 dividend was paid. Had the $20 special distribution been reinvested

Exhibit 13.22   continued

in Shoney's stub shares, an investor would have realized a return of 74% from the time of the recapitalization to the end of 1989. The S&P 500, assuming reinvestment of all dividends, returned only 41% over this same period.

In 1988, the year of the recapitalization, Shoney's added nearly $200 million to the value of its capital employed (i.e., its MVA), and another $125 million in 1989. However it is measured, a tremendous value has been created by the restructuring. Shoney's stock market performance anticipated the across-the-board operating improvements that followed. Although the overall sales growth continued in the range of 11% to 12% in 1988 and 1989, the return on capital increased, reaching 21% in 1989, the first full year after the recapitalization, versus 19.2% in 1988 and 18.6% in 1987. EVA tripled, the result of improved returns and, more significantly, a reduction in the weighted average cost of capital brought about by the aggressive use of debt.

Shoney's Performance
in the Wake of the Recapitalization (1987–89)
(Dollars in Millions)

	1987	1988	1989
Sales	$ 690	$770	$852
Growth	10.8 %	11.7 %	10.7 %
EBIT	$ 79.7	$ 87.6	$115.6
Percent of sales	12.7 %	13.0 %	13.6 %
Return on capital	18.6 %	19.2 %	21.0 %
EVA	$ 10.8	$ 30.4	$ 34.9
Free cash flow	$ (0.1)	$ 61.1	$ 79.9
Market value added	$ 460	$650	$776
Increase in MVA	(161)	191	126

The profitability of restaurant operations reversed an historic decline. For the 33 weeks after the restructuring became effective, the operating profit margin improved over the comparable period the year before, from 10.5% to 11.5%. Same-store sales, which were off by 0.5% in the period before the announcement, increased by 1.3% afterward.

The biggest change occurred in free cash flow. Averaging just $10 million 1984–87, FCF grew to $61 million in 1988 and to $80 million in 1989 as new investment spending was contained. Of course, generating more cash was a necessity. It was needed to amortize debt and pay interest. But generating more cash had an importance that superseded the paydown of debt. It was a measure of management's success at improving profitability and holding back on growth, the two goals of the new business strategy.

Conclusion

The Shoney's case illustrates the necessity of changing with the times. The transition from a dynamic Z to a more mature Y or X firm requires a shift in strategy, incentives, and financial structure. Leverage slows the momentum of operating people and reorders their priorities from unbridled expansion to a focus on profitability. The Shoney's leveraged recapitalization is noteworthy not so much as financial engineering but as a mechanism to reorient the energies and incentives for directors, officers, and employees and thereby to generate substantial rewards for shareholders.

David M. Glassman
Partner, Stern Stewart & Co.

The Benefits of Preemptive
Restructuring

The management of FMC Corporation of Chicago initiated a leveraged recap at a time when no hostile offer was on the table. As a pre-preemptive strike to deter a raider, its restructuring followed the masochist's creed: Be the first to do unto yourself as others would do unto you. No competing offer was forthcoming, and today FMC operates very successfully as an independent, publicly traded entity. Let's see why.

On February 20, 1986, FMC proposed to exchange a package of cash and new shares for each common share held. There were three parties to the transaction and three exchange offers:

The public	$ 70	+	1 new share
The thrift plan	$ 25	+	4 new shares
Management and PAYSOP	$ 0	+	$5\frac{2}{3}$ new shares

The public stockholders were to receive $70 in cash and one new share. Not coincidentally, FMC's shares were selling for $70 at the time. Hence, the term "leveraged cash-out" arises from giving the public stockholders cash proceeds equal to the current market value of their shares (or something close to it). In effect, current shareholders get a lump sum payment equal to the present value of the dividends that they expected the company to pay over its entire future life.

Taking less cash but more new shares than the public, the insiders increased their ownership in FMC from 19% to 41%. By concentrating more equity in the hands of management and employees, the recapitalization strengthened the incentive to perform (and to sell the company, should an attractive offer be made, though that has not been necessary). The heightened incentives for the insiders may be illustrated by plotting the exchange offers (exhibit 13.23).

The horizontal axis in exhibit 13.23 represents the value of the new FMC shares (the so-called stub equity), and the vertical axis is the corresponding value of the proposed exchange offer. The points of intersection on the vertical axis are the cash portions of the offers: $70 for the public to fully cash out the current market

Exhibit 13.23   FMC Exchange Offer

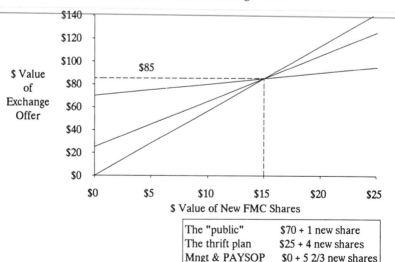

The "public"	$70 + 1 new share
The thrift plan	$25 + 4 new shares
Mngt & PAYSOP	$0 + 5 2/3 new shares

value of their shares, $25 for the thrift, and nothing for management. The slopes of the lines drawn from those points simply add the value of the new shares on top of the cash portion (1 share for the public, 4 for the thrift, and 5⅔ for management).

All three exchange offers intersect at a common point that represents the "intrinsic" value of the transaction. Should the new shares sell for $15, all three parties would emerge with an $85 package of value. The public, at one extreme, has $70 of cash and one new share worth $15. Management, at the other end, holds 5⅔ shares also worth $85.

Should the new shares sell for more than $15 each, management would be the greatest beneficiary. For example, if the new shares sold for $20, management's 5⅔ new shares would be worth $113.33, whereas the public's combination of $70 plus 1 new share would sum to a value of just $90. On the other hand, should the new shares sell for less than $15 each, management would stand to lose the most. If the new shares sold for, say, $10, management's package would come to a meager $56.67. Investors need to believe only in the rationality of management to understand that the exchange offer insists that a greater value than before be placed on the company. The aggressive payoff schedule shows that the insiders hold a "leveraged equity stake" in FMC. They will receive an unlimited and amplified reward for success and a genuine penalty for failure, the two true dimensions of an incentive.

The message to investors is compelling. By volunteering to take on a leveraged equity stake in the new FMC, management expressed its commitment to and confidence in creating at least $85 worth of share value out of a company that was selling for $70 a share before the recapitalization. The message was heeded by the market: As the recapitalization was first announced, FMC's shares rose from a price of $70 to just about the $85 value implied by the structure of the exchange offer (exhibit 13.24). Is that not fascinating! Does it not bear witness to the influence of astute lead-steer investors in pricing shares, when not one investor in a thousand would understand the true significance of the restructuring offer?

Exhibit 13.24 FMC Recapitalization

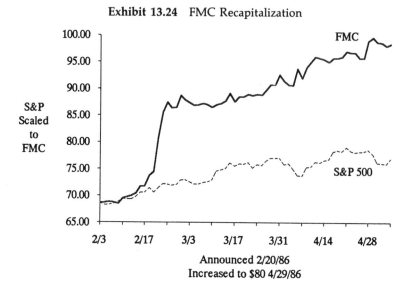

Announced 2/20/86
Increased to $80 4/29/86

Before the deal was sealed, however, FMC's shares nearly touched $100. Apparently Ivan Boesky, as a result of sound financial analysis (and perhaps some inside information), was buying up FMC shares and putting pressure on the company to enrich the offer. With FMC's share value approaching $100, the implied value for new shares was $30 (investors who paid $100 could expect to receive $70 in cash and one new share worth $30). Management's 5⅔ new shares times $30 a share would give them $170 in value, an obvious inequity. To gain shareholder approval (the restructuring plan was submitted to a shareholders' vote at the May 29 annual meeting), management had to increase the offer to the public shareholders from $70 to $80 plus the one new share. The implied new share value then became $20. Management's 5⅔ shares times $20 a share is $113.33, leaving it still somewhat ahead of the pack, but then, the managers were the ones to step up to the plate to propose the plan and they would have far more at risk in the aftermath. I say God bless them.

As FMC increased the cash offer to the public shareholders, Ivan Boesky, who had taken a 7.5% stake in FMC, commented to *The Wall Street Journal,* "It is always gratifying when a management team awakens to the realization that outside shareholders ought to be treated with relative fairness compared to insiders." Whether he was speaking as an "outside shareholder" or an "insider" was something Boesky did not elaborate upon at the time.

With nearly 25 million shares outstanding, the recapitalization boosted FMC's total market value by $750 million ($30 price increase, from $70 to $100 a share, times 25 million shares). I almost forgot to mention that FMC paid some $60 million in professional fees. Thus, FMC's market value was enhanced by some $800 million, but only $750 million was permitted to show up in the company's stock price. What could account for the remarkable increase in value, given that FMC remained essentially the same company afterward as before, with the same businesses, management, prospects, and risks? Some analysts could not imagine. "I think people think it's a better deal than it is," said Sean St. Clair, a Duff & Phelps analyst who recommended selling FMC shares. "The plan is gimmicky. Too bad it doesn't do anything to improve the company's fundamentals."[17]

But my answer is that the restructuring plan did change the company's fundamentals in three important respects, all related to the magical consequences of aggressive debt financing:

1. Operating profits for the foreseeable future will be sheltered almost entirely from corporate taxation. In effect, FMC became a partnership for tax purposes.

2. With discretionary cash flow dedicated to debt service, the risk of an unproductive reinvestment has been eliminated for some time. (Now that is an understatement.)

3. Management and employees were given a far greater incentive to perform well and more obvious penalties for failure.

To finance the cash payments, FMC became *very* highly leveraged. Debt increased from 25% to over 125% of combined debt and equity capital. Because the $80 in cash per share paid to the public investors was approximately 1.8 times the accounting book value of FMC's shares, the company exited from the recapitalization with a negative accounting net worth. (Not to worry, however, because market equity capitalization was around $500 million.) How would it be possible for FMC to service such an astounding increase in leverage?

First, FMC announced that the new shares would not pay dividends. By conserving cash that otherwise would flow to its shareholders, FMC strengthened its ability to retire debt. Non-tax-deductible dividends were converted to fully deductible interest payments. But far more important than dividend retention is the fact that every important measure of corporate health, except growth, improved in the years following the recapitalization (exhibit 13.25).

The carrot of incentives and the stick of potential bankruptcy spurred FMC's management and employees to exceptional performances (see exhibit 13.25). Widening profit margins and a more efficient management of working capital improved profitability. Free cash flow, the single best indicator of ability to service debt, exploded. The combination of slower growth and improved profitability opened the floodgates on the cash generated to pay down debt. The money that FMC disgorged will pour back into our economy to be invested in promising ventures. The stock price performance since the recapitalization is yet another indication of FMC's exceptional performance. Management and employees are to be congratulated.

An additional appeal of FMC's leveraged cash-out is that it avoided many of the ethical complications of a leveraged buy-

Exhibit 13.25   FMC Operating Performance Since Recapitalization

	Before Recap 5-Year Avg	After Recap		
		1986	1987	1988
Revenue Growth	(1.3)%	(7.9)%	4.5 %	4.7 %
EBIT/Beginning Capital	12.9 %	17.8 %	18.9 %	21.4 %
EBIT/Sales	7.1 %	10.1 %	9.6 %	9.8 %
Working Capital/Sales	13.1 %	5.3 %	1.8 %	7.1 %
Free Cash Flow	$256	$320	$204	($45)
Total Debt/Total Capital	19 %	101 %	84 %	78 %
EBIT/Interest	6.6x	1.2x	1.5x	1.8x
Stock Price Increase	16.5 %	61.5 %	31.0 %	(5.2)%

out. In an LBO, management benefits richly if the value of the company can be increased beyond the price offered to buy out the public shareholders. That creates a conflict between management's responsibility to shareholders and its self-interest. There is no way to get around the suspicion that management steals the company from the public shareholders in an LBO that subsequently performs well, even though much academic evidence dispels this myth. (I suspect that Ross Johnson, the ex-chairman of RJR, would be willing to testify at length to the risks entailed in lowballing a bid for a company.)

With a leveraged cash-out, however, investors participate in the value created after the recapitalization because they retain shares in the sponsoring company. Moreover, any one shareholder could, if desired, duplicate management's stake. In the original FMC proposal, the $70 of cash that a public shareholder was to receive could have been used to purchase 4⅔ new shares (at the targeted stub share price of $15). When those new shares are added to the one new share issued in the exchange, the public shareholder, like the insiders, would hold 5⅔ new shares.

A public shareholder also could reverse the recapitalization. By using the cash from the exchange offer to buy the junk bonds issued by FMC to finance the exchange offer, shareholders could recreate the claim they held on FMC's earnings before the recapitalization. By so doing, their original common equity stake in FMC just divides into a lower risk for lower expected reward, interest-earning claim (the junk debt), and a higher risk for higher expected reward, non-dividend-paying claim (the new FMC shares). Thus, such a leveraged recapitalization cannot change the risk in the underlying assets, nor can it force a shareholder, or society at large, to bear more risk.

The benefit of hindsight indicates that joining management— maximizing the equity stake in FMC—would have been the wiser decision. Since the recapitalization, the new FMC shares have traded for a value in excess of $60, giving management's 5⅔ new shares a peak value of $340, certainly not a bad return for a stock that sold for $70 before the recapitalization was announced.

Now for the bad news. FMC did not escape the October 1987 market meltdown. FMC's common shares plummeted from the mid-$60 range to the mid-$30 range, a decline of 50% in market value. The S&P 500 had dropped a mere 30% during the period surrounding the crash. Does this disparity indict FMC's leveraged cash-out? Not at all.

FMC's shares fell further in value than the S&P 500 because of their far greater financial risk, making the comparison grossly unfair. Investment risk must be the same in order to compare return outcomes meaningfully. To properly compare how well FMC's public shareholders would have done with and without the leveraged cash-out, it must be assumed that the cash proceeds they received in the exchange offer were used to purchase FMC's junk debt. Comparing the return on $80 worth of FMC junk debt and 1 new $20 FMC share with the S&P 500 is a fair measure of the wisdom of the leveraged cash-out.

In the event, FMC's junk bonds fell only about 10% in market value during the crash. With 80% of the investors' money tied up in junk bonds and 20% at risk in FMC's stub shares, the overall value of an investment in FMC fell only about 18%. The facts show that FMC's total market value held up better, was indeed more resilient, than the typical less-leveraged company trading on the market. All the incentives to perform and the obligation to pay off the debt remained intact.

It is all well and good for the fortunate public shareholders to come out so far ahead. But what about managers who, by design of the exchange offer, were forced to convert their old shares wholly into the new FMC shares? Of course the crash hurt them more than shareholders who could place the cash proceeds from the exchange offer into lower-risk investments. But do not weep for management. Even the marked-down $35 value for the new shares was 75% more than the initial $20 value. The 5⅔ shares management received in the recapitalization were still worth nearly $200, a 185% gain from the original $70 share value. Granted, not all recapitalizations will work this well for the insiders. But that is the point. Fear that it will not work is one reason most recapitalizations do succeed in creating value. Robert Malott, FMC's chairman, has given the press his perspective on the voluntary plan of recapitalization.

Mr. Malott admits to some trepidation when he undertook the recap. "We leveraged from $300 million to $2.3 billion and took net worth down from $1 billion to a negative 500 or 600 million dollars. Anyone who says he would not be concerned about that has got to be crazy. That kind of capital structure gets your attention."

Mr. Mallott says the FMC board decided to do the recapitalization because the company was in mature industries but generating a lot of cash. "Basically we had fairly good market positions in most of the markets we are in. Most of them are not growing very rapidly. All of them with a few exceptions were generating more cash than we could use internally.

"We made a very aggressive effort to look for acquisitions as a way of intelligently using shareholder money and weren't very successful. We looked at a lot of them and the market was such that the greater fools would outbid us. We could have used our money that way. We could have closed some of those deals but I—and I think my associates—felt it was not in the shareholders' best interests to overpay. So therefore we bought very few.

"We couldn't use all the cash we were generating. So I was casting around for some way of using this money effectively. The idea of a public LBO, where we leave the shareholders in but leverage the company and pay the public stockholders a substantial amount of cash, was the alternative I chose."

Mr. Malott thinks the rise in employee ownership has been positive. "I think ideally every company should be run as if those who own it run it. I think you tend to get better management and a better company."

"Why FMC Shareholders Do the Diversifying"
The Wall Street Journal
August 16, 1988

The Ultimate Incentive. To completely traverse the compensation risk map, the most equity-like, risk-filled compensation package provides no wage, pension, profit sharing, or ESOP. It reminds me of the plan my partners and I at Stern Stewart & Co. have adopted. We have no wages (remember, we are partners); we have no pension plan (I have not told my wife about this just yet); we have no bonus or profit-sharing plans either. All we have is the ownership of equity in a highly leveraged financial advisory firm. You see, I just had to write this book to keep my family off the streets at night.

IV. Fit and Focus

After a company undergoes a dramatic leveraging, it often is said that the debt load is "intolerable." Quite right and deliberately so! Management's response to a staggering debt load frequently must be to sell unrelated and underperforming assets and businesses, thereby reaping the dual benefits of fit and focus.

Fit.   When a business or asset is worth more to another company or with a different management team, it can be sold for a value greater than it contributes to the seller, a tangible reward for finding a better fit. A shrewd seller will first look at a divestiture from the buyer's perspective. When scrutinizing an acquisition candidate, a buyer will figure into the potential purchase price the value of all the synergies he expects to derive and then will try to pay something less than that. In the heat of battle, however, buyers often will let their natural enthusiasm for expansion overrule pure economic logic. The sad truth is that many buyers overpay.

For the seller, the buyer's logic and emotion are reversed: The seller receives, up front and in cash, much (if not all or more than all) of the value that the buyer expects to create, whereas the buyer is left with hopeful expectations and risk. Not long ago I met with a company whose managers said to me, "Bennett, you would not believe the synergies we are deriving from this recent acquisition."

I said, "I believe you, because I just saw the seller over there spending it."

Who gets the value of the synergies? Mostly, the sellers do. Is it any wonder, then, that for this reason alone the breakup values of conglomerate companies exceed the current trading prices?

Take Beatrice, for example. After its LBO, Beatrice was saddled with $7.5 billion of debt and just over $400 million of equity. Don Kelley, recalled from semiretirement to run the company, had to sell assets quickly. Two prominent divestitures were the sale of the Coca-Cola Bottling Company of Los Angeles to the Coca-Cola Company and the sale of the dairy business to Borden. Coca-Cola subsequently packaged the Los Angeles franchise with other bottling properties into a new, highly leveraged company, Coca-Cola Enterprises, and sold a 51% stake in it to the public. Some of the benefits that Coca-Cola obtained by restructuring its bottling network in this way were passed back to Beatrice through the premium price Coke paid to acquire Coke of LA. Borden likewise rewarded Beatrice with part of the value it expected to create by combining Beatrice's dairy operation with its own. It becomes clear only now with the benefit of hindsight that the banks which financed Beatrice's LBO were lending not against Beatrice's assets, nor its cash flow, but against the value of its businesses in the hands of other, more productive owners.

If, as I am arguing, the seller is rewarded for the value that the buyer expects to create, then what counts in a divestiture is the question of relative, not absolute, value: Is this asset or business worth more in someone else's hands than it is in ours? It does not matter whether a business has bright or deteriorating prospects (it will have those same prospects for the buyer); what does matter is whether the buyer possesses a distinct advantage the seller cannot duplicate. Unfortunately, this simple principle of fit can be one of the most difficult for managers to follow in practice because it means that even healthy, core, promising, and profitable businesses ought to be candidates for sale if they are worth more to others.

As a result, such logic is not widely followed in practice. If a broad cross section of corporate managers were asked to identify candidates for divestiture, many would ignore considerations of relative worth and would instead simply rank their business units from the best- to worst-performing and offer to dispose of the ones at the bottom of the heap. This kind of mistaken thinking has been derided by Warren Buffett as "gin-rummy divestitures," simply discarding the worst card at each turn. But as Buffett well knows, selling dogs may not be the best way to create value, for the seller gets only what buyers are willing to pay for them.

Union Carbide provides a good illustration of the importance of weighing relative instead of absolute values. To defeat GAF's all-cash bid, Union Carbide had to go deeply into debt to retire shares at a premium price. If Carbide's management had been asked, before the debt gun was pointed to its head, which of its businesses it would be willing to sell, it probably would have offered up the company's traditional chemicals business.

But in the heat of battle, and with debt to repay, Carbide sold Eveready Battery and its home and automotive consumer businesses, widely regarded as the company's crown jewels. Did this move make sense? Robert D. Kennedy, who became the company's chairman in the wake of the restructuring, seems to think so:

> Did we like parting with a billion-dollar battery products business that was a leader in its field? I'd be lying if I said it was something we would have done without a gun to our heads. But if your mission is getting value to your shareholders, a good case can be made that it was the right thing to do *even before the gun was drawn*. In fact, I'm inclined to think that all strategic planning should be done as if somebody had a gun to your head. It forces you to make the tough choices.
>
> Now, after the fact, I can tell you that it might have been time to sell battery products precisely because it was a *good* business, and there wasn't much *we* could do to make it better. . . . As for the purchaser, Ralston Purina—a total consumer products company with broad consumer distribution, with wholesaler leverage, with consumer-marketing smarts, and the ability to look at a mega-buck consumer advertising budget without feeling faint—the battery business is in a much more congenial environment than it ever was at Carbide. That's a fact. And a lesson learned.
>
> Robert D. Kennedy, Chairman and CEO of
> Union Carbide
> "The New Union Carbide: Some Assembly Required, Batteries
> Not Included"
> *Planning Review,* May/June 1987, page 10

As Kennedy tells it, the divestiture of Eveready arose not from a failing on the part of management, nor because the business was performing poorly. Instead, it represented a harvesting of the fruits of a past successful investment and a transfer to another company in a position to carry Eveready up to an even higher plateau of value. In the event, the added value was split between Ralston and Carbide, buyer and seller. Both companies enjoyed appreciating stock values vis-à-vis the market about the date the deal was first announced, the hallmark of a win-win transaction (exhibit 13.26). For another example of build and harvest, see exhibit 13.27.

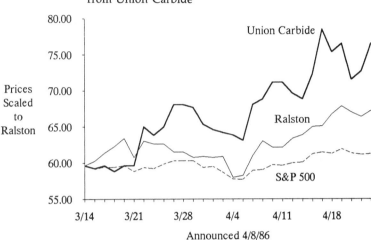

Exhibit 13.26 Ralston Buys Eveready from Union Carbide

Announced 4/8/86

Exhibit 13.27 Build and Harvest

Another company that illustrates the benefit of selling winners to more productive owners is Minnetonka (no, not the toy company), a firm whose main asset may well have been its founder Robert Taylor, a consumer marketing genius if there ever was one. The story of how Minnetonka came to adopt a build and harvest strategy is a restructuring classic.

Bob Taylor's first big hit was Softsoap, the original pump-dispensed liquid soap. After several years of skyrocketing growth in the early 1980s, Minnetonka nearly went bankrupt when Proctor & Gamble and Colgate-Palmolive launched competing products backed by overwhelming advertising blitzes. Necessity being the mother of invention, Taylor dreamed up Check-Up, the first pump-dispensed toothpaste to emphasize plaque control. That timely success, and the stabilization of Softsoap's market share, saved the company.

Having slugged it out on the low plains with the mass-marketing

Exhibit 13.27   continued

merchants, Taylor decided to move to higher ground. His new strategy was to emphasize upscale beauty products less susceptible to attack by the giants. He had acquired Calvin Klein's floundering cosmetics business for $1 million in 1980, and he set to work on new product development and marketing once again. Surely not even the most phlegmatic couch potato could have missed Minnetonka's sexually charged advertisements for the Obsession line of perfumes and colognes. Like the ads or not, Obsession was another big winner for Minnetonka, ringing up over $100 million in sales and piles of profits within 2 years of its introduction.

Taylor bankrolled the 1985 launch with an advertising budget estimated at $15 million—an unusually large sum at the time. "It revolutionized the way fragrances were launched in the United States," said Lawrence Appel of Horvitz & Appel Associates, a marketing consultant specializing in the beauty business. "They used a packaged-goods technique in a business that doesn't normally use packaged-goods marketing strategies."[18]

Encouraged by this success, Taylor decided to complete the transition from mass to class. In early 1987, Minnetonka sold Softsoap to Colgate-Palmolive and Check-Up toothpaste to S. C. Johnson, leaving behind Calvin Klein, new product ventures, and a focus on upscale cosmetics. Where most founders may have difficulty cutting the apron strings that tie them to their original businesses, Taylor understood the logic and necessity for his actions. As he put it to me once, "Our strength is not in watching the nickels and dimes roll in. Our forte is new product development, positioning, and advertising. Once the initial market share for a product has been achieved, our job is done."

Softsoap and Check-Up had settled into a stable share of their markets. Generating incremental profitability depended upon manufacturing efficiencies and international expansion—areas in which the buyers held a comparative advantage. Departing from those established businesses left Minnetonka free to concentrate on exploiting growth opportunities in the upscale market. As with Carbide's sale of its battery business, Minnetonka's divestitures had more to do with success than with failure, but most of all, they had to do with the benefits of comparative advantage.

But the sale of the two mature product lines had significance beyond the transactions themselves. Investors discovered that Minnetonka had in effect adopted a new strategy: It would concentrate on developing new, upscale products and leave ongoing product manage-

[18]"Ego Clash: Calvin Klein vs. Bob Taylor," *The Wall Street Journal,* April 12, 1989.

ment to others. Presumably as the company's new product lines become established, they too would become subject to harvest through sales to more productive owners. If Minnetonka could extend its successful track record by bringing still more successful consumer products to market and selling the resulting businesses for premium values, the recurring gains on such sales would enter the company's stock price with a manufacturing multiple. That would be the ultimate benefit of a build-and-harvest strategy.

Minnetonka's build-and-harvest strategy brought still other benefits that spill over into the advantages of an improved focus, our next topic. For example, by cashing out the value of the unyielding annuity streams generated by the mature product lines, the value of Minnetonka's common shares would become far more responsive to management's success in bringing new products to market, thereby making equity ownership a stronger incentive to perform.

Without the restructuring, moreover, Minnetonka might have adopted a capital structure that had both too little and too much debt—too little to take full advantage of the debt capacity of its mature product lines and too much to provide Minnetonka with the flexibility to carry out its aggressive plans for growth. By disposing of its leverageable businesses, Minnetonka could safely adopt a conservative financial posture—one relying heavily on equity to finance risky new product development and acquisitions—without attracting the attention of raiders. Thus, it became possible for appropriate financial structures to be set for businesses in different stages of their life cycles, an important benefit, too.

The motivation for a build-and-harvest strategy finds a voice in Gabriele Rico, a student of mental processes and a teacher of creative writing. In her book, *Writing the Natural Way* (J.P. Tarcher, Inc., 1983), Ms. Rico described the importance of isolating right- and left-brain thinking:

> Most teachers of creative writing, and certainly all investigators of the creative process, tend to agree that there are two distinctly different aspects of any creative act that sometimes come into conflict: the productive, generative, or "unconscious" phase, and the highly conscious, critical phase, which edits, refines, and revises what has been produced. Call it unconscious and conscious, artist and critic, but whatever the nomenclature the task is to reserve these functions for their appropriate phases and to have them work harmoniously rather than conflict with one another.

The necessity for separating the established from the incipient, left- from right-brain thinking, apparently arises from a logic deeply

Exhibit 13.27   continued

> rooted in our human psyche. Whatever the reason, building up a business to the point of diminishing returns and then selling it to others best able to carry it to a higher plateau is a proven formula for value creation.
>
> Taylor has carried build and harvest to its ultimate conclusion. The entire company, Calvin Klein cosmetics and all, was sold to Unilever N.V. in the latter half of 1989. Unilever saw the acquisition as a chance to strengthen its prestige fragrance business in the United States, where the company already marketed Elizabeth Taylor's Passion, White Shoulders, and Prince Machiabelli fragrances. A company spokesman said that the company also believes the Calvin Klein Obsession and Eternity lines, which had been sold mostly in the United States, had "a lot of potential in the international market." These are the benefits of a better business fit.
>
> So what now for Bob Taylor? With the $25 million he will receive from the sale of Minnetonka, the 53-year old company founder intends to start over. Build and harvest, build and harvest, that is the mantra of the entrepreneur.

Focus.   Focus is the benefit that comes when a company's unrelated activities have been divested and management can concentrate its energies on solving problems and exploiting opportunities in the remaining businesses (exhibits 13.28 and 13.29). One of the theories espoused by conglomerates was that good managers could manage anything. Maybe. But even if true, not even good managers can effectively manage everything at the same time. Several years ago, at a roundtable discussion my firm sponsored on the topic of effective financial communication with investors, an investment banker suggested that conglomerates sold at a discount because securities analysts found them difficult to follow. Michael Sherman, head of investment strategy for Shearson Lehman Brothers, bristled. "It's not that conglomerates are difficult for analysts to understand. We worry that conglomerates are too difficult for management to understand," he countered. Perhaps investment bankers are just being politic when they blame the market for management's shortcomings, but in doing so, they obscure the real motives to restructure and the advantage of improving focus.

| Exhibit 13.28 | A Case of Focus |

Several years ago I had the pleasure of meeting Michael Higgins, who was then the chief financial officer of Rollins, Inc., of Atlanta, Georgia. At that time Rollins was engaged in four highly interrelated business activities: termite and pest control through the Orkin Exterminating Company, oil and gas services, media (radio and TV stations and cable), and Rollins Protective Services. As I said, there were four highly synergistic lines of business.

Orkin and the media outfit were consistently profitable, but in 1983 oil and gas services took a big hit and protective services was losing money as well. Higgins admitted to me that the media and Orkin managers were upset (I recall the language being somewhat stronger than that) that their Rollins stock options were under water because the oil and gas and protective services people were not pulling their weight. Instead of providing an incentive, the options were only a constant source of irritation to the managers of the performing units.

On December 16, 1983, Rollins announced that it would split up into three companies by spinning off the oil and gas operation and the media operation into separate, publicly traded companies. That left in one company, Orkin Exterminating and Rollins Protective Services, both of which market directly to the home. Another synergy between them, according to Mike, was that Protective Services put the bugs in the homes and then Orkin took them out. (I believe that he was only kidding.)

> Rollins said the reorganization would separate three dissimilar businesses and allow management to concentrate its energies and skills on the respective businesses in which they are employed.
> "Rollins Inc. Board Approves Reorganization of Company"
> *The Wall Street Journal*
> December 16, 1983

Recognizing the benefits of the improved focus, including a more precise and powerful incentive for managers (who received stock options in their respective units), Rollins' investors bid up the company's stock price by approximately 20% from $16.50 to $19.50, in a flat market.

The increase in value is striking because the same group of shareholders would own the same group of businesses after the restructuring as before. Also, no advantage was to be derived from writing up assets for tax purposes (nor would any tax be imposed). Moreover, the increase in Rollins' share price occurred when the plan was first

Exhibit 13.28   continued

> announced, well before any new information on the business units was disclosed. The share price appreciation, therefore, cannot be ascribed to achieving a better business fit, to saving taxes, or to improving the market's understanding of the businesses. It was due, quite simply, to the benefits of an improved focus and incentive for management.

In addition to concentrating management's energies, a corporate streamlining often justifies slashing superfluous bureaucratic layers, speeding decision making, and promoting initiative. Moreover, without a lot of peripheral businesses to muddy the waters, management and employees can see the fruits of their labors more clearly reflected in the movements of the company's stock price. As a result, stock options and other equity-linked incentives become more meaningful incentive devices, an important competitive advantage. A clearer focus also may facilitate the adoption of capital structures more appropriate for businesses in different stages of their life cycle and for assets with varying degrees of standardization and tradability. The absence of those benefits are among the real reasons why conglomerates sell for a discount.

Evidence of the relative inefficiency of complex organizations abounds. For example, Frank R. Lichtenberg, who teaches at the Columbia Business School, has shown that diversification dulls performance.

> My research, based upon data for more than 17,000 manufacturing plants, indicates that diversification has a negative effect on productivity (output produced per unit of inputs employed): In other words, the greater the number of industries in which a plant's parent firm operates, the lower the productivity of the plant. . . . Studies by other researchers have shown that corporate profitability also suffered as a result of diversification.
>
> "Want More Productivity? Kill That Conglomerate"
> *The Wall Street Journal*
> January 15, 1989

Here is the proof that the market discounts the value of conglomerates with good reason. Those who blame market ineptitude are just plain ignorant of established facts.

Fortunately for the United States, Lichtenberg documents a

Exhibit 13.29 Focus Is Fractal

Chaos, James Gleick's fascinating book (Viking, 1987), tells about the development of a new science to describe complexity in nature. One of the important new mathematical concepts to come out of the field are fractals,[19] which is something in nature—a geometrical shape, a stream of data, the weather—which is self-similar at every level of magnification. The coastline of a country is fractal. It exhibits the same jagged-edge complexity in a satellite picture as it does to someone walking a rocky shore. Stock prices, too, are self-similar. Plot separate distributions of yearly, monthly, weekly, and daily data, and they all look the same. A fractal is like peeling an onion. Pull away one layer of skin, and the same-shaped onion appears again and again. There is a symmetry across scales.

The restructuring motive of focus is fractal. Breaking down a large conglomerate into its constituent business units is focus at one level. But, like the military organizations after which they are patterned, conglomerates are self-similar at smaller scales further down the chain of command. The benefits to be derived by improving focus within any one of the company's large business units are probably as great as, and similar to, the ones available to the parent. At the next scale down, within what appear to be discrete lines of business, there may be opportunities to clarify and atomize the business activities to the betterment of value by breaking down complex integrated business activities into decentralized networks, and so on, and so on, until an indivisible individual person is reached.

Nike is a company to which the principle of focus applies at many levels, beginning at the top. As a company, Nike is devoted to just one line of business: It designs, develops, and markets footwear, apparel, and accessories for athletic and leisure activities. Apparel and accessories may seem to be a distraction from a pure focus on footwear, but they are designed to complement the company's athletic footwear products, they feature the same trademarks, and they are sold through the same marketing and distribution channels. Thus, the company concentrates on one (horizontally integrated) line of business to the exclusion of all others (if the 1988 acquisition of Cole-Haan, a fashion footwear company, is excused as a peccadillo).

Within its one well-defined business, Nike's management has concentrated the company's energies and resources on just the critical

---

[19]"Fractal" is a name and concept devised by Benoit Mandelbrot while employed by IBM.

Exhibit 13.29   continued

activities in which stock market value is added, and it has farmed out the perfunctory, undifferentiated functions for which the company possesses no comparative advantage. By doing so, Nike is able to lavish its resources on new product development and advertising and promotion. New products germinate from a permanent staff of specialists in biomechanics, exercise physiology, and engineering and design practices. The company anticipates consumer needs and preferences by cultivating advisory boards made up of athletes, coaches, and doctors. The few retail outlets Nike does own give Nike yet another way to keep in touch with its consumers' emerging needs and tastes. Nike is perhaps best known, however, for its high-powered national advertising campaigns that feature prominent sports stars. Nike, like Coca-Cola, recognizes that a large part of its products' value added is an image conveyed through clever advertising.

But Nike is no Bo Jackson of all trades. Nike, for example, does no manufacturing. Almost all production is subcontracted to independent manufacturers, mainly in Korea, Taiwan, and Hong Kong. The Asian subcontractors have the advantage of being geographically close to the sources of rubber and other raw materials and enjoy low labor costs. For another thing, Nike does no heavy lifting. Instead, the company hires a Japanese trading company (Nissho Iwai) to arrange transportation of its products from the Far East and to finance goods in transit. The arrangement with Nissho Iwai began in 1972. And Nike does no selling. Nike products are sold through 16,800 retail outlets and just 22 company-owned stores, 10 of which sell reject and discontinued merchandise. Nike does maintain four sales-distribution centers in the United States. But sales to the retail outlets are made by two independent regional sales representative agencies as well as by fifteen company-owned sales agencies.

Nike's extreme focus enables the company to be successful in a business fraught with terrific complexity and risk. Its success points the way for other companies engaged in businesses characterized by rapid technological change, globalization, a high degree of product differentiation, the need for great manufacturing flexibility, and increasing demands for quality. Nike's concept of extreme focus might go a long way if it were applied in earnest to a GM or an IBM, for example.

Another company whose business success over the years is partly attributable to extreme focus is The Coca-Cola Company. Ever since 1886, Coke has concentrated on advertising, promotion, and new product development in the soft drink business—creating intangible values—leaving the brutish business of production and distribution to its independently owned and operated bottler franchises. Coke's de-integration strategy maintains a clarity of purpose, separates risks and responsibilities, enhances debt capacity, improves incentives, establishes a meaningful transfer price, and in the early years gave the company a way to grow without the need to raise capital. Faithful to this long-standing policy, Coca-Cola was quick to sell to the public a majority interest in Coca-Cola Enterprises shortly after it had been formed with the bottling assets Coke acquired from Beatrice and J.T. Lupton.

Another example of a vertical deintegration focus is the restructuring of Courage, a British brewer. Elders, an Australian brewing, food, and financial services conglomerate, purchased Courage Brewing from Hanson Trust for $2.1 billion cash in September 1986. Elders borrowed over $2 billion to finance the purchase. Courage, the United Kingdom's sixth largest brewer with a 9% market share, owned approximately 5,000 public houses (pubs) through which most of its brew is sold.

In January 1987, Elders announced a plan to convert 1,300 of the pubs to tenancies. A tenancy is a franchise-like arrangement in which the owner-manager leases the pub from Courage and manages it as his or her own business. Close contractual ties were retained with the parent to ensure that Courage had enough outlets for its brew production. In announcing the plan, Courage commented that "Research has shown that large formal organizations are slower to react to local market changes and needs. Individual entrepreneur licensees are often best placed to identify and seize the opportunities afforded by their local communities. This creativity and speed of reaction is essential in today's leisure market."

The fractal dimensions of meaningful focus are limited only by one's imagination. In our consulting practice we have found a broad range of focus financial restructurings to yield increases in corporate performance and value:

- Separating the entrepreneurial, value-creating activities from the commodity end of the business
- Segmenting creative development activities from the ownership and operation of the resulting assets
- Separating proven, low-risk earnings streams from unproven, speculative investment opportunities
- Isolating activities with different success factors and cultural requirements

Exhibit 13.29   continued

- Vertically deintegrating
- Compartmentalizing different stages of the product and business life cycle
- Cutting off cash generators from cash users
- Separating leverageable assets and businesses from those requiring equity

That such focus strategies work is a consequence of the power of specialization and an irreversible trend toward increasing market sophistication. The more efficient markets become, the more able they are to process information and impound it quickly and accurately into a multitude of prices. A more decentralized, disaggregated, atomistic economy generates more prices—both stock prices and transfer prices—to guide resource allocation, improve operating efficiency, and sharpen incentives.

Thus, if you are really serious about creating value, next time, don't split your stock. Split your company.

reduction in corporate diversity over the latter half of the 1980s and a corresponding increase in manufacturing productivity. From January 1985 to November 1989, the number of different industries in which the typical U.S. firm operated fell from 5.5 to 4.7, a 14% decline. Furthermore, the proportion of firms operating in just one industry increased from 16.5 percent to 25.4%, a 54% increase in just 5 years. The corporate clarification has paid a dividend, Lichtenberg notes. Manufacturing productivity, stagnant from 1977 to 1982, swelled by 25% between 1982 and 1987.

Though the progress in making U.S. companies more focused is heartening, it does seem meager in comparison with the remaining opportunity. In light of the evidence, companies that continue to operate in more than one line of business cannot claim to be concerned with maximizing their shareholders' values. If this country is serious about improving its productivity, it ought to encourage corporate managers to swallow the Lichtenberg pill and kill that conglomerate.

To conclude, a divestiture can create value in two ways:

- The seller receives, in cash and in advance, a part if not more than all of the value that a buyer expects to create.

- Management can devote its undivided attention to creating value with the businesses left behind.

An Example of Fit and Focus. One clear illustration of the dual benefits of fit and focus comes from Libbey-Owens-Ford (now Trinova). LOF's original flat-glass business carried the company's lowest profit margin and required substantial capital investment to remain competitive. The company's other businesses, fluid power and plastics, offered far brighter growth prospects and higher profitability. Meanwhile, Pilkington Brothers, a British glass company, had acquired a 30% stake in LOF. The restructuring, first announced on February 27 and then confirmed on March 10, 1986, saw LOF swap the flat-glass business for the shares Pilkington held. Upon the announcement, LOF's shares increased in value from approximately $60 a share to just over $75, a 25% gain, or a little more than $200 million in total (exhibit 13.30).

The impressive value added by this financial restructuring can be attributed to fit and focus. Start with the fact that, because of operating economies, the glass business was more valuable in Pilkington's hands than in LOF's. As a consequence, Pilkington Brothers could afford to pay, through the value of the shares surrendered, a price that more than adequately compensated LOF and still come out ahead. That is the hallmark of a win-win

Exhibit 13.30 Fit and Focus: Libbey-Owens-Ford Splits Off Glass Business

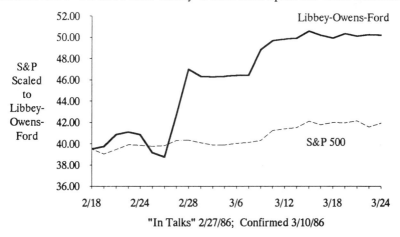

transaction: The value created by a more efficient use of assets is shared by the two parties.

But in our desire to congratulate fit, let us not forget focus. After the spin-off of glass, LOF could more reliably and aggressively realize the full value of its other businesses:

> We like the deal . . . By divesting itself of the unit, LOF will be able to concentrate its efforts on the fluid power and plastics businesses [which] offer far better growth potential than does the glass industry.
>
> *Value Line Survey*
> May 23, 1986

LOF, as Trinova, has been so successful in growing since the divestiture that it is now even larger than its predecessor. Management has admitted to me that, without the spin-off, growth in fluid power and plastics probably would have been stunted by the diversion of time and capital resources to glass. In life, it's the squeaking wheel that gets the oil. So get rid of that wheel.

Debt admittedly was not a part of LOF's restructuring. All the better, really. Parting with businesses worth more to others, and concentrating on the remaining opportunities, is a maxim that should not need debt for proof. Of necessity, however, debt is needed to instill a vital organizational drive for excellence (if not survival), our next and final restructuring topic.

V. Organizational Imperative

The last reason why Bennett Stewart loves debt is the psychological difference between debt and equity. Equity is soft; debt is hard. Equity is forgiving; debt is insistent. Equity is a pillow; debt is a dagger. Equity and debt are the Yin and Yang of corporate finance. Equity lulls a company's management to sleep, forgiving its sins more readily than a deathbed priest. A surplus of stock muffles the alarms that should be heard when earnings decline. Forgive and forget is equity's creed.

But put a load of debt on that same company's books and then watch what happens when its operating profits begin to fall off even a little bit. *All of a sudden there's a crisis to fix that problem.* But the actual problem is the same no matter whether debt or equity is on the company's books. It just *feels* a lot more pressing if debt is at the door. The substitution of debt for equity is just a ruse, a theatrical ploy to make people believe they can and must perform to their fullest potential. What a perfect device for the land of Disney and Coca-Cola, where illusion is more important than reality.

"With leverage," say Nelson Peltz and Peter May, "managements get tougher, they go out and make sales, and they do all the things that built America." (*Business Week,* September 15, 1986). Peltz and May relied almost exclusively on debt to finance their acquisitions of National Can and American Can, building their flagship company, Triangle Industries, from a pipsqueak juke box concern to a powerful industrial empire in just 3 years. Their experience confirmed the advantage to living on the razor's edge with debt instead of slumbering upon an equity pillow.

The Japanese know this, too. In fact, they learned the lesson first. By now the benefits of the Japanese just-in-time production system are widely acknowledged. Adopting precise, seemingly impossible, production schedules and keeping inventories to an absolute minimum (inventory, like equity, is another reserve to cosset poor management) forces workers to iron out operating problems as they arise and at their source. By purposely taking all flexibility out of it, the system must be fine-tuned to work better.

Can the corollary benefit of the highly leveraged Japanese financial structures go unnoticed? Debt is the just-in-time financial system. The obligation to deliver precise packets of cash to the banks is another mechanism to squeeze out operating inefficiencies. Leaving no margin for error guarantees that fewer errors will be committed. Enlarging the consequences of making a mistake ensures that fewer mistakes are made. The result is a more valuable enterprise.

> "When you get higher levels of debt, it really sharpens your focus," says Holiday Corporation Chairman Michael D. Rose. "It makes for better managers since there is less margin for error."
>
> "Learning to Live with Leverage"
> *Business Week*
> November 7, 1988

Aggressive leveraging, Japanese style, is much like the Oscar de la Renta diet popular with many of the New York women we know: They purchase expensive designer wardrobes a size too small, and then they cannot afford *not* to lose weight.

Incentives are the carrot. The threat of bankruptcy is the stick. Both are important motivators.

Earnings or Cash Flow. Besides giving the impetus to perform exceptionally well, debt compels managers to reckon with the most fundamental question of corporate value: Is it earnings or cash flow that really matters?

Many senior managers of publicly traded companies, captivated by the cant of the popular press, securities analysts, and investment bankers, believe in the myth that the market wants earnings and wants them now. To satisfy their shareholders' supposedly irrational longing for reported profits, they feel compelled to capitalize outlays that should be expensed to save taxes, to give short shrift to sensible R&D and market-building expenditures, to stay the execution of dying businesses, and, perhaps worst of all, to fuel earnings growth by overinvesting in mature businesses.

Put a load of debt on their books and sight is restored to the blind. With the earnings myth vanquished, management's attention turns to the wellspring of all corporate values: the generation of cash. It was many years ago that I first witnessed this magical transformation, and my faith has been fortified many times since. It happened first when I questioned the CFO of a midwestern company that had gone private, asking about his management's attitude toward the LBO:

"Very positive," he said. "At one time we thought there was an income statement and a balance sheet to manage. Now we see that there is only one statement that matters—sources and uses of cash. Can we pay back the banks?"

"And," he said, "we are now looking three to five years out, to a time when we can take the company public or sell it. It's long-run value creation that concerns us. Before the LBO we were preoccupied with quarterly earnings-per-share growth.

"One last thing. We are *increasing* our research and development in selected areas. We were reluctant to do that before the LBO because it would have reduced our earnings. But now we can see the real benefit."

I said, "It's nice to know that you are making the right decisions for your shareholders, now that you are the shareholders of the company. Why weren't you making those same decisions before."

He said, "Well, Bennett, we certainly didn't have anything near the incentive we do now, and we didn't believe in your lead-steer theory of the stock market. Now we do, though, because the lead steers are sitting on our board."

A scene in the book *The Barbarians at the Gate* perfectly illustrates the wasteful practices that can be eliminated when generating cash becomes more important than reporting steady earnings. The exchange is between John Greeniaus, the head of the Nabisco unit, and Paul Raether, General Partner, Kohlberg Kravis Roberts & Co. Raether is asking Greeniaus if there is anything that could be done to make Nabisco operate more efficiently.

"Look," Greeniaus said, "nobody's ever asked us how we'd run this business for cash. Let me tell you, there are a whole lot of things that can be done."

Nabisco, Greeniaus stated confidently, could increase its operating income 40 percent in a single year if necessary. Profit margins could be taken to 15 percent from 11. Cash flow, he said, could be taken to $1.1 billion a year from $816 million.

"Come on . . ." Raether said in disbelief.

"No, you don't understand," Greeniaus replied. "Our charter is to run this company on a steady basis. There was really no good reason for the earnings in this group to go up fifteen or twenty percent. In fact, I'd be in trouble if they did. Twelve percent is about what I'm supposed to give every quarter. The biggest problem I'll have is disposing of all the additional cash these businesses generate. The earnings are going to be too big. Christ, I've got to spend money to keep them down." It was all done, Greeniaus explained, because Wall Street craved predictability.

Raether was dumbfounded. "What are you going to spend it on?"

"Product promotion, marketing."

"Is that money well spent."

Greeniaus chuckled. "No, not really."

"You guys better believe those numbers," Raether told Greeniaus as they left, "because you may have to deliver them."

It seems a shame that only by going private can management be brought to see the light. It is a pity, indeed, because no matter what Greeniaus may think Wall Street craves, there is strong evidence that share values for public companies are maximized by generating as much cash as possible, and not by reporting steady earnings.

Eliminate Cross-Subsidies.   The urgency debt instills to perform well often leads management to ferret out previously overlooked opportunities to create value. One important form of damage control is the elimination of cross-subsidies, inefficiencies that sap companies of their vitality (exhibit 13.31).

- An *operating* cross-subsidy occurs when an individual unit within a consolidated company loses money and, without a

---

Exhibit 13.31   "Close the Show and Keep the Store Open at Night":
A Cross-Subsidy Robert Campeau Could Appreciate

One of the best known show business anecdotes concerns Alfred Bloomingdale, one of the brothers who founded Bloomingdale's department store in New York in 1872.

Having lost a bundle as an angel backing Broadway flops, he decided to shed his wings and became a full-fledged producer. He poured a vast deal of money into a musical comedy called *Allah Be Praised!* The show was in trouble and, during its Boston tryout, Bloomingdale called in his friend Cy Howard as a play doctor to see if he could work a miracle cure. Howard sat through the comedy in silence. After the final curtain, the lights went on and Howard found himself looking at the producer's anxious face:

"Well, what do you think?"

"Al," he gave his considered advice, "close the show and keep the store open at night."

Adapted from *The Book of Business Anecdotes* by Peter Hay. Copyright © 1988 by Peter Hay. Reprinted with the permission of Facts on File, Inc., New York.

chance for a turnaround anytime soon, draws value from the company's other profitable activities.

- A *strategic* cross-subsidy is more subtle but nonetheless serious. It happens when a company persists in investing cash into business units that are unlikely to earn sufficient rates of return over time (or, the opposite, when businesses with promising opportunities are denied the capital that they need and deserve).

- An *economic* cross-subsidy arises when there is a higher-valued alternative use for the assets that underlie a business.

Operating Cross-Subsidies

Trans World Airlines (TWA) provides a good example of the value that can be created through the elimination of an operating cross-subsidy. Its parent, Trans World Corporation (TWC), which also owned Hilton International, Century 21, Canteen and Spartan Food Systems, was consistently profitable. TWA, on the other hand, had been losing money each year since the deregulation of airlines in 1978, in large measure because of uneconomic wage levels for employees. With a strong parent behind them, TWA's employees were in no hurry to make necessary wage concessions. In effect, TWC's shareholders were being forced to subsidize TWA's employees, an obvious inequity.

The curtain started to rise when Odyssey Partners, a New York investment group, acquired a stake in TWA and claimed that TWC's breakup value exceeded its actual market value by a wide margin. Not only would TWC's businesses benefit from a better fit with other owners but, more to the point, the apparent perpetual subsidization of TWA's losses would be alleviated. Although impossible for a whole company, an individual business unit within a profitable company can have a negative value.

Thinking that the market simply failed to understand the company's inherent values, TWC's first restructuring step was the sale of a 19% stake in TWA to the public in February 1983. Management reasoned that if a money-losing business could be demonstrated to have a positive market value, investors would be more alert to the true worth of the overall firm. But because this restructuring move did not address the real problem at hand, the company continued to sell at a wide discount from its breakup value.

In April of that same year, Odyssey Partners waged an unsuccessful proxy fight to force TWC to separate its various units, claiming again that the sum would be greater than the whole. Pressed on all sides by impatient investors, TWC on September 23 distributed the remaining 81% stake in TWA to its shareholders through a tax-free spin-off, thereby creating a separate, publicly trading entity. Upon the announcement, TWA's stock fell nearly 4% while that of its parent, TWC, rose more than 11% (exhibit 13.32). These share price reactions correspond to the severance of the subsidy and the creation of overall value. TWA's president, C. B. Meyer, Jr., cited competitive industry conditions as the reasons why TWA employees "must reduce labor costs and make permanent changes to gain greater productivity. TWA's employees for too long have felt they could rely on a rich and fat parent. They may currently see that their fate remains in their own hands."

TWA's problem was caused by employees' unwillingness to reconcile themselves to the competitive forces unleashed by deregulation. Operating cross-subsidies are more frequently caused by management insistence on turning around businesses better left face down.

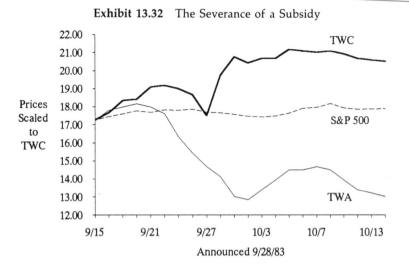

Exhibit 13.32   The Severance of a Subsidy

Prices Scaled to TWC

Announced 9/28/83

Strategic Cross-Subsidies

Strategic cross-subsidies occur when management invests in business units unlikely to earn attractive returns (or denies others the access to capital they desperately need and deserve). When a company conditions the market to expect a pattern of capital misallocation to continue, a vast discount gets subtracted from current market value. That is the only way that new investors can be enticed to buy shares without fearing the harmful consequences of management's future investment decisions. Eliminating this depressing discount is a prime objective of any raider worth his salt.

It was with the objective of turning off an egregious cross-subsidy that Asher Edelman made Lucky Stores the target of a hostile bid in late 1986. Although Lucky presented an experienced raider like Edelman with many reasons to push for a restructuring, the continued misallocation of capital to the Gemco membership discount department stores unit (yes, you had to pay to get in, for reasons its patrons were at a loss to explain) was the most prominent. Gemco's business segment data bear witness to the operating problems there.

For years on end Gemco had been earning a very inadequate rate of return on assets (refer to the after-tax operating profits as a percent of assets in exhibit 13.33). Nevertheless, Lucky's management continued to shovel capital into Gemco in amounts far in excess of its earnings, thereby draining the parent of cash flow. If management persisted in pursuing such a policy, Gemco might well be construed to have a negative value. Here is all the evidence astute investors would need in order to justify their worst fears:

> During the year [1985], Gemco's new president, Stan Brenner, and the outstanding team of merchants he has assembled have begun the implementation of Gemco's plan for the future. This is most visible in the attractive shopping environment and merchandising created within the three new prototype stores and three retrofitted Gemco stores opened during the year. . . . During 1986, the priorities will be to accelerate the retrofit program with 16 major remodels and to complete a chain-wide point-of-sale merchandise data

capture system to allow the merchants to rapidly respond to customer desires.

John M. Lillie
President and Chief Executive Officer
Report to Shareholders
Lucky Stores, Inc. 1985 Annual Report

Exhibit 13.33   Operating Results for Gemco

	1985	1984	1983
Sales	$2,428.1	$2,326.2	$2,135.0
Pretax Oper Profits	$ 15.9	$ 22.8	$ 47.5
Assets	$ 578.2	$ 480.2	$ 438.3
Aft-Tax Op Profits*	$ 9.5	$ 13.7	$ 28.5
Percent of Assets	1.6%	2.9%	6.5%
Aft-Tax Op Profits	$ 9.5	$ 13.7	$ 28.5
— Incr in Assets	$ 98.0	$ 41.9	
Free Cash Flow	$ −88.5	$ −28.2	

*The effective corporate income tax rate is assumed to be 40%

Source: Lucky Stores, Inc. 1985 Annual Report, Business Segment Information, page 24

If at first you don't succeed, try, try again (at shareholders' expense nonetheless). Fortunately for Lucky's investors, management's plan for a complete overhaul of Gemco was not to come to pass. To repel Edelman's offer, Lucky closed the Gemco division and sold most of the empty stores to Dayton Hudson for net proceeds of $450 million. The new owner completely gutted and remodeled the stores and reopened them as new Target discount department stores, an established, profitable chain. Eliminating the strategic cross-subsidy of Gemco was part of a broader-based restructuring that netted Lucky's investors a market value gain of approximately $500 million, and Gemco's customers a better place to shop. Thank you, Mr. Edelman.

In the mid-1980s, Peter Grace, chairman, W. R. Grace, would at various intervals announce his intention to think about the possibility of some day evaluating whether it would be advisable to split up his empire—or vague statements to that effect. On such occasions, W. R. Grace's stock price would leap on the order of 20% to 25%. Capital misallocation within the firm had been so rife over the years, all excused with the wave of Mr. Grace's conglomerate wand, that the prospect of subjecting the business units to the discipline of a market test for new capital made the shareholders salivate. The increase in the company's market value following these intermittent signs of sanity was only a conservative measure of the cost of internal capital misallocations suffered by the company's investors.

The event that finally tipped Grace's hand was the sale of the Flick Group of West Germany, a friendly holder of a 26% block of W. R. Grace stock. To prevent it from falling into unfriendly hands, Grace purchased the block for nearly $600 million, incurring an onerous load of debt that forced an acceleration of a restructuring program to the nearly hysterical applause of investors (exhibit 13.34). Grace subsequently divested all retail and restaurant operations and, most significantly, its fertilizer business into which mounds of cash had been shoveled over the years for a very unsatisfactory rate of return. Grace's stock market value climbed again from $55 to $65 a share, or some $415 million in market value, with the announcement the fertilizer unit would be sold.

Strategic cross-subsidies need not be so blatant as those pre-

Exhibit 13.34 W. R. Grace Leverages Up

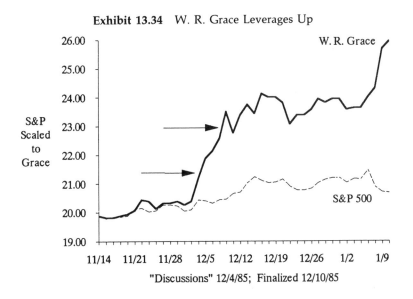

"Discussions" 12/4/85; Finalized 12/10/85

sided over by Lucky Stores or W. R. Grace to be important. Often they arise from decisions to invest capital unwisely because of a preoccupation with uncertain, long-term payoffs.

One of the accusations hurled at raiders is that they force management to focus on shorter-term payoffs to the detriment of longer-term values. The raiders are guilty as charged. But they are also to be applauded for righting a wrong that arises from a common confusion between gross future values and net present values. If less money is invested in a business, the future value of the business is reduced. The inevitable consequences of trimming investment spending are smaller size, fewer products, a less commanding market position, and, indeed, a lower long-run value for any business. And yet, even though all those consequences are real, none provide a sufficient justification for investing capital.

All those statements focus myopically on gross future values: the value of a business at some future point as envisioned by an empire builder. By that time, all of the outlays required to achieve the enviable position management foresees will be sunk costs, irrelevant to computing value in the mind's eye. The way to maximize the long-run value of any business, to build an empire, is to spend as much money as possible—hardly a meaningful capital budgeting prescription.

The stock market, raiders—indeed, all value builders—focus on net present values: the anticipated value of the future position discounted to the present and net of all outlays required to fuel growth. Net present value calculations ought to drive corporate decisions because they implicitly consider the benefit that may be derived from deploying resources to grow other businesses and seek the highest ratio between gross future values and the outlays required to produce them. By undertaking the projects holding the prospect of generating the greatest net present values, management ensures the greatest future value for society at large from investing our limited capital resources.

Capital budgeting is the process of deciding which businesses ought not to grow as rapidly, so that other, more promising ones, can grow even more rapidly. A failure to hew to this basic corporate finance principle when making internal capital budgeting decisions will attract raiders like bees to flowers.

Economic Cross-Subsidies

An economic cross-subsidy arises when the assets that support a business are worth more than the business itself—a sign that there is a more highly valued alternative use for the assets. For example, when I met with the CFO of one of the largest grocery store chains in the nation, he said that the value of the real estate beneath his stores exceeded the company's current market value. "Where does the value of our real estate appear in the market value of this company?" he asked. "Why, we could liquidate our real estate and realize far more than our current stock price."

In view of the facts, I suggested that liquidation sounded like the appropriate strategy. "Well, I was just speaking hypothetically," he said.

But that was the point. So long as their real estate supported their grocery operations, its value would be limited to the cash flow the grocery stores could be expected to generate. Because management had conditioned the market to expect a continuation of the grocery operations, the company sold for less than its breakup value.

Part of the CFO's confusion arose from his belief that, in figuring the worth of his company, investors should add the value of the real estate to the value of the grocery business when, in fact, any company's value is an either-or proposition. A company can either realize the value of its assets or generate the value of its business, but not both. That our client's stock price reflected the lower of the two values was due to management's decision to use fortuitous gains from asset appreciation to subsidize unrecorded but nevertheless real operating losses.

How so? Imagine, first, that the assets of the company are held in a separate financing subsidiary. This subsidiary leases the assets to internal operating units at fair market rental rates. The operating units, in turn, use the assets in the grocery business, receiving all revenues, paying all operating expenses (including rents), without owning any assets.

This division into operating and ownership units, and the introduction of a market-driven transfer price between them, permits the company's overall profits to be divided into two components. The income of the financing subsidiary—namely, the rents—is set so as to provide just a fair return on a current appraised value of the assets. By design, the financing subsidiary just breaks even in economic terms. The income recorded by the operating subsidiaries, in contrast, is a residual that reflects management's ability to add value to the assets employed in its business. In other words, it is a measure of the residual income (or economic value added, to use our term) from operations after subtracting the cost of the capital tied up in the business.

Consider, for example, a company that records $75 million of income on $500 million of book assets, giving the appearance of a respectable 15% return ($75/$500), quality management, and no vulnerability to a hostile takeover. If, however, the assets supporting the business have a current appraised value of $1 billion and the prevailing cost of capital is 10%, the internal lease rate from owner to operator is $100 million (10% applied to $1 billion), leaving a deficit of $25 million from operations ($75−$100). The $75 million of consolidated reported profits divides into $100 million attributable to the ownership of appreciated assets, and a true operating loss of $25 million, a cross-subsidy that any raider would be pleased to eliminate by selling the assets to a more highly valued alternative use.

That our hypothetical company can earn an attractive return on the original cost but not the current value of its assets simply indicates that the optimal use of its assets has changed over time. What may have started as an isolated grocery store built on a paved-over cornfield may today be in the midst of a burgeoning office park. The value of that location has appreciated as its preferred use has changed, an important development that the company's accounting books have failed to record and its management to act on.

An economic cross-subsidy is yet another manifestation of Joseph Schumpeter's "creative destruction": capitalism constantly sowing the seeds of its own undoing through progress. Being attuned to the changing value of assets, and their most productive current use, is an important management responsibility, one that is too frequently delegated to a raider.

The Evidence

Fortunately, broad-based evidence is mounting to support my proposition that debt is good and more debt is even better. A study performed by Frank R. Lichtenberg (of the Columbia University Graduate School of Business) and Donald Siegel (of the National Bureau of Economic Research) is one of the most impressive and comprehensive of the lot.[20] Using Census Bureau data, they investigated the effects of LBOs at the level of individual plants, the very firing line of an industrial company's competitiveness. About 5%, or 1100, of the manufacturing plants in their sample were involved in LBOs during 1981 to 1986. The performances of those plants were compared with those of plants in the same industry that did not undergo LBOs. The conclusions are startling even to a visceral believer in the benefits of debt such as myself.

- Plants involved in LBOs had significantly higher rates of total-factor productivity growth than other plants in the same industry.

- The productivity gains are due not to generating more output than non-LBO plants (nor do they produce less), but to the more effective utilization of labor and particularly of capital inputs (but not materials).

- The mix and compensation of employees changed after the LBO in a very significant way. Wage rates of production workers increased, whereas both the employment and wages of supervisory personnel declined sharply. The authors note that these changes suggest an increasing reliance on the carrot of higher wages as an incentive, and less emphasis on the stick of close supervision, to elicit effort on the part of production workers, an important restructuring of compensation that complements the leveraging of the balance sheet. (This evidence showing that LBOs liberate the floor worker

[20]Frank R. Lichtenberg and Donald Siegel, "The Effects of Leveraged Buyouts on Productivity and Related Aspects of Firm Behavior," Columbia University working paper (revised June 1989).

from the tyranny of close supervision is one of the most satisfying of the findings to me.)

- Productivity growth was found to be even higher in LBOs in which the preceding management participated.
- Plants involved in management LBOs were less likely to subsequently close than other plants in the same industry.
- The average R&D intensity of firms involved in LBOs increased at least as much from 1978 to 1986 as did the average R&D intensity of all firms responding to the National Science Foundation/Census Bureau survey of industrial R&D.

Sounds too good to be true, does it not? Nevertheless, this, and not the popular opinion, is the truth about LBOs.

So What about Bloomies?

Despite Lichtenberg and Siegel's compelling evidence, many people believe that LBOs are not good because a few highly publicized deals are now experiencing financial difficulty. Campeau's problems with his highly leveraged acquisitions of the Federated and Allied department stores is the example most frequently thrown out as proof that LBOs do not work. Let me say a few things about that.

First, the bondholders' loss is the shareholders' gain. The decline in value that Campeau's bondholders are suffering is just surrendering *some* of the premium that Campeau paid to the Allied and Federated shareholders when those companies were acquired. But value has not been lost, on net. As far as judging the social desirability of LBOs is concerned, the question is whether the assets that make up Federated and Allied are being operated more or less efficiently now than before, and not whether the junk bonds are holding their value. Consistent with the Lichtenberg-Siegel findings, Campeau's LBOs have indeed spurred greater efficiency at the level of the individual stores.

Bloomingdale's, the crown jewel of Federated Department Stores, Inc., is a good example. Though Bloomingdale's is in bankruptcy as I write, it is operating more efficiently now than ever before. One reason is the shift in pay away from wages to commissions, from a management by mandate to a management by motivation, just as Lichtenberg and Siegel documented to be the case with other LBOs.

John L. Palmerio, a 25-year veteran of the men's shoe salon at Bloomingdale's flagship store in Manhattan, thought working on commission would prove lucrative. He hasn't been disappointed. Since February [1989], when his department switched from an hourly wage scale to a 10% commission on sales, Palmerio has been pulling in an extra $175, or 25%, in his average weekly paycheck. And overall sales in the nine-person department have increased 22%. "So far, everybody has done much better than we anticipated," he says.

While department stores see it as an investment that should boost sales, converting to commissions is expensive at first. The process costs $700,000 to $1 million per store, estimates James M. Zimmerman, president of Campeau's Federated and Allied chains. That includes training programs, computer changes, and pay, which often goes up immediately. Still, Campeau Corporation plans to have 90 percent of its sales associates in its nine department store chains on some form of commission by the end of 1990.

"Now Salespeople Must Really Sell for Their Supper"
Business Week
July 31, 1989

A publicly traded company, with its preoccupation with near-term earnings, would probably be reluctant to make that productive change in incentives, or at least to make it happen so fast. But not Campeau.

So if the Allied and Federated stores are operating more efficiently now than before, and are more valuable, why is Campeau in trouble? The answer is shockingly simple: He overpaid. Campeau's LBO of Federated and Allied has increased value enormously for many of the reasons I have outlined in this chapter, but just not by enough to recover the outrageous premiums that Campeau paid. There is justice in all this, however. No one individual will suffer as much of a personal loss from his rash acquisitions as Robert Campeau himself. It has been estimated that his personal net worth dropped from about $500 million in 1988 to (only) $35 million by the end of 1989.[21] (I should not be too quick

---

[21]"Campeau: Who Won and Who Lost," *Fortune,* February 12, 1990.

in laying blame at poor Robert's door. After all, he had the misfortune of having "Bid-Em-Up Brucie" Wasserstein as his financial advisor on price and structure. When will Brucie's day of reckoning come?)

Campeau's problems are symptomatic of larger forces at work in the LBO market. Sure Campeau overpaid, but so have others. Is there any reason why the LBOs since 1986 have not worked out as well as the ones before that? Ted Forstmann (of Forstmann, Little, a prominent LBO sponsor) thinks the culprit was the proliferation of junk bond financing, particularly payment-in-kind bonds that tempted LBO sponsors to finance takeovers even when the target's current cash flow was insufficient to cover interest. But Ted is confusing a symptom for the disease.

Performing LBOs is a business like any other, and the profitability of LBOs has followed the classic evolution of an industry subjected to an innovation followed by free entry. In the early 1980s, only a relative handful of firms had the insight, expertise, reputation, and access to capital to perform LBOs. The early birds get the worms. The fantastic returns earned by those astute LBO entrepreneurs attracted other birds into the business. Unfortunately for Ted Forstmann, the barriers to entry into his business are not too great. In fact, the way in which Ted Forstmann himself entered the fray shows just how easy a business it is to enter.

One of Forstmann's golfing buddies at Long Island's Deepdale Golf Club was Derald Ruttenberg, then president of an industrial company named Studebaker-Worthington. Forstmann's younger brother, Nick, who worked at a start-up firm named Kohlberg Kravis Roberts, asked Ted (Forstmann) to arrange a meeting.

That meeting changed Ted Forstmann's life. He and Ruttenberg listened to Henry Kravis and Jerry Kohlberg propose something they called a leveraged buyout. Forstmann was familiar with the concept but had never tried anything like it. Ruttenberg listened politely; after the meeting broke up, he asked Forstmann, "Isn't that kind of what you were talking about?"

Forstmann wasn't quite sure what Ruttenberg meant. "Well," he said guardedly. "Yeah, sort of."

"Well," Ruttenberg continued, "what do those guys have that you and I don't have?"

"Nothing."

"Okay. How would you go about doing this?"

"Well, I would need some money first."

The conversation led to Ruttenberg's proposing to bankroll Forstmann in a new firm. Ruttenberg and a group of his friends would chip in, and Forstmann and brother Nick would try their hand at leveraged buyouts.

Barbarians at the Gate: The Fall of RJR Nabisco

By 1986, so much capital had flocked into the LBO game that even the early birds found worms difficult to find. There is one market truism in which it is safe to say every capitalist economist believes: the more bidders, the higher the price. The fabulous LBO returns of the early years were competed away in wide-open auctions passed on, as in any market, to the consumer (this time, the shareholders of companies that performed LBOs) in the form of higher premiums. But the LBO business wasn't just competitive; it was downright crowded. In all of 1987, Ted Forstmann could not close on one deal. Not a single one. Too many players spurred by the prospect of garnering front-end fees and chasing too few deals kept him from winning even once, and that was a formula for disaster in the business. Hockey-stick forecasts replaced any sense of reality. By this time commercial bankers had become so dependent on feeding at the LBO trough that they could not stomach the thought of imposing a discipline on the market. The junk bond investors too had become addicted. They swallowed lower and lower quality paper trusting in the word of previously reputable LBO sponsors. Now it is clear. LBO prices got too high. They became unhinged from reality. The LBOs became victims of their own success. I believe that LBOs are good, maybe even great, but LBOs cannot turn lead into gold.

For now the market is taking a breather from LBOs. But the merits of LBOs are so overwhelming for many companies that I am forced to predict a resurrection of the business. To paraphrase Mark Twain: Rumors of its death are greatly exaggerated.

The question is why the LBOs have stopped all of a sudden. Is it because lenders are no longer willing to lend and equity investors no longer willing to invest? To a certain extent, that is true, at least for a time. Wholly unwarranted clampdowns by regulators on LBO financing by banks and insurance companies is another, more troublesome, factor. But I believe the real reason for the slowdown is that the managers who might participate in LBOs are no longer comfortable doing so. They read the newspapers and have seen what happened to Campeau. Understandably, they are unwilling to stake their own hard-earned money and business reputations in an LBO in which they might lose it all. What will persuade the managers to come back? Time heals all wounds. But some adjustments in the business will help, too.

The financiers, the commercial banks, and the junk bond buyers will return chastened by their experience. They will demand more equity, more stringent control and repayment terms, and more reality in the forecasts. That is healthy, and a natural market adjustment. LBO prices will come down to reflect the new reality, so fewer will be done, but a greater proportion will succeed in repaying all their debt. This, obviously, is the development that astute managers will wait for. But they should insist upon one more thing before returning to the game. The LBO sponsors, the KKRs and Forstmann, Littles of the world, and their merchant banking friends, must stop getting such large up-front fees that they no longer care whether the deals are economic. Their fees must fall so that their returns are geared to the successful paydown of the LBO debt and the harvesting of the residual equity value added. That, and not the abolition of junk bonds or PIK bonds, is what is needed. Only then would I as a manager be willing to stake my money in the transaction. But don't wait too long. Remember, it is the early bird that catches the worm.

A Qualification.   Unlike KKR, however, the return of the LBO is really not the development I am waiting for. Management-initiated leveraged recapitalizations, which leave the current shareholders in place, are generally more equitable and viable transactions than LBOs are. But even a leveraged recapitalization may not be the best structure, for it bluntly burdens all of a company's assets with debt. In the next chapter I propose that, instead of recapitalizing at the corporate level, the subsidiary units within an overall company be recapitalized with a surgical precision that is sensitive to the strategic challenges that each one faces: debt for the mature, cash-rich operations and partial public equity capitalization for the promising, risky ventures. What I am proposing is that companies replicate internally the disciplinary and incentive advantages that external capital markets offer. If that vision is carried out, it is my opinion that raiders, and KKR, will become an unnecessary evil and corporations will be even better managed than they are now.

Summary

Just in the process of discussing leverage, many of the most prominent of the methods and motives of financial restructuring have surfaced (my real objective). I have illustrated how financial restructurings often lead to strengthened incentives for success and more painful penalties for failure, a cure for the risk of an unproductive reinvestment of surplus cash flow, the achievement of a better business fit and an improved focus, a renewed sense of urgency, a commitment to cash flow above profits, the elimination of wasteful cross-subsidies, and last and maybe least, tax savings. My partner David Glassman and I are convinced that these motives are the real reasons why financial restructurings create value. Our conviction is strengthened by the observation that companies that restructured without clearly addressing the motives we identified did not increase their market values. In such cases where there was form without function, the market wisely eschewed any interest in mere financial maneuverings.

I also have discussed, if only briefly, partnerships, partial public stock offerings, spin-offs and divestitures, share repurchases, leveraged ESOPs, leveraged cash-outs, leveraged buy-outs, and split-ups. These tax-driven techniques are among the many methods available to unleash the rewards of the restructuring motives. We found the most effective financial restructurings to be those initiated by management and not an outsider, either all at once as a preemptive strike (FMC) or, maybe even better, as a natural complement to the company's ongoing business strategy (Exxon). A voluntary restructuring produces a company that is more cohesive, more valuable, and more financially flexible than those in which a third party has set the agenda.

It also appears to us that managers overestimate the risk of precipitating a hostile offer by performing a financial restructuring on their own. For example, we have found not a single instance in which a management-initiated leveraged recapitalization triggered a subsequent successful hostile offer. Most managers do not realize that they are playing a zero-sum game with the hostile suitors. But the evidence shows that the target's gains are the raider's losses, and vice versa. The more value a company can produce by restructuring, and the sooner the better, the less likely it is ever to be taken over and the more value it will preserve for its own shareholders. In the restructuring game, the best defense is a good offense.

In chapter 14, the offense takes the field against the arch nemesis, Kohlberg Kravis Roberts & Co., or KKR, the dreaded white whale of LBOs. Financial restructuring reaches a crescendo with my three-part plan to turn back the persistent advances of the great leviathan.

14

Remaking the Public Corporation from Within

The Whiteness of the Whale

Kohlberg Kravis Roberts & Co. is a great leviathan that has swallowed companies with combined sales of over $60 billion, and its appetite remains unsated. Though its record is not unblemished, KKR has proved remarkably adept at creating value through a long string of premium-priced, highly publicized, and wholly unrelated acquisitions. What has made KKR so successful in comparison with most conventional companies? Mostly a unique financial structure and a distinctive management style.

To begin with, *KKR is essentially a holding company that owns majority equity stakes in a vast array of highly leveraged and unrelated subsidiary business units (the LBOs).* These units include such prominent companies as RJR, the tobacco giant, Safeway, one of the largest grocery chains in the country, Owens-Illinois, the nation's largest glass manufacturer, Duracell, the battery company, and Jim Walter, a large building products concern, among many others.

KKR is almost totally decentralized. It must be. KKR itself consists of just 60 people. It does not have a corporate bureaucracy, does not have corporate meetings, does not have corporate goals. There is no allocation of corporate overhead. Without a corporate bureaucracy to keep close tabs on its units, *KKR manages by motivation, not by mandate; by empowerment, not by punishment.*

The CEOs of KKR's business units have a significant equity ownership interest in the units they manage, an incentive that is much more precise and powerful than is usual for the managers of most other companies (Professor Michael Jensen of Harvard has shown that the average CEO in a sample of LBOs receives $6.40 of every $100 change in corporate value, whereas the average CEO in the Forbes 1000 experiences a total wealth change of about $0.20 per $100). The opportunity to create personal wealth is generally a more compelling incentive than that provided by even the most ingenious annual or long-term bonus system.

KKR uses debt aggressively. But it does not borrow at the consolidated, or parent, level, and it is unconcerned with an overall bond rating. Instead, *KKR borrows at the subsidiary level, with the debts of the individual LBO units having no recourse to one another.* Much like a boat whose hull is divided into separate chambers, compartmentalizing debt and equity ensures that a leak in any one unit cannot sink the equity invested in any of the other units. By limiting exposure to risk in this way, the cost of equity is held down and financing flexibility is enhanced. Though it operates with a consolidated leverage ratio that would lock a public LDC out of the market, KKR has no trouble floating new debt and equity to finance new deals. The increased cost of debt is a small price to pay for these advantages.

This decentralized financing policy prevents wasteful cross-subsidization among the units. Cash generated in one cannot be passed freely to another. It also ensures that surplus cash flow is dedicated to debt service and is repatriated to equity investors, thereby reining in the natural temptation to reinvest in businesses that may lack the potential for real growth. The substitution of debt for equity on a unit's balance sheet also makes it easier to concentrate a significant equity stake in the hands of the unit's management. Making unit managers face the burden of meeting interest and principal payments on their own instills a sense of urgency and a dedication to cash flow rather than to accounting profits.

KKR's debt policy departs from common practice in one other important way. *KKR's use of debt is dynamic, not static.* Instead of attempting to maintain a reasonably fixed blend of debt and equity in its capital structure as most companies do, KKR's objective is to repay its LBO debt, and the sooner the better. This fluid debt policy resembles the classic Bob Hope and Bing Crosby road movies in which the journey is more important than the destination, the action along the way more important than getting there. In their drive to pay down LBO debt, the managers of KKR's units bring about operational efficiencies and asset sales that in turn make for more valuable businesses. Ironically, the companies that complete the journey and successfully pay down their debt often will volunteer to try the treacherous LBO route once again. Thus the *dynamic* use of debt itself becomes dynamic—not one cycle of debt and debt repayment, but a series of such cycles that each time wrings out inefficiencies, breathes in value, and bootstraps more managers into the ranks of owners. *For KKR, LBOs are not one-shot transactions. They are a way of life.*

KKR does not buy companies so much as it leases them. KKR controls a company for only as long as it takes to prove it has enhanced value, normally a period of 3 to 7 years. Afterward, it has a strategy to "exit," to sell the business unit to a third party or to the public or to releverage the unit once again to wind up the spring that propels the creation of value. KKR's philosophy is best described as one of *buy, build, and harvest* (build value, that is) and not the buy and hold or buy and sell mindsets that dominate conventional U.S. management thinking. Knowing that they have a finite horizon over which to create and then to realize exceptional value provides unit managers with a special incentive often denied to those within LDCs.

KKR leases talent too. For example, KKR installed Lou Gerstner, the former president of American Express, as head of its RJR subsidiary and brought Karl von der Heyden from H. J. Heinz to serve as the unit's CFO. As the world's largest single user of executive search firms, KKR helps to put the scarcest of resources—talented and motivated managers—to their highest-valued use.

KKR uses other peoples' money. The debt and most of the equity it uses comes from outside investors. KKR derives its return by taking 20% of the profits earned after the debt has been repaid and the equity holders have received a return of their original capital. By offering to stand last in line for payout along with the residual equity investors, KKR makes a credible statement about its commitment to and confidence in creating value (notwith-standing its significant up-front fees).

KKR achieves its comparative advantages mostly through a strategy of decentralization: the decentralization of debt, of equity, of incentives, of decision making. But I come not to praise KKR; I come to bury it. I see no reason why the managers of conventional companies cannot capture the benefits of KKR's highly decentralized organization for themselves and their shareholders and still stay public if they wish. What follows is a simple, three-step procedure. If you have the will, here is the way.

A Game Plan for Creating Value

How can a company avoid becoming the next breakfast snack of the great white whale?

First, make the senior corporate officers, a skeletal supporting staff, and influential board members into significant owners of equity in the corporate parent. It is unlikely that any of the profound changes this new structure requires will happen without involving the people at the top *first.*

Making senior managers and board members into significant owners runs headlong into a fundamental contradiction: How can insiders with limited financial resources acquire a large equity stake *without* unfairly diluting the value of the current shareholders' investment? Hand them a large number of stock options or shower them with restricted stock, and the shareholders will suffer, notwithstanding the incentive it may provide. I propose a new, leveraged stock option to reconcile these conflicting objectives.

Second, selectively decentralize the use of debt. Certain individual business units, those in a position to distribute substantial levels of cash without impairing their intrinsic value, should borrow *without recourse* and up to their full *dynamic* debt capacity and pass the proceeds to the corporate parent. The parent will, in turn, pay down its debt, make a special distribution of cash to its shareholders, or accumulate a war chest for acquisitions.

Incentives and decision-making authority must be decentralized into those units at the same time. The business unit managers should obtain a significant equity stake in the units they manage and should be delegated the authority, autonomy, and responsibility to maximize unit value. Not only does this make good economic sense; the lenders to the units probably will insist on it.

Decentralization should be underscored by turning corporate staff functions into profit centers, with staff bonuses tied to measurable results. When it is practical, explicit, market-based transfer prices should be charged to the units. The corporate staff should be free to sell their services outside the boundaries of the corporation to maximize the value of their offerings, and the business units should be able to contract with third parties for staff services if they choose.

Once debt has been decentralized, an option is equity decentralization, the disposition of some or all of the common stock in the recapitalized subsidiary units. Equity in the leveraged subsidiary units could be distributed to the parent company's stockholders in a tax-free spin-off, used as a currency for tax-free acquisitions of other related companies, or sold in whole or in part to the public, to a strategic business buyer or to a savvy financial player such as a KKR. Chief among the advantages of equity decentralization are to reduce risk, to gain a synergistic partner, and to raise even more cash for the parent.

Third, selectively decentralize just the equity in certain business units, a process I call venture capitalization. Just as KKR is the model for debt decentralization, a venture capital fund is the model for the decentralization of equity alone. Applicable to high-potential, entrepreneurial businesses—ones whose growth and risk preclude aggressive leverage—venture capitalization can involve offering or distributing a minority interest in a promising but risky unit to the public or making managers and employees into partial owners of their venture without creating a public market for the stock. No matter how it is done, the objective is to keep the flame of start-up entrepreneurism flickering under the protective umbrella of a large corporate infrastructure.

In sum, I recommend that, after they are made into significant owners of parent equity, the senior corporate officers tailor a financial decentralization strategy suitable for each of the firm's individual business units depending upon the stage in its life cycle: debt for the mature, cash-rich sunset operations and equity for the rapidly growing, cash-starved sunrise ventures. The ensuing sections of this chapter spell out in greater detail the specific steps in this plan and illustrate many of the individual elements with case examples.

Step 1: Make Senior Corporate Managers (and the Board) into Owners

The Leveraged Equity Purchase Plan.   To begin with, senior corporate executives and board members should acquire a large equity stake in the parent company through a technique I call a leveraged equity purchase plan (LEPP) whereby:

- 90% of the purchase price is financed through a loan from the company that is secured solely by a pledge of the stock itself but which has no recourse to management's personal assets.
- The 10% balance is paid by management and is put at risk.

Suppose that a company's common shares have a $1 billion market value and it is desired to provide insiders with a 10% stake. With a LEPP, the $100 million purchase price is 90% financed through a $90 million loan from the company, and the $10 million balance is invested by the executive and board group from their personal resources. The investments that managers make should be sizable enough to matter but not be so sizable that they cannot afford to lose them, because that might happen.

Should the company's market value subsequently fall beneath the face value of the loan, management will cancel the loan by tendering the shares back to the company, and it can lose only the initial $10 million investment. I will say that again: Management can lose *only* the original $10 million investment. Preventing that from happening is likely to be a top priority.

I frequently meet with senior executives who complain that their company's common shares are undervalued. The company's complexity, the lack of a meaningful following, or their investors' preoccupation with the short term are just a few of the reasons advanced to account for this. Sometimes whole string quartets come out of their closet to play me a very sad song. It's then that

I say, "Well then, this would seem to be a particularly opportune moment for you to introduce a leveraged equity purchase plan for upper management."

"Oh," they respond, "we are not quite that undervalued."

During one of Stern Stewart & Co.'s public forums a representative from a major midwestern manufacturing company (whom I can no longer identify because she wrote to tell me that she was embarrassed by what she said at that time) interrupted me to say, "Bennett, we took a very close look at the leveraged equity purchase plan, and there are only two problems with it."

Stunned by the possibility that I had missed some crucial legal or tax issue, I asked what those two problems were. She said, "Well, you must have great confidence in your management team, and you must expect your stock to perform well over a brief period of time."

I said, "Yes, that would all be true."

And then she said, "Well, we're not."

But she made a good point. There can be no question that in light of the risk they are taking with their own money, just by announcing their willingness to participate in such a plan, a management team powerfully expresses to shareholders its commitment to and confidence in creating value. And that is one reason why the initiation of such a plan often will send a company's stock price rising. Another reason is that management will not be rewarded for any increase in value, because the loan used to purchase the stock accrues interest. Only if the company's value grows at a rate faster than interest accrues on the loan will management come out ahead. Indeed, if the loan bears interest at a rate equal to the company's cost of capital, the leveraged equity purchase plan rewards management for generating a spread between the rate of return earned on the funds employed to purchase the stock and the cost of the capital (as reflected by the interest on the loan), a concept at the heart of effective capital budgeting.

All of these are valuable protections and assurances for investors. But what a LEPP threatens to give management is equally important. A LEPP is a powerful motivator because it doubly amplifies management's rewards for exceptional performance. The potential payoff is magnified, once because the shares management acquires through the LEPP will discount to a present value all of the projected payoffs resulting from current management actions; twice because such potential share value gains are financially leveraged 10 to 1. A mere 10% increase in the market value of the company's equity will generate a 100% increase in the value of management's investment. Of course, a 10% decline will wipe it out.

As KKR and other financiers have shown repeatedly, a true incentive must provide managers with *an unlimited and an amplified reward for success and a genuine penalty for failure.* Faced with this stark choice, most people will choose to succeed. Count among them Peter Magowan, chairman and chief executive of Safeway, a large grocery store chain that underwent a KKR-sponsored LBO.

> We have our money involved. Corporate management is given large salaries, stock options and that sort of thing but they haven't got their own money at risk. We have. If this thing fails, we are going to lose a substantial portion of what we've invested. That's a powerful incentive to get better performance. We've tried to carry that down with incentive plans to the level of store management.
>
> *The Wall Street Journal*
> December 5, 1989

After three years, Magowan rates the company's LBO a success. Safeway went through a major downsizing program, shedding $2.3 billion in low-profit supermarkets and other assets. It is now only 60% of its former size, but it will make more money in 1989 than it made before the LBO, and it is now set to grow once again. That's great, but why should KKR be the one to benefit if revitalizing incentives explains a large part of the LBO's success?

Why, indeed, for a LEPP creates the incentives of an LBO for management without necessitating an LBO of the company itself. In a typical LBO, 90% of the purchase price is financed with debt carried on the company's books that has no recourse to management, and then management is invited to acquire a stake in the equity that stands beneath the corporate debt. A LEPP shrinks the typical leverage and ownership structure of an LBO down to a size that fits just management. That way, shareholders can have the luxury of owning stock in a healthy, publicly traded company while management can pretend it is going through an LBO.

Henley's Leveraged Equity Purchase Plan. Michael Dingman, chairman of the Henley Group of San Diego, is one who believes that KKR can be beaten at its own game. Henley was formed in early 1986 by the spin-off of 35 poorly performing businesses from Allied-Signal. The company floated to an initial market value of $1.8 billion, remarkable considering that, as a group, the businesses that comprised Henley had lost $23 million the year before the spin-off occurred. Investors were banking on the track record of Michael Dingman, who became Henley's chairman, and his reputation for giving his talented managers a tremendous personal incentive to create value for shareholders. It was widely anticipated that Dingman would introduce a very powerful incentive scheme for them, and he did.

On October 10, 1986, Dingman announced that 20 of Henley's top executives had agreed to purchase freshly issued shares in the Henley Group sufficient in number to give them about a 5% stake in the company. Of the $108 million purchase price, $97 million, or 90%, was to be financed with a loan from the company that would have no recourse to management. The loan would be secured solely by a pledge of the shares. The 10% balance, $11 million, would be contributed by management and put at risk. (The plan is diagrammed in exhibit 14.1.) The $97 million loan bears interest at the company's bank borrowing rate,[1] but it will be accrued and not actually paid. Instead, in each of the third to seventh years of the plan, one-fifth of the accumulated loan balance will come due against one-fifth of the common shares.

Management will exercise its option to acquire the shares only if Henley's share value compounds at a rate that surpasses the rate at which interest accrues on the loan. Failing that, management will surrender the shares to the company to cancel the loan, and forfeit its 10% down payment. The payoff profile duplicates that of an LBO. There is an unlimited and accentuated reward, a genuine penalty for failure. Michael Dingman also saw the plan in those stark terms:

---

[1]Dividends paid on the common shares are credited against the accrued interest and the loan balance.

Exhibit 14.1   The Henley Leveraged Equity Purchase Plan (LEPP)

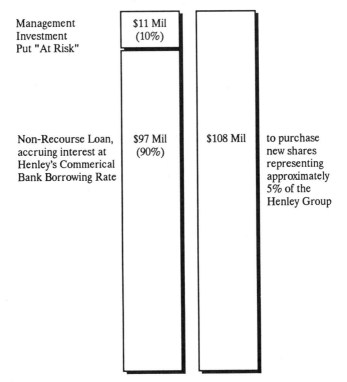

Management Investment Put "At Risk" — $11 Mil (10%)

Non-Recourse Loan, accruing interest at Henley's Commerical Bank Borrowing Rate — $97 Mil (90%)

$108 Mil to purchase new shares representing approximately 5% of the Henley Group

"We believe that substantial borrowing and equity risk taking by key executives will create the entrepreneurial conditions that are critical to Henley's success."

Dingman said the leveraged equity purchase program was modeled on the way executives participate in a leveraged buyout and was preferable to a stock option plan because executives make an up-front investment and can watch that investment fluctuate with the stock price.

"Henley Group Says 20 Officials to Buy 5.1 Million Shares in Unusual Program"
The Wall Street Journal
October 10, 1986

As the plan was first announced, Henley's share value surged almost 10% versus the S&P 500 (exhibit 14.2), undoubtedly a

Exhibit 14.2   Henley Initiates Leveraged Equity Purchase Plan

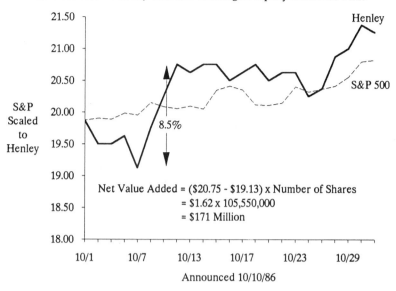

Announced 10/10/86

pleasing prospect for the participating managers even if they did have 3 years to go before they could first taste the fruits of their labors. Granted, a 10% gain is short of the premium normally associated with an LBO. But investors had previously bid Henley's market value to a premium because clever actions of just this sort were expected. That the company's stock price rose as much as it did suggests that the LEPP was an incentive plan even better than investors had expected.

Great idea, Michael. So who needs KKR?

An Even Better Mousetrap

Henley's ingenious leveraged equity purchase plan can be replicated by a special type of stock option. In practice, I recommend implementing a LEPP through a nonqualified stock option plan whereby (1) the exercise price for the options is set at a 10% discount from the current market price, (2) management purchases the options at a price equal to the in-the-money discount, and (3) the exercise price increases by a predetermined rate of interest (less dividends paid on the common shares), thereby preserving a minimum acceptable return for shareholders before management participates.[2]

For a company whose common shares currently trade for, say, $30, a LEPP option would set the initial exercise price at $27, a 10% discount. The options would be sold to management for $3 each. The $27 exercise price would increase at a rate equal to the projected cost of equity capital, but less any dividends paid on the common shares (and possibly less a discount to compensate managers for illiquidity and bearing market risk). If, for example, the cost of equity is 15% and the common dividend yield is 5%, the exercise price will rise 10% per annum, becoming $29.70 after the first year, $32.67 the year after, etc.[3] (See exhibit 14.3 for an illustration of the potential payoff from the LEPP option plan.)

In contrast to conventional stock options, LEPP options are in the money and not at the money, are bought and not granted, and index the exercise price to grow instead of standing still. The comparison shows stock options (or worse, restricted stock) for what they really are, just additional compensation. LEPP options, by contrast, provide a real incentive to perform, or else.

The most important reason to use LEPP options, however, is a quantitative advantage. A board of directors is unquestionably justified in selling management a *very* large number of them because, unlike ordinary options, LEPP options are nondilutive unless and until the shareholders realize a return that exceeds the rate at which interest is added to the exercise price (see exhibit 14.3). Thus, the appeal for the corporate executives is that they will be able to acquire many times more LEPP options than they would be granted ordinary options, like 5 to 10 times as many. LEPP options, in other words, must be used aggressively, not half-heartedly, in order to entice managers with the prospect of becoming very wealthy.

Some managers still may be reluctant to jump at the chance to

[2]Alternatively, the exercise price on the LEPP option may be tied to the change in the market value of a portfolio of competing companies or of a broader index such as the S&P 500. Then management will not be rewarded or penalized for changes in value due to exogenous factors beyond its control.
[3]The LEPP options cannot be exercised right away. As with the Henley plan, one-fifth of the LEPP option becomes exercisable after the end of each of the third through seventh year from purchase, emulating the time horizon to exit an LBO. As with qualified options, the final maturity of the LEPP options is 10 years.

Exhibit 14.3   Look Before You LEPP

Let's consider an individual willing to gamble $30,000 on a **LEPP** plan. If the current stock price is $30 a share and the exercise price is set at a 10% discount, or $27, then the LEPP option has a $3 in-the-money value. A $30,000 investment buys 10,000 of these special LEPP options. The payoff 5 years out is modeled in the table below, assuming that the exercise price is indexed to increase at 10% per annum.

In the first section of the table the current $30 stock price is projected 5 years hence at various rates of return. Next, the initial $27 exercise price is compounded 5 years at a 10% rate, yielding $43.48. In effect, the managers are guaranteeing this minimum future stock price before they participate. For any future share value less than $43.48, the managers will let their LEPP options lapse unexercised and worthless. The spread between the prospective value of the shares and the projected exercise price, if positive, is multiplied by 10,000 options to determine the future value of the original $30,000 investment. The last line in the table reports the compound average annual rate of return on the managers' investment in the LEPP option program.

If the common stock fails to compound at least at 9.2% per annum on average, the managers' investment is erased. The breakeven return is 10%, the rate at which the managers will realize the same return as the shareholders. Managers will not enjoy an exceptional return unless and until the shareholders receive this minimum acceptable return on their investments, an important assurance. After a 10% return for the shareholders has been secured, the managers' return on investment accelerates because it is financially leveraged 10:1. A common stock return of 20% per annum, for instance, produces a 60% per annum return on the LEPP, or $312,000 from a measly $30,000 investment. Anyone who has ever played a state lottery understands the appeal of gambling a small sum for the prospect of a huge payoff. The LEPP does that too, except that in this game, the managers can swing the odds in their favor by their exceptional efforts. Mortgage the house, anyone?

Exhibit 14.3 continued

Initial stock price	$30.00	$30.00	$30.00	$30.00	$30.00	$30.00
At compound growth rate	0.0 %	7.7 %	9.2 %	10.0 %	15.0 %	20.0 %
Stock price in 5 years	$30.00	$43.48	$46.48	$48.32	$60.34	$74.65
Initial exercise price	$27.00	$27.00	$27.00	$27.00	$27.00	$27.00
At compound growth rate	10.0 %	10.0 %	10.0 %	10.0 %	10.0 %	10.0 %
Exercise price in 5 years	$43.48	$43.48	$43.48	$43.48	$43.48	$43.48
Amount in the money	$0.00	$0.00	$3.00	$4.83	$16.86	$31.17
× Number of options	10,000	10,000	10,000	10,000	10,000	10,000
Aggregate in the money	0	0	$30,000	$48,315	$168,569	$311,658
Total equity invested	$30,000	$30,000	$30,000	$30,000	$30,000	$30,000
Participants' annual return on investment	−100%	−100%	0%	10%	41%	60%

buy LEPP options because of a concern over the challenge of keeping the stock price ahead of the rising exercise price. Such a concern is unwarranted to a great degree, however, because stock prices are *expected* to appreciate in value over time. Current stock prices reflect a discounting of future cash flows, and hence, of future stock prices, to a present value. As time passes, and the discount on cash flow lifts, stock prices will tend to rise in order to provide investors with returns that compensate for risk. The share price appreciation is just the reverse of the discounting process. Indexing the exercise price thus subtracts from future stock price appreciation that part which could be expected, leaving the part which is exceptional. The LEPP option, in other words, will reward managers for outperforming the forward plan that already is reflected in the current stock price. That is exactly what an incentive compensation plan is supposed to do but rarely does.

In conclusion, I believe LEPP options are the best way to make managers into significant owners and to initiate a wholesale change in the corporate culture from the top down, our first objective. A LEPP is one harpoon in the back of the mighty whale. Its time now to bring out the big guns.

Step 2: Decentralize Debt Through "Internal LBOs"

The next challenge is to push debt and the incentive of ownership down into certain of the individual business units within the company. One powerful way to accomplish this objective is a financial restructuring technique I call an internal LBO, in which a corporate parent sells its existing business units back to itself and unit management and escapes almost all tax in the process.

For example, consider an individual business unit which, as a result of discounting its likely future cash flow, is thought to contribute $100 million to its parent's market value. The corporate parent will simultaneously sell and buy the unit at a price reflecting a typical LBO premium, say, 30% over intrinsic value, or for $130 million. The parent will finance the acquisition of its own unit like an LBO whereby, for example (refer, please, to exhibit 14.4):

- Of the purchase price, 50%, or $65 million, is obtained from commercial banks at a rate of, say, prime plus 1½%.
- 30%, or approximately $40 million, is financed with subordinated debt paying a rate close to the normal cost of equity (say, 15%), but which is tax-deductible.
- The remaining 20%, or $25 million, is common equity, of which 80%, or $20 million, is retained by the corporate parent and 20% is acquired by the unit's management for $5 million.

To further amplify its incentive, management's investment may be financed with a LEPP option leveraged by a factor of, say, 5 to 1. In other words, it pays $1 million for an option that entitles it to acquire $5 million worth of shares at an exercise price of $4 million plus interest.

By following this blueprint for an internal LBO transaction, the parent company pulls out $105 million in cash from a business

Exhibit 14.4   Anatomy of an Internal LBO

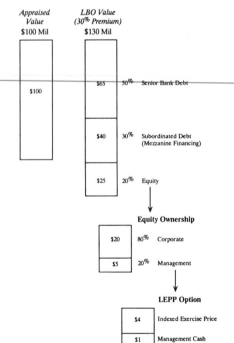

unit that had an apparent $100 million value, money that the parent can invest or return to its investors. Furthermore, because the debt raised by the unit has no recourse, the parent's overall debt capacity is increased, and its financing flexibility is preserved. Yet, even with these benefits, the parent still retains 80% of the potential upside equity rewards while the lenders bear the brunt of the downside risk.

One thing that has made lenders willing to participate in internal LBOs so heavily debt-financed is knowing that the management of the unit, and occasionally managers of the corporate parent, stake a substantial portion of their own net worth to purchase shares in the unit and will get back their money only when and if the debt is substantially repaid.

What makes the deal appeal to management is that, for a total investment of $1 million, or just 1% of the original $100 million appraised value, management will gain 20% of the value it creates with the unit after a 30% premium is surpassed. Of course, if its efforts fail to create a value sufficient to cover the premium paid, its investment will be completely erased. The all-or-nothing payoff profile of an LBO (or a LEPP, for that matter) is a powerful and proven motivator.

Definitive evidence is pouring in to prove the effectiveness of putting a leveraged equity stake into the hands of management. As but one example, Professor Abbie Smith of the University of Chicago investigated the performance of 58 leveraged management buy-outs (MBOs) completed during 1977 to 1986. She discovered "a substantial increase in profitability following the MBO" which "does not appear to be due to industry-wide trends." One reason is that "resources tied up in working capital are reduced after the MBO." The evidence provides "little support that the increased operating cash flows are due to pervasive cutbacks in 'discretionary expenditures' such as maintenance and repairs, advertising, or research and development which might lead to a longer run decline in cash flows." Professor Smith concludes by observing:

> The estimated coefficients on the change in the ratio of debt/ tangible assets, and the change in the percent of common stock held by corporate officers, outside board members, and other

major stockholders are positive as expected, and tend to be highly significant in the regression model of the change in the relative return on assets (before and after tax).

Corporate Ownership Structure and Performance:
The Case of Management Buyouts
Abbie Smith
The University of Chicago
January 1989

In other words, the more leverage a company employs—as a means of instilling a sense of urgency and to make the cost of capital explicit and obvious to all—and the more equity is concentrated in the hands of people who are able to increase its value, the greater is the improvement in the rate of return, and hence in value, relative to other companies operating in the same industry. Here is the proof that the leveraged ownership of equity works.

It's What's Left Over That Counts.   The internal LBO (or LEPP for that matter) gives managers essentially the same incentive as a compensation plan that rewards residual income, which is the profit from operations left after subtracting a charge for the use of capital (both debt and equity). The hypothetical capital charge contained within a residual income calculation is made explicit by the interest that must be paid on the LBO debt (which is essentially all of capital) and that accrues on management's LEPP loan. Thus, making managers into leveraged owners of equity gives them the incentive to maximize residual income, whether they realize it or not.

One good way to make managers grasp the importance of residual income would be to supplement the internal LBO and LEPP with a long-range bonus plan that rewards residual income (or economic value added, which is Stern Stewart's specific version of residual income). Maximizing residual income as an internal performance measure will lead to the maximization of share value and a successful LBO. That is because residual income will increase only if operating profits can be made to grow without tying up more capital, new capital is invested to earn a rate of return in excess of the cost of capital, or capital is withdrawn from activities not covering their cost of capital. The evidence shows that these are the three ways to create value that managers strive for even more diligently and aggressively when they are made into leveraged owners of equity.

A Balanced Budget Amendment. Besides bringing about powerful and proper incentives, another reason an internal LBO creates value is that a debt repayment schedule substitutes for counterproductive budget negotiations.

Business unit managers often hold the upper hand in negotiating easily achievable budget targets with their corporate parents. In many a company poor performance is simply institutionalized year after year in an undemanding budget that the parent feels powerless to change. What's worse, by budgeting for profits but only rarely for cash flow, most companies do not encourage managers to discover the many truly exceptional opportunities to create value that raiders unearth. The larger and more diverse the company, the more aggravated these budgetary problems are likely to be.

While serving as an advisor to a huge integrated oil company, I learned just how frustrating this can be. My colleagues and I were shocked to learn that our request for financial data on one of the company's major operating units could not be fulfilled by our contacts at the head office. Apparently the unit's senior executives had negotiated the right to control the release of detailed information to the parent, and they certainly were not about to share it with outside consultants. The corporate officers we dealt with conceded that this policy put them at a disadvantage around the time of budget negotiations.

An internal LBO repeals these problems. The level of LBO debt and its repayment schedule spell out a challenging, multiyear, cash flow budget for the unit managers to achieve in which there is no chance for hedging or renegotiation. The bankers' earnest intent to lend no more money to the LBO than they can be repaid, and the competitive pressure they feel to lend enough money to win the bid are opposing forces that negotiate a debt repayment schedule likely to be neither too aggressive nor too lax. Management by exception now takes on a new meaning: So long as the debt is being repaid, there is no need for the parent to get involved, for the budget is being achieved.

Seen in this light, an internal LBO makes it possible for a CEO to extract better performance from the business units by externalizing the budgeting and bonus systems. It engages outside parties to set a cash flow budget that is highly demanding but still realistic, one that arises from the full value of the unit, converts those lofty performance expectations into an unyielding debt repayment schedule, and offers unit managers an exceptional reward for exceeding that budget and extracts from them a penalty for falling short.

Moreover, once their incentive switches from beating a budget negotiated with the parent to one of paying down debt and earning out their equity, managers will devise and carry out aggressive budgets and plans without fear that their ambitious goals and aggressive performances will be used against them in the next round of negotiations. Their budgets and strategies, in other words, will become a means to an end, and not ends unto themselves. This shift in the use of budgets and strategies brought about by an LBO is the ultimate rejection of the accounting mentality that emphasizes control over delegation, variances instead of vision, questions instead of answers. Weaving a web of overlapping ownership interests rather than managing through an archaic accounting model of financial control is a primary reason why all LBOs, internal ones included, enhance operating performance and market value.

Now we have driven to the very heart of the beast. An internal LBO will create value by forcing unit managers to "dividend" a challenging cash flow budget to the parent, capitalizing that commitment into a bond they must repay, and freeing them to devise and prosecute budgets and strategies that will maximize the long-run value of their equity investment. Very clever, that KKR.

A Partial Internal LBO

It may be possible to stop short of conducting a complete internal LBO and still derive many of the potential benefits. For example, the parent may take back subordinated debt (or a preferred stock) from the unit in addition to retaining an 80% common equity stake. With such a partial internal LBO, only the commercial bank debt will actually be raised and the proceeds repatriated to the parent.

The parent still is guaranteed a preferred takeout of profits before the unit's managers will participate, but if the unit's earnings fall short of expectations so that all of the financial charges cannot be serviced as they come due, the parent and not some third party will negotiate to convert some or all of the subordinated debt (or preferred stock) into equity. Unit management will be penalized to the extent that its equity stake in the unit is diluted as a result of the exchange. But unless the unit's performance deteriorates quite severely, it will still be possible to repay the senior bank debt and thereby keep the real creditors at bay.

A Simulated Internal LBO

Carrying the illusion one step further, the corporate parent could provide the senior debt financing too. Such a simulated internal LBO is performed just on paper and is truly internal; it completely bypasses the need to bring in outside parties for financing. All that happens is that operating managers purchase phantom stock in their unit which they earn out as they repay a hypothetical senior and subordinated debt burden with the cash flows generated by their units. This version of an internal LBO is essentially just another way of presenting managers with a residual income bonus, or EVA, bonus plan.

An advantage of a simulated internal LBO is that there is no external creditor to threaten bankruptcy. The parent remains the one and only true investor in the unit. Moreover, the details of the scheme can be kept from unwanted public scrutiny. But, as in many things, these apparent advantages are also potential shortcomings.

Without involving external investors, it may be difficult for the parent to know the true debt capacity and value of the unit. Will corporate management be any better at negotiating the price and structure of an internal LBO with unit managers than it is at negotiating a budget? Moreover, there is a risk that, without the threat of intervention by external creditors and without a clear mechanism to capitalize the value it creates, unit management will not take the plan as seriously as it should. No matter how realistic, war games are not war.

Equity Decentralization.   For the reasons given, there may be a benefit after all to bringing in a third party to purchase a stake in the equity of the recapitalized unit. Selling a partial stake in the recapitalized unit to a savvy financial player has the advantage of convincing lenders to the LBO that the business values are real and not fabricated. It also may reassure the managers of the unit to know that a sophisticated investor is acquiring equity at the same price that they are, is concerned with maximizing the value of the unit, and will help to arbitrate conflicts of interest with the parent. For the parent, selling some of the equity in the unit will cash out even more of its remaining investment and further reduce risk (and, correspondingly, the opportunity for an exceptional reward).[4] Must there be a role for a KKR after all?

Perhaps. But it also can be costly to bring in a third-party investor, at least to any significant degree.[5] Doing so can trigger

[4]If the parent winds up owning less than 50%, it will not be obligated to consolidate the unit for accounting purposes, thereby keeping its leverage and performance off the books. That is worthy of mention in a footnote, but I fail to understand why it might be beneficial to the parent company when sophisticated lead-steer investors and creditors see through accounting fictions anyway.

[5]Bringing in a third-party investor, at least to any significant extent, can trigger a tax on any gain that arises from distributing cash to the parent in excess of the parent's tax basis in the stock of the subsidiary (a difference that gives rise to an excess loss account [ELA] for tax purposes). If more than 20% of the stock in the subsidiary unit is sold, the parent can no longer consolidate it for tax purposes. Then the entire gain (in the excess loss account) will be taxed right away even though the parent may retain a large part of its original equity investment in the unit.

However, so long as the subsidiary sells new shares and the parent retains more than an 80% ownership interest in the unit, thereby continuing to consolidate the subsidiary for tax purposes, the gain (in the excess loss account) will not be taxed at all. (If the parent sells existing shares, the ELA will be taxed in the proportion of the interest sold; if 10% of the subsidiary stock is sold, 10% of the ELA is taxed.) Thus an internal LBO in which the unit's management and a third party in tandem purchase new shares entitling them to no more than a 20% interest can be tax advantageous.

To qualify for consolidation, and avoid the tax on gain, the parent is required to own 80% of the subsidiary's voting stock (vote is defined in terms of electing the board) and 80% of its equity value. (Options, warrants, and convertible debt are not included in the value of equity if, when issued, they are sufficiently out of the money to make them not equivalent to common; straight, nonvoting, nonconvertible preferred also is excluded, but convertible preferred is included in the value of the equity.)

Until recently, there had been a loophole in the federal tax code through which the parent could escape paying a tax on the entire gain when more than a 20% interest in the stock of the subsidiary is sold. It worked as follows: If the parent company already happened to own the operating subsidiary (OS) through an intermediate subsidiary (IS) (a two-tier structure that is not uncommon, incidentally), the OS shares were contributed to the parent, giving the parent a basis in the shares stepped up to fair market value. But any gain the IS would recognize by giving its parent shares that had a value a tax on the gain that arises from distributing cash to the parent in excess of the parent's tax basis in the stock of the subsidiary. Tax can be avoided, though, if the parent continues to own at least 80% of the stock in the subsidiary after the dust has settled and consolidates it for federal income tax purposes. Once unit management is provided with the first helping of equity, most third-party investors will not be willing to settle for the scrap of equity left on the table. Well, so be it.

Another reason to leave third-party equity investors out is that the concerns of management and lenders probably can be addressed satisfactorily without them. The unit's managers and lenders can commission or undertake their own independent appraisals of the value of the unit as the basis for making their investment decisions. And, as happens with all private companies that use ESOPs, an independent appraisal of the unit can be arranged in each succeeding year as a way to determine a cashout value for the shares that the managers purchase.

Besides, selling equity in the recapitalized unit to a third-party

---

in excess of tax basis was deferred because it was consolidated with the parent for income tax purposes.

Now if the subsidiary sold new shares and the parent ended up owning less than an 80% interest because of dilution, the deferred gain remained deferred. It was not taxed until the parent sold some of its existing shares in the OS. Then the IS would be taxed on the deferred gain to the extent of the proportion of the OS stock sold. (If 45% of the parent's interest was sold, 45% of the gain was taxed.) Thus, a sale of new shares in the subsidiary unit to a third party escaped tax even if the parent wound up owning less than 80% so long as it was preceded by an upstream distribution of the subsidiary to the parent (and the two steps were not considered one transaction). Unfortunately, on March 14, 1990, the Treasury issued temporary regulations making such a transaction taxable upon deconsolidation to the same extent as if there had been no upstream distribution and, thus, no basis step-up.

The first step, upstream distribution, continues to have one benefit, however: So long as the parent continues to own at least 80%, neither a sale of new shares by the subsidiary nor *a sale of existing shares by the parent will trigger the deferred gain into income.*

Another way that potentially exists for a parent to avoid tax when it lets go of more than a 20% interest would be for it to contribute the unit's assets to a partnership. Then (after the partnership leverages up to pass a distribution to the parent) a third party contributes cash to acquire a partnership interest that may dilute the parent below an 80% ownership stake. Under section 721 of the code, partners do not recognize gains when they contribute property to a partnership. Thus, this disguised sale transaction avoids tax on gain. Unfortunately, it too will come under attack with the Treasury's reexamination of the Disguised Sale rule of section 707(a)(2)(B).

If this loophole also is closed, then it will be a question of comparing no tax if less than 20% is sold against a proportionate tax (or a complete tax) on the gain if more than 20% is sold. Thus, retaining more than 80% ownership will in most cases be advantageous from a tax standpoint.

investor is only one option among many to decentralize equity in the recapitalized unit. Other choices include, for example, a partial or complete distribution of the unit's shares to shareholders in the parent company (considered to be a nonqualifying stock dividend or a qualifying spin-off for tax purposes), a partial or full sale of common stock in the unit to the public, or an issuance of the unit's stock to facilitate a tax-free merger or joint venture combination. Deciding which route is the best will depend very much on the specific facts and circumstances at hand.

But implementation details should not lead us too far astray from addressing the central elements of my plan. Let's examine a transaction that is a model internal LBO.

The Internal LBO of Union Texas Petroleum

In April 1985, Allied Chemical Corporation performed an internal LBO of Union Texas Petroleum (UTP), a wholly owned subsidiary that is the largest independent (nonintegrated) oil and gas company in the United States. The significant elements of the transaction unfolded in this manner:

- UTP paid a $2 billion cash dividend to its parent by borrowing $1.7 billion in senior bank debt and $300 million in subordinated debentures. The debt had no recourse to Allied.

- UTP gave Allied a $300 million issue of redeemable preferred stock. Allied held onto the preferred in addition to retaining a common equity stake, making this a partial internal LBO.

- New common shares representing a 0.6% interest in UTP were purchased by UTP's management for $3 million. UTP's managers were also granted options to purchase UTP common shares representing an approximate 2.5% interest in the company.

- In a move to decentralize equity, new common shares representing a 49.7% interest in the recapitalized unit were sold for $250 million to, you guessed it, the great white whale itself, Kohlberg Kravis Roberts. UTP's senior management bought their UTP shares for the same price as KKR, and the options they obtained were exercisable at the same price, too (about $7.50 a share).

- The $253 million in cash raised by the sale of the new UTP shares was retained by UTP to support its future capital expenditure requirements.

Although distributing the cash and the preferred stock to its parent reduced UTP's common stockholders' equity to a negative $320 million for financial accounting purposes, if the price that KKR paid for its shares is any indication, the market value of UTP's common equity actually was $503 million, broken down as follows:

UTP management	$ 3 million	0.6 %
KKR	$250 million	49.7 %
Allied	$250 million	49.7 %
Total	$503 million	100.0 %

Carving KKR and the managers into new shares left Allied with a 49.7% stake worth $250 million. Maximizing the subsequent return on this investment would appear to be a goal to which KKR and UTP management would be even more committed than Allied. After all, they put fresh cash at risk, while Allied did not have to. When the other financings are added to the common equity value, UTP's total transaction value sums to $2.803 billion, as follows (see exhibit 14.5).[6]

Senior bank debt	$1.700 billion	60%
Subordinated debt	$ 300 million	10%
Preferred stock	$ 300 million	10%
Common equity	$ 503 million	20%
Total value	$2.803 billion	100%

The financial structure reflects classic LBO proportions: 80% was new debt and preferred stock, and only 20% was common equity.

---

[6]The depiction of the transaction presented here simplifies several of the actual facts of the deal structure. Of the reported $2 billion in cash Allied received, approximately $850 million actually was realized by Allied as a result of UTP forgiving a net intercompany receivable. Accordingly, instead of raising $1.7 billion in senior bank debt, UTP actually needed to raise only $850 million.

Exhibit 14.5   Allied Corporation: Internal LBO of Union Texas Petroleum
(Dollars in Millions)

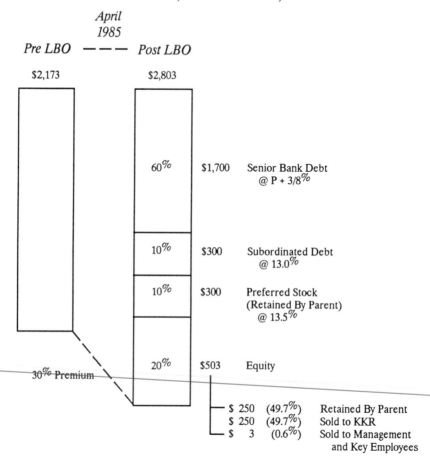

Allied's common share price around the time of the initial announcement of the LBO is plotted in exhibit 14.6 The shares leaped $7.59 in price versus the market (the S&P 500), an increase in total market value of approximately $630 million.[7] Assuming that the increase in Allied's market value is due solely to the recapitalization of UTP, it can be inferred that UTP had an intrinsic value to Allied of $2.173 billion before the deal (by subtracting the $630 million improvement in the parent company's value

[7] Allied's $7.59 relative share price increase times the 83 million Allied shares outstanding at the time is $630 million in added value.

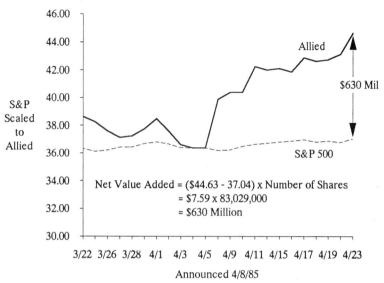

Exhibit 14.6 Allied Corporation:
Leveraged 50% Sale of Union Texas Petroleum

from UTP's $2.803 billion transaction value). The increase in UTP's value, from $2.173 billion to $2.803 billion, is almost precisely 30%, the gain typically associated with LBOs.

Reflecting the KKR philosophy of buy, build, and harvest, new shares in UTP were taken public in September 1987 (exhibit 14.7). The $14 offering price indicates that the value of the shares Allied, UTP management, and KKR held had risen from $503 million to $953 million over this brief 2½-year period, a compound annual rate of return of 30%, or 90% cumulatively.

Was Allied adequately compensated for carving KKR into a mouthwatering 30% return, or should the LBO have been completely internal? With the benefit of hindsight, keeping it all within the family would have been better, obviously. But it is hard to fault Allied in any event because, after all, the company did cart away $2 billion in cash from a business unit that apparently had a value of $2.173 billion before the LBO, established a preferred takeout of $300 million in value above that, raised $253 million for UTP to invest by selling stock to management and to KKR, and realized a 30% compound annual rate of return

Exhibit 14.7   Allied Corporation: Return on Union Texas Petroleum
(Dollars in Millions)

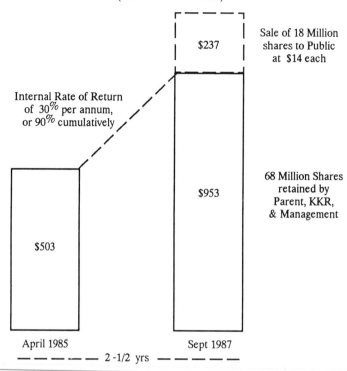

on the $250 million common equity stake left behind in the recapitalized unit. Benefits like these make me wonder why internal LBO's are not embraced more openly than they are.

That is not to say that internal LBOs are not being used at all. As a matter of fact, they already have been employed in a variety of different formats to accommodate specific restructuring objectives, among them:

- USX performed an internal LBO of a transportation unit that is highly vertically integrated with the company's other operations (exhibit 14.8).
- Building upon the USX theme, Stone Container's internal LBO recapitalized and expanded an individual mill in a transaction that in many respects is similar to the time-tested technique of project finance (exhibit 14.9).

Exhibit 14.8 An Internal LBO of a Vertically Integrated
Business Unit:
The Case of USX's Transportation Business

USX's transportation operation consisted of seven railroads, a barge line, a dock company, and a lake fleet. A significant portion of the $380 million revenues in 1987 was derived from carrying raw materials (coal and ore) to USX's steel mills and transporting finished products, a classic, no-growth business forgotten in a company the size and diversity of USX.

In December 1988, USX sold the transportation unit to a new company formed for the purpose of conducting an internal LBO. The senior management of the transportation unit acquired 5% of the new company's common equity shares and a third-party investor purchased a 51% interest, leaving USX a 44% owner after pulling out the $500 million in proceeds from the new, nonrecourse debt the unit took on.

The USX transaction shows that it is possible to perform an internal LBO of business units that are highly integrated with the company's other operations. The trick is to negotiate contracts that spell out the operating relationship between the parent and subsidiary, and a mechanism for adjudicating any disputes, before the transaction takes place.

Exhibit 14.9 An Internal LBO as Project Finance:
The Case of Stone Container

Stone Container's internal LBO financed growth while recapitalizing an individual mill in a transaction that is similar to project finance. In December 1988, Stone transferred its Port Wentworth, Georgia, linerboard mill to a new company called Stone Savannah River. Then, instead of leveraging to distribute cash to its parent, the new company borrowed $335 million in nonrecourse senior and subordinated debt to finance a major expansion and capital improvement project. Since Stone agreed to take all of the mill's production for at least 12 years, the new company has a guaranteed captive customer to generate funds to pay down its debt. In the final step of the restructuring, outside investors paid Stone $115 million in cash to acquire a 50% stake in the new company. Stone reinvested $35 million of those proceeds into Savannah River preferred stock, leaving it with $80 million for reduc-

Exhibit 14.9   continued

ing its own debt and improving its balance sheet.[8] Stone will continue to manage the mill operations under a long-term contract and will receive an annual management fee for its efforts.

Stone's transaction illustrates that an internal LBO can be used to finance growth while recapitalizing all the way down at the level of individual, vertically integrated production facilities.

[8]The Stone transaction was profiled in the November 1988 issue of *Corporate Restructuring.*

Exhibit 14.10   An Internal LBO and the Public Decentralization
of Equity:
The Case of IMC's Fertilizer Group

International Minerals & Chemical Corporation (IMC) followed an internal LBO of its fertilizer business with the decentralization of equity in a public offering.

On January 7, 1987, IMC contributed its worldwide fertilizer operations (phosphate mining and production of phosphate chemical fertilizers) to a new, wholly owned subsidiary called IMC Fertilizer Group, Inc. IMC swapped the shares it held in the group for 10 million shares of new common stock and $200 million in preferred stock in the group. IMC directed the new company to pay two special dividends on the new common shares:

1. A special $370 million cash dividend to be paid with the proceeds of a bank borrowing
2. A cash dividend payable out of the proceeds of an insurance settlement (estimated to be $51.7 million)

The preferred stock also was designed to deliver cash to the parent. In addition to paying ongoing participating dividends (equal to 40% of the fertilizer group's profits in excess of $40 million), the $200 million preferred stock issue entitled IMC to receive a special dividend equal to the proceeds raised in a public offering of new shares in the fertilizer group.

On January, 26, 1988, the fertilizer group was taken public. The sale of 11 million new shares at $22 each netted $229.2 million (after the underwriters' 5.3% discount). But no sooner had the fertilizer group cashed the check than it was obligated to turn over the proceeds to IMC. Issuing the shares diluted IMC's original 100% interest to

47%. Still, IMC's ownership was sufficient to retain effective control of the company, a distinction that separates this transaction from an outright sale.

The pro forma capitalization of the fertilizer group presented below includes the $370 million bank debt incurred to finance the special common dividend and the $200 million preferred stock held by IMC. Ironically, the issuance of new shares to the public did not change common equity because the proceeds were offset by the special dividend paid on the preferred stock.

IMC Fertilizer Group Pro Forma Book Capitalization (September 30, 1987)		
Short-term bank debt	$ 370.0	
Long-term debt	$ 117.9	
Total debt	$ 487.9	(45%)
Preferred stock	$ 200.0	(18%)
Common equity	$ 409.4	(37%)
Total capital	$1,097.3	(100%)

Dollars in Millions

Although not highly leveraged by the standards of most LBOs, IMC had reason to be conservative. The fertilizer business is highly cyclical. As a matter of fact, had the new capital structure been in place the year before (FYE June 30, 1987) the fertilizer group's earnings would have been not much more than breakeven. Even this seemingly conservative capital structure would put the managers of the new unit under pressure to perform right away.

IMC introduced new incentives to compensate the managers for the heightened risk they faced. Formerly participating in bonus plans that rewarded IMC's progress in meeting corporate-wide goals, the unit's managers would henceforth receive a cash bonus that depended upon the performance of the fertilizer group alone. Moreover, instead of share option grants in IMC (whose other businesses are Mallinckrodt, a major supplier of medical products, specialty chemicals, and flavors and fragrances, and Pitman-Moore, a leading animal health and nutrition outfit), senior managers were slated to receive options and restricted shares in the new fertilizer group, an important change.

The new stock option plan set aside 1 million options (representing 4.7% of the 21.3 million shares outstanding) for grant at the discretion of the board. Of this number, 270,000 (representing 1.3% of the

Exhibit 14.10   continued

outstanding) were granted to managers upon the initial public offering and were exercisable at the initial offering price of $22 a share. Moreover, 270,000 restricted shares and 270,000 contingent stock units also were granted to fertilizer group managers upon the offering. Of the restricted shares and stock units, 30% vested with continued service (10% a year for 3 years, with the first tranche vesting immediately). More important, however, the remaining 70% would be earned depending upon the fertilizer group's attainment of cumulative operating cash flow objectives for the 3 fiscal years ending June 30, 1991. All together, the new bonus plan and equity rewards offered key executives and managers a far more powerful and precise incentive than was the case before the restructuring occurred, an important benefit.

IMC's share price appreciated sharply as the restructuring plan was announced (see below). Adjusted for movements in the S&P 500, IMC's shares rose from $43.75 to $50 a share, a gain of $170 million ($6.25 a share × 27.2 million IMC shares), or nearly 15%. Chalk up this transaction as another success in the quest for value.

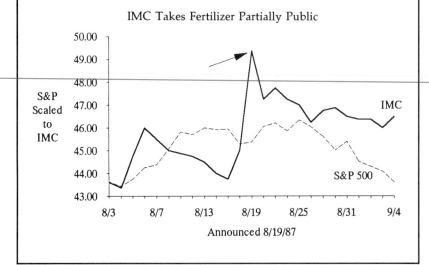

IMC Takes Fertilizer Partially Public

Exhibit 14.11 An Internal LBO and an External Recapitalization: SPX's OEM Business

SPX used an internal LBO in a recapitalization of the corporate parent. SPX (the former Sealed Power Corporation) makes automotive parts for sale to the original equipment market (OEM) and the aftermarket. SPX's problem was that the OEM business is not as profitable as is the aftermarket operation. The potential for harmful cross-subsidization, the lack of focus, and the absence of precise and powerful incentives are some of the reasons why SPX sold for a discounted value and was the subject of recurring takeover rumors. An internal LBO was the answer.

SPX contributed its OEM operations to a new partnership with the name Sealed Power Technologies (SPT). The partnership raised senior and subordinated debt without recourse to SPX to finance a $260 million distribution to its corporate parent. Next, the OEM unit's management purchased a 2% interest in the partnership (which could grow to 10% if the partnership achieves certain performance objectives). Finally, in an equity decentralization move, an outside investor purchased for $15 million new units in the partnership representing a 49% interest, leaving SPX too with a 49% percent stake.

Though it will have no effect on its corporate parent, the capital structure of Sealed Power Technologies was very heavily laden with debt.

The capital structure resembles a house perched on the very edge of a cliff. With debt 90% of market value, this is a rather highly leveraged transaction no matter how one looks at it. Understandably, the $100 million senior subordinated debentures were rated B— by Standard & Poor's. In commenting on the company's financial condition, S&P observed that "cash interest coverage is weak and free cash flow is expected to be barely sufficient to meet principal payments."[9] Of some assurance was the fact that Sealed Power had spent $100 million over the past 5 years to modernize and expand its facilities, so that capital spending in the unit could be significantly less in the future. Furthermore, the closing of a high-cost piston ring plant was expected to improve margins. In addition, the company's dominant positions in many of its product lines, including piston rings and automatic transmission filters, and the fact that its products are used on several different models of each carmaker, mitigates the risk of shrinking sales. Last, S&P observed, the company has discrete busi-

[9] Standard & Poor's *Creditweek,* May 8, 1989, p. 35.

Exhibit 14.11   continued

Sealed Power Technologies
Pro Forma Book Capitalization*
(December 31, 1988; Dollars in Millions)

Short-term debt	$ 4.5
Long-term debt	
Bank ·debt	155.5
Senior subordinated debentures	100.0
Other	1.5
Total long-term debt	$257.0
Partners' capital	(97.9)
Total capital	$163.6

*Negative equity resulted because SPX received cash in excess of the book value of the OEM business it contributed to the partnership. Given the price paid by the outside investors, however, the implicit value of the partners' equity was $30.6 million.[10]

Sealed Power Technologies
Market Value Capitalization
(Dollars in Millions)

Total debt	$261.5	(90%)
Equity value	$ 30.6	(10%)
Total	$292.1	(100%)

ness units which can be sold if the company encounters financial stress. It is attributes such as these that make a highly leveraged internal LBO possible even in a cyclical and intensely competitive business.

SPX used the cash proceeds[11] from the internal LBO of the OEM operation to repay $100 million of its debt and to pay a special, one-time dividend of $13 to each its shareholders (a total dividend of $175 million on 13.5 million shares outstanding). Thus, the new theme in the SPX restructuring is a recapitalization of the corporate parent financed by an internal LBO of a subsidiary unit.

Instead of bluntly burdening the entire company with debt, this surgical leveraging of an underperforming unit preserved the parent

[10]If 49% of the partnership's equity was purchased for $15 million by an outside investor, total equity has an implicit value of $15 million/0.49, or $30.6 million.
[11]The proceeds were augmented by the sale of several peripheral businesses.

company's overall financial flexibility. It also created an incentive for the managers of the OEM unit that is much more precise and powerful than if the corporate parent alone had restructured in a similar manner. Being optimistic for a moment (what the heck, if the Berlin Wall can come down, anything is possible), I believe that the SPX transaction could represent a new wave in financial restructuring (though it probably did not go far enough, as I explain in the body of the text).

- International Minerals & Chemical Corporation (IMC) followed an internal LBO of its fertilizer business with the decentralization of equity in a public offering (exhibit 14.10).
- SPX used an internal LBO of a subsidiary unit to finance a recapitalization of the corporate parent, a transaction that comes close to representing the wave in financial restructurings I am advocating (exhibit 14.11).

Picky, Picky, Picky.   All of the internal LBO examples chronicled in the exhibits, as innovative and successful as they might turn out to be, leave something to be desired. Using SPX (exhibit 14.11) to illustrate the shortcomings throughout, incentives for corporate management and the management of the aftermarket business were not powerfully strengthened at the same time.[12] Why should the managers of the OEM unit be the only ones to receive a powerful new incentive? Related to this problem is the fact that SPX continues to use debt at a centralized, or parent, level to finance its profitable aftermarket operations instead of pushing all of it down into the operating units.

Second, in almost all cases the third party apparently was invited to purchase equity in the recapitalized unit largely for an accounting reason that is without economic merit. SPX, for example, by reducing ownership in the OEM unit below 51%, will no longer be required to consolidate it for financial reporting purposes. Although earnings are not affected, deconsolidating the OEM unit's debt will reduce the financial leverage that appears on SPX's balance sheet.

---

[12]Though SPX did implement a leveraged ESOP, this did not, in my opinion, provide a precise and powerful enough incentive for the managers of the corporation and the aftermarket unit.

It is a mistake, however, to think that the improvement in the parent company's reported leverage will bring SPX better financing terms and more debt capacity. What matters to the parent company's creditors is not whether the unit's debt is consolidated but whether the unit's debt has a legal recourse to the assets and earnings of the parent company. In all of the internal LBOs discussed here, the debt raised by the unit had no recourse to the parent. That fact alone, and not accounting deconsolidation, is what makes the parent company's credit risk and financial capacity independent of the leveraging of the unit.[13] Therefore, if these companies introduced a third party just to make their accounting books look more appealing, then a severe error may have been made in the structuring of these transactions (particularly if, as I mentioned earlier, it triggered a tax that might have been avoided).

A final criticism is that the internal LBOs were episodic (in SPX's case a response to an immediate threat of a raider) and were used to decouple unrelated or underperforming business from the parent (except Stone's). I am advocating the use of internal LBOs as a systematic and voluntary part of a company's strategy, applicable to healthy, core businesses as much as to underperforming, peripheral ones. I am looking for a KKR wrapped in publicly traded clothing.

Bringing It All Together.   The company that currently comes closest to my ideal of a public KKR is Bairnco, a name evoking the Scottish expression for children. On the surface Bairnco looks to be an uninspiring little conglomerate hardly worth a second glance. For example, the company currently consists of four com-

[13]Rating agencies and other senior institutional lenders take great pains to assess the true creditworthiness of a parent company by deconsolidating nonrecourse debt (and associated assets). One relatively straightforward way to demonstrate this is by examining the consequences of FASB No. 94, an unhelpful accounting pronouncement that required manufacturing companies to begin to consolidate their finance and insurance arms. Though complying with this new principle dramatically increased the leverage ratios of such prominent companies as GE (which began in 1988 to consolidate onto its books the debt of GE Financial Services—including GE Capital Corporation, Employers Reinsurance Corporation, and The Kidder, Peabody Group—even though the debt has no legal recourse to GE) the rating agencies did not downgrade a single one of the affected companies for this reason. Here is a proof that the agencies continue to assess the creditworthiness of these companies based upon the economic substance of company situations and not according to an unreliable and shifting accounting representation of the facts.

pletely unrelated lines of business ($ in parentheses are 1988 sales in millions):

- Keene Corporation ($24): a manufacturer of advanced composites materials
- Kasco ($41): a provider of cutting products and services to retail butchers
- Arlon ($83): a producer of laminated and coated products
- SSC ($79): a maker of shielding and radar-absorbing products

Scratch beneath the surface, though, and Bairnco emerges as quite distinctly better than the run-of-the-mill conglomerate. One reason is the company's ardent belief in the benefits of decentralization. Glenn W. Bailey, chairman and president (and company founder), summarizes this element of the Bairnco philosophy:

> Big companies kill the entrepreneurial spirit. I'd much rather have five $200 million companies with highly motivated management than a single institutionalized $1 billion one.
> "Bairnco: An Empire That Spins Off Companies to Grow"
> *Business Week*
> April 30, 1984

Making managers into owners, the foundation of a strategy of decentralization, starts at the top. Bailey owns nearly 10% of Bairnco's stock. That gives him a tremendous personal incentive to grow the company's value, something he has done quite successfully over the years.

But, as important, Bairnco pushes the benefits of ownership down into the organization through a unique strategy of decentralizing debt and equity in individual business units. Bairnco's articulated philosophy is to acquire a family of separate companies with single or focused product lines, nurture them to the point where they may stand successfully on their own, and then spin them off to its shareholders (exhibit 14.12). "Buy, build and harvest," a KKR motto, is Bairnco's strategy too.

Prior to spinning off its qualifying businesses, Bairnco structures an internal LBO, thereby recovering a substantial portion of

---

Exhibit 14.12   The Internal LBO and Spin-off of Kaydon:
The First of Bairnco's Debt and Equity Decentralizations

Kaydon Corporation, a Muskegon, Michigan, maker of specialty bearings, rings, and seals, left the Bairnco fold in April 1984 through a one-for-one stock dividend to Bairnco stockholders. Prior to its spin-off from Bairnco, Kaydon performed an internal LBO. Kaydon paid Bairnco, its parent, a special $56 million cash dividend, financed by borrowing $52.8 million and selling new Kaydon shares to management for $3.2 million. The recapitalization reduced Kaydon's equity from $63 million to $10 million and increased its debt to 87% of capital employed (debt plus equity).

Kaydon Partial Internal LBO
(Pro Forma Balance Sheet as of December 31, 1983)

	Beginning	Plus	Minus	Ending
Senior Debt	$ 14.0	$46.8		$ 60.8
Subordinated Debt	$ 0.0	$ 6.0		$ 6.0
Stockholders' Investment	$ 63.2	$ 3.2	($56.0)	$ 10.4
Capital	$ 77.2	$56.0	($56.0)	$ 77.2
Total Debt/Capital	18%			87%

Dollars in Millions

Source: Form S-1 Prospectus (March 21, 1984)

Of the $52.8 million in debt raised, $46.8 million was senior debt having no recourse to Bairnco and $6 million was a subordinated issue placed with Bairnco, making this a partial internal LBO in my lexicon. Bairnco's acquisition of the subordinated debt staked out a claim to future cash flow and value that is senior to Kaydon's common stockholders, including Kaydon's managers. Furthermore, should Kaydon's cash flow be insufficient to service the subordinated debt, the former parent will be the one responsible to step in and negotiate a financial restructuring of Kaydon, an important assurance for lenders.

Kaydon's managers as a group invested $3.1 million to acquire 18.7% of the stock in the unit for a purchase price that was 1.6 times book value. Certain officers of Bairnco and its other subsidiaries invested $100,000 to purchase 0.6% of Kaydon's shares at the same price. Without the recapitalization, the $3.2 million the managers and officers invested would have bought less than a 4% interest in the company. Thus, one benefit of leveraging Kaydon in this way is that it made it easier to make the managers into significant owners of equity in the enterprise.

Once the internal LBO was completed, Bairnco distributed the shares it held in Kaydon, representing an 80.7% interest, to its own shareholders as a stock dividend. Kaydon's shares commenced trading on NASDAQ (National Market System) with the symbol KDON.

Through his ownership of Bairnco and as a result of the spin-off, Glenn Bailey received shares in Kaydon giving him an approximate 10% interest. No doubt his interest in the newly public company was heightened by the fact that he was elected the chairman of Kaydon's board of directors, a post he relinquished in April 1987 to the then president and chief operating officer of Kaydon, Richard Shantz.

With the spin-off of Kaydon, Bairnco launched a publicly traded LBO predating the leveraged recapitalization of FMC (widely held to be the first such transaction) by more than 2 years. Like FMC, Kaydon has performed exceptionally well since its initial launch.

Kaydon operates in competitive, limited-growth markets. Nevertheless, sales grew sharply in 1986 and 1987, the result of two acquisitions. In June 1986, Kaydon acquired for $29.6 million the Piston Ring and Seal division of Koppers Company, Inc., and in July 1987, it acquired for $5.1 million the Spirolox specialty retaining ring business from TRW, Inc. The myth is that LBO companies are not supposed to grow, particularly through acquisitions. That all depends, for this one did.

Kaydon's leverage, which started at LBO proportions, was substantially paid down over 5 years, a dynamic use of debt partly responsible for the drive for greater efficiency. Debt dropped from $70 million to about $20 million by the end of 1988 while common stockholders' equity rose from $10 million to nearly $70 million. The rapid unleveraging occurred for three reasons.

First, by emphasizing higher value added product lines, and dropping commodity products, Kaydon's operating profit margin widened from 20% to over 26%. That brought in more cash from operations to service debt.

Second, the sales focus facilitated an increasingly efficient use of fixed assets. Kaydon was able to hold capital spending to less than depreciation while still supporting sales. The ratio of sales to net property, plant, and equipment rose from a turnover of $1.8\times$ to $2.8\times$. (Somewhat surprisingly, however, working capital efficiency did not improve, as it does in many LBOs.) Widening profit margins and conservative capital spending gave Kaydon operating cash flow after

Exhibit 14.12   continued

Kaydon Corporation
Summary of Performance since Spin-Off (April 1984)

	1984	1985	1986	1987	1988
Operating Results					
Sales	$ 86.0	$ 84.8	$112.6	$133.5	$135.0
Growth	19%	−1%	33%	19%	1%
Operating profits	$ 17.2	$ 19.6	$ 23.7	$ 33.9	$ 35.6
Profit margin	20.0%	23.1%	21.0%	25.4%	26.3%
Working investment[14]	$ 19.4	$ 21.2	$ 32.5	$ 30.0	$ 33.0
Working	22.6%	25.0%	24.8%	22.5%	24.4%
investment/sales					
Sales/net PP&E	1.8×	1.9×	2.6×	2.7×	2.8×
Capital					
Total debt	$ 72.8	$ 59.3	$ 62.7	$ 40.4	$ 22.5
Stockholder's investment	16.1	23.9	33.6	50.3	69.9
Capital	$ 88.9	$ 83.2	$ 96.3	$ 90.7	$ 92.4
Increase in capital	$ 11.7	$ −5.7	$ 13.1	$ −5.6	$ 1.7
Acquisition expenditures	$NA	$ 0.0	$ 29.6	$ 5.1	$ 0.0
Capital expenditures, net	$ 4.4	$ 5.1	$ 2.8	$ 3.3	$ 4.8
Depreciation	$ 4.9	$ 4.6	$ 5.5	$ 6.2	$ 6.4
Financial Policy					
Total debt/capital	82%	71%	65%	45%	24%
Free cash flow[15]	$ −2.3	$ 16.1	$ −0.9	$ 24.7	$ 20.8
Cash dividends	$ 0.0	$ 0.0	$ 0.4	$ 0.8	$ 1.7
Percent of net income	0%	0%	4%	5%	9%
Economic Value Added					
Return on Average					
capital employed[16]	12.0%	12.1%	13.0%	20.8%	24.1%
Cost of capital[17]	12.0%	12.0%	12.0%	12.0%	12.0%
Spread	0.0%	0.1%	1.0%	8.8%	12.1%
Average capital	$ 83.1	$ 86.0	$ 89.8	$ 93.5	$ 91.6
Economic value added	$ 0.0	$ 0.1	$ 0.9	$ 8.2	$ 11.1
Market Value Added					
Year-end share price	$ 6.88	$ 11.50	$ 14.63	$ 24.75	$ 26.88
Econ Book val per share	1.96	2.91	4.06	6.02	8.25
Spread	$ 4.92	$ 8.59	$ 10.57	$ 18.73	$ 18.63
Common shares	8.2	8.2	8.3	8.4	8.5
outstanding					
Market value added	$ 40.3	$ 70.5	$ 87.5	$156.6	$157.9

[14]Working investment is (net) accounts receivable plus inventories minus accounts payable (except income taxes) and accrued expenses.

Kaydon Corporation continued

[15]Free cash flow is the after-tax cash flow from operations that is free of all capital investments for incremental working capital and acquisitions, including acquisitions.

[16]Kaydon computes the return on capital employed by taking an approximate measure of net operating profits after taxes (NOPAT) and dividing by the (monthly if not weekly) average of capital employed (interest-bearing debt plus stockholders' equity). NOPAT is computed as the sum of net income plus interest expense after taxes.

[17]The cost of capital is an estimate of the minimum rate of return that debt and equity investors combined are seeking to compensate for risk. While our calculations reveal that Kaydon's weighted average cost of debt and equity capital did change over this 5-year period, due to changes in the general level of interest rates and the company's own changing mix of debt and equity, 12% was chosen as an approximate average cost of capital in order to provide a stationary benchmark against which to judge the company's performance over this time frame.

taxes and after new capital investment (free cash flow) that was strongly positive for the most part and was used to repay debt.

Third, Kaydon did not pay dividends until 3 years after the recapitalization, and even then the payout was immaterial (though I predict Kaydon will rue the day it ever started paying dividends). By not paying dividends, Kaydon's stockholders' equity increased by the entire amount earned, and more cash was available to repay debt.

The best internal measure of Kaydon's progress is EVA, or residual income, which grew substantially over the period of the LBO; it rose from essentially breakeven to $11.1 million. Sharing EVA with employees through the company's bonus plan certainly didn't hurt.

> An important element in Kaydon's relations with its people is a sharing in the financial results of the company. All Kaydon employees participate in a bonus which is based on the specific operation and is over and above their competitive wage. Each bonus system is tailored to suit the specific needs of the individual operation, but in general, *each one allocates a portion of the operation's profit over a minimum return on investment to the employees.* Bonuses in excess of 20% of base wages can and are being earned by successful performance. Financial results, upon which all bonuses are built, are posted in all plants for the people to read and to understand where the payments come from and how they flow from their efforts.
>
> Kaydon 1987 Annual Report

Using residual income as the basis of its reward system was a smart choice because it fired up a premium in the company's stock market

Exhibit 14.12 continued

value. From an initial value of $5, Kaydon's shares have skyrocketed to over $25 a share, a 1,000% increase directly benefiting the Bairnco shareholders who held onto the Kaydon shares they received. The company's exceptional stock market performance was also reflected in its market value added (MVA). Kaydon built a premium into its market value by creating a positive and growing economic value added, and the expectation among investors that it would continue. By any measure, the restructuring of Kaydon was a tremendous success.

its investment by leveraging the subsidiary and distributing the proceeds to the parent, and then sells subsidiary management up to 20% of the stock in the unit.

The first such restructuring was performed on Kaydon Corporation, a subsidiary engaged in the manufacture of bearings. Kaydon went heavily into debt to pay for a cash distribution to Bairnco, its parent. After substantially reducing the equity through leverage, nearly 20% of the common stock in the unit was sold to management. Kaydon's remaining shares, distributed to Bairnco's shareholders in April 1984, have gone from an initial $5 to over $25 in 5 years (exhibit 14.12).

Kaydon, like UTP, was a very successful internal LBO. Both generated substantial amounts of cash for the parent while preserving the parent's financial flexibility. Both created a tremendous personal incentive for managers and employees to perform well. Both kept the parent company's shareholders as investors in the LBO (either directly or indirectly). And both subsequently generated handsome rewards for investors. There the similarities end, though, and three important differences emerge.

First, Kaydon's LBO proceeded in full view of the public; UTP's was submerged in private hands. It is possible that making managers perform in a goldfish bowl may accentuate the pain of failure and satisfaction of success. Second, Bairnco decentralized equity by putting Kaydon's shares into the hands of the company's own shareholders. They, not some third party, benefited from the successful aftermath of the transaction. Allied, on the other hand, saw fit to carve KKR into the return on nearly half of UTP's common shares. Last, there are some important tax differences. A spin-off to shareholders, if it qualifies, can be tax-free to the parent company and to the shareholders on the receiving end. A third-party sale to a KKR, by contrast, can trigger an up-front tax on part or all of the gain implicit in the transaction. Also, should Allied decide to sell its UTP shares to harvest its gain, Allied will be stuck with a corporate capital gains tax. But when Bairnco investors choose to harvest the gain in Kaydon's value by selling shares in the market, only they will have to pay taxes on the capital gain. Bairnco will escape tax at the corporate level, and that is an important advantage.

Another difference is that Allied used the internal LBO to isolate an unwanted unit in a one-off transaction. For Bairnco, the decentralization of debt and equity is an integral part of the company's growth strategy, as the subsequent spin-off of Genlyte indicates.

Genlyte

Bairnco's second decentralization move was the tax-free spin-off on August 8, 1989 of the stock in the Genlyte Group, Inc., a lighting products concern Bairnco built up after acquiring Lightolier in 1981. The formula is familiar. Prior to spin-off, Bairnco aggressively leveraged Genlyte to recover its investment (77% debt to capital) and sold Genlyte management 16% of the shares in the recapitalized unit.

> A key element of Bairnco's philosophy is that the motivation of management through significant entrepreneurial reward (and risk) leads to superior operating and financial performance. The establishment of an independent company in which Genlyte's management has made a significant direct investment is consistent with this philosophy.
>
> > Genlyte Information Statement
> > August 1, 1988

Stock market investors concurred. When the intention to distribute shares in Genlyte was first announced (April 29, 1988), Bairnco's common shares appreciated nearly 10% in value vis-à-vis the S&P 500 (exhibit 14.13)

Exhibit 14.13   Bairnco Considers Spin-off of Genlyte

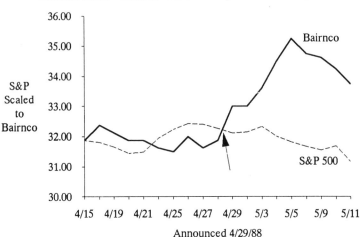

Announced 4/29/88

Who's Next?

Given Bairnco's track record, managers of the remaining units, who realize that they may eventually share in the value they help to create while they are with Bairnco, have a special motivation to perform—one that is usually not offered to managers of most companies.

> In our group our morale and determination are at an all-time high. It's not everyday that you get an opportunity as a manager to become [associated with] a publicly held company. That's what we're aiming for.
>
> William Roy, Chairman of Arlon
> Bairnco Corporation
> A Report to Stockholders
> April 13, 1989

There are other aspects of Bairnco's modus operandi consistent with my recommended strategy. For example, in keeping with a policy of extreme decentralization, Bairnco maintains a lean organization trimmed of bureaucratic fat:

> It is a basic Bairnco philosophy that fewer people, well trained and motivated, can produce better results and thereby earn more for

themselves, for the company and for stockholders. In pursuing this philosophy, the company attracts and develops higher-caliber, experienced management personnel, delegates responsibility to them and compensates them well for superior performance. This has helped to create the results-oriented and profit-driven environment that exists at Bairnco.

Bairnco 1988 Annual Report

Implementation starts right at the top, as this exchange between shareholder John Gilbert and Glenn Bailey during the company's 1989 annual meeting illustrates:

> *John Gilbert:* How do you feel about serving as both chairman and president? Shouldn't these two jobs be filled by two people?
>
> *Glenn Bailey:* Well, we are not a normal company. If you'll note, I believe that we are the only one of the top thousand companies in the United States that builds companies to dividend them off to shareholders so they can increase their portfolio of excellently run companies. We are different. And because we're different, we have to structure ourselves differently. We don't need a separate chairman and president because our subsidiaries operate independently.

Bairnco Corporation
A Report to Stockholders
April 13, 1989

Bairnco also has the discipline not to spend its surplus free cash flow unwisely. For instance, even as he sat on top of a pile of cash from the Genlyte restructuring, Bailey was not seduced by growth for growth's sake.

> As a result of the Genlyte spin-off, Bairnco has substantial excess cash and unutilized borrowing capacity. Normally, we would use these resources to make new acquisitions, but our ongoing search for acquisition opportunities indicates current prices are not justified. We will continue our search but will pursue acquisitions only where our goals for return on capital employed can be achieved through application of Bairnco's management and financial control systems.

Glenn W. Bailey
Report to Stockholders
Bairnco 1988 Annual Report

Bailey's philosophizing (and hard work) has paid off hand-somely for his shareholders. An investor who owned Bairnco shares from 1978 to 1988, and who held on to the Kaydon and Genlyte shares distributed, would have realized a 31% compound average annual rate of return, almost double the return from a similar investment in the S&P 500 (see exhibit 14.14). Not bad for an uninspiring little conglomerate.[18]

So What's the Matter Now?   Bairnco illustrates in many respects the three-step plan I outlined at the beginning of this chapter (exhibit 14.15). The top corporate officers do have a meaningful interest in the parent company's common equity. The corporate bureaucracy is skeletal because the responsibility to perform has been delegated to the operating units. The company relates well to its people and lets them share materially in the financial success of their individual operations, properly measured in terms of residual income (or economic value added). Debt and equity in the individual business units is systematically decentralized through internal LBOs followed by a spin-off of shares. The best testimony to the efficacy of the company's strategy is the exceptional return Bairnco has produced for its shareholders over a long time frame.

As much as I admire what Bailey has done with Bairnco, his strategy still is somewhat different from what I am advocating. Why, for example, does Bairnco wait until it spins off the businesses it acquires before leveraging them and selling management an equity stake? What I am calling for is the use of internal LBOs without selling or distributing equity—private, self-contained recapitalizations between the parent company and unit management—as a means of improving the performance and value of individual business units. To my knowledge, this plan has not yet been carried out by any publicly traded company on a systematic basis. Will there be no one to challenge KKR head-on?

[18]In the first months of 1989, Bairnco's stock price fell as it was disclosed that insurance to cover asbestos litigation exposure was lost. While an unfortunate development, this does not alter the conclusions reached about the benefits of Bairnco company's financial and incentive structures.

Exhibit 14.14   Bairnco Corporation 10-Year Average Return to Investors

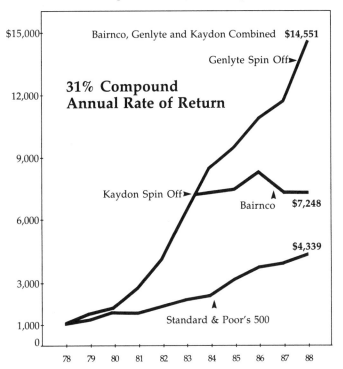

A $1,000 investment on December 31, 1978 would have provided you with about 77 Bairnco shares. Ten years later, on December 31, 1988, after two Bairnco stock splits, both the Kaydon and Genlyte stock dividends, and with all cash dividends reinvested, you would have owned about 293 Bairnco shares, 178 Kaydon shares, and 288 Genlyte shares — with a combined value of $14,551. This is a 31 percent compound annual rate of return, almost double the return from a similar investment in the S&P 500, which would have grown in value only to $4,339.

Exhibit 14.15   Bairnco's Objective and Philosophy

Bairnco's objective is to grow a family of separate companies with single, or focused, product lines. To help develop its companies, Bairnco evolved a unique management system that:

- Attracts and rewards entrepreneurial managers.
- Uses sound management and financial controls.

Exhibit 14.15   continued

- Fosters new products to meet market needs.
- Increases penetration in niche markets.
- Emphasizes return on capital employed.

Bairnco also provides financial resources to its businesses, allocating Bairnco capital to growth opportunities.

As an operating group assimilates Bairnco's management style and more fully develops its potential, it can "spin off" as an independent company through distribution of its shares to Bairnco stockholders. The cash Bairnco invests in an operation over time is repaid by the operation as it spins off, giving Bairnco the capital to reinvest in new acquisitions. To obtain this cash, the spun-off operation incurs substantial external debt and becomes highly leveraged.

Through this process, Bairnco stockholders have an opportunity to build a diversified portfolio of equities in well-managed, profitable companies that continue to grow as industry leaders.

The first spin-off occurred in 1984 when Kaydon Corporation became an independent public company through a one-for-one stock dividend to Bairnco stockholders. In 1988, The Genlyte Group Inc. became an independent public company in a tax-free distribution of one share of Genlyte for each share of Bairnco.

To qualify for a spin-off, a Bairnco company must first build a strong entrepreneurial management team and meet demanding standards for finance, marketing, manufacturing and human resources. For example:

- In finance—dependable P&L performance, ability to handle a leveraged balance sheet, good cash flow and effective controls.
- In marketing—competitive pricing, results-oriented product development programs and widespread recognition of the company as a market leader.
- In manufacturing—modern, safe and efficient facilities that assure excellent quality and service.
- In human resources—effective recruiting, management development and incentive programs that attract the best people at all levels and spur outstanding performance.

Philosophy

Bairnco's business is built on very few specific principles. First and foremost, Bairnco maintains a lean organization in which all employees work together to achieve maximum results for the company and themselves as well as for stockholders. To encourage top performance, managers are rewarded through effective, goal-oriented incentive programs.

From Bairnco's 1988 annual report.

Step 3: Venture Capitalization

The aggressive decentralization of debt will work fine for stable, slow-growth businesses. But loading debt on the shoulders of promising new ventures or rapidly expanding companies will snuff out flexibility to grow and ever attain full potential. Businesses whose risk and growth preclude aggressive leveraging may benefit instead from venture capitalization, that is, the decentralization of equity alone.

Thermo Electron. Thermo Electron exemplifies a strategy of decentralizing equity in individual business units to promote start-up entrepreneurism within a large company. Essentially a publicly traded venture capital group, Thermo Electron has sold a minority interest in a whole range of subsidiaries formed to develop and exploit promising new technologies. George Hatsopoulos, chairman, president, and founder, gave his reasons for doing this in the company's 1988 annual report.

To provide for effective management for our fast-growing and diverse businesses, we have created a new type of corporate structure comprising a mix of wholly owned operations and majority-owned subsidiary companies. We believe that the strategy of forming separate public subsidiaries for the pursuit of highly promising new ventures provides the best of both worlds; it allows us to combine the growth-oriented entrepreneurial environment of a venture capital start-up operation with the financial, managerial, and technological strengths of a mature, well-established company.

The sale of minority stock interests in our public subsidiaries provides the necessary resources for aggressive development of new businesses. It also allows stockholders to concentrate their investments in the specific opportunities that most interest them. Finally, through the mechanism of stock options in the subsidiaries, we create the targeted incentives needed to attract and retain top-quality people.

George Hatsopoulos
Chairman and President
Thermo Electron 1988 Annual Report

Hatsopoulos founded Thermo Electron in 1956 with an investment of $50,000. An MIT-educated engineer, his first invention was a thermionics converter, a device that converts heat directly into electricity. Though never commercialized, the thermionics technology was the foundation for a host of applications that bloomed with the environmental and social concerns of the 1970s.

> They work on an idea for a decade and, then when it comes to fruition, they are well-positioned as the dominant player. They put together money and resources early on, so they are not just trying to get up to speed when it suddenly becomes the thing to do.[19]

Tina Rizopoulos
Senior Securities Analyst
Paine Webber
New York

Today, Thermo Electron is a $500 million sales company (1988). The company's vast array of products and services derive from a common pool of technology but also reflect the founder's desire to improve the quality of life (exhibit 14.16). They encompass better ways to produce energy, the detection and elimination of noxious elements in the environment, heat-based process and pollution control equipment, and medical advances to prolong life (exhibit 14.17).

The company's commercial offerings flow from its advanced research laboratories at Waltham, Massachusetts, and San Diego, California. As a new technology approaches commercial application, Thermo Electron will deposit the newly hatched business into a separate subsidiary, and will then sell some of its shares to the public. The process began in 1983, and by the end of 1988 it had spawned five partially public business units (exhibit 14.18).

[19]Samuel Greengard, "Perpetual Notion Machine," *American Way Magazine.*

Exhibit 14.16   The Thinking Man's CEO:
An Interview with George Hatsopoulos

I wanted to create a team of people who were dedicated to a common objective—to create an environment in which talented people could continually learn from one another. One of my main jobs is to worry about the development of people.

The other big part of my job is figuring out which businesses we should be in—deciding between areas that are already commercial and those that haven't yet developed. Some of them may be 10 or more years away, so it's not easy to do. Among other things, you have to understand the long-range needs of customers—even if they don't.

Unlike most companies, we're not product-driven. I had made a decision that I wanted to build a company that would be technologically oriented, always looking for new ventures. I would have a company that had a certain core technology, then look around to identify what needs existed, and try to invent things that met those needs.

Finding out what these emerging problems are is my job. I have to be out there all the time, talking with people, taking part in public-policy discussions, anything that will enable me to see broad changes before the other guy. If you do a little studying, reading the newspapers, and following things, you will begin to see what problems are coming up. I spend a lot of my time figuring out what makes the economy tick. How can we fill some of the holes that have been created?

If you don't think this way, you're forced into being reactive, into focusing on short-term problems, because other companies have learned to think longer term and therefore have defined the market for you. The stakes are too high to let that happen.

In a market like steel, which has been developing since the turn of the century, many people are already competing. What are my chances of success in that? I think that if you are going to develop new products or services, it is much more beneficial to do it in a market that is in its infancy, where the needs are only now being understood.

We found that industry in this country was about 50% less energy-efficient than industry in Japan or West Germany in producing almost any product. We were using more energy because it was so much cheaper here. I called in the general manager of Holcroft and said, "Let's create a new generation of furnaces that will be 50% more efficient. We'll have the corporate lab support you, and I'll give you all the money."

Exhibit 14.16   continued

As it turned out in 1976, natural gas was rationed to the automobile companies. So, they started purchasing more efficient gas furnaces. For example, when General Motors asked us what we could do for them, I said we could give them metallurgical furnaces that are 50% more efficient.

Later we developed an altogether new energy-based venture known as cogeneration—the simultaneous production of electrical and thermal energy from a single fuel source. We structured the company in the '70s to pursue energy efficiency. Within seven years, the sales of the furnace division went from $5 million to $50 million.

I'd been curious about economics for a while, but my interest became more pronounced in the '70s. I couldn't figure out why American industry was so energy-inefficient, and why Germany's was so much more efficient. The reason was simple: economics dictated that. Our energy prices were much lower. So energy efficiency is not just a matter of technology, it's a matter of economics.

I have gone much further in trying to decentralize than any company I know. In an effort to try to do that and make people responsible, I have set up many of our divisions as publicly owned organizations. I think that structure has tremendous benefits. Managers of each subsidiary know that what they do gets scrutinized not only by corporate management but also by their own stockholders.

I really believe in small companies. But small companies have a big disadvantage. They don't have the support, the financial and management resources, that big companies have. So, you have to find a new structure for U.S. industry that combines the advantages of small companies and the support of large companies. My own answer is to have a bunch of small companies in a family, which gives them financial and management support and strategic direction. But at the same time they are acting as though they are independent companies with their own constituency or stockholders.

I want Thermo Electron to grow to more than $10 billion, maybe in the year 2000, but it will be a company that consists of many smaller companies. Right now, we have 17 business units, and 5 of them have minority public ownership—I hope that in 10 years most of them will.

You have to be very gutsy and adventuresome. I always liked taking risks—but within limits. One way to limit your risks is the way you get financial support.

There's no way to implement this strategy without having tremendous people around you. What I consider my major job is to get the

> right people and to convey to them a sense of responsibility. I try to create an environment in which people in the company feel that they are partners, regardless of the reporting hierarchy.
>
> It takes a lot of time and effort, but people are very flattered and get to feel they are participating in decision making—and they are.
>
> Reprinted with permission, *Inc.* magazine, November 1988. Copyright © 1988 by Goldhirsh Group, Inc., 38 Commercial Wharf, Boston, MA 02110.

- **Thermedics** houses the biomedical products.
- **Thermo Environmental** performs environmental services.
- **Thermo Process** designs, manufactures, and markets heat-based process equipment.
- **Thermo Instruments** makes environmental monitoring equipment.
- **Tecogen** produces prepackaged cogeneration systems.

The initial public offerings were quite small, raising from less than $4 million to just over $10 million. At the time of their IPOs, most of the units had sales on the order of $10 to $20 million and were barely profitable (Thermo Instruments is the exception). With initial market capitalizations ranging from $15 to $70 million, their returns lay ahead of them, or so investors were hoping.

The combined sales for the five companies were $242.2 million in 1988, or approximately half of Thermo Electron's $500 million total. Two years earlier the sales of the gang of five were only $137.2 million, indicating a composite compound annual growth rate of around 33%. Operating income for the group increased over the same period from $17.7 to $32.6 million, a growth rate of better than 35%. Needless to say, these are start-up, growing businesses, hungry for new capital.

With a voracious appetite for funds to satisfy, none of the subsidiaries pays a dividend (and neither does Thermo Electron). Furthermore, many of the satellite subsidiaries have tapped the markets since becoming public companies in order to raise more capital. Thermo Instrument, for example, in 1988 completed the sale in Europe of $30 million of 6¾% convertible subordinated debentures due in 2003. The shares are convertible into Thermo

---

Exhibit 14.17   Thermo Electron Business Activities

Energy Systems

- Leading market position in cogeneration, biomass power generation, trash-to-energy, and other, related technologies
- World leader in small-scale, factory-built cogeneration systems

Environmental

- Air pollution, nuclear radiation, and toxic materials detection and monitoring instruments
- Environmental management services (hazardous and radioactive wastes management, radon contamination detection, and water quality control)

Process Equipment

- Metallurgical heat-treating equipment (Ford and Caterpillar are customers), thermal hazardous waste incineration systems (e.g., for on-site cleanup of petroleum-laced soils), web-processing dryers (for papermaking), and pollution abatement equipment (for printing and paper-converting operations)

Biomedical Products

- Heart assist device for people awaiting transplants
- New plastics compatible with human implantation
- The first "sterile" enteral nutritional delivery system
- The first walk-through explosive detector
- The first monitor to detect drugs (cocaine and heroin) without requiring a blood sample

Research and Development

- Commercial applications of lasers and electro/optical devices
- Alternative fuels technology
- "Clean coal" burning technologies
- Low-cost spark-ignition gas-fueled engines

Exhibit 14.18 Thermo Electron Venture Capitalization
(Dollars in Millions)

	Ther-medics	Thermo Environ-mental	Thermo Process Systems	Thermo Instru-ments	Tecogen
IPO date	6/83	11/85	8/86	8/86	6/87
IPO proceeds	$ 4.0	$ 9.6	$ 3.6	$11.7	$12.3
Initial Mkt capitalization	$50.7	$32.6	$16.5	$68.0	$70.0
Sales					
1986	$15.8	$16.6	$22.9	$69.3	$12.6
1987	$20.1	$23.3	$26.6	$85.2	$14.4
1988	$25.4	$51.8	$43.5	$101.8	$19.7
Operating Income					
1986	$ 0.8	$ 2.0	$ 1.8	$12.3	$ 0.7
1987	$ 2.0	$ 2.5	$ 1.6	$15.9	$ 0.3
1988	$ 2.7	$ 5.7	$ 4.3	$19.0	$ 0.9
Financing Activity					
1986	$ 9.3 CS(A) $30.0 CSD	$23.0 CSD	$ 3.6 CS	$25.0 CSD(TE) $11.7 CS	
1987	$ 2.0 CS(A)	$ 3.7 CS(TE)	$ 5.8 CS(TE)		$13.9 CS, W $ 3.0 CSD(TE)

Exhibit 14.18 continued

	Ther-medics	Thermo Environ-mental	Thermo Process Systems	Thermo Instru-ments	Tecogen
1988	$ 4.8	$ 0.2	$ 2.6	$30.0	
	CS	CS(A)	CS(TE)	CSD	
Thermo Electron					
Interest (%)					
1986	72	68	73	85	95
1987	67	81	87	87	74
1988	65	85	89	86	78
Ownership (as of 1988 FYE)					
Stock options outstanding	559	637	396	552	88
Common shares outstanding	16,728	8,743	7,362	15,046	7,774
Percent	3.3 %	7.3 %	5.4 %	3.7 %	1.1 %

CS: common stock issue

CSD: convertible subordinated debenture

W: warrants

(A): issued in an acquisition

(TE): issued to Thermo Electron

Instrument common shares, but (and this is in contradiction to the principle of decentralization) they are guaranteed on a subordinated basis by Thermo Electron.

Several of the subsidiaries have issued common shares to acquire related companies in order to build up to critical mass in a shorter period of time. In 1987, for instance, Thermedics acquired the enteral food products of the Navaco division of Lifetime Industries, Inc. for approximately $810,000 in cash and $2 million of its common stock (245,000 shares). The product line dovetailed with Corepak, a wholly owned subsidiary of Thermedics engaged in the production of enteral food delivery systems for patients who are unable or unwilling to eat normally. Now Corepak has the first closed sterile system for dispensing enteral food directly into the body and thereby limiting the potential for contamination.

On more than one occasion a subsidiary has issued shares to acquire a business from Thermo Electron itself. For example, on August 5, 1987, Thermo Environmental acquired Thermo Water Management from Thermo Electron in exchange for 2.4 million of its shares. Thermo Process acquired Thermo Process Services (1987) and Thermo Process Services Midwest (1988) from Thermo Electron by using its shares. Besides the economic advantages of the combinations, this tactic enabled Thermo Electron to take public the businesses it sold while avoiding the expense of an underwriting. It also increased Thermo Electron's ownership interest in the public subsidiary. For instance, from 1986 to 1988 the share of Thermo Process in its parent's hands increased from 73% to 89% as a result of the share exchanges.

All told, the subsidiaries have raised nearly $60 million worth of common stock through public offerings and $110 million of convertible subordinated debentures. But while Thermo Electron has given them the independence to access capital on their own, the scale benefits of a large organization have not been lost to the units. "They feel it's their company, but they also have a large company to provide advice and support,"[20] says John Hatsopoulos, senior vice president, brother to George and the architect of the company's unique financial structure. Here, for instance, are some of the ways in which the strong corporate parent lends a hand to its fledgling offspring.

[20]David Wessel, "Partial Spinoffs Offer Investors a Chance to Get in on a Real Winner—or Real Flop," *The Wall Street Journal,* July 17, 1986.

- Cash management is centralized; Thermo Electron credits the individual subsidiary companies with a return on their funds based upon prevailing interest rates.

- Thermo Electron's corporate staff provides certain administrative services[21] in exchange for a fee that amounts to 1% of each unit's gross revenues.

- For identifiable overhead costs,[22] Thermo Electron charges back to the units based upon the costs directly attributable to each company.

- These service agreements can be canceled by the subsidiary companies with 4 months' notice.

- Thermo Electron funds certain research and development efforts in the subsidiary companies. For example, Thermo Electron has agreed to reimburse up to $4 million of the costs that Thermedics incurs to develop and commercialize its drug and explosive-detection products. Thermedics will have the exclusive right to obtain a license from Thermo Electron to produce and market the products that result from the research and development effort, in exchange for the payment of royalties to Thermo Electron on the sales of such products.

- Thermo Electron manufactures certain products for its subsidiary companies under cost plus fixed profit contracts. For example, Tecogen's small-scale cogeneration units are manufactured by Thermo Electron's Crusader Engine Division, a leading supplier of inboard marine engines. The contract is cancelable upon 1 year's notice to Thermo Electron.

- Thermo Electron has drawn experienced and well-connected individuals to serve as board members. For example, Frank Borman is a director of Thermo Instrument and Paul Tsongas is a director of Thermo Environmental and Tecogen.

- Thermo Electron marries incentives for individual performance with the benefits of corporate-wide diversification of

[21]These include risk management, legal services, employee benefits administration, tax advice and preparation of tax returns, corporate communications, and certain corporate development, financial, and other services.
[22]Items such as pension, property, casualty, and employee health, life, and disability insurance coverage.

risk. Employees of the subsidiary companies are eligible to participate both in their own company's stock purchase plan and in Thermo Electron's defined contribution retirement and employee stock ownership plan. Certain officers and key employees of the subsidiary companies may participate in Thermo Electron's incentive and nonqualified stock option plans as well as their own.

The entrepreneurs who are concentrating on developing new technologies and building their businesses appreciate Thermo Electron's big company infrastructure. "There's the adventure of working for a small start-up but the resources of a huge corporation," says John Wood, president of Thermedics, Inc.[23]

Thermo Electron's unique structure also has enhanced the company's ability to attract talent. "We have a much easier time recruiting new people," says John Hatsopoulos. "They feel they become a large part of a small thing rather than being a small cog in a big machine."[24] A targeted financial reward is part of it too. The managers of the public subsidiary units participate in stock option plans that give them from over 1% to more than 7% of upside value in the unit (see bottom of exhibit 14.18). In general, the ownership in the hands of the unit managers increases with the length of time that the subsidiary has been public. Stock options in these start-up ventures, it should be noted, are more valuable than they are for more mature companies because the companies pay no dividends and have great upside potential.

By taking the units public, Thermo Electron also has done a favor for investors. They can pick and choose which of the company's many ventures has the greatest investment appeal to them. In addition, they receive high-quality information about the prospects and risks of the individual businesses. The information flow is strengthened in both directions, too. The valuation the market places on the units gives unit managers an unbiased judgment of their performance and a reaction to their future investment plans.

Thermo Electron's practice of equity decentralization recently

[23]Samuel Greengard, "Perpetual Notion Machine," *American Way Magazine.*
[24]David Wessel, "Partial Spinoffs Offer Investors a Chance to Get in on a Real Winner—or Real Flop," *The Wall Street Journal,* July 17, 1986.

cascaded another level lower. Thermo Cardiosystems, a wholly owned subsidiary of Thermedics (which is 65% owned by Thermo Electron), was formed to develop a permanently implantable heart assist device. It was taken public in January 1989, leaving Thermedics a 60% owner (and Thermo Electron with 39%). Such a practice puts pressure on Thermo Cardiosystems to perform and challenges Thermedic's management to come up with yet another winner instead of resting on its laurels.

Of course, the ultimate test of an organizational strategy is stock market performance. Thermo Electron has not disappointed in this regard. The company's market value added increased smartly from 1984 to 1988, the period over which the strategy has been implemented (exhibit 14.19).

Exhibit 14.19   Thermo Electron Market Value Added

	1984	1985	1986	1987	1988
Year-end share price	$8.89	$13.42	$17.00	$13.63	$ 20.25
Economic book value*	10.11	10.65	11.32	12.48	14.15
Spread	−$1.23	$ 2.77	$ 5.58	$ 1.14	$ 6.10
Common shares outstanding	13.6	14.5	17.4	17.2	17.4
Market value added	−$16.7	$40.1	$99.1	$19.6	$106.4

*Economic book value is a measure of the cash investment shareholders have made in the business. It is computed by taking the reported accounting book value of the firm's common equity and backing out non-cash charges and credits and capitalizing R&D. For this purpose, the company's R&D expense has been capitalized and straight-line-amortized over 5 years. Another problem is that Thermo Electron has recorded accounting gains when it has taken subsidiaries public at market values above their accounting book values. This gain has been eliminated from book value because it did not represent a cash investment in the business.

Thermo Electron's economic book value (per share) was $14.15 at the end of 1988. A stock price in excess of $14.15 indicates that Thermo Electron has added value to the capital shareholders have placed at its disposal.

Reported common equity	$184.4
Plus:	
Deferred income tax reserve	4.3
Bad-debt reserve	3.4
Cumulative goodwill amortization	0.3
Net capitalized R&D	74.1
Minus:	
Cumulative after-tax accounting gain	17.6
Economic book value	$246.5
Shares outstanding	17.4
Economic book value per share	$14.15

There is no reason why Thermo Electron's equity decentralization strategy should be applicable only to firms whose businesses are predominantly high-tech. Carving out from any larger company those separable business activities that could be characterized as being developmental or entrepreneurial in nature should bring about similar benefits (exhibit 14.20).

Internal Venture Capitalization. Like Bairnco's Glenn Bailey, T. J. Rodgers, chairman and founder of Cypress Semiconductor, an upstart chipmaker, believes that big companies kill the entrepreneurial spirit. "Large companies do not bring new technologies to the marketplace very efficiently," he says. "Big organizations spend too much time justifying why they shouldn't be doing something rather than working to meet a new goal or objective."[25]

So in his drive to make Cypress the largest semiconductor manufacturer in the United States, and a billion dollar company to boot, Rodgers wants to keep small company entrepreneurism alive within the support structure of a larger company. Entrepreneurism is particularly important because of the company's product market strategy. "Our recipe is to stay away from commodity parts that big Japanese and American companies make, and instead make a variety of high-performance, value-added parts."[26] "The high-speed niche products we make yield good profitability, but their markets are much smaller than mass markets, so we need more of them."[27] (See exhibit 14.21.)

Cypress's niche strategy is highly profitable, but it makes the company complex and dependent upon continuous innovation. Rodgers found these problems compounding as the company grew larger. "At about $50 million in revenues I felt I could run it," he says. "I could name everybody in the company. But as it grew large I found myself stretched. There had to be a change."[28] After finding that divisionalizing only led to political infighting, Rodgers searched for ways to regain the sense of camaraderie and the penny-pinching focus of a start-up.

[25]"Is Your Company Too Big?" *Business Week,* March 27, 1989.
[26]"Cypress Semiconductor Sees Higher 4th Quarter, Year Net," *Dow Jones News Wire,* December 19, 1986.
[27]"Cypress Semiconductor Interview," *Dow Jones News Wire,* December 19, 1986.
[28]"Is Your Company Too big?" *Business Week,* March 27, 1989.

Exhibit 14.20   A Summary of the Benefits of Thermo Electron's Venture Capitalization

The practice of selling shares of stock in promising subsidiary units to the public has benefited Thermo Electron in many ways:

- The incentives for management and employees are precise and powerful.
- The units are able to attract, retain, and motivate key executives through stock options and other equity-linked compensation devices.
- Autonomy and entrepreneurism within the units has been encouraged.
- The unit managers' attention has been focused on a well-defined business opportunity; in other words, it created some order out of chaos.
- Experienced board members have been drafted for guidance and influence.
- Transfer prices for important corporate resources have been made explicit.
- The potential for wasteful subsidies passing between units has been minimized.
- The units can access capital outside the parent company's usual capital budgeting process.
- The units have a currency to consummate tax-free acquisitions without diluting ownership in the corporate parent.
- Excessive business risks are syndicated, thereby making the parent more willing to fund its share of promising but risky new investments.
- Unit managers are provided with a market feedback for past performance and a market test for critical new investment decisions.
- Investors are furnished with high-quality information about the prospects and risks of individual activities in a diversified company.
- Investors are assured that new funds raised will be devoted to an identifiable and particularly promising purpose instead of being spread unaccountably throughout the consolidated company.
- Investors concentrate their investments in the specific opportunities holding the greatest appeal to them (the so-called pure-play benefit).

Exhibit 14.21 Cypress Semiconductor
Marketing and Product Strategy

For the purpose of strategic planning, the Company separates the CMOS (complementary metal oxide silicon) integrated circuit market into four quadrants based on product market size (niche vs. mass markets) and process technology (high performance vs. low performance) as illustrated below:

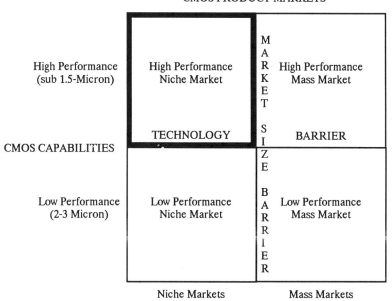

CMOS PRODUCT MARKETS

High Performance (sub 1.5-Micron)	High Performance Niche Market	High Performance Mass Market
	TECHNOLOGY	BARRIER
CMOS CAPABILITIES		
Low Performance (2-3 Micron)	Low Performance Niche Market	Low Performance Mass Market

MARKET SIZE BARRIER

Niche Markets   Mass Markets

SINGLE PRODUCT MARKET SIZE

☐ CYPRESS TARGET

The "market size barrier" relates to the relative economic efficiency with which different semiconductor companies can address various product markets based on their relative size, corporate structure, and strategic focus. The "technology barrier" is based on the level of design and process technology required to produce various levels of performance in semiconductor products. Currently, the Company believes that sub 1.5-micron CMOS process technology is needed to

Exhibit 14.21   continued

produce high-performance integrated circuit products while the more common 2–3 micron CMOS process technologies produce lower-performance products.

Based on this view of the semiconductor market, the Company believes that its optimal product and market strategy is achieved by focusing its product and process development efforts on the high-performance niche market quadrant. The Company has implemented this strategy and plans to maintain its position with the following tactics:

- Design and market high-performance products which, because of their critical importance to the performance of sophisticated electronic systems, can command premium pricing.

- Differentiate within product market niches by using other Company capabilities such as special packaging, access to military markets, and advanced design for proprietary features.

- Protect the Company's product markets using its advanced process technologies as a "technology barrier" against companies attempting to gain access to such markets and maintain the barrier to competition with continual investment in process technology improvements.

- Protect the Company's product markets from large U.S., Japanese, and other semiconductor manufacturers which have the technological capability to compete in the high-performance segments with "market size barriers" created by selecting individual niche product markets which are small enough to be unattractive to the mass production economies of the larger companies.

- Create a large aggregate market for the Company and concurrently reduce the impact of competitive movement across the "technology" and "market size barriers" by establishing multiple product lines, each consisting of numerous products.

Common Stock Prospectus
March 4, 1987

Cypress has lived up to its word. By the end of 1988, the company was shipping 103 products diversified into six product lines. In 1988, Cypress introduced 26 new products, up dramatically over the 9 introduced in 1987 and 14 in 1986.

His solution: establish separate and autonomous companies under the Cypress Semiconductor umbrella to concentrate on individual new products and singular production functions; invest them with separate boards of directors and their own CEOs free to pursue their vision of a new business; and give local managers and employees a piece of the equity action.

> I would rather see our billion-dollar company of the 1990's be ten $100 million companies, all strong, growing, healthy, and aggressive as hell. The alternative is an aging billion-dollar company that spends more time defending its turf than growing.
>
> "The New Innovators"
> *Fortune*
> July 3, 1989

The sentiment (and even some of the words) echoes Bairnco's Bailey. But though the concern is much the same, the solution is different. Rodgers's businesses could not support the leverage Bailey piles onto his. Venture capitalization, that is, equity decentralization alone, is the answer for his high-tech outfits. But instead of taking them public, as Thermo Electron does, Rodgers has kept the equity decentralization strictly internal, a benefit if it can be made to work.

So far, Rodgers has created four companies within his company (exhibit 14.22). Each is autonomous. Its president can change product design and add capacity, raise money, including issuing equity, and set wages, even hire and fire employees, without head office approval. Each unit has carved employees into a significant share of the common stock in the unit (through options), a powerful incentive. The second, third, and fourth companies listed have developed new semiconductors. Ross Technology has been

Exhibit 14.22 Cypress Semiconductor Start-up Corporations

Company	Established	Employee Ownership
Cypress Semiconductor (Texas), Inc.	1986	11%
Aspen Semiconductor	1986	11%
Multichip Technology Corporation	1987	9%
Ross Technology, Inc.	1988	n.a.

funded with a seed loan that will convert into equity once its business plan is accepted by Cypress. Cypress Semiconductor (Texas) is a chip factory that serves as a separate, arm's-length supplier to the other units and to outsiders. Its genesis is one of those success stories that can define the culture for a new company. After several years of heady success as a start-up, by 1987 Cypress's growth had become severely production-constrained. Rodgers needed a new plant on line, fast. Incentives through equity decentralization was the answer.

> This company got a major new plant on stream very quickly, about twice as fast as the industry norm. Rodgers was instrumental here. . . . He did a very clever thing when he incorporated the factory and its management as a separate subsidiary and gave the factory managers stock options that would gain in value if the factory came on stream in time. Factory management, as a result, had a tremendous personal financial incentive.
>
> An (unidentified) institutional investor
> *The Wall Street Transcript*
> May 23, 1988
> page 89,543

The plant was up and running in record time; it was producing $400,000 of revenues within 12 months of its ground breaking in 1987. Typically it takes a new plant 2 years to record significant sales.

Rodgers wants his board of directors to become owners, too. The 1988 Directors Stock Option Plan reserved up to 200,000 shares to be issued upon exercise of options granted to three *outside* board members. The options expire 3 months after a director leaves the board. In addition, Cypress established The Directors' Warrant Plan, which granted each outside director warrants to purchase 40,000 shares of stock at a price equal to the company's market value at the time of the grant, $6.25 a share.

Cypress has proved its mettle in a tough business right from its initial public offering in 1986 (exhibit 14.23). Sales are more than doubling every 2 years (sales for 1989 are expected to top $200 million). The company's niche strategy shows through in the very high ratio of R&D to sales, around 25%. Cypress's investment in R&D and in tangible assets outstrips internally

Exhibit 14.23 Cypress Semiconductor
Performance
Since Going Public

	1985	1986	1987	1988
Operating Results				
Sales	$17.4	$50.9	$77.3	$139.4
Growth		193%	52%	80%
R&D	$5.2	$10.4	$18.9	$33.7
Percent of sales	30%	20%	24%	24%
NOPAT*		$10.9	$21.6	$40.8
Investment†		$30.9	$33.8	$59.6
Free cash flow		−$20.0	−$12.2	−$18.8
Financial Policies				
Marketable securities		$74.0	$107.4	$89.5
Total debt/total capital		21%	16%	12%
Dividend payout ratio		0%	0%	0%
Economic Value Added				
Return on beginning capital‡		25.3%	29.2%	37.8%
Cost of capital§		20.0%	20.0%	20.0%
Spread		5.3%	9.2%	17.8%
Beginning capital		$43.1	$73.9	$107.8
Economic value added		$2.3	$6.8	$19.2
Market Value Added				
Year-end share price		$7.13	$11.63	$10.88
Economic book value per share		3.60	5.00	6.22
Spread		$3.52	$6.62	$4.66
Common shares outstanding		32.7	36.3	36.4
Market value added		$115.2	$240.7	$169.6

*NOPAT is net operating profit after taxes. For the purpose of this computation, Cypress's R&D expense has been capitalized onto its books as an asset and depreciated evenly over an arbitrarily chosen 5-year period.

†Investment is the additional capital invested in net operating assets from the beginning to the end of the period. For these purposes, Cypress's periodic R&D expense was treated as an asset expenditure.

‡The rate of return on capital is computed by dividing NOPAT by the capital tied up in net operating assets.

§The cost of capital is an estimate of the minimum rate of return that debt and equity investors combined are seeking to compensate for risk. While our calculations reveal that Cypress's weighted average cost of debt and equity capital did vary over this 3-year period, 20% was chosen as an approximate average cost of capital in order to provide a stationary benchmark against which to judge the company's performance over this time frame.

generated sources of cash, producing a *deficit* free cash flow. Cypress justifiably employs conservative financial policies. In view of its cash needs, risk, and high potential, management wisely keeps on hand a sizable hoard of marketable securities, restrains debt to less than 20% of all capital, and pays no cash dividends.

The company's rate of return on capital has soared well above an extremely high cost of capital (high because of the reliance on equity and the great risk of the business[29]). A broadening spread combined with the growth of the business to triple residual income, or EVA, in each of the past 2 years. Market value added, a measure of the net present value of all past and projected capital projects, loomed large right out of the starting gate, and it has grown bigger still since then in appreciation of the prospect for more economic value added.

Cypress's stock market value anticipates great things to come. But Rodgers will need all the help he can get if he is to build the world's most profitable semiconductor company. Growing big by thinking small is the name of his game. If his track record thus far is any indication, the decentralization of equity is the play for him to call again and again.

The Atomistic Decentralization of Equity.

Cypress Semiconductor shows that equity decentralization can work even if ownership is kept just within the company and among its employees. Riding that thought to infinity is Wal-Mart, the world's greatest retailer, which has made entrepreneurs out of each of the managers of its "stores within a store."

> Wal-Mart chief David Glass expects managers for each of the 34 departments within a typical Wal-Mart store to run their operations as if they were running their own businesses. The managers are supported with detailed financial statements that show costs and profit margins. Says Glass: "Instead of having one entrepreneur who founded the business, we have got 250,000 entrepreneurs out there running their part of the business."
>
> "Leaders of the Most Admired"
> *Fortune*
> January 29, 1990

[29]Cypress's beta, a measure of investment risk, is about 2.0. The company's common shares are twice as risky as the typical publicly traded firm.

The spirit of Sam Walton lives on in every individual who oversees every department in every Wal-Mart store. Here is the benefit of making managers into owners carried to its most atomistic, and productive, level.

Structure Follows Strategy

Alfred Chandler, in his landmark book *Structure Follows Strategy,* wrote that a company's organization structure should complement and support its business strategy. A business likewise benefits from having a financial, or ownership, structure that is suitably matched to its rate of growth and level of risk. For those purposes, most businesses can be roughly divided into two camps.[30]

The first category are the seasoned and stable businesses which generate more cash than they can productively reinvest (classic X, X-Minus, and to a certain extent, Y outfits). KKR has become very nearly the world's largest and certainly the most successful conglomerate by developing and perfecting a new and more effective ownership structure for operations of this type. LBOs apparently are a superior way to stimulate them to create value.

Rather than fall prey to the advances of KKR, I have argued that firms whose units exhibit these characteristics can re-create for themselves the elements of KKR's structure that are most vital to building up value and still remain public if they wish. The most important facet of this strategy is to make managers at all levels, outside board directors, and ultimately rank-and-file employees too, into significant owners of the firm, or better, of the specific enterprise with which their labors are associated.

To facilitate the process of making the doers into financial owners, debt should be decentralized into the mature units. This makes it easier to concentrate equity in the hands of the executives and employees in the units, amplifies the reward for success and the penalty for failure, and instills a sense of urgency to

[30]The exceptions are those businesses which, while not offering the prospect of exceptional growth, are too cyclical to support the aggressive use of debt. It is likely, however, that a financial market innovation will make it possible to LBO firms sensitive to business fluctuations. Indeed, subordinated payment-in-kind bonds may have been just the ticket.

generate cash at a rate that covers the cost of capital insistently accruing on the debts. It has the effect of capitalizing a challenging, multiyear cash flow budget into a bond that must be repaid and then freeing managers to devise and prosecute aggressive plans to maximize value. The obligation to repay the debt will focus everyone's efforts on the task of maximizing profitability and will help them to let go the natural urge to keep investing aggressively in a business that no longer has exceptional growth opportunities. It may also trigger the sale of certain assets worth more to others.

Decentralizing debt in the manner I am prescribing should not impair the parent company's financial flexibility, however. So long as the debt of the units is nonrecourse, the parent will be able to raise additional capital, though funding will be more dependent on the merits of the proposed new investments. Forcing the parent to tap external capital markets for funds, rather than just consume internally generated cash, is an important check on the inclination to spend wantonly. It is the microeconomic equivalent of a budget deficit.

For sunrise ventures, ones whose leverage would snuff out the value that is glimmering in the eyes of entrepreneurs (i.e., Pre-Z and Z enterprises), a decentralization of equity alone, through either a partial public stock offering, or better if it can be done, completely internal, is advisable. The trick is to keep the flame of a start-up flickering under the protective umbrella of a larger infrastructure.

To turn back the KKR and venture capitalist challenge, I am proposing that conventionally structured companies internally replicate the disciplinary and incentive advantages that external capital markets offer. The decentralization of debt, of equity, of ownership and decision making is part of the answer. Companies that fail to decentralize not only run the risk of being swallowed whole and digested in parts by the great white whale but, and this is more important, forfeit the opportunity to create more value for their shareholders and society at large.

PART IV

The Capstone Case

15

A Recipe for Reviving The Campbell Soup Company

The Campbell Soup Company has been embroiled in a fractious family brawl ever since John T. Dorrance, Jr., the son of the founder, died. Dorrance's three children are determined to preserve the company's independence. Opposing them are cousins who, unhappy with the company's performance, want to sell their shares or swap them for stock in a larger company. Though the arrival of David Johnson from Gerber has quenched the fiery dispute for now, real differences still simmer below the surface, and they will need to be addressed before long. This chapter shows how. (I must admit my real objective is to illustrate how to apply the concepts and analytical methods introduced in this book, rather than to actually resolve Campbell's dilemma.)

To set the stage, the events since John Dorrance passed away are chronicled first. Next comes a tedious but necessary task: a review of Campbell's past performance in relation to its cost of capital and business peers. Bear with me through this hard plowing, for the fruits of this labor are soon harvested.

To establish a base case valuation, a forecast for Campbell is prepared at the consolidated level. It reflects an extrapolation of past trends and also closely parallels the *Value Line* projection. It solves for $34 per share. From that base a quest for greater value is launched in two directions (exhibit 15.1). In the first lies *value planning* (a moniker I prefer to the hackneyed "value-based plan-

Exhibit 15.1   The Quest for Value

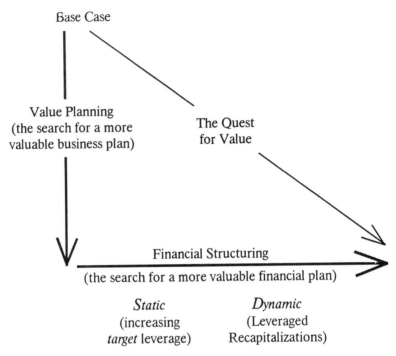

ning")—the search for a more valuable business strategy. Ralston Purina serves as a model for Campbell in this regard. Starting with a bouillabaisse of businesses in the early 80s, Ralston's Chairman William Stiritz chopped, sliced, and diced his way to a more streamlined and valuable company, a procedure I have inelegantly entitled a focus strategy. A projection is prepared for Campbell to simulate the outcome of pursuing a similar corporate plan. In comparison with the base projection, it yields lower sales, earnings, and returns early on, but also more cash flow, debt capacity, and value. Trimmed of bureaucratic fat, Campbell's intrinsic share value is now $37 per share, a gain of $405 million overall.

The dogleg of our crusade is *financial structuring:* the tailoring of a financial strategy to support the most value-adding business strategy. Operating decisions should be separated from financing ones, but the converse is not true. Once the operating game plan is set, the financial structure should be tailored to support it.

Financial structuring itself branches in two. The more conservative route is static debt policy: the adoption of a target capital structure that balances the cost and benefit of debt financing. Even here, Campbell could be more adventuresome. Management could justifiably stoke up leverage from a tepid 25% ratio of total debt to total capital to a searing 55% ratio, from a capital structure deserving a Aa bond rating to one corresponding to just a strong Baa bond rating. Stepping up leverage will increase Campbell's borrowing rate, but it will reduce the cost of capital by 1.5%, increase Campbell's intrinsic share value to $44, and commit the company to a series of debt-financed share repurchases, or minileveraged recapitalizations.

To really spice things up, however, and complete our recipe for corporate revival, Campbell should proceed with a maxileveraged recapitalization. This dynamic use of debt entails borrowing to make a substantial, one-time distribution of cash to shareholders and then working like the dickens to pay it down. If only because of the additional corporate income taxes saved, Campbell's intrinsic share value will rise to $45, a gain of $8 in value. That does not include the benefit of making the managers into owners, a process facilitated by using debt aggressively to replace equity. Perhaps the most important advantage to the leveraged recapitalization is that it makes it possible to restructure the share ownership interests, thereby consolidating control in the hands of the Dorrances who want to keep Campbell independent while providing liquidity to the dissident family members who crave that. There are many ways to cook a goose, but here is one recipe that should satisfy the conflicting tastes of all the guests at Campbell's party (if only they can swallow their aversion to debt).

Campbell's predicament raises many of the issues that confront all companies in the quest for value. Value planning, financial structuring, and incentive compensation—all are ingredients in the bubbling stew. To address them, this chapter is organized into the following sections.

I. The Hatfields and The McCoys

II. Let Bygones Be Long Gone

III. The Base Case

Tie on your apron. It's time to break some eggheads.

I. The Hatfields and The McCoys

The death of John T. Dorrance, Jr., on April 9, 1989, set off a heated contest for control of Campbell Soup that has not yet cooled. Campbell's stock price ignited from $33 to about $50 as arbitrageurs hoped for a quick sale or restructuring. Not without good reason. Since March 1989, Campbell Chairman Robert Vlasic had been working behind the scenes to arrange a merger with Quaker Oats. Further fueling the takeover fires, R. Gordon McGovern, Campbell's CEO, abruptly quit on November 1, 1989. Dissatisfied with his oversight of the company, the board and family members had pressured McGovern to leave.

Enraged that the proposed merger called for swapping Campbell's common stock for Quaker shares valued only in the $40 range, disgusted by their lack of influence over the company's affairs, and concerned about The Campbell Soup Company's poor performance this past decade, a disgruntled slate of family members went on record on December 28, 1989 to press for a sale of the company under favorable terms. Led by board member Dorrance ("Dodo") Hamilton, the 61-year-old niece of the deceased John Dorrance, Jr., the dissident group holds 17.4% of Campbell's stock (they are labeled D for "dissidents" in exhibit 15.2). Two other family members, who together control a 7.3% Campbell's block, sympathized with the goals of the dissidents but stated in a letter to the board their preference to convert their Campbell holdings into stock of a much larger entity in a tax-free transaction (they are labeled S for "sympathizers").

Dead set against the dissidents are the three children of John Dorrance led by elder son John ("Ipy") T. Dorrance III. (They are labeled L for "loyalists.") At present, they are prevailing, for

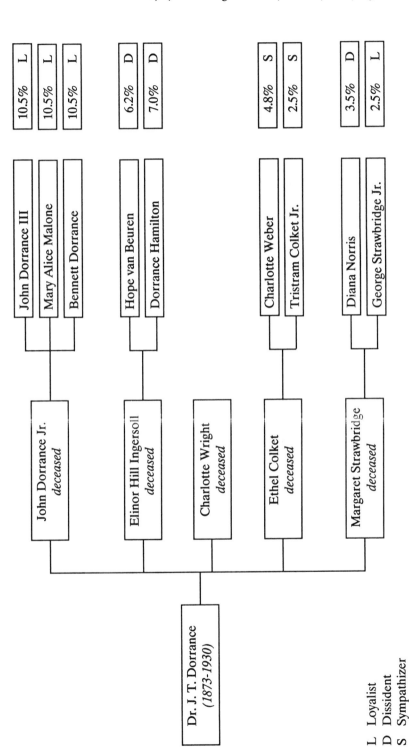

Campbell Stake	Position
10.5%	L
10.5%	L
10.5%	L
6.2%	D
7.0%	D
4.8%	S
2.5%	S
3.5%	D
2.5%	L

John Dorrance III
Mary Alice Malone
Bennett Dorrance

Hope van Beuren
Dorrance Hamilton

Charlotte Weber
Tristram Colket Jr.

Diana Norris
George Strawbridge Jr.

John Dorrance Jr.
deceased

Elinor Hill Ingersoll
deceased

Charlotte Wright
deceased

Ethel Colket
deceased

Margaret Strawbridge
deceased

Dr. J. T. Dorrance
(1873-1930)

L Loyalist
D Dissident
S Sympathizer

Reprinted by permission of the *Wall Street Journal*
© 1990 Dow Jones & Company, Inc.
All Rights Reserved Worldwide.

together the three hold 31.5% of the Campbell shares (10.5% each). George Strawbridge, a cousin and director who controls about 2.5% of Campbell's stock, also is determined to see Campbell remain independent. He has stated flatly, "my shares are not for sale."[1]

A tenuous truce between the feuding family members has set in since David W. Johnson, former chairman and CEO of Gerber products, agreed to take over as Campbell CEO. Highly regarded for the turnaround of Gerber, Johnson wants to set a torch under Campbell's management. He intends to replace the paternalistic style of the past with a results-oriented work ethic. "M'm M'm Good" shall become "M'm M'm Great" in the 90s, he declared upon his arrival. Johnson conceded that some divestitures will be inevitable. True to his word, in one of his first official acts, on January 31, 1990, Johnson announced that Campbell will sell its Juice Bowl products unit and will close its frozen food plant in the United Kingdom, where the Campbell PLC unit overbuilt. Johnson sees no benefit to making a large acquisition: "The underlying assumption that we have to get bigger than what we are is a fallacy."[2] As for resolving the simmering family dispute, Johnson's initial pronouncement was not very helpful: "Perhaps they [the dissidents] could sell a small percentage [of their holdings] to accommodate their aims, whatever they are."[3]

IIa. Let Bygones be Long Gone (Stock Performance)

The dissidents have reason to complain, given Campbell's stock market performance. Starting with a share worth $17.38 at the end of 1984 and assuming subsequent dividends were reinvested, an investor in Campbell's stock would hold 1.13 shares worth $35.48 by the end of 1988 (exhibit 15.3). A $17.38 investment in an equally weighted portfolio of 12 food competitors[4] would

[1]"Campbell's picks Gerber's Chief for Top Post," *The Wall Street Journal,* January 3, 1990.
[2]"Hot Kitchen Awaits Campbell Chief," *The Wall Street Journal,* January 4, 1990.
[3]"Hot Kitchen Awaits Campbell Chief," *The Wall Street Journal,* January 4, 1990.
[4]The industry composite consisted of Borden, CPC International, ConAgra, General Mills, Gerber, H. J. Heinz, Kellogg, Quaker Oats, Ralston Purina, Sara Lee, Smuckers, and Tasty Baking.

Exhibit 15.3 Campbell Soup Stock Performance vs. Index of Food Companies

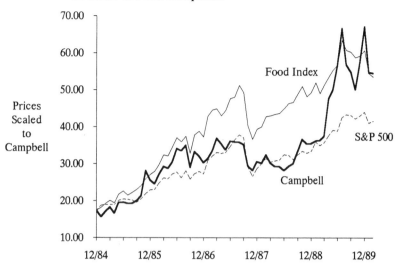

have cumulated to a value of $49.32 in the same time frame. The only consolation was that Campbell's shares did keep pace with the S&P 500.

With the passing of John Dorrance in April, Campbell's shares jumped from $33.25 to $42.00. (Prices quoted here are actual prices as opposed to those displayed in exhibit 15.3, which assume dividend reinvestment.) Takeover speculation reached fever pitch in July. Campbell's soared to $58.50 that month, a value exceeded only at the end of the year when, with the departure of CEO McGovern, arbitrageurs bet on a sure thing only to be disappointed once again. Johnson's arrival upon the new year doused the takeover rumors, at least for awhile.

IIb. Let Bygones Be Long Gone (Operating Performance)

Campbell's disappointing stock market valuation has been a reflection of the company's operating performance. Results this past decade for Campbell and the composite group of 12 competitors are presented in exhibits 15.4 and 15.5. All of the results have been standardized by dividing dollar values by the capital out-

Exhibit 15.4 Campbell Soup Co.: Summary of Operating Performance
(Scaled to 1980 Beginning Capital = $100)

(Aug-Jul)	1980	1981	1982	1983	1984	1985	1986	1987	1988	1989	10 year Summary Growth/Avg
Operating Results											
Sales	244.4	267.0	281.0	314.1	349.0	380.6	417.8	428.4	464.6	541.2	9.2%
Sales Growth	13.9%	9.3%	5.3%	11.8%	11.1%	9.1%	9.8%	2.6%	8.4%	16.5%	9.8%
NOPBT	31.0	29.5	27.0	32.6	35.5	35.3	40.5	42.4	43.7	49.8	5.4%
Pct. of Sales	12.7%	11.1%	9.6%	10.4%	10.2%	9.3%	9.7%	9.9%	9.4%	9.2%	10.1%
NOPAT	19.1	17.7	14.3	19.0	22.8	24.3	27.9	30.2	30.4	25.1	3.1%
Oper. Cash Tax Rate	38%	40%	47%	42%	36%	31%	31%	29%	30%	50%	37%
Capital	124.3	132.3	125.0	142.1	166.0	175.9	182.0	205.2	271.6	302.7	10.4%
Sales/Beg Capital	2.4x	2.1x	2.1x	2.5x	2.5x	2.3x	2.4x	2.4x	2.3x	2.0x	2.3x
Net Working Cap/Sales	20.2%	18.7%	14.8%	12.9%	15.8%	14.1%	11.8%	11.9%	13.0%	11.4%	14.5%

(Aug-Jul)	1980	1981	1982	1983	1984	1985	1986	1987	1988	1989	10 year Summary
FCF & Leverage											*Cumulative*
NOPAT	19.1	17.7	14.3	19.0	22.8	24.3	27.9	30.2	30.4	25.1	231.0
Increase in Capital(I)	24.3	7.9	(7.3)	17.1	24.0	9.8	6.1	23.3	66.3	31.1	202.8
Free Cash Flow	(5.2)	9.8	21.6	1.9	(1.0)	14.5	21.8	7.1	(35.9)	(6.1)	28.2
Debt/Total Capital	18%	18%	20%	18%	18%	18%	19%	18%	22%	26%	20%
Internal Performance											*Average*
NOPAT/Beg Capital r	19.1%	14.3%	10.8%	15.2%	16.1%	14.7%	15.8%	16.6%	14.8%	9.2%	14.7%
Wtd Avg Cap Cost c*	12.3%	14.0%	13.1%	11.7%	12.8%	13.0%	11.2%	11.8%	12.5%	11.6%	12.4%
Spread r-c*	6.9%	0.3%	-2.3%	3.6%	3.3%	1.7%	4.6%	4.8%	2.3%	-2.3%	2.3%
x Beginning Capital	100.0	124.3	132.3	125.0	142.1	166.0	175.9	182.0	205.2	271.6	162.4
Economic Value Added	6.9	0.3	(3.1)	4.5	4.7	2.8	8.1	8.8	4.7	(6.3)	3.1
External Performance											*Growth/Avg*
Year End Share Price	$7.75	$7.16	$12.09	$15.25	$17.38	$24.69	$28.50	$27.88	$31.50	$58.63	25.2%
Adj Book Value Per Shr	8.92	9.74	10.09	10.91	12.01	13.23	14.77	16.67	18.22	18.86	8.7%
Price - Adj Book	($1.17)	($2.59)	$2.01	$4.34	$5.37	$11.46	$13.73	$11.21	$13.28	$39.76	$9.74
x No. Shares Outst'g	10.1	9.9	9.9	9.9	9.9	9.9	10.0	10.0	9.9	10.0	10.0
Market Value Added	(11.7)	(25.6)	19.9	43.0	53.2	113.7	136.8	111.8	131.5	395.4	96.8

Exhibit 15.5 Consolidated Food Group (12 Companies): Summary of Operating Performance (Scaled to 1979 Beginning Capital = $100)

	1979	1980	1981	1982	1983	1984	1985	1986	1987	1988	10 year Summary Growth/Avg
Operating Results											
Sales	287.6	329.2	348.4	353.6	372.3	403.7	438.3	483.8	540.2	601.2	8.5%
Sales Growth	16.9%	14.5%	5.8%	1.5%	5.3%	8.4%	8.6%	10.4%	11.7%	11.3%	9.4%
NOPBT	24.1	28.0	30.2	31.4	33.6	35.1	38.4	45.1	49.5	58.9	10.4%
Pct. of Sales	8.4%	8.5%	8.7%	8.9%	9.0%	8.7%	8.8%	9.3%	9.2%	9.8%	8.9%
NOPAT	14.9	17.1	18.3	19.6	21.0	22.8	23.6	28.3	30.5	37.7	10.9%
Oper. Cash Tax Rate	38%	39%	39%	38%	37%	35%	39%	37%	38%	36%	38%
Capital	114.7	124.4	134.3	142.3	142.7	155.6	157.4	190.4	208.4	234.9	8.3%
Sales/Beg Capital	2.9x	2.9x	2.8x	2.6x	2.6x	2.8x	2.8x	3.1x	2.8x	2.9x	2.8x
Net Working Cap/Sales	13.6%	12.7%	12.2%	11.6%	10.1%	11.6%	7.8%	7.6%	7.3%	6.8%	10.1%

	1979	1980	1981	1982	1983	1984	1985	1986	1987	1988	10 year Summary
FCF & Leverage											Cumulative
NOPAT	14.9	17.1	18.3	19.6	21.0	22.8	23.6	28.3	30.5	37.7	233.9
Increase in Capital(I)	14.7	9.8	9.8	8.0	0.5	12.8	1.8	33.0	18.0	26.4	134.8
Free Cash Flow	0.2	7.3	8.5	11.6	20.6	10.0	21.8	(4.8)	12.5	11.2	99.0
Debt/Total Capital	30%	29%	29%	28%	27%	32%	32%	40%	38%	37%	32%
Internal Performance											Average
NOPAT/Beg Capital r	14.9%	14.9%	14.7%	14.6%	14.8%	16.0%	15.2%	18.0%	16.0%	18.1%	15.7%
Wtd Avg Cap Cost c*	10.7%	12.4%	14.3%	13.7%	12.4%	13.4%	12.1%	9.8%	11.0%	11.4%	12.1%
Spread r-c*	4.1%	2.5%	0.5%	0.9%	2.4%	2.6%	3.1%	8.1%	5.0%	6.7%	3.6%
x Beginning Capital	100.0	114.7	124.4	134.3	142.3	142.7	155.6	157.4	190.4	208.4	147.0
Economic Value Added	4.1	2.8	0.6	1.2	3.4	3.7	4.8	12.8	9.5	14.0	5.7
External Performance											Average
Market Value Added	1.0	4.6	6.0	31.9	43.2	68.5	146.9	217.3	227.8	250.2	99.7

standing at the beginning of the first year and multiplying by $100. One complication is that Campbell's fiscal year ends on July 31. (For example, "history 1989" contains the results for the year that ends July 31, 1989.) Thus, for purposes of comparison, Campbell's results are matched with those of business peers with a 1-year lag. (Campbell's 1989 year is matched with the food peers' 1988, and so forth.)

Rate of Return.   During a decade in which the competitors increased their rate of return, Campbell's slipped. A preoccupation with growth at the expense of profitability, or reinvestment risk, has been the culprit.

> In recent years, Campbell has developed a reputation for overemphasizing new products, while underemphasizing the importance of its core offerings and of manufacturing and distributional efficiencies, at the expense of profits.
>
> Stephen E. Grant
> *Value Line*
> November 24, 1989

For the first 5 years, Campbell's rate of return was on a par with the industry's, an average of 15.1% for Campbell versus 14.8% for the composite. But for the most recent 5 years, Campbell's average return dipped to 14.2% while the peer group managed to pull its average up to 16.7%. The unfavorable comparison boils down to differences in operating profit margin, capital turns, and growth.

Operating Profit Margin.   Campbell's operating profit margin (NOPBT as a percent of sales) fell from a range of 11% to 12% in the early 80s to 9% to 10% over the most recent 5 years. The industry's profit margin, by contrast, rose from a range of 8% to 9% in the early 80s to 9% to 10% more recently.

Capital Turns.   The most striking comparison is capital efficiency. For every dollar of capital invested, the peer group turned out approximately $2.80 of sales versus only $2.30 at Campbell. Over the 10-year period, Campbell Soup and the peer companies sharply improved the efficiency of their working capital management, essentially cutting in half the ratio of net working capital to sales. The trouble is that Campbell's working capital intensivity remains almost twice as high as it is for the typical food company. Here there is room for improvement.

Growth and Investment. For every $100 to start, Campbell's finished with $302.70 of capital, a growth rate of 10.4%. The industry, on the other hand, ended with capital of only $234.90, a growth rate of just 8.3%. Sales also expanded faster at Campbell's, 9.2% on average versus 8.5% for its peers. The emphasis on growth, however, was a flawed strategy. Choosing to rationalize and focus on profitability, the competition ended with greater value added (in part because of their managements' concerns over hostile takeovers, a pressure not exerted upon Campbell's management).

Free Cash Flow and Leverage. By investing comparatively less and earning higher rates of return, Campbell's competitors generated more free cash flow, another measure of their superiority. Over the 10 years the food group invested less than 60% of their cumulative NOPAT back into the business versus almost 90% for Campbell's. The food companies stepped up leverage in the face of strong positive cash flow, a proactive policy designed to reduce their overall cost of capital. Their ratio of total debt to total capital increased from about 30% in the early 80s to a range of 35% to 40% more recently, the result of hefty share repurchases and conscious management strategy. Campbell, on the other hand, held its debt ratio essentially flat at 20%, except for the most recent year, when it rose to about 25%. The company's conservative financial structure can be attributed in part to a preoccupation with maintaining a Aaa rating on its bonds.

Ironically, Campbell already has lost the Aaa rating in the market if not in the eyes of the rating agencies. Its bonds trade at a yield on a par with that paid by the typical Aa if not A-rated companies, and with good reason, as we shall see.

Value Added. The bottom line in any economic analysis is value added. Campbell's EVA, the internal measure of value added, remained essentially flat over the decade, except for two brief shining moments in fiscal 1986 and 1987. Standardized EVA was $2.7 on average for the first 5 years and $3.6 on average for the most recent 5 years, an insignificant shift. The industry's EVA rose materially, from $2.4 to $9.0 on average from the first to the most recent 5-year period. To compare the most recent 3 years alone is telling. While the industry's EVA climbed to a higher plateau, Campbell's plummeted.

The food industry's standardized MVA, the external measure of added value, rose in line with the growing EVA from about breakeven in the early 80s to $250 by the end of 1988. Campbell's MVA, on the other hand, progressed from slightly deficit to only about $130 by the end of its 1988 fiscal year, a level just about half that reached by the industry. With takeover speculation powering Campbell's stock price to $58.63 by the end of its 1989 fiscal year, MVA soared to $395, a measure meaningful only to arbitrageurs.

Conclusion.   Let's not be too hard on Campbell. After all, the company's strategy did produce more sales. Unfortunately, the extra sales were purchased at the expense of a dissipating profit margin, relatively slower capital turns, shrunken rates of return, and anemic value added. Exacerbating the unfavorable perform-ance comparison, Campbell is less leveraged than its peers, and as a result it must pay a higher overall cost for its capital. The analysis so far suggests that the opportunity to rationalize the business and to gear up the balance sheet may answer the prayers of shareholders clamoring for more performance and greater li-quidity at one and the same time. Before investigating the poten-tial for restructuring Campbell, however, we will need a baseline forecast that reflects the status quo.

Perhaps now would be a good time to issue a disclaimer. All of the analysis and simulations presented in this chapter are based upon my independent review of The Campbell Soup Com-pany and its competitors by using publicly available information. Absolutely no input has been sought from nor has any been provided by any representative of the company or its peers. Now that that is out of the way, let's continue to stir the pot.

IIIa. The Base Case (Forecast)

A forecast reflecting *Value Line* assumptions will be used as the starting point for an analysis of alternatives. Analyst Stephen E. Grant, in a release dated November 24, 1989, forecast various items for Campbell for the 1990 fiscal year and for the period 1992 to 1994. His expectations, along with the results of the base case forecast that I prepared to replicate his estimates, are presented in exhibit 15.6. My base case forecast turned out to be only a touch more optimistic than Grant's—a few more sales, a wee bit better cash operating profit margin [the ratio of earnings before depreciation, interest, and taxes (EBDIT) to sales], and a little higher capital expenditures to support it all—reflecting my natural ebullience (and love of Campbell's Homestyle Cream of Tomato soup).

A full summary of the base case forecast, along with the preceding 5 years' history, is given in exhibit 15.7. This time the results have not been standardized, in order to make them comparable to *Value Line* and to satisfy your pent-up demand for real numbers.

Exhibit 15.6   Baseline Forecast Assumptions

		1992–94		
Value Line	1990			
Base case	1990	1992	1993	1994
Sales				
Value Line	$6,250		$8,000	
Base case	$6,250	$7,563	$8,319	$9,151
EBDIT/Sales				
Value Line	13.5%		13.5%	
Base case	13.5%	13.5%	13.6%	13.6%
Net Profit				
Value Line	$335		$440	
Base case	$344	$430	$486	$551
Capital Expenditures				
Value Line	$427.2		$375.0	
Base case	$427.2	$387.8	$388.7	$381.4

Exhibit 15.7 Campbell Soup Base Case: Summary of Operating Performance

FINANSEER (Data in Millions) (August-July)	History 1985	History 1986	History 1987	History 1988	History 1989	Forecast 1990	Forecast 1991	Forecast 1992	Forecast 1993	Forecast 1994	5-Year Summary
Operating Results											Growth/Avg
Sales	$3,988.7	$4,378.7	$4,490.4	$4,868.9	$5,672.1	$6,250.0	$6,875.0	$7,562.5	$8,318.8	$9,150.6	10.0%
Sales Growth	9.1%	9.8%	2.6%	8.4%	16.5%	10.2%	10.0%	10.0%	10.0%	10.0%	10.0%
NOPBT	$369.6	$424.4	$443.8	$457.7	$521.9	$677.5	$744.6	$820.2	$903.3	$997.6	10.2%
Percent of Sales	9.3%	9.7%	9.9%	9.4%	9.2%	10.8%	10.8%	10.8%	10.9%	10.9%	10.9%
NOPAT	$255.4	$291.7	$317.2	$318.9	$262.7	$534.7	$541.9	$584.1	$637.1	$693.8	6.7%
Oper. Cash Tax Rate	31%	31%	29%	30%	50%	21%	27%	29%	29%	30%	27%
Capital	$1,843.0	$1,907.1	$2,150.8	$2,846.1	$3,172.4	$3,410.4	$3,698.4	$3,950.2	$4,189.1	$4,408.1	6.6%
Sales/Beg Capital	2.3	2.4	2.4	2.3	2.0	2.0	2.0	2.0	2.1	2.2	2.1
PPE Expenditures	$153.0	$214.8	$317.4	$337.0	$172.0	$427.2	$411.6	$387.8	$388.7	$381.4	$399.3
Net Working Cap/Sales	14.1%	11.8%	11.9%	13.0%	11.4%	10.3%	10.3%	10.3%	10.3%	10.3%	10.3%

FINANSEER
(Data in Millions)
(August-July)

	History 1985	History 1986	History 1987	History 1988	History 1989	Forecast 1990	Forecast 1991	Forecast 1992	Forecast 1993	Forecast 1994	5-Year Summary
Free Cash Flow											Cumulative
NOPAT	$255.4	$291.7	$317.2	$318.9	$262.7	$534.7	$541.9	$584.1	$637.1	$693.8	$2,991.6
Increase in Capital(I)	103.3	64.1	243.7	695.3	326.3	238.0	288.0	251.8	238.9	219.1	1,235.7
Free Cash Flow	152.1	227.6	73.6	(376.5)	(63.6)	296.7	253.9	332.3	398.3	474.7	1,755.9
Invest Rate (I/NOPAT)	40.4%	22.0%	76.8%	218.1%	124.2%	44.5%	53.1%	43.1%	37.5%	31.6%	41.3%
Internal Performance											Average
NOPAT/Beg Capital r	14.7%	15.8%	16.6%	14.8%	9.2%	16.9%	15.9%	15.8%	16.1%	16.6%	16.2%
Wtd Avg Cap Cost c*	13.0%	11.2%	11.8%	12.5%	11.6%	11.6%	11.6%	11.6%	11.6%	11.6%	11.6%
Index r/c*	1.13	1.41	1.41	1.18	0.80	1.46	1.37	1.37	1.39	1.43	1.40
Spread r-c*	1.7%	4.6%	4.8%	2.3%	-2.3%	5.3%	4.3%	4.2%	4.6%	5.0%	4.7%
x Beginning Capital	$1,739.7	$1,843.0	$1,907.1	$2,150.8	$2,846.1	$3,172.4	$3,410.4	$3,698.4	$3,950.2	$4,189.1	$3,684.1
Economic Value Added	29.4	84.9	91.8	49.2	(66.3)	168.0	147.7	156.6	180.5	209.5	172.5
Change in EVA	(19.9)	55.6	6.9	(42.7)	(115.5)	234.3	(20.3)	8.9	23.9	29.0	55.2

c* based upon target Debt/Capital = 25%.

- Sales are projected to grow at a 10% rate (except in the first year, because I wanted to precisely match the *Value Line* estimate for 1990), in line with the 9.8% average sales growth rate of the prior decade.

- Profit margin (measured this time by NOPBT, not EBDIT, to sales) reverses its historic slide. As implied by the *Value Line* estimates, it is forecast to be 10.8% to 10.9% versus a prior 10-year average of 10.1%.

- The effective cash tax rate on operating profits is projected to be well below the marginal corporate income tax rate in 1990 for two reasons. First, Campbell wrote down operations in fiscal 1989 and thereby incurred a $344 million charge against earnings, an expense that will become tax-deductible in fiscal 1990. Second, according to *Value Line,* Campbell plans to step up its capital spending in 1990, a decision that will generate additional accelerated depreciation charges to defer taxes. Thereafter, the effective cash tax rate rises to a more normal level as capital spending, and the associated deferral of taxes, slows.

- The turnover rate of capital, steady at two times in the first three forecast years, improves in 1993 and 1994 as plant utilization rates increase. Working capital utilization also is expected to become more efficient.

This base case forecast produces a strong, positive free cash flow. Instead of investing 90% of NOPAT as in the past, Campbell is projected to plow back just about 40% of its after-tax operating profits. Of greater significance, Campbell's rate of return is expected to rise to 16.5%, an improvement in profitability that teams up with an expanding capital base to produce a positive and generally improving EVA.

Campbell's 11.6% cost of capital is based upon the assumption that management will continue to employ a debt to capital ratio of 25% as a target. Campbell's c, or cost of capital for business risk, is 12.8%, a 4.5% premium over the 8.3% average yield to maturity on long-term government bonds prevailing during June 1989. Taking into account the tax benefit of adopting a 25% target debt ratio at a 38% corporate marginal income tax rate, c drops to a c^*, or weighted average cost of capital, of 11.6%.

$$c^* = c\ (1-t\ \times\frac{\text{debt}}{\text{capital}})$$

$$11.6\% = 12.8\%\ (1-38\%\ \times\ 25\%)$$

IIIb. The Base Case (Valuation)

A valuation of the base case forecast is given in exhibit 15.8 The present value of projected EVA is $1.82 billion, representing a 54% premium over the $3.35 billion capital base installed at the end of fiscal 1989 (as adjusted for a half-year's rate of interest).

To solve for the share value implied by the forecast, the value of assets not included in capital, i.e., marketable securities ($84.8 million) and construction in progress ($162.2 million), are added, and debt and leases ($900.7 million), other liabilities ($19.6 million), and minority interest ($54.9 million) are subtracted. The implied common equity value is $4.44 billion, or $34.30 per share (130 million shares are outstanding, net of treasury stock). Absent takeover speculation, this appears to be a reasonable valuation for Campbell in light of the company's stock market performance up until the time of John Dorrance's death and the company's operating performance since that time.

The base case projection, the 25% target capital structure, and the $34.30 common stock valuation together represent one of many possibilities for Campbell. It will now be our challenge to search for more valuable alternative business strategies and financial structures that also take into account the dissident shareholders' desire for liquidity. Before diving in, however, let's take a moment to scrutinize Ralston Purina, which is one of Campbell's business peers and a company that has successfully changed the focus and structure of its operations to the betterment of market value.

IV. Comparison with a Winner

Over the period from 1981 to 1988, Ralston Purina added $4.4 billion to the market value of its capital employed. Under the leadership of Chairman and CEO William P. Stiritz, Ralston was

Exhibit 15.8 Campbell Soup Base Case: Target D/Cap = 25%
Economic Value Added Valuation (Dollars in Millions)

Year	(1) Return on Capital r	(2) Wtd Avg Cap Cost c*	(3)=(1)-(2) Perform Spread r-c*	(4) Beginning Capital	(5)=(3)x(4) EVA	(6) Present Value Factor	(7)=(5)x(6) Present Value of EVA	A.
1990	16.9%	11.6%	5.3%	$3,172.4	$168.0	0.947	$159.1	
1991	15.9%	11.6%	4.3%	3,410.4	147.7	0.849	125.3	
1992	15.8%	11.6%	4.2%	3,698.4	156.6	0.761	119.1	
1993	16.1%	11.6%	4.6%	3,950.2	180.5	0.682	123.1	
1994	16.6%	11.6%	5.0%	4,189.1	209.5	0.611	128.1	
1995 &							B.	
Beyond	16.6%	11.6%	5.0%	4,408.1	220.5	5.288	1,166.0	

Premium (Discount)	$1,820.8
+ Capital	C. 3,350.7
Intrinsic Operating Value	$5,171.5
+ Marketable Securities	84.8
+ Construction in Progress	162.2
Intrinsic Total Value	$5,418.5
- Total Debt & Leases	900.7
- Other Liabilities	19.6
- Minority Interest	54.9
Intrinsic Common Equity Value	$4,443.3
Number of Shares Outstanding	129.6
Intrinsic Share Value	$34.29
	======

A. EVA discounted from mid-year.
B. Present value of $1 in perpetuity beginning in 1995.
C. Beginning Capital of $3,172.4 adjusted for mid-year discounting by
    multiplying by (1+c*)**.5, where c* = 11.6% in the first forecast period.

transformed through a series of interrelated and mutually reinforcing strategies and actions, including (exhibits 15.9 and 15.10):

- Focusing upon cash flow and economic returns as the paramount corporate goal, even when doing so penalized near-
  term accounting results
- Selling off a whole series of unrelated and underperforming
  assets and businesses to others better able to increase their
  value
- Making selective acquisitions of sizable businesses in which
  the company's consumer marketing and management skills
  could be leveraged and then working to build up the value
  of those businesses
- Decentralizing management responsibility and accountability into the units and making corporate staff functions into
  service businesses that are subjected to outside competition
  where possible
- Leveraging up the balance sheet and aggressively buying
  back stock in the open market in order to reduce the cost of
  capital

Ralston's Financial Results.   Reconfiguring its business portfolio and changing its management and financial structures paid
Ralston handsome dividends (exhibit 15.11 presents the absolute
dollar results and in exhibit 15.12 the results are standardized).
Though overall sales growth over the past decade was much
slower than it was for the peer group (only 3.5% per annum
versus 8.5%), Ralston did manage a far greater increase in its
EVA. From breakeven in the early 80s, Ralston's standardized
EVA climbed to over $20 in the most recent 2 years, the result of
a rate of return on capital that ascended to over 20%, a precipi-
tous drop in the weighted average cost of capital brought about
by an intentional strategy of leveraging the balance sheet and a
near doubling of the company's capital base.

Leverage Strategy.   Continuing a policy begun in 1982, over
just the most recent 5 years Ralston bought back 29 million of its
common shares on the open market, or a third of the potential
shares outstanding, for about $1.8 billion. Combined with the

---

Exhibit 15.9   Ralston Purina:
Statement of Objectives, Strategy, and Structure

Our objective is to effectively manage the assets entrusted to us for the benefit of the shareholder. Our strategy to do this has not changed—that is, to build on the strengths of our primary businesses, redeploy unproductive assets, and to add to our strength by acquiring businesses where management can add value. Increasing the size of the company is not an objective unless it makes a positive contribution to value.

We are also committed to successful innovation, not only in terms of new product development, which is the lifeblood of the Company, but also in terms of finding better ways to manage our businesses.

> William P. Stiritz
> Chairman and Chief Executive Officer
> Letter to Shareholders November 22, 1985

We believe that a *decentralized organization structure* [italics added] is the most rational way to manage the corporation. Our operating units are sized to stand alone and each has the scale required to compete in its respective market. All of our operating units are strong cash providers; high achievers do not subsidize underperformers.

We maintain a corporate staff which is limited in size and scope. Most of the staff functions that support the operations are organized as independent service businesses and, where possible, subjected to outside competition. Managers are rewarded for the quality and value of services provided, not for the size of their departments. The intent is to constrain bureaucratic behavior and keep overhead costs low.

We try to keep the operating environment simple and straightforward. We keep management layers to a minimum—there are no group officers or staff and no management committee of consequence. As a result, the lines of communication throughout the company are short. Moreover, we do not impose a standardized regimen of management systems and processes upon the operating companies. In this way we try to avoid the type of organization structure that focuses excessively on control in favor of one that encourages creative thinking and innovation.

Within a flexible organization structure our only rigid bias is to *manage the business for economic rather than accounting rates of return* [italics added]. At times this focus on cash generation penalizes the more generally accepted, although in the view of many, outdated measures of corporate performance. It is not coincidental that we have been a reliable and strong generator of excess cash in recent years.

> William P. Stiritz
> Chairman and Chief Executive Officer Letter to Shareholders
> November 18, 1988

Exhibit 15.10   The Restructuring of Ralston Purina

---

*Ralston Purina Company, founded in 1894, is the world's largest produ-
cer of dry dog and dry and soft-moist cat foods. Other consumer products
include cereal and canned tuna. The Company is also the world's largest
producer of commercial feed for livestock and poultry. The Company
operates a chain of fast-service restaurants. It is also a major producer
of isolated soy protein* [italics added].

   1984 Ralston Purina Company Annual Report to Shareholders

Starting with that potpourri, management almost completely over-
hauled Ralston's business portfolio over the next 5 years, as follows.

Streamlining

Sep 1984   Sold Foodservice Division.

Oct 1984   Reduced ownership in Keystone Colorado resort from
            100% to 50% via a leveraged limited partnership, though
            Ralston continues as the general partner and manager.

1/2/85   Sold soybean processing operations, a commodity busi-
            ness.

7/1/84   Closed San Diego tuna cannery, $19.9 million after-tax
            charge.

1985   Wrote down tuna cannery and related operations in Ecua-
            dor and tuna boats and related operations for a loss of
            $32.3 million, or $24.5 million after taxes.

11/15/88   Sold Van Camp Seafood (Chicken of the Sea tuna) for
            $260 million, a gain of $70.2 million after taxes.

10/21/85   Sold the 800-restaurant Jack-in-the-Box chain to Food-
            maker, an LBO company formed by Jack-in-the-Box
            management and Gibbons Green van Amerongen, for
            $450 million, a gain of $113.4 million, or $68.2 million
            after taxes. The payment included a $34.7 million junior
            subordinated note, and Ralston retained 20% of the eq-
            uity in the LBO.

Sep 1986   Sold remaining 20% equity interest and junior subor-
            dinated note back to Foodmaker for $55 million, a gain
            of $35.4 million after taxes.

Oct 1986   Sold domestic animal-feed-producing subsidiary to Brit-
            ish Petroleum (the world's largest such supplier) for $545
            million, an after-tax gain of $209.3 million.

Exhibit 15.10 continued

Building and Rationalizing

10/9/84	Acquired Continental Baking, the largest baker in the United States, from ITT for $475 million.
FYE 88	Continental Baking purchased a large, state-of-the-art bakery in Philadelphia from Acme Markets, and subsequently closed bakeries in Norristown, Pa., and Washington, D.C., in a consolidation move.
4/30/86	Acquired Eveready Battery, the world's largest such concern, for $1.415 billion from Union Carbide.
1/18/89	Acquired Cofinea, a French-based battery products company, for $124.0 million.
1989	Closed or restructured certain battery, bakery, and administrative operations, taking a $31.4 million write-down, or $19.5 million after taxes.
7/12/86	Acquired Drake Bakeries for $115 million from Borden.
10/27/87	Sold Drake Bakeries to a leveraged management buy-out for $176 million, an after-tax gain of $43 million, because of an antitrust suit that sought to prohibit Ralston from merging the operations of Drake with those of Continental Baking.
1987	Acquired Benco Pet Foods.
11/3/89	Acquired Beechnut, the second largest manufacturer of baby food in the United States with sales of about $150 million, from Nestlé.

Financial Maneuverings

FYE 85	Bought 5.4 million common shares for $270 million.
FYE 86	Bought 7.6 million common shares for $265 million.
FYE 87	Bought 6.5 million common shares for $490 million.
FYE 88	Bought 2.6 million common shares for $180 million.
FYE 89	Bought 6.9 million common shares for $550 million.
2/1/89	Issued $500 million of convertible preferred stock to a leveraged ESOP.

Exhibit 15.11 Ralston Purina Co.: Summary of Operating Performance
(Dollars in Millions)

(Oct-Sep)	1980	1981	1982	1983	1984	1985	1986	1987	1988	1989	10 year Summary Growth/Avg
Operating Results											
Sales	$4,886.0	$5,224.7	$4,802.6	$4,872.4	$4,980.1	$5,863.9	$5,514.6	$5,868.0	$5,875.9	$6,658.3	3.5%
Sales Growth	6.2%	6.9%	-8.1%	1.5%	2.2%	17.7%	-6.0%	6.4%	0.1%	13.3%	4.0%
NOPBT	$352.3	$398.6	$396.9	$506.2	$524.3	$615.4	$712.1	$746.9	$883.1	$879.9	10.7%
Pct. of Sales	7.2%	7.6%	8.3%	10.4%	10.5%	10.5%	12.9%	12.7%	15.0%	13.2%	10.8%
NOPAT	$207.0	$233.7	$173.5	$323.8	$291.6	$324.8	$356.2	$418.9	$581.0	$587.7	12.3%
Oper. Cash Tax Rate	41%	41%	56%	36%	44%	47%	50%	44%	34%	33%	43%
Capital	$1,757.1	$1,873.2	$1,772.5	$1,658.0	$1,649.1	$2,083.1	$3,234.9	$2,801.9	$2,926.6	$3,226.2	7.0%
Sales/Beg Capital	3.2x	3.0x	2.6x	2.7x	3.0x	3.6x	2.6x	1.8x	2.1x	2.3x	2.7x
Net Working Cap/Sales	9.0%	8.3%	5.5%	4.4%	5.0%	1.5%	5.8%	5.7%	8.4%	8.0%	6.2%

Exhibit 15.11 continued

(Oct-Sep)	1980	1981	1982	1983	1984	1985	1986	1987	1988	1989	10 year Summary
FCF & Leverage											Cumulative
NOPAT	$207.0	$233.7	$173.5	$323.8	$291.6	$324.8	$356.2	$418.9	$581.0	$587.7	$3,498.4
Increase in Capital(I)	237.1	116.1	(100.7)	(114.5)	(8.9)	434.0	1,151.8	(433.0)	124.7	299.6	1,706.2
Free Cash Flow	(30.1)	117.6	274.2	438.3	300.5	(109.2)	(795.6)	851.9	456.4	288.1	1,792.1
Debt/Total Capital	32%	28%	28%	23%	23%	45%	60%	57%	54%	61%	41%
Internal Performance											Average
NOPAT/Beg Capital r	13.6%	13.3%	9.3%	18.3%	17.6%	19.7%	17.1%	12.9%	20.7%	20.1%	16.3%
Wtd Avg Cap Cost c*	12.4%	14.4%	13.9%	12.8%	13.9%	11.2%	8.6%	9.0%	9.3%	9.2%	11.5%
Spread r-c*	1.2%	-1.1%	-4.6%	5.5%	3.6%	8.5%	8.5%	4.0%	11.4%	10.9%	4.8%
x Beginning Capital	$1,520.0	$1,757.1	$1,873.2	$1,772.5	$1,658.0	$1,649.1	$2,083.1	$3,234.9	$2,801.9	$2,926.6	$2,127.6
Economic Value Added	$18.3	($18.6)	($87.0)	$97.6	$60.5	$139.6	$177.9	$128.1	$320.2	$317.6	$115.4
External Performance											Growth/Avg
Year End Share Price	$11.63	$10.50	$14.50	$24.75	$31.50	$45.13	$63.00	$80.88	$80.13	$88.88	25.4%
Adj Book Value Per Shr	12.11	13.17	13.27	14.69	15.26	15.60	17.91	15.77	18.95	18.66	4.9%
Price - Adj Book	($0.48)	($2.67)	$1.23	$10.06	$16.24	$29.53	$45.09	$65.11	$61.17	$70.22	$29.55
x No. Shares Outst'g	107.9	107.9	101.5	95.1	86.4	80.2	76.2	70.2	69.2	61.6	85.6
Market Value Added	($52.0)	($288.7)	$124.6	$956.4	$1,402.7	$2,367.7	$3,437.5	$4,568.4	$4,233.1	$4,325.3	$2,107.5

Exhibit 15.12 Ralston Purina Co.: Summary of Operating Performance
(Scaled to 1980 Beginning Capital = $100)

(Oct-Sep)	1980	1981	1982	1983	1984	1985	1986	1987	1988	1989	10 year Summary Growth/Avg	
Operating Results												
Sales	321.5	343.7	316.0	320.6	327.6	385.8	362.8	386.1	386.6	438.1	3.5%	
Sales Growth	6.2%	6.9%	-8.1%	1.5%	2.2%	17.7%	-6.0%	6.4%	0.1%	13.3%	4.0%	
NOPBT	23.2	26.2	26.1	33.3	34.5	40.5	46.9	49.1	58.1	57.9	10.7%	
Pct. of Sales	7.2%	7.6%	8.3%	10.4%	10.5%	10.5%	12.9%	12.7%	15.0%	13.2%	10.8%	
NOPAT	13.6	15.4	11.4	21.3	19.2	21.4	23.4	27.6	38.2	38.7	12.3%	
Oper. Cash Tax Rate	41%	41%	56%	36%	44%	47%	50%	44%	34%	33%	43%	
Capital	115.6	123.2	116.6	109.1	108.5	137.0	212.8	184.3	192.5	212.3	7.0%	
Sales/Beg Capital	3.2x	3.0x	2.6x	2.7x	3.0x	3.6x	2.6x	1.8x	2.1x	2.3x	2.7x	
Net Working Cap/Sales	9.0%	8.3%	5.5%	4.4%	5.0%	1.5%	5.8%	5.7%	8.4%	8.0%	6.2%	

Exhibit 15.12 continued

(Oct-Sep)	1980	1981	1982	1983	1984	1985	1986	1987	1988	1989	10 year Summary
FCF & Leverage											Cumulative
NOPAT	13.6	15.4	11.4	21.3	19.2	21.4	23.4	27.6	38.2	38.7	230.2
Increase in Capital(I)	15.6	7.6	(6.6)	(7.5)	(0.6)	28.6	75.8	(28.5)	8.2	19.7	112.3
Free Cash Flow	(2.0)	7.7	18.0	28.8	19.8	(7.2)	(52.3)	56.0	30.0	19.0	117.9
Debt/Total Capital	32%	28%	28%	23%	23%	45%	60%	57%	54%	61%	41%
Internal Performance											Average
NOPAT/Beg Capital r	13.6%	13.3%	9.3%	18.3%	17.6%	19.7%	17.1%	12.9%	20.7%	20.1%	16.3%
Wtd Avg Cap Cost c*	12.4%	14.4%	13.9%	12.8%	13.9%	11.2%	8.6%	9.0%	9.3%	9.2%	11.5%
Spread r-c*	1.2%	-1.1%	-4.6%	5.5%	3.6%	8.5%	8.5%	4.0%	11.4%	10.9%	4.8%
x Beginning Capital	100.0	115.6	123.2	116.6	109.1	108.5	137.0	212.8	184.3	192.5	140.0
Economic Value Added	1.2	(1.2)	(5.7)	6.4	4.0	9.2	11.7	8.4	21.1	20.9	7.6
External Performance											Growth/Avg
Year End Share Price	$11.63	$10.50	$14.50	$24.75	$31.50	$45.13	$63.00	$80.88	$80.13	$88.88	25.4%
Adj Book Value Per Shr	12.11	13.17	13.27	14.69	15.26	15.60	17.91	15.77	18.95	18.66	4.9%
Price - Adj Book	($0.48)	($2.67)	$1.23	$10.06	$16.24	$29.53	$45.09	$65.11	$61.17	$70.22	$29.55
x No. Shares Outst'g	6.1	6.1	5.8	5.4	4.9	4.6	4.3	4.0	3.9	3.5	4.9
Market Value Added	(3.0)	(16.4)	7.1	54.4	79.8	134.8	195.6	260.0	240.9	246.2	119.9

policy of using debt to finance acquisitions, the share repurchases raised Ralston's ratio of total debt to total capital from about 30% in the early 80s to nearly 60% over the past 4 years. As a result of this intentional financial policy shift, Ralston's bond rating was marked down from Aa3 to Baa1 by Moody's and from AA to A— by Standard & Poor's. Ralston professed a justifiable lack of concern. "Our feeling is that the change in rating isn't due to any weakness in the company; we don't see it as a big deal," said a company spokesman after one of the many downgrades.[5]

Cost of Capital. Far from a cause for concern, the increase in leverage reduced Ralston's overall financing cost. Doubling the use of debt from 30% to 60% of capital brought down the weighted average cost of capital from 12.5% to 10.9% for the 1989 fiscal year.

$$c^* = c \ (1 - t \times \frac{\text{debt}}{\text{capital}})$$

Early 80s Policy

$$12.5\% = 14.1\% \ (1 - 38\% \times 30\%)$$

Late 80s Policy

$$10.9\% = 14.1\% \ (1 - 38\% \times 60\%)$$

Ralston can justify its aggressive debt target because its diverse operations produce attractive and stable returns and cash flows. But then, so do Campbell's, if only to a lesser extent.

Market Value Added. Ralston's MVA, the market mirror of EVA, increased from breakeven to about $250 in standardized terms, almost exactly the same as the level attained by the food composite and double that reached by Campbell before the takeover fever hit the company (exhibit 15.13).

The Opportunity. In contrast to Ralston's focused, large-scale, and highly decentralized operations, Campbell's business activi-

[5]"Ralston's Ratings on $750 Million Debt Are Lowered by S&P," *The Wall Street Journal,* July 15, 1985.

Exhibit 15.13   Storm Warnings

Ralston's strategy of leverage, decentralization, and a focus on value-added consumer products has been a success. But dark clouds may be forming on the horizon. Ralston's stock price, a sensitive barometer of coming corporate performance, has not moved much over the last 3 years. The real improvement in the company's market value occurred over the prior 6 years, from fiscal 1981 to 1987. That suggests that the increase in Ralston's market value this past decade may have had as much, if not more, to do with the decision to exit businesses in which Ralston lacked a competitive advantage as it did to improving the performance of newly acquired ones. If that is the case, any further exceptional increases in market value must come from the hard task of making businesses that have become valuable even more valuable, if that is possible, or acquiring still more businesses and attempting to perform the same transforming magic. The recent acquisition of Beechnut, the baby food concern, suggests that Ralston is determined to try its hand at improving yet another business. If so, Ralston will grow larger and still more complex, thereby straining the company's ability to manage a portfolio of nonoverlapping operations.

Therefore, at this juncture it might be beneficial for Ralston to adopt a buy, build, and harvest strategy. Once the acquired units have been repaired and revitalized, with strong management, systems, and incentives in place, Ralston should dispose of them through a sale to a value-adding merger partner, or, if such an opportunity does not present itself, spin them off into separate, public companies.

Related to this strategy, Ralston could decentralize its debt into the individual business units, preferably as they are acquired or later on through an internal recapitalization. The decentralization of debt into the units would spread out the company's financial risk. Furthermore, it would be wholly consistent with Ralston's espoused philosophy of management decentralization. It would put the onus on operating people to cover the cost of capital with the cash flows generated in their units, and it would facilitate the process of making the managers of individual business units into owners, a powerful incentive.

So far, Ralston's strategy seems to have worked well without buy, build, and harvest and the decentralization of debt. That's so far. As the company continues to grow and to increase in complexity, however, the multiplying management challenges may be simplified by making these two changes.

ties are spread over too vast an array of unrelated food products, are burdened by a thicket of bureaucratic entanglements and are overly vertically integrated (see exhibit 15.14).

Though it is still called The Campbell Soup Company, its name belies its business. Campbell's food products go well beyond just soup to include sauces, spaghetti, frozen foods, bakery goods, canned goods, condiments, juices, salads, seafoods, poultry, chocolates, and chewing gum. Starting from condensed soups, a marvelous core business, Campbell's growth over its long history has been a model of reinvestment risk, cross-subsidization, and dilettantism. At present, the company is largely unfocused and many of its product offerings lack the scale to possess a meaningful competitive advantage.

Given the small size and unrelated nature of many of the company's acquisitions, a dense bureaucracy has grown up to oversee the sprawling empire. The company's four divisions divide into groups which in turn are comprised of business units, with each layer in the hierarchy outfitted with its own contingent of management and staff.

Reminiscent of Henry Ford's River Rouge plant, a manufacturing complex so completely vertically integrated that iron ore would be hauled in one end and shiny black automobiles would drive out the other, Campbell manufactures most of the cans for its soup and a substantial portion of the plastic and paper containers for its frozen foods. Sensible as a strategy to minimize costs in settled markets, vertical integration becomes uneconomic in times of rapid technological changes and shifting consumer tastes. With packaging technology undergoing rapid change, with two-piece cans replacing three-piece ones, and with aluminum and plastics substituting for steel, to say nothing of the competitive turmoil in the soup and frozen food business, Campbell's extreme vertical integration may be more a hindrance than a help at this point.

Va. The New Focus Plan (Projection)

Ralston Purina points the way to a new and potentially more valuable course of action for Campbell's. A focus plan might consist of pruning overlapping product lines, disposing of periph-

---

Exhibit 15.14   Campbell's Business Activities

The principal brands and products manufactured and sold by the company are as follows:

United States

Campbell's	Soups, ready-to-serve canned entrees, ketchup, bean products, tomato juice
Home Cookin'	Soups
Franco-American	Spaghetti, ravioli and macaroni products, and gravies
Prego	Spaghetti sauce
Swanson	Frozen prepared foods, canned poultry and meat products
Le Menu	Premium frozen dinners
Great Starts	Frozen breakfasts
Pepperidge Farm	Bakery goods
V-8	Vegetable juice
Juice Bowl	Fruit juices
Godiva	Chocolates
Barringer's	Chocolates
Vlasic	Pickles, peppers, relishes, sauerkraut, specialty items
Milwaukee's	Pickles
Durkee	Olives and cherries
Early California	Olives
Campbell's Fresh	Mushrooms
Mrs. Kinser's	Refrigerated salads
Mrs. Giles	Refrigerated salads
Swiss Maid	Refrigerated salads
Marie's	Salad dressing
Win Schuler	Cheese spreads, melba rounds, salad dressing
Mrs. Paul's	Frozen seafood and vegetables
Domsea	Seafood
Plump & Juicy	Frozen poultry
Bounty	Canned entrees, canned chili, and meat products
Open Pit	Barbecue sauce

Foreign

Granny's	Semicondensed soups
Lacroix	Soups, patés, sauces
La Forest Perigord	Gourmet patés
Freshbake	Frozen convenience foods
Beeck	Premium refrigerated foods
Groko	Frozen vegetables, potato croquettes
Target	Canned food
Swift	Canned food
Exeter	Canned meat products
Unger	Formulated meat products
Casera	Canned beans, tomato sauce, olive oil
Gattuso	Pasta products, olives, oils, tomato sauces, pickles, canned tomatoes
Betis	Olive oil
Devos-Lemmens	Pickles, sauces, mustard, mayonnaise
Imperial	Flour products
Lazzaroni	Premium biscuits
Leo	Confectionery products
Borsari	Seasonal (holiday) cakes
NOBO	Cookies
Delacre	Cookies, pastries, chocolates
Lutti	Chocolates
Lamy	Chocolates
Kwatta	Chocolate spread
Tubble Gum	Chewing Gum

The company's operations are managed by four major divisions: Campbell USA, Pepperidge Farm, Campbell Enterprises, and Campbell International. Within each there are groups and business units; as an example, within Campbell USA the major groups are Soups, Convenience Meals, Groceries, Condiments, and Seafood. In the U.S. the company manufactures most of the metal containers for its canned products. It also manufactures substantial quantities of plastic containers and some paper containers for its frozen products.

The company operates 83 retail bakery thrift stores throughout the country; it also operates 69 retail candy stores in the U.S. and Europe. From its Clinton, Connecticut facility, the company offers specialty foods for sale by direct mail.

Source: *Moody's Industrial Manual* (1989 edition)

eral lines of business, vertically deintegrating to a certain extent, reorganizing the company around sizable, focused operating units, and giving managers the autonomy, responsibility, and incentive to create value, among other things. Without being any more specific than that (after all, this is only an example), a hypothetical outcome of these actions is presented in exhibit 15.15.

The first effect of implementing such a focus plan would be to reduce top-line growth. In this case, sales are projected to grow at a rate of only 8% per annum, off from the 10% rate projected in the base case. Sales reach a level of $8.33 billion in fiscal 1994 versus $9.15 billion in the base case, a difference of about $820 million, or 9%. The operating profit margin is projected to dip early on, reflecting the expense of rationalizing and reorganizing. (Cash expenses only; mere bookkeeping write-offs are ignored in this analysis.) Eventually, however, the margin widens as efficiencies are realized. Higher capacity utilization, flowing from a consolidation of production and the sale or shuttering of low-volume businesses, plus greater working capital efficiency brought about by a streamlining of product lines, increases capital turnover, in the example, up to a level of 2.3 to 2.4 times.

The new focus plan produces a greater free cash flow from operations than was previously projected. Net new investment (I) uses up only 14% of NOPAT (vs. 40% in the base case), leaving a cumulative free cash flow of $2.4 billion (vs. $1.75 billion) over the 5-year forecast. The surplus cash enhances the company's capacity to borrow and then to amortize debt, a coincidental benefit that makes the strategy doubly rewarding.

Though suffering in comparison with the base case for the first 2 years, Campbell's rate of return and EVA roar ahead in the third year out, never to look back. Such is the power of projecting.

Vb. The New Focus Plan (Valuation)

The valuation of The Campbell Soup Company under the hypothetical focus plan is given in exhibit 15.16. The present value of projected EVA is now $2.22 billion versus $1.82 billion before. The nearly $400 million difference is the value to be gained by

Exhibit 15.15 Campbell Soup Focus Scenario:
Summary of Operating Performance (Dollars in Millions)

FINANSEER (Data in Millions) (August-July)	History 1985	History 1986	History 1987	History 1988	History 1989	Forecast 1990	Forecast 1991	Forecast 1992	Forecast 1993	Forecast 1994	5-Year Summary
											Growth/Avg
Operating Results											
Sales	$3,988.7	$4,378.7	$4,490.4	$4,868.9	$5,672.1	$6,125.9	$6,615.9	$7,145.2	$7,716.8	$8,334.2	8.0%
Sales Growth	9.1%	9.8%	2.6%	8.4%	16.5%	8.0%	8.0%	8.0%	8.0%	8.0%	8.0%
NOPBT	$369.6	$424.4	$443.8	$457.7	$521.9	$582.1	$685.4	$815.3	$920.2	$995.0	14.3%
Percent of Sales	9.3%	9.7%	9.9%	9.4%	9.2%	9.5%	10.4%	11.4%	11.9%	11.9%	11.0%
NOPAT	$255.4	$291.7	$317.2	$318.9	$262.7	$439.0	$478.6	$561.5	$631.6	$683.6	11.7%
Oper. Cash Tax Rate	31%	31%	29%	30%	50%	25%	30%	31%	31%	31%	30%
Capital	$1,843.0	$1,907.1	$2,150.8	$2,846.1	$3,172.4	$3,130.1	$3,226.6	$3,331.5	$3,442.7	$3,560.5	3.3%
Sales/Beg Capital	2.3	2.4	2.4	2.3	2.0	1.9	2.1	2.2	2.3	2.4	2.2
PPE Expenditures	$153.0	$214.8	$317.4	$337.0	$172.0	$174.6	$248.2	$268.1	$289.5	$312.7	$258.6
Net Working Cap/Sales	14.1%	11.8%	11.9%	13.0%	11.4%	10.1%	9.8%	9.4%	9.1%	8.8%	9.4%

Exhibit 15.15   continued

FINANSEER

(Data in Millions) (August-July)	History 1985	History 1986	History 1987	History 1988	History 1989	Forecast 1990	Forecast 1991	Forecast 1992	Forecast 1993	Forecast 1994	5-Year Summary
Free Cash Flow											Cumulative
NOPAT	$255.4	$291.7	$317.2	$318.9	$262.7	$439.0	$478.6	$561.5	$631.6	$683.6	$2,794.3
Increase in Capital(I)	103.3	64.1	243.7	695.3	326.3	(42.3)	96.5	104.9	111.2	117.8	388.2
Free Cash Flow	152.1	227.6	73.6	(376.5)	(63.6)	481.3	382.1	456.6	520.4	565.8	2,406.1
Invest Rate (I/NOPAT)	40.4%	22.0%	76.8%	218.1%	124.2%	-9.6%	20.2%	18.7%	17.6%	17.2%	13.9%
Internal Performance											Average
NOPAT/Beg Capital r	14.7%	15.8%	16.6%	14.8%	9.2%	13.8%	15.3%	17.4%	19.0%	19.9%	17.1%
Wtd Avg Cap Cost c*	13.0%	11.2%	11.8%	12.5%	11.6%	11.6%	11.6%	11.6%	11.6%	11.6%	11.6%
Index r/c*	1.13	1.41	1.41	1.18	0.80	1.20	1.32	1.51	1.64	1.72	1.48
Spread r-c*	1.7%	4.6%	4.8%	2.3%	-2.3%	2.3%	3.7%	5.8%	7.4%	8.3%	5.5%
x Beginning Capital	$1,739.7	$1,843.0	$1,907.1	$2,150.8	$2,846.1	$3,172.4	$3,130.1	$3,226.6	$3,331.5	$3,442.7	$3,260.7
Economic Value Added	29.4	84.9	91.8	49.2	(66.3)	72.3	116.8	188.5	246.5	285.7	182.0
Change in EVA	(19.9)	55.6	6.9	(42.7)	(115.5)	138.6	44.4	71.8	58.0	39.1	70.4

c* based upon target Debt/Capital = 25%.

Exhibit 15.16   Campbell Soup Focus Case: Target D/Cap = 25%
Economic Value Added Valuation (Dollars in Millions)

Year	(1) Return on Capital r	(2) Wtd Avg Cap Cost c*	(3)=(1)-(2) Perform Spread r-c*	(4) Beginning Capital	(5)=(3)x(4) EVA	(6) Present Value Factor	(7)=(5)x(6) Present A. Value of EVA
1990	13.8%	11.6%	2.3%	$3,172.4	$72.3	0.947	$68.5
1991	15.3%	11.6%	3.7%	3,130.1	116.8	0.849	99.1
1992	17.4%	11.6%	5.8%	3,226.6	188.5	0.761	143.4
1993	19.0%	11.6%	7.4%	3,331.5	246.5	0.682	168.1
1994	19.9%	11.6%	8.3%	3,442.7	285.7	0.611	174.6
1995 &							B.
Beyond	19.9%	11.6%	8.3%	3,560.5	295.5	5.288	1,562.4

Premium (Discount)	$2,216.1
+ Capital	C. 3,350.7
Intrinsic Operating Value	$5,566.8
+ Marketable Securities	84.8
+ Construction in Progress	162.2
Intrinsic Total Value	$5,813.8
- Total Debt & Leases	900.7
- Other Liabilities	19.6
- Minority Interest	54.9
Intrinsic Common Equity Value	$4,838.6
Number of Shares Outstanding	129.6
Intrinsic Share Value	$37.34

A. EVA discounted from mid-year.

B. Present value of $1 in perpetuity beginning in 1995.

C. Beginning Capital of $3,172.4 adjusted for mid-year discounting by
   multiplying by $(1+c*)^{**}.5$, where c* = 11.6% in the first forecast period.

pursuing the focus plan instead of the base business strategy. If the base and focus projections were realistic representations of two alternative courses of action, management should choose the focus plan despite the fact that it leads to sharply lower sales over the indefinite future and produces lower profits and returns in the first 2 years. It creates more value.

Here, then, is the benefit of value planning. It is possible to make better business decisions when, instead of scrutinizing any of the imperfect accounting or strategic proxies or relying upon gut instinct, the value of different courses of action is simulated.

Putting the potential value-planning gain in terms of the benefit to the shareholders, the implied common share price is $37.34 with the focus plan, or about 10% more than the $34.29 base case share value. That the gain is not relatively larger is testimony to my extreme conservatism in forecasting the benefits of implementing a focus plan.

VI. The *Static* Use of Debt

Having now completed, if only illustratively, the value-planning process for Campbell,[6] the next challenge is to identify an appropriate financial structure for the company and its business units. In this section the use of debt will be approached from a static perspective, that is, in terms of an optimal capital structure, deferring until the next and final section a consideration of the possible dynamic uses of debt. Also, for the sake of simplicity, we will concentrate on the corporate, or centralized use of debt, instead of the more powerful *decentralized* use of debt, which is what I really advocate.

A static analysis examines the trade-off of debt and equity by assuming that a relatively fixed blend of the two financing forms will be adopted as a target capital structure. Another way to express such a financial policy is in terms of a bond-rating objective, which, in turn, requires that certain financial conditions and ratios be maintained.

---

[6]In practice, a greater number of potential alternatives would be explored in greater depth, and ideally not just at the corporate level, but preferably at the level of the individual business units—a "bottoms-up" as opposed to "tops-down" approach.

Assessing Campbell's Current Bond Rating. At present, Campbell's overriding financial policy objective appears to be to maintain its Aaa rating from Moody's (Campbell is not rated by Standard & Poor's). That is a false god to worship in any event, but particularly so when the company already has lost the credit quality of a Aaa company.

An indication of Campbell's true credit standing is the Stern Stewart Bond Rating Score (see exhibit 15.17). The result of weighting five key risk factors, Campbell's senior debt score at the end of fiscal 1989 places the company at the weak end of Aa on the creditworthiness scale, well shy of the score needed to qualify for Aaa standing. As a matter of fact, the last time Campbell's score did qualify as Aaa was as far back as 1980. Since then, profitability has eroded (both the level and the stability of the total return on total capital have deteriorated) and leverage has increased. The 3-year average ratio of long term debt to total capital has tripled, adjusted total liabilities to net worth has about doubled, and investments and advances to unconsolidated subsidiaries now comprises fully 6% of capital. With financials like these, Campbell can no longer be considered a Aaa-rated credit, no matter what Moody's may say.

> Many professionals in the market view the ratings of the three agencies [Moody's, Standard & Poor's, and Fitch] as "rearview mirror" analysis. "These are lagging indicators of credit quality," says Bruce N. Lehmann, an associate professor at Columbia University business school. "I have never known a portfolio manager who goes by the ratings."
>
> "Why the Rating Agencies Get Low Marks on the Street"
> *Business Week*
> March 12, 1990

The rating agencies apparently are all too human. They detest being the bearers of bad news or having to admit to errors in judgment. Time and again they have been reluctant to downgrade a company long after it has become obvious to the market that creditworthiness has deteriorated.

Another indication of Campbell's weakened credit standing is the yield to maturity prevailing on its publicly traded bonds.

Exhibit 15.17   Campbell Soup Co.: Bond Rating Summary (Dollars in Millions)

FINANSEER (August-July)	1980	1981	1982	1983	1984	1985	1986	1987	1988	1989
Size										
Assets	$1,627.6	$1,722.9	$1,865.5	$1,991.5	$2,210.1	$2,437.5	$2,762.8	$3,090.0	$3,609.6	$3,932.1
Asset Size Rating	BB	BB	BB	BB	BB	BB	BBB	BBB	BBB	BBB
Profitability & Risk										
TPAT/Beg Total Capital	17.9%	13.3%	10.1%	12.5%	14.4%	14.2%	14.4%	13.9%	12.7%	9.4%
Trailing 3-5 Year Avg	15.5%	15.3%	14.5%	13.7%	13.7%	12.9%	13.1%	13.9%	13.9%	12.9%
Standard Deviation	1.6%	1.9%	3.0%	2.9%	2.9%	1.7%	1.9%	0.8%	0.7%	2.1%
Risk Adjusted Return	14.0%	13.4%	11.5%	10.9%	10.8%	11.2%	11.3%	13.1%	13.2%	10.8%
Profit & Risk Rating	AAA	AAA	AAA	AA	AA	AA	AA	AAA	AAA	AA
Leverage										
Long-term Debt/Tot Cap	9.5%	9.7%	14.4%	15.3%	14.7%	13.9%	15.1%	14.2%	17.2%	18.4%
3 Yr Avg LTD/Total Cap	5.6%	7.5%	11.2%	13.2%	14.8%	14.7%	14.6%	14.4%	15.5%	16.6%
Cap Structure Rating	AAA	AAA	AAA	AAA	AAA	AAA	AAA	AAA	AA	AA

FINANSEER
(August-July)

	1980	1981	1982	1983	1984	1985	1986	1987	1988	1989
Tot Liabs/Net Worth	0.63	0.65	0.69	0.63	0.65	0.64	0.64	0.60	0.72	1.01
Bankruptcy Risk Rating	AAA	AAA	AAA	AAA	AAA	AAA	AAA	AAA	AAA	AA
Inv&Adv Subs/Total Cap	0.0%	0.0%	0.0%	2.2%	0.9%	4.1%	3.8%	4.0%	6.1%	6.2%
Double Leverage Rating	AAA	AAA	AAA	AAA	AAA	AAA	AAA	AAA	AAA	AAA
Bond Rating										
Senior Debt Score	5.2	5.0	4.7	4.5	4.5	4.5	4.6	4.8	4.8	4.5
Senior Debt Rating	AAA/AA	AAA/AA	AA	AA	AA	AA	AA	AA	AA	AA

Bond Rating Score Ranges

B	BB	BBB	A	AA	AAA
I————————————I————I————I————I————I—I

-2.1   0.0   1.5   2.8   4.1   5.2   6.2

Reflecting the judgment of the lead steers in the bond market, Campbell's Euro-issues trade at yields typical of A-rated companies. For example, the company's Aaa-rated 10.5% Euronotes due 1995 closed January 1990 at a price of $102⅜, indicating a yield to maturity of 9.9%. A second Aaa-rated issue, the 9.125% Eurobonds due 1993, closed at $99⅛, or a yield to maturity of 9.4%. A far cry from the 8.9% yield paid by Aaa-rated companies at the time, the 9.4% to 9.9% yield on these Campbell's bonds actually falls in line with the yield the market required of A-rated companies, or lower.

	Aaa	Aa	A	Baa
Yield to Maturity on a Sample of Bonds Rated by Moody's (As of January 1990)				
Yield to maturity	8.9%	9.1%	9.5%	10.1%

But the market yield may be too harsh a judgment. The yield prevailing on Campbell's bonds probably understates the company's actual creditworthiness. To the extent that the buyers of Campbell's bonds are concerned about "event risk"—the chance that Campbell may recapitalize and thereby force the bondholders into a riskier position—the current yield will overstate the true credit risk of the company in its present condition. That the yield on Campbell's bonds did *not* increase following the passing of John T. Dorrance, an event that certainly raised the chances for the recapitalization, suggests that Campbell's bonds have for some time impounded an extra premium for such a risk.

All things considered, the best indicator of Campbell's current creditworthiness probably is the bond score, which signals a middling to weak Aa rating. Though it is not as high a rating as Aaa, an Aa rating still may be overly conservative. In light of Campbell's strong and stable cash flow and relatively slow growth in the focus strategy, it is a costly luxury to operate with a bond rating any higher than A or strong Baa. By adopting a more aggressive though still prudent leverage target, Campbell's can more fully capture the tax benefits of substituting debt for equity financing.

Campbell's Potential Debt Target.   To test Campbell's potential for leveraging its balance sheet to the equivalent of an A or strong Baa rating, the company's historical bond score is simulated for various debt configurations in exhibit 15.18. The exhibit shows that, based upon historical results through the 1989 fiscal year, Campbell's could adopt a target total debt to total capital ratio of 45% and be rated middle A and that adopting a target ratio of 55% would likely produce a strong Baa rating.

In the simulations, the company's size and profitability and the investments in unconsolidated subsidiaries are held constant as the ratio of total debt to total capital is stepped up from 0% to 70%. As prospective leverage increases, the ratios of long-term debt to total capital and of adjusted total liabilities to net worth are revised and figured into the bond score. (It is assumed that 5% of total capital is financed with short-term debt, a typical proportion.) The point at which the score drops to 3.4, a score midway in the A range, is deemed to be the company's debt capacity for an A rating. It occurs when total debt reaches 45% of total capital. The point at which the score drops to 2.7, the highest score in the Baa range, is the company's debt capacity for a strong Baa rating. It occurs when total debt reaches 55% of total capital.

Ralston Purina's bond score and bond rating also provide indirect support for the conclusion that Campbell could leverage its balance sheet to the extent of a 45% to 55% ratio and still garner an A or strong Baa rating (exhibit 15.19). Ralston Purina currently is rated A— by Standard & Poor's and Baa1 by Moody's even though its ratio of total debt to total capital has been running at close to 60% for the past 4 years. (About 10% of Ralston's total capital has been financed through short-term debt.) Ralston's bond score shows why. Exceptional risk adjusted returns compensate for high leverage to produce a score of 3.2 that rightly places Ralston at the weak end of the A-rated companies. Ralston can leverage up even further than Campbell can and still obtain a weak A or strong Baa rating because of its greater profitability in recent years. Allowing for that difference, however, it seems eminently plausible that Campbell could leverage to and maintain a 45% to 55% leverage ratio as a target.

The feasibility of adopting a target in that range also is sub-

Exhibit 15.18   Campbell Soup Co.: Bond Rating Simulation (Dollars in Millions)

FINANSEER (August-July)	1989

Factors Held Constant

Assets	$3,932.1
Asset Size Rating	BBB
Risk Adjusted Return	10.8%
Profit & Risk Rating	AA
Inv&Adv Subs/Total Cap	6.2%
Double Leverage Rating	AAA

Total Debt /Total Capital	
0%	5.3
5%	5.3
10%	5.2
15%	5.0
20%	4.7
25%	4.5
30%	4.2
35%	3.9
40%	3.7
45%	3.4
50%	3.0
55%	2.7
60%	2.1
65%	1.3
70%	1.1

Bond Rating Score Ranges

```
          B        BB     BBB    A     AA  AAA
     I----------------I-----------I-----------I----------I--------I------I
    -2.1            0.0      1.5       2.8     4.1   5.2  6.2
```

Exhibit 15.19   Ralston Purina Co.: Bond Rating Summary (Dollars in Millions)

FINANSEER (October-September)	1980	1981	1982	1983	1984	1985	1986	1987	1988	1989
Size										
Assets	$2,246.5	$2,218.5	$2,113.8	$2,101.2	$2,004.2	$2,637.3	$4,209.9	$3,863.7	$4,044.4	$4,381.7
Asset Size Rating	BBB	BBB	BB	BB	BB	BBB	A	BBB	BBB	BBB
Profitability & Risk										
TPAT/Beg Total Capital	11.5%	12.2%	8.7%	17.2%	16.1%	18.5%	15.2%	11.4%	18.6%	17.6%
Trailing 3-5 Year Avg	12.5%	12.3%	11.4%	12.3%	13.2%	14.6%	15.2%	15.7%	16.0%	16.3%
Standard Deviation	0.8%	0.7%	1.6%	3.1%	3.5%	4.0%	3.8%	2.7%	3.0%	3.1%
Risk Adjusted Return	11.7%	11.6%	9.8%	9.2%	9.7%	10.5%	11.4%	13.0%	13.0%	13.2%
Profit & Risk Rating	AAA	AAA	AA	AA	AA	AA	AA	AAA	AAA	AAA
Leverage										
Long-term Debt/Tot Cap	24.9%	23.4%	24.6%	20.3%	16.7%	43.0%	44.7%	47.9%	47.2%	51.1%
3 Yr Avg LTD/Total Cap	26.5%	24.8%	24.3%	22.8%	20.5%	26.6%	34.8%	45.2%	46.6%	48.8%
Cap Structure Rating	A	A	A	A	AA	A	BBB	B	B	B

Exhibit 15.19 continued

FINANSEER

(October-September)	1980	1981	1982	1983	1984	1985	1986	1987	1988	1989
Tot Liabs/Net Worth	0.95	0.76	0.90	0.84	0.94	1.85	3.19	2.42	2.20	3.06
Bankruptcy Risk Rating	AA	AAA	AA	AAA	AA	BBB	BB	BB	BBB	BB
Inv&Adv Subs/Total Cap	4.1%	5.3%	10.7%	7.2%	6.9%	6.4%	1.7%	1.7%	1.3%	1.4%
Double Leverage Rating	AAA	AAA	BBB	AA	AAA	AAA	AAA	AAA	AAA	AAA
Bond Rating										
Senior Debt Score	4.1	4.1	3.9	3.9	4.0	3.8	3.7	3.4	3.3	3.2
Senior Debt Rating	AA/A	AA/A	AA/A	AA/A	AA/A	A	A	A	A	A

Bond Rating Score Ranges

B	BB	BBB	A	AA	AAA
I——————I——————I——————I——————I——————I——————I
-2.1	0.0	1.5	2.8	4.1	5.2	6.2

stantiated by computing the bond score for the focus plan (exhibit 15.20). Holding constant projected size, profitability, and investment in unconsolidated subsidiaries, a 45% target produces a 3.3 to 3.4 score in the third to fifth projected period, corresponding to a middle A rating, and a 55% target produces a score of 2.7, right on the borderline separating A and Baa. Adopting a more aggressive leverage target will have two consequences, one affecting cash flow and the other the cost of capital.

Projected Sources and Uses of Free Cash Flow.

First, because sources and uses of cash flows must balance, borrowing more funds to maintain a target capital structure requires a compensating reduction in equity. One outlet for surplus equity would be to increase dividends. A better strategy, though, would be to repurchase shares on the open market as Ralston Purina has done.

Projected sources and uses of free cash flow for Campbell are presented in exhibit 15.21. The top portion, operating activities, shows the free cash flow from operations projected by the focus plan. Investing less than it will earn, Campbell will generate an average of $480 million in free cash flow each year. This is reduced by an investment in construction in progress that averages about $17.5 million each year, leaving more than $460 million on average as the net financial liquidity generated by operations.

Two financial strategies are presented; they correspond to a 25% and a 55% target capital structure. Both assume that marketable securities of $100 million will be held in reserve on the balance sheet, that debt will amortize according to the schedule contained in the company's 1989 annual report, and that dividends will equal 38% of income available to common, the traditional policy.

Even maintaining a modest 25% leverage target requires common stock to be repurchased. In fact, $1.275 billion of common stock cumulatively over the 5 years, or about $255 million on average each year, will have to be repurchased to maintain a 25% leverage target. In all but the first forecast year, Campbell will raise debt simultaneously with retiring common equity. *Thus, maintaining the 25% target debt policy is tantamount to a commitment to undertake a series of subsequent leveraged recapitalizations.*

Exhibit 15.20   Campbell Soup Focus Scenario: Bond Rating Summary
D/Cap 45% vs. 55%

FINANSEER

(Data in Millions) (August-July)	History 1989	Forecast 1990	Forecast 1991	Forecast 1992	Forecast 1993	Forecast 1994
Factors Held Constant						
Assets	$3,932	$4,026	$4,169	$4,317	$4,472	$4,633
Asset Size Rating	BBB	BBB	BBB	BBB	BBB	BBB
Risk Adjusted Return	10.8%	10.6%	10.5%	11.0%	11.9%	13.7%
Profit & Risk Rating	AA	AA	AA	AA	AAA	AAA
Inv&Adv Subs/Total Cap	6.2%	6.3%	6.1%	5.9%	5.7%	5.5%
Double Leverage Rating	AAA	AAA	AAA	AAA	AAA	AAA
Variable Factors						
45% D/Cap:						
Long-term Debt/Tot Cap	18.4%	41.4%	38.9%	42.0%	44.7%	44.5%
3 Yr Avg LTD/Total Cap	16.6%	25.7%	32.9%	40.7%	41.8%	43.7%
Cap Structure Rating	AA	A	BBB	BB	BB	BB
55% D/Cap:						
Long-term Debt/Tot Cap	18.4%	51.4%	48.9%	52.0%	54.7%	54.5%
3 Yr Avg LTD/Total Cap	16.6%	29.0%	39.5%	50.7%	51.8%	53.7%
Cap Structure Rating	AA	A	BB	B	B	B
45% D/Cap:						
Tot Liabs/Net Worth	1.01	2.27	2.35	2.44	2.53	2.63
Bankruptcy Risk Rating	AA	BBB	BB	BB	BB	BB
55% D/Cap:						
Tot Liabs/Net Worth	1.01	3.64	3.83	4.03	4.25	4.51
Bankruptcy Risk Rating	AA	BB	BB	B	B	B
Bond Rating						
45% D/Cap:						
Senior Debt Score	4.5	3.9	3.6	3.3	3.3	3.4
Senior Debt Rating	AA	AA/A	A	A	A	A
55% D/Cap:						
Senior Debt Score	4.5	3.7	3.1	2.7	2.7	2.7
Senior Debt Rating	AA	A	A	A/BBB	A/BBB	A/BBB

Exhibit 15.21 Campbell Soup Focus Scenario: Projected Sources and Uses of Free Cash Flow

FINANSEER
(Data in Millions)
(August-July)

	History 1989	Target D/Cap = 25%					Target D/Cap = 55%				
		Forecast 1990	Forecast 1991	Forecast 1992	Forecast 1993	Forecast 1994	Forecast 1990	Forecast 1991	Forecast 1992	Forecast 1993	Forecast 1994
Operating Activities											
NOPAT	$262.7	$439.0	$478.6	$561.5	$631.6	$683.6	$439.0	$478.6	$561.5	$631.6	$683.6
Depreciation & Amort	175.9	175.2	189.2	204.4	220.7	238.4	175.2	189.2	204.4	220.7	238.4
Operating Sources	438.6	614.2	667.8	765.8	852.3	922.0	614.2	667.8	765.8	852.3	922.0
Net Working Capital	12.5	(26.6)	27.6	28.0	28.4	28.6	(26.6)	27.6	28.0	28.4	28.6
PPE Expenditures	172.0	174.6	248.2	268.1	289.5	312.7	174.6	248.2	268.1	289.5	312.7
Goodwill	(29.7)	0.0	0.0	0.0	0.0	0.0	0.0	0.0	0.0	0.0	0.0
Other Assets	347.4	(15.1)	9.9	13.1	14.0	14.9	(15.1)	9.9	13.1	14.0	14.9
Operating Uses	502.2	132.9	285.7	309.2	331.9	356.2	132.9	285.7	309.2	331.9	356.2
Free Cash Flow	(63.6)	481.3	382.1	456.6	520.4	565.8	481.3	382.1	456.6	520.4	565.8
(Incr) Construc in Progr	(35.6)	(21.6)	(14.7)	(15.9)	(17.1)	(18.5)	(21.6)	(14.7)	(15.9)	(17.1)	(18.5)
Cash Flow Bef Financ'g	($99.2)	$459.7	$367.4	$440.7	$503.3	$547.3	$459.7	$367.4	$440.7	$503.3	$547.3

Exhibit 15.21   continued

FINANSEER
(Data in Millions)
(August-July)

	History 1989	Target D/Cap = 25%					Target D/Cap = 55%				
		Forecast 1990	Forecast 1991	Forecast 1992	Forecast 1993	Forecast 1994	Forecast 1990	Forecast 1991	Forecast 1992	Forecast 1993	Forecast 1994
Financing Activities											
Interest Income AT	($23.7)	($4.6)	($5.0)	($5.0)	($5.0)	($5.0)	($4.6)	($5.0)	($5.0)	($5.0)	($5.0)
Interest Expense AT	58.3	53.1	51.9	53.0	54.3	56.0	85.4	117.7	121.9	126.3	130.9
Debt Amortization	22.5	30.9	123.6	216.2	109.9	13.2	30.9	123.6	216.2	109.9	13.2
Common Dividends	116.4	114.8	138.8	168.0	191.8	208.4	102.6	113.8	141.8	164.5	179.9
Financing Payments	173.5	194.3	309.3	432.3	351.0	272.6	214.2	350.2	475.0	395.7	319.0
(Reqd)Surpls Financing	(272.7)	265.4	58.0	8.4	152.2	274.7	245.5	17.2	(34.2)	107.6	228.3
Marketable Securities	2.4	(15.2)	0.0	0.0	0.0	0.0	(15.2)	0.0	0.0	0.0	0.0
Total Debt & Leases	259.4	(16.3)	151.4	246.4	142.0	47.3	1,007.9	184.8	282.6	180.5	88.2
Other Liabilities	4.0	0.0	0.0	0.0	0.0	0.0	0.0	0.0	0.0	0.0	0.0
Minority Interest	20.3	(24.3)	(3.7)	(4.0)	(4.3)	(4.6)	(24.3)	(3.7)	(4.0)	(4.3)	(4.6)
Common Stock	(13.4)	(209.7)	(205.7)	(250.9)	(289.9)	(317.4)	(1,213.8)	(198.3)	(244.4)	(283.8)	(311.8)
Net Financing	$272.7	($265.5)	($58.0)	($8.4)	($152.2)	($274.7)	($245.5)	($17.2)	$34.2	($107.6)	($228.3)

Raising the leverage target to 55% affects only the financial side of free cash flow. The operating projections remain precisely the same. Adopting a 55% target changes the financial flows in three respects. Substantially more debt is raised, particularly in the first year, in order to bring debt immediately up to 55% of total capital. Interest expense (after taxes), a use of funds, is correspondingly higher. But now $2.25 billion of common stock will be repurchased, almost double the amount retired with the 25% target. Thus, *adhering to the 55% target commits the company to an immediate substantial recapitalization followed by a series of smaller but nevertheless still significant ones.* Implementing a 45% target brings about much the same financial consequences, only to a lesser extent.

Because sources and uses of cash must balance, choosing to implement a 45% to 55% target capital structure requires making a simultaneous commitment to repurchase shares in significant amounts (or to increase the dividend). Thus, when the intention to increase target leverage is communicated to investors, it will also be important to discuss how the surplus equity cash flow the new policy brings about will be handled.

The Cost of Capital and Value. The second important consequence to adopting a more aggressive leverage policy would be to reduce Campbell's cost of capital and increase its intrinsic market value.

The weighted average cost of capital c^* will decline from the 11.6% cost associated with a 25% leverage target to 10.6% by adopting a 45% target and to 10.1% with a 55% target, saving between 1% and 1.5% on overall financing costs (exhibit 15.22). A lower cost of capital increases the EVA of a given business plan and more gently discounts it to a present value. For instance, should management adopt a 55% target in place of the current 25% one, the value of the focus plan increases by $860 million, from $5.57 to $6.43 billion, or from $37.34 to $43.98 a share, an increase of nearly 18% (see exhibit 15.23). Thus, though Campbell will have to pay more to borrow funds (an increase of between 0.5% to 1%) and though its common shares will sell for a lower P/E multiple as shareholders are put into a riskier position, the company's overall cost of capital will fall and its share price will rise. Despite the appeal of such a

Exhibit 15.22   Campbell Soup Co.: Weighted Average Cost of Capital

	c^*		c			t		$\dfrac{\text{Debt}}{\text{Capital}}$
Aa	11.6%	=	12.8%	(1	−	38%	×	25%)
A	10.6%	=	12.8%	(1	−	38%	×	45%)
Strong Baa	10.1%	=	12.8%	(1	−	38%	×	55%)

Exhibit 15.23 Leverage Creates Value.
Campbell Soup Focus Scenario: Economic Value Added Valuation
(Dollars in Millions)

Target D/Cap = 25%; c* = 11.6%

Year	(1) Return on Capital r	(2) Wtd Avg Cap Cost c*	(3)=(1)-(2) Perform Spread r-c*	(4) Beginning Capital	(5)=(3)x(4) EVA	(6) Present Value Factor	(7)=(5)x(6) Present Value of EVA	A.
1990	13.8%	11.6%	2.3%	$3,172.4	$72.3	0.947	$68.5	
1991	15.3%	11.6%	3.7%	3,130.1	116.8	0.849	99.1	
1992	17.4%	11.6%	5.8%	3,226.6	188.5	0.761	143.4	
1993	19.0%	11.6%	7.4%	3,331.5	246.5	0.682	168.1	
1994	19.9%	11.6%	8.3%	3,442.7	285.7	0.611	174.6	
1995 &							B.	
Beyond	19.9%	11.6%	8.3%	3,560.5	295.5	5.288	1,562.4	

Premium (Discount)		$2,216.1
+ Capital	C.	3,350.7
Intrinsic Operating Value		$5,566.8
+ Marketable Securities		84.8
+ Construction in Progress		162.2
Intrinsic Total Value		$5,813.8
- Total Debt & Leases		900.7
- Other Liabilities		19.6
- Minority Interest		54.9
Intrinsic Common Equity Value		$4,838.6
Number of Shares Outstanding		129.6
Intrinsic Share Value		$37.34

A. EVA discounted from mid-year.
B. Present value of $1 in perpetuity beginning in 1995.
C. Beginning Capital of $3,172.4 adjusted for mid-year discounting by multiplying by $(1+c*)**.5$, where c* = 11.6% in the first forecast period.

Exhibit 15.23   continued

Target D/Cap = 55%; c* = 10.1%

Year	(1) Return on Capital r	(2) Wtd Avg Cap Cost c*	(3)=(1)-(2) Perform Spread r-c*	(4) Beginning Capital	(5)=(3)x(4) EVA	(6) Present Value Factor	(7)=(5)x(6) Present Value of EVA	A.
1990	13.8%	10.1%	3.7%	$3,172.4	$118.6	0.953	$113.0	
1991	15.3%	10.1%	5.2%	3,130.1	162.4	0.866	140.6	
1992	17.4%	10.1%	7.3%	3,226.6	235.6	0.786	185.2	
1993	19.0%	10.1%	8.9%	3,331.5	295.1	0.714	210.7	
1994	19.9%	10.1%	9.8%	3,442.7	335.9	0.649	217.9	
1995 &							B.	
Beyond	19.9%	10.1%	9.8%	3,560.5	347.4	6.421	2,230.8	

Premium (Discount)		$3,098.2
+ Capital	C.	3,328.8
Intrinsic Operating Value		$6,427.0
+ Marketable Securities		84.8
+ Construction in Progress		162.2
Intrinsic Total Value		$6,674.0
- Total Debt & Leases		900.7
- Other Liabilities		19.6
- Minority Interest		54.9
Intrinsic Common Equity Value		$5,698.8
Number of Shares Outstanding		129.6
Intrinsic Share Value		$43.98
		======

A. EVA discounted from mid-year.

B. Present value of $1 in perpetuity beginning in 1995.

C. Beginning Capital of $3,172.4 adjusted for mid-year discounting by multiplying by $(1+c^*)^{**}.5$, where $c^* = 10.1\%$ in the first forecast period.

policy, however, it may not go far enough, for it does not address the immediate liquidity needs and control concerns of the influential shareholders.

VII. The *Dynamic* Use of Debt

The dynamic use of debt coupled with a plan for an immediate and substantial share repurchase may help to satisfy the desire of some of Campbell's shareholders for liquidity at a premium price while cementing control in the hands of those who wish to preserve the company's independence.

The dynamic use of debt entails *temporarily* borrowing more than the company's long-range target capital structure dictates is prudent, using the proceeds to distribute cash to investors, and then dedicating all future operating cash flow to pay down debt. In effect, the dynamic use of debt simply accelerates to a present value the distribution of cash to investors that would otherwise flow through as dividends and share repurchases over time. By raising debt to retire equity, moreover, it will be easier to concentrate a substantial equity ownership in the hands of insiders, thereby strengthening the reward for success and the penalty for failure. The obligation to pay down debt will also urge an even more efficient and aggressive rationalization of Campbell's business activities, the primary goal of the focus plan.

Engineering the Share Repurchase. Two criteria will guide the design of a leverage share repurchase plan for Campbell:

- Common stock should be bought back in an amount sufficient to concentrate control in the hands of the loyalists.
- The buy-back price should be high enough to induce shareholders to tender and to compensate the dissidents for forgoing a sale to a third party.

The loyalists hold 34% of the Campbell shares (10.5% each for Dorrance's three children plus the 2.5% held by George Strawbridge, their cousin). Buying back one-third of the company's shares would increase their share to 51% (34/66.66) and give them an absolute veto over the sale of Campbell, assuming, naturally, that they do not sell any of their shares. As their shares are dispersed into the hands of the next generation, the possibility of selling the company will resurface, as well it should.

To buy back shares, the board of directors must choose among open-market share repurchases, premium-priced tender offers, "Dutch auctions," or repurchase rights, a relatively new technique first used by Gillette in a restructuring to fend off Coniston Partners. Each approach has pluses and minuses, but all things considered, repurchase rights may be the most suitable for Campbell's situation. They certainly will be the most fun to discuss, in any event.

The Repurchase Rights Plan.   One way for the board of directors to force the retirement of a third of the shares would be to distribute repurchase rights to shareholders, one right for each three shares outstanding. Each repurchase right will entitle the holder to sell one share of common stock back to the company at a set price within a certain period of time, normally about one month. The stipulated price must be sufficiently above the actual stock price to induce shareholders either to exercise their rights, thereby selling shares back to the company at the premium price, or to sell the rights in the market to other investors who will exercise them.

For the purposes of this exercise, the repurchase price will be set at $55 a share, a 10% premium over the company's current $50 stock price (current, that is, as I write), and well above the company's intrinsic market value in the absence of a takeover. Each right would thus appear to have a value of $5, the difference between the current $50 a share value and the $55 buy-back price. In fact, a right will be more valuable than that for two reasons.

First, the very act of distributing the right will reduce the value of the shares, making the right more valuable. If each right is thought to be worth $5 initially and one right is distributed for every three shares, then each share would have to fall in price by $1.67 ($5/3), from $50 to $48.33. But once that happens, a right to sell a share for $55 is worth $6.67, which means that the shares must fall by more than $1.67, and so on, until an equilibrium value for the shares and the rights is reached.

The right also will be more valuable than $5 because the stock price will fall once control is consolidated in the hands of the loyalists. The takeover premium incorporated in the current share price will disappear. Campbell's shares will begin to sell for their intrinsic stand-alone value. Suppose, for example, that the intrinsic value of the company is $45 a share in the absence of a takeover. Then each right would turn out to be worth $15. With one right parceled out for every three shares, each share would fall in price by the value of a third of a right, or by $5. In other words, the shares would fall from an intrinsic value of $45 to a value of $40 once the rights had been distributed, and then the right to sell a share to the company for $55 would in fact be worth $15. It all checks out.

For both of those reasons, the distribution of rights to sell shares back to the company at what appears to be only a modest premium to the current share value should be sufficient to make the rights too valuable to ignore. Investors will be compelled to exercise or to sell them. It is expected that the loyalists would not exercise their rights, but would instead sell them in the market and receive cash proceeds per share equal to about 5 years' worth of dividends (as will be demonstrated later). The cash proceeds from the sale of the right will compensate them fairly for forfeiting the opportunity to sell shares to the company for a premium price.

The dissidents and sympathizers, on the other hand, would exercise their rights and sell one-third of their shares to the company for $55 each, giving them cash to cover estate taxes when necessary. Though they will sell a third of their shares, the total number of Campbell shares outstanding also will shrink by a third, so that they will retain the same ownership proportion they had before the repurchase. Should a sale of the company occur at some future time, they will be entitled to a share of proceeds that is the same as it would have been in the absence of the buy-back. The one drawback of this plan, and it is not inconsequential, is that the dissidents and sympathizers will have to pay taxes on the proceeds from the repurchase of their shares. Liquidity has its price.

The consequences of the repurchase rights plan are summarized in the following table. Before the repurchase, the dissidents and sympathizers together held 24.7% of the shares, the loyalists

34%, and others 41.3% (column 1). The dissidents and sympathizers exercise their rights and sell one-third of their holdings;
the loyalists sell the rights and none of their shares; and the other
investors are forced to sell a third of their shares plus the third
that the loyalists did not sell (column 4). In the aftermath of the
repurchase, the dissidents and sympathizers retain their 24.7%
stake, the loyalists hold a controlling 51% interest, and the other
investors are diluted from 41.3% to 24.3% (column 4).

Shareholders	(1) Before, %	(2) Sell	(3) After	(4) After, %
Dissidents and sympathizers	24.7	8.2	16.5	24.7
Loyalists	34.0	0.0	34.0	51.0
Others	41.3	25.1	16.2	24.3
	100.0	33.3	66.7	100.0

Campbell has about 130 million common shares outstanding, net
of those in treasury. With one repurchase right distributed for
every three shares, the company will repurchase 43.33 million
shares (130/3) at $55 each for a total cash outlay of about
$2.4 billion. Financing a distribution of this magnitude would
vigorously stir up Campbell's balance sheet and income statement.

The Balance Sheet Consequences.   As a basis for comparison,
the balance sheet projected for the focus case, assuming that a
25% target debt ratio is maintained, is presented in the left-hand
portion of exhibit 15.24. About $1.8 billion of common equity
initially supports the firm, and total debt and leases gently rise
from about $850 million to just about $1 billion by the end of the
fifth forecast year, a financial picture that is a model of tranquility
and contentment. Now let's turn on the debt dynamo and see
what cooks up.

Paying out $2.4 billion to buy back shares reduces common
equity to −$420 million by the end of the first forecast year, and
it increases total debt and leases to over $3 billion right away (see
the right-hand portion of exhibit 15.24). The deficit net worth,
while superficially worrisome, is, for three reasons, an accounting
illusion with little economic significance:

Exhibit 15.24 Campbell Soup Focus Scenario: Liabilities and Net Worth

FINANSEER (Data in Millions) (August-July)	History 1989	Target D/Cap = 25%					$55/sh Leveraged Recap				
		Forecast 1990	Forecast 1991	Forecast 1992	Forecast 1993	Forecast 1994	Forecast 1990	Forecast 1991	Forecast 1992	Forecast 1993	Forecast 1994
Short-Term Debt	$240.6	$0.0	$0.0	$0.0	$0.0	$0.0	$0.0	$0.0	$0.0	$0.0	$0.0
Current Portion LTD	30.9	123.6	216.2	109.9	13.2	20.0	123.6	216.2	109.9	13.2	20.0
NIBCLs	960.6	1,067.1	1,108.2	1,148.9	1,189.2	1,228.5	1,067.1	1,108.2	1,148.9	1,189.2	1,228.5
Total Current Liabs	1,232.1	1,190.7	1,324.4	1,258.8	1,202.4	1,248.5	1,190.7	1,324.4	1,258.8	1,202.4	1,248.5
Existing Debt & Leases	629.2	505.6	289.4	179.5	166.3	146.3	505.6	289.4	179.5	166.3	146.3
New Long-Term Debt	0.0	224.3	375.7	622.1	764.1	811.3	2,399.9	2,366.8	2,340.7	2,127.1	1,747.4
Total Senior Liabs	1,861.3	1,920.6	1,989.4	2,060.4	2,132.7	2,206.1	4,096.2	3,980.6	3,779.0	3,495.8	3,142.2
Subordinated Liabs	19.6	19.6	19.6	19.6	19.6	19.6	19.6	19.6	19.6	19.6	19.6
Total Liabilities	1,880.9	1,940.2	2,009.0	2,080.0	2,152.3	2,225.7	4,115.8	4,000.2	3,798.6	3,515.4	3,161.8
Deferred Income Taxes	218.0	293.6	343.4	394.4	450.2	511.3	293.6	343.4	394.4	450.2	511.3
Minority Interest	54.9	36.8	39.7	42.9	46.3	50.0	36.8	39.7	42.9	46.3	50.0
Common Equity	1,778.3	1,756.0	1,776.7	1,799.9	1,823.0	1,845.6	(419.7)	(214.5)	81.3	459.9	909.5
Total Liab & Net Worth	$3,932.1	$4,026.5	$4,168.8	$4,317.2	$4,471.8	$4,632.6	$4,026.5	$4,168.8	$4,317.2	$4,471.8	$4,632.6
Total Debt & Leases	$900.7	$853.5	$881.3	$911.5	$943.6	$977.6	$3,029.1	$2,872.4	$2,645.1	$2,306.6	$1,913.7
Total Debt/Total Capital	26%	25%	25%	25%	25%	25%	89%	82%	72%	61%	49%
Cum Stock Distributions		$324.5	$669.0	$1,087.9	$1,569.6	$2,095.4	$2,417.3	$2,417.3	$2,417.3	$2,417.3	$2,417.3

1. The sum of total liabilities and net worth is the same each year in both the dynamic and the static cases. The dynamic use of debt modeled here merely *recapitalizes* existing and projected assets, leaving the basic business plan unchanged.

2. Campbell's equity is projected to recover swiftly and its debt to amortize quickly (see exhibit 15.24), double signs of Campbell's strong operating cash flow and inherent value. This rapid unleveraging is by far more important as a sign of the company's strength than is a negative accounting net worth as a sign of weakness.

3. Cumulative distributions to shareholders through cash dividends and share repurchases are almost the same over 5 years in the static and the dynamic cases (see the bottom line of exhibit 15.24). It comes to $2.1 billion in the static case version and $2.4 billion in the dynamic case. The recapitalization merely accelerates to a present value the cash that would otherwise flow through to investors over time. Thus, there is no need to take the negative net worth seriously. It is compensated for by retaining all subsequent equity distributions to pay down debt.

The Income Statement Consequences. The recapitalization whips up Campbell's income statement, too. Again, as a basis for comparison, the income statement projected for the focus case assuming that a 25% target debt ratio is maintained is presented in the left-hand portion of exhibit 15.25. The conventional EBIT to interest coverage ratio is 6 times in the first forecast year, and it improves to more than 10 times by the end of the 5-year forecast next-to-last line. Covering interest is one thing, but smothering it as Campbell's does here is another kettle of fish.

By contrast, EBIT covers interest by just 1.6 times in the latter half of the first year of the recapitalization,[7] though it smartly recovers to 2 times, then 3 times, and to a positively robust 4 times coverage by the last forecast year (see the right-hand por-

[7]The recapitalization was assumed to occur halfway through the company's 1990 fiscal year (i.e., as of January 31, 1990), so that interest on the new debt is incurred in only the second half of the year. The coverage ratio has been adjusted so that the interest expense projected for the later half of the 1990 fiscal year is compared with just half of that year's earnings. The interest rate on the debt raised is assumed to be 12%.

Exhibit 14.23 Campbell Soup Focus Scenario: Income Statement

FINANSEER (Data in Millions) (August-July)	History 1989	Target D/Cap = 25%					$55/sh Leveraged Recap				
		Forecast 1990	Forecast 1991	Forecast 1992	Forecast 1993	Forecast 1994	Forecast 1990	Forecast 1991	Forecast 1992	Forecast 1993	Forecast 1994
Net Sales	$5,672.1	$6,125.9	$6,615.9	$7,145.2	$7,716.8	$8,334.2	$6,125.9	$6,615.9	$7,145.2	$7,716.8	$8,334.2
Operating Expenses	4,960.7	5,378.5	5,754.5	6,142.0	6,593.3	7,119.0	5,378.5	5,754.5	6,142.0	6,593.3	7,119.0
Depreciation	175.9	175.2	189.2	204.4	220.7	238.4	175.2	189.2	204.4	220.7	238.4
Net Operating Profit	535.5	572.2	672.2	798.8	902.9	976.8	572.2	672.2	798.8	902.9	976.8
Int Exp--Existing Debt	94.1	75.3	55.8	39.1	23.1	17.0	75.3	55.8	39.1	23.1	17.0
Int Exp--New Debt	0.0	10.4	27.9	46.4	64.5	73.3	144.0	286.0	282.4	268.1	232.5
Other Income	(13.4)	(10.7)	(11.3)	(11.3)	(11.3)	(11.3)	(10.7)	(11.3)	(11.3)	(11.3)	(11.3)
Income Before Taxes	454.8	497.2	599.8	724.7	826.7	897.8	363.6	341.7	488.6	623.1	738.6
Income Tax Provision	175.4	188.9	227.9	275.4	314.1	341.2	138.2	129.8	185.7	236.8	280.7
Income After Taxes	279.4	308.2	371.9	449.3	512.5	556.6	225.4	211.8	302.9	386.3	457.9
Minority Interest	5.3	6.1	6.6	7.1	7.7	8.3	6.1	6.6	7.1	7.7	8.3
A/T Extra Loss(Gain)	261.0	0.0	0.0	0.0	0.0	0.0	0.0	0.0	0.0	0.0	0.0
Income Avail to Common	13.1	302.1	365.2	442.1	504.8	548.3	219.3	205.2	295.8	378.6	449.6
Cash Dividends	116.4	114.8	138.8	168.0	191.8	208.4	2,417.3	0.0	0.0	0.0	0.0
Adjust to Ret Earnings	26.4	0.0	0.0	0.0	0.0	0.0	0.0	0.0	0.0	0.0	0.0
To Retained Earnings	($129.7)	$187.3	$226.5	$274.1	$313.0	$340.0	($2,198.0)	$205.2	$295.8	$378.6	$449.6
EBIT	$548.9	$582.9	$683.5	$810.2	$914.2	$988.1	$582.9	$683.5	$810.2	$914.2	$988.1
EBDIT	724.8	758.1	872.7	1,014.6	1,134.9	1,226.5	758.1	872.7	1,014.6	1,134.9	1,226.5
EBIT/Interest Expense	5.8	6.1	8.2	9.5	10.4	10.9	1.6	2.0	2.5	3.1	4.0
EBDIT/Interest Expense	7.7	7.9	10.4	11.9	13.0	13.6	2.1	2.6	3.2	3.9	4.9

tion of exhibit 15.25). The rapid recovery of the coverage ratios along with the swift reversal of leverage makes this recapitalization a slam dunk.

Change in Value.   The dynamic use of debt can increase value for many reasons. The most obvious, and readily quantifiable, is the additional taxes saved by deducting even more interest expense. To estimate this benefit, the additional taxes saved are discounted to a present value at the rate the company pays to raise the new debt.

Exhibit 15.26   Campbell Soup Co.:
The Tax Benefit of Dynamic Debt Financing
(Dollars in Millions)

	(1) Income Tax Provision Static 55%	(2) Dynamic $55/sh	(3)=(1)-(2) Tax Benefit of Interest Expense	(4)* Present Value Factor	(5)=(3)x(4) Present Value
1990	$169.2	$138.2	$31.0	0.945	$29.3
1991	187.6	129.8	57.8	0.844	48.8
1992	233.2	185.7	47.5	0.753	35.8
1993	270.0	236.8	33.2	0.673	22.3
1994	295.3	280.7	14.6	0.601	8.8
Total					$144.9

*Reflects mid-year discounting at the pre-tax borrowing rate of 12%.

The recapitalization saves a present value of $144.9 million in corporate taxes over 5 years, or about $1.12 per share, over and above the taxes that would be sheltered by adopting a 55% target capital structure (exhibit 15.26). Adding this incremental benefit to $43.98, which is the intrinsic value when a 55% target capital structure was used to finance the focus plan, produces an intrinsic share value of $45.10 for the recapitalization plan.

Post-Rights Value.   Though $45.10 is the hypothetical share value after the recapitalization, the shares actually will be worth less than that once the buy-back occurs. After the company acquires one-third of its shares for $55, the remaining shares will trade for only \$40.15 because the combination must equate to \$45.10, as follows:

$$\$45.10 = \frac{1}{3}\,(\$55.00) + \frac{2}{3}\,(x)$$

$$\$45.10 = \frac{1}{3}\,(\$55.00) + \frac{2}{3}\,(\$40.15)$$

The \$40.15 post-buy-back share value also can be explained by subtracting the per share value of the right from the \$45.10 share value before the rights are distributed. By providing investors with the opportunity to sell shares for \$55 that will end up being worth only \$40.15, each right will be worth \$15.85, the difference. With one right distributed for every three shares, each share will fall by the value of a third of a right, or by \$4.95 (\$14.85/3), from \$45.10 to \$40.15. It all checks out, as well it must.

A Share Repurchase without a Premium. The true significance of the repurchase rights plan now becomes clear. It is equivalent to making a dividend of \$4.95 to all shareholders and then *forcing* a sale back to the company of a third of the shares at \$40.15, the post-rights intrinsic value. Investors who sell the right receive \$14.85 for every three shares, or \$4.95 in cash per share, equivalent to a dividend. Those who exercise the right receive \$55 from the company for every third share, which is equivalent to \$4.95 for each of the three shares, or \$14.85 in total, plus the sale of one of the three shares for \$40.15, the post-rights intrinsic value. Thus, the repurchase rights plan is an effective way to give all investors a special cash dividend equal to the per share value of the right and to force the sale of a fraction of the shares back to the company at intrinsic value.[8] Unlike tender offers or Dutch auctions, no premium needs to be paid to induce investors to sell

[8]Distributing a repurchase right is not only the economic equivalent of a dividend; the right is also taxed as a dividend. Investors will have dividend income equal to the value of the right on the close of the first day of trade, even though they receive no cash. But, in exchange, they will have a basis in the right equal to the right's initial market value. If the investor sells the right, capital gain or loss will be measured relative to the initial market value of the right. An investor who exercises the right will apply the initial value of the right as an offset to the share repurchase proceeds in figuring the gain to be taxed. Thus, the IRS also treats the rights plan as a dividend coupled with a share repurchase.

shares to the company. That makes the procedure eminently fair to all investors, even those who, for one reason or another, choose not to sell. The only drawbacks are the additional complexity and the extra transactions costs necessary to make a market for the rights.

Dividend Equivalence.   Campbell currently pays a dividend of about $1 per share, and the dividend is increasing at the rate of approximately 10% per year. Thus, the investors who decide to sell their rights and receive $4.95 per share will collect the present value of almost 5 years' worth of dividends up front and will prepay 5 years' worth of taxes (assuming the appropriate discount rate is on the order of 10%). Campbell offers a prime example of the maxim that a company in a position to pay dividends at all would do even better to pay them all at once.

Not Good Enough.   The recapitalization plan just outlined may be a very appealing opportunity for Campbell and its shareholders (though I do not expect them to follow it, because the Dorrances are reputed to dislike debt intensely). It would increase value by more fully sheltering operating profits from taxation and by hurrying along a necessary streamlining of business activities. It would cement control in the hands of shareholders who are concerned about preserving independence. And it would provide liquidity to those who want it but without taking away from them the opportunity to realize a sale premium down the road. And yet . . .

And yet, as an action plan, it still is inadequate in many important respects. Incentives for managers and employees could be strengthened; the recapitalization could be financed by decentralizing debt into the units through internal LBOs instead of by burdening the entire company with corporate debt; units could be clustered into sizable and related groups and then certain ones spun off to investors in tax-free share distributions; and certain business units could be sold to buyers in a better position to maximize their value. Furthermore, opportunities for Campbell to grow profitability and to capitalize more fully upon its brand strengths even as it goes about its rationalization program could be investigated. And to ensure that promising enterprises are not lost in the shuffle, some of these units could be venture-capitalized in the manner I described in chapter 14. Simulating these important modifications I will leave as a challenge to the interested reader, if not to the company itself.

VIII. Summary

The Campbell Soup Company case illustrates a tops-down, corporate approach to value planning and financial structuring. Actually, a bottoms-up, unit-by-unit appraisal is generally a more effective way to search for additional value. But then, if I had illustrated that approach for Campbell, this book would have to come out in installments, and I would once again be a bachelor.

Starting in the upper left-hand corner of exhibit 15.27, Campbell's intrinsic value is only $5,172.5 million *if* a business-as-usual plan is pursued and *if* a conservative but traditional 25% target capital structure is adopted. It was from this uninspiring platform that our crusade for greater value was launched.

The appropriate business opportunities to be explored will depend very much upon the specific company and its individual operating units. Some paths will be more worthwhile to trace out than others, and the challenge is to prune the options to just those few significant departures from the current practice that are truly promising. Trying to go down too many roads is one good way to get lost in the quest for value.

Thus, the first step in value planning is to review past performance in relevant economic terms and in comparison with business peers. The goal at the outset is to identify important strengths and weaknesses, needs and opportunities. Once that's done, the next step is to define alternative business strategies that will resolve the critical needs and capitalize upon the opportunities and then simulate the likely outcome over the time horizon necessary for the opportunities to bear fruit. The optimal plan is the one which produces the greatest expected present value to EVA, without regard to sales, size, market share, growth, earnings, return, or any of the other imperfect proxies for value.

For Campbell, our research suggested that the most obvious *corporate* strategy would be to streamline and focus. As projected, this strategy adds $394.3 million in value, or $3.04 per share (see

Exhibit 15.27   Campbell Soup Co.: Summary of Restructuring Alternatives

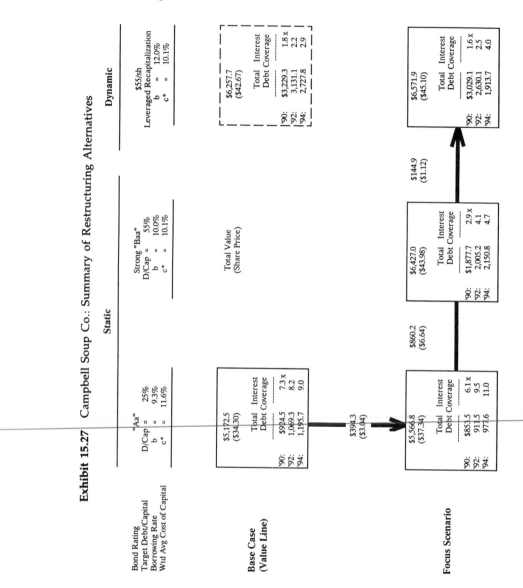

	Static		Dynamic
	"Aa"	Strong "Baa"	$55/sh Leveraged Recapitalization
Bond Rating	D/Cap = 25%	D/Cap = 55%	b = 12.0%
Target Debt/Capital	b = 9.3%	b = 10.0%	c* = 10.1%
Borrowing Rate	c* = 11.6%	c* = 10.1%	
Wtd Avg Cost of Capital			

Total Value
(Share Price)

**Base Case
(Value Line)**

$5,172.5
($34.30)

	Total	Interest	
	Debt	Coverage	
'90:	$924.5	7.3 x
'92:	1,069.3	8.2
'94:	1,195.7	9.0

$394.3
($3.04)

$6,257.7
($42.67)

	Total	Interest	
	Debt	Coverage	
'90:	$3,229.3	1.8 x
'92:	3,131.1	2.2
'94:	2,727.8	2.9

Focus Scenario

$5,565.8
($37.34)

	Total	Interest	
	Debt	Coverage	
'90:	$853.5	6.1 x
'92:	911.5	9.5
'94:	977.6	11.0

$860.2
($6.64)

$6,427.0
($43.98)

	Total	Interest	
	Debt	Coverage	
'90:	$1,877.7	2.9 x
'92:	2,005.2	4.1
'94:	2,150.8	4.7

$144.9
($1.12)

$6,571.9
($45.10)

	Total	Interest	
	Debt	Coverage	
'90:	$3,029.1	1.6 x
'92:	2,630.1	2.5
'94:	1,913.7	4.0

lower left-hand box of exhibit 15.27), despite the fact that it will produce lower sales, earnings, and returns early on.

Once the business campaign has been mapped out, a suitable financial strategy should be devised, one which minimizes the cost of capital while still preserving adequate flexibility to undertake all value-adding investment opportunities. Financial structuring progresses from left to right in exhibit 15.27. With its strong and stable cash flow, Campbell could justifiably employ more leverage than it has used in the past. Stepping up leverage to a 55% target capital structure, for example, would add at least $860.2 million to value, or $6.64 per share, by driving down the overall, or weighted average, cost of capital from 11.6% to 10.1%.

But Campbell may be better off abandoning any pretense of a target capital structure. Borrowing to finance a special distribution to shareholders can address liquidity and control concerns, save taxes, strengthen incentives, cure the risk of an unproductive reinvestment of surplus cash flow, and spur an even more efficient use of corporate assets, among other things.

Paying $55 a share for a third of the shares, or a total outlay of $2.38 billion, for example, would increase value by an additional $144.9 million, or $1.12 per share, just on the basis of the additional taxes saved (see the lower right-hand corner of exhibit 15.27). A distribution of that size appears to be financially feasible so long as the company successfully executes the focus plan. The pace of debt amortization and the coverage of interest would not be acceptable, however, if Campbell continues business as usual (see upper right-hand corner of exhibit 15.27). Cash flow is not strong enough to pay down debt swiftly, and profits do not rebound sufficiently to cover interest with a degree of comfort. Thus, the repayment of debt takes on a significance beyond merely meeting a contractual financial obligation. It is a measure of management's success at achieving the most-value-adding business strategy. Here is the integration of value planning and financial structuring at its best.

Throughout the case there was no mention of earnings per share. In the quest for value, earnings per share don't count. And that is the final word!

Glossary

Type A rough and ready characterization of corporate performance on average over the five fiscal years from 1984 to 1988:

- An "X-Minus" company earned a rate of return on capital that was at least 2.5% less than its cost of capital (e.g., United Technologies, number 893).

- An "X" company earned a return within plus or minus 2.5% of its cost of capital (e.g., James River, number 854).

- A "Y" company earned a return at least 2.5% more than its cost of capital, but could manage an average growth rate in its capital that was not more than 25% per annum (e.g., Bristol-Myers, number 9).

- A "Z" company also earned at least 2.5% more than its cost of capital but expanded its capital at a growth rate above 25% per annum (e.g., Wal-Mart, number 4).

- A "Pre-Z" company earned at least 2.5% less than its cost of capital, but exhibited such explosive capital growth (at least 25% per annum) that management and the market may be hoping for a payoff to materialize down the road. (e.g., McCaw Cellular, number 36).

Market Value Added (MVA) The difference between a firm's market value and its capital employed, MVA is a measure of the value a company has created in excess of the resources already committed to the enterprise. In theory, MVA represents the net present value of all past and projected capital investment projects.

Change in MVA   The creation or destruction of value is measured by calculating the change in MVA over the past 5- and 10-year periods. MVA will increase if value expands by more than the amount of new capital committed to the business, and vice versa.

Economic Value Added (EVA)   A fundamental measure of corporate performance, it is computed by taking the spread between the return on capital and the cost of capital, and multiplying by the capital outstanding at the beginning of the year (or the average over the year if that was used in computing the return on capital; see below). It is the residual income that remains after operating profits cover a full and fair return on capital (i.e., the cost of capital). In theory, a company's market value added at a point in time is equal to the discounted present value of all the EVA it can be expected to generate in the future. To the extent that it is unanticipated, a change in EVA will tend to explain a contemporaneous change in MVA. Often, however, a change in MVA will anticipate a subsequent change in EVA.

Change in EVA   A company's internal progress in creating value is measured by taking the change in EVA over the prior 5- and 10-year periods. EVA will increase if profits improve without tying up any more capital, if new capital is invested in projects that earn attractive rates of return, and if capital is withdrawn from uneconomic activities yielding less than the cost of capital. Changes in capital structure and in the level of interest rates also can influence EVA by altering the cost of capital.

Return on Capital r   A measure of the periodic, after-tax, cash-on-cash yield earned in the business, it is computed by taking net operating profits after taxes, or NOPAT, and dividing by capital outstanding at the beginning of the fiscal year, or by the simple year-to-year average of capital if assets declined by more than 20% over the year or if acquisition expenditures totaled more than 20% of average assets. For this purpose, NOPAT is defined as:

- reported net operating profits
- plus the increase in the bad debt reserve
- plus the increase in the LIFO reserve
- plus the amortization of goodwill
- plus the increase in net capitalized R&D
- plus other operating income (excluding passive investment income)
- less cash operating taxes, i.e., taxes payable, in cash, on the company's net operating profits (as adjusted), defined as:
    - the provision for income taxes

- less the increase in the deferred income tax reserve
- plus the tax saved by deducting any unusual loss (gain) at a marginal corporate income tax rate
- plus the tax saved by deducting interest expense at a marginal rate
- less the tax imposed on passive investment income at a marginal rate

The marginal tax rate employed was 48% through 1986; 44% in 1987, and 38% for 1988.

Cost of Capital c^* As the minimum rate of return on capital required to compensate debt and equity investors for bearing risk, it is the cutoff rate to create value. The cost of capital is computed by weighting the after-tax cost of debt and equity by the relative proportions employed in the firm's capital structure on average over the trailing three years. The before-tax cost of debt is determined by the yield prevailing on long-term bonds issued by companies of equivalent credit risk. The after-tax cost is the before-tax cost times 1 less the marginal corporate income tax rate (assumed to 48% through 1986; 44% in 1987, and 38% for 1988). The cost of equity is computed by adding a premium for risk to the 1-year average of the daily yield-to-maturity on long-term government bonds. The risk premium is estimated by multiplying beta, a measure of stock volatility relative to the market, by 6%, the risk premium typical of common equities in general.

r **to** c^* The ratio of the rate of return on capital r divided by the cost of capital c^* is an index of the productivity of capital relative to risk. Abstracting from growth, cycles, or turnaround potential, the r to c^* ratio should account for the ratio of value-to-capital.

Value to Capital   The ratio of market value divided by capital is a measure of the efficiency with which capital translates into market value.

Market Value   An approximation of the fair market value of a company's entire debt and equity capitalization (net of passive investments). It is computed as:

1. The actual market value of common equity (approximated by taking the closing stock price as of December 31, 1988 times the number of shares outstanding for the quarter end closest to December 31, 1988)

2. Plus the book value (as of the fiscal reporting date closest to December 31, 1988) of:

- preferred stock
- minority interests
- long-term non-interest-bearing liabilities (except the deferred income tax reserve)
- all interest-bearing liabilities and capitalized leases and
- the present value of noncapitalized leases (estimated by discounting the minimum rents projected for the next 5 years by 10%)

3. Less the book value of marketable securities and of construction in progress (because these items also are subtracted from capital, there is no effect on MVA; the intent is to produce more accurate measures of returns earned in active business activities)

Book value was used to approximate the market value of all items except common equity due to the absence of broad availability of quoted prices.

Capital   An approximation of the economic book value of all cash invested in going-concern business activities, capital is essentially a company's net assets (total assets less non-interest-bearing current liabilities), but with three adjustments:

1. Marketable securities and construction in progress are subtracted.

2. The present value of noncapitalized leases is added to net property, plant, and equipment.

3. Certain equity equivalent reserves are added to assets:
   - Bad debt reserve is added to receivables.
   - LIFO reserve is added to inventories.
   - The cumulative amortization of goodwill is added back to goodwill.
   - R&D expense is capitalized as a long-term asset and smoothly depreciated over 5 years (a period chosen to approximate the economic life typical of an investment in R&D).
   - Cumulative unusual losses (gains) after taxes is considered to be a long-term investment.

For the last three items, data was cumulated since 1973, or since the subsequent year in which data first became publicly available. Even after making these adjustments there is a distortion in measuring MVA. Companies that made acquisitions accounted for as pooling of interests probably understated the true cost of the acquisition.

As a result of recording the seller's book value as the acquisition cost instead of the market value of the shares offered to consummate the transaction, the MVA of pooling acquisitors is overstated to the extent of this "unrecorded goodwill."

To conform with FASB #94, in 1988 many industrial and service companies were forced to consolidate previously unconsolidated finance and insurance activities for the first time. In order to measure rates of return on capital more accurately and consistently over the 10-year period covered by this survey, these activities were deconsolidated for a number of companies. The companies are listed in groups arranged by the quality of information available for restating their financial statements:

Excellent information (The statements of the parent company and the finance subsidiary have been disaggregated or separate statements for the equity method of accounting have been furnished):

Caterpillar Inc.	General Motors Corp.
Chrysler Corp.	Greyhound Corp.
Ethyl Corp.	Harcourt Brace Jovanovich
Figgie International Inc.	Paccar Inc.
Ford Motor Co.	Quaker State Corp.
General Dynamics Corp.	Westinghouse Electric Corp.
General Electric Co.	Weyerhaeuser Co.

Typical quality (Some information on the financial subsidiary was shown, but some judgment on the part of Stern Stewart & Co. was required):

Allied Products Corp.	ITT Corp.
American Brands Inc.	Jacobson Stores
Amoco Corp.	Kerr-Mcgee Corp.
ATT	The Limited Inc.
Blount Inc.	Mack Trucks Inc.
Carter Hawley Hale Stores	Martin Marietta Corp.
Cincinnati Milacron Inc.	McDonnell Douglas Corp.
Coca-Cola Co.	Mobil Corp.
Crown Cork & Seal Co.	Motorola Inc.
Dana Corp.	Nalco Chemical Co.
Federal Signal Corp.	Penney (J. C.) Co.
Forest City Enterprises Inc.	Philip Morris Cos.
Honeywell Inc.	Pitney-Bowes Inc.
Illinois Tool Works	Raytheon Co.
International Business Machines Inc.	The Ryland Group
	Sequa Group

Southern New Eng Telecom
Talley Industries Inc.
Tandy Corp.
Temple-Inland Inc.
Texaco Inc.
Textron Inc.
UAL Corp.

Unisys Corp.
U S Home Corp.
USX Corp.
Wendy's International Inc.
Whirlpool Corp.
Xerox Corp.

Negligible impact (Although these companies switched to FASB #94, the
   overall impact of the change was reported to be negligible, and thus
   was ignored):

American Information Tech
Ametek Inc
Anheuser-Busch Cos.
Butler Mgr Co.
Champion International Corp.
Dairy Mart Convenience Stores
Eastman Kodak Co.
Eaton Corp.
GTE Corp.

Heinz (H. J.) Co.
Hubbell Inc.
Lin Broadcasting
Lukens Inc.
Meredith Corp.
Nynex Corp.
Smith (A. O.) Corp.
Stewart & Stevenson Services
United Telecom

Not restated (The data needed for restatement was generally incomplete
   or too complex. As a result, the financial statements for these companies were not restated even though they should be):

Bell Atlantic Corp.
Castle & Cooke
Lonestar Industries Inc.
Pacific Telesis Group
U.S. West

The MVA of companies for which deconsolidation was impossible or
imprecise will not be affected (since the equity in the finance subsidiary
is contained both in value and in capital). The only consequence will be
to alter and generally understate the rate of return on capital. Some
companies, Sears (number 872) and Household International (number
267) among them, traditionally have consolidated their insurance and
finance activities, making it impossible to separate them from the rest
of the company. As a result, their rates of return cannot be meaningfully
compared with the rest of the companies, and thus are not presented in
the survey.

Capital Growth Rate   The compound average annual rate of growth
   in capital over the past five years (or over the longest period for which
   such data was publicly available).

The Stern Stewart Performance 1000

The Stern Stewart Performance 1000

1988 MVA Rank	Company	Type	Industry	1988	Change from 1983	1978
	Company Profile			**Market Value Added (MVA)**		
1	Intl Business Machines Corp	Y	Computers & Peripherals	20,330	-25,893	-7,133
2	Merck & Co	Y	Drugs & Research	18,557	15,398	15,271
3	General Electric Co	X	Conglomerates	17,213	6,111	15,718
4	Wal-Mart Stores	Z	Discount & Fashion Retailing	14,341	9,940	14,152
5	Philip Morris Cos Inc	Z	Tobacco	13,937	10,640	11,842
6	Coca-Cola Co	Y	Beverages	12,585	8,483	9,061
7	RJR Nabisco Inc	X	Tobacco	11,793	12,183	12,803
8	Johnson & Johnson	Y	Medical Products	9,224	5,401	6,895
9	Bristol-Myers	Y	Medical Products	8,722	5,277	7,617
10	American Home Products Corp	Y	Drugs & Research	8,586	3,262	5,513
11	Exxon Corp	X	Oil & Gas	7,933	16,581	13,188
12	Dun & Bradstreet Corp	Z	Publishing	7,928	3,833	7,262
13	Abbott Laboratories	Y	Medical Products	7,218	3,606	6,135
14	Eli Lilly & Co	Y	Drugs & Research	7,109	5,809	5,332
15	Waste Management Inc	X	Pollution Control	6,935	5,592	6,817
16	Minnesota Mining & Mfg Co	Y	Conglomerates	6,852	1,890	2,556
17	Dow Chemical	Y	Chemicals	6,247	6,615	6,444
18	Kellogg Co	Y	Food Processing	6,038	4,677	5,302
19	Hewlett-Packard Co	X	Computers & Peripherals	5,938	-895	4,631
20	Walt Disney Company	X	Entertainment	5,820	5,689	5,484
21	PepsiCo Inc	Y	Beverages	5,805	4,720	4,712
22	McDonald's Corp	Y	Eating Places	5,124	2,997	4,121
23	Procter & Gamble Co	X	Personal Care	5,099	1,849	1,572
24	Anheuser-Busch Cos Inc	Y	Beverages	4,553	3,908	4,474
25	Squibb Corp	Y	Drugs & Research	4,370	3,512	4,132
26	Ralston Purina Co	Y	Food Processing	4,270	3,056	4,132
27	Time Inc	X	Publishing	4,241	1,515	4,275
28	Pfizer Inc	Y	Drugs & Research	4,071	1,095	3,230
29	Schering-Plough	Y	Drugs & Research	3,968	3,762	3,458
30	H.J. Heinz Co	Y	Food Processing	3,851	2,486	3,849
31	Limited Inc	Z	Discount & Fashion Retailing	3,711	2,495	3,651
32	MCI Communications	X-	Telephone Equip. & Services	3,678	1,486	3,602
33	Emerson Electric Co	Y	Electrical Products	3,598	949	2,464
34	Gannett Co	Y	Publishing	3,538	1,580	2,601
35	Syntex Corp	Y	Drugs & Research	3,512	2,545	3,288
36	McCaw Cellular Communication	Pre Z	Telephone Equip. & Services	3,448	.	.
37	Schlumberger Ltd	X-	Petroleum Services	3,367	-4,693	-2,585
38	Capital Cities/ABC Inc	Z	Broadcasting	3,290	2,099	3,030
39	Toys R Us Inc	Z	Discount & Fashion Retailing	3,285	1,858	3,247
40	Apple Computer Inc	Z	Computers & Peripherals	3,261	2,326	.

1988 MVA Rank	Economic Value Added (EVA)			Profitability (1988)				Size (1988)		
		Change from		Rtn on Cap	Wtd Avg Cost Cap	r to	Value to			5-Year Growth in
	1988	1983	1978	r (%)	c* (%)	c*	Capital	Value	Capital	Cap (Avg %)
1	-1,784	-4,766	-3,765	9.7	12.8	0.8	1.3	80,706	60,376	17
2	657	404	450	27.2	12.6	2.2	5.5	22,651	4,094	2
3	-475	64	-940	11.9	13.4	0.9	1.5	53,783	36,570	14
4	534	415	515	25.2	12.6	2.0	3.7	19,574	5,233	32
5	-135	-541	-396	10.3	10.9	0.9	1.5	41,038	27,101	28
6	524	455	294	19.9	10.6	1.9	3.9	16,936	4,352	3
7	667	1,124	524	17.1	12.2	1.4	1.8	25,778	13,985	8
8	416	358	265	20.3	12.9	1.6	2.4	15,648	6,424	9
9	500	304	395	30.1	13.0	2.3	3.6	12,087	3,365	11
10	561	163	304	31.5	13.8	2.3	3.4	12,194	3,609	11
11	-2,273	-1,047	-3,048	8.9	12.4	0.7	1.1	75,132	67,199	7
12	221	201	190	23.0	14.2	1.6	4.0	10,544	2,616	35
13	521	300	462	28.5	13.3	2.1	2.9	11,082	3,865	11
14	156	16	-11	18.5	14.7	1.3	2.6	11,623	4,514	9
15	162	186	158	19.6	14.0	1.4	2.6	11,147	4,212	30
16	329	229	50	18.3	13.6	1.3	2.0	13,978	7,126	6
17	1,388	2,433	1,285	24.1	12.8	1.9	1.4	20,307	14,060	6
18	355	226	257	34.8	11.8	3.0	4.0	8,064	2,026	16
19	237	117	187	20.1	15.8	1.3	1.9	12,505	6,566	14
20	64	101	56	17.5	15.4	1.1	2.9	8,857	3,036	8
21	360	132	186	16.1	10.5	1.5	1.7	13,926	8,121	20
22	234	92	132	14.2	10.7	1.3	1.7	12,876	7,752	16
23	236	25	60	13.7	11.7	1.2	1.4	17,506	12,406	14
24	291	136	219	18.2	12.1	1.5	1.9	9,792	5,239	11
25	276	313	281	32.2	14.9	2.2	3.4	6,184	1,814	2
26	283	185	218	19.4	9.3	2.1	2.5	7,160	2,890	12
27	57	321	78	13.7	12.1	1.1	2.0	8,508	4,268	20
28	145	-9	75	16.2	13.5	1.2	1.6	10,377	6,305	18
29	297	245	178	24.1	11.4	2.1	2.6	6,510	2,542	6
30	168	75	108	18.1	11.9	1.5	2.2	6,948	3,096	14
31	109	70	100	18.8	13.4	1.4	2.6	6,040	2,329	41
32	231	263	227	14.8	9.5	1.5	1.8	8,481	4,803	17
33	42	-23	-33	14.9	13.9	1.1	1.8	7,861	4,263	19
34	73	26	32	14.5	12.1	1.2	2.0	7,013	3,475	18
35	236	157	223	45.2	15.4	2.9	4.9	4,402	890	5
36	-170	.	.	-11.3	9.3	-1.2	3.2	4,986	1,538	87
37	-201	-508	-533	8.9	13.8	0.6	1.8	7,552	4,185	-1
38	73	30	52	12.8	11.1	1.2	1.8	7,664	4,374	44
39	109	69	105	21.6	14.4	1.5	2.8	5,128	1,843	39
40	483	387	.	71.5	16.6	4.3	3.2	4,744	1,483	29

1988 MVA Rank	Company Profile			Market Value Added (MVA)		
					Change from	
	Company	Type	Industry	1988	1983	1978
41	Newmont Gold Company	Z	Other Metals	3,218	.	.
42	American Brands Inc	X	Tobacco	3,195	2,161	3,344
43	Smithkline Beckman Corp	Y	Drugs & Research	3,190	1,061	1,115
44	LIN Broadcasting	Y	Broadcasting	3,178	2,865	3,141
45	Tele-Communications	X	Broadcasting	3,007	2,409	.
46	Browning-Ferris Industries	X	Pollution Control	2,942	1,971	2,922
47	Kroger Co	X	Food Retailing	2,911	2,748	3,066
48	Gillette Co	Y	Personal Care	2,897	2,339	2,841
49	Warner-Lambert Co	Y	Drugs & Research	2,862	2,572	2,604
50	General Mills Inc	Y	Food Processing	2,856	1,954	2,446
51	Burlington Northern Inc	X-	Railroads	2,854	4,183	4,444
52	Newmont Mining Corp	X	Other Metals	2,829	2,711	3,032
53	American TV & Commun	X	Broadcasting	2,807	.	.
54	Warner Communications Inc	X	Entertainment	2,796	2,283	2,846
55	Sara Lee Corp	Y	Food Processing	2,788	2,490	2,895
56	AMP Inc	X	Semiconductors	2,763	-239	2,200
57	Whitman Corp	X-	Conglomerates	2,586	3,265	3,382
58	CPC International Inc	X	Food Processing	2,572	2,283	2,441
59	Quantum Chemical Corp	X	Chemicals	2,556	2,947	2,915
60	Quaker Oats Co	Y	Food Processing	2,553	2,197	2,674
61	Food Lion Inc	Z	Food Retailing	2,532	2,133	.
62	Upjohn Co	X	Drugs & Research	2,502	2,381	2,005
63	Westinghouse Electric Corp	X	Electrical Products	2,417	2,794	4,475
64	Marion Labs	Z	Drugs & Research	2,416	1,856	2,389
65	Affiliated Publications	Y	Publishing	2,399	2,219	2,388
66	Eastman Kodak Co	X	Other Leisure	2,383	385	-820
67	Microsoft Corp	Z	Software	2,380	.	.
68	Gulf & Western Inc	X-	Conglomerates	2,362	1,962	3,035
69	Borden Inc	X	Food Processing	2,262	2,389	2,722
70	Melville Corp	Y	Discount & Fashion Retailing	2,232	1,287	1,949
71	Atlantic Richfield Co	X-	Oil & Gas	2,217	6,785	2,506
72	Marriott Corp	X	Hotel & Motel	2,202	1,164	2,237
73	Digital Equipment	Y	Computers & Peripherals	2,179	2,449	1,137
74	Boeing Co	X-	Aerospace	2,158	3,130	1,207
75	Times Mirror Co	X	Publishing	2,116	832	1,767
76	Tandy Corp	X	Computers & Peripherals	2,021	-1,350	1,505
77	American Tele & Telegraph	X-	Telephone Companies	2,010	.	.
78	Kimberly-Clark Corp	Y	Paper	2,002	1,718	2,276
79	Pennzoil Co	X-	Oil & Gas	1,953	2,062	1,794
80	Chemical Waste Management	Y	Pollution Control	1,939	.	.
81	McGraw-hill Inc	X	Publishing	1,933	546	1,736
82	Washington Post	Y	Publishing	1,857	1,190	1,689
83	Harcourt Brace Jovanovich	X	Publishing	1,848	1,835	1,847
84	Genuine Parts Co	Y	Industrial Distn Services	1,843	852	1,406
85	Masco Corp	X	Building Materials	1,782	693	1,616
86	Dow Jones & Co Inc	Z	Publishing	1,753	-907	1,423
87	Nordstrom Inc	Y	Discount & Fashion Retailing	1,750	1,339	1,691
88	Campbell Soup Co	Y	Food Processing	1,722	1,162	1,558
89	UST Inc	Y	Tobacco	1,708	888	1,564
90	Automatic Data Processing	Y	Software	1,686	973	1,426
91	Intel Corp	X-	Semiconductors	1,664	-1,537	1,298
92	Raytheon Co	Y	Electronics	1,659	446	1,067
93	May Department Stores Co	X	Discount & Fashion Retailing	1,657	1,601	1,995
94	Albertson's Inc	Y	Food Retailing	1,600	1,178	1,485
95	Hilton Hotels Corp	Y	Hotel & Motel	1,570	759	1,326

1988 MVA Rank	Economic Value Added (EVA)			Profitability (1988)				Size (1988)		
		Change from		Rtn on Cap	Wtd Avg Cost Cap	r to	Value to			5-Year Growth in
	1988	1983	1978	r (%)	c* (%)	c*	Capital	Value	Capital	Cap (Avg %)
41	85	.	.	40.0	10.6	3.8	7.3	3,733	515	45
42	102	33	55	13.2	11.6	1.1	1.5	9,610	6,415	13
43	171	-98	39	17.4	12.3	1.4	1.7	7,748	4,558	13
44	62	49	56	36.5	13.8	2.7	11.5	3,481	302	18
45	-12	11	-10	9.1	9.3	1.0	1.3	11,602	8,595	50
46	49	45	57	17.5	14.1	1.2	2.7	4,651	1,709	23
47	75	-23	44	10.2	8.2	1.2	1.7	6,805	3,894	5
48	152	139	126	16.8	10.4	1.6	2.2	5,308	2,411	13
49	101	124	41	16.7	13.0	1.3	1.9	5,924	3,062	2
50	126	110	26	17.8	11.3	1.6	2.4	4,953	2,098	-1
51	-884	-1,247	-513	1.4	11.9	0.1	1.4	9,337	6,483	-7
52	9	220	101	10.3	9.3	1.1	5.3	3,493	664	-16
53	6	.	.	12.0	11.5	1.0	2.8	4,388	1,581	17
54	238	1,010	235	25.5	13.6	1.9	2.0	5,585	2,788	2
55	103	50	62	16.2	12.3	1.3	1.9	6,006	3,218	14
56	56	23	-8	19.1	16.1	1.2	2.4	4,761	1,997	13
57	-89	142	16	8.9	11.4	0.8	1.9	5,587	3,001	-3
58	63	102	-14	14.6	11.8	1.2	2.0	5,164	2,592	5
59	265	330	243	22.1	10.3	2.1	3.1	3,758	1,202	-9
60	51	85	28	13.0	10.8	1.2	2.1	4,933	2,380	14
61	74	63	67	20.5	10.8	1.9	3.5	3,547	1,016	31
62	61	73	13	16.5	14.3	1.2	1.9	5,424	2,922	5
63	44	501	138	14.7	14.0	1.0	1.3	10,065	7,647	5
64	152	147	147	48.1	14.5	3.3	5.1	3,004	588	31
65	-129	-141	-132	-19.1	14.8	-1.3	8.4	2,725	326	18
66	129	263	-392	12.7	12.0	1.1	1.1	23,759	21,375	17
67	145	.	.	90.8	17.9	5.1	7.4	2,752	372	62
68	36	256	157	12.7	11.7	1.1	1.6	6,393	4,030	3
69	93	55	52	14.7	11.6	1.3	1.6	5,796	3,534	10
70	172	57	103	20.8	13.1	1.6	1.8	4,862	2,631	12
71	310	1,489	376	12.5	10.7	1.2	1.1	21,737	19,519	-2
72	-34	-84	-28	9.5	10.4	0.9	1.5	6,499	4,298	20
73	674	810	609	25.6	15.7	1.6	1.3	10,818	8,639	15
74	-111	779	-301	12.5	14.5	0.9	1.3	9,129	6,971	5
75	66	74	12	16.0	13.8	1.2	1.6	5,403	3,287	9
76	92	-12	56	17.7	13.2	1.3	1.9	4,342	2,321	11
77	-3,548	4,529	-4,310	2.4	11.8	0.2	1.1	39,493	37,483	-23
78	145	133	107	16.2	11.7	1.4	1.6	5,354	3,352	8
79	301	438	285	22.1	8.6	2.6	5.1	2,426	473	-31
80	48	.	.	23.2	14.3	1.6	3.5	2,720	781	22
81	-32	-63	-60	12.1	14.4	0.8	2.4	3,311	1,378	10
82	60	54	33	18.1	12.2	1.5	3.1	2,743	886	15
83	25	36	24	10.3	8.8	1.2	1.9	4,013	2,165	38
84	94	73	70	25.8	13.7	1.9	3.1	2,729	886	8
85	74	64	50	16.0	12.8	1.2	1.7	4,343	2,561	21
86	20	-37	-6	16.5	15.2	1.1	2.0	3,463	1,710	33
87	18	6	14	15.2	13.2	1.1	2.5	2,946	1,196	25
88	49	3	-16	14.8	12.5	1.2	1.6	4,568	2,846	14
89	114	75	100	36.5	12.8	2.9	4.5	2,199	491	7
90	73	57	53	20.3	13.5	1.5	2.4	2,867	1,181	13
91	160	188	112	24.4	16.1	1.5	1.7	4,106	2,442	11
92	143	11	26	17.7	13.0	1.4	1.4	5,357	3,698	14
93	-41	-11	-41	12.2	13.0	0.9	1.2	8,767	7,110	26
94	75	44	51	18.6	11.6	1.6	2.2	2,955	1,356	14
95	55	25	26	16.4	11.2	1.5	2.5	2,644	1,074	7

	Company Profile			Market Value Added (MVA)		
1988 MVA Rank	Company	Type	Industry	1988	Change from 1983	Change from 1978
96	MCA Inc	X-	Entertainment	1,553	683	1,304
97	Pitney Bowes Inc	X	Business Machines	1,546	1,307	1,575
98	Tribune Co	X-	Publishing	1,541	1,230	.
99	Deluxe Corp	Y	Business Machines	1,523	952	1,322
100	Tenneco Inc	X-	Conglomerates	1,503	4,105	2,363
101	Colgate-Palmolive Co	X-	Personal Care	1,481	1,410	1,454
102	Computer Associates Intl Inc	Z	Software	1,454	1,312	.
103	CBS Inc	X	Broadcasting	1,454	1,097	1,098
104	Citizens Utilities	X-	Telephone Equip. & Services	1,442	1,248	1,373
105	United Telecommunications	X-	Telephone Equip. & Services	1,427	2,065	1,619
106	Knight-Ridder Inc	X	Publishing	1,427	606	1,218
107	UAL Corp	X-	Airlines	1,427	1,596	2,172
108	J.C. Penney Co	X	Discount & Fashion Retailing	1,408	1,470	1,922
109	Turner Broadcasting	Pre Z	Broadcasting	1,373	877	.
110	Price Co	Z	Discount & Fashion Retailing	1,362	709	.
111	Compaq Computer Corp	Z	Computers & Peripherals	1,357	1,136	.
112	Bellsouth Corp	X	Telephone Companies	1,352	.	.
113	Carnival Cruise Lines	Y	Other Leisure	1,340	.	.
114	Owens Corning Fiberglas	Y	Building Materials	1,291	1,279	1,286
115	Multimedia Inc	Y	Broadcasting	1,273	918	.
116	Viacom Inc	Pre Z	Broadcasting	1,253	1,067	1,212
117	Rubbermaid Inc	Y	General Manufacturing	1,248	825	1,213
118	Woolworth Corp	X	Discount & Fashion Retailing	1,242	1,312	1,937
119	Holiday Corp	Y	Hotel & Motel	1,241	580	1,329
120	Polaroid Corp	X-	Other Leisure	1,220	1,381	608
121	American Information Tech	X	Telephone Companies	1,195	.	.
122	Gap Inc	Y	Discount & Fashion Retailing	1,180	1,131	1,183
123	Home Depot Inc	Z	Discount & Fashion Retailing	1,179	592	.
124	ConAgra Inc	Y	Food Processing	1,175	962	1,182
125	Sysco Corp	Y	Food Distribution	1,165	642	1,136
126	Dayton Hudson Corp	X	Discount & Fashion Retailing	1,164	-111	.
127	Pan Am Corp	X-	Airlines	1,155	446	1,242
128	General Cinema Corp	Z	Beverages	1,139	878	1,114
129	Corning Inc	X-	General Manufacturing	1,135	1,007	1,153
130	Arco Chemical Co	Z	Chemicals	1,132	.	.
131	American Cyanamid Co	X	Chemicals	1,131	973	1,558
132	Federal Express Corp	X	Transportation Services	1,109	-101	995
133	Interco Inc	X-	Apparel	1,108	1,213	1,303
134	Burlington Resources Inc	X-	Oil & Gas	1,105	.	.
135	Teledyne Inc	X	Conglomerates	1,104	876	1,000
136	NCR Corp	Y	Computers & Peripherals	1,097	269	1,059
137	US West Newvector Group	X-	Telephone Equip. & Services	1,081	.	.
138	TJX Cos Inc	Y	Discount & Fashion Retailing	1,077	.	.
139	New York Times Co	Y	Publishing	1,074	440	951
140	WM. Wrigley Jr Co	Y	Food Processing	1,072	964	1,047
141	Intl Flavors & Fragrances	Y	Personal Care	1,064	482	506
142	Contel Cellular Inc	Pre Z	Telephone Equip. & Services	1,061	.	.
143	Freeport-McMoRan Inc	X	Chemicals	1,052	541	957
144	GAF Corp	Y	Chemicals	1,052	949	1,306
145	Ethyl Corp	X	Chemicals	1,050	1,173	1,383
146	Liz Claiborne Inc	Z	Apparel	1,046	753	.
147	Fluor Corp	X-	Construct. & Eng. Services	1,019	1,727	961
148	PPG Industries Inc	X-	Building Materials	1,012	1,249	1,835
149	Illinois Tool Works	X	General Manufacturing	1,000	704	921
150	Rouse Co	X-	Construction & R.E.	999	608	.

1988 MVA Rank	Economic Value Added (EVA)			Profitability (1988)				Size (1988)		5-Year Growth in Cap (Avg %)
	1988	Change from 1983	1978	Rtn on Cap r (%)	Wtd Avg Cost Cap c* (%)	r to c*	Value to Capital	Value	Capital	
96	-182	-222	-286	6.9	13.2	0.5	1.5	4,748	3,196	24
97	-49	-44	-78	12.4	14.7	0.8	1.7	3,651	2,106	14
98	36	.	.	14.9	13.1	1.1	1.7	3,739	2,198	10
99	61	11	43	23.4	13.5	1.7	3.4	2,159	636	22
100	-1,219	-480	-1,226	1.6	9.8	0.2	1.1	14,488	12,985	-3
101	-34	-66	-84	10.2	11.4	0.9	1.6	3,933	2,453	7
102	204	197	.	42.2	15.2	2.8	2.2	2,705	1,251	71
103	-107	-7	-223	7.2	12.3	0.6	1.5	4,505	3,051	8
104	-117	-108	-119	-1.7	12.0	-0.1	2.6	2,351	909	11
105	-54	68	-109	9.1	10.0	0.9	1.2	9,556	8,129	13
106	19	32	-3	13.1	11.9	1.1	1.7	3,443	2,016	17
107	146	273	41	13.0	9.6	1.4	1.4	5,460	4,033	4
108	-129	-217	-289	10.1	11.3	0.9	1.1	11,334	9,926	9
109	-176	-181	-178	-1.0	9.2	-0.1	1.8	3,036	1,662	62
110	56	45	.	32.5	15.1	2.1	4.4	1,764	402	48
111	246	.	.	66.3	14.9	4.5	2.4	2,297	940	79
112	-551	.	.	8.7	11.0	0.8	1.1	26,806	25,453	5
113	122	.	.	47.4	14.0	3.4	4.9	1,683	343	7
114	142	270	78	19.9	9.1	2.2	2.0	2,586	1,294	-2
115	67	51	61	26.6	8.8	3.0	4.4	1,643	370	3
116	-289	-268	-290	1.4	9.4	0.2	1.4	4,743	3,490	41
117	42	32	34	24.1	15.7	1.5	3.1	1,854	605	24
118	73	119	95	14.5	12.1	1.2	1.3	4,869	3,627	8
119	105	130	130	13.6	7.9	1.7	1.7	3,134	1,893	3
120	-117	18	-135	6.4	15.0	0.4	1.9	2,632	1,412	3
121	-238	.	.	8.9	10.3	0.9	1.1	17,829	16,634	2
122	24	21	21	18.5	14.0	1.3	2.9	1,789	609	20
123	39	31	.	20.7	12.0	1.7	2.9	1,814	635	55
124	134	107	119	19.3	11.2	1.7	1.7	2,945	1,770	16
125	14	8	12	15.9	13.4	1.2	2.7	1,865	699	17
126	-75	-108	-113	10.4	12.0	0.9	1.2	6,406	5,242	14
127	-120	39	-162	-1.8	8.8	-0.2	2.0	2,329	1,174	-7
128	-9	-30	-19	10.5	11.2	0.9	1.6	2,981	1,842	29
129	-94	65	-125	9.9	14.0	0.7	1.4	3,788	2,652	9
130	350	.	.	41.1	13.2	3.1	1.6	3,002	1,870	49
131	31	171	16	14.4	13.4	1.1	1.3	4,737	3,606	6
132	23	-51	5	10.5	9.7	1.1	1.2	6,214	5,105	32
133	-91	-55	-115	4.8	9.8	0.5	1.7	2,729	1,621	3
134	-322	.	.	4.4	12.3	0.4	1.2	6,068	4,963	21
135	93	139	-56	15.4	12.1	1.3	1.2	6,583	5,479	13
136	253	389	239	23.8	14.7	1.6	1.3	4,394	3,297	5
137	-37	.	.	-6.0	11.3	-0.5	5.1	1,346	265	23
138	22	.	.	13.6	11.0	1.2	2.8	1,691	614	-13
139	24	7	27	15.7	13.8	1.1	1.8	2,400	1,326	19
140	64	55	49	41.2	14.1	2.9	5.3	1,321	248	2
141	54	29	14	25.4	15.8	1.6	2.8	1,668	604	11
142	-8	.	.	4.5	13.0	0.3	9.2	1,190	130	32
143	154	305	187	17.0	11.1	1.5	1.4	4,039	2,987	18
144	113	159	142	39.1	10.1	3.9	5.8	1,273	221	-5
145	42	140	33	16.2	14.0	1.2	1.5	3,116	2,066	8
146	71	56	.	44.2	17.3	2.6	5.0	1,310	264	37
147	-169	239	-201	3.5	13.6	0.3	1.7	2,549	1,530	-13
148	-78	76	-76	12.9	14.5	0.9	1.2	5,834	4,822	7
149	30	37	15	16.7	13.8	1.2	1.9	2,087	1,087	27
150	-44	-21	-41	6.8	9.5	0.7	1.5	3,022	2,023	22

1988 MVA Rank	Company	Type	Industry	1988	Change from 1983	1978
151	Metro Mobile Cts Inc	Pre Z	Telephone Equip. & Services	974	.	.
152	R.R. Donnelley & Sons Co	X	Printing & Advertising	967	473	945
153	Valhi Inc	Z	Conglomerates	964	.	.
154	Tyco Laboratories Inc	Z	Special Machinery	962	904	976
155	Sonoco Products Co	Y	Paper Containers	962	764	996
156	Alexander & Baldwin Inc	X	Trucking & Shipping	950	920	1,053
157	Giant Food Inc	Y	Food Retailing	935	842	992
158	Hershey Foods Corp	Y	Food Processing	934	709	1,069
159	Sigma-Aldrich	Y	Medical Products	915	601	.
160	Comcast Corp	Pre Z	Broadcasting	912	797	.
161	Pennwalt Corp	X-	Chemicals	903	1,069	1,084
162	C.R. Bard Inc	Y	Medical Products	901	609	901
163	Vulcan Materials Co	Y	Building Materials	900	716	902
164	Himont Inc	Y	Chemicals	897	.	.
165	Humana Inc	Y	Health Care Services	894	-443	769
166	Cray Research	Z	Computers & Peripherals	892	318	.
167	United Artists Entmnt	X	Entertainment	889	768	.
168	Oracle Systems Corp	Z	Software	888	.	.
169	Tambrands Inc	Y	Personal Care	885	447	695
170	Brown-Forman	Y	Beverages	878	671	713
171	AMAX Gold Inc	Z	Other Metals	876	.	.
172	Castle & Cooke Inc	X-	Food Processing	876	795	906
173	Super Valu Stores Inc	X	Food Distribution	867	256	763
174	Winn-Dixie Stores Inc	X	Food Retailing	864	414	511
175	Great Atlantic & Pac Tea Co	X	Food Retailing	863	839	1,219
176	Premier Industrial Cp	Y	Industrial Distn Services	861	352	805
177	Maytag Corp	Z	Appliances & Furnishings	846	428	714
178	Sterling Chemicals Inc	Y	Chemicals	842	.	.
179	K Mart Corp	X	Discount & Fashion Retailing	837	237	164
180	Hospital Corp Of America	X-	Health Care Services	836	-634	653
181	Dover Corp	Y	Special Machinery	823	387	714
182	Walgreen Co	X	Drug Distribution	819	162	858
183	Texas Instruments Inc	X-	Semiconductors	815	-737	24
184	Cablevision Systems	Pre Z	Broadcasting	806	.	.
185	Clorox Co	Y	Personal Care	795	512	774
186	Snap-On Tools Corp	Y	Machine & Hand Tools	791	444	600
187	Cellular Communications Inc	Pre Z	Telephone Equip. & Services	773	.	.
188	Nalco Chemical Co	X	Chemicals	744	-23	489
189	Motorola Inc	X-	Electronics	743	-1,997	645
190	Becton, Dickinson & Co	X	Medical Products	742	765	590
191	FMC Corp	X	Special Machinery	740	1,403	1,414
192	Gerber Products Co	X	Food Processing	737	541	750
193	Weis Markets Inc	Y	Food Retailing	736	292	665
194	Rohm & Haas Co	X	Chemicals	728	314	1,025
195	Bandag Inc	Y	Tire & Rubber	726	372	707
196	Battle Mountain Gold Co	Z	Other Metals	726	.	.
197	Sun Microsystems Inc	Z	Computers & Peripherals	723	.	.
198	Contel Corp	X	Telephone Companies	719	1,063	1,015
199	Circus Circus Enterpr Inc	Y	Hotel & Motel	718	563	.
200	Ogden Corp	X-	Conglomerates	717	579	888
201	VF Corp	Z	Apparel	713	149	773
202	Stone Container Corp	Y	Paper Containers	710	481	768
203	Texas Air Corp	Pre Z	Airlines	703	463	687
204	Pall Corp	Y	Conglomerates	697	182	626
205	Jefferson Smurfit Corp	Y	Paper Containers	696	568	.

1988 MVA Rank	Economic Value Added (EVA)			Profitability (1988)				Size (1988)		
		Change from		Rtn on Cap	Wtd Avg Cost Cap	r to	Value to			5-Year Growth in
	1988	1983	1978	r (%)	c* (%)	c*	Capital	Value	Capital	Cap (Avg %)
151	-35	.	.	-20.9	10.6	-2.0	5.8	1,179	205	57
152	-18	-48	-32	14.3	15.3	0.9	1.5	2,792	1,825	16
153	-12	.	.	11.1	11.8	0.9	1.6	2,501	1,537	117
154	48	49	46	18.4	11.5	1.6	1.9	1,998	1,036	31
155	42	40	28	18.3	11.8	1.5	2.3	1,707	745	19
156	19	41	30	13.8	11.7	1.2	1.9	1,955	1,005	9
157	58	41	48	20.6	10.8	1.9	2.4	1,588	653	14
158	83	63	66	19.0	13.5	1.4	1.6	2,631	1,697	14
159	24	19	20	23.2	13.7	1.7	4.0	1,216	301	21
160	-121	-122	-122	1.3	9.7	0.1	1.4	2,996	2,084	80
161	-119	-67	-129	1.5	13.8	0.1	2.7	1,447	544	-9
162	29	24	30	20.5	14.1	1.5	2.8	1,401	500	15
163	48	68	20	18.9	12.4	1.5	2.0	1,776	876	5
164	290	.	.	51.8	14.3	3.6	1.9	1,871	974	24
165	34	-41	0	12.3	11.0	1.1	1.3	3,607	2,713	11
166	53	59	51	23.2	16.2	1.4	2.1	1,731	839	27
167	6	11	7	9.6	9.1	1.1	1.4	2,910	2,020	40
168	104	.	.	68.5	14.9	4.6	2.9	1,352	464	103
169	40	4	18	27.6	15.2	1.8	3.6	1,222	337	24
170	34	20	12	17.6	13.4	1.3	2.1	1,684	806	-2
171	34	.	.	59.8	12.1	4.9	8.1	1,001	124	103
172	-16	90	-39	9.9	11.0	0.9	1.5	2,484	1,608	10
173	46	25	19	13.3	10.3	1.3	1.5	2,635	1,768	19
174	19	-20	-34	11.9	10.6	1.1	1.6	2,427	1,563	9
175	37	73	140	13.1	10.7	1.2	1.5	2,728	1,865	16
176	33	17	22	30.8	15.8	1.9	4.8	1,088	227	5
177	67	28	43	23.1	13.6	1.7	1.8	1,946	1,100	33
178	205	.	.	108.3	11.5	9.4	5.0	1,053	211	4
179	80	30	-107	13.0	12.1	1.1	1.1	11,333	10,496	11
180	-169	-221	-188	7.5	11.0	0.7	1.2	5,842	5,007	8
181	76	70	51	21.3	13.6	1.6	1.6	2,110	1,288	17
182	19	8	22	14.0	12.7	1.1	1.5	2,316	1,497	16
183	-187	196	-208	10.4	15.8	0.7	1.2	4,302	3,487	12
184	-83	.	.	1.5	8.9	0.2	1.6	2,247	1,441	68
185	57	33	40	23.2	13.8	1.7	2.1	1,537	742	12
186	35	31	15	23.0	16.6	1.4	2.2	1,424	633	20
187	-12	.	.	1.1	10.8	0.1	5.3	953	179	83
188	17	7	-8	17.9	15.4	1.2	2.1	1,445	701	10
189	-110	15	-96	13.7	15.9	0.9	1.1	6,808	6,066	16
190	38	148	34	14.3	12.0	1.2	1.4	2,655	1,913	13
191	77	250	35	13.5	9.3	1.5	1.4	2,821	2,082	-0
192	25	8	16	16.2	12.2	1.3	2.2	1,337	601	8
193	62	29	45	43.0	12.9	3.3	4.0	984	248	10
194	38	77	107	17.2	14.9	1.2	1.4	2,600	1,872	8
195	44	23	39	32.9	13.7	2.4	3.7	994	268	11
196	48	.	.	77.2	13.1	5.9	7.1	845	119	29
197	122	.	.	44.1	10.2	4.3	2.0	1,417	694	99
198	-27	-27	-89	9.8	10.4	0.9	1.1	5,893	5,174	6
199	39	23	.	19.9	11.3	1.8	2.5	1,202	484	15
200	-19	90	-20	8.5	11.9	0.7	1.5	2,134	1,417	13
201	-3	-79	-7	13.5	13.6	1.0	1.4	2,348	1,635	35
202	163	247	170	20.6	12.7	1.6	1.3	2,761	2,051	18
203	-724	-491	-729	-0.8	8.9	-0.1	1.1	8,379	7,676	50
204	2	-6	-6	13.7	13.2	1.0	2.6	1,120	423	19
205	101	.	.	32.4	13.9	2.3	2.0	1,360	664	19

1988 MVA Rank	Company	Type	Industry	1988	Change from 1983	Change from 1978
	Company Profile				Market Value Added (MVA)	
206	Amdahl Corp	Y	Computers & Peripherals	683	579	232
207	Community Psychiatric Cntrs	Y	Health Care Services	680	157	659
208	Cincinnati Bell Inc	X	Telephone Companies	679	863	805
209	IMC Fertilizer Group	NA	Chemicals	674	.	.
210	Hillenbrand Industries	Y	General Manufacturing	664	407	633
211	Kelly Services Inc	Y	Other Services	658	459	.
212	Avon Products	X-	Personal Care	657	19	-1,597
213	W.W. Grainger Inc	Y	Industrial Distn Services	656	281	450
214	Novell Inc	Z	Software	650	.	.
215	Prime Motor Inns Inc	X	Hotel & Motel	649	442	635
216	Unocal Corp	X-	Oil & Gas	647	2,144	1,593
217	Georgia Gulf Corp	Y	Chemicals	646	.	.
218	Reebok International Ltd	Z	Apparel	641	.	.
219	Rorer Group	X	Drugs & Research	635	277	476
220	Cooper Industries Inc	X-	Electrical Products	634	868	483
221	FMC Gold Company	Y	Other Metals	626	.	.
222	Consolidated Papers Inc	Y	Paper	610	490	571
223	Phillips Petroleum Co	X-	Oil & Gas	607	3,552	97
224	Tyson Foods Inc	Z	Food Processing	603	542	.
225	Alco Standard Corp	X-	Conglomerates	601	365	630
226	Union Texas Petro Hldgs Inc	X-	Oil & Gas	598	.	.
227	King World Productions Inc	Y	Entertainment	598	.	.
228	John H. Harland Co	Z	Business Machines	593	373	565
229	Rite Aid Corp	Z	Drug Distribution	578	6	514
230	Genentech Inc	Pre Z	Drugs & Research	575	207	.
231	A.H. Robins Co	Pre Z	Medical Products	575	498	628
232	Rockwell Intl Corp	Y	Conglomerates	574	-1,610	1,021
233	American Stores Co	X	Food Retailing	569	-67	487
234	TW Services Inc	X	Eating Places	568	-145	807
235	Worthington Industries	Y	Steel	562	234	.
236	Lubrizol Corp	X-	Chemicals	560	320	23
237	Safety-Kleen Corp	Z	Industrial Distn Services	556	332	.
238	Commerce Clearing House Inc	Y	Publishing	556	154	406
239	Molex Inc	Z	Semiconductors	553	-93	.
240	Neutrogena Corp	Z	Personal Care	544	472	.
241	P.H. Glatfelter Co	Y	Paper	544	528	555
242	Archer-Daniels-Midland Co	X-	Food Processing	542	438	619
243	Koger Properties	Pre Z	Construction & R.E.	542	428	503
244	Neiman-Marcus Group Inc	X-	Discount & Fashion Retailing	539	.	.
245	Occidental Petroleum Corp	X-	Oil & Gas	532	1,531	620
246	Autodesk Inc	Z	Software	528	.	.
247	Circuit City Stores Inc	Z	Appliances & Furnishings	525	418	527
248	Brunos Inc	Z	Food Retailing	521	341	.
249	National Health Laboratories	NA	Health Care Services	521	.	.
250	Alza Corp	Pre Z	Drugs & Research	521	334	.
251	Bausch & Lomb Inc	Y	Personal Care	521	138	516
252	U S Shoe Corp	X-	Discount & Fashion Retailing	519	115	544
253	Mercantile Stores Co Inc	X	Discount & Fashion Retailing	516	286	633
254	USX Corp	X-	Conglomerates	514	4,140	6,411
255	Holly Farms Corp	Y	Food Processing	512	489	517
256	Homestake Mining	X-	Other Metals	510	-479	362
257	Freeport-McMoRan Copper Co	NA	Other Metals	505	.	.
258	Dillard Department Stores	Z	Discount & Fashion Retailing	505	372	557
259	Caesars World	X	Hotel & Motel	502	388	443
260	Scripps Howard Broadcasting	Z	Broadcasting	500	327	.

	Economic Value Added (EVA)			Profitability (1988)				Size (1988)		
1988 MVA Rank	1988	Change from		Rtn on Cap r (%)	Wtd Avg Cost Cap c* (%)	r to c*	Value to Capital	Value	Capital	5-Year Growth in Cap (Avg %)
		1983	1978							
206	143	145	75	34.1	16.8	2.0	1.6	1,843	1,159	10
207	32	19	30	24.3	14.1	1.7	2.8	1,052	372	22
208	-10	-4	-34	9.6	10.5	0.9	1.6	1,775	1,095	8
209	.	.	.	.	.	.	1.6	1,815	1,141	.
210	40	34	35	19.1	12.2	1.6	2.0	1,345	682	22
211	45	36	39	53.8	14.9	3.6	6.7	773	115	10
212	-26	-4	-200	9.2	10.4	0.9	1.4	2,334	1,677	-2
213	24	32	5	18.0	14.8	1.2	1.8	1,446	789	6
214	35	.	.	52.6	15.7	3.3	4.7	824	175	164
215	1	-5	1	11.6	11.5	1.0	1.7	1,537	888	48
216	-1,127	-454	-1,070	-1.5	10.3	-0.1	1.1	9,084	8,437	-0
217	171	.	.	94.8	16.3	5.8	3.0	978	331	15
218	71	.	.	25.6	15.4	1.7	1.7	1,503	862	157
219	27	6	19	13.9	11.7	1.2	1.5	1,921	1,286	30
220	-113	136	-125	9.3	12.9	0.7	1.2	4,252	3,618	13
221	44	.	.	61.0	13.4	4.5	6.9	732	106	-0
222	66	66	44	24.1	14.4	1.7	1.8	1,360	750	13
223	278	746	199	13.4	10.4	1.3	1.1	9,401	8,794	-4
224	187	186	179	47.4	10.1	4.7	1.9	1,306	703	31
225	5	35	-22	13.9	13.4	1.0	1.6	1,661	1,060	5
226	-104	.	.	2.3	10.6	0.2	1.5	1,763	1,165	-8
227	54	.	.	140.8	13.0	10.8	63.3	607	10	-7
228	33	23	30	38.7	14.8	2.6	3.8	802	208	25
229	5	-25	-4	11.4	11.1	1.0	1.4	2,190	1,612	25
230	-19	-15	.	13.1	16.0	0.8	1.8	1,327	752	41
231	-266	-282	-271	6.3	19.8	0.3	1.3	2,551	1,976	39
232	299	224	291	20.6	14.6	1.4	1.1	6,614	6,040	21
233	-20	-38	-32	10.2	10.7	1.0	1.1	6,312	5,743	38
234	-7	172	81	10.5	10.9	1.0	1.3	2,603	2,036	20
235	16	10	7	20.6	15.8	1.3	2.6	912	350	7
236	-31	1	-70	11.0	15.0	0.7	1.8	1,284	724	6
237	7	1	.	16.4	13.7	1.2	2.8	870	313	27
238	6	-4	0	13.4	11.9	1.1	2.1	1,066	510	13
239	13	3	7	21.7	17.3	1.3	2.5	921	368	28
240	20	18	19	96.9	15.1	6.4	13.4	588	44	37
241	-7	-5	-13	12.2	13.7	0.9	2.3	975	431	21
242	127	241	160	18.4	14.0	1.3	1.2	3,734	3,192	10
243	-25	-19	-17	1.8	9.0	0.2	1.9	1,149	608	29
244	-58	.	.	3.1	12.8	0.2	1.8	1,186	647	8
245	-385	336	-78	6.9	9.7	0.7	1.0	17,272	16,739	12
246	27	.	.	67.8	19.2	3.5	8.3	600	72	92
247	34	28	32	21.6	12.6	1.7	2.1	999	474	42
248	59	52	58	34.3	12.3	2.8	2.0	1,034	513	48
249	.	.	.	.	.	.	2.8	816	295	.
250	12	14	23	35.8	17.6	2.0	6.0	626	105	33
251	14	20	4	15.2	13.1	1.2	1.6	1,381	861	13
252	-78	-82	-75	5.6	11.8	0.5	1.4	1,845	1,326	13
253	-13	-26	-24	12.5	13.6	0.9	1.4	1,773	1,257	12
254	-469	3,335	-43	7.4	10.1	0.7	1.0	16,393	15,878	-3
255	34	21	17	17.4	11.6	1.5	1.9	1,101	589	18
256	-11	17	-13	10.2	12.2	0.8	1.7	1,220	710	17
257	.	.	.	.	.	.	4.1	670	165	.
258	44	26	40	15.7	12.1	1.3	1.3	2,266	1,761	38
259	19	73	24	16.5	13.4	1.2	1.9	1,083	581	3
260	14	5	3	11.3	8.5	1.3	1.9	1,052	552	37

1988 MVA Rank	Company Profile Company	Type	Industry	Market Value Added (MVA) 1988	Change from 1983	1978
261	Noxell	Y	Personal Care	495	251	479
262	E.W. Scripps Co	X	Publishing	491	.	.
263	US Cellular Corp	Pre Z	Telephone Equip. & Services	490	.	.
264	Lee Enterprises	Y	Publishing	488	299	400
265	Interpublic Group Of Cos	Y	Printing & Advertising	487	383	454
266	Baxter International Inc	Pre Z	Medical Products	485	-1,415	-211
267	Household International Inc	X-	Conglomerates	484	1,055	1,084
268	Flightsafety International	Y	Transportation Services	482	188	418
269	Tandem Computers Inc	X	Computers & Peripherals	480	-525	.
270	Charming Shoppes	Z	Discount & Fashion Retailing	480	255	.
271	Rollins Environmental Svcs	Z	Pollution Control	480	442	.
272	Associated Communications	X-	Telephone Equip. & Services	473	403	.
273	Vista Chemical Co	Y	Chemicals	470	.	.
274	Jostens Inc	Y	General Manufacturing	469	246	411
275	Hubbell Inc	Y	Electrical Products	467	357	476
276	Anadarko Petroleum Corp	X-	Oil & Gas	466	.	.
277	Acuson Corp	Z	Medical Products	465	.	.
278	EG&G Inc	Y	Construct. & Eng. Services	462	-257	355
279	Lands' End Inc	Z	Discount & Fashion Retailing	460	.	.
280	Centel Corp	X-	Telephone Companies	459	668	594
281	Crown Cork & Seal Co Inc	X	Glass, Metal & Plastics	458	606	496
282	Mead Corp	X	Paper	454	509	771
283	Dean Foods Co	Y	Food Processing	451	276	.
284	Adobe Systems Inc	Z	Software	451	.	.
285	Roadway Services Inc	Z	Trucking & Shipping	447	-379	255
286	Telephone & Data Systems	X-	Telephone Equip. & Services	447	454	.
287	Pacific Telesis Group	X	Telephone Companies	445	.	.
288	Freeport-McMoRan Gold Co	Y	Other Metals	442	.	.
289	Great Lakes Chemical Corp	Y	Chemicals	442	110	346
290	A.T. Cross & Co	Y	General Manufacturing	438	261	376
291	Thomas & Betts Corp	Y	Semiconductors	438	84	257
292	Betz Laboratories Inc	Y	Chemicals	438	21	285
293	Flowers Industries Inc	Y	Food Processing	435	249	424
294	Rexene Corp	Z	Chemicals	434	.	.
295	Envirodyne Industries Inc	X	General Manufacturing	428	363	.
296	Media General	X	Publishing	425	346	447
297	Nucor Corp	X	Steel	419	165	391
298	National Education Corp	Z	Other Services	417	302	431
299	Millipore Corp	Y	Instruments	415	272	.
300	Medtronic Inc	Y	Medical Products	413	172	341
301	Tejon Ranch Co	X-	Food Processing	412	316	392
302	Calgon Carbon Corp	Y	Pollution Control	409	.	.
303	MGM/UA Communications Inc	X-	Entertainment	406	.	.
304	Blockbuster Enmnt Corp	Pre Z	Other Leisure	405	403	.
305	GTE Corp	X-	Telephone Companies	400	2,585	2,090
306	Chambers Development Co Inc	X	Pollution Control	397	.	.
307	Lance Inc	Y	Food Processing	392	215	.
308	Paccar Inc	X-	Cars & Trucks	391	128	509
309	National Service Inds Inc	X	Electrical Products	391	135	420
310	Longview Fibre Co	Y	Paper Containers	391	307	311
311	Nike Inc	Y	Apparel	390	152	.
312	GenCorp Inc	X-	Aerospace	390	912	1,028
313	Air Products & Chemicals Inc	X-	Chemicals	383	312	384
314	Chris-Craft Industries	X	Broadcasting	381	240	398
315	Alltel Corp	X	Telephone Companies	377	517	445

1988 MVA Rank	Economic Value Added (EVA)			Profitability (1988)				Size (1988)		5-Year Growth in Cap (Avg %)
	1988	Change from 1983	1978	Rtn on Cap r (%)	Wtd Avg Cost Cap c* (%)	r to c*	Value to Capital	Value	Capital	
261	31	20	25	32.3	14.4	2.2	3.6	687	192	12
262	-3	.	.	12.1	12.3	1.0	1.3	1,936	1,445	7
263	-15	.	.	-8.2	12.5	-0.7	5.1	610	120	65
264	19	14	13	19.8	11.9	1.7	2.9	739	251	11
265	32	37	22	19.1	12.4	1.5	1.8	1,119	631	13
266	-232	-324	-262	8.8	12.2	0.7	1.1	8,054	7,568	35
267	.	.	.	.	.	.	1.0	25,039	24,555	21
268	23	5	20	22.6	13.9	1.6	2.6	789	307	22
269	-7	8	-9	16.0	16.7	1.0	1.4	1,792	1,313	25
270	5	-4	-1	15.9	14.6	1.1	2.4	831	352	25
271	14	16	.	26.5	16.2	1.6	4.1	633	153	28
272	-5	0	.	40.4	17.8	2.3	-21	451	-22	.
273	106	.	.	35.6	13.1	2.7	1.9	998	528	9
274	17	-2	5	21.8	12.7	1.7	3.7	640	171	4
275	32	38	26	23.9	15.0	1.6	2.2	873	406	10
276	-64	.	.	5.5	10.1	0.5	1.3	1,848	1,382	4
277	28	.	.	67.4	16.3	4.1	5.4	571	106	64
278	16	-3	10	17.7	13.7	1.3	2.1	880	418	17
279	29	.	.	71.2	14.5	4.9	6.5	544	84	34
280	-228	-217	-276	3.0	10.5	0.3	1.1	3,906	3,447	11
281	-21	27	-37	12.9	15.6	0.8	1.6	1,196	738	2
282	64	326	45	16.1	13.6	1.2	1.2	3,378	2,924	9
283	22	14	17	19.3	13.0	1.5	2.2	843	392	20
284	22	.	.	134.7	15.3	8.8	12.9	489	38	77
285	-14	-62	-55	13.6	16.2	0.8	1.6	1,169	722	42
286	-24	-14	-23	5.1	10.6	0.5	1.9	961	514	13
287	-578	.	.	7.6	10.7	0.7	1.0	19,580	19,135	3
288	19	.	.	42.9	11.2	3.8	5.1	551	109	22
289	47	43	40	24.4	15.3	1.6	1.8	1,031	589	24
290	23	20	15	41.6	14.7	2.8	5.7	532	93	5
291	16	23	3	19.1	14.4	1.3	2.0	866	428	15
292	15	7	8	20.7	14.9	1.4	2.5	730	292	9
293	25	17	21	17.9	10.2	1.7	2.2	784	350	18
294	116	.	.	48.5	13.9	3.5	1.9	903	469	134
295	29	23	51	23.9	12.8	1.9	2.4	733	306	.
296	-8	-10	-9	11.6	12.6	0.9	1.5	1,205	780	15
297	15	26	-3	20.1	16.1	1.2	1.7	1,015	595	15
298	45	85	45	28.0	11.9	2.4	2.0	835	419	34
299	4	17	-1	15.6	14.9	1.0	1.6	1,069	654	21
300	36	10	24	20.1	13.5	1.5	1.6	1,102	689	14
301	-3	0	-1	1.9	13.8	0.1	20.6	433	21	-9
302	14	.	.	25.7	13.7	1.9	3.8	555	146	13
303	-156	.	.	-0.9	13.2	-0.1	1.3	1,693	1,287	25
304	10	11	.	27.1	14.9	1.8	3.0	604	199	125
305	-825	-618	-712	7.3	10.4	0.7	1.0	28,674	28,274	5
306	-0	.	.	12.4	12.6	1.0	2.5	669	272	70
307	24	8	16	29.8	13.4	2.2	3.1	575	183	9
308	68	186	16	25.1	15.5	1.6	1.5	1,219	828	0
309	9	-13	2	16.6	14.9	1.1	1.7	978	587	9
310	49	82	57	24.0	13.5	1.8	1.7	953	562	8
311	92	88	.	32.0	15.9	2.0	1.6	1,023	633	5
312	-11	126	-54	10.2	11.6	0.9	1.4	1,340	950	-10
313	-17	68	-31	12.9	13.6	0.9	1.1	3,097	2,714	9
314	-30	-28	-30	8.2	12.6	0.7	1.5	1,090	710	53
315	71	26	58	16.1	11.1	1.4	1.2	2,207	1,831	9

1988 MVA Rank	Company	Type	Industry	1988	Change from 1983	Change from 1978
	Company Profile			Market Value Added (MVA)		
316	E-Systems Inc	X	Electronics	375	-304	361
317	Vanguard Cellular Sys	Pre Z	Telephone Equip. & Services	374	.	.
318	Intergraph Corp	Z	Software	371	-407	.
319	Pep Boys-Manny Moe & Jack	X	Auto Parts & Equipment	362	241	384
320	Wellman Inc	Z	Chemicals	361	.	.
321	Ashland Oil Inc	X-	Oil & Gas	358	1,347	494
322	Lotus Development Corp	Z	Software	358	-65	.
323	Amgen Inc	Pre Z	Drugs & Research	355	338	.
324	Bell Atlantic Corp	X	Telephone Companies	353	.	.
325	Loctite Corp	Y	Chemicals	352	87	194
326	Medco Containment Svcs Inc	X	Drug Distribution	352	.	.
327	Geo. A. Hormel & Co	X	Food Processing	352	370	414
328	Stratus Computer Inc	Z	Computers & Peripherals	351	194	.
329	Alberto-Culver Co	X	Personal Care	350	354	377
330	J.B. Hunt Transport Svcs Inc	Z	Trucking & Shipping	349	174	.
331	3Com Corp	Z	Software	348	.	.
332	AMAX Inc	X-	Aluminum	347	398	454
333	Yellow Freight System	X-	Trucking & Shipping	347	80	327
334	Computer Sciences Corp	X	Software	345	244	256
335	Newell Companies	X	General Manufacturing	344	315	358
336	Masco Industries Inc	X	Auto Parts & Equipment	341	.	.
337	Comdisco Inc	X	Software	339	-1	302
338	Universal Foods Corp	X	Food Processing	335	302	293
339	Cintas Corp	Y	Other Services	334	.	.
340	Raychem Corp	X-	Electrical Products	330	-6	229
341	Nordson Corp	Y	Special Machinery	330	298	.
342	Biomet Inc	Z	Medical Products	330	292	.
343	Black & Decker Corp	X-	Machine & Hand Tools	329	-216	145
344	Scott Paper Co	X	Paper	329	522	866
345	Stanley Works	X	Machine & Hand Tools	329	150	426
346	Thiokol Corp	X	Chemicals	327	-244	308
347	St Jude Medical Inc	Y	Medical Products	324	269	.
348	Trinity Industries	X-	General Manufacturing	324	146	331
349	Sherwin-Williams Co	X	Building Materials	323	197	515
350	Topps Co Inc	Y	Publishing	323	.	.
351	Longs Drug Stores Inc	Y	Drug Distribution	319	60	155
352	Pioneer Hi-Bred Intl	Y	Food Processing	318	-229	.
353	Century Telephone Enterprise	X	Telephone Equip. & Services	318	374	338
354	Avery International	X	General Manufacturing	318	364	347
355	Armor All Products Corp	Y	Other Services	317	.	.
356	Hamilton Oil Corp	X	Oil & Gas	315	303	.
357	Rollins Inc	Y	Other Services	315	127	229
358	Parker-Hannifin Corp	X-	Aerospace	314	-9	262
359	Calmat Co	Z	Building Materials	313	204	329
360	Dana Corp	X-	Auto Parts & Equipment	313	78	195
361	Bolar Pharmaceutical Co Inc	Z	Drugs & Research	312	236	.
362	Ametek Inc	X	Electrical Products	310	-47	288
363	Telecom USA Inc	Z	Telephone Equip. & Services	310	.	.
364	Keystone International	X	General Manufacturing	309	79	256
365	Sotheby's Holdings	Y	Other Services	309	.	.
366	Chicago Milwaukee Corp	X-	Railroads	307	47	250
367	Mapco Inc	X	Oil & Gas	305	465	122
368	Navistar International	X	Cars & Trucks	305	-237	1,351
369	Hercules Inc	X-	Chemicals	301	-42	608
370	New England Business Svc Inc	Y	Business Machines	300	53	.

1988 MVA Rank	Economic Value Added (EVA)			Profitability (1988)				Size (1988)		
		Change from		Rtn on Cap	Wtd Avg Cost Cap	r to	Value to			5-Year Growth in
	1988	1983	1978	r (%)	c* (%)	c*	Capital	Value	Capital	Cap (Avg %)
316	6	-17	4	15.0	13.9	1.1	1.6	1,016	641	21
317	-29	.	.	-44.1	10.4	-4.3	3.9	502	127	142
318	13	-5	.	19.6	17.4	1.1	1.5	1,058	687	29
319	1	1	-0	11.9	11.8	1.0	1.7	865	503	32
320	20	.	.	23.9	12.8	1.9	2.8	566	206	27
321	-295	51	-154	2.2	11.4	0.2	1.1	3,367	3,008	0
322	90	.	.	50.6	14.8	3.4	1.9	739	382	98
323	-36	-26	.	-12.1	17.2	-0.7	3.1	521	166	39
324	170	.	.	11.0	10.1	1.1	1.0	22,429	22,077	8
325	21	20	8	24.5	14.6	1.7	2.6	573	221	10
326	3	.	.	16.9	15.0	1.1	2.3	627	275	67
327	-4	0	-12	11.8	12.5	0.9	1.7	835	483	7
328	26	25	.	35.1	15.9	2.2	2.7	561	210	59
329	7	16	10	16.9	12.8	1.3	2.9	538	188	7
330	20	13	.	20.9	11.6	1.8	2.4	602	252	48
331	37	36	.	38.2	14.8	2.6	2.3	610	262	91
332	336	1,475	506	22.4	12.2	1.8	1.1	3,645	3,298	-4
333	-22	-22	-44	11.2	14.1	0.8	1.4	1,167	820	18
334	-0	2	-6	13.8	13.8	1.0	1.7	845	500	14
335	-12	-15	-15	12.9	14.6	0.9	1.5	1,008	664	31
336	-24	.	.	8.5	10.2	0.8	1.2	2,194	1,854	45
337	-69	-65	-63	9.9	12.2	0.8	1.1	4,901	4,563	41
338	-8	-16	-19	9.6	12.0	0.8	1.9	687	353	9
339	8	4	.	18.4	12.6	1.5	3.2	488	154	24
340	17	45	19	15.6	13.5	1.1	1.3	1,291	961	15
341	22	32	14	32.2	13.5	2.4	3.4	467	137	9
342	15	13	.	34.7	17.4	2.0	4.3	429	100	43
343	-49	30	-49	10.2	13.5	0.8	1.2	1,851	1,522	15
344	125	311	180	15.6	12.2	1.3	1.1	4,248	3,919	12
345	-25	8	-22	11.4	13.4	0.9	1.2	1,666	1,338	15
346	17	-35	3	16.1	14.9	1.1	1.2	1,998	1,671	13
347	25	23	25	79.3	15.9	5.0	7.0	378	54	16
348	62	113	62	25.8	13.1	2.0	1.4	1,239	916	20
349	37	61	93	19.7	14.7	1.3	1.3	1,268	945	8
350	33	.	.	49.0	9.5	5.1	4.9	405	83	3
351	16	5	4	17.7	13.6	1.3	1.8	744	425	10
352	-18	-32	-32	10.9	13.1	0.8	1.4	1,143	824	9
353	-6	-2	-9	9.4	10.9	0.9	1.7	765	447	7
354	18	12	17	14.7	12.5	1.2	1.3	1,267	949	20
355	13	.	.	30.0	17.4	1.7	3.5	445	128	23
356	-65	-53	-70	1.2	11.1	0.1	1.6	880	565	13
357	7	39	-1	18.4	12.5	1.5	3.3	454	139	-14
358	-32	41	-49	12.4	15.0	0.8	1.2	1,868	1,554	18
359	9	11	10	13.9	12.2	1.1	1.5	937	624	46
360	-11	91	-85	11.4	11.9	1.0	1.1	2,788	2,475	7
361	24	20	23	50.0	18.7	2.7	4.5	401	89	36
362	-32	-27	-43	3.2	12.3	0.3	2.0	621	311	6
363	37	.	.	48.5	14.0	3.5	2.1	587	278	169
364	-3	3	-9	10.8	12.0	0.9	2.2	558	248	23
365	45	.	.	35.1	13.5	2.6	2.4	531	222	7
366	40	39	39	-9.0	10.3	-0.9	-14	286	-20	.
367	26	116	-0	13.8	11.1	1.2	1.3	1,326	1,020	-6
368	69	976	104	22.1	16.6	1.3	1.2	1,683	1,377	-12
369	-51	112	7	10.6	13.4	0.8	1.1	2,435	2,134	3
370	14	10	.	35.9	14.1	2.6	5.2	372	72	16

1988 MVA Rank	Company	Type	Industry	Market Value Added (MVA) 1988	Change from 1983	Change from 1978
371	Martin Marietta Corp	X	Aerospace	298	396	603
372	McCormick & Co	X	Food Processing	297	148	260
373	TCA Cable TV Inc	Z	Broadcasting	296	227	.
374	Consolidated Freightways Inc	X	Trucking & Shipping	295	135	367
375	Houghton Mifflin Co	X	Publishing	294	254	270
376	ITEL Corp	Pre Z	Conglomerates	292	239	257
377	Measurex Corp	Y	Instruments	290	272	248
378	Louisiana-Pacific Corp	X-	Forest Products	290	215	365
379	Costco Wholesale Corporation	X	Discount & Fashion Retailing	287	.	.
380	McKesson Corp	X	Drug Distribution	286	318	397
381	Baker-Hughes Inc	X-	Petroleum Services	285	320	-180
382	Dress Barn Inc	Z	Discount & Fashion Retailing	282	243	.
383	Ohio Mattress Co	X	Appliances & Furnishings	280	159	276
384	Noble Affiliates Inc	X-	Petroleum Services	278	70	108
385	J.M. Smucker Co	Y	Food Processing	277	217	294
386	Philips Industries Inc	Y	General Manufacturing	277	181	296
387	Luby's Cafeterias Inc	Y	Eating Places	277	6	.
388	Allegheny International Inc	X-	Appliances & Furnishings	276	316	638
389	Businessland Inc	Pre Z	Business Machines	275	43	.
390	Grossmans Inc	X-	Discount & Fashion Retailing	273	.	.
391	Columbia Pictures Entmnt Inc	Pre Z	Entertainment	271	.	.
392	West Point-Pepperell	Pre Z	Textiles	270	300	454
393	Pier 1 Imports Inc	Z	Appliances & Furnishings	270	186	.
394	San Juan Basin Royalty Trust	Y	Oil & Gas	269	-73	.
395	Fleming Companies Inc	X	Food Distribution	266	42	273
396	Tiffany & Co	Z	Discount & Fashion Retailing	265	.	.
397	New Plan Realty Trust	Z	Construction & R.E.	263	190	255
398	Intl Dairy Queen	Y	Eating Places	262	200	.
399	Precision Castparts Corp	Z	Other Metals	261	221	.
400	Allegheny Ludlum Corp	Z	Steel	261	.	.
401	Eaton Corp	X-	Auto Parts & Equipment	258	12	664
402	Aristech Chemical Corp	X-	Chemicals	258	.	.
403	Weingarten Realty Invst	X-	Construction & R.E.	258	.	.
404	Wetterau Inc	X	Food Distribution	256	246	261
405	Hechinger Co	Z	Discount & Fashion Retailing	254	108	.
406	Blair Corp	Y	Discount & Fashion Retailing	252	144	238
407	Systematics Inc	Y	Software	250	84	.
408	Home Shopping Network	Z	Discount & Fashion Retailing	250	.	.
409	Block Drug	Y	Personal Care	250	221	.
410	Carter Hawley Hale Stores	X-	Discount & Fashion Retailing	250	346	439
411	Whirlpool Corp	X-	Appliances & Furnishings	248	-241	348
412	Pic 'N' Save Corp	Z	Discount & Fashion Retailing	245	-241	.
413	Century Communications Corp	X	Broadcasting	243	.	.
414	Alexander's Inc	X-	Discount & Fashion Retailing	242	240	285
415	Mattel Inc	X	Other Leisure	238	56	262
416	Service Corp International	X	Other Services	237	87	269
417	Greif Bros Corp	X	Paper Containers	237	157	.
418	Gerber Scientific Inc	X	Software	234	98	238
419	Forest City Enterprises	X-	Building Materials	233	157	247
420	Atari Corp	Z	Computers & Peripherals	232	.	.
421	Russell Corp	Y	Apparel	232	118	251
422	Danaher Corp	X	Auto Parts & Equipment	231	182	248
423	Hecla Mining Co	Pre Z	Other Metals	229	-202	149
424	Forest Laboratories	X	Drugs & Research	229	122	233
425	First Union Real Estate	X	Construction & R.E.	229	65	220

1988 MVA Rank	Economic Value Added (EVA)			Profitability (1988)				Size (1988)		5-Year Growth in Cap (Avg %)
	1988	Change from		Rtn on Cap r (%)	Wtd Avg Cost Cap c* (%)	r to c*	Value to Capital	Value	Capital	
		1983	1978							
371	-92	148	-91	9.9	14.1	0.7	1.1	2,812	2,515	4
372	-7	-12	-7	9.6	10.9	0.9	1.5	866	569	13
373	2	-2	.	12.2	10.9	1.1	3.3	426	130	31
374	-11	-15	-43	12.7	13.8	0.9	1.3	1,377	1,082	15
375	6	6	2	18.4	14.4	1.3	2.4	502	208	14
376	18	95	-27	10.4	9.4	1.1	1.1	3,914	3,622	31
377	19	30	24	32.8	16.3	2.0	3.6	403	113	4
378	-73	53	-163	7.5	12.9	0.6	1.3	1,126	837	-2
379	-5	.	.	8.7	10.3	0.8	1.9	607	321	69
380	-71	-29	-62	6.9	11.5	0.6	1.2	1,792	1,506	8
381	-230	42	-262	3.3	14.2	0.2	1.1	2,212	1,927	-2
382	11	9	.	32.5	13.8	2.4	4.6	361	79	46
383	3	-2	2	12.8	12.2	1.1	1.6	780	500	67
384	-50	26	-60	2.2	12.6	0.2	1.6	725	447	-7
385	16	13	15	26.7	13.1	2.0	3.1	408	130	15
386	16	13	17	20.9	15.0	1.4	1.7	660	383	23
387	12	5	9	22.6	13.1	1.7	2.9	423	147	18
388	-99	125	-24	-1.1	13.8	-0.1	1.4	968	691	-14
389	6	.	.	16.9	13.4	1.3	2.1	515	240	72
390	29	.	.	-633	7.7	-82	6.3	325	52	17
391	-256	.	.	2.8	12.8	0.2	1.1	3,528	3,257	28
392	-5	15	17	11.9	12.1	1.0	1.1	2,565	2,295	28
393	10	8	.	13.0	9.7	1.3	1.7	643	374	40
394	-0	-23	.	12.1	12.6	1.0	3.7	367	98	-3
395	37	33	34	15.1	11.1	1.4	1.1	2,063	1,797	33
396	17	.	.	29.0	12.3	2.4	2.7	419	153	25
397	10	5	10	17.2	10.1	1.7	2.6	432	169	32
398	12	9	11	22.3	11.1	2.0	3.4	371	108	18
399	12	14	11	19.3	13.4	1.4	2.0	526	265	30
400	140	.	.	44.1	14.9	3.0	1.4	869	608	27
401	-274	-206	-329	3.7	12.8	0.3	1.1	2,931	2,673	8
402	76	.	.	31.5	16.7	1.9	1.5	825	567	8
403	-1	4	1	9.4	9.7	1.0	1.7	609	351	11
404	11	20	10	12.0	10.0	1.2	1.3	1,063	808	20
405	22	15	20	18.7	12.2	1.5	1.5	797	543	33
406	13	11	11	27.2	13.8	2.0	3.4	357	105	10
407	10	5	.	28.0	14.2	2.0	4.3	326	76	17
408	-10	.	.	10.1	12.8	0.8	1.5	734	484	158
409	10	5	-2	15.7	12.3	1.3	1.7	591	341	14
410	-21	33	-31	6.8	8.3	0.8	1.2	1,598	1,348	-6
411	-103	-156	-145	10.5	15.4	0.7	1.1	2,414	2,166	17
412	23	-3	19	29.5	16.0	1.8	2.1	468	223	37
413	35	.	.	13.7	9.2	1.5	1.2	1,271	1,028	70
414	-18	-10	-14	-2.5	9.8	-0.3	2.6	393	151	-1
415	3	57	-7	11.7	11.2	1.0	1.5	734	496	1
416	-77	-72	-73	5.4	12.5	0.4	1.1	1,856	1,620	41
417	10	15	10	16.6	11.8	1.4	2.0	465	229	8
418	-0	1	-2	17.4	17.4	1.0	2.1	452	218	19
419	-8	3	-10	6.9	10.1	0.7	1.8	534	302	12
420	6	.	.	18.3	15.0	1.2	3.3	334	101	34
421	22	25	15	18.0	12.2	1.5	1.4	753	521	15
422	23	64	47	14.7	9.9	1.5	1.6	615	384	53
423	2	-9	9	14.6	13.0	1.1	2.7	365	136	25
424	5	6	6	21.7	17.7	1.2	2.4	395	166	35
425	4	2	7	10.6	9.5	1.1	1.6	587	359	2

1988 MVA Rank	Company	Type	Industry	1988	Change from 1983	Change from 1978
	Company Profile			Market Value Added (MVA)		
426	Watts Industries	Y	General Manufacturing	228	.	.
427	United Television Inc	Y	Broadcasting	227	108	.
428	Bob Evans Farms	Y	Eating Places	227	-47	.
429	TCBY Enterprises Inc	Z	Eating Places	226	.	.
430	Omnicom Group	Z	Printing & Advertising	225	177	.
431	Echlin Inc	X-	Auto Parts & Equipment	225	-11	107
432	Hannaford Brothers Co	Y	Food Retailing	225	188	234
433	A. Schulman Inc	X	Chemicals	224	240	.
434	Vons Companies Inc	Pre Z	Food Retailing	223	.	.
435	Brunswick Corp	Z	Other Leisure	222	-19	481
436	Morrison Inc	X	Eating Places	222	115	150
437	Symbol Technologies	Z	Computers & Peripherals	220	192	.
438	Oshkosh B'Gosh Inc	Z	Apparel	219	.	.
439	Harsco Corp	X-	General Manufacturing	219	242	273
440	Figgie International	X	Conglomerates	216	302	326
441	Combustion Engineering Inc	X-	Construct. & Eng. Services	215	418	510
442	Cabot Corp	X-	Chemicals	214	412	315
443	Armstrong World Inds Inc	X	Appliances & Furnishings	212	362	468
444	Mentor Graphics Corp	X	Software	210	.	.
445	Bemis Co	X	Paper Containers	209	336	363
446	Wallace Computer Svcs Inc	Y	Business Machines	209	32	205
447	Oryx Energy Co	X-	Oil & Gas	207	.	.
448	Family Dollar Stores	Z	Discount & Fashion Retailing	205	-118	191
449	Louisiana Land & Exploration	X-	Oil & Gas	204	244	-6
450	Johnson Controls Inc	X	Instruments	204	51	202
451	Applied Biosystems Inc	Z	Instruments	204	142	.
452	Intl Lease Finance Corp	X	Transportation Services	203	183	.
453	Ideal Basic Industries Inc	X-	Building Materials	203	357	265
454	Emhart Corp	X	General Manufacturing	202	152	275
455	Olsten Corp	Z	Other Services	199	174	.
456	Ashton-Tate Co	Z	Software	196	130	.
457	Service Merchandise Co	X	Discount & Fashion Retailing	196	-36	.
458	Ocean Drilling & Exploration	X-	Petroleum Services	195	-295	114
459	Stryker Corp	Z	Medical Products	194	100	.
460	Park Communications Inc	X	Publishing	194	91	.
461	U S Surgical Corp	X	Medical Products	194	129	.
462	Stride Rite Corp	Y	Apparel	194	106	196
463	Ecolab Inc	X	Personal Care	193	-6	80
464	RPM Inc	X	Building Materials	191	130	.
465	Carter-Wallace Inc	X	Drugs & Research	189	252	293
466	Sealed Air Corp	Y	General Manufacturing	187	107	183
467	Chaparral Steel Company	Y	Steel	187	.	.
468	Albany International Corp	Y	Textiles	186	.	.
469	Square D Co	X	Electrical Products	184	-215	109
470	AAR Corp	X	Industrial Distn Services	183	206	189
471	Teleflex Inc	Y	General Manufacturing	182	86	177
472	Stanhome Inc	Y	Personal Care	181	188	203
473	Manor Care Inc	X	Health Care Services	181	-15	182
474	Shaw Industries Inc	X	Textiles	180	79	193
475	Morrison Knudsen Corp	X-	Construct. & Eng. Services	180	253	245
476	IBP Inc	X-	Food Processing	176	.	198
477	W.R. Grace & Co	X-	Chemicals	176	666	710
478	Fuqua Industries Inc	X	Conglomerates	176	147	333
479	Litton Industries Inc	X-	Electronics	175	-515	604
480	Universal Corp-Va	X	Tobacco	174	120	161

1988 MVA Rank	Economic Value Added (EVA)			Profitability (1988)				Size (1988)		5-Year Growth in Cap (Avg %)
	1988	Change from 1983	1978	Rtn on Cap r (%)	Wtd Avg Cost Cap c* (%)	r to c*	Value to Capital	Value	Capital	
426	9	.	.	22.2	12.9	1.7	3.0	340	112	14
427	-0	-4	.	11.8	12.0	1.0	2.5	382	155	15
428	6	1	2	16.7	13.6	1.2	2.1	432	205	21
429	12	.	.	43.2	16.0	2.7	4.1	299	73	77
430	5	5	1	11.7	10.9	1.1	1.4	788	563	34
431	-36	-29	-44	9.8	14.7	0.7	1.3	1,062	837	20
432	9	8	9	16.3	12.6	1.3	1.7	561	336	24
433	5	3	5	19.1	15.7	1.2	2.3	389	166	15
434	-65	.	.	3.5	9.4	0.4	1.2	1,551	1,329	56
435	108	123	119	21.8	14.5	1.5	1.1	1,916	1,694	30
436	-1	-4	-7	11.4	11.9	1.0	1.8	498	277	8
437	18	20	.	89.9	16.1	5.6	4.9	277	57	69
438	8	.	.	25.0	16.3	1.5	2.7	346	128	28
439	-38	10	-62	7.0	12.9	0.5	1.3	916	698	6
440	6	38	4	14.0	13.0	1.1	1.3	927	711	12
441	-602	-442	-762	-23.6	13.2	-1.8	1.2	1,494	1,279	7
442	-134	12	-147	1.0	12.9	0.1	1.2	1,426	1,212	-1
443	28	81	31	18.3	16.2	1.1	1.1	2,061	1,850	15
444	12	.	.	28.7	20.8	1.4	2.2	389	179	26
445	6	35	4	14.5	13.3	1.1	1.4	747	538	7
446	5	4	5	16.3	14.0	1.2	1.9	446	237	19
447	-780	.	.	-6.3	11.3	-0.6	1.1	3,932	3,725	-28
448	5	-2	2	15.1	12.8	1.2	1.7	482	277	28
449	-238	-121	-275	-4.1	11.7	-0.3	1.1	1,621	1,417	0
450	17	11	8	13.6	12.3	1.1	1.1	1,775	1,571	24
451	11	12	.	29.0	17.8	1.6	3.0	307	103	35
452	-17	-22	.	8.3	9.8	0.8	1.1	1,930	1,727	44
453	-58	90	-76	-2.6	10.6	-0.2	1.5	643	440	-16
454	-29	23	-76	10.6	12.2	0.9	1.1	2,461	2,259	20
455	12	11	11	36.1	14.7	2.5	3.2	290	91	27
456	56	48	.	49.9	18.1	2.8	1.7	476	279	66
457	33	17	16	14.3	10.6	1.3	1.2	1,034	839	21
458	-162	-39	-118	-5.3	13.5	-0.4	1.2	987	792	-8
459	8	6	.	23.2	15.8	1.5	2.5	328	133	32
460	-1	-1	.	10.7	11.1	1.0	1.9	411	217	13
461	10	39	7	14.4	10.4	1.4	1.7	482	288	9
462	23	18	21	27.1	13.3	2.0	1.8	423	229	6
463	-3	2	-11	11.5	11.9	1.0	1.2	1,100	908	24
464	4	3	0	13.3	11.7	1.1	1.8	437	246	18
465	7	17	17	17.4	15.1	1.2	1.5	542	353	8
466	7	7	5	17.8	13.5	1.3	2.0	378	192	18
467	29	.	.	24.1	13.4	1.8	1.7	470	284	5
468	10	.	.	14.5	11.9	1.2	1.4	649	463	20
469	100	133	60	22.3	13.3	1.7	1.1	1,443	1,259	8
470	21	26	21	22.2	13.4	1.7	1.6	494	311	26
471	-1	-2	-0	12.9	13.5	1.0	2.0	367	185	22
472	26	24	22	31.6	14.9	2.1	2.1	341	160	6
473	-9	-21	-10	8.9	10.3	0.9	1.3	872	692	8
474	10	14	10	17.1	13.7	1.2	1.4	635	455	28
475	-99	-40	-103	-5.6	13.3	-0.4	1.5	570	390	-6
476	12	2	-2	13.1	11.8	1.1	1.2	1,017	840	13
477	-149	215	-104	8.5	12.4	0.7	1.0	4,567	4,391	-1
478	2	4	-19	12.5	12.1	1.0	1.2	1,073	897	16
479	-49	14	48	9.1	11.2	0.8	1.1	2,964	2,789	11
480	5	3	-0	11.6	10.9	1.1	1.2	955	781	19

	Company Profile			Market Value Added (MVA)		
1988 MVA Rank	Company	Type	Industry	1988	Change from 1983	Change from 1978
481	Chemed Corp	X	Personal Care	173	-56	20
482	First Financial Mgmt Corp	Z	Software	173	145	.
483	United Stationers Inc	X	Industrial Distn Services	171	54	.
484	Willamette Industries	X	Forest Products	170	142	146
485	Lyphomed Inc	Z	Drugs & Research	170	112	.
486	Brush Wellman Inc	X-	Other Metals	170	-137	206
487	Cypress Semiconductor Corp	Z	Semiconductors	170	.	.
488	JWP Inc	Z	Other Services	169	115	.
489	CPI Corp	Z	Other Leisure	169	18	.
490	Bergen Brunswig Corp	X	Drug Distribution	168	-2	188
491	Trans World Music Corp	Z	Other Leisure	165	.	.
492	Caesars New Jersey Inc	X	Hotel & Motel	165	5	.
493	Kinder-Care Learning Centers	X-	Other Services	165	.	.
494	Meredith Corp	X-	Publishing	162	6	213
495	Ogilvy Group	Y	Printing & Advertising	160	51	135
496	Hon Industries	X	Business Machines	160	55	.
497	Thermo Electron Corp	X-	Construct. & Eng. Services	159	122	.
498	Santa Fe Pacific Corp	X-	Railroads	159	2,944	2,008
499	Reynolds Metals Co	X-	Aluminum	159	1,266	1,155
500	First Mississippi Corp	X-	Chemicals	155	124	170
501	NCH Corp	Y	Personal Care	154	130	122
502	Fleetwood Enterprises	Z	Other Leisure	153	-230	164
503	Stone & Webster Inc	X	Construct. & Eng. Services	153	117	147
504	Golden Nugget Inc	X	Hotel & Motel	152	5	104
505	Goulds Pumps Inc	X-	Special Machinery	151	-13	87
506	Ball Corp	X-	Glass, Metal & Plastics	151	144	215
507	Conner Peripherals	Z	Software	149	.	.
508	U S Healthcare Inc	Y	Health Care Services	149	-4	.
509	Standard Products Co	Y	Auto Parts & Equipment	142	58	158
510	Herman Miller Inc	Y	Business Machines	142	-109	.
511	Loral Corp	X	Electronics	141	-205	103
512	Intertan Inc	X-	Appliances & Furnishings	140	.	.
513	Ross Stores Inc	X-	Discount & Fashion Retailing	139	.	.
514	Cooper Tire & Rubber	Y	Tire & Rubber	139	177	200
515	Crane Co	X	General Manufacturing	138	150	338
516	Western Publishing Group Inc	Z	Publishing	138	.	.
517	United Brands	X	Food Processing	138	287	537
518	Gibson Greetings Inc	Y	Other Leisure	138	-6	.
519	Consolidated Stores Corp	Z	Discount & Fashion Retailing	137	.	.
520	Petrie Stores Corp	X-	Discount & Fashion Retailing	136	-142	-250
521	Carl Karcher Enterprises	X	Eating Places	134	5	.
522	Lowe's Cos	X	Discount & Fashion Retailing	132	-345	51
523	Circle K Corp	X	Food Retailing	131	-25	106
524	CVN Companies Inc	X	Discount & Fashion Retailing	130	.	.
525	Rohr Industries	X	Aerospace	126	-11	96
526	Cetus Corp	X-	Drugs & Research	126	38	.
527	Leggett & Platt Inc	Y	Appliances & Furnishings	125	60	125
528	Rochester Telephone Co	Y	Telephone Companies	123	94	132
529	A.H. Belo Corp	X	Publishing	119	-80	.
530	Greyhound Corp	X-	Conglomerates	119	38	437
531	Diebold Inc	X	Software	117	-306	116
532	Adia Services Inc	Z	Other Services	117	.	.
533	Dresser Industries Inc	X-	Special Machinery	117	1,050	211
534	Brown Group Inc	X-	Apparel	116	-68	225
535	Honeywell Inc	X-	Instruments	116	311	478

1988 MVA Rank	Economic Value Added (EVA)			Profitability (1988)				Size (1988)		
	1988	Change from 1983	1978	Rtn on Cap r (%)	Wtd Avg Cost Cap c* (%)	r to c*	Value to Capital	Value	Capital	5-Year Growth in Cap (Avg %)
481	0	-5	-5	13.2	13.1	1.0	1.6	450	277	10
482	4	2	.	13.3	12.0	1.1	1.5	521	349	101
483	8	9	.	15.8	12.1	1.3	1.7	417	246	25
484	55	140	44	19.1	13.9	1.4	1.1	1,383	1,212	7
485	-21	-24	.	3.9	16.1	0.2	1.8	372	201	73
486	-12	-7	-11	12.0	15.6	0.8	1.5	514	345	7
487	21	.	.	37.8	18.3	2.1	2.0	337	167	57
488	4	5	6	12.9	11.8	1.1	1.3	671	501	49
489	14	5	.	29.1	16.2	1.8	2.2	309	140	31
490	4	0	5	13.2	12.2	1.1	1.4	571	402	22
491	7	.	.	18.1	11.4	1.6	2.2	303	138	121
492	5	9	.	15.7	13.6	1.2	1.8	363	198	8
493	-17	.	.	7.6	10.8	0.7	1.3	806	641	21
494	-61	-51	-59	2.5	14.6	0.2	1.3	750	588	11
495	12	5	6	14.4	11.7	1.2	1.3	677	516	20
496	7	8	-5	15.4	11.5	1.3	1.9	329	169	0
497	1	23	2	13.2	12.8	1.0	1.6	443	284	14
498	-1,406	-2,515	-1,125	-4.8	11.7	-0.4	1.0	6,368	6,209	-8
499	345	1,038	415	21.4	12.4	1.7	1.0	4,427	4,268	6
500	-28	-1	-14	5.6	15.7	0.4	1.5	442	288	-2
501	11	16	-3	18.0	12.5	1.4	1.7	375	221	7
502	26	-24	19	27.1	16.5	1.6	1.2	998	846	39
503	-4	-4	-9	13.1	14.1	0.9	1.4	555	402	8
504	2	-57	-1	10.8	10.0	1.1	1.2	792	640	13
505	-6	15	-17	10.8	13.0	0.8	1.5	463	312	10
506	-48	-43	-51	5.6	12.8	0.4	1.2	915	764	10
507	17	.	.	40.4	15.0	2.7	2.0	294	145	111
508	7	3	.	-44.4	16.2	-2.7	4.9	188	39	.
509	15	13	17	22.1	14.0	1.6	1.8	331	188	16
510	-7	-17	-16	12.0	13.8	0.9	1.3	595	454	16
511	-9	-29	-16	9.9	10.6	0.9	1.1	1,390	1,249	34
512	-5	.	.	11.1	12.9	0.9	1.5	433	293	2
513	1	.	.	12.5	12.2	1.0	1.5	417	277	18
514	14	18	17	16.9	12.8	1.3	1.3	544	406	13
515	-11	80	6	10.3	12.1	0.8	1.2	733	595	4
516	16	.	.	19.1	12.7	1.5	1.5	419	281	42
517	-4	47	95	10.1	10.5	1.0	1.1	1,321	1,183	6
518	12	-3	.	15.7	11.2	1.4	1.5	439	301	12
519	-2	.	.	13.2	14.1	0.9	1.5	394	258	55
520	-89	-110	-132	4.4	12.6	0.4	1.2	1,032	896	15
521	12	7	.	15.3	9.8	1.6	1.5	391	257	10
522	-32	-47	-44	10.4	14.3	0.7	1.2	947	815	19
523	-12	-12	-15	8.5	9.3	0.9	1.1	2,140	2,009	37
524	-3	.	.	12.3	14.0	0.9	1.6	335	205	81
525	-12	-15	-3	10.2	13.1	0.8	1.2	722	595	30
526	-49	-37	.	-16.4	16.0	-1.0	2.2	235	109	11
527	26	27	23	21.5	12.8	1.7	1.3	526	401	19
528	12	5	10	11.3	9.6	1.2	1.2	927	804	14
529	-13	-31	.	8.6	10.5	0.8	1.2	800	681	38
530	-51	135	-9	9.2	11.8	0.8	1.1	1,956	1,837	2
531	-12	-35	-9	10.8	14.4	0.7	1.3	463	346	10
532	11	.	.	26.0	14.6	1.8	1.7	281	163	49
533	-316	285	-367	2.3	15.3	0.1	1.0	2,482	2,366	-6
534	-23	-23	-34	8.2	11.1	0.7	1.1	932	815	4
535	-802	-481	-786	-6.5	12.3	-0.5	1.0	3,699	3,583	-1

1988 MVA Rank	Company Profile Company	Type	Industry	Market Value Added (MVA) 1988	Change from 1983	1978
536	Inspiration Resources Corp	X-	Other Metals	116	309	.
537	Interface Inc	X	Textiles	115	-55	.
538	Fedders Corp	Y	Building Materials	114	23	172
539	CDI Corp	Y	Construct. & Eng. Services	113	102	114
540	Standard Register Co	Y	Business Machines	112	77	155
541	Norton Co	X-	General Manufacturing	112	143	155
542	Hills Department Stores Inc	X	Discount & Fashion Retailing	112	.	.
543	Dexter Corp	X	Chemicals	111	55	88
544	La-Z-Boy Chair Co	X	Appliances & Furnishings	111	30	.
545	Valspar Corp	Z	Building Materials	111	84	128
546	Cyclops Industries Inc	Z	Steel	110	.	.
547	Westvaco Corp	X	Paper	107	108	318
548	Banta Corp	Z	Printing & Advertising	107	69	124
549	Collins Foods International	X	Eating Places	107	52	118
550	Rykoff-Sexton Inc	X	Food Distribution	106	92	127
551	McClatchy Newspapers	X	Publishing	106	.	.
552	Avnet Inc	X-	Industrial Distn Services	105	-980	142
553	Rockefeller Center Pptys Inc	X-	Construction & R.E.	104	.	.
554	Handleman Co	Y	Other Services	102	6	87
555	Analog Devices	X	Semiconductors	101	-436	91
556	Unifi Inc	Y	Textiles	101	53	.
557	Shared Medical Systems Corp	Y	Software	99	-571	.
558	Braniff Inc	Pre Z	Airlines	99	.	.
559	Tecumseh Products Co	Y	Building Materials	98	32	59
560	Willcox & Gibbs Inc	Z	Industrial Distn Services	97	62	.
561	Nashua Corp	X	Business Machines	95	117	141
562	PHH Corp	Pre Z	Transportation Services	95	-119	117
563	Pentair Inc	X	Paper	95	42	.
564	Union Pacific Corp	X-	Railroads	92	-70	563
565	General Nutrition Inc	X-	Food Retailing	90	-225	.
566	Premark International Inc	X-	Conglomerates	88	.	.
567	Kaufman & Broad Home Corp	X	Construction & R.E.	87	.	.
568	Kellwood Co	X	Apparel	87	107	123
569	Pittston Co	X-	Coal	85	190	144
570	Getty Petroleum Corp	Y	Industrial Distn Services	84	70	90
571	Fisher Scientific Group Inc	X-	Medical Products	84	.	.
572	National Convenience Stores	X-	Food Retailing	84	-154	68
573	Western Digital Corp	Z	Software	84	-25	.
574	Cincinnati Milacron Inc	X-	Machine & Hand Tools	83	-188	151
575	Kimball International	Y	Appliances & Furnishings	83	-5	.
576	Federal-Mogul Corp	X-	Auto Parts & Equipment	83	16	194
577	Jacobs Engineering Group Inc	X-	Construct. & Eng. Services	82	76	74
578	FHP International Corp	Y	Health Care Services	81	.	.
579	General Signal Corp	X-	Instruments	80	-308	11
580	Coca-Cola Enterprises	X	Beverages	79	.	.
581	Ryder System Inc	X	Transportation Services	79	-297	82
582	America West Airlines Inc	Pre Z	Airlines	79	51	.
583	Ferro Corp	X	Chemicals	79	82	112
584	Univar Corp	X-	Industrial Distn Services	79	83	125
585	General Host Corp	X-	Conglomerates	78	36	90
586	Super Food Services Inc	X	Food Distribution	78	48	73
587	CRSS Inc	X-	Construct. & Eng. Services	78	39	84
588	Jepson Corp	Y	Building Materials	78	.	.
589	Formica Corp	X	Building Materials	77	.	.
590	Applied Materials	X	Special Machinery	73	-92	.

| 1988 MVA Rank | Economic Value Added (EVA) | | | Profitability (1988) | | | | Size (1988) | | 5-Year Growth in Cap (Avg %) |
	1988	Change from 1983	1978	Rtn on Cap r (%)	Wtd Avg Cost Cap c* (%)	r to c*	Value to Capital	Value	Capital	
536	-34	184	.	7.7	13.0	0.6	1.2	649	534	-10
537	-5	-8	.	10.2	11.7	0.9	1.3	524	409	70
538	9	12	29	33.7	13.7	2.5	2.7	182	69	3
539	1	1	-1	11.7	11.2	1.0	1.7	281	168	22
540	3	-1	-1	14.2	13.4	1.1	1.3	510	398	17
541	-26	85	-36	10.5	13.0	0.8	1.1	1,213	1,101	5
542	14	.	.	12.1	10.0	1.2	1.1	966	854	19
543	-8	-8	-22	12.3	13.9	0.9	1.2	686	575	10
544	-4	-9	-3	11.3	12.8	0.9	1.4	402	291	19
545	5	2	5	15.1	12.9	1.2	1.5	332	222	29
546	23	.	.	22.4	12.3	1.8	1.3	478	368	60
547	31	130	34	14.4	12.7	1.1	1.1	2,023	1,915	10
548	10	9	11	19.4	13.1	1.5	1.3	424	317	28
549	-21	-23	-24	7.9	13.7	0.6	1.3	491	384	12
550	-1	-4	-1	10.6	11.0	1.0	1.3	448	342	15
551	-3	.	.	12.8	14.0	0.9	1.4	407	301	5
552	-40	12	-32	9.0	14.8	0.6	1.1	893	788	11
553	-42	.	.	6.2	9.0	0.7	1.1	1,559	1,455	7
554	18	13	14	28.2	15.8	1.8	1.5	296	194	24
555	-24	-25	-25	10.8	15.9	0.7	1.2	592	490	18
556	13	12	13	26.7	13.2	2.0	2.1	195	94	10
557	1	-13	-6	12.2	11.8	1.0	1.3	431	332	15
558	-21	.	.	-64.5	8.5	-7.6	1.4	357	258	31
559	20	12	-2	16.7	12.1	1.4	1.2	648	550	11
560	12	7	10	23.7	12.5	1.9	1.7	238	141	32
561	4	23	-9	14.5	13.1	1.1	1.3	440	345	10
562	-594	-512	-559	0.7	10.5	0.1	1.0	6,263	6,168	34
563	12	10	6	15.2	11.7	1.3	1.2	692	598	34
564	-530	157	-326	8.2	13.4	0.6	1.0	10,933	10,841	6
565	-8	-17	.	8.4	11.5	0.7	1.4	315	225	-0
566	-1	.	.	12.2	12.3	1.0	1.1	1,328	1,240	8
567	-1	.	.	13.2	13.4	1.0	1.1	707	620	12
568	11	3	17	17.9	13.9	1.3	1.2	440	354	8
569	-75	188	-15	4.8	12.5	0.4	1.1	1,076	991	2
570	25	30	25	24.9	10.0	2.5	1.4	272	188	23
571	-38	.	.	7.2	14.4	0.5	1.2	637	553	4
572	-28	-33	-31	3.2	9.8	0.3	1.2	585	501	16
573	46	49	.	34.8	16.3	2.1	1.2	570	487	56
574	-70	37	-73	4.7	14.8	0.3	1.1	739	656	3
575	13	13	6	19.0	13.2	1.4	1.3	337	254	15
576	-42	-18	-66	7.5	12.7	0.6	1.1	880	798	7
577	1	17	-1	12.0	10.4	1.2	1.8	182	100	1
578	12	.	.	27.1	10.3	2.6	2.4	140	59	-11
579	-132	-91	-140	4.5	14.3	0.3	1.1	1,405	1,324	3
580	-16	.	.	9.6	10.0	1.0	1.0	4,510	4,431	90
581	-247	-231	-282	6.3	11.4	0.6	1.0	5,179	5,100	22
582	-42	.	.	4.0	9.0	0.4	1.1	942	863	61
583	7	22	-6	16.0	14.3	1.1	1.2	559	481	10
584	9	44	13	14.7	11.3	1.3	1.3	352	274	5
585	-31	-52	-31	-0.9	10.8	-0.1	1.3	356	277	-3
586	-2	0	-1	11.2	12.2	0.9	1.4	280	201	11
587	-2	-4	-4	10.2	12.4	0.8	2.0	156	77	15
588	5	.	.	12.4	10.2	1.2	1.3	330	252	9
589	-2	.	.	9.9	10.8	0.9	1.3	319	242	-0
590	17	22	16	29.3	19.9	1.5	1.3	292	218	21

1988 MVA Rank	Company Profile			Market Value Added (MVA)		
					Change from	
	Company	Type	Industry	1988	1983	1978
591	General Instrument Corp	X	Electronics	73	-237	96
592	Phillips-Van Heusen	X	Apparel	73	87	128
593	Savannah Foods & Inds	X	Food Processing	73	49	.
594	Casey's General Stores Inc	X	Food Retailing	72	57	.
595	Kennametal Inc	X-	Machine & Hand Tools	70	-54	55
596	Union Camp Corp	X	Paper	70	-353	-155
597	Georgia-Pacific Corp	X-	Forest Products	68	222	-294
598	Donaldson Co Inc	X-	Auto Parts & Equipment	67	65	31
599	Pilgrims Pride Corp	X	Food Processing	66	.	.
600	Fays Inc	X	Drug Distribution	66	-49	69
601	Apogee Enterprises Inc	Y	Construct. & Eng. Services	64	10	.
602	Esselte Business Systems Inc	X	Business Machines	64	.	.
603	Western Union Corp	X-	Telephone Equip. & Services	64	-21	435
604	Delchamps Inc	X	Food Retailing	63	19	.
605	Interlake Corp	X	Special Machinery	63	304	359
606	Edison Brothers Stores	X	Discount & Fashion Retailing	63	-93	-83
607	Harley-Davidson Inc	X	Other Leisure	62	.	.
608	Winnebago Industries	X	Other Leisure	61	-171	72
609	Standex International Corp	X	Building Materials	61	-2	36
610	TBC Corp	Y	Tire & Rubber	60	43	.
611	Hexcel Corp	X	General Manufacturing	58	48	46
612	Midway Airlines Inc	X-	Airlines	56	15	.
613	Federal Signal Corp	X	Cars & Trucks	55	10	61
614	Merry-Go-Round Entprs	Z	Discount & Fashion Retailing	54	-19	.
615	Durr-Fillauer Medical	X	Drug Distribution	53	13	.
616	Ryland Group Inc	X	Construction & R.E.	53	-25	64
617	Tosco Corp	X	Oil & Gas	53	97	91
618	Hartmarx Corp	X-	Apparel	53	-44	170
619	Wendy's International Inc	X-	Eating Places	53	-466	.
620	Coastal Corp	X-	Oil & Gas	52	679	613
621	Drug Emporium Inc	Y	Drug Distribution	51	.	.
622	Smithfield Foods Inc	X	Food Processing	51	70	.
623	Genlyte Group Inc	NA	Electrical Products	50	.	.
624	Barnes Group Inc	X	Building Materials	50	52	74
625	Toro Co	X	Appliances & Furnishings	48	65	69
626	Fred Meyer Inc	X	Discount & Fashion Retailing	47	.	.
627	Harnischfeger Industries Inc	X-	Special Machinery	47	138	115
628	Di Giorgio Corp	X-	Food Distribution	46	83	68
629	Perkin-Elmer Corp	X-	Instruments	45	-550	-188
630	SPX Corp	X	Auto Parts & Equipment	45	-26	57
631	American Business Prods	X	Business Machines	44	-13	53
632	Ruddick Corp	X	Food Retailing	44	48	70
633	Curtice-Burns Food	X	Food Processing	42	4	44
634	Vermont American	X-	Machine & Hand Tools	42	30	50
635	Stewart & Stevenson Services	X	Special Machinery	42	106	.
636	Hovnanian Enterprises Inc	X	Construction & R.E.	40	14	.
637	Gaylord Container Cp	NA	Paper Containers	40	.	.
638	Centex Corp	X-	Construction & R.E.	40	52	54
639	C M L Group	X	Discount & Fashion Retailing	39	30	.
640	Carlisle Cos Inc	X-	Tire & Rubber	39	-22	66
641	Great Northern Nekoosa Corp	X	Paper	39	128	191
642	Texas Industries Inc	X-	Building Materials	38	-8	76
643	Amer Bldg Maintenance Inds	X-	Other Services	37	13	43
644	Lafarge Corp	X	Building Materials	35	113	.
645	Witco Corp	X-	Chemicals	35	12	167

1988 MVA Rank	Economic Value Added (EVA)			Profitability (1988)				Size (1988)		5-Year Growth in Cap (Avg %)
	1988	Change from		Rtn on Cap r (%)	Wtd Avg Cost Cap c* (%)	r to c*	Value to Capital	Value	Capital	
		1983	1978							
591	-3	59	-4	15.1	15.5	1.0	1.1	973	899	6
592	2	5	11	12.5	11.9	1.0	1.2	389	316	12
593	-2	-7	-3	8.8	9.7	0.9	1.3	318	245	18
594	-2	-2	.	10.7	12.3	0.9	1.5	210	138	33
595	-19	62	-35	8.4	14.2	0.6	1.2	432	362	1
596	51	122	24	15.4	13.4	1.2	1.0	2,757	2,687	8
597	51	393	-34	13.7	12.7	1.1	1.0	6,329	6,260	7
598	-5	20	-10	12.5	15.5	0.8	1.4	236	168	5
599	-12	.	.	2.2	9.8	0.2	1.3	281	215	34
600	4	-0	2	12.9	10.5	1.2	1.4	226	160	11
601	5	6	4	18.1	13.8	1.3	1.4	223	159	21
602	1	.	.	12.5	12.3	1.0	1.1	951	887	24
603	-551	-308	-457	-29.8	11.6	-2.6	1.1	1,230	1,166	-11
604	3	.	.	11.8	10.1	1.2	1.3	283	220	17
605	-5	58	17	12.0	13.1	0.9	1.1	521	458	-5
606	2	-4	-23	11.3	10.9	1.0	1.1	577	515	0
607	23	.	.	19.3	10.7	1.8	1.2	341	279	48
608	-28	-29	-13	-0.5	18.1	-0.0	1.5	188	126	10
609	1	5	-2	11.9	11.4	1.0	1.3	291	231	7
610	8	10	.	23.3	14.2	1.6	1.6	161	101	21
611	-2	8	-3	11.2	12.2	0.9	1.2	340	282	20
612	-9	11	.	6.5	10.2	0.6	1.2	322	266	21
613	3	6	1	13.9	12.3	1.1	1.3	253	199	8
614	3	-5	.	13.7	11.6	1.2	1.4	191	137	28
615	1	1	2	14.6	13.6	1.1	1.4	184	130	15
616	-19	-39	-22	8.7	15.5	0.6	1.1	416	362	26
617	-9	302	-3	10.6	12.3	0.9	1.1	538	485	-15
618	-15	-6	-6	9.6	11.9	0.8	1.1	808	755	8
619	-41	-53	-61	7.5	13.2	0.6	1.1	776	724	10
620	-95	154	-31	8.0	9.5	0.8	1.0	6,275	6,223	19
621	4	.	.	14.9	10.9	1.4	1.4	166	115	21
622	-2	-1	-1	10.2	11.6	0.9	1.3	202	152	12
623	.	.	.	.	.	.	1.2	293	242	.
624	-5	10	-13	10.4	12.4	0.8	1.2	312	263	3
625	10	26	2	18.3	13.3	1.4	1.2	268	220	7
626	-4	.	.	10.6	11.1	1.0	1.1	804	757	6
627	-40	51	-28	8.1	13.6	0.6	1.1	781	734	17
628	-9	3	-4	7.6	11.7	0.7	1.3	221	175	-11
629	-115	-49	-116	5.4	14.9	0.4	1.0	1,400	1,355	14
630	4	7	1	14.0	13.3	1.1	1.1	704	659	20
631	-1	-2	-2	12.5	13.0	1.0	1.3	172	128	11
632	3	1	-1	10.8	9.8	1.1	1.1	401	357	19
633	-3	-3	-4	8.5	9.3	0.9	1.1	353	311	13
634	-3	12	-7	11.2	12.6	0.9	1.2	281	239	16
635	12	40	16	20.7	13.0	1.6	1.2	249	207	1
636	-4	-5	.	10.2	11.5	0.9	1.1	458	417	31
637	.	.	.	.	.	.	1.1	618	578	.
638	-82	-26	-78	-0.2	12.4	-0.0	1.0	943	903	2
639	-1	.	.	10.8	11.2	1.0	1.2	282	242	31
640	-11	6	-14	10.3	14.4	0.7	1.1	304	265	5
641	42	117	40	15.3	14.0	1.1	1.0	3,557	3,518	16
642	-1	22	-23	10.1	10.3	1.0	1.1	603	565	10
643	-4	-4	-4	7.6	11.3	0.7	1.3	179	142	13
644	8	.	.	14.5	13.6	1.1	1.0	1,044	1,008	1
645	-15	31	-25	11.6	13.5	0.9	1.0	872	836	4

1988 MVA Rank	Company	Type	Industry	1988	Change from 1983	Change from 1978
	Company Profile			**Market Value Added (MVA)**		
646	Helmerich & Payne	X-	Petroleum Services	35	-22	-73
647	Jerrico Inc	X	Eating Places	34	-67	49
648	Guilford Mills Inc	X	Textiles	34	-84	49
649	House Of Fabrics Inc	X	Discount & Fashion Retailing	34	2	48
650	Morgan Products Ltd	Z	Industrial Distn Services	33	.	.
651	Dennison Mfg Co	X-	Business Machines	33	-12	81
652	Softsel Computer Prods Inc	Z	Business Machines	33	.	.
653	Leslie Fay Companies Inc	Y	Apparel	33	.	.
654	Pace Membership Warehouse	Pre Z	Discount & Fashion Retailing	31	.	.
655	Carson Pirie Scott	X-	Discount & Fashion Retailing	30	71	92
656	TRW Inc	X-	Conglomerates	29	-459	290
657	Kaman Corp	X	Aerospace	28	-17	44
658	Chesapeake Corp	X	Paper	27	-14	46
659	H.B. Fuller Co	X	Chemicals	27	-33	47
660	Burlington Coat Factory Wrhs	X	Discount & Fashion Retailing	26	-160	.
661	Communications Transmission	X	Telephone Equip. & Services	26	.	.
662	Terex Corp	X	Special Machinery	26	.	.
663	Anchor Glass Container Corp	Z	Glass, Metal & Plastics	26	.	.
664	LSI Logic Corp	X	Semiconductors	25	-308	.
665	Helene Curtis Industries	X	Personal Care	25	-35	42
666	Dollar General	X-	Discount & Fashion Retailing	24	-102	.
667	Phelps Dodge Corp	X-	Other Metals	23	491	723
668	Ramada Inc	X-	Hotel & Motel	23	-52	8
669	Pope & Talbot Inc	X-	Forest Products	23	-15	39
670	AM International Inc	X-	Software	23	-29	103
671	Valmont Industries	X	General Manufacturing	22	25	.
672	Standard Motor Products	X	Auto Parts & Equipment	22	-119	21
673	Owens & Minor Inc	Pre Z	Medical Products	22	23	.
674	VWR Corp	X	Industrial Distn Services	21	.	.
675	Airborne Freight Corp	Pre Z	Transportation Services	21	-65	-26
676	Lukens Inc	X-	Steel	20	97	92
677	Village Super Market	X	Food Retailing	18	27	.
678	Tyler Corp	X-	Building Materials	17	-36	-20
679	Huffy Corp	X-	Other Leisure	16	11	32
680	Nacco Industries	X	Machine & Hand Tools	16	-20	14
681	Florida East Coast Industrie	X-	Railroads	15	56	42
682	Hudson Foods Inc	Z	Food Processing	15	.	.
683	Marshall Industries	Y	Industrial Distn Services	13	-52	16
684	Foster Wheeler Corp	X-	Construct. & Eng. Services	12	-106	-20
685	J P Industries Inc	X	Auto Parts & Equipment	11	-20	.
686	Oneida Ltd	X	General Manufacturing	11	-44	33
687	Jacobson Stores	X	Discount & Fashion Retailing	11	23	.
688	Strawbridge & Clothier	X	Discount & Fashion Retailing	11	43	.
689	Genovese Drug Stores	X	Drug Distribution	10	-32	14
690	Reynolds & Reynolds	X	Business Machines	8	-68	-53
691	Constar International Inc	X-	Glass, Metal & Plastics	7	6	54
692	LDI Corp	X	Business Machines	7	.	.
693	Quanex Corp	X	Steel	7	43	3
694	Culbro Corp	X-	Tobacco	6	33	63
695	Maxtor Corp	Z	Software	5	.	.
696	Wholesale Club Inc	Pre Z	Discount & Fashion Retailing	5	.	.
697	Oshman's Sporting Goods	X-	Discount & Fashion Retailing	4	-86	.
698	Spiegel Inc	X	Discount & Fashion Retailing	3	.	.
699	Perry Drug Stores	X-	Drug Distribution	3	-21	7
700	JM Peters Co Inc	Z	Construction & R.E.	3	.	.

| 1988 MVA Rank | Economic Value Added (EVA) | | | Profitability (1988) | | | | Size (1988) | | 5-Year Growth in Cap (Avg %) |
| | | Change from | | Rtn on Cap | Wtd Avg Cost Cap | r to | Value to | | | |
	1988	1983	1978	r (%)	c* (%)	c*	Capital	Value	Capital	
646	-43	1	-47	4.1	12.8	0.3	1.1	455	420	-3
647	-3	-1	-4	11.4	12.3	0.9	1.1	442	408	11
648	-2	3	-11	12.2	12.8	1.0	1.1	368	334	19
649	-4	-4	-0	9.0	10.8	0.8	1.1	274	240	14
650	-7	.	.	7.9	13.1	0.6	1.2	183	149	30
651	4	3	-4	13.7	12.8	1.1	1.1	471	438	5
652	5	.	.	24.4	11.8	2.1	1.4	108	75	92
653	9	.	.	13.7	10.4	1.3	1.1	352	320	12
654	-3	.	.	9.3	10.9	0.9	1.2	225	195	54
655	-32	-7	-29	5.7	11.2	0.5	1.0	666	636	7
656	-171	65	-223	8.0	12.5	0.6	1.0	3,836	3,807	7
657	6	1	7	13.8	11.8	1.2	1.1	375	347	20
658	19	38	23	15.4	12.0	1.3	1.0	621	594	17
659	1	1	-0	13.4	13.0	1.0	1.1	364	337	12
660	-1	-10	.	11.6	12.2	1.0	1.1	333	307	26
661	-0	.	.	9.9	10.1	1.0	1.0	708	682	70
662	9	19	12	18.5	11.5	1.6	1.1	207	182	71
663	-11	.	.	8.0	10.0	0.8	1.0	649	624	53
664	-20	-25	.	11.0	15.3	0.7	1.0	638	612	58
665	5	3	8	17.7	14.3	1.2	1.1	232	208	19
666	-15	-20	-14	6.0	12.2	0.5	1.1	252	229	10
667	299	774	498	30.6	14.3	2.1	1.0	2,347	2,323	5
668	-69	-13	-49	3.9	10.8	0.4	1.0	950	927	4
669	6	18	1	20.6	17.4	1.2	1.1	271	247	5
670	-63	-0	-44	2.2	11.6	0.2	1.0	619	596	17
671	8	12	8	17.3	11.6	1.5	1.1	188	166	18
672	-8	-17	-10	8.5	12.2	0.7	1.1	314	292	18
673	-3	-2	-3	10.4	12.5	0.8	1.1	196	175	25
674	-4	.	.	9.7	12.7	0.8	1.1	181	159	18
675	-51	-55	-57	-3.2	11.6	-0.3	1.1	419	398	26
676	-3	47	1	13.9	14.9	0.9	1.1	284	264	1
677	1	2	1	12.3	10.7	1.1	1.2	121	103	23
678	-27	-10	-34	4.6	10.9	0.4	1.1	350	332	-7
679	-4	11	-7	9.9	13.9	0.7	1.1	149	133	5
680	5	36	10	11.1	10.1	1.1	1.0	668	652	-4
681	-37	-85	-37	7.0	15.4	0.5	1.0	485	470	7
682	39	.	.	28.9	9.8	2.9	1.1	287	272	84
683	4	-4	4	16.8	14.3	1.2	1.1	182	169	16
684	-73	-43	-93	4.3	15.1	0.3	1.0	535	523	8
685	-10	.	.	8.7	11.9	0.7	1.0	414	402	71
686	-0	29	-8	11.7	11.8	1.0	1.0	246	235	6
687	-2	-3	-2	10.5	12.0	0.9	1.1	210	199	14
688	-5	3	-0	10.1	11.2	0.9	1.0	555	545	9
689	3	1	3	12.4	9.6	1.3	1.1	137	127	20
690	-14	-10	-17	10.3	14.0	0.7	1.0	400	392	23
691	-5	0	-7	10.3	12.8	0.8	1.0	212	204	5
692	-5	.	.	8.9	11.0	0.8	1.0	443	436	94
693	15	71	10	20.4	13.5	1.5	1.0	199	192	-7
694	-23	-14	-7	4.2	10.7	0.4	1.0	365	359	10
695	-5	.	.	10.0	13.1	0.8	1.0	227	222	57
696	1	.	.	13.6	11.6	1.2	1.1	65	60	59
697	-4	-7	-7	9.4	12.6	0.7	1.0	133	129	6
698	87	100	105	20.7	11.2	1.9	1.0	1,102	1,098	22
699	-27	-27	-29	1.0	9.9	0.1	1.0	265	262	21
700	18	.	.	19.7	11.2	1.8	1.0	388	385	60

1988 MVA Rank	Company	Type	Industry	Market Value Added (MVA)		
					Change from	
				1988	1983	1978
701	Coleman Co Inc	X-	Other Leisure	3	-45	38
702	Intl Multifoods Corp	X	Food Processing	3	-6	52
703	Dairy Mart Convenience Strs	X	Food Retailing	2	-6	
704	LPL Technologies Inc	Z	Telephone Equip. & Services	2		
705	Great American Mgmt & Invt	Pre Z	Chemicals	2	-65	
706	Foodarama Supermarkets	X	Food Retailing	2	9	15
707	Scientific-Atlanta Inc	X-	Telephone Equip. & Services	2	-126	-55
708	Foxboro Co	X-	Instruments	1	6	30
709	Weyerhaeuser Co	X	Forest Products	-2	-504	-429
710	Briggs & Stratton	X	Special Machinery	-2	-126	-175
711	Wyle Laboratories	X-	Industrial Distn Services	-2	-99	9
712	IMO Industries Inc	Pre Z	Special Machinery	-3		
713	Sudbury Inc	X	Auto Parts & Equipment	-3		
714	Thorn Apple Valley Inc	X-	Food Processing	-3	10	
715	Vicorp Restaurants Inc	X-	Eating Places	-4	-102	
716	Seaway Food Town Inc	X-	Food Retailing	-5	23	9
717	Southwest Airlines	X-	Airlines	-7	-443	-21
718	Trinova Corp	X-	Auto Parts & Equipment	-7	193	244
719	Highland Superstores Inc	Z	Appliances & Furnishings	-7		
720	Ames Department Stores Inc	X	Discount & Fashion Retailing	-8	-203	-3
721	Hughes Supply Inc	X	Building Materials	-9	-26	
722	Commtron Corp	Z	Other Services	-10		
723	Carolina Freight Corp	X-	Trucking & Shipping	-10	-98	7
724	Scotty's Inc	X-	Building Materials	-10	-64	-25
725	Commercial Intertech	X-	Special Machinery	-12	-30	
726	Hasbro Inc	X	Other Leisure	-15	-107	5
727	Quaker State Corp	X-	Oil & Gas	-16	19	29
728	Lionel Corp	X-	Discount & Fashion Retailing	-17	-49	-9
729	De Soto Inc	X-	Building Materials	-19	-16	48
730	Amoco Corp	X-	Oil & Gas	-20	3,359	1,235
731	Bindley Western Inds	Z	Drug Distribution	-20	-39	
732	Dekalb Genetics Corp	X-	Food Processing	-21		
733	Bearings Inc	X-	Industrial Distn Services	-22	0	-29
734	Brendle's Inc	X	Discount & Fashion Retailing	-23		
735	Southern New Eng Telecomm	X	Telephone Companies	-23	204	337
736	Volt Info Sciences Inc	X-	Other Services	-23	-74	
737	Alaska Air Group Inc	X	Airlines	-23	-74	-24
738	Advo-System Inc	X-	Printing & Advertising	-27		
739	Federal Paper Board Co	X	Paper Containers	-27	-78	25
740	S.E. Nichols	X-	Discount & Fashion Retailing	-28	-37	-23
741	National Medical Enterprises	X	Health Care Services	-29	-613	-2
742	DSC Communications Corp	Z	Telephone Equip. & Services	-29	-1,044	
743	Talley Industries Inc	X-	Aerospace	-29	2	31
744	AVX Corp	X-	Semiconductors	-30	-154	-36
745	Commercial Metals Co	X-	Steel	-30	-32	14
746	Standard Shares Inc	Z	Conglomerates	-30	-14	
747	Preston Corp	X-	Trucking & Shipping	-31	-40	
748	Crystal Brands	Pre Z	Apparel	-32		
749	Potlatch Corp	X-	Paper Containers	-32	65	23
750	Bell Industries Inc	X-	Industrial Distn Services	-32	-151	-28
751	Oshkosh Truck	Y	Cars & Trucks	-33		
752	Greenman Brothers Inc	Pre Z	Discount & Fashion Retailing	-33	-42	-19
753	Butler Mfg Co	X-	Construct. & Eng. Services	-34	23	-49
754	Champion Spark Plug Co	X-	Auto Parts & Equipment	-34	10	-3
755	Delta Woodside Industries	Z	Textiles	-34		

	Economic Value Added (EVA)			Profitability (1988)				Size (1988)		
1988 MVA Rank	1988	Change from 1983	1978	Rtn on Cap r (%)	Wtd Avg Cost Cap c* (%)	r to c*	Value to Capital	Value	Capital	5-Year Growth in Cap (Avg %)
701	-12	-1	-12	10.2	13.3	0.8	1.0	432	429	11
702	-28	-28	-33	6.9	11.0	0.6	1.0	586	584	8
703	-3	-3	.	7.2	9.0	0.8	1.0	145	142	56
704	-8	.	.	7.8	9.0	0.9	1.0	627	625	129
705	0	-5	55	8.3	8.3	1.0	1.0	964	962	58
706	-0	4	1	10.2	10.7	1.0	1.0	94	92	12
707	-17	9	-22	10.3	16.4	0.6	1.0	286	284	5
708	-64	8	-66	1.4	15.1	0.1	1.0	521	520	3
709	-66	477	-150	12.7	13.8	0.9	1.0	6,913	6,915	5
710	-6	-1	-34	13.2	14.8	0.9	1.0	426	428	9
711	-8	-2	-5	8.3	14.1	0.6	1.0	154	156	7
712	-18	.	.	9.6	13.0	0.7	1.0	666	669	55
713	-28	-28	-25	1.3	10.0	0.1	1.0	281	284	48
714	-2	2	-2	7.6	10.9	0.7	1.0	70	73	-6
715	-13	-16	.	7.0	12.2	0.6	1.0	251	255	23
716	-5	-1	-5	5.5	10.3	0.5	0.9	81	86	-4
717	-25	-34	-41	9.1	11.9	0.8	1.0	1,059	1,066	20
718	-65	-7	-64	8.8	14.1	0.6	1.0	1,341	1,348	14
719	-10	.	.	7.8	11.8	0.7	1.0	283	290	44
720	-39	-48	-43	7.8	10.9	0.7	1.0	1,759	1,767	53
721	-4	-2	-5	9.2	11.5	0.8	0.9	166	176	18
722	-3	.	.	12.0	17.5	0.7	0.8	54	63	29
723	-14	-20	-14	6.8	12.2	0.6	1.0	247	257	21
724	-17	-18	-19	5.5	11.8	0.5	1.0	251	261	15
725	-3	14	-17	11.6	13.0	0.9	1.0	254	266	14
726	-16	-31	-11	12.0	13.8	0.9	1.0	876	891	73
727	-67	-31	-61	3.6	14.1	0.3	1.0	605	621	5
728	-2	23	-3	9.8	10.9	0.9	0.9	192	209	8
729	-26	-20	-23	1.2	12.5	0.1	0.9	215	234	9
730	-288	1,063	-651	9.9	11.3	0.9	1.0	26,637	26,656	5
731	-4	-8	.	8.3	10.9	0.8	0.8	114	134	55
732	-19	.	.	5.4	13.2	0.4	0.9	177	198	-28
733	-7	11	-12	10.7	13.9	0.8	0.9	220	242	3
734	-3	.	.	7.9	11.3	0.7	0.8	70	94	17
735	-2	42	-22	9.9	10.0	1.0	1.0	2,672	2,695	8
736	-28	-30	-31	-0.3	11.7	-0.0	0.9	189	213	9
737	-10	-24	-16	8.9	10.3	0.9	1.0	805	828	34
738	-14	.	.	2.4	14.0	0.2	0.8	102	129	9
739	41	67	46	17.8	13.6	1.3	1.0	1,160	1,188	18
740	-16	-18	-16	0.1	12.0	0.0	0.8	95	123	6
741	0	-44	-1	10.8	10.8	1.0	1.0	3,660	3,689	14
742	-42	-66	.	6.4	16.5	0.4	0.9	452	480	42
743	-22	-16	-18	4.9	10.7	0.5	0.9	444	473	24
744	-13	-7	-16	11.4	15.3	0.8	0.9	347	377	20
745	19	29	23	23.9	13.3	1.8	0.9	184	214	7
746	-18	-25	.	9.0	12.3	0.7	0.9	549	580	32
747	-13	-7	-13	6.2	10.9	0.6	0.9	240	271	20
748	-36	.	.	4.8	13.0	0.4	1.0	619	650	41
749	2	103	-8	13.5	13.3	1.0	1.0	1,086	1,118	1
750	-14	-7	-14	6.4	15.2	0.4	0.8	123	155	9
751	-1	.	.	15.1	15.9	1.0	0.8	100	133	12
752	-8	-7	-5	6.9	12.8	0.5	0.8	101	135	32
753	-7	23	-22	8.4	11.3	0.7	0.8	191	225	0
754	-50	-0	-71	5.8	14.4	0.4	0.9	478	513	1
755	23	.	.	32.1	11.3	2.8	0.7	83	118	64

Company Profile				Market Value Added (MVA)		
					Change from	
1988 MVA Rank	Company	Type	Industry	1988	1983	1978
756	Cooper Companies Inc	X	Medical Products	-36	-177	.
757	Jamesway Corp	X-	Discount & Fashion Retailing	-36	-55	-25
758	Caterpillar Inc	X-	Special Machinery	-37	1,764	-650
759	Temple-Inland Inc	X	Paper Containers	-39	25	.
760	A.M. Castle & Co	X	Industrial Distn Services	-41	2	10
761	Allied Products	Pre Z	Special Machinery	-42	-9	14
762	Oxford Industries Inc	X-	Apparel	-48	-110	0
763	Westmark International Inc	X-	Medical Products	-49	.	.
764	American President Cos Ltd	X	Trucking & Shipping	-50	-52	.
765	Nerco Inc	Y	Coal	-50	.	.
766	H.H. Robertson Co	X-	General Manufacturing	-50	-104	-4
767	Earle M. Jorgensen Co	X-	Industrial Distn Services	-51	1	2
768	Noland Co	X-	Building Materials	-51	-1	.
769	Genesco Inc	X-	Discount & Fashion Retailing	-53	-55	-35
770	M.A. Hanna Co	X	Chemicals	-55	122	53
771	Child World Inc	X-	Discount & Fashion Retailing	-55	.	.
772	Subaru Of America	X-	Transportation Services	-56	-389	.
773	AST Research Inc	Z	Computers & Peripherals	-59	.	.
774	Blount Inc	X-	Construction & R.E.	-60	-110	-50
775	Tonka Corp	Z	Other Leisure	-60	-47	-39
776	Arvin Industries Inc	X	Auto Parts & Equipment	-62	-38	2
777	Kansas City Southern Inds	X-	Railroads	-63	-180	21
778	Apollo Computer Inc	Z	Computers & Peripherals	-64	-632	.
779	Mine Safety Appliances Co	X-	Medical Products	-66	-17	.
780	B.F. Goodrich Co	X-	Chemicals	-70	696	798
781	DWG Corp	X-	Textiles	-70	36	-7
782	SSMC Inc	X-	Appliances & Furnishings	-71	.	.
783	Westmoreland Coal Co	X-	Coal	-73	-26	-45
784	Arrow Electronics Inc	X-	Industrial Distn Services	-77	-172	-65
785	Maxus Energy Corp	X-	Oil & Gas	-78	705	95
786	CBI Industries Inc	X-	Petroleum Services	-78	17	-147
787	Pacific Telecom Inc	X-	Telephone Equip. & Services	-78	-293	.
788	American Petrofina	X	Oil & Gas	-79	117	73
789	Mark IV Industries Inc	Z	Instruments	-81	-85	.
790	Cameron Iron Works	X-	Petroleum Services	-83	140	-91
791	Penn Central Corp	X-	Conglomerates	-85	294	.
792	Overseas Shipholding Group	X-	Trucking & Shipping	-87	30	9
793	Teradyne Inc	X-	Instruments	-91	-630	-85
794	Rose's Stores	X	Discount & Fashion Retailing	-93	2	.
795	Rowan Cos Inc	X-	Petroleum Services	-93	-18	-166
796	Murphy Oil Corp	X-	Oil & Gas	-94	151	-60
797	Texaco Inc	X-	Oil & Gas	-95	9,928	5,296
798	American Maize-Prods	X-	Food Processing	-96	-42	-31
799	American Medical Intl	X	Health Care Services	-101	-607	-196
800	Ingersoll-Rand Co	X-	Special Machinery	-102	466	233
801	Prime Computer	X	Computers & Peripherals	-104	-528	-233
802	American Greetings	X-	Other Leisure	-113	-483	-49
803	Sundstrand Corp	X-	Aerospace	-117	-322	-88
804	Boise Cascade Corp	X	Forest Products	-118	168	283
805	Gordon Jewelry Corp	X-	Discount & Fashion Retailing	-120	-101	-92
806	Wyman-Gordon Co	X-	General Manufacturing	-121	-261	.
807	Eagle-Picher Inds	Pre Z	Auto Parts & Equipment	-122	-120	-146
808	Wheeling-Pittsburgh Steel	X	Steel	-123	132	309
809	M/A-Com Inc	X-	Telephone Equip. & Services	-130	-531	-178
810	Fruit Of The Loom Inc	X-	Apparel	-131	.	.

	Economic Value Added (EVA)			Profitability (1988)				Size (1988)		
1988 MVA Rank	1988	Change from 1983	1978	Rtn on Cap r (%)	Wtd Avg Cost Cap c* (%)	r to c*	Value to Capital	Value	Capital	5-Year Growth in Cap (Avg %)
756	-137	-145	.	-2.1	10.2	-0.2	1.0	912	948	41
757	-9	-11	-11	9.1	12.4	0.7	0.9	295	331	17
758	-43	1,456	-344	13.3	13.9	1.0	1.0	8,092	8,129	-0
759	18	.	.	14.5	13.3	1.1	1.0	1,665	1,705	11
760	27	47	24	30.3	11.5	2.6	0.8	168	209	9
761	-25	-7	-18	4.9	12.0	0.4	0.9	305	347	28
762	-12	-20	-14	7.2	12.8	0.6	0.8	152	199	0
763	-18	.	.	7.6	14.8	0.5	0.8	215	264	-8
764	4	.	.	12.0	11.6	1.0	1.0	1,378	1,428	17
765	43	.	.	14.8	9.9	1.5	1.0	1,002	1,052	15
766	-43	-32	-43	-7.0	10.7	-0.7	0.7	148	198	-2
767	6	40	-7	14.0	11.1	1.3	0.8	227	277	3
768	-6	1	-3	7.8	11.1	0.7	0.7	150	202	12
769	-18	24	13	7.4	13.8	0.5	0.8	243	295	-6
770	-8	94	10	10.7	11.6	0.9	0.9	831	886	12
771	-8	.	.	10.8	13.7	0.8	0.9	323	378	13
772	-88	-123	-101	-12.8	14.0	-0.9	0.9	340	396	24
773	11	.	.	30.2	17.9	1.7	0.7	145	204	67
774	-79	-80	-84	-9.7	11.2	-0.9	0.7	147	207	9
775	-11	0	-6	9.7	11.2	0.9	0.9	659	719	72
776	-52	-41	-59	5.5	12.0	0.5	0.9	852	913	27
777	-106	-126	-94	-1.3	12.8	-0.1	0.9	697	760	3
778	-32	-44	.	7.9	13.9	0.6	0.9	550	613	56
779	-12	-5	-20	9.0	12.6	0.7	0.8	284	350	11
780	-39	242	43	13.5	15.9	0.9	1.0	1,508	1,579	-6
781	-47	-40	-39	3.6	10.1	0.4	0.9	844	915	16
782	-31	.	.	7.8	15.9	0.5	0.8	332	403	-0
783	-43	-18	-25	-0.4	11.4	-0.0	0.8	297	370	3
784	-7	0	-9	8.7	11.1	0.8	0.8	359	436	14
785	-320	390	-328	-3.1	12.1	-0.3	1.0	1,891	1,969	-19
786	-15	-3	-36	10.1	11.5	0.9	0.9	1,100	1,178	21
787	-41	-39	-41	5.5	9.2	0.6	0.9	1,078	1,156	7
788	70	184	104	13.4	9.4	1.4	1.0	1,990	2,069	13
789	42	41	43	15.5	9.5	1.6	0.9	925	1,007	123
790	-128	25	-129	-4.2	14.1	-0.3	0.9	667	751	-8
791	-8	442	.	10.7	11.5	0.9	0.9	1,402	1,487	-7
792	-67	18	-71	6.2	12.2	0.5	0.9	969	1,056	-1
793	-55	-56	-53	5.8	17.4	0.3	0.8	443	534	13
794	-12	-18	-14	8.4	11.0	0.8	0.8	402	495	17
795	-167	-88	-175	-5.1	15.0	-0.3	0.9	647	740	-1
796	-216	94	-164	1.5	13.9	0.1	0.9	1,572	1,665	-4
797	-1,206	2,071	-471	5.8	10.8	0.5	1.0	23,553	23,648	1
798	-21	-10	-15	6.3	11.8	0.5	0.8	290	386	11
799	-308	-354	-309	1.8	11.3	0.2	1.0	2,863	2,964	18
800	-133	261	-133	8.6	14.8	0.6	1.0	2,170	2,271	1
801	-20	-7	-33	12.1	13.6	0.9	0.9	1,597	1,701	30
802	-25	-30	-29	10.0	12.2	0.8	0.9	949	1,062	13
803	-85	-59	-82	8.1	14.2	0.6	0.9	1,391	1,508	13
804	-15	203	3	12.7	13.2	1.0	1.0	2,933	3,051	6
805	-41	-21	-44	2.1	10.2	0.2	0.7	340	460	4
806	-39	11	-58	2.5	13.4	0.2	0.7	257	378	-1
807	-166	-144	-174	-19.2	16.2	-1.2	0.9	790	913	25
808	5	218	41	16.6	16.1	1.0	0.9	848	970	-2
809	-57	-34	-57	2.6	13.9	0.2	0.7	284	414	-6
810	-37	.	.	9.1	11.6	0.8	0.9	1,556	1,687	7

1988 MVA Rank	Company Profile Company	Type	Industry	Market Value Added (MVA) 1988	Change from 1983	1978
811	Diamond Shamrock R & M Inc	Z	Oil & Gas	-131	.	.
812	Crown Central Petroleum	X-	Oil & Gas	-135	125	-25
813	CNW Corp	X-	Railroads	-137	-529	-114
814	Outboard Marine Corp	X-	Other Leisure	-140	-104	77
815	Lone Star Technologies	Pre Z	Steel	-140	.	.
816	U S Home Corp	X-	Construction & R.E.	-142	-135	-91
817	Southdown Inc	X	Building Materials	-144	-139	-166
818	Clark Equipment Co	X-	Machine & Hand Tools	-147	32	115
819	Seagate Technology	Z	Software	-148	-634	.
820	Varian Associates Inc	X-	Electronics	-154	-832	-23
821	Storage Technology Cp	X-	Software	-163	89	-385
822	Bowater Inc	X	Paper	-166	.	.
823	Sequa Corp	Pre Z	Instruments	-172	-142	-131
824	Springs Industries	X	Textiles	-172	49	85
825	Allied Signal Inc	X-	Conglomerates	-175	156	831
826	Northrop Corp	X-	Aerospace	-179	-331	-218
827	Pittway Corp	X-	Conglomerates	-184	-69	-174
828	Kerr-McGee Corp	X-	Oil & Gas	-189	456	-119
829	Harris Corp	X-	Electronics	-189	-859	-599
830	Bally Mfg Corp	X-	Other Leisure	-198	-118	-528
831	McDermott Intl Inc	X-	Construct. & Eng. Services	-198	632	407
832	Carpenter Technology	X-	Steel	-200	-194	-128
833	Soo Line Corp	X-	Railroads	-214	-19	-130
834	Olin Corp	X-	Chemicals	-225	293	225
835	Timken Co	X-	Special Machinery	-236	32	-15
836	Zenith Electronics Corp	X-	Computers & Peripherals	-236	-459	-112
837	Amerada Hess Corp	X-	Oil & Gas	-243	78	270
838	Beverly Enterprises	X-	Health Care Services	-247	-450	-263
839	Sprague Technologies Inc	X-	Semiconductors	-253	.	.
840	A.O. Smith Corp	X-	Auto Parts & Equipment	-257	-66	-57
841	Intl Minerals & Chemical	X-	Chemicals	-259	-266	-119
842	Grumman Corp	X-	Aerospace	-260	-236	-162
843	Halliburton Co	X-	Petroleum Services	-281	-961	-1,856
844	NYNEX Corp	X-	Telephone Companies	-291	.	.
845	Engelhard Corp	X-	Chemicals	-298	-699	.
846	Lone Star Industries	X-	Building Materials	-300	-171	-150
847	Cummins Engine Co Inc	X-	Auto Parts & Equipment	-305	-226	28
848	Communications Satellite	X-	Telephone Equip. & Services	-307	-94	-147
849	GATX Corp	X-	Transportation Services	-307	211	118
850	E.I. Du Pont De Nemours	X-	Chemicals	-313	2,428	-79
851	Mitchell Energy & Dev	X-	Oil & Gas	-350	-599	-331
852	Deere & Co	X-	Special Machinery	-358	1,038	327
853	National Semiconductor Corp	X-	Semiconductors	-364	-713	-331
854	James River Corp Of Virginia	X	Paper	-366	-705	-357
855	Mack Trucks Inc	X-	Cars & Trucks	-383	-314	.
856	Delta Air Lines Inc	X	Airlines	-390	-632	-116
857	Intl Paper Co	X-	Paper	-394	299	466
858	Valero Energy Corp	X-	Oil & Gas	-395	-130	.
859	Unisys Corp	Y	Computers & Peripherals	-430	46	-1,173
860	Tektronix Inc	X-	Instruments	-432	-686	-737
861	Advanced Micro Devices	X-	Semiconductors	-466	-1,825	.
862	Asarco Inc	X	Other Metals	-474	103	431
863	NWA Inc	Pre Z	Airlines	-483	-339	-14
864	AMR Corp	X	Airlines	-512	-920	6
865	Cyprus Minerals Co	X-	Coal	-551	.	.

	Economic Value Added (EVA)			Profitability (1988)				Size (1988)		
1988 MVA Rank	1988	Change from 1983	1978	Rtn on Cap r (%)	Wtd Avg Cost Cap c* (%)	r to c*	Value to Capital	Value	Capital	5-Year Growth in Cap (Avg %)
811	114	.	.	27.0	10.3	2.6	0.8	630	761	28
812	-13	80	-18	10.7	14.0	0.8	0.6	219	354	-9
813	-34	8	-16	9.1	11.3	0.8	0.9	1,360	1,497	6
814	-5	6	6	14.2	14.9	1.0	0.9	873	1,013	17
815	-108	.	.	-4.6	13.6	-0.3	1.0	3,725	3,865	55
816	-62	-13	-54	2.3	11.6	0.2	0.8	512	654	-2
817	25	38	14	14.7	11.6	1.3	0.9	959	1,102	22
818	-78	67	-112	3.8	12.8	0.3	0.8	695	842	-1
819	60	48	.	30.9	15.1	2.0	0.8	673	822	49
820	-56	-38	-40	8.6	16.0	0.5	0.8	635	789	11
821	-95	98	-120	4.9	15.6	0.3	0.8	727	890	-6
822	58	.	.	17.7	14.0	1.3	0.9	1,414	1,580	16
823	-42	-16	-46	9.1	12.2	0.7	0.9	1,157	1,328	26
824	-20	2	23	10.1	12.5	0.8	0.8	771	943	10
825	-181	102	-69	9.4	11.7	0.8	1.0	7,450	7,625	5
826	-352	-379	-424	-1.8	12.0	-0.1	0.9	2,325	2,504	17
827	-20	-20	-33	9.3	13.3	0.7	0.7	374	558	15
828	-245	101	-237	4.2	12.9	0.3	0.9	2,687	2,876	-3
829	-201	-50	-225	1.5	15.3	0.1	0.9	1,182	1,372	10
830	-190	-154	-213	2.7	10.5	0.3	0.9	2,516	2,714	16
831	-536	-257	-791	-9.3	11.9	-0.8	0.9	2,077	2,275	-2
832	32	104	31	18.0	13.3	1.4	0.7	573	773	11
833	-46	-39	-49	5.4	11.2	0.5	0.7	623	838	13
834	-30	93	-11	11.1	12.9	0.9	0.9	1,787	2,013	6
835	-55	105	-84	9.8	13.7	0.7	0.8	1,264	1,500	8
836	-136	-118	-110	3.0	14.7	0.2	0.8	914	1,150	14
837	-259	277	-131	5.5	11.2	0.5	0.9	4,397	4,641	-2
838	-183	-172	-185	2.3	10.1	0.2	0.9	1,901	2,149	9
839	-66	.	.	3.7	16.9	0.2	0.5	272	525	6
840	-67	-23	-64	4.8	14.9	0.3	0.7	490	747	11
841	10	172	-25	12.6	11.9	1.1	0.7	743	1,002	-8
842	-84	-128	-67	5.7	10.3	0.6	0.9	1,733	1,993	18
843	-583	-55	-765	2.8	15.6	0.2	1.0	5,562	5,843	7
844	-1,200	.	.	4.8	10.7	0.4	1.0	22,473	22,765	7
845	-63	27	.	8.1	13.3	0.6	0.8	1,071	1,369	10
846	-44	94	-38	8.5	12.4	0.7	0.8	924	1,225	-1
847	-223	-59	-248	1.2	14.6	0.1	0.8	1,430	1,735	11
848	-3	-7	14	11.2	11.6	1.0	0.5	367	674	2
849	-111	211	-68	5.8	10.2	0.6	0.9	2,878	3,185	4
850	-911	302	-976	10.5	14.0	0.8	1.0	28,892	29,205	6
851	-301	-210	-311	-4.2	11.3	-0.4	0.8	1,516	1,866	2
852	-246	640	-313	8.1	13.1	0.6	0.9	5,144	5,502	-1
853	-357	-334	-380	-9.6	17.0	-0.6	0.7	913	1,277	7
854	32	-32	27	13.1	12.3	1.1	0.9	4,363	4,729	32
855	-83	82	-110	3.8	13.4	0.3	0.6	545	928	3
856	-203	183	-214	7.4	11.2	0.7	0.9	5,013	5,404	11
857	143	583	289	15.2	13.3	1.1	1.0	7,717	8,112	11
858	-75	24	.	5.5	13.3	0.4	0.6	568	963	-7
859	318	565	289	15.6	11.7	1.3	1.0	9,429	9,858	23
860	-151	-102	-203	1.8	14.0	0.1	0.6	796	1,229	-0
861	-195	-266	-201	1.6	18.2	0.1	0.6	641	1,107	18
862	23	357	169	16.1	14.7	1.1	0.8	1,473	1,948	-2
863	-165	-67	-132	6.4	10.7	0.6	0.9	3,373	3,857	26
864	-27	-55	-29	10.6	11.0	1.0	0.9	6,662	7,174	21
865	-63	.	.	13.3	17.7	0.8	0.7	1,133	1,683	8

Company Profile				Market Value Added (MVA)		
1988 MVA Rank	Company	Type	Industry	1988	Change from 1983	1978
866	Data General Corp	X-	Computers & Peripherals	-560	-746	-903
867	Wickes Cos Inc	X-	Conglomerates	-618	-709	-482
868	Adolph Coors Co	X-	Beverages	-633	-287	-398
869	Wang Laboratories	X-	Computers & Peripherals	-634	-4,348	-889
870	National Intergroup Inc	X-	Conglomerates	-634	189	903
871	Goodyear Tire & Rubber Co	X-	Tire & Rubber	-679	424	1,031
872	Sears Roebuck & Co	X-	Discount & Fashion Retailing	-726	-1,256	551
873	Union Carbide Corp	X-	Chemicals	-730	1,834	2,252
874	Inland Steel Industries Inc	X	Steel	-735	209	340
875	Textron Inc	X-	Conglomerates	-737	-313	-351
876	Armco Inc	X-	Steel	-828	-46	472
877	Southwestern Bell Corp	X	Telephone Companies	-831	.	.
878	USAIR Group	X	Airlines	-874	-932	-846
879	Champion International Corp	X	Paper	-905	-559	-412
880	Xerox Corp	X-	Computers & Peripherals	-1,008	-116	-2,011
881	Lockheed Corp	Y	Aerospace	-1,088	-2,469	-879
882	Bethlehem Steel Corp	X-	Steel	-1,096	268	1,739
883	Control Data Corp	X-	Computers & Peripherals	-1,191	-467	-530
884	Monsanto Co	X-	Chemicals	-1,235	-353	495
885	Mobil Corp	X-	Oil & Gas	-1,331	6,475	2,480
886	Sun Co Inc	X-	Oil & Gas	-1,391	888	24
887	McDonnell Douglas Corp	X	Aerospace	-1,519	-1,263	-1,278
888	General Dynamics Corp	X	Aerospace	-1,595	-2,361	-1,368
889	Consolidated Rail Corp	X-	Railroads	-1,597	.	.
890	U S West Inc	X	Telephone Companies	-1,696	.	.
891	ITT Corp	X	Conglomerates	-1,886	-1,086	956
892	Manville Corp	X-	Building Materials	-1,886	-962	-1,267
893	United Technologies Corp	X-	Aerospace	-1,912	-739	-1,163
894	Aluminum Co of America	X	Aluminum	-1,970	-884	-521
895	Norfolk Southern Corp	X-	Railroads	-2,272	-159	-1,439
896	CSX Corp	X-	Railroads	-3,113	-802	-2,124
897	Chrysler Corp	Z	Cars & Trucks	-3,208	-5,316	-450
898	Chevron Corp	X-	Oil & Gas	-3,941	3,383	-1,998
899	Ford Motor Co	Y	Cars & Trucks	-5,459	-166	2,917
900	General Motors Corp	X-	Cars & Trucks	-19,892	-14,687	-13,349
.	Total ($ in billions)			552	328	462

| 1988 MVA Rank | Economic Value Added (EVA) | | | Profitability (1988) | | | | Size (1988) | | 5-Year Growth in Cap (Avg %) |
| | 1988 | Change from | | Rtn on Cap r (%) | Wtd Avg Cost Cap c* (%) | r to c* | Value to Capital | Value | Capital | |
		1983	1978							
866	-120	-53	-155	4.6	15.5	0.3	0.5	604	1,164	14
867	-277	-58	-284	2.4	10.8	0.2	0.8	2,316	2,934	17
868	-97	-53	-81	5.6	14.1	0.4	0.5	616	1,249	9
869	-165	-217	-172	7.6	13.3	0.6	0.8	2,359	2,993	14
870	-187	341	-86	3.1	13.1	0.2	0.6	1,127	1,761	-8
871	-255	-136	-196	7.7	11.8	0.7	0.9	5,628	6,307	2
872	.	.	.	.	.	.	1.0	89,598	90,325	11
873	282	1,514	421	14.4	10.9	1.3	0.9	7,578	8,308	-4
874	71	661	71	16.2	13.6	1.2	0.7	2,059	2,794	1
875	-34	189	-90	11.4	12.2	0.9	0.8	3,892	4,629	21
876	-117	934	-55	9.9	14.5	0.7	0.7	1,709	2,537	-7
877	-544	.	.	7.6	10.4	0.7	1.0	18,295	19,126	5
878	-237	-262	-240	6.4	11.0	0.6	0.8	4,769	5,642	41
879	-85	290	-89	11.8	13.4	0.9	0.8	4,818	5,723	14
880	-461	-82	-728	9.0	13.1	0.7	0.9	13,017	14,025	10
881	58	-211	-2	14.2	12.8	1.1	0.7	3,229	4,317	18
882	-157	1,218	229	12.4	15.8	0.8	0.8	3,456	4,552	-2
883	-277	164	-211	2.1	12.9	0.2	0.6	1,596	2,787	-20
884	-147	173	-135	11.6	13.2	0.9	0.9	7,750	8,985	10
885	-739	1,817	-355	9.6	11.9	0.8	1.0	28,302	29,633	1
886	-1,894	-537	-1,632	-11.6	11.3	-1.0	0.8	5,361	6,752	-6
887	-68	-43	-117	10.3	11.5	0.9	0.8	5,023	6,542	23
888	89	-104	75	17.1	14.9	1.2	0.7	3,262	4,856	16
889	-231	73	.	8.6	13.1	0.7	0.7	3,770	5,367	4
890	117	.	.	11.4	10.7	1.1	0.9	18,292	19,989	8
891	-344	439	-91	9.2	12.1	0.8	0.9	14,151	16,037	5
892	-117	145	-109	3.1	8.5	0.4	0.5	1,711	3,596	12
893	-470	-265	-518	9.5	14.4	0.7	0.8	8,358	10,269	6
894	111	868	69	14.6	13.4	1.1	0.8	7,496	9,466	9
895	-448	-676	-187	9.8	15.2	0.6	0.7	6,283	8,555	6
896	-1,075	-1,111	-851	4.4	13.2	0.3	0.8	9,751	12,864	6
897	7	61	790	15.3	15.3	1.0	0.8	9,863	13,071	38
898	-795	1,787	-618	8.8	11.9	0.7	0.9	22,893	26,834	6
899	1,967	2,165	813	23.6	15.4	1.5	0.8	22,667	28,126	12
900	-2,570	-2,912	-5,501	9.4	13.0	0.7	0.7	56,629	76,522	19
.	-25	39	-35	10.9	12.2	0.9	1.3	2,704	2,153	10